FOUNDATIONS OF MATHEMATICS

with Geometry, Trigonometry, and Statistics

Online Lessons

- Contain highly engaging and interactive videos that use cutting-edge Cloud Learning technologies.
- Break down mathematical concepts into logical and intuitive steps that enhance the learning process.
- Prepare students for upcoming classes, labs, and quizzes through self-study lessons.
- Contain lessons that are self-paced and are excellent for visual learners.

Online Labs

- Contain a comprehensive test-bank of real-world problems, which may be used as an assessment tool.
- Break down every answer into dynamic, step-by-step solutions.
- Provide unlimited amount of practice through algorithmically generated problems.
- Contain numerous statistical tools to analyze students' strengths and weaknesses.

FOUNDATIONS OF MATHEMATICS

with Geometry, Trigonometry, and Statistics

Third Edition

Thambyrajah Kugathasan, Seneca College

Erin Kox, Fanshawe College

ISBN 978-1-927737-31-6

Foundations of Mathematics with Geometry, Trigonometry, and Statistics, Third Edition

Textbook printed in Canada.

Authors: Thambyrajah Kugathasan and Erin Kox

Textbook Editor: Lakshmi Kugathasan
Development Editor: Arbana Miftari
Copy Editor: Connor Peebles
Art Director: Aleksandar Vozarevic
Solution Manuals Editor: Ana Carranza

PowerPoint Presentations: Ali Alavi
Instructional Design: Casey McFadyen
Technology Systems: Zach Williams
Operations: Harsha Varlani
Marketing: Jacob Pucar

Expert Advice: TK Academic Consulting Inc.
Turning Technologies' Student Response System (Clickers) Integrated into PowerPoint Presentations
Online Resources: Vretta's Cloud Learning Technologies

Disclaimer

Vretta Inc. has taken complete care to trace the ownership of copyright material contained in these resources. However, if you have any information which would enable us to rectify any reference or credit for subsequent editions and/or identify any errors or omissions which require correction, please email us at copyright@vretta.com.

The examples and exercises in the Foundations of Mathematics resources are fictitious, unless otherwise stated. Any resemblance to real life people, businesses, organizations, institutions, facts or circumstances is purely coincidental.

Preface

The *Foundations of Mathematics* textbook/e-textbook, along with its award-winning interactive online resources, have been designed, developed, and perfected for *you*. Whether you are an aspiring marketer, human resource professional, engineer, business analyst, economist, artist, or on a different professional path, these resources will help you achieve success in mathematics.

Mathematics encompasses such a diverse range of applications, and each student arrives at the doorstep of this field with unique experiences, aspirations, goals, and learning styles. As you embark on this journey through the Foundations of Mathematics, know that even with all of the different types of students that this subject attracts, we have designed these resources to meet *your individual needs.*

We achieve this by providing you with various ways to approach your education. We have developed, and integrated into this resource, a variety of cutting-edge technologies, mediums of deliveries, and innovative tools that support the diverse learning styles of the 21st century learner. Specifically, we have given you access to four distinct methods of learning: interactive real-world lessons, dynamic assessments, media-rich PowerPoint presentations, and this comprehensive textbook and e-textbook. Combined, these methods allow you to progress in an immersive, engaging, and personalized learning environment.

We designed these resources to work for every student because we passionately believe that *all students* can be successful in mathematics.

The notion that mathematical skills are something that you are born with and that can only be mastered by a select few is a common misconception that perpetuates the negative associations that so many students develop with mathematics. The outcry from students who feel overwhelming anxiety and frustration at even the thought of math was too loud for us to ignore. We were moved to do something about it.

We asked ourselves: How can we boost your confidence in mathematics? How can we help reduce the number of students who dropout of their programs because of poor math grades? How can we ensure that every student, despite their different goals or levels of understanding, has the best chance to succeed in mathematics?

The *Foundations of Mathematics* resource is here to provide you with the most innovative and personalized learning experience for mathematics available. By taking into consideration every learner type and diverse teaching styles, these resources ensure that you are personally engaged, motivated, and confident throughout your learning experience. These resources put you, the student, at the centre of your journey through mathematics and with the tools and support to help you get one step closer to mastering this crucial life skill.

Kuga, Erin, and Team Vretta

Brief Contents

Contents

Chapter 3

Chapter 4

Chapter 5

Chapter 6

Chapter 7

Chapter 8

Chapter 9

Chapter 10

Chapter 11

Chapter 12

List of Tables and Exhibits

Tables

Exhibits

ACKNOWLEDGMENTS

The authors and Vretta would like to thank the following professors for their detailed feedback on helping us update the Third Edition of the Foundations of Mathematics textbook and its accompanying online resources:

Adam Wojtus, Northern College

Isaac Haque, Fanshawe College

Larry White, Georgian College

Margaret Dancy, Fanshawe College

Paul Hansuld, Lambton College

Soobia Siddiqui, Fleming College

Resources

Textbook

Language

The language used in this textbook is simple and straight-forward, while maintaining the levels of sophistication required to thoroughly prepare students for the next stage in their academic and professional careers.

Pedagogies and Learning Methods

Numerous pedagogies and learning methods that have been developed and proven over 60 years are incorporated into the textbook. These pedagogies have succeeded in simplifying critical mathematical concepts and significantly improving retention of concepts. The different learning methods to solve problems have also proven to cater to the varied student learning styles.

Exercises

The textbook has 3,000+ exercises, review exercises, and self-test exercises, as well as 400+ solved examples. Problems are designed to test students on real-world, practical applications and are presented in increasing levels of difficulty, with the most difficult problems being indicated by a dot (•). The problems are categorized into pairs of similar questions to provide professors with an opportunity to solve the even-numbered problems in class and assign the odd-numbered problems as homework.

Solution Manual

All problems in the end-of-section exercises, review exercises, and self-test exercises have been solved using detailed step-by-step methods, as demonstrated in the solved examples. The solution manual is available online.

PowerPoint Presentations

The animated PowerPoint presentations are available for professors to use in class. The PowerPoint presentations are designed to work with clickers in class to gauge student understanding of concepts.

Test Bank

A comprehensive test bank, of 3,000+ problems in varying levels of difficulty, that covers all concepts in the textbook is provided for professors to use as a database for exercises, quizzes, cases, group projects, or assignments.

Online Lessons

The online lessons are created as a pre-study component for students. They contain pedagogies that are highly interactive and engaging, and which teach concepts in a very logical and intuitive way. These lessons are not PowerPoint presentations but are interactive videos that have been created to enrich and enhance the learning experience. Every frame is locked to ensure that students go through the lessons sequentially as they are designed to build on learning concepts in succession. The system automatically records students' progress and performance. Once students complete a lesson, the frame unlocks itself, allowing students to navigate back and forth through the lesson. Professors, on the other hand, have administrative access which allows them to navigate through the online lessons without any restrictions.

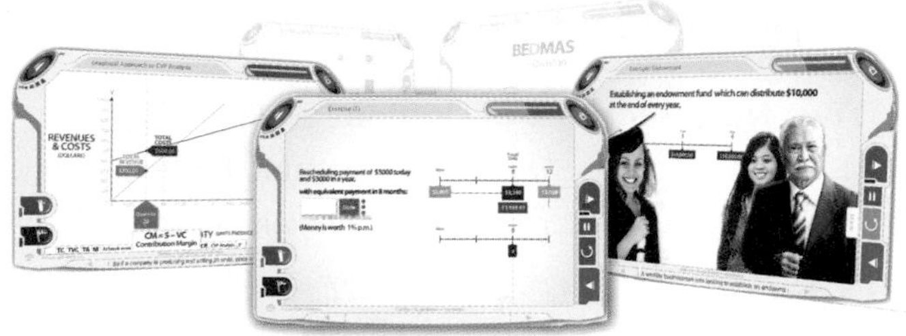

Online Labs

The online lab assessment system contains a rich comprehensive test-bank of real-world problems that are algorithmically generated and that provide students with dynamic feedback on their responses. The labs can also be customized based on course requirements. A few of the customizable features include: previewing and selecting questions, setting the number of questions, setting and modifying start and due dates, opening, closing and re-opening labs, creating new labs and quizzes, and determining the weighting and number of attempts for each question.

Administrative Tools

The following administrative tools will provide professors with the ability to monitor overall class performance and individual student performance on online lessons and labs.

Performance Dashboard for Professors

The lesson performance dashboard provides professors with the average completion percentage per chapter, including a lesson-by-lesson percentage completed visualization for the entire class. The lab performance dashboard provides them with the average percentage mark on each lab for the class. Professors can also download or export individual grades for lessons and labs to a spreadsheet or to the college's course management system.

Performance Dashboard for Students

The lesson performance dashboard provides students with their chapter completion mark, including a lesson-by-lesson percentage completed visualization. The lab performance dashboard provides them with their lab percentage marks.

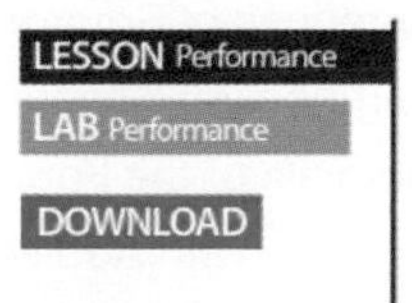

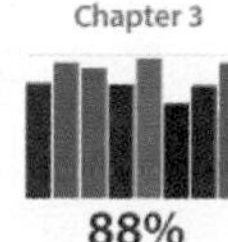

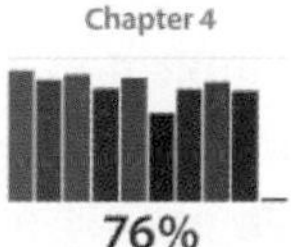

Lab Management System The lab management system is provided for administrators or subject leaders to create new labs, quizzes and case studies, preview and select questions, set the number of questions, set and modify start and due dates, open, close and re-open labs, and determine the weighting and number of attempts for each question.

Updates in the Third Edition

The content of the Third Edition textbook, along with its 400+ solved problems and 3,000+ exercises, has been carefully reviewed by professors at various colleges in Canada. In addition to the updates to the texbook, accompanying online resources have also been updated to reflect the changes.

New Exercise Questions

Over **200 New Exercise Questions** added throughout the textbook.

New Content

Two **New Sections of Content** added.

Includes new content, examples, and exercises on the following topics:

- Factoring Polynomials using the Greatest Common Factor (GCF)
- Factoring Polynomials with Four Terms using Grouping
- Factoring Differences of Squares
- Factoring Trinomials of the Form: $x^2 + bx + c$
- Factoring Trinomials of the Form: $ax^2 + bx + c$
- Factoring Perfect Square Tinomials

Includes new content, examples, and exercises on the following topics:

- Methods of Optimization
- Two-Dimensional Optimization Problems
- Three-Dimensional Optimization Problems

New Examples

Examples revised, updated, and expanded throughout the textbook, with over **30 New Solved Examples** added.

Modified Content

Chapter 4: Expanded the content and reordered the chapter for better flow

Chapter 5: Application problems for Percent and Percent Change included within the chapter

Chapter 6: Application problems for Ratios and Proportions included within the chapter

Chapters 11 & 12: Revised and expanded the content from the Statistics chapter to create two chapters:

- Chapter 11: Basic Statistics
- Chapter 12: Basic Probability

FOUNDATIONS OF MATHEMATICS

with Geometry, Trigonometry, and Statistics

Third Edition

Thambyrajah Kugathasan, Seneca College

Erin Kox, Fanshawe College

Chapter

1 WHOLE NUMBERS

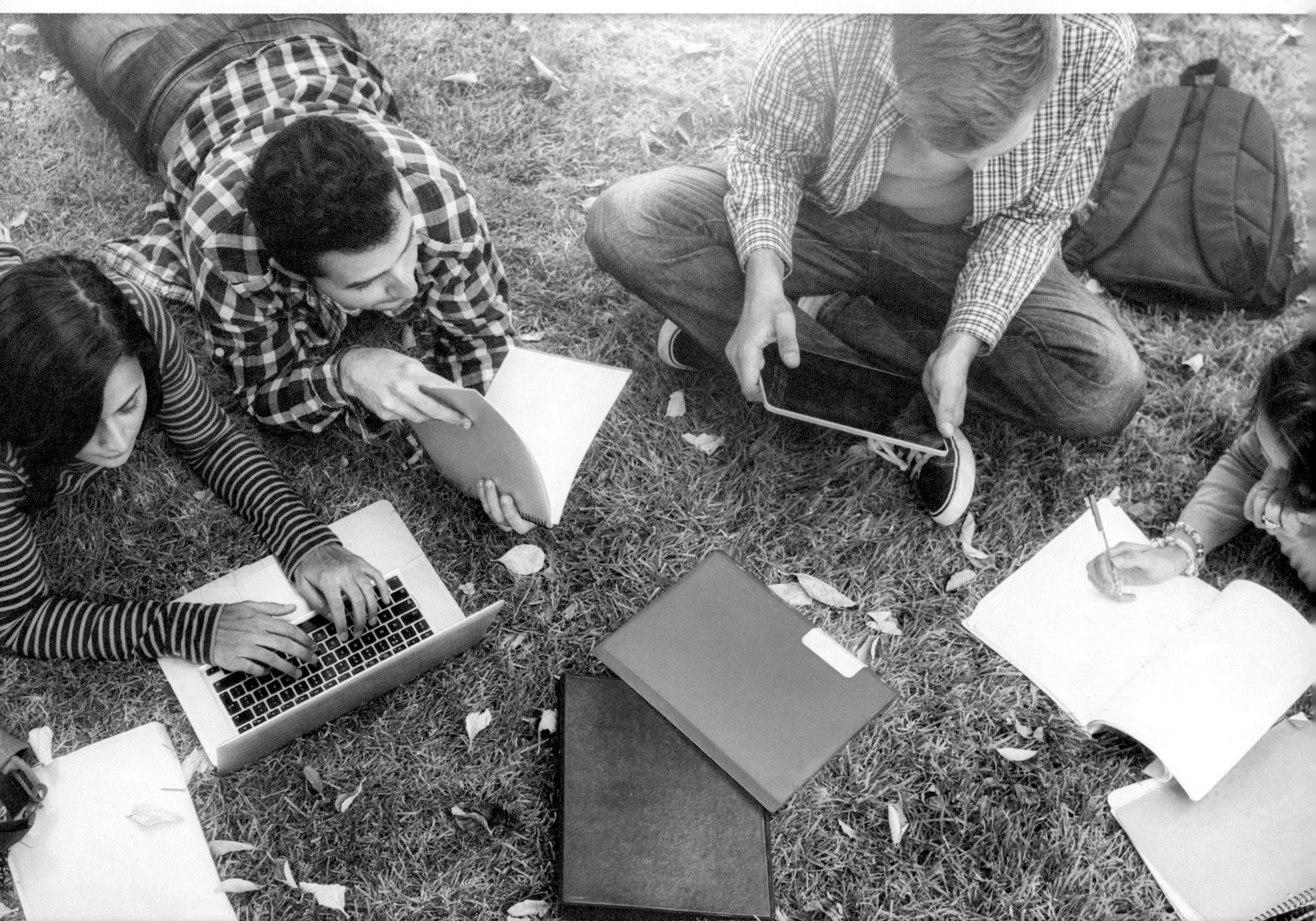

LEARNING OBJECTIVES

- Identify whole numbers.
- Read, write, and round whole numbers correctly.
- Solve problems involving arithmetic operations with whole numbers.
- Determine the least common multiple (LCM) and greatest common factor (GCF).
- Perform order of operations with whole numbers.

CHAPTER OUTLINE

Introduction

Arithmetic is the elementary branch of mathematics that we use in everyday life, in such tasks as buying, selling, estimating expenses, and checking bank balances. When we count, we use arithmetic; when we perform the simple operations of addition, subtraction, multiplication, and division, we use principles of arithmetic. Arithmetic is woven into our general interaction with the real world, and as such, it forms the basis of all science, technology, engineering, and business.

Whole numbers are simply the numbers 0, 1, 2, 3, 4,... They include all counting numbers, also known as natural numbers or positive integers (1, 2, 3, 4,...), and zero (0).

All whole numbers are integers. However, whole numbers and integers are not the same because integers include counting numbers (positive integers) and their negatives (negative integers).

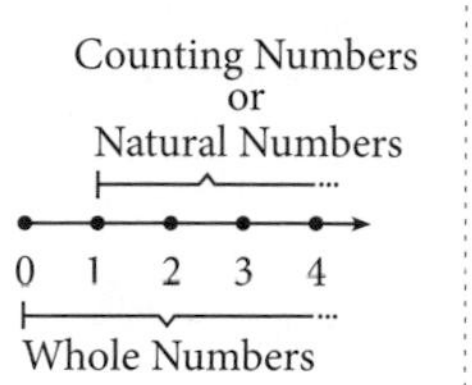

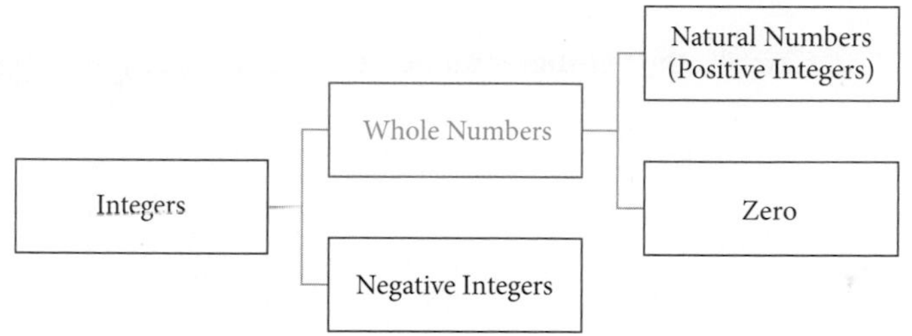

In this chapter, we will learn how to perform arithmetic operations with whole numbers, including powers and roots of perfect squares.

1.1 | Understanding Whole Numbers

Place Value of Whole Numbers

All numbers can be made up using the digits **0, 1, 2, 3, 4, 5, 6, 7, 8,** and **9**. Numbers may consist of one or more digits. When a number is written using the above digits, it is said to be in **standard form**.

For example, 7, 85, and 2,349 are examples of numbers in their standard form, where 7 is a single-(one) digit number, 85 is a two-digit number, and 2,349 is a four-digit number.

The position of each digit in a whole number determines the **place value** for the digit.

Exhibit 1.1-a illustrates the place value of each of the ten digits in the whole number: 3,867,254,129. In this whole number, 4 occupies the 'thousands' place value and represents 4 thousand (or 4,000), whereas 7 occupies the 'millions' place value and represents 7 million (or 7,000,000).

The place value of 'ones' is 10^0 (= 1) and each position has a value of 10 times the place value to its right, as shown in Table 1.1.

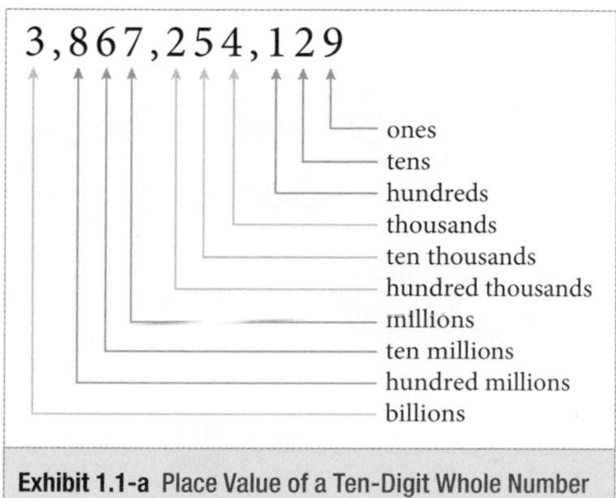

Exhibit 1.1-a Place Value of a Ten-Digit Whole Number

Table 1.1 **Place Value Chart of Whole Numbers**

10^9	10^8	10^7	10^6	10^5	10^4	10^3	10^2	10^1	10^0
1,000,000,000	100,000,000	10,000,000	1,000,000	100,000	10,000	1,000	100	10	1
Billions	Hundred millions	Ten millions	Millions	Hundred thousands	Ten thousands	Thousands	Hundreds	Tens	Ones

We read and write numbers from left to right. A number in standard form is separated into groups of three digits using commas. The vertical red lines in Table 1.1 denote the positions of the commas that separate the groups of three digits, starting from the place value for 'ones'.

For example, the ten-digit number in Exhibit 1.1-a is written as 3,867,254,129 in its standard form.

3	8	6	7	2	5	4	1	2	9
Billions	Hundred millions	Ten millions	Millions	Hundred thousands	Ten thousands	Thousands	Hundreds	Tens	Ones

Numbers can also be written in **expanded form,** by writing the number as the sum of what each place value represents.

For example, the number 3,867,254,129 in standard form can be written in expanded form as follows:

3,000,000,000 + 800,000,000 + 60,000,000 + 7,000,000 + 200,000 + 50,000 + 4,000 + 100 + 20 + 9

Or,

3 billion + 800 million + 60 million + 7 million + 200 thousand
+ 50 thousand + 4 thousand + 1 hundred + 2 tens + 9 ones

Example 1.1-a **Identifying the Place Value of a Digit and the Amount it Represents**

What is the place value of the digit 5 in each of the following numbers and what amount does it represent?

(i) $2,543 (ii) $75,342 (iii) $6,521,890 (iv) $915,203,847

Solution

	(i) $2,543	(ii) $75,342	(iii) $6,521,890	(iv) $915,203,847
Place value of the digit 5:	Hundreds	Thousands	Hundred thousands	Millions
Amount it represents:	$500	$5,000	$500,000	$5,000,000

Example 1.1-b **Identifying the Digit of a Number Given its Place Value**

In the number 5,320,948, identify the digit that occupies the following place values:

(i) Hundred thousands (ii) Ten thousands (iii) Thousands
(iv) Tens (v) Hundreds (vi) Millions

Solution

(i) 5,320,948 ↑ Hundred thousands
(ii) 5,320,948 ↑ Ten thousands
(iii) 5,320,948 ↑ Thousands
(iv) 5,320,948 ↑ Tens
(v) 5,320,948 ↑ Hundreds
(vi) 5,320,948 ↑ Millions

Example 1.1-c

Writing Numbers in Expanded Form

Write the following numbers in expanded form:

(i) 698	(ii) 8,564	(iii) 49,005
(iv) 521,076	(v) 9,865,323	(vi) 43,583,621

Solution

(i) 698

600 + 90 + 8

(ii) 8,564

8,000 + 500 + 60 + 4

(iii) 49,005

40,000 + 9,000 + 5

(iv) 521,076

500,000 + 20,000 + 1,000 + 70 + 6

(v) 9,865,323

9,000,000 + 800,000 + 60,000 + 5,000 + 300 + 20 + 3

(vi) 43,583,621

40,000,000 + 3,000,000 + 500,000 + 80,000 + 3,000 + 600 + 20 + 1

Reading and Writing Whole Numbers

To make it easier to read and write numbers, any number larger than three digits is separated into smaller groups of three digits, starting from the last digit of the number. Each of these groups of three digits has a name.

- The first group of three digits on the right is the "**Units**" group.
- The second group from the right is the "**Thousands**" group.
- The third group from the right is the "**Millions**" group.
- The fourth group from the right is the "**Billions**" group.
- The fifth group from the right is the "**Trillions**" group and so on, as shown in the following chart.

Trillions			Billions			Millions			Thousands			Units		
Hundreds	Tens	Ones	Hundreds	Tens	Ones	Hundreds	Tens	Ones	Hundreds	Tens	Ones	Hundreds	Tens	Ones

Follow these steps to write large numbers in **word form**:

Step 1: Start from the group furthest to the left and write the number formed by the digits in that group, followed by the name of the group.

Step 2: Moving to the next group (to the right), write the numbers formed by this next group, followed by its name. Continue to do this for each of the groups.

Step 3: For the last group (i.e., the group furthest to the right), write the numbers formed by the group; however, for this group, do not write the name of it.

Note: When a group contains all zeros, that group is neither read nor written.

Also, commas and hyphens are used when expressing numbers in word form.

- Commas (,) are used between the groups to separate them.
- Hyphens (-) are used to express two-digit numbers in each group;

  i.e., 21 to 29, 31 to 39, 41 to 49,...91 to 99.

For example, 2,835,197,000,642 expressed in word form using the above rules would be as follows:

Trillions			Billions			Millions			Thousands			Units		
Hundreds	Tens	Ones	Hundreds	Tens	Ones	Hundreds	Tens	Ones	Hundreds	Tens	Ones	Hundreds	Tens	Ones
		2	8	3	5	1	9	7	0	0	0	6	4	2
Two trillion,			eight hundred thirty-five billion,			one hundred ninety-seven million,						six hundred forty-two		

The word 'and' does not appear in the word form of whole numbers.

When writing numbers in word form, the names of the groups remain in their singular forms, irrespective of the number preceeding; i.e., hundred, thousand, million, billion, trillion, etc.

For example:

- Eight **hundred** thirty-five **billion**
- One **hundred** ninety-seven **million**

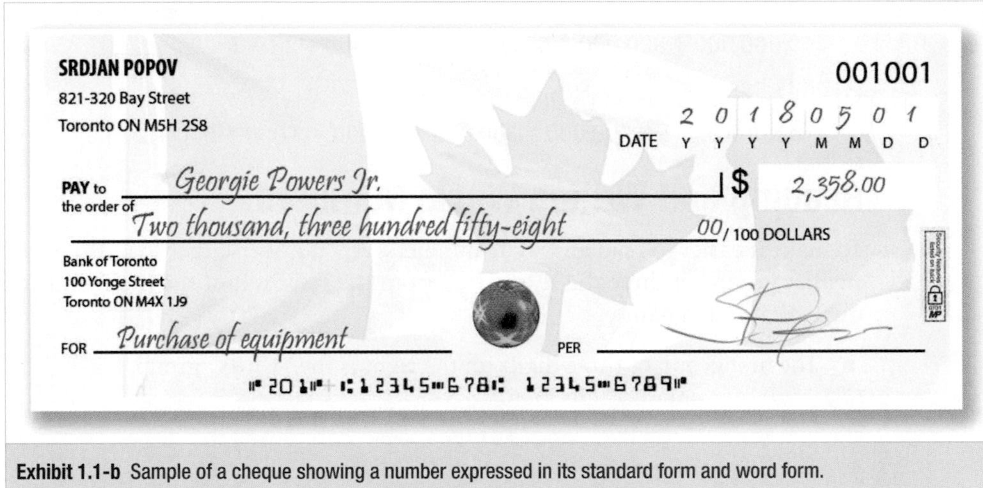

Exhibit 1.1-b Sample of a cheque showing a number expressed in its standard form and word form.

Example 1.1-d Writing Numbers in Word Form Given their Standard Form

Write the following numbers in word form:

(i) 743	(ii) 5,006	(iii) 15,017
(iv) 800,629	(v) 6,783,251	(vi) 52,630,042

Solution

(i) 743 Seven hundred forty-three

(ii) 5,006 Five thousand, six

(iii) 15,017 Fifteen thousand, seventeen

(iv) 800,629 Eight hundred thousand, six hundred twenty-nine

(v) 6,783,251 Six million, seven hundred eighty-three thousand, two hundred fifty-one

(vi) 52,630,042 Fifty-two million, six hundred thirty thousand, forty-two

Example 1.1-e **Writing Numbers In Standard Form Given their Word Form**

Write the following numbers in standard form:

(i) Two hundred five

(ii) Six thousand, four

(iii) Thirty-five thousand, eight hundred twenty-five

(iv) Eight hundred thousand, five

(v) Two million, three hundred forty-two thousand, six hundred seventeen

(vi) Half of a million

(vii) One-quarter of a billion

Solution

(i)	Two hundred five	205
(ii)	Six thousand, four	6,004
(iii)	Thirty-five thousand, eight hundred twenty-five	35,825
(iv)	Eight hundred thousand, five	800,005
(v)	Two million, three hundred forty-two thousand, six hundred seventeen	2,342,617
(vi)	Half of a million	$\frac{1{,}000{,}000}{2} = 500{,}000$
(vii)	One-quarter of a billion	$\frac{1{,}000{,}000{,}000}{4} = 250{,}000{,}000$

Representing Whole Numbers on a Number Line

Whole numbers can be represented graphically as a point on a horizontal line, called the **number line**, as shown below.

The arrowhead at the end shows that the line continues indefinitely in that direction.

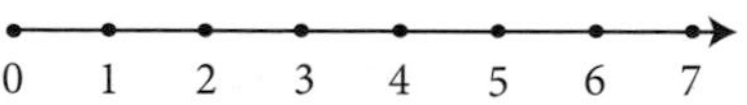

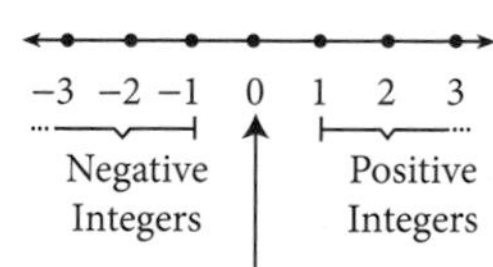

The smallest whole number is zero (0). It is not possible to find the largest whole number because for any given number, there will always be another number greater than that number.

Writing numbers on a number line helps in comparing and identifying numbers that are smaller or larger than other numbers. Numbers that lie to the left of a number on the number line are less than (i.e., smaller than) that number, and numbers that lie to the right of a number on the number line are greater than (i.e., larger than) that number.

For example,

- 6 is greater than 2 (or 2 is less than 6). 0 1 2 3 4 5 6 7 8
- 5 is less than 7 (or 7 is greater than 5). 0 1 2 3 4 5 6 7 8

The signs used to show the relative position of two numbers (or quantities) are:

The signs '>' and '<' always point towards the smaller number.

- '>' read as "**greater than**", meaning that the number on the left of the sign has a value greater than that on the right.

  For example, "6 is greater than 2" is written as $6 > 2$.

  This is the same as "2 is less than 6" which is written as $2 < 6$.

- '<' read as "**less than**", meaning that the number on the left of the sign has a value less than that on the right.

  For example, "5 is less than 7" is written as $5 < 7$.

  This is the same as "7 is greater than 5" which is written as $7 > 5$.

Example 1.1-f **Plotting Numbers on a Number Line and Using Signs to Show the Relative Positions of the Numbers**

Plot the following numbers on a number line and place the correct sign of inequality, '>' or '<', in the space between the numbers.

(i) 7 ☐ 11	(ii) 7 ☐ 5	(iii) 11 ☐ 5
(iv) 5 ☐ 12	(v) 3 ☐ 5	(vi) 12 ☐ 11

Solution

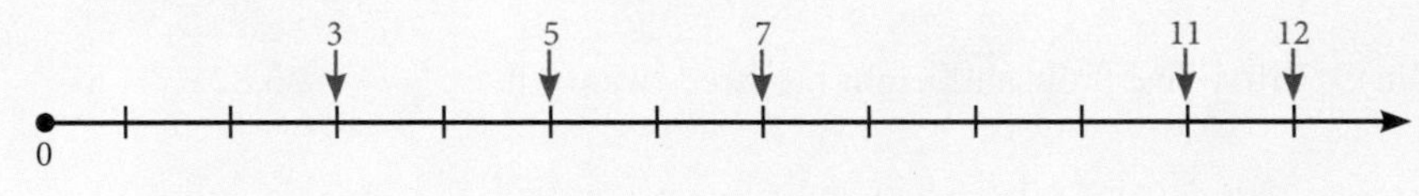

(i) $7 < 11$	(ii) $7 > 5$	(iii) $11 > 5$
(iv) $5 < 12$	(v) $3 < 5$	(vi) $12 > 11$

Example 1.1-g **Writing a Statement to Represent '>' or '<'**

Write statements using the words "greater than" or "less than" for the following expressions:

(i) $24 > 22$ (ii) $36 < 39$ (iii) $9 > 0$ (iv) $0 < 5$

Solution

(i) $24 > 22$

24 is greater than 22, or 22 is less than 24.

(ii) $36 < 39$

36 is less than 39, or 39 is greater than 36.

(iii) $9 > 0$

9 is greater than 0, or 0 is less than 9.

(iv) $0 < 5$

0 is less than 5, or 5 is greater than 0.

Rounding Whole Numbers

Rounding numbers makes them easier to work with and easier to remember. Rounding changes some of the digits in a number but keeps its value close to the original. It is used in reporting large quantities or values that change often, such as population, income, expenses, etc.

For example, the population of Canada is approximately 37 million, or Henry's car expense for this month is approximately $700.

Rounding numbers also makes arithmetic operations faster and easier, especially when determining the exact answer is not required.

For example, if you are required to estimate the area of a rectangular plot of land that measures 114 m by 97 m, you would have to multiply 114 × 97, which would result in 11,058 m^2. However, rounding the measurements to the nearest ten can provide a quick estimate.

Rounding Whole Numbers to the Nearest Ten, Hundred, Thousand, etc.

Rounding whole numbers refers to changing the value of the whole number to the nearest ten, hundred, thousand, etc. It is also referred to as rounding whole numbers to a multiple of 10, 100, 1,000, etc.

- Rounding a whole number to the nearest ten is the same as rounding it to a multiple of 10.
- Rounding a whole number to the nearest hundred is the same as rounding it to a multiple of 100.
- Rounding an amount to the nearest \$1,000 is the same as rounding the amount to a multiple of \$1,000.

For example, rounding the measurements of the above mentioned plot of land to the nearest ten (or multiple of 10):

- Rounding 114 to the nearest ten results in 110.

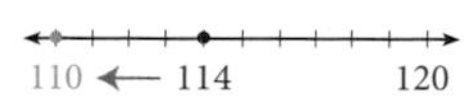

114 is closer to 110 than 120. Therefore, round down to 110.

- Rounding 97 to the nearest ten results in 100.

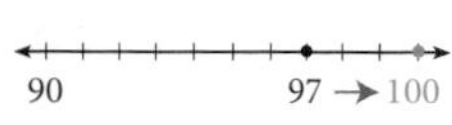

97 is closer to 100 than 90. Therefore, round up to 100.

Therefore, rounding the measurements to the nearest ten results in an estimated area of $110 \text{ m} \times 100 \text{ m} = 11{,}000 \text{ m}^2$.

Example 1.1-h **Rounding Numbers Using a Number Line (Visual Method)**

Round the following numbers to the indicated place value using a number line:

(i) 624 to the nearest ten (multiple of 10).

(ii) 150 to the nearest hundred (multiple of 100).

(iii) 1,962 to the nearest hundred (multiple of 100).

Solution

We can visualize these numbers on a number line to determine the nearest number to round to:

(i) 624 to the nearest ten (multiple of 10)

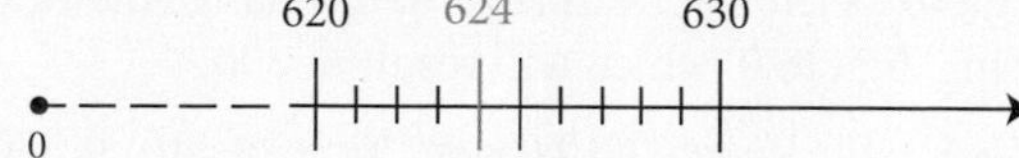

624 is closer to 620 than it is to 630.

Therefore, 624 rounded to the nearest ten is 620.

(ii) 150 to the nearest hundred (multiple of 100)

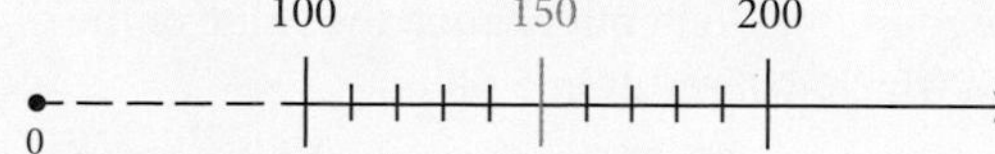

150 is exactly midway between 100 and 200. By convention, if a number is exactly in the middle, we round up.

Therefore, 150 rounded to the nearest hundred is 200.

(iii) 1,962 to the nearest hundred (multiple of 100)

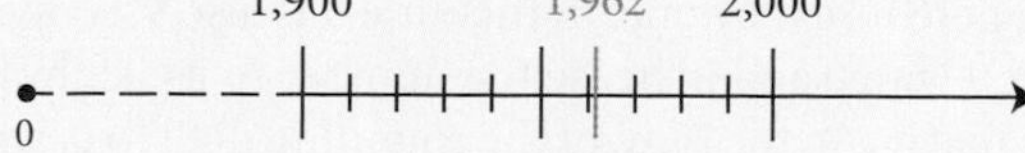

1,962 is closer to 2,000 than it is to 1,900.

Therefore, 1,962 rounded to the nearest hundred is 2,000.

Follow these steps to round whole numbers:

Step 1: Identify the digit to be rounded (this is the place value for which the rounding is required).

Step 2: If the digit to the immediate right of the required rounding digit is less than 5 (0, 1, 2, 3, 4), do not change the value of the rounding digit.

If the digit to the immediate right of the required rounding digit is 5 or greater than 5 (5, 6, 7, 8, 9), increase the value of the rounding digit by one (i.e., round up by one number).

Step 3: Change the value of all digits to the right of the rounding digit to 0.

If the digit to the **right** of the rounding digit is:

0 1 2 3 4	5 6 7 8 9
do not change rounding digit	increase rounding digit by one

Example 1.1-i Rounding to Indicated Place Values

Round the following to the indicated place values:

(i) $568 to the nearest $10.

(ii) $795 to the nearest $10.

(iii) $5,643 to the nearest $100.

(iv) $19,958 to the nearest $100.

Solution

(i) Rounding $568 to the nearest $10:

Identify the rounding digit in the tens place: 568 (6 is the digit in the tens place).

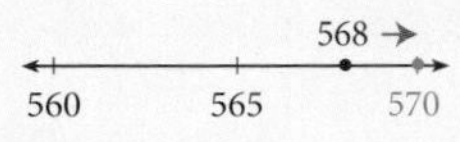

The digit to the immediate right of the rounding digit is 8, which is greater than 5; therefore, increase the value of the rounding digit by one, from 6 to 7, and change the value of the digits that are to the right of the rounding digit to 0, which will result in 570.

Therefore, $568 rounded to the nearest $10 (or multiple of $10) is $570.

(ii) Rounding $795 to the nearest $10:

Identify the rounding digit in the tens place: 795 (9 is the digit in the tens place).

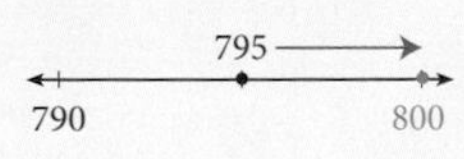

The digit to the immediate right of the rounding digit is 5; therefore, increase the value of the rounding digit by one, from 9 to 10. This is done by replacing the rounding digit 9 with 0, and increasing the next digit to its left by one, from 7 to 8. Change the value of the digits that are to the right of the rounding digit to 0, which will result in 800.

Therefore, $795 rounded to the nearest $10 (or multiple of $10) is $800.

(iii) Rounding $5,643 to the nearest $100:

Identify the rounding digit in the hundreds place: 5,643 (6 is the digit in the hundreds place).

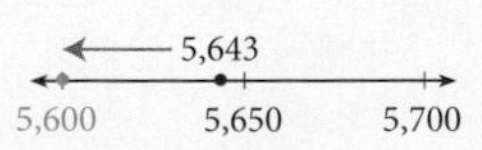

The digit to the immediate right of the rounding digit is 4, which is less than 5; therefore, do not change the value of the rounding digit, but change the value of the digits that are to the right of the rounding digit to 0, which will result in 5,600.

Therefore, $5,643 rounded to the nearest $100 (or multiple of $100) is $5,600.

(iv) Rounding $19,958 to the nearest $100:

Identify the rounding digit in the hundreds place: 19,958 (9 is the digit in the hundreds place).

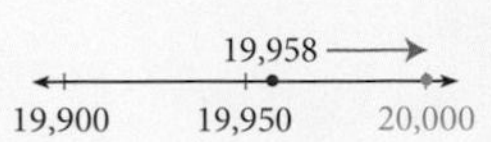

The digit to the immediate right of the rounding digit is 5; therefore, increase the value of the rounding digit by one, from 9 to 10. This is done by replacing the rounding digit 9 with 0 and increasing the next digit to its left by one. In this case it is also 9, so increase again from 9 to 10, by replacing that digit 9 with 0 and increase the number to its left by one, from 1 to 2. Change the value of the digits that are to the right of the rounding digit to 0, which will result in 20,000.

Therefore, $19,958 rounded to the nearest $100 (or multiple of $100) is $20,000.

1.1 | Exercises

Answers to odd-numbered problems are available at the end of the textbook.

For Problems 1 to 4, write (i) the place value of the underlined digit and (ii) the value it represents.

1. a. $4{,}7\underline{9}2$ b. $5{,}\underline{3}52$ c. $45{,}\underline{7}21$
2. a. $7{,}\underline{6}28$ b. $4{,}6\underline{8}7$ c. $\underline{9}4{,}083$
3. a. $3\underline{1}9{,}526$ b. $7{,}8\underline{2}5{,}500$ c. $1\underline{6}{,}702{,}555$
4. a. $20\underline{4}{,}095$ b. $3\underline{5}{,}217{,}123$ c. $4{,}\underline{3}85{,}207$

For Problems 5 to 10, write the numbers in their (i) expanded form and (ii) word form.

5. a. 407 b. 2,056
6. a. 860 b. 7,805
7. a. 29,186 b. 464,448
8. a. 94,975 b. 684,137
9. a. 2,604,325 b. 15,300,604
10. a. 9,084,351 b. 23,006,045

For Problems 11 to 16, write the numbers in their (i) standard form and (ii) word form.

11. a. 600 + 70 + 9 b. 3,000 + 100 + 40 + 7
12. a. 400 + 50 + 6 b. 1,000 + 900 + 30 + 2
13. a. 2,000 + 600 + 5 b. 9,000 + 20 + 4
14. a. 5,000 + 300+1 b. 7,000 + 80 + 8
15. a. 40,000 + 900 + 90 b. 10,000 + 50 + 3
16. a. 60,000 + 700 + 80 b. 20,000 + 100 + 4

For Problems 17 to 24, write the numbers in their (i) standard form and (ii) expanded form.

17. a. Five hundred seventy
    b. Eight hundred three
18. a. One thousand, five
    b. Seven thousand, twenty
19. a. Eighty thousand, six hundred thirty
    b. Seventy-five thousand, twenty-five
20. a. Sixty-five thousand, two hundred forty-four
    b. Eight hundred thirty-three thousand, six hundred forty-one
21. a. Twelve million, four hundred fifty-two thousand, eight hundred thirty-two
    b. Thirty-two million, six hundred eighty-four thousand, two hundred fifty-six
22. a. Two billion, one thousand
    b. One billion, twenty-five thousand
23. a. One-eighth of a million
    b. One-quarter of a million
24. a. Half of a billion
    b. One-tenth of a billion

For Problems 25 and 26, plot the numbers on a number line.

25. a. 14, 19, 15, 7 b. 12, 8, 17, 5
26. a. 18, 9, 6, 11 b. 4, 10, 7, 16

For Problems 27 and 28, place the correct sign '>' or '<' in the space between the numbers.

27. a. 7 $\square$ 15 b. 19 $\square$ 14 c. 0 $\square$ 5 d. 19 $\square$ 0
28. a. 12 $\square$ 17 b. 8 $\square$ 5 c. 17 $\square$ 0 d. 0 $\square$ 8

For Problems 29 and 30, express the relationship between the numbers using the statements (i) "less than" and (ii) "greater than".

29. a. 6 < 9 b. 18 > 11 c. 5 < 11 d. 11 > 0

30. a. 4 < 7 b. 16 > 7 c. 10 < 16 d. 0 < 4

For Problems 31 to 34, arrange the numbers in order from least to greatest.

31. a. 87; 108; 99; 103; 96 b. 159; 141; 108; 139; 167

32. a. 58; 129; 147; 49; 68 b. 836; 820; 805; 873; 875

33. a. 2,067; 2,040; 2,638; 2,533 b. 79,487; 79,534; 79,468; 78,812

34. a. 2,668; 2,630; 2,579; 2,759 b. 68,336; 69,999; 69,067; 68,942

For Problems 35 and 36, create the (i) least and (ii) greatest possible numbers using all the given digits.

35. a. 9, 2, 5 b. 7, 9, 1, 8 c. 3, 5, 4, 8

36. a. 6, 1, 7 b. 9, 4, 8, 5 c. 4, 7, 2, 6, 5

For Problems 37 and 38, round the numbers to (i) nearest ten, (ii) nearest hundred, and (iii) nearest thousand.

37.

	Number	Nearest Ten	Nearest Hundred	Nearest Thousand
a.	524			
b.	1,645			
c.	53,562			
d.	235,358			

38.

	Number	Nearest Ten	Nearest Hundred	Nearest Thousand
a.	895			
b.	9,157			
c.	25,972			
d.	139,835			

For Problems 39 and 40, round the numbers to (i) nearest ten thousand, (ii) nearest hundred thousand, and (iii) nearest million.

39.

	Number	Nearest Ten Thousand	Nearest Hundred Thousand	Nearest Million
a.	875,555			
b.	1,656,565			
c.	3,368,850			
d.	4,568,310			

40.

	Number	Nearest Ten Thousand	Nearest Hundred Thousand	Nearest Million
a.	759,850			
b.	3,254,599			
c.	7,555,450			
d.	2,959,680			

1.2 | Arithmetic Operations with Whole Numbers

Addition of Whole Numbers

Addition can be performed in any order and the sum will be the same.

A + B = B + A

For example,

9 + 5 = 14, and 5 + 9 = 14

This is known as the **commutative property** of addition.

Addition of whole numbers refers to combining two or more whole numbers to find the total.

The numbers that are added are referred to as the **addends**, and the result or answer is called the **total** or **sum**. The symbol '+' denotes addition.

For example, 9 + 5 refers to adding 9 and 5. This is read as 'nine plus five'.

```
                  9 ←——— Addends
Plus sign ——→ +   5 ←—
              ————
                 14 ←——— Total or sum
```

Follow these steps to add whole numbers:

Step 1: Write the numbers one under the other by aligning the place values (ones, tens, hundreds, etc.) of the numbers and draw a horizontal line underneath.

Step 2: Starting from the ones place value, add all the numbers in the column.

- If the total is less than 10, write the total under the horizontal line in the same column.
- If the total is 10 or more, write the 'ones' digit of the total under the horizontal line in the same column, and write the 'tens' digit of the total above the column to the left. This is called 'carrying'.

Step 3: Add the numbers in the tens column, followed by the hundreds column, etc., by following the same procedure for each column.

Example 1.2-a **Adding Whole Numbers**

Perform the following additions:

(i) 3,514 + 245

(ii) 8,578 + 3,982 + 564 + 92

Solution

(i) 3,514 + 245

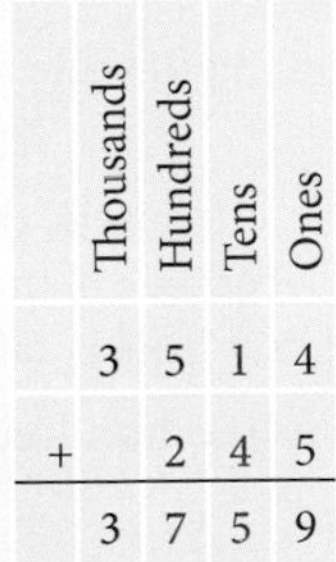

	Thousands	Hundreds	Tens	Ones
	3	5	1	4
+		2	4	5
	3	7	5	9

The sum of the digits in the **ones column** is 9 since 4 + 5 = 9. There are 9 ones, so we write 9 in the ones column below the horizontal line.

The sum of the digits in the **tens column** is 5 since 10 + 40 = 50. There are 5 tens, so we write 5 in the tens column below the horizontal line.

The sum of the digits in the **hundreds column** is 7 since 500 + 200 = 700. There are 7 hundreds, so we write 7 in the hundreds column below the horizontal line.

As only 3 is in the thousands column, the sum of the digits in the **thousands column** is 3. Write 3 in the thousands column below the horizontal line.

Therefore, adding 3,514 and 245 results in 3,759.

Solution continued

(ii) 8,578 + 3,982 + 564 + 92

	Ten Thousands	Thousands	Hundreds	Tens	Ones
		2	3	1	
		8	5	7	8
		3	9	8	2
			5	6	4
+				9	2
	1	3	2	1	6

The sum of the digits in the **ones column** is 16 since 8 + 2 + 4 + 2 = 16, which is 1 ten and 6 ones. Write 6 in the ones column below the horizontal line and carry the 1 above the tens column.

The sum of the digits in the **tens column** is 31 since 70 + 80 + 60 + 90 + **10** (carried from the ones column) = 310, which is 3 hundreds and 1 ten. Write 1 in the tens column below the horizontal line and carry the 3 above the hundreds column.

The sum of the digits in the **hundreds column** is 22 since 500 + 900 + 500 + **300** (carried from the tens column) = 2,200, which is 2 thousands and 2 hundreds. Write 2 in the hundreds column below the horizontal line and carry the 2 above the thousands column.

The sum of the digits in the **thousands column** is 13 since 8,000 + 3,000 + **2,000** (carried from the hundreds column) = 13,000, which is 1 ten thousand and 3 thousands. Write 3 in the thousands column below the horizontal line and 1 in the ten thousands column.

Therefore, adding 8,578, 3,982, 564, and 92 results in 13,216.

Subtraction of Whole Numbers

Subtraction of whole numbers refers to finding the difference between numbers. This is the reverse process of addition.

Subtraction must be performed in the written order.

A – B ≠ B – A

For example,

8 – 5 = 3, but 5 – 8 = –3

i.e., 5 – 8 results in the negative answer of 8 – 5.

The number from which another number is subtracted is referred to as the **minuend** and the number that is being subtracted is referred to as the **subtrahend**. The result or answer is called the **difference**. The symbol '–' denotes subtraction.

For example, 8 – 5 refers to subtracting 5 from 8. This is read as 'eight minus five'.

8 ⟵ Minuend
Minus sign ⟶ – 5 ⟵ Subtrahend
3 ⟵ Difference

Follow these steps to subtract a whole number from another whole number:

Step 1: Write the numbers one under the other by aligning the place values (ones, tens, hundreds, etc.) of the numbers and draw a horizontal line underneath. Ensure that the number that is being subtracted from (the minuend) is in the top row and that the number that is being subtracted (the subtrahend) is below.

Step 2: Starting from the ones place value, subtract the bottom number from the top number.

- If the top digit is greater than (or equal to) the bottom digit, write the difference under the horizontal line in the same column.
- If the top digit is less than the bottom digit, borrow 'one' from the digit to the left in the top number, and add 'ten' to the digit in the current place value of the top number. Then, find the difference and write it under the horizontal line. This is called 'borrowing'.

Step 3: Subtract the numbers in the tens column, followed by the hundreds column, etc., by following the same procedure for each column.

Note: To check your answer, add the difference to the number subtracted (subtrahend); the result should be the number from which it was subtracted (minuend). e.g., 8 – 5 = 3; *therefore* 3 + 5 = 8

Example 1.2-b **Subtracting Whole Numbers**

Perform the following subtractions:

(i) Subtract 1,314 from 3,628

(ii) Subtract 789 from 8,357

Solution

(i) Subtract 1,314 from 3,628

	Thousands	Hundreds	Tens	Ones
	3	6	2	8
−	1	3	1	4
	2	3	1	4

The difference of the digits in the **ones column** is 4 since 8 – 4 = 4. There are 4 ones, so we write 4 in the ones column below the horizontal line.

The difference of the digits in the **tens column** is 1 since 20 – 10 = 10. There is 1 ten, so we write 1 in the tens column below the horizontal line.

The difference of the digits in the **hundreds column** is 3 since 600 – 300 = 300. There are 3 hundreds, so we write 3 in the hundreds column below the horizontal line.

The difference of the digits in the **thousands column** is 2 since 3,000 – 1,000 = 2,000. There are 2 thousands, so we write 2 in the thousands column below the horizontal line.

Check your answer:

2,314 + 1,314 = 3,628

Therefore, subtracting 1,314 from 3,628 results in 2,314.

(ii) Subtract 789 from 8,357

	Thousands	Hundreds	Tens	Ones
	7	12	14	17
	~~8~~	~~3~~	~~5~~	~~7~~
−		7	8	9
	7	5	6	8

In the **ones column**, the ones digit on the top (7) is smaller than the ones digit on the bottom (9). Borrow one ten from the tens digit on the top row and add it to the 7 ones to get 17 ones. 17 – 9 = 8, so we write 8 in the ones column below the horizontal line.

In the **tens column**, the tens digit on the top (4, after borrowing 1 for the ones column) is smaller than the tens digit on the bottom (8). Borrow one hundred from the hundreds digit on the top row and add it to the 4 tens to get 14 tens. 14 – 8 = 6, so we write 6 in the tens column below the horizontal line.

In the **hundreds column**, the hundreds digit on the top (2, after borrowing 1 for the tens column) is smaller than the hundreds digit on the bottom (7). Borrow one thousand from the thousands digit on the top row and add it to the 2 hundreds to get 12 hundreds. 12 – 7 = 5, so we write 5 in the hundreds column below the horizontal line.

As only 7 (after borrowing 1 for the hundreds column) is in the **thousands column**, we write 7 in the thousands column below the horizontal line.

Therefore, subtracting 789 from 8,357 results in 7,568.

Note: If a larger whole number is subtracted from a smaller whole number, the result will be a negative number. To do this, reverse the question to deduct the smaller number from the larger number following the above steps, and set the answer to be negative.

Multiplication of Whole Numbers

Multiplication is the process of finding the product of two numbers. Multiplication of whole numbers can be thought of as repeated additions. The symbol '×' denotes multiplication.

For example, 5 × 4 refers to repeatedly adding 5, four times. This is read as 'five times four', and can also be written as 5 · 4 or 5(4).

Multiplication can be performed in any order and the product will be the same.

A × B = B × A

For example,
5 × 4 = 20, and 4 × 5 = 20

This is known as the **commutative property** of multiplication.

5 × 4 can be represented pictorially as:

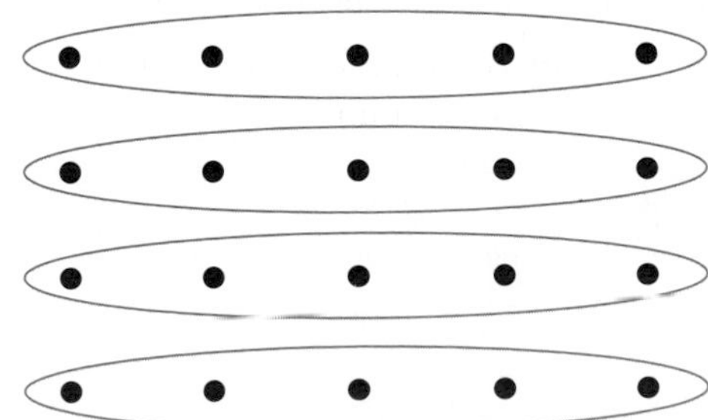

Here, the size of the set is 5 and it is repeated 4 times:
5 + 5 + 5 + 5 = 20

This can also be viewed as 4 × 5:

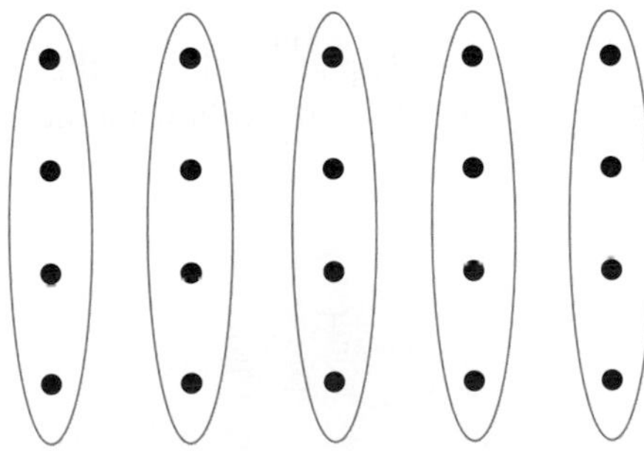

Here, the size of the set is 4 and it is repeated 5 times:
4 + 4 + 4 + 4 + 4 = 20

The numbers that are being multiplied are referred to as **factors** and the result is referred to as the **product**.

	5 ←	Factors
Multiplication sign →	× 4 ←	
	20 ←	Product

In this example, 5 and 4 are factors of 20.

Follow these steps to multiply one whole number by another whole number:

Step 1: Write the numbers one under the other by aligning the place values and draw a horizontal line underneath, as done for addition and subtraction.

Step 2: Starting from the ones digit of the bottom factor, multiply the digit by each digit of the top factor, starting with the right-most digit.

- If the product is less than 10, write the product under the horizontal line.
- If the product is 10 or more, write the 'ones' digit of the product under the horizontal line, carry the 'tens' digit, and add it to the subsequent product.

Step 3: Multiply the next digit of the bottom factor by each digit of the top factor by following the same procedure, and write the product below the first product, but one place value to the left. Continue for each digit of the bottom factor.

Step 4: Sum all the products to obtain the answer.

The above steps for multiplying numbers are provided in detail in Example 1.2-c below.

Example 1.2-c **Multiplying Whole Numbers**

Perform the following multiplications:

(i) Multiply 38 by 6 (ii) Multiply 36 by 24 (iii) Multiply 263 by 425

Solution

(i) Multiply 38 by 6

	Hundreds	Tens	Ones
		4	
		3	8
×			6
	2	2	8

Multiplying 8 ones by 6 results in 48 ones. This is 4 tens and 8 ones. Write 8 in the ones column below the horizontal line and 4 above the tens column.

Multiplying 3 tens by 6 results in 18 tens. Add the 4 tens carried from the previous step to 18 to obtain 22 tens. Write 2 in the tens column and 2 in the hundreds column below the horizontal line.

Therefore, multiplying 38 by 6 results in 228.

(ii) Multiply 36 by 24

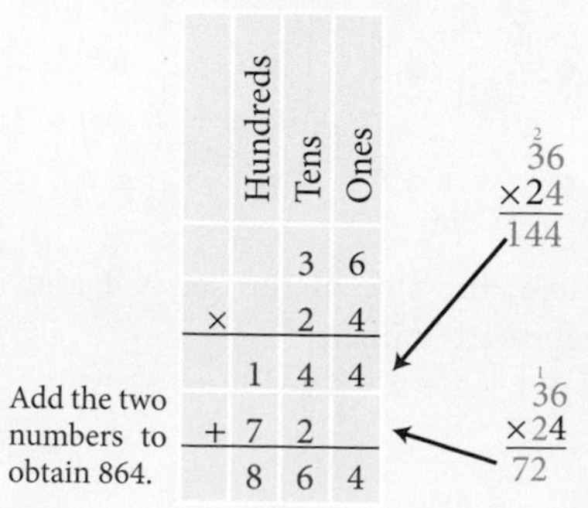

Hundreds
Tens
Ones
3 6
× 2 4
1 4 4
+ 7 2
8 6 4
Add the two numbers to obtain 864.
2
36
×24
144
1
36
×24
72

Multiply 36 by 4 ones, as shown, to obtain 144.

Multiply 36 by 2 tens. To do this, write a '0' under the horizontal line in the ones column (or simply leave it blank, as shown) and multiply 36 by 2 to obtain 72.

Therefore, multiplying 36 by 24 results in 864.

Solution
continued

(iii) Multiply 263 by 425

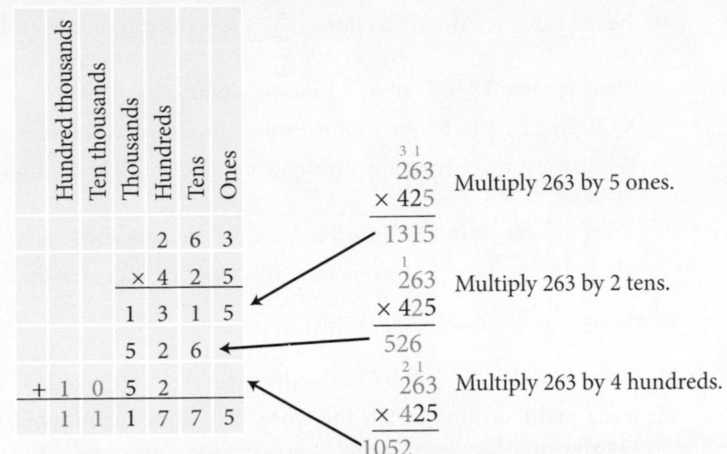

Therefore, multiplying 263 by 425 results in 111,775.

Division of Whole Numbers

Division must be performed in the written order.

$A \div B \neq B \div A$

For example,

$20 \div 5 = 4$, but $5 \div 20 = \frac{1}{4}$

i.e., $5 \div 20$ results in the reciprocal of $20 \div 5$.

Division is the process of determining how many times one number is contained in another. This is the inverse process of multiplication. When a larger number is divided by a smaller number, this division can be thought of as repeated subtractions. The symbol '÷' denotes division.

For example, $20 \div 5$ refers to repeatedly subtracting 5 from 20. This is read as 'twenty divided by five', and can also be written as $5\overline{)20}$.

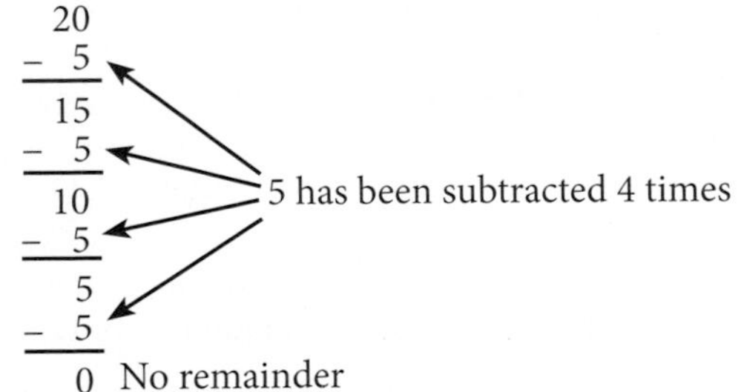

In a set of 20 items, we can create four groups of 5:

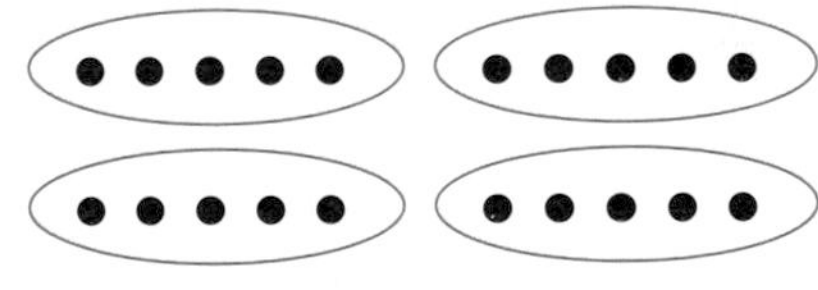

Therefore, $20 \div 5 = 4$.

The number that is being divided is referred to as the **dividend**, and the number by which the dividend is divided is referred to as the **divisor**. The result or answer is called the **quotient**. If the dividend cannot be divided evenly by the divisor, the number left over is referred to as the **remainder**.

For example, consider $25 \div 7$:

$$\begin{array}{r} 3 \\ 7\overline{)25} \\ -21 \\ \hline 4 \end{array}$$

Divisor ⟶ 7; 3 ⟵ Quotient; 25 ⟵ Dividend; 4 ⟵ Remainder

The following relationship exists between the four components of a division problem:

$$\text{Dividend} = \text{Divisor} \times \text{Quotient} + \text{Remainder}$$

$$25 = 7 \times 3 + 4$$

The steps to be followed in dividing whole numbers are provided in detail in Example 1.2-d below.

Example 1.2-d **Dividing Whole Numbers**

Perform the following divisions and state the quotient and remainder:

(i) Divide 76 by 3 (ii) Divide 637 by 25 (iii) Divide 6,543 by 12

Solution (i) Divide 76 by 3

$$\begin{array}{r} 25 \\ 3\overline{)76} \\ -6\downarrow \\ \hline 16 \\ -15 \\ \hline 1 \end{array}$$

7 can be divided by 3. Therefore, determine the number of multiples of 3 there are in 7.

There are two 3's in 7. Write 2 in the quotient area above 7.

Multiply 2 by 3 (= 6) and subtract this from 7. Write the remainder 1.

Bring down the 6 from the dividend and determine the number of multiples of 3 there are in 16.

There are five 3's in 16. Write 5 in the quotient area above 6.

Multiply 5 by 3 (= 15) and subtract this from 16 to get the final remainder of 1.

Therefore, the quotient is 25 and the remainder is 1.

(ii) Divide 637 by 25

$$\begin{array}{r} 25 \\ 25\overline{)637} \\ -50\downarrow \\ \hline 137 \\ -125 \\ \hline 12 \end{array}$$

6 cannot be divided by 25. Therefore, determine the number of multiples of 25 there are in 63.

There are two 25's in 63. Write 2 in the quotient area above 3.

Multiply 2 by 25 (= 50) and subtract this from 63. Write the remainder 13.

Bring down the 7 from the dividend and determine the number of multiples of 25 there are in 137.

There are five 25's in 137. Write 5 in the quotient area above 7.

Multiply 5 by 25 (= 125) and subtract this from 137 to get the final remainder of 12.

Therefore, the quotient is 25 and the remainder is 12.

(iii) Divide 6,543 by 12

$$\begin{array}{r} 545 \\ 12\overline{)6543} \\ -60\downarrow\, \\ \hline 54\, \\ -48\downarrow \\ \hline 63 \\ -60 \\ \hline 3 \end{array}$$

6 cannot be divided by 12. Therefore, determine the number of multiples of 12 there are in 65.

There are five 12's in 65. Write 5 in the quotient area above 5. Multiply 5 by 12 (= 60) and subtract this from 65. Write the remainder 5. Bring down the 4 from the dividend and determine the number of multiples of 12 there are in 54.

There are four 12's in 54. Write 4 in the quotient area above 4. Multiply 4 by 12 (= 48) and subtract this from 54. Write the remainder 6. Bring down the 3 from the dividend and determine the number of multiples of 12 there are in 63.

There are five 12's in 63. Write 5 in the quotient area above 3. Multiply 5 by 12 (= 60) and subtract this from 63 to get the final remainder of 3.

Therefore, the quotient is 545 and the remainder is 3.

Arithmetic Operations with Zero and One

Table 1.2-a **Arithmetic Operations with Zero**

Operation	Description	Examples
Addition	When 0 is added to a number, or when a number is added to 0, there will be no change to that number.	$25 + 0 = 25$ $0 + 25 = 25$
Subtraction	When 0 is subtracted from a number, there will be no change to that number.	$16 - 0 = 16$
	When a number is subtracted from 0, the answer will be the negative value of that number.	$0 - 16 = -16$

Operation	Description	Examples
Multiplication	When 0 is multiplied by a number, or when a number is multiplied by 0, the answer will be 0.	$0 \times 35 = 0$ $35 \times 0 = 0$
Division	When 0 is divided by a number, the answer will be 0.	$0 \div 25 = 0$
	When a number is divided by 0, the answer is undefined.	$25 \div 0 =$ Undefined

Table 1.2-b **Arithmetic Operations with One**

Operation	Description	Examples
Multiplication	When 1 is multiplied by a number, or when a number is multiplied by 1, there will be no change to that number.	$1 \times 12 = 12$ $12 \times 1 = 12$
Division	When 1 is divided by a number, the answer is the reciprocal of that number.	$1 \div 35 = \frac{1}{35}$
	When a number is divided by 1, there will be no change to that number.	$35 \div 1 = \frac{35}{1} = 35$

Powers of Whole Numbers

We learned previously that multiplication is a shorter way to write repeated additions of a number. Similarly, when a number is multiplied by itself repeatedly, we can represent this repeated multiplication using **exponential notation.**

When 2 is multiplied 5 times, in repeated multiplication, it is represented by:

$$2 \times 2 \times 2 \times 2 \times 2$$

However, it can be tedious to represent repeated multiplication using this notation. Instead, exponential notation can be used.

When 2 is multiplied 5 times, in exponential notation, it is represented by:

base ⟶ 2^5 ⟵ exponent

In this example, 2 is known as the **base**, 5 is known as the **exponent**, and the whole representation 2^5 is known as the **power**. The exponent is written in superscript to the right of the base, and represents the number of times that the base is multiplied by itself. The whole representation is read as "2 raised to the power of 5" or "2 to the 5th power".

1 raised to any exponent = 1

0 raised to any positive exponent = 0

Example 1.2-e **Converting Exponential Notation to Repeated Multiplication and Evaluating**

Expand 8^2 to show the repeated multiplication and evaluate.

Solution

$$8^2 = \overbrace{8 \times 8}^{\text{Repeated Multiplication}} = 64$$

8^2: Exponential Notation; 64: Standard Notation

Example 1.2-f **Converting Repeated Multiplication to Exponential Notation**

Express the repeated multiplication $9 \times 9 \times 9 \times 9 \times 9 \times 9$ in exponential notation.

Solution

The number 9 is being multiplied repeatedly 6 times.

In exponential notation, the **base** is **9** and the **exponent** is **6**.

Therefore, $9 \times 9 \times 9 \times 9 \times 9 \times 9 = \mathbf{9^6}$.

Example 1.2-g **Evaluating Expressions by Writing in Standard Form**

Express the following in standard form and then evaluate:

(i) 5×3^4 (ii) $2^3 \times 3^2$ (iii) $5^4 + 2^2$ (iv) $5^2 - 4^2$

Solution

(i) $5 \times 3^4 = 5 \times [\,3 \times 3 \times 3 \times 3\,] = 5 \times 81 = 405$

(ii) $2^3 \times 3^2 = [\,2 \times 2 \times 2\,] \times [\,3 \times 3\,] = 8 \times 9 = 72$

(iii) $5^4 + 2^2 = [\,5 \times 5 \times 5 \times 5\,] + [\,2 \times 2\,] = 625 + 4 = 629$

(iv) $5^2 - 4^2 = [\,5 \times 5\,] - [\,4 \times 4\,] = 25 - 16 = 9$

Example 1.2-h **Evaluating Powers using a Different Power of the Same Base**

Use the equation $6^5 = 7{,}776$ to evaluate the following expressions:

(i) 6^6 (ii) 6^4

Solution

(i) $6^5 = 6 \times 6 \times 6 \times 6 \times 6 = 7{,}776$

$$6^6 = \underbrace{6 \times 6 \times 6 \times 6 \times 6}_{6^5} \times 6$$

$$= 6^5 \times 6$$

$$= 7{,}776 \times 6$$

$$= 46{,}656$$

(ii) $6^5 = \underbrace{6 \times 6 \times 6 \times 6}_{6^4} \times 6 = 7{,}776$

$$6^5 = 6^4 \times 6$$

$$7{,}776 = 6^4 \times 6$$

$$\frac{7{,}776}{6} = 6^4$$

$$6^4 = 1{,}296$$

Table 1.2-c **Examples of Powers with Exponents of 2, 3, 4, and 5**

Powers of 2		Powers of 3	Powers of 4	Powers of 5
$1^2 = 1$	$11^2 = 121$	$1^3 = 1$	$1^4 = 1$	$1^5 = 1$
$2^2 = 4$	$12^2 = 144$	$2^3 = 8$	$2^4 = 16$	$2^5 = 32$
$3^2 = 9$	$13^2 = 169$	$3^3 = 27$	$3^4 = 81$	$3^5 = 243$
$4^2 = 16$	$14^2 = 196$	$4^3 = 64$	$4^4 = 256$	$4^5 = 1{,}024$
$5^2 = 25$	$15^2 = 225$	$5^3 = 125$	$5^4 = 625$	$5^5 = 3{,}125$
$6^2 = 36$	$16^2 = 256$	$6^3 = 216$	$6^4 = 1{,}296$	$6^5 = 7{,}776$
$7^2 = 49$	$17^2 = 289$	$7^3 = 343$	$7^4 = 2{,}401$	$7^5 = 16{,}807$
$8^2 = 64$	$18^2 = 324$	$8^3 = 512$	$8^4 = 4{,}096$	$8^5 = 32{,}768$
$9^2 = 81$	$19^2 = 361$	$9^3 = 729$	$9^4 = 6{,}561$	$9^5 = 59{,}049$
$10^2 = 100$	$20^2 = 400$	$10^3 = 1{,}000$	$10^4 = 10{,}000$	$10^5 = 100{,}000$

Perfect Squares and Square Roots

Any whole number base with an exponent of 2 is known as a **perfect square**. For example, 9 is the perfect square produced by 3 raised to an exponent 2. The first twenty perfect squares are shown in Table 1.2-c under Powers of 2.

The **square root** of a number is one of two identical factors that, when multiplied together, result in that number.

Finding the **square root** of a perfect square is the inverse of raising a whole number to the power of 2.

For example,

- 2 is the square root of 4 because $2^2 = 4$ or $2 \times 2 = 4$
- 5 is the square root of 25 because $5^2 = 25$ or $5 \times 5 = 25$

That is, a whole number multiplied by itself results in a perfect square. The whole number multiplied by itself to get that perfect square is called the square root of that perfect square.

For example,

- 16 is a perfect square because it is the product of two identical factors of 4; i.e., $16 = 4 \times 4$.
- Therefore, 4 is the square root of 16.

The radical sign $\sqrt{\ }$ indicates the root of a number (or expression). The square root of 16, using the radical sign, is represented by $\sqrt[2]{16}$, where 2 is the index. The index indicates which root is to be taken, and is written as a small superscript number to the left of the radical symbol. For square roots, the index 2 does not need to be written as it is understood to be there; i.e. $\sqrt[2]{16}$ is written as $\sqrt{16}$.

Note: In future chapters, we will discuss roots with indexes other than 2.

Example 1.2-i **Determining the Square Root of Perfect Squares**

Determine the square root of the following:

(i) $\sqrt{36}$ (ii) $\sqrt{81}$ (iii) $\sqrt{144}$

Solution

(i) $\sqrt{36} = \sqrt{6 \times 6}$ (Using $36 = 6 \times 6$)

$= 6$

(ii) $\sqrt{81} = \sqrt{9 \times 9}$ (Using $81 = 9 \times 9$)

$= 9$

(iii) $\sqrt{144} = \sqrt{12 \times 12}$ (Using $144 = 12 \times 12$)

$= 12$

1.2 | Exercises

Answers to odd-numbered problems are available at the end of the textbook.

For the addition Problems 1 to 8, (i) estimate the answer by rounding each number to the nearest ten, and (ii) calculate the exact answer.

1. a. 48 + 29 b. 38 + 95
2. a. 16 + 79 b. 69 + 47
3. a. 875 + 48 b. 574 + 79
4. a. 459 + 27 b. 356 + 65
5. a. 286 + 109 + 15 b. 839 + 645 + 27
6. a. 989 + 215 + 25 b. 798 + 237 +12
7. a. 195 + 459 + 8 b. 996 + 816 + 6
8. a. 896 + 642 + 9 b. 995 + 724 + 8

For the addition Problems 9 to 14, (i) estimate the answer by rounding each number to the nearest hundred, and (ii) calculate the exact answer.

9. a. 745 + 668 b. 427 + 225
10. a. 357 + 245 b. 451 + 645
11. a. 1,883 + 5,466 b. 2,157 + 3,459
12. a. 6,950 + 2,367 b. 3,765 + 1,992
13. a. 2,635 + 372 + 1,524 b. 653 + 2,188 + 891
14. a. 1,650 + 1,647 + 875 +167 b. 3,869 + 1,967 + 550 + 745

For the subtraction Problems 15 to 22, (i) estimate the answer by rounding each number to the nearest ten, and (ii) calculate the exact answer.

15. a. 62 – 25 b. 33 – 18
16. a. 43 – 27 b. 71 – 59
17. a. 208 – 79 b. 315 – 47
18. a. 327 – 28 b. 500 – 73
19. a. 767 – 159 b. 804 – 308
20. a. 904 – 629 b. 584 – 167
21. a. 8,302 – 7,244 b. 2,927 – 888
22. a. 9,185 – 6,728 b. 5,765 – 777

For the subtraction Problems 23 to 28, (i) estimate the answer by rounding each number to the nearest hundred, and (ii) calculate the exact answer.

23. a. 946 – 452 b. 855 – 251
24. a. 868 – 745 b. 495 – 357
25. a. 2,950 – 2,275 b. 3,961 – 1,833
26. a. 2,955 – 1,350 b. 1,967 – 352
27. a. 3,513 – 2,846 b. 3,981 – 1,657
28. a. 7,676 – 3,969 b. 5,789 – 5,626

For the multiplication Problems 29 to 34, (i) estimate the answer by rounding each number to the nearest ten, and (ii) calculate the exact answer.

29. a. 58 × 75 b. 63 × 59
30. a. 35 × 97 b. 95 × 71
31. a. 764 × 53 b. 799 × 68
32. a. 482 × 95 b. 755 × 55
33. a. 1,995 × 37 b. 2,150 × 59
34. a. 2,996 × 32 b. 2,995 × 38

For the division Problems 35 to 44, (i) estimate the answer by rounding each number to the nearest ten, and (ii) perform the exact division and state the quotient and the remainder.

35. a. 78 ÷ 5 b. 36 ÷ 8
36. a. 69 ÷ 7 b. 85 ÷ 9
37. a. 86 ÷ 27 b. 78 ÷ 19
38. a. 59 ÷ 12 b. 95 ÷ 18
39. a. 654 ÷ 14 b. 396 ÷ 24
40. a. 777 ÷ 16 b. 255 ÷ 19
41. a. 2,562 ÷ 18 b. 1,225 ÷ 28
42. a. 2,097 ÷ 55 b. 1,795 ÷ 64
43. a. 3,004 ÷ 204 b. 6,501 ÷ 498
44. a. 3,895 ÷ 264 b. 5,195 ÷ 255

For Problems 45 to 48, express the repeated multiplication in exponential notation.

45. a. 6 × 6 × 6 × 6 b. 12 × 12
46. a. 5 × 5 × 5 b. 7 × 7 × 7 × 7 × 7
47. a. 3 × 3 × 3 × 3 × 3 × 3 b. 9 × 9 × 9 × 9
48. a. 8 × 8 × 8 × 8 × 8 b. 4 × 4 × 4 × 4 × 4

For Problems 49 to 52, write the base and exponent for the powers.

49. a. 2^9 b. 5^7
50. a. 6^2 b. 10^9
51. a. 1^{20} b. 8^3
52. a. 7^5 b. 12^1

For Problems 53 and 54, express the powers in standard notation and then evaluate.

53. a. 10^6 b. 3^5
54. a. 2^8 b. 5^4
55. If 3^{10} = 59,049, evaluate 3^9 and 3^{11}
56. If 5^8 = 390,625, evaluate 5^7 and 5^9

For Problems 57 to 62, determine the square root.

57. a. $\sqrt{64}$ b. $\sqrt{121}$
58. a. $\sqrt{25}$ b. $\sqrt{225}$
59. a. $\sqrt{1}$ b. $\sqrt{324}$
60. a. $\sqrt{100}$ b. $\sqrt{400}$
61. a. $\sqrt{8^2}$ b. $\sqrt{20^2}$
62. a. $\sqrt{12^2}$ b. $\sqrt{45^2}$
63. a. What amount is \$65 less than \$784? b. What amount is \$35 more than \$98?
64. a. What amount is \$79 less than \$487? b. What amount is \$97 more than \$52?

65. a. What amount is $515 increased by $847? b. What amount is $745 decreased by $125?

66. a. What amount is $745 increased by $1,274? b. What amount is $526 decreased by $346?

67. a. If there are 24 pens in a box, how many pens are there in 15 boxes?
    b. A wire of length 420 centimetres is to be cut into 35-centimetre pieces. How many 35-centimetre pieces can be cut?

68. a. If you save $125 every month, how much will you save in one year?
    b. If 8 people can be seated at a dinner table, how many tables are required to seat 280 people?

69. a. If you save $15 a week, how many weeks will it take you to save $675?
    b. If there are 16 chairs in a row, how many chairs are there in 22 rows?

70. a. If you work 25 hours per week, how many weeks will it take you to complete a job that requires 450 hours?
    b. If you earn $18 per hour, how much will you earn in a week in which you have worked 32 hours?

71. Mythili went to a bookstore and bought a dictionary. She gave the cashier a $100 note and received $47 as change. How much did the dictionary cost?

72. There were 744 students in a primary school. In May, after some students left to join another school, 576 students remained. How many students left for the other school?

73. Andy has $1,238 and Bill has $346 less than Andy. How much money do both of them have together?

74. A television costs $649 more than a Blu-ray player. If the Blu-ray player costs $235, how much will it cost to buy the TV and the Blu-ray player?

75. Peter earns $18 per hour. If he worked 25 hours last week, calculate his earning for that week.

76. Sam's overtime rate is $37 per hour. If he worked 29 hours overtime last week, calculate his overtime pay for that week.

77. Earl wants to save $3,150. If he saves $75 per week, how many weeks will it take for him to achieve his goal?

78. How long will it take to travel 1,190 km at 85 km per hour?

79. A large group of students visited an exhibition on Friday. The first 275 students were given one free balloon each. 487 students were disappointed that they did not receive any balloons. How many students visited the exhibition?

80. There were 2,415 boys and 1,875 girls that attended a fair. The first 2,650 visitors to the fair received gifts. How many visitors did not receive gifts?

• 81. There were 450 passengers on a train. Half of them were men, 125 were children, and the rest were women. How many more men than women were there on the train?

• 82. Out of the 3,678 visitors at an art exhibition, 1,469 were men, 1,234 were women, and the rest were children. How many more adults than children went to the exhibition?

• 83. Aran had some money saved up. On his birthday, Aran's grandparents gave him $125. After spending $98 on toys and $75 on clothes, he had $115 remaining. What amount did Aran have in his savings before his birthday?

• 84. Girija had some biscuits. She ate 19 and gave 27 to her brother and 5 to her parents. She had 12 biscuits left. How many biscuits did Girija have originally?

• 85. There are 19 girls in a class of 43 students. 15 of the girls and 11 of the boys are wearing eyeglasses.
    a. How many boys are there in the class?
    b. How many students do not wear eyeglasses?

• 86. There are 22 players on a soccer field. 10 players are wearing blue and 2 are wearing green. The rest of the players are wearing red. How many players are wearing red?

1.3 | Factors and Multiples

Factors of a number are whole numbers that can divide the number evenly (i.e., with no remainder).

For example, to find factors of 12, divide the number 12 by 1, 2, 3, 4,...; the numbers that divide 12 evenly are its factors.

1 is a factor of every number and every number is a factor of itself.

$$12 \div 1 = 12$$
$$12 \div 2 = 6$$
$$12 \div 3 = 4$$
$$12 \div 4 = 3$$
$$12 \div 6 = 2$$
$$12 \div 12 = 1$$

Therefore, 1, 2, 3, 4, 6, and 12 are factors of 12.

A number is **divisible** by another number if it divides evenly with no remainder.

Note: 5, 7, 8, 9, 10, and 11 do not divide 12 evenly. Therefore, they are not factors of 12.

We can also express factors of a number by showing how the product of two factors results in the number.

$12 = 1 \times 12$	or	12×1
$12 = 2 \times 6$	or	6×2
$12 = 3 \times 4$	or	4×3

Multiples of a number are the products of the number and the natural numbers (1, 2, 3, 4,...).

For example, multiples of 10:

$10 \times 1 = 10$ $\quad 10 \times 2 = 20$ $\quad 10 \times 3 = 30$ $\quad 10 \times 4 = 40$ $\quad 10 \times 5 = 50$

Therefore, multiples of 10 are 10, 20, 30, 40, 50, etc.

Note: Multiples of a number can be divided by the number with no remainder.

Prime Numbers and Composite Numbers

A **prime number** is a whole number that has only two factors: 1 and the number itself; i.e., prime numbers can be divided evenly only by 1 and the number itself.

For example, 7 is a prime number because it only has two factors: 1 and 7.

A **composite number** is a whole number that has at least one factor other than 1 and the number itself; i.e., all whole numbers that are not prime numbers are composite numbers.

For example, 8 is a composite number because it has more than two factors: 1, 2, 4, and 8.

Note: 0 and 1 are neither prime numbers nor composite numbers.

Example 1.3-a Identifying Prime Numbers

Identify all the prime numbers less than 25.

Solution

All the prime numbers less than 25 are:

2, 3, 5, 7, 11, 13, 17, 19, and 23.

Example 1.3-b Identifying Composite Numbers

Identify all the composite numbers less than 25.

Solution

All the composite numbers less than 25 are:

4, 6, 8, 9, 10, 12, 14, 15, 16, 18, 20, 21, 22, and 24.

Example 1.3-c **Finding Factors of Prime Numbers**

Find all the factors of 13.

Solution

1 and 13 are the only factors of 13.

Example 1.3-d **Finding All Factors of Composite Numbers**

Find all the factors of:

(i) 16 (ii) 20

Solution

(i) The factors of 16 are: 1, 2, 4, 8, and 16. (ii) The factors of 20 are: 1, 2, 4, 5, 10, and 20.

Example 1.3-e **Finding the Prime Factors of Composite Numbers**

Find all the prime factors of 24.

Solution

All the factors of 24 are: 1, 2, 3, 4, 6, 8, 12, and 24.

Of the above factors, only 2 and 3 are prime numbers.

Therefore, the prime factors of 24 are 2 and 3.

Factor Tree

A factor tree helps to find all of the prime factors of a number. It also shows the number of times that each prime factor appears when writing that number as a product of its prime factors.

The following steps illustrate creating a factor tree for the number 24:

Step 1: Write 24. Draw two short lines down from the number at diverging angles, as shown.

24

Step 2: 24 is divisible by the first prime number 2; i.e. $24 = 2 \times 12$.

Write these factors at the end of the two lines. Now 24 is at the top and 2×12 is the 2nd layer below it, as shown.

24

2×12

Step 3: Now, 12 is divisible by the prime number 2; i.e. $12 = 2 \times 6$.

Write these factors below 12; i.e., the 3rd layer is $2 \times 2 \times 6$, as shown.

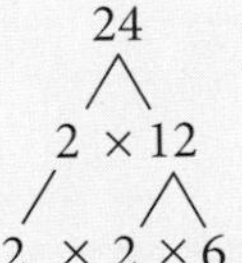

Step 4: Next, 6 is divisible by the prime number 2; i.e. $6 = 2 \times 3$.

Write these factors below 6; i.e., the 4th layer is $2 \times 2 \times 2 \times 3$, as shown.

Step 5: The factors at the 4th layer are all prime numbers and cannot be factored any more. Therefore, writing 24 as a product of its prime factors: $24 = 2 \times 2 \times 2 \times 3$.

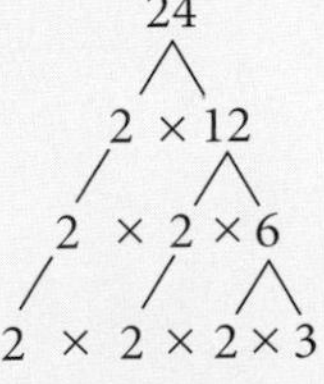

Note: It is not necessary to do every step starting with a prime number. You may start with any two factors that multiply together to get the number.

For example, $24 = 4 \times 6$

Then continue factoring until you are left with only prime numbers on the bottom layer, as shown. The answer will be same.

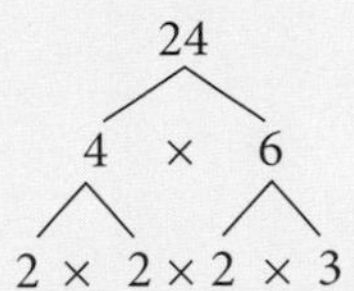

Least or Lowest Common Multiple (LCM)

LCM is the smallest integer that is a common multiple of two or more numbers.

The **Least Common Multiple (LCM)** of two or more whole numbers is the smallest multiple that is common to those numbers. The LCM can be determined using one of the following methods:

Method 1:

- First, select the largest number and check to see if it is divisible by all the other numbers. If it divides, then the largest number is the LCM.

  For example, in finding the LCM of 2, 3, and 12, the largest number 12 is divisible by the other numbers 2 and 3. Therefore, the LCM of 2, 3, and 12 is 12.

- If none of the numbers have a common factor, then the LCM of the numbers is the product of all the numbers.

  For example, in finding the LCM of 2, 5, and 7, none of these numbers have a common factor. Therefore, the LCM of 2, 5, and 7 is $2 \times 5 \times 7 = 70$.

- If the largest number is not divisible by the other numbers and there is a common factor between some of the numbers, then find a multiple of the largest number that is divisible by all the other numbers.

  For example, in finding the LCM of 3, 5, and 10, the largest number 10 is not divisible by 3, and 5 and 10 have a common factor of 5. Multiples of 10 are 10, 20, 30, 40, etc. 30 is divisible by both 3 and 5. Therefore, the LCM of 3, 5, and 10 is 30.

A number is divisible by 2 if the last digit of the number ends in a 0, 2, 4, 6, or 8.

A number is divisible by 3 if the sum of all the digits of a number is divisble by 3.

A number is divisible by 5 if the last digit of the number is a 0 or 5.

Method 2:

Step 1: Find the prime factors of each of the numbers using a factor tree and list the different prime numbers.

Step 2: Count the number of times each different prime number appears in each of the factorizations.

Step 3: Find the largest of these counts for each prime number.

Step 4: List each prime number as many times as you counted it in Step 3. The LCM is the product of all the prime numbers listed.

Example 1.3-f **Finding the Least Common Multiple**

Find the LCM of 9 and 15.

Solution

Method 1: The largest number, 15, is **not** divisible by 9.

Multiples of 15 are: 15, 30, 45...

45 is divisible by 9.

Therefore, 45 is the LCM of 9 and 15.

Method 2:

1	9 → 3×3	15 → 3×5
2	Number of 3's = 2	Number of 3's = 1 Number of 5's = 1
3	Largest count for the prime number 3 = 2 Largest count for the prime number 5 = 1	
4	LCM = $3 \times 3 \times 5 = 45$	

Example 1.3-g **Finding the Least Common Multiple**

Find the LCM of 3, 5, and 8.

Solution

Method 1: The largest number, 8, is **not** divisible by 3 and 5.

Since 3, 5, and 8 have no common factors, the LCM is the product of the three numbers: $3 \times 5 \times 8 = 120$.

Therefore, 120 is the LCM of 3, 5, and 8.

Method 2:

1

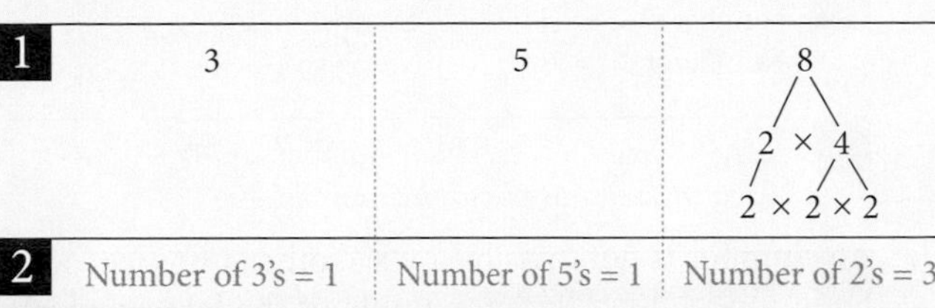

2 Number of 3's = 1 | Number of 5's = 1 | Number of 2's = 3

3 Largest count for the prime number 2 = 3
Largest count for the prime number 3 = 1
Largest count for the prime number 5 = 1

4 LCM = $2 \times 2 \times 2 \times 3 \times 5 = 120$

Example 1.3-h **Finding the Least Common Multiple**

Find the LCM of 3, 6, and 18.

Solution

Method 1: The largest number, 18, is divisible by both 6 and 3.
Therefore, 18 is the LCM of 3, 6, and 18.

Method 2:

1

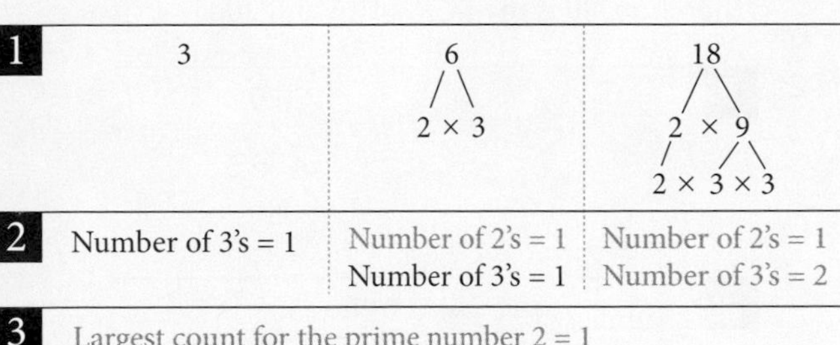

2 Number of 3's = 1 | Number of 2's = 1, Number of 3's = 1 | Number of 2's = 1, Number of 3's = 2

3 Largest count for the prime number 2 = 1
Largest count for the prime number 3 = 2

4 LCM = $2 \times 3 \times 3 = 18$

Example 1.3-i **Finding the Least Common Multiple**

Find the LCM of 24, 36, and 48.

Solution

Method 1: The largest number, 48, is divisible by 24 but **not** by 36.
Multiples of 48 are: 48, 96, 144, ...
144 is divisible by both 24 and 36.
Therefore, 144 is the LCM of 24, 36, and 48.

Solution *continued*

Method 2:

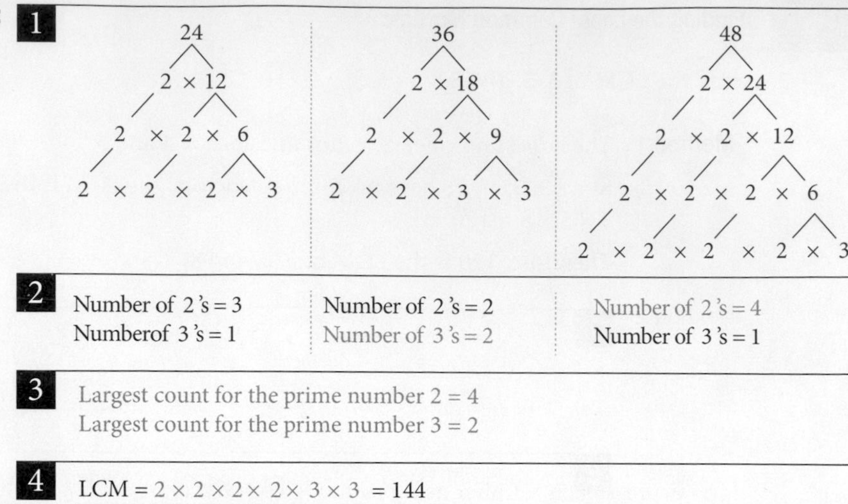

1. (Factor trees for 24, 36 and 48)

2. Number of 2's = 3, Number of 3's = 1 | Number of 2's = 2, Number of 3's = 2 | Number of 2's = 4, Number of 3's = 1

3. Largest count for the prime number 2 = 4
Largest count for the prime number 3 = 2

4. LCM = $2 \times 2 \times 2 \times 2 \times 3 \times 3 = 144$

Example 1.3-j **Finding the Least Common Multiple to Solve a Word Problem**

Two flashing lights are turned on at the same time. One light flashes every 16 seconds and the other flashes every 20 seconds. How often will they flash together?

Solution

In this example, we are required to find the least common interval for both lights to flash together. Thereafter, both lights will continue to flash together at this interval (multiple).

Method 1: The largest number, 20, is **not** divisible by 16.

Multiples of 20 are: 20, 40, 60, 80,...

80 is divisble by 16.

Therefore, 80 is the LCM of 16 and 20.

Method 2:

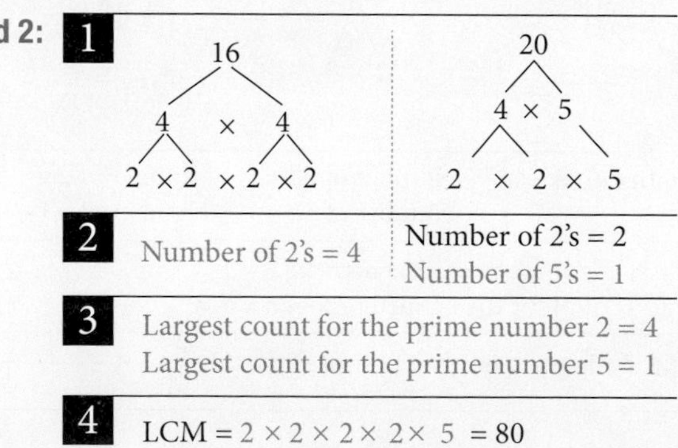

1. (Factor trees for 16 and 20)

2. Number of 2's = 4 | Number of 2's = 2, Number of 5's = 1

3. Largest count for the prime number 2 = 4
Largest count for the prime number 5 = 1

4. LCM = $2 \times 2 \times 2 \times 2 \times 5 = 80$

Therefore, the two flashing lights will flash together every 80 seconds.

Greatest Common Factor (GCF)

GCF is the largest integer that divides the set of numbers without remainder.

The factors that are common to two or more numbers are called **common factors** of those numbers.

The **Greatest Common Factor (GCF)** of two or more numbers is the largest common number that divides the numbers with no remainder. In other words, the GCF is the largest of all the common factors.

The GCF can be determined using one of the following methods:

Method 1:

First list all the factors of all the numbers. Then select all the common factors of the numbers. The highest value of the common factors is the GCF.

For example, in finding the GCF of 12 and 18:

- The factors of 12 are 1, 2, 3, 4, 6, and 12.
- The factors of 18 are 1, 2, 3, 6, 9, and 18.

The common factors are 2, 3, and 6.

Therefore, the GCF is 6.

*Note: 1 is a factor that is common to **all** numbers, and therefore we do not bother to include it in the list of common factors. If there are no common factors other than 1, then 1 is the greatest common factor.*

For example, 1 is the only common factor of 3, 5, 7, and 9, and therefore the GCF = 1.

Method 2:

First express each number as a product of prime factors. Then identify the set of prime factors that is common to **all** the numbers (including repetitions). The product of these prime factors is the GCF.

For example, in finding the GCF of 12 and 18:

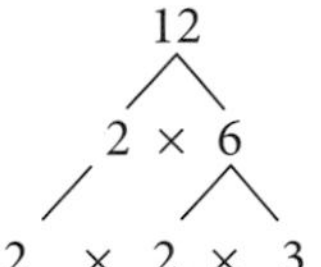

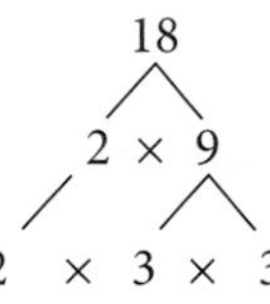

Number	Prime Factors of:	
	2	3
12	2, 2	3
18	2	3, 3

The set of prime factors which is common to 12 and 18 is one 2 and one 3.

Therefore, the GCF is 2 × 3 = 6.

Example 1.3-k **Finding the Greatest Common Factor**

Find the GCF of 36 and 60.

Solution

Method 1: Factors of 36 are: 1, 2, 3, 4, 6, 9, 12, 18, and 36.

Factors of 60 are: 1, 2, 3, 4, 5, 6, 10, 12, 15, 20, 30, and 60.

The common factors are: 2, 3, 4, 6, and 12.

Therefore, the GCF is 12.

Method 2:

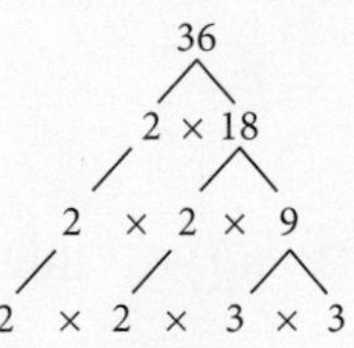

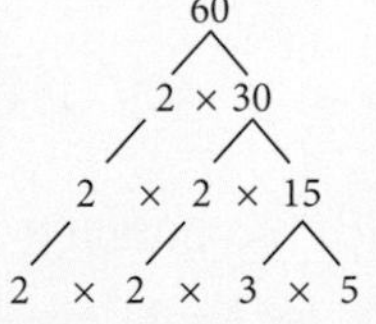

Number	Prime Factors of:		
	2	3	5
36	2, 2	3, 3	
60	2, 2	3	5

The set of prime factors which is common to 36 and 60 is two 2's and one 3. Therefore, the GCF is 2 × 2 × 3 = 12.

Example 1.3-l **Finding the Greatest Common Factor**

Find the GCF of 72, 126, and 216.

Solution

Method 1: Factors of 72 are: 1, 2, 3, 4, 6, 8, 9, 12, 18, 24, 36, and 72.

Factors of 126 are: 1, 2, 3, 6, 7, 9, 14, 18, 21, 42, 63, and 126.

Factors of 216 are: 1, 2, 3, 4, 6, 8, 9, 12, 18, 24, 27, 36, 54, 72, 108, and 216.

The common factors are: 2, 3, 6, 9, and 18.

Therefore, the GCF is 18.

Solution
continued

Method 2:

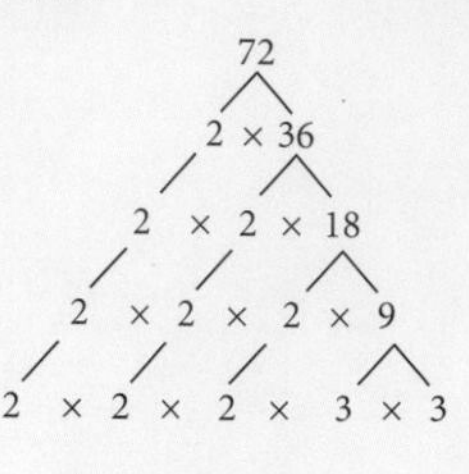

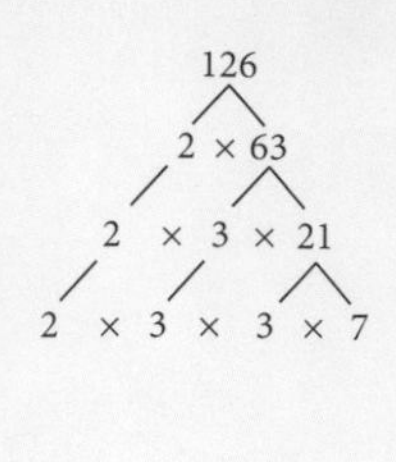

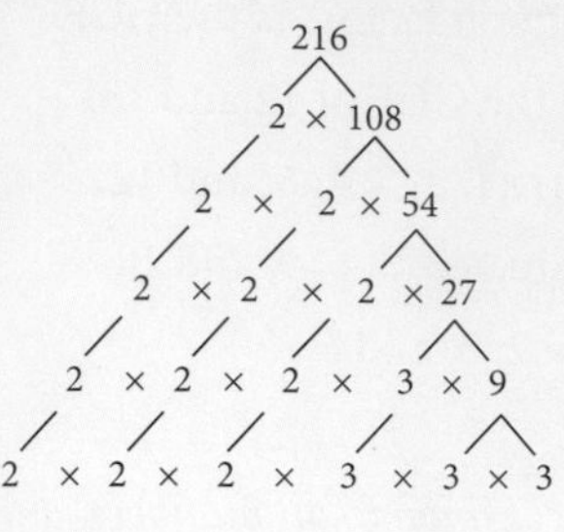

Number	Prime Factors of:		
	2	3	7
72	2, 2, 2	3, 3	
126	2	3, 3	7
216	2, 2, 2	3, 3, 3	

The set of prime factors which is common to 72, 126, and 216 is one 2 and two 3's.

Therefore, the GCF is $2 \times 3 \times 3 = 18$.

Example 1.3-m

Finding the Greatest Common Factor to Solve a Word Problem

Three pieces of timber with lengths 48 cm, 72 cm, and 96 cm are to be cut into smaller pieces of equal length without remainders.

(i) What is the greatest possible length of each piece?

(ii) How many pieces of such equal lengths are possible?

Solution

Method 1: Factors of 48 are: 1, 2, 3, 4, 6, 8, 12, 16, 24, and 48.

Factors of 72 are: 1, 2, 3, 4, 6, 8, 9, 12, 18, 24, 36, and 72.

Factors of 96 are: 1, 2, 3, 4, 6, 8, 12, 16, 24, 32, 48, and 96.

The common factors are: 2, 3, 4, 6, 8, 12, and 24.

Therefore, the GCF is 24.

Method 2:

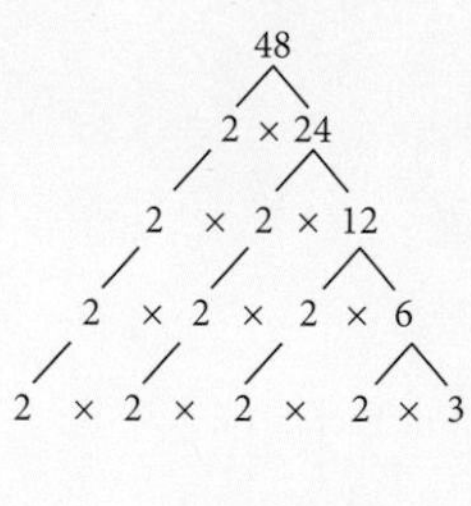

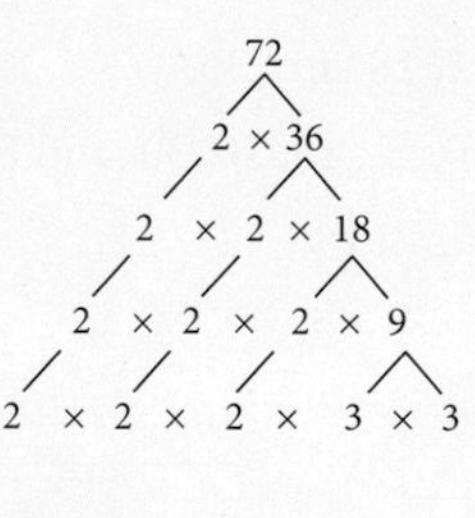

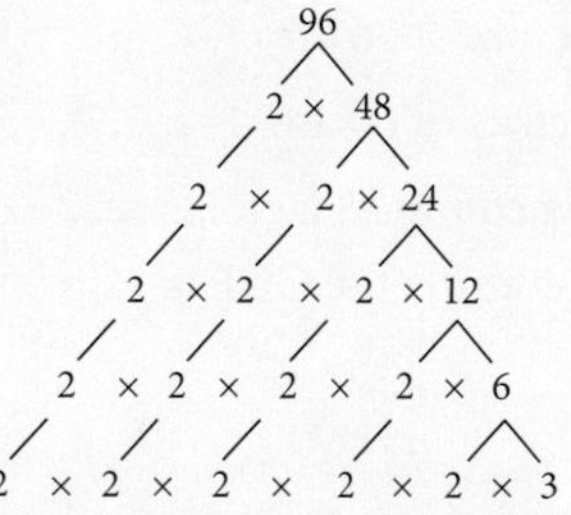

Number	Prime Factors of:	
	2	3
48	2, 2, 2, 2	3
72	2, 2, 2	3, 3
96	2, 2, 2, 2, 2	3

The set of prime factors which is common to 48, 72, and 96 is three 2's and one 3.

Therefore, the GCF $= 2 \times 2 \times 2 \times 3 = 24$.

(i) Therefore, the greatest possible length of each piece is 24 cm.

(ii) The total number of equal pieces is the number of multiples of 24 cm in each piece:

$$48 = 24 \times 2$$

$$72 = 24 \times 3$$

$$96 = 24 \times 4$$

Therefore, the total number of equal pieces of 24 cm possible is $2 + 3 + 4 = 9$.

1.3 | Exercises

Answers to odd-numbered problems are available at the end of the textbook.

1. List all the prime numbers less than 20.
2. List all the prime numbers between 20 and 40.
3. List all the composite numbers greater than 10 and less than 30.
4. List all the composite numbers greater than 30 and less than 50.
5. Identify the prime numbers in the given sets of numbers: a. 13, 19, 36, 47, 49 b. 11, 14, 29, 35, 43
6. Identify the prime numbers in the given sets of numbers: a. 31, 39, 41, 59, 63 b. 23, 37, 45, 51, 53

For Problems 7 to 14, (i) find all the factors and (ii) list the prime factors of the numbers.

7. a. 15 b. 34
8. a. 18 b. 35
9. a. 64 b. 54
10. a. 56 b. 60
11. a. 21 b. 25
12. a. 30 b. 42
13. a. 36 b. 65
14. a. 40 b. 49

For Problems 15 to 18, find the first six multiples of the numbers.

15. a. 6 b. 8
16. a. 5 b. 12
17. a. 9 b. 10
18. a. 7 b. 15

For Problems 19 to 24, find the least common multiple (LCM) of each pair of the numbers.

19. a. 10, 15 b. 15, 18
20. a. 12, 16 b. 21, 36
21. a. 18, 24 b. 35, 45
22. a. 10, 25 b. 45, 60
23. a. 16, 64 b. 8, 60
24. a. 12, 90 b. 25, 30

For Problems 25 to 32, find the least common multiple (LCM) of the sets of numbers.

25. a. 2, 3, 8 b. 4, 9, 10
26. a. 8, 5, 12 b. 5, 15, 20
27. a. 10, 15, 25 b. 6, 27, 36
28. a. 4, 8, 40 b. 3, 16, 2
29. a. 14, 21, 28 b. 3, 18, 27
30. a. 4, 6, 21 b. 12, 28, 42
31. a. 24, 36, 12 b. 6, 15, 18
32. a. 5, 12, 15 b. 12, 40, 48

For Problems 33 to 38, find the (i) factors, (ii) common factors, and (iii) greatest common factor (GCF) of each pair of numbers.

33. a. 15, 25 b. 18, 32
34. a. 14, 35 b. 8, 36
35. a. 18, 48 b. 32, 60
36. a. 16, 30 b. 36, 42
37. a. 25, 80 b. 40, 120
38. a. 35, 75 b. 24, 64

For Problems 39 to 44, find the (i) factors, (ii) common factors, and (iii) greatest common factor (GCF) of the sets of numbers.

39. a. 8, 12, 15 b. 6, 15, 20
40. a. 6, 8, 10 b. 10, 15, 25
41. a. 12, 18, 24 b. 12, 30, 42
42. a. 24, 36, 40 b. 12, 36, 48
43. a. 40, 50, 80 b. 30, 75, 90
44. a. 50, 75, 125 b. 60, 90, 120
45. Two wires of lengths 96 cm and 160 cm are to be cut into pieces of equal length, without wastage. Find the greatest possible length of each piece.
46. Two ribbons of lengths 112 cm and 154 cm are to be cut into pieces of equal length, without wastage. Find the greatest possible length of each piece.
47. Tahrell has music lessons every 6th day and swimming lessons every 8th day. If he had music and swimming lessons on February 4th, on which date will he have both lessons again?
48. Enea has skating lessons every 8th day and ballet lessons every 10th day. If she had skating and ballet lessons on March 3rd, on which date will she have both lessons again?

• 49. Three wires measuring 18 m, 45 m, and 36 m are to be cut into pieces of equal length, without wastage. What is the maximum possible length of each piece?

• 50. A store has 54 green marbles, 72 yellow marbles, and 90 red marbles. The owner decides to package all the marbles into bags, such that each bag contains the same number of marbles. As well, each bag has to contain marbles of the same colour. Find the maximum possible number of marbles in each bag.

• 51. Three lights, red, blue, and green, flash at intervals of 15, 18, and 40 seconds, respectively. If they begin flashing at the same time, how long will it take (in minutes) until all three flash at the same time again?

• 52. Three bells ring simultaneously. If they ring at intervals of 24, 36, and 40 seconds, respectively, how long will it take (in minutes) until they ring together again?

1.4 | Order of Operations

In this chapter, we have learned how to perform addition, subtraction, multiplication, division, powers, and square roots with whole numbers. In this section, we will learn the correct order (or sequence) for performing the combined arithmetic operations of whole numbers.

When there are no groupings (operations within brackets or a radical sign), the six arithmetic operations are performed in the following sequence:

1. Exponents (Powers) and Roots
2. Division and Multiplication, in order from left to right
3. Addition and Subtraction, in order from left to right

Example 1.4-a **Evaluating Expressions with Mixed Arithmetic Operations**

Evaluate the following arithmetic expressions:

(i) $16 \div 2^2 + 44 - 3^3$ (ii) $12 \div 3 \times 2 + 5^2$

Solution

(i) $16 \div \mathbf{2^2} + 44 - \mathbf{3^3}$ Evaluating the exponents,

$= \mathbf{16 \div 4} + 44 - 27$ Dividing,

$= \mathbf{4 + 44} - 27$
$= \mathbf{48 - 27}$ } Adding and subtracting from left to right,

$= 21$

(ii) $12 \div 3 \times 2 + \mathbf{5^2}$ Evaluating the exponent,

$= \mathbf{12 \div 3} \times 2 + 25$
$= \mathbf{4 \times 2} + 25$ } Dividing and multiplying from left to right,

$= \mathbf{8 + 25}$ Adding,

$= 33$

When there are groupings, the arithmetic operations within the groupings are to be evaluated first. Common symbols used for groupings are brackets ( ), [ ], { }, and the radical sign $\sqrt{\ }$.

When there are groupings with more than one bracket, start by evaluating the innermost bracket, and move outwards to evaluate all expressions within the brackets by following the order of operations explained earlier.

In summary, arithmetic expressions that contain multiple operations, with brackets, exponents, divisons, multiplications, additions, and subtractions, are performed in the following sequence:

1. Brackets
2. Exponents (Powers) and Roots
3. Division and Multiplication, in order from left to right
4. Addition and Subtraction, in order from left to right

The above Order of Operations, Brackets, Exponents, Division and Multiplication, and Addition and Subtraction, can be remembered by the following acronym:

B E D M A S

D M: Performed together, in order from left to right

A S: Performed together, in order from left to right

Example 1.4-b **Evaluating Expressions with Square Roots**

Evaluate the following expressions:

(i) $\sqrt{49} + \sqrt{25}$ (ii) $\sqrt{64} - \sqrt{16}$ (iii) $\sqrt{4} \times \sqrt{9}$

Solution

(i) $\sqrt{49} + \sqrt{25}$ Evaluating the square roots,

$= 7 + 5$ Adding,

$= 12$

(ii) $\sqrt{64} - \sqrt{16}$ Evaluating the square roots,

$= 8 - 4$ Subtracting,

$= 4$

(iii) $\sqrt{4} \times \sqrt{9}$ Evaluating the square roots,

$= 2 \times 3$ Multiplying,

$= 6$

Example 1.4-c **Evaluating Expressions with Square Roots**

Evaluate the following expressions:

(i) $5 \times \sqrt{121}$ (ii) $\sqrt{100} \div 5$ (iii) $35 + \sqrt{49} - \sqrt{9}$

Solution

(i) $5 \times \sqrt{121}$ Evaluating the square root,

$= 5 \times 11$ Multiplying,

$= 55$

(ii) $\sqrt{100} \div 5$ Evaluating the square root,

$= 10 \div 5$ Dividing,

$= 2$

(iii) $35 + \sqrt{49} - \sqrt{9}$ Evaluating the square roots,

$= 35 + 7 - 3$ Adding and subtracting from left to right,

$= 39$

Example 1.4-d Evaluating Expressions with Groupings

Evaluate the following arithmetic expressions:

(i) $4 \times 50 \div (8 - 3)^2 - 1$

(ii) $(100 - 3 \times 24) + 8(6 - 3) \div 6$

(iii) $\sqrt{3^2 + 4^2} \times (7 - 4) + 2$

(iv) $35 \div 7 + \sqrt{4^2 + 9}$

(v) $4^2 - \sqrt{13^2 - 5^2} + 3^2\sqrt{25}$

Solution

(i) $4 \times 50 \div \mathbf{(8 - 3)}^2 - 1$ — Evaluating the operation within the bracket,

$= 4 \times 50 \div \mathbf{5^2} - 1$ — Evaluating the exponent,

$= \mathbf{4 \times 50} \div 25 - 1$

$= \mathbf{200 \div 25} - 1$ — Dividing and multiplying from left to right,

$= \mathbf{8 - 1}$ — Subtracting,

$= 7$

(ii) $(100 - \mathbf{3 \times 24}) + 8\mathbf{(6 - 3)} \div 6$

$= \mathbf{(100 - 72)} + 8(3) \div 6$ — Evaluating the operations within the brackets in the order of operations,

$= 28 + \mathbf{8(3)} \div 6$

$= 28 + \mathbf{24 \div 6}$ — Dividing and multiplying from left to right,

$= \mathbf{28 + 4}$ — Adding,

$= 32$

(iii) $\sqrt{\mathbf{3^2 + 4^2}} \times \mathbf{(7 - 4)} + 2$

$= \sqrt{\mathbf{9 + 16}} \times 3 + 2$ — Evaluating the operations within the groupings (radical sign and bracket) in the order of operations,

$= \sqrt{\mathbf{25}} \times 3 + 2$ — Evaluating the square root,

$= \mathbf{5 \times 3} + 2$ — Multiplying,

$= \mathbf{15 + 2}$ — Adding,

$= 17$

(iv) $35 \div 7 + \sqrt{\mathbf{4^2 + 9}}$

$= 35 \div 7 + \sqrt{\mathbf{16 + 9}}$ — Evaluating the operations within the radical sign in the order of operations,

$= 35 \div 7 + \sqrt{\mathbf{25}}$ — Evaluating the square root,

$= \mathbf{35 \div 7} + 5$ — Dividing,

$= \mathbf{5 + 5}$ — Adding,

$= 10$

(v) $4^2 - \sqrt{\mathbf{13^2 - 5^2}} + 3^2\sqrt{25}$

$= 4^2 - \sqrt{\mathbf{169 - 25}} + 3^2\sqrt{25}$ — Evaluating the operations within the radical sign in the order of operations,

$= \mathbf{4^2} - \sqrt{\mathbf{144}} + \mathbf{3^2}\sqrt{\mathbf{25}}$ — Evaluating the exponents and square roots,

$= 16 - 12 + \mathbf{9 \times 5}$ — Multiplying,

$= \mathbf{16 - 12} + 45$

$= \mathbf{4 + 45}$ — Adding and subtracting from left to right,

$= 49$

Example 1.4-e **Evaluating Expressions with More than One Bracket**

Evaluate the following arithmetic expressions:

(i) $4 \times 50 \div [(8-3)^2 - 5]$ (ii) $100 - 3\,[24 \div 2(6-3)] \div 2$ (iii) $[10^2 \times 4 + 50] \div [(8-3)^2 - 4^2]$

Solution

(i) $4 \times 50 \div [(\mathbf{8-3})^2 - 5]$ — Evaluating the operation within the inner bracket,

$= 4 \times 50 \div [\mathbf{5^2} - 5]$

$= 4 \times 50 \div [\mathbf{25 - 5}]$

— Evaluating the operations within the outer bracket in the order of operations,

$= \mathbf{4 \times 50} \div 20$

$= \mathbf{200 \div 20}$

— Dividing and multiplying from left to right,

$= 10$

(ii) $100 - 3\,[24 \div 2(\mathbf{6-3})] \div 2$ — Evaluating the operation within the inner bracket,

$= 100 - 3[\mathbf{24 \div 2} \times 3] \div 2$

$= 100 - 3[\mathbf{12 \times 3}] \div 2$

— Dividing and multiplying from left to right within the outer bracket,

$= 100 - \mathbf{3 \times 36} \div 2$

$= 100 - \mathbf{108 \div 2}$

— Dividing and multiplying from left to right,

$= \mathbf{100 - 54}$ — Subtracting,

$= 46$

(iii) $[10^2 \times 4 + 50] \div [(\mathbf{8-3})^2 - 4^2]$ — Evaluating the operation within the inner bracket,

$= [\mathbf{10^2} \times 4 + 50] \div [\mathbf{5^2} - \mathbf{4^2}]$ — Evaluating the exponents within the brackets,

$= [\mathbf{100 \times 4 + 50}] \div [\mathbf{25 - 16}]$

$= [\mathbf{400 + 50}] \div 9$

— Evaluating the operations within the brackets in the order of operations,

$= \mathbf{450 \div 9}$ — Dividing,

$= 50$

1.4 | Exercises

Answers to odd-numbered problems are available at the end of the textbook.

For Problems 1 to 12, evaluate the expressions with mixed arithmetic operations.

1. a. $5 \times 4 + 25 \div 25$ b. $64 \div 8 \times 2$
2. a. $7 \times 5 + 20 \div 4$ b. $36 \div 4 \times 9$
3. a. $100 \div 25 \times 4$ b. $18 \div 2 \times 3 + 5$
4. a. $80 \div 10 \times 8$ b. $50 \times 2 \times 5 + 10$
5. a. $32 \div 4 \div 2 \times 4$ b. $96 \div 12 \times 2 + 4$
6. a. $20 \div 4 \times 5 + 2$ b. $56 \div 4 \div 2 \times 5$
7. a. $4^2 \times 2^4$ b. $3^2 \times 2^3$
8. a. $5^2 \times 2^3$ b. $4^2 \times 3^3$
9. a. $2^3 + 3^3$ b. $5^2 - 4^2$
10. a. $5^2 + 6^2$ b. $8^2 - 6^2$
11. a. $6^2 \times 2 - 2$ b. $100 - 5^2 \times 3$
12. a. $5^2 \times 3 - 15$ b. $144 - 3^3 \times 4$

For Problems 13 to 22, evaluate the expressions with square roots.

13. a. $\sqrt{100} + \sqrt{25}$ b. $\sqrt{81} - \sqrt{16}$
14. a. $\sqrt{121} + \sqrt{36}$ b. $\sqrt{144} - \sqrt{9}$
15. a. $\sqrt{9 \times 16}$ b. $\sqrt{36 \times 49}$
16. a. $\sqrt{25 \times 64}$ b. $\sqrt{81 \times 121}$
17. a. $\sqrt{40 - 24}$ b. $\sqrt{75 - 11}$
18. a. $\sqrt{125 - 76}$ b. $\sqrt{48 - 23}$
19. a. $\sqrt{3^2 + 4^2}$ b. $\sqrt{13^2 - 5^2}$
20. a. $\sqrt{5^2 - 4^2}$ b. $\sqrt{12^2 + 5^2}$
21. a. $\sqrt{100 \div 25}$ b. $\sqrt{196 \div 4}$
22. a. $\sqrt{256 \div 4}$ b. $\sqrt{225 \div 25}$

For Problems 23 to 46, evaluate the expressions with groupings.

23. a. $(7 - 4)^2$ b. $(3 + 2)^3$

24. a. $(8 - 5)^3$ b. $(4 + 1)^2$

25. a. $5^2 \sqrt{16} + 10 - 2$ b. $19 - 2^2 \sqrt{9} + 3$

26. a. $40 - 3^2 \sqrt{16} + 1$ b. $6^2 \sqrt{25} + 16 - \sqrt{100}$

27. a. $(4 + 3)^2 - 5^2 + 2^3$ b. $6^2 + 2^3 - (12 - 8)^2$

28. a. $(9 - 6)^2 - 2^2 + 3^3$ b. $3^2 + 2^4 - (15 - 9)^2$

29. $12^2 - 5 \times 27 \div (5 - 2)^2 - 3$

30. $16 \div 8 \times 10^2 + (12 - 7)^2 \times 2$

31. $3^2[(9 - 6)^2 \div 9 + 7 - 4]$

32. $3^2[(12^2 + 8)^2 \div 4 + 6 - 2]$

33. $7 + (3\sqrt{49} - 1)^2$

34. $15 + (5\sqrt{10^2} - 8)^2$

35. $16 \div \sqrt{64} + \sqrt{10^2 - 6^2}$

36. $\sqrt{12^2 + 5^2} - 27 \div \sqrt{81}$

37. $[(20 \div 5) \times 8] \div (2^2 + 4)$

38. $[(6^2 \div 4) \times 5] \div (2^2 + 5)$

39. $(64 \div 8 \div 4)^2 + (3^2 + 6^0)$

40. $(81 \div 9 \div 3)^2 + (9^0 + 2^2)$

41. $[(11 - 2)^2 + 3] + (16 \div 2)^2$

42. $(20 \div 2)^2 + [(13 - 6) + 4^2]$

43. $(45 - \sqrt{9^2 + 12^2}) \div (4^2 - \sqrt{36})$

44. $(27 + \sqrt{15^2 - 12^2}) \div (5^2 - \sqrt{49})$

45. $\sqrt{144} - 3^2 + (64 \div 4^2)^2 \div (18 \div 3^2)$

46. $\sqrt{81} + 2^2 - (36 \div 3^2)^2 \div (16 \div 2^2)$

1 | Review Exercises

Answers to odd-numbered problems are available at the end of the textbook.

For Problems 1 and 2, write the numbers in (i) expanded form and (ii) word form.

1. a. 7,502 b. 25,047 c. 620,025 d. 3,054,705

2. a. 9,024 b. 38,024 c. 405,037 d. 2,601,071

For Problems 3 and 4, write the the numbers in (i) standard form and (ii) expanded form.

3. a. Five thousand, six hundred seven
b. Thirty-seven thousand, forty
c. Four hundred eight thousand, one hundred five
d. One million, seventy thousand, fifty-five

4. a. Nine thousand, nine hundred three
b. Fifty-nine thousand, three hundred three
c. Seven hundred thousand, eight hundred eighty-eight
d. Seven million, seventy-six thousand, fifty-five

For Problems 5 and 6, insert the proper sign of inequality (< or >) between each pair of numbers.

5. a. 167 ☐ 176 b. 2,067 ☐ 2,097 c. 79,084 ☐ 79,087 d. 162,555 ☐ 162,507

6. a. 159 ☐ 139 b. 1,838 ☐ 1,868 c. 52,109 ☐ 51,889 d. 379,847 ☐ 397,487

For Problems 7 and 8, (i) estimate the answer by rounding each number to the nearest hundred, and (ii) calculate the exact answer.

7. a. 3,495 + 276 + 85 b. 5,555 + 157 + 60 c. 7,836 – 655 d. 6,405 – 2,769

8. a. 8,655 + 348 + 75 b. 3,450 + 645 + 50 c. 5,245 – 876 d. 2,056 – 444

For Problems 9 and 10, perform the arithmetic operation.

9. a. 465×23 b. 365×24 c. $315 \div 5$ d. $2{,}532 \div 12$

10. a. 345×34 b. 237×25 c. $276 \div 6$ d. $4{,}785 \div 15$

For Problems 11 and 12, find the LCM of the numbers.

11. a. 12 and 20 b. 16 and 72 c. 16, 18, and 33

12. a. 16 and 40 b. 36 and 54 c. 8, 24, and 32

For Problems 13 and 14, find the GCF of the numbers.

13. a. 8 and 12 b. 42 and 48 c. 24, 30, and 32

14. a. 4 and 9 b. 40 and 72 c. 12, 16, and 60

For Problems 15 to 28, perform the arithmetic operations.

15. a. $6 + 8 - 6 \times 2 \div 4$ b. $15 - (7 - 5) \div 2$

16. a. $9 + 2 - 4 \times 3 \div 2$ b. $10 - (7 - 4) \div 3$

17. a. $12 - 2(9 - 6) + 10 \div 5 + 5$ b. $9 - 8(7 - 5) \div (6 + 2)$

18. a. $8 - 4(6 - 4) + 16 \div 4 + 4$ b. $10 - 4(9 - 7) \div (5 + 3)$

19. a. $8(7 + 3) + 6^2 \div 4$ b. $8^2 \div 4 - 6(5 - 3)$

20. a. $7(6 + 4) + 4^2 \div 2$ b. $9^2 \div 3(8 - 5) - 4(5 + 3)$

21. a. $24 \div 2^2 \times 3 + (5 - 2)^2$ b. $8(7 - 3)^2 \div 4 - 5$

22. a. $64 \div (8 - 4)^2 + 5^2$ b. $9(8 - 5) \div 3 + (7 - 4)^2$

23. a. $(16 + 4 \times 2) \div (4^2 - 8)$ b. $6^2 - 2[(6 - 3)^2 + 4]$

24. a. $(6 + 3 \times 2) \div (2^2 - 1)$ b. $8^2 - 3[(7 - 3)^2 + 2]$

25. a. $\sqrt{9} - (8 - 5) + 10 \div 5 + 7$
b. $15 - 15(8 - 6) \div \sqrt{36} + 15$

26. a. $\sqrt{49} - 7(6 - 4) \div (5 - 3)$
b. $\sqrt{16} + (10 - 7) + 20 \div 4 - 3$

27. a. $6^2 \div 9 + 6(5^2 - 2^2)$
b. $3[(7 - 4)^2 + 4] - (2 + 3)^2$

28. a. $5(12^2 - 2^2) + 48 \div 4^2$
b. $(6 + 2)^2 - 4[(12 - 9)^2 + 3]$

29. After Martha gave 175 stamps to her brother, she had 698 stamps left. How many stamps did she have at the beginning?

30. Amy spent $349 and had $167 left. How much did she have at the beginning?

31. Each ticket for a concert costs $25. A total of $35,000 was collected from ticket sales for Saturday and Sunday. If 550 tickets were sold on Saturday, how many were sold on Sunday?

32. A company manufactured printers for $40 a unit. Over two weeks, $46,000 was spent on manufacturing printers. If 500 printers were manufactured in the first week, how many printers were manufactured in the second week?

33. At a concert, 245 tickets were sold for $125 each and 325 tickets were sold for $68 each. How much money was collected altogether?

34. Susie held a bake sale. She sold 45 cookies for $2 each and 63 brownies for $3 each. How much money did she make altogether?

35. Allan and Babar have a total of $2,550. Allan has $800 more than Babar. How much money does each of them have?

36. Ayesha saved $5,500 more than Beth. If they saved $32,450 together, how much did each of them save?

• 37. An elevator can carry a maximum of 540 kg. Two workers want to move 20 boxes of tiles, each weighing 24 kg. One of the workers weighs 72 kg and the other weighs 65 kg. What is the largest number of boxes that can be carried in the elevator if both workers are in it?

• 38. A delivery truck can carry a maximum of 2,000 kg. Two workers want to move 100 planks of wood, each weighing 30 kg. One of the workers weighs 85 kg and the other weighs 77 kg. What is the largest number of planks that can be carried by the truck if both workers are in the truck?

• 39. Three balls of yarn measuring 24 metres, 60 metres, and 36 metres are to be cut into pieces of equal lengths, without wastage. What is the maximum possible length of each piece?

• 40. A store has 32 oranges, 48 bananas, and 72 apples. The owner decides to make fruit baskets each containing an equal number of fruits, without any left over. It was required that each basket have only one type of fruit in it. Find the maximum possible number of fruits in each basket.

• 41. Amy, Bob, and Cathy go for a swim every 3rd, 7th, and 14th day, respectively. If they met each other on a particular day at the pool, how many days later would they meet again?

• 42. Three gentlemen decided to go for a walk around a circular park. The first man takes 6 minutes, the second takes 10 minutes, and the third takes 8 minutes. If they start together, when will they meet again?

Self-Test | Chapter 1

Answers to all problems are available at the end of the textbook.

For Problem 1, (i) estimate the answer by rounding each number to the nearest hundred, and (ii) calculate the exact answer.

1. a. $5{,}475 + 1{,}260 + 179 - 50$

   b. $1{,}274 \times 350$

   c. $6{,}720 \div 112$

For Problems 2 to 5, evaluate the expressions.

2. a. $5(3^2 - 4) + (5^2 - 4^2)$

   b. $(5 + 4)^2 \div (5 - 2)^3$

   c. $4[12 - (6 - 3)(2)] \div 12$

3. a. $8 + (8 \times 5 + 4) + 11 - 7$

   b. $(5 + 1)^2\,[(11 - 9)^2 - 6 \div 2]$

   c. $100 \div [5 \times 4 + (8 - 3)^2 + 5]$

4. a. $\sqrt{(4^2 \times 5 + 1)} - \sqrt{6^2 \div 3^2}$

   b. $16 \times 8 - (4^2 + 8) + \sqrt{(16^2 \div 4)^2}$

   c. $5(5^2 - 3^2) \div (5 - 3)$

5. a. $(4 \times 8 - 4^2) \div \sqrt{10^2 - 6^2}$

   b. $[(12^2 - 4 \times 3) + 8] \div 7$

   c. $12^2 \div 4 - 3 \times 3^2$

6. Bob and Hari saved a total of $7,650. If Bob saved five times as much as Hari, how much money do each of them have?

7. A truck can hold 1,275 cartons of milk. Each carton weighs 18 -kg and the empty truck weighs 3,045 kg. Calculate the total weight of the truck when it is fully loaded with milk.

8. Caroline's take home pay for last year was $48,880. Calculate her pay for each week. (Assume 1 year = 52 weeks).

9. A carpark has 9 rows and each row has 47 parking spaces. How many cars are in the carpark if there were 29 empty parking spaces?

• 10. 4,256 people visited the Toronto Zoo on Sunday. 1,968 were adults and the rest were children. How many more children than adults visited the zoo?

• 11. Four lights, red, blue, green, and yellow, flash at intervals of 12, 16, 18, and 21 seconds, respectively. If they begin flashing at the same time, when will they flash together again?

• 12. Four wires measuring 12 m, 18 m, 24 m, and 42 m are to be cut into pieces of equal lengths, without wastage. What is the maximum possible length of each piece?

Chapter 2

FRACTIONS AND DECIMALS

LEARNING OBJECTIVES

- Identify the types of fractions and perform computations with them.
- Determine the least common denominator (LCD).
- Read, write, and round decimal numbers.
- Solve problems involving fractions and decimal numbers.
- Determine the relationship between fractions and decimal numbers.
- Perform arithmetic operations combined with fractions and decimal numbers.

CHAPTER OUTLINE

Introduction

In the previous chapter, we learned about whole numbers and how to perform basic arithmetic operations with whole numbers. However, measurements and calculations of quantities, values, amounts, etc., cannot always be represented by whole numbers. Most of these involve portions of whole numbers, which are represented by **fractions** and **decimal numbers**.

Fractions and decimal numbers are used to express values that are a portion of a whole number. Fractions are widely used throughout mathematics, including in measurement, probability, and data applications. Decimal numbers are a special type of fraction that express numbers as a portion of powers of 10 (10, 100, 1,000, etc.).

Fractions and decimal numbers have different benefits. Fractions can be more precise than decimal numbers; for example, it is impossible to exactly represent the fraction $\frac{1}{3}$ as a decimal number.

However, it is easier to read, write, and perform arithmetic operations with decimal numbers than it is with fractions. In addition, it is easier to determine the magnitude of numbers when they are expressed as decimal numbers rather than as fractions. For example, it is easier to recognize that the decimal number 7.75, as opposed to its fractional form $\frac{31}{4}$, lies between the whole numbers 7 and 8.

In this chapter, we will learn about the different types of fractions and decimal numbers and the methods to convert them from one form to the other. As well, we will learn to perform arithmetic operations with fractions and decimal numbers, including powers and square roots.

2.1 | Fractions

If we divide one whole unit into several equal portions, then one or more of these equal portions can be represented by a **fraction**.

Fractions represent division. For example, $\frac{3}{8}$ is the same as $3 \div 8$.

A fraction is composed of the following three parts:

1. **Numerator:** the number of equal parts of a whole unit.
2. **Fraction bar:** the division sign, meaning 'divided by'.
3. **Denominator:** the total number of equal parts into which the whole unit is divided.

For example, $\frac{3}{8}$ is a fraction.

fraction bar → $\frac{3}{8}$ ← numerator (3), ← denominator (8)

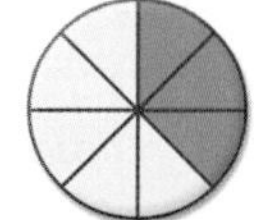

The **numerator '3'** indicates that the fraction represents 3 equal parts of a whole unit and the **denominator '8'** indicates that the whole unit is divided into 8 equal parts, as shown above. The **fraction bar** indicates that the numerator '3' is divided by the denominator '8'.

$\frac{3}{8}$ is read as "three divided by eight", "three-eighths", or "three over eight". All of these indicate that 3 is the numerator, 8 is the denominator, and the fraction represents 3 of 8 pieces of the whole. The numerator and denominator are referred to as the **terms** of the fraction.

Note: The denominator of a fraction cannot be zero, since a number cannot be divided into zero equal parts.

Any number that can be represented as a fraction is known as a **rational number**.

For example,

- $\frac{2}{3}$, $\frac{5}{2}$, and $\frac{7}{1}$ are rational numbers.
- The whole number 7 can be written as the fraction $\frac{7}{1}$; therefore, 7 is also a rational number.

Fractions can be represented on a number line. They are plotted in-between whole numbers.

For example, $\frac{1}{2}$ is represented on a number line as:

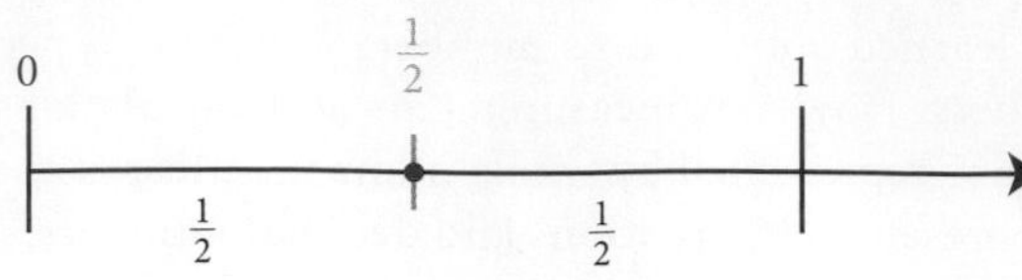

When one unit is divided into two equal portions, each portion represents one-half of that unit. One of such equal portions is written as $\frac{1}{2}$.

Example 2.1-a **Representing Fractions on a Number Line**

Represent the following fractions on a number line:

(i) $\frac{2}{3}$ (ii) $\frac{3}{5}$

Solution

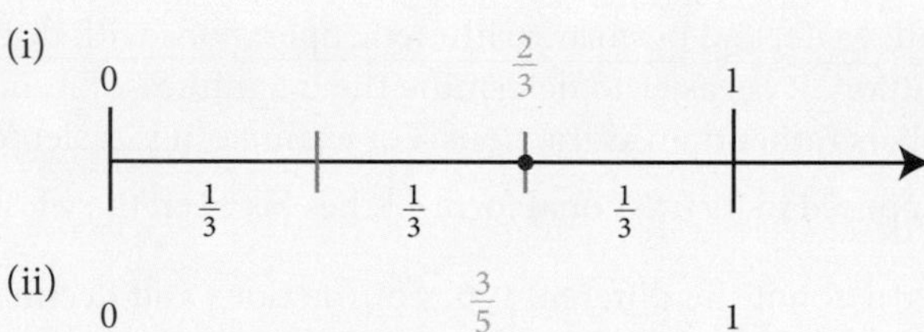

(i) When one unit is divided into three equal portions, each portion represents one-third of that unit. Two of such equal portions is two-thirds and is written as $\frac{2}{3}$.

(ii) When one unit is divided into five equal portions, each portion represents one-fifth of that unit. Three of such equal portions is three-fifths and is written as $\frac{3}{5}$.

Types of Fractions

Proper Fractions

A **proper fraction** is a fraction in which the numerator is less than the denominator.

For example,

- $\frac{3}{8}$ is a proper fraction because the numerator, 3, is less than the denominator, 8.

three-eighths

Improper Fractions

An **improper fraction** is a fraction in which the numerator is greater than the denominator; i.e., the value of the entire fraction is more than 1.

For example,

- $\frac{7}{4}$ is an improper fraction because the numerator 7 is greater than the denominator 4 (i.e., $7 > 4$, or $\frac{7}{4} > 1$).

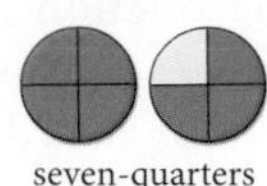

seven-quarters

Mixed Numbers (or Mixed Fractions)

A **mixed number** consists of both a whole number and a proper fraction, written side-by-side, which implies that the whole number and the proper fraction are added.

For example,

- $3\frac{5}{8}$ is a mixed number, where 3 is the whole number, and $\frac{5}{8}$ is the proper fraction.

  $3\frac{5}{8}$ implies $3 + \frac{5}{8}$

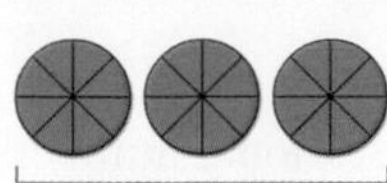

three

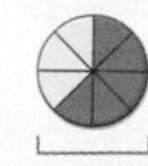

five-eighths

Relationship Between Mixed Numbers and Improper Fractions

Converting a Mixed Number to an Improper Fraction

Follow these steps to convert a mixed number to an improper fraction:	**Example:** **Convert $3\frac{5}{8}$ to an improper fraction.**
Step 1: Multiply the whole number by the denominator of the fraction and add this value to the numerator of the fraction.	$\underbrace{3(8)}_{24} + 5 = 29$
Step 2: The resulting answer will be the numerator of the improper fraction.	The numerator will be 29.
Step 3: The denominator of the improper fraction is the same as the denominator of the original fraction in the mixed number.	The denominator will be 8. Therefore, $3\frac{5}{8} = \frac{29}{8}$.

Note: You can perform the above steps in a single line of arithmetic, as follows:

$$3\frac{5}{8} = \frac{3(8) + 5}{8} = \frac{24 + 5}{8} = \frac{29}{8}$$

There is a total of 29 pieces, each piece being one-eighth in size.

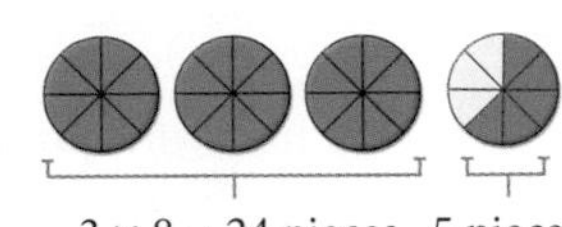

3 × 8 = 24 pieces 5 pieces

Converting an Improper Fraction to a Mixed Number

Follow these steps to convert an improper fraction to a mixed number:	**Example:** **Convert $\frac{29}{8}$ to a mixed number.**
Step 1: Divide the numerator by the denominator.	$8\overline{)29}$ = 3 ← Quotient; −24; 5 ← Remainder
Step 2: The quotient becomes the whole number and the remainder becomes the numerator of the fraction portion of the mixed number.	
Step 3: The denominator of the fraction portion of the mixed number is the same as the denominator of the original improper fraction.	Therefore, $\frac{29}{8} = 3\frac{5}{8}$.

Equivalent Fractions

When both the numerator and denominator of a fraction are either multiplied by the same number or divided by the same number, the result is a new fraction known as an **equivalent fraction**. Equivalent fractions have the same value.

That is, the same part (or portion) of a whole unit can be represented by different fractions.

For example,

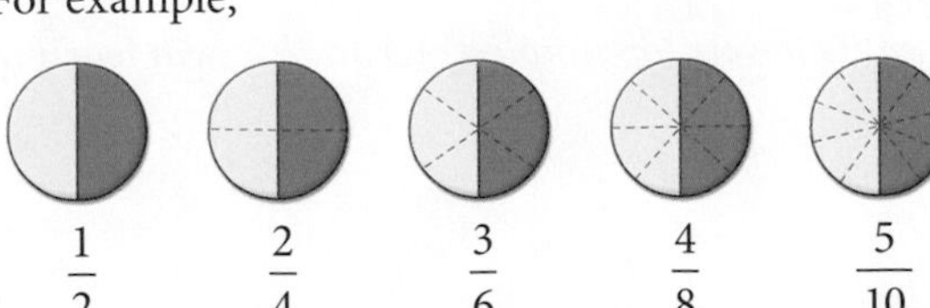

$\frac{1}{2}$ $\frac{2}{4}$ $\frac{3}{6}$ $\frac{4}{8}$ $\frac{5}{10}$

$\frac{1}{2}, \frac{2}{4}, \frac{3}{6}, \frac{4}{8}, \frac{5}{10}, \ldots$ are equivalent fractions.

Example 2.1-b Finding Equivalent Fractions by Raising to Higher Terms

Find two equivalent fractions of $\frac{2}{5}$ by raising to higher terms.

Solution

$\frac{2}{5}$ (2 portions of 5 equal parts of the whole)

$\frac{2}{5} = \frac{2 \times 2}{5 \times 2}$ Multiplying both the numerator and denominator by 2,

$= \frac{4}{10}$ (4 portions of 10 equal parts of the whole)

$\frac{2}{5} = \frac{2 \times 3}{5 \times 3}$ Multiplying both the numerator and denominator by 3,

$= \frac{6}{15}$ (6 portions of 15 equal parts of the whole)

Therefore, $\frac{4}{10}$ and $\frac{6}{15}$ are equivalent fractions of $\frac{2}{5}$.

Example 2.1-c Finding Equivalent Fractions by Reducing to Lower Terms

Find two equivalent fractions of $\frac{12}{30}$ by reducing to lower terms.

Solution

$\frac{12}{30}$ (12 portions of 30 equal parts of the whole)

$\frac{12}{30} = \frac{12 \div 3}{30 \div 3}$ Dividing both the numerator and denominator by 3,

$= \frac{4}{10}$ (4 portions of 10 equal parts of the whole)

$= \frac{4 \div 2}{10 \div 2}$ Further dividing both the numerator and denominator by 2,

$= \frac{2}{5}$ (2 portions of 5 equal parts of the whole)

$\frac{12}{30} = \frac{12 \div 6}{30 \div 6}$ Or, the lowest terms can be found by dividing both the numerator and denominator of the original fraction, $\frac{12}{30}$, by 6,

$= \frac{2}{5}$

Therefore, $\frac{4}{10}$ and $\frac{2}{5}$ are equivalent fractions of $\frac{12}{30}$.

Note: The fraction $\frac{2}{5}$ cannot be further reduced, as 2 and 5 do not have any common factors. Therefore, $\frac{2}{5}$ is a fraction in its lowest (or simplest) terms. We will learn more about this further in the section.

Identifying Equivalent Fractions Using Cross Products

If the **cross products** of two fractions are equal, then the two fractions are equivalent fractions, and vice versa (i.e., if the fractions are equivalent, then their cross products are equal).

That is, if $\frac{a}{b} = \frac{c}{d}$, then $a \times d = b \times c$ $\qquad$ $\boldsymbol{a \times d}$ and $\boldsymbol{b \times c}$ are known as cross products

For example, $\frac{3}{5}$ and $\frac{12}{20}$ are equivalent fractions because their cross products, 3×20 and 5×12, are equal:

$3 \times 20 = 60$

$5 \times 12 = 60$

Example 2.1-d **Classifying Fractions as Equivalent or Not Equivalent**

Classify the pair of fractions as 'equivalent' or 'not equivalent' by using their cross products.

(i) $\frac{2}{5}$ and $\frac{12}{30}$ $\qquad$ (ii) $\frac{5}{4}$ and $\frac{20}{12}$ $\qquad$ (iii) $\frac{3}{8}$ and $\frac{9}{24}$

Solution

(i) $\frac{2}{5}$ and $\frac{12}{30}$ $\qquad$ The cross products are 2×30 and 5×12.

$2 \times 30 = 60$

$5 \times 12 = 60$

} The cross products are equal.

Therefore, the two fractions are equivalent.

(ii) $\frac{5}{4}$ and $\frac{20}{12}$ $\qquad$ The cross products are 5×12 and 4×20.

$5 \times 12 = 60$

$4 \times 20 = 80$

} The cross products are not equal.

Therefore, the two fractions are not equivalent.

(iii) $\frac{3}{8}$ and $\frac{9}{24}$ $\qquad$ The cross products are 3×24 and 8×9.

$3 \times 24 = 72$

$8 \times 9 = 72$

} The cross products are equal.

Therefore, the two fractions are equivalent.

Fractions in Lowest (or Simplest) Terms

Dividing both the numerator and denominator of a fraction by the same number, which results in an equivalent fraction, is known as **reducing** or **simplifying** the fraction.

For example, we saw in Example 2.1-c that $\frac{4}{10}$ and $\frac{2}{5}$ are reduced fractions of $\frac{12}{30}$.

A fraction in which the numerator and denominator have no factors in common (other than 1) is said to be a fraction in its **lowest (or simplest) terms.**

Any fraction can be **fully reduced** to its lowest terms by one of the following two methods:

Method 1: Dividing both the numerator and denominator by the greatest common factor (GCF).

Method 2: Writing the numerator and denominator as products of prime factors and reducing by the common prime factors.

Example 2.1-e **Reducing Fractions to their Lowest Terms**

Reduce the following fractions to their lowest terms.

(i) $\frac{40}{45}$ (ii) $\frac{54}{24}$

Solution

(i) $\frac{40}{45}$

Method 1: Factors of 40 are: 1, 2, 4, 5, 8, 10, 20, and 40

Factors of 45 are: 1, 3, 5, 9, 15, and 45

The GCF is 5.

Dividing the numerator and denominator by the GCF, 5,

$$\frac{40}{45} = \frac{40 \div 5}{45 \div 5} = \frac{8}{9}$$

Method 2: Prime factors of 40 are: $2 \times 2 \times 2 \times 5$
Prime factors of 45 are: $3 \times 3 \times 5$
} The common prime factor is one 5.

$$\frac{40}{45} = \frac{2 \times 2 \times 2 \times \cancel{5}^{1}}{3 \times 3 \times \cancel{5}_{1}} = \frac{8}{9}$$

Therefore, $\frac{40}{45}$ is equal to $\frac{8}{9}$ reduced to its lowest terms.

(ii) $\frac{54}{24}$

Method 1: Factors of 54 are: 1, 2, 3, 6, 9, 18, 27, and 54

Factors of 24 are: 1, 2, 3, 4, 6, 8, 12, and 24

The GCF is 6.

Dividing the numerator and denominator by the GCF, 6,

$$\frac{54}{24} = \frac{54 \div 6}{24 \div 6} = \frac{9}{4}$$

Method 2: Prime factors of 54 are: $2 \times 3 \times 3 \times 3$
Prime factors of 24 are: $2 \times 2 \times 2 \times 3$
} The common prime factors are one 2 and one 3.

$$\frac{54}{24} = \frac{{}^{1}\cancel{2} \times \cancel{3}^{1} \times 3 \times 3}{{}_{1}\cancel{2} \times 2 \times 2 \times \cancel{3}_{1}} = \frac{9}{4}$$

Therefore, $\frac{54}{24}$ is equal to $\frac{9}{4}$ reduced to its lowest terms.

Reciprocals of Fractions

Two numbers whose product is equal to 1 are known as **reciprocals** of each other. Every non-zero real number has a reciprocal.

For example,

- $\frac{2}{3}$ and $\frac{3}{2}$ are reciprocals of each other, because $\frac{2}{3} \times \frac{3}{2} = 1$.

When the numerator and denominator of a fraction are interchanged, the resulting fraction is the reciprocal of the original fraction.

For example,

- 5 and $\frac{1}{5}$ are reciprocals (5 can also be written as $\frac{5}{1}$).
- Similarly, the reciprocal of $\frac{-2}{5}$ is $\frac{5}{-2} = -\frac{5}{2}$

The reciprocal of a number has the same sign as that number.

The reciprocal of a positive number is always positive and the reciprocal of a negative number is always negative.

Note:

(i) *The reciprocal of a number is not the negative of that number.*

(*The reciprocal of* $3 \neq -3$. *The reciprocal of* $3 = \frac{1}{3}$.)

(ii) *The reciprocal of a fraction is not an equivalent fraction of that fraction.*

(*The reciprocal of* $\frac{2}{5} \neq \frac{4}{10}$. *The reciprocal of* $\frac{2}{5} = \frac{5}{2}$.)

Table 2.1 **Examples of Numbers with their Negatives and Reciprocals**

When any number is multiplied by its reciprocal, the answer is always 1.

When any number is added to its negative, the answer is always 0.

Number	5	-3	$\frac{2}{3}$	$-\frac{3}{8}$
Negative of the Number	-5	3	$-\frac{2}{3}$	$\frac{3}{8}$
Reciprocal of the Number	$\frac{1}{5}$	$-\frac{1}{3}$	$\frac{3}{2}$	$-\frac{8}{3}$

2.1 | Exercises

Answers to odd-numbered problems are available at the end of the textbook.

For Problems 1 to 6, classify the fractions as proper fractions, improper fractions, or mixed numbers.

1. a. $\frac{16}{35}$ b. $3\frac{2}{9}$
2. a. $2\frac{7}{10}$ b. $15\frac{12}{13}$ b. $\frac{29}{30}$

3. a. $\frac{19}{16}$ b. $9\frac{7}{8}$
4. a. $\frac{21}{22}$ b. $\frac{52}{25}$
5. a. $4\frac{2}{5}$ b. $\frac{7}{3}$
6. a. $6\frac{1}{2}$ b. $\frac{20}{75}$

For Problems 7 to 10, convert the mixed numbers to improper fractions.

7. a. $2\frac{2}{7}$ b. $3\frac{1}{8}$
8. a. $3\frac{2}{5}$ b. $7\frac{5}{8}$
9. a. $5\frac{4}{5}$ b. $6\frac{3}{4}$
10. a. $4\frac{3}{7}$ b. $9\frac{5}{6}$

For Problems 11 to 14, convert the improper fractions to mixed numbers.

11. a. $\frac{19}{7}$ b. $\frac{45}{8}$
12. a. $\frac{23}{7}$ b. $\frac{34}{3}$
13. a. $\frac{23}{3}$ b. $\frac{31}{6}$
14. a. $\frac{26}{4}$ b. $\frac{29}{5}$

For Problems 15 to 22, classify the pair of fractions as 'equivalent' or 'not equivalent' by first converting the mixed numbers to improper fractions.

15. $\frac{44}{5}$ and $4\frac{4}{5}$ 16. $\frac{47}{8}$ and $5\frac{7}{8}$ 17. $11\frac{5}{7}$ and $7\frac{5}{7}$ 18. $\frac{41}{4}$ and $10\frac{3}{4}$

19. $\frac{54}{7}$ and $7\frac{5}{7}$ 20. $\frac{17}{8}$ and $2\frac{3}{8}$ 21. $\frac{37}{9}$ and $4\frac{1}{9}$ 22. $\frac{45}{11}$ and $4\frac{3}{11}$

For Problems 23 to 30, classify the pair of fractions as 'equivalent' or 'not equivalent' by first converting the improper fractions to mixed numbers.

23. $\frac{15}{4}$ and $3\frac{1}{4}$ 24. $\frac{43}{6}$ and $7\frac{5}{6}$ 25. $\frac{18}{5}$ and $3\frac{3}{5}$ 26. $\frac{45}{7}$ and $6\frac{3}{7}$

27. $3\frac{8}{9}$ and $\frac{35}{9}$ 28. $\frac{34}{8}$ and $4\frac{1}{8}$ 29. $\frac{41}{12}$ and $3\frac{5}{12}$ 30. $7\frac{3}{9}$ and $\frac{67}{9}$

For Problems 31 to 36, (i) reduce the fractions to their lowest terms and (ii) write their reciprocals.

31. a. $\frac{30}{20}$ b. $\frac{48}{84}$ 32. a. $\frac{44}{12}$ b. $\frac{42}{70}$

33. a. $\frac{56}{48}$ b. $\frac{84}{21}$ 34. a. $\frac{75}{105}$ b. $\frac{144}{48}$

35. a. $\frac{36}{63}$ b. $\frac{60}{96}$ 36. a. $\frac{131}{84}$ b. $\frac{54}{126}$

For Problems 37 to 44, classify the pair of fractions as 'equivalent' or 'not equivalent'.

37. $\frac{6}{12}$ and $\frac{15}{30}$ 38. $\frac{6}{10}$ and $\frac{9}{15}$ 39. $\frac{8}{10}$ and $\frac{15}{12}$ 40. $\frac{12}{18}$ and $\frac{18}{27}$

41. $\frac{15}{12}$ and $\frac{36}{45}$ 42. $\frac{35}{15}$ and $\frac{28}{12}$ 43. $\frac{20}{25}$ and $\frac{24}{30}$ 44. $\frac{16}{24}$ and $\frac{25}{30}$

For Problems 45 to 50, determine the missing values.

45. a. $\frac{4}{9} = \frac{?}{27}$ b. $\frac{4}{9} = \frac{20}{?}$ 46. a. $\frac{42}{36} = \frac{14}{?}$ b. $\frac{42}{36} = \frac{?}{30}$

47. a. $\frac{9}{12} = \frac{18}{?}$ b. $\frac{9}{12} = \frac{?}{4}$ 48. a. $\frac{45}{75} = \frac{?}{25}$ b. $\frac{45}{75} = \frac{18}{?}$

49. a. $\frac{3}{2} = \frac{12}{?}$ b. $\frac{3}{2} = \frac{?}{12}$ 50. a. $\frac{25}{15} = \frac{?}{3}$ b. $\frac{25}{15} = \frac{35}{?}$

For Problems 51 to 58, express the answer as a fraction reduced to its lowest terms.

51. What fraction of 1 year is 4 months?
52. What fraction of 1 hour is 25 minutes?
53. Karen cut a pizza into 16 equal slices and served 12 slices to her friends. What fraction of the pizza was served?
54. Out of 35 students in a math class, 15 received an 'A' in their final exam. What fraction of the students in the class received an 'A' grade?
55. In a survey of 272 people, 68 people responded 'yes' and the remaining responded 'no'. What fraction of the people responded 'no'?
56. In a finance math course with 490 students, 70 students failed the final exam. What fraction of the students passed the final exam in this course?
57. Out of the 480 units in a condominium tower, 182 are rented. What fraction of the units are not rented?
58. In a community of 6,000 people, 1,800 were 60 years or older. What fraction of the people were below the age of 60 years?

2.2 | Arithmetic Operations with Fractions

Least or Lowest Common Denominator (LCD)

The **Least Common Denominator (LCD)** of a set of two or more fractions is the smallest whole number that is divisible by each of the denominators. It is the least common multiple (LCM) of the denominators of the fractions. There are two methods of finding the LCM, as explained in Chapter 1, Section 1.3.

In performing addition and subtraction of fractions, it is necessary to determine equivalent fractions with common denominators. The best choice for a common denominator is the LCD, because it makes any further simplification easier.

Example 2.2-a

Determining the Least Common Denominator

Determine the LCD of $\frac{4}{9}$ and $\frac{7}{15}$.

Solution

The LCD of the fractions $\frac{4}{9}$ and $\frac{7}{15}$ is the same as the LCM of the denominators 9 and 15.

Using one of the methods from Chapter 1, Section 1.3:

- The largest number, 15, is **not** divisible by 9.
- Multiples of 15 are: 15, 30, 45, ...
- 45 is divisible by 9.
- Thus, the LCM of 9 and 15 is 45.

Therefore, the LCD of $\frac{4}{9}$ and $\frac{7}{15}$ is 45.

It is best to convert a mixed number into an improper fraction before performing any basic arithmetic operations.

Comparing Fractions

Fractions can easily be compared when they have the same denominator. If they do not have the same denominator, first determine the LCD of the fractions and convert them into equivalent fractions with the LCD as the denominator.

Example 2.2-b

Comparing Fractions

Which of the fractions, $\frac{5}{12}$ or $\frac{3}{8}$, is greater?

Solution

Step 1: Since the fractions do not have the same denominator, we need to first determine the LCD of the fractions, which is the same as the LCM of the denominators. The LCM of 12 and 8 is 24.

Step 2: Convert each of the fractions to its equivalent fraction with 24 as the denominator.

Solution
continued

To convert $\frac{5}{12}$ to its equivalent fraction with 24 as the denominator, multiply the denominator by 2 to obtain the LCD of 24, and multiply the numerator by 2 as well to maintain an equivalent fraction.

$$\frac{5}{12} = \frac{5 \times 2}{12 \times 2} = \frac{10}{24}$$

5 portions of 12 equal parts of a whole is equal to 10 portions of 24 equal parts of that whole.

Similarly, convert $\frac{3}{8}$ to an equivalent fraction with 24 as the denominator:

$$\frac{3}{8} = \frac{3 \times 3}{8 \times 3} = \frac{9}{24}$$

3 portions of 8 equal parts of a whole is equal to 9 portions of 24 equal parts of that whole.

Step 3: Since the denominators are the same, we can now compare the numerators of the fractions to identify the greater fraction.

Since 10 > 9, it implies: $\frac{10}{24} > \frac{9}{24}$.

Therefore, $\frac{5}{12} > \frac{3}{8}$.

Addition of Fractions

The denominator of a fraction indicates the number of parts into which an item is divided. Therefore, addition of fractions requires that the denominators of every fraction be the same. If the demoninators are different, they must first be made the same by determining the LCD and changing each fraction to its equivalent fraction with the LCD as the denominator.

When the fractions have the same denominator, the numerators of each of the fractions may be added. The numerator of the resulting fraction is equal to this sum, and the denominator is equal to the common denominator of the fractions being added.

Express the final answer reduced to lowest terms and as a mixed number, where applicable.

Example 2.2-c **Adding Fractions that have the Same Denominator**

Add $\frac{2}{9}$ and $\frac{5}{9}$.

Solution

$\frac{2}{9} + \frac{5}{9}$

$= \frac{2 + 5}{9}$

$= \frac{7}{9}$

The denominators of the fractions are the same. Adding the numerators and keeping the common denominator,

$\frac{2}{9}$ + $\frac{5}{9}$ = $\frac{7}{9}$

Therefore, the result from adding $\frac{2}{9}$ and $\frac{5}{9}$ is $\frac{7}{9}$.

Example 2.2-d **Adding Fractions that have Different Denominators**

Add $\frac{3}{4}$ and $\frac{2}{3}$.

Solution

$\frac{3}{4} + \frac{2}{3}$ LCM of 4 and 3 is 12 (i.e., LCD = 12). Determining the equivalent fractions with a denominator of 12,

$= \frac{9}{12} + \frac{8}{12}$ Adding the numerators and keeping the common denominator,

$= \frac{9 + 8}{12}$

$= \frac{17}{12}$ Converting the improper fraction to a mixed number,

$= 1\frac{5}{12}$

Therefore, the result from adding $\frac{3}{4}$ and $\frac{2}{3}$ is $1\frac{5}{12}$.

Example 2.2-e **Adding a Mixed Number and a Proper Fraction**

Add $3\frac{5}{6}$ and $\frac{4}{9}$.

Solution

Method 1:

$3\frac{5}{6} + \frac{4}{9}$ Converting the mixed number to an improper fraction,

$= \frac{(3 \times 6) + 5}{6} + \frac{4}{9} = \frac{23}{6} + \frac{4}{9}$ LCM of 6 and 9 is 18 (i.e., LCD = 18). Determining the equivalent fractions with a denominator of 18,

$= \frac{69}{18} + \frac{8}{18}$ Adding the numerators and keeping the common denominator,

$= \frac{77}{18}$ Converting the improper fraction to a mixed number,

$= 4\frac{5}{18}$

Method 2:

$3\frac{5}{6} + \frac{4}{9}$ Separating the whole number and the fractions,

$= 3 + \left(\frac{5}{6} + \frac{4}{9}\right)$ LCM of 6 and 9 is 18 (i.e., LCD = 18). Determining the equivalent fractions with a denominator of 18,

$= 3 + \left(\frac{15}{18} + \frac{8}{18}\right)$ Adding the numerators and keeping the common denominator,

$= 3 + \frac{23}{18}$ Converting the improper fraction to a mixed number,

$= 3 + 1\frac{5}{18}$

$= 3 + 1 + \frac{5}{18}$ Adding the whole numbers and then the fraction,

$= 4 + \frac{5}{18}$

$= 4\frac{5}{18}$

Therefore, the result from adding $3\frac{5}{6}$ and $\frac{4}{9}$ is $4\frac{5}{18}$.

Example 2.2-f **Adding Mixed Numbers**

Add: (i) $2\frac{1}{6}$ and $4\frac{3}{4}$ (ii) $15\frac{2}{3}$ and $3\frac{3}{5}$

Solution

(i) $2\frac{1}{6} + 4\frac{3}{4}$

LCM of 6 and 4 is 12 (i.e., LCD = 12). Determining the equivalent mixed numbers with a denominator of 12,

$= 2\frac{2}{12} + 4\frac{9}{12}$

Separating the whole numbers and the fractions,

$= (2 + 4) + \left(\frac{2}{12} + \frac{9}{12}\right)$

Adding the whole numbers and the fractions,

$= 6\frac{11}{12}$

Therefore, the result from adding $2\frac{1}{6}$ and $4\frac{3}{4}$ is $6\frac{11}{12}$.

(ii) $15\frac{2}{3} + 3\frac{3}{5}$

LCM of 3 and 5 is 15 (i.e., LCD = 15). Determining the equivalent mixed numbers with a denominator of 15,

$= 15\frac{10}{15} + 3\frac{9}{15}$

Separating the whole numbers and the fractions,

$= (15 + 3) + \left(\frac{10}{15} + \frac{9}{15}\right)$

Adding the whole numbers and the fractions,

$= 18 + \frac{19}{15}$

Converting the improper fraction to a mixed number,

$= 18 + 1\frac{4}{15}$

Adding the whole numbers and then the fraction,

$= 19\frac{4}{15}$

Therefore, the result from adding $15\frac{2}{3}$ and $3\frac{3}{5}$ is $19\frac{4}{15}$.

Subtraction of Fractions

The process for subtraction of fractions is the same as that of addition of fractions. First, determine a common denominator and change each fraction to its equivalent fraction with the common denominator. When the fractions have the same denominator, the numerators of the fractions may be subtracted. The numerator of the resulting fraction is equal to this difference, and the denominator is equal to the common denominator of the fractions being subtracted.

Express the final answer reduced to lowest terms and as a mixed number, where applicable.

Example 2.2-g **Subtracting Fractions that have the Same Denonimator**

Subtract $\frac{3}{8}$ from $\frac{7}{8}$.

Solution

$\frac{7}{8} - \frac{3}{8}$

The denominators of the fractions are the same. Subtracting the numerators and keeping the common denominator,

$= \frac{7-3}{8}$

Solution *continued*

$= \frac{4}{8} = \frac{\cancel{4}^{1}}{\cancel{8}_{2}}$ Reducing to lowest terms,

$= \frac{1}{2}$

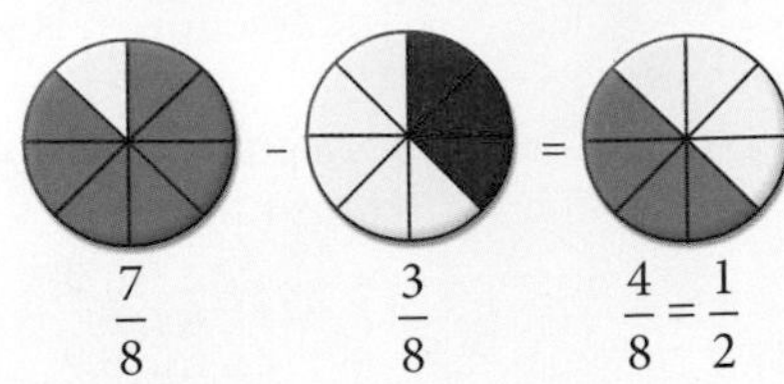

$\frac{7}{8}$ $\frac{3}{8}$ $\frac{4}{8} = \frac{1}{2}$

Therefore, the result from subtracting $\frac{3}{8}$ from $\frac{7}{8}$ is $\frac{1}{2}$.

Example 2.2-h **Subtracting Fractions that have Different Denominators**

Subtract $\frac{2}{8}$ from $\frac{7}{10}$.

Solution

$\frac{7}{10} - \frac{2}{8}$ LCM of 8 and 10 is 40 (i.e., LCD = 40). Determining the equivalent fractions with a denominator of 40,

$= \frac{28}{40} - \frac{10}{40}$ Subtracting the numerators and keeping the common denominator,

$= \frac{28 - 10}{40}$

$= \frac{18}{40} = \frac{\cancel{18}^{9}}{\cancel{40}_{20}}$ Reducing to lowest terms,

$= \frac{9}{20}$

Therefore, the result from subtracting $\frac{2}{8}$ from $\frac{7}{10}$ is $\frac{9}{20}$.

Example 2.2-i **Subtracting Mixed Numbers**

Subtract $7\frac{2}{3}$ from $12\frac{1}{2}$.

Solution

Method 1: $12\frac{1}{2} - 7\frac{2}{3}$ Converting the mixed numbers to improper fractions,

$= \frac{(12 \times 2) + 1}{2} - \frac{(7 \times 3) + 2}{3}$

$= \frac{25}{2} - \frac{23}{3}$ LCM of 2 and 3 is 6 (i.e., LCD = 6). Determining the equivalent fractions with a denominator of 6,

$= \frac{75}{6} - \frac{46}{6}$ Subtracting the numerators and keeping the common denominator,

$= \frac{29}{6}$ Converting the improper fraction to a mixed number,

$= 4\frac{5}{6}$

Solution *continued*

Method 2: $12\frac{1}{2} - 7\frac{2}{3}$

LCM of 2 and 3 is 6 (i.e., LCD = 6). Determining the equivalent mixed numbers with a denominator of 6,

$= 12\frac{3}{6} - 7\frac{4}{6}$

The fraction $\frac{4}{6}$ is greater than $\frac{3}{6}$. Therefore, we have to regroup the mixed number $12\frac{3}{6}$ by borrowing 1 from 12:

$12\frac{3}{6} = \underbrace{11 + 1}_{} + \frac{3}{6} = 11 + \underbrace{\frac{6}{6} + \frac{3}{6}}_{} = 11\frac{9}{6}$

$= 11\frac{9}{6} - 7\frac{4}{6}$

Subtracting the whole numbers and then the fractions,

$= 4\frac{(9 - 4)}{6}$

$= 4\frac{5}{6}$

Therefore, the result from subtracting $7\frac{2}{3}$ from $12\frac{1}{2}$ is $4\frac{5}{6}$.

Multiplication of Fractions

To multiply two or more fractions, first convert any mixed number to its improper fraction. Then, simply multiply the numerators together to get the new numerator and multiply the denominators together to get the new denominator.

When multiplying fractions, you can reduce any numerator term with any denominator term. Reduce as much as possible before multiplying the numerators together and the denominators together, in order to keep the numbers as simple as possible.

Express the final answer reduced to lowest terms and as a mixed number, where applicable.

Note: When multiplying mixed numbers, it is incorrect to multiply the whole number parts separately from the fractional parts to arrive at the answer.

Example 2.2-j **Multiplying Fractions**

Multiply:

(i) $\frac{3}{2} \times \frac{4}{11}$ (ii) $15 \times \frac{2}{5}$ (iii) $3\frac{1}{8} \times 2\frac{4}{5}$

Solution

(i) $\frac{3}{2} \times \frac{4}{11} = \frac{3}{{}_1\cancel{2}} \times \frac{\cancel{4}^{\,2}}{11}$ Reducing the fractions,

$= \frac{3}{1} \times \frac{2}{11}$ Multiplying the numerators together and denominators together,

$= \frac{6}{11}$

Therefore, the result of $\frac{3}{2} \times \frac{4}{11}$ is $\frac{6}{11}$.

(ii) $15 \times \frac{2}{5} = \frac{{}^3\cancel{15}}{1} \times \frac{2}{\cancel{5}_1}$ Reducing the fractions,

$= \frac{3}{1} \times \frac{2}{1}$ Multiplying the numerators together and denominators together,

$= \frac{6}{1} = 6$

Therefore, the result of $15 \times \frac{2}{5}$ is 6.

Solution *continued*

(iii) $3\frac{1}{8} \times 2\frac{4}{5}$ Converting the mixed numbers to improper fractions,

$$= \frac{(3 \times 8) + 1}{8} \times \frac{(2 \times 5) + 4}{5}$$

$$= \frac{25}{8} \times \frac{14}{5} = \frac{{}^{5}\cancel{25}}{{}_{4}\cancel{8}} \times \frac{\cancel{14}^{7}}{\cancel{5}_{1}}$$ Reducing the fractions,

$$= \frac{5}{4} \times \frac{7}{1}$$ Multiplying the numerators together and denominators together,

$$= \frac{35}{4}$$ Converting the improper fraction to a mixed number,

$$= 8\frac{3}{4}$$

Therefore, the result of $3\frac{1}{8} \times 2\frac{4}{5}$ is $8\frac{3}{4}$.

Division of Fractions

When a fraction is inverted, the resulting fraction is known as the 'reciprocal' of the original fraction.

When dividing fractions, as in multiplication, first convert any mixed number to its improper fraction. The division of fractions is done by multiplying the first fraction by the reciprocal of the second fraction. Then, follow the procedure used in multiplication to arrive at the final result.

Express the final answer reduced to lowest terms and as a mixed number, where applicable.

Note:

(i) *Dividing by 2 is the same as multiplying by the reciprocal of 2, which is* $\frac{1}{2}$.

(ii) *When multiplying or dividing mixed numbers, it is incorrect to multiply or divide the whole number parts separately from the fractional parts to arrive at the answer.*

Example 2.2-k **Dividing Fractions**

Divide $\frac{15}{16}$ by $\frac{9}{20}$.

Solution

$$\frac{15}{16} \div \frac{9}{20}$$ Multiplying $\frac{15}{16}$ by the reciprocal of $\frac{9}{20}$, which is $\frac{20}{9}$,

$$= \frac{15}{16} \times \frac{20}{9} = \frac{{}^{5}\cancel{15}}{{}_{4}\cancel{16}} \times \frac{\cancel{20}^{5}}{\cancel{9}_{3}}$$ Reducing the fractions,

$$= \frac{5}{4} \times \frac{5}{3}$$ Multiplying the numerators together and denominators together,

$$= \frac{25}{12}$$ Converting the improper fraction to a mixed number,

$$= 2\frac{1}{12}$$

Therefore, the result of $\frac{15}{16}$ divided by $\frac{9}{20}$ is $2\frac{1}{12}$.

Example 2.2-l **Dividing Mixed Numbers**

Divide $3\frac{3}{20}$ by $1\frac{4}{5}$.

Solution

$3\frac{3}{20} \div 1\frac{4}{5}$ Converting the mixed numbers to improper fractions,

$= \frac{(3 \times 20) + 3}{20} \div \frac{(1 \times 5) + 4}{5}$

$= \frac{63}{20} \div \frac{9}{5}$ Multiplying $\frac{63}{20}$ by the reciprocal of $\frac{9}{5}$, which is $\frac{5}{9}$,

$= \frac{63}{20} \times \frac{5}{9} = \frac{\cancel{63}^{7}}{_{4}\cancel{20}} \times \frac{\cancel{5}^{1}}{\cancel{9}_{1}}$ Reducing the fractions,

$= \frac{7}{4}$ Converting the improper fraction to a mixed number,

$= 1\frac{3}{4}$

Therefore, the result of $3\frac{3}{20}$ divided by $1\frac{4}{5}$ is $1\frac{3}{4}$.

Complex Fractions

A **complex fraction** is a fraction in which one or more fractions are found in the numerator or denominator.

For example,

- $\frac{1}{\left(\frac{5}{8}\right)}$ is a complex fraction because it has a fraction in the denominator.
- $\frac{\left(\frac{2}{3}\right)}{6}$ is a complex fraction because it has a fraction in the numerator.
- $\frac{\left(\frac{2}{5} + \frac{1}{4}\right)}{3}$ is a complex fraction because it has two fractions in the numerator.
- $\frac{\left(\frac{5}{6}\right)}{\left(\frac{1}{8}\right)}$ is a complex fraction because it has a fraction in both the numerator and the denominator.

A complex fraction can be converted into a proper or an improper fraction by dividing the numerator by the denominator and then simplifying the expression.

For example,

$$\frac{1}{\left(\frac{5}{8}\right)} = 1 \div \frac{5}{8} = 1 \times \frac{8}{5} = \frac{8}{5}$$

$$\frac{\left(\frac{2}{3}\right)}{6} = \frac{2}{3} \div 6 = \frac{\cancel{2}^{1}}{3} \times \frac{1}{\cancel{6}_{3}} = \frac{1}{9}$$

Example 2.2-m

Simplifying Complex Fractions

Express the following complex fractions as a proper fraction or mixed number, where applicable.

(i) $\dfrac{\left(\dfrac{7}{2}\right)}{5}$ (ii) $\dfrac{6}{\left(\dfrac{9}{8}\right)}$

Solution

(i) $\dfrac{\left(\dfrac{7}{2}\right)}{5} = \dfrac{7}{2} \div 5 = \dfrac{7}{2} \times \dfrac{1}{5} = \dfrac{7}{10}$

(ii) $\dfrac{6}{\left(\dfrac{9}{8}\right)} = 6 \div \dfrac{9}{8} = \dfrac{\cancel{6}^{2}}{1} \times \dfrac{8}{\cancel{9}_{3}} = \dfrac{16}{3} = 5\frac{1}{3}$

Powers and Square Roots of Fractions

Powers of fractions are expressed the same way as whole numbers. When the base of a power is a fraction, it is written within brackets.

For example, $\left(\dfrac{2}{3}\right)^2$ is read as "two-thirds squared".

- This means that $\dfrac{2}{3}$ is used as a factor two times.
- i.e., $\left(\dfrac{2}{3}\right)^2 = \dfrac{2}{3} \times \dfrac{2}{3} = \dfrac{4}{9}$

A mixed number that is raised to a power is evaluated by first converting it into an improper fraction, and then following the same procedure explained above.

For example, $\left(1\frac{2}{3}\right)^4$ is evaluated by first converting $1\frac{2}{3}$ into an improper fraction.

$$\left(1\tfrac{2}{3}\right)^4 = \left(\frac{1(3)+2}{3}\right)^4 = \left(\frac{5}{3}\right)^4 = \left(\frac{5}{3}\right)\left(\frac{5}{3}\right)\left(\frac{5}{3}\right)\left(\frac{5}{3}\right) = \frac{625}{81} = 7\tfrac{58}{81}$$

Example 2.2-n

Evaluating Powers of Fractions

Evaluate the following powers:

(i) $\left(\dfrac{4}{5}\right)^4$ (ii) $\left(1\frac{1}{2}\right)^5$

Solution

(i) $\left(\dfrac{4}{5}\right)^4$ Expanding by using $\dfrac{4}{5}$ as a factor four times,

$= \left(\dfrac{4}{5}\right)\left(\dfrac{4}{5}\right)\left(\dfrac{4}{5}\right)\left(\dfrac{4}{5}\right) = \dfrac{256}{625}$

(ii) $\left(1\frac{1}{2}\right)^5$ Converting the mixed number into an improper fraction,

$= \left(\dfrac{1(2)+1}{2}\right)^5 = \left(\dfrac{3}{2}\right)^5$ Expanding by using $\dfrac{3}{2}$ as a factor five times,

$= \left(\dfrac{3}{2}\right)\left(\dfrac{3}{2}\right)\left(\dfrac{3}{2}\right)\left(\dfrac{3}{2}\right)\left(\dfrac{3}{2}\right) = \dfrac{243}{32}$ Converting back to a mixed number,

$= 7\frac{19}{32}$

$\sqrt{\frac{a}{b}}$ is equal to $\frac{\sqrt{a}}{\sqrt{b}}$

Square roots of fractions are calculated the same way as square roots of whole numbers, but the numerators and denominators are evaluated separately.

For example, $\sqrt{\frac{9}{16}}$ is the same as $\frac{\sqrt{9}}{\sqrt{16}} = \frac{3}{4}$.

Example 2.2-o **Evaluating Square Roots of Fractions**

Evaluate the square root: $\sqrt{\frac{25}{144}}$

Solution

$\sqrt{\frac{25}{144}}$

Determining the square root of the numerator and denominator separately,

$= \frac{\sqrt{25}}{\sqrt{144}} = \frac{5}{12}$

2.2 | Exercises

Answers to odd-numbered problems are available at the end of the textbook.

For Problems 1 to 8, identify the greater fraction in each pair.

1. $\frac{2}{5}$ or $\frac{3}{8}$
2. $\frac{4}{3}$ or $\frac{6}{5}$
3. $\frac{12}{15}$ or $\frac{35}{45}$
4. $\frac{5}{4}$ or $\frac{7}{6}$
5. $\frac{8}{7}$ or $\frac{13}{12}$
6. $\frac{5}{13}$ or $\frac{16}{39}$
7. $\frac{8}{9}$ or $\frac{39}{45}$
8. $\frac{3}{8}$ or $\frac{25}{48}$
9. Which of the following fractions are less than $\frac{2}{3}$?

   $\frac{5}{8}, \frac{6}{7}, \frac{3}{5}, \frac{7}{9}$
10. Which of the following fractions are greater than $\frac{3}{4}$?

    $\frac{4}{5}, \frac{7}{9}, \frac{5}{7}, \frac{9}{11}$

For Problems 11 to 18, perform the addition, reduce to lowest terms, and express the answer as a mixed number, whenever possible.

11. a. $\frac{5}{8} + \frac{7}{8}$ b. $\frac{7}{12} + \frac{3}{4}$
12. a. $\frac{5}{9} + \frac{7}{9}$ b. $\frac{7}{10} + \frac{9}{20}$
13. a. $\frac{4}{3} + \frac{5}{6}$ b. $12\frac{3}{4} + 5\frac{1}{3}$
14. a. $\frac{23}{12} + \frac{1}{3}$ b. $18\frac{5}{7} + 2\frac{2}{5}$
15. a. $9\frac{3}{4} + 6\frac{1}{6}$ b. $8\frac{2}{3} + 5\frac{3}{4}$
16. a. $11\frac{1}{4} + 5\frac{2}{3}$ b. $7\frac{1}{12} + 5\frac{3}{4}$
17. a. $\frac{1}{10} + \frac{17}{100} + \frac{39}{1,000}$ b. $\frac{3}{5} + \frac{7}{10} + \frac{9}{15}$
18. a. $\frac{3}{10} + \frac{47}{100} + \frac{241}{1,000}$ b. $\frac{2}{3} + \frac{3}{4} + \frac{5}{8}$

For Problems 19 to 24, perform the subtraction, reduce to lowest terms, and express the answer as a mixed number, whenever possible.

19. a. $\frac{2}{3} - \frac{1}{9}$ b. $\frac{9}{12} - \frac{3}{5}$
20. a. $\frac{1}{6} - \frac{1}{8}$ b. $\frac{19}{20} - \frac{3}{10}$
21. a. $\frac{5}{3} - \frac{3}{8}$ b. $16\frac{1}{8} - 1\frac{1}{2}$
22. a. $\frac{17}{9} - \frac{5}{6}$ b. $5\frac{2}{3} - 1\frac{5}{12}$
23. a. $8\frac{5}{6} - 5\frac{3}{9}$ b. $9\frac{2}{5} - 7\frac{3}{10}$
24. a. $8\frac{5}{12} - 4\frac{3}{6}$ b. $5\frac{5}{8} - 4\frac{5}{6}$

For Problems 25 and 26, perform the mixed additions and subtractions, reduce to lowest terms, and express the answer as a mixed number, whenever possible.

25. a. $\frac{32}{100} - \frac{8}{1,000} + \frac{3}{25}$ b. $\frac{5}{8} + \frac{13}{16} - \frac{3}{4}$

26. a. $\frac{3}{10} - \frac{4}{1,000} + \frac{5}{100}$ b. $\frac{7}{12} + \frac{5}{6} - \frac{2}{3}$

For Problems 27 to 32, perform the multiplication, reduce to lowest terms, and express the answer as a mixed number, whenever possible.

27. a. $\frac{16}{5} \times \frac{5}{4}$ b. $3 \times \frac{7}{9}$

28. a. $\frac{12}{5} \times \frac{25}{3}$ b. $\frac{6}{9} \times \frac{19}{12}$

29. a. $\frac{3}{8} \times \frac{5}{11}$ b. $9\frac{3}{5} \times 1\frac{29}{96}$

30. a. $\frac{4}{5} \times \frac{23}{9}$ b. $11\frac{3}{4} \times 1\frac{1}{74}$

31. a. $\frac{9}{38} \times \frac{19}{63}$ b. $2\frac{2}{9} \times 1\frac{1}{2}$

32. a. $\frac{15}{27} \times \frac{18}{45}$ b. $2\frac{3}{7} \times \frac{25}{45}$

For Problems 33 to 38, perform the division, reduce to lowest terms, and express the answer as a mixed number, whenever possible.

33. a. $\frac{2}{3} \div \frac{4}{9}$ b. $\frac{3}{8} \div 4$

34. a. $\frac{3}{5} \div \frac{3}{4}$ b. $\frac{1}{7} \div \frac{3}{5}$

35. a. $\frac{10}{15} \div \frac{3}{7}$ b. $23\frac{1}{2} \div 8\frac{13}{16}$

36. a. $\frac{8}{12} \div \frac{2}{4}$ b. $10\frac{1}{4} \div 2\frac{27}{48}$

37. a. $5\frac{1}{5} \div 13$ b. $18 \div 4\frac{4}{5}$

38. a. $5\frac{1}{4} \div 7$ b. $15 \div 3\frac{1}{3}$

For Problems 39 and 40, express the complex fractions as a proper fraction or a mixed number, where possible.

39. a. $\frac{1}{\left(\frac{9}{4}\right)}$ b. $\frac{4\frac{3}{4}}{\left(\frac{3}{8}\right)}$

40. a. $\frac{1}{\left(\frac{11}{2}\right)}$ b. $\frac{8\frac{4}{9}}{\left(\frac{14}{3}\right)}$

For Problems 41 to 46, evaluate the powers of the fractions.

41. a. $\left(\frac{3}{5}\right)^2$ b. $\left(\frac{6}{7}\right)^2$

42. a. $\left(\frac{3}{4}\right)^2$ b. $\left(\frac{2}{9}\right)^2$

43. a. $\left(\frac{3}{4}\right)^3$ b. $\left(\frac{5}{3}\right)^4$

44. a. $\left(\frac{2}{7}\right)^3$ b. $\left(\frac{6}{5}\right)^4$

45. a. $\left(1\frac{1}{3}\right)^2$ b. $\left(3\frac{1}{2}\right)^3$

46. a. $\left(2\frac{1}{4}\right)^2$ b. $\left(1\frac{2}{3}\right)^3$

For Problems 47 to 52, evaluate the square roots of the fractions.

47. a. $\sqrt{\frac{1}{9}}$ b. $\sqrt{\frac{1}{49}}$

48. a. $\sqrt{\frac{1}{16}}$ b. $\sqrt{\frac{1}{10,000}}$

49. a. $\sqrt{\frac{4}{25}}$ b. $\sqrt{\frac{81}{16}}$

50. a. $\sqrt{\frac{36}{100}}$ b. $\sqrt{\frac{144}{81}}$

51. a. $\sqrt{3\frac{1}{16}}$ b. $\sqrt{6\frac{1}{4}}$

52. a. $\sqrt{1\frac{11}{25}}$ b. $\sqrt{1\frac{21}{100}}$

For Problems 53 to 74, express your answers as a proper fraction or a mixed number, where appropriate.

53. Peter spent $\frac{5}{12}$ of his money on rent and $\frac{1}{4}$ on food. What fraction of his money did he spend on rent and food?

54. Alan walked $\frac{3}{5}$ km to his friend's house and from there, he walked another $\frac{3}{4}$ km to his school. How far did Alan walk?

55. Last night, Amy spent $3\frac{1}{6}$ hours on her math project and $2\frac{3}{10}$ hours on her design project. How much time did she spend on both projects altogether?

56. A bag contains $2\frac{3}{5}$ kg of red beans and $1\frac{1}{8}$ kg of green beans. What is the total weight of the bag?

57. Thomas baked a $2\frac{1}{2}$ pound cake. He gave $1\frac{5}{8}$ pounds of it to his friend Yan. How much was left?

58. Alexander bought $4\frac{2}{5}$ litres of milk and drank $1\frac{2}{3}$ litres of it. How much milk was left?

59. Sarah had $\frac{3}{4}$ kg of cheese. She used $\frac{2}{7}$ kg of the cheese while baking. How many kilograms of cheese was left?

60. Cassidy bought $\frac{5}{8}$ litres of olive oil and used $\frac{1}{3}$ litre of the oil while cooking. What quantity of olive oil was left?

61. David spent $\frac{7}{10}$ of his money on toys and $\frac{1}{3}$ of the remainder on food. What fraction of his money was spent on food?

62. Mary spent $\frac{2}{5}$ of her money on a school bag. She then spent $\frac{1}{3}$ of the remainder on shoes. What fraction of her money was spent on shoes?

63. After selling $\frac{2}{5}$ of its textbooks, a bookstore had 810 books left. How many textbooks were in the bookstore initially?

64. Rose travelled $\frac{3}{5}$ of her journey by car and the remaining 20 km by bus. How far did she travel by car?

65. Cheng can walk $5\frac{1}{4}$ km in $1\frac{1}{2}$ hours. How many kilometres can he walk in 1 hour?

66. $2\frac{3}{4}$ litres of juice weighs $4\frac{2}{3}$ kg. Determine the weight (in kilograms) of 1 litre of juice.

67. A chain of length $\frac{7}{8}$ metres is cut into pieces measuring $\frac{1}{16}$ metres each. How many pieces are there?

68. A cake that weighs $\frac{2}{3}$ kg is cut into slices weighing $\frac{1}{12}$ kg each. How many slices are there?

69. A bottle of medicine contains 80 mg of medicine. Each dose of the medicine is $\frac{2}{5}$ mg. How many doses are there in the bottle?

70. A box of cereal contains 917 grams of cereal. How many bowls of cereal will there be if each serving is $32\frac{3}{4}$ grams?

71. Out of 320 bulbs, $\frac{1}{20}$ of the bulbs are defective. How many of them are not defective?

72. If $\frac{4}{15}$ of the 1,800 students in a school enrolled for a mathematics course, how many students did not enroll for the course?

73. The product of two numbers is 9. If one number is $3\frac{3}{4}$, what is the other number?

74. If a wire that is $42\frac{3}{4}$ cm long is cut into several $2\frac{1}{4}$ cm equal pieces, how many pieces would exist?

2.3 | Decimal Numbers

Decimal numbers, also simply known as **decimals**, represent a part or a portion of a whole, similar to fractions as outlined in the previous sections.

Decimal numbers are used in situations that require more precision than whole numbers can provide. We use decimal numbers frequently in our daily lives; a good example of this is money. For example, a nickel is worth 5¢, which is equal to \$0.05, and bus fare for a city may be \$3.25; 0.05 and 3.25 are both examples of decimal numbers.

A decimal number contains a whole number portion and a decimal portion. The decimal point (**.**) is used to separate these two portions: the whole number portion is comprised of the digits to the left of the decimal point, and the decimal portion is comprised of the digits to the right of the decimal point. The decimal portion represents a value less than 1.

When a number is less than 1, it is usually expressed in its decimal form with 0 in its ones place. For example, .25 is expressed as 0.25.

For example,

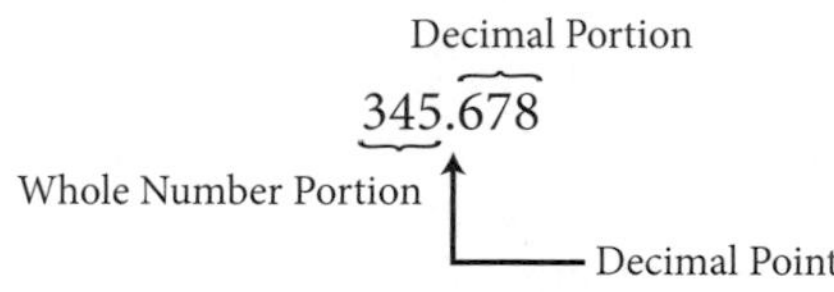

The decimal portion of a decimal number can be represented as a fraction with a denominator that is a power of 10 (i.e., 10, 100, 1,000, etc.). These fractions are referred to as **decimal fractions**.
For example,

- The decimal number 0.3 is $\frac{3}{10}$ as a decimal fraction.
- The decimal number 0.07 is $\frac{7}{100}$ as a decimal fraction.
- The decimal portion of the decimal number 345.678 is $\frac{678}{1{,}000}$ as a decimal fraction.

When decimal numbers are expressed as a decimal fraction with a denominator that is a power of 10, we do not reduce to their lowest terms.

For example, $\frac{678}{1{,}000}$ if reduced to $\frac{339}{500}$ is no longer expressed with a denominator that is a power of 10, and therefore is not a decimal fraction.

Similarly,

- $1.2 = 1\frac{2}{10}$
- $23.45 = 23\frac{45}{100}$
- $75.378 = 75\frac{378}{1{,}000}$

Every whole number can be written as a decimal number by placing a decimal point to the right of the units digits.

For example, the whole number 5 written as a decimal number is 5. or 5.0 or 5.00, etc.

The number of decimal places in a decimal number is the number of digits written to the right of the decimal point.

For example,

- 5. No decimal places
- 5.0 One decimal place
- 5.00 Two decimal places
- 1.250 Three decimal places
- 2.0050 Four decimal places

Types of Decimal Numbers

There are three different types of decimal numbers.

Repeating, non-terminating decimal numbers are commonly expressed with a horizontal bar over the decimal places which are infinitely repeated.

1. Non-repeating, terminating decimals numbers:
   For example, 0.2, 0.3767, 0.86452
2. Repeating, non-terminating decimal numbers:
   For example, 0.222222.... ($0.\overline{2}$), 0.255555.... ($0.2\overline{5}$), 0.867867.... ($0.\overline{867}$)
3. Non-repeating, non-terminating decimal numbers:
   For example, 0.453740...., π (3.141592...), e (2.718281...)

Place Value of Decimal Numbers

The position of each digit in a decimal number determines the place value of the digit. Exhibit 2.3 illustrates the place value of the five-digit decimal number: 0.35796.

The place value of each digit as you move right from the decimal point is found by decreasing powers of 10. The first place value to the right of the decimal point is the tenths place, the second place value is the hundredths place, and so on, as shown in Table 2.3.

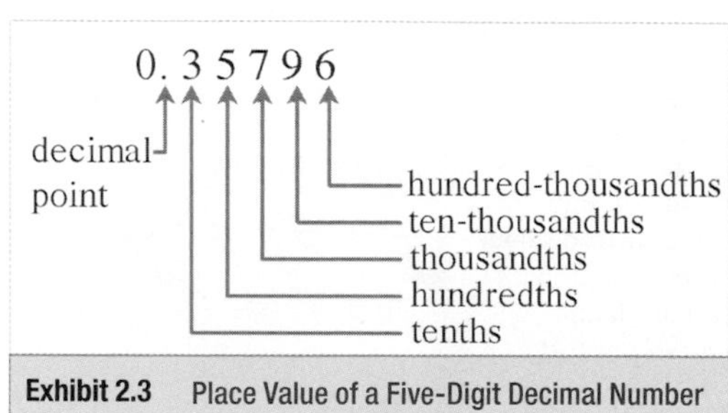

Exhibit 2.3 Place Value of a Five-Digit Decimal Number

Table 2.3 Place Value Chart of Decimal Numbers

$10^{-1} = \frac{1}{10}$	$10^{-2} = \frac{1}{100}$	$10^{-3} = \frac{1}{1,000}$	$10^{-4} = \frac{1}{10,000}$	$10^{-5} = \frac{1}{100,000}$
0.1	0.01	0.001	0.0001	0.00001
Tenths	Hundredths	Thousandths	Ten-thousandths	Hundred-thousandths

The five-digit number in Exhibit 2.3 is written as 0.35796 in its **standard form**.

0.	3	5	7	9	6
	Tenths	Hundredths	Thousandths	Ten-thousandths	Hundred-thousandths

The decimal number 0.35796 can also be written in **expanded form** as follows:

0.3 + 0.05 + 0.007 + 0.0009 + 0.00006

Or,

3 tenths + 5 hundredths + 7 thousandths + 9 ten-thousandths + 6 hundred-thousandths

Or,

$\frac{3}{10} + \frac{5}{100} + \frac{7}{1,000} + \frac{9}{10,000} + \frac{6}{100,000}$ (0.35796 as a decimal fraction is $\frac{35,796}{100,000}$)

	0.3
	0.05
	0.007
	0.0009
+	0.00006
	0.35796

Reading and Writing Decimal Numbers

The word 'and' is used to represent the decimal point (.)

Follow these steps to read and write decimal numbers in **word form**:

Step 1: Read or write the number to the left of the decimal point as a whole number.

Step 2: Read or write the decimal point as "and".

Step 3: Read or write the number to the right of the decimal point also as a whole number, but followed by the name of the place value occupied by the right-most digit.

For example, 745.023 is written in word form as:

Seven hundred forty-five and twenty-**three** thousandths

Whole Number Portion	Decimal Point	Decimal Portion
Seven hundred forty-five	and	twenty-three thousandths

The last digit, three, ends in the thousandths place. Therefore, the decimal fraction is $\frac{23}{1,000}$.

There are other ways of reading and writing decimal numbers as noted below.

- Use the word "point" to indicate the decimal point and thereafter, read or write each digit individually.

  For example, 745.023 can also be read or written as: Seven hundred forty-five point zero, two, three.

- Ignore the decimal point of the decimal number and read or write the number as a whole number followed by the name of the place value occupied by the right-most digit of the decimal portion.

  For example, 745.023 can also be read or written as: Seven hundred forty-five thousand, twenty-three thousandths (i.e., $\frac{745,023}{1,000}$).

Note: The above two representations are not used in the examples and exercise questions within this chapter.

Use of Hyphens to Express Decimal Numbers in Word Form

- A hyphen (-) is used to express the two-digit numbers, 21 to 29, 31 to 39, 41 to 49, ... 91 to 99, in each group in their word form.
- A hyphen (-) is also used while expressing the place value portion of a decimal number, such as ten-thousandths, hundred-thousandths, ten-millionths, hundred-millionths, and so on.

The following examples illustrate the use of hyphens to express numbers in their word form:

- 0.893 Eight hundred ninety-three thousandths
- 0.0506 Five hundred six ten-thousandths
- 0.00145 One hundred forty-five hundred-thousandths

Example 2.3-a **Writing Decimal Numbers in Standard Form**

Write the following decimal numbers in standard form:

(i) Two hundred and thirty-five hundredths

(ii) Three and seven tenths

(iii) Eighty-four thousandths

Solution

(i)

Whole Number Portion		Decimal Portion	
Two hundred	and	thirty-five hundredths	The last digit, five, ends in the hundredths place.
200	.	$\frac{35}{100} = 0.35$	

Therefore, the number is written in standard form as **200.35**.

(ii)

Whole Number Portion		Decimal Portion	
Three	and	seven tenths	The last digit, seven, ends in the tenths place.
3	.	$\frac{7}{10} = 0.7$	

Therefore, the number is written in standard form as **3.7**.

Solution *continued*

(iii)

Whole Number Portion		Decimal Portion	
		Eighty-four thousandths	The last digit, four, ends in the thousandths place.
0	.	$\frac{84}{1,000} = 0.084$	

Therefore, the number is written in standard form as **0.084**.

Example 2.3-b

Writing Decimal Numbers in Word Form

Write the following decimal numbers in word form:

(i) 23.125 (ii) 7.43

(iii) 20.3 (iv) 0.2345

Solution

(i) 23.125 — The last digit, 5, is in the thousandths place.

$= 23\frac{125}{1,000}$ — Twenty-three and one hundred twenty-five thousandths

(ii) 7.43 — The last digit, 3, is in the hundredths place.

$= 7\frac{43}{100}$ — Seven and forty-three hundredths

(iii) 20.3 — The last digit, 3, is in the tenths place.

$= 20\frac{3}{10}$ — Twenty and three tenths

(iv) 0.2345 — The last digit, 5, is in the ten-thousandths place.

$= \frac{2,345}{10,000}$ — Two thousand, three hundred forty-five ten-thousandths

Rounding Decimal Numbers

Rounding Decimal Numbers to the Nearest Whole Number, Tenth, Hundredth, etc.

Rounding decimal numbers refers to changing the value of the decimal number to the nearest whole number, tenth, hundredth, thousandth, etc. It is also referred to as rounding to a specific number of decimal places, indicating the number of decimal places that will be left when the rounding is complete.

- Rounding to the nearest whole number is the same as rounding without any decimals.
- Rounding to the nearest tenth is the same as rounding to one decimal place.
- Rounding to the nearest hundredth is the same as rounding to two decimal places.
- Rounding to the nearest cent refers to rounding the amount to the nearest hundredth, which is the same as rounding to two decimal places.

Follow these steps to round decimal numbers:

Step 1: Identify the digit to be rounded (this is the place value for which the rounding is required).

Step 2: If the digit to the immediate right of the identified rounding digit is less than 5 (0, 1, 2, 3, 4), do not change the value of the rounding digit.

If the digit to the immediate right of the identified rounding digit is 5 or greater than 5 (5, 6, 7, 8, 9), increase the value of the rounding digit by one (i.e., round up by one number).

Step 3: Drop all digits to the right of the rounding digit.

Example 2.3-c **Rounding Decimal Numbers**

Round the following decimal numbers to the indicated place value:

(i) 268.143 to the nearest tenth

(ii) 489.679 to the nearest hundredth

(iii) $39.9985 to the nearest cent

Solution

(i) Rounding 268.143 to the nearest tenth:

1 is the rounding digit in the tenths place: 268.143.

The digit to the immediate right of the rounding digit is less than 5; therefore, do not change the value of the rounding digit. Drop all of the digits to the right of the rounding digit. This will result in 268.1.

Therefore, 268.143 rounded to the nearest tenth is 268.1.

(ii) Rounding 489.679 to the nearest hundredth:

7 is the rounding digit in the hundredths place: 489.679.

The digit to the immediate right of the rounding digit is greater than 5; therefore, increase the value of the rounding digit by one, from 7 to 8, and drop all of the digits to the right of the rounding digit. This will result in 489.68.

Therefore, 489.679 rounded to the nearest hundredth is 489.68.

(iii) Rounding $39.9985 to the nearest cent:

9 is the rounding digit in the hundredths place: $39.9985.

The digit to the immediate right of the rounding digit is greater than 5; therefore, increase the value of the rounding digit by one, from 9 to 10, by replacing the rounding digit 9 with 0 and carrying the one to the tenths place, then to the ones, and then to the tens, to increase the digit 3 to 4. Finally, drop all digits that are to the right of the rounding digit. This will result in $40.00

Therefore, $39.9985 rounded to the nearest cent is $40.00.

2.3 | Exercises

Answers to odd-numbered problems are available at the end of the textbook.

For Problems 1 to 8, express the decimal fractions as decimal numbers.

1. a. $\frac{6}{10}$ b. $\frac{7}{1,000}$
2. a. $\frac{9}{10,000}$ b. $\frac{41}{1,000}$
3. a. $\frac{12}{100}$ b. $\frac{29}{1,000}$
4. a. $\frac{75}{100}$ b. $\frac{3}{10}$
5. a. $7\frac{5}{10}$ b. $9\frac{503}{1,000}$
6. a. $9\frac{3}{10}$ b. $6\frac{207}{1,000}$
7. a. $\frac{367}{100}$ b. $\frac{2,567}{1,000}$
8. a. $\frac{475}{10}$ b. $\frac{2,972}{1,000}$

For Problems 9 to 24, write the numbers in (i) standard form and (ii) expanded form.

9. Eighty-seven and two tenths
10. Thirty-five and seven tenths
11. Three and four hundredths
12. Nine and seven hundredths

13. Four hundred one ten-thousandths

14. Two hundred eight thousandths

15. Eighty-nine and six hundred twenty-five ten-thousandths

16. Fifty-two and three hundred five thousandths

17. One thousand, seven hundred eighty-seven and twenty-five thousandths

18. Seven thousand, two hundred sixty and fifteen thousandths

19. Four hundred twelve and sixty-five hundredths

20. Nine hundred eighty-seven and twenty hundredths

21. One million, six hundred thousand and two hundredths

22. Six million, two hundred seventeen thousand and five hundredths

23. Twenty-three and five tenths

24. Twenty-nine hundredths

For Problems 25 to 32, express the decimal numbers in their word form.

25. a. 42.55 b. 734.125

26. a. 7.998 b. 12.77

27. a. 0.25 b. 9.5

28. a. 0.987 b. 311.2

29. a. 7.07 b. 15.002

30. a. 11.09 b. 9.006

31. a. 0.062 b. 0.054

32. a. 0.031 b. 0.073

33. Arrange the following decimal numbers from least to greatest.

    0.034, 0.403, 0.043, 0.304

34. Arrange the following decimal numbers from greatest to least.

    1.014, 1.011, 1.104, 1.041

For Problems 35 to 42, round the numbers to one decimal place (nearest tenth).

35. 415.1654

36. 7.8725

37. 264.1545

38. 25.5742

39. 24.1575

40. 112.1255

41. 10.3756

42. 0.9753

For Problems 43 to 50, round the numbers to two decimal places (nearest hundredth, or nearest cent).

43. 14.3585

44. 0.0645

45. 181.1267

46. 19.6916

47. $16.775

48. $10.954

49. $9.987

50. $24.995

2.4 | Arithmetic Operations with Decimal Numbers

Addition of Decimal Numbers

Addition of decimal numbers refers to combining decimal numbers to find the **total** or **sum**. It is similar to adding whole numbers.

Follow these steps to add decimal numbers:

Step 1: Write the numbers one under the other by aligning the decimal points of the numbers.

Step 2: Add zeros to the end of any decimal number that has fewer decimal places, if necessary, to ensure that each number has the same number of decimal places. Draw a horizontal line underneath.

Step 3: Starting from the right-most place value, add all the numbers in that column.

- If the total is less than 10, write the total under the horizontal line in the same column.
- If the total is 10 or more, write the 'ones' digit of the total under the horizontal line in the same column, and write the 'tens' digit of the total above the column to the left.

Step 4: Follow this procedure for each column going from right to left. Write the decimal point in the answer, aligned with the other decimal points in the sum.

Example 2.4-a

Adding Decimal Numbers

Perform the following additions:

(i) 25.125 + 7.14

(ii) 741.87 + 135.456

(iii) 127 + 68.8 + 669.95

Solution

(i) 25.125 + 7.14

$$\begin{array}{r} \overset{1}{2}5.125 \\ +\ \ 7.140 \\ \hline 32.265 \end{array}$$ ← Add a zero to match the number of decimal places.

Therefore, adding 25.125 and 7.14 results in 32.265.

(ii) 741.87 + 135.456

$$\begin{array}{r} 74\overset{1}{1}.\overset{1}{8}70 \\ +\ 135.456 \\ \hline 877.326 \end{array}$$ ← Add a zero to match the number of decimal places.

Therefore, adding 741.87 and 135.456 results in 877.326.

(iii) 127 + 68.8 + 669.95

$$\begin{array}{r} \overset{1}{1}\overset{2}{2}\overset{1}{7}.00 \\ 68.80 \\ +\ 669.95 \\ \hline 865.75 \end{array}$$

127.00 ← Add two zeros to match the number of decimal places.

68.80 ← Add a zero to match the number of decimal places.

Therefore, adding 127, 68.8, and 669.95 results in 865.75.

Subtraction of Decimal Numbers

Subtraction of decimal numbers refers to finding the **difference** between decimal numbers. It is similar to subtracting whole numbers.

Follow these steps to subtract a decimal number from another decimal number:

Step 1: Write the numbers one under the other by aligning the decimal points of the numbers. Ensure that the number from which subtraction is indicated (the minuend) is in the top row and that the number that is being subtracted (the subtrahend) is below.

Step 2: Add zeros to the end of any decimal number that has fewer decimal places, if necessary, to ensure that each number has the same number of decimal places. Draw a horizontal line underneath.

Step 3: Starting from the right-most place value, subtract the bottom number from the top number.

- If the top digit is greater than (or equal to) the bottom digit, write the difference under the horizontal line in the same column.
- If the top digit is less than the bottom digit, borrow 'one' from the digit to the left in the top number, and add 'ten' to the digit in the current place value of the top number. Then, find the difference and write it under the horizontal line.

Step 4: Follow this procedure for each column going from right to left. Write the decimal point in the answer, aligned with the other decimal points in the difference.

Example 2.4-b

Subtracting Decimal Numbers

Perform the following subtractions:

(i) Subtract 29.02 from 135.145

(ii) Subtract 38.7 from 457

Solution

(i) Subtract 29.02 from 135.145

```
   2 15
  135.145
-  29.020
  106.125
```

Therefore, subtracting 29.02 from 135.145 results in 106.125.

(ii) Subtract 38.7 from 457

```
    16
   4 6 10
  457.0
-  38.7
  418.3
```

Therefore, subtracting 38.7 from 457 results in 418.3

Multiplication of Decimal Numbers

Multiplication of decimal numbers refers to finding the **product** of two decimal numbers.

Follow these steps to multiply one decimal number by another decimal number:

Step 1: Line up the numbers on the right without aligning the decimal points.

Step 2: Multiply the number assuming that there are no decimal points; i.e., multiply each digit in the top number by each digit in the bottom number and add the products, just like the process for multiplying whole numbers.

Step 3: Count the total number of decimal places in the numbers that are being multiplied (the factors).

Step 4: The number obtained in Step 3 is equal to the number of decimal places in the answer. Starting at the right of the answer, move towards the left by the total number of decimal places counted, and place the decimal point there.

Example 2.4-c

Multiplying Decimal Numbers

Multiply 12.56 and 1.8.

Solution

```
   12.56   (2 Decimal places) } Total of 3 Decimal places
×   1.8    (1 Decimal places) }
   10048
   12560
   22.608  (3 Decimal places)
```

Therefore, multiplying 12.56 and 1.8 results in 22.608.

Division of Decimal Numbers

Division of decimal numbers is the process of determining how many times one decimal number is contained in another decimal number.

Follow these steps to divide a decimal number:

Step 1: If the divisor is not a whole number, convert it to a whole number by moving the decimal point to the right. Move the decimal point in the dividend by the same number of places.

Step 2: Divide by following a similar process to the process of dividing whole numbers. Add zeros to the right of the last digit of the dividend and keep dividing until there is no remainder or a repeating pattern shows up in the quotient.

Example 2.4-d **Dividing Decimal Numbers**

Perform the following divisions:

(i) Divide 8.25 by 0.6

(ii) Divide: 0.166 by 0.03

Solution

(i) Step 1: Since the denominator contains one decimal place, move the decimal point one decimal place to the right for both the numerator and the denominator.

$$8.25 \div 0.6 = \frac{8.25}{0.6} = \frac{82.5}{6}$$

This is the same as multiplying both the numerator and denominator by 10.

$$8.25 \div 0.6 = \frac{8.25 \times 10}{0.6 \times 10} = \frac{82.5}{6}$$

Step 2:

```
      13.75
  6 |82.50
    -6
     22
    -18
      45
     -42
       30   <-- Add a Zero
      -30
        0
```

Position the decimal point within the quotient directly above the decimal point within the dividend.

Therefore, when 8.25 is divided by 0.6, the quotient is 13.75.

(ii) Step 1: Since the denominator contains two decimal places, move the decimal point two decimal places to the right for both the numerator and the denominator.

$$0.166 \div 0.03 = \frac{0.166}{0.03} = \frac{16.6}{3}$$

This is the same as multiplying both the numerator and denominator by 100.

$$0.166 \div 0.03 = \frac{0.166 \times 100}{0.03 \times 100} = \frac{16.6}{3}$$

Step 2:

```
      5.533
  3 |16.600
    -15
      16
     -15
       10   <-- Add a Zero
       -9
        10  <-- Add a Zero
        -9
         1
```

Position the decimal point within the quotient directly above the decimal point within the dividend.

If we continue to add 0's to the end of the dividend, the pattern will repeat and we will continually add 3's to the end of the quotient. Therefore, the quotient is a repeating, non-terminating decimal number.

Therefore, when 0.166 is divided by 0.03, the quoitent is $5.5\overline{3}$.

Powers and Square Roots of Decimal Numbers

Similar to fractions, powers of decimal numbers are usually written within brackets.

For example, $(0.12)^3$ is read as "twelve hundredths raised to the power of three".

- This means that 0.12 is used as a factor three times.
- i.e., $(0.12)^3 = (0.12)(0.12)(0.12) = 0.001728$

Example 2.4-e **Evaluating Powers of Decimal Numbers**

Evaluate the power: $(1.25)^3$

Solution

$(1.25)^3$ Expanding by using 1.25 as a factor three times,

$= (1.25)(1.25)(1.25) = 1.953125$

Determining square roots of decimal numbers is simple if the decimal number can first be converted to a decimal fraction with an even power of ten as the denominator (i.e., $10^2 = 100$, $10^4 = 10{,}000$, etc.). Then, follow the procedure for evaluating the square root of a fraction.

For example, $\sqrt{0.25} = \sqrt{\frac{25}{100}} = \frac{\sqrt{25}}{\sqrt{100}} = \frac{5}{10} = \frac{1}{2} = 0.5$

Example 2.4-f **Evaluating Square Roots of Decimal Numbers**

Evaluate the square root: $\sqrt{0.49}$

Solution

$\sqrt{0.49}$ Converting the decimal number into a decimal fraction,

$= \sqrt{\frac{49}{100}}$ Determining the square root of the numerator and denominator separately,

$= \frac{\sqrt{49}}{\sqrt{100}} = \frac{7}{10} = 0.7$

2.4 | Exercises

Answers to odd-numbered problems are available at the end of the textbook.

For Problems 1 to 8, perform the additions.

1. 927.896 + 659.50 + 128.649
2. 619.985 + 52.82 + 3.187
3. 74 + 129.258 + 0.32 + 666.015
4. 17 + 3.48 + 0.278 + 78.24
5. 292.454 + 121.69 + 65.3
6. 396.716 + 191.68 + 90.6
7. 948.684 + 15.17 + 0.717
8. 625.365 + 27.97 + 0.613
9. Calculate the sum of the following numbers:
   Twenty and ninety-five hundredths; Two hundred and seventy-two thousandths; Nineteen and nine tenths.
10. Calculate the sum of the following numbers:
    Six and thirty-nine thousandths; Eighty and fourteen hundredths; Sixteen and eight tenths.

For Problems 11 to 18, perform the subtractions.

11. 423.92 – 185.728
12. 9.555 – 7.18
13. 29.28 – 13.4
14. 15.7 – 7.92
15. 539.64 – 258.357
16. 848.62 – 495.476
17. 409.5 – 179.832
18. 475.3 – 281.375
19. Subtract three hundred five and thirty-nine hundredths from seven hundred twenty and four tenths.
20. Subtract eight hundred twenty and four hundredths from one thousand, one hundred one and six tenths.

For Problems 21 to 28, perform the multiplications.

21. 137.89 × 5.4
22. 189.945 × 6.3
23. 62.095 × 4.18
24. 92.74 × 3.25
25. 0.43 × 0.8
26. 0.59 × 0.9
27. 109.78 × 2.91
28. 145.75 × 3.74

For Problems 29 to 36, perform the divisions.

29. 67.78 ÷ 9
30. 261.31 ÷ 7
31. 732.6 ÷ 8
32. 413.9 ÷ 6
33. 14.6 ÷ 0.6
34. 9.155 ÷ 0.7
35. 3.1 ÷ 0.25
36. 2.7 ÷ 0.15

For Problems 37 to 40, evaluate the powers of the decimal numbers.

37. a. $(0.1)^3$ b. $(0.3)^2$

38. a. $(1.1)^3$ b. $(1.2)^3$

39. a. $(0.4)^2$ b. $(0.02)^3$

40. a. $(0.9)^2$ b. $(0.05)^3$

For Problems 41 to 46, evaluate the square roots of the decimal numbers.

41. a. $\sqrt{0.25}$ b. $\sqrt{0.49}$

42. a. $\sqrt{0.36}$ b. $\sqrt{0.64}$

43. a. $\sqrt{1.21}$ b. $\sqrt{1.69}$

44. a. $\sqrt{2.56}$ b. $\sqrt{1.44}$

45. a. $\sqrt{0.01}$ b. $\sqrt{0.0049}$

46. a. $\sqrt{0.09}$ b. $\sqrt{0.0004}$

For Problems 47 to 54, formulate arithmetic expressions and evaluate.

47. Find the amount that is $248.76 less than $627.40.

48. Find the amount that is $45.27 less than $90.75.

49. Find the difference in the amounts $30.75 and $15.89.

50. Find the difference in the amounts $235.62 and $115.75.

51. Find the sum of $52.43 and $23.95.

52. Find the sum of $252.34 and $297.90.

53. Find the amount that is $38.89 more than $25.67.

54. Find the amount that is $412.78 more than $634.25.

55. The cost of an item is $88.46. If you gave $90.00 to the cashier, how much change would you receive?

56. The cost of an item is $125.69. If Arun gave $150.00 to the cashier, how much change would Arun receive?

57. Bill saved $578.50 this week. He saved $124.85 more last week than this week. How much did Bill save during the two-week period?

58. Last week Carol spent $96.75 more on food than on transportation. She spent $223.15 on transport. How much did Carol spend on both food and transportation last week?

59. The normal selling price of an item is $237.75. When this item was on sale Dave paid $49.89 less for it. How much did Dave pay for that item?

60. A car driver filled gas when the odometer reading was 35,894.9 km. The odometer reading now is 39,894.4 km. How many kilometres did the driver travel, rounded to the nearest kilometre?

61. After spending $38.96 on toys and $1.75 on wrapping paper, Ann still had $45.75. How much money did Ann have initially?

62. After paying $515.09 for a car lease and $379.92 for property tax, Elisa's bank balance was $675.45. How much money did Elisa have initially?

63. Simon bought a camera that was on sale for $799.99. He agreed to pay $70.35 every month for 12 months. How much more money than the sale price did Simon pay for the camera?

64. Andy bought a TV that was on sale for $2,249.95. He agreed to pay $130.45 every month for 18 months. How much more money than the sale price did Andy pay for the TV?

65. A salesperson earns a salary of $725.35 every week. During the past three weeks, he also received commissions of $375.68, $578.79, and $338.57. Calculate his total income for the past three weeks.

66. Danny leased a car on a four-year term at $694.38 per month. At the end of the lease period, she paid an additional $18,458.74 to purchase the car. Calculate the total amount Danny paid for the car.

67. John bought two shirts at $20.95 each and three pairs of pants at $34.55 each. He gave $200 to the cashier. Calculate the balance he should receive from the cashier.

68. Taylor bought 3 kg of walnuts at \$8.69 per kg and 4 kg of almonds at \$7.72 per kg. He gave the cashier a \$100 bill. How much change should Taylor receive from the cashier?

69. A string that measured 0.875 m was cut into pieces of 0.0625 m each. How many pieces were there?

70. A cake that weighed 0.82 kg was cut into slices that weighed 0.1025 kg each. How many slices were there?

71. Marion bought three dresses at \$22.49 per dress and two pairs of shoes at \$14.99 per pair. She gave a \$100 bill to the cashier. What change should she expect to receive from the cashier?

72. Gilbert bought 2 kg of grapes at \$3.29 per kg and 1.5 kg of strawberries at \$5.99 per kg. He gave a \$20 bill to the cashier. How much should he expect to receive in change from the cashier?

2.5 | Converting Between Fractions and Decimal Numbers and Combined Order of Operations

Converting Decimal Numbers to Fractions

It is possible to convert **terminating** decimal numbers (e.g., 0.275) and **repeating, non-terminating** decimal numbers (e.g., 0.333333...) to fractions. However, there is no exact equivalent fraction for **non-repeating, non-terminating** decimal numbers (e.g., 0.837508...).

Converting Terminating Decimal Numbers to Fractions

Any non-repeating, terminating decimal number can be converted to a fraction by following these steps:

Step 1: Count the number of decimal places in the decimal number.

Step 2: Move the decimal point by that many places to the right, making it a whole number, and divide this whole number by 10 raised to the power of the number of decimal places counted in Step 1; for example, if there were 2 decimal places in the original number, we divide by $10^2 = 100$.

Step 3: Simplify (or reduce) the fraction.

Example 2.5-a **Converting Terminating Decimal Numbers to Fractions**

Convert the following decimal numbers to their fractional equivalents:

(i) 3.75

(ii) 0.015

Solution

(i) Converting 3.75 to its fractional equivalent:

3.75 — 3.75 contains two decimal places. Therefore, move the decimal point two places to the right and divide by $10^2 = 100$.

$= \frac{3.75}{100}$ — (This is the same as multiplying by 100 and dividing by 100: $\frac{3.75 \times 100}{100} = \frac{375}{100}$)

$= \frac{375}{100}$ (÷25 numerator and denominator) — Dividing by 25 to simplify,

$= \frac{15}{4} = 3\frac{3}{4}$

Therefore, 3.75 converted to its fractional equivalent is $\frac{15}{4}$ or $3\frac{3}{4}$.

Solution *continued*

(ii) Converting 0.015 to its fractional equivalent:

0.015 — 0.015 contains three decimal places. Therefore, move the decimal point three places to the right and divide by $10^3 = 1{,}000$.

$= \frac{0.015}{1{,}000}$ — (This is the same as multiplying by 1,000 and dividing by 1,000: $\frac{0.015 \times 1{,}000}{1{,}000} = \frac{15}{1{,}000}$)

$= \frac{15}{1{,}000}\ {\scriptstyle \div 5}$ — Dividing by 5 to simplify,

$= \frac{3}{200}$

Therefore, 0.015 converted to its fractional equivalent is $\frac{3}{200}$.

Converting Repeating Decimal Numbers to Fractions

Any repeating, non-terminating decimal number can be converted to a fraction by following the procedure illustrated in the following examples.

Example 2.5-b **Converting Repeating Decimal Numbers to Fractions**

Convert 0.777777... to a fraction.

Solution

Let 0.777777... be equal to a fraction x.

Therefore,

(a) $x = 0.777777... = 0.\overline{7}$ — Multiplying both sides by 10,

(b) $10x = 7.777777... = 7.\overline{7}$ — We now have two repeating decimal numbers, each with the same decimal portion.

Subtracting (a) from (b),

$10x - x = 7.\overline{7} - 0.\overline{7}$

$9x = 7$ — Dividing both sides by 9,

$x = \frac{7}{9}$

This method makes use of **algebra**, which will be covered in detail in Chapter 4.

Therefore, $0.777777... = \frac{7}{9}$.

Example 2.5-c **Converting Repeating Decimal Numbers to Fractions**

Convert 0.655555... to a fraction.

Solution

Let 0.655555... be equal to a fraction x.

Therefore,

(a) $x = 0.655555... = 0.6\overline{5}$ — Multiplying both sides by 10,

(b) $10x = 6.555555... = 6.\overline{5}$ — The decimal portions of the two decimal numbers are different. Multiplying both sides by 10 again,

(c) $100x = 65.555555... = 65.\overline{5}$ — We now have two repeating decimal numbers with the same decimal portion ((b) and (c)).

Solution *continued*

Subtracting (b) from (c),

$100x - 10x = 65.\overline{5} - 6.\overline{5}$

$90x = 59$ Dividing both sides by 90,

$x = \frac{59}{90}$

Therefore, $0.655555... = \frac{59}{90}$.

Example 2.5-d **Converting Repeating Decimal Numbers to Fractions**

Convert 0.353535... to a fraction.

Solution

Let 0.353535... be equal to a fraction x.

Therefore,

(a) $x = 0.353535... = 0.\overline{35}$ Multiplying both sides by 10,

(b) $10x = 3.535353... = 3.\overline{53}$ The decimal portions of the two decimal numbers are different. Multiplying both sides by 10 again,

(c) $100x = 35.353535... = 35.\overline{35}$ We now have two repeating decimal numbers with the same decimal portion ((a) and (c)).

Subtracting (a) from (c),

$100x - x = 35.\overline{35} - 0.\overline{35}$

$99x = 35$ Dividing both sides by 99,

$x = \frac{35}{99}$

Therefore, $0.353535... = \frac{35}{99}$.

Rational numbers can be represented by $\frac{a}{b}$, whereas irrational numbers cannot be represented by $\frac{a}{b}$, where 'a' and 'b' are integers and $b \neq 0$.

From Examples 2.5-a to 2.5-d, we have learned that it is possible to convert terminating decimal numbers (e.g., 0.015) and repeating, non-terminating decimal numbers (e.g., $0.6\overline{5}$) into fractions. Therefore, such decimal numbers are **rational numbers**.

However, it is not possible to convert non-repeating, non-terminating decimal numbers (e.g., $\sqrt{2}$, π, 5.81271...) to fractions. Such decimal numbers are referred to as **irrational numbers**.

These rational numbers and irrational (non-rational) numbers together form the **real numbers** in the number system.

Converting Fractions to Decimal Numbers

Converting Proper and Improper Fractions to Decimal Numbers

A proper or improper fraction can be converted to its equivalent decimal number by dividing the numerator by the denominator, as shown in the following examples.

Example 2.5-e **Converting Proper and Improper Fractions to Decimal Numbers**

Convert the following fractions to their decimal number equivalents:

(i) $\frac{3}{8}$ (ii) $\frac{15}{11}$

Solution

(i) $\frac{3}{8}$

$= 3 \div 8$

$= 0.375$

$$\begin{array}{r} .375 \\ 8\overline{)3.000} \\ -24 \\ \hline 60 \\ -56 \\ \hline 40 \\ -40 \\ \hline 0 \end{array}$$

A remainder of zero indicates that the decimal equivalent of the fraction is a terminating decimal number.

Therefore, 0.375 is the decimal equivalent of $\frac{3}{8}$.

(ii) $\frac{15}{11}$

$= 15 \div 11$

$= 1.363636....$

$= 1.\overline{36}$

$$\begin{array}{r} 1.3636 \\ 11\overline{)15.0000} \\ -11 \\ \hline 40 \\ -33 \\ \hline 70 \\ -66 \\ \hline 40 \\ -33 \\ \hline 70 \\ -66 \\ \hline 4 \end{array}$$

If we continue to add 0's to the end of the dividend, the pattern will repeat and we will continually add '36' to the end of the quotient. Therefore, the decimal equivalent of the fraction is a repeating, non-terminating decimal number.

Therefore, $1.\overline{36}$ is the decimal equivalent of $\frac{15}{11}$.

Converting Mixed Numbers to Decimal Numbers

A mixed number can be converted to its decimal form by first converting it to an improper fraction, then dividing the numerator by the denominator, as shown in the following example.

Example 2.5-f **Converting Mixed Numbers to Decimal Numbers**

Convert the following mixed numbers to their decimal number equivalents:

(i) $3\frac{2}{5}$ (ii) $11\frac{3}{7}$

Solution

(i) $3\frac{2}{5}$ Coverting to an improper fraction,

$= \frac{3(5) + 2}{5} = \frac{17}{5}$ Dividing the numerator by the denominator,

$= 3.4$

Therefore, the decimal number equivalent of $3\frac{2}{5}$ is 3.4.

(ii) $11\frac{3}{7}$ Coverting to an improper fraction,

$= \frac{11(7) + 3}{7} = \frac{80}{7}$ Dividing the numerator by the denominator,

$= 11.428571... = 11.43$

Therefore, the decimal number equivalent of $11\frac{3}{7}$, rounded to two decimal places, is 11.43.

Combined Order of Operations

The Order of Operations **(BEDMAS)**, as learned in Chapter 1, Section 1.4, is also used in evaluating expressions with fractions and decimal numbers.

Arithmetic expressions with fractions and decimal numbers that contain multiple operations are performed in the following sequence:

1. Evaluate the expressions within grouping symbols (i.e., **B**rackets and radical signs).
2. Evaluate powers (i.e., **E**xponents) and roots.
3. Perform **D**ivision and **M**ultiplication, in order from left to right.
4. Perform **A**ddition and **S**ubtraction, in order from left to right.

Note: For multiplication, division, powers, and roots of mixed numbers, they must first be converted to improper fractions before proceeding with the Order of Operations.

Example 2.5-g **Evaluating Expressions Using Order of Operations (BEDMAS)**

Evaluate the following expressions:

(i) $\left(1\frac{1}{3}\right)^2 + \sqrt{\frac{5}{16} + \frac{20}{16}}$ (ii) $\left(\frac{2}{3}\right)^2 + \frac{1}{2}\left(4\frac{1}{2}\right)^2 \div \sqrt{81}$

(iii) $\left(\frac{4}{5}\right)^2 + \left(\frac{11}{9} + \sqrt{\frac{49}{81}}\right) \times \frac{3}{25}$ (iv) $\sqrt{1\frac{69}{100}} + \sqrt{0.09} + \sqrt{\frac{64}{25}}$

(v) $\left(1 + \frac{0.08}{4}\right)^2 - 1$

Solution

(i) $\left(1\frac{1}{3}\right)^2 + \sqrt{\frac{5}{16} + \frac{20}{16}}$

$= \left(\frac{4}{3}\right)^2 + \sqrt{\frac{25}{16}}$

$= \left(\frac{4}{3}\right)\left(\frac{4}{3}\right) + \frac{\sqrt{25}}{\sqrt{16}}$

$= \frac{16}{9} + \frac{5}{4}$

$= \frac{64}{36} + \frac{45}{36}$

$= \frac{109}{36} = 3\frac{1}{36}$

(ii) $\left(\frac{2}{3}\right)^2 + \frac{1}{2}\left(4\frac{1}{2}\right)^2 \div \sqrt{81}$

$= \left(\frac{2}{3}\right)\left(\frac{2}{3}\right) + \frac{1}{2}\left(\frac{9}{2}\right)\left(\frac{9}{2}\right) \div 9$

$= \frac{4}{9} + \frac{\overset{9}{\cancel{81}}}{8} \times \frac{1}{\cancel{9}_1}$

$= \frac{4}{9} + \frac{9}{8}$

$= \frac{32}{72} + \frac{81}{72}$

$= \frac{113}{72} = 1\frac{41}{72}$

(iii) $\left(\frac{4}{5}\right)^2 + \left(\frac{11}{9} + \sqrt{\frac{49}{81}}\right) \times \frac{3}{25}$

$= \left(\frac{4}{5}\right)^2 + \left(\frac{11}{9} + \frac{\sqrt{49}}{\sqrt{81}}\right) \times \frac{3}{25}$

$= \left(\frac{4}{5}\right)^2 + \left(\frac{11}{9} + \frac{7}{9}\right) \times \frac{3}{25}$

$= \left(\frac{4}{5}\right)^2 + \frac{18}{9} \times \frac{3}{25}$

(iv) $\sqrt{1\frac{69}{100}} + \sqrt{0.09} + \sqrt{\frac{64}{25}}$

$= \sqrt{\frac{169}{100}} + \sqrt{\frac{9}{100}} + \sqrt{\frac{64}{25}}$

$= \frac{\sqrt{169}}{\sqrt{100}} + \frac{\sqrt{9}}{\sqrt{100}} + \frac{\sqrt{64}}{\sqrt{25}}$

$= \frac{13}{10} + \frac{3}{10} + \frac{8}{5}$

Solution *continued*

$= \left(\frac{4}{5}\right)\left(\frac{4}{5}\right) + 2 \times \frac{3}{25}$

$= \frac{16}{25} + \frac{6}{25}$

$= \frac{22}{25}$

$= \frac{13}{10} + \frac{3}{10} + \frac{16}{10}$

$= \frac{32}{10}$

$= \frac{16}{5} = 3\frac{1}{5}$

(v) $\left(1 + \frac{0.08}{4}\right)^2 - 1$

$= (1 + 0.02)^2 - 1$

$= (1.02)^2 - 1$

$= (1.02)(1.02) - 1$

$= 1.0404 - 1$

$= 0.0404$

Example 2.5-h **Evaluating Expressions by Using the Order of Operations (BEDMAS)**

Evaluate: $\frac{4}{2^3}[(0.5 \times 5^2 + 2.5)^2 \div 3^2] + \sqrt{25}$

Solution

$\frac{4}{2^3}[(0.5 \times 5^2 + 2.5)^2 \div 3^2] + \sqrt{25}$

$= \frac{4}{2^3}[(0.5 \times 25 + 2.5)^2 \div 3^2] + \sqrt{25}$

$= \frac{4}{2^3}[(12.5 + 2.5)^2 \div 3^2] + \sqrt{25}$

$= \frac{4}{2^3}[15^2 \div 3^2] + \sqrt{25}$

$= \frac{4}{2^3}[225 \div 9] + \sqrt{25}$

$= \frac{4}{2^3} \times 25 + \sqrt{25}$

$= \frac{4}{8} \times 25 + 5$

$= 0.5 \times 25 + 5$

$= 12.5 + 5$

$= 17.5$

2.5 | Exercises

Answers to odd-numbered problems are available at the end of the textbook.

For Problems 1 to 8, convert the decimal numbers to proper fractions and the proper fractions to decimal numbers.

1.

	Decimal Number	Proper Fraction
a.	0.2	?
b.	?	$\frac{3}{4}$
c.	0.06	?

2.

	Decimal Number	Proper Fraction
a.	0.26	?
b.	?	$\frac{41}{50}$
c.	0.92	?

3.

	Decimal Number	Proper Fraction
a.	?	$\frac{9}{25}$
b.	0.004	?
c.	?	$\frac{7}{50}$

4.

	Decimal Number	Proper Fraction
a.	?	$\frac{16}{25}$
b.	0.225	?
c.	?	$\frac{19}{20}$

5.

	Decimal Number	Proper Fraction
a.	?	$\frac{1}{2}$
b.	0.4	?
c.	?	$\frac{3}{50}$

6.

	Decimal Number	Proper Fraction
a.	?	$\frac{13}{20}$
b.	0.425	?
c.	?	$\frac{14}{25}$

7.

	Decimal Number	Proper Fraction
a.	0.005	?
b.	?	$\frac{9}{25}$
c.	0.01	?

8.

	Decimal Number	Proper Fraction
a.	0.66	?
b.	?	$\frac{43}{50}$
c.	0.78	?

For Problems 9 to 12, convert the decimal numbers to improper fractions and the improper fractions to decimal numbers.

9.

	Decimal Number	Improper Fraction
a.	3.5	?
b.	?	$\frac{8}{5}$
c.	5.6	?

10.

	Decimal Number	Improper Fraction
a.	7.2	?
b.	?	$\frac{37}{5}$
c.	8.4	?

11.

	Decimal Number	Improper Fraction
a.	?	$\frac{101}{20}$
b.	6.8	?
c.	?	$\frac{11}{4}$

12.

	Decimal Number	Improper Fraction
a.	?	$\frac{107}{50}$
b.	4.8	?
c.	?	$\frac{23}{4}$

For Problem 13 to 16, convert the decimal numbers to mixed numbers and the mixed numbers to decimal numbers.

13.

	Decimal Number	Mixed Number
a.	2.25	?
b.	?	$1\frac{3}{4}$
c.	4.02	?

14.

	Decimal Number	Mixed Number
a.	5.04	?
b.	?	$12\frac{3}{5}$
c.	14.025	?

15.

	Decimal Number	Mixed Number
a.	?	$8\frac{7}{20}$
b.	16.005	?
c.	?	$15\frac{1}{2}$

16.

	Decimal Number	Mixed Number
a.	?	$3\frac{5}{8}$
b.	4.75	?
c.	?	$5\frac{9}{20}$

For Problems 17 to 20, convert the repeating decimal numbers to proper fractions and the proper fractions to repeating decimal numbers.

17.

	Decimal Number	Proper Fraction
a.	$0.\overline{6}$	?
b.	?	$\frac{23}{90}$
c.	$0.\overline{25}$	?

18.

	Decimal Number	Proper Fraction
a.	$0.\overline{27}$	?
b.	?	$\frac{4}{7}$
c.	$0.8\overline{3}$	?

19.

	Decimal Number	Proper Fraction
a.	?	$\frac{5}{11}$
b.	$0.\overline{2}$	?
c.	?	$\frac{2}{7}$

20.

	Decimal Number	Proper Fraction
a.	?	$\frac{4}{99}$
b.	$0.\overline{75}$	?
c.	?	$\frac{11}{15}$

For Problems 21 to 52, evaluate the expressions.

21. a. $\left(\frac{3}{5}\right)^2\left(\frac{2}{3}\right)^3$ b. $\left(\frac{3}{4}\right)^3\left(\frac{1}{6}\right)^2$

22. a. $\left(\frac{5}{2}\right)^3\left(\frac{1}{3}\right)^2$ b. $\left(\frac{3}{8}\right)^2\left(\frac{4}{3}\right)^3$

23. a. $\left(\frac{1}{4}\right)^2 \div \left(\frac{2}{3}\right)^3$ b. $\left(\frac{5}{3}\right)^2 \div \left(\frac{10}{9}\right)^2$

24. a. $\left(\frac{1}{2}\right)^2 \div \left(\frac{1}{3}\right)^2$ b. $\left(\frac{2}{3}\right)^2 \div \left(\frac{4}{9}\right)^2$

25. a. $\sqrt{\frac{5}{9}+\frac{4}{9}}$ b. $\sqrt{\frac{15}{36}+\frac{5}{18}}$

26. a. $\sqrt{\frac{2}{25}+\frac{14}{25}}$ b. $\sqrt{\frac{1}{16}+\frac{1}{2}}$

27. a. $\left(2\frac{1}{6}+1\frac{2}{3}\right) \div 5\frac{3}{4}$ b. $8\frac{1}{2} \div \left(2\frac{2}{5}+2\right)$

28. a. $\left(5\frac{1}{4}+2\frac{5}{6}\right) \div 1\frac{1}{2}$ b. $2\frac{2}{3} \div \left(1\frac{7}{15}+\frac{2}{3}\right)$

29. a. $\left(\frac{3}{5}\right)^2 + \left(1\frac{1}{5}\right)(\sqrt{144})$ b. $\left(\frac{2}{5}\right)^2 + \left(\frac{3}{2}\right)^3$

30. a. $\left(\frac{4}{7}\right)^2 + \sqrt{\frac{3}{9}+\frac{1}{9}}$ b. $\left(\frac{3}{8}\right)^2 + \left(\frac{1}{2}\right)^3$

31. a. $\sqrt{4\frac{21}{25}} \times \left(\frac{5}{3}\right)^2$ b. $\left(\frac{1}{4}\right)^2 \times \left(\frac{1}{8}\right)^2$

32. a. $\sqrt{1\frac{9}{16}} \times \left(\frac{4}{5}\right)^2$ b. $\left(\frac{1}{3}\right)^2 \div \left(\frac{1}{6}\right)^2$

33. a. $(1.3)^2 \times \sqrt{0.04}$ b. $(0.1)^3 \div \sqrt{\frac{1}{100}}$

34. a. $(0.01)^2 \times \sqrt{0.09}$ b. $(0.5)^3 \div \sqrt{\frac{1}{100}}$

35. $\left(\frac{5}{8}\right)^2 + \frac{3}{16} + \frac{5}{12} + 1\frac{2}{3}$

36. $\left(\frac{6}{7}\right)^2 + 1\frac{5}{9} + \frac{5}{6} + 4\frac{1}{2}$

37. $\sqrt{\frac{7}{9}-\frac{2}{3}} \div \left(\frac{1}{12}+\frac{1}{9}\right)$

38. $\left(\frac{5}{12}+\frac{3}{8}\right) \div \sqrt{\frac{4}{18}+\frac{1}{36}}$

39. $10\frac{1}{2} \div 4\frac{1}{5} + \frac{9}{10} \times 2\frac{2}{5} - \frac{3}{4}$

40. $7\frac{2}{3} \div 2\frac{1}{3} + \frac{3}{5} \times 4\frac{2}{3} - \frac{2}{5}$

41. $13\frac{3}{7} \times \frac{5}{94} + 6\frac{4}{5} \div \frac{4}{15} + 7\frac{1}{5}$

42. $2\frac{1}{6} \div \frac{26}{45} + 3\frac{1}{4} \times 4\frac{1}{2} + \frac{3}{8}$

43. $[0.8 - (7.2 - 6.5)] \div [3 \div (3.4 - 0.4)]$

44. $(9.9 \div 1.1) \div (8.1 \div 1.5) + (9.2 - 7.7 + 1.5)$

45. $(9.2 + 2.8)\ 0.25 \div (5.6 - 2.3 + 1.7)$

46. $(9.1 - 7.3)\ 0.5 \div (5.8 + 8.6 - 5.4)$

• 47. $\sqrt{49} + \frac{8}{4^2}(0.4 \times 6^2 \div 1.2)^2$

• 48. $\sqrt{81} + \frac{12.5}{5^2}(0.3 \times 5^2 \div 1.5)^2$

• 49. $\sqrt{2\frac{25}{100}} + \sqrt{0.16} + \sqrt{\frac{49}{16}}$

• 50. $\sqrt{1\frac{21}{100}} + \sqrt{0.25} + \sqrt{\frac{25}{36}}$

• 51. $\frac{9}{50}\left(\sqrt{\frac{49}{81}} + 1\frac{4}{9}\right) + \left(1\frac{3}{5}\right)^2$

• 52. $\frac{16}{25}\left(\sqrt{\frac{25}{16}} + 2\frac{1}{4}\right) + \left(1\frac{2}{5}\right)^2$

2 | Review Exercises

Answers to odd-numbered problems are available at the end of the textbook.

For Problems 1 and 2, determine the missing values.

1. a. $\frac{6}{12}=\frac{?}{6}=\frac{24}{?}$ b. $\frac{12}{45}=\frac{?}{15}=\frac{16}{?}$

   c. $\frac{20}{25}=\frac{?}{5}=\frac{12}{?}$ d. $\frac{36}{48}=\frac{?}{36}=\frac{18}{?}$

2. a. $\frac{9}{15}=\frac{?}{10}=\frac{15}{?}$ b. $\frac{18}{27}=\frac{?}{18}=\frac{10}{?}$

   c. $\frac{21}{35}=\frac{?}{25}=\frac{12}{?}$ d. $\frac{12}{28}=\frac{?}{70}=\frac{15}{?}$

For Problems 3 and 4, place the appropriate symbol (<, >, or =) between each of the fractions.

3. a. $\frac{24}{21}\ \square\ \frac{11}{5}$ b. $\frac{20}{44}\ \square\ \frac{6}{15}$

   c. $\frac{18}{45}\ \square\ \frac{16}{4}$ d. $\frac{15}{25}\ \square\ \frac{63}{105}$

4. a. $\frac{15}{18}\ \square\ \frac{30}{42}$ b. $\frac{21}{24}\ \square\ \frac{35}{40}$

   c. $\frac{40}{48}\ \square\ \frac{35}{42}$ d. $\frac{8}{38}\ \square\ \frac{12}{57}$

For Problems 5 and 6, convert the improper fractions into mixed numbers in simplest form.

5. a. $\frac{15}{10}$ b. $\frac{39}{26}$

   c. $\frac{88}{12}$ d. $\frac{102}{9}$

6. a. $\frac{18}{8}$ b. $\frac{98}{12}$

   c. $\frac{88}{10}$ d. $\frac{48}{15}$

For Problems 7 and 8, reduce the fractions to their lowest terms.

7. a. $\frac{75}{345}$ b. $\frac{124}{48}$

   c. $\frac{70}{14}$ d. $\frac{292}{365}$

8. a. $\frac{36}{144}$ b. $\frac{68}{10}$

   c. $\frac{80}{12}$ d. $\frac{61}{366}$

For Problems 9 to 12, express the decimal numbers in their word form.

9. a. 0.5 b. 0.007

   c. 0.12 d. 0.029

10. a. 0.75 b. 0.3

    c. 0.008 d. 0.04

11. a. 32.04 b. 200.2

    c. 45,005.001 d. 1,005,071.25

12. a. 27.602 b. 470.5

    c. 32,010.07 d. 3,500,007.45

For Problems 13 and 14, perform the indicated arithmetic operations.

13. a. 478.82 + 85.847 b. 65.09 – 24.987

    c. 54.37 × 1.46 d. 77.09 ÷ 8

14. a. 716.03 + 49.936 b. 15.71 – 3.509

    c. 15.71 × 3.26 d. 39.83 ÷ 9

15. What is the difference between the least and the greatest numbers of the following?

    0.012, 0.201, 0.02, 0.102

16. What is the sum of the least and the greatest numbers of the following?

    0.041, 0.011, 0.014, 0.01

17. Which of the following is closest to 2?

    2.011, 2.005, 1.996, 1.995

18. Which of the following is closest to 2?

    2.011, 2.004, 1.997, 1.996

For Problems 19 and 20, convert the decimal numbers to proper fractions in lowest terms and the fractions to decimal numbers.

19.

	Decimal Number	Proper Fraction
a.	0.025	?
b.	?	$\frac{5}{8}$
c.	0.08	?
d.	?	$\frac{7}{25}$
e.	0.002	?
f.	?	$\frac{39}{50}$

20.

	Decimal Number	Proper Fraction
a.	0.06	?
b.	?	$\frac{23}{50}$
c.	0.075	?
d.	?	$\frac{27}{40}$
e.	0.004	?
f.	?	$\frac{17}{25}$

21. Find the total weight of three items that weigh $3\frac{2}{3}$ kg, $4\frac{1}{2}$ kg, and $5\frac{3}{8}$ kg.

22. Alex used $2\frac{1}{5}$ litres of paint for his bedroom, $1\frac{1}{4}$ litres for his study room, and $7\frac{1}{3}$ litres for his living room. How many litres of paint did he use for the three rooms?

23. Henry is $8\frac{1}{4}$ years old. Amanda is $2\frac{5}{12}$ years old. How many years younger is Amanda than Henry?

24. Harsha purchased $12\frac{1}{3}$ hectares of land and sold $4\frac{2}{5}$ hectares. How many hectares does she now own?

25. A car can travel $8\frac{1}{4}$ km with one litre of gas. How many kilometres can it travel using $45\frac{3}{5}$ litres of gas?

26. Samantha can walk $5\frac{3}{8}$ km in one hour. How far can she walk in $4\frac{1}{3}$ hours?

27. Alisha and Beyonce saved a total of $580. Two-fifths of Alisha's savings equals $144. How much did each of them save?

28. Andy and Bob had $128. One-third of Bob's amount is $25. How much did each of them have?

29. Lakshmi had $2,675.68 in her chequing account. She deposited 2 cheques in the amounts of $729.27 and $72.05 and withdrew $1,275.60. How much did she have in her account after the withdrawal?

30. George's car had 12.47 litres of gas at the start of his trip to the United States. He added the following quantities of gas during his trip: 34.25 litres, 15.2 litres, and 20.05 litres. At the end of the trip, there were 7.9 litres of gas left in the car. How much gas was used during the trip?

31. Barbie's hourly pay is $23.07. If Barbie worked 37.75 hours last week, calculate her gross pay for last week.

32. Carol's overtime rate of pay is $57.45 per hour. If Carol worked 12.5 hours overtime last week, calculate her gross overtime pay for last week.

33. Three-fourths of the number of boys at a school is equal to half of the number of girls. The school has 480 students in total. How many more girls are there than boys?

34. There are 3,400 spectators at a soccer match. Three-fifths of the number of men equals six-sevenths of the number of women. How many spectators are women?

For Problems 35 to 46, evaluate the expressions.

35. $5 + \left(\frac{6}{10}\right)^3 + \sqrt{6^2 + 8^2}$

36. $\left(\frac{5}{7}\right)^2 \div 5 + \sqrt{3^2 + 4^2}$

37. $\sqrt{1.21} - (0.5)^2 + \sqrt{\frac{4}{25}}$

38. $\sqrt{0.81} - (0.2)^2 + \sqrt{\frac{9}{36}}$

39. $\left(\frac{1}{5}\right)^3 + \left(\frac{4}{25}\right)^2$

40. $\left(\frac{2}{3}\right)^3 + \left(\frac{2}{9}\right)^2$

41. $\left(\frac{5}{12}\right)^3 \left(\frac{4}{5}\right)^2$

42. $\left(\frac{4}{7}\right)^2 \left(\frac{1}{4}\right)^3$

43. $\left(2\frac{4}{5} - \frac{7}{10}\right) \div 2\frac{4}{5}$

44. $\left(2\frac{5}{8} + 1\frac{5}{12}\right) \div 1\frac{1}{2}$

45. $3\frac{1}{5} \div \left(1\frac{1}{5} + 1\right)$

46. $2\frac{2}{3} \div \left(2\frac{2}{5} + 6\right)$

Self-Test | Chapter 2

Answers to all problems are available at the end of the textbook.

1. Determine the missing values:

   a. $\frac{5}{5} = \frac{?}{20} = \frac{24}{?}$ b. $\frac{12}{22} = \frac{6}{?} = \frac{?}{55}$

   c. $\frac{48}{72} = \frac{12}{?} = \frac{?}{144}$ d. $\frac{11}{12} = \frac{?}{72} = \frac{22}{?}$

2. Reduce the following fractions to their lowest terms:

   a. $\frac{225}{30}$ b. $\frac{156}{18}$

   c. $\frac{256}{144}$ d. $\frac{135}{825}$

3. Perform the indicated operations:

   a. $7\frac{1}{2} + 6\frac{1}{4}$ b. $5\frac{1}{3} - 3\frac{7}{15}$

   c. $\frac{3}{4} \times \frac{26}{27} \times \frac{9}{13}$ d. $2\frac{1}{4} \div \frac{3}{8}$

4. Perform the indicated operations:

   a. $0.165 + 10.8478 + 14.7 + 2.19$

   b. $34.09 - 25.957$

   c. 0.524×4.08

   d. $6.893 \div 3$

5. Express the following numbers in word from:

   a. 0.004 b. 6.05

   c. 300.02 d. 7.071

6. Convert the decimal numbers to fractions in lowest terms and fractions to decimal numbers:

	Decimal Number	Fraction
a.	0.625	?
b.	3.2	?
c.	$0.\overline{72}$	?
d.	?	$\frac{7}{20}$
e.	?	$1\frac{4}{5}$
f.	?	$\frac{16}{15}$

7. On a certain map, 1 cm represents 125 km. How many km are represented by 4.75 cm? How many cm on the map will represent a distance of 4,725 km?

8. Kyle had $4,000 and gave half of it to Bob. Bob spent a quarter of the money he received from Kyle. How much money does Bob have left?

For Problems 9 and 10, evaluate the expressions.

9. a. $\sqrt{\frac{81}{64}} - \left(\frac{5}{4}\right)^3 \div \left(\frac{25}{16}\right)^2 + \sqrt{7^2 + 24^2}$

   b. $\left(\frac{3}{5}\right)^3 \left(\frac{25}{6}\right)^2 + (\sqrt{0.25})\sqrt{100}$

   c. $\sqrt{5^2 + 12^2} - (\sqrt{0.49})\sqrt{\frac{25}{144}}$

10. a. $\left(4\frac{9}{10} \div \frac{7}{15} \times 1\frac{3}{5}\right) \div 1\frac{9}{10}$

    b. $3\frac{1}{2} \div 1\frac{2}{5} + \frac{9}{10} \times 2\frac{2}{5} - \frac{3}{4}$

    c. $\left(3\frac{4}{15} + 2\frac{3}{5}\right) \times \left(\frac{5}{6} + \frac{1}{9}\right) - 1\frac{1}{2}$

• 11. Henry took 3 days to make 69 deliveries. On the first day, he completed one-third of the deliveries. On the second day, he made 10 more deliveries than on the first day. How many deliveries did he make on the third day?

• 12. Niveda spent one-third of her money on a handbag and half of the remainder on shoes. What fraction of her money did she spend on shoes? If she has $40 left, how much did she spend?

• 13. The cost per day to rent a car is $24.45 plus $0.37 per kilometre driven. What would be the cost to rent a car for 5 days if Sally plans to drive 325.50 km?

• 14. Ana walked for $\frac{3}{4}$ hour at $5\frac{1}{2}$ km per hour and jogged for $\frac{1}{2}$ hour at 10 km per hour. What was the total distance that she covered?

Chapter 3 | OPERATIONS WITH EXPONENTS AND INTEGERS

LEARNING OBJECTIVES

- Identify the types and properties of exponents.
- Perform arithmetic operations with exponents.
- Identify types of roots.
- Perform computations with roots and fractional exponents.
- Perform arithmetic operations with signed numbers.
- Apply rounding rules using significant digits.
- Perform calculations involving scientific notation.

CHAPTER OUTLINE

3.1 Exponents and Properties (Rules) of Exponents

3.2 Roots, Fractional Exponents, and Negative Exponents

3.3 Arithmetic Operations with Signed Numbers

3.4 Significant Digits and Scientific Notation

Introduction

In Chapters 1 and 2, we learned that **exponents** are used to indicate that a number or expression is to be multiplied by itself a certain number of times. Exponents allow us to perform arithmetic operations more simply than having to use the standard form of a number. A practical application of exponents is used in calculating compound interest on loans and investments. In this chapter, we will expand upon our knowledge of exponents, and look further into the properties of exponents, the relationship between exponents and roots, and how to use exponents to represent extremely large and extremely small numbers through scientific notation.

Furthermore, all of the numbers we have been working with so far have been positive numbers; that is, they lie to the right of zero on the number line. However, every positive whole number, fraction, and decimal number has a negative number known as its opposite, which lies the same distance to the left of zero on the number line. **Integers** are made up of zero (0), all counting numbers (1, 2, 3, 4, ...), and their opposites (–1, –2, –3, –4, ...). In this chapter, we will also expand our knowledge of arithmetic operations to include both positively '+' and negatively '–' signed numbers.

3.1 | Exponents and Properties (Rules) of Exponents

In Chapters 1 and 2, we learned about powers of whole numbers, fractions, and decimal numbers.

Recall that when a number is raised to a whole number exponent, we can think of it as repeated multiplication. Powers are a simpler way to indicate repeated multiplication, similar to how multiplication is a simpler way to indicate repeated addition. Powers are expressed using exponential notation.

For example, the whole number 2 multiplied by itself 5 times is written in exponential notation as:

base → 2^5 ← exponent

2 is the base, 5 is the exponent, and the whole representation 2^5 is known as the power.

$$\underbrace{2^5}_{\text{Exponential Notation}} = \underbrace{2 \times 2 \times 2 \times 2 \times 2}_{\text{Repeated Multiplication}} = \underbrace{32}_{\text{Standard Notation}}$$

Similarly, the fraction $\frac{3}{4}$ multiplied by itself 4 times is written in exponential notation as:

base → $\left(\frac{3}{4}\right)^4$ ← exponent

$\frac{3}{4}$ is the base, 4 is the exponent, and the whole representation $\left(\frac{3}{4}\right)^4$ is the power.

$$\underbrace{\left(\frac{3}{4}\right)^4}_{\text{Exponential Notation}} = \underbrace{\frac{3}{4} \times \frac{3}{4} \times \frac{3}{4} \times \frac{3}{4}}_{\text{Repeated Multiplication}} = \underbrace{\frac{81}{256}}_{\text{Standard Notation}}$$

Similarly, the decimal number 1.2 multiplied by itself 3 times is written in exponential notation as:

base → $(1.2)^3$ ← exponent

1.2 is the base, 3 is the exponent, and the whole representation $(1.2)^3$ is the power.

$$\underbrace{(1.2)^3}_{\text{Exponential Notation}} = \underbrace{1.2 \times 1.2 \times 1.2}_{\text{Repeated Multiplication}} = \underbrace{1.728}_{\text{Standard Notation}}$$

Properties (Rules) of Exponents

The following properties of exponents, known as the **rules** or **laws** of exponents, are used to simplify expressions that involve exponents.

Product of Powers (Product Rule)

When multiplying powers of the same base, add the exponents.

To multiply powers with the same base, add their exponents.

For example, $7^5 \times 7^3 = \underbrace{(7 \times 7 \times 7 \times 7 \times 7)}_{\text{5 Factors of 7}} \times \underbrace{(7 \times 7 \times 7)}_{\text{3 Factors of 7}}$

$$= \underbrace{7 \times 7 \times 7 \times 7 \times 7 \times 7 \times 7 \times 7}_{\text{8 Factors of 7}}$$

$$= 7^8, \text{ which is the same as } 7^{(5+3)}$$

You will note that the resulting exponent, 8, can be obtained by adding the exponents 5 and 3 since the powers have the same base.

In general, for powers with base '*a*' and exponents '*m*' and '*n*',

$$\boldsymbol{a^m \times a^n = a^{(m+n)}}$$

Note: $a^m + a^n \neq a^{(m+n)}$

Example 3.1-a **Simplifying Exponential Expressions Using the Product Rule**

Express the following as a single power:

(i) $2^3 \times 2^4 \times 2^2$ (ii) $\left(\frac{3}{5}\right)^6 \times \left(\frac{3}{5}\right)^2$ (iii) $(0.2)^3 \times (0.2)^2$

Solution

(i) $2^3 \times 2^4 \times 2^2$

$= 2^{(3+4+2)}$

$= 2^9$

(ii) $\left(\frac{3}{5}\right)^6 \times \left(\frac{3}{5}\right)^2$

$= \left(\frac{3}{5}\right)^{(6+2)}$

$= \left(\frac{3}{5}\right)^8$

(iii) $(0.2)^3 \times (0.2)^2$

$= (0.2)^{(3+2)}$

$= (0.2)^5$

Quotient of Powers (Quotient Rule)

When dividing powers of the same base, subtract the exponent of the denominator from that of the numerator.

To divide two powers with the same base, subtract their exponents.

For example, $4^7 \div 4^2 = \dfrac{\overbrace{4 \times 4 \times 4 \times 4 \times 4 \times 4 \times 4}^{\text{7 Factors of 4}}}{\underbrace{4 \times 4}_{\text{2 Factors of 4}}}$

$$= \frac{4 \times 4}{4 \times 4} \times 4 \times 4 \times 4 \times 4 \times 4$$

$$= 1 \times \underbrace{4 \times 4 \times 4 \times 4 \times 4}_{\text{5 Factors of 4}}$$

$$= 4^5, \text{ which is the same as } 4^{(7-2)}$$

You will note that the resulting exponent, 5, can be obtained by subtracting the exponent of the denominator from the exponent of the numerator (7 – 2 = 5) since the powers have the same base.

In general, for powers with a non-zero base '*a*' and exponents '*m*' and '*n*',

$$\boldsymbol{\frac{a^m}{a^n} = a^{(m-n)}}, \text{ where } \boldsymbol{a \neq 0}$$

Note: $a^m - a^n \neq a^{(m-n)}$

Example 3.1-b **Simplifying Exponential Expressions Using the Quotient Rule**

Express the following as a single power:

(i) $3^9 \div 3^5$ (ii) $\left(\frac{2}{3}\right)^6 \div \left(\frac{2}{3}\right)^4$ (iii) $(1.15)^5 \div (1.15)^2$

Solution

(i) $3^9 \div 3^5$

$= 3^{(9-5)}$

$= 3^4$

(ii) $\left(\frac{2}{3}\right)^6 \div \left(\frac{2}{3}\right)^4$

$= \left(\frac{2}{3}\right)^{(6-4)}$

$= \left(\frac{2}{3}\right)^2$

(iii) $(1.15)^5 \div (1.15)^2$

$= (1.15)^{(5-2)}$

$= (1.15)^3$

Power of a Product (Power of a Product Rule)

To raise the product of factors 'a' and 'b' to the power 'n', raise each factor to the nth power.

To determine the power of a product, each factor of the product is raised to the indicated power.

For example, $(3 \times 5)^4 = (3 \times 5)(3 \times 5)(3 \times 5)(3 \times 5)$

$$= \underbrace{3 \times 3 \times 3 \times 3}_{\text{4 Factors of 3}} \times \underbrace{5 \times 5 \times 5 \times 5}_{\text{4 Factors of 5}}$$

$$= 3^4 \times 5^4$$

You will note from the result that each factor of the product is raised to the power of 4.

In general, for any product of factors **'*a*'** and **'*b*'** that is raised to the power **'*n*'**,

$$(a \times b)^n = a^n \times b^n$$

Example 3.1-c **Expanding Exponential Expressions Using the Power of a Product Rule**

Express the following in expanded form using the Power of a Product Rule:

(i) $(8 \times 6)^3$ (ii) $\left(\frac{3}{5} \times \frac{2}{7}\right)^3$ (iii) $(1.12 \times 0.6)^3$

Solution

(i) $(8 \times 6)^3$

$= 8^3 \times 6^3$

(ii) $\left(\frac{3}{5} \times \frac{2}{7}\right)^3$

$= \left(\frac{3}{5}\right)^3 \times \left(\frac{2}{7}\right)^3$

(iii) $(1.12 \times 0.6)^3$

$= (1.12)^3 \times (0.6)^3$

Power of a Quotient (Power of a Quotient Rule)

To raise a fraction to the power 'n', raise both the numerator and denominator to the nth power.

The Power of a Quotient Rule is similar to the Power of a Product Rule. To determine the power of a quotient, raise the numerator to the indicated power and divide by the denominator raised to the indicated power.

For example, $\left(\frac{5}{8}\right)^3 = \underbrace{\left(\frac{5}{8}\right) \times \left(\frac{5}{8}\right) \times \left(\frac{5}{8}\right)}_{\text{3 Factors of } \left(\frac{5}{8}\right)}$

$$= \frac{5 \times 5 \times 5}{8 \times 8 \times 8} \quad \begin{matrix} \leftarrow \text{3 factors of 5} \\ \leftarrow \text{3 factors of 8} \end{matrix}$$

$$= \frac{5^3}{8^3}$$

You will note from the result that the numerator and the denominator of the expression is raised to the power of 3.

In general, for any quotient with numerator '*a*' and non-zero denominator '*b*' that is raised to the power '*n*',

$$\left(\frac{a}{b}\right)^n = \frac{a^n}{b^n}, \text{ where } b \neq 0$$

Example 3.1-d

Expanding Exponential Expressions Using the Power of a Quotient Rule

Express the following in expanded form using the Power of a Quotient Rule:

(i) $\left(\frac{7}{4}\right)^3$ (ii) $\left[\frac{\left(\frac{2}{3}\right)}{\left(\frac{3}{5}\right)}\right]^4$ (iii) $\left(\frac{1.05}{0.05}\right)^3$

Solution

(i) $\left(\frac{7}{4}\right)^3$

$= \frac{7^3}{4^3}$

(ii) $\left[\frac{\left(\frac{2}{3}\right)}{\left(\frac{3}{5}\right)}\right]^4$

$= \left(\frac{2}{3} \div \frac{3}{5}\right)^4$

$= \left(\frac{2}{3}\right)^4 \div \left(\frac{3}{5}\right)^4$

$= \frac{2^4}{3^4} \div \frac{3^4}{5^4}$

(iii) $\left(\frac{1.05}{0.05}\right)^3$

$= \frac{(1.05)^3}{(0.05)^3}$

Power of a Power (Power of a Power Rule)

To raise a power to a power, multiply the exponents.

In order to determine the power of a power of a number, multiply the two exponents of the powers together to obtain the new exponent of the power.

For example, $(9^3)^2$

$= (9^3) \times (9^3)$

$= (9 \times 9 \times 9) \times (9 \times 9 \times 9)$

$= \underbrace{9 \times 9 \times 9 \times 9 \times 9 \times 9}_{\text{6 Factors of 9}}$

$= 9^6$, which is the same as $9^{(3 \times 2)}$

You will note that the resulting exponent, 6, can be obtained by multiplying the exponents 3 and 2.

In general, to raise the power of a number '*a*' to a power '*m*', and then raise it to a power '*n*',

$$(a^m)^n = a^{(m \times n)}$$

Example 3.1-e

Simplifying Exponential Expressions Using the Power of a Power Rule

Express the following as a single power:

(i) $(5^4)^3$ (ii) $\left[\left(\frac{3}{8}\right)^3\right]^2$ (iii) $[(1.04)^4]^2$

Solution

(i) $(5^4)^3$

$= 5^{(4 \times 3)}$

$= 5^{12}$

(ii) $\left[\left(\frac{3}{8}\right)^3\right]^2$

$= \left(\frac{3}{8}\right)^{(3 \times 2)}$

$= \left(\frac{3}{8}\right)^6$

(iii) $[(1.04)^4]^2$

$= (1.04)^{(4 \times 2)}$

$= (1.04)^8$

Example 3.1-f **Solving Expressions Using the Power of a Power Rule, Product Rule, and Quotient Rule**

Solve the following:

(i) $(2^2)^3 \times 2^7 \div 2^9$ (ii) $7^5 \div (7^3)^2 \times 7^2$

Solution

(i) $(2^2)^3 \times 2^7 \div 2^9$
$= 2^6 \times 2^7 \div 2^9$
$= 2^{(6+7-9)}$
$= 2^4$
$= 16$

(ii) $7^5 \div (7^3)^2 \times 7^2$
$= 7^5 \div 7^6 \times 7^2$
$= 7^{(5-6+2)}$
$= 7^1$
$= 7$

Table 3.1-a summarizes the properties (rules) of exponents.

Table 3.1-a **Properties (Rules) of Exponents**

Property (Rule)	Rule in Exponential Form	Example
Product Rule	$a^m \times a^n = a^{(m+n)}$	$3^5 \times 3^4 = 3^{(5+4)} = 3^9$
Quotient Rule	$\frac{a^m}{a^n} = a^{(m-n)}$	$\frac{3^7}{3^4} = 3^{(7-4)} = 3^3$
Power of a Product Rule	$(a \times b)^n = a^n \times b^n$	$(3 \times 5)^2 = 3^2 \times 5^2$
Power of a Quotient Rule	$\left(\frac{a}{b}\right)^n = \frac{a^n}{b^n}$	$\left(\frac{3}{5}\right)^3 = \frac{3^3}{5^3}$
Power of a Power Rule	$(a^m)^n = a^{(m \times n)}$	$(3^2)^3 = 3^{(2\times 3)} = 3^6$

Note:
$(a+b)^n \neq a^n + b^n$
$(a-b)^n \neq a^n - b^n$

Properties of Exponents and Bases of One and Zero

Table 3.1-b summarizes the properties of powers with exponents and bases of one and zero.

Table 3.1-b **Exponents and Bases of One (1) and Zero (0)**

Property (Rule)	Description	Rule in Exponential Form	Example
Base 'a' Exponent 1	Any base 'a' raised to the exponent '1' equals the base itself.	$a^1 = a$	$8^1 = 8$
Base 'a' Exponent 0	Any non-zero base 'a' raised to the exponent '0' equals 1.	$a^0 = 1$	$8^0 = 1$
Base '1' Exponent 'n'	A base of '1' raised to any exponent 'n' equals 1.	$1^n = 1$	$1^5 = 1$
Base '0' Exponent 'n'	A base of '0' raised to any positive exponent 'n' equals 0.	$0^n = 0$	$0^5 = 0$
Base '0' Exponent '0'	A base of '0' raised to the exponent '0' is indeterminate.	0^0 = indeterminate	

Addition and Subtraction of Powers

For the addition and subtraction of powers, there is **no** special rule for powers with either the same or different bases. Evaluate each operation separately and then perform the addition or subtraction.

For example,

- Addition of exponential expressions with the same base:

  $2^3 + 2^4$ Evaluating 2^3 and 2^4 separately and then adding,

  $= 8 + 16 = 24$

- Addition of exponential expressions with different bases:

  $2^2 + 3^3$ Evaluating 2^2 and 3^3 separately and then adding,

  $= 4 + 27 = 31$

- Subtraction of exponential expressions with the same base:

  $5^3 - 5^2$ Evaluating 5^3 and 5^2 separately and then subtracting,

  $= 125 - 25 = 100$

- Subtraction of exponential expressions with different bases:

  $4^3 - 2^3$ Evaluating 4^3 and 2^3 separately and then subtracting,

  $= 64 - 8 = 56$

Example 3.1-g **Adding and Subtracting Powers**

Evaluate the following:

(i) $3^3 + 3^2$ (ii) $5^2 + 3^2$ (iii) $5^4 - 5^2$ (iv) $6^2 - 4^2$

Solution

(i) $3^3 + 3^2$

$= 27 + 9$

$= 36$

Note: $a^m + a^n \neq a^{(m+n)}$

$3^3 + 3^2 \neq 3^5$

(ii) $5^2 + 3^2$

$= 25 + 9$

$= 34$

Note: $a^m + b^m \neq (a+b)^m$

$5^2 + 3^2 \neq 8^2$

(iii) $5^4 - 5^2$

$= 625 - 25$

$= 600$

Note: $a^m - a^n \neq a^{(m-n)}$

$5^4 - 5^2 \neq 5^2$

(iv) $6^2 - 4^2$

$= 36 - 16$

$= 20$

Note: $a^m - b^m \neq (a-b)^m$

$6^2 - 4^2 \neq 2^2$

Multiplication and Division of Powers with Different Bases

There is also **no** special rule for the product or quotient of powers having different bases. Evaluate each operation separately and then perform the multipication or division.

For example,

- Product of exponential expressions with different bases:

  $2^4 \times 3^2$ Evaluating 2^4 and 3^2 separately and then multiplying,

  $= 16 \times 9 = 144$

- Quotient of exponential expressions with different bases:

$\frac{3^3}{2^4}$ Evaluating 3^3 and 2^4 separately and then dividing,

$= \frac{27}{16} = 1.6875$

Example 3.1-h **Multiplying and Dividing Powers that have Different Bases**

Evaluate the following:

(i) $5^3 \times 4^2$ (ii) $5^3 \div 3^2$ (iii) $9^2 \times 5^1$ (iv) $4^2 \times 5^0$

Solution

(i) $5^3 \times 4^2$

$= 125 \times 16$

$= 2{,}000$

(ii) $5^3 \div 3^2$

$= 125 \div 9$

$= \frac{125}{9}$

$= 13\frac{8}{9}$

(iii) $9^2 \times 5^1$

$= 81 \times 5$

$= 405$

(iv) $4^2 \times 5^0$

$= 16 \times 1$

$= 16$

Evaluating Expressions with Exponents Using a Calculator

The exponent key on different calculators can be identified by symbols such as

, etc.

In the following examples '∧' will be used to to represent the exponent key.

Example 3.1-i **Evaluating Exponential Expressions using a Calculator**

Evaluate the following using a calculator:

(i) 5^6 (ii) $\left(\frac{3}{2}\right)^3$ (iii) $(1.02)^4$

Solution

(i) 5^6

(ii) $\left(\frac{3}{2}\right)^3$

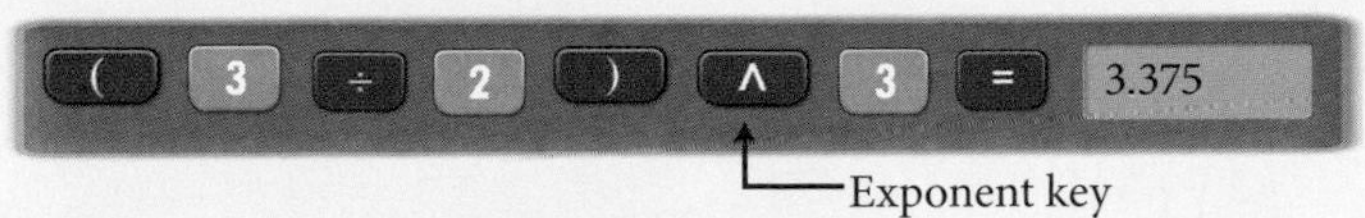

(iii) $(1.02)^4$

3.1 | Exercises

Answers to odd-numbered problems are available at the end of the textbook.

For Problems 1 and 2, identify the values in the empty columns for Repeated Multiplication, Base, Exponent, and Power (Exponential Notation).

1.

	Repeated Multiplication	Base	Exponent	Power (Exponential Notation)
a.	$7 \times 7 \times 7 \times 7$			
b.				9^5
c.		3	4	
d.	$\frac{2}{5} \times \frac{2}{5} \times \frac{2}{5} \times \frac{2}{5} \times \frac{2}{5} \times \frac{2}{5}$			
e.				$\left(\frac{5}{7}\right)^5$
f.		$\left(\frac{4}{7}\right)$	3	
g.	$(1.15) \times (1.15) \times (1.15) \times (1.15)$			
h.				$(1.6)^3$
i.		(1.25)	5	

2.

	Repeated Multiplication	Base	Exponent	Power (Exponential Notation)
a.	$2 \times 2 \times 2 \times 2 \times 2 \times 2 \times 2 \times 2$			
b.				6^7
c.		5	3	
d.	$\frac{2}{7} \times \frac{2}{7} \times \frac{2}{7} \times \frac{2}{7} \times \frac{2}{7}$			
e.				$\left(\frac{3}{8}\right)^4$
f.		$\left(\frac{2}{9}\right)$	4	
g.	$(2.5) \times (2.5) \times (2.5) \times (2.5) \times (2.5)$			
h.				$(1.1)^5$
i.		(0.75)	4	

Express Problems 3 to 22 as a single power and then evaluate using a calculator. Round the answer to two decimal places, wherever applicable.

3. $4^3 \times 4^6$
4. $5^5 \times 5^6$
5. $\left(\frac{1}{2}\right)^4\left(\frac{1}{2}\right)^3$
6. $\left(\frac{2}{3}\right)^2\left(\frac{2}{3}\right)^3$
7. $\left(\frac{5}{2}\right)^2\left(\frac{5}{2}\right)^3$
8. $\left(\frac{5}{3}\right)^3\left(\frac{5}{3}\right)^2$
9. $(3.25)^4\,(3.25)^2$
10. $(0.75)^3\,(0.75)^4$
11. $6^8 \div 6^3$
12. $3^7 \div 3^5$
13. $\left(\frac{2}{5}\right)^3 \div \left(\frac{2}{5}\right)^1$
14. $\left(\frac{3}{2}\right)^4 \div \left(\frac{3}{2}\right)^3$
15. $(1.4)^5 \div (1.4)^2$
16. $(3.25)^6 \div (3.25)^5$
17. $[(6)^2]^3$
18. $[(5)^3]^2$
19. $\left[\left(\frac{2}{3}\right)^4\right]^3$
20. $\left[\left(\frac{3}{4}\right)^4\right]^2$
21. $[(2.5)^2]^3$
22. $[(1.03)^3]^2$

Express Problems 23 to 34 as a power of the indicated base value.

23. 4^5 as a power of 2
24. 9^6 as a power of 3
25. $9(27)^2$ as a power of 3
26. $8(16)^2$ as a power of 2
27. $\frac{3^9 \times 3^2}{3^5}$ as a power of 3
28. $\frac{2^9 \times 2^1}{2^5}$ as a power of 2
29. $\frac{(2^5)^4}{4^6}$ as a power of 2
30. $\frac{(2^5)^4}{16^3}$ as a power of 2
31. $\frac{10^6}{10^0}$ as a power of 10
32. $\frac{3^7}{27}$ as a power of 3
33. $\frac{8^5}{8^3}$ as a power of 2
34. $\frac{5^6}{125}$ as a power of 5

Evaluate Problems 35 to 70.

35. $5^2 + 5^3$
36. $4^3 + 4^2$
37. $5^4 - 2^4$
38. $6^3 - 4^3$
39. $4^4 - 4^2$
40. $6^3 - 6^1$
41. $7^2 + 3^2$
42. $6^2 - 4^2$
43. $3^5 + 5^3$
44. $4^3 + 3^4$
45. $2^5 - 5^2$
46. $2^6 - 6^2$
47. $5^4 - 4^2$
48. $10^3 - 7^2$
49. $4^0 + 4^4$
50. $3^0 + 3^4$
51. $(5 \times 4)^3$
52. $(10 \times 2)^4$
53. $(1.25 \times 4)^4$
54. $(5 \times 0.8)^3$
55. $\left(\frac{2}{3} + 6\right)^5$
56. $\left(\frac{3}{5} + 1\right)^3$
57. $3^4 + 3^2 + 3^0$
58. $4^2 + 4^4 + 4^0$
59. $2^4 + 3^4 - 1^4$
60. $3^3 + 2^3 - 1^3$
61. $\left(\frac{1}{2}\right)^3 + \left(\frac{1}{2}\right)^2 + \left(\frac{1}{2}\right)^0$
62. $\left(\frac{1}{5}\right)^2 + \left(\frac{1}{5}\right)^0 + \left(\frac{1}{5}\right)^4$
63. $(2.1)^2 + (2.1)^0$
64. $(3.2)^2 + (3.2)^1$
65. $4^3 \times 3^4$
66. $7^2 \times 2^2$
67. $6^4 \div 5^4$
68. $8^2 \div 7^2$
69. $(2 \times 3^2)^4$
70. $(5 \times 2^2)^3$

3.2 | Roots, Fractional Exponents, and Negative Exponents

Roots

Roots are the inverse operation of exponents.

In the previous chapters, we learned that taking the square root of a number is the inverse of raising a number to the power of 2.

For example,

- The square of 2 is $2^2 = 4$. Therefore, the square root of 4 is $\sqrt{4} = 2$.
- The square of 3 is $3^2 = 9$. Therefore, the square root of 9 is $\sqrt{9} = 3$.

We can also use roots to express the inverse of raising a number to a power that is greater than 2.

We know that, $9 = 3 \times 3 = 3^2$ Therefore, the square root (2nd root) of 9 is 3.

Similarly, $125 = 5 \times 5 \times 5 = 5^3$ Therefore, the cube root (3rd root) of 125 is 5.

$16 = 2 \times 2 \times 2 \times 2 = 2^4$ Therefore, the 4th root of 16 is 2.

The following notation is used to represent roots, also known as **radicals**:

$$\sqrt[n]{a}$$

Radical sign

Index of the root

'*a*' can be any positive number

The index is written as a small number to the left of the radical sign. It indicates which root is to be taken.

For example,

- $\sqrt[3]{125}$ indicates the cube root (3rd root) of 125.
- $\sqrt[4]{16}$ indicates the 4th root of 16.

Note: Recall that for square roots, the index 2 does not need to be written as it is understood to be there; i.e., $\sqrt[2]{9} = \sqrt{9}$.

Perfect Roots

Roots of a whole number may not be a whole number. A whole number is a **perfect root** if its root is also a whole number.

For example,

- 4 is a perfect square root of 16 because $4^2 = 16$; i.e., $\sqrt{16} = 4$
- 3 is a perfect cube root of 27 because $3^3 = 27$; i.e., $\sqrt[3]{27} = 3$

Table 3.2 **Examples of Perfect Roots**

Roots	1	2	3	4	5	6	7	8	9	10
Square Roots	$\sqrt{1}$	$\sqrt{4}$	$\sqrt{9}$	$\sqrt{16}$	$\sqrt{25}$	$\sqrt{36}$	$\sqrt{49}$	$\sqrt{64}$	$\sqrt{81}$	$\sqrt{100}$
Cube Roots	$\sqrt[3]{1}$	$\sqrt[3]{8}$	$\sqrt[3]{27}$	$\sqrt[3]{64}$	$\sqrt[3]{125}$	$\sqrt[3]{216}$	$\sqrt[3]{343}$	$\sqrt[3]{512}$	$\sqrt[3]{729}$	$\sqrt[3]{1,000}$
Fourth Roots	$\sqrt[4]{1}$	$\sqrt[4]{16}$	$\sqrt[4]{81}$	$\sqrt[4]{256}$	$\sqrt[4]{625}$	$\sqrt[4]{1,296}$	$\sqrt[4]{2,401}$	$\sqrt[4]{4,096}$	$\sqrt[4]{6,561}$	$\sqrt[4]{10,000}$

Simplifying Roots Using Perfect Roots

Just like we can simplify a power of a product, we can simplify a root of a product as follows:

$$\sqrt[n]{ab} = \sqrt[n]{a} \times \sqrt[n]{b}$$

For example, $\sqrt{10} = \sqrt{2 \times 5} = \sqrt{2} \times \sqrt{5}$.

We can use this rule and our knowledge of perfect roots to simplify square roots, cube roots, etc.

For example,

- To simplify $\sqrt{12}$, we can write 12 as the product 4×3, where one of the factors, 4, is a perfect square. Therefore,

  $\sqrt{12} = \sqrt{4 \times 3} = \sqrt{4} \times \sqrt{3} = 2\sqrt{3}$

- To simplify $\sqrt[3]{54}$, we can write 54 as the product 27×2, where one of the factors, 27, is a perfect cube. Therefore,

  $\sqrt[3]{54} = \sqrt[3]{27 \times 2} = \sqrt[3]{27} \times \sqrt[3]{2} = 3\sqrt[3]{2}$

Example 3.2-a **Simplifying Using Perfect Roots**

Simplify using perfect roots of a number:

(i) $\sqrt{72}$ (ii) $\sqrt[3]{40}$

Solution

(i) $\sqrt{72}$

$= \sqrt{36 \times 2}$ — $72 = 36 \times 2$

$= \sqrt{36} \times \sqrt{2}$ — 36 is a perfect square of 6.

$= 6\sqrt{2}$

(ii) $\sqrt[3]{40}$

$= \sqrt[3]{8 \times 5}$ — $40 = 8 \times 5$

$= \sqrt[3]{8} \times \sqrt[3]{5}$ — 8 is a perfect cube of 2.

$= 2\sqrt[3]{5}$

Fractional Exponents

A radical can also be represented using **fractional exponents**. Fractional exponents are often easier to write and perform operations with than radicals.

Index of the Root ⟶ $\sqrt[n]{a} = a^{\frac{1}{n}}$ ⟵ Fractional Exponent

For example,

- The **square (2nd) root** of a number can be written as the number raised to the power of $\frac{1}{2}$.

  e.g., $\sqrt{5} = 5^{\frac{1}{2}}$

- The **cube (3rd) root** of a number can be written as the number raised to the power of $\frac{1}{3}$.

  e.g., $\sqrt[3]{8} = 8^{\frac{1}{3}}$

- The **fourth (4th) root** of a number can be written as the number raised to the power of $\frac{1}{4}$.

  e.g., $\sqrt[4]{5^3} = (5^3)^{\frac{1}{4}} = 5^{\left(3 \times \frac{1}{4}\right)} = 5^{\frac{3}{4}}$

An appropriate radical will "undo" an exponent.

For example,

$$\sqrt{5^2} = (5^2)^{\frac{1}{2}} = 5^{\left(2 \times \frac{1}{2}\right)} = 5$$

$$\sqrt[3]{7^3} = (7^3)^{\frac{1}{3}} = 7^{\left(3 \times \frac{1}{3}\right)} = 7$$

Example 3.2-b **Expressions in Radical Form**

Express the following in radical form:

(i) $2^{\frac{5}{6}}$ (ii) $3^{\frac{2}{5}}$ (iii) $\left(\frac{2}{3}\right)^{\frac{3}{4}}$

Solution

(i) $2^{\frac{5}{6}}$

$= \sqrt[6]{2^5}$

(ii) $3^{\frac{2}{5}}$

$= \sqrt[5]{3^2}$

(iii) $\left(\frac{2}{3}\right)^{\frac{3}{4}}$

$= \sqrt[4]{\left(\frac{2}{3}\right)^3}$

Evaluating Expressions with Fractional Exponents Using a Calculator

When entering a fractional exponent in a calculator, **brackets** must be used.

For example, to evalute $25^{\frac{2}{5}}$ using a calculator, enter it as follows:

Note: Without the brackets, the operation will mean $(25)^2 \div 5$, *which is incorrect.*

Example 3.2-c **Evaluating Expressions with Fractional Exponents Using a Calculator**

Evaluate the following using a calculator:

(i) $15^{\frac{3}{2}}$ (ii) $\left(\frac{3}{5}\right)^{\frac{1}{4}}$ (iii) $(2.5)^{\frac{3}{7}}$

Solution

(i) $15^{\frac{3}{2}} =$ 15 ^ (3 ÷ 2) =

58.094750... $= 58.09$

(ii) $\left(\frac{3}{5}\right)^{\frac{1}{4}} =$ (3 ÷ 5) ^ (1 ÷ 4) =

0.880111... $= 0.88$

(iii) $(2.5)^{\frac{3}{7}} =$ (2.5) ^ (3 ÷ 7) =

1.480968... $= 1.48$

Arithmetic Operations with Fractional Exponents

All the rules of exponents, Product Rule, Quotient Rule, Power of a Product Rule, Power of a Quotient Rule, Power of a Power Rule, etc., learned in Section 3.1 and as outlined in Tables 3.1-a and 3.1-b are applicable to fractional exponents.

Example 3.2-d **Evaluating Expressions with Fractional Exponents using the Product Rule**

Simplify the following using the Product Rule to express as a single power, and then evaluate to two decimal places, where applicable.

(i) $2^{\frac{1}{2}} \times 2^{\frac{1}{3}}$ (ii) $3^{\frac{3}{4}} \times 3^{\frac{9}{4}} \times 3^0$ (iii) $\left(\frac{3}{5}\right)^{\frac{7}{3}} \times \left(\frac{3}{5}\right)^{\frac{2}{3}}$

Solution

(i) $2^{\frac{1}{2}} \times 2^{\frac{1}{3}}$

$= 2^{\left(\frac{1}{2}+\frac{1}{3}\right)}$

$= 2^{\left(\frac{3+2}{6}\right)}$

$= 2^{\frac{5}{6}}$

$= 1.781797... = 1.78$

(ii) $3^{\frac{3}{4}} \times 3^{\frac{9}{4}} \times 3^0$

$= 3^{\left(\frac{3}{4}+\frac{9}{4}+0\right)}$

$= 3^{\frac{12}{4}}$

$= 3^3$

$= 27$

(iii) $\left(\frac{3}{5}\right)^{\frac{7}{3}} \times \left(\frac{3}{5}\right)^{\frac{2}{3}}$

$= \left(\frac{3}{5}\right)^{\left(\frac{7}{3}+\frac{2}{3}\right)}$

$= \left(\frac{3}{5}\right)^{\frac{9}{3}}$

$= \left(\frac{3}{5}\right)^3$

$= 0.216 = 0.22$

Example 3.2-e **Evaluating Expressions with Fractional Exponents using the Quotient Rule**

Simplify the following using the Quotient Rule to express as a single power, and then evaluate to two decimal places, where applicable.

(i) $2^{\frac{4}{3}} \div 2^{\frac{2}{3}}$ (ii) $(1.2)^{\frac{5}{2}} \div (1.2)^{\frac{1}{2}}$ (iii) $\left(\frac{1}{3}\right)^{\frac{6}{4}} \div \left(\frac{1}{3}\right)^{\frac{3}{4}}$

Solution

(i) $2^{\frac{4}{3}} \div 2^{\frac{2}{3}}$

$= 2^{\left(\frac{4}{3} - \frac{2}{3}\right)}$

$= 2^{\frac{2}{3}}$

$= 1.587401... = 1.59$

(ii) $(1.2)^{\frac{5}{2}} \div (1.2)^{\frac{1}{2}}$

$= (1.2)^{\left(\frac{5}{2} - \frac{1}{2}\right)}$

$= (1.2)^{\frac{4}{2}}$

$= (1.2)^2$

$= 1.44$

(iii) $\left(\frac{1}{3}\right)^{\frac{6}{4}} \div \left(\frac{1}{3}\right)^{\frac{3}{4}}$

$= \left(\frac{1}{3}\right)^{\left(\frac{6}{4} - \frac{3}{4}\right)}$

$= \left(\frac{1}{3}\right)^{\frac{3}{4}}$

$= 0.438691... = 0.44$

Example 3.2-f **Evaluating Expressions with Fractional Exponents using the Power of a Product Rule**

Simplify the following using the Power of a Product Rule, and then evaluate to two decimal places, where applicable.

(i) $(4^2 \times 3^2)^{\frac{1}{2}}$ (ii) $\left(7^2 \times \frac{1}{3^2}\right)^{\frac{1}{2}}$ (iii) $(2^6 \times 3^2)^{\frac{3}{2}}$

Solution

(i) $(4^2 \times 3^2)^{\frac{1}{2}}$

$= (4^2)^{\frac{1}{2}} \times (3^2)^{\frac{1}{2}}$

$= 4 \times 3$

$= 12$

(ii) $\left(7^2 \times \frac{1}{3^2}\right)^{\frac{1}{2}}$

$= (7^2)^{\frac{1}{2}} \times \left(\frac{1}{3^2}\right)^{\frac{1}{2}}$

$= \frac{7}{3}$

$= 2.333333... = 2.33$

(iii) $(2^6 \times 3^2)^{\frac{3}{2}}$

$= (2^6)^{\frac{3}{2}} \times (3^2)^{\frac{3}{2}}$

$= 2^{\left(6 \times \frac{3}{2}\right)} \times 3^{\left(2 \times \frac{3}{2}\right)}$

$= 2^9 \times 3^3$

$= 512 \times 27$

$= 13{,}824$

Example 3.2-g **Evaluating Expressions with Fractional Exponents using the Power of a Quotient Rule**

Simplify the following using the Power of a Quotient Rule, and then evaluate to two decimal places, where applicable.

(i) $\left(\frac{4^2}{3^2}\right)^{\frac{1}{2}}$ (ii) $\left(\frac{5^3}{2^6}\right)^{\frac{1}{3}}$

Solution

(i) $\left(\frac{4^2}{3^2}\right)^{\frac{1}{2}}$

$= \frac{(4^2)^{\frac{1}{2}}}{(3^2)^{\frac{1}{2}}}$

$= \frac{4}{3}$

$= 1.333333... = 1.33$

(ii) $\left(\frac{5^3}{2^6}\right)^{\frac{1}{3}}$

$= \frac{(5^3)^{\frac{1}{3}}}{(2^6)^{\frac{1}{3}}}$

$= \frac{5}{2^{\frac{6}{3}}}$

$= \frac{5}{2^2}$

$= \frac{5}{4}$

$= 1.25$

Example 3.2-h

Evaluating Expressions with Fractional Exponents using the Power of a Power Rule

Simplify the following using the Power of a Power Rule to express as a single power, and then evaluate to two decimal places, where applicable.

(i) $\left(6^{\frac{1}{2}}\right)^3$ (ii) $\left(18^{\frac{1}{3}}\right)^{\frac{1}{4}}$ (iii) $\left[\left(\frac{2}{3}\right)^3\right]^2$

Solution

(i) $\left(6^{\frac{1}{2}}\right)^3$

$= 6^{\left(\frac{1}{2} \times 3\right)}$

$= 6^{\frac{3}{2}}$

$= 14.696938... = 14.70$

(ii) $\left(18^{\frac{1}{3}}\right)^{\frac{1}{4}}$

$= 18^{\left(\frac{1}{3} \times \frac{1}{4}\right)}$

$= 18^{\frac{1}{12}}$

$= 1.272348... = 1.27$

(iii) $\left[\left(\frac{2}{3}\right)^3\right]^2$

$= \left(\frac{2}{3}\right)^{(3 \times 2)}$

$= \left(\frac{2}{3}\right)^6$

$= \frac{2^6}{3^6}$

$= \frac{64}{729}$

$= 0.087791... = 0.09$

Example 3.2-i

Evaluating Expressions with Fractional Exponents and Different Bases

Evaluate the following to two decimal places, where applicable.

(i) $16^{\frac{1}{2}} + 8^{\frac{1}{2}}$ (ii) $25^{\frac{1}{2}} - 27^{\frac{1}{3}}$ (iii) $\left(\frac{7}{8}\right)^{\frac{1}{4}} - \left(\frac{2}{3}\right)^{\frac{1}{3}}$

(iv) $5^{\frac{1}{2}} \times 3^{\frac{1}{2}}$ (v) $2^{\frac{3}{4}} \div 3^{\frac{1}{2}}$ (vi) $5^{\left(2\frac{3}{4}\right)}$

Solution

(i) $16^{\frac{1}{2}} + 8^{\frac{1}{2}}$

$= 4 + 2.828427...$

$= 6.828427... = 6.83$

(ii) $25^{\frac{1}{2}} - 27^{\frac{1}{3}}$

$= 5 - 3$

$= 2$

(iii) $\left(\frac{7}{8}\right)^{\frac{1}{4}} - \left(\frac{2}{3}\right)^{\frac{1}{3}}$

$= 0.967168... - 0.873580...$

$= 0.093587... = 0.09$

(iv) $5^{\frac{1}{2}} \times 3^{\frac{1}{2}}$

$= 2.236067... \times 1.732050...$

$= 3.872983... = 3.87$

(v) $2^{\frac{3}{4}} \div 3^{\frac{1}{2}}$

$= 1.681792... \div 1.732050...$

$= 0.970983... = 0.97$

(vi) $5^{\left(2\frac{3}{4}\right)}$

$= 5^{\frac{11}{4}}$

$= 83.592538... = 83.59$

Negative Exponents

In exponential notation, the base of the number may be raised to a negative exponent. We can represent this as a^{-n}. A power with a negative exponent is the **reciprocal** of the power with the positive exponent.

Positive Exponent: $a^n = a \times a \times a \times ... \times a$ (multiplication of 'n' factors of 'a')

Negative Exponent: $a^{-n} = \frac{1}{a^n} = \frac{1}{a \times a \times a \times ... \times a}$ (division of 'n' factors of 'a')

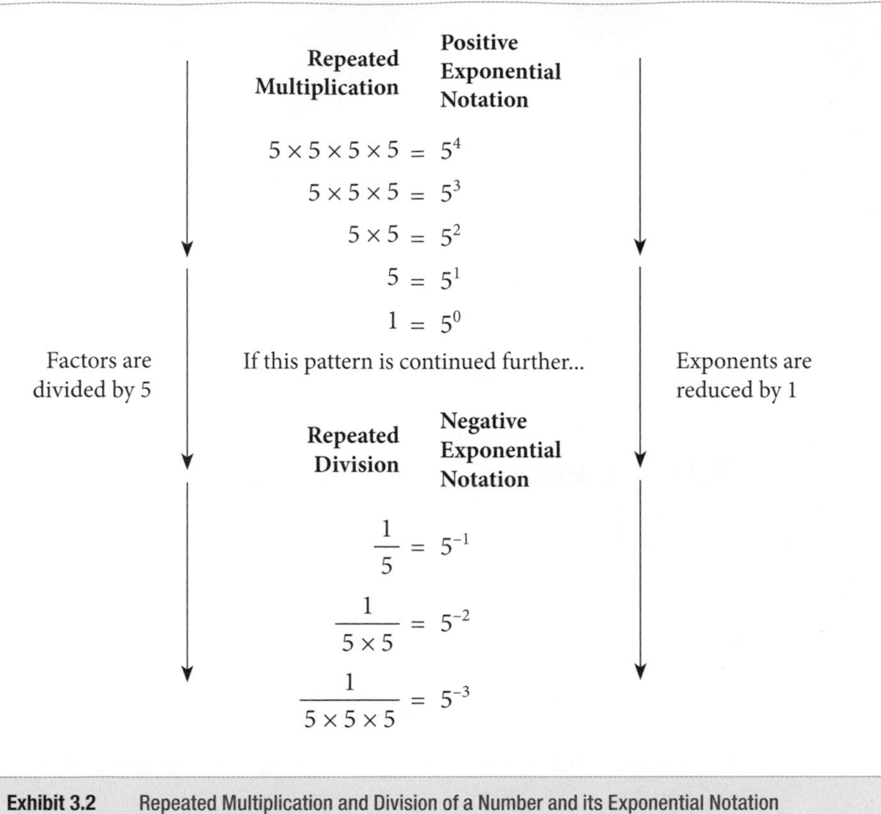

Repeated Multiplication
Positive Exponential Notation
5 × 5 × 5 × 5 = 5^4
5 × 5 × 5 = 5^3
5 × 5 = 5^2
5 = 5^1
1 = 5^0
Factors are divided by 5
If this pattern is continued further...
Exponents are reduced by 1
Repeated Division
Negative Exponential Notation
1/5 = 5^-1
1/(5 × 5) = 5^-2
1/(5 × 5 × 5) = 5^-3

Exhibit 3.2 Repeated Multiplication and Division of a Number and its Exponential Notation

$a^{-n} = \frac{1}{a^n}$, and $\frac{1}{a^{-n}} = a^n$ Therefore, a^n and a^{-n} are reciprocals.

Any positive base with a **negative** exponent will always result in a **positive** answer.

For example, as illustrated in Exhibit 3.2 above,

Negative Exponential Notation	Positive Exponential Notation	Repeated Division	Standard Notation
5^{-1}	$\frac{1}{5^1}$	$\frac{1}{5}$	$\frac{1}{5}$
5^{-2}	$\frac{1}{5^2}$	$\frac{1}{5 \times 5}$	$\frac{1}{25}$
5^{-3}	$\frac{1}{5^3}$	$\frac{1}{5 \times 5 \times 5}$	$\frac{1}{125}$

The properties (rules) of exponents in Section 3.1 of this chapter (summarized in Table 3.1-a) also apply to all negative exponents. We can use these properties to simplify powers with negative exponents and then convert negative exponents to positive exponents.

Example 3.2-j

Multiplying and Dividing Powers with Negative Exponents

Simplify the following and express the answer in exponential form with positive exponents:

(i) $2^{-2} \times 2^{-3}$ (ii) $\frac{3^{-4}}{3^{-2}}$ (iii) $(3 \times 5)^{-2}$ (iv) $(3^{-2})^3$

Solution

(i) $2^{-2} \times 2^{-3}$ Using Product Rule,

$= 2^{-2+(-3)}$

$= 2^{-2-3}$

$= 2^{-5}$ Expressing with a positive exponent,

$= \frac{1}{2^5}$

(ii) $\frac{3^{-4}}{3^{-2}}$ Using Quotient Rule,

$= 3^{-4-(-2)}$

$= 3^{-4+2}$

$= 3^{-2}$ Expressing with a positive exponent,

$= \frac{1}{3^2}$

Arithmetic operations with signed numbers are covered in Section 3.3.

(iii) $(3 \times 5)^{-2}$ Using Power of a Product Rule,

$= 3^{-2} \times 5^{-2}$ Expressing with positive exponents,

$= \frac{1}{3^2} \times \frac{1}{5^2}$

(iv) $(3^{-2})^3$ Using Power of a Power Rule,

$= 3^{-2(3)}$

$= 3^{-6}$ Expressing with a positive exponent,

$= \frac{1}{3^6}$

Fractions with Negative Exponents

When a fraction has a negative exponent, change the fraction to its reciprocal and drop the negative sign from the exponent. After this change, the exponent simply indicates the number of times the numerator and denominator should be multiplied.

$$\left(\frac{a}{b}\right)^{-n} = \left(\frac{b}{a}\right)^{n}$$

For example,

$$\left(\frac{2}{5}\right)^{-3} = \left(\frac{5}{2}\right)^{3} = \left(\frac{5}{2}\right)\left(\frac{5}{2}\right)\left(\frac{5}{2}\right) = \frac{5 \times 5 \times 5}{2 \times 2 \times 2} = \frac{125}{8}$$

Note: The reciprocal of $\frac{2}{5}$ *is* $\frac{5}{2}$.

Example 3.2-k **Evaluating Fractions with Negative Exponents**

Evaluate the following to two decimal places, where applicable.

(i) $\left(\frac{5}{4}\right)^{-2} \times \left(\frac{2}{3}\right)^{-3}$

(ii) $\left(\frac{3}{5}\right)^{-3} \div \left(\frac{2}{5}\right)^{-2}$

Solution

(i) $\left(\frac{5}{4}\right)^{-2} \times \left(\frac{2}{3}\right)^{-3}$

$= \left(\frac{4}{5}\right)^{2} \times \left(\frac{3}{2}\right)^{3}$

$= \frac{4^2}{5^2} \times \frac{3^3}{2^3}$

$= \frac{{}^{2}\cancel{16}}{25} \times \frac{27}{\cancel{8}_{1}}$

$= \frac{2}{25} \times \frac{27}{1}$

(ii) $\left(\frac{3}{5}\right)^{-3} \div \left(\frac{2}{5}\right)^{-2}$

$= \left(\frac{5}{3}\right)^{3} \div \left(\frac{5}{2}\right)^{2}$

$= \frac{5^3}{3^3} \div \frac{5^2}{2^2}$

$= \frac{125}{27} \div \frac{25}{4}$

$= \frac{{}^{5}\cancel{125}}{27} \times \frac{4}{\cancel{25}_{1}}$

Solution
continued

$= \dfrac{54}{25}$

$= 2\frac{4}{25} = 2.16$

$= \dfrac{5}{27} \times \dfrac{4}{1}$

$= \dfrac{20}{27}$

$= 0.740740... = 0.74$

3.2 | Exercises

Answers to odd-numbered problems are available at the end of the textbook.

Express Problems 1 to 4 in their radical form and evaluate.

1. a. $64^{\frac{1}{2}}$ b. $\left(\dfrac{25}{16}\right)^{\frac{1}{2}}$
2. a. $81^{\frac{1}{2}}$ b. $\left(\dfrac{8}{25}\right)^{\frac{1}{2}}$
3. a. $8^{\frac{1}{3}}$ b. $\left(\dfrac{27}{64}\right)^{\frac{1}{3}}$
4. a. $64^{\frac{1}{3}}$ b. $\left(\dfrac{125}{8}\right)^{\frac{1}{3}}$

Express Problems 5 to 10 in their fractional exponent form and then evaluate. Round to two decimal places, wherever applicable.

5. a. $\sqrt{144}$ b. $\sqrt[3]{64}$
6. a. $\sqrt{81}$ b. $\sqrt[3]{125}$
7. a. $\sqrt{2^6}$ b. $\sqrt{40}$
8. a. $\sqrt{3^4}$ b. $\sqrt{50}$
9. a. $\sqrt{8} \times \sqrt{12}$ b. $\sqrt{7} \times \sqrt{14}$
10. a. $\sqrt{12} \times \sqrt{10}$ b. $\sqrt{9} \times \sqrt{27}$

Express Problems 11 and 12 in their fractional exponent form and then evaluate. Express your answer as a simplified fraction.

11. a. $\sqrt{\dfrac{25}{49}}$ b. $\sqrt{\dfrac{64}{9}}$
12. a. $\sqrt{\dfrac{36}{64}}$ b. $\sqrt{\dfrac{169}{16}}$

Express Problems 13 and 14 in their fractional exponent form with a single base, and then evaluate. Round to two decimal places, wherever applicable.

13. a. $\sqrt[4]{2^2 \times 2}$ b. $\sqrt[4]{5^2 \times 25^2}$
14. a. $\sqrt{3^4 \times 3^2}$ b. $\sqrt[6]{9^3 \times 27^4}$

Simplify Problems 15 to 24 by expressing the powers using a single exponent and then evaluate. Round to two decimal places, wherever applicable.

15. a. $5^{\frac{1}{2}} \times 5^{\frac{3}{4}}$ b. $3^{\frac{7}{8}} \times 3^{\frac{5}{9}}$
16. a. $3^{\frac{1}{2}} \times 3^{\frac{1}{4}}$ b. $11^{\frac{3}{4}} \times 11^{\frac{2}{3}}$
17. a. $8^{\frac{4}{5}} \times 8^{\frac{2}{5}} \times 8^{\frac{1}{5}}$ b. $5^{\frac{1}{3}} \times 5^{\frac{1}{2}} \times 5^0$
18. a. $5^{\frac{4}{7}} \times 5^{\frac{4}{7}} \times 5^{\frac{6}{7}}$ b. $9^{\frac{5}{8}} \times 9^{\frac{2}{3}} \times 9^0$
19. a. $8^{\frac{1}{3}} \times 8^{\frac{2}{3}} \times 8^1$ b. $\dfrac{3^{\frac{8}{3}}}{3^2}$
20. a. $2^{\frac{2}{3}} \times 2^{\frac{1}{2}} \times 2^1$ b. $\dfrac{6^{\frac{7}{2}}}{6^2}$
21. a. $\dfrac{4^{\frac{5}{7}}}{4^{\frac{2}{7}}}$ b. $(3^2)^{\frac{1}{3}}$
22. a. $\dfrac{2^{\frac{4}{5}}}{2^{\frac{3}{5}}}$ b. $(10^3)^0$
23. a. $\left(12^{\frac{1}{2}}\right)^4$ b. $\left(7^{\frac{1}{4}}\right)^8$
24. a. $\left(5^{\frac{2}{3}}\right)^6$ b. $\left(4^{\frac{2}{3}}\right)^6$

Evaluate Problems 25 to 32. Round to two decimal places, wherever applicable.

25. a. $5^{\frac{1}{2}} + 7^{\frac{1}{2}}$ b. $16^{\frac{1}{2}} - 9^{\frac{1}{2}}$
26. a. $125^{\frac{1}{3}} + 64^{\frac{1}{3}}$ b. $50^{\frac{1}{2}} - 40^{\frac{1}{2}}$
27. a. $5 \times 3^{\frac{1}{2}} + 2^{\frac{1}{2}}$ b. $(2^5)^{\frac{1}{2}} - (5^2)^{\frac{1}{2}}$
28. a. $12 \times 10^{\frac{1}{2}} + 5^{\frac{1}{2}}$ b. $(3^4)^{\frac{1}{3}} - (4^3)^{\frac{1}{4}}$

29. a. $8^{\frac{1}{2}} \times 9^{\frac{1}{2}}$ b. $45^{\frac{1}{2}} \times 60^{\frac{1}{2}}$

30. a. $6^{\frac{1}{2}} \times 3^{\frac{1}{2}}$ b. $24^{\frac{1}{2}} \times 75^{\frac{1}{2}}$

31. a. $\dfrac{5 + 4^{\frac{1}{2}}}{36^{\frac{1}{2}}}$ b. $\dfrac{10^{\frac{1}{2}} - 5^{\frac{1}{2}}}{25^{\frac{1}{2}}}$

32. a. $\dfrac{6^{\frac{1}{2}} + 6^{\frac{1}{2}}}{9^{\frac{1}{2}}}$ b. $\dfrac{7 - 7^{\frac{1}{2}}}{4^{\frac{1}{2}}}$

Simplify Problems 33 to 42 by expressing the powers using a single exponent and as a radical (where applicable), and then evaluate. Round to two decimal places, wherever applicable.

33. a. $6^{-\frac{5}{4}} \times 6^{\frac{3}{4}}$ b. $7^{\frac{4}{3}} \times 7^{-\frac{2}{3}}$

34. a. $5^{\frac{4}{9}} \times 5^{-\frac{2}{9}}$ b. $3^{-\frac{6}{7}} \times 3^{\frac{2}{7}}$

35. a. $\dfrac{10^{-\frac{3}{5}} \times 10^{\frac{4}{5}}}{10^{\frac{2}{5}}}$ b. $\dfrac{2^{\frac{5}{7}} \times 2^{-\frac{6}{7}}}{2^{-\frac{8}{7}}}$

36. a. $\dfrac{5^{\frac{2}{7}} \times 5^{\frac{4}{7}}}{5^{-\frac{6}{7}}}$ b. $\dfrac{3^{\frac{2}{3}} - 3^{-\frac{4}{3}}}{3^{\frac{5}{3}}}$

37. a. $\dfrac{6^{-\frac{5}{9}} \times 6^{0}}{6^{\frac{7}{9}}}$ b. $\dfrac{7^{\frac{7}{8}} \times 7^{\frac{8}{3}}}{7^{2}}$

38. a. $\dfrac{9^{\frac{2}{5}} \times 9^{0}}{9^{\frac{3}{5}}}$ b. $\dfrac{5^{\frac{5}{6}} \times 5^{\frac{2}{3}}}{5^{2}}$

39. a. $(5^{-2})^{\frac{4}{3}}$ b. $\left(6^{-\frac{1}{2}}\right)^{-6}$

40. a. $(4^{-2})^{\frac{5}{2}}$ b. $\left(2^{-\frac{4}{5}}\right)^{-5}$

41. a. $\left(8^{-\frac{2}{3}}\right)^{-6}$ b. $\left(7^{-\frac{1}{3}}\right)^{9}$

42. a. $\left(6^{-\frac{2}{3}}\right)^{-3}$ b. $\left(3^{-\frac{4}{9}}\right)^{0}$

Evaluate Problems 43 to 48. Round to two decimal places, wherever applicable.

43. a. $\dfrac{3^{-1}}{2^{-1}}$ b. $3^{-1} + 2^{-1}$

44. a. $\dfrac{2^{-2}}{3^{-1}}$ b. $2^{-2} + 3^{-1}$

45. a. $3^{-1} \times 3^{2} \times 3^{-2}$ b. $[2^{-3}]^{-1}$

46. a. $5^{-2} \times 5^{2} \times 5^{3}$ b. $[5^{-2}]^{-2}$

47. a. $\dfrac{2^{\frac{2}{5}} + 3^{0} \times 2^{-1}}{\left(\frac{1}{2}\right)^{-1}}$ b. $2^{-2} + \dfrac{1}{2^{-1}}$

48. a. $\dfrac{3^{-1} + 2 \times 3^{-1}}{\left(\frac{1}{3}\right)^{-1}}$ b. $3^{-2} + \dfrac{1}{3^{-1}}$

3.3 | Arithmetic Operations with Signed Numbers

In the previous chapters, we learned that positive real numbers can be represented by points on a number line from zero to the right of the zero. That is, whole numbers and positive rational and irrational numbers can be represented on a number line from zero to the right of the zero.

Every positive number has a negative number known as its opposite, which lies to the left of zero on the number line. We use the negative sign '–' to represent negative numbers, and the positive sign '+' to represent positive numbers. Zero, '0', is neither positive nor negative.

For example, plotting the positive numbers $\frac{3}{4}$, 4, and 6.5 and their opposites on the number line:

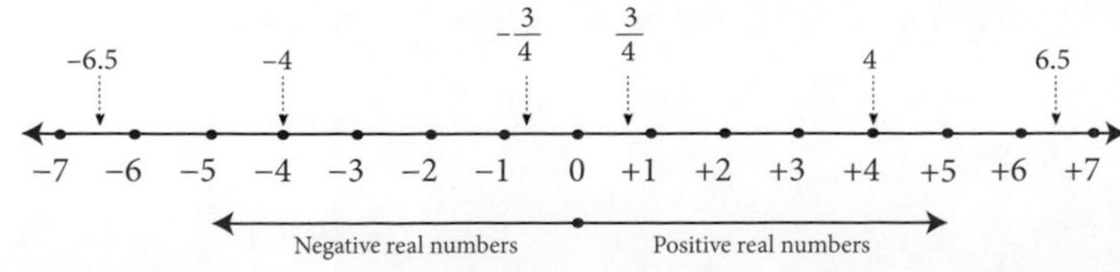

The arrowhead on either end shows that the number line continues indefinitely in both the positive and negative directions.

A negative number is the opposite of a positive number. For example, −3 is the opposite of +3.

Positive and negative numbers are collectively referred to as **signed numbers**. Since numbers are naturally positive, when we read or write positive numbers, we usually omit the word **'positive'** or the positive sign (+). However, when the number is negative, we must read or write it as **'negative'** or include the negative sign (−). For example, '+7' is read as **'seven'** and written as '7'. However, '−7' is read as **'negative seven'** and written with the negative sign as '−7'.

Any positive number and its negative (opposite) will be at an equal distance from zero (origin) on the number line.

Two integers that are at equal distances from the origin and in opposite directions are opposites.

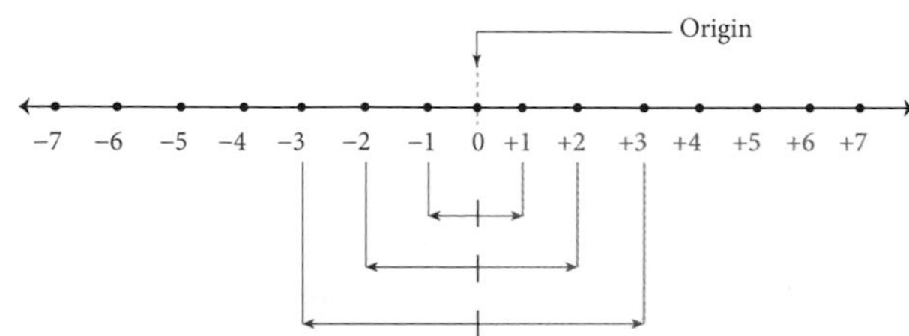

Numbers that lie to the left of a number on the number line are **less than** that number, and numbers that lie to the right of a number on a number line are **greater than** that number.

For example,

- 3 is greater than −2, i.e., $3 > -2$
- −3 is greater than −5, i.e., $-3 > -5$
- −5 is less than −4, i.e., $-5 < -4$
- −1 is less than 2 i.e., $-1 < 2$

Absolute Value

Absolute value is the magnitude of the number.

The **absolute value** of a number is its distance from the origin '0' on the number line. Since it is a distance, it is always positive and the direction does not matter.

For example, −5 and +5 are both 5 units from the origin '0'.

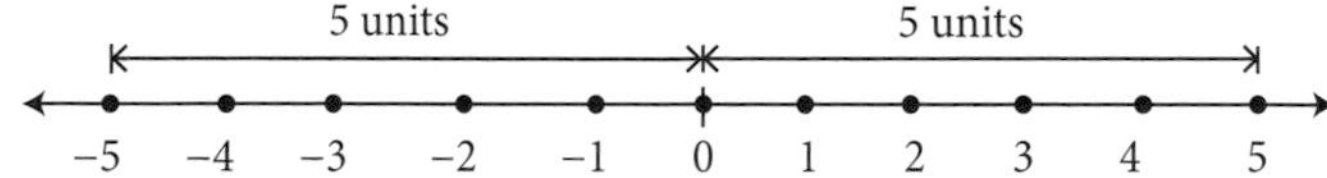

Therefore, the absolute value of both −5 and +5 is 5.

The absolute value of a number 'a' is denoted by $|a|$. The vertical bars used in the representation of the absolute value differ from how brackets are used.

For example, $|-4| = 4$, whereas $(-4) = -4$

Example 3.3-a **Simplifying Arithmetic Expressions Involving Absolute Values**

Simplify the following expressions:

(i) $-\left|\frac{-4}{3}\right|$ (ii) $-|8(-2)|$

Solution

(i) $-\left|\frac{-4}{3}\right|$ Simplifying the absolute value portion,

$= -\left(\frac{4}{3}\right)$

(ii) $-|8(-2)|$ Simplifying within the absolute value portion,

$= -|-16|$ Simplifying the absolute value portion,

Solution *continued*

$= -\dfrac{4}{3}$

Therefore, $-\left|\dfrac{-4}{3}\right| = -\dfrac{4}{3}$.

$= -(16)$

$= -16$

Therefore, $-|8(-2)| = -16$.

Example 3.3-b **Adding and Subtracting Arithmetic Expressions Involving Absolute Values**

Simplify the following expressions:

(i) $10 - |8 - 15|$ (ii) $-5 + |-10 + 8|$

Solution

(i) $10 - |8 - 15|$ Simplifying within the absolute value portion,

$= 10 - |-7|$ Simplifying the absolute value portion,

$= 10 - 7$ Subtracting,

$= 3$

Therefore, $10 - |8 - 15| = 3$.

(ii) $-5 + |-10 + 8|$ Simplifying within the absolute value portion,

$= -5 + |-2|$ Simplifying the absolute value portion,

$= -5 + 2$ Adding,

$= -3$

Therefore, $-5 + |-10 + 8| = -3$.

Note: In the previous two examples, we performed arithmetic with signed numbers. The rules we follow when adding, subtracting, multiplying, and dividing signed numbers are explained in detail below.

Addition and Subtraction of Signed Numbers

- When adding two positive numbers, the answer is always positive (+).
  For example,

  Adding +5 and +3:
  $(+5) + (+3) = 5 + 3 = \mathbf{8}$
  This is the same as **+8.**

- When adding two negative numbers, the answer is always negative (–).
  For example,

  Adding –4 and –3:
  $(-4) + (-3) = -4 - 3 = \mathbf{-7}$

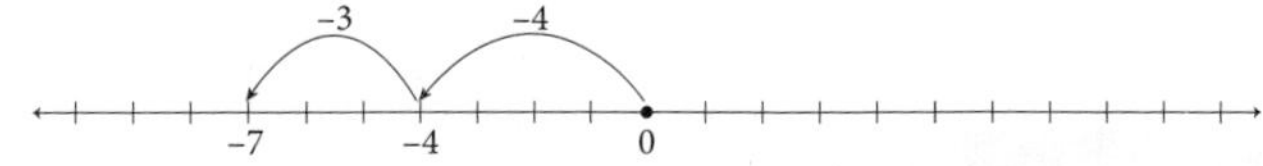

- When adding numbers that have different signs, subtract the smaller absolute value from the larger absolute value, and keep the sign of the number with the larger absolute value.
  For example,

  (i) Adding +8 and –12 (or –12 and +8):
  $(+8) + (-12) = 8 - 12 = \mathbf{-4}$

  (ii) Adding –5 and +8 (or +8 and –5):
  $(-5) + (+8) = -5 + 8 = \mathbf{3}$ (or **+3**)

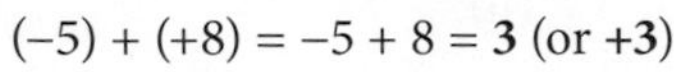

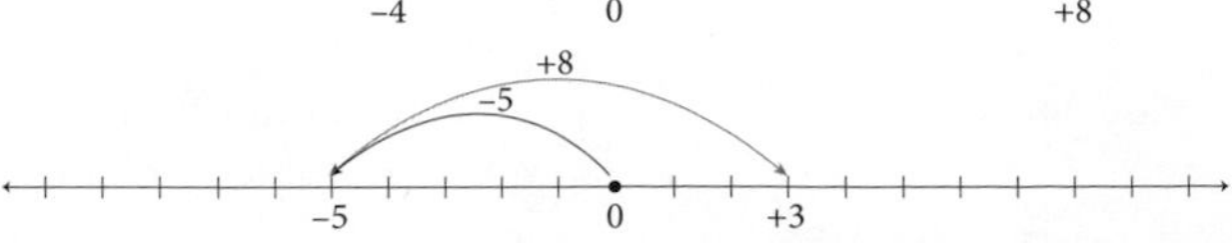

- When subtracting negative numbers, first change all the subtraction problems to addition problems by adding the opposite, and then follow the rules for addition of signed numbers.

For example,

(i) Subtracting 12 from 18:

$18 - 12 = 18 + (-12) = 6$

(ii) Subtracting −12 from 18:

$18 - (-12) = 18 + 12 = 30$

(iii) Subtracting 12 from −18:

$-18 - 12 = -18 + (-12) = -30$

(iv) Subtracting −12 from −18:

$-18 - (-12) = -18 + 12 = -6$

Multiplication and Division of Signed Numbers

Multiplying two signed numbers:

$(+)(+) = (+)$

$(-)(-) = (+)$

$(+)(-) = (-)$

$(-)(+) = (-)$

When multiplying two signed numbers:

- The product of two numbers with the **same sign** is **positive**.

  For example,

  (i) $(+5)(+4) = +20$

  (ii) $(-5)(-4) = +20$

- The product of two numbers with **different signs** is **negative**.

  For example,

  (i) $(+5)(-4) = -20$

  (ii) $(-5)(+4) = -20$

Dividing two signed numbers:

$\frac{(+)}{(+)} = (+)$

$\frac{(-)}{(-)} = (+)$

$\frac{(-)}{(+)} = (-)$

$\frac{(+)}{(-)} = (-)$

When dividing two signed numbers:

- The quotient of two numbers with the **same sign** is **positive**.

  For example,

  (i) $\frac{+12}{+8} = \frac{3}{2}$

  (ii) $\frac{-12}{-8} = \frac{3}{2}$

- The quotient of two numbers with **different signs** is **negative**.

  For example,

  (i) $\frac{-12}{+8} = -\frac{3}{2}$

  (ii) $\frac{+12}{-8} = -\frac{3}{2}$

When multiplying or dividing more than two signed numbers, group them into pairs to determine the sign using the rules for multiplication and division of signed numbers.

For example,

(i) $\underbrace{(-3)(-2)}\,\underbrace{(+4)(-1)}(-5)$

$= \underbrace{(6)(-4)}(-5)$

$= (-24)(-5)$

$= 120$

(ii) $\frac{\overbrace{(-15)(+8)}(-50)}{\underbrace{(-25)(14)}}$

$= \frac{\overbrace{-(15 \times 8)(-50)}}{-(25 \times 14)}$

$= \frac{+(15 \times 8 \times 50)}{-(25 \times 14)} = \frac{(15 \times \overset{4}{\cancel{8}} \times \overset{2}{\cancel{50}})}{-(\underset{1}{\cancel{25}} \times \underset{7}{\cancel{14}})}$

$= -\frac{15 \times 4 \times 2}{7}$

$= -\frac{120}{7}$

Powers with Negative Bases

When a power has a negative base, there are four possible scenarios, as outlined in the following table:

Table 3.3-a **Powers with Negative Bases**

Sign and Parity of Exponent	Example	Sign of Answer
Positive and Even	$(-2)^6 = \underbrace{(-2)\,(-2)}\,\underbrace{(-2)\,(-2)}\,\underbrace{(-2)\,(-2)} = 64$	+
Positive and Odd	$(-2)^5 = \underbrace{(-2)\,(-2)}\,\underbrace{(-2)\,(-2)}\,(-2) = -32$	–
Negative and Even	$(-2)^{-6} = \frac{1}{(-2)^6} = \frac{1}{\underbrace{(-2)(-2)}\underbrace{(-2)(-2)}\underbrace{(-2)(-2)}} = \frac{1}{64} = 0.015625$	+
Negative and Odd	$(-2)^{-5} = \frac{1}{(-2)^5} = \frac{1}{\underbrace{(-2)(-2)}\underbrace{(-2)(-2)}(-2)} = \frac{1}{-32} = -0.03125$	–

From the above scenarios you will note:

- A negative base with an even exponent produces a positive result (because pairs of negatives become positive).
- A negative base with an odd exponent produces a negative result (because after negatives are paired, one negative will be left over).

A negative base of a power expressed within a bracket, as in $(-a)^n$, results in a different answer than a negative base expressed without a bracket, as in $-a^n$.

In $(-a)^n$, the exponent applies to both the negative sign and a.

In $-a^n$, the exponent applies only to a and the negative sign is applied to the answer.

For example,

(i) In $(-5)^4$, (-5) is multiplied 4 times; i.e., $(-5)^4 = (-5)(-5)(-5)(-5) = 625$

(ii) In $(-5)^3$, (-5) is multiplied 3 times; i.e., $(-5)^3 = (-5)(-5)(-5) = -125$

(iii) In -5^4, only 5 is multiplied 4 times and the answer is negative; i.e., $-5^4 = -[5 \times 5 \times 5 \times 5] = -625$

(iv) In -5^3, only 5 is multiplied 3 times and the answer is negative; i.e., $-5^3 = -[5 \times 5 \times 5] = -125$

Example 3.3-c **Evaluating Expressions with Negative Bases using the Product Rule**

Evaluate the following expressions:

(i) $(-5)^4 \times (-5)^{-1}$ (ii) $(-2)^5 \times (-2)^2 \times (-2)^0 \times 2$

Solution

(i) $(-5)^4 \times (-5)^{-1}$

$= (-5)^{(4-1)}$

$= (-5)^3$

$= -125$

(ii) $(-2)^5 \times (-2)^2 \times (-2)^0 \times 2$

$= (-2)^{(5+2+0)} \times 2$

$= (-2)^7 \times 2$

$= -128 \times 2$

$= -256$

Example 3.3-d **Evaluating Expressions with Negative Bases using the Quotient Rule**

Evaluate the following expressions:

(i) $(-3)^7 \div (-3)^2$ (ii) $(-5)^3 \div (-5)^0$

Solution

(i) $(-3)^7 \div (-3)^2$
$= (-3)^{(7-2)}$
$= (-3)^5$
$= -243$

(ii) $(-5)^3 \div (-5)^0$
$= (-5)^{(3-0)}$
$= (-5)^3$
$= -125$

Example 3.3-e **Evaluating Expressions with Negative Bases using the Power of a Product Rule**

Evaluate the following expressions:

(i) $(-5 \times 2)^3$ (ii) $(-3 \times 2)^{-2}$

Solution

(i) $(-5 \times 2)^3$
$= (-5)^3 \times 2^3$
$= -125 \times 8$
$= -1{,}000$

or

$(-5 \times 2)^3$
$= (-10)^3$
$= -1{,}000$

(ii) $(-3 \times 2)^{-2}$
$= (-3)^{-2} \times 2^{-2}$
$= \frac{1}{(-3)^2} \times \frac{1}{2^2}$
$= \frac{1}{9} \times \frac{1}{4}$
$= \frac{1}{36}$

or

$(-3 \times 2)^{-2}$
$= (-6)^{-2}$
$= \frac{1}{(-6)^2}$
$= \frac{1}{36}$

Example 3.3-f **Evaluating Expressions with Negative Bases using the Power of a Quotient Rule**

Evaluate the following expressions:

(i) $(-2 \div 3)^{-2}$ (ii) $(3 \div (-2))^{-3}$

Solution

(i) $(-2 \div 3)^{-2}$
$= \left(\frac{-2}{3}\right)^{-2}$
$= \left(\frac{3}{-2}\right)^{2}$
$= \frac{3^2}{(-2)^2}$
$= \frac{9}{4}$

(ii) $(3 \div (-2))^{-3}$
$= \left(\frac{3}{-2}\right)^{-3}$
$= \left(\frac{-2}{3}\right)^{3}$
$= \frac{(-2)^3}{3^3}$
$= \frac{-8}{27} = -\frac{8}{27}$

Example 3.3-g **Evaluating Expressions with Negative Bases using the Power of a Power Rule**

Evaluate the following expressions:

(i) $(-2^3)^3$ (ii) $(-3^3)^2$

Solution

(i) $(-2^3)^3$

$= (-2)^{3 \times 3}$

$= (-2)^9$

$= -512$

(ii) $(-3^3)^2$

$= (-3)^{3 \times 2}$

$= (-3)^6$

$= 729$

Principal Roots

Roots of Positive Numbers

- When the index of the root is **even**, any positive number will have two real number solutions, with one being the negative of the other. The positive solution is known as its **principal root**.
  - For example, $\sqrt{9}$ has two roots: +3 and –3, because $(3) \times (3) = 9$ and $(-3) \times (-3) = 9$
    This is usually written as ±3 and read as "plus or minus 3", and the principal root is 3.
  - $\sqrt[4]{16}$ has two roots: +2 and –2, because $(2) \times (2) \times (2) \times (2) = 16$ and $(-2) \times (-2) \times (-2) \times (-2) = 16$
    i.e., the roots are ±2 and the principal root is 2.
- When the index of the root is **odd**, there is only one real number solution and it is positive. This positive solution is the **principal root.**
  - For example, $\sqrt[3]{27} = 3$ because $(3) \times (3) \times (3) = 27$; i.e., the principal root is 3.
  - Similary, $\sqrt[5]{32} = 2$ because $(2) \times (2) \times (2) \times (2) \times (2) = 32$; i.e., the principal root is 2.

Roots of Negative Numbers

- When the index of the root is **even,** there is **no real number solution** to any negative number.
  - For example, $\sqrt[4]{-81}$ has no real roots.
- When the index of the root is **odd**, there is only one real number solution to any negative number and it is negative. This negative solution is the **principal root.**
  - For example, $\sqrt[5]{-32} = -2$ because $(-2)\,(-2)\,(-2)\,(-2)\,(-2) = -32$; i.e., the principal root is –2.

Real Numbers

Real numbers include all positive numbers and negative numbers. A summary of the types of real numbers, which we have learned about in the last three chapters, is provided below:

Table 3.3-b **Types of Real Numbers**

Natural numbers are positive integers. Zero is neither positive nor negative.

Type	Description	Examples
Natural Numbers	Counting numbers (numbers starting from 1).	Counting Numbers or Natural Numbers; 0 1 2 3 4; Whole Numbers
Whole Numbers	Natural numbers, including zero.	
Integers	Natural numbers (positive integers), their negatives (negative integers), and zero.	–4 –3 –2 –1 0 1 2 3 4; Negative Integers; Positive Integers; Zero is neither positive nor negative

Rational numbers can be expressed as $\frac{a}{b}$, whereas irrational numbers cannot be expressed as $\frac{a}{b}$, where a and b are integers and $b \neq 0$.

Type	Description	Examples
Rational Numbers	Numbers that can be expressed as one integer divided by another non-zero integer; i.e., numbers that can be written as a quotient of integers with non-zero divisors.	$-\frac{5}{2}$, 0.75, $\frac{3}{2}$
Irrational Numbers	Numbers that cannot be expressed as a rational number.	$\sqrt{2}$, π, 2.718281...

Note: Terminating decimals (decimals that end) and repeating decimals (decimals that do not end but show a repeating pattern) are also rational numbers because they can be expressed as a quotient of integers.

For example,

- 0.375 *can be expressed as* $\frac{3}{8}$.
- 0.185185... *is usually written as* $0.\overline{185}$ *and can be expressed as* $\frac{5}{27}$.

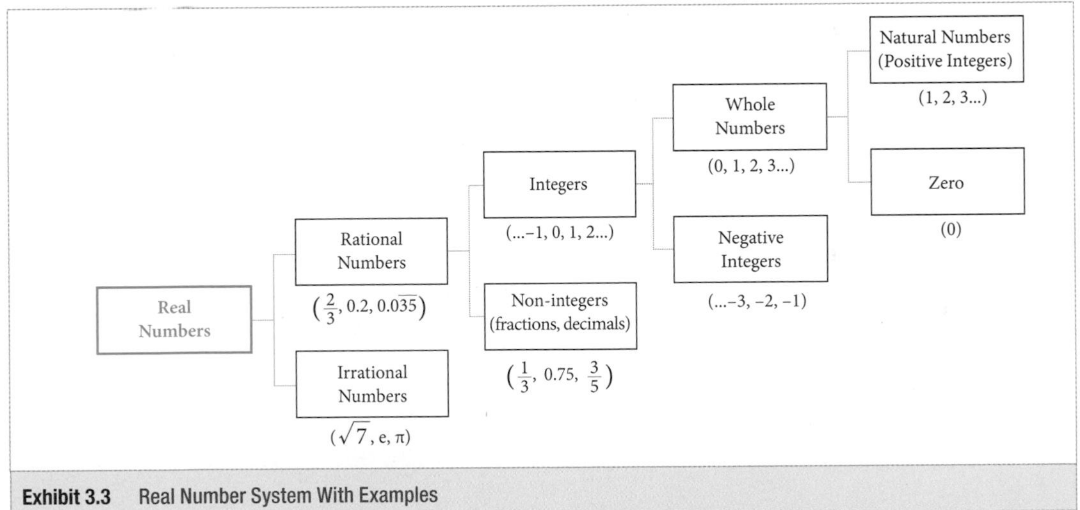

Exhibit 3.3 Real Number System With Examples

3.3 | Exercises

Answers to odd-numbered problems are available at the end of the textbook.

For Problems 1 to 6, place the correct sign '<' or '>' in the space between the following pairs of numbers.

1. a. −5 ☐ 0 b. −2 ☐ +6
2. a. 0 ☐ −3 b. −5 ☐ +3
3. a. +8 ☐ −3 b. +1 ☐ −2
4. a. −5 ☐ +4 b. +3 ☐ −7
5. a. −6 ☐ −8 b. −5 ☐ −2
6. a. −7 ☐ −9 b. −8 ☐ −4

For Problems 7 to 10, arrange the numbers in order from least to greatest.

7. a. 5, −6, 8, −8, −5, 2 b. −8, 4, −6, 3, −9, 7
8. a. −2, −3, 5, 2, −1, 4 b. 15, −14, 17, 4, −5, −7
9. a. 9, −5, −8, 3, 7, 10 b. 12, −13, 15, 2, −8, −3
10. a. −3, 6, 1, −7, −1, 7 b. −12, 0, 12, −16, 15, −5

Evaluate Problems 11 to 20.

11. a. $|-16|$ b. $-|3|$
12. a. $|-8|$ b. $-|12|$
13. a. $-|-5|$ b. $-[-|-9|]$
14. a. $-|-7|$ b. $-[-|-3|]$
15. a. $|-4| - |-7|$ b. $-|-8| + |-3|$
16. a. $-|-15| - |-3|$ b. $|-5| + |-4|$

17. a. $|-10| \times |-5|$ b. $|-15| \div |-3|$

18. a. $|-10| \times |-2|$ b. $|-12| \div |-4|$

19. a. $-|6| \times |-3|$ b. $-|-20| \div |-5|$

20. a. $|-8| \times |4|$ b. $-|-24| \div |-6|$

Evaluate Problems 21 to 44.

21. a. $-8 + (-5 - 7)$ b. $2 - (-3) + 1$

22. a. $-9 + (-3 - 8)$ b. $5 - (-7) + 8$

23. a. $-3 - (-7) + 8$ b. $(-4 + 9) - (-3 - 6)$

24. a. $-7 - (-9) - 1$ b. $(-5 + 3) + (-4 - 9)$

25. a. $4 + (-3) - [5 + (-11)]$ b. $-6 + (-4) - [-(15 - 8)]$

26. a. $5 + (-4) - [7 + (-9)]$ b. $-8 + (-15) - [-(6 - 7)]$

27. a. $2(-3)(-5)$ b. $-4(-3)(-2)$

28. a. $6(-2)(-4)$ b. $-5(-3)(-2)$

29. a. $-64 \div (-8)$ b. $45 \div (-5)$

30. a. $-48 \div (-6)$ b. $36 \div (-4)$

31. a. $-5 + (-2)(-5) - (6 - 3)$ b. $7(2 - 3) - 4(-7 + 1)$

32. a. $-8(5 - 6) - 3(-6 + 2)$ b. $-7 + (-3)(-4) - (-8 - 3)$

33. a. $(5 + 7)^2 - 5^2 - 7^2$ b. $2^2 - 2^4 - 20 \times 3$

34. a. $(9 - 12)^2 - 9^2 - 12^2$ b. $7 \times 8 - 3^2 - 2^3$

35. a. $(20 \times 4 - 8^2)^2 + 9$ b. $(3 \times 9 - 3^2) + 12$

36. a. $-12 \div 4 - 3 \times 2^4$ b. $-5 \times 3^3 \div 9 + 5^2$

37. $-11^2 - 4 \times 54 \div (5 - 2)^3 - 3$

38. $[(1 + 12)(1 - 5)]^2 \div (5 - 3 \times 2^2 - 4)$

39. $-31 - [(15 \div 3) \times 32] \div \left(2^2 \times \dfrac{23}{46}\right)$

40. $3(7^2 + 2 \times 15 \div 3) - (1 - 3 \times 4)^2$

41. $[(-8) + 4]^3 \times (-2) \div (6 + |-5| \times 2)$

42. $|-7 + 3|^3 \times (-3) \div (4 + |-2| \times 4)$

43. $|-3 - 1|^2 \div (-2 + 2 \times |-3|) - (-3 - 2)$

44. $|-2 - 1|^3 \div |3 - 6| \times (-4 + |-5| \times 3)$

Express Problems 45 to 50 as a single power and then evaluate.

45. a. $(-6)^5 \times (-6)^3$ b. $8^{-6} \times 8^9$

46. a. $(-2)^5 \times (-2)^6$ b. $4^{-7} \times 4^8$

47. a. $(-4)^5 \div (-4)^3$ b. $-5^4 \div (-5)^2$

48. a. $(-2)^7 \div (-2)^4$ b. $-4^6 \div (-4)^4$

49. a. $(-2^3)^2 \div (-2)^5$ b. $-(3^2) \div (-3)^6$

50. a. $(-3^2)^3 \div (-3)^7$ b. $-(2^2)^2 \div (-2)^3$

Evaluate Problems 51 to 54.

51. a. $(-2)^2 + (-3)^3$ b. $(-3)^2 - (-2)^3$

52. a. $(-4)^2 + (-5)^3$ b. $(-5)^2 - (-4)^2$

53. a. $(-2)^3 - (-3)^2 - 1^5$ b. $(-7)^1 + (5)^0 - (-3)^2$

54. a. $(-3)^0 + (-4)^1 - (-2)^3$ b. $(-3)^2 - (-2)^3 - 2^2$

3.4 | Significant Digits and Scientific Notation

Significant Digits

Significant digits are critical when reporting data as they provide information on how well the data is measured or reported.

The **accuracy** of a number is determined by the number of significant digits in the number. The **precision** of a number is based on the place value of the rightmost significant digit.

For example,

- 4,700 is accurate to 2 significant digits and precise to the nearest hundred.
- 12.25 is accurate to 4 significant digits and precise to the nearest hundredth.

Note: The number of significant digits in a number is calculated by following the rules outlined in Table 3.4-a.

Determining the Number of Significant Digits in a Number

The general rules for determining the number of significant digits are as follows:

Table 3.4-a **Determining the Number of Significant Digits**

	General Rule	Example	
1.	All non-zero digits are significant.	270 31.4	2 significant digits 3 significant digits
2.	All zeros between two significant digits are significant.	3005 105.03	4 significant digits 5 significant digits
3.	Leading zeros are **not** significant.	0.05 0.00325	1 significant digit 3 significant digits
4.	Trailing zeros in any number with a decimal point are significant.	250.0 0.00380	4 significant digits 3 significant digits
5.	Trailing zeros in a whole number are **ambiguous** and therefore should not be counted as significant.	25000 1580	assume 2 significant digits assume 3 significant digits

Trailing zeros in a whole number with the decimal point at the end are significant.

For example, the number 250. has 3 significant digits as there is a decimal point at the end of the number.

Example 3.4-a **Identifying Significant Digits**

Identify the number of significant digits in the following numbers:

(i) 89,000 (ii) 138.750 (iii) 706.00 (iv) 30.9
(v) 0.075 (vi) 0.00875 (vii) 0.750 (viii) 0.04070

Solution

(i) 89, 000 — Number of significant digits = 2 (Rules 1 and 5)

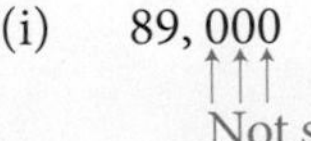

Not significant

(ii) 138.750 — All digits are significant — Number of significant digits = 6 (Rules 1 and 4)

Significant

(iii) 706.00 — All digits are significant — Number of significant digits = 5 (Rules 1, 2, and 4)

Significant

(iv) 30.9 — All digits are significant — Number of significant digits = 3 (Rules 1 and 2)

Significant

(v) 0.075 — Number of significant digits = 2 (Rules 1 and 3)

Not significant

(vi) 0.00875 — Number of significant digits = 3 (Rules 1 and 3)

Not significant

(vii) 0.750 — Number of significant digits = 3 (Rules 1, 3, and 4)

Significant
Not significant

(viii) 0.04070 — Number of significant digits = 4 (Rules 1, 2, 3, and 4)

Significant
Not significant

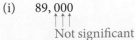

Note:

- *4,500 has 2 significant digits (Rules 1 and 5).*
- *4,500. has 4 significant digits (Rules 1 and 4).*
- *4,500.0 has 5 significant digits (Rules 1 and 4).*
- *4,500.00 has 6 significant digits (Rules 1 and 4).*

Rounding Numbers to Required Significant Digits

It is often necessary to round the result of calculations to a required number of significant digits. The general methods for rounding numbers to required significant digits are as follows:

Table 3.4-b **Rules for Rounding Numbers to Significant Digits**

Start with the left-most digit of the number and count from left to right until the required number of significant digits and identify the last significant digit.

	If the digit immediately to the right of the identified digit is:	Rounding Whole Numbers to required significant digits	Rounding Decimal Numbers to required significant digits
1.	Less than 5	Leave the identified digit unchanged and replace all digits to the right of it with zeros.	Leave the identified digit unchanged and drop all digits to the right of it.
	Example: (Rounding to 3 significant digits)	278,312 = 278,000 (digit after identified digit 8: <5)	3.0723 = 3.07 (digit after identified digit 7: <5)
2.	Greater than 5, or equal to 5 but followed by at least one non-zero digit	Add 1 to the identified digit and replace all digits to the right of it with zeros.	Add 1 to the identified digit and drop all digits to the right of it.
	Example: (Rounding to 3 significant digits)	i. 308,765 = 309,000 (>5) ii. 296,572 = 297,000 (= 5, >0)	i. 21.476 = 21.5 (>5) ii. 13. 3502 = 13.4 (= 5, >0)
3. a	Equal to 5, but followed by all zero digits or no other digits **and** the identified digit is even	If the identified digit is even, leave the identified digit unchanged and replace all digits to the right of it with zeros. *Note: Zero is an even digit.*	If the identified digit is even, leave the identified digit unchanged and drop all digits to the right of it. *Note: Zero is an even digit.*
	Example: (Rounding to 3 significant digits)	i. 408,500 = 408,000 (even; = 5; = 0) ii. 7,465 = 7,460 (even; = 5)	i. 7.0450 = 7.04 (even; = 5; = 0) ii. 24.85 = 24.8 (even; = 5)
3. b	Equal to 5, but followed by all zero digits or no other digits **and** the identified digit is odd	If the identified digit is odd, add 1 to the identified digit to make it even and replace all digits to the right of it with zeros.	If the identified digit is odd, add 1 to the identified digit to make it even and drop all digits to the right of it.

Example:
(Rounding to 3 significant digits)

i. 383,500 = 384,000 (odd; = 5; = 0)

ii. 7,415 = 7,420 (odd; = 5)

i. 43.7500 = 43.8 (odd; = 5; = 0)

ii. 9.395 = 9.40 (odd; = 5)

Example 3.4-b

Rounding Whole Numbers to Indicated Significant Digits

Round the following numbers to the indicated significant digits:

(i) 62,578 to 3 significant digits (ii) 124,390 to 2 significant digits

(iii) 704,534 to 3 significant digits (iv) 8,047,500 to 4 significant digits

(v) 340,650 to 4 significant digits (vi) 500,067 to 4 significant digits

Solution

(i) Rounding 62,578 to 3 significant digits: 62,578 = 62,600 (>5)

(ii) Rounding 124,390 to 2 significant digits: 124,390 = 120,000 (<5)

(iii) Rounding 704,534 to 3 significant digits: 704,534 = 705,000 (=5; >0)

(iv) Rounding 8,047,500 to 4 significant digits: 8,047,500 = 8,048,000 (odd; =5; =0)

(v) Rounding 340,650 to 4 significant digits: 340,650 = 340,600 (even; =5; =0)

(vi) Rounding 500,067 to 4 significant digits: 500,067 = 500,100 (>5)

Example 3.4-c

Rounding Decimal Numbers to Indicated Significant Digits

Round the following numbers to the indicated significant digits:

(i) 0.8090 to 2 significant digits (ii) 1.0621 to 3 significant digits (iii) 0.0635 to 2 significant digits

(iv) 0.08250 to 2 significant digits (v) 0.043517 to 2 significant digits (vi) 4,257.25 to 3 significant digits

Solution

(i) Rounding 0.8090 to 2 significant digits: 0.8090 = 0.81 (>5)

(ii) Rounding 1.0621 to 3 significant digits: 1.0621 = 1.06 (<5)

(iii) Rounding 0.0635 to 2 significant digits: 0.0635 = 0.064 (odd; =5)

Solution *continued*

(iv) Rounding 0.08250 to 2 significant digits: 0.08250 = 0.082 (=5, =0, even)

(v) Rounding 0.043517 to 2 significant digits: 0.043517 = 0.044 (=5, >0)

(vi) Rounding 4,257.25 to 3 significant digits: 4,257.25 = 4,260 (>5)

Rounding Rules for Addition and Subtraction of Decimal Numbers

When adding or subtracting decimal numbers, the final answer should have the same number of **decimal places** as the number with the least number of decimal places (i.e., the number with the least precision). The rules for rounding to a given precision are the same as the rules for rounding decimal numbers, as learned in Chapter 2.

Example 3.4-d

Rounding to a Number with the Least Number of Decimal Places

Perform the following operations and round the answer using the rounding rules for addition and subtraction of decimal numbers.

(i) Add 565.346 and 6.35 (ii) Subtract 3.9 from 34.45

Solution

(i)

```
    1
 565.346 <------ 3 decimal places
+  6.35  <------ 2 decimal places
 571.696
```

565.346 has 3 decimal places and 6.35 has 2 decimal places. The least number of decimal places is 2.

Therefore, rounding the answer 571.696 to 2 decimal places results in 571.70.

(ii)

```
 3 14
 34.45 <------ 2 decimal places
-  3.9 <------ 1 decimal place
 30.55
```

34.45 has 2 decimal places and 3.9 has 1 decimal place. The least number of decimal places is 1.

Therefore, rounding the answer 30.55 to 1 decimal place results in 30.6.

Rounding Rules for Multiplication and Division of Decimal Numbers

When multiplying or dividing decimal numbers, the final answer should have the same number of **significant digits** as the number with the least number of significant digits (i.e., the number with the least accuracy). Here, we must use the rules for rounding with significant digits introduced earlier in Table 3.4-b.

Example 3.4-e

Rounding to a Number with the Least Number of Significant Digits

Perform the following operations and round the answer using the rounding rules for multiplication and division of decimal numbers.

(i) Multiply 10.46 and 1.2 (ii) Divide 370.25 by 10.5

Solution

(i)

```
   10.46 <------ 4 significant digits
×   1.2  <------ 2 significant digits
   2092
  10460
  12.552
```

Solution *continued*

10.46 has 4 significant digits and 1.2 has 2 significant digits. The least number of significant digits is 2.

Therefore, rounding the answer 12.552 to 2 significant digits results in 13.

(ii) $\frac{370.25}{10.5}$ ← 5 significant digits (370.25); 3 significant digits (10.5)

= 35.261904...

370.25 has 5 significant digits and 10.5 has 3 significant digits. The least number of significant digits is 3.

Therefore, rounding the answer 35.261904... to 3 significant digits results in 35.3.

Special Situation in Rounding to Indicated Significant Digits

Consider the multiplication: 3,906.25 × 115.2

3,906.25 has 6 significant digits and 115.2 has 4 significant digits. Therefore, the answer should be rounded to 4 significant digits. However, when we multiply these numbers, the answer is 450,000 which has only 2 significant digits.

To indicate that the answer has 4 significant digits, we can place the symbol '~' above the second zero that is to be included as a significant digit to indicate that the answer has a total of 4 significant digits; i.e., place the symbol '~' above the 4th digit (second zero), to indicate it as a significant digit.

450,000 — 2 significant digits

$450,0\tilde{0}0$ — Now it has 4 significant digits

We may also use scientific notation (which we will learn later in this section), to indicate the number of significant digits.

$$450,0\tilde{0}0 = \underbrace{4.500}_{\text{4 significant digits}} \times 10^5$$

Example 3.4-f

Rounding Numbers to Indicated Significant Digits

Round the number 50,040.365 first to 6, then to 5, 4, and 3 significant digits.

Solution

50,040.365 = 50,040.4 (6 significant digits) $= 5.00404 \times 10^4$

50,040.365 = 50,040. or $50,04\tilde{0}$ (5 significant digits) $= 5.0040 \times 10^4$

50,040.365 = 50,040 (4 significant digits) $= 5.004 \times 10^4$

50,040.365 = $50,\tilde{0}00$ (3 significant digits) $= 5.00 \times 10^4$

Note: The second solution to each of the rounding problems above is expressed in scientific notation, which is discussed in detail below.

Scientific Notation

Scientific notation is a method of expressing numbers using decimal numbers with one non-zero digit to the left of the decimal point multiplied by the power of 10; i.e., scientific notation is based on the base number 10.

For example, 52,500 in scientific notation is written as 5.25×10^4.

$$52{,}500 = \underbrace{5.25}_{\text{Coefficient}} \times 10^{4}$$

(Exponent: 4; Base: 10)

Note:

- *The base is always 10.*
- *The exponent is always an integer.*
- *The coefficient should always be greater than or equal to 1, and less than 10.*

Converting Numbers between Standard Notation and Scientific Notation

Table 3.4-c **Converting Numbers from Standard Notation to Scientific Notation**

Any number raised to the power of 0 is 1. Therefore, $10^0 = 1$.

	Rule	Example
1.	For numbers 1 up to 10, the exponent will be 0. For example, to convert 9.5 to scientific notation, multiply 9.5 by the factor $10^0 = 1$.	9.5 9.5×10^0
2.	For numbers 10 and above, the exponent will be positive. For example, to convert 525.6 to scientific notation, follow these steps: Move the decimal point to the left and place it after the first non-zero digit in the number. This will be the coefficient. Count the number of places the decimal point moved to the left. This will be the exponent on the power of 10, and it will be positive. Write the number in scientific notation as: Coefficient $\times$ 10^{Exponent}	525.6 525.6 Coefficient = 5.256 2 decimal places to the left Exponent = 2 5.256×10^2
3.	For numbers less than 1, the exponent will be negative. For example, to convert 0.00752 to scientific notation, follow these steps: Move the decimal point to the right and place it after the first non-zero digit in the number. This will be the coefficient. Count the number of places the decimal point moved to the right. This will be the exponent on the power of 10, and it will be negative. Write the number in scientific notation as: Coefficient $\times$ 10^{Exponent}	0.00752 0.00752 Coefficient = 7.52 3 decimal places to the right Exponent = –3 7.52×10^{-3}

Example 3.4-g Converting Numbers from Standard Notation to Scientific Notation

Convert the following numbers from standard notation to scientific notation.

(i) 6,526 (ii) 135.275 (iii) 0.000058 (iv) 7.2

Solution

(i) $6526 = 6.526 \times 10^3$

(ii) $135.275 = 1.35275 \times 10^2$

(iii) $0.000058 = 5.8 \times 10^{-5}$

(iv) $7.2 = 7.2 \times 10^0$

Table 3.4-d Converting Numbers from Scientific Notation to Standard Notation

	Rule	Example
1.	When the exponent of base 10 is 0: To convert to standard notation, simply drop the factor 10^0.	8.75×10^0 $= 8.75$
2.	When the exponent of base 10 is a postive number: The answer will be a larger number. To convert to standard notation, move the decimal point to the right by the same number of places as the exponent.	3.45×10^4 Exponent of base 10 = 4 $= 3.45$ ← 4 places to the right $= 34,500$
3.	When the exponent of base 10 is a negative number: The answer will be a smaller number. To convert to standard notation, move the decimal point to the left by the same number of places as the exponent.	2.45×10^{-3} Exponent of base 10 = −3 $= 2.45$ ← 3 places to the left $= 0.00245$

Example 3.4-h Coverting Numbers from Scientific Notation to Standard Notation

Convert the following numbers from scientific notation to standard notation.

(i) 2.07×10^3 (ii) 5.18×10^{-4} (iii) 9×10^0 (iv) 7.29×10^0

Solution

(i) 2.07×10^3 Moving the decimal point 3 places to the right,

$= 2.07$

$= 2,070$

(ii) 5.18×10^{-4} Moving the decimal point 4 places to the left,

$= 5.18$

$= 0.000518$

(iii) 9×10^0 Dropping the factor 10^0,

$= 9$

(iv) 7.29×10^0 Dropping the factor 10^0,

$= 7.29$

Addition and Subtraction of Numbers in Scientific Notation

Numbers in scientific notation have the same base 10. However, they may or may not have the same exponent.

- To add or subtract numbers in scientific notation whose exponents are the same, factor out the power and add or subtract the coefficients within the brackets.

For example,

(i)	$4 \times \mathbf{10^5} + 3 \times \mathbf{10^5}$	Taking 10^5 as a common factor,
	$= (4 + 3) \times \mathbf{10^5}$	Adding the coefficients within brackets,
	$= 7 \times \mathbf{10^5}$	
(ii)	$9 \times \mathbf{10^6} - 5 \times \mathbf{10^6}$	Taking 10^6 as a common factor,
	$= (9 - 5) \times \mathbf{10^6}$	Subtracting the coefficients within brackets,
	$= 4 \times \mathbf{10^6}$	

- To add or subtract numbers in scientific notation whose exponents are the not the same, they must first be converted to have the same exponent. It is easier to convert the lesser exponent to have it equal the greater exponent.

Follow these steps to add (or subtract) numbers in scientific notation:

Steps	Example
1. Determine the number by which the lesser exponent needs to be increased to have it equal the greater exponent.	$9.8 \times 10^5 + 6.2 \times 10^4$ Greater exponent = 5 Lesser exponent = 4 $5 - 4 = 1$
2. Increase the lesser exponent by this number and move the decimal point of the coefficient of the number to the left by the same number of places.	$9.8 \times 10^5 + 6.2 \times 10^{(4+1)}$ $= 9.8 \times 10^5 + 0.62 \times 10^5$
3. Add (or subtract) the new coefficient and factor out the common power of 10.	$(9.8 + 0.62) \times 10^5$ $= 10.42 \times 10^5$ (This answer is not in scientific notation).
4. If the answer is not in scientific notation (i.e., if the coefficient is not between 1 and 10), then convert it to scientific notation. If the coefficient is 10 or greater, move the decimal point to the left until the coefficient is between 1 and 10. For each place the decimal point is moved, increase the exponent by 1. If the coefficient is less than 1, move the decimal point to the right until the coefficient is between 1 and 10. For each place the decimal point is moved, decrease the exponent by 1.	$10.42 \times 10^{(5+1)}$ $= 1.042 \times 10^6$

Example 3.4-i **Adding Numbers in Scientific Notation**

Add the following:

(i) $5.1 \times 10^{-2} + 6.3 \times 10^{-2}$ (ii) $8.74 \times 10^{-3} + 5.28 \times 10^{-1}$ (iii) $7.41 \times 10^{2} + 2.6 \times 10^{-3}$

Solution

(i) $5.1 \times 10^{-2} + 6.3 \times 10^{-2}$ — Exponents are equal. Taking the common factor 10^{-2},

$= (5.1 + 6.3) \times 10^{-2}$ — Adding the coefficients within brackets,

$= 11.4 \times 10^{-2}$ — Answer **not** in scientific notation.

$= 11.4 \times 10^{(-2+1)}$ — Converting to scientific notation by increasing the exponent by 1 and moving the decimal point 1 place to the left,

$= 1.14 \times 10^{-1}$ — Answer in scientific notation.

(ii) $8.74 \times 10^{-3} + 5.28 \times 10^{-1}$ — Exponents are not equal.
Greater exponent – lesser exponent $= -1 - (-3) = -1 + 3 = 2$

$= 8.74 \times 10^{(-3+2)} + 5.28 \times 10^{-1}$ — Increasing the lesser exponent by 2 and moving the decimal point of its coefficient 2 places to the left,

$= 0.0874 \times 10^{-1} + 5.28 \times 10^{-1}$ — Taking the common factor 10^{-1},

$= (0.0874 + 5.28) \times 10^{-1}$ — Adding the coefficients within brackets,

$= 5.3674 \times 10^{-1}$ — Answer in scientific notation.

(iii) $7.41 \times 10^{2} + 2.6 \times 10^{-3}$ — Exponents are not equal.
Greater exponent – lesser exponent $= 2 - (-3) = 2 + 3 = 5$

$= 7.41 \times 10^{2} + 2.6 \times 10^{(-3+5)}$ — Increasing the lesser exponent by 5 and moving the decimal point of its coefficient 5 places to the left,

$= 7.41 \times 10^{2} + 0.000026 \times 10^{2}$ — Taking the common factor 10^{2},

$= (7.41 + 0.000026) \times 10^{2}$ — Adding the coefficients within brackets,

$= 7.410026 \times 10^{2}$ — Answer in scientific notation.

Example 3.4-j **Subtracting Numbers in Scientific Notation**

Subtract the following:

(i) $7.24 \times 10^{-4} - 2.5 \times 10^{-4}$ (ii) $5.28 \times 10^{-2} - 9.59 \times 10^{-5}$ (iii) $4.78 \times 10^{3} - 6.5 \times 10^{-2}$

Solution

(i) $7.24 \times 10^{-4} - 2.5 \times 10^{-4}$ — Exponents are equal. Taking the common factor 10^{-4},

$= (7.24 - 2.5) \times 10^{-4}$ — Subtracting the coefficients within brackets,

$= 4.74 \times 10^{-4}$ — Answer in scientific notation.

Solution *continued*

(ii) $5.28 \times 10^{-2} - 9.59 \times 10^{-5}$ — Exponents are not equal.

Greater exponent – lesser exponent = $-2 - (-5) = -2 + 5 = 3$

$= 5.28 \times 10^{-2} - 9.59 \times 10^{(-5+3)}$ — Increasing the lesser exponent by 3 and moving the decimal point of its coefficient 3 places to the left,

$= 5.28 \times 10^{-2} - 0.00959 \times 10^{-2}$ — Taking the common factor 10^{-2},

$= (5.28 - 0.00959) \times 10^{-2}$ — Subtracting the coefficients within brackets,

$= 5.27041 \times 10^{-2}$ — Answer in scientific notation.

(iii) $4.78 \times 10^{3} - 6.5 \times 10^{-2}$ — Exponents are not equal.

Greater exponent – lesser exponent = $3 - (-2) = 3 + 2 = 5$

$= 4.78 \times 10^{3} - 6.5 \times 10^{(-2+5)}$ — Increasing the lesser exponent by 5 and moving the decimal point of its coefficient 5 places to the left,

$= 4.78 \times 10^{3} - 0.000065 \times 10^{3}$ — Taking the common factor 10^{3},

$= (4.78 - 0.000065) \times 10^{3}$ — Subtracting the coefficients within brackets,

$= 4.779935 \times 10^{3}$ — Answer in scientific notation.

Example 3.4-k **Combined Addition and Subtraction of Numbers in Scientific Notation**

Evaluate:

$2.5 \times 10^{5} + 8.2 \times 10^{4} - 4.7 \times 10^{3}$

Solution

$2.5 \times 10^{5} + 8.2 \times 10^{4} - 4.7 \times 10^{3}$ — Greatest exponent = 5. Converting all exponents to 5 by moving the decimal points to the left and increasing the exponents,

$= 2.5 \times 10^{5} + 8.2 \times 10^{(4+1)} - 4.7 \times 10^{(3+2)}$

$= 2.5 \times 10^{5} + 0.82 \times 10^{5} - 0.047 \times 10^{5}$ — Taking the common factor 10^{5},

$= (2.5 + 0.82 - 0.047) \times 10^{5}$ — Performing the arithmetic operations within brackets,

$= 3.273 \times 10^{5}$ — Answer in scientific notation.

Multiplication of Numbers in Scientific Notation

Recall that multiplying two powers with the same base is equivalent to adding their exponents.

Numbers in scientific notation have the same base: 10.

Therefore, to multiply numbers in scientific notation, multiply their coefficients and add their exponents on the power of 10. If the answer is not in scientific notation (i.e., coefficient is not between 1 and 10), convert it to scientific notation.

For example,

$(6.02 \times 10^{3}) \times (4 \times 10^{5})$ — Multiplying the coefficients and adding the exponents,

$= (6.02 \times 4) \times 10^{(3+5)}$ — Performing the arithmetic operations within brackets,

$= 24.08 \times 10^{8}$ — Answer **not** in scientific notation.

$= 24.08 \times 10^{(8+1)}$	Converting to scientific notation,
$= 2.408 \times 10^{9}$	Answer in scientific notation.

*Note: Moving the decimal point one place to the left is equivalent to dividing the number by 10; therefore, to maintain the value of the number, for each place the decimal point is moved to the **left** in the coefficient, we **increase** the exponent on the power of 10 by 1.*

Example 3.4-I **Multiplying Numbers in Scientific Notation**

Multiply the following:

(i) $(5.4 \times 10^{-3}) \times (2.2 \times 10^{-5})$ (ii) $(4.75 \times 10^{6}) \times (1.5 \times 10^{-2})$ (iii) $(7.5 \times 10^{-6}) \times (5.0 \times 10^{4})$

Solution

(i)	$(5.4 \times 10^{-3}) \times (2.2 \times 10^{-5})$	Multiplying the coefficients and adding the exponents,
	$= (5.4 \times 2.2) \times 10^{[-3+(-5)]}$	Performing the arithmetic operations within brackets,
	$= 11.88 \times 10^{-8}$	Answer **not** in scientific notation.
	$= 11.88 \times 10^{(-8+1)}$	Converting to scientific notation,
	$= 1.188 \times 10^{-7}$	Answer in scientific notation.
(ii)	$(4.75 \times 10^{6}) \times (1.5 \times 10^{-2})$	Multiplying the coefficients and adding the exponents,
	$= (4.75 \times 1.5) \times 10^{[6+(-2)]}$	Performing the arithmetic operations within brackets,
	$= 7.125 \times 10^{4}$	Answer in scientific notation.
(iii)	$(7.5 \times 10^{-6}) \times (5.0 \times 10^{4})$	Multiplying the coefficients and adding the exponents,
	$= (7.5 \times 5.0) \times 10^{(-6+4)}$	Performing the arithmetic operations within brackets,
	$= 37.5 \times 10^{-2}$	Answer **not** in scientific notation.
	$= 37.5 \times 10^{(-2+1)}$	Converting to scientific notation,
	$= 3.75 \times 10^{-1}$	Answer in scientific notation.

Division of Numbers in Scientific Notation

Recall that dividing two powers with the same base is equivalent to subtracting their exponents.

Numbers in scientific notation have the same base: 10.

Therefore, to divide two numbers in scientific notation, divide their coefficients and subtract their exponents on the power of 10. If the answer is not in scientific notation (i.e., coefficient is not between 1 and 10), convert it to scientific notation.

For example,

$(2.48 \times 10^{6}) \div (8.0 \times 10^{2})$	Dividing the coefficients and subtracting the exponents,
$= \frac{2.48}{8.0} \times 10^{(6-2)}$	Performing the arithmetic operations,

$= 0.31 \times 10^4$ Answer **not** in scientific notation.

$= 0.31 \times 10^{(4-1)}$ Converting to scientific notation,

$= 3.1 \times 10^3$ Answer in scientific notation.

Note: Moving the decimal point one place to the right is equivalent to multiplying the number by 10; therefore, to maintain the value of the number, for each place the decimal point is moved to the ***right*** *in the coefficient, we* ***decrease*** *the exponent on the power of 10 by 1.*

Example 3.4-m **Dividing Numbers in Scientific Notation**

Divide the following:

(i) $(4.68 \times 10^{-3}) \div (6.5 \times 10^{-5})$ (ii) $(3.5 \times 10^{8}) \div (4.0 \times 10^{-4})$ (iii) $(9.2 \times 10^{-3}) \div (1.15 \times 10^{2})$

Solution

(i) $(4.68 \times 10^{-3}) \div (6.5 \times 10^{-5})$ Dividing the coefficients and subtracting the exponents,

$= \frac{4.68}{6.5} \times 10^{[-3-(-5)]}$ Performing the arithmetic operations,

$= 0.72 \times 10^2$ Answer **not** in scientific notation.

$= 0.72 \times 10^{(2-1)}$ Converting to scientific notation,

$= 7.2 \times 10^1$ Answer in scientific notation.

(ii) $(3.5 \times 10^{8}) \div (4.0 \times 10^{-4})$ Dividing the coefficients and subtracting the exponents,

$= \frac{3.5}{4.0} \times 10^{[8-(-4)]}$ Performing the arithmetic operations,

$= 0.875 \times 10^{12}$ Answer **not** in scientific notation.

$= 0.875 \times 10^{(12-1)}$ Converting to scientific notation,

$= 8.75 \times 10^{11}$ Answer in scientific notation.

(iii) $(9.2 \times 10^{-3}) \div (1.15 \times 10^{2})$ Dividing the coefficients and subtracting the exponents,

$= \frac{9.2}{1.15} \times 10^{(-3-2)}$ Performing the arithmetic operations,

$= 8 \times 10^{-5}$ Answer in scientific notation.

Example 3.4-n **Combined Multiplication and Division of Numbers in Scientific Notation**

Evaluate:

$$\frac{(7.4 \times 10^6) \times (3.75 \times 10^5)}{2.5 \times 10^4}$$

Solution

$\frac{(7.4 \times 10^6) \times (3.75 \times 10^5)}{2.5 \times 10^4}$ Multiplying the coefficients within the numerator and dividing by the coefficient in the denominator, then adding the exponents within the numerator and subtracting the exponent in the denominator,

Solution
continued

$= \frac{(7.4 \times 3.75)}{2.5} \times 10^{(6+5-4)}$ Performing the arithmetic operations,

$= 11.1 \times 10^{7}$ Answer **not** in scientific notation.

$= 11.1 \times 10^{(7+1)}$ Converting to scientific notation,

$= 1.11 \times 10^{8}$ Answer in scientific notation.

3.4 | Exercises

Answers to odd-numbered problems are available at the end of the textbook.

For Problems 1 to 10, determine the number of significant digits in each of the numbers.

1. a. 700 b. 9,070
2. a. 40,600 b. 10,200
3. a. 5.70 b. 30.40
4. a. 9.00 b. 20.80
5. a. 6.250 b. 70.0164
6. a. 4.530 b. 20.325
7. a. 0.4700 b. 24.805
8. a. 0.2010 b. 15.407
9. a. 0.008 b. 0.0224
10. a. 0.000004 b. 0.0825

For Problems 11 to 20, round the numbers to (i) 3 significant digits and (ii) 2 significant digits.

11. a. 5,065 b. 1,982
12. a. 5,460 b. 1,978
13. a. 589.025 b. 57.3892
14. a. 821.782 b. 40.9055
15. a. 48.4848 b. 25.859
16. a. 99.0999 b. 91.555
17. a. 0.7850 b. 6.07344
18. a. 0.8090 b. 9.0085
19. a. 0.98901 b. 6.6666
20. a. 0.5555 b. 7.7777

For Problems 21 to 26, perform the indicated arithmetic operations and round the answer to the same number of decimal places as the number with the least number of decimal places.

21. a. 142.135 + 9.12 b. 324.761 + 28.4
22. a. 215.241 + 6.37 b. 532.863 + 59.9
23. a. 287.657 – 6.42 b. 466.945 – 54.8
24. a. 354.657 – 7.89 b. 465.976 – 99.7
25. a. 30.6 + 4.703 – 9.009 b. 44.9 – 1.906 – 0.61
26. a. 50.7 + 9.856 – 21.05 b. 27.02 – 9.005 – 0.081

For Problems 27 to 32, perform the indicated arithmetic operations and round the answer to the same number of significant digits as the number with the least number of significant digits.

27. a. 67.86×9.8 b. 152.92×45.5
28. a. 59.43×8.2 b. 253.15×38.4
29. a. $99.33 \div 9.9$ b. $225.25 \div 25.5$
30. a. $46.66 \div 0.6$ b. $315.15 \div 15.15$
31. a. $54.75 \times 1.21 \times 4{,}500$ b. $1.90 \times 380 \div 0.95$
32. a. $25.5 \times 1.8 \times 3{,}600$ b. $5.07 \times 4{,}500 \div 13.5$

For Problems 33 to 42, write the numbers in scientific notation.

33. a. 235 b. 42,300
34. a. 745 b. 15,700
35. a. 0.58 b. 0.048
36. a. 0.74 b. 0.089
37. a. 0.0038 b. 0.0002
38. a. 0.0096 b. 0.0007
39. a. 0.06×10^{8} b. 0.0025×10^{-9}
40. a. 0.03×10^{5} b. 0.0046×10^{-10}
41. a. 0.003×10^{7} b. 0.036×10^{-5}
42. a. 0.04×10^{6} b. 0.0038×10^{-7}

For Problems 43 to 52, write the numbers in standard notation.

43. a. 4.6×10^4 b. 2.9×10^0
44. a. 3.7×10^3 b. 4.75×10^1
45. a. 3.09×10^6 b. 4.654×10^4
46. a. 7.54×10^4 b. 8.015×10^5
47. a. 8.9×10^{-1} b. 2.16×10^{-4}
48. a. 6.8×10^{-2} b. 4.65×10^{-3}
49. a. 3.15×10^{-3} b. 6.15×10^{-5}
50. a. 1.29×10^{-4} b. 9.17×10^{-3}
51. a. 0.0056×10^3 b. 406.5×10^{-6}
52. a. 0.0076×10^4 b. 675.7×10^{-5}

For Problems 53 to 62, perform the arithmetic operations and write the answer in scientific notation. Do not round your answer.

53. $(8.5 \times 10^5) + (3.84 \times 10^4)$
54. $(6.35 \times 10^6) + (5.07 \times 10^7)$
55. $(9.82 \times 10^{-3}) + (1.58 \times 10^{-4})$
56. $(7.92 \times 10^{-5}) + (9.72 \times 10^{-3})$
57. $(3.1 \times 10^9) - (2.6 \times 10^8)$
58. $(8.2 \times 10^7) - (4.7 \times 10^6)$
59. $(7.54 \times 10^{-2}) - (3.25 \times 10^{-3})$
60. $(2.58 \times 10^{-2}) - (1.99 \times 10^{-1})$
61. $(2.5 \times 10^4) + (8.9 \times 10^2) - (1.5 \times 10^3)$
62. $(6.7 \times 10^3) + (7.4 \times 10^2) - (8.6 \times 10^1)$

For Problems 63 to 72, perform the arithmetic operation and write the answer in scientific notation. Do not round your answer.

63. $(2.0 \times 10^5) \times (8.6 \times 10^8)$
64. $(4.75 \times 10^4) \times (2.0 \times 10^6)$
65. $(7.5 \times 10^{-12}) \times (4.2 \times 10^5)$
66. $(8.25 \times 10^3) \times (4 \times 10^{-6})$
67. $(4.8 \times 10^5) \div (1.5 \times 10^8)$
68. $(9.25 \times 10^{10}) \div (5.0 \times 10^4)$
69. $(3.84 \times 10^{-2}) \div (7.68 \times 10^{-4})$
70. $(6.48 \times 10^{-4}) \div (9.72 \times 10^{-6})$
71. $(9.8 \times 10^{-4}) \times (5 \times 10^{-3}) \div (3.5 \times 10^{-9})$
72. $(5.4 \times 10^{-5}) \times (8 \times 10^{-6}) \div (7.2 \times 10^{-14})$

3 | Review Exercises

Answers to odd-numbered problems are available at the end of the textbook.

1. Calculate the difference between 2^5 and 5^2.
2. Calculate the difference between 3^4 and 4^3.
3. Express 243 as a power of 3 and then evaluate $243^{\frac{3}{5}}$.
4. Express 512 as a power of 2 and then evaluate $512^{\frac{4}{9}}$.

Express Problems 5 to 8 as a single power and then evaluate.

5. a. $(2^6)^{\frac{1}{3}}$ b. $(5^{15})^{\frac{1}{5}}$
6. a. $\left(\frac{3^9}{3^3}\right)^{\frac{1}{3}}$ b. $\left(\frac{2^{12}}{2^4}\right)^{\frac{1}{4}}$
7. a. $(3^2)^{\frac{1}{2}} \times (3^3)^{\frac{2}{3}}$ b. $(6^2)^{\frac{1}{3}} \times (6^3)^{\frac{1}{9}}$
8. a. $(2^2)^{\frac{1}{4}} \times (2^5)^{\frac{3}{10}}$ b. $(5^3)^{\frac{2}{3}} \times (5^2)^{\frac{1}{2}}$

For Problems 9 to 16, simplify using laws of exponents and then evaluate.

9. a. $\frac{2^3 \times 3^4 \times 2^2}{3 \times 2^5}$ b. $\frac{(5^2) \times 5^4}{5^7}$
10. a. $\frac{5^2 \times 7^3 \times 5^4}{7 \times 5^6}$ b. $\frac{(2^5) \times 2^2}{2^{17}}$
11. a. $(-5)^2 \times (4)^2$ b. $-10^4 \times 10^3$
12. a. $(-2)^2 \times (3)^2$ b. $-2^4 \times 2^2$
13. a. $(125)^{-\frac{1}{3}}$ b. $(49)^{-\frac{1}{2}}$ c. $\sqrt{\frac{64}{81}}$
14. a. $(16)^{-\frac{1}{4}}$ b. $(27)^{-\frac{1}{3}}$ c. $\sqrt{\frac{25}{49}}$
15. a. $\sqrt{7^4}$ b. $\sqrt{\frac{25}{36}}$ c. $\sqrt[3]{\frac{216}{125}}$
16. a. $\sqrt{5^6}$ b. $\sqrt{\frac{49}{64}}$ c. $\sqrt[3]{\frac{64}{27}}$

Evaluate Problems 17 to 32 and express the answers rounded to two decimal places, wherever applicable.

17. a. $\frac{16 + 4(-3)}{10 - 4 + 1} + \frac{(16 + 4) - 3}{10 - (4 + 1)}$

b. $14 - 3\,[(6 - 9)(-4) + 12] \div (-2)$

18. a. $\frac{2(-6) + 4}{24 - (7 + 3)} + \frac{2(-6 + 4)}{24 - 7 + 3}$

b. $5(-4) - 3[(-9 + 6) + (-3) - 4]$

19. a. $[(1 + 12)(1 - 5)]^2 \div [(5 + 3) \times 2^2 - (-2)^2]$

b. $2^2[(9 - 7) \div 2 + 9 - 4]$

20. a. $8 \div 4 + (4 - 6^2) \div (13 - 5) \times (-2)^6$

b. $6 \div [4 \times (2 - 8) \div (3^2 + 3)] \div 4$

21. a. $64 \div (-2)^4 + 4\,(-3^2) \div 2 - 5$

b. $(-6)^2 - 9^2 \div 3^3 - (-3)(-2)$

22. a. $8 \div (-2)^3(-9) + 6(-5)^3 \div (-5)^2$

b. $(-8)^2 - 4^3 \div 2^2 - (-6)(-2)$

23. a. $6{,}000\left(1 + \frac{0.06}{12}\right)^{36}$

b. $2{,}000(1 + 0.004)^{-24}$

24. a. $4{,}000\left(1 + \frac{0.075}{12}\right)^{60}$

b. $5{,}000(1 + 0.003)^{-48}$

25. $\frac{3{,}000[(1.06)^{25} - 1]}{0.06}$

26. $\frac{1{,}400[(1.03)^{30} - 1]}{0.03}$

27. $\frac{950[1 - (1.03)^{15}]}{0.03}$

28. $\frac{1{,}200[1 - (1.04)^{20}]}{0.04}$

29. a. $-15 - (-15)$

b. $-14 - (-7)$

30. a. $13 - (-11) + 0$

b. $22 - (-4) - 6$

31. a. $8 + |2 - 7|$

b. $-|-23| - |10 - 15|$

32. a. $15 - |3 - 9|$

b. $-|-42| - |35 - 18|$

33. Determine the number of significant digits in each of the following numbers and write them in scientific notation:

a. 7,101.1 b. 54.001 c. 0.0072

34. Determine the number of significant digits in each of the following numbers and write them in scientific notation:

a. 54,020 b. 0.2055 c. 0.09081

35. Write the numbers in standard form.

a. 8.9×10^2 b. 5.6×10^{-2} c. 9.64×10^{-4}

36. Write the numbers in standard form.

a. 5.1×10^3 b. 6.8×10^{-4} c. 4.75×10^{-4}

For Problems 37 to 44, perform the arithmetic operations and write the answers in scientific notation. Do not round the answer.

37. a. $4.65 \times 10^{14} + 9.95 \times 10^{12}$

b. $7.02 \times 10^{-2} + 6.95 \times 10^{-3}$

38. a. $7.28 \times 10^6 + 4.35 \times 10^5$

b. $1.64 \times 10^{-12} + 5.5 \times 10^{-10}$

39. a. $4.01 \times 10^6 - 3.56 \times 10^4$

b. $3.56 \times 10^{-3} - 8.01 \times 10^{-4}$

40. a. $1.25 \times 10^7 - 9.75 \times 10^5$

b. $2.85 \times 10^{-1} - 7.45 \times 10^{-3}$

41. a. $(6.0 \times 10^4) \times (4.0 \times 10^7)$

b. $(7.5 \times 10^{-6}) \times (6.0 \times 10^{-5})$

42. a. $(7.75 \times 10^6) \times (2.0 \times 10^8)$

b. $(9.45 \times 10^{-5}) \times (3.0 \times 10^{-7})$

43. a. $(2.0 \times 10^5) \div (4.0 \times 10^8)$

b. $(1.45 \times 10^{-9}) \div (5.8 \times 10^{-3})$

44. a. $(1.75 \times 10^4) \div (3.50 \times 10^{-6})$

b. $(1.61 \times 10^{-7}) \div (4.83 \times 10^{-2})$

Self-Test | Chapter 3

Answers to all problems are available at the end of the textbook.

1. Express the following as a power of the indicated bases:

   a. 729 as a power of 3.

   b. 128 as a power of 2.

   c. $(9)^{\frac{3}{2}}$ as a power of 3.

   d. $(16)^{\frac{3}{4}}$ as a power of 2.

2. Express the following as a single power:

   a. $3^4 \times 3^{(4+2)}$ b. $10^4 \times 10^{(3+2)}$

3. Simplify using the laws of exponents and then evaluate, rounding to two decimal places, wherever applicable.

   a. $\dfrac{2^3 \times (3)^3 \times 3^4}{2^3 \times (2^3)^2 \times 3^5}$ b. $\dfrac{2^4 \times (3^2)^4 \times 2^2}{2^5 \times (3^3)^2 \times 2^0}$

Evaluate Problems 4 to 12. Round to two decimal places, wherever applicable.

4. a. $(2^2 \times 3^3 \times 5^0)^{-1}$ b. $(3^2 \times 2^{-2} \times 5)^0$

5. a. $\left(\dfrac{3}{2}\right)^2 \times \dfrac{3}{8}$ b. $4 \times \dfrac{8}{5} \div \dfrac{4}{3} + \sqrt{4} - 1$

6. a. $\dfrac{2}{5} \times \sqrt{100} + 2^4 \div \dfrac{5}{3}$ b. $\sqrt{36} \times \dfrac{4}{3} \div \dfrac{8}{6} - 7 + 2$

7. a. $\left(\dfrac{2}{3} + \dfrac{4}{3}\right)^5$ b. $\left(\dfrac{9^{\frac{2}{5}}}{9^{\frac{3}{5}}}\right) \times 3^2$

8. a. $-5^3(-25)^3$ b. $3^{-2} \times 3^3$

9. a. $(-3)^3 - (-1)^3$ b. $(-2)^5 \times (4-5)^3 - (-10)$

10. a. $(-5)^3 - (-4)^3$ b. $(-4)^5 \div (-2)^6$

11. a. $-9 + |(-4) + (-2)|$ b. $|12 - 8 \times 2| - |-4|$

12. a. $\dfrac{16^{\frac{1}{2}} \times 6}{81^{\frac{1}{2}}}$ b. $\dfrac{9^{\frac{1}{2}} \times 81^{\frac{1}{2}}}{13^2 - 5^2}$

13. Write the numbers in scientific notation:

    a. 10.09 b. 0.005 c. 60,200

14. Write the numbers in standard form:

    a. 2.7×10^3 b. 4.15×10^{-3} c. 3.0405×10^{-2}

For Problems 15 and 16, perform the arithmetic operations and express the answers in scientific notation. Do not round the answers.

15. a. $4.01 \times 10^4 + 9.99 \times 10^3$

    b. $4.06 \times 10^{-8} - 9.94 \times 10^{-7}$

16. a. $(6.50 \times 10^7) \times (8.0 \times 10^{-9})$

    b. $(1.225 \times 10^{14}) \div (8.75 \times 10^{-6})$

Chapter 4 BASIC ALGEBRA

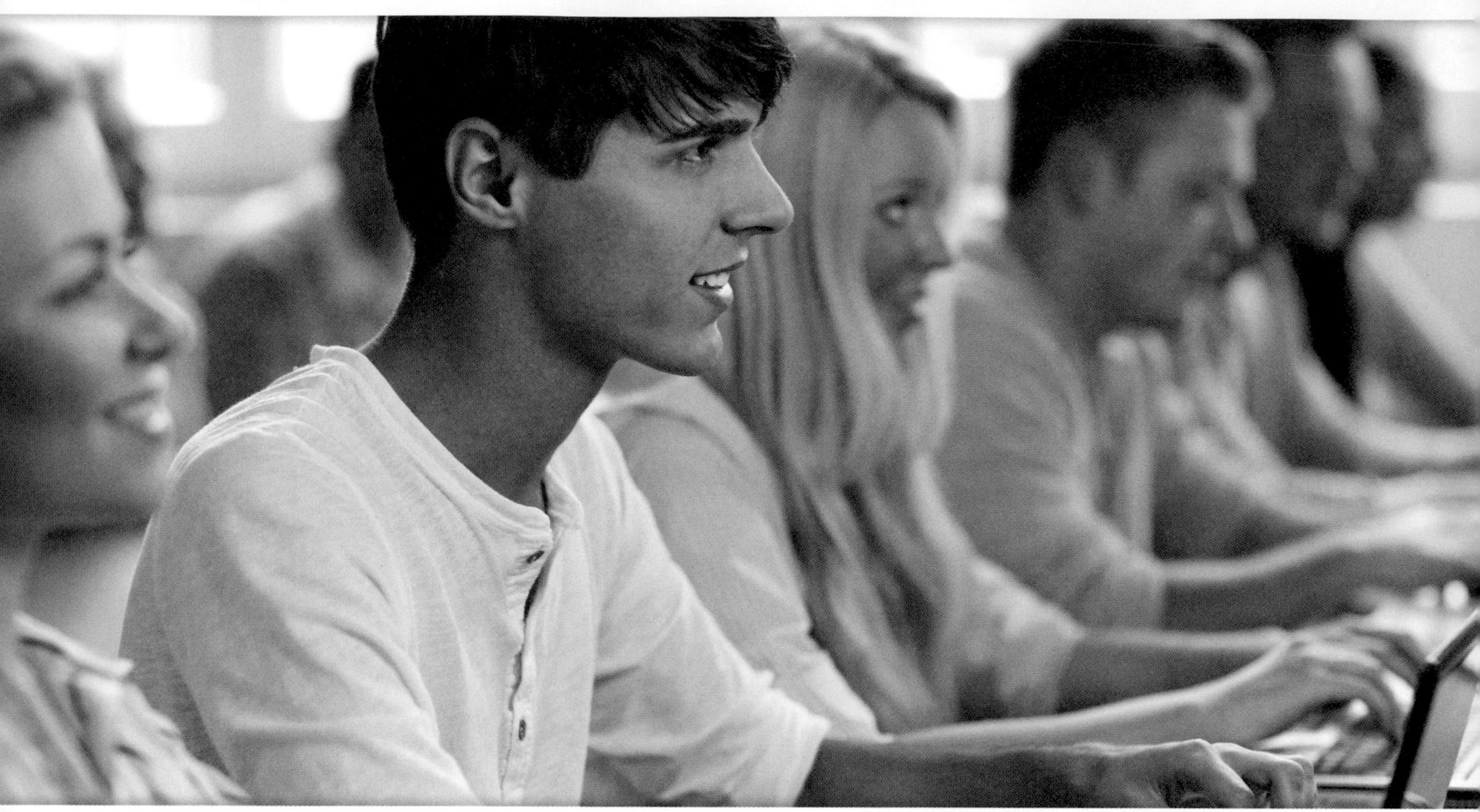

LEARNING OBJECTIVES

- Identify exponents and evaluate exponents using rules of exponents.
- Perform basic arithmetic operations on algebraic expressions.
- Factor algebraic expressions using a variety of methods.
- Set up basic linear equations with one variable.
- Solve linear equations with one variable using various arithmetic operations.
- Create, rearrange, and use equations to solve for unknown vairables.
- Convert between exponential and logarithmic form.
- Simplify and evaluate logarithmic expressions using properties of logarithms.
- Solve exponential equations using common logarithms (log) and natural logarithms (ln).

CHAPTER OUTLINE

Introduction

Algebra is a branch of mathematics that is used to analyze and solve practical problems by using letters and symbols, known as variables, to represent numbers. These variables, together with numbers and operations, can be combined to create algebraic expressions and equations. Algebra provides a framework from which formulas are derived to solve general problems, and helps develop logical-thinking and problem-solving skills in a systematic and analytical way. The study of algebra is required in any occupational field, including business and sciences.

In this chapter, we will learn how to evaluate and perform arithmetic with algebraic expressions, how to form and solve algebraic equations, and how to rearrange equations and formulas to isolate a particular variable.

4.1 | Algebraic Expressions

In arithmetic, we use numbers and operations in expressions. The following are examples of arithmetic expressions:

$$25 + 15, \quad 75 - 22, \quad 8 \times 9, \quad \frac{9}{5}$$

In algebra, we use numbers, operations, and **variables** (letters and symbols that represent various numbers) in expressions. The following are examples of algebraic expressions:

$$2x + 5, \quad 30 - 5y, \quad 6(2a + 5), \quad \frac{b+3}{2}$$

We can use algebra to translate a statement (using words) into an expression (using numbers, operations, and variables). The following key words will help in translating written statements into algebraic expressions:

Table 4.1 **Arithmetic Operations and their Meanings**

Operations	Key Words
Addition (+)	add, sum, total, and, plus, more than, increased by, appreciate, rise
Subtraction (−)	subtract, difference, minus, less than, decreased by, depreciate, fall
Multiplication (×), (·)	multiply, product, times, of
Division (÷)	divide, ratio, divided by, quotient, per

For example,

In words	As an algebraic expression
• Ten more than a number	$x + 10$
• A number more than ten	$10 + x$
• Twenty less than a number	$x - 20$
• A number less than twenty	$20 - x$
• Product of five and a number	$5x$
• Divide a number by twenty	$\frac{x}{20}$
• Divide twenty by a number	$\frac{20}{x}$

- Half of a number $\frac{1}{2}x$ or $\frac{x}{2}$
- Twice a number $2x$
- Ten more than the product of two numbers $xy + 10$
- 'x' less than 'y' or 'y' minus 'x' $y - x$
- 'y' less than 'x' or 'x' minus 'y' $x - y$
- Seventy decreased by three times a number $70 - 3x$
- 'm' subtracted from 'n' $n - m$

Terminology used in Algebraic Expressions

Terminology	Description	Examples
Variable	A letter or symbol used in expressions to represent a varying or unknown quantity.	x, y, a, b In the expression $2m + 5n - 6$, m and n are variables.
Term	A number, variable, or a combination of numbers and variables which are multiplied or divided together.	$5, x, 5x^2y, 2xy, \frac{4}{a}, \frac{b}{3}$ are all single terms. The expression $5x + y$ has 2 terms. The expression $\frac{x}{4} - y^2 + \frac{x}{y} - \frac{1}{x}$ has 4 terms.
Constant	A term that only has a number with no variables.	In the expression $2x + 3y + 5$, the 3rd term, +5, is a constant. In the expression $5x^2 - 8$, the 2nd term, −8, is a constant.
Coefficient	The product of all numerical factors in a single term involving a variable. If a coefficient is not present, its value is 1.	In the expression $x^3 + 5x^2 - 3(2y^3)$, the coefficient of the 1st term is 1, the coefficient of the 2nd term is 5, and the coefficient of the 3rd term is −6.
Expression	A mathematical phrase made up of a combination of terms and operations.	Expressions with one variable: $(2x + 5)$, $(9x - 3)$ Expressions with two variables: $(5x - 7y + 5)$, $(xy + 3x + 7)$
Like terms	Terms that have the same variables and exponents. They differ only in their numerical coefficient. Constant terms are like terms.	$5x$ and $9x$ are like terms. $30a^2$, $-4a^2$, and $9a^2$ are like terms. 5 and −9 are like terms.
Unlike terms	Terms that have different variables or the same variables with different exponents.	$12y$ and $3y^2$ are unlike terms. x, y, and 1 are unlike terms. $5xy$, $-3x^2y$, and $7xy^2$ are unlike terms.
Factors	Refer to each of the combinations of variables and/or numbers multiplied together in a term.	5 and x are factors of the term $5x$. 3, x, and y are factors of the term $3xy$.
Monomial	An algebraic expression that has only one term.	8, $7x$, $4y$, and $2xy$ are monomials.

Terminology	Description	Examples
Polynomial	An algebraic expression that has two or more terms.	$(8x^2 - 5x + 3)$ is a polynomial with 3 terms, where the 1st term is $8x^2$, the 2nd term is $-5x$, and the 3rd term is 3. The coefficient of the 1st term is 8, and the coefficient of the 2nd term is –5. The 3rd term is a constant.
Binomial	A polynomial with 2 terms.	$(4x - 3y)$, $(x - 5)$, $(4xy + 7x)$ are binomials.
Trinomial	A polynomial with 3 terms.	$(2x + 3y + 5)$, $(xy + x - 2)$, $(2x + xy + 3z)$ are trinomials.

Example 4.1-a **Identifying Components of an Algebraic Expression**

Given: $7x^2 - 4x + 7 - 12x$

Identify the following (if applicable):

(i) the expression (ii) the terms (iii) any like terms

(iv) the coefficients (v) the constant

Solution

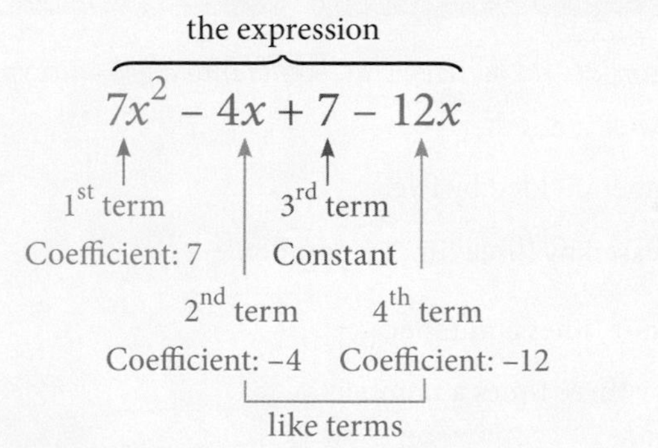

Evaluating Algebraic Expressions

In an algebraic expression, the process of replacing all the variables with numerical values and simplifying the expression is referred to as evaluating the algebraic expression. The simplified answer is the value of the expression.

Example 4.1-b **Evaluating Algebraic Expressions**

Evaluate the following expressions:

(i) $2x + y$, where $x = 10$ and $y = 5$

(ii) $\frac{3xy + 3x}{2y + 5}$, where $x = 3$ and $y = 2$

Solution

(i) $2x + y$ — Substituting $x = 10$ and $y = 5$,

$= 2(10) + 5$ — [$2x$ means $2(x)$]

$= 20 + 5 = 25$

(ii) $\frac{3xy + 3x}{2y + 5}$ — Substituting $x = 3$ and $y = 2$,

$= \frac{3(3)(2) + 3(3)}{2(2) + 5}$

$= \frac{18 + 9}{4 + 5} = \frac{27}{9} = 3$

Example 4.1-c **Evaluating Algebraic Expressions with Exponents**

Evaluate the following expressions:

(i) $\frac{(5x)^2 \times 4y}{50}$, where $x = 2$ and $y = 3$

(ii) $2(x^2 + 3x) - 5y$, where $x = 4$ and $y = -3$

Solution

(i) $\frac{(5x)^2 \times 4y}{50}$ Substituting $x = 2$ and $y = 3$,

$= \frac{[5(2)]^2 \times 4(3)}{50}$

$= \frac{10^2 \times 12}{50} = \frac{100 \times 12}{50} = 24$

(ii) $2(x^2 + 3x) - 5y$ Substituting $x = 4$ and $y = -3$,

$=2[(4)^2 + 3(4)] - 5(-3)$

$= 2(16 + 12) + 15 = 56 + 15 = 71$

4.1 | Exercises

Answers to odd-numbered problems are available at the end of the textbook.

For Problems 1 and 2, translate the written statements into algebraic expressions.

1. a. Three less than twice a number.

   b. Two times a number divided by five.

   c. Twenty-five increased by three times a number.

2. a. Seven less than four times a number.

   b. Fifteen divided by three times a number.

   c. Twenty increased by twice a number.

For Problems 3 to 6, (i) identify the number of terms in each expression, (ii) identify the constant term (if applicable), and (iii) state the coefficients of each of the variable terms.

3. a. $3x^2 + 7xy - 4y$ b. $x^2 - 5x$ c. $9xy + 7x - 6y + 2$

4. a. $-x^2 + 9xy + y + 7$ b. $7xy$ c. $10x^2 + 5xy - 7y^2$

5. a. $5x^2 - 3xy + 5$ b. $-2y^2 + 3x + 1$ c. $-2xy^2 - 2x^2y + 7$

6. a. $-2y^2 + 3y - 4$ b. $y^5 - 2y^7 - 2$ c. $2x^3 - 3x^2 + 1$

For Problems 7 to 10, identify any like terms in the expressions.

7. a. $12A + 4B - 7A - B$ b. $6x + 8y - 5x - 3y + 7$

8. a. $6B + 8A - A - 2B$ b. $14 - 3x + 10y + 4y$

9. a. $-2x + 5x - 12x + 8 + 7y - 3$ b. $6xy^2 - 2x^2y - 4x^2 + 2xy^2 + 3x^2y + 2x^2 + 4$

10. a. $3 + 6x - 20x + 8y + 8y + 5x + 12$ b. $3x^2y - 12xy^2 - 6x^2y - 5xy - 2xy - 4xy^2$

For Problems 11 to 14, evaluate the expressions.

11. $2a + 14b - 12c + 2$, where $a = 3$, $b = 2$, $c = 1$

12. $x + 2y - 13z + 1$, where $x = 5$, $y = 8$, $z = 2$

13. $3x^2 - 2x$, where $x = 5$

14. $2a^2 + a$, where $a = 15$

For Problems 15 to 18, evaluate the expressions, given $x = 2$ and $y = 3$.

15. a. $\dfrac{19x - 5y}{9}$ b. $x^2 + 6x + 8$

16. a. $\dfrac{7x - 5y}{3}$ b. $-x^2 + 10x + 7$

17. a. $\dfrac{(3x)^2(5y)}{6y}$ b. $-2x^2 + 3x + 8y$

18. a. $\dfrac{(2x)^2(2y)}{5y}$ b. $4x^2 + 10x - 4y$

4.2 | Properties (Rules) of Exponents in Algebraic Expressions

The concept of exponents was covered in Chapter 3, where integer-valued exponents were used to express repeated multiplication or division of the same numbers.

For example,

$$\underbrace{(2)(2)(2)(2)(2)}_{\text{5 factors of 2}} = 2^5 \quad (\text{2: base, 5: exponent})$$

$$\frac{1}{\underbrace{(8)(8)(8)}_{\text{3 factors of 8}}} = \frac{1}{8^3} = 8^{-3} \quad (\text{8: base, }-3\text{: exponent})$$

The above exponential principle is applied to express repeated multiplication or division of a variable or an algebraic term.

In algebra, when 'n' is a positive integer, the general form for writing exponential expressions using variables is represented by:

$$\underbrace{(x)(x)(x)\ldots(x)}_{\text{'}n\text{' factors of '}x\text{'}} = x^n \qquad \frac{1}{\underbrace{(x)(x)(x)\ldots(x)}_{\text{'}n\text{' factors of '}x\text{'}}} = \frac{1}{x^n} = x^{-n}$$

Some useful applications of the above with examples are provided below:

	Exponential Form	Expanded Form	Example
(i)	ax^n	$a(x)(x)(x)\ldots(x)$	$2x^5 = 2(x)(x)(x)(x)(x)$
(ii)	$(ax)^n$	$(ax)(ax)(ax)\ldots(ax)$	$(2x)^5 = (2x)(2x)(2x)(2x)(2x) = 32x^5$
(iii)	$-ax^n$	$-a(x)(x)(x)\ldots(x)$	$-2x^5 = -2(x)(x)(x)(x)(x)$
(iv)	$(-ax)^n$	$(-ax)(-ax)(-ax)\ldots(-ax)$	$(-2x)^5 = (-2x)(-2x)(-2x)(-2x)(-2x) = -32x^5$ $(-2x)^4 = (-2x)(-2x)(-2x)(-2x) = 16x^4$
(v)	$-x^n$	$-1 \cdot (x)(x)(x)\ldots(x)$	$-x^5 = -1 \cdot (x)(x)(x)(x)(x)$

	Exponential Form	Expanded Form	Example
(vi)	$(-x)^n$	$(-x)(-x)(-x)...(-x)$	$(-x)^5 = (-x)(-x)(-x)(-x)(-x) = -x^5$ $(-x)^4 = (-x)(-x)(-x)(-x) = x^4$
(vii)	ax^{-n}	$a \cdot \dfrac{1}{(x)(x)(x)...(x)}$	$2x^{-5} = 2 \cdot \dfrac{1}{(x)(x)(x)(x)(x)} = \dfrac{2}{x^5}$
(viii)	$(ax)^{-n}$	$\dfrac{1}{(ax)(ax)(ax)...(ax)}$	$(2x)^{-5} = \dfrac{1}{(2x)(2x)(2x)(2x)(2x)} = \dfrac{1}{32x^5}$

Note: The examples above assume that x is a positive number.

Properties (Rules) of Exponents

The properties of exponents introduced in Chapter 3 (also referred to as rules or laws of exponents) all apply to algebraic terms and expressions in the same way as they do to numbers. The following table revisits and summarizes the basic properties of exponents.

Table 4.2-a **Rules of Exponents**

Summary of Rules:

$(x^m)(x^n) = x^{(m+n)}$

$\dfrac{x^m}{x^n} = x^{(m-n)}$

$(x^m)^n = x^{mn}$

$(xy)^m = x^m y^m$

$\left(\dfrac{x}{y}\right)^m = \dfrac{x^m}{y^m}$

$x^{-1} = \dfrac{1}{x}$

$\left(\dfrac{x}{y}\right)^{-m} = \left(\dfrac{y}{x}\right)^m$

$x^0 = 1$

$x^1 = x$

	Rule	Description	Example
1.	Product Rule	To multiply powers of the same base, write the base and add the exponents. $x^m \cdot x^n = x^{(m+n)}$	$x^4 \cdot x^3 = x^{(4+3)} = x^7$
2.	Quotient Rule	To divide powers of the same base, write the base and subtract the exponents. $\dfrac{x^m}{x^n} = x^{(m-n)}$	$\dfrac{x^5}{x^2} = x^{(5-2)} = x^3$
3.	Power of a Power Rule	To raise a power to another power, write the base and multiply the exponents. $(x^m)^n = x^{mn}$	$(x^4)^2 = x^{(4 \cdot 2)} = x^8$
4.	Power of a Product Rule	To simplify a power of a product, raise each factor to the same exponent. $(xy)^m = x^m \cdot y^m$	$(x \cdot y)^5 = x^5 \cdot y^5$
5.	Power of a Quotient Rule	To simplify a power of a quotient, raise each factor in the numerator and the denominator to the same exponent. $\left(\dfrac{x}{y}\right)^m = \dfrac{x^m}{y^m}$	$\left(\dfrac{x}{y}\right)^4 = \dfrac{x^4}{y^4}$

	Rule	Description	Example
6.	Negative Exponent Rule	To simplify negative exponents, write the reciprocal of the base and use a positive exponent. $x^{-m} = \frac{1}{x^m}$, $\frac{1}{x^{-m}} = x^m$ $\left(\frac{x}{y}\right)^{-m} = \left(\frac{y}{x}\right)^m$	$x^{-5} = \frac{1}{x^5}$ $\frac{1}{x^{-4}} = x^4$ $\left(\frac{x}{y}\right)^{-3} = \left(\frac{y}{x}\right)^3$
7.	Exponent of Zero Rule	Any base (except 0) raised to an exponent of zero is equal to 1. $x^0 = 1$	$5^0 = 1$ $(xy)^0 = 1$ $\left(\frac{x}{y}\right)^0 = 1$
8.	Exponent of One Rule	Any base raised to an exponent of 1 is equal to itself. $x^1 = x$	$7^1 = 7$ $(xy)^1 = xy$ $\left(\frac{x}{y}\right)^1 = \frac{x}{y}$

Note:

(i) *There are no rules for addition or subtraction of powers, with or without the same base.*

i.e., $x^m + x^n \neq x^{(m+n)}$

$x^m - x^n \neq x^{(m-n)}$

(ii) *There are no rules for the power of a sum or difference.*

i.e., $(x + y)^m \neq x^m + y^m$

$(x - y)^m \neq x^m - y^m$

Simplifying Algebraic Terms

Recall from the previous section that an algebraic term is defined as a number, variable, or a combination of numbers and variables which are multiplied or divided together.

We can use the properties of exponents to simplify algebraic terms. Once all the terms in algebraic expressions are simplified, we are able to perform arithmetic operations with the expressions (which we will learn in the following section).

When simplifying algebraic terms, the factors may be regrouped to allow the numerical factors to be grouped together and the variable factors to be grouped together, as shown in the following examples.

Example 4.2-a **Simplifying Terms Using the Product Rule**

Simplify each of the following terms:

(i) $3x^2 \cdot 4x^5$

(ii) $-2x \cdot 4x^3 \cdot 2x^4$

(iii) $2x^2 \cdot y^4 \cdot 3x^2 \cdot y^2$

(iv) $x^n \cdot x^{2n} \cdot x^{(n-1)}$

Solution

(i) $3x^2 \cdot 4x^5$ — Regrouping the factors,

$= 3 \cdot 4 \cdot x^2 \cdot x^5$ — Applying the Product Rule and simplifying,

$= 12 \cdot x^{(2+5)}$

$= 12x^7$

(ii) $-2x \cdot 4x^3 \cdot 2x^4$ — Regrouping the factors,

$= -2 \cdot 4 \cdot 2 \cdot x \cdot x^3 \cdot x^4$ — Applying the Product Rule and simplifying,

$= -16 \cdot x^{(1+3+4)}$

$= -16x^8$

(iii) $2x^2 \cdot y^4 \cdot 3x^2 \cdot y^2$ — Regrouping the factors,

$= 2 \cdot 3 \cdot x^2 \cdot x^2 \cdot y^4 \cdot y^2$ — Applying the Product Rule and simplifying,

$= 6 \cdot x^{(2+2)} \cdot y^{(4+2)}$

$= 6x^4y^6$

(iv) $x^n \cdot x^{2n} \cdot x^{(n-1)}$ — Applying the Product Rule,

$= x^{[n+2n+(n-1)]}$

$= x^{4n-1}$

Example 4.2-b **Simplifying Terms Using the Product and Quotient Rules**

Simplify each of the following terms:

(i) $\dfrac{6x^5}{8x^2}$ (ii) $\dfrac{-15x^4 \cdot 8x^2}{10x^3}$

(iii) $\dfrac{-25x^2 \cdot 3y^3}{-5xy^2}$ (iv) $\dfrac{2x^n \cdot 3x^{2n}}{4x^{n-1}}$

Solution

(i) $\dfrac{6x^5}{8x^2}$ — Regrouping the factors,

$= \dfrac{6}{8} \cdot \dfrac{x^5}{x^2}$ — Applying the Quotient Rule and simplifying,

$= \dfrac{3}{4} \cdot x^{(5-2)}$

$= \dfrac{3}{4}x^3 = \dfrac{3x^3}{4}$

(ii) $\dfrac{-15x^4 \cdot 8x^2}{10x^3}$ — Regrouping the factors,

$= \dfrac{-15 \cdot 8}{10} \cdot \dfrac{x^4 \cdot x^2}{x^3}$ — Applying the Product and Quotient Rules and simplifying,

$= -12 \cdot x^{(4+2-3)}$

$= -12x^3$

(iii) $\dfrac{-25x^2 \cdot 3y^3}{-5xy^2}$ — Regrouping the factors,

$= \dfrac{-25 \cdot 3}{-5} \cdot \dfrac{x^2}{x} \cdot \dfrac{y^3}{y^2}$ — Applying the Product and Quotient Rules and simplifying,

$= 15 \cdot x^{(2-1)} \cdot y^{(3-2)}$

$= 15xy$

Solution *continued*

(iv) $\dfrac{2x^n \cdot 3x^{2n}}{4x^{n-1}}$ Regrouping the factors,

$= \dfrac{2 \cdot 3}{4} \cdot \dfrac{x^n \cdot x^{2n}}{x^{n-1}}$ Applying the Product and Quotient Rules and simplifying,

$= \dfrac{3}{2} \cdot x^{[n + 2n - (n - 1)]}$

$= \dfrac{3}{2} \cdot x^{(3n - n + 1)}$

$= \dfrac{3}{2}x^{2n+1} = \dfrac{3x^{2n+1}}{2}$

Example 4.2-c **Simplifying Terms Using the Power of a Product and Power of a Power Rules**

Simplify each of the following terms:

(i) $(2x^2)^4$

(ii) $(2x^3 \cdot 3y^2)^3$

(iii) $(-3x^3)^2$

(iv) $(-2x^2 \cdot y^4)^3$

Solution

(i) $(2x^2)^4$ Applying the Power of a Product Rule,

$= (2)^4 \cdot (x^2)^4$ Applying the Power of a Power Rule and simplifying,

$= 16 \cdot x^{(2 \cdot 4)}$

$= 16x^8$

(ii) $(2x^3 \cdot 3y^2)^3$ Regrouping the factors,

$= (2 \cdot 3 \cdot x^3 \cdot y^2)^3$ Applying the Power of a Product Rule,

$= (6)^3 \cdot (x^3)^3 \cdot (y^2)^3$ Applying the Power of a Power Rule and simplifying,

$= 216 \cdot x^{(3 \cdot 3)} \cdot y^{(2 \cdot 3)}$

$= 216x^9y^6$

(iii) $(-3x^3)^2$ Applying the Power of a Product Rule,

$= (-3)^2 \cdot (x^3)^2$ Applying the Power of a Power Rule and simplifying,

$= 9 \cdot x^{(3 \cdot 2)}$

$= 9x^6$

(iv) $(-2x^2 \cdot y^4)^3$ Applying the Power of a Product Rule,

$= (-2)^3 \cdot (x^2)^3 \cdot (y^4)^3$ Applying the Power of a Power Rule and simplifying,

$= -8 \cdot x^{(2 \cdot 3)} \cdot y^{(4 \cdot 3)}$

$= -8x^6y^{12}$

Example 4.2-d **Simplifying Terms Using the Power of a Quotient and Power of a Power Rules**

Simplify each of the following terms:

(i) $\left(\dfrac{x^5}{y^2}\right)^4$

(ii) $\left(\dfrac{x^3 \cdot y^4}{x^5 y}\right)^2$

Solution

(i) $\left(\frac{x^5}{y^2}\right)^4$ — Applying the Power of a Quotient Rule,

$= \frac{(x^5)^4}{(y^2)^4}$ — Applying the Power of a Power Rule and simplifying,

$= \frac{x^{(5 \cdot 4)}}{y^{(2 \cdot 4)}}$

$= \frac{x^{20}}{y^8}$

(ii) $\left(\frac{x^3 \cdot y^4}{x^5 y}\right)^2$ — Regrouping the factors,

$= \left(\frac{x^3}{x^5} \cdot \frac{y^4}{y}\right)^2$ — Simplifying using the Quotient Rule,

$= \left(x^{(3-5)} \cdot y^{(4-1)}\right)^2$ — Applying the Negative Exponent Rule,

$= \left(\frac{y^3}{x^2}\right)^2$ — Applying the Power of a Quotient Rule,

$= \frac{(y^3)^2}{(x^2)^2}$ — Applying the Power of a Power Rule and simplifying,

$= \frac{y^{(3 \cdot 2)}}{x^{(2 \cdot 2)}}$

$= \frac{y^6}{x^4}$

Example 4.2-e **Simplifying Terms Using the Negative Exponent Rule**

Simplify each of the following terms. Express your answer using only positive exponents.

(i) $(x^{-5})^2$ (ii) $x^{-4} \cdot y^{-2}$ (iii) $\frac{5x^{-4} \cdot y^{-3}}{x^2 y}$

Solution

(i) $(x^{-5})^2$

$= x^{-10}$

$= \frac{1}{x^{10}}$

(ii) $x^{-4} \cdot y^{-2}$

$= \frac{1}{x^4} \cdot \frac{1}{y^2}$

$= \frac{1}{x^4 y^2}$

(iii) $\frac{5x^{-4} \cdot y^{-3}}{x^2 y}$

$= 5 \cdot \frac{x^{-4}}{x^2} \cdot \frac{y^{-3}}{y}$

$= 5 \cdot x^{(-4-2)} \cdot y^{(-3-1)}$

$= 5 \cdot x^{-6} \cdot y^{-4}$

$= 5 \cdot \frac{1}{x^6} \cdot \frac{1}{y^4}$

$= \frac{5}{x^6 y^4}$

Fractional Exponents

Recall that **fractional exponents** are another way of expressing radicals, without using the radical sign $\sqrt{\ }$.

For example,

- The square root of $x = \sqrt{x} = x^{\frac{1}{2}}$.
- The cube root of $x = \sqrt[3]{x} = x^{\frac{1}{3}}$.
- Similarly, the nth root of $x = \sqrt[n]{x} = x^{\frac{1}{n}}$.

Fractional exponents obey all the rules of exponents.

Table 4.2-b **Rules of Fractional Exponents**

Summary of Rules:

$x^{\frac{1}{n}} = \sqrt[n]{x}$

$x^{-\frac{1}{n}} = \frac{1}{x^{\frac{1}{n}}} = \frac{1}{\sqrt[n]{x}}$

$x^{\frac{m}{n}} = \left(x^{\frac{1}{n}}\right)^m = \left(\sqrt[n]{x}\right)^m$

$x^{-\frac{m}{n}} = \frac{1}{x^{\frac{m}{n}}} = \frac{1}{\left(\sqrt[n]{x}\right)^m}$

	Rule	Example
1.	$x^{\frac{1}{n}} = \sqrt[n]{x}$	If $x = 16$ and $n = 4$: $x^{\frac{1}{n}} = 16^{\frac{1}{4}} = \sqrt[4]{16} = 2$
2.	$x^{-\frac{1}{n}} = \frac{1}{x^{\frac{1}{n}}} = \frac{1}{\sqrt[n]{x}}$	If $x = 27$ and $n = 3$: $x^{-\frac{1}{n}} = 27^{-\frac{1}{3}} = \frac{1}{27^{\frac{1}{3}}} = \frac{1}{\sqrt[3]{27}} = \frac{1}{3}$
3.	$x^{\frac{m}{n}} = \left(x^{\frac{1}{n}}\right)^m = (\sqrt[n]{x})^m$	This refers to finding the nth root of x, then raising the result to the power of m. If $x = 16$, $m = 3$, and $n = 4$: $x^{\frac{m}{n}} = 16^{\frac{3}{4}} = \left(16^{\frac{1}{4}}\right)^3 = (\sqrt[4]{16})^3 = (2)^3 = 8$
	$x^{\frac{m}{n}} = (x^m)^{\frac{1}{n}} = \sqrt[n]{x^m}$	This refers to raising x to the power of m, then finding the nth root of the result. If $x = 16$, $m = 3$, and $n = 4$: $x^{\frac{m}{n}} = 16^{\frac{3}{4}} = (16^3)^{\frac{1}{4}} = \sqrt[4]{16^3} = \sqrt[4]{4{,}096} = 8$
	Note: The first method is typically easier to compute because finding the nth root first results in a smaller number, which is then easier to raise to the power of m.	
4.	$x^{-\frac{m}{n}} = \frac{1}{x^{\frac{m}{n}}} = \frac{1}{(\sqrt[n]{x})^m}$	If $x = 27$, $m = 4$, and $n = 3$: $x^{-\frac{m}{n}} = 27^{-\frac{4}{3}} = \frac{1}{27^{\frac{4}{3}}} = \frac{1}{(\sqrt[3]{27})^4} = \frac{1}{(3)^4} = \frac{1}{81}$

Example 4.2-f **Simplifying Terms with Fractional Exponents**

Simplify each of the following terms:

(i) $\left(\frac{\sqrt[4]{x^8}}{\sqrt[2]{x^3}}\right)^2$ (ii) $\left(\sqrt[3]{x^{12}}\right)^{-\frac{1}{2}}$

Solution

(i) $\left(\dfrac{\sqrt[4]{x^8}}{\sqrt[2]{x^3}}\right)^2$ Rewriting the radicals as powers with fractional exponents,

$= \left(\dfrac{x^{\frac{8}{4}}}{x^{\frac{3}{2}}}\right)^2$ Applying the Quotient Rule and simplifying,

$= \left(x^{\left(2-\frac{3}{2}\right)}\right)^2$

$= \left(x^{\frac{1}{2}}\right)^2$ Applying the Power of a Power Rule and simplifying,

$= x^{\left(\frac{1}{2}\cdot 2\right)}$

$= x$

(ii) $\left(\sqrt[3]{x^{12}}\right)^{-\frac{1}{2}}$ Rewriting the radical as a power with a fractional exponent,

$= \left(x^{\frac{12}{3}}\right)^{-\frac{1}{2}}$ Applying the Power of a Power Rule and simplifying,

$= x^{\left(4\cdot -\frac{1}{2}\right)}$

$= x^{-2}$ Applying the Negative Exponent Rule,

$= \dfrac{1}{x^2}$

4.2 | Exercises

Answers to odd-numbered problems are available at the end of the textbook.

For Problems 1 to 76, simplify the terms and write the answers with positive exponents. Express any radicals as fractional exponents.

1. $x^3 \cdot x^7$
2. $x^5 \cdot x^4$
3. $4x^4 \cdot 2x$
4. $3x^3 \cdot 5x^2$
5. $(-5x^6)(-3x^2)$
6. $(-4x^3)(-2x)$
7. $(-2x^3)(3x^5)$
8. $(4x^6)(-3x^3)$
9. $x^2 \cdot x^5 \cdot x^7$
10. $x^6 \cdot x^4 \cdot x$
11. $2x^3 \cdot 3x^2 \cdot 4x$
12. $3x^5 \cdot 4x^4 \cdot 5x$
13. $x^7 \div x^4$
14. $x^5 \div x^2$
15. $6x^6 \div 2x^2$
16. $8x^5 \div 4x^2$
17. $x^8 \cdot x^2 \div x^7$
18. $x^3 \cdot x^7 \div x^6$
19. $(x^2)^4 \cdot (x^3)^5$
20. $(3x^3)^2 \cdot (2x)^3$
21. $(4x^0)^4$
22. $(3x^0)^3$
23. $\left(\dfrac{2x^4}{5y^2}\right)^3$
24. $\left(\dfrac{3x^3}{2y^4}\right)^4$
25. $\left(\dfrac{2x^3}{5y^2}\right)^2$
26. $\left(\dfrac{3x^4}{5y^3}\right)^4$
27. $\dfrac{x^2y^2}{(xy)^2}$
28. $\dfrac{x^5y^6}{(x^2y^3)^2}$
29. $(2x^2)^{-4}$
30. $(3x^3)^{-2}$
31. $(x^{-5} \cdot 2y^{-1})^{-1}$
32. $(2x^{-3} \cdot y^{-2})^{-1}$
33. $(3x^{-3} \cdot y^3)^{-2}$
34. $(4x^4 \cdot y^{-3})^{-3}$
35. $(2x^2 \cdot y^{-4})^3$
36. $(2x^{-3} \cdot y^2)^4$

37. $\left(\frac{x}{y}\right)^{-2}\left(\frac{x}{y}\right)^{3}$

38. $\left(\frac{x}{y}\right)^{-3}\left(\frac{x}{y}\right)^{5}$

39. $\left(\frac{x}{y}\right)^{2}\left(\frac{x}{y}\right)^{3}\left(\frac{x}{y}\right)^{-4}$

40. $\left(\frac{x}{y}\right)^{4}\left(\frac{x}{y}\right)^{3}\left(\frac{x}{y}\right)^{-5}$

41. $(x^3)^2\,(x^2)^3\,(x^3)^{-1}$

42. $(x^5)^{-1}\,(x^3)^2\,(x^2)^{-3}$

43. $-2x^2\,(-2x)^2$

44. $3x^3\,(-3x)^3$

45. $\left(\frac{2x \cdot 5y}{16xy^4}\right)^2$

46. $\left(\frac{2x^3y^2}{12xy^3}\right)^3$

47. $\frac{(-x^2y)^3}{-x^2y^3}$

48. $\frac{(-xy)^3}{-xy^2}$

49. $\frac{(-2^2y^3)^3}{(xy)^2}$

50. $\frac{(-3x^3y^2)^2}{(xy)^3}$

51. $\frac{(3xy)^2}{3y^6}$

52. $\frac{(2xy)^3}{4y^6}$

53. $\frac{(3x^2y^3)^2}{9xy}$

54. $\frac{(5x^4y)^3}{25xy}$

55. $\frac{(-4x^5y^2)^2}{16x^2y^2}$

56. $\frac{(-2x^2y^2)^4}{8x^3y^3}$

57. $\sqrt[5]{x}$

58. $\sqrt[4]{x^2}$

59. $\sqrt[6]{x^5}$

60. $\sqrt[5]{x^3}$

61. $\frac{1}{\sqrt[3]{x}}$

62. $\frac{1}{\sqrt{x^3}}$

63. $\frac{1}{\sqrt[4]{x^3}}$

64. $\frac{1}{\sqrt[3]{x^4}}$

65. $\left(\sqrt[4]{x^3}\right)^8$

66. $\left(\sqrt[3]{x^5}\right)^{10}$

67. $(2x)^{-\frac{1}{3}}$

68. $(3x)^{-\frac{1}{4}}$

69. $\sqrt[4]{x^6x^{10}}$

70. $\sqrt[6]{x^8x^4}$

71. $\sqrt[3]{x^9y^{12}}$

72. $\sqrt[4]{x^{12}y^8}$

73. $\sqrt[3]{x^9x^6}$

74. $\sqrt[2]{x^{10}y^{-6}}$

75. $(27x^2)^{\frac{1}{3}}$

76. $(81x^8)^{\frac{1}{4}}$

4.3 | Arithmetic Operations with Algebraic Expressions

All arithmetic operations can be applied to algebraic expressions by following the rules that we have learned thus far, including the order of operations (BEDMAS), properties of exponents, and operations with signed numbers.

Addition and Subtraction

Addition and Subtraction of Monomials

Addition and subtraction of monomials can be performed by adding and subtracting the coefficients of like terms, according to the rules of signed numbers.

Note: Recall that if a coefficient of a term is not written, it is 1.

Example 4.3-a **Adding and Subtracting Monomials**

(i) Add $6x$ and $3x$

(ii) Add $4x^2y$ and x^2y

(iii) Subtract $5x^3$ from $7x^3$

(iv) Subtract $8x$ from the sum of $7x$ and $4x$

(v) Add $5x$ and $6y$

(vi) Subtract $2y^2$ from $7y^3$

Solution

(i) $6x + 3x$ Adding like terms,

$= 9x$

(ii) $4x^2y + x^2y$ Adding like terms,

$= 5x^2y$

Solution
continued

(iii) $7x^3 - 5x^3$ — Subtracting like terms,

$= 2x^3$

(iv) $(7x + 4x) - (8x)$ — Adding like terms inside the brackets,

$= 11x - 8x$ — Subtracting like terms,

$= 3x$

(v) $5x + 6y$ — Since these are not like terms, we cannot simplify the expression at all.

(vi) $7y^3 - 2y^2$ — Since these are not like terms, we cannot simplify the expression at all.

Addition and Subtraction of Polynomials

When adding or subtracting algebraic expressions, first collect the like terms and group them, then add or subtract the coefficients of the like terms.

- For **addition of polynomials** (indicated by a plus '+' sign outside the brackets), brackets can be removed without changing any of the signs of the terms within the brackets.
- For **subtraction of polynomials** (indicated by a negative '–' sign outside the brackets), brackets can be removed by distributing the negative sign to the terms within the brackets; this is equivalent to multiplying every term within the brackets by –1, resulting in the signs changing on each term within the brackets.

Example 4.3-b **Adding and Subtracting Algebraic Expressions**

Evaluate the following expressions:

(i) Add $(3x + 7)$ and $(5x + 3)$

(ii) Add $(4y^2 - 8y - 9)$ and $(2y^2 + 6y - 2)$

(iii) Subtract $(x^2 + 5x - 7)$ from $(2x^2 - 2x + 3)$

(iv) Subtract $[5x - (x + 8)]$ from $(x - 3)$

Solution

When a bracket is preceded by a positive sign (+), drop the brackets.

(i) $(3x + 7) + (5x + 3)$ — Removing the brackets,

$= 3x + 7 + 5x + 3$ — Grouping like terms,

$= \underbrace{3x + 5x}\underbrace{+ 7 + 3}$ — Adding like terms,

$= 8x + 10$

(ii) $(4y^2 - 8y - 9) + (2y^2 + 6y - 2)$ — Removing the brackets,

$= 4y^2 - 8y - 9 + 2y^2 + 6y - 2$ — Grouping like terms,

$= \underbrace{4y^2 + 2y^2}\underbrace{- 8y + 6y}\underbrace{- 9 - 2}$ — Adding and subtracting like terms,

$= 6y^2 - 2y - 11$

When a bracket is preceded by a negative sign (–), change the sign of every term within the brackets, then drop the brackets.

(iii) $(2x^2 - 2x + 3) - (x^2 + 5x - 7)$ — Removing the brackets by distributing the negative sign to all the terms within the bracket,

$= 2x^2 - 2x + 3 - x^2 - 5x + 7$ — Grouping like terms,

$= \underbrace{2x^2 - x^2}\underbrace{- 2x - 5x}\underbrace{+ 3 + 7}$ — Adding and subtracting like terms,

$= x^2 - 7x + 10$

Solution *continued*

(iv) $(x - 3) - [5x - (x + 8)]$ — Removing the brackets by distributing the negative sign to all the terms within the bracket,

$= x - 3 - [5x - x - 8]$

$= x - 3 - 5x + x + 8$ — Grouping like terms,

$= \underbrace{x - 5x + x}\underbrace{- 3 + 8}$ — Adding and subtracting like terms,

$= -3x + 5$

Multiplication

Multiplying a Monomial by a Monomial

Multiplying a monomial by another monomial is just simplifying an algebraic term, as we did in the previous section. Multiply the coefficients together and multiply the variables together using the properties of exponents, where applicable.

Example 4.3-c Multiplying Monomials by Monomials

Evaluate the following expressions:

(i) Multiply $6x^2y$ and $5xy$

(ii) Multiply $(3a^3)$, $(-4ab)$, and $(2b^2)$

Solution

(i) $(6x^2y)(5xy)$

$= (6)(5)(x^2)(x)(y)(y)$

$= 30x^3y^2$

(ii) $(3a^3)(-4ab)(2b^2)$

$= (3)(-4)(2)(a^3)(a)(b)(b^2)$

$= -24a^4b^3$

Multiplying a Polynomial by a Monomial

When multiplying a polynomial by a monomial, multiply the monomial by **each term** of the polynomial. This is also known as the distributive property of multiplication, as shown below.

$$a(b + c) = ab + ac$$

Then, group the like terms and simplify using addition and subtraction.

Example 4.3-d Multiplying Polynomials by Monomials

(i) Multiply: $2x^3$ and $(3x^2 + 2x - 5)$

(ii) Expand and simplify: $8x(x + 3) + 4x(x - 4)$

(iii) Expand and simplify: $\frac{1}{5}\{5y - 15[2 - 3(y - 2)] + 25\}$

Solution

(i) $2x^3(3x^2 + 2x - 5)$ — Expanding, by following the Product Rule of Exponents,

$= 6x^5 + 4x^4 - 10x^3$

(ii) $8x(x + 3) + 4x(x - 4)$ — Expanding,

$= 8x^2 + 24x + 4x^2 - 16x$ — Grouping like terms,

$= \underbrace{8x^2 + 4x^2}\underbrace{+ 24x - 16x}$ — Adding and subtracting like terms,

$= 12x^2 + 8x$

Solution
continued

(iii) $\frac{1}{5}\{5y - 15[2 - 3(y - 2)] + 25\}$ Expanding the inner brackets,

$= \frac{1}{5}\{5y - 15[2 - 3y + 6] + 25\}$

$= \frac{1}{5}\{5y - 30 + 45y - 90 + 25\}$ Grouping like terms,

$= \frac{1}{5}\{5y + 45y - 30 - 90 + 25\}$ Adding and subtracting like terms,

$= \frac{1}{5}\{50y - 95\}$ Expanding the outer brackets,

$= 10y - 19$

Multiplying a Binomial by a Binomial

When multiplying two binomials, each term of the first binomial is multiplied by each term of the second binomial. This is the same as adding the products of the **F**irst terms, **O**utside terms, **I**nside terms, and **L**ast terms of each binomial, which can be remembered by the acronym "**FOIL**".

$$(a + b)(c + d) = a \cdot c + a \cdot d + b \cdot c + b \cdot d$$

F O I L

The same result is obtained by using the distributive property to expand.

$$(a + b)(c + d) = a(c + d) + b(c + d)$$

$$= a \cdot c + a \cdot d + b \cdot c + b \cdot d$$

Then, group the like terms and simplify using addition and subtraction.

Example 4.3-e **Multiplying Two Binomials**

(i) Multiply $(x + 5)$ and $(x + 6)$

(ii) Multiply $(2x + 3)$ and $(3x - 4)$

Solution

(i) $(x + 5)(x + 6)$

$(x + 5)(x + 6)$ F O I L

$= x^2 + 6x + 5x + 30$

$= x^2 + 11x + 30$

or

$x(x + 6) + 5(x + 6)$

$= x^2 + 6x + 5x + 30$

$= x^2 + 11x + 30$

(ii) $(2x + 3)(3x - 4)$

$(2x + 3)(3x - 4)$ F O I L

$= 6x^2 - 8x + 9x - 12$

$= 6x^2 + x - 12$

or

$2x(3x - 4) + 3(3x - 4)$

$= 6x^2 - 8x + 9x - 12$

$= 6x^2 + x - 12$

Special Products of Binomials

$(a+b)^2 = a^2 + 2ab + b^2$

$(a-b)^2 = a^2 - 2ab + b^2$

- **Squaring a binomial:** the product of a binomial with itself

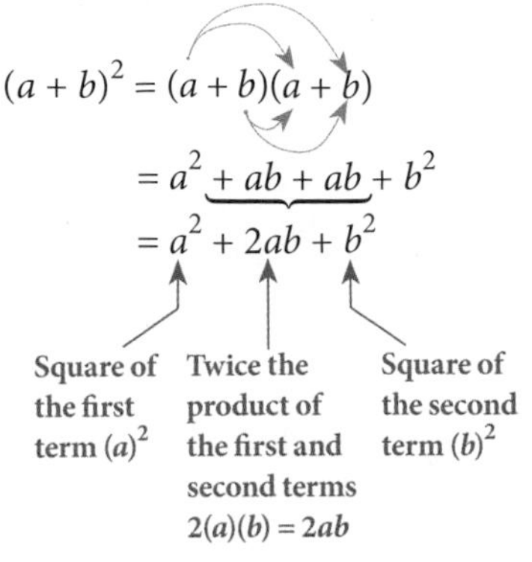

$$(a-b)^2 = (a-b)(a-b)$$
$$= a^2 - ab - ab + (-b)^2$$
$$= a^2 - 2ab + b^2$$

Square of the first term $(a)^2$ | Twice the product of the first and second terms $2(a)(-b) = -2ab$ | Square of the second term $(-b)^2 = b^2$

$(a+b)(a-b) = a^2 - b^2$

- **Difference of squares:** the product of two binomials having the same two terms but opposite signs separating the terms; i.e., the product of the sum and difference of two terms.

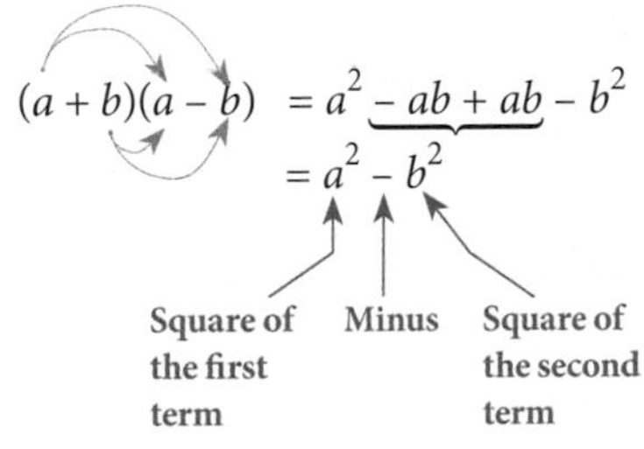

Example 4.3-f **Squaring a Binomial**

Multiply the following expressions using the special product of binomials.

(i) $(2x+y)(2x+y)$ (ii) $(3x+4)(3x+4)$

(iii) $(3x-2y)(3x-2y)$ (iv) $(5x-6)(5x-6)$

Solution

(i) $(2x+y)(2x+y)$

$= (2x+y)^2$ Using $(a+b)^2 = a^2 + 2ab + b^2$,

Note: Common error $(a+b)^2 \neq a^2 + b^2$

$= (2x)^2 + 2(2x)(y) + (y)^2$

$= 4x^2 + 4xy + y^2$

(ii) $(3x+4)(3x+4)$

$= (3x+4)^2$ Using $(a+b)^2 = a^2 + 2ab + b^2$,

$= (3x)^2 + 2(3x)(4) + (4)^2$

$= 9x^2 + 24x + 16$

(iii) $(3x-2y)(3x-2y)$

$= (3x-2y)^2$ Using $(a-b)^2 = a^2 - 2ab + b^2$,

Note: Common error $(a-b)^2 \neq a^2 - b^2$

$= (3x)^2 - 2(3x)(2y) + (2y)^2$

$= 9x^2 - 12xy + 4y^2$

(iv) $(5x-6)(5x-6)$

$= (5x-6)^2$ Using $(a-b)^2 = a^2 - 2ab + b^2$,

$= (5x)^2 - 2(5x)(6) + (6)^2$

$= 25x^2 - 60x + 36$

Example 4.3-g **Multiplying the Sum and Difference of Two Terms (Difference of Squares)**

Multiply the following expressions using the special product of binomials.

(i) $(3x + y)(3x - y)$

(ii) $(2x + 5)(2x - 5)$

Solution

(i) $(3x + y)(3x - y)$ Using $(a + b)(a - b) = a^2 - b^2$,

$= (3x)^2 - (y)^2$

$= 9x^2 - y^2$

(ii) $(2x + 5)(2x - 5)$ Using $(a + b)(a - b) = a^2 - b^2$,

$= (2x)^2 - (5)^2$

$= 4x^2 - 25$

Multiplying a Polynomial by a Polynomial

When multiplying a polynomial by a polynomial, multiply each term of the first polynomial by each term of the second polynomial. Then, using the distributive property, group the like terms and simplify using addition and subtraction.

Example 4.3-h **Multiplying Polynomials by Polynomials**

(i) Multiply: $(x^2 + 7)$ and $(2x^2 + 5x + 2)$

(ii) Multiply: $(x - 4)$ and $(2x^2 - x - 3)$

(iii) Expand and simplify: $(x + 5)(2x - 6) + (3x - 4)(x - 5)$

(iv) Expand and simplify: $(x - 3)(3x - 1) - (2x - 3)(x + 4)$

Solution

(i) $(x^2 + 7)(2x^2 + 5x + 2)$

$= x^2(2x^2 + 5x + 2) + 7(2x^2 + 5x + 2)$ Expanding,

$= 2x^4 + 5x^3 \underbrace{+ 2x^2 + 14x^2} + 35x + 14$ Adding like terms,

$= 2x^4 + 5x^3 + 16x^2 + 35x + 14$

(ii) $(x - 4)(2x^2 - x - 3)$

$= x(2x^2 - x - 3) - 4(2x^2 - x - 3)$ Expanding,

$= 2x^3 - x^2 - 3x - 8x^2 + 4x + 12$ Grouping like terms,

$= 2x^3 \underbrace{- x^2 - 8x^2} \underbrace{- 3x + 4x} + 12$ Adding and subtracting like terms,

$= 2x^3 - 9x^2 + x + 12$

(iii) $(x + 5)(2x - 6) + (3x - 4)(x - 5)$

$= [x(2x - 6) + 5(2x - 6)] + [3x(x - 5) - 4(x - 5)]$ Expanding,

$= (2x^2 - 6x + 10x - 30) + (3x^2 - 15x - 4x + 20)$ Removing the brackets,

$= 2x^2 - 6x + 10x - 30 + 3x^2 - 15x - 4x + 20$ Grouping like terms,

$= \underbrace{2x^2 + 3x^2} \underbrace{- 6x + 10x - 15x - 4x} \underbrace{- 30 + 20}$ Adding and subtracting like terms,

$= 5x^2 - 15x - 10$

Solution *continued*

(iv) $(x - 3)(3x - 1) - (2x - 3)(x + 4)$

$= [x(3x - 1) - 3(3x - 1)] - [2x(x + 4) - 3(x + 4)]$ Expanding,

$= (3x^2 - x - 9x + 3) - (2x^2 + 8x - 3x - 12)$ Removing the brackets by distributing the negative sign,

$= 3x^2 - x - 9x + 3 - 2x^2 - 8x + 3x + 12$ Grouping like terms,

$= \underbrace{3x^2 - 2x^2}\underbrace{- x - 9x - 8x + 3x}\underbrace{+ 3 + 12}$ Adding and subtracting like terms,

$= x^2 - 15x + 15$

Division

Dividing a Monomial by a Monomial

Dividing a monomial by another monomial is also just simplifying an algebraic term, as we did in the previous section. Divide the coefficients and divide the variables using the properties of exponents, where applicable.

Example 4.3-i **Dividing Monomials by Monomials**

(i) Divide $8x^2y$ by $6x$

(ii) Divide $-9x^2$ by $3x^3$

Solution

(i) $\frac{8x^2y}{6x} = \frac{8}{6} \cdot \frac{x^2}{x} \cdot y = \frac{4}{3}xy$ or $\frac{4xy}{3}$

(ii) $\frac{-9x^2}{3x^3} = \frac{-9}{3} \cdot \frac{x^2}{x^3} = \frac{-3}{1} \cdot \frac{1}{x} = \frac{-3}{x}$

Dividing a Polynomial by a Monomial

When dividing a polynomial by a monomial, divide **each term** of the polynomial by the monomial. The process is similar to dividing a monomial by a monomial.

Example 4.3-j **Dividing Polynomials by Monomials**

(i) Divide $(9x^3 + 12x^2)$ by $6x$

(ii) Divide $(4x^4 + 2x^3 - 7x)$ and $4x^4$

Solution

(i) $\frac{9x^3 + 12x^2}{6x} = \frac{9x^3}{6x} + \frac{12x^2}{6x} = \frac{3x^2}{2} + 2x$

(ii) $\frac{4x^4 + 2x^3 - 7x}{4x^4} = \frac{4x^4}{4x^4} + \frac{2x^3}{4x^4} - \frac{7x}{4x^4} = 1 + \frac{1}{2x} - \frac{7}{4x^3}$

4.3 | Exercises

Answers to odd-numbered problems are available at the end of the textbook.

For Problems 1 to 8, simplify and evaluate the expressions.

1. $6y + 4y - 7y$, where $y = 10$
2. $3x + 5x - 8x$, where $x = 4$
3. $2z - z + 7z$, where $z = 7$
4. $3A - A + 6A$, where $A = 10$

5. $(6x)(3x) - (5x)(4x)$, where $x = 3$

6. $(10x \times 4.5x) - (11x \times 4x)$, where $x = 50$

7. $(2x)(0.5x + 4x)(5x + x)$, where $x = 5$

8. $(4x)(12x + 0.25x)(0.5x + x)$, where $x = 3$

For Problems 9 to 28, simplify the expressions.

9. $13x^2 + 8x - 2x^2 + 9x$

10. $7x + 12x^2 - 4x + 5x^2$

11. $-18y - 5y^2 + 19y - 2y^2$

12. $-14y - 2y^2 + 7y + 7y^2$

13. $6x - 3x + 2y^2 + y^2$

14. $9x^2 - 6x^2 + 7y - 6y$

15. $4xy^2 - x^2y^2 - 3xy^2 + 2x^2y^2$

16. $3x^2y^2 - 2xy^2 - 8x^2y^2 + xy^2$

17. $3[(5-3)(4-x)] - 2 - 5[3(5x-4) + 8] - 9x$

18. $(5-14)\{x - 8[3 - 5(2x-3) + 3x] - 3\}$

19. $6[4(8-y) - 5(3+3y)] - 21 - 7[3(7+4y) - 4] + 198y$

20. $\frac{1}{2}\{y - 15[2 - 3(3y-2) - 7y] - 4\}$

21. $y - \{4x - [y - (2y-9) - x] + 2\}$

22. $2y + \{-6y - [3x + (-4x + 3)] + 5\}$

23. $(x-1) - \{[x - (x-3)] - x\}$

24. $9x - \{3y + [4x - (y - 6x)] - (x + 7y)\}$

25. $5\{-2y + 3[4x - 2(3+x)]\}$

26. $4\{-7y + 8[5x - 3(4x+6)]\}$

27. $2y + \{8[3(2y-5) - (8y+9) + 6]\}$

28. $7x - \{5[4(3x-8) - (9x+10)] + 14\}$

For Problems 29 to 38, expand and simplify the expressions.

29. $(2y-1)(y-4) - (3y+2)(3y-1)$

30. $(y+4)(y-3) + (y-2)(y-3)$

31. $(2x+3)(2x-1) - 4(x^2 - 7)$

32. $4(2x-1)(x+3) - 3(x-2)(3x-4)$

33. $3(x-2)(4-3x) + 4(2x-1)(3-x)$

34. $2(3x+2)(1-3x) + 3(2x-1)(4-x)$

35. $4(3x^2 + 4) - 2(x+3)(x+5)$

36. $3(5x^2 - 1) - (2x-4)(3x+5)$

37. $3(2-3x)(2+x) - (1-x)(x-3)$

38. $(x-2)(3x+2) - (3x+2)(x-5)$

For Problems 39 to 54, expand the expressions by using special products of binomials.

39. $(x+5)^2$

40. $(x+7)^2$

41. $(2x+3y)^2$

42. $(3x+4y)^2$

43. $(3-x)^2$

44. $(7-x)^2$

45. $(3x-2y)^2$

46. $(2x-3y)^2$

47. $(1-3x)^2$

48. $(6x-1)^2$

49. $(3-2x)^2$

50. $(2y-1)^2$

51. $(x+5)(x-5)$

52. $(12x-1)(12x+1)$

53. $(3+7x)(3-7x)$

54. $(2a+9b)(2a-9b)$

For Problems 55 to 62, expand and simplify the expressions.

55. $(x+3)^2 + (x-2)^2$

56. $(x+5)^2 + (x-4)^2$

57. $(4+x)^2 - (x-3)(x+3)$

58. $(3+x)^2 + (x+5)(x-5)$

59. $(3x-2)^2 + (2x-3)(2x+3)$

60. $(2x+5)(2x-5) + (1-4x)^2$

61. $(2x-4)^2 - (y+3)^2$

62. $(5x-6)^2 - (x+5)^2$

For Problems 63 to 72, simplify the expressions.

63. $\frac{(16y)(8x)}{(4x)(8y)}$

64. $\frac{(20y)(4x)}{(2x)(5y)}$

65. $\frac{(6x)(-18y)}{(3x)(-24y)}$

66. $\frac{(7x)(18y)}{(14x)(-27y)}$

67. $\frac{-x^2y - xy^2}{xy}$

68. $\frac{x^2y - 3xy^2}{xy}$

69. $\frac{x^2y - 3xy^2 + 4x^2y + xy}{xy}$

70. $\frac{3x^3y^3 - 6x^2y + 3xy^2 + 3xy}{3xy}$

71. $\frac{6xy^2}{7} \cdot \frac{21x^2}{y} \cdot \frac{1}{36xy^2}$

72. $\frac{12x^2y^3}{5} \cdot \frac{15x^2}{4xy} \cdot \frac{1}{30x^3y}$

4.4 | Factoring Algebraic Expressions

In the previous section, we learned how to multiply a polynomial by another polynomial to determine the product; the product of two polynomials is another polynomial. In this section, we will learn how to determine the original polynomials, known as **factors**, that when multiplied together, will result in a given product. This process is known as **factorization**, and is the opposite of multiplying (or expanding) polynomials.

For example, multiplying the two polynomials $(x + 2)$ and $(x + 1)$ results in the polynomial $x^2 + 3x + 2$ (as learned in the previous section). Factorization is the process of determining the factors, $(x + 2)$ and $(x + 1)$, that can be multiplied together to result in the given polynomial $x^2 + 3x + 2$.

Multiplying and factoring polynomials are opposite operations. All factorizations can be verified by multiplying the factors.

Multiplying (or Expanding)

$$(x + 2)(x + 1) = x^2 + 3x + 2$$

Factors

Factoring

Factoring Polynomials using the Greatest Common Factor (GCF)

Algebraic expressions can be factored by using the **greatest common factor (GCF)** for both the coefficients and the variables in all the terms of the expression.

For example, consider the expression $15x^2 - 20x$. It has two terms.

First, identify the GCF of the coefficients of the two terms.

- The coefficients of the terms are 15 and –20.

  $15 = 3 \times 5$

  $-20 = (-1) \times 2 \times 2 \times 5$

  Therefore, the GCF of the coefficients is 5.

Next, look for variables that are common to each term, and identify the lowest exponents of those variables.

- All terms contain the variable x. The lowest exponent on the variable x is 1 ($x^1 = x$).

  Therefore, the GCF of the variables is x.

The GCF of the expression is the product of the GCF of the coefficients and the variables that are common to each term.

- Therefore, for the expression $15x^2 - 20x$, the GCF $= 5 \times x = 5x$.

Example 4.4-a **Identifying the GCF of Algebraic Expressions**

Identify the greatest common factors of the following expressions:

(i) $24x^4 + 12x^3 - 8x^2$ (ii) $15x^2y^3z^2 + 10x^2yz^2 - 5x^2y$

Solution

(i) The coefficients of the terms are 24, 12, and –8.

$24 = 2 \times 2 \times 2 \times 3$

$12 = 2 \times 2 \times 3$

$-8 = (-1) \times 2 \times 2 \times 2$

The GCF of the coefficients is $2 \times 2 = 4$.

All the terms contain the variable x. The lowest exponent on the variable x is 2.

Therefore, the GCF of the expression is $4x^2$.

(ii) The coefficients of the terms are 15, 10, and –5.

$15 = 3 \times 5$

$10 = 2 \times 5$

$-5 = (-1) \times 5$

The GCF of the coefficients is 5.

All the terms contain the variable x. The lowest exponent on the variable x is 2.

All the terms contain the variable y. The lowest exponent on the variable y is 1.

Therefore, the GCF of the expression is $5x^2y$.

Although the first two terms contain the variable z, the last one does not!

Once the GCF is identified, we can factor the expression by dividing it by the GCF, as learned in the previous section. The GCF is the first factor of the expression, and the resulting quotient is the second factor. This process is demonstrated in the following example.

Example 4.4-b **Factoring Algebraic Expressions**

Factor the following expressions:

(i) $12x + 18y$ (ii) $8y^2 + 20y$

(iii) $3x^2y^3 + 6xy^4 - 15x^3y^5$ (iv) $x(x + 4) - y(4 + x)$

Solution

(i) $12x + 18y$

$12x = 2 \cdot 2 \cdot 3 \cdot x$

$18y = 2 \cdot 3 \cdot 3 \cdot y$

The GCF is $2 \cdot 3 = 6$.

Divide the original expression by the GCF of 6 to determine the second factor:

$$\frac{12x + 18y}{6} = \frac{12x}{6} + \frac{18y}{6} = 2x + 3y$$

i.e., the second factor is $(2x + 3y)$.

Therefore, $12x + 18y = 6(2x + 3y)$.

(ii) $8y^2 + 20y$

$8y^2 = 2 \cdot 2 \cdot 2 \cdot y \cdot y$

$20y = 2 \cdot 2 \cdot 5 \cdot y$

The GCF is $2 \cdot 2 \cdot y = 4y$.

Solution *continued*

Divide the original expression by the GCF of $4y$ to determine the second factor:

$$\frac{8y^2 + 20y}{4y} = \frac{8y^2}{4y} + \frac{20y}{4y} = 2y + 5$$

i.e., the second factor is $(2y + 5)$.

Therefore, $8y^2 + 20y = 4y(2y + 5)$.

(iii) $3x^2y^3 + 6xy^4 - 15x^3y^5$

The GCF is $3xy^3$.

Divide the original expression by the GCF of $3xy^3$ to determine the second factor:

$$\frac{3x^2y^3 + 6xy^4 - 15x^3y^5}{3xy^3} = \frac{3x^2y^3}{3xy^3} + \frac{6xy^4}{3xy^3} - \frac{15x^3y^5}{3xy^3} = x + 2y - 5x^2y^2$$

i.e., the second factor is $(x + 2y - 5x^2y^2)$.

Therefore, $3x^2y^3 + 6xy^4 - 15x^3y^5 = 3xy^3(x + 2y - 5x^2y^2)$.

(iv) $x(x + 4) - y(4 + x)$

The GCF is $(x + 4)$. $[(x + 4) = (4 + x)]$

Divide the original expression by the GCF of $(x + 4)$ to obtain the second factor:

$$\frac{x(x + 4) - y(4 + x)}{(x + 4)} = \frac{x(x + 4)}{(x + 4)} - \frac{y(4 + x)}{(x + 4)} = x - y$$

i.e., the second factor is $(x - y)$.

Therefore, $x(x + 4) - y(4 + x) = (x + 4)(x - y)$.

Multiplying and dividing algebraic expressions is easier once all the expressions are factored. The following example illustrates how factoring can be used to simplify products and quotients of polynomials.

Example 4.4-c Simplifying Algebraic Expressions by Factoring

Simplify the following expressions:

(i) $[14(2x + y) - 7x(2x + y)] \div (2x + y)$ (ii) $\frac{(x^2 + xy)}{(7x - 14)} \times \frac{(14x - 28)}{(x + y)}$

Solution

(i) $[14(2x + y) - 7x(2x + y)] \div (2x + y)$ Rewriting the question,

$= \frac{14(2x + y) - 7x(2x + y)}{(2x + y)}$ The GCF of the numerator is $7(2x + y)$. Factoring,

$= \frac{7(2x + y)(2 - x)}{(2x + y)}$ Reducing,

$= 7(2 - x)$

Alternatively, when there is a common binomial, such as $(2x + y)$, it may be simpler to factor it out first.

Therefore, $[14(2x + y) - 7x(2x + y)] \div (2x + y) = 7(2 - x)$.

(ii) $\frac{(x^2 + xy)}{(7x - 14)} \times \frac{(14x - 28)}{(x + y)}$ The GCF of the first numerator is x. Factoring,

$= \frac{x(x + y)}{(7x - 14)} \times \frac{(14x - 28)}{(x + y)}$ The GCF of the second numerator is 14. Factoring,

Solution *continued*

$$= \frac{x(x+y)}{(7x-14)} \times \frac{14(x-2)}{(x+y)}$$

The GCF of the first denominator is 7. Factoring,

$$= \frac{x(x+y)}{7(x-2)} \times \frac{14(x-2)}{(x+y)}$$

Reducing,

$$= \frac{14x}{7}$$

$$= 2x$$

Therefore, $\frac{(x^2+xy)}{(7x-14)} \times \frac{(14x-28)}{(x+y)} = 2x.$

Factoring Polynomials with Four Terms using Grouping

When the polynomial to be factored has four terms, but does not have a common factor among all terms, these polynomials can sometimes be factored into products of binomials by **grouping** the terms into pairs.

Once grouped into pairs, determine the greatest common factor (GCF) of each group, as previously learned, and then factor out the common binomial factor. Some four-term polynomials can be factored by grouping the first two terms and the last two terms; others may need to be rearranged in order to identify a common binomial factor.

The following example outlines a technique for factoring four-term polynomials by grouping.

Example 4.4-d **Factoring by Grouping**

Factor the following expressions:

(i) $9x^2 + 6x + 12x + 8$ (ii) $15x^2 - 10x - 6x + 4$

Solution

(i) $9x^2 + 6x + 12x + 8$

Grouping the first two terms and the last two terms,

$$= \underbrace{9x^2 + 6x}_{1^{st}\text{ group}} \underbrace{+ 12x + 8}_{2^{nd}\text{ group}}$$

The GCF of the first group is $3x$. Factoring out $3x$ from the first group,

$$= 3x(3x+2) \underbrace{+ 12x + 8}$$

The GCF of the second group is 4. Factoring out 4 from the second group,

$$= 3x(3x+2) + 4(3x+2)$$

We now have a common binomial factor of $(3x + 2)$. Factoring out $(3x + 2)$ from the expression,

$$= (3x+2)(3x+4)$$

Therefore, $9x^2 + 6x + 12x + 8 = (3x + 2)(3x + 4)$.

(ii) $15x^2 - 10x - 6x + 4$

Grouping the first two terms and the last two terms,

$$= \underbrace{15x^2 - 10x}_{1^{st}\text{ group}} \underbrace{- 6x + 4}_{2^{nd}\text{ group}}$$

The GCF of the first group is $5x$. Factoring out $5x$ from the first group,

$$= 5x(3x-2) \underbrace{- 6x + 4}$$

The GCF of the second group is 2. However, if we factor out 2 from the second group, the resulting binomial would be $(-3x + 2)$. Therefore, in order to obtain a binomial that matches the one from the first group, $(3x - 2)$, we factor out -2 from the second group,

$$= 5x(3x-2) - 2(3x-2)$$

We now have a common binomial factor of $(3x - 2)$. Factoring out $(3x - 2)$ from the expression,

$$= (3x-2)(5x-2)$$

Therefore, $15x^2 - 10x - 6x + 4 = (3x - 2)(5x - 2)$.

Factoring Differences of Squares

In the previous section, we learned that the product of two binomials having the same two terms but opposite signs separating the terms is equal to the square of the first term minus the square of the second term; this resulting polynomial is called a **difference of squares**.

That is:

$$(a+b)(a-b) = \underbrace{(a)^2 - (b)^2}_{\text{Difference of Squares}}$$

Therefore, when two perfect squares are subtracted, its factors are equal to the sum and difference of the square roots of the terms.

That is, the **factors** of $(a)^2 - (b)^2$ are $(a + b)$ and $(a - b)$.

When factoring a difference of two terms, the first step is to check whether both terms are perfect squares.

Multiplying (or Expanding)

$$(a+b)(a-b) = (a)^2 - (b)^2$$

Factoring

Note: The "sum of squares", i.e., $(a)^2 + (b)^2$, cannot be factored using this method. It may be factorable using the GCF method.

Example 4.4-e **Factoring Differences of Squares**

Factor the following expressions:

(i) $x^2 - 49$ (ii) $16 - x^2$ (iii) $9x^2 - 25y^2$ (iv) $36x^2y^2 - 1$

Solution

(i) $x^2 - 49$ 49 is a perfect square of 7.

$= (x)^2 - (7)^2$

$= (x + 7)(x - 7)$

(ii) $16 - x^2$ 16 is a perfect square of 4.

$= (4)^2 - (x)^2$

$= (4 + x)(4 - x)$

(iii) $9x^2 - 25y^2$ $9x^2$ is a perfect square of $3x$, and $25y^2$ is a perfect square of $5y$.

$= (3x)^2 - (5y)^2$

$= (3x + 5y)(3x - 5y)$

(iv) $36x^2y^2 - 1$ $36x^2y^2$ is a perfect square of $6xy$, and 1 is a perfect square of 1.

$= (6xy)^2 - (1)^2$

$= (6xy + 1)(6xy - 1)$

Example 4.4-f **Factoring Differences of Squares with Additional Steps**

Factor the following expressions:

(i) $(x + y)^2 - 36$ (ii) $5x^2 - 20$ (iii) $x^4 - 16$ (iv) $81x^4 - 1$

Solution

(i) $(x + y)^2 - 36$ $(x + y)^2$ is a perfect square of the binomial $(x + y)$, and 36 is a perfect square of 6.

$= (x + y)^2 - (6)^2$ Factoring using differences of squares,

$= (x + y + 6)(x + y - 6)$

Solution
continued

(ii) $5x^2 - 20$ — Factoring out the common factor 5,

$= 5(x^2 - 4)$ — 4 is a perfect square of 2.

$= 5[(x)^2 - (2)^2]$ — Factoring using differences of squares,

$= 5(x + 2)(x - 2)$

(iii) $x^4 - 16$ — x^4 is a perfect square of x^2, and 16 is a perfect square of 4.

$= (x^2)^2 - (4)^2$ — Factoring using differences of squares,

$= (x^2 + 4)(x^2 - 4)$ — $(x^2 - 4)$ can also be written as a difference of squares. The expression can be factored further.

Recall: a sum of squares $(x^2 + 4)$ cannot be factored using the same method as a difference of squares $(x^2 - 4)$.

$= (x^2 + 4)[(x)^2 - (2)^2]$

$= (x^2 + 4)(x + 2)(x - 2)$ — *Note:* $(x^2 + 4)$ *cannot be factored.*

(iv) $81x^4 - 1$ — $81x^4$ is a perfect square of $9x^2$, and 1 is a perfect square of 1.

$= (9x^2)^2 - (1)^2$ — Factoring using differences of squares,

$= (9x^2 + 1)(9x^2 - 1)$ — $(9x^2 - 1)$ can also be written as a difference of squares. The expression can be factored further.

$= (9x^2 + 1)[(3x)^2 - (1)^2]$

$= (9x^2 + 1)(3x + 1)(3x - 1)$ — *Note:* $(9x^2 + 1)$ *cannot be factored.*

Factoring Trinomials of the Form: $x^2 + bx + c$

Some trinomials of the form $x^2 + bx + c$ can be factored as a product of two binomials.

For example, let the factors of $x^2 + bx + c$ be $(x + m)$ and $(x + n)$. Then,

$x^2 + bx + c = (x + m)(x + n)$ — Expanding,

$= x^2 + \underbrace{nx + mx} + mn$ — Regrouping,

$= x^2 + (m + n)x + mn$

Comparing the results, we see that the sum $(m + n)$ is equal to b, and the product mn is equal to c.

$$\begin{aligned} &\mathbf{x^2 + \quad bx \quad + c} \\ &\mathbf{= x^2 + (m + n)x + mn} \end{aligned}$$

Therefore, a trinomial of the form $x^2 + bx + c$ can be factored by finding two terms whose sum is equal to b and whose product is equal to c. This process is demonstrated in the following examples.

Example 4.4-g **Factoring Trinomials of the Form $x^2 + bx + c$**

Factor the following expressions:

(i) $x^2 + 5x + 4$ (ii) $x^2 + 3x - 18$

Solution

(i) $x^2 + 5x + 4$

Here, $b = +5$ and $c = +4$.

Therefore, we need to find two integers, m and n, whose sum is 5 and whose product is 4.

Listing all possible two factors of $c = +4$:

m	n	mn	$m + n$
4	**1**	**4**	**5**
−4	−1	4	−5
2	2	4	4
−2	−2	4	−4

← $4(1) = 4$ and $4 + 1 = 5$

$m = +4$ and $n = +1$ satisfy the conditions.

Therefore, $x^2 + 5x + 4 = (x + 4)(x + 1)$.

Recall: you can verify your factorization by multiplying the factors:

$$(x + 4)(x + 1) = x^2 + x + 4x + 4$$
$$= x^2 + 5x + 4$$

(ii) $x^2 + 3x - 18$

Here, $b = +3$ and $c = -18$.

Therefore, we need to find two integers, m and n, whose sum is 3 and whose product is −18.

Listing all possible two factors of $c = -18$:

m	n	mn	$m + n$
18	−1	−18	17
−18	1	−18	−17
9	−2	−18	7
−9	2	−18	−7
6	**−3**	**−18**	**3**
−6	3	−18	−3

← $6(-3) = -18$ and $6 + (-3) = 3$

$m = +6$ and $n = -3$ satisfy the conditions.

Therefore, $x^2 + 3x - 18 = (x + 6)(x - 3)$.

Example 4.4-h **Factoring Trinomials with Additional Steps**

Factor the following expressions:

(i) $x^3 - 3x^2 - 40x$ (ii) $x^2 - 3xy + 2y^2$

Solution

(i) $x^3 - 3x^2 - 40x$

Factoring out the common factor x,

$= x(x^2 - 3x - 40)$

We now have a trinomial of the form $x^2 + bx + c$. We need two integers, m and n, whose sum is $b = -3$ and whose product is $c = -40$.

$m = -8$ and $n = 5$ satisfy the conditions $mn = -8(5) = -40$ and $m + n = -8 + 5 = -3$.

$= x(x - 8)(x + 5)$

Solution
continued

(ii) $x^2 - 3xy + 2y^2$

Although there is an additional variable y, we still have a trinomial of the form $x^2 + bx + c$. We need two terms, m and n, whose sum is $b = -3y$ and whose product is $c = +2y^2$.

$m = -2y$ and $n = -y$ satisfy the conditions $mn = -2y(-y) = 2y^2$ and $m + n = -2y + (-y) = -3y$.

$= (x - 2y)(x - y)$

Factoring Trinomials of the Form: $ax^2 + bx + c$

Some trinomials of the form $ax^2 + bx + c$ can be factored as a product of two binomials.

The process is similar to factoring trinomials of the form $x^2 + bx + c$; we are still attempting to find two terms, m and n, whose **sum** is equal to $\boldsymbol{b}$, but whose **product** is now equal to $\boldsymbol{ac}$ (as opposed to just c).

Then, since $m + n = b$, we can split the middle term, $+bx$, into the two terms $+mx + nx$.

$$\boldsymbol{ax^2 + bx + c}$$

$$= \boldsymbol{ax^2 + mx + nx + c}$$

This results in a polynomial with four terms, which we can factor by grouping. This process is demonstrated in the following example.

Example 4.4-i **Factoring Trinomials of the Form $ax^2 + bx + c$**

Factor the following expressions:

(i) $3x^2 + 8x + 4$

(ii) $2x^2 + 7x - 15$

Solution

(i) $3x^2 + 8x + 4$

Here, $a = +3$, $b = +8$, and $c = +4$.

Therefore, we need to find two integers, m and n, whose sum is 8 and whose product is $3(4) = 12$.

Listing all possible two factors of $ac = +12$:

m	n	mn	$m + n$
12	1	12	13
−12	−1	12	−13
6	**2**	**12**	**8**
−6	−2	12	−8
4	3	12	7
−4	−3	12	−7

$6(2) = 12$ and $6 + 2 = 8$

$m = +6$ and $n = +2$ satisfy the conditions.

$3x^2 + 8x + 4$

Splitting the middle term, $+8x$, into $+6x + 2x$,

$= 3x^2 + 6x + 2x + 4$

Grouping the first two terms and the last two terms,

$= \underbrace{3x^2 + 6x}_{1^{st}\text{ group}} + \underbrace{2x + 4}_{2^{nd}\text{ group}}$

The GCF of the first group is $3x$. Factoring out $3x$ from the first group,

Solution
continued

$= 3x(x + 2) \underbrace{+ 2x + 4}$ — The GCF of the second group is 2. Factoring out 2 from the second group,

$= 3x(x + 2) + 2(x + 2)$ — We now have a common binomial factor of $(x + 2)$. Factoring out $(x + 2)$ from the expression,

$= (x + 2)(3x + 2)$

Therefore, $3x^2 + 8x + 4 = (x + 2)(3x + 2)$.

> Verify your factorization by multiplying the factors:
>
> $(x + 2)(3x + 2) = 3x^2 + 2x + 6x + 4$
>
> $= 3x^2 + 8x + 4$

(ii) $2x^2 + 7x - 15$

Here, $a = +2$, $b = +7$, and $c = -15$.

Therefore, we need to find two integers, m and n, whose sum is 7 and whose product is $2(-15) = -30$.

Listing all possible two factors of $ac = -30$:

m	n	mn	$m + n$
30	−1	−30	29
−30	1	−30	−29
15	−2	−30	13
−15	2	−30	−13
10	**−3**	**−30**	**7**
−10	3	−30	−7
6	−5	−30	1
−6	5	−30	−1

← $10(-3) = -30$ and $10 + (-3) = 7$
$m = +10$ and $n = -3$ satisfy the conditions.

$2x^2 + 7x - 15$ — Splitting the middle term, $+7x$, into $+10x - 3x$,

$= 2x^2 + 10x - 3x - 15$ — Grouping the first two terms and the last two terms,

$= \underbrace{2x^2 + 10x}_{1^{st}\text{ group}} \underbrace{- 3x - 15}_{2^{nd}\text{ group}}$ — The GCF of the first group is $2x$. Factoring out $2x$ from the first group,

$= 2x(x + 5) \underbrace{- 3x - 15}$ — The GCF of the second group is 3. Factoring out −3 from the second group,

> If we factor out +3 from the second group, the resulting binomial would be $(-x - 5)$. Therefore, to obtain $(x + 5)$, we factor out −3 from the second group.

$= 2x(x + 5) - 3(x + 5)$ — We now have a common binomial factor of $(x + 5)$. Factoring out $(x + 5)$ from the expression,

$= (x + 5)(2x - 3)$

Therefore, $2x^2 + 7x - 15 = (x + 5)(2x - 3)$.

Factoring Perfect Square Trinomials

In the previous section, we learned rules for products when squaring a binomial. The resulting trinomial formed by squaring a binomial is known as a **perfect square trinomial**.

That is:

$$(a + b)^2 = \underbrace{a^2 + 2ab + b^2}_{\text{Perfect Square Trinomial}} \qquad (a - b)^2 = \underbrace{a^2 - 2ab + b^2}_{\text{Perfect Square Trinomial}}$$

A perfect square trinomial, $a^2 + 2ab + b^2$ and $a^2 - 2ab + b^2$, has the following two properties:

1. The first and last terms are perfect squares (a^2 and b^2).
2. The middle term is twice the product of the square roots of the first and last terms ($2ab$).

Therefore, once an expression is identified as a perfect square trinomial, it has two equal factors: the square root of the first term *plus or minus* the square root of the last term; the sign *plus or minus* follows the sign of the middle term.

That is, the **factors** of $a^2 + 2ab + b^2$ are $(a + b)$ and $(a + b)$; i.e., $(a + b)^2$.

Similarly, the **factors** of $a^2 - 2ab + b^2$ are $(a - b)$ and $(a - b)$; i.e., $(a - b)^2$.

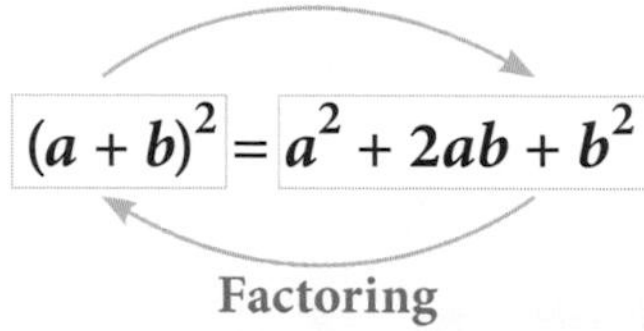

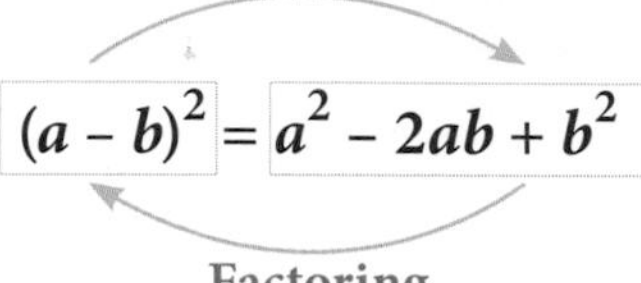

Example 4.4-j **Factoring Perfect Square Trinomials**

Factor the following expressions:

(i) $x^2 + 6x + 9$ (ii) $9x^2 - 30x + 25$

Solution

(i) $x^2 + 6x + 9$ — The first and last terms are perfect squares and the middle term is twice the product of the square roots of the first and last terms.

$= (x)^2 + 2(x)(3) + (3)^2$ — Therefore, the expression is a perfect square trinomial.

$= (x + 3)(x + 3) = (x + 3)^2$ — The sign of the middle term of the trinomial is plus (+).

(ii) $9x^2 - 30x + 25$ — The first and last terms are perfect squares and the middle term is twice the product of the square roots of the first and last terms.

$= (3x)^2 - 2(3x)(5) + (5)^2$ — Therefore, the expression is a perfect square trinomial.

$= (3x - 5)(3x - 5) = (3x - 5)^2$ — The sign of the middle term of the trinomial is minus (–).

Summary of Factoring Methods

When factoring polynomials, perform the factoring methods in the following order:

1. First look for the **greatest common factor (GCF)** among all the terms, and factor the GCF out of the expression.
2. If there are **four terms**, identify whether the terms can be grouped to factor out a common binomial factor.
3. If there are **two terms**, identify whether the terms are a difference of squares: $a^2 - b^2$.
4. If there are **three terms**, identify whether one of the following patterns applies to the expression:
   (i) $x^2 + bx + c$
   (ii) $ax^2 + bx + c$
   (iii) Perfect Square Trinomial: $a^2 + 2ab + b^2$ or $a^2 - 2ab + b^2$

Note: Not all polynomials are factorable. However, all polynomials presented in the Exercises can be factored using one/multiple of these methods.

4.4 | Exercises

Answers to odd-numbered problems are available at the end of the textbook.

For Problems 1 to 10, factor the expressions using the greatest common factor (GCF).

1. $8x^2 + 4x$
2. $2x^2 + 10x$
3. $7xy - 35x^2y$
4. $45x^2y - 25y$
5. $3x^2y + 6x^3y^2$
6. $8x^3y^2 + 4x^2y$
7. $30x^3 + 5xy - 15x^2$
8. $30x^3 + 15xy^2 - 25x$
9. $10y^2 + 70xy^2 + 50x^2y$
10. $18x^2 + 3x^3 + 21x + 3$

For Problems 11 to 16, simplify the expressions.

11. $\frac{(3x^2 + 9)}{14} \cdot \frac{(7x + 21)}{x + 3}$
12. $\frac{16}{(3x^2y + 4x)} \cdot \frac{(6x^2y + 8x)}{12}$
13. $\frac{(x^2 - 5x)}{(2x + 10)} \cdot \frac{(3x + 15)}{4x}$
14. $\frac{(3xy - 5x)}{8x} \cdot \frac{12y^2}{(9y - 15)}$
15. $\frac{(15xy - 5x)}{(4x + 12)} \cdot \frac{(3x - 9)}{(4x - 12)}$
16. $\frac{(x^2 - xy)}{(7x - 14)} \cdot \frac{(14x - 28)}{(x + y)}$

For Problems 17 to 26, factor the expressions by grouping.

17. $x^2 + 3x - 2xy - 6y$
18. $x^2 + x + x + 1$
19. $x^2 + 3x + 5x + 15$
20. $x^2 + 3x + xy + 3y$
21. $6x - 9y + 2xz^2 - 3yz^2$
22. $9x - 18y + xz^3 - 2yz^3$
23. $x^2 - 6xy + 5x - 30y$
24. $5x + 10y - ax - 2ay$
25. $5xy - 3y + 10x - 6$
26. $14x - 4y + 7xz - 2yz$

For Problems 27 to 38, factor the differences of squares.

27. $x^2 - 36$
28. $x^2 - 9$
29. $1 - x^2$
30. $x^2 - 1$
31. $100x^2 - 900$
32. $25x^2 - 400$
33. $16x^2 - 9y^2$
34. $4x^2 - 49y^2$
35. $(x + 2)^2 - 9$
36. $(x - 3)^2 - 16$
37. $625 - x^4$
38. $1 - 256x^4$

For Problems 39 to 70, factor the trinomials.

39. $x^2 + 11x + 30$
40. $x^2 + 8x + 15$
41. $x^2 + x - 12$
42. $x^2 + 5x - 6$
43. $x^2 - 7x + 6$
44. $x^2 - 12x + 20$
45. $x^2 - x - 30$
46. $x^2 - 10x - 24$
47. $x^2 + 16xy + 63y^2$
48. $x^2 - 6xy - 27y^2$
49. $x^3 + 7x^2 - 18x$
50. $x^3 + 18x^2 + 80x$
51. $5x^2 + 8x + 3$
52. $2x^2 + 15x + 7$
53. $2x^2 - 5x - 3$
54. $2x^2 + 5x - 3$

55. $3x^2 + x - 10$

56. $3x^2 + 11x + 10$

57. $5x^2 - 22x - 15$

58. $9x^2 - 30x + 25$

59. $4x^2 - 8x - 60$

60. $5x^2 + 40x + 60$

61. $x^2 + 12x + 36$

62. $x^2 + 8x + 16$

63. $x^2 + 4x + 4$

64. $x^2 + 2x + 1$

65. $25x^2 - 10x + 1$

66. $4x^2 - 20x + 25$

67. $1 - 6x + 9x^2$

68. $1 - 14x + 49x^2$

69. $25x^2 + 30x + 9$

70. $4x^2 - 28x + 49$

4.5 | Simple Algebraic Equations and Word Problems

An **algebraic equation** is a mathematical sentence expressing equality between two algebraic expressions (or an algebraic expression and a number).

All equations have an equal (=) sign that separates the equation into two equal parts: the left side (LS) and right side (RS).

When two expressions are joined by an equal (=) sign, it indicates that the expression to the left of the equal sign is identical in value to the expression to the right of the equal sign.

For example, when two algebraic expressions, such as $5x + 7$ and $x + 19$, are equal, the two expressions are joined by an equal (=) sign and the equation is written as:

$$\underbrace{5x + 7}_{\text{'Left side' (LS)}} = \underbrace{x + 19}_{\text{'Right side' (RS)}}$$

The value of the variable that makes both sides (LS and RS) equal is the solution to the equation.

The **solution** to the equation is the value of the variable that makes the left side (LS) evaluate to the same number as the right side (RS).

Note: You need an equation to solve for an unknown variable - you cannot solve for a variable in an algebraic expression that is not part of an equation.

- *If you have an* ***expression****, it needs to be* ***simplified****.*
- *If you have an* ***equation****, it needs to be* ***solved****.*

In algebra, there are a variety of equations. In this section, we will learn one category of equations, known as **linear equations with one variable**.

Examples of linear equations with one variable are:

$$2x = 8, \qquad 3x + 5 = 14, \qquad 5x + 7 = x + 19$$

An equation is either true or false depending on the value of the variable.

For example, consider the equation $2x = 8$:

- If $x = 4$, LS = 2(4) = 8, RS = 8; therefore, the equation is true.
- If $x = 3$, LS = 2(3) = 6, RS = 8; therefore, the equation is false.

Equations may be classified into the following three types:

1. **Conditional Equation** - these equations are only true when the variable has a specific value.

   For example, $2x = 8$ is a conditional equation, true if and only if $x = 4$.
2. **Identity** - these equations are true for any value for the variable.

   For example, $2x + 10 = 2(x + 5)$ is an identity, true for any value of x.
3. **Contradiction** - these equations are not true for any value of the variable.

   For example, $x + 5 = x + 4$ is a contradiction, not true for any value of x.

Equivalent Equations

Equations with the same solutions are called **equivalent equations**.

For example, $2x + 5 = 9$ and $2x = 4$ are equivalent equations because the solution $x = 2$ satisfies each equation.

Similarly, $3x - 4 = 5$, $2x = x + 3$, and $x + 1 = 4$ are equivalent equations because the solution $x = 3$ satisfies each equation.

Properties of Equality

Performing the same operation on both sides of an equation will result in an equivalent equation.

If $a = b$, then,

$b = a$	Symmetric Property	Interchanging LS and RS.
$a + c = b + c$	Addition Property	Adding the same quantity to both sides.
$a - c = b - c$	Subtraction Property	Subtracting the same quantity from both sides.
$a \cdot c = b \cdot c$	Multiplication Property	Multiplying by the same quantity on both sides.
$\frac{a}{c} = \frac{b}{c}$	Division Property, $c \neq 0$	Dividing by the same quantity on both sides.

The above properties are used to solve equations.

Equations with Fractional Coefficients

If an equation contains fractional coefficients, then the fractional coefficients can be changed to whole numbers by multiplying both sides of the equation by the least common denominator (LCD) of all the fractions, using the Multiplication Property.

For example,

$\frac{2}{3}x = \frac{5}{2} + 4$	Since the LCD of the denominators 3 and 2 is 6, multiply both sides of the equation by 6.
$6\left(\frac{2}{3}x\right) = 6\left(\frac{5}{2} + 4\right)$	This is the same as multiplying each term by the LCD of 6.
$6\left(\frac{2}{3}x\right) = 6\left(\frac{5}{2}\right) + 6(4)$	Simplifying,
$4x = 15 + 24$	Now, the equation has only whole number coefficients.
$4x = 39$	

Equations with Decimal Coefficients

If an equation contains decimal coefficients, then the decimal coefficients can be changed to whole numbers by multiplying both sides of the equation by an appropriate power of 10, using the Multiplication Property.

For example,

$1.25x = 0.2 + 4$	Since there is at most 2 decimal places in any of the coefficients or constants, multiply both sides of the equation by $10^2 = 100$.
$100(1.25x) = 100(0.2 + 4)$	This is the same as multiplying each term by 100.
$100(1.25x) = 100(0.2) + 100(4)$	Simplifying,
$125x = 20 + 400$	Now, the equation has only whole number coefficients.
$125x = 420$	

Steps to Solve Algebraic Equations with One Variable

Step 1: If the equation contains fraction and/or decimal coefficients, it is possible to work with them as they are - in that case, proceed onto Step 2. Alternatively, the equation may be rewritten in whole numbers, as explained above, to make calculations and rearrangements easier.

Step 2: Expand and clear brackets in the equation, if present, by following the order of arithmetic operations (BEDMAS).

Step 3: Use the addition and subtraction properties to collect and group all **variable** terms on the **left side** of the equation and all **constants** on the **right side** of the equation. Then, simplify both sides.

Note: If it is more convenient to gather all the variable terms on the right side and the constants on the left side, you may do so, and then use the symmetric property and switch the sides of the equation to bring the variables over to the left side and the constants to the right side.

Step 4: Use the division and multiplication properties to ensure that the coefficient of the variable is +1.

Step 5: After completing Step 4, there should be a single variable with a coefficient of +1 on the left side and a single constant term on the right side - that constant term is the solution to the equation.

Step 6: Verify the answer by substituting the solution from Step 5 back into the original problem.

Step 7: State the answer.

Example 4.5-a Solving Equations Using the Addition and Subtraction Properties

Solve the following equations and verify the solutions:

(i) $x - 11 = 4$ (ii) $8 + x = 20$

Solution

(i) $x - 11 = 4$

Adding **11** to both sides,

$x - 11 + \mathbf{11} = 4 + \mathbf{11}$

$x = \mathbf{15}$

Verify by substituting $x = 15$:

$\text{LS} = x - 11$	$\text{RS} = 4$
$= \mathbf{15} - 11$	
$= 4$	

LS = RS

Therefore, the solution is $x = 15$.

(ii) $8 + x = 20$

Subtracting **8** from both sides,

$8 - \mathbf{8} + x = 20 - \mathbf{8}$

$x = \mathbf{12}$

Verify by substituting $x = 12$:

$\text{LS} = 8 + x$	$\text{RS} = 20$
$= 8 + \mathbf{12}$	
$= 20$	

LS = RS

Therefore, the solution is $x = 12$.

Example 4.5-b **Solving Equations Using the Multiplication and Division Properties**

Solve the following equations and verify the solutions:

(i) $5x = 20$ (ii) $\frac{3}{8}x = 12$

Solution

(i) $5x = 20$ Dividing both sides by **5**,

$$\frac{5x}{\mathbf{5}} = \frac{20}{\mathbf{5}}$$

$$x = \mathbf{4}$$

Verify by substituting $x = 4$:

LS = $5x$	RS = 20
$= 5(\mathbf{4})$	
$= 20$	

LS = RS

Therefore, the solution is $x = 4$.

(ii) $\frac{3}{8}x = 12$ Multiplying both sides by $\frac{\mathbf{8}}{\mathbf{3}}$ (the reciprocal of $\frac{3}{8}$),

$$\left(\frac{\mathbf{8}}{\mathbf{3}}\right)\cdot\frac{3}{8}x = \left(\frac{\mathbf{8}}{\mathbf{3}}\right)\cdot 12$$

$$x = 8 \times 4$$

$$x = \mathbf{32}$$

or

$\frac{3}{8}x = 12$ Multiplying both sides by **8**,

$$(\mathbf{8})\cdot\frac{3}{8}x = (\mathbf{8})\cdot 12$$

$3x = 96$ Dividing both sides by **3**,

$$\frac{3x}{\mathbf{3}} = \frac{96}{\mathbf{3}}$$

$$x = \mathbf{32}$$

Verify by substituting $x = 32$:

LS = $\frac{3}{8}x$	RS = 12
$= \frac{3}{8} \times \mathbf{32}$	
$= 12$	

LS = RS

Therefore, the solution is $x = 32$.

Example 4.5-c **Solving Equations with Variables on Both Sides**

Solve the following equations and verify the solutions:

(i) $3x - 8 = 12 - 2x$ (ii) $15 + 6x - 4 = 3x + 31 - x$

Solution

(i) $3x - 8 = 12 - 2x$ Adding **2x** to both sides,

$$3x + \mathbf{2x} - 8 = 12 - 2x + \mathbf{2x}$$

$5x - 8 = 12$ Adding **8** to both sides,

$$5x - 8 + \mathbf{8} = 12 + \mathbf{8}$$

$5x = 20$ Dividing both sides by **5**,

$$\frac{5x}{\mathbf{5}} = \frac{20}{\mathbf{5}}$$

$$x = \mathbf{4}$$

Verify by substituting $x = 4$ back into the original equation:

LS = $3x - 8$	RS = $12 - 2x$
$= 3(\mathbf{4}) - 8$	$= 12 - 2(\mathbf{4})$
$= 12 - 8$	$= 12 - 8$
$= 4$	$= 4$

LS = RS

Therefore, the solution is $x = 4$.

Solution
continued

(ii)

$$15 + 6x - 4 = 3x + 31 - x$$ Combining like terms (LS: 15 – 4 = 11, and RS: $3x - x = 2x$),

$$11 + 6x = 2x + 31$$ Subtracting **2*x*** from both sides,

$$11 + 6x - \mathbf{2x} = 2x - \mathbf{2x} + 31$$

$$11 + 4x = 31$$ Subtracting **11** from both sides,

$$11 - \mathbf{11} + 4x = 31 - \mathbf{11}$$

$$4x = 20$$ Dividing both sides by **4**,

$$\frac{4x}{\mathbf{4}} = \frac{20}{\mathbf{4}}$$

$$x = \mathbf{5}$$

Verify by substituting $x = 5$ back into the original equation:

$LS = 15 + 6x - 4$	$RS = 3x + 31 - x$
$= 15 + 6(\mathbf{5}) - 4$	$= 3(\mathbf{5}) + 31 - \mathbf{5}$
$= 15 + 30 - 4$	$= 15 + 31 - 5$
$= 41$	$= 41$

LS = RS

Therefore, the solution is $x = 5$.

Example 4.5-d **Solving Equations with Fractions**

Solve the following equation and verify the solution:

$$\frac{x}{3} - \frac{1}{12} = \frac{1}{6} + \frac{x}{4}$$

Solution

$$\frac{x}{3} - \frac{1}{12} = \frac{1}{6} + \frac{x}{4}$$ LCD of 3, 4, 6, and 12 is 12. Multiplying each term by **12**,

$$\mathbf{12}\left(\frac{x}{3}\right) - \mathbf{12}\left(\frac{1}{12}\right) = \mathbf{12}\left(\frac{1}{6}\right) + \mathbf{12}\left(\frac{x}{4}\right)$$

$$4x - 1 = 2 + 3x$$ Subtracting **3*x*** from both sides,

$$4x - \mathbf{3x} - 1 = 2 + 3x - \mathbf{3x}$$

$$x - 1 = 2$$ Adding **1** to both sides,

$$x - 1 + \mathbf{1} = 2 + \mathbf{1}$$

$$x = \mathbf{3}$$

Verify by substituting $x = 3$ back into the original equation:

$LS = \frac{x}{3} - \frac{1}{12}$	$RS = \frac{1}{6} + \frac{x}{4}$
$= \frac{\mathbf{3}}{3} - \frac{1}{12}$	$= \frac{1}{6} + \frac{\mathbf{3}}{4}$
$= \frac{12}{12} - \frac{1}{12}$	$= \frac{2}{12} + \frac{9}{12}$
$= \frac{11}{12}$	$= \frac{11}{12}$

LS = RS

Therefore, the solution is $x = 3$.

Example 4.5-e Solving Equations with Decimals

Solve the following equation and verify the solution:
$0.15x + 1.2 = 0.4x - 0.8$

If we do not interchange the LS and RS, we will still obtain the correct solution of $x = 8$. We simply end up working with negative coefficients and constants instead of positive ones.

$$0.15x + 1.2 = 0.4x - 0.8$$

Greatest number of decimal places is 2 (i.e., hundredths). Multiplying all the terms by $10^2 = \mathbf{100}$,

$$\mathbf{100}(0.15x) + \mathbf{100}(1.2) = \mathbf{100}(0.4x) - \mathbf{100}(0.8)$$

$$15x + 120 = 40x - 80$$

Interchanging the LS and RS using the Symmetric Property to have the larger x term on the LS,

$$40x - 80 = 15x + 120$$

Subtracting $\mathbf{15x}$ from both sides,

$$40x - \mathbf{15x} - 80 = 15x - \mathbf{15x} + 120$$

$$25x - 80 = 120$$

Adding **80** to both sides,

$$25x - 80 + \mathbf{80} = 120 + \mathbf{80}$$

$$25x = 200$$

Dividing both sides by **25**,

$$\frac{25x}{\mathbf{25}} = \frac{200}{\mathbf{25}}$$

$$x = \mathbf{8}$$

Verify by substituting $x = 8$ back into the original equation:

LS	RS
$\text{LS} = 0.15x + 1.2$	$\text{RS} = 0.4x - 0.8$
$= 0.15(\mathbf{8}) + 1.2$	$= 0.4(\mathbf{8}) - 0.8$
$= 1.2 + 1.2$	$= 3.2 - 0.8$
$= 2.4$	$= 2.4$

LS = RS

Therefore, the solution is $x = 8$.

Note: For the rest of the examples in this section, we will not show the verification by substitution step.

Example 4.5-f Solving Equations Using All the Properties

Solve the following equations by using the properties of equality, and express the answer as a fraction in its lowest terms, or as a mixed number, wherever applicable:

(i) $8x + 7 - 3x = -6x - 15 + x$

(ii) $2(3x - 7) = 28 - 3(x + 1)$

(iii) $\frac{1}{4}(x + \frac{2}{3}) = \frac{1}{2}(x - 3) + x$

(iv) $0.45(2x + 3) - 2.55 = 0.6(3x - 5)$

(v) $\frac{x + 2}{3} = \frac{5 - 2x}{7}$

Solution

(i)

$$8x + 7 - 3x = -6x - 15 + x$$

Grouping like terms on both sides,

$$8x - 3x + 7 = -6x + x - 15$$

$$5x + 7 = -5x - 15$$

Adding $\mathbf{5x}$ to both sides,

$$5x + \mathbf{5x} + 7 = -5x + \mathbf{5x} - 15$$

$$10x + 7 = -15$$

Subtracting **7** from both sides,

$$10x + 7 - \mathbf{7} = -15 - \mathbf{7}$$

$$10x = -22$$

Dividing both sides by **10**,

$$\frac{10x}{\mathbf{10}} = -\frac{22}{\mathbf{10}}$$

$$x = -\frac{11}{5} = -2\frac{1}{5}$$

Solution
continued

(ii) $2(3x - 7) = 28 - 3(x + 1)$ — Expanding both sides,

$6x - 14 = 28 - 3x - 3$ — Grouping like terms,

$6x - 14 = 28 - 3 - 3x$

$6x - 14 = 25 - 3x$ — Adding $\mathbf{3x}$ to both sides,

$6x + \mathbf{3x} - 14 = 25 - 3x + \mathbf{3x}$

$9x - 14 = 25$ — Adding **14** to both sides,

$9x - 14 + \mathbf{14} = 25 + \mathbf{14}$

$9x = 39$ — Dividing both sides by **9**,

$$\frac{9x}{\mathbf{9}} = \frac{39}{\mathbf{9}}$$

$$x = \frac{13}{3} = 4\frac{1}{3}$$

(iii) $\frac{1}{4}(x + \frac{2}{3}) = \frac{1}{2}(x - 3) + x$ — Expanding both sides,

$\frac{1}{4}x + \frac{1}{6} = \frac{1}{2}x - \frac{3}{2} + x$ — Multiplying each term by the LCD **12**,

$$\mathbf{12}\left(\frac{1}{4}x\right) + \mathbf{12}\left(\frac{1}{6}\right) = \mathbf{12}\left(\frac{1}{2}x\right) - \mathbf{12}\left(\frac{3}{2}\right) + \mathbf{12}\,(x)$$

$3x + 2 = 6x - 18 + 12x$ — Grouping like terms,

$3x + 2 = 6x + 12x - 18$

$3x + 2 = 18x - 18$ — Interchanging the LS and RS using the Symmetric Property to have the larger x term on the LS,

$18x - 18 = 3x + 2$ — Subtracting $\mathbf{3x}$ from both sides,

$18x - \mathbf{3x} - 18 = 3x - \mathbf{3x} + 2$

$15x - 18 = 2$ — Adding **18** to both sides,

$15x - 18 + \mathbf{18} = 2 + \mathbf{18}$

$15x = 20$ — Dividing both sides by **15**,

$$\frac{15x}{\mathbf{15}} = \frac{20}{\mathbf{15}}$$

$$x = \frac{4}{3} = 1\frac{1}{3}$$

(iv) $0.45(2x + 3) - 2.55 = 0.6(3x - 5)$ — Expanding both sides,

$0.90x + 1.35 - 2.55 = 1.8x - 3.0$ — Greatest number of decimal places is 2 (i.e., hundredths). Multiplying all the terms by $10^2 = \mathbf{100}$,

$$\mathbf{100}(0.90x) + \mathbf{100}(1.35) - \mathbf{100}(2.55) = \mathbf{100}(1.8x) - \mathbf{100}(3.0)$$

$90x + \underbrace{135 - 255} = 180x - 300$ — Grouping like terms,

$90x - 120 = 180x - 300$ — Interchanging the LS and RS using the Symmetric Property to have the larger x term on the LS,

$180x - 300 = 90x - 120$ — Subtracting $\mathbf{90x}$ from both sides,

$180x - \mathbf{90x} - 300 = 90x - \mathbf{90x} - 120$

Solution *continued*

$$90x - 300 = -120$$ Adding **300** to both sides,

$$90x - 300 + \mathbf{300} = -120 + \mathbf{300}$$

$$90x = 180$$ Dividing both sides by **90**,

$$\frac{90x}{\mathbf{90}} = \frac{180}{\mathbf{90}}$$

$$x = 2$$

(v) $$\frac{x+2}{3} = \frac{5-2x}{7}$$ Cross-multiplying,

$$7(x+2) = 3(5-2x)$$ Expanding both sides,

$$7x + 14 = 15 - 6x$$ Adding **6x** to both sides,

$$7x + \mathbf{6x} + 14 = 15 - 6x + \mathbf{6x}$$

$$13x + 14 = 15$$ Subtracting **14** from both sides,

$$13x + 14 - \mathbf{14} = 15 - \mathbf{14}$$

$$13x = 1$$ Dividing both sides by **13**,

$$\frac{13x}{\mathbf{13}} = \frac{1}{\mathbf{13}}$$

$$x = \frac{1}{13}$$

Steps to Solve Word Problems

Step 1: Read the entire problem and ensure you understand the situation.

Step 2: Identify the given information and the question to be answered.

Step 3: Look for key words. Some words indicate certain mathematical operations (see Table 4.1).

Step 4: Choose a variable to represent the unknown(s) and state what that variable represents, including the unit of measure.

Note: For now, if there is more than one unknown, try to identify all the unknowns in terms of one variable, as all the questions in this chapter can be solved with only one variable.

Step 5: Where necessary, draw a simple sketch to identify the information. This helps with envisioning the question more clearly.

Step 6: Create an equation (or set of equations) to describe the relationship between the variables and the constants in the question.

Step 7: Group like terms, isolate the variable, and solve for the unknown(s).

Step 8: State the solution to the given problem.

Example 4.5-g Solving a Word Problem Using Algebraic Equations

If Harry will be 65 years old in 5 years, how old is he today?

Solution

Let Harry's age today be x years.

Therefore, in 5 years, Harry's age will be:

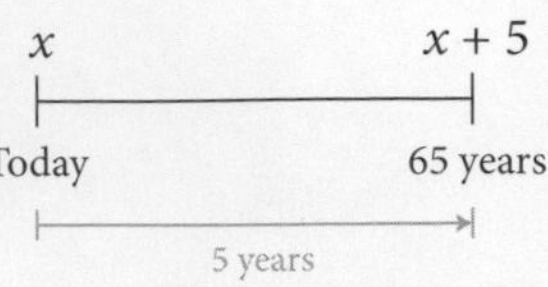

$$x + 5 = 65$$

Solving for x, $x = 65 - 5$

$= 60$

Therefore, Harry is 60 years old today.

Example 4.5-h Solving a Geometry Problem Using Algebraic Equations

The perimeter of a rectangular garden is 50 metres. The length is 5 metres more than the width. Find the dimensions of the garden. *Hint: Perimeter = 2(length) + 2(width)*

Solution

Let the width be w metres.

Therefore, the length is $(w + 5)$ metres.

$w + 5$

w w

$w + 5$

Perimeter = 50 m

$$Perimeter = 2(length) + 2(width)$$

$$50 = 2(w + 5) + 2w$$

$$50 = 2w + 10 + 2w$$

$$2w + 10 + 2w = 50$$

$$4w + 10 = 50$$

$$4w = 50 - 10$$

$$4w = 40$$

$$w = \frac{40}{4}$$

$$w = 10$$

We can verify our solution by substituting the values for length and width into the original equation:

Perimeter = 2(*length*) + 2(*width*)

LS = 50

RS = 2(15) + 2(10) = 30 + 20 = 50

Therefore, the width of the garden is 10 metres and the length is (10 + 5) = 15 metres.

Example 4.5-i Solving a Finance Problem Using Algebraic Equations

A TV costs \$190 more than a Blu-ray player. The total cost of the TV and the Blu-ray player is \$688. Calculate the cost of the TV and the cost of the Blu-ray player.

Solution

Let the cost of the Blu-ray player be $\$x$.

Therefore, the cost of the TV is $\$(x + 190.00)$.

The total cost is \$688.00.

$$x + (x + 190.00) = 688.00$$

$$x + x + 190.00 = 688.00$$

$$2x + 190.00 = 688.00$$

$$2x = 688.00 - 190.00$$

$$2x = 498.00$$

$$x = \frac{498.00}{2}$$

$$x = \$249.00$$

Therefore, the cost of the Blu-ray player is \$249.00 and the cost of the TV is (249.00 + 190.00) = \$439.00.

Example 4.5-j Solving a Mixture Problem Using Algebraic Equations

How many litres of water need to be added to 30 litres of a 15% saline solution to make a saline solution that is 10% saline?

Solution

	# of Litres	% Saline	Total Litres of Saline
Water	x	0	0
15% Saline Solution	30	0.15	$0.15 \times 30 = 4.5$
10% Saline Solution	$30 + x$	0.10	$0.10 \times (30 + x)$

From the last column, we get the equation for the saline mix. The number of litres of saline in the 15% solution must be the same as the number of litres in the final 10% solution, as only water is being added, which does not contribute any additional saline to the solution. Therefore,

$$4.5 = 0.10 \times (30 + x)$$

$$4.5 = 3 + 0.10x$$

$$1.5 = 0.10x$$

$$x = 15$$

Therefore, 15 litres of water need to be added to the 15% saline solution to make the solution 10% saline.

4.5 | Exercises

Answers to odd-numbered problems are available at the end of the textbook.

For Problems 1 to 8, write and solve the algebraic equations.

1. The sum of a number and six is ten.
2. A number decreased by fifteen is five.
3. Six times a number is seventy-two.
4. The product of a number and four is twenty-eight.
5. A number divided by five is four.
6. A number divided by three is three.
7. Two-thirds of a number is twelve.
8. Two-fifths of a number is six.

For Problems 9 to 30, solve the algebraic equations using the properties of equality, and express the answer as a fraction in its lowest terms or as a mixed number, wherever applicable.

9. $x - 20 = 10$
10. $x - 25 = 17$
11. $22 = 40 - x$
12. $54 = 23 - x$
13. $21 + x = 4$
14. $50 + x = 45$
15. $16 + x = 22$
16. $12 + x = 38$
17. $11x + 4 = 17$
18. $7x - 16 = 22$
19. $x - \frac{4}{5} = \frac{3}{5}$
20. $x - \frac{1}{6} = 1$

21. $\frac{10}{15} = x - \frac{4}{3}$

22. $\frac{x}{7} + 15 = 24$

23. $x + \frac{2}{5} = \frac{1}{4}$

24. $2x - \frac{2}{3} = \frac{5}{6}$

25. $5x = 20$

26. $4x = 24$

27. $\frac{2x}{3} + 1 = \frac{5x}{8} + 2$

28. $\frac{x}{2} - \frac{1}{6} = \frac{1}{3} + \frac{3x}{5}$

29. $\frac{7x}{8} - 4 = \frac{x}{4} + 6$

30. $\frac{8x}{3} - 5 = \frac{x}{3} + 2$

For Problems 31 to 54, solve the algebraic equations using the properties of equality, and round the answer to 2 decimal places, wherever applicable.

31. $10y - 0.09y = 17$

32. $x + 0.13x = 70$

33. $0.3x - 3.2 = 0.4 - 0.6x$

34. $4 + 0.2x = 0.7x - 0.5$

35. $0.4x - 1.38 = 0.3x - 1.2$

36. $1.2 - 0.7x = 2.7 - 0.5x$

37. $0.43x + 0.25 = 0.29x - 0.03$

38. $0.6x - 1.2 = 0.9 - 1.5x$

39. $8x + 7 - 3x = -6x - 15 + x$

40. $x - 2 - 4x = -3x - 8 + 5x$

41. $2(3x - 7) = 28 - 3(x + 1)$

42. $4(2x - 5) = 32 - 4(x - 2)$

43. $(4 + 6)(2 + 4x) = 45 - 2.5(x + 3)$

44. $(5 + 0.5x)(1 + 3) = -1.2(2x + 4) + 25$

45. $15 + 5(x - 10) = 3(x - 1)$

46. $2(x - 3) + 3(x - 5) = 4$

47. $4(y + 7) - 2(y - 4) = 3(y - 2)$

48. $8(2y + 4) - 6(3y + 7) = 3y$

49. $\frac{x - 7}{2} + \frac{x + 2}{3} = 41$

50. $\frac{7}{12}(2x + 1) + \frac{3}{4}(x + 1) = 3$

51. $\frac{5}{y + 4} = \frac{3}{y - 2}$

52. $\frac{3}{x + 1} = \frac{2}{x - 3}$

53. $\frac{7}{5x - 3} = \frac{5}{4x}$

54. $\frac{5}{y + 2} = \frac{3}{y}$

For Problems 55 to 76, solve the word problems using algebraic equations.

55. If three times a number plus twenty is seven times that number, what is the number?

56. Fifteen less than three times a number is twice that number. What is the number?

57. A 25-metre long wire is cut into two pieces. One piece is 7 metres longer than the other. Find the length of each piece.

58. A 9-metre long pipe is cut into two pieces. One piece is twice the length of the other piece. Find the length of each piece.

59. \$500 is shared between Andy and Becky. Andy's share is \$150 less than Becky's share. Calculate the amount of each of their shares.

60. \$200 is shared between Bill and Ann. Ann's share is \$50 more than Bill's share. Calculate the size of each of their shares.

61. Movie tickets that were sold to each child was \$3 cheaper than those sold to each adult. If a family of two adults and two children paid \$34 to watch a movie at the cinema, what was the price of each adult ticket and each child ticket?

62. Giri had twice the number of quarters (25 cents) in his bag than dimes (10 cents). If he had a total of 54 coins, how many of them were quarters? What was the total dollar value of these coins?

63. A square garden, with sides of length x metres, is widened by 4 metres and lengthened by 3 metres. Write the equation for the area (A) of the expanded garden. If each side was originally 10 metres in length, find the new area. (*Hint: Area of a Rectangle = Length × Width*)

64. A square garden, with sides of length x metres, has had its width reduced by 4 metres and its length reduced by 2 metres. Write the equation for the Area (A) of the smaller garden. If each side was originally 20 metres in length, find the new area.

65. Aran bought a shirt and a pair of pants for $34.75. The pair of pants cost $9.75 more than the shirt. Calculate the cost of the shirt.

66. Mythili bought a schoolbag and a toy for $30.45. The school bag cost $5.45 more than the toy. Calculate the cost of the school bag.

67. Sam is paid $720 a week. He worked 9 hours of overtime last week and he received $954. Calculate his overtime rate per hour.

68. Lisa is paid $840 a week. Her overtime rate is $28 per hour. Last week she received $1,036. How many hours of overtime did she work last week?

69. The sum of the three angles of any triangle is 180°. If $3x$, $7x$, and $8x$ are the measures of the three angles of a triangle, calculate the measure of each angle of the triangle.

70. The sum of the three angles of any triangle is 180°. If $3x$, $4x$, and $5x$ are the measures of the three angles of a triangle, calculate the measure of each angle of the triangle.

71. The perimeter of a triangle is the sum of the lengths of the three sides of the triangle. The perimeter of a triangle with sides x cm, $(x + 10)$ cm, and $2x$ cm is 70 cm. Calculate the length of each side of the triangle.

72. The perimeter of a triangle is the sum of the lengths of the three sides of the triangle. The perimeter of a triangle with sides $x + 10$, $2x + 10$, and $3x$ is 110 cm. Calculate the length of each side of the triangle.

73. After completing a weight-loss program, a patient weighs 160 lb. His dietician observes that the patient has lost 15% of his original weight. What was the patient's starting weight?

74. A beaker in a chemistry lab contains 3 litres of water. While conducting an experiment, the chemistry professor removes three-fifths of the water from the beaker. He then adds three-fifths of the remaining volume to the beaker. How much water is left in the beaker at the end of the experiment?

75. A researcher wants to make 4 L of a 7% acid solution. She has a beaker of 15% acid solution in stock. How much of the 15% solution does she need to use and how much water must she add in order to prepare her desired solution?

76. A chemist wants to make a 10% acid solution. She has 5 L of 25% acid solution. How many litres of water should she add to the 25% solution in order to prepare her desired solution?

4.6 | Rearranging Equations and Formulas

Equations are mathematical statements formed by placing an equal (=) sign between two expressions to indicate that the expression on the left side of the equal sign is equal to the expression on the right side of the equal sign.

For example, $5x + 3 = y - x$

Formulas are similar to equations. In formulas, the relationship among many variables is written as a rule for performing calculations. Formulas are written so that a single variable, known as the subject of the formula, is on the left side of the equation, and everything else is on the right side.

For example, $I = Prt$

Isolating Variables

To isolate a particular variable in an equation or a formula, rearrange the terms and simplify so that the required variable is on the left side of the equation and all the other variables and numbers are on the right side of the equation. Rearrangement can be performed by using the rules that we have learned in the previous sections of this chapter, summarized in the following guidelines:

- Expand brackets and collect like terms.
- Remove fractions by multiplying both sides by the LCD.
- Add or subtract the same quantity to or from both sides.
- Multiply or divide both sides by the same quantity.
- Take powers or roots on both sides.

For example, consider the formula for simple interest: $I = Prt$.

To solve for any of the variables, 'P', 'r', or 't' in this formula, we can rearrange the variables as shown below:

$$I = Prt \qquad \text{is the same as } Prt = I$$

Solving for 'P':

$$\frac{Prt}{rt} = \frac{I}{rt} \qquad \text{Dividing both sides by '}rt\text{',}$$

$$P = \frac{I}{rt}$$

Solving for 'r':

$$\frac{Prt}{Pt} = \frac{I}{Pt} \qquad \text{Dividing both sides by '}Pt\text{',}$$

$$r = \frac{I}{Pt}$$

Solving for 't':

$$\frac{Prt}{Pr} = \frac{I}{Pr} \qquad \text{Dividing both sides by '}Pr\text{',}$$

$$t = \frac{I}{Pr}$$

Example 4.6-a

Rearranging Formulas to Isolate Variables

Rearrange the following formulas to isolate the variables indicated in the brackets:

(i) $S = C + E + P$ (P)

(ii) $P = RB$ (R)

(iii) $y = mx + b$ (m)

(iv) $S = P(1 + rt)$ (P)

Solution

(i) $S = C + E + P$ (P)

$$C + E + P = S \qquad \text{Subtracting '}C\text{' and '}E\text{' from both sides,}$$

$$C + E + P - C - E = S - C - E$$

$$P = S - C - E$$

(ii) $P = RB$ (R)

$$RB = P \qquad \text{Dividing both sides by '}B\text{',}$$

$$\frac{RB}{B} = \frac{P}{B}$$

$$R = \frac{P}{B}$$

Solution
continued

(iii) $y = mx + b$ (m)

$$mx + b = y$$

Subtracting 'b' from both sides,

$$mx + b - b = y - b$$

$$mx = y - b$$

Dividing both sides by 'x',

$$\frac{mx}{x} = \frac{y - b}{x}$$

$$m = \frac{y - b}{x}$$

(iv) $S = P(1 + rt)$ (P)

$$P(1 + rt) = S$$

Dividing both sides by '$(1 + rt)$',

$$\frac{P(1 + rt)}{(1 + rt)} = \frac{S}{(1 + rt)}$$

$$P = \frac{S}{(1 + rt)}$$

Example 4.6-b **Rearranging Formulas Involving Fractions**

Rearrange the following formulas to isolate the variables indicated in the brackets:

(i) $R = \dfrac{Vd}{t}$ (t)

(ii) $F = \left(\dfrac{9}{5}\right)C + 32$ (C)

(iii) $M = \dfrac{1}{3}S + \dfrac{2}{3}D$ (D)

Solution

(i) $R = \dfrac{Vd}{t}$ (t)

$$R = \frac{Vd}{t}$$

Multiplying both sides by 't',

$$Rt = Vd$$

Dividing both sides by 'R',

$$t = \frac{Vd}{R}$$

(ii) $F = \left(\dfrac{9}{5}\right)C + 32$ (C)

$$\frac{9}{5}C + 32 = F$$

Subtracting 32 from both sides,

$$\frac{9}{5}C = F - 32$$

Multiplying both sides by $\frac{5}{9}$ (the reciprocal of $\frac{9}{5}$),

$$\frac{5}{9}\left(\frac{9}{5}C\right) = \frac{5}{9}(F - 32)$$

$$C = \frac{5}{9}(F - 32)$$

Solution continued

(iii) $M = \frac{1}{3}S + \frac{2}{3}D$ (D)

$\frac{1}{3}S + \frac{2}{3}D = M$ Multiplying both sides by the LCD 3,

$S + 2D = 3M$ Subtracting 'S' from both sides,

$2D = 3M - S$ Dividing both sides by 2,

$D = \frac{3M - S}{2}$

Example 4.6-c

Rearranging Formulas Involving Powers and Roots

Rearrange the following formulas to isolate the variables indicated in the brackets:

(i) $F = \frac{mV^2}{r}$ (V)

(ii) $y = \sqrt{x - a}$ (x)

Solution

(i) $F = \frac{mV^2}{r}$ (V)

$\frac{mV^2}{r} = F$ Multiplying both sides by 'r',

$mV^2 = Fr$ Dividing both sides by 'm',

$V^2 = \frac{Fr}{m}$ Taking the square root on both sides,

$V = \sqrt{\frac{Fr}{m}}$

(ii) $y = \sqrt{x - a}$ (x)

$\sqrt{x - a} = y$ Squaring both sides,

$x - a = y^2$ Adding 'a' to both sides,

$x = a + y^2$

Example 4.6-d

Rearranging Formulas Involving Expanding and Factoring

Rearrange the following formulas to isolate the variables indicated in the brackets:

(i) $y = \frac{x + a}{x - a}$ (x)

(ii) $y = (x + y)(x - y)$ (x)

Solution

(i) $y = \frac{x + a}{x - a}$ (x)

$y = \frac{x + a}{x - a}$ Multiplying both sides by '$(x - a)$',

$y(x - a) = x + a$ Expanding the bracket,

$xy - ay = x + a$ Adding 'ay' to both sides,

Solution *continued*

$$xy = x + a + ay$$ Subtracting 'x' from both sides,

$$xy - x = ay + a$$ Factoring 'x' on the left side and 'a' on the right side,

$$x(y - 1) = a(y + 1)$$ Dividing both sides by '$(y - 1)$',

$$x = \frac{a(y + 1)}{(y - 1)}$$

(ii) $y = (x + y)(x - y)$ (x)

$$(x + y)(x - y) = y$$ Expanding the brackets,

$$x^2 - y^2 = y$$ Adding 'y^2' to both sides,

$$x^2 = y^2 + y$$ Taking square roots on both sides,

$$x = \sqrt{y^2 + y}$$ Factoring 'y' on the right side within the root,

$$x = \sqrt{y(y + 1)}$$

Example 4.6-e **Rearranging the Formula and Evaluating to Find the Value of a Subject**

The area 'A' of a rectangle of length 'l' and width 'w' is given by the formula $A = l \cdot w$

(i) Rearrange the formula to find 'w' as the subject.

(ii) Calculate the width (w) of a rectangle whose area is 200 cm^2 and whose length is 25 cm.

Solution

(i) $A = l \cdot w$ (w)

$$l \cdot w = A$$ Dividing both sides by 'l',

$$w = \frac{A}{l}$$

(ii) Substituting the values for 'A' and 'l' in the rearranged formula,

$$w = \frac{200}{25} = 8 \text{ cm}$$

Example 4.6-f **Rearranging a Formula and Evaluating to Find the Value of a Subject**

The area 'A' of a circle is given by the formula $A = \pi r^2$, where 'r' is the radius of the circle.

(i) Rearrange the formula to find 'r' as the subject.

(ii) Calculate the radius (r) of a circle whose area is 400 cm^2. Use $\pi = 3.14$. (Round the answer to two decimal places).

Solution

(i) $A = \pi r^2$ (r)

$$\pi r^2 = A$$ Dividing both sides by 'π',

$$r^2 = \frac{A}{\pi}$$ Taking the square root on both sides,

$$r = \sqrt{\frac{A}{\pi}}$$

Solution
continued

(ii) Substituting the values for 'A' and 'π' in the rearranged formula,

$$r = \sqrt{\frac{400}{3.14}}$$

$$= 11.286652... = 11.29 \text{ cm}$$

4.6 | Exercises

Answers to odd-numbered problems are available at the end of the textbook.

For Problems 1 to 46, rearrange the formulas to isolate the variables indicated in the brackets.

1. $4x + 5 = y$ (x)
2. $x + 6y = 15$ (y)
3. $3x - y = 7$ (x)
4. $2y - x = 5$ (y)
5. $S = C + M$ (C)
6. $L - N = d \cdot L$ (d)
7. $N = L(1 - d)$ (L)
8. $C = 2\pi r$ (r)
9. $C + E + P = S$ (E)
10. $S - P - E = C$ (P)
11. $5x - 6 = 2x + y$ (x)
12. $3 - 5x = x + y$ (x)
13. $b = \dfrac{ac}{1 + a}$ (a)
14. $b = \dfrac{ac}{1 - a}$ (c)
15. $c = \dfrac{a - c}{b}$ (b)
16. $c = \dfrac{a + c}{b}$ (a)
17. $b = \dfrac{c + ac}{a - 2}$ (a)
18. $b = \dfrac{c - ac}{a + 2}$ (c)
19. $c = \dfrac{ab - b}{4 + a}$ (a)
20. $c = \dfrac{ab + b}{4 - a}$ (a)
21. $6(a - x) = y$ (x)
22. $4(x + a) = y$ (x)
23. $3(a + x) = x$ (x)
24. $5(y + a) = y$ (y)
25. $V^2 = u^2 + 2as$ (u)
26. $V^2 = u^2 + 2as$ (s)
27. $x^2 + y^2 = r^2$ (y)
28. $S = ut + at^2$ (u)
29. $x - y = xy$ (x)
30. $x - xy = y$ (y)
31. $y = \dfrac{x + 5}{x - 5}$ (x)
32. $x = \dfrac{y + 2}{y - 2}$ (y)
33. $y = \sqrt{2x - 5}$ (x)
34. $y = \sqrt{7 - 3x}$ (x)
35. $y = 8 - \sqrt{x}$ (x)
36. $y = \sqrt{x} + 4$ (x)
37. $r = \sqrt{\dfrac{A}{4\pi}}$ (A)
38. $C = \sqrt{a^2 + b^2}$ (a)
39. $\dfrac{x}{y} + 5 = x$ (y)
40. $7 - \dfrac{x}{y} = x$ (y)
41. $A = \dfrac{(a + b)h}{2}$ (a)
42. $A = \dfrac{(a + b)h}{2}$ (h)
43. $y = (x - 4)(x + 4)$ (x)
44. $y = (3 - x)(3 + x)$ (x)
45. $\dfrac{P_1V_1}{T_1} = \dfrac{P_2V_2}{T_2}$ (P_2)
46. $\dfrac{P_1V_1}{T_1} = \dfrac{P_2V_2}{T_2}$ (T_2)

47. The formula for the area, 'A', of a square is $A = s^2$, where 's' is the length of the side.

    a. Rearrange the formula to find 's' as the subject.

    b. Calculate the side length of a square whose area is 441 cm^2.

48. The formula for the area, 'A', of a triangle is $A = \frac{bh}{2}$, where 'b' is the base and 'h' is the height.

    a. Rearrange the formula to find 'h' as the subject.

    b. Calculate the height of the triangle whose area is 198 cm^2 and base is 18 cm.

49. The formula for the surface area, 'A', of a sphere is $A = 4\pi r^2$, where 'r' is the radius of the sphere.

    a. Rearrange the formula to find 'r' as the subject.

    b. Calculate the radius of a sphere with an area of 800 cm^2. (Use $\pi = 3.14$ and round the answer to 2 decimal places.)

50. The formula for the volume 'V' of a cone is given by the formula $V = \frac{1}{3}\pi r^2 h$, where 'r' is the radius of the base and 'h' is the perpendicular height.

    a. Rearrange the formula to find 'r' as the subject.

    b. Calculate the base radius of a cone whose volume is 900 cm^3 and perpendicular height is 10 cm. (Use $\pi = 3.14$ and round the answer to 2 decimal places.)

4.7 | Logarithms and Properties (Rules) of Logarithms

Recall from earlier chapters that roots are used to isolate and solve for the *base* of a power. We will introduce an algebraic concept used to isolate and solve for the *exponent* of a power: the **logarithm**.

Exponential Form vs Logarithmic Form

Exponential Form

Recall that a **power** is comprised of a base, a, raised to an exponent, x, to produce a number, y.

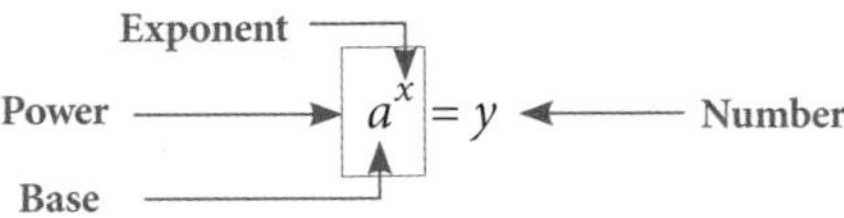

Read as: base 'a' raised to the exponent 'x' is 'y', or 'a' to the power of 'x' is 'y'.

In exponential form	Base	Exponent
$a^x = y$	a	x
$10^3 = 1{,}000$	10	3
$5^2 = 25$	5	2

Logarithmic Form

A **logarithm** is the exponent, x, to which a base, a, must be raised to obtain the number, y.

Any positive number not equal to 1 can be used as the base for logarithms.

Number

$\log_a y = x$ ← Logarithm (exponent)

Base

Read as: logarithm of 'y' to the base 'a' is 'x', or log-base-'a' of 'y' is 'x'.

In logarithmic form	Base	Exponent	In exponential form
$\log_a y = x$	a	x	$a^x = y$
$\log_{10} 1{,}000 = 3$	10	3	$10^3 = 1{,}000$
$\log_5 25 = 2$	5	2	$5^2 = 25$

Converting between Exponential and Logarithmic Forms

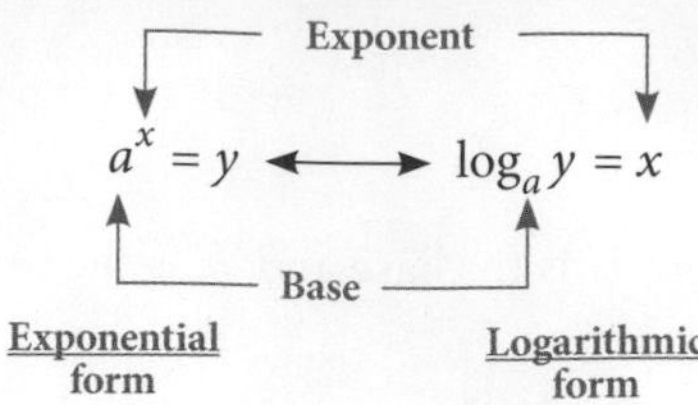

$$x \underset{\log_a y}{\overset{a^x}{\rightleftarrows}} y$$

Exponents and logarithms are inverse functions.

For example,

- $10^3 = 1{,}000$ (Exponential Form) is the same as $\log_{10} 1{,}000 = 3$ (Logarithmic Form)

$$3 \underset{\log_{10} 1{,}000}{\overset{10^3}{\rightleftarrows}} 1{,}000$$

- $5^2 = 25$ (Exponential Form) is the same as $\log_5 25 = 2$ (Logarithmic Form)

$$2 \underset{\log_5 25}{\overset{5^2}{\rightleftarrows}} 25$$

Example 4.7-a

Converting from Exponential Form to Logarithmic Form

Convert the following to logarithmic form:

(i) $6^2 = 36$ (ii) $2^6 = 64$ (iii) $7^3 = 343$

(iv) $2^{-5} = \frac{1}{32}$ (v) $16^{\frac{3}{4}} = 8$ (vi) $a^b = c$

Solution

Using $a^x = y \longleftrightarrow \log_a y = x$,

(i) $6^2 = 36$
$\log_6 36 = 2$

(ii) $2^6 = 64$
$\log_2 64 = 6$

(iii) $7^3 = 343$
$\log_7 343 = 3$

(iv) $2^{-5} = \frac{1}{32}$
$\log_2 \left(\frac{1}{32}\right) = -5$

(v) $16^{\frac{3}{4}} = 8$
$\log_{16} 8 = \frac{3}{4}$

(vi) $a^b = c$
$\log_a c = b$

Example 4.7-b

Converting from Logarithmic Form to Exponential Form

Convert the following to exponential form:

(i) $\log_3 81 = 4$ (ii) $\log_2 128 = 7$ (iii) $\log_3 2{,}187 = 7$

(iv) $\log_2 \left(\frac{1}{16}\right) = -4$ (v) $\log_{27} 9 = \frac{2}{3}$ (vi) $\log_a b = c$

Solution

Using $\log_a y = x \longleftrightarrow a^x = y$,

(i) $\log_3 81 = 4$
$3^4 = 81$

(ii) $\log_2 128 = 7$
$2^7 = 128$

(iii) $\log_3 2{,}187 = 7$
$3^7 = 2{,}187$

(iv) $\log_2 \left(\frac{1}{16}\right) = -4$
$2^{-4} = \frac{1}{16}$

(v) $\log_{27} 9 = \frac{2}{3}$
$27^{\frac{2}{3}} = 9$

(vi) $\log_a b = c$
$a^c = b$

Common Logarithms (log)

Common logarithms always have a base of 10. If no base is shown in a logarithmic expression, it is assumed to be a common logarithm of base 10 and is referred to simply by the symbol '**log**'.

Common Logarithmic Form	Exponential Form
$\log_{10} 1{,}000 = \log 1{,}000 = 3$	$10^3 = 1{,}000$
$\log_{10} 100 = \log 100 = 2$	$10^2 = 100$
$\log_{10} 10 = \log 10 = 1$	$10^1 = 10$
$\log_{10} 1 = \log 1 = 0$	$10^0 = 1$
$\log_{10} 0.1 = \log 0.1 = -1$	$10^{-1} = 0.1$
$\log_{10} 0.01 = \log 0.01 = -2$	$10^{-2} = 0.01$
$\log_{10} y = \log y = x$	$10^x = y$

Example 4.7-c Calculating the Common Logarithm of Powers of 10

Calculate the following, without the use of a calculator:

(i) log 1,000,000 (ii) log 1 (iii) log 0.001 (iv) $\log (10^n)$

Solution

(i) log 1,000,000

$10^6 = 1{,}000{,}000$ in exponential form; hence, in logarithmic form, log 1,000,000 = 6

(ii) log 1

$10^0 = 1$ in exponential form; hence, in logarithmic form, log 1 = 0

(iii) log 0.001

$10^{-3} = 0.001$ in exponential form; hence, in logarithmic form, log 0.001 = –3

(iv) $\log (10^n)$

Using the previous three examples as a pattern, we can deduce that $\log 10^n = n$.

Example 4.7-d Estimating and Calculating Common Logarithms using a Calculator

First, estimate the following common logarithms without the use of a calculator. Then, calculate the exact value of each of the logarithms using a calculator, rounded to 4 decimal places (as needed).

(i) log 10,000 (ii) log 40 (iii) log 6.5 (iv) log 0.25

Solution

We can use the log button on a scientific calculator to solve common logarithms.

(i) Since $10^4 = 10{,}000$, we can compute exactly that log 10,000 = 4 using the method above. Using the calculator, we confirm that log 10,000 = 4.

(ii) Since $10^1 = 10$ and $10^2 = 100$, we can estimate that log 40 will be between 1 and 2. Using the calculator, we confirm that log 40 = 1.602059… = 1.6021.

(iii) Since $10^0 = 1$ and $10^1 = 10$, we can estimate that log 6.5 will be between 0 and 1. Using the calculator, we confirm that log 6.5 = 0.812913… = 0.8129.

(iv) Since $10^{-1} = 0.1$ and $10^0 = 1$, we can estimate that log 0.25 will be between –1 and 0. Using the calculator, we confirm that log 0.25 = –0.602059… = –0.6021.

Natural Logarithms (ln)

Natural logarithms are always to the base 'e' where the constant $e = 2.718281...$

e is a special irrational number in mathematics (similar to π, which is equal to 3.141592...) and is found by $\left(1 + \frac{1}{n}\right)^n$, where '$n$' is a very large number.

Assume n = 100,000. Then $e \approx \left(1 + \frac{1}{100{,}000}\right)^{100{,}000} \approx 2.718281...$

If the base of a logarithmic expression is 'e', then it is called the **natural logarithm**, and is expressed by the symbol '**ln**' (pronounced "lawn").

We know $x^0 = 1$

Thus, $10^0 = 1$ and $e^0 = 1$

Therefore,

$\log_{10} 1 = 0 \longrightarrow \log 1 = 0$

$\log_e 1 = 0 \longrightarrow \ln 1 = 0$

Natural Logarithmic Form			Exponential Form	
$\log_e 1$	$= \ln 1$	$= 0$	e^0	$= 1$
$\log_e e$	$= \ln e$	$= 1$	e^1	$= e$ (= 2.718281...)
$\log_e 10$	$= \ln 10$	$= 2.302585...$	$e^{2.302585...}$	$= 10$
$\log_e 0.01$	$= \ln 0.01$	$= -4.605170...$	$e^{-4.605170...}$	$= 0.01$

Example 4.7-e Calculating Natural Logarithms using a Calculator

Calculate the following using a calculator, rounded to 4 decimal places (as needed):

(i) ln 1,000 (ii) ln 50 (iii) ln 0.50 (iv) $\ln e^2$

Solution

Using the LN button on the calculator,

(i) ln 1,000 = 6.907755... = 6.9078

(ii) ln 50 = 3.912023... = 3.9120

(iii) ln 0.50 = −0.693147... = −0.6931

(iv) $\ln e^2 = 2$

Note: From Example 4.7-e (iv), we can deduce that $\ln e^n = n$.

Rules of Logarithms

The following rules apply to logarithms of any positive base $a \neq 1$, including common logarithms (**log**, base 10) and natural logarithms (**ln**, base e).

Table 4.7 Rules of Logarithms

	Rule	Description	Rule in Common Logarithmic Form
1.	Product Rule	The logarithm of a product equals the sum of the logarithms of the factors.	$\log_a (AB) = \log_a A + \log_a B$
2.	Quotient Rule	The logarithm of a quotient equals the difference between the logarithm of the numerator (dividend) and the logarithm of the denominator (divisor).	$\log_a \left(\frac{A}{B}\right) = \log_a A - \log_a B$

	Rule	Description	Rule in Common Logarithmic Form
3.	Power Rule	The logarithm of a number raised to an exponent equals the product of the exponent and the logarithm of the number.	$\log_a (A)^n = n \log_a A$
4.	Logarithm of 1 Rule	The logarithm of 1 is zero.	$\log_a 1 = 0$
5.	Logarithm of the Base Rule	The logarithm of a number that is the same as the base is one.	$\log_a a = 1$
6.	Logarithm of a Base Raised to a Power Rule	The logarithm of the base raised to a power is equal to the power.	$\log_a (a)^n = n$
7.	"Change of Base" Rule	The logarithm of a number with any arbitrary (positive) base is equal to the common (or natural) logarithm of the number, divided by the common (or natural) logarithm of the original base.	$\log_a A = \frac{\log A}{\log a} = \frac{\ln A}{\ln a}$

*Note: Be aware of the following **common errors**:*

(i) $\log_a (A + B) \neq \log_a A + \log_a B$

(ii) $\log_a (A - B) \neq \log_a A - \log_a B$

(iii) $(\log_a A)(\log_a B) \neq \log_a A + \log_a B$

(iv) $\frac{\log_a A}{\log_a B} \neq \log_a A - \log_a B$

The rules of logarithms can be used to combine two or more logarithmic expressions into a single logarithmic expression, as seen in the following examples.

Example 4.7-f **Evaluating Logarithms Using Rules of Logarithms, without a Calculator**

Evaluate the following common and natural logarithms without using a calculator.

(i) $\log (100 \times 100)$

(ii) $\log 200 + \log 5{,}000$

(iii) $\log 35{,}000 - \log 7 - \log 50$

(iv) $\log 8 + 3\log 5$

(v) $\log_2 32^3 - \log_3 81^4 + \log_5 125^2$

Solution

(i) $\log (100 \times 100)$ Expressing 100 as a power of 10,

$= \log (10^2 \times 10^2)$

$= \log 10^4$ Using the Power Rule,

$= 4 \log 10$

$= 4$

or

$\log (100 \times 100)$ Using the Product Rule,

$= \log 100 + \log 100$

$= \log 10^2 + \log 10^2$

$= 2 \log 10 + 2 \log 10$

$= 2 + 2$

$= 4$

(ii) $\log 200 + \log 5{,}000$ Using the Product Rule,

$= \log(200 \times 5{,}000)$

$= \log(1{,}000{,}000)$ Expressing 1,000,000 as a power of 10,

$= \log 10^6$ Using the Power Rule,

$= 6 \log 10$

$= 6$

Solution
continued

(iii) $\log 35{,}000 - \log 7 - \log 50$ — Using the Quotient Rule,

$$= \log\left[\frac{\left(\frac{35{,}000}{7}\right)}{50}\right]$$

$= \log (100)$ — Expressing 100 as a power of 10 and using the Power Rule,

$= \log 10^2 = 2 \log 10 = 2$

(iv) $\log 8 + 3\log 5$ — Using the Power Rule,

$= \log 8 + \log 5^3$

$= \log 8 + \log 125$ — Using the Product Rule,

$= \log (8 \times 125)$

$= \log (1{,}000)$ — Expressing 1,000 as a power of 10 and using the Power Rule,

$= \log 10^3 = 3 \log 10 = 3$

(v) $\log_2 32^3 - \log_3 81^4 + \log_5 125^2$ — Using the Power Rule,

$= 3\log_2 32 - 4\log_3 81 + 2\log_5 125$ — Expressing 32, 81, and 125 as powers of 2, 3, and 5, respectively,

$= 3\log_2 (2^5) - 4\log_3 (3^4) + 2\log_5 (5^3)$ — Using the Logarithm of a Base Raised to a Power Rule,

$= 3(5) - 4(4) + 2(3)$

$= 5$

Example 4.7-g — **Evaluating Logarithms Using Rules of Logarithms, with a Calculator**

Evaluate the following common and natural logarithms using a calculator, rounded to 4 decimal places (as needed).

(i) $\log\left(\frac{75}{50}\right)$ (ii) $\log (125)^5$ (iii) $\ln (275 \times 75)$

(iv) $\ln\left(\frac{4{,}750}{3{,}275}\right)$ (v) $\ln (4.25)^6$

Solution

> $\log\left(\frac{75}{50}\right)$ is equivalent to $\log\left(\frac{3}{2}\right)$ (the simplified fraction), and log 1.5 (the decimal equivalent).

(i) $\log\left(\frac{75}{50}\right)$ — Using the Quotient Rule,

$= \log 75 - \log 50$

$= 1.875061... - 1.698970...$

$= 0.176091... = 0.1761$

(ii) $\log (125)^5$ — Using the Power Rule,

$= 5 \cdot \log (125)$

$= 5 \cdot (2.096910...)$

$= 10.484550... = 10.4846$

(iii) $\ln (275 \times 75)$ — Using the Product Rule,

$= \ln 275 + \ln 75$

$= 5.616771... + 4.317488...$

$= 9.934259... = 9.9343$

Solution *continued*

(iv) $\ln\left(\frac{4,750}{3,275}\right)$ Using the Quotient Rule,

$= \ln 4,750 - \ln 3,275$

$= 8.465899... - 8.094073...$

$= 0.371826... = 0.3718$

(v) $\ln (4.25)^6$ Using the Power Rule,

$= 6 \cdot \ln (4.25)$

$= 6 \cdot (1.446918...)$

$= 8.681513... = 8.6815$

Example 4.7-h **Evaluating Logarithms with Different Bases**

Evaluate the following logarithms of various bases using natural logarithms and a calculator, rounded to 4 decimal places (as needed).

(i) $\log_2\left(\frac{4,750}{3,275}\right)$ (ii) $\log_7 (4.25)^6$ (iii) $\log_{0.25} (125)^2 + \log_{0.25} (10)^{-6}$

Solution

(i) $\log_2\left(\frac{4,750}{3,275}\right)$ Using the Quotient Rule,

$= \log_2 4,750 - \log_2 3,275$ Using the Change of Base Rule,

$= \frac{\ln 4,750}{\ln 2} - \frac{\ln 3,275}{\ln 2}$

$= \frac{\ln 4,750 - \ln 3,275}{\ln 2}$

$= \frac{8.465899... - 8.094073...}{0.693147...}$

$= \frac{0.371826...}{0.693147...}$

$= 0.536432... = 0.5364$

(ii) $\log_7 (4.25)^6$ Using the Power Rule,

$= 6 \cdot \log_7 (4.25)$ Using the Change of Base Rule,

$= \frac{6 \ln (4.25)}{\ln (7)}$

$= \frac{6(1.446918...)}{1.945910...}$

$= 4.461415... = 4.4614$

(iii) $\log_{0.25} (125)^2 + \log_{0.25} (10)^{-6}$ Using the Power Rule,

$= 2 \cdot \log_{0.25} (125) - 6 \cdot \log_{0.25} (10)$ Using the Change of Base Rule,

$= \frac{2\ln (125)}{\ln (0.25)} - \frac{6\ln (10)}{\ln (0.25)}$

$= \frac{2\ln (125) - 6\ln (10)}{\ln (0.25)}$

$= \frac{2(4.828313...) - 6(2.302585...)}{-1.386294...}$

$= \frac{-4.158883...}{-1.386294...}$

$= 3$

Example 4.7-i **Writing a Simple Logarithm**

First, write each of the following as a single logarithm. Then, evaluate the logarithm using a calculator, rounded to 4 decimal places (as needed).

(i) $2\log 3 + \log 5$ (ii) $3\log 4 - \log 8$ (iii) $5\log 2 + \log 5 - \log 10$ (iv) $\log \sqrt[3]{216}$

Solution

(i) $2\log 3 + \log 5$

$= \log 3^2 + \log 5$

$= \log (3^2 \times 5)$

$= \log 45$

$= 1.653212... = 1.6532$

(ii) $3\log 4 - \log 8$

$= \log 4^3 - \log 8$

$= \log \left(\frac{4^3}{8}\right)$

$= \log 8$

$= 0.903089... = 0.9031$

(iii) $5\log 2 + \log 5 - \log 10$

$= \log 2^5 + \log 5 - \log 10$

$= \log 32 + \log 5 - \log 10$

$= \log \left(32 \times \frac{5}{10}\right)$

$= \log 16$

$= 1.204119... = 1.2041$

(iv) $\log \sqrt[3]{216}$

$= \log (216)^{\frac{1}{3}}$

$= \log (6^3)^{\frac{1}{3}}$

$= \log 6$

$= 0.778151... = 0.7782$

Solving Algebraic Equations using Logarithms

Earlier in this chapter, we learned how to solve algebraic equations with one variable, by isolating the variable using the addition, subtraction, multiplication, and division properties of equality. However, what if the algebraic equation contains a variable in the exponent?

An equation with a variable exponent can be solved by taking the **logarithm** on **both sides** of the equation, and applying the power rule to express the unknown exponent as a multiplication factor. This is demonstrated in the following example.

Example 4.7-j **Solving Algebraic Equations using Logarithms**

Solve for n in the following equations (rounded to 4 decimal places, as needed):

(i) $1{,}024 = 2^n$ (ii) $3{,}749 = 1{,}217(1.005)^n$

Solution

Using natural logarithms:

(i) $1{,}024 = 2^n$ Taking ln on both sides,

$\ln 1{,}024 = \ln 2^n$ Using Power Rule,

$\ln 1{,}024 = n \ln 2$ Isolating n,

$n = \frac{\ln 1{,}024}{\ln 2}$

$= \frac{6.931471...}{0.693147...}$

$= 10$

or

Using common logarithms:

$1{,}024 = 2^n$ Taking log on both sides,

$\log 1{,}024 = \log 2^n$ Using Power Rule,

$\log 1{,}024 = n\log 2$ Isolating n,

$n = \frac{\log 1{,}024}{\log 2}$

$= \frac{3.010299...}{0.301029...}$

$= 10$

Solution *continued*

(ii) $3{,}749 = 1{,}217(1.005)^n$ Dividing both sides by 1,217,

$$\frac{3{,}749}{1{,}217} = (1.005)^n \quad \text{Taking ln on both sides,}$$

$$\ln\left(\frac{3{,}749}{1{,}217}\right) = \ln(1.005)^n \quad \text{Using Power Rule,}$$

$$\ln\left(\frac{3{,}749}{1{,}217}\right) = n\ln(1.005) \quad \text{Isolating } n,$$

$$n = \frac{\ln\left(\frac{3{,}749}{1{,}217}\right)}{\ln 1.005}$$

$$= \frac{1.125100...}{0.004987...}$$

$$= 225.582147... = 225.5821$$

or

$3{,}749 = 1{,}217(1.005)^n$ Dividing both sides by 1,217,

$$\frac{3{,}749}{1{,}217} = (1.005)^n \quad \text{Taking log on both sides,}$$

$$\log\left(\frac{3{,}749}{1{,}217}\right) = \log(1.005)^n \quad \text{Using Power Rule,}$$

$$\log\left(\frac{3{,}749}{1{,}217}\right) = n\log(1.005) \quad \text{Isolating } n,$$

$$n = \frac{\log\left(\frac{3{,}749}{1{,}217}\right)}{\log 1.005}$$

$$= \frac{0.488624...}{0.002166...}$$

$$= 225.582147... = 225.5821$$

4.7 | Exercises

Answers to odd-numbered problems are available at the end of the textbook.

For Problems 1 to 6, express the equations in logarithmic form.

1. a. $10^5 = 100{,}000$ b. $4^5 = 1{,}024$
2. a. $10^4 = 10{,}000$ b. $4^4 = 256$
3. a. $2^6 = 64$ b. $6^5 = 7{,}776$
4. a. $2^3 = 8$ b. $6^4 = 1{,}296$
5. a. $3^2 = 9$ b. $9^4 = 6{,}561$
6. a. $3^3 = 27$ b. $8^2 = 64$

For Problems 7 to 12, express the equations in exponential form.

7. a. $\log_{10}100 = 2$ b. $\log_4 64 = 3$
8. a. $\log_{10}1{,}000 = 3$ b. $\log_4 4{,}096 = 6$
9. a. $\log_2 32 = 5$ b. $\log_5 625 = 4$
10. a. $\log_2 4 = 2$ b. $\log_5 125 = 3$
11. a. $\log_3 729 = 6$ b. $\log_6 216 = 3$
12. a. $\log_3 243 = 5$ b. $\log_6 1{,}296 = 4$

For Problems 13 to 20, calculate the following (rounding to 4 decimal places):

13. a. log 225 b. log 1.54
14. a. log 27 b. log 2.5
15. a. log 35 b. log 0.25
16. a. log 155 b. log 0.75
17. a. ln 10.05 b. ln 1.005
18. a. ln 0.675 b. ln 750
19. a. ln 0.165 b. ln 1.02
20. a. ln 12.51 b. ln 72

For Problems 21 to 32, express the following as a sum or difference of two or more natural logarithms:

21. $\ln\left(\frac{3}{7}\right)$
22. $\ln\left(\frac{40}{13}\right)$
23. $\ln(4 \times 9)$
24. $\ln(7 \times 8)$
25. $\ln\left(\frac{AB}{C}\right)$
26. $\ln\left(\frac{x}{ab}\right)$
27. $\ln\left(\frac{X}{YZ}\right)$
28. $\ln\left(\frac{xy}{c}\right)$
29. $\ln\left(\frac{3x}{2yz}\right)$
30. $\ln\left(\frac{5x}{2ab}\right)$
31. $\ln\left(\frac{xy}{\sqrt{z}}\right)$
32. $\ln\left(\frac{x}{\sqrt{yz}}\right)$

For Problems 33 to 44, if $\log_a x = M$ and $\log_a y = N$, express the value of each of the following in terms of M and N:

33. $\log_a\left(\frac{x}{y}\right)$
34. $\log_a\left(\frac{y}{x}\right)$
35. $\log_a(xy^2)$
36. $\log_a(x^2y)$
37. $\log_a\left(\frac{x^2}{y}\right)$
38. $\log_a\left(\frac{x}{y^2}\right)$
39. $\log_a(xy)^{-\frac{1}{2}}$
40. $\log_a(yx)^{-\frac{1}{2}}$
41. $\log_a(\sqrt[5]{x^4})$
42. $\log_a\left(\frac{1}{\sqrt[3]{x^2y^2}}\right)$
43. $\log_a\left(\frac{1}{\sqrt[3]{xy}}\right)$
44. $\log_a\left(\frac{1}{\sqrt{xy^3}}\right)$

For Problems 45 to 52, calculate the following (rounding to 4 decimal places):

45. $\log_2 60$
46. $\log_{12} 2{,}100$
47. $\log_5(16.5)^3$
48. $\log_7(2.2)^{20}$
49. $\log_{0.25}\left(\frac{12{,}600}{80}\right)$
50. $\log_{0.5}\left(\frac{96{,}785}{12}\right)$
51. $\log_{20}(200)^5 + \log_{20}(80)^{-5}$
52. $\log_8(1{,}255)^4 - \log_8(950)^{-6}$

For Problems 53 to 72, express the following as a single natural logarithm:

53. $\ln 8 + \ln 5$
54. $\ln 25 + \ln 4$
55. $\ln 15 - \ln 3$
56. $\ln 60 - \ln 15$
57. $2\ln 5 + 3\ln 3$
58. $2\ln 8 + 3\ln 3$
59. $5\ln 2 - 2\ln 3$
60. $4\ln 5 - 3\ln 2$
61. $2\ln 5$
62. $5\ln 2$
63. $3\ln 6$
64. $6\ln 3$
65. $2\ln\left(\frac{x}{y}\right)$
66. $5\ln\left(\frac{a}{b}\right)$
67. $4\ln(a \times b)$
68. $3\ln(xy)$
69. $3\ln a + 2\ln b - 5\ln c$
70. $4\ln x - 2\ln y + 3\ln z$
71. $3\ln 2 + 4\ln 3 - 2\ln 4$
72. $2\ln 3 + 3\ln 2 - 4\ln 2$

For Problems 73 to 80, simplify the expressions by writing them without exponents or radicals, and then evaluate without the use of a calculator.

73. $\log_{10}\left(\sqrt{1{,}000}\right)$
74. $\log_{10}\left(\sqrt[4]{10{,}000}\right)$
75. $\log_2\left(\sqrt{64}\right)$
76. $\log_5\left(\sqrt{625}\right)$
77. $\log_3\left(\sqrt[3]{9^2}\right)$
78. $\log_2\left(\sqrt[5]{32^3}\right)$
79. $\log_{27}\left(\sqrt[4]{\frac{1}{81}}\right)$
80. $\log_{36}\left(\sqrt[3]{\frac{1}{216}}\right)$

For Problems 81 to 88, evaluate for 'n' (rounding to 4 decimal places).

81. $n = \ln\left(\frac{4{,}285}{4{,}000}\right)$
82. $n = \ln\left(\frac{6{,}750}{3{,}200}\right)$
83. $n = \ln\left(\frac{3{,}645}{2{,}175}\right)$
84. $n = \ln\left(\frac{75{,}000}{2{,}200}\right)$
85. $n = \frac{\ln\left(\frac{7{,}200}{4{,}725}\right)}{\ln(1.01)}$
86. $n = \frac{\ln\left(\frac{5{,}120}{2{,}250}\right)}{\ln(1.005)}$
87. $n = \frac{\ln(2.5)}{\ln(1.03)}$
88. $n = \frac{\ln(3)}{\ln(1.02)}$

For Problems 89 to 96, solve for 'n' (rounding to 4 decimal places).

89. $250 = (30)^n$
90. $320 = (15)^n$
91. $(1.05)^n = 1.31$
92. $2.5 = (1.05)^n$
93. $7{,}500 = (45)^n + 500$
94. $8{,}000 = (35)^n + 1{,}500$
95. $10{,}000 = 2{,}000(1.2)^n$
96. $15{,}000 = 5{,}000(1.04)^n$

4 | Review Exercises

Answers to odd-numbered problems are available at the end of the textbook.

For Problems 1 to 4, write the algebraic expression.

1. a. Twelve increased by three times a number.
   b. The difference between a number and five.
2. a. Eight decreased by twice a number.
   b. Six less than the total of a number and ten.
3. a. The product of three more than a number and the number.
   b. Sum of ten times a number and fifteen.
4. a. Sum of fifteen and half of a number.
   b. Product of two times a number and seven.

For Problems 5 to 20, simplify the algebraic terms, and express the answer with a positive exponent.

5. a. $(-x)^2 \cdot (x)^{-4}$ b. $(-x)^3 \cdot (x)^4$
6. a. $(-x)^3 \cdot (x)^{-6}$ b. $x^3 \cdot (-x)^4$
7. a. $\frac{x^8}{x^4}$ b. $\frac{x^{-6}}{x^{-4}}$
8. a. $\frac{x^7}{x^5}$ b. $\frac{x^{-2}}{x^{-3}}$
9. a. $\left(\frac{x^3}{y^{-2}}\right)^{\frac{1}{2}}$ b. $\sqrt[3]{x^6}$
10. a. $\left(\frac{x^{-3}}{y^{-2}}\right)^{\frac{2}{3}}$ b. $\sqrt[5]{x^{10}}$

11. a. $\frac{x^9}{x^5 \cdot x^2}$ b. $\frac{x^{-4}}{x^5 \cdot x^{-9}}$

12. a. $\frac{x^4 \cdot x^2}{x^3}$ b. $\frac{x^{-5}}{x^4 \cdot x^{-3}}$

13. a. $(x^4)(3x^3)$ b. $\frac{x^6}{x^2}$

14. a. $(x^3)(2x^5)$ b. $\frac{x^9}{x^6}$

15. a. $\left(\frac{x^2}{y}\right)\left(\frac{x}{2y^2}\right)^2$ b. $\frac{2x^{-4}y^6}{x^3y^{-4}}$

16. a. $\left(\frac{2x^2}{y}\right)\left(\frac{3x}{y^2}\right)^2$ b. $\frac{12x^{-5}y^2}{6x\,6y^{-8}}$

17. a. $\left(\frac{4x^3}{2y^2}\right)^3$ b. $(8x^6)^{\frac{1}{3}}$

18. a. $\left(\frac{3x^2}{4y^3}\right)^2$ b. $\left(\frac{x^0}{y^3}\right)^3$

19. a. $\left(\frac{x^7}{x^0}\right)^2$ b. $\left(\frac{3x^{-2}y^7}{6x^3y^{-5}}\right)^2$

20. a. $(4x^2)^{\frac{1}{2}}$ b. $\left(\frac{3x^{-3}y^4}{6xy^{-2}}\right)^{-3}$

For Problems 21 to 26, simplify the expressions, then evaluate for the given value of the variables in the brackets.

21. a. $-4x^2 + 3x - 5 + 7x^2 - 2x + 3$ $(x = 2)$
    b. $4x^2 - 5 + 7x - 2x^2 - x - 3$ $(x = -1)$

22. a. $3x^2 - x + 2 + x^2 - 5x - 2$ $(x = 3)$
    b. $-5y^2 - 7y + 3 + y^2 - 5y + 2$ $(y = -2)$

23. a. $-y^2 + 4xy + x^2 - 6y^2 - xy - 11x^2$ $(x = 1, y = 2)$
    b. $(x - 4)(x + 2) + 3(x + 2)$ $(x = 3)$

24. a. $-4x^2 + 6xy - 6y^2 + 6x^2 - 2xy + 3y^2$ $(x = 2, y = 1)$
    b. $(y - 2)(y - 3) + 2(y - 2)$ $(y = 4)$

25. a. $(2x - 3)^2 - (x + 3)^2$ $(x = 4)$
    b. $(5 + x)^2 + (4 - x)(4 + x)$ $(x = 5)$

26. a. $(2x + 1)^2 - (x - 2)^2$ $(x = 1)$
    b. $(3 - x)^2 + (x - 3)(x + 3)$ $(x = 2)$

For Problems 27 and 28, factor the expressions using the GCF, then evaluate for the given value of the variables in the brackets.

27. a. $6x^2 - 4x$ $(x = 1)$
    b. $7xy + 14x^2$ $(x = 3, y = 2)$

28. a. $8y^2 - 64y$ $(y = 2)$
    b. $15y^2 + 10xy$ $(x = -1, y = 2)$

For Problems 29 and 30, factor the expressions by grouping.

29. a. $6x^3 - 2x^2 + 15x - 5$
    b. $xy - 3y + 5x - 15$

30. a. $6x^3 + 12x^2 + 3x + 6$
    b. $y^2 - xy + 2y - 2x$

For Problems 31 and 32, factor the differences of squares.

31. a. $4x^2 - 9$
    b. $25x^2 - 64y^2$

32. a. $1 - 16x^2$
    b. $81x^2 - 144y^2$

For Problems 33 to 36, factor the trinomials.

33. a. $x^2 + 5x - 36$
    b. $4x^2 + 16x + 15$

34. a. $x^2 - 4x - 77$
    b. $5x^2 + 20x - 60$

35. a. $x^2 + 16x + 64$
    b. $9x^2 - 24x + 16$

36. a. $4x^2 + 4x + 1$
    b. $x^2 - 8xy + 7y^2$

For Problems 37 to 40, write the algebraic equation and solve.

37. a. Seventeen more than five times a number is forty-two.
    b. A number divided by fifteen is forty-five.

38. a. The product of five and a number is seventy-five.
    b. Three more than two times a number is nine.

39. a. The difference between a number and ten is ten.
    b. The product of four times a number and three is thirty-six.

40. a. The sum of two times a number and eight is one hundred.
    b. A number divided by three is seven.

For Problems 41 to 44, solve for the unknown variable, x, using the principles of equality.

41. a. $5x - 5 = 10$ b. $\frac{x}{3} + 4 = 10$

42. a. $3x - 5 = -17$ b. $\frac{x}{4} - 2 = 1$

43. a. $12 - 3x = 3 - 4x$ b. $4(x + 4) = 24$

44. a. $4x - 2 = 13 - 6x$ b. $3(2x - 5) = 3$

45. The formula for the circumference of a circle is $C = 2\pi r$.

a. Rearrange to isolate the variable 'r'.

b. Calculate 'r' to 2 decimal places when $C = 75$ cm.

46. The formula for the volume of a cylinder is $V = \pi r^2 h$.

a. Rearrange to isolate the variable 'r'.

b. Calculate 'r' when $V = 300$ cm^3 and $h = 15$ cm. Round to 2 decimal places.

47. The formula for the volume of a cone is $V = \frac{1}{3}\pi r^2 h$.

a. Rearrange to isolate the variable 'h'.

b. Calculate 'h', when $r = 11$ cm and $V = 4{,}560$ cm^3. Round the answer to 2 decimal places.

48. The formula for the volume of a cone is $V = \frac{1}{3}\pi r^2 h$.

a. Rearrange to isolate the variable 'r'.

b. Calculate 'r', when $V = 2{,}280$ cm^3 and $h = 15$ cm. Round the answer to 2 decimal places.

For Problems 49 to 52, evaluate for 'n'. Round to 4 decimal places.

49. a. $n = \dfrac{\ln\left(\dfrac{2{,}775}{1{,}200}\right)}{\ln(1.03)}$ b. $n = \dfrac{\ln(3)}{\ln(1.02)}$

50. a. $n = \dfrac{\ln\left(\dfrac{4{,}950}{1{,}250}\right)}{\ln(1.005)}$ b. $n = \dfrac{\ln(1{,}200)}{\ln(5)}$

51. a. $n = \dfrac{\log(500)}{\log(2)}$ b. $n = \dfrac{\log(2)}{\log(1.05)}$

52. a. $n = \dfrac{\log\left(\dfrac{4{,}235}{1{,}615}\right)}{\log(1.048)}$ b. $n = \dfrac{\log(320)}{\log(4)}$

For Problems 53 to 58, express the following as a single natural logarithm:

53. a. $\ln 3 + \ln 11$ b. $\ln 16 - \ln 4$

54. a. $\ln 7 + \ln 2$ b. $\ln 45 - \ln 15$

55. a. $2\ln\left(\dfrac{2}{3}\right)$ b. $3\ln(2 \times 5)$

56. a. $3\ln\left(\dfrac{4a}{2b}\right)$ b. $6\ln(2ab)$

57. $4\ln s + 5\ln t - 3\ln r$

58. $3\ln a + 4\ln b - 7\ln a$

For Problems 59 to 62, solve for 'n'. Round to 4 decimal places.

59. a. $2{,}060 = 1{,}225(1.02)^n$ b. $5{,}215 = (1.005)^n + 600$

60. a. $6{,}075 = 4{,}150(1.03)^n$ b. $4{,}815 = (1.04)^n + 900$

61. a. $2{,}187 = 3^n$ b. $1{,}000 = 7^n - 1{,}401$

62. a. $15{,}625 = 5^n$ b. $6{,}000 = 3^n - 561$

Self-Test | Chapter 4

Answers to all problems are available at the end of the textbook.

For Problems 1 and 2, write the algebraic expression.

1. a. Twenty-five less than three times a number.
   b. A number increased by eighteen.

2. a. The difference between twice a number and six.
   b. A number divided by three.

For Problems 3 to 5, simplify the algebraic terms, and express the answer with a positive exponent.

3. a. $(-x)^3(-x)^4$ b. $\frac{(-x)^{-5}(-x)^3}{(-x)^{-4}}$

4. a. $(x^{-6})^{\frac{1}{3}}$ b. $\sqrt[3]{x^6}$

5. a. $(16x^0y^4)^{\frac{1}{2}}$ b. $(-2x^{-2}y^{-4})^{-1}(2x^{-2})^2$

For Problems 6 and 7, simplify the expressions, then evaluate for the given value of the variables in the brackets.

6. a. $-3x^2 + 2x + 2x^2 - 8x + 10$ $(x = -3)$
   b. $5(2x - 3y) - 2(3x - 2y) + 7$ $(x = 2 \text{ and } y = 1)$

7. a. $(x + 3)^2 - (x + 2)(x - 2)$ $(x = 3)$
   b. $(2x + 5)^2 - (3x - 1)^2$ $(x = 1)$

For Problems 8 to 11, factor the expressions.

8. a. $8xy^2 - 6x^2y$
   b. $10ab - 8bc$

9. a. $4xy - 20y - x^2 + 5x$
   b. $1 - 121x^2$

10. a. $2x^2 - 22x + 56$
    b. $4x^2 - 9x - 9$

11. a. $x^2 + 10x + 25$
    b. $x^2 + 6xy - 16y^2$

For Problems 12 and 13, write the algebraic equation and solve.

12. a. Nine less than twice a number is twenty-one.
    b. Twenty-two is five times a number less than three.

13. a. Four times eight is sixteen times a number.
    b. Thirty is a product of six and a number.

For Problems 14 and 15, solve for the unknown variable, x, using the principles of equality.

14. a. $24 - 5x = 4$ b. $\frac{x}{3} - 2 = 4$

15. a. $8 + 2x = 4 - 5x$ b. $3(3x - 3) = 33$

16. Given the formula $C = \frac{5}{9}(F - 32)$:
    a. Rearrange to isolate the variable 'F'.
    b. Calculate the value of 'F' when $C = 30$ °C. Round to 2 decimal places.

17. Given the formula $A = 2\pi r(r + h)$:
    a. Rearrange to isolate the variable 'h'.
    b. Calculate the value of 'h' when $A = 1{,}200$ cm^2 and $r = 10$ cm. Round to 2 decimal places.

18. Solve for 'n'. Round to 4 decimal places.
    a. $n = \frac{\ln\left(\frac{2{,}200}{1{,}200}\right)}{\ln(1.04)}$ b. $n = \frac{\log(5{,}000)}{\log(3)}$

19. Express the following as a single natural logarithm:
    $2\ln 3 + 3\ln 2 - 5\ln 3$

20. Solve for 'n'. Round to 4 decimal places.
    a. $460 = 240(1.05)^n$ b. $750 = (1.05)^n + 600$

Chapter 5 PERCENTS, PERCENT CHANGES, AND APPLICATIONS

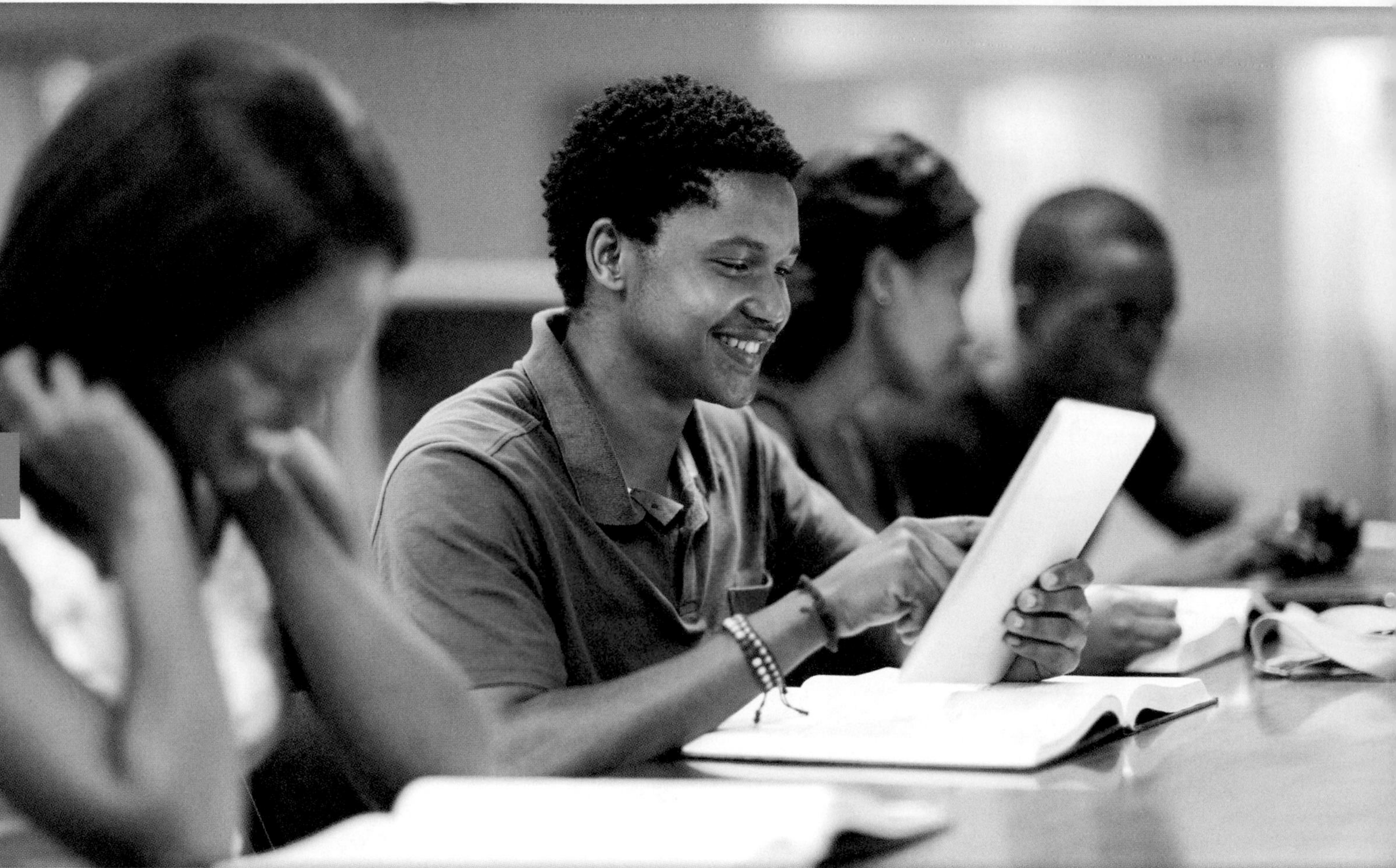

LEARNING OBJECTIVES

- Convert percents to equivalent fractions and decimal numbers.
- Solve percent problems using different methods.
- Calculate bases, rates, or portions of quantities, expressed in percents.
- Identify the terminology used in percent change.
- Use percents to measure percent increase and decrease.
- Calculate the amount and rate of simple interest, principal, time period, and maturity value of investments and loans.
- Calculate gross pay based on annual salary, sales commissions, and hourly rate.

CHAPTER OUTLINE

Introduction

In Chapter 2, we learned that fractions and decimal numbers are used to represent portions of a whole number or quantity. In this chapter, we will learn about another form used to represent a part of a whole: **percents**.

Percents are used to represent the number of parts per one hundred. Due to their simplicity, percents are a widely accepted measure for expressing fractions and decimal numbers. They make comparisons easy, and are used often in our daily lives and in making business decisions; some examples of the use of percents include the interest rate charged by a bank on a loan, the discount offered at a store, the sales tax charged on items purchased, and the commission received by a sales representative.

In this chapter, we will learn the relationship between fractions, decimal numbers, and percents, and learn to solve problems related to percents and percent changes, including business applications such as calculating simple interest and payroll.

5.1 | Percents

Percent is the number of parts per hundred:

$C\% = \frac{C}{100} = 0.01C$

Percent (per cent or per hundred in the literal meaning) is used to express a quantity out of 100 units and is represented by the symbol '%'.

For example, 5% means 5 **per** hundred, or 5 out of 100, or $\frac{5}{100}$ ($5\% = \frac{5}{100} = 0.05$).

- 100% means 100 out of 100 (i.e, the whole quantity)
- 75% means 75 out of 100 (i.e., $\frac{75}{100} = \frac{3}{4}$ or 0.75)
- 50% means 50 out of 100 (i.e., $\frac{50}{100} = \frac{1}{2}$ or 0.50)
- 25% means 25 out of 100 (i.e., $\frac{25}{100} = \frac{1}{4}$ or 0.25)

Note: A percent greater than 100 *is typically expressed as a comparison to the original amount, rather than as parts of a whole.*

For example, 200% *means* 2 *times (or double, or twice) the whole quantity; although technically correct, it is not meaningful to say* 200% *means* 200 *out of* 100 *(since the total number of parts exceeds the whole). Similarly,* 350% *means* $3\frac{1}{2}$ *times the whole quanity.*

Relationship Among Percents, Fractions, and Decimal Numbers

Fractions and decimal numbers can be converted to percents and vice-versa. For example, 3 out of 4 equal parts of a quantity can be represented as a fraction, decimal number, or in percent form, as follows:

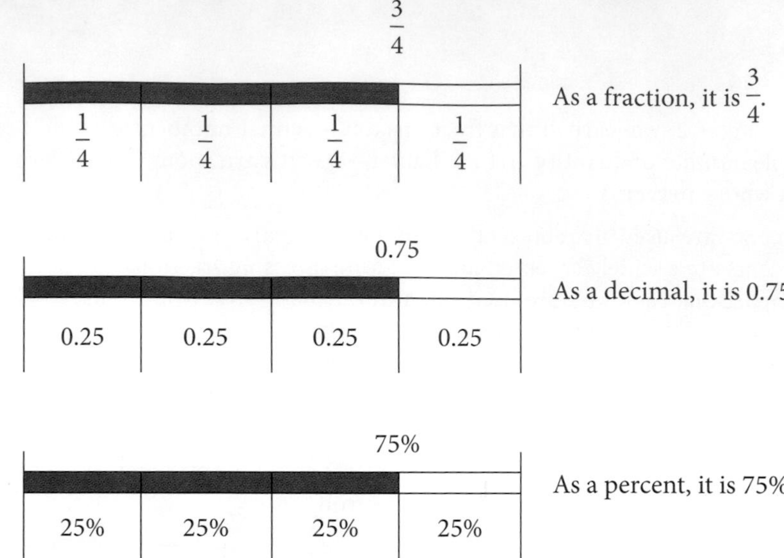

In day-to-day business, percents are commonly used to represent interest rates, sales, discounts, commissions, comparison of changes in quantity, etc. However, in actual calculations, fractions or decimal equivalents are used. Therefore, it is necessary to know the methods for converting from one form to the other.

Converting Percents to Decimal Numbers

- **If the percent is a whole number or a decimal number,** remove the '%' sign and move the decimal point two places to the left. This is the same as dividing the number by 100 and removing the '%' sign.

For example,

- To convert 45% to a decimal number,

$45\% = 45.0$	Remove the % sign and move the decimal point two places to the left.
$= 0.45$	This is the same as $\frac{45\%}{100\%} = 0.45$.

Therefore 45% = 0.45.

- To convert 0.38% to a decimal number,

$0.38\% = 0.38$	Remove the % sign and move the decimal point two places to the left.
$= 0.0038$	This is the same as $= \frac{0.38\%}{100\%} = 0.0038$.

Therefore 0.38% = 0.0038.

- **If the percent is a fraction or a mixed number**, change it to its decimal equivalent and follow the steps as shown above.

For example,

If the fraction produces a decimal number which is non-terminating, a horizontal bar should be used to show repeating decimal places.

e.g., $8\frac{1}{3}\% = 8.\overline{3}\% = 0.08\overline{3}$

- To convert $2\frac{1}{2}\%$ to a decimal number,

$2\frac{1}{2}\% = 2.5\%$	Convert the mixed number to a decimal number.
$= 2.5$	Remove the % sign and move the decimal point two places to the left.
$= 0.025$	This is the same as $\frac{2.5\%}{100\%} = 0.025$.

Therefore, $2\frac{1}{2}\% = 0.025$.

Example 5.1-a

Converting Percents to Decimal Numbers

Convert each percent to its equivalent decimal number.

(i) 85% (ii) $5\frac{1}{4}\%$ (iii) 20.75% (iv) 225% (v) $\frac{2}{3}\%$

Solution

(i) 85% = 85.0% = 85.0 = 0.85 (ii) $5\frac{1}{4}\%$ = 5.25% = 5.25 = 0.0525

(iii) 20.75% = 20.75 = 0.2075 (iv) 225% = 225.0% = 225.0 = 2.25

(v) $\frac{2}{3}\% = 0.666666...\% = 0.\overline{6}\% = 0.\overline{6} = 0.00\overline{6}$

Converting Decimal Numbers to Percents

- To convert a decimal number or a whole number to a percent, move the decimal point two places to the right and insert the '%' sign. This is the same as multiplying the number by 100 and inserting the '%' sign.

For example,

- To convert 0.35 to a percent,

0.35 = 0.35%	Move the decimal point two places to the right and insert the % sign.
= 35%	This is the same as 0.35 × 100% = 35%.

Therefore 0.35 = 35%.

- To convert 5 to a percent,

5 = 5.00%	Move the decimal point two places to the right and insert the % sign.
= 500%	This is the same as 5 × 100% = 500%.

Therefore, 5 = 500%.

Example 5.1-b

Converting Decimal Numbers to Percents

Convert each decimal number to its equivalent percent.

(i) 0.45 (ii) 0.03 (iii) 5.25 (iv) 0.002

Solution

(i) 0.45 = 0.45% = 45% (ii) 0.03 = 0.03% = 3%

(iii) 5.25 = 5.25% = 525% (iv) 0.002 = 0.002% = 0.2%

Example 5.1-c

Application of Converting from Decimal to Percent

If Alexander earns three times the amount that Emma earns, what percent is Alexander's earnings compared to Ema's earnings?

Solution

Here, '3 times' when converted to a percent = 3 × 100% = 300%.

Therefore, Alexander's earnings are 300% of Emma's.

Note: This also means that Alexander earns 200% ***more than*** *Emma. It is important not to confuse these two statements!*

Converting Percents to Fractions

- **If the percent is a whole number,** remove the percent sign and divide by 100 (or multiply by $\frac{1}{100}$). Reduce the resulting fraction to its lowest terms.

For example, to convert 60% to a fraction in its lowest terms,

$60\% = \frac{60}{100}$ Reduce the fraction to its lowest terms.

$= \frac{3}{5}$

Therefore, $60\% = \frac{3}{5}$.

If the percent is a repeating decimal number, the decimal number must first be converted into a fraction using the method described in Section 2.5.

- **If the percent is a decimal number**, remove the percent sign and divide by 100; eliminate the decimal in the numerator of the resulting fraction by multiplying both the numerator and denominator by an appropriate power of 10. Reduce the fraction to its lowest terms.

For example, to convert 42.5% to a fraction,

$42.5\% = \frac{42.5}{100}$ Eliminate the decimal in the numerator by multiplying both the numerator and the denominator by 10.

$= \frac{425}{1{,}000}$ Reduce the fraction to its lowest terms.

$= \frac{17}{40}$

Therefore, $42.5\% = \frac{17}{40}$.

- **If the percent is a fraction or a mixed number,** either convert it to its decimal equivalent and follow the steps outlined above, or convert it to an improper fraction (if required), remove the percent sign, and multiply the fraction by $\frac{1}{100}$.

For example, to convert $6\frac{1}{2}\%$ to a fraction,

Method 1: By converting it to its decimal equivalent

$6\frac{1}{2}\% = 6.5\%$ Remove the percent sign and divide by 100.

$= \frac{6.5}{100}$ Eliminate the decimal in the numerator by multiplying both the numerator and the denominator by 10.

$= \frac{65}{1{,}000}$ Reduce the fraction to its lowest terms.

$= \frac{13}{200}$

If the decimal equivalent of a fraction is a repeating decimal number, Method 2 must be used.

e.g., $2\frac{2}{3}\% = \frac{8}{3}\% = \frac{8}{3} \times \frac{1}{100}$

$= \frac{8}{300} = \frac{2}{75}$

Method 2: By converting it to its improper fractional equivalent

$6\frac{1}{2}\% = \frac{13}{2}\%$ Remove the percent sign and multiply the fraction by $\frac{1}{100}$.

$= \frac{13}{2} \times \frac{1}{100}$ Simplify.

$= \frac{13}{200}$

Therefore, $6\frac{1}{2}\% = \frac{13}{200}$.

Example 5.1-d **Converting Percents to Fractions**

Convert each percent to its equivalent fraction or mixed number and simplify to lowest terms.

(i) 45% (ii) $8\frac{1}{3}\%$ (iii) 6.25% (iv) 175% (v) $\frac{1}{5}\%$

Solution

(i) $45\% = \frac{45}{100} = \frac{9}{20}$

(ii) $8\frac{1}{3}\% = \frac{25}{3}\% = \frac{\overset{1}{\cancel{25}}}{3} \times \frac{1}{\cancel{100}_4} = \frac{1}{3} \times \frac{1}{4} = \frac{1}{12}$

(iii) $6.25\% = \frac{6.25}{100} = \frac{6.25}{100} \times \frac{100}{100} = \frac{625}{10{,}000} = \frac{1}{16}$

(iv) $175\% = \frac{175}{100} = \frac{7}{4} = 1\frac{3}{4}$

(v) $\frac{1}{5}\% = \frac{1}{5} \times \frac{1}{100} = \frac{1}{500}$

Converting Fractions or Mixed Numbers to Percents

- To convert a fraction or a mixed number to a percent, first convert the fraction or the mixed number to a decimal number. Then, convert the decimal number to a percent by moving the decimal point two places to the right and inserting the '%' sign. This is the same as multiplying the decimal by 100 and inserting the '%' sign.

For example,

- To convert $\frac{3}{8}$ to a percent,

$\frac{3}{8} = 0.375$	Convert the fraction to its decimal equivalent.
$= 0.375\%$	Convert the decimal to percent, by moving the decimal point two places to the right and inserting the % sign.
$= 37.5\%$	This is the same as $0.375 \times 100\% = 37.5\%$.

Therefore $\frac{3}{8} = 37.5\%$.

- To convert $5\frac{1}{2}$ to a percent

$5\frac{1}{2} = 5.50$	Convert the fraction to its decimal equivalent.
$= 5.50\%$	Convert the decimal to percent, by moving the decimal point two places to the right and inserting the % sign.
$= 550\%$	This is the same as $5.50 \times 100\% = 550\%$.

Therefore $5\frac{1}{2} = 550\%$.

Example 5.1-e **Converting Fractions or Mixed Numbers to Percents**

Convert each of the following fractions to its equivalent percent.

(i) $\frac{3}{25}$ (ii) $5\frac{1}{4}$ (iii) $\frac{18}{5}$ (iv) $\frac{1}{200}$

Solution

(i) $\frac{3}{25} = 0.12$

$= 0.12\% = 12\%$

(ii) $5\frac{1}{4} = 5.25$

$= 5.25\% = 525\%$

(iii) $\frac{18}{5} = 3.60$

$= 3.60\% = 360\%$

(iv) $\frac{1}{200} = 0.005$

$= 0.005\% = 0.5\%$

Example 5.1-f **Application of Converting from Fractions to Percents**

Peter and Angela study Business Mathematics, but at different colleges. Peter scored 46 out of 60 on his final exam, while Angela scored 63 out of 75 on her exam. Who received a better grade on their exam?

Solution

It is not possible to answer the question by simple observation, because Peter's score is expressed out of 60, while Angela's score is expressed out of 75. To compare their scores, we can convert them to their percent equivalents, as shown below:

$$\text{Peter's score: } \frac{46}{60} = 0.766666... = 76.67\%$$

$$\text{Angela's score: } \frac{63}{75} = 0.84 = 84\%$$

Therefore, Angela received a better grade than Peter on the exam.

Example 5.1-g **Comparing Fractions and Percents**

Out of 54 students in Class A, 43 students passed the final exam. In Class B, 78% of the students passed the final exam. Which class had the better pass rate?

Solution

$$\text{Class A: Fraction of students passed} = \frac{43}{54}$$

$$\text{Percent of students passed} = \frac{43}{54} \times 100\%$$

$$= 0.796296... \times 100\%$$

$$= 79.63\%$$

Class B: Percent of students passed = 78%

Therefore, Class A had a better pass rate.

Solving Percent Problems

Many methods may be used to solve percent problems. Described below are three common methods:

Method 1: Formula Method

Every percent problem will contain three variables: *B*, *P*, and *R*.

Base (*B*): Whole quantity or value (100%). It usually follows the word 'of', or 'percent of'.

R% converted to a fraction is $\frac{R}{100}$ and converted to a decimal is $0.01R$.

Portion (P): Portion of the whole quantity or value (i.e., portion of the base).

Rate (R): Relationship between the base and portion, usually expressed as a percent. It usually carries the percent sign (%) or the word '**percent**'.

Every percent statement can be expressed as: ***P* is *R*% of *B*.** The value of ***R*** is used as a decimal or fractional equivalent in calculations.

The relationship between these variables can be expressed as follows:

$$\textit{Portion} = \textit{Rate} \times \textit{Base}$$

Or,

Formula 5.1

Portion

$$P = R \times B$$

Rearranging, we obtain $R = \frac{P}{B}$ and $B = \frac{P}{R}$.

Therefore, if any two of these quantities are known, then the third quantity can be calculated.

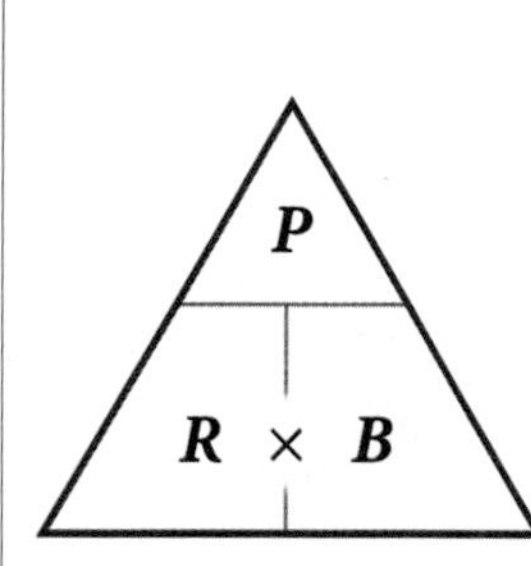

***P, R, B* triangle**

Here is a triangle that can be used to help in rearranging the formula $P = R \times B$ to solve for the variable R or B.

Variables beside each other at the bottom are multiplied, ($R \times B$, as shown).

Variable P is divided by the variables at the bottom.

Cover the variable for which you want to solve to see the new formula.

For example, if you want to solve for R, the formula can be found by covering R and reading the remaining variables in the triangle, to obtain $R = \frac{P}{B}$

Method 2: Algebraic Method

Solving problems using algebraic methods involve forming an equation for an unknown 'x' and then solving for 'x'. In this method, we assume that the unknown is 'x', and form equation(s) for the given problem (or statement) using key words to represent certain arithmetic operations.

The following are key words and phrases that are commonly used to indicate various arithmetic operations.

Operation	Key words
Addition (+)	Add, sum, total, and, plus, more than, increased by, appreciate, rise
Subtraction (−)	Subtract, difference, minus, less than, decreased by, depreciate, fall
Multiplication (× or () or ·)	Multiply, product, times, of
Division (÷ or /)	Divide, ratio, divided by, quotient, per
Equal (=)	Is, was, gives, given by
Unknown value (denoted by a variable, such as 'x')	What, how much

For example, we can use these key words to form the algebraic equations for the following:

- What percent of 200 is 60

  $x\% \quad \times 200 = 60$

  $x\% \times 200 = 60$

- \$52 is 13% of what amount

  $\$52 = 13\% \times \quad x$

  $\$52 = 13\%(x)$

- 40% of what amount is \$280

  $40\% \times \quad x \quad = \$280$

  $40\%(x) = \$280$

- How much is 2% of 75

  $x \quad = 2\% \times 75$

  $x = 2\% \times 75$

Method 3: Ratio-Proportion Method

The whole amount or quantity is represented by 100% and is known as the **base** (*B*). The **portion** (*P*) is a part of the base and it forms a percent, or **rate** (*R*%), of the base. Thus, in the ratio-proportion method, we first identify the base, portion, and rate in the problem, then solve for the unknown using the following proportion equation:

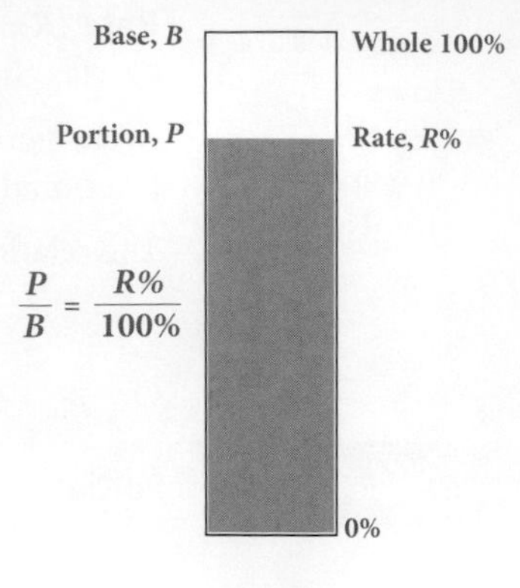

$$\text{Portion} : \text{Base} = \text{Rate} : 100\%$$

$$P : B = R\% : 100\%$$

$$\frac{P}{B} = \frac{R\%}{100\%}$$

$$\frac{P}{B} = \frac{R}{100}$$

Note: We will learn more about ratios, proportions, and their applications in Chapter 6.

Example 5.1-h **Calculating the Portion of a Whole Quantity**

What is 75% of \$250? (Or, 75% of \$250 is how much?)

Solution

Method 1: Using the Formula Method

$R\% = 75\%$ (value with % sign); i.e., $R = 0.75$

$B = \$250$ (value that follows the word 'of')

$P = ?$ (the other value)

Using Formula 5.1, $P = R \times B$ — Substituting values for R and B,

$P = 0.75 \times 250.00$ — Simplifying,

$= \$187.50$

Method 2: Using the Algebraic Method

What is 75% of \$250?

$x = 75\% \times 250.00$ — Expressing the percent as a decimal,

$x = 0.75 \times 250.00$ — Simplifying,

$= \$187.50$

Method 3: Using the Ratio-Proportion Method

Here, the whole amount of \$250 is the base and is represented by 100%. 75% is a portion of the base, as illustrated:

$$\text{Portion} : \text{Base} = \text{Rate} : 100\%$$

$$P : B = R\% : 100\%$$

$$P : \$250 = 75\% : 100\%$$

$$\frac{P}{\$250} = \frac{75\%}{100\%}$$

$$\frac{P}{250.00} = \frac{75}{100}$$ Cross-multiplying,

$$100P = 250.00 \times 75$$ Solving for P,

$$P = \frac{250.00 \times 75}{100}$$ Simplifying,

$$= \$187.50$$

B = \$250
100%
P = ?
R% = 75%
0%

Therefore, 75% of \$250.00 is \$187.50.

Note: The following examples use the formula method; however, you can solve them using any of the three methods described above.

Example 5.1-i Calculating Portion When Rate is More Than 100%

What is 150% of 200?

Solution

$R\% = 150\%$ (value with % sign); i.e., $R = 1.50$

$B = 200$ (value that follows the word 'of')

$P = ?$ (the other value)

Using Formula 5.1, $P = R \times B$ — Substituting values for R and B,

$P = 1.50 \times 200$ — Simplifying,

$= 300$

Therefore, 150% of 200 is 300.

Example 5.1-j Calculating Rate When Portion and Base are Known

What percent of \$775 is \$1,250? (Or, \$1,250 is what percent of \$775?)

Solution

$B = \$775$ (value that follows the word 'of')

$P = \$1,250$ (the other value)

$R = ?$ (value for the word 'percent')

Using Formula 5.1, $P = R \times B$ — Rearranging for R,

$R = \frac{P}{B}$ — Substituting values for P and B,

$R = \frac{1,250.00}{775.00}$ — Simplifying,

$R = 1.612903...$ — Converting the decimal to a percent,

$R\% = 1.612903... \times 100\%$

$= 161.29\%$

Therefore, 161.29% of \$775.00 is \$1,250.00.

Note: It is tempting to treat \$1,250 as the base, since it is the larger value. However, in this question \$775 is the base, since it follows the word 'of'. This illustrates the importance of reading these types of questions carefully!

Example 5.1-k Calculating Base When Portion and Rate are Known

50% of what number is 200?

Solution

$R\% = 50\%$ (value with % sign); i.e., $R = 0.50$

$P = 200$ (the other value)

$B = ?$ (value that follows the word 'of')

Using Formula 5.1, $P = R \times B$ — Rearranging for B,

$B = \frac{P}{R}$ — Substituting values for P and R,

$B = \frac{200}{0.50}$ — Simplifying,

$= 400$

Therefore, 50% of 400 is 200.

Example 5.1-l Application Problem with a Fractional Rate

Sandra owns $25\frac{1}{3}\%$ of a web development company. If the company is valued at \$180,000 what is the value of Sandra's ownership in the company?

Solution

Do not round values calculated in intermediary steps. Store these values in your calculator and recall them for subsequent calculations.

$R\% = 25\frac{1}{3}\%$ (value with % sign)

$= 25.333333...\%$; i.e., $R = 0.253333...$

$B = \$180,000$ (the whole value)

$P = ?$ (the other value)

Using Formula 5.1, $P = R \times B$ Substituting values for R and B,

$= 0.253333... \times 180,000.00$ Simplifying,

$= \$45,600.00$

Alternatively, instead of performing calculations with repeating decimals, this question can be solved by converting the percent into a fraction:

$R\% = 25\frac{1}{3}\%$ Converting the mixed number into an improper fraction,

$= \frac{76}{3}\%$ Converting the percent into a fraction,

$R = \frac{76}{3} \times \frac{1}{100}$

$= \frac{76}{300}$

Using Formula 5.1, $P = R \times B$ Substituting values for R and B,

$= \frac{76}{300} \times 180,000.00$ Simplifying,

$= \$45,600.00$

Therefore, the value of Sandra's ownership in the company is \$45,600.00.

5.1 | Exercises

Answers to odd-numbered problems are available at the end of the textbook.

For Problems 1 to 18, calculate the missing values.

		Percents	Decimals	Fractions (or mixed numbers) in lowest terms
1.	a.	75%		
	b.		0.30	
	c.			$\frac{1}{4}$
3.	a.	5%		
	b.		0.2	
	c.			$\frac{3}{5}$

		Percents	Decimals	Fractions (or mixed numbers) in lowest terms
2.	a.	50%		
	b.		0.70	
	c.			$\frac{1}{5}$
4.	a.	2%		
	b.		0.8	
	c.			$\frac{3}{8}$

		Percents	Decimals	Fractions (or mixed numbers) in lowest terms
5.	a.	150%		
	b.		0.175	
	c.			$\frac{12}{25}$
7.	a.	12.5%		
	b.		0.05	
	c.			$4\frac{1}{2}$
9.	a.	0.6%		
	b.		0.005	
	c.			$4\frac{3}{5}$
11.	a.	0.05%		
	b.		0.0025	
	c.			$1\frac{1}{8}$
13.	a.	$\frac{3}{5}\%$		
	b.		1.08	
	c.			$\frac{3}{55}$
15.	a.	$1\frac{3}{4}\%$		
	b.		2.025	
	c.			$\frac{1}{400}$
17.	a.	$6\frac{1}{2}\%$		
	b.		2.5	
	c.			$\frac{4}{25}$

		Percents	Decimals	Fractions (or mixed numbers) in lowest terms
6.	a.	225%		
	b.		0.225	
	c.			$\frac{7}{20}$
8.	a.	7.5%		
	b.		0.03	
	c.			$3\frac{3}{4}$
10.	a.	0.8%		
	b.		0.003	
	c.			$1\frac{1}{5}$
12.	a.	0.08%		
	b.		0.075	
	c.			$2\frac{3}{8}$
14.	a.	$\frac{3}{8}\%$		
	b.		2.04	
	c.			$\frac{22}{75}$
16.	a.	$2\frac{3}{4}\%$		
	b.		1.075	
	c.			$\frac{1}{250}$
18.	a.	$10\frac{3}{5}\%$		
	b.		7.5	
	c.			$\frac{13}{50}$

For the following problems, express the answers rounded to two decimal places, wherever applicable.

For Problems 19 to 48, calculate the value.

19. a. 20% of 350 b. 12.5% of 800

20. a. 45% of 180 b. 2.5% of 960

21. a. 0.25% of 75 b. $\frac{1}{4}\%$ of 200 km

22. a. 0.755% of 120 b. $\frac{1}{8}\%$ of 450 km

23. a. 130% of 40 b. $5\frac{1}{3}\%$ of $1,000

24. a. 285% of 110 b. $12\frac{3}{4}\%$ of $1,260

25. What is 2.5% of 80?

26. What is 40% of 160?

27. $8\frac{1}{4}\%$ of $200 is how much?

28. $25\frac{3}{4}\%$ of $2,680 is how much?

29. How much is $\frac{1}{4}$% of $108?

30. How much is $\frac{3}{4}$% of 350 kg?

31. What number is 125% of 6?

32. What number is 250% of 12?

33. 12 is what percent of 30?

34. 18 is what percent of 40?

35. What percent of 4 is 16?

36. What percent of 9 is 45?

37. What percent of 220 is 100?

38. What percent of 22.10 is 110.50?

39. 280 metres is what percent of a kilometre?

40. 180 grams is what percent of 3 kilograms?

41. 400 is 50% of what number?

42. 225 is 25% of what number?

43. 15% of what amount is $27.90?

44. 30% of what amount is 708?

45. 120% of what amount is 156?

46. 215% of what amount is 258?

47. $16.50 is 0.75% of what amount?

48. $16.40 is 0.5% of what amount?

49. How much tax was charged on a table that costs $250, if the tax rate is 13%?

50. The monthly gross salary of an employee is $6,250. 26% of the salary was deducted for taxes. How much money was deducted for taxes?

51. 5% of commission on sales was $1,250. How much was the sales amount?

52. 3% interest on a loan was $210. How much was the loan?

53. In a survey of 450 people, 117 responded 'yes'. What percent of the people surveyed responded 'no'?

54. 144 out of 600 students took Business Mathematics. What percent of students did not take the course?

55. A company that makes games sets sales targets at $280,000 per year for each of its salespeople. If Amanda, an excellent salesperson, achieved 250% of her target this year, calculate her sales for the year.

56. If the population of Canada was estimated to be 36,910,000 in May 2018, and the population of Ontario was estimated to be $38\frac{1}{4}$% of Canada's population, calculate the estimated population of Ontario.

• 57. When there was a boom in the real estate market, Lucy sold her property for $410,440, which was 130% of the amount she originally paid. Calculate the amount she originally paid for the property.

• 58. Ronald, an investment banker sold his shares for $18,568.50 when there was a boom in the stock market. Calculate the amount he paid for the shares if his selling price was 180.65% of the amount he paid for the shares originally.

• 59. Evan, a business development representative of a leading pharmaceutical firm, took his client out for a dinner that cost $180.75 before taxes. If the tax was $23.50, calculate the tax rate.

• 60. A leading information technology company donated $87,790 out of its 2017 fiscal revenue of $17,558,643 towards socially-responsible causes. What percent of its revenue did it contribute towards these causes?

• 61. Neel Plastics Manufacturing Corporation targets to obtain $120,000 of funding from their investors to purchase new machinery. If they were only able to obtain 25.5% of their total target, calculate the amount of money that is yet to be received.

• 62. Pamela and Martha run a business that made a profit of $12,750. As Pamela invested a higher amount in the business, she received 57.5% of the profits and Martha received the remaining. Calculate Martha's share of the profit, in dollars.

5.2 | Percent Changes

The percent by which a quantity increases or decreases from its initial (original) value is known as **percent change (%C)**; i.e., the amount of change (increase or decrease) is calculated as a percent (%C) of its initial value.

$$Amount\ of\ Change = \%C \times Initial\ Value$$

The amount of change is the difference between the final value (V_f) and the initial value (V_i); i.e., the amount of change can also be calculated by subtracting the initial value from the final value.

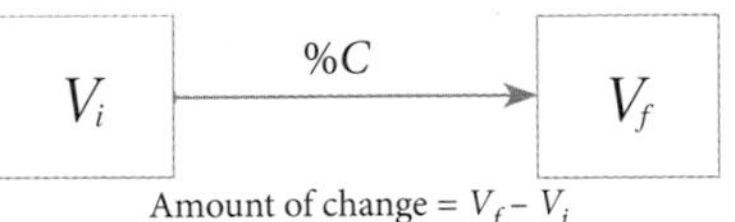

$$Amount\ of\ Change = Final\ Value - Initial\ Value$$

Therefore, $\%C \times Initial\ Value = Final\ Value - Initial\ Value$

To calculate a percent increase or decrease, determine the amount of increase or decrease and then determine its percent value compared to the initial value.

$$\%C = \frac{(Final\ Value - Initial\ Value)}{Initial\ Value}$$

Percent Change ⟶ $\%C = \frac{(V_f - V_i)}{V_i}$ ⟵ Amount of Change (numerator), ⟵ Initial Value (denominator)

Therefore, percent change is equal to the amount of change divided by the initial value. It is expressed as a percent, by multiplying the value by 100 and inserting a '%' sign, as shown below.

Formula 5.2-a **Percent Change**

$$\%C = \frac{(V_f - V_i)}{V_i} \times 100\%$$

Percent change is measured as either a percent increase (profit, rise, appreciation, etc.) or a percent decrease (loss, fall, depreciation, etc.) compared to the initial value.

- If the final value is **greater than** the initial value, then the percent change is a **percent increase**, which results in a positive value for %C.
- If the final value is **less than** the initial value, then the percent change is a **percent decrease**, which results in a negative value for %C.

Using the amount of change formulas, we can derive the formula for the final value (V_f) as follows:

$$Amount\ of\ Change = Final\ Value - Initial\ Value$$ Rearranging,

$$Final\ Value = Initial\ Value + Amount\ of\ Change$$ Therefore,

$$V_f = V_i + \%C \times V_i$$ Factoring out the common factor V_i,

$$V_f = V_i(1 + \%C)$$

Formula 5.2-b **Final Value**

$$V_f = V_i (1 + \%C)$$

Using Formula 5.2-b, the formula for the initial value (Vi) can be derived as follows:

$$V_f = V_i (1 + \%C)$$ Interchanging LS and RS,

$$V_i (1 + \%C) = V_f$$ Solving for V_i,

$$V_i = \frac{V_f}{(1 + \%C)}$$

Formula 5.2-c **Initial Value**

$$V_i = \frac{V_f}{(1 + \%C)}$$

Example 5.2-a **Calculating the Amount of Increase and Final Value**

The price of an item that originally sells at $150 is increased by 20%. Calculate the dollar amount of the increase and the price after the increase.

Solution

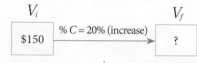

V_i = $150 → %C = 20% (increase) → V_f = ?

Method 1:

Amount of Change = %C × *Initial Value*

= 20% × 150.00

= 0.20 × 150.00

= $30.00 (increase)

Final Value = *Inital Value* + *Amount of Increase*

= 150.00 + 30.00

= $180.00

Method 2:

Using Formula 5.2-b,

$V_f = V_i (1 + \%C)$ Substituting values,

= 150.00(1 + 20%) Converting % to decimal,

= 150.00(1 + 0.20) Solving,

= 150.00(1.20)

= $180.00

Amount of Change = *Final Value* – *Initial Value*

= 180.00 – 150.00

= $30.00 (increase)

Helpful Check:
If the %*C* is positive (i.e., there is a percent increase), then the final value must be greater than the initial value.

Therefore, the amount of increase is $30.00 and the price after the increase is $180.00.

Example 5.2-b **Calculating the Amount of Decrease and Final Value**

An item normally sells for $400 and is discounted (reduced in price) by 15% during a sale. Calculate the dollar amount of discount and the price after the discount.

Solution

V_i = $400 → %C = –15% (decrease) → V_f = ?

Method 1:

Amount of Change = %C × *Initial Value*

= –15% × 400.00

= –0.15 × 400.00

= –$60.00 (decrease)

Final Value = *Initial Value* – *Amount of Decrease*

= 400.00 – 60.00

= $340.00

Method 2:

Using Formula 5.2-b,

$V_f = V_i (1 + \%C)$ Substituting values,

= 400.00(1 – 15%) Converting % to decimal,

= 400.00(1 – 0.15) Solving,

= 400.00(0.85)

= $340.00

Amount of Change = *Final Value* – *Initial Value*

= 340.00 – 400.00

= –$60.00 (decrease)

Helpful check:
If the %*C* is negative (i.e., there is a percent decrease), then the final value must be less than the initial value.

Therefore, the amount of discount is $60.00 and the price after discount is $340.00.

Example 5.2-c Calculating Percent Increase

A store had sales of \$50,000 in July and \$80,000 in August. Calculate the percent change in sales from July to August.

Solution

Initial Value, V_i = \$50,000.00

Final Value, V_f = \$80,000.00

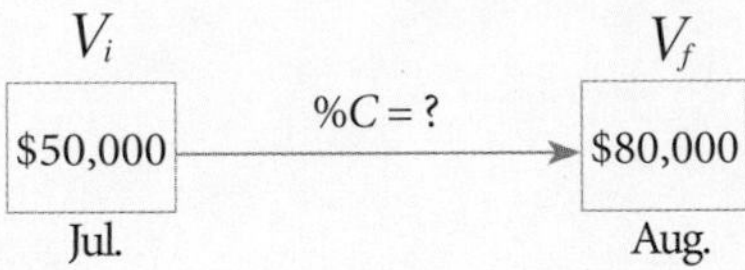

Using Formula 5.2-a, $\%C = \frac{(V_f - V_i)}{V_i} \times 100\%$ Substituting values,

$= \frac{80{,}000.00 - 50{,}000.00}{50{,}000.00} \times 100\%$ Solving,

$= \frac{30{,}000.00}{50{,}000.00} \times 100\%$

$= 0.6 \times 100\% = 60\%$ (increase)

Therefore, the percent change in sales from July to August is an increase of 60%.

Example 5.2-d Calculating Percent Decrease

A store's total expenses were \$2,400 in September and \$1,800 in October. Calculate the percent change in expenses from September to October.

Solution

Initial Value, V_i = \$2,400.00

Final Value, V_f = \$1,800.00

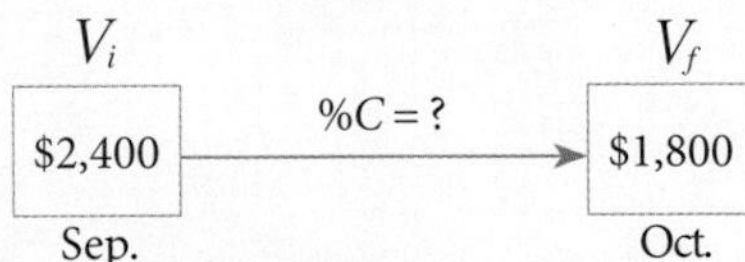

Using Formula 5.2-a, $\%C = \frac{(V_f - V_i)}{V_i} \times 100\%$ Substituting values,

$= \frac{1{,}800.00 - 2{,}400.00}{2{,}400.00} \times 100\%$ Solving,

$= \frac{-600.00}{2{,}400.00} \times 100\%$

$= -0.25 \times 100\% = -25\%$ (decrease)

Therefore, the percent change in expenses from September to October is a decrease of 25%.

Example 5.2-e Calculating Initial Value When the Percent Change is Positive

The value of a stock increased by 35% since it was purchased. If the stock is now selling at \$81, what was its value when it was purchased?

Solution

%C = 35% (increase)

V_f = \$81.00

V_i → V_f: ? —(%C = 35% (increase))→ \$81

Solution *continued*

Using Formula 5.2-c, $V_i = \frac{V_f}{(1 + \%C)}$ Substituting values,

$= \frac{81.00}{(1 + 35\%)}$ Converting % to decimal,

$= \frac{81.00}{(1 + 0.35)}$ Solving,

$= \frac{81.00}{1.35}$

$= \$60.00$

Therefore, the value of the stock when it was purchased was $60.00.

Example 5.2-f **Calculating Initial Value When the Percent Change is Negative**

After a discount of 25%, an item was sold at $450. Calculate the price of this item before the discount.

Solution

$\%C = -25\%$ (decrease)

$V_f = \$450.00$

V_i		V_f
?	$\%C = -25\%$ (decrease) →	$450

Using Formula 5.2-c, $V_i = \frac{V_f}{(1 + \%C)}$ Substituting values,

$= \frac{450.00}{(1 - 25\%)}$ Converting % to decimal,

$= \frac{450.00}{(1 - 0.25)}$ Solving,

$= \frac{450.00}{0.75}$

$= \$600.00$

Therefore, the price of the item before the discount was $600.00.

Example 5.2-g **Understanding Relative Percent Change**

Company A's profit increased from $165,000 to $170,000 last year. Company B's profit increased from $122,000 to $126,000 in the same year. Which company showed a better relative change in profit?

Solution

At first instinct, you may think that you only need to calculate the differences in profits of the two companies and compare them to arrive at the answer. That is,

$$\text{Amount of Change}_{\text{Company } A} = 170{,}000.00 - 165{,}000.00 = \$5{,}000.00$$

$$\text{Amount of Change}_{\text{Company } B} = 126{,}000.00 - 122{,}000.00 = \$4{,}000.00$$

Therefore, Company A showed a greater increase in profit; however, we need to determine which company showed a better **relative change** in profit.

To compare the relative change in profits, we have to calculate the **percent change** in profits of Companies A and B last year.

Solution
continued

In financial applications, it is often more important to calculate percent changes and associated values instead of relying on a mere difference between two values.

Using Formula 5.2-a, $\%C = \frac{(V_f - V_i)}{V_i} \times 100\%$

$$\%C_{\text{Company A}} = \frac{170{,}000.00 - 165{,}000.00}{165{,}000.00} \times 100\%$$

$$= \frac{5{,}000.00}{165{,}000.00} \times 100\%$$

$$= 0.030303... \times 100\% = 3.03\%$$

V_i: \$165,000 → %C = ? (Company A) → V_f: \$170,000

$$\%C_{\text{Company B}} = \frac{126{,}000.00 - 122{,}000.00}{122{,}000.00} \times 100\%$$

$$= \frac{4{,}000.00}{122{,}000.00} \times 100\%$$

$$= 0.032786... \times 100\% = 3.28\%$$

V_i: \$122,000 → %C = ? (Company B) → V_f: \$126,000

Therefore, even though Company B had a smaller increase in profit than Company A during the year, Company B had a better relative growth (3.28%) compared to Company A (3.03%).

Example 5.2-h

Calculating Percent Change When Initial and Final Values are Given as Percents

If the Bank of Canada increases its prime lending rate from 2.25% to 3.35%, calculate the percent increase in the prime rate.

Solution

Initial Value, $V_i = 2.25\%$

Final Value, $V_f = 3.35\%$

V_i: 2.25% → %C = ? → V_f: 3.35%

Using Formula 5.2-a, $\%C = \frac{(V_f - V_i)}{V_i} \times 100\%$ Substituting the values,

$$\%C = \frac{3.35\% - 2.25\%}{2.25\%} \times 100\%$$ Solving,

$$= \frac{1.10\%}{2.25\%} \times 100\%$$

$$= \frac{0.0110}{0.0225} \times 100\%$$

$$= 0.488888... \times 100\% = 48.89\%$$

Therefore, the percent increase in prime rate is 48.89%.

Note: It is incorrect to say that the percent increase in the prime rate is 3.35% – 2.25% = 1.10%. *Use caution when calculating percent change of percent values!*

Example 5.2-i Calculating Percent Change of Unit Rates

A jeweler made and sold 500 g of silver chains for $90.00. If he reduced the weight of the silver in the chain to 450 g and reduced the price to $85.50, by what percent did the price per gram of silver (i.e., unit price) change?

Solution

Unit price of the 500 g silver chain: $\frac{\$90.00}{500\text{ g}} = \$0.18$ per gram of silver

Unit price of the 450 g silver chain: $\frac{\$85.50}{450\text{ g}} = \$0.19$ per gram of silver

There is an increase in the unit price of the chain.

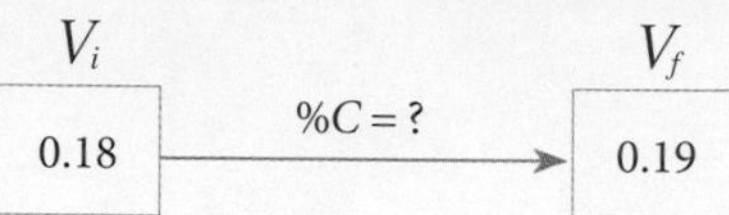

Using Formula 5.2-a, $\%C = \frac{(V_f - V_i)}{V_i} \times 100\%$ Substituting values,

$\%C = \frac{0.19 - 0.18}{0.18} \times 100\%$ Solving,

$= 0.055555... \times 100\% = 5.56\%$ (increase)

Therefore, the unit price increased by 5.56%.

There are many methods used in calculating percent change problems. So far, our solutions have focused on using the formulas presented at the beginning of this section. In the following example, we will demonstrate three common methods used to solve a percent change problem, including a ratio-proportion method, which we will study more in depth in the next chapter.

Example 5.2-j Calculating Final Value When Percent Change is Positive Using Different Methods

If a $20 hourly rate of pay is increased by 10%, what is the new hourly rate?

Solution

V_i: $20 → %C = 10% (increase) → V_f: ?

Method 1: Using the Definition of Amount of Change

Initial Value + Amount of Increase = Final Value

$V_i + \%C \times V_i = V_f$ Substituting values,

$20.00 + 0.1(20.00) = V_f$ Solving,

$20.00 + 2.00 = V_f$

$V_f = \$22.00$

Method 2: Using the Formula Method

Using Formula 5.2-b,

$V_f = V_i(1 + \%C)$ Substituting values,

$= 20.00(1 + 10\%)$ Converting % to decimal,

$= 20.00(1 + 0.10)$ Solving,

$= 20.00(1.10)$

$= \$22.00$

Method 3: Using the Ratio-Proportion Method

In this method, we compare the original value and final value using ratios and proportions to determine the unknown.

The original value of $20 represents 100%. This is increased by 10% to a final value of 110%, as illustrated:

Solution
continued

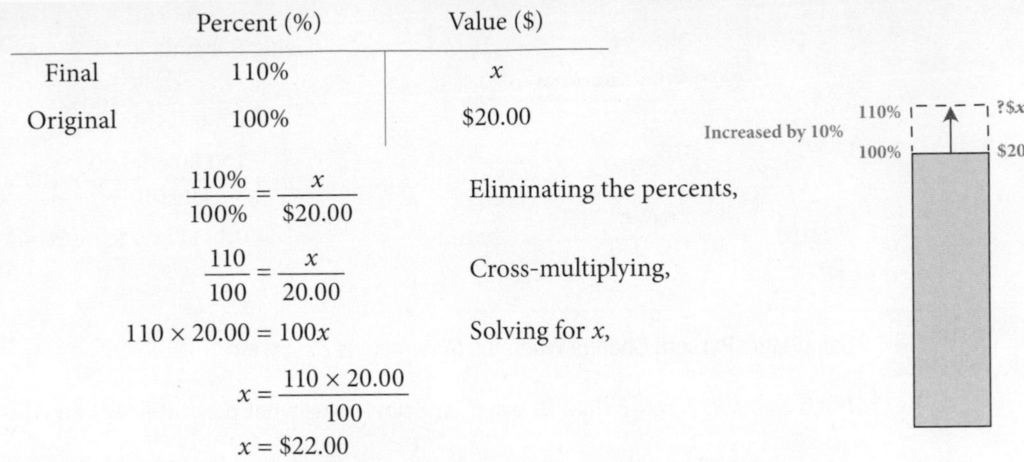

	Percent (%)	Value ($)
Final	110%	x
Original	100%	$20.00

$$\frac{110\%}{100\%} = \frac{x}{\$20.00}$$ Eliminating the percents,

$$\frac{110}{100} = \frac{x}{20.00}$$ Cross-multiplying,

$$110 \times 20.00 = 100x$$ Solving for x,

$$x = \frac{110 \times 20.00}{100}$$

$$x = \$22.00$$

Therefore, the new hourly rate is $22.00.

'Reversing' a Percent Increase/Decrease

- **Percent increase cannot be reversed by the same percent decrease.**

$100.00 increased by 10% = $110.00.

But, $110.00 decreased by 10% ≠ $100.00

For example,

$100 increased by 10% results in $110.

$V_f = 100.00(1 + 0.10) = \$110.00$

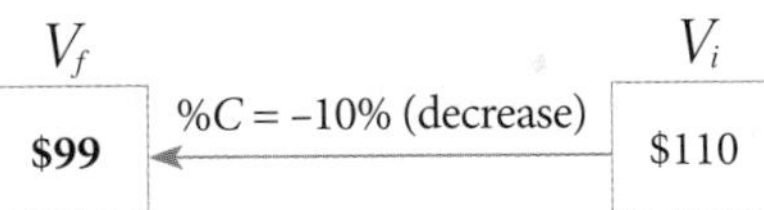

However, $110 decreased by 10% results in $99.

$V_f = 110.00(1 - 0.10) = \$99.00$

V_f $99 ← %C = –10% (decrease) ← V_i $110

- **Similarly, percent decrease cannot be reversed by the same percent increase.**

$100.00 decreased by 10% = $90.00.

But, $90.00 increased by 10% ≠ $100.00

For example,

$100 decreased by 10% results in $90.

$V_f = 100.00(1 - 0.10) = \$90.00$

V_i $100 → %C = –10% (decrease) → V_f **$90**

However, $90 increased by 10% results in $99.

$V_f = 90.00(1 + 0.10) = \$99.00$

V_f **$99** ← %C = 10% (increase) ← V_i $90

- **To reverse a percent increase or percent decrease, the proper percent change method should be used, as shown below.**

V_i $100 → %C = 10% (increase) → V_f $110

V_f $100 ← %C = ? ← V_i $110

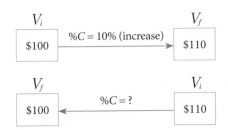

Using Formula 5.2-a,

$$\%C = \frac{(V_f - V_i)}{V_i} \times 100\%$$

$$= \frac{100.00 - 110.00}{110.00} \times 100\%$$

$$= -0.090909... \times 100\% = -9.09\% \text{ (decrease)}$$

V_i		V_f
\$100	%C = –10% (decrease) →	\$90

V_f		V_i
\$100	← %C = ?	\$90

Using Formula 5.2-a,

$$\%C = \frac{(V_f - V_i)}{V_i} \times 100\%$$

$$= \frac{100.00 - 90.00}{90.00} \times 100\%$$

$$= 0.111111... \times 100\% = 11.11\% \text{ (increase)}$$

Example 5.2-k **Calculating Percent Change When the Statement is Reversed**

If Ali earns 25% more than Brian, then Brian earns what percent less than Ali?

Solution

Method 1: Using the Algebraic Method

Let Ali's earnings be A and Brian's earnings be B.

$A = B + (25\% \text{ of } B)$

$A = 125\% \text{ of } B$ Converting % to decimal,

$A = 1.25B$ Expressing B as a fraction of A,

$$B = \frac{1}{1.25}A$$

$B = 0.80A$

That is, Brian earns 80% of Ali's earnings, which is the same as stating that Brian earns 20% less than Ali.

Method 2: Using the Formula Method, Assuming a Value for Brian

Let Brian's earnings = \$1,000

Then Ali's earnings = \$1,000 + (25% of \$1,000)

= 1,000.00 + (0.25 × 1,000.00)

= 1,000.00 + 250.00

= \$1,250.00

V_i		V_f
\$1,250	%C = ? →	\$1,000

Using Formula 5.2-a, $\%C = \frac{(V_f - V_i)}{V_i} \times 100\%$ Substituting values,

$$\%C = \frac{1{,}000.00 - 1{,}250.00}{1{,}250.00} \times 100\%$$ Solving,

$$= \frac{-250.00}{1{,}250.00} \times 100\%$$

$$= -0.20 \times 100\% = -20\%$$

Therefore, if Ali earns 25% more than Brian, then Brian earns 20% less than Ali.

Example 5.2-l **Calculating Percent Change When the Value of a Currency Increases (Appreciates) or Decreases (Depreciates) Against Another Currency**

If the US dollar appreciated by 10% relative to the Canadian dollar, by what percent has the Canadian dollar depreciated relative to the US dollar?

Solution

Assume US\$1 = C\$$x$.

If the US dollar appreciated by 10%, then,

$$\text{US\$1} = \text{C\$}1.10x$$ Dividing both sides by 1.10,

$$\text{US\$}\frac{1}{1.10} = \text{C\$}x$$

$$\text{C\$}x = \text{US\$}0.909090...$$

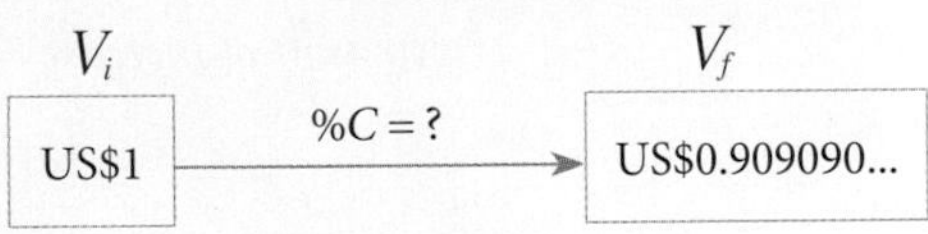

Therefore, after the US dollar appreciated by 10% relative to the Canadian dollar, US\$0.909090... = C\$$x$.

Using Formula 5.2-a, $$\%C = \frac{(V_f - V_i)}{V_i} \times 100\%$$ Substituting the values,

$$\%C = \frac{\text{US\$}0.909090... - \text{US\$}1}{\text{US\$}1} \times 100\%$$ Solving,

$$= -0.090909... \times 100\% = -9.09\%$$

Therefore, if the US dollar appreciated by 10% relative to the Canadian dollar, then the Canadian dollar depreciated by 9.09% relative to the US dollar.

Percent Change When the Initial Value (V_i) is Negative

In the equation, $V_i + \textit{Amount of Change} = V_f$

where, $\textit{Amount of Change} = \%C \times V_i$

- **When the *Amount of Change* is positive (i.e., there is an amount of increase),** regardless of the value or sign for V_i, we add the amount of increase to V_i to determine V_f; i.e., the amount that is **added** to V_i is **positive.**

$$V_i + \textit{Amount of Increase} = V_f$$

- **When the *Amount of Change* is negative (i.e., there is an amount of decrease),** regardless of the value or sign for V_i, we subtract the amount of decrease from V_i to determine V_f; i.e., the amount that is **subtracted** from V_i is **positive.**

$$V_i - \textit{Amount of Decrease} = V_f$$

Therefore, the amount that is added (amount of increase) or subtracted (amount of decrease) should always be a positive quantity.

When the original quantity (V_i) is negative, we use the absolute value of V_i to calculate the amount of increase or decrease. This ensures that the amount of increase or decrease will be a positive answer.

Therefore, when V_i is negative,

$$\textit{Amount of Increase or Decrease} = \%C \times \textit{Absolute value of } V_i$$
$$= \%C\,|V_i|$$

The absolute value of a number 'a', written as $|a|$, will always be a positive number (regardless of the sign for 'a').

For example, $|-5| = 5$ and $|5| = 5$.

If the final value is greater than the initial value,

Initial Value + Amount of Increase = Final Value

$$V_i + \%C\,|V_i| = V_f$$

$$\%C = \frac{(V_f - V_i)}{|V_i|}$$

Therefore, the value of %C will be positive.

If the final value is less than the initial value,

Initial Value – Amount of Decrease = Final Value

$$V_i - \%C\,|V_i| = V_f$$

$$\%C = -\frac{(V_f - V_i)}{|V_i|}$$

Therefore, the value of %C will be negative.

Example 5.2-m **Percent Change When Initial Value is a Negative Value**

The average temperature in Toronto last winter was –4 °C. If the average temperature this winter increased by 1.15 °C, calculate the percent change in this year's winter temperature from last year's winter.

Solution

Method 1:

Since V_i is negative,

$Amount\ of\ Increase = \%C\,|V_i|$ — Substituting values,

$1.15 = \%C\,|-4|$ — Taking the absolute value of –4,

$1.15 = \%C(4)$ — Solving,

$\%C = \frac{1.15}{4}$

$= 0.2875 \times 100\% = 28.75\%$ (increase)

Method 2:

Since V_i is negative,

$\%C = \frac{(V_f - V_i)}{|V_i|} \times 100\%$ — Substituting values ($V_f - V_i = 1.15$ and $V_i = -4$),

$\%C = \frac{1.15}{|-4|} \times 100\%$ — Taking the absolute value of –4,

$= \frac{1.15}{4} \times 100\%$ — Solving,

$= 0.2875 \times 100\% = 28.75\%$ (increase)

Therefore, this year's winter temperature increased by 28.75% from last year's winter.

5.2 | Exercises

Answers to odd-numbered problems are available at the end of the textbook.

For the following problems, express the answers rounded to two decimal places, wherever applicable.

For Problems 1 to 4, calculate the missing values.

1.

	Initial Value	Percent Increase	Final Value
a.	$270	45%	?
b.	$4,500	137.5%	?
c.	?	25%	$600
d.	?	262.5%	$2,250
e.	$150	?	$225
f.	$3,400	?	$9,200

2.

	Initial Value	Percent Increase	Final Value
a.	$250	35%	?
b.	$3,500	112.5%	?
c.	?	40%	$800
d.	?	187.5%	$6,950
e.	$170	?	$204
f.	$7,500	?	$24,500

3.

	Initial Value	Percent Decrease	Final Value
a.	$145	45%	?
b.	$1,275	112.5%	?
c.	?	25%	$412.5
d.	?	23.75%	$3,400
e.	$740	?	$400
f.	$5,200	?	$1,600

4.

	Initial Value	Percent Decrease	Final Value
a.	$525	35%	?
b.	$6,800	137.5%	?
c.	?	40%	$525
d.	?	18.75%	$4,800
e.	$222	?	$120
f.	$8,125	?	$2,500

5. If Harley's salary of $2,000 per month is increased by 5.5%, what is his new monthly salary?

6. Revenues of Python Graphics Corporation rose by 280% from last year. If the revenue last year was $860,760, calculate the revenue this year.

7. After a discount of $12\frac{1}{2}$%, a publishing company purchased an offset printing press for $245,000. Calculate the original price of the machine.

8. A clothing retail outlet purchased clothes in bulk from a wholesaler for $86,394. This was after a discount of $10\frac{3}{4}$% on the purchase. Calculate the original price of the clothes.

9. If calculators that sell in stores for $30 each are being offered online for $24 each, calculate the percent discount offered online.

10. If Lilo's student loan of $12,000 will increase to $12,860 by the end of the year, calculate the percent increase in her debt.

11. Dawson purchased a pair of shoes on Boxing Day that was discounted by 10% from the original price of $50. Calculate the amount he paid for the pair of shoes.

12. Jamie went to the mall during the holiday season to purchase a wall painting for his mother. He liked a painting that was selling for $199.99 and which had a seasonal discount of 18% on its selling price. How much would this painting cost Jamie after the discount?

13. A sales tax of 13% increased the cost of a meal at a restaurant to $34.50. What was the cost of the meal before taxes?

14. After paying income taxes of 45%, Carla's take-home annual income was $45,000. Calculate her income before deducting income taxes.

15. The average daytime summer temperature in Calgary increased by 3.0 °C this year. If the average daytime summer temperature last year was 29 °C, calculate the percent change in the average daytime summer temperature this year.

16. The average yearly snowfall in Vancouver increased by 3 cm this year. If the average yearly snowfall last year was 47.5 cm, calculate the percent change in average yearly snowfall this year.

17. The value of a car depreciated by 18.5% from the purchase price of $36,450 a year ago. What is its current price?

18. A company laid off 12% of its 675 employees. How many are currently employed?

19. The current average price for an airline ticket from Toronto to Vancouver is $812. This is an increase of 12.5% from last year's average price. What was the average price last year?

20. The current price for the monthly Metro Pass is $141.50. This is 7.4% more than last year's price. What was last year's price?

21. During a sale, a TV regulary priced at $999 was sold at $779. What was the percent discount?

22. Sales at the store dropped from $83,570 to $69,500 over a two-year period. What was the percent decrease in sales during this period?

23. A shirt regularly priced at $37.50 was sold at a 17.5% discount. Calculate the discounted price of the shirt.

24. A town's population increased by 13.5% from 27,000 people. What is the current population?

25. James' current annual salary is $63,536. This is an increase of 4.5% from last year's salary. What was his salary last year?

26. The current enrollment at a college is 22,575, and represents an increase of 7.5% from last year. What was the enrollment last year?

27. If the current fixed mortgage rate of 5.4% rises to 6.6%, calculate the percent increase in the mortgage rate.

28. If the prime rate of 3.5% increased to 4.2%, calculate the percent increase in the prime rate.

29. If Roger scored 20% more than Judie, by what percent is Judie's score less than Roger's?

30. If Harry earns 15% more than Beary per hour, by what percent is Beary's earning less than Harry's?

31. Last month, a 750 g box of cereal was sold at a grocery store for $3.00. However, this month, the cereal manufacturer has launched the same cereal in a 600 g box, which is being sold at $2.50. By what percent did the unit price change?

32. A 450 g stick of butter was sold for $3.50. If the manufacturer reduced the size of the stick to 250 g and sold it at a reduced price of $2.00, by what percent did the unit price change?

33. If the Canadian dollar appreciated by 5% relative to the British pound, by what percent has the British pound depreciated relative to the Canadian dollar?

34. If the Australian dollar appreciated by 15% relative to the British pound, by what percent has the British pound depreciated relative to the Australian dollar?

35. Gabrielle's portfolio of shares comprised of investments of $8,600 and $12,400 in the telecommunication and information technology industries, respectively. If the market price of her telecommunication shares dropped by 65% and that of information technology grew by 25%, by what percent did the total value of her investments change?

36. Kemi had her money invested in two types of mutual funds: $2,800 in low-risk funds and $700 in high-risk funds. If the value of her high-risk funds grew by 30% and that of the low-risk funds decreased by 10%, by what percent did the total value of her investments change?

37. Sandra posted an advertisement on an auction site to sell her phone for 50% more than what she had paid for it. Since it did not sell within a month, she decreased the advertised price by 50% and it sold immediately. By what percent, more or less than her purchase price, did she sell the phone?

38. If the temperature rose by 12% from the average temperature, then fell by 12%, by what percent did the final temperature increase or decrease from the average temperature?

39. The average winter temperature in Toronto increased by 2.0 °C this year. If the average winter temperature last year was –15 °C, calculate the percent change in average winter temperature this year.

40. The average winter temperature in Montreal increased by 1.15 °C this year. If the average winter temperature last year was –10 °C, calculate the percent change in the average winter temperature this year.

• 41. The price of a telecommunications share dropped by $2.50 at the end of the first year and dropped by a further $3.45 at the end of the second year. If the price of the share at the end of the second year was $12.55, calculate the percent change in the price of the share at the end of each year from its price at the beginning of each year. What was the percent drop in the price over the two-year period?

• 42. Amtex Computers Inc. sells refurbished laptops online. At the beginning of the year, a particular model was being sold at $400. However, by the end of the first year, the price was reduced by $80. At the end of the second year, the price was increased by $64. Calculate the percent change in the price of this model at the end of each year from its price at the beginning of each year. Calculate the percent discount offered in the second year from the original price of $400.

• 43. The labour cost for manufacturing a $30,000 car increased by 5%. If the cost of labour was 30% of the total cost for manufacturing the car, by what amount did the cost of the car increase?

• 44. The material cost for manufacturing a $2,000 TV decreased by 10%. If the cost of material was 40% of the total cost for manufacturing the TV, by what amount did the cost of the TV decrease?

• 45. Tudor and Rani, two sales representatives in a company, were earning $2,815 per month and $2,875 per month, respectively. After a yearly appraisal, if Tudor's salary increased by 14% and Rani's increased by 11%, who had the higher salary?

• 46. Reggie's annual salary increased from $42,000.00 to $46,830.00 this year and his colleague Gerald's annual salary increased from $39,500.00 to $44,437.50. Who received a higher rate of increase this year?

5.3 | Simple Interest

Interest is a fee that borrowers pay to lenders for using their money temporarily for a period of time. For example, when we invest money, a financial institution uses our money, and therefore pays us interest for the time period it has been invested. Similarly, when we borrow money from a financial institution, we pay interest to them for the time period borrowed.

Calculations Involving Simple Interest

In simple interest calculations, the amount of **interest (I)**, for a period of **time (t)**, is calculated as a percent, or **rate (r)**, of the initial amount of money invested or borrowed, known as the **principal (P)**. Therefore,

$$\textit{Interest} = \textit{Principal} \times \textit{Interest Rate} \times \textit{Time}$$

$$I = P \times r \times t$$

This can be rearranged to solve for the variables **P**, **r**, and **t** as follows:

$$P = \frac{I}{r \times t} \qquad r = \frac{I}{P \times t} \qquad t = \frac{I}{P \times r}$$

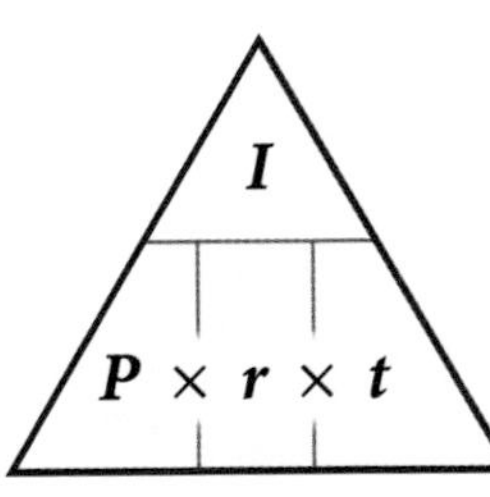

P, r, t triangle

Here is a triangle that can be used to help in rearranging the formula $I = P \times r \times t$ to solve for the variable P, r, or t.

Variables beside each other at the bottom are multiplied, ($P \times r \times t$, as shown).

Variable I is divided by the variables at the bottom.

Cover the variable for which you want to solve to see the new formula.

For example, if you want to solve for P, the formula can be found by covering P and reading the remaining variables in the triangle, to obtain $P = \dfrac{I}{r \times t}$

Interest rate is usually expressed as a percent per annum (r% p.a.) or percent per month (r% p.m.) and time (t) is expressed in days, months, or years.

- If 'r' is expressed as per annum (r% p.a.), then 't' should be in years.
- If 'r' is expressed as per month (r% p.m.), then 't' should be in months.

In calculations, 'r' is used as the decimal or fractional equivalent of the percent 'r%'.

In this section, we will use annual interest rates (r% p.a.) and time periods (t) expressed in years (or converted to years) when performing simple interest calculations. Examples of converting time periods from months or days to years are as follows:

The unit of 't' is converted to match the unit of 'r' using 1 year = 12 months or 1 year = 365 days.

- $t = 4 \text{ months} = \dfrac{4}{12} \text{ years}$
- $t = 1 \text{ year and } 3 \text{ months} = 15 \text{ months} = \dfrac{15}{12} \text{ years}$
- $t = 125 \text{ days} = \dfrac{125}{365} \text{ years}$

Example 5.3-a

Calculating the Amount of Interest

Calculate the amount of interest earned from a six-month investment of \$2,250 at an interest rate of 4.2% p.a.

Solution

$P = \$2{,}250.00$

$r = 4.2\% \text{ p.a.} = 0.042 \text{ p.a.}$

$t = 6 \text{ months} = \frac{6}{12} \text{ years}$

Calculating I, $I = P \times r \times t$

$$= 2{,}250.00 \times 0.042 \times \frac{6}{12} = \$47.25$$

Therefore, the amount of interest earned is \$47.25.

Example 5.3-b

Calculating Principal

Calculate the amount of money that should be invested for three years at an annual interest rate of 6% to earn an interest of \$675.

Solution

$I = \$675.00$

$r = 6\% \text{ p.a.} = 0.06 \text{ p.a.}$

$t = 3 \text{ years}$

Calculating P, $P = \frac{I}{r \times t}$

$$= \frac{675.00}{(0.06 \times 3)} = \$3{,}750.00$$

Therefore, \$3,750.00 should be invested.

As time goes by, the value of money increases by the amount of interest earned for that period. Therefore, when money is returned after a period of time, interest is added to the principal and the accumulated value is known as the **maturity value (S)**.

Maturity Value = Principal + Interest

$$S = P + I$$

This formula can be rearranged to solve for the variables I and P, as follows:

$$I = S - P$$

$$P = S - I$$

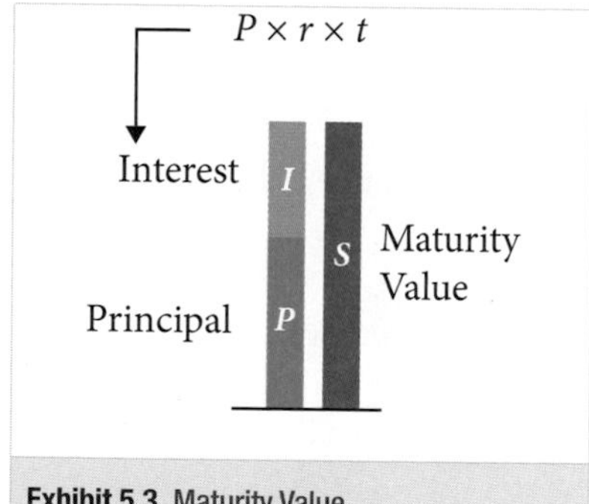

Exhibit 5.3 Maturity Value

Example 5.3-c

Calculating the Amount of Interest and Maturity Value

Tony invested \$7,500 for two years at an annual interest rate of 4.8%. Calculate:

(i) The amount of interest earned from this investment.

(ii) The maturity value at the end of two years.

Solution

$P = \$7{,}500.00$

$r = 4.8\% \text{ p.a.} = 0.048 \text{ p.a.}$

$t = 2 \text{ years}$

(i) $I = P \times r \times t$

$$= 7{,}500.00 \times 0.048 \times 2 = \$720.00$$

Therefore, the amount of interest earned in two years is \$720.00.

Solution continued

(ii) $S = P + I$

$= 7{,}500.00 + 720.00 = \$8{,}220.00$

Therefore, the maturity value at the end of two years is $8,220.00.

Example 5.3-d **Calculating the Amount of Interest and Interest Rate**

An investment of $4,500.00 resulted in a maturity value of $4,938.75 after 18 months. Calculate:

(i) The amount of interest earned.

(ii) The annual interest rate.

Solution

$P = \$4{,}500.00$

$S = \$4{,}938.75$

$t = 18 \text{ months} = \frac{18}{12} \text{ years}$

(i) $I = S - P$

$= 4{,}938.75 - 4{,}500.00 = \$438.75$

Therefore, the amount of interest earned in 18 months is $438.75.

(ii) $r = \frac{I}{P \times t}$

$$= \frac{438.75}{\left(4{,}500.00 \times \frac{18}{12}\right)} = 0.065 \times 100\% = 6.50\% \text{ p.a.}$$

Therefore, the annual interest rate is 6.50%.

5.3 | Exercises

Answers to odd-numbered problems are available at the end of the textbook.

For the following problems, express the answers rounded to two decimal places, wherever applicable.
For Problems 1 to 6, calculate the Interest (I) and the Maturity Value (S).

	Principal (**P**)	Rate (**r**)	Time (**t**)	Interest (**I**)	Maturity Value (**S**)
1.	$900	5% p.a.	3 years	?	?
2.	$6,250	4% p.a.	2 years	?	?
3.	$1,480	4.5% p.a.	18 months	?	?
4.	$2,500	3.5% p.a.	15 months	?	?
5.	$5,840	6% p.a.	75 days	?	?
6.	$7,300	3% p.a.	250 days	?	?

7. Calculate the amount of interest earned on a two-year, $2,600 investment at 3.5% p.a.

8. Calculate the amount of interest charged on a four-year, $1,250 loan borrowed at 4.25% p.a.

9. How much interest is owed on a $1,500 loan borrowed for 1 year and 9 months at 4.8% p.a.?

10. How much interest is earned from an investment of $2,400 made for 2 years and 3 months at 3.6% p.a.?

11. Khan borrowed $1,460 at 5% p.a. for 200 days. Calculate the amount of interest due on the loan and the maturity value of the loan.

12. Ann invested $4,380 for 100 days in an account that pays 3% p.a. Calculate the amount of interest earned and the maturity value of the investment.

13. An amount of $3,600 is borrowed at a simple interest rate of 6% p.a. for 2 years and 7 months. Calculate the amount of interest and the maturity value of the loan.

14. Saul borrowed $1,750 for 9 months at a simple interest rate of 5% p.a. Calculate the amount of interest and the maturity value of the loan.

For Problems 15 to 24, calculate the missing values.

	Principal (*P*)	Rate (*r*)	Time (*t*)	Interest (*I*)	Maturity Value (*S*)
15.	$750	?	3 years	?	$930
16.	$1,300	?	2 years	?	$1,404
17.	$5,000	4% p.a.	? years	$500	?
18.	$8,000	3.5% p.a.	? years	$1,120	?
19.	?	?	9 months	$60	$2,600
20.	?	?	15 months	$120	$1,720
21.	$1,600	4% p.a.	? months	?	$1,792
22.	$1,000	3% p.a.	? months	?	$1,050
23.	?	6% p.a.	120 days	$36	?
24.	?	5% p.a.	180 days	$63	?

25. At what annual interest rate will a $6,000 investment result in a maturity value of $6,600 in 2 years?

26. At what annual interest rate will a $1,250 investment result in a maturity value of $1,625 in 5 years?

27. In how many years will $3,000 invested at 3% p.a. result in a maturity value of $3,360?

28. How many years will it take for a $5,000 deposit to mature to $6,500 at 6% p.a.?

29. How much needs to be invested for four years at 4% p.a. to earn an interest amount of $400?

30. The amount of interest charged on a three-year loan at 6% p.a. is $810. Calculate the amount of the loan.

31. A loan of $4,800 was paid off at the end of five months with a payment of $4,940. Calculate the annual interest rate charged on the loan.

32. John deposited $3,600 in a savings account. The balance in this account after nine months was $3,681. Calculate the annual interest rate earned from this investment.

• 33. The maturity value of an investment is $4,460, which included a 5.5% p.a. simple interest for 1 year and 4 months. Calculate the amount invested and the amount of interest earned from this investment.

• 34. Shaunti paid off a loan by making a payment of $5,058, which included simple interest at 6% p.a. If she obtained the loan eight months ago, calculate the amount borrowed and the the amount of interest paid on this loan.

• 35. An amount of $3,200 is borrowed for 180 days. At the end of the term, $3,420 is paid to settle the loan. Calculate the annual simple interest rate charged on the loan.

• 36. Jane borrowed $900 and paid $960 after 145 days to settle the loan. Calculate the annual simple interest rate charged on the loan.

• 37. How many days will it take for an investment of $6,000 to accumulate to $6,700 at 5% p.a. simple interest?

• 38. If the maturity value of a $2,000 loan at 4.2% p.a. simple interest was $2,250, determine the term of the loan to the nearest day.

• 39. If the simple interest charged on a $2,500 loan for a period of 1 year and 8 months was $180, what was the annual simple interest rate charged on this loan?

• 40. If the maturity value of an investment of $10,000.00 for 1 year and 2 months is $10,437.50, calculate the the annual simple interest rate.

5.4 | Payroll

Employees of an organization receive payment from their employers for their services. In this section, we will calculate (or use) the gross pay given to employees based on an annual salary, hourly rate of pay, or commission.

Annual Salary

Annual salary employees are usually supervisory, managerial, or professional employees who work on an annual basis and are not paid an hourly rate. If you are employed by an organization paying you an annual salary, this is the amount that you will be paid for your service over a period of one year.

Pay Period

Pay period refers to the frequency of payments (how often payments are being made). The most common pay periods are:

One monthly payment is **not** equal to four weekly payments.

A semi-monthly payment is **not** equal to a bi-weekly payment.

- **Monthly:** Once a month; 12 payments per year. (1 year = 12 months)
- **Semi-monthly:** Twice per month; 24 payments per year. (1 year = 12 months; 2 × 12 = 24)
- **Weekly:** Once a week; 52 payments per year. (1 year = 52 weeks)
- **Bi-weekly:** Once every two weeks; 26 payments per year. (1 year = 52 weeks; 52 ÷ 2 = 26)

Note: In the examples and exercises in this section, we will be using 52 weekly pay periods or 26 bi-weekly pay periods. However, it is possible to have 53 weekly pay periods or 27 bi-weekly pay periods depending on the year and the payment days.

The pay for the pay period is calculated using the following formula:

$$\textit{Pay for a pay period} = \frac{\textit{Annual salary}}{\textit{Number of pay periods}}$$

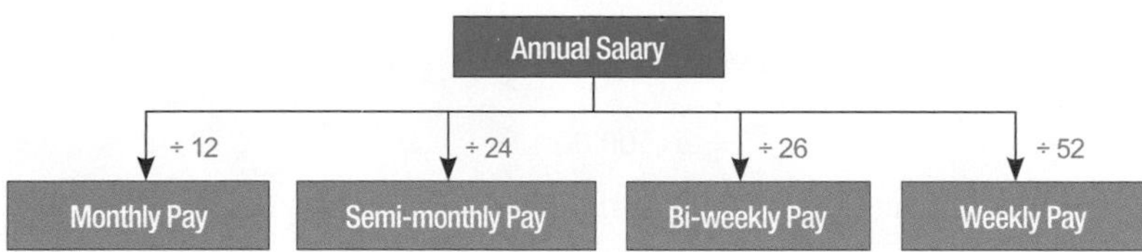

We can rearrange the above formula to calculate annual salary as follows:

$$\textit{Annual salary} = \textit{Pay for a pay period} \times \textit{Number of pay periods}$$

Example 5.4-a **Calculating Payment for a Pay Period, Given the Annual Salary**

Ann works for a publishing company and receives an annual salary of $62,400. Calculate her gross pay for a pay period, if paid:

(i) monthly (ii) semi-monthly (iii) weekly (iv) bi-weekly

Solution

$$\textit{Pay for a pay period} = \frac{\textit{Annual salary}}{\textit{Number of pay periods}}$$

(i) $\textit{Monthly pay} = \frac{\textit{Annual salary}}{\textit{12 pay periods}} = \frac{62{,}400.00}{12} = \$5{,}200.00$

Therefore, if paid monthly, her pay would be $5,200.00.

Solution *continued*

(ii) $\textit{Semi-monthly pay} = \dfrac{\textit{Annual salary}}{\textit{24 pay periods}} = \dfrac{62{,}400.00}{24} = \$2{,}600.00$

Therefore, if paid semi-monthly, her pay would be \$2,600.00.

(iii) $\textit{Weekly pay} = \dfrac{\textit{Annual salary}}{\textit{52 pay periods}} = \dfrac{62{,}400.00}{52} = \$1{,}200.00$

Therefore, if paid weekly, her pay would be \$1,200.00.

(iv) $\textit{Bi-weekly pay} = \dfrac{\textit{Annual salary}}{\textit{26 pay periods}} = \dfrac{62{,}400.00}{26} = \$2{,}400.00$

Therefore, if paid bi-weekly, her pay would be \$2,400.00.

Example 5.4-b Calculating Annual Salary, the Equivalent Monthly and Semi-Monthly Pay, Given the Weekly Pay

Sam is paid \$1,500 weekly. Calculate the:

(i) Annual salary (ii) Equivalent monthly pay (iii) Equivalent semi-monthly pay

Solution

(i) Number of weekly payments per year = 52

$$\textit{Annual salary} = \textit{Pay for a pay period} \times \textit{Number of pay periods}$$
$$= 1{,}500.00 \times 52$$
$$= \$78{,}000.00$$

Therefore, the annual salary is \$78,000.00.

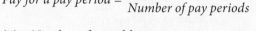

Weekly Pay → × 52 → (i) Annual Salary → ÷ 12 → Monthly Pay (ii); Annual Salary → ÷ 24 → Semi-Monthly Pay (iii)

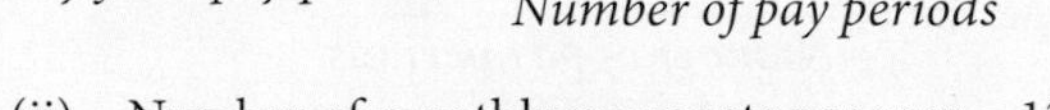

$$\textit{Pay for a pay period} = \frac{\textit{Annual salary}}{\textit{Number of pay periods}}$$

(ii) Number of monthly payments per year = 12

$$\textit{Monthly pay} = \frac{78{,}000.00}{12}$$
$$= \$6{,}500.00$$

Therefore, the equivalent monthly pay is \$6,500.00.

(iii) Number of semi-monthly payments per year = 24

$$\textit{Semi-monthly pay} = \frac{78{,}000.00}{24}$$
$$= \$3{,}250.00$$

Therefore, the equivalent semi-monthly pay is \$3,250.00.

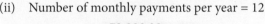

Example 5.4-c Calculating Semi-Monthly Pay Given the Bi-Weekly Pay

James' bi-weekly pay is \$2,700. Calculate his equivalent semi-monthly pay.

Solution

Number of bi-weekly payments per year = 26

$$\textit{Annual salary} = \textit{Pay for a period} \times \textit{Number of pay periods}$$
$$= 2{,}700.00 \times 26$$
$$= \$70{,}200.00$$

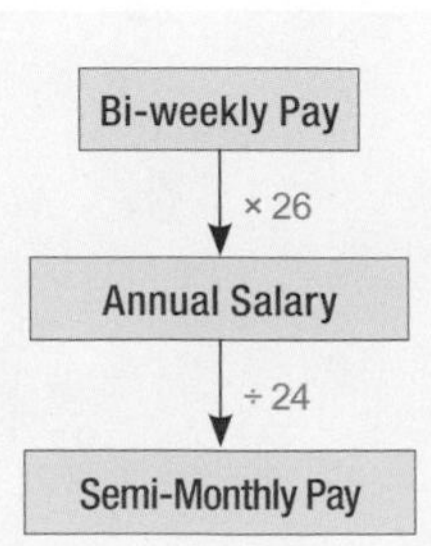

Solution *continued*

Number of semi-monthly payments per year = 24

$$\text{Semi-monthly pay} = \frac{\text{Annual salary}}{\text{24 pay periods}}$$

$$= \frac{70{,}200.00}{24}$$

$$= \$2{,}925.00$$

Therefore, his equivalent semi-monthly pay is $2,925.00.

Example 5.4-d **Calculating the Weekly Pay Given the Semi-Monthly Pay**

Lisa's semi-monthly pay is $1,892.80. Calculate her equivalent weekly pay.

Solution

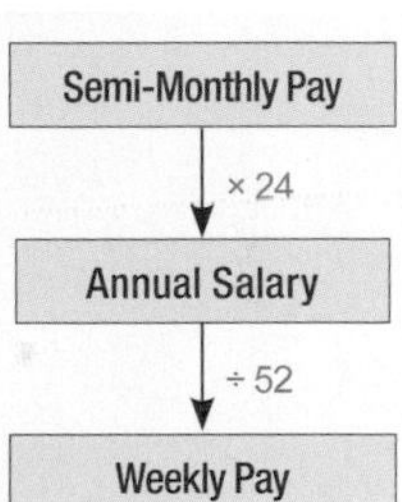

Number of semi-monthly payments per year = 24

$$\text{Annual salary} = \text{Pay for a period} \times \text{Number of pay periods}$$

$$= 1{,}892.80 \times 24$$

$$= \$45{,}427.20$$

Number of weekly payments per year = 52

$$\text{Weekly pay} = \frac{\text{Annual salary}}{\text{52 pay periods}}$$

$$= \frac{45{,}427.20}{52}$$

$$= \$873.60$$

Therefore, her equivalent weekly pay is $873.60.

Hourly Rate of Pay

Hourly rate of pay employees usually have a variable and unpredictable workload. They receive payment based on an hourly rate of pay for the number of hours worked during the pay period.

By knowing the hourly rate of pay and the number of hours worked during a pay period, you can calculate the total gross pay for that pay period.

$$\textbf{Pay for a pay period} = \textbf{Hourly rate} \times \textbf{Number of hours worked}$$

Depending on the type of profession/job, the number of working hours per week (workweek) may vary. The most common workweeks are: 40 hours, 37.5 hours, 35 hours, and 32.5 hours.

$$\textbf{Weekly pay} = \textbf{Hourly rate} \times \textbf{Workweek}$$

$$\textbf{Hourly rate} = \frac{\textbf{Weekly pay}}{\textbf{Workweek}}$$

Example 5.4-e **Calculating Bi-Weekly Pay, Given the Hourly Rate and the Workweek**

Aran is paid bi-weekly. His workweek is 35 hours and his hourly rate is $29.50. Calculate his:

(i) Bi-weekly pay

(ii) Equivalent semi-monthly pay

Solution

(i) Number of working hours for 2 weeks = 2 × 35 = 70 hours

$$\textit{Pay for 2 weeks} = \textit{Hourly rate} \times \textit{Number of hours worked for 2 weeks}$$
$$= 29.50 \times 70$$
$$= \$2{,}065.00$$

Therefore, his bi-weekly pay is $2,065.00.

(ii) Number of bi-weekly payments per year = 26

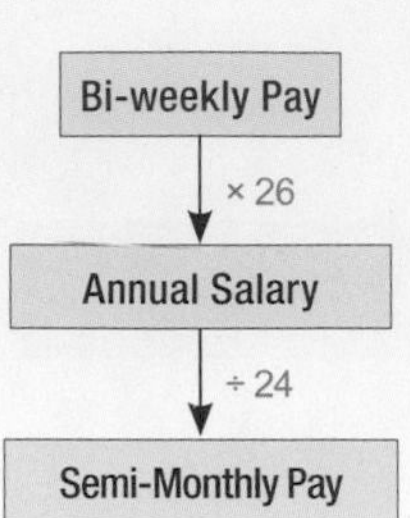

$$\textit{Annual salary} = \textit{Pay for a period} \times \textit{Number of pay periods}$$
$$= 2{,}065.00 \times 26$$
$$= \$53{,}690.00$$

Number of semi-monthly payments per year = 24

$$\textit{Semi-monthly pay} = \frac{\textit{Annual salary}}{\textit{24 pay periods}}$$
$$= \frac{53{,}690.00}{24}$$
$$= 2{,}237.083333... = \$2{,}237.08$$

Therefore, his equivalent semi-monthly pay is $2,237.08.

Example 5.4-f **Calculating Weekly Pay and Hourly Rate, Given the Annual Pay and the Workweek**

Mythili is being paid $39,000 per annum. Her workweek is 40 hours. Calculate her:

(i) Weekly pay

(ii) Hourly rate of pay

Solution

(i)
$$\textit{Weekly pay} = \frac{\textit{Annual salary}}{\textit{52 pay periods}}$$
$$= \frac{39{,}000.00}{52}$$
$$= \$750.00$$

Therefore, her weekly pay is $750.00.

(ii)
$$\textit{Hourly rate} = \frac{\textit{Weekly pay}}{\textit{Workweek}}$$
$$= \frac{750.00}{40}$$
$$= \$18.75$$

Therefore, her hourly rate is $18.75.

Example 5.4-g **Calculating Workweek and Annual Salary, Given the Bi-Weekly Pay and the Hourly Rate**

Albert is paid $1,687.50 bi-weekly. His hourly rate of pay is $22.50. Calculate his:

(i) Regular workweek

(ii) Equivalent annual salary

Solution

(i)
$$\textit{Pay for 2 weeks} = \textit{Hourly rate} \times \textit{Number of hours worked for 2 weeks}$$
$$1{,}687.50 = 22.50 \times \textit{Number of hours worked for 2 weeks}$$
$$\textit{Number of hours worked for 2 weeks} = \frac{1{,}687.50}{22.50}$$
$$= 75 \text{ hours}$$
$$\textit{Number of hours worked per week} = \frac{75}{2}$$
$$= 37.5 \text{ hours}$$

Therefore, his regular workweek is 37.5 hours.

Solution
continued

(ii) $\textit{Annual salary} = \textit{Pay for a pay period} \times \textit{Number of pay periods}$

$= 1{,}687.50 \times 26$

$= \$43{,}875.00$

Therefore, his equivalent annual salary is $43,875.00.

Overtime Rate of Pay

If you work more than the specified number of hours per week (workweek), you will be eligible for overtime payment for the additional hours worked. This extra payment is calculated using an overtime rate. The overtime rate of pay is usually $1\frac{1}{2}$ times the regular hourly rate (time-and-a-half) or 2 times the regular hourly rate (double). This factor (1.5 times or 2 times) that employers use to calculate the overtime rate is known as the **overtime factor**.

Overtime rate = Overtime factor × Hourly rate

Overtime pay = Overtime rate × Number of hours worked overtime

Example 5.4-h **Calculating Regular Rate of Pay and Overtime Rate of Pay**

Cindy earns $46,800 per year. Her workweek is 40 hours and her overtime factor is 1.5. Calculate her:

(i) Regular rate of pay (ii) Overtime rate of pay

Solution

(i) $\textit{Pay for a pay period} = \dfrac{\textit{Annual salary}}{\textit{Number of pay periods}}$

$\textit{Weekly pay} = \dfrac{46{,}800.00}{52}$

$= \$900.00$

$\textit{Hourly rate} = \dfrac{\textit{Weekly pay}}{\textit{Workweek}}$

$= \dfrac{900.00}{40}$

$= \$22.50$ per hour

Therefore, her regular rate of pay is $22.50 per hour.

Annual Salary
÷ 52
Weekly Pay
÷ Workweek
Hourly Rate
× Overtime Factor
Overtime Rate

(ii) $\textit{Overtime rate} = \textit{Overtime factor} \times \textit{Hourly rate}$

$= 1.5 \times 22.50$

$= \$33.75$

Therefore, her overtime rate of pay is $33.75 per hour.

Example 5.4-i **Calculating Pay for a Pay Period Including Overtime Pay**

Fred earns $58,500 annually and is paid bi-weekly. His regular workweek is 37.5 hours. Overtime is paid at 1.5 times the regular rate. Calculate his pay for the last pay period in which he worked 85 hours.

Solution

$$\textit{Pay for a pay period} = \frac{\textit{Annual salary}}{\textit{Number of pay periods}}$$

$$\textit{Bi-weekly pay} = \frac{58{,}500.00}{26} = \$2{,}250.00$$

$$\textit{Weekly pay} = \frac{\textit{Bi-weekly pay}}{2} = \frac{2{,}250.00}{2} = \$1{,}1250.00$$

$$\textit{Hourly rate} = \frac{\textit{Weekly pay}}{\textit{Workweek}} = \frac{1{,}125.00}{37.5} = \$30.00 \text{ per hour}$$

$$\textit{Overtime factor} = 1.5$$

$$\textit{Overtime rate} = \textit{Overtime factor} \times \textit{Hourly rate} = 1.5 \times 30.00 = \$45.00 \text{ per hour}$$

$$\textit{Number of hours worked overtime} = 85 - (37.5 \times 2) = 85 - 75 = 10 \text{ hours}$$

$$\textit{Overtime pay} = \textit{Overtime rate} \times \textit{Number of hours worked overtime} = 45.00 \times 10 = \$450.00$$

$$\textit{Total Pay} = \textit{Bi-weekly pay} + \textit{Overtime pay} = 2{,}250.00 + 450.00 = \$2{,}700.00$$

Therefore, Fred's pay for the last pay period is $2,700.00.

Commissions

If the employment is based on commission, then the gross pay for a given pay period is calculated based on a percent of sales, known as the commission rate. Sales commissions are usually given to sales people to encourage them to sell more, because the more they sell, the more they will earn.

In this section we will use only a straight (single) commission rate in calculating the gross pay for a pay period.

$$\textbf{\textit{Commission}} = \textbf{\textit{Commission rate}} \times \textbf{\textit{Amount of sales}}$$

Example 5.4-j **Calculating Salary Based on a Straight (Single) Commission Rate**

David's salary is 5% of the sales that he makes for the month. If he makes $50,000 in sales in one month, what is his salary for that month?

Solution

$$\textit{Commission} = \textit{Commission rate} \times \textit{Amount of sales} = 0.05 \times 50{,}000.00 = \$2{,}500.00$$

Therefore, David's salary for the month is $2,500.00.

Example 5.4-k **Calculating the Amount of Sales, Given the Amount and the Rate of Commission**

Mercy is paid 4.5% sales commission. She earned $2,025 in commission last month. Calculate her sales for last month.

Solution

$$\text{Commission} = \text{Commission rate} \times \text{Amount of sales}$$

$$\text{Amount of sales} = \frac{\text{Commission}}{\text{Commission rate}}$$

$$= \frac{2{,}025.00}{0.045}$$

$$= \$45{,}000.00$$

Therefore, Mercy's sales for last month were $45,000.00.

Example 5.4-l **Calculating the Rate of Commission, Given the Amount of Commission and the Amount of Sales**

Carol earned a commission of $11,375 from the sale of a house which sold for $650,000. Calculate the rate of commission she charged for the sale of the house.

Solution

$$\text{Commission} = \text{Commission rate} \times \text{Amount of sales}$$

$$\text{Commission rate} = \frac{\text{Commission}}{\text{Amount of sales}}$$

$$\text{Commission rate} = \frac{11{,}375.00}{650{,}000.00}$$

$$= 0.0175$$

$$= 1.75\%$$

Therefore, she charged a rate of commission of 1.75%.

5.4 | Exercises

Answers to odd-numbered problems are available at the end of the textbook.

For the following problems, express the answers rounded to two decimal places, wherever applicable.

For Problems 1 to 10, calculate the missing values.

	Annual Salary ($)	Monthly Pay ($)	Semi-Monthly Pay ($)	Bi-Weekly Pay ($)	Weekly Pay ($)
1.	$48,750.00	?	?	?	?
2.	$32,760.00	?	?	?	?
3.	?	$3,380.00	?	?	?
4.	?	$4,550.00	?	?	?
5.	?	?	$1,787.50	?	?
6.	?	?	$2,047.50	?	?
7.	?	?	?	$1,350.00	?
8.	?	?	?	$1,540.50	?
9.	?	?	?	?	$673.50
10.	?	?	?	?	$864.00

11. Scott is paid an annual salary of $36,400. Calculate his bi-weekly pay and the equivalent monthly pay.
12. Judy receives an annual salary of $45,000. Calculate her weekly pay and the equivalent monthly pay.
13. Floyd's bi-weekly pay is $1,912.50. Calculate his annual salary and the equivalent monthly pay.
14. Barb receives a weekly pay of $936. Calculate her annual salary and the equivalent monthly pay.
15. Joyce receives a monthly pay of $4,143.75. Calculate her annual salary and the equivalent weekly pay.
16. Chris receives a monthly pay of $2,625. Calculate his annual salary and the equivalent bi-weekly pay.

17. Lionel receives a bi-weekly pay of $1,980 from his employer. If the employer changed the pay period to semi-monthly instead of bi-weekly, calculate the semi-monthly payment he would receive.

18. An employee receives a weekly pay of $720. Calculate the equivalent semi-monthly pay this employee would receive.

19. Calculate the bi-weekly pay and the equivalent semi-monthly pay of an employee receiving an annual salary of $68,640.

20. Calculate the semi-monthly pay and equivalent bi-weekly pay of an employee receiving an annual salary of $42,900.

For Problems 21 to 28, calculate the missing values.

	Annual Salary ($)	Weekly Pay ($)	Workweek (Hours/Week)	Hourly Rate ($/hour)	Overtime Factor	Overtime Rate ($/hour)
21.	$57,200.00	?	40.0	?	1.50	?
22.	$47,775.00	?	47.5	?	2.00	?
23.	?	$747.50	32.5	?	?	$34.50
24.	?	$938.00	35.0	?	?	$40.20
25.	?	$519.75	?	$15.75	1.50	?
26.	?	$890.00	?	$22.25	2.00	?
27.	?	?	37.5	$17.20	2.25	?
28.	?	?	32.5	$24.00	1.75	?

29. Susan's annual salary of $68,000 is based on a 35-hour workweek and she is paid weekly. Calculate:

    a. Her weekly pay.

    b. Her overtime rate of pay at 1.5 times the regular rate of pay.

    c. Her gross pay for a week in which she worked 6 hours overtime.

30. James receives an annual salary of $46,800. His workweek is 37.5 hours. Calculate:

    a. His weekly pay.

    b. His overtime rate of pay at 2 times the regular rate of pay.

    c. His gross pay for a week in which he worked 9 hours overtime.

31. Terry receives a weekly pay of $1,267.50. He has a 32.5-hour workweek. Calculate his hourly rate of pay and his equivalent annual salary.

32. Ron's weekly pay of $918.75 is based on a 37.5-hour workweek. Calculate his hourly rate of pay and his equivalent annual salary.

33. Alex earns an hourly rate of pay of $23.70 for a 35-hour workweek. Calculate his weekly pay and his equivalent annual salary.

34. Tom earns $25 per hour and his workweek is 40 hours. Calculate his weekly pay and his equivalent annual salary.

For Problems 35 to 40, calculate the missing values.

	Sales ($)	Commission Rate (%)	Commission ($)
35.	$45,500	4.5%	?
36.	$21,375	7.5%	?
37.	?	5.0%	$2,925
38.	?	7.0%	$1,775
39.	$46,500	?	$1,395
40.	$35,000	?	$1,925

41. Tracy is paid a fixed commission of 5.5% on her sales in a month. How much will she be paid in a month in which her sales are $47,500?

42. Nancy is paid a fixed commission of 3.75% on all sales during the month. Sales for last month were $38,550. What were her gross earnings for last month?

43. Dianne is paid a commission of 4.5% on all sales in a month. Determine her sales for the month in which she earned $2,317.50 in commission.

44. Joana receives a commission of 6.5% on all sales during that period. Last week she earned $1,935.05. What were her sales for last week?

45. Bill is paid on a fixed commission rate basis. His gross pay in September was $2,730 on sales totalling $42,000. Calculate his rate of commission.

46. Jennifer is paid on a fixed commission rate based on her sales. Calculate her rate of commission if she earned $3,696 in a month when her sales were $67,200.

5 | Review Exercises

Answers to odd-numbered problems are available at the end of the textbook.

For Problems 1 and 2, calculate the missing values.

1.

	Percent	Decimal	Fraction (or mixed number) in lowest terms
a.	80%	?	?
b.	?	0.25	?
c.	?	?	$1\frac{1}{2}$
d.	$6\frac{1}{3}$%	?	?
e.	?	0.048	?
f.	?	?	$\frac{2}{25}$

2.

	Percent	Decimal	Fraction (or mixed number) in lowest terms
a.	2%	?	?
b.	?	0.245	?
c.	?	?	$\frac{5}{12}$
d.	$12\frac{2}{5}$%	?	?
e.	?	1.075	?
f.	?	?	$\frac{3}{80}$

For the following problems, express the answers rounded to two decimal places, wherever applicable.

For Problems 3 and 4, calculate the value.

3. a. 125% of what number is 45?

b. What percent of $180 is $36?

c. How much is $\frac{3}{8}$% of $60?

4. a. 225% of what number is 180?

b. What percent of $750 is $300?

c. How much is $\frac{2}{5}$% of $30?

5. Paul sold a property for $575,000, which was 125% of the purchase price. Calculate the purchase price.

6. Peter sold his shares for $14,437.50. Calculate the amount he paid for the shares if his selling price was 275% of the amount he paid for the shares.

7. Lian scored 45 out of 60 on a math test. What was his percent grade on the test?

8. There were 48 questions in a test. Ann answered 40 questions correctly. What percent of the questions did she answer correctly?

9. The total expenditure for the construction of a highway was $1,280,000. If this is 111% of the budgeted amount, calculate the amount budgeted to build the highway.

10. If Henry's business expenditures were $14,480 in March and $14,806.50 in April, which were 112% and 122% of his budgeted expenditure for March and April respectively, calculate his total budgeted expenditure for the two months.

11. Assume that out of the 350,000 people who immigrated to Canada in 2016, 12.25% were from China, 9.75% were from the Philippines, and the rest were from other countries.

    a. Calculate the number of people who immigrated to Canada from China.

    b. If the combined number of immigrants from China and the Philippines constituted 0.2% of the population of Canada, calculate the population of Canada in 2016. (Round the answer up to the next whole number.)

12. A dinner at a restaurant cost you $27.80 and you tipped the waiter 15% of the cost.

    a. What was the value of the tip?

    b. If the tip that you gave the waiter was 2% of all the money he made from tips that night, calculate the amount that the waiter earned from tips that night.

13. a. What is 180 increased by 70%?

    b. $90 decreased by 90% is how much?

    c. How much is $4,500 increased by 150%?

    d. What amount increased by 25.75% is 855.10 kg?

14. a. What is 2,680 increased by 85%?

    b. $880.45 decreased by 85% is how much?

    c. How much is $1,850.50 increased by 300%?

    d. What amount increased by $90\frac{1}{2}$% is 110.49 kg?

15. a. What amount decreased by 10% is $477?

    b. What amount increased by 180% is $20.65?

    c. $1,200 decreased by what percent is $300?

    d. 750 kg is what percent less than 1,000 kg?

16. a. What amount increased by 28% is $231.75?

    b. What amount increased by 600% is $24.92?

    c. $800 increased by what percent is $1,800?

    d. 102 km is what percent more than 85 km?

17. The sales tax of 13% increased the cost of a dinner at a restaurant to $55.37. What was the cost of dinner before taxes?

18. After paying income taxes of 32%, Sally's annual pay was $35,600. Calculate Sally's income before deducting income taxes.

19. If toner cartridges that sell in stores for $45 each are being offered online for $36 each, calculate the percent discount offered online.

20. A college tuition fee of $4,500 increases to $4,900. Calculate the percent increase of the fee.

21. The average summer temperature in Toronto increased by 3.5 °C this year. If the average daytime temperature last year was 28 °C, calculate the percent change in the average summer temperature this year.

22. The average winter snowfall in Montreal increased by 2.5 cm this year. If the average winter snowfall last year was 50 cm, calculate the percent change in average winter snowfall this year.

23. The selling price of an apartment was $335,000. This is 34% more than the purchase price. Calculate the original purchase price.

24. The selling price of a home was $663,000. This is 23.5% more than the purchase price. Calculate the original purchase price.

25. A car dealer reduced the price of a car by 8.75%. The current price of the car is $38,000. What was the price of the car before the reduction in price?

26. A property developer reduced the price of a house by 6.25%. The current price of the house is $703,125. What was the price of the house before the reduction?

27. A marketing department's expenses rose by 30% from last year. If this year's expenses are $234,260, calculate last year's expenses.

28. Following a discount, a manufacturing company paid $56,400 for a heavy-duty packing machine from Japan. If they received a 21% discount, calculate the original price of the machine.

29. On a math quiz, Chelsea scored 15% more than Zane. By what percent is Zane's score less than Chelsea's?

30. If Sabrina's annual salary is 10% more than Christina's, by what percent is Christina's annual earnings less than Sabrina's?

• 31. Holistic Energy Ltd. spends $1,200, $1,400, $800, and $1,700 on average on replacing printer cartridges for their black & white inkjet printers, colour inkjet printers, black & white laser printers, and colour laser printers, respectively, every month.

a. What percent of the total expenditures on printer cartridges do they spend on colour laser printers every month?

b. If they decide to reduce the expenses on both colour inkjet printers and colour laser printers by 50%, what percent of the total expenditures would they spend on black & white laser printers?

• 32. A manufacturing company has 280 production people, 21 quality inspectors, 15 sales people, 6 marketing people, and 15 people in other departments such as HR, Finance, etc.

a. What percent of the total employees is quality inspectors?

b. If 15% of the production people quit their jobs, what percent of the total remaining employees is quality inspectors?

• 33. Katelyn's financial manager invested her savings in a portfolio of shares that comprised of investments of $2,000, $1,800, and $3,100 in the infrastructure, hi-tech, and garment industries, respectively. Towards the end of 2017, if the value of her shares in the infrastructure industry rose by 20% while the rest remained the same, calculate the percent change in the value of her total investments.

• 34. Preston's website company invests their annual savings in different mutual funds. In 2016, they invested $12,500 in high-growth funds, $5,000 in medium-growth funds, and $2,000 in low-growth funds. If the value of their low-growth funds dropped by 10% this year while the rest stayed the same, by what percent did the total value of their investments change?

35. Calculate the amount of interest earned from an eight-month investment of $7,500 at 4.5% p.a.

36. Steve borrowed $4,250 for 15 months at 3.2% p.a. How much interest would he have to pay on the loan?

37. What amount must be invested now to earn $375 in interest in three years at 4% p.a.?

38. An investment at 3% p.a. earned interest of $225 over a period of two years. Calculate the amount invested.

39. At what annual interest rate will an investment of $2,400 earn interest of $660 in five years?

40. The interest on a loan of $3,600 for three years is $486. Calculate the annual interest rate charged on the loan.

41. Ram's bi-weekly pay is $1,750. Calculate his annual salary and the equivalent monthly pay.

42. Sam's monthly pay is $4,680. Calculate his annual salary and the equivalent bi-weekly pay.

43. Rodney's weekly pay is $787.50 and his workweek is 35 hours. If his overtime factor is 2, calculate his hourly rate of pay and the overtime rate of pay.

44. John's bi-weekly pay is $1,820 and his regular workweek is 40 hours. If his overtime factor is 1.5, calculate his hourly rate of pay and the overtime rate of pay.

45. A secretary is paid $14.50 per hour and her workweek is 37.5 hours. Calculate her annual salary and her semi-monthly pay.

46. A bank teller is paid $17.25 per hour and her workweek is 35 hours. Calculate her annual salary and her semi-monthly pay.

47. Chris receives a semi-monthly pay of $2,246.40. Calculate his annual salary and the equivalent bi-weekly pay.

48. Lisa receives a bi-weekly pay of $2,121.60. Calculate her annual salary and the equivalent semi-monthly pay.

49. Amy receives a commission rate of 6% on all sales in a month. Last month she earned $2,160. Calculate her sales during last month.

50. Roger, a real estate agent, receives a 2% commission on the sales of houses. He earned a commission of $8,500 from the sale of a house. Calculate the selling price of the house.

Self-Test | Chapter 5

Answers to all problems are available at the end of the textbook.

1. Calculate the missing values:

	Percent	Decimal	Fraction (or mixed number) in lowest terms
a.	$10\frac{3}{5}\%$	?	?
b.	?	2.25	?
c.	?	?	$\frac{1}{400}$
d.	$\frac{1}{2}\%$	?	?
e.	?	0.002	?
f.	?	?	$\frac{53}{200}$

For the following problems, express the answers rounded to two decimal places, wherever applicable.

2. a. What percent of $30 is $3.75?

   b. 22.5% of $1,500 is how much?

   c. $75 is 15% of what number?

3. Colton's store expenses for the month of July and August were $33,480 and $36,580, which were 110% and 90% of the budgeted expenditure for the months of July and August, respectively. Calculate the total budgeted expenses for the two months.

4. Sandra earns an annual salary of $60,000. Every month, she spends $1,400 on rent, $600 on car expenses, $200 on loan repayment, $800 on miscellaneous expenses, and saves $2,000.

   a. What percent of her annual salary is her annual expenses?

   b. If she invests 25% of the $2,000 savings in a mutual fund every month, what percent of the annual salary is invested in the fund over the year.

5. Calculate the missing values:

	Initial value	Percent change	Final value
a.	$80	?	$125
b.	$725	13%	?
c.	?	0.5%	$4.75
d.	$60	?	$45
e.	$150	–20%	?
f.	?	–4%	$297.60

6. What is the amount of decrease if the initial value was 75 and the percent decrease is 28%?

7. If a discount of $51 is equivalent to a 60% decrease from the initial value, calculate the initial value.

• 8. In 2017, a stock lost 60% of its value. In 2018, the stock's value increased by 80%. Calculate the percent change in the stock's value over the two-year period.

• 9. The overall increase in the price of a house from 2016 to 2018 was 4%. If the price increased by 5% from 2016 to 2017 and its value in 2017 was $472,500, calculate the value of the house in 2018.

• 10. The price of a share that was purchased for $20 increased by 30% during the first year and decreased by 30% during the second year.

   a. Calculate the value of the share at the end of the two years.

   b. Calculate the percent change in the share price over the two-year period.

• 11. The value of a share dropped by $1.25 at the end of the first year, and a further $2.50 at the end of the second year. If the price of the share at the end of the second year was $12.55, calculate the percent change in the price of the share:

   a. For each of the two years.

   b. Over the two-year period.

12. At what annual interest rate will $650 earn interest of $62.40 in two years?

13. Calculate the principal which will earn interest of $202.50 at 3.6% p.a. in 15 months.

14. How much interest would you have to pay on a 180-day loan of $2,190 at 4.2% p.a.?

15. Ruben's weekly pay is $810. Calculate his annual salary and the equivalent monthly pay.

16. Kathy's annual salary is $34,944, based on a 35-hour workweek.

   a. What would be her bi-weekly pay?

   b. What is her hourly rate of pay?

17. An emloyee was receiving a bi-weekly pay of $2,340. If the employer changed the pay period to semi-monthly, instead bi-weekly, calculate the employee's semi-monthly pay.

18. Warren is paid a commission on all his sales. He is paid monthly. Last month his pay was $2,400 and his sales were $32,000. Calculate the commission rate.

Chapter 6 RATIOS, PROPORTIONS, AND APPLICATIONS

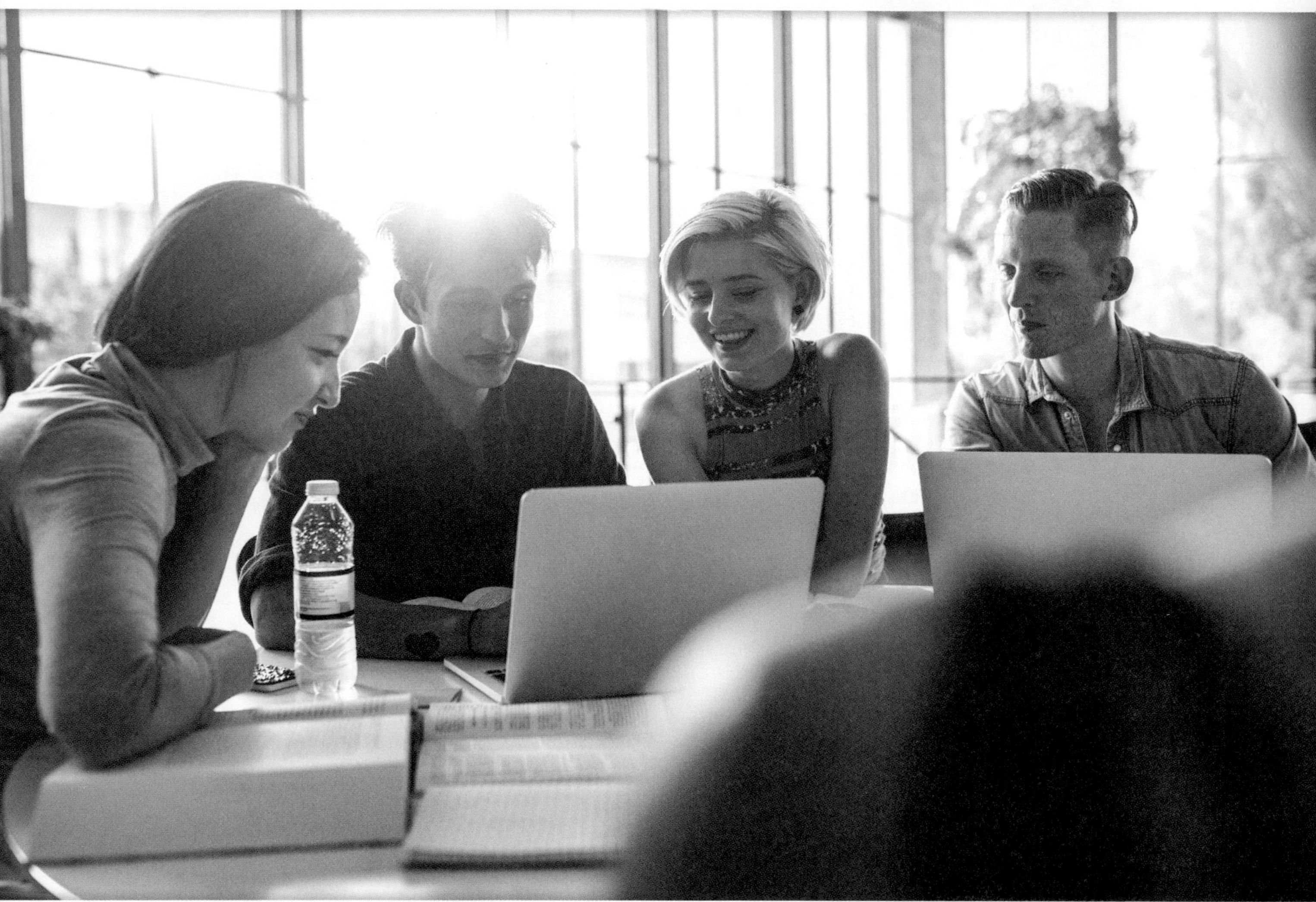

LEARNING OBJECTIVES

- Identify ratios and rates to compare quantities.
- Set up ratios and use them to solve problems involving allocation and sharing of quantities.
- Solve problems by determining unknown quantities using proportions as equivalent sets of ratios.
- Allocate quantities on a proportional basis using pro-ration as an application of proportions.
- Convert currencies between countries using exchange rates.
- Determine index numbers and their applications.

CHAPTER OUTLINE

Introduction

One of the ways in which we use mathematics in our daily lives is through the comparison of numbers and quantities of two or more items. Numbers and quantities are more meaningful and easier to work with when relevant comparisons can be made between them. A **ratio** is a comparison or relationship between two or more quantities. An example of how ratios can be used in our daily lives is in grocery shopping: if a 260 gram box of cereal costs $2.67, and a 400 gram box of the same cereal costs $3.99, we can use ratios to calculate the unit prices and determine which box of cereal is more economical.

When two sets of ratios are equal, we say that they are **proportional** to each other. We can use proportions to calculate unknown quantities that would otherwise be difficult to estimate. For example, if you wanted to calculate the amount of gas needed to travel 375 km, knowing that the fuel efficiency of your car is 9.8 litres per 100 km, then you could set up a proportion equation to determine the amount of gas needed for the trip.

In this chapter, we will learn the concepts related to ratios to be able to solve problems involving ratios, proportions, and pro-rations, including business applications such as currency conversions and index numbers.

6.1 | Ratios

A ratio is a comparison or relationship between two or more quantities.

A **ratio** is a comparison or relationship between two or more quantities with the same units. Therefore, ratios are not expressed with units.

For example, if Andy (A) invested $5,000 and Barry ($B$) invested $4,000 in a business, the comparison of A's investment to B's investment in the same order is known as the ratio of their investments.

Expressing Ratios

Expressing a Ratio of Two Quantities

When comparing two quantities, there are different ways to express the ratio. In the example above, the ratio of A's investment to B's may be expressed in any of the following forms:

5,000 to 4,000 (separate the quantities using the word 'to')

5,000 : 4,000 (using a colon and read as '5,000 is to 4,000')

$\frac{5,000}{4,000}$ (as a fraction and read as '5,000 over 4,000')

In the above example, the decimal equivalent of the fraction $\frac{5,000}{4,000}$ is 1.25; therefore, we can state that "A's invesment is 1.25 times B's investment".

Note: When representing a ratio as a fraction, if the denominator is 1, the denominator (1) *must still be written. For example, if the ratio of two quantities is* $\frac{3}{1}$, *then it is incorrect to say that the ratio is 3. It should be stated as* $\frac{3}{1}$ *or* 3 : 1.

Expressing a Ratio of More than Two Quantities

When comparing more than two quantities, the ratio is expressed using colons.

For example, if A's investment is $5,000, B's investment is $4,000, and C's investment is $1,000 in a business, then the ratio of their investments, respectively, is expressed as:

5,000 : 4,000 : 1,000

Terms of a Ratio

The quantities in a ratio are known as the **terms** of the ratio.

For example, the terms of the ratio 5 : 7 : 19 are 5, 7, and 19.

Equivalent Ratios

When all the terms of the ratio are multiplied by the same number or divided by the same number, the result will be an **equivalent ratio**.

For example, when the terms of the ratio 12 : 15 are multiplied by 2, we obtain an equivalent ratio of 24 : 30.

$$12 : 15$$
$$12 \times \mathbf{2} : 15 \times \mathbf{2}$$
$$24 : 30$$

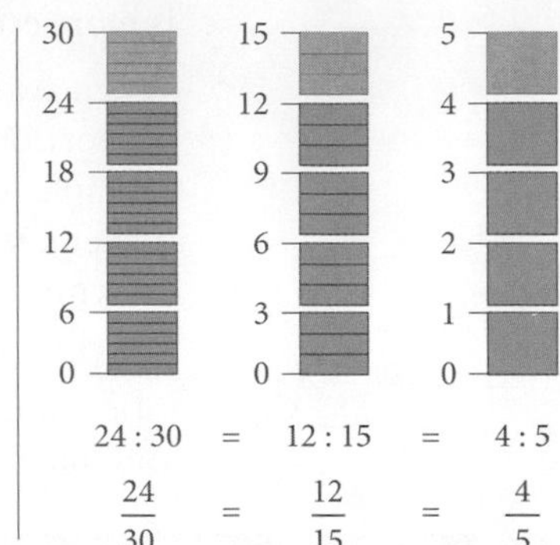

When the terms of the ratio 12 : 15 are divided by the common factor 3, we obtain the equivalent ratio of 4 : 5.

$$12 : 15$$
$$12 \div \mathbf{3} : 15 \div \mathbf{3}$$
$$4 : 5$$

Therefore, the ratios 12 : 15, 24 : 30, and 4 : 5 are equivalent ratios.

Reducing a Ratio to its Simplest or Lowest Terms

Comparisons are easier when ratios are reduced to their **lowest terms**. When all the terms of a ratio are integers, the ratio can be reduced to its lowest terms by dividing all the terms by their common factors.

For example, if A earns \$3,000, B earns \$4,500, and C earns \$6,000, then the equivalent ratio of their earnings reduced to its lowest terms is calculated as follows:

A ratio is in its simplest form when the terms do not have a common factor other than one.

A : B : C	
3,000 : 4,500 : 6,000	Dividing each term by the common factor 100,
30 : 45 : 60	Dividing each term by the common factor 15,
2 : 3 : 4	The ratio is now in its lowest terms.

By reducing the ratio to lowest terms, we can say that the earnings of A, B, and C are in the ratio of 2 : 3 : 4.

When two ratios are equivalent, they result in the same answer when reduced to lowest terms.

Example 6.1-a **Determining Equivalent Ratios**

Determine whether the given pairs of ratios are equivalent by reducing them to lowest terms.

(i) 18 : 12 and 12 : 8 (ii) 20 : 24 and 15 : 20

Solution

(i)

18 : 12	12 : 8
18 ÷ 6 : 12 ÷ 6	12 ÷ 4 : 8 ÷ 4
3 : 2	3 : 2

Therefore, the ratios 18 : 12 and 12 : 8 are equivalent.

(ii)

20 : 24	15 : 20
20 ÷ 4 : 24 ÷ 4	15 ÷ 5 : 20 ÷ 5
5 : 6	3 : 4

Therefore, the ratios 20 : 24 and 15 : 20 are **not** equivalent.

Reducing Ratios When One or More of the Terms of the Ratio Are Fractions

To reduce a ratio with fractions, first convert all the terms to integers by multiplying all the terms by the least common denominator, and then reduce to lowest terms.

For example,

The ratio remains the same when all the terms are multiplied or divided by the same number.

$\frac{2}{3} : \frac{4}{5} : 2$	Multiplying each term by the least common denominator 15,
$10 : 12 : 30$	Dividing each term by the common factor 2,
$5 : 6 : 15$	

Reducing Ratios When One or More of the Terms of the Ratio Are Decimal Numbers

To reduce a ratio with decimal numbers, first convert all the terms to integers by moving the decimal point of all the terms to the right by the same number of places, and then reduce to lowest terms.

For example,

$2.25 : 3.5 : 5$	Moving the decimal point of each term two places to the right,
$225 : 350 : 500$	Dividing each term by the common factor 25,
$9 : 14 : 20$	

Reducing Ratios When the Terms of the Ratio Are a Combination of Fractions and Decimal Numbers

To reduce a ratio with both fractions and decimal numbers, first convert all the fractional terms to integers, and then convert all the decimal terms to integers. Finally, reduce to lowest terms.

For example,

$5.8 : \frac{9}{2} : 4$	Multiplying each term by 2,
$11.6 : 9 : 8$	Moving the decimal point of each term one place to the right,
$116 : 90 : 80$	Dividing each term by the common factor 2,
$58 : 45 : 40$	

Reducing Ratios to an Equivalent Ratio Where the Smallest Term is 1

To make the comparison of quantities easier, we can also reduce a ratio to its equivalent ratio where the smallest term is equal to 1, by dividing all the terms by the smallest term.

For example, if the investment amounts of three partners A, B, and C are \$35,000, \$78,750, and \$59,500, respectively, then the equivalent ratio of their investments, where the smallest term is 1, is calculated as follows:

$A : B : C$	
$35{,}000 : 78{,}750 : 59{,}500$	Dividing each term by the smallest term, 35,000,
$1 : 2.25 : 1.7$	The ratio is now reduced to its equivalent ratio with the smallest term equal to 1.

By reducing the ratio so that the smallest term is equal to 1, we can state: (i) B's investment is 2.25 times A's investment, and (ii) C's investment is 1.7 times A's investment.

Example 6.1-b **Reducing Ratios to Lowest Terms**

Express the following ratios as equivalent ratios in their lowest terms (as whole numbers) and then reduce them to ratios where the smallest term is 1.

(i) $2\frac{7}{9} : 3\frac{1}{3} : 5$ (ii) $2.5 : 1.75 : 0.625$ (iii) $1.25 : \frac{5}{6} : 2$

Solution

(i) $2\frac{7}{9} : 3\frac{1}{3} : 5$ — Converting the terms with mixed numbers to improper fractions,

$\frac{25}{9} : \frac{10}{3} : 5$ — Multiplying each term by the least common denominator 9,

$25 : 30 : 45$ — Dividing each term by the common factor 5,

$5 : 6 : 9$ — Dividing each term by the smallest term 5,

$1 : 1.2 : 1.8$

Therefore, $2\frac{7}{9} : 3\frac{1}{3} : 5$ reduced to its lowest terms is 5 : 6 : 9 and the equivalent ratio where the smallest term is 1 is 1 : 1.2 : 1.8.

(ii) $2.5 : 1.75 : 0.625$

$2.5 : 1.75 : 0.625$ — Moving the decimal point of each term three places to the right,

$2,500 : 1,750 : 625$ — Dividing each term by the common factor 125,

$20 : 14 : 5$ — Dividing each term by the smallest term 5,

$4 : 2.8 : 1$

Therefore, 2.5 : 1.75 : 0.625 reduced to its lowest terms is 20 : 14 : 5 and the equivalent ratio where the smallest term is 1 is 4 : 2.8 : 1.

(iii) $1.25 : \frac{5}{6} : 2$ — Multiplying each term by 6,

$7.5 : 5 : 12$ — Moving the decimal point of each term one place to the right,

$75 : 50 : 120$ — Dividing each term by the common factor 5,

$15 : 10 : 24$ — Dividing each term by the smallest term 10,

$1.5 : 1 : 2.4$

Therefore, $1.25 : \frac{5}{6} : 2$ reduced to its lowest terms is 15 : 10 : 24 and the equivalent ratio where the smallest term is 1 is 1.5 : 1 : 2.4.

Order of a Ratio

The order of presenting terms in a ratio is important. For example, if A saves \$800, B saves \$1,500, and C saves \$1,200, then the ratio of the savings of A to B to C is:

A	:	B	:	C	
800	:	1,500	:	1,200	Dividing each term by the common factor 100,
8	:	15	:	12	

In the previous example, the ratio of the savings of C to B to A is:

C	:	B	:	A	
1,200	:	1,500	:	800	Dividing each term by the common factor 100,
12	:	15	:	8	

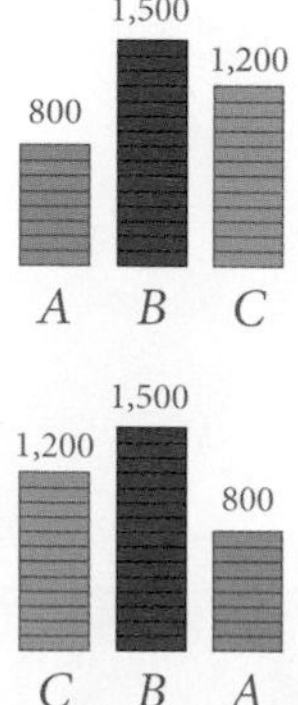

Notice that $C : B : A$ is not the same as $A : B : C$.

Ratios compare the numbers in order. The ratio 12 : 15 : 8 expresses a different comparison than the ratio 8 : 15 : 12.

Comparing Quantities

When using ratios to compare quantities of items that have the same kind of measure, the units have to be the same.

For example, the ratio of 45 minutes to 2 hours is not 45 : 2. We are comparing 'time' in both these cases; therefore, the units used have to be the same.

45 minutes : 2 hours	Converting 2 hours to minutes using 1 hour = 60 minutes,
45 minutes : 120 minutes	Dividing by the common factor 15,
3 : 8	

Similarly, we determine the ratio of 2.5 kilometres to 3,000 metres as follows:

2.5 km : 3,000 m	Converting km to m using 1 km = 1,000 m,
2,500 m : 3,000 m	Dividing by the common factor 100,
25 : 30	Dividing by the common factor 5,
5 : 6	

Example 6.1-c

Comparing Quantities that have the Same Kind of Measure but Different Units

Express each of the following ratios in its simplest form:

(i) 1.2 L to 800 mL (ii) 16 weeks to 2 years

Solution

(i)

1.2 L : 800 mL	Converting 1.2 L to mL using 1 L = 1,000 mL,
1,200 mL : 800 mL	Dividing both terms by the common factor 400,
3 : 2	

Therefore, the ratio of 1.2 L to 800 mL is 3 : 2.

(ii)

16 weeks : 2 years	Converting 2 years to weeks using 1 year = 52 weeks,
16 weeks : 104 weeks	Dividing both terms by the common factor 8,
2 : 13	

Therefore, the ratio of 16 weeks to 2 years is 2 : 13.

When using ratios to compare quantities of items that have different kinds of measure, the units of measurement of each quantity must be included in the ratio.

For example, when baking a cake, Maggie uses 4 kilograms of flour, 2 litres of water, and 6 eggs. Therefore, the ratio of flour to water to eggs is,

flour	:	water	:	eggs	
(kg)		(L)		(number)	
4	:	2	:	6	Dividing each term by the common factor 2,
2	:	1	:	3	i.e., 2 kg flour : 1 L water : 3 eggs

Rate, Unit Rate, and Unit Price

Rate

A **rate** is a special ratio that is used to compare two quantities or amounts that have different kinds of measure. The units of measurement of both quantities are included when expressing a rate.

For example, if a car travels 100 km using 9 L of gas, then the rate of kilometres per litres is 100 km : 9 L. The first term of the ratio is measured in kilometres and the second term is measured in litres. The word 'per' indicates that it is a rate and is usually denoted by a slash "/". Therefore, 100 km : 9 L is usually written as 100 km per 9 L or 100 km/9 L.

Rates are used in our day-to-day activities such as travelling, working, shopping, etc.

For example,

- travelling 90 kilometres in 1.5 hours: 90 km/1.5 hours
- working 75 hours in 2 weeks: 75 hours/2 weeks
- paying $4.80 for 4 litres of milk: $4.80/4 L

Example 6.1-d **Expressing Rate as a Ratio of Different Units of Measurement**

A laser printer printed 88 pages in 6 minutes. Express the rate in lowest terms.

Solution

The unit of the first term is in number of pages and the unit of the second term is in minutes.

88 pages : 6 minutes — Dividing each term by the common factor 2,

44 pages : 3 minutes — This is expressed as a rate as 44 pages/3 minutes.

Therefore, the printing rate is 44 pages/3 minutes.

Unit Rate

If the denominator of a **ratio** is 1, the 1 must be written in the denominator.
If the denominator of a **rate** is 1, we usually do not write the 1 in the denominator.

Unit rate represents the number of units of the first quantity (or measurement) that corresponds to one unit of the second quantity (or measurement). That is, unit rate is a rate which has a denominator of 1.

Rate can be converted to unit rate simply by dividing the first term by the second term.

For example, a rate of 90 kilometres in 1.5 hours, converted to unit rate:

$$90 \text{ km}/1.5 \text{ hours}$$
$$= \frac{90 \text{ km}}{1.5 \text{ hours}}$$
$$= 60 \text{ km/hour}$$

Similarly, a rate of 75 hours in 2 weeks, converted to unit rate:

$$75 \text{ hours}/2 \text{ weeks}$$
$$= \frac{75 \text{ hours}}{2 \text{ weeks}}$$
$$= 37.5 \text{ hours/week}$$

Example 6.1-e **Calculating Unit Rate**

A car travelled 300 kilometres in 5 hours. Calculate its average speed in km/h.

Solution

The rate of speed is 300 kilometres in 5 hours.

$$\frac{300 \text{ km}}{5 \text{ h}}$$ Dividing the first term by the second term to obtain the **unit rate**,

$$= 60 \text{ km/h}$$

Therefore, the average rate of speed is 60 kilometres per hour, or 60 km/h.

Example 6.1-f **Calculating Hourly Rate of Pay**

Peter worked 9 hours and earned $247.50. Calculate his hourly rate of pay.

Solution

The rate of pay is \$247.50 for 9 hours.

$\frac{\$247.50}{9\text{ h}}$ Dividing the first term by the second term to obtain the **unit rate**,

$= \$27.50/\text{h}$

Therefore, his hourly rate of pay is \$27.50 per hour, or \$27.50/h.

Example 6.1-g

Using Unit Rates to Solve a World Problem

A car travels 90 km in 1.5 hours. At this rate, how many kilometres will it travel in 5 hours?

Solution

This question can be solved by first determining the unit rate.

The rate of speed is 90 kilometres in 1.5 hours.

Therefore, the number of km travelled per hour $= \frac{90\text{ km}}{1.5\text{ h}}$

$= 60\text{ km/h}$

That is, the distance travelled in 1 hour = 60 km.

Therefore, the distance travelled in 5 hours = $60 \times 5 = 300$ km.

Example 6.1-h

Comparing Unit Rates

Car A requires 8.9 litres of gas to travel 100 km. Car B requires 45 litres of gas to travel 475 km. Which car has the better fuel economy?

Solution

Car A : 100 km requires 8.9 litres of gas.

Therefore, the number of km travelled per litre $= \frac{100\text{ km}}{8.9\text{ L}}$

$= 11.235955... = 11.24$ km/L of gas

Car B : 475 km requires 45 litres of gas.

Therefore, the number of km travelled per litre $= \frac{475\text{ km}}{45\text{ L}}$

$= 10.555555... = 10.56$ km/L of gas

Therefore, Car A has the better fuel economy.

Unit Price

Unit price is the unit rate that expresses the cost of an item (in dollars, cents, etc.) per one unit of that item. The price is always the numerator and the unit quantity is the denominator. That is, price is expressed per quantity of 1.

Examples of unit price are:

- Price of gas is \$1.36 per litre (\$1.36/L)
- Price of grapes is \$2 per kilogram (\$2/kg)
- Price of juice is \$0.75 per can

If the total price for a given quantity of an item is known, to determine its unit price, divide the total price of the item by its quantity.

Unit price is used in comparing and making decisions in purchasing items when various options are available. We save money when we compare the unit prices of the same item in different sized containers or different packages to determine the cheaper price per unit for our purchases.

Example 6.1-i **Calculating the Unit Price of an Item**

If 4 litres of milk cost \$4.80, then what is the unit price of milk?

Solution

To determine the unit price of milk, divide the total price by the given quantity.

That is, divide \$4.80 by 4 litres.

$$\text{Unit price} = \frac{\$4.80}{4\text{ L}} = \$1.20/\text{L}$$

Therefore, the unit price of milk is \$1.20 per litre (\$1.20/L).

Example 6.1-j **Comparing Unit Prices**

5 kg of almonds cost \$43.50 and 4 kg of almonds cost \$34.20. Which is cheaper to buy based on its unit price?

Solution

5 kg of almonds cost \$43.50.

$$\text{Therefore, unit price} = \frac{\$43.50}{5\text{ kg}} = \$8.70/\text{kg}$$

4 kg of almonds cost \$34.20

$$\text{Therefore, unit price} = \frac{\$34.20}{4\text{ kg}} = \$8.55/\text{kg}$$

Therefore, based on unit price, buying 4 kg of almonds for \$34.20 is cheaper than buying 5 kg of almonds for \$43.50.

Note: Unit rate and unit price problems can also be solved using the method of proportions as demonstrated in the next section.

Sharing Quantities Using Ratios

Sharing quantities refers to the allocation or distribution of a quantity into two or more portions (or units) based on a given ratio.

For example, to allocate last year's \$1,000 profit among persons *A*, *B*, and *C* in the ratio of 2 : 3 : 5, first add the terms of the ratio (i.e., 2, 3, and 5), which results in a total of 10 units. These 10 units represent the total profit of \$1,000, where *A*'s share constitutes 2 units, *B*'s 3 units, and *C*'s 5 units, as shown in the diagram below.

Each person's share can then be calculated, as follows:

$$A\text{'s share} = \frac{2}{10} \times 1{,}000.00 = \$200.00$$

$$B\text{'s share} = \frac{3}{10} \times 1{,}000.00 = \$300.00$$

$$C\text{'s share} = \frac{5}{10} \times 1{,}000.00 = \$500.00$$

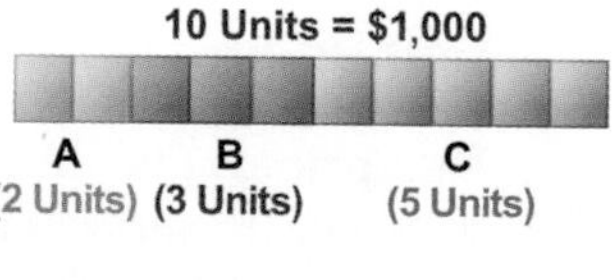

The total of the individual shares will be equal to the original amount.

- The total of *A*, *B*, and *C*'s shares is equal to the profit amount of \$1,000. That is, the shares of $A + B + C = 200 + 300 + 500 = 1{,}000$.

The ratio of the individual shares, when reduced, will be equal to the original ratio.

- If we reduce the ratio of the amounts shared by *A*, *B*, and *C* to its lowest terms, the result would be the original ratio. That is, 200 : 300 : 500 reduced to lowest terms is 2 : 3 : 5.

If this year, the ratio of *A*'s share : *B*'s share : *C*'s share is changed to 5 : 3 : 2 (instead of last year's 2 : 3 : 5), and the profit of \$1,000 remained the same, then their individual shares will change.

Their shares are recalculated as follows:

$$A\text{'s share} = \frac{5}{10} \times 1{,}000.00 = \$500.00$$

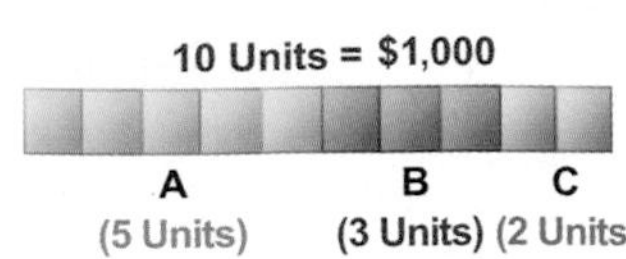

$$B\text{'s share} = \frac{3}{10} \times 1{,}000.00 = \$300.00$$

$$C\text{'s share} = \frac{2}{10} \times 1{,}000.00 = \$200.00$$

- The total of *A*, *B*, and *C*'s shares this year is still equal to the profit amount of $1,000. That is, the shares of $A + B + C = 500 + 300 + 200 = 1{,}000$.
- If we reduce the ratio of the amounts shared by *A*, *B*, and *C* to its lowest terms, the result would be the original ratio. That is, 500 : 300 : 200 reduced to lowest terms is 5 : 3 : 2.

Example 6.1-k **Sharing Quantities Using Ratios**

A, *B*, and *C* start a business and invest $3,500, $2,100, and $2,800, respectively. After a few months, *C* decides to sell his share of the business to *A* and *B*. How much would *A* and *B* have to pay for *C*'s shares if *A* and *B* want to maintain their initial investment ratio?

Solution

The investments of *A*, *B*, and *C* are in the ratio of 3,500 : 2,100 : 2,800, which can be reduced to 5 : 3 : 4.

If *A* and *B* want to maintain their initial investment ratio of 5 : 3, then *C*'s share (of $2,800) has to be paid for by *A* and *B* in the same ratio, 5 : 3.

By adding the terms of *A* and *B*, we know that *C*'s share is to be divided into a total of 8 units, as illustrated:

$$A \text{ would have to pay } C: \frac{5}{8} \times 2{,}800.00 = \$1{,}750.00$$

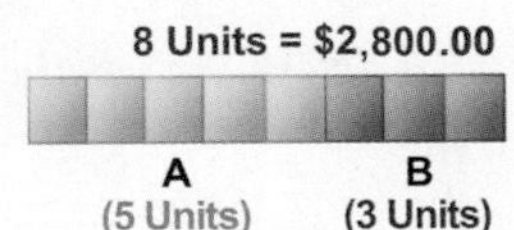

$$B \text{ would have to pay } C: \frac{3}{8} \times 2{,}800.00 = \$1{,}050.00$$

Therefore, *A* would have to pay *C* $1,750 and *B* would have to pay *C* $1,050 in order to maintain their initial investment ratio.

Example 6.1-l **Sharing Quantities Using Fractional Ratios**

The sum of all three angles of a triangle is 180 degrees. If the three angles of a triangle are in the ratio of $\frac{1}{6} : \frac{1}{3} : \frac{1}{4}$, calculate each angle of the triangle.

Solution

First, convert all the terms in the ratio to integers.

$\frac{1}{6} : \frac{1}{3} : \frac{1}{4}$ Multiplying each term by the least common denominator 12,

2 : 4 : 3 This ratio is in lowest terms.

By adding all the terms, we know that the 180 degrees is to be divided into a total of $2 + 4 + 3 = 9$ units.

1st angle: $\frac{2}{9} \times 180° = 40°$

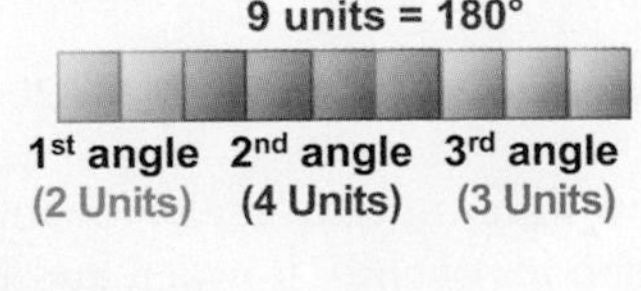

2nd angle: $\frac{4}{9} \times 180° = 80°$

3rd angle: $\frac{3}{9} \times 180° = 60°$

Therefore, the three angles of the triangle are 40°, 80°, and 60°, which sum to $40° + 80° + 60° = 180°$.

Example 6.1-m **Application Using Equivalent Ratios**

A fashion boutique is split into three departments: Clothing, Beauty products, and Accessories. Each department takes up a different area in the boutique. The ratio of the areas of Accessories to Beauty is 2 : 3, and that of Beauty to Clothing is 4 : 5. What is the ratio of the department areas of Accessories : Beauty : Clothing?

Solution

$A : B = 2 : \mathbf{3}$ and $B : C = \mathbf{4} : 5$

Determine the equivalent ratios for $A : B$ and $B : C$ such that the number of units in B is the same in both ratios.

$A : B = 2 : 3$ Multiplying each term by 4,

$= 8 : \mathbf{12}$

$B : C = 4 : 5$ Multiplying each term by 3,

$= \mathbf{12} : 15$

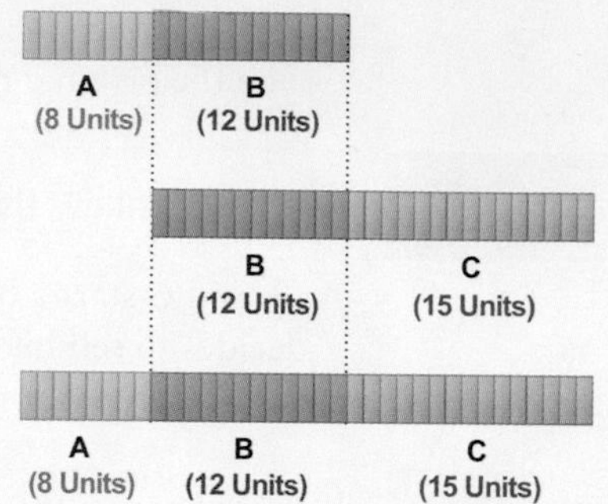

Therefore, the ratio of the department areas of Accessories : Beauty : Clothing in the boutique is 8 : 12 : 15.

6.1 | Exercises

Answers to odd-numbered problems are available at the end of the textbook.

For Problems 1 and 2, determine whether the given pairs of ratios are equivalent.

1. a. 4 : 6 and 6 : 10 b. 8 : 10 and 28 : 35 c. 6 : 8 and 27 : 32 d. 16 : 22 and 64 : 88

2. a. 16 : 20 and 24 : 30 b. 10 : 12 and 35 : 42 c. 12 : 14 and 30 : 42 d. 12 : 26 and 30 : 65

3. Determine if the following ratios are equivalent or not equivalent to the ratio 6 : 9 : 12.
   a. 4 : 6 : 8 b. 2 : 3 : 4 c. 1 : 3 : 2 d. 8 : 12 : 16

4. Determine if the following ratios are equivalent or not equivalent to the ratio 16 : 24 : 12.
   a. 20 : 30 : 15 b. 8 : 12 : 6 c. 28 : 42 : 21 d. 24 : 36 : 18

For Problems 5 to 8, express the ratios as (i) equivalent ratios in their lowest terms (as whole numbers), and (ii) equivalent ratios where the smallest term is 1.

5. a. 18 : 48 : 30 b. 175 : 50 : 125 c. 0.45 : 1 : 2

6. a. 27 : 45 : 72 b. 180 : 60 : 150 c. 2.4 : 0.75

7. a. $\frac{2}{3} : \frac{1}{5}$ b. $12 : \frac{5}{3} : 3$ c. $1.7 : 8.5 : \frac{34}{3}$

8. a. $\frac{3}{2} : \frac{2}{5}$ b. $65 : 91 : \frac{13}{2}$ c. $12 : 1.5 : \frac{3}{2}$

For Problems 9 and 10, express the ratios in lowest terms.

9. a. 9 months to 2 years b. 750 g to 3 kg c. 30 minutes to 1 hour and 15 minutes

10. a. 3 weeks to 126 days b. 120 g to 2 kg c. 55 minutes to 2 hours and 45 minutes

11. Emily was planning to make an authentic Indian dish for her guests. She planned to use 36 eggs, 6 litres of water, 3 tablespoons of chilli powder, and 12 tomatoes.
    a. What is the ratio of the ingredients in her recipe, expressed in lowest terms?
    b. If she decides to reduce the quantity of chilli powder to $1\frac{1}{2}$ tablespoons, calculate the new ratio of the ingredients in her recipe, expressed in lowest terms.

12. In Murphy's battery manufacturing company, 600 kg of lead, 45 kg of carbon, 30 litres of battery acid, and 120 kg of rubber are used per day to make batteries.
    a. What is the ratio of the raw materials used per day to make batteries, expressed in lowest terms?
    b. If they alter the quantity of carbon used in the batteries and utilize 30 kg of carbon per day, calculate the new ratio of raw materials used per day, expressed in lowest terms.

For Problems 13 to 20, determine the unit rate.

13. 525 kilometres in 7 hours = ? km/h
14. 680 kilometres in 8 hours = ? km/h
15. 154 kilometres to 14 litres = ? km/L
16. 228 kilometres to 19 litres = ? km/L
17. 450 words typed in 6 minutes = ? words/min
18. 496 words typed in 8 minutes = ? words/min
19. 261 pages in 9 minutes = ? pages/min
20. 192 pages in 8 minutes = ? pages/min

For Problems 21 to 26, identify the option with the lower cost, based on unit price.

21. 2 kg of flour for $3.30, or 5 kg of flour for $8.40.
22. 3 kg of sugar for $3.90, or 5 kg of sugar for $6.25.
23. 12 pencils for $4.44, or 8 pencils for $2.88.
24. 6 litres of paint for $45.60, or 5 litres of paint for $37.25.
25. 1.2 litres of juice for $2.16, or 0.8 litres of juice for $1.40.
26. 2.2 kg of jam for $11.00, or 1.5 kg of jam for $7.20.
27. In a race, participants are required to swim 3,850 metres and bike 7 kilometres. Calculate the ratio of the distance covered by swimming to the distance covered by biking, in its lowest terms.
28. Adam, a hardware engineer, wants to install a microchip that is 38.2 mm in length into his laptop. The length of the installation space provided in his laptop is 4.8 cm. Calculate the ratio of the length of the microchip to the installation space, in its lowest terms.
29. An aircraft travels a distance of 3,105 km in 5 hours and 45 minutes. Calculate the ratio of the distance traveled to the time taken, reduced to a rate of kilometres per hour.
30. Speed is defined as the ratio of the distance travelled to the time taken. If Mary, who lives in Toronto, took 6 hours and 15 minutes to reach her parent's home in Montreal, which is 575 km away, calculate the average speed at which she was travelling in kilometres per hour.
31. If *A* earns $196 for working 8 hours and *B* earns $98 for working 5 hours, whose hourly rate is higher?
32. If Amanda travelled 325 km in 4 hours and 15 minutes and Ashton travelled 290 km in 3 hours and 30 minutes, whose average speed was greater?
33. Kate earned $210 for 7.5 hours of work and Susan earned $249.75 for 9 hours of work.
    a. Calculate their hourly rates.
    b. Whose hourly rate was higher and by how much?
34. Jack's monthly pay is $4,200. Steve's weekly pay is $975.
    a. Calculate their annual salaries. (1 year = 12 months = 52 weeks)
    b. Whose annual salary is more and by how much?
35. A TV cable bill of $90 is shared between two housemates, Mike and Sarah, in the ratio of $2 : 2\frac{1}{2}$. How much did each person pay?
36. Alexander and Alyssa invested a total of $10,000 in a web-design business. If the ratio of their investments is 3 : 5, what were their investments?
37. Amy and two of her friends received the first prize for a marketing case competition. They received an amount of $7,500; however, they decided to share the prize in the ratio of the amount of time each of them spent on the marketing case. If Amy spent 5 hours, Gary spent 8 hours, and Andrew spent 2 hours, what would be each person's share of the prize?
38. Three friends, Andy, Berry, and Cassandra, jointly insured a commercial property in the ratio of 10 : 9 : 6, respectively. How will an annual premium of $8,000 be distributed among the three of them?

39. The lengths of the three sides of a triangle are in the ratio of $\frac{3}{4} : \frac{2}{5} : \frac{1}{2}$. If the perimeter of the triangle (i.e., the sum of the three sides lengths) is 66 cm, calculate the length of each side.

40. The lengths of the three sides of a triangle are in the ratio of $\frac{2}{3} : \frac{5}{6} : \frac{4}{5}$. If the perimeter of the triangle (i.e., the sum of the three sides lengths) is 128 cm, calculate the length of each side.

• 41. Three friends, Alex, Brooks, and Charlie, have decided to invest $4,000, $6,000, and $2,000, respectively, to start a software development business. If Charlie decided to leave the business, how much would Alex and Brooks have to pay for Charlie's share if they want to maintain their initial investment ratio?

• 42. Chuck decided to build a yacht with his two friends Rob and Bob; they invested $9,000, $11,000, and $6,500, respectively. After the yacht was built, Bob decided to sell his share of the investment to Chuck and Rob. How much would each of them have to pay if they want to maintain the same ratio of their investments in the yacht?

• 43. A box contains red, green, and blue marbles. $\frac{1}{3}$ of the marbles are red, $\frac{2}{5}$ of the marbles are green, and the remaining marbles are blue.

   a. What fraction of the marbles in the box are blue?

   b. Calculate the ratio of red to green to blue ($R : G : B$) marbles in the box, expressed in its lowest terms (as whole numbers).

   c. If there are 75 marbles in the box, how many of each colour are there?

• 44. A box contains black, white, and yellow marbles. $\frac{1}{4}$ of the marbles are black, $\frac{1}{3}$ of the marbles are white, and the remaining marbles are yellow.

   a. What fraction of the marbles in the box are yellow?

   b. Calculate the ratio of black to white to yellow ($B : W : Y$) marbles in the box, expressed in its lowest terms (as whole numbers).

   c. If there are 72 marbles in the box, how many of each colour are there?

• 45. Abey and Baxter invested equal amounts of money in a business. A year later, Abey withdrew $7,500, making the ratio of their investments 5 : 9. How much money did each of them invest in the beginning?

• 46. Jessica and Russel invested equal amounts to start a business. Two months later, Jessica invested an additional $3,000 in the business, making the ratio of their investments 11 : 5. How much money did each of them invest in the beginning?

• 47. If $A : B = 4 : 3$ and $B : C = 6 : 5$, determine $A : B : C$.

• 48. If $X : Y = 5 : 2$ and $Y : Z = 7 : 6$, determine $X : Y : Z$.

6.2 | Proportions

The Proportion Equation

When two ratios are equivalent, we say that they are **proportional** to each other. In the proportion equation, the ratio on the left side of the equation is equivalent to the ratio on the right side of the equation.

Consider an example where $A : B$ is 50 : 100 and $C : D$ is 30 : 60.

Reducing the ratios to lowest terms, we obtain the ratio of $A : B$ as 1 : 2 and the ratio of $C : D$ as 1 : 2.

Since these ratios are equivalent, they are proportional to each other, and their proportion equation is:

$$A : B = C : D$$

The proportion equation can also be formed by representing the ratios as fractions.

Equating the fraction obtained by dividing the first term by the second term on the left side, to the one obtained by dividing the first term by the second term on the right side, we obtain:

$$\frac{A}{B}=\frac{C}{D}$$

This proportion equation can be simplified by multiplying both sides of the equation by the product of both denominators, which is $B \times D$.

$\frac{A}{B}=\frac{C}{D}$ Multiplying both sides by $(B \times D)$,

$\frac{A}{B}(B \times D)=\frac{C}{D}(B \times D)$ Simplifying,

$AD = BC$

If two fractions are equivalent, then the product obtained by cross-multiplying the fractions will be equal.

The same result can be obtained by equating the product of the numerator of the first ratio and the denominator of the second ratio with the product of the denominator of the first ratio and the numerator of the second ratio. This is referred to as cross-multiplication and is shown below:

$\frac{A}{B} \times \frac{C}{D}$ Cross-multiplying,

$AD = BC$

If $A : B = C : D$, then, $\frac{A}{B}=\frac{C}{D}$ or, $\frac{A}{C}=\frac{B}{D}$

Notice that the cross-multiplication of $\frac{A}{C}=\frac{B}{D}$ also gives the same result of $AD = BC$. Therefore, $A : B = C : D$ is equivalent to both $\frac{A}{B}=\frac{C}{D}$ and $\frac{A}{C}=\frac{B}{D}$. If any three terms of the proportion equation are known, the fourth term can be calculated.

Proportion Equation With Sets of Ratios Having More Than Two Terms

Consider the proportion equation $A : B : C = D : E : F$.

This proportion equation can also be expressed using fractions: $\frac{A}{B}=\frac{D}{E}$, $\frac{B}{C}=\frac{E}{F}$, and $\frac{A}{C}=\frac{D}{F}$

Cross-multiplying leads to: $AE = BD$, $BF = CE$, and $AF = CD$

The proportion $A : B : C = D : E : F$ can be illustrated by the table,

1st Term	2nd Term	3rd Term
A	B	C
D	E	F

and expressed as, $A : D = B : E = C : F$

A : B : C = D : E : F

If $A : B : C = D : E : F$, then, $\frac{A}{B}=\frac{D}{E}$, $\frac{B}{C}=\frac{E}{F}$, $\frac{A}{C}=\frac{D}{F}$ or, $\frac{A}{D}=\frac{B}{E}=\frac{C}{F}$

Expressing using fractions, $\frac{A}{D} = \frac{B}{E} = \frac{C}{F}$

Cross-multiplying leads to the same result as shown above:

$AE = BD$, $BF = CE$, and $AF = CD$

Therefore, $A : B : C = D : E : F$ is equivalent to both

(i) $\frac{A}{B}=\frac{D}{E}$, $\frac{B}{C}=\frac{E}{F}$, $\frac{A}{C}=\frac{D}{F}$, and

(ii) $\frac{A}{D}=\frac{B}{E}=\frac{C}{F}$.

Example 6.2-a Solving for the Unknown Quantity in Proportions

Determine the missing term in the following proportions:

(i) $4 : 5 = 8 : x$ (ii) $6 : x = 10 : 25$ (iii) $x : 1.9 = 2.6 : 9.88$ (iv) $3 : 3\frac{3}{4} = x : 5\frac{1}{4}$

Solution

(i) $4 : 5 = 8 : x$

Using fractional notation, $\frac{4}{5} = \frac{8}{x}$ **or** $\frac{4}{8} = \frac{5}{x}$

Cross-multiplying, $4x = 40$

Simplifying, $x = \frac{40}{4}$

Therefore, $x = 10$

1st Term	2nd Term
4	5
8	x

(ii) $6 : x = 10 : 25$

Using fractional notation, $\frac{6}{x} = \frac{10}{25}$ **or** $\frac{6}{10} = \frac{x}{25}$

Cross-multiplying, $150 = 10x$

Simplifying, $x = \frac{150}{10}$

Therefore, $x = 15$

1st Term	2nd Term
6	x
10	25

(iii) $x : 1.9 = 2.6 : 9.88$

Using fractional notation, $\frac{x}{1.9} = \frac{2.6}{9.88}$ **or** $\frac{x}{2.6} = \frac{1.9}{9.88}$

Cross-multiplying, $9.88x = 4.94$

Simplifying, $x = \frac{4.94}{9.88}$

Therefore, $x = 0.5$

1st Term	2nd Term
x	1.9
2.6	9.88

(iv) $3 : 3\frac{3}{4} = x : 5\frac{1}{4}$

Rewriting as an improper fraction, $3 : \frac{15}{4} = x : \frac{21}{4}$

Multiplying both sides by 4, $12 : 15 = 4x : 21$

Using fractional notation, $\frac{12}{15} = \frac{4x}{21}$ **or** $\frac{12}{4x} = \frac{15}{21}$

Cross-multiplying, $252 = 60x$

Simplifying, $x = \frac{252}{60}$

Therefore, $x = \frac{21}{5} = 4\frac{1}{5}$

1st Term	2nd Term
12	15
$4x$	21

Example 6.2-b Solving Word Problems Using Proportions

Ben can walk a distance of 9 km in 2 hours. Calculate:

(i) The distance (in km) that Ben can walk in $3\frac{1}{2}$ hours.

(ii) How long (in hours and minutes) will it take him to walk 15 km?

Solution

(i) Calculating the distance (in km) he can walk in $3\frac{1}{2}$ hours:

$$\textbf{km : h = km : h}$$

$$9:2 = x:3\frac{1}{2}$$

Rewriting as an improper fraction, $9:2 = x:\frac{7}{2}$

Multiplying both sides by 2, $18:4 = 2x:7$

Using fractional notation, $\frac{18}{4} = \frac{2x}{7}$ **or** $\frac{18}{2x} = \frac{4}{7}$

Cross-multiplying, $126 = 8x$

Simplifying, $x = \frac{126}{8}$

$$x = 15.75 \text{ km}$$

Therefore, Ben can walk a distance of 15.75 km in $3\frac{1}{2}$ hours.

1st Term	2nd Term
18	4
$2x$	7

(ii) Calculating the time (in hours and minutes) that it will take him to walk 15 km:

$$\textbf{km : h = km : h}$$

$$9:2 = 15:x$$

Using fractional notation, $\frac{9}{2} = \frac{15}{x}$ **or** $\frac{9}{15} = \frac{2}{x}$

Cross multiplying, $9x = 30$

Simplifying, $x = \frac{30}{9} = 3\frac{1}{3} \text{ h}$

$$x = 3 \text{ h} + \left(\frac{1}{3} \times 60\right) \text{ min}$$

$$x = 3 \text{ h } 20 \text{ min}$$

Therefore, Ben can walk 15 km in 3 hours and 20 minutes.

1st Term	2nd Term
9	2
15	x

Example 6.2-c Sharing Using Proportions

Andrew (A), Brandon (B), and Chris (C) decide to form a partnership to start a snow removal business together. A invests \$31,500, B invests \$42,000, and C invests \$73,500. They agree to share the profits in the same ratio as their investments.

(i) What is the ratio of their investments, expressed in lowest terms?

(ii) In the first year of running the business, A's profit was \$27,000. What were B's and C's profits?

(iii) In the second year, their total profit was \$70,000. How much would each of them receive from this total profit?

Solution

(i) Ratio of their investments:

A : B : C	
31,500 : 42,000 : 73,500	Dividing each term by the common factor of 100,
315 : 420 : 735	Dividing each term by the common factor of 5,
63 : 84 : 147	Dividing each term by the common factor of 7,
9 : 12 : 21	Dividing each term by the common factor of 3,
3 : 4 : 7	

Therefore, the ratio of their investments is 3 : 4 : 7.

Solution
continued

(ii) *A*'s profit was $27,000. *B*'s and *C*'s profits are calculated using one of the two methods, as follows:

Method 1:

$$\text{Ratio of Investment} = \text{Ratio of Profit}$$
$$A : B : C = A : B : C$$

Substituting terms,
$$3 : 4 : 7 = 27{,}000 : x : y$$

Using fractional notation,
$$\frac{3}{4} = \frac{27{,}000}{x} \quad \text{and} \quad \frac{3}{7} = \frac{27{,}000}{y}$$

Cross-multiplying,
$$3x = 108{,}000 \qquad 3y = 189{,}000$$

Simplifying,
$$x = \$36{,}000.00 \qquad y = \$63{,}000.00$$

Method 2:

$$\text{Ratio of Investment} = \text{Ratio of Profit}$$
$$A : B : C = A : B : C$$

Substituting terms,
$$3 : 4 : 7 = 27{,}000 : x : y$$

Using fractional notation,
$$\frac{3}{27{,}000} = \frac{4}{x} = \frac{7}{y}$$

1st Term	2nd Term	3rd Term
3	4	7
27,000	x	y

Hence,
$$\frac{3}{27{,}000} = \frac{4}{x} \quad \text{and} \quad \frac{3}{27{,}000} = \frac{7}{y}$$

Cross-multiplying,
$$3x = 108{,}000 \qquad 3y = 189{,}000$$

Simplifying,
$$x = \$36{,}000.00 \qquad y = \$63{,}000.00$$

Therefore, *B*'s profit is $36,000 and *C*'s profit is $63,000.

(iii) In the second year, their total profit was $70,000. The profit that each of them would receive is calculated by using one of the methods, as follows:

Method 1:

Since *A*, *B*, and *C* agreed to share profits in the same ratio as their investments, the ratio of their individual investments to their individual profits should be equal to the ratio of the total investment to the total profit.

By adding the ratio of their investments (3 + 4 + 7), we know that the total profit of $70,000 should be distributed over 14 units. Therefore,

$$\text{Ratio of Investment} = \text{Ratio of Profit}$$
$$A : B : C : \text{Total} = A : B : C : \text{Total}$$

Substituting terms,
$$3 : 4 : 7 : 14 = A : B : C : 70{,}000$$

Using fractional notation,
$$\frac{3}{14} = \frac{A}{70{,}000}, \qquad \frac{4}{14} = \frac{B}{70{,}000}, \qquad \frac{7}{14} = \frac{C}{70{,}000}$$

Cross-multiplying,
$$14A = 210{,}000 \qquad 14B = 280{,}000 \qquad 14C = 490{,}000$$

Simplifying,
$$A = \$15{,}000.00 \qquad B = \$20{,}000.00 \qquad C = \$35{,}000.00$$

Solution *continued*

Method 2:

			1st Term	2nd Term	3rd Term	4th Term
	Ratio of Investment = Ratio of Profit					
	$A : B : C : \text{Total} = A : B : C : \text{Total}$					
Substituting terms,	$3 : 4 : 7 : 14 = A : B : C : 70{,}000$		3	4	7	14
Using fractional notation,	$\frac{3}{A} = \frac{4}{B} = \frac{7}{C} = \frac{14}{70{,}000}$		A	B	C	70,000

Hence, $\frac{3}{A} = \frac{14}{70{,}000}$ $\quad \frac{4}{B} = \frac{14}{70{,}000}$ $\quad \frac{7}{C} = \frac{14}{70{,}000}$

Cross-multiplying, $14A = 210{,}000$ $\quad 14B = 280{,}000$ $\quad 14C = 490{,}000$

Simplifying, $A = \$15{,}000.00$ $\quad B = \$20{,}000.00$ $\quad C = \$35{,}000.00$

Method 3:

Sharing Quantities Using Ratios:

A's share $= \frac{3}{14} \times 70{,}000.00 = \$15{,}000.00$

B's share $= \frac{4}{14} \times 70{,}000.00 = \$20{,}000.00$

C's share $= \frac{7}{14} \times 70{,}000.00 = \$35{,}000.00$

Therefore, A, B, and C will receive profits of \$15,000, \$20,000, and \$35,000, respectively.

Pro-rations

Pro-ration is defined as sharing or allocating quantities, usually amounts of money, on a proportional basis.

Consider an example where Sarah paid \$690 for a math course but decided to withdraw from the course after attending only half of it. As she attended only half the course, the college decided to refund half of her tuition fee, $\left(\frac{\$690}{2} = \$345\right)$. As the college calculated the refund amount proportional to the time she attended the course, we say that the college refunded her tuition fee on a **pro-rata basis**.

A few examples where pro-rated calculations are used are:

- When a propery is sold, the property tax paid in advance will be refunded on a pro-rata basis.
- When an insurance is cancelled before the end of the period for which the premiums were paid, the amount refunded is calculated on a pro-rata basis.
- Employees' overtime pay, part-time pay, and vacation time are calculated on a pro-rata basis.

Example 6.2-d **Calculating the Pro-rated Amount of a Payment**

Calculate the pro-rated insurance premium for seven months if the annual premium paid for car insurance is \$2,250.

Solution

Ratio of the premiums paid:

Premium (\$) : Time (months) = Premium (\$) : Time (months)

Substituting terms, $2{,}250 : 12 = x : 7$

Using fractional notation, $\frac{2{,}250}{12} = \frac{x}{7}$ **or** $\frac{2{,}250}{x} = \frac{12}{7}$

1st Term	2nd Term
2,250	12
x	7

Solution *continued*

Cross-multiplying, $15{,}750 = 12x$

Simplifying, $x = \dfrac{15{,}750}{12}$

$x = \$1{,}312.50$

Therefore, the pro-rated premium for seven months is $1,312.50.

Example 6.2-e Calculating the Pro-rated Amount of a Refund

Johnson paid $350 for a two-year, weekly subscription of a health journal. After receiving 18 issues of the journal in his second year, he decided to cancel his subscription. What should be the amount of his pro-rated refund? Assume 1 year = 52 weeks.

Solution

Johnson paid for 104 issues (2 × 52) and received 70 issues (52 + 18); therefore, he should be refunded for 34 issues (104 – 70).

Issues (#) : Cost ($) = Issues (#) : Cost ($)

Substituting terms, $104 : 350 = 34 : x$

Using fractional notation, $\dfrac{104}{350} = \dfrac{34}{x}$ **or** $\dfrac{104}{34} = \dfrac{350}{x}$

1st Term	2nd Term
104	350
34	x

Cross-multiplying, $104x = 11{,}900$

Simpifying, $x = \dfrac{11{,}900}{104}$

$x = 114.423076... = \$114.42$

Therefore, his refund should be $114.42.

6.2 | Exercises

Answers to odd-numbered problems are available at the end of the textbook.

For Problems 1 and 2, determine whether the pairs of ratios are in proportion or not.

1. a. 6 : 9 and 14 : 21 b. 5 : 15 and 2 : 8 c. 18 : 24 and 12 : 16 d. 12 : 60 and 6 : 24
2. a. 9 : 12 and 4 : 3 b. 10 : 30 and 8 : 24 c. 14 : 20 and 28 : 42 d. 15 : 12 and 24 : 30

For Problems 3 to 6, solve the proportion equations for the unknown value.

3. a. $x : 4 = 27 : 36$ b. $24 : x = 6 : 9$ c. $5 : 9 = x : 3$ d. $1 : 2 = 5 : x$
4. a. $x : 8 = 6 : 24$ b. $3 : x = 18 : 42$ c. $15 : 5 = x : 15$ d. $28 : 35 = 4 : x$
5. a. $x : 18\frac{1}{4} = 8 : 11\frac{3}{4}$ b. $7\frac{1}{5} : x = 5\frac{4}{3} : 3\frac{2}{5}$ c. $1 : 4\frac{1}{2} = x : 2\frac{3}{4}$ d. $1\frac{1}{2} : 2\frac{1}{4} = 1\frac{3}{4} : x$
6. a. $x : 3.65 = 5.5 : 18.25$ b. $2.2 : x = 13.2 : 2.5$ c. $4.25 : 1.87 = x : 2.2$ d. $2.4 : 1.5 = 7.2 : x$
7. A truck requires 96 litres of gas to cover 800 km. How many litres of gas will it require to cover 1,500 km?
8. Based on Alvin's past experience, it would take his team five months to complete two projects. How long would his team take to complete eight similar projects?
9. Eric paid a property tax of $3,600 for his land that measures 330 square metres. Using the same tax rate, what would his neighbour's property tax be if the size of the house is 210 square metres and is taxed at the same rate?
10. The city of Brampton charges $1,750 in taxes per year for a 2,000 square metre farm. How much would Maple Farms have to pay in taxes if they had a 12,275 square metre farm in the same area?

11. On a map, 4 cm represents 5.0 km. If the distance between Town A and Town B on the map is 9.3 cm, how many kilometres apart are these towns?

12. On a house plan, 1.25 cm represents 3 metres. If the actual length of a room is 5.4 metres, how will this length be represented in the plan in cm?

13. Steve invested his savings in a GIC, mutual funds, and a fixed deposit in the ratio of 5 : 4 : 3, respectively. If he invested $10,900 in mutual funds, calculate his investments in the GIC and the fixed deposit.

14. The ratio of the distance from Ann's house to Mark, Jeff, and Justin's houses is 3 : 5.25 : 2, respectively. If the distance from Ann's house to Mark's is 9.50 km, calculate the distance from Ann's house to Justin's and Ann's house to Jeff's.

15. *A*, *B*, and *C*, started a business with investments in the ratio of 5 : 4 : 3, respectively. *A* invested $25,000, and all three of them agreed to share profits in the ratio of their investments.

    a. Calculate *B* and *C*'s investments.

    b. If *A*'s profit was $30,000 in the first year, calculate *B* and *C*'s profits.

    c. How much would each of them receive if, in the second year, the total profit was $135,000?

16. *A*, *B*, and *C* formed a partnership and invested in the ratio of 7 : 9 : 5, respectively. They agreed to share the profit in the ratio of their investments. *A* invested $350,000.

    a. Calculate *B* and *C*'s investments in the partnership.

    b. In the first year, if *A* made $38,500 in profit from the partnership, how much did *B* and *C* make?

    c. If the partnership made a profit of $126,000 in the second year, calculate each partner's share of the profit.

17. *A*, *B*, and *C* invested $35,000, $42,000, and $28,000, respectively, to start an e-learning business. They realized that they required an additional $45,000 for operating the business. How much did each of them have to individually invest to maintain their original investment ratio?

18. Three wealthy business partners decided to invest $150,000, $375,000, and $225,000, respectively, to purchase an industrial plot on the outskirts of the city. They required an additional $90,000 to build an industrial shed on the land. How much did each of them have to individually invest to maintain their original investment ratio?

19. Chris, Diane, and David invested a total of $520,000 in the ratio of 3 : 4 : 6, respectively, to start a business. Two months later, each of them invested an additional $25,000 into the business. Calculate their new investment ratio after the additional investments.

20. Michael and his two sisters purchased an office for $720,000. Their individual investments in the office were in the ratio of 5 : 4 : 3, respectively. After the purchase, they decided to renovate the building and purchase furniture, so each of them invested an additional $60,000. Calculate their new investment ratio after the additional investments.

21. A student pays $620 for a course that has 25 classes. Calculate the pro-rated refund she would receive if she only attends 5 classes before withdrawing from the course.

22. Megan joined a driving school that charges $375 for 12 classes. After attending 7 classes, she decided that she did not like the training and wanted to cancel the remaining classes. Calculate the pro-rated refund she should receive.

23. Frank bought a brand new car on August 01, 2018 and obtained pre-paid insurance of $1,058 for the period of August 01, 2018 to July 31, 2019. After two months of using the car, he sold it and cancelled his insurance. Calculate the pro-rated refund he should receive from the insurance company.

24. The owner of a new gaming business decided to insure his servers and computers. His insurance company charged him a premium of $2,000 per quarter, where the first quarter starts on January 01. If his insurance is to start on February 01, how much pro-rated insurance premium did he have to pay for the rest of the first quarter? *(Hint: A 'quarter' of a year is three months).*

25. If the annual salary of an employee is $45,000, calculate his bi-weekly salary using pro-rations. Assume that there are 52 weeks in a year and 26 bi-weekly payments.

26. Ashley received a job offer at a company that would pay her $2,800, bi-weekly. What would her annual salary be, assuming that she would receive 26 payments in a year?

27. Charles set up a new charity fund to support children in need. For every $10 collected by the charity, the government donated an additional grant of $5 to the charity. At the end of three months, if his charity fund had a total of $135,000, including the government grant, calculate the amount the charity received from the government.

28. The tax on education materials sold in Ontario is such that for every $1.00 worth of materials sold, the buyer would have to pay an additional $0.05 in taxes. If $25,000 worth of textbooks were sold at a bookstore before taxes, calculate the total amount of tax to be paid by the purchasers.

• 29. A first semester class in a college has six more girls than boys, and the ratio of the number of girls to boys in the class is 8 : 5.

a. How many students are there in the class?

b. If four girls and three boys joined the class, determine the new ratio of girls to boys in the class.

• 30. The advisory board of a public sector company has ten more men than women, and the ratio of the number of men to women is 8 : 3.

a. How many people are there on the board?

b. If four men and four women joined the board, determine the new ratio of men to women.

• 31. To estimate the number of tigers in a forest, a team of researchers tagged 84 tigers and released them into the forest. Six months later, 30 tigers were spotted, out of which 7 had tags. How many tigers were estimated to be in the forest?

• 32. Researchers were conducting a study to estimate the number of frogs in a pond. They put a bright yellow band on the legs of 60 frogs and released them into the pond. A few days later, 15 frogs were spotted, out of which 5 had bands. How many frogs were estimated to be in the pond?

6.3 | Currency Conversion

Exchange Rates

Exchange rates are used to convert currencies between countries.

Exchange rates, also known as foreign exchange rates or forex rates, are used for converting currencies between countries. They allow us to calculate the amount of a currency that is required to purchase one unit of another currency.

For example, to convert Canadian currency to US currency, it is important to know the amount in Canadian dollars that is equivalent to one US dollar, or vice versa.

The value of a currency may fluctuate constantly during the day and the exchange rate may vary accordingly. For example, at 1:00 PM EST on March 01, 2017, US$1 was equal to C$1.3342 and C$1 was equal to US$0.7495. Therefore, the exchange rates on that date and time were US$1 = C$1.3342 and C$1 = US$0.7495.

Currency Cross-Rate Table

Currency exchange rates are generally displayed in a Currency Cross-Rate Table for quick reference. Below is a currency cross-rate table from March 01, 2017 at 1:00 PM EST.

Table 6.3-a

Currency Cross-Rate Table as of March 01, 2017

Common currencies and their symbols

Canadian dollar:	C$
US dollar:	US$
Euro:	€
British pound:	£
Australian dollar:	A$

One Unit of (columns); Equivalent to (rows)

Symbol	C$	US$	€	£	A$
C$	-	1.3342	1.4095	1.6435	1.0226
US$	0.7495	-	1.0565	1.2318	0.7665
€	0.7095	0.9466	-	1.1660	0.7255
£	0.6085	0.8118	0.8576	-	0.6222
A$	0.9779	1.3047	1.3784	1.6072	-

The vertical columns of the table represent one unit of the currency to be converted and the horizontal rows represent its equivalent value in another currency.

For example, US$1 = A$1.3047 and £1 = US$1.2318, as highlighted in the table.

Based on the exchange rates given in Table 6.3-a, the exchange rates of foreign currency per Canadian dollars (C$) and vice versa are given in Table 6.3-b for easy reference.

Table 6.3-b

Exchange Rates of Foreign Currency per C$ and C$ per Unit of Foreign Currency

Currency	Symbol	Units of Foreign Currency per C$	C$ per Unit of Foreign Currency
US dollar	US$	0.7495	1.3342
Euro	€	0.7095	1.4095
British pound	£	0.6085	1.6435
Australian dollar	A$	0.9779	1.0226

For calculations involving conversion from one currency to another, we will either use the cross-rate table or the exchange rates provided in the question. We will be using the method of proportions to solve examples that follow.

Example 6.3-a

Currency Conversion from Canadian Dollar to US Dollar

Based on the exchange rates provided in Table 6.3-a (Currency Cross-Rate Table), calculate the amount in US dollars that you will receive when you convert C$400.

Solution

From the cross-rate table, US$1 = C$1.3342

US$: C$ = US$: C$

$1 : 1.3342 = x : 400$

US$	C$
1	1.3342
x	400

In fractional form, $\frac{1}{x} = \frac{1.3342}{400}$ **or** $\frac{1}{1.3342} = \frac{x}{400}$

Cross-multiplying and solving for x,

$$400.00 = 1.3342x$$

$$x = \frac{400.00}{1.3342}$$

$$= 299.805126... = \text{US\$}299.81$$

Therefore, you will receive US$299.81 when you convert C$400.00.

Example 6.3-b **Currency Conversion from C$ to US$ and from US$ to C$**

If US$1 = C$1.3342, calculate:

(i) the amount that you will receive if you convert US$1,000 to Canadian dollars.

(ii) the amount that you will receive if you convert C$1,000 to US dollars.

Solution

(i) US$: C$ = US$: C$

1 : 1.3342 = 1,000 : x

US$	C$
1	1.3342
1,000	x

In fractional form, $\frac{1}{1{,}000} = \frac{1.3342}{x}$ **or** $\frac{1}{1.3342} = \frac{1{,}000}{x}$

Cross-multiplying and solving for x,

$x = 1{,}000.00 \times 1.3342$

$= \text{C\$}1{,}334.20$

Therefore, you will receive C$1,334.20 when you convert US$1,000.00.

(ii) US$: C$ = US$: C$

1 : 1.3342 = x : 1,000

US$	C$
1	1.3342
x	1,000

In fractional form, $\frac{1}{x} = \frac{1.3342}{1{,}000}$ **or** $\frac{1}{1.3342} = \frac{x}{1{,}000}$

Cross-multiplying and solving for x,

$1{,}000.00 = 1.3342x$

$x = \frac{1{,}000.00}{1.3342}$

$= 749.512816... = \text{US\$}749.51$

Therefore, you will receive US$749.51 when you convert C$1,000.00.

Example 6.3-c **Converting from One Currency to Another Currency, Given Exchange Rates**

Samantha is travelling from Canada to London on vacation. If £1 = C$1.6435, how much will she receive if she converts C$1,000 to British pounds?

Solution

£ : C$ = £ : C$

1 : 1.6435 = x : 1,000

£	C$
1	1.6435
x	1,000

In fractional form, $\frac{1}{x} = \frac{1.6435}{1{,}000}$ **or** $\frac{1}{1.6435} = \frac{x}{1{,}000}$

Cross-multiplying and solving for x,

$1{,}000.00 = 1.6435x$

$x = \frac{1{,}000.00}{1.6435}$

$= 608.457560... = £608.46$

Therefore, she will receive £608.46 when she converts C$1,000.00.

Example 6.3-d **Series of Currency Conversions**

If US$1 = C$1.3342 and C$1 = A$0.9779, calculate the amount of US dollars you will receive with 100 Australian dollars.

Solution

First, determine the amount in Canadian dollars that you will receive with A$100.

C$: A$ = C$: A$

$1 : 0.9779 = x : 100$

C$	A$
1	0.9779
x	100

In fractional form, $\frac{1}{x} = \frac{0.9779}{100}$ **or** $\frac{1}{0.9779} = \frac{x}{100}$

Cross-multiplying and solving for x,

$$100.00 = 0.9779x$$

$$x = \frac{100.00}{0.9779}$$

$$= \text{C\$}102.259944...$$

Now, determine the amount in US dollars that you will receive with C$102.259944...

US$: C$ = US$: C$

$1 : 1.3342 = x : 102.259944...$

US$	C$
1	1.3342
x	102.259944...

In fractional form, $\frac{1}{x} = \frac{1.3342}{102.259944...}$ **or** $\frac{1}{1.3342} = \frac{x}{102.259944...}$

Cross-multiplying and solving for x,

$$102.259944... = 1.3342x$$

$$x = \frac{102.259944...}{1.3342}$$

$$= 76.645139... = \text{US\$}76.65$$

Therefore, you will receive US$76.65 when you convert A$100.00.

Buying and Selling Currencies

If you would like to convert currencies, you should go to a bank or another financial institution that is authorized to buy and sell currencies. These financial institutions usually have different exchange rates for buying and selling currencies, which they refer to as their 'buy rate' and 'sell rate'. They use the actual currency exchange rates and their rate of commission to create their own buying and selling rates for each currency. Commission is charged for their services on these transactions.

- Buying rate (buy rate) is the rate at which the financial institution buys a particular foreign currency from the customers.
- Selling rate (sell rate) is the rate at which the financial institution sells a particular foreign currency to the customers.

Example 6.3-e **Currency Conversion Including Commission in Buying or Selling Currencies**

Sarah plans to travel to the US from Canada and approaches a local bank to purchase US$1,000. Assume US$1 = C$1.3342 and that the bank charges a commission of 0.75% to sell or buy US dollars.

(i) How much in Canadian dollars would Sarah have to pay for US$1,000?

(ii) If Sarah changes her plan and wishes to convert US$1,000 back to Canadian dollars, how much will she receive from the same bank, assuming the same exchange rate and the same commission rate?

Solution

(i) US\$: C\$ = US\$: C\$

1 : 1.3342 = 1,000 : x

When buying or selling currencies, it does not matter if you calculate the commission first and then convert the value, or vice versa. You will always obtain the same answer.

US\$	C\$
1	1.3342
1,000	x

In fractional form, $\frac{1}{1,000} = \frac{1.3342}{x}$ **or** $\frac{1}{1.3342} = \frac{1,000}{x}$

Cross-multiplying and solving for x,

$$x = 1,000.00 \times 1.3342$$
$$= \text{C\$}1,334.20$$

US\$1,000 =	C\$1,334.20	Amount in C\$ before the bank's commission.
0.0075 × 1,334.20 =	+C\$10.0065	Adding bank's 0.75% commission,
Total =	C\$1,344.21	Amount that Sarah will pay the bank.

When you buy currencies, you will pay the converted amount and the financial institution's commission.

Or,

C\$1,334.20(1 + 0.0075) = 1,344.2065 = C\$1,344.21

Therefore, Sarah would have to pay C\$1,344.21 for US\$1,000.00.

(ii)

US\$1,000 =	C\$1,334.20	As calculated in (i).
0.0075 × 1,334.20 =	–C\$10.0065	Subtracting bank's 0.75% commission,
Total =	C\$1,324.19	Amount the bank will pay Sarah.

When you sell currencies, you will receive the converted amount less the financial institution's commission.

Or,

C\$1,334.20(1 – 0.0075) = 1,324.1935 = C\$1,324.19

Therefore, Sarah will receive C\$1,324.19 from the bank.

Example 6.3-f Calculating Bank's Rate of Commision to Buy and Sell Foreign Currency

When the exchange rate is US\$1 = C\$1.3342, a bank has the following buy rate and sell rate for US dollars:

- Buy rate: US\$1 = C\$1.3242
- Sell rate: US\$1 = C\$1.3509

Calculate the following:

(i) Bank's rate of commision to buy US\$

(ii) Bank's rate of commision to sell US\$

Solution

(i) Assume you want to sell US\$1,000 to the bank (i.e., bank is buying from you: **buy rate**).

Using the exchange rate, US\$1 = C\$1.3342:

US\$	C\$
1	1.3342
1,000	x

$$\frac{1}{1,000} = \frac{1.3342}{x}$$
$$x = 1,000.00 \times 1.3342$$
$$= \text{C\$}1,334.20$$

Using the bank's buy rate, you will receive: 1,000.00 × 1.3242 = C\$1,324.20.

Therefore, the bank's commision = C\$(1,334.20 – 1,324.20)

= C\$10.00

Solution
continued

$$\text{Bank's rate of commision to buy} = \frac{\textit{Amount of commision}}{\textit{Amount based on exchange rate}} \times 100\%$$

$$= \frac{\text{C\$10.00}}{\text{C\$1,334.20}} \times 100\%$$

$$= 0.007495... \times 100\%$$

$$= 0.75\%$$

Therefore, the bank's rate of commision to buy US$ is 0.75%.

(ii) Assume you want to buy US$1,000 from the bank (i.e., the bank is selling to you: **sell rate**)

From part (i), using the exchange rate, US$1,000 = C$1,334.20

Using the bank's sell rate, you will pay: 1,000.00 × 1.3509 = C$1,350.90

Therefore, the bank's commision = C$(1,350.90 – 1,334.20)

= C$16.70

$$\text{Bank's rate of commision to sell} = \frac{\textit{Amount of commision}}{\textit{Amount based on exchange rate}} \times 100\%$$

$$= \frac{\text{C\$16.70}}{\text{C\$1,334.20}} \times 100\%$$

$$= 0.012516... \times 100\%$$

$$= 1.25\%$$

Therefore, the bank's rate of commison to sell US$ is 1.25%.

6.3 | Exercises

Answers to odd-numbered problems are available at the end of the textbook.

Use the following exchange rates to perform the conversions in Problems 1 to 4:

£1 = A$1.6072, US$1 = C$1.3342, €1 = US$1.0565, C$1 = £0.6085

1. Convert A$200 to British pounds (£).
2. Convert C$3,000 to US dollars (US$).
3. Convert US$5,000 to Euros (€).
4. Convert £10 to Canadian dollars (C$).

Use the following exchange rates to perform the conversions in Problems 5 to 8:

€1 = C$1.4095, A$1 = US$0.7665, US$1 = £0.8118, C$1 = A$0.9779

5. Convert C$2,500 to Euros (€).
6. Convert US$2,850 to Australian dollars (A$).
7. Convert £18 to US dollars (US$).
8. Convert A$300 to Canadian dollars (C$).
9. If C$1 = A$0.9779 and A$1 = US$0.7665, how many Canadian dollars would you receive with US$1,000?
10. If C$1 = £0.6085 and £1 = US$1.2318, how many Canadian dollars would you receive with US$1,000?
11. A bank in Ottawa charges 2.5% commission to buy and sell currencies. Assume the exchange rate is US$1 = C$1.3342.

    a. How many Canadian dollars would you have to pay to purchase US$1,500?

    b. How much commission in Canadian dollars (C$) would you pay the bank for the above transaction?

12. A bank in Montreal charges 2.25% commission to buy and sell currencies. Assume the exchange rate is US$1 = C$1.3342.

    a. How many Canadian dollars would you receive from the bank if you sell US$1,375?

    b. How much commission would you pay the bank for this transaction?

13. Mark converted US$4,500 into Canadian dollars at a bank that charged him a commission of 0.25%. How much did he receive from the bank? Assume that the exchange rate was C$1 = US$0.7495.

14. Carmin converted £2,000 into Canadian dollars. If the commission the bank was charging was 0.90%, calculate the amount that she received in Canadian dollars. Assume that the exchange rate was C$1 = £0.6085.

• 15. Dell left Canada for the UK with C$8,000. When he reached the UK, he converted all his cash into British pounds. The conversion rate was £1 = C$1.6435. After spending £1,000 in the UK, he returned to Canada. Calculate the the amount that he received in Canadian dollars when he converted the remaining British pounds into Canadian dollars at an exchange rate of £1 = C$1.6500.

• 16. Jason travelled from Toronto to Australia, where he converted C$3,000 to Australian dollars at an exchange rate of C$1 = A$0.9779. He spent A$2,000 in Australia before returning to Toronto. How many Canadian dollars did he receive when he converted the remaining Australian dollars into Canadian dollars at an exchange rate of C$1 = A$1.0200?

• 17. David planned to travel to Australia from Canada and purchased A$5,000. A week later, he decided to cancel his trip and wanted to convert his Australian dollars back into Canadian dollars at the same bank. How much money did he lose or gain? Assume that the bank charged a commission of 0.5% to buy and sell currencies, and that the exchange rate was C$1 = A$0.9779.

• 18. Lisa purchased US$10,000 from a bank in America, which charged her a commission of 0.80%, and sold the US dollars to a bank in Canada, which charged her 0.80% commission. How much money did she lose or gain? Assume that the exchange rate was C$1 = US$0.7495.

• 19. A bank in London, Ontario has a selling rate of £1 = C$1.6912. If the exchange rate is £1 = C$1.6435, calculate the rate of commission that the bank charges.

• 20. A bank in London, Ontario has a buying rate of A$1 = C$1. If the exchange rate is A$1 = C$1.0226, calculate the rate of commission that the bank charges.

6.4 | Index Numbers

The price of various items constantly fluctuates at different points in time. You may have noticed that the cost of transportation, entertainment, education, housing, etc., have consistently been on the rise. Index numbers are used to quantify such economic changes over time.

An **index number** is a comparison of the value of an item on a selected date to the value of the same item on a designated date, known as the base date. This can be expressed using a proportion equation, as follows:

$$\textit{Index Number on selected date} : \textit{Value on selected date} = \textit{Index Number on base date} : \textit{Value on base date}$$

The index number on the base date is usually set as 100 to align the index numbers with percents.

Therefore, representing the above proportion in fractional form, we obtain,

$$\frac{\textit{Index Number on selected date}}{100} = \frac{\textit{Value on selected date}}{\textit{Value on base date}} \quad \textbf{or} \quad \frac{\textit{Index Number on selected date}}{\textit{Value on selected date}} = \frac{100}{\textit{Value on base date}}$$

Rearranging the above equations, the index number on a selected date can be calculated as follows:

$$\textbf{\textit{Index Number on selected date}} = \frac{\textbf{\textit{Value on selected date}}}{\textbf{\textit{Value on base date}}} \times \mathbf{100}$$

The index number on the base date is 100 and is the comparative centre of the index numbers. That is, if the index number is less than 100, the value of that item has decreased since the base date; if the index number is greater than 100, the value of that item has increased since the base date.

The difference between the index number of an item on a selected date and 100 represents the percent change in value of that item between the selected date and the base period. For example, if the index number for an item on a selected date is 120.5, then the value of the item is 20.5% above the base period price of 100 for the same item.

Example 6.4-a Calculating the Index Number in Price of Gasoline in 2016 Using 2010 as the Base Year

The price of gasoline in 2010 was $0.91 per litre and in 2016 it increased to $1.05 per litre. Calculate the index number for the price of gas in 2016 using 2010 as the base year.

Solution

	Year	Index	Price ($)
Base Year	2010	100	0.91
	2016	x	1.05

In fractional form, $\frac{100}{x} = \frac{0.91}{1.05}$

Cross-multiplying, $105 = 0.91x$

$$x = \frac{105}{0.91}$$

$$= 115.384615...$$

$$= 115.38$$

or

$$\textit{Index Number on selected date} = \frac{\textit{Value on selected date}}{\textit{Value on base date}} \times 100$$

$$\textit{Index Number}_{2016} = \frac{1.05}{0.91} \times 100$$

$$= 115.384615... = 115.38$$

Therefore, the index number for the price of gas in 2016 is 115.38 using 2010 as the base year.

Note: Since 2010 is the base year, its index number is set to 100. Since the index number for 2016 is greater than 100, the value of the item has increased.

% Change = 115.38 – 100 = 15.38%

Therefore, the price of gas has increased by 15.38% from its price in 2010.

Example 6.4-b

Calculating the Index Number in the Price of Basic Cable TV in 2018 Using 2005 as the Base Year

The price of basic cable TV in 2005 was $39 per month and it decreased to $25 per month in 2018. Calculate the index number for the price of basic cable TV in 2018 using 2005 as the base year.

Solution

	Year	Index	Price ($)
Base Year	2005	100	39
	2018	x	25

In fractional form, $\frac{100}{x} = \frac{39}{25}$

Cross multiplying, $2{,}500 = 39x$

$$x = \frac{2{,}500}{39}$$

$$= 64.102564...$$

$$= 64.10$$

or

$$\text{Index Number on selected date} = \frac{\text{Value on selected date}}{\text{Value on base date}} \times 100$$

$$\text{Index Number}_{2018} = \frac{25.00}{39.00} \times 100$$

$$= 64.102564... = 64.10$$

Therefore, the index number for basic cable TV in 2018 is 64.10 using 2005 as the base year.

Note: Since 2005 is the base year, its index number is set to 100. Since the index number for 2018 is less than 100, the value of the item has decreased.

% Change = 64.10 – 100 = –35.90%

Therefore, the price of basic cable TV has decreased by 35.90% from its price in 2005.

Consumer Price Index (CPI)

The Consumer Price Index (CPI) is an indicator of changes in consumer prices experienced by Canadians.

The Consumer Price Index (CPI) is a good example of how useful index numbers can be in day-to-day life. CPI is an indicator of changes in consumer prices. In Canada, Statistics Canada obtains this number by calculating the cost of a fixed basket of goods and services purchased by consumers and comparing this cost over time. This basket is composed of around 600 different goods and services classified under eight major categories: food, shelter, recreation, health, transportation, clothing, housing, and alcohol and tobacco products.

Statistics Canada calculates and issues the CPI for Canada on a monthly basis and releases it during the third week of the following month (around the 20th). The CPI is usually rounded to one decimal place.

For example, CPI for March 2018 was released on April 20, 2018. (CPI for March 2018 = 132.9).

When there are considerable changes in consumer spending patterns, the base period for CPI is adjusted periodically by Statistics Canada. In 2004, the base period was changed from 1992 to 2002, which is the current base period used in CPI calculations (CPI for 2002 = 100). The annual CPI from 2002 to 2017 is provided in Table 6.4 below.

Table 6.4

CPI from the Years 2002 to 2017

Year	2002	2003	2004	2005	2006	2007	2008	2009	2010	2011	2012	2013	2014	2015	2016	2017
CPI	100.0	102.8	104.7	107.0	109.1	111.5	114.1	114.4	116.5	119.9	121.7	122.8	125.2	126.6	128.4	130.4

Example 6.4-c **Calculating the Cost of the Basket of Goods and Services in 2016 and Percent Change from the Base Year**

The basket of goods and services cost $16,500 in 2002. Using the CPI for 2016 from Table 6.4:

(i) Calculate the cost of the basket of goods and services in 2016.

(ii) What is the percent change in the cost of the basket of goods and services from 2002 to 2016?

Solution

(i)

	Year	Index	Price ($)
Base Year	2002	100	16,500
	2016	128.4	x

In fractional form, $\frac{100}{128.4} = \frac{16{,}500.00}{x}$

Cross multiplying, $x = \frac{128.4 \times 16{,}500.00}{100}$

$= \$21{,}186.00$

or

$$\frac{\text{Index Number}}{\text{on selected date}} = \frac{\text{Value on selected date}}{\text{Value on base date}} \times 100$$

$$128.4 = \frac{x}{16{,}500.00} \times 100$$

$$x = \frac{128.4 \times 16{,}500.00}{100}$$

$$= \$21{,}186.00$$

Therefore, the cost of the basket of goods and services in 2016 is $21,186.00.

(ii) CPI for 2002 is 100.

CPI for 2016 is 128.4.

Percent change = (128.4 – 100)% = 28.4%

or

Using the percent change formula,

$$\%C = \frac{V_f - V_i}{V_i} \times 100\%$$

$$= \frac{21{,}186.00 - 16{,}500.00}{16{,}500.00} \times 100\%$$

$$= 0.284 \times 100\% = 28.4\%$$

Therefore, the percent change in the cost from 2002 to 2016 is 28.4%.

Example 6.4-d **Calculating the Value of an Item after a Time Period Based on a Given Index**

An item was worth $1,750 in year 2005. How much was it worth in 2017 if the index for year 2005 was 107.0 and that for year 2017 was 130.4?

Solution

(i)

Year	Index	Price ($)
2005	107.0	1,750
2017	130.4	x

In fractional form, $\frac{107.0}{130.4} = \frac{1{,}750.00}{x}$

or

$$\frac{\text{Index Number}}{\text{on selected date}} = \frac{\text{Value on selected date}}{\text{Value on base date}} \times 100$$

$$107.0 = \frac{1{,}750.00}{\text{Value on base date}} \times 100 \quad (1)$$

$$130.4 = \frac{x}{\text{Value on base date}} \times 100 \quad (2)$$

(1) divided by (2): $\frac{107.0}{130.4} = \frac{1{,}750.00}{x}$

Cross multiplying, $107.0x = 130.4 \times 1{,}750.00$

$$x = \frac{130.4 \times 1{,}750.00}{107.0}$$

$$= 2{,}132.710280...$$

$$= \$2{,}132.71$$

Therefore, the item was worth $2,132.71 in 2017.

Purchasing Power of a Dollar and Inflation

The purchasing power of money is the number of goods/services that can be purchased with a unit of currency.

CPI is used to measure the purchasing power of a dollar and inflation. Wages of workers, private and public pension programs, personal income tax deductions, social and welfare payments, spousal and child support payments, etc., are adjusted periodically based on the changes in CPI.

The purchasing power of a dollar is the value of one dollar expressed in terms of the amount of goods or services that one dollar can buy. We use CPI to measure the purchasing power of a dollar:

$$\textit{Purchasing power of a dollar} = \frac{\$1}{CPI} \times 100$$

Inflation is a rise on the general level of prices of goods and services in an economy over time.

Inflation is the rate at which the price of goods and services increases. When prices increase, CPI increases and the purchasing power of a dollar decreases. Inflation rate is the rate of change in CPI over a period of time, and is calculated as follows:

$$\textit{Inflation rate (from Year A to Year B)} = \frac{CPI_{Year\ B} - CPI_{Year\ A}}{CPI_{Year\ A}} \times 100\%$$

$100 today does not buy the same amount of goods and services as it did before. Similarly, $100 to be received in the future will be worth less than $100 received today. Unless our income rises to match the price increase (inflation), we will not be able to maintain the same standard of living as before. Therefore, inflation is crucial in financial planning.

Real income is the income after adjusting for inflation and is calculated as follows:

$$\textit{Real income} = \frac{\textit{Money income}}{CPI} \times 100$$

Example 6.4-e **Calculating Purchasing Power of a Dollar Given CPI**

If the CPI was 125.2 for 2014 and 130.4 for 2017, determine the purchasing power of a dollar for the two years. Compare with the base year 2002 (CPI = 100).

Solution

$$\textit{Purchasing power in 2014} = \frac{\$1}{125.2} \times 100 = 0.798722...$$

$$\textit{Purchasing power in 2017} = \frac{\$1}{130.4} \times 100 = 0.766871...$$

Therefore, the dollar in 2014 could purchase 79.87% of what could be purchased in 2002, and the dollar in 2017 could purchase 76.69% of what could be purchased in 2002.

Example 6.4-f **Calculating Inflation Rate Given CPI**

If the CPI was 126.6 in 2015 and 128.4 at the end of 2016, what was the inflation rate from 2015 to 2016?

Solution

$$\textit{Inflation rate (from 2015 to 2016)} = \frac{CPI_{2016} - CPI_{2015}}{CPI_{2015}} \times 100\%$$

$$= \frac{128.4 - 126.6}{126.6} \times 100\%$$

$$= 0.014218... \times 100\%$$

$$= 1.42\%$$

Therefore, the inflation rate from 2015 to 2016 was 1.42%.

Example 6.4-g

Calculating Real Income Given CPI

Peter's income was $26,000 in 2002 (base year), $38,000 in 2010, and $40,000 in 2016. The CPI was 116.5 in 2010 and 128.4 in 2016. Determine Peter's real income in 2010 and 2016.

Solution

$$\text{Real income} = \frac{\text{Money income}}{\text{CPI}} \times 100$$

$$\text{Real income in 2010} = \frac{38{,}000.00}{116.5} \times 100$$

$$= 32{,}618.02575... = \$32{,}618.03$$

$$\text{Real income in 2016} = \frac{40{,}000.00}{128.4} \times 100$$

$$= 31{,}152.64798... = \$31{,}152.65$$

Therefore, Peter's real income in 2010 was $32,618.03 and his real income in 2016 was $31,152.65.

When compared to the purchasing power of Peter's $26,000 salary in 2002, his real income escalated considerably by 2010, due to his significantly higher salary of $38,000 earned at that time.

However, between 2010 and 2016, the rate of inflation, as determined by the CPI values for those years, exceeded the rate of his salary increase, resulting in a slight reduction in his 2016 real income.

Stock Index

S&P/TSX is an index of stock prices of the largest companies on the Toronto Stock Exchange.

A stock index is an application of index numbers that is used to measure the performance of stock markets. For example, the Standard and Poor's Toronto Stock Exchange Composite (S&P/TSX) index reflects the share prices of all the companies trading on the Toronto Stock Exchange. Here, the "basket" composed of ordinary goods and services that all consumers use on average is replaced by a portfolio composed of the shares of the big companies that are listed on the Toronto Stock Exchange. This index is an indicator of the health of the Toronto Stock Exchange. If the S&P/TSX increases, it means that the overall value of the shares in the Exchange is increasing; it is important to note that individually, some companies will be performing better than others, but collectively, the companies are performing well. The base value used for the S&P/TSX is 1,000, set in 1975. S&P/TSX is calculated as follows:

$$\textbf{S\&P/TSX Composite Index} = \frac{\textbf{Value of portfolio on selected date}}{\textbf{Value of portfolio on base date}} \times \mathbf{1{,}000}$$

In June 2018, the S&P/TSX index reached 16,000, which means that the value of the portfolio in 2018 was 16 times its value in 1975.

Example 6.4-h

Calculating S&P/TSX

If an S&P/TSX portfolio cost $200,000 in 1975, and the same portfolio cost $2,729,000 in 2015, calculate the S&P/TSX Composite Index.

Solution

$$\text{S\&P/TSX Composite Index} = \frac{\text{Value of portfolio on selected date}}{\text{Value of portfolio on base date}} \times 1{,}000$$

$$= \frac{2{,}729{,}000.00}{200{,}000.00} \times 1{,}000$$

$$= 13{,}645$$

Therefore, in 2015, the S&P/TSX Composite Index was 13,645.

6.4 | Exercises

Answers to odd-numbered problems are available at the end of the textbook.

1. Determine the index number for 2011 and 2016 for the value of a car using 2005 as the base year.

Year	2005	2011	2016
Value of Car	\$32,000	\$37,000	\$43,000

2. Determine the index number for 2010 and 2015 for the price of a tire using 2002 as the base year.

Year	2002	2010	2015
Price of a Tire	\$35	\$60	\$86

3. Determine the index number for 2016 for the price of a monthly metro pass for adults and students using 2002 as the base year.

Year	Metro Pass Adult	Metro Pass Student
2002	\$98.75	\$83.25
2016	\$141.50	\$112.00

4. Determine the index number for 2016 for the cost of an adult and child movie ticket using 2006 as the base year.

Year	Movie Ticket Adult	Movie Ticket Child
2006	\$9.00	\$6.00
2016	\$13.50	\$9.00

Use the index given below to answer Problems 5 to 8.

Year	1	2	3	4	5	6	7
Index	100.0	105.0	107.5	111.0	110.0	118.5	120.0

5. If an item was worth \$2,500 in year 3, how much was it worth in year 5 and year 7?
6. If an item was worth \$4,000 in year 2, how much was it worth in year 4 and year 6?
7. If an item was worth \$2,000 in year 5, how much was it worth in year 2 and year 3?
8. If an item was worth \$5,000 in year 6, how much was it worth in year 3 and year 4?

Use the CPI values from years 2002 to 2017 provided in Table 6.4 to answer Problems 9 to 16.

9. What real income in 2017 would be equivalent to an income of \$60,000 in 2006?
10. What real income in 2017 would be equivalent to an income of \$50,000 in 2007?
11. Calculate the inflation rate for the period 2010 to 2017.
12. Calculate the inflation rate for the period 2011 to 2017.
13. The college tuition fee for the year 2008 was \$3,200. What would the tuition fee be for the year 2017 if the tuition fee increased with the inflation rate during this period?
14. Tony earned \$58,000 in 2004. How much would he have earned in 2017 if his earnings grew with the inflation rate during this period?
15. Calculate the purchasing power of a dollar for 2015 and 2016 relative to the base year 2002.
16. Calculate the purchasing power of a dollar for 2012 and 2013 relative to the base year 2002.

Use the following data for Problems 17 to 20.

End of the Year	2009	2010	2011	2012	2013	2014	2015	2016
S&P/TSX Index	11,746	13,443	11,955	12,541	13,622	14,754	13,010	15,288

17. If you had invested $25,000 at the end of 2010, what would have been the value at the end of 2016?

18. If you had invested $75,000 at the end of 2009, what would have been the value at the end of 2016?

19. What amount invested at the end of 2012 would have resulted in a value of $50,000 at the end of 2016?

20. What amount invested at the end of 2011 would have resulted in a value of $150,000 at the end of 2016?

6 | Review Exercises

Answers to odd-numbered problems are available at the end of the textbook.

For Problems 1 and 2, determine whether the given pairs of ratios are equivalent.

1. a. 6 : 8 and 18 : 24
   b. 30 : 25 and 36 : 48
   c. 10 : 35 and 14 : 49
   d. 24 : 30 and 12 : 18

2. a. 16 : 20 and 18 : 30
   b. 4 : 10 and 10 : 24
   c. 35 : 50 and 21 : 36
   d. 20 : 16 and 30 : 24

3. What is the ratio of a Canadian quarter (25¢) to a Canadian $5 bill, reduced to lowest terms?

4. What is the ratio of 12 minutes to 2 hours, reduced to lowest terms?

5. Ali can run 12 km in 40 minutes.
   a. Calculate his speed in km/hour.
   b. At this speed, how far can he run in 1.5 hours?

6. A car can travel 486 km using 45 litres of gas.
   a. Calculate the fuel efficency of the car in km/litre.
   b. At this rate, how many litres of gas is required for a trip of 810 km?

7. Jeffrey and Gina were classmates who graduated together from college. Jeffrey found a job as a banker that pays him $189 for 9 hours and Gina found a job as a freelance artist that pays her $174 for 8 hours of work. Who is being paid a higher hourly rate and by how much?

8. Gregory purchased a racing motorbike and Chris purchased a cruising motorbike. Jeffery travelled 765 km from Toronto to New York City in 8 hours and 20 minutes. Chris travelled 165 km from Toronto to Buffalo in 2 hours and 10 minutes. Based on this information, whose average speed was greater and by how much (in km/h)?

9. Which is the better buy based on the unit price: 360 grams for $2.99 or 480 grams for $3.75?

10. Which is the better buy based on the unit price: 125 grams for $4.75 or 175 grams for $5.95?

For Problems 11 and 12, calculate the unit prices to determine which offer is best.

11. a. 3 kg of oranges for $7.99
    b. 4 kg of oranges for $9.99
    c. 5 kg of oranges for $11.99

12. a. 5 kg of rice for $4.99
    b. 8 kg of rice for $7.99
    c. 10 kg of rice for $9.49

13. If the ratio of sugar to flour in a pie is 3 : 5 and that of flour to eggs is 3 : 1, calculate the ratio of sugar : flour : eggs in the pie.

14. If the ratio of sales people to marketing people in an organization is 5 : 4 and the ratio of marketing people to finance people is 5 : 2, what is the ratio of sales people : marketing people : finance people in the organization?

15. The number of computers sold in a store in the last three weeks are in the ratio of $\frac{3}{5} : \frac{2}{3} : \frac{7}{15}$, respectively.

    If a total of 520 computers were sold in the three weeks, how many computers were sold during the last week?

16. The number of magazines sold in a store in the last three weeks are in the ratio of $\frac{1}{2} : \frac{1}{3} : \frac{3}{5}$, respectively.

    If a total of 1,060 magazines were sold in the three weeks, how many magazines were sold during the last week?

For Problems 17 and 18, solve the proportion equations for the unknown value.

17. a. $x : 9 = 26 : 39$
    b. $16 : 24 = 12 : x$
    c. $x : 0.45 = 0.16 : 1.20$

18. a. $x : 15 = 24 : 36$
    b. $8 : 14 = x : 35$
    c. $12.5 : 70 = x : 1.4$

19. A 450 gram loaf of bread costs $3.15 and has 15 slices.
   a. Determine the cost per 100 grams of bread.
   b. Determine the cost per slice of bread.

20. 250 grams of sliced cheese costs $4.50 and has 6 slices.
   a. Determine the cost per 100 grams of cheese.
   b. Determine the cost per slice of cheese.

21. If Christina, a graphic designer, receives an annual salary of $55,000, calculate her weekly salary using pro-rations. Assume that there are 52 weeks in a year.

22. As the CFO of a technology company, every year Tyler would receive 26 bi-weekly payments of $6,000 each. Calculate his monthly salary.

23. The sales tax on an item costing $350.00 is $45.50. What will be the sales tax on an item costing $1,250.00?

24. Peter works 5.5 hours per day and his salary per day is $112.75. At this rate, how much will he receive if he works 7.5 hours per day?

25. Alexander, an investment banker, invests all his yearly earnings in stocks of high-tech, mining, and real-estate in the ratio of 4 : 5 : 3, respectively. Calculate his investment in mining stocks if his investment in high-tech stocks was $10,900.

26. The ratio of the driving distance from London to Hamilton, Mississauga, and Toronto is 3 : 4 : 5, respectively. If the distance from London to Hamilton is 125 km, calculate the distance from London to Mississauga and from London to Toronto.

27. Three college classmates, Khan, Thomas, and Lee decided to start a small business and invested $1,000, $2,500, and $3,500, respectively. If Lee decided to leave the business, how much would Khan and Thomas have to pay for Lee's shares if they wanted to maintain their initial investment ratio?

28. Calvin decided to build a shopping complex with his two brothers, Kevin and Alex. They invested $200,000, $350,000, and $450,000, respectively. After the complex was built, Kevin decided to sell his share of the investment to Calvin and Alex. How much would each of them have to pay if they wanted to maintain the same ratio of their investments in the complex?

29. *A*, *B*, and *C* invested a total of $900 in the ratio of 3 : 4 : 5, respectively, to purchase a billiards table for their club house. After the table was delivered, each invested an additional $200 to purchase balls and cue sticks. Calculate their new investment ratio after their additional investments.

30. Samuel, his wife, and his mother jointly purchased an estate for $1,350,000. Their individual investments in the estate were in the ratio of 5 : 3 : 1 , respectively. Each of them decided to invest an additional $250,000 to develop the estate into a small family resort. Calculate their new investment ratio after the additional investments.

31. Anton, Cheryl, and Ellen invested $4,000, $7,500, and $6,000, respectively, to start a video production studio. The company did very well in the first year and they wanted to invest an additional $5,250 in total to expand their business. How much would each of them have to individually invest to maintain their original investment ratio?

32. Russel, an investment banker, invested $8,000, $12,000, and $4,000 in stocks of three different companies. The market showed potential to grow so he decided to invest an additional $1,500 in total in stocks of the same companies. How did he invest this amount into stocks of the three companies to maintain the original investment ratio?

Use the following exchange rates to answer Problems 33 to 36:

£1 = A$1.6072, C$1 = £0.6085, €1 = C$1.4095,
A$1 = US$0.7665

33. Convert A$1,500 to British pounds (£).

34. Convert £2,500 to Canadian dollars (C$).

35. Convert C$1,250 to Euros (€).

36. Convert US$2,000 to Australian dollars (A$).

37. Charles converted US$3,000 into Canadian dollars at a bank that charged him a commission rate of 0.75%. How much did he receive from the bank? Use the exchange rate C$1 = US$0.7495.

38. Dylan converted £2,000 into US dollars. If the bank was charging a commission rate of 0.50%, calculate the amount he received from the bank. Use the exchange rate US$1 = £0.8118.

Use the CPI values in Table 6.4 to answer Problems 39 to 44.

39. If an item was worth $25,000 in 2010, how much was it worth in 2016?

40. If an item was worth $7,500 in 2009, how much was it worth in 2017?

41. What real income in 2017 would be equivalent to an income of $5,000 in 2010?

42. What real income in 2016 would be equivalent to an income of $4,000 in 2011?

43. Calculate the purchasing power of a dollar in 2011 relative to the base year 2002.

44. Calculate the purchasing power of a dollar in 2010 relative to the base year 2002.

Self-Test | Chapter 6

Answers to all problems are available at the end of the textbook.

1. Which is cheaper: a 240 gram box of cereal for \$3.69, or a 360 gram box of cereal for \$4.89?

2. A 500 km trip by car took 6 hours and 45 minutes. Calculate the average speed of the car in km/h.

3. The average speed of a car is 75 km/h. At this speed, how many hours will it take to travel 700 km?

For Problems 4 and 5, solve the proportion equations for the unknown value.

4. a. $35 : 7 = 60 : x$

   b. $45 : x = 70 : 63$

5. a. $25 : 9 = x : 2.7$

   b. $x : 8 = 2\frac{1}{4} : 2\frac{1}{2}$

6. The scale on a map is 3 cm = 50 km. Calculate the actual distance between two cities that are 12.75 cm apart on the map.

7. An investment of \$1,500 earned \$820 in interest in one year. What amount should be invested at this rate to earn \$1,459 in interest?

8. A car travelled 250 km. If the fuel efficency of the car is 9 litres per 100 km, calculate the amount of gas used for the trip.

9. Which offer is the best based on the unit price?

   a. 75 grams of chocolate for \$1.49

   b. 100 grams of choclate for \$1.99

   c. 125 grams of chocolate for \$2.25

10. Andrew's earnings to Bill's was in the ratio of 3 : 5 and Bill's to Cathy's was in the ratio of 4 : 6. What was the ratio of the earnings of Andrew : Bill : Cathy?

11. For every \$25 that a not-for-profit foundation transferred to a relief fund, the government donated \$10 towards the same cause. After two months of fundraising, the foundation had a total of \$9,450, including the government's contribution. Calculate the amount donated by the government.

12. Georgia paid a yearly subscription amount of \$250 to receive a business magazine monthly. After receiving two issues, she cancelled her subscription. Calculate the pro-rated refund she should receive from the magazine company.

13. *A*, *B*, and *C* invested \$9,000, \$15,000, and \$12,000 respectively, to start a small business. An additional \$6,000 is required for operating the business. How much must each of them invest to mantain their original investment ratio?

14. Nabil and Mohammad invested a total of \$100,000 in the ratio of 3 : 5, respectively. After onc year, both of them withdrew \$10,000 from the invesment. Calculate the ratio of their investments after the withdrawal.

15. Profits are distributed to the three partners, Alice, Bill, and Carol, based on their investments of \$60,000, \$40,000 and \$96,000, respectively. If the profit last year was \$58,800, calculate their share of the profits.

16. Anil wants to convert US\$2,250 to Canadian dollars. If the exchange rate is C\$1 = US\$0.7495 and the bank's commission rate is 0.75%, how many Canadian dollars will he receive?

17. A bank has a buying rate of £1 = C\$1.65. If the exchange rate is £1 = C\$1.6435, calculate the rate of commision that the bank charges to buy British pounds.

Use the CPI values in Table 6.4 to answer Problems 18 to 20.

18. If an item was worth \$32,500 in 2014, how much was it worth in 2017?

19. What real income in 2017 would be equivalent to an income of \$80,000 in 2010?

20. What amount in 2014 had the same purchasing power as \$10,000 in 2016?

Chapter 7

UNITS OF MEASUREMENT

LEARNING OBJECTIVES

- Read, write, and interpret symbols and prefixes used in the metirc and US Customary systems of units.
- Convert within metric units of length, mass, and capacity.
- Convert within US Customary units of length, mass, and capactiy.
- Convert between metric and US Customary units of length, mass, and capacity.
- Convert units of temperature between the Celsius scale, Fahrenheit scale, and Kelvin scale.

CHAPTER OUTLINE

Introduction

Three common ways to describe an object are by its length (how long is it?), its mass (how heavy is it?), and its capacity (how much space/volume does it occupy?). Each of these types of measurement can be expressed using different units. It is important that these units are well defined so that measurements made in different units may be converted to a common unit for easy comparison.

The two measurement systems generally in use are the **metric system** and the **US customary system**. The metric system is widely used in science, medicine, technology, and engineering. It is simple to use and easy to understand as all the units within the system are related by powers of ten. Most of the world now uses the metric system of measurement; however, the US and two other countries (Liberia and Myanmar) have not fully adapted to the metric system.

In this chapter, we will learn the units of measurement for length, mass, and capacity used within both the metric and US customary systems, and to convert units within each system. We will also learn to covert between the two systems, in order to understand and interpret how 90 kilometres compares to 60 miles, how 70 kilograms compares to 145 pounds, how 55 litres compares to 20 gallons, etc. In addition, conversions among units of temperature will be discussed.

7.1 | Metric System of Measurement

Converting within Metric Units of Measurement

The **metric system** uses the metre (m), gram (g), and litre (L) as the base units for measurements of length, mass, and capacity, respectively. In this section, we will learn to convert within the following common metric units:

- **Length:** kilometre (km), metre (m), centimetre (cm), and millimetre (mm)
- **Mass:** kilogram (kg), gram (g), and milligram (mg)
- **Capacity:** litre (L) and millilitre (mL)

The conversion factors that relate to the different units in the metric system, including the prefixes used, are shown in Table 7.1.

The prefix and symbol for units from kilo- to milli- are written in lowercase.

Base Units
length: metre (m)
mass: gram (g)
capacity: litre (L)

Table 7.1 **Conversion Factors**

Prefix	Symbol	Factor	Factor (in Words)	Factor as a Power of 10
kilo-	k	1,000	Thousand	10^3
hecto-	h	100	Hundred	10^2
deca-	da	10	Ten	10^1
	Base Unit	**1**		
deci-	d	$\frac{1}{10} = 0.1$	One-tenth	10^{-1}
centi-	c	$\frac{1}{100} = 0.01$	One-hundredth	10^{-2}
milli-	m	$\frac{1}{1,000} = 0.001$	One-thousandth	10^{-3}

Note: The prefixes hecto-, deca-, and deci- are not commonly used as units of measurement for length, mass, and capacity. The prefix centi- is only commonly used in the measurement of length, as in centimetre.

Converting units within the metric system involves moving the decimal point to the right or to the left by the appropriate number of places (which is the same as multiplying or dividing by the appropriate power of 10).

This conversion process can be shown using the following horizontal line diagram, with the units ordered from largest to smallest.

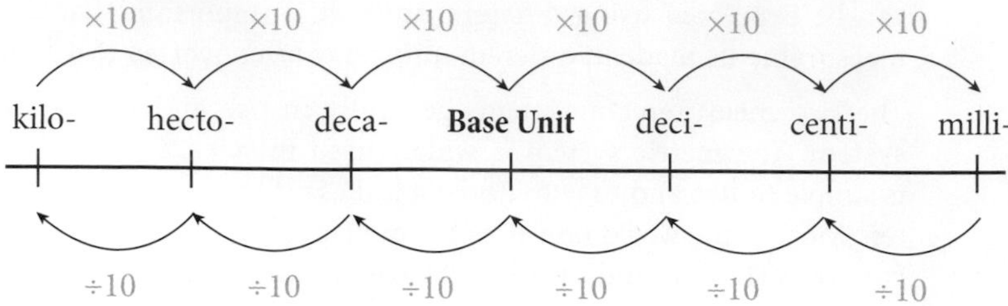

The conversion from a larger unit to a smaller unit involves moving the decimal point to the right or multiplying by powers of 10, as required.

For example, to convert 10.5 kilometres (km) to metres (m), move the decimal point 3 places to the right or multiply by 10^3 (= 1,000).

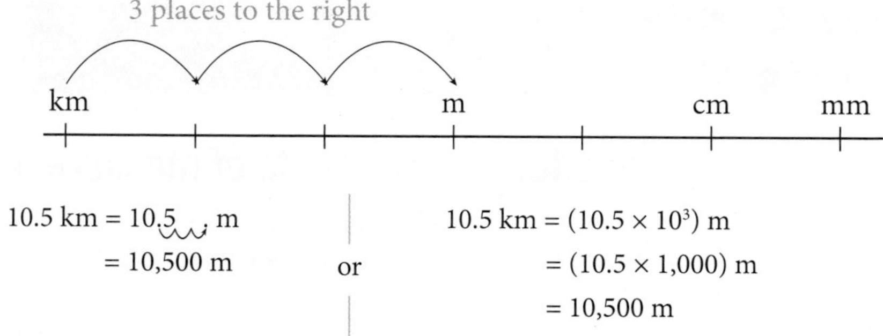

$$10.5 \text{ km} = 10.5\_\_\_ \text{ m} = 10{,}500 \text{ m}$$

or

$$10.5 \text{ km} = (10.5 \times 10^3) \text{ m} = (10.5 \times 1{,}000) \text{ m} = 10{,}500 \text{ m}$$

The conversion from a smaller unit to a larger unit involves moving the decimal point to the left or dividing by powers of 10, as required.

For example, to convert 425 centimetres (cm) to metres (m), move the decimal point 2 places to the left or divide by 10^2 (= 100).

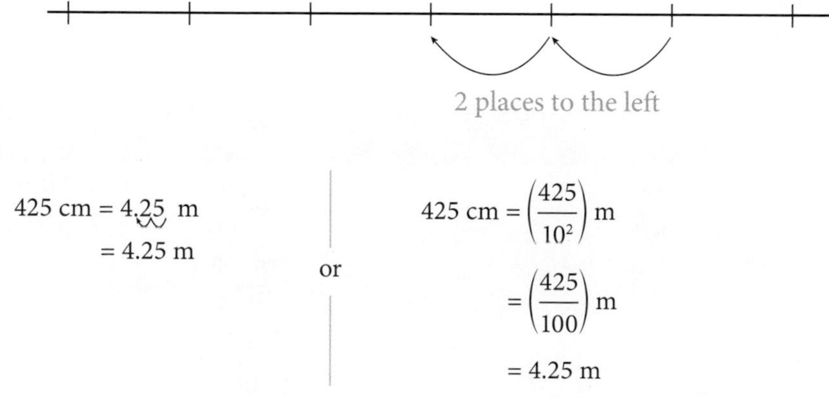

$$425 \text{ cm} = 4.25 \text{ m} = 4.25 \text{ m}$$

or

$$425 \text{ cm} = \left(\frac{425}{10^2}\right) \text{ m} = \left(\frac{425}{100}\right) \text{ m} = 4.25 \text{ m}$$

Length

Converting from larger units to smaller units	Converting from smaller units to larger units
1 km = (1 × 1,000) m = 1,000 m	$1\text{ m} = \left(\frac{1}{1{,}000}\right)\text{ km} = 0.001\text{ km}$
1 m = (1 × 100) cm = 100 cm	$1\text{ cm} = \left(\frac{1}{100}\right)\text{ m} = 0.01\text{ m}$
1 cm = (1 × 10) mm = 10 mm	$1\text{ mm} = \left(\frac{1}{10}\right)\text{ cm} = 0.1\text{ cm}$

Mass

1 metric ton or metric tonne

(t) = 1,000 kg

Converting from larger units to smaller units	Converting from smaller units to larger units
1 kg = (1 × 1,000) g = 1,000 g	$1\text{ g} - \left(\frac{1}{1{,}000}\right)\text{ kg} = 0.001\text{ kg}$
1 g = (1 × 1,000) mg = 1,000 mg	$1\text{ mg} = \left(\frac{1}{1{,}000}\right)\text{ g} = 0.001\text{ g}$

The capitalized 'L' is used to represent litre in order to avoid confusion with the number 1.

Capacity

1 cubic metre or metre cube (m^3) = 1,000 L

Converting from larger units to smaller units	Converting from smaller units to larger units
1 L = (1 × 1,000) mL = 1,000 mL	$1\text{ mL} = \left(\frac{1}{1{,}000}\right)\text{ L} = 0.001\text{ L}$

Example 7.1-a

Converting Metric Measurements

Convert the following measurements:

(i) 7.5 cm to millimetres

(ii) 1,120 cm to metres

(iii) 2.56 kg to grams

(iv) 21,750 mL to litres

Solution

(i) 7.5 cm to millimetres:

7.5 cm = (7.5 × 10) mm = 75 mm

(same as 7.5 = 75 mm)

(ii) 1,120 cm to metres:

$$1{,}120\text{ cm} = \left(\frac{1{,}120}{100}\right)\text{ m} = 11.2\text{ m}$$

(same as 1120 = 11.2 m)

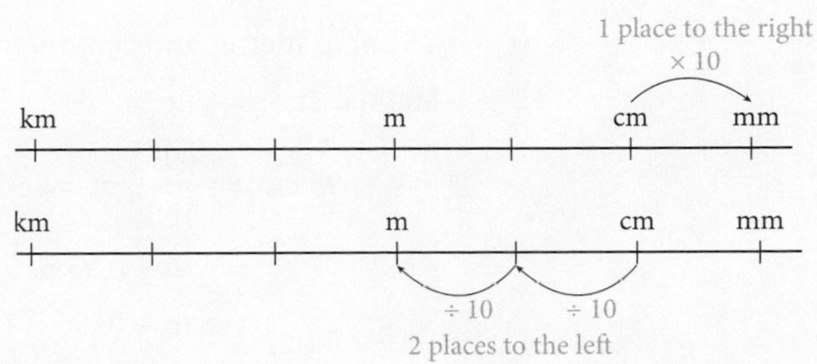

(iii) 2.56 kg to grams:

2.56 kg = (2.56 × 1,000) g = 2,560 g

(same as 2.56 = 2,560 g)

(iv) 21,750 mL to litres:

$$21{,}750\text{ mL} = \left(\frac{21{,}750}{1{,}000}\right)\text{ L} = 21.75\text{ L}$$

(same as 21750 = 21.75 L)

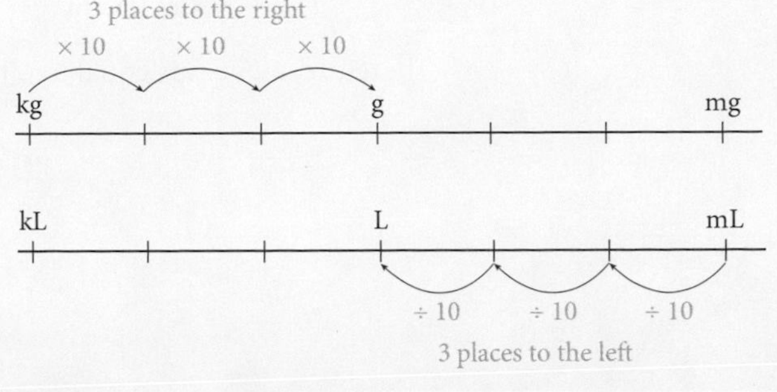

Example 7.1-b **Converting Metric Measurements Expressed in Multiple Units**

Convert the following measurements:

(i) 12 m 25 cm to centimetres (ii) 2 kg 456 g to grams (iii) 3 L 75 mL to millilitres

Solution

(i) 12 m 25 cm to centimetres:

12 m 25 cm = 12 m + 25 cm

= (12 × 100) cm + 25 cm

= 1,200 cm + 25 cm

= 1,225 cm

Therefore, 12 m 25 cm is equal to 1,225 cm.

(ii) 2 kg 456 g to grams:

2 kg 456 g = 2 kg + 456 g

= (2 × 1,000) g + 456 g

= 2,000 g + 456 g

= 2,456 g

Therefore, 2 kg 456 g is equal to 2,456 g.

(iii) 3 L 75 mL to millilitres:

3 L 75 mL = 3 L + 75 mL

= (3 × 1,000) mL + 75 mL

= 3,000 mL + 75 mL

= 3,075 mL

Therefore, 3 L 75 mL is equal to 3,075 mL.

Example 7.1-c **Converting Metric Measurements and Expressing in Multiple Units**

Convert the following measurements:

(i) 695 cm to metres and centimetres (ii) 2,275 mL to litres and millilitres

Solution

(i) 695 cm to metres and centimetres:

Method 1:

$$695 \text{ cm} = \left(\frac{695}{100}\right) \text{m} = 6.95 \text{ m}$$

= 6 m + 0.95 m

= 6 m + (0.95 × 100) cm

= 6 m + 95 cm

= 6 m 95 cm

Method 2:

695 cm = 600 cm + 95 cm

$$= \left(\frac{600}{100}\right) \text{m} + 95 \text{ cm}$$

= 6 m 95 cm

Therefore, 695 cm is equal to 6 m 95 cm.

Solution *continued*

(ii) 2,275 mL to litres and millilitres:

Method 1:

$$2{,}275 \text{ mL} = \left(\frac{2{,}275}{1{,}000}\right) \text{L} = 2.275 \text{ L}$$
$$= 2 \text{ L} + 0.275 \text{ L}$$
$$= 2 \text{ L} + (0.275 \times 1{,}000) \text{ mL}$$
$$= 2 \text{ L} + 275 \text{ mL}$$
$$= 2 \text{ L } 275 \text{ mL}$$

Method 2:

$$2{,}275 \text{ mL} = 2{,}000 \text{ mL} + 275 \text{ mL}$$
$$= \left(\frac{2{,}000}{1{,}000}\right) \text{L} + 275 \text{ mL}$$
$$= 2 \text{ L } 275 \text{ mL}$$

Therefore, 2,275 mL is equal to 2 L 275 mL.

Example 7.1-d Converting Metric Measurements Involving Two Steps

Convert the following measurements:

(i) 5 km 20 m to centimetres

(ii) 3,125,000 mg to kilograms and grams

Solution

(i) 5 km 20 m to centimetres:

Method 1:

Step 1: Convert 5 km 20 m to metres

$$5 \text{ km } 20 \text{ m} = 5 \text{ km} + 20 \text{ m}$$
$$= (5 \times 1{,}000) \text{ m} + 20 \text{ m}$$
$$= 5{,}000 \text{ m} + 20 \text{ m}$$
$$= 5{,}020 \text{ m}$$

Step 2: Convert 5,020 m to centimetres

$$5{,}020 \text{ m} = (5{,}020 \times 100) \text{ cm}$$
$$= 502{,}000 \text{ cm}$$

Method 2:

$$5 \text{ km } 20 \text{ m} = 5 \text{ km} + 20 \text{ m}$$
$$= (5 \times 10^5) \text{ cm} + (20 \times 10^2) \text{ cm}$$
$$= 500{,}000 \text{ cm} + 2{,}000 \text{ cm}$$
$$= 502{,}000 \text{ cm}$$

Therefore, 5 km 20 m is equal to 502,000 cm.

(ii) 3,125,000 mg to kilograms and grams:

Method 1:

Step 1: Convert 3,125,000 mg to grams

$$3{,}125{,}000 \text{ mg} = \left(\frac{3{,}125{,}000}{1{,}000}\right) \text{g}$$
$$= 3{,}125 \text{ g}$$

Step 2: Convert 3,125 g to kilograms and grams

$$3{,}125 \text{ g} = \left(\frac{3{,}125}{1{,}000}\right) \text{kg}$$
$$= 3.125 \text{ kg}$$
$$= 3 \text{ kg} + 0.125 \text{ kg}$$
$$= 3 \text{ kg} + (0.125 \times 1{,}000) \text{ g}$$
$$= 3 \text{ kg} + 125 \text{ g}$$
$$= 3 \text{ kg } 125 \text{ g}$$

Method 2:

$$3{,}125{,}000 \text{ mg} = \left(\frac{3{,}125{,}000}{10^6}\right) \text{kg}$$
$$= 3.125 \text{ kg}$$
$$= 3 \text{ kg} + 0.125 \text{ kg}$$
$$= 3 \text{ kg} + (0.125 \times 10^3) \text{ g}$$
$$= 3 \text{ kg} + 125 \text{ g}$$
$$= 3 \text{ kg } 125 \text{ g}$$

Therefore, 3,125,000 mg is equal to 3 kg 125 g.

Example 7.1-e Word Problems Involving Conversion of Metric Measurements

Megan bought 1.5 kg of flour and used 925 g of it. Calculate the quantity of flour remaining, in grams.

Solution

Since the answer needs to be expressed in grams, convert all measurements into grams.

$$1.5 \text{ kg} = (1.5 \times 1{,}000) \text{ g} \quad [\text{using } 1 \text{ kg} = 1{,}000 \text{ g}]$$
$$= 1{,}500 \text{ g}$$

Since she used 925 g of flour, this needs to be subtracted from the total.

$$\text{Remaining flour} = (1{,}500 - 925) \text{ g}$$
$$= 575 \text{ g}$$

Therefore, the quantity of flour remaining is 575 g.

7.1 | Exercises

Answers to odd-numbered problems are available at the end of the textbook.

For Problems 1 to 8, calculate the missing values.

1.

	metres (m)	centimetres (cm)	millimetres (mm)
a.	2.40	?	?
b.	?	860	?
c.	?	?	34,420

2.

	metres (m)	centimetres (cm)	millimetres (mm)
a.	1.20	?	?
b.	?	975	?
c.	?	?	23,170

3.

	metres (m)	centimetres (cm)	millimetres (mm)
a.	0.25	?	?
b.	?	58	?
c.	?	?	8,470

4.

	metres (m)	centimetres (cm)	millimetres (mm)
a.	0.67	?	?
b.	?	95	?
c.	?	?	5,200

5.

	kilometres (km)	metres (m)	centimetres (cm)
a.	1.62	?	?
b.	?	2,390	?
c.	?	?	2,320

6.

	kilometres (km)	metres (m)	centimetres (cm)
a.	1.25	?	?
b.	?	1,454	?
c.	?	?	1,190

7.

	kilometres (km)	metres (m)	centimetres (cm)
a.	0.65	?	?
b.	?	154	?
c.	?	?	1,770

8.

	kilometres (km)	metres (m)	centimetres (cm)
a.	0.17	?	?
b.	?	230	?
c.	?	?	9,400

For Problems 9 to 12, convert the measurements to the units indicated.

9. a. 23 m 21 cm = ____ cm b. 16 cm 7 mm = ____ mm c. 5 km 252 m = ____ m

10. a. 7 m 49 cm = ____ cm b. 45 cm 8 mm = ____ mm c. 2 km 725 m = ____ m

11. a. 335 cm = ____ m ____ cm b. 603 mm = ____ cm ____ mm c. 1,487 m = ____ km ____ m

12. a. 793 cm = ____ m ____ cm b. 379 mm = ____ cm ____ mm c. 6,745 m = ____ km ____ m

13. Arrange the following measurements in order from smallest to largest:
    0.15 km, 150,800 mm, 155 m, 15,200 cm

14. Arrange the following measurements in order from largest to smallest:
    19,750 cm, 1.97 km, 1,950 m, 195,700 mm

15. The distance between Howard's house and his office is 1.7 km. If he leaves home and walks 925 m toward his office, how many more metres would he have to walk to reach his office?

16. In a 2.5 km race, there is a checkpoint at 875 m from the finish line. Calculate the distance, in metres, that you would have to run to reach the checkpoint.

17. Ali is 1.75 m tall. Eric is 30 mm taller than Ali. Calculate Eric's height, in centimetres.

18. Five-year-old Aran's height is 1.2 m. His sister Girija is 40 mm taller than him. Calculate Girija's height, in centimetres.

For Problems 19 to 26, calculate the missing values.

19.

	kilograms (kg)	grams (g)
a.	2.62	?
b.	?	6,750

20.

	kilograms (kg)	grams (g)
a.	3.79	?
b.	?	8,620

21.

	kilograms (kg)	grams (g)
a.	0.84	?
b.	?	580

22.

	kilograms (kg)	grams (g)
a.	0.32	?
b.	?	930

23.

	kilograms (kg)	grams (g)	milligrams (mg)
a.	1.65	?	?
b.	?	4,950	?
c.	?	?	6,440

24.

	kilograms (kg)	grams (g)	milligrams (mg)
a.	2.45	?	?
b.	?	8,700	?
c.	?	?	3,890

25.

	kilograms (kg)	grams (g)	milligrams (mg)
a.	0.76	?	?
b.	?	35,760	?
c.	?	?	50,300

26.

	kilograms (kg)	grams (g)	milligrams (mg)
a.	0.45	?	?
b.	?	25,090	?
c.	?	?	20,080

For Problems 27 to 30, convert the measurements to the units indicated.

27. a. 18 kg 79 g = ___ g b. 2 kg 116 mg = ___ mg c. 3 t 74 kg = ___ kg

28. a. 7 kg 89 g = ___ g b. 14 kg 547 mg = ___ mg c. 15 t 90 kg = ___ kg

29. a. 5,903 g = ___ kg ___ g b. 2,884 mg = ___ g ___ mg c. 9,704 kg = ___ t ___ kg

30. a. 5,014 g = ___ kg ___ g b. 6,629 mg = ___ g ___ mg c. 3,075 kg = ___ t ___ kg

31. Arrange the following measurements in order from smallest to largest:
0.075 t, 123,200 g, 850,250 mg, 125 kg

32. Arrange the following measurements in order from largest to smallest:
0.025 t, 50,750 mg, 125,700 g, 27 kg

33. If one tablespoon of salt weighs 5.5 g, how many tablespoons of salt are there in a box containing 1.1 kg of salt?

34. If a bowl can hold 40 g of cereal, how many bowls of cereal will you obtain from a box that has 1.35 kg of cereal?

35. Linda is baking a cake. She bought 0.75 kg of sugar and used 575 g of it. Calculate the quantity of sugar left, in grams.

36. Ben bought 1.3 kg of meat and cooked 650 g of it for dinner. Calculate the quantity of meat left, in grams.

37. 450 g of butter cost $3.25. At this price, how much will it cost to buy 2.25 kg of butter?

38. 250 g of cheese cost $2.75. At this price, how much will it cost to buy 2 kg of cheese?

For Problems 39 to 42, calculate the missing values.

39.

	litres (L)	millilitres (mL)
a.	3.25	?
b.	?	5,060

40.

	litres (L)	millilitres (mL)
a.	1.75	?
b.	?	1,975

41.

	litres (L)	millilitres (mL)
a.	0.045	?
b.	?	220

42.

	litres (L)	millilitres (mL)
a.	0.015	?
b.	?	5,730

For Problems 43 to 46, convert the measurements to the units indicated.

43. a. 5 L 85 mL = ___ L　　b. 2 L 5 mL = ___ L

44. a. 9 L 25 mL = ___ L　　b. 1 L 205 mL = ___ L

45. a. 2,708 mL = ___ L ___ mL　　b. 12,080 mL = ___ L ___ mL

46. a. 6,503 mL = ___ L ___ mL　　b. 32,096 mL = ___ L ___ mL

47. A bottle can hold 900 mL of orange juice. Calculate the total volume of orange juice in five bottles. Express the answer in litres.

48. Andy drinks 250 mL of milk every day. Calculate the quantity of milk he will require for seven days. Express the answer in litres.

49. A milk carton contains 1.75 L of milk. If three glasses with a volume of 320 mL each are filled with milk from the carton, how much milk will be left in the carton? Express the answer in millilitres.

50. A bottle can hold 1.5 L of wine. If four glasses with a volume of 280 mL each are filled with wine from the bottle, how much wine will be left in the bottle? Express the answer in millilitres.

7.2 | US Customary System of Measurement

In the United States, measurements are primarily in units of the **US customary system**. For example, road distance is measured in miles, butter is measured in pounds, and gasoline is measured in gallons. Related to the US customary system, is the **Imperial system**, which was historically used in the British Commonwealth countries. Though very similar, there are a number of differences between these two systems.

For example,

- 1 US ton is approximately 0.893 imperial tons.
- 1 US gallon is approximately 0.833 imperial gallons.

In this section, we will only be focusing on the US customary system of measurement, which uses the yard (yd), pound (lb), and gallon (gal) as the base units for measurements of length, mass, and capacity, respectively.

Base Units

length: yard (yd)

mass: pound (lb)

capacity: gallon (gal)

We will learn to convert within the following common US customary units:

- **Length:** mile (mi), yard (yd), foot (ft), and inch (in)
- **Mass:** ton (ton), pound (lb), and ounce (oz)
- **Capacity:** gallon (gal), quart (qt), pint (pt), cup (c), and fluid ounce (fl oz)

Converting within US Customary Units of Measurement

Length

- 1 mile is 1,760 yd or 5,280 feet — 1 mi = 1,760 yd = 5,280 ft
- 1 yard is 3 feet — 1 yd = 3 ft
- 1 foot is 12 inches — 1 ft = 12 in

Mass

- 1 US ton is 2,000 pounds — 1 ton = 2,000 lb
- 1 pound is 16 ounces — 1 lb = 16 oz

Note: The US Customary unit for ton is called 'short ton' and is represented by the word 'ton'. This is to distinguish it from the metric ton that has the symbol 't', where t = 1,000 kg.

Capacity

- 1 gallon is 4 quarts — 1 gal = 4 qt
- 1 quart is 2 pints — 1 qt = 2 pt
- 1 pint is 2 cups — 1 pt = 2 c
- 1 cup is 8 fluid ounces — 1 c = 8 fl oz

There are a number of methods for converting measurements from one unit to another. In Section 7.1, to convert units within the metric system, we multiplied or divided by powers of 10 because the units are related by factors of 10, 100, 1,000, $\frac{1}{10}$, $\frac{1}{100}$, $\frac{1}{1,000}$, etc. Conversions within the US customary system can also be performed using direct multiplication or division, using the conversion factors as shown in the diagram below:

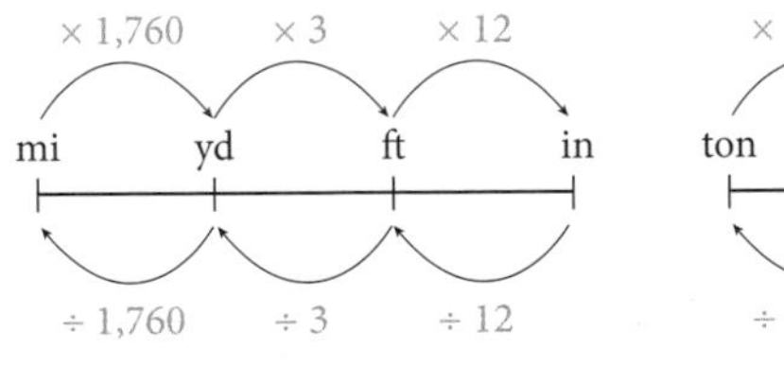

Length

× 2,000 × 16

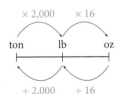

ton lb oz

÷ 2,000 ÷ 16

Mass

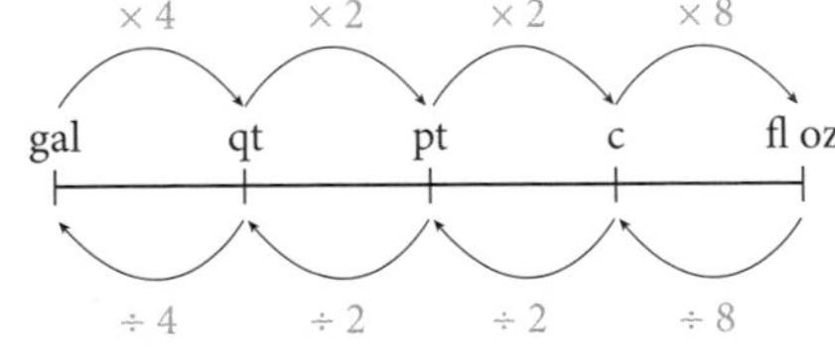

Capacity

For example, since 1 yd = 3 ft and 1 ft = 12 in, in order to convert 5 yards to inches, multiply by first converting yards to feet and then feet to inches.

i.e., 5 yd = (5 × 3) ft = 15 ft

= (15 × 12) in = 180 in

Example 7.2-a **Converting US Customary Measurements Expressed in Multiple Units Using Direct Multiplication**

Convert the following measurements:

(i) 2 ft 10 in to inches (ii) 5 lb 9 oz to ounces (iii) 2 gal 3 qt to quarts

Solution

(i) 2 ft 10 in to inches:

$$\begin{aligned} 2 \text{ ft } 10 \text{ in} &= 2 \text{ ft} + 10 \text{ in} \\ &= (2 \times 12) \text{ in} + 10 \text{ in} \qquad [\text{using } 1 \text{ ft} = 12 \text{ in}] \\ &= 24 \text{ in} + 10 \text{ in} \\ &= 34 \text{ in} \end{aligned}$$

Therefore, 2 ft 10 in is equal to 34 in.

(ii) 5 lb 9 oz to ounces:

$$\begin{aligned} 5 \text{ lb } 9 \text{ oz} &= 5 \text{ lb} + 9 \text{ oz} \\ &= (5 \times 16) \text{ oz} + 9 \text{ oz} \qquad [\text{using } 1 \text{ lb} = 16 \text{ oz}] \\ &= 80 \text{ oz} + 9 \text{ oz} \\ &= 89 \text{ oz} \end{aligned}$$

Therefore, 5 lb 9 oz is equal to 89 oz.

(iii) 2 gal 3 qt to quarts:

$$\begin{aligned} 2 \text{ gal } 3 \text{ qt} &= 2 \text{ gal} + 3 \text{ qt} \\ &= (2 \times 4) \text{ qt} + 3 \text{ qt} \qquad [\text{using } 1 \text{ gal} = 4 \text{ qt}] \\ &= 8 \text{ qt} + 3 \text{ qt} \\ &= 11 \text{ qt} \end{aligned}$$

Therefore, 2 gal 3 qt is equal to 11 qt.

Example 7.2-b **Converting US Customary Measurements Using Direct Division and Expressing in Multiple Units**

Convert the following measurements:

(i) 6,730 ft to miles and feet (ii) 73 oz to pounds and ounces (iii) 95 qt to gallons and quarts

Solution

Divide the given, smaller unit by the known conversion factor using the method of long division. The quotient will be the larger unit and the remainder will be the smaller unit.

(i) 6,730 ft to miles and feet:

$$6{,}730 \text{ ft} = \left(\frac{6{,}730}{5{,}280}\right) \text{mi} \qquad [\text{using } 1 \text{ mi} = 5{,}280 \text{ ft}]$$

$$\begin{array}{r} 1 \text{ mi} \\ 5{,}280 \overline{)\, 6{,}730} \\ -\underline{5{,}280} \\ 1{,}450 \text{ ft} \end{array}$$

Therefore, 6,730 ft is equal to 1 mi 1,450 ft.

(ii) 73 oz to pounds and ounces:

$$73 \text{ oz} = \left(\frac{73}{16}\right) \text{lb} \qquad [\text{using } 1 \text{ lb} = 16 \text{ oz}]$$

$$\begin{array}{r} 4 \text{ lb} \\ 16 \overline{)\, 73} \\ -\underline{64} \\ 9 \text{ oz} \end{array}$$

Therefore, 73 oz is equal to 4 lb 9 oz.

Solution
continued

(iii) 95 qt to gallons and quarts:

$$95 \text{ qt} = \left(\frac{95}{4}\right) \text{ gal} \qquad \text{[using 1 gal = 4 qt]}$$

$$\begin{array}{r} 23 \text{ gal} \\ 4 \overline{)\,95} \\ -8\downarrow \\ \hline 15 \\ -12 \\ \hline 3 \text{ qt} \end{array}$$

Therefore, 95 qt is equal to 23 gal 3 qt.

When converting between units within the US customary system, especially when multiple conversions are necessary, it can be helpful to apply one of the following more formally-defined methods:

(i) the conversion factor (ratio) method (also known as dimensional analysis), and

(ii) the proportion method.

Conversion Factor (Ratio) Method

For any known relationship between two units, we can find two conversion factors to use in converting units.

For example, consider the relationship 1 foot = 12 inches.

Dividing both sides of the equation by 1 foot,

$$\frac{1 \cancel{\text{foot}}}{1 \cancel{\text{foot}}} = \frac{12 \text{ inches}}{1 \text{ foot}}$$

$$1 = \frac{12 \text{ inches}}{1 \text{ foot}}$$

Dividing both sides of the equation by 12 inches,

$$\frac{1 \text{ foot}}{12 \text{ inches}} = \frac{12 \cancel{\text{inches}}}{12 \cancel{\text{inches}}}$$

$$\frac{1 \text{ foot}}{12 \text{ inches}} = 1$$

Therefore, the relationship between two units can be written as two conversion factors (or ratios):

$$\frac{12 \text{ inches}}{1 \text{ foot}} \text{ or } \frac{1 \text{ foot}}{12 \text{ inches}}$$

Since the conversion factors are equal to 1, they can be used to multiply the given measurement to convert it from one unit to another. The following examples will illustrate how to use them in conversions.

Example 7.2-c **Finding Conversion Factors for a Given Relationship**

Find the two conversion factors for the following known relationship: 1 yard = 3 feet.

Solution

1 yard = 3 feet

Dividing both sides of the equation by 1 yard: $1 = \frac{3 \text{ feet}}{1 \text{ yard}}$

Dividing both sides of the equation by 3 feet: $\frac{1 \text{ yard}}{3 \text{ feet}} = 1$

Therefore, the two conversion factors are $\frac{3 \text{ feet}}{1 \text{ yard}}$ and $\frac{1 \text{ yard}}{3 \text{ feet}}$.

Example 7.2-d **Using a Conversion Factor to Convert Units of Measurements**

Convert 90 in. to feet. Use the relationship 1 foot = 12 inches.

Solution

90 in. to feet:

Step 1: Write the two conversion factors: $\frac{1 \text{ foot}}{12 \text{ inches}}$ and $\frac{12 \text{ inches}}{1 \text{ foot}}$

Step 2: Write the measurement to be converted: 90 inches

Step 3: Identify the correct conversion factor that will cancel the unit to be converted (in this case, the conversion factor that has the unit 'inches' in its denominator): $\frac{1 \text{ foot}}{12 \text{ inches}}$

Step 4: Multiply the measurement to be converted by this conversion factor:

$$90 \text{ inches} \times \frac{1 \text{ foot}}{12 \text{ inches}}$$

Step 5: Cross-cancel the units that appear in both the numerator and denominator and simplify the fraction to obtain the answer:

$$\begin{aligned} 90 \text{ inches} &= 90 \cancel{\text{inches}} \times \frac{1 \text{ foot}}{12 \cancel{\text{inches}}} \\ &= \left(\frac{90}{12}\right) \text{feet} \\ &= 7.5 \text{ feet} \end{aligned}$$

Therefore, 90 inches is equal to 7.5 feet.

The conversion factor method can be expanded to perform multi-step conversions in a single step. For example, knowing that 1 foot = 12 inches and 1 yard = 3 feet, the conversion factor can be expanded as follows:

$$\frac{1 \text{ foot}}{12 \text{ inches}} \times \frac{1 \text{ yard}}{3 \text{ feet}}$$

When simplified,

$$\frac{1 \cancel{\text{foot}}}{12 \text{ inches}} \times \frac{1 \text{ yard}}{3 \cancel{\text{feet}}} = \frac{1 \text{ yard}}{36 \text{ inches}}$$

Therefore, this results in a new conversion factor of $\frac{1 \text{ yard}}{36 \text{ inches}}$; i.e., 1 yard = 36 inches.

Example 7.2-e **Using an Expanded Conversion Factor to Convert Units of Measurements**

Convert the following measurements:

(i) 5.9 yd to inches

(ii) 72 c to gallons

Solution

(i) 5.9 yd to inches:

Multiply with the conversion factors $\left(\frac{3 \text{ feet}}{1 \text{ yard}}\right)$ and $\left(\frac{12 \text{ inches}}{1 \text{ foot}}\right)$ to cross-cancel the units 'yd' and 'ft'.

$$\begin{aligned} 5.9 \text{ yd} &= 5.9 \cancel{\text{yards}} \times \left(\frac{3 \cancel{\text{feet}}}{1 \cancel{\text{yard}}}\right) \times \left(\frac{12 \text{ inches}}{1 \cancel{\text{foot}}}\right) \\ &= 5.9 \times 3 \times 12 \text{ inches} \\ &= 212.4 \text{ in} \end{aligned}$$

Therefore, 5.9 yd is equal to 212.4 in.

Solution
continued

(ii) 72 c to gallons:

Multiply with the conversion factors $\left(\frac{1 \text{ pint}}{2 \text{ cups}}\right), \left(\frac{1 \text{ quart}}{2 \text{ pints}}\right)$, and $\left(\frac{1 \text{ gallon}}{4 \text{ quarts}}\right)$ to cross-cancel the units 'c', 'pt', and 'qt'.

$$72 \text{ c} = 72 \text{ cups} \times \left(\frac{1 \text{ pint}}{2 \text{ cups}}\right) \times \left(\frac{1 \text{ quart}}{2 \text{ pints}}\right) \times \left(\frac{1 \text{ gallon}}{4 \text{ quarts}}\right)$$

$$= \frac{72}{2 \times 2 \times 4} \text{ gallons}$$

$$= \frac{72}{16} \text{ gallons}$$

$$= 4.5 \text{ gal}$$

Therefore, 72 c is equal to 4.5 gal

Proportion Method

When forming the proportion equation, the order in which the units of the terms in the ratio are written should be consistent on either side of the equation;

e.g., km : m = km : m

This is similar to the method learned in the previous chapter (Ratios, Proportions, and Applications).

In this method, we equate two ratios, where one of the ratios is formed from a known relationship, and the second ratio is formed from the question asked, using the value for the unit to be converted and the unit required. These two ratios are equated to form the proportion equation and the unknown unit is solved using cross-multiplication and simplification.

Example 7.2-f **Using the Proportion Method to Convert Units of Measurements**

Convert the following measurements:

(i) 8.5 mi to feet (ii) 25 pt to gallons

Solution

(i) 8.5 mi to feet:

$$\text{mi} : \text{ft} = \text{mi} : \text{ft}$$

$$8.5 : x = 1 : 5{,}280 \qquad \text{[Using 1 mi = 5,280 ft]}$$

In fractional form, $\frac{8.5}{x} = \frac{1}{5{,}280}$

Cross-multiplying, $x = 8.5 \times 5{,}280 = 44{,}880 \text{ ft}$

Therefore, 8.5 mi is equal to 44,880 ft.

(ii) 25 pt to gallons:

First, converting from pints to quarts,

$$\text{qt} : \text{pt} = \text{qt} : \text{pt}$$

$$x : 25 = 1 : 2 \qquad \text{[Using 1 qt = 2 pt]}$$

In fractional form, $\frac{x}{25} = \frac{1}{2}$

Cross-multiplying, $2x = 25$

$$x = \frac{25}{2} = 12.5 \text{ qt}$$

Therefore, 25 pt is equal to 12.5 qt.

Converting from quarts to gallons,

$$\text{gal} : \text{qt} = \text{gal} : \text{qt}$$

$$x : 12.5 = 1 : 4 \qquad \text{[Using 1 gal = 4 qt]}$$

Solution
continued

In fractional form, $\frac{x}{12.5} = \frac{1}{4}$

Cross-multiplying, $4x = 12.5$

$$x = \frac{12.5}{4} = 3.125 \text{ gal}$$

Therefore, 25 pt is equal to 3.125 gal (25 pt = 12.5 qt = 3.125 gal).

The conversion factor method is preferable over the proportion method when two or more steps are involved in the conversion.

For example, converting 25 pt to gallons, as in Example 7.2-f, can be performed using the conversion factor method, as follows:

1st conversion factor from 1 qt = 2 pt
2nd conversion factor from 1 gal = 4 qt

$$25 \text{ pt} = 25 \text{ pt} \times \left(\frac{1 \text{ qt}}{2 \text{ pt}}\right) \times \left(\frac{1 \text{ gal}}{4 \text{ qt}}\right)$$

$$= \left(\frac{25}{2 \times 4}\right) \text{gal} = 3.125 \text{ gal}$$

Example 7.2-g

Converting Measurements in a Word Problem

A wire of length 10.5 yd is cut into seven equal pieces. Calculate the length of each piece, in feet.

Solution

Since the answer needs to be measured in feet, convert all measurements into feet before doing any calculations.

$$\text{yd} : \text{ft} = \text{yd} : \text{ft}$$

$$10.5 : x = 1 : 3 \qquad \text{[Using 1 yd = 3 ft]}$$

$$\frac{10.5}{x} = \frac{1}{3}$$

$$x = 10.5 \times 3 = 31.5 \text{ ft}$$

If the wire is cut into seven equal pieces, then the total length needs to be divided by seven.

$$\frac{31.5 \text{ ft}}{7} = 4.5 \text{ ft}$$

Therefore, the length of each piece is 4.5 ft.

Note: It is also correct to divide the wire into seven pieces first, and then convert that length from yards to feet.

7.2 | Exercises

Answers to odd-numbered problems are available at the end of the textbook.

For Problems 1 to 8, calculate the missing values.

1.

	yard (yd)	feet (ft)	inch (in.)
a.	42	?	?
b.	?	48	?
c.	?	?	648

2.

	yard (yd)	feet (ft)	inch (in.)
a.	84	?	?
b.	?	72	?
c.	?	?	540

3.

	yard (yd)	feet (ft)	inch (in.)
a.	46.5	?	?
b.	?	22.5	?
c.	?	?	2,880

4.

	yard (yd)	feet (ft)	inch (in.)
a.	67.5	?	?
b.	?	37.5	?
c.	?	?	3,960

5.

	miles (mi)	yard (yd)	feet (ft)
a.	3	?	?
b.	?	6,160	?
c.	?	?	10,560

6.

	miles (mi)	yard (yd)	feet (ft)
a.	2	?	?
b.	?	9,680	?
c.	?	?	18,480

7.

	miles (mi)	yard (yd)	feet (ft)
a.	2.25	?	?
b.	?	2,200	?
c.	?	?	6,192

8.

	miles (mi)	yard (yd)	feet (ft)
a.	42.5	?	?
b.	?	3,080	?
c.	?	?	25,080

For Problems 9 to 12, convert the measurements to the units indicated.

9. a. 12 yd 1.5 ft = ___ ft b. 11 ft 10 in. = ___ in. c. 1 mi 121 yd = ___ yd

10. a. 15 yd 7.5 ft = ___ ft b. 12 ft 11 in. = ___ in. c. 2 mi 45 yd = ___ yd

11. a. 78 ft = ___ yd ___ ft b. 570 in. = ___ ft ___ in. c. 5,705 yd = ___ mi ___ yd

12. a. 56 ft = ___ yd ___ ft b. 420 in. = ___ ft ___ in. c. 7,350 yd = ___ mi ___ yd

13. A sheet of paper is 7 ft long. A piece that is 5 ft 9 in. long is cut from it. Calculate the length of the paper left, in inches.

14. An iron rod is 7 ft in length. One piece of 5 ft 3 in. is cut from it. Calculate the length of the remaining portion of the rod, in inches.

15. A rope of length 13.5 yd is cut into nine equal pieces. Calculate the length of each piece, in feet.

16. A wooden fence of length 32 yd is made up of twelve equal panels. Calculate the length of each panel, in feet.

17. The length of a river is 39,600 ft. Calculate the length of the river, in miles.

18. The height of a mountain is 81,840 ft. Calculate the height of the mountain, in miles.

For Problems 19 to 26, calculate the missing values.

19.

	pound (lb)	ounce (oz)
a.	?	288
b.	8	?

20.

	pound (lb)	ounce (oz)
a.	?	384
b.	12	?

21.

	pound (lb)	ounce (oz)
a.	?	232
b.	25.25	?

22.

	pound (lb)	ounce (oz)
a.	?	296
b.	19.75	?

23.

	ton (ton)	pound (lb)
a.	35	?
b.	?	14,500

24.

	ton (ton)	pound (lb)
a.	37	?
b.	?	23,500

25.

	ton (ton)	pound (lb)
a.	12.75	?
b.	?	65,000

26.

	ton (ton)	pound (lb)
a.	17.25	?
b.	?	47,000

For Problems 27 to 30, convert the measurements to the units indicated.

27. a. 11 lb 10 oz = ___ oz b. 2 ton 1,250 lb = ___ lb

28. a. 9 lb 3 oz = ___ oz b. 5 ton 1,175 lb = ___ lb

29. a. 55,825 lb = ___ ton ___ lb b. 150 oz = ___ lb ___ oz

30. a. 79,125 lb = ___ ton ___ lb b. 200 oz = ___ lb ___ oz

31. Arrange the following measurements in order from largest to smallest:
34,400 oz, 1.2 ton, 2,250 lb

32. Arrange the following measurements in order from smallest to largest:
0.95 ton, 1,920 lb, 29,760 oz

33. A cake weighing 2 lb 8 oz is cut into eight equal portions. Calculate the weight of each portion, in ounces.

34. The weight of twelve cans of softdrink is 5 lb 4 oz. Calculate the weight of each can of soft drink, in ounces.

35. A wholesaler bought 1.25 tons of cashews. He wants to sell them in packages of 2.5 pounds, each. Calculate the number of packages that can be made.

36. A bookstore received a shipment of 1,600 mathematics textbooks. The total weight of the shipment is 2.2 tons. Calculate the weight of each book, in pounds.

For Problems 37 to 44, calculate the missing values.

37.

	quart (qt)	pint (pt)	cup (c)
a.	22	?	?
b.	?	38	?
c.	?	?	68

38.

	quart (qt)	pint (pt)	cup (c)
a.	28	?	?
b.	?	26	?
c.	?	?	74

39.

	quart (qt)	pint (pt)	cup (c)
a.	32.5	?	?
b.	?	45	?
c.	?	?	94

40.

	quart (qt)	pint (pt)	cup (c)
a.	47.5	?	?
b.	?	51	?
c.	?	?	102

41.

	gallon (gal)	quart (qt)	pint (pt)
a.	12	?	?
b.	?	18	?
c.	?	?	56

42.

	gallon (gal)	quart (qt)	pint (pt)
a.	15	?	?
b.	?	24	?
c.	?	?	64

43.

	gallon (gal)	quart (qt)	pint (pt)
a.	7.5	?	?
b.	?	14	?
c.	?	?	50

44.

	gallon (gal)	quart (qt)	pint (pt)
a.	9.5	?	?
b.	?	22	?
c.	?	?	30

For Problems 45 to 48, convert the measurements to the units indicated.

45. a. 9 qt 1 pt = ___ pt b. 15 pt 3 c = ___ c c. 12 gal 1 qt = ___ qt

46. a. 14 qt 1 pt = ___ pt b. 27 pt 1 c = ___ c c. 17 gal 1 qt = ___ qt

47. a. 19 pt = ___ qt ___ pt b. 39 c = ___ pt ___ c c. 86 qt = ___ gal ___ qt

48. a. 23 pt = ___ qt ___ pt b. 55 c = ___ pt ___ c c. 75 qt = ___ gal ___ qt

49. Arrange the following measurements in order from smallest to largest:
29 c, 6 qt, 14 pt, 2 gal

50. Arrange the following measurements in order from largest to smallest:
    45 c, 23 pt, 10 qt, 3 gal

51. Mythili drinks 2 c of milk every day. How many gallons of milk will she require for a month of 30 days?

52. If a family uses an average of 8 c of milk everyday, how many gallons of milk will be required for a week?

53. A juice container had 12 pt of juice. If 15 c of juice was used from the container, how many cups of juice are left in the container?

54. A water bottle contained 8 qt of spring water. If 25 c of water was used from the bottle, how many cups of water are left in the bottle?

7.3 | Conversion Between Metric and US Customary Units

Conversion of units between the metric and US customary systems is achieved by using conversion tables and either the conversion factor method or the proportion method, as discussed is Section 7.2. For the examples in this section, the conversion factor approach will be used.

Conversion tables between the commonly used metric and US customary units of measurement are provided below (all the conversions provided are from US to metric, as metric is the preferred system of measurement in Canada; there is a quick metric to US conversion provided later in this section).

Length

- **Metric units:** kilometre (km), metre (m), centimetre (cm), and millimetre (mm)
- **US Customary units:** mile (mi), yard (yd), foot (ft), and inch (in.)

Conversion Table

US Customary Units	Metric Units
1 mi	1.609 km
1 yd	0.9144 m
1 ft	30.48 cm
1 in.	2.54 cm

1 in. = 2.54 cm is an exact conversion.

Example 7.3-a **Converting Metric Units of Length to US Customary Units**

Convert the following measurements (round your answers to the nearest hundredth, as appropriate):

(i) 250 km to miles (ii) 45 m to feet

Solution

(i) 250 km to miles:

Use $\left(\frac{1 \text{ mi}}{1.609 \text{ km}}\right)$ as the conversion factor to cross-cancel the unit 'km'.

$$250 \text{ km} = 250 \cancel{\text{km}} \times \left(\frac{1 \text{ mi}}{1.609 \cancel{\text{km}}}\right)$$

$$= \frac{250}{1.609} \text{ mi}$$

$$= 155.376009... = 155.38 \text{ mi}$$

Therefore, 250 km is equal to 155.38 mi.

Solution *continued*

(ii) 45 m to feet:

Use $\left(\dfrac{100 \text{ cm}}{1 \text{ m}}\right)$ as the first conversion factor to cross-cancel the unit 'm' and $\left(\dfrac{1 \text{ ft}}{30.48 \text{ cm}}\right)$ as the second conversion factor to cross-cancel the unit 'cm'.

$$45 \text{ m} = 45 \cancel{\text{m}} \times \left(\frac{100 \cancel{\text{cm}}}{1 \cancel{\text{m}}}\right) \times \left(\frac{1 \text{ ft}}{30.48 \cancel{\text{cm}}}\right)$$

$$= \frac{45 \times 100}{30.48} \text{ ft}$$

$$= 147.637795... = 147.64 \text{ ft}$$

Therefore, 45 m is equal to 147.64 ft.

Example 7.3-b **Converting US Customary Units of Length to Metric Units**

Convert the following measurements (round your answers to the nearest hundredth, as appropriate):

(i) 8.75 yd to centimetres (ii) 2.5 mi to metres

Solution

(i) 8.75 yd to centimetres:

Use $\left(\dfrac{0.9144 \text{ m}}{1 \text{ yd}}\right)$ as the first conversion factor to cross-cancel the unit 'yd' and $\left(\dfrac{100 \text{ cm}}{1 \text{ m}}\right)$ as the second conversion factor to cross-cancel the unit 'm'.

$$8.75 \text{ yd} = 8.75 \cancel{\text{yd}} \times \left(\frac{0.9144 \cancel{\text{m}}}{1 \cancel{\text{yd}}}\right) \times \left(\frac{100 \text{ cm}}{1 \cancel{\text{m}}}\right)$$

$$= 8.75 \times 0.9144 \times 100 \text{ cm}$$

$$= 800.1 \text{ cm}$$

Therefore, 8.75 yd is equal to 800.1 cm.

(ii) 2.5 mi to metres:

Use $\left(\dfrac{1.609 \text{ km}}{1 \text{ mi}}\right)$ as the first conversion factor to cross-cancel the unit 'mi' and $\left(\dfrac{1{,}000 \text{ m}}{1 \text{ km}}\right)$ as the second conversion factor to cross-cancel the unit 'km'.

$$2.5 \text{ mi} = 2.5 \cancel{\text{mi}} \times \left(\frac{1.609 \cancel{\text{km}}}{1 \cancel{\text{mi}}}\right) \times \left(\frac{1{,}000 \text{ m}}{1 \cancel{\text{km}}}\right)$$

$$= 2.5 \times 1.609 \times 1{,}000 \text{ m}$$

$$= 4{,}022.5 \text{ m}$$

Therefore, 2.5 mi is equal to 4,022.5 m.

Mass

- **Metric units:** kilogram (kg), gram (g), and milligram (mg)
- **US Customary units:** US ton (ton), pound (lb), and ounce (oz)

Conversion Table

US Customary Units	Metric Units
1 ton	907.2 kg
1 lb	0.4536 kg
1 oz	28.35 g

Example 7.3-c Converting Metric Units of Mass to US Customary Units

Convert the following measurements (round your answers to the nearest hundredth, as appropriate):

(i) 2.5 kg to pounds (ii) 400 g to ounces

Solution

(i) 2.5 kg to pounds:

Use $\left(\frac{1 \text{ lb}}{0.4536 \text{ kg}}\right)$ as the conversion factor to cross-cancel the unit 'kg'.

$$2.5 \text{ kg} = 2.5 \text{ kg} \times \left(\frac{1 \text{ lb}}{0.4536 \text{ kg}}\right)$$

$$= \frac{2.5}{0.4536} \text{ lb}$$

$$= 5.511463... = 5.51 \text{ lb}$$

Therefore, 2.5 kg is equal to 5.51 lb.

(ii) 400 g to ounces:

Use $\left(\frac{1 \text{ oz}}{28.35 \text{ g}}\right)$ as the conversion factor to cross-cancel the unit 'g'.

$$400 \text{ g} = 400 \text{ g} \times \left(\frac{1 \text{ oz}}{28.35 \text{ g}}\right)$$

$$= \frac{400}{28.35} \text{ oz}$$

$$= 14.109347... = 14.11 \text{ oz}$$

Therefore, 400 g is equal to 14.11 oz.

Example 7.3-d Converting US Customary Units of Mass to Metric Units

Convert the following measurements (round your answers to the nearest hundredth, as appropriate):

(i) 1.75 lb to grams (ii) 225 oz to kilograms

Solution

(i) 1.75 lb to grams:

Use $\left(\frac{0.4536 \text{ kg}}{1 \text{ lb}}\right)$ as the first conversion factor to cross-cancel the unit 'lb' and $\left(\frac{1{,}000 \text{ g}}{1 \text{ kg}}\right)$ as the second conversion factor to cross-cancel the unit 'kg'.

$$1.75 \text{ lb} = 1.75 \text{ lb} \times \left(\frac{0.4536 \text{ kg}}{1 \text{ lb}}\right) \times \left(\frac{1{,}000 \text{ g}}{1 \text{ kg}}\right)$$

$$= 1.75 \times 0.4536 \times 1{,}000 \text{ g}$$

$$= 793.8 \text{ g}$$

Therefore, 1.75 lb is equal to 793.8 g.

(ii) 225 oz to kilograms:

Use $\left(\frac{28.35 \text{ g}}{1 \text{ oz}}\right)$ as the first conversion factor to cross-cancel the unit 'oz' and $\left(\frac{1 \text{ kg}}{1{,}000 \text{ g}}\right)$ as the second conversion factor to cross-cancel the unit 'g'.

$$225 \text{ oz} = 225 \text{ oz} \times \left(\frac{28.35 \text{ g}}{1 \text{ oz}}\right) \times \left(\frac{1 \text{ kg}}{1{,}000 \text{ g}}\right)$$

$$= \frac{225 \times 28.35}{1{,}000} \text{ kg}$$

$$= 6.37875 = 6.38 \text{ kg}$$

Therefore, 225 oz is equal to 6.38 kg.

Capacity

- **Metric units:** litre (L) and millilitre (mL)
- **US Customary units:** gallon (gal), quart (qt), pint (pt), cup (c), and fluid ounce (fl oz)

Conversion Table

US Customary Units	Metric Units
1 gal	3.785 L
1 qt	0.9464 L
1 pt	473.2 mL
1 c	236.6 mL
1 fl oz	29.57 mL

Example 7.3-e **Converting Metric Units of Capacity to US Customary Units**

Convert the following measurements (round your answers to the nearest hundredth, as appropriate):

(i) 60 L to gallons (ii) 425 mL to fluid ounces

Solution

(i) 60 L to gallons:

Use $\left(\frac{1 \text{ gal}}{3.785 \text{ L}}\right)$ as the conversion factor to cross-cancel the unit 'L'.

$$60 \text{ L} = 60 \not{\text{L}} \times \left(\frac{1 \text{ gal}}{3.785 \not{\text{L}}}\right)$$

$$= \frac{60}{3.785} \text{ gal}$$

$$= 15.852047... = 15.85 \text{ gal}$$

Therefore, 60 L is equal to 15.85 gal.

(ii) 425 mL to fluid ounces:

Use $\left(\frac{1 \text{ fl oz}}{29.57 \text{ mL}}\right)$ as the conversion factor to cross-cancel the unit 'mL'.

$$425 \text{ mL} = 425 \not{\text{mL}} \times \left(\frac{1 \text{ fl oz}}{29.57 \not{\text{mL}}}\right)$$

$$= \frac{425}{29.57} \text{ fl oz}$$

$$= 14.372675... = 14.37 \text{ fl oz}$$

Therefore, 425 mL is equal to 14.37 fl oz.

Example 7.3-f **Converting US Customary Units of Capacity to Metric Units**

Convert the following measurements (round your answers to the nearest hundredth, as appropriate):

(i) 2.5 gal to litres (ii) 30 fl oz to millilitres

Solution

(i) 2.5 gal to litres:

Use $\left(\frac{3.785\text{ L}}{1\text{ gal}}\right)$ as the conversion factor to cross-cancel the unit 'gal'.

$$2.5\text{ gal} = 2.5\text{ gal} \times \left(\frac{3.785\text{ L}}{1\text{ gal}}\right)$$
$$= 2.5 \times 3.785\text{ L}$$
$$= 9.4625 = 9.46\text{ L}$$

Therefore, 2.5 gal is equal to 9.46 L.

(ii) 30 fl oz to millilitres:

Use $\left(\frac{29.57\text{ mL}}{1\text{ fl oz}}\right)$ as the conversion factor to cross-cancel the unit 'fl oz'.

$$30\text{ fl oz} = 30\text{ fl oz} \times \left(\frac{29.57\text{ mL}}{1\text{ fl oz}}\right)$$
$$= 30 \times 29.57\text{ mL}$$
$$= 887.1\text{ mL}$$

Therefore, 30 fl oz is equal to 887.1 mL.

Quick Metric to US Customary Conversions

The following approximate conversions from metric units to US Customary units are useful to conceptualize the magnitude of the US Customary units.

- 1 km is a little more than half a mile (1 km ≈ 0.6 mi).
- 1 m is a little more than a yard, or 3 feet (1 m ≈ 1.1 yd, or 3.3 ft).
- 1 cm is a little less than half an inch (1 cm ≈ 0.4 in.).
- 1 kg is a little more than 2 pounds (1 kg ≈ 2.2 lb).
- 1 L is a little more than a quart (1 L ≈ 1.1 qt).

*Note: Do **not** use these approximate conversions in the Exercise Problems in this chapter. Use the exact conversions as given in the length, mass, and capacity Conversion Tables in this section.*

Conversion of Rates

Recall from the previous chapter that a rate is a ratio that is used to compare two quantities or amounts that have different units of measure. For example, a speed limit on a road of 60 kilometres per hour, or 60 km/h, is a rate.

We can use the method of conversion factors to express a rate using different units. For example, if we wanted to express the speed limit of 60 km/h in metres per second (m/s):

$$60\text{ km/h} = \frac{60\text{ km}}{1\text{ h}}$$

1st conversion factor of 1 km = 1,000 m
2nd conversion factor of 1 h = (60 × 60) s

$$= \frac{60\text{ km}}{1\text{ h}} \times \left(\frac{1{,}000\text{ m}}{1\text{ km}}\right) \times \left(\frac{1\text{ h}}{60 \times 60\text{ s}}\right)$$

$$= \frac{60 \times 1{,}000\text{ m}}{60 \times 60\text{ s}} = \frac{1{,}000}{60}\text{ m/s}$$

$$= 16.666666... = 16.67\text{ m/s}$$

Therefore, 60 km/h is equal to 16.67 m/s.

The following two examples demonstrate the conversion of a rate expressed in metric units to US customary units.

Example 7.3-g **Converting a Rate Expressed in Metric Units to US Customary Units**

The fuel efficiency of a car is 12 km/L. What is the fuel efficiency of the car in miles per gallon (mi/gal), rounded to the nearest hundredth?

Solution

Use $\left(\frac{1 \text{ mi}}{1.609 \text{ km}}\right)$ as the first conversion factor to cross-cancel the unit 'km' and $\left(\frac{3.785 \text{ L}}{1 \text{ gal}}\right)$ as the second conversion factor to cross-cancel the unit 'L'.

$$12 \text{ km/L} = \frac{12 \text{ km}}{1 \text{ L}}$$

$$= \frac{12 \cancel{\text{km}}}{1 \cancel{\text{L}}} \times \left(\frac{1 \text{ mi}}{1.609 \cancel{\text{km}}}\right) \times \left(\frac{3.785 \cancel{\text{L}}}{1 \text{ gal}}\right)$$

$$= \frac{12 \times 3.785 \text{ mi}}{1.609 \text{ gal}}$$

$$= 28.228713... = 28.23 \text{ mi/gal}$$

Therefore, a fuel efficiency of 12 km/L is equal to 28.23 mi/gal.

Example 7.3-h **Converting Rates to Solve a Word Problem**

A train is travelling at a speed of 150 km/h. How long, in minutes, will it take to reach the station which is 40 miles away? Round your answer to the nearest hundredth.

Solution

First, convert the given rate from km/h to miles per minute (mi/min).

Use $\left(\frac{1 \text{ mi}}{1.609 \text{ km}}\right)$ as the first conversion factor to cross-cancel the unit 'km' and $\left(\frac{1 \text{ h}}{60 \text{ min}}\right)$ as the second conversion factor to cross-cancel the unit 'h'.

$$150 \text{ km/h} = \frac{150 \text{ km}}{1 \text{ h}}$$

$$= \frac{150 \cancel{\text{km}}}{1 \cancel{\text{h}}} \times \left(\frac{1 \text{ mi}}{1.609 \cancel{\text{km}}}\right) \times \left(\frac{1 \cancel{\text{h}}}{60 \text{ min}}\right)$$

$$= \frac{150 \text{ mi}}{1.609 \times 60 \text{ min}}$$

$$= 1.553760... \text{ mi/min}$$

Now, use proportions to determine how long it will take to travel 40 miles.

$$\text{mi} : \text{min} = \text{mi} : \text{min}$$

$$1.553760... : 1 = 40 : x$$

$$\frac{1.553760...}{1} = \frac{40}{x}$$

$$(1.553760...)x = 40$$

$$x = \frac{40}{1.553760...} = 25.744 = 25.74 \text{ min}$$

Therefore, it will take 25.74 minutes for the train to reach the station.

Conversion of Temperature Scales

There are three common scales used when measuring temperature:

1. °C, the Celsius scale
2. °F, the Fahrenheit scale
3. K, the Kelvin scale

The Celsius scale (°C) is part of the metric system, and is the standard used by most countries, including Canada. The Fahrenheit scale is primarily used in the US. The Kelvin scale is an extension of the Celsius scale, and is used frequently in physics and chemistry.

Celsius and Fahrenheit Scales

The Celsius scale (°C) derives from the basis that pure water, at sea level pressure, freezes at 0 °C and boils at 100 °C. The Fahrenheit scale (°F) derives from the basis that pure water, at sea level pressure, freezes at 32 °F and boils at 212 °F.

Therefore, the difference between the freezing and boiling points of water is 100 °C (100 °C – 0 °C) and 180 °F (212 °F – 32 °F).

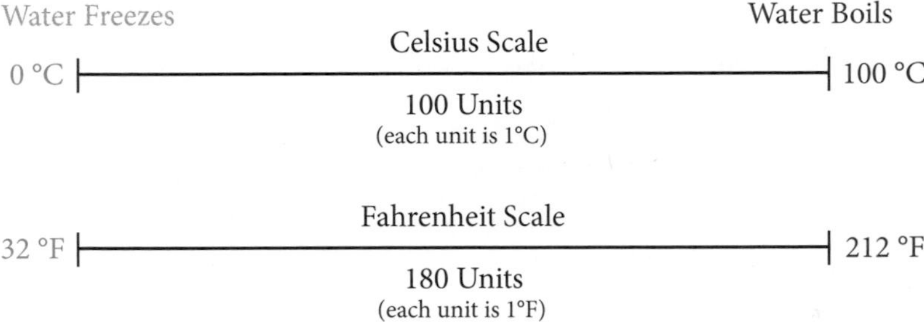

100 units in the Celsius scale, starting from 0 °C, is equivalent to 180 units in the Fahrenheit scale, starting from 32 °F.

Therefore, to convert from °C to °F, multiply °C by a factor of $\frac{180}{100} = \frac{9}{5} = 1.8$ and add 32 °F.

$$\mathbf{°F = 1.8(°C) + 32}$$

Similarly, to convert from °F to °C, subtract 32 °F and divide by 1.8.

$$\mathbf{°C = \frac{(°F - 32)}{1.8}}$$

Conversion Table

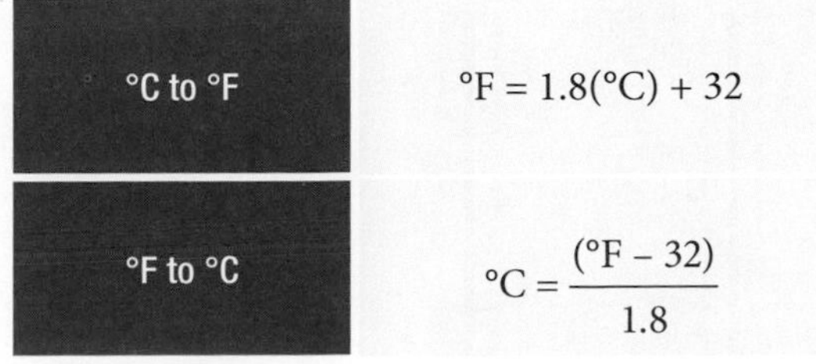

°C to °F	$°F = 1.8(°C) + 32$
°F to °C	$°C = \frac{(°F - 32)}{1.8}$

Example 7.3-i **Converting Between the Celsius (°C) and Fahrenheit (°F) Scales**

Convert the following (round to the nearest hundredth, as needed):

(i) 25 °C to Fahrenheit (ii) 90 °F to Celsius

Solution

(i) 25 °C to Fahrenheit:

$$°F = 1.8(°C) + 32$$
$$= 1.8(25) + 32$$
$$= 77\ °F$$

Therefore, 25 °C is equal to 77 °F.

(ii) 90 °F to Celsius:

$$°C = \frac{(°F - 32)}{1.8}$$
$$= \frac{(90 - 32)}{1.8}$$
$$= 32.222222... = 32.22\ °C$$

Therefore, 90 °F is equal to 32.22 °C.

Example 7.3-j **Comparing Temperatures Measured Using Different Scales**

Which is the higher temperature: 80 °C or 175 °F?

Solution

Convert 80 °C to °F and compare with 175 °F.

$$°F = 1.8(°C) + 32$$
$$= 1.8(80) + 32$$
$$= 176\ °F$$

i.e., 80 °C = 176 °F > 175 °F

i.e., 80 °C > 175 °F

or

Convert 175 °F to °C and compare with 80 °C.

$$°C = \frac{(°F - 32)}{1.8} = \frac{(175 - 32)}{1.8}$$
$$= 79.444444... = 79.44\ °C$$

i.e., 175 °F = 79.44 °C < 80 °C

i.e., 80 °C > 175 °F

Therefore, 80 °C is a (slightly) higher temperature than 175 °F.

Kelvin Scale

Another unit of measure for temperature is the Kelvin scale, symbolized by K (*not* °K). The Kelvin scale does not have negative numbers; i.e., its zero point is "absolute zero", at which point there is complete absence of heat energy. It is for this reason that the Kelvin scale is frequently used in physics and chemistry.

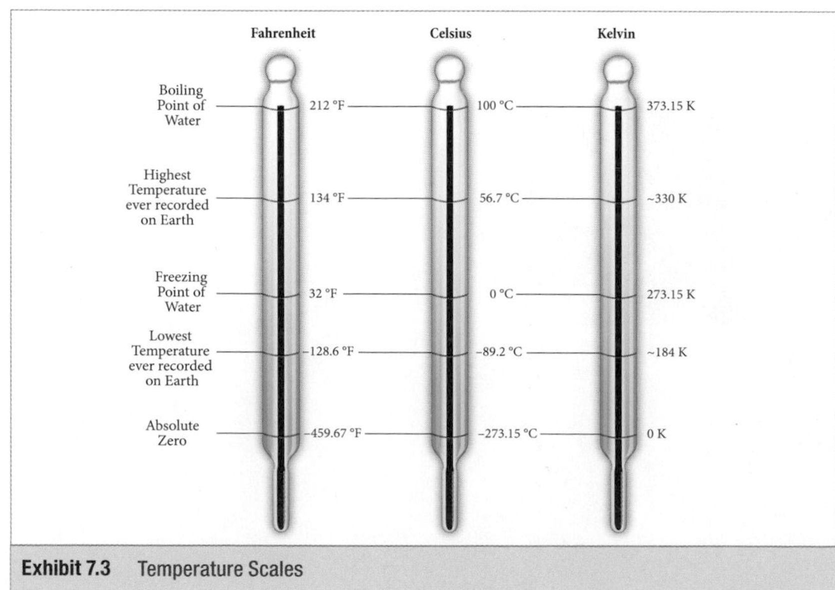

Exhibit 7.3 Temperature Scales

To convert between Celsius (°C) and Kelvin (K) measurements and to convert between Fahrenheit (°F) and Kelvin (K), use the conversion tables below.

Conversion Table

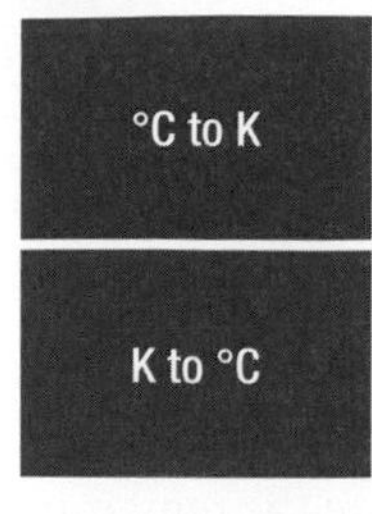
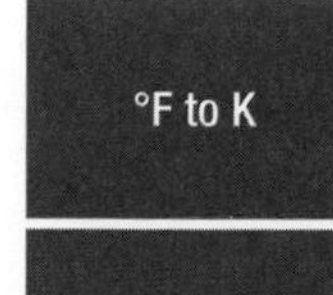

°C to K	$K = °C + 273.15$	°F to K	$K = \dfrac{(°F - 32)}{1.8} + 273.15$
K to °C	$°C = K - 273.15$	K to °F	$°F = 1.8(K - 273.15) + 32$

Example 7.3-k **Converting Between the Celsius (°C) , Fahrenheit (°F), and Kelvin (K) Scales**

Convert the following (round to the nearest hundredth, as needed):

(i) 25 °C to Kelvin (ii) 300 K to Celsius

(iii) 75 °F to Kelvin (iv) 350 K to Fahrenheit

Solution

(i) 25 °C to Kelvin:

$$K = °C + 273.15$$
$$= 25 + 273.15$$
$$= 298.15 \text{ K}$$

Therefore, 25 °C is equal to 298.15 K.

(ii) 300 K to Celsius:

$$°C = K - 273.15$$
$$= 300 - 273.15$$
$$= 26.85 \text{ °C}$$

Therefore, 300 K is equal to 26.85 °C.

(iii) 75 °F to Kelvin:

$$K = \frac{(°F - 32)}{1.8} + 273.15$$
$$= \frac{(75 - 32)}{1.8} + 273.15$$
$$= \frac{43}{1.8} + 273.15$$
$$= 297.038888... = 297.04 \text{ K}$$

Therefore, 75 °F is equal to 297.04 K.

(iv) 350 K to Fahrenheit:

$$°F = 1.8(K - 273.15) + 32$$
$$= 1.8(350 - 273.15) + 32$$
$$= 1.8(76.85) + 32$$
$$= 170.33 \text{ °F}$$

Therefore, 350 K is equal to 170.33 °F.

7.3 | Exercises

Answers to odd-numbered problems are available at the end of the textbook.

For the following problems, express your answers rounded to two decimal places, wherever applicable.

For Problems 1 to 8, calculate the missing values.

1.

	Metric Units	US Customary Units
a.	250 km	? mi
b.	? km	120 mi

2.

	Metric Units	US Customary Units
a.	175 km	? mi
b.	? km	80 mi

3.

	Metric Units	US Customary Units
a.	17.5 m	? yd
b.	? m	22 yd

4.

	Metric Units	US Customary Units
a.	11 m	? yd
b.	? m	12.5 yd

5.

	Metric Units	US Customary Units
a.	250 m	? ft
b.	? m	75 ft

6.

	Metric Units	US Customary Units
a.	12 m	? ft
b.	? m	45.5 ft

7.

	Metric Units	US Customary Units
a.	100 cm	? in.
b.	? cm	3.5 in.

8.

	Metric Units	US Customary Units
a.	80 cm	? in.
b.	? cm	7.5 in.

9. Arrange the following measurements in order from largest to smallest:
   82.5 ft, 900 in., 4,250 cm, 28 yd, 24 m

10. Arrange the following measurements in order from smallest to largest:
    1,280 cm, 44 ft, 15 yd, 450 in., 12 m

11. June bought 5.5 metres of fabric and used 10 feet of it to make a curtain. Calculate the remaining quantity of fabric, in metres.

12. A swimming pool is 12.5 metres wide. It is divided into five lanes of equal width. Calculate the width of each lane, in feet.

13. The distance from Toronto to Niagara Falls is 320 km. After driving 100 miles from Toronto, calculate the distance left to reach Niagara Falls, in kilometres.

14. The distance from Niagara Falls to New York is 410 miles. After driving 550 kilometres from Niagara Falls, what is the distance to be travelled, in kilometres, to reach New York?

For Problems 15 to 22, calculate the missing values.

15.

	Metric Units	US Customary Units
a.	3,500 kg	? tons
b.	? kg	2.5 tons

16.

	Metric Units	US Customary Units
a.	4,250 kg	? tons
b.	? kg	4 tons

17.

	Metric Units	US Customary Units
a.	15.5 kg	? lb
b.	? kg	45 lb

18.

	Metric Units	US Customary Units
a.	70 kg	? lb
b.	? kg	135.5 lb

19.

	Metric Units	US Customary Units
a.	1,200 g	? lb
b.	? g	6.5 lb

20.

	Metric Units	US Customary Units
a.	750 g	? lb
b.	? g	4.5 lb

21.

	Metric Units	US Customary Units
a.	200 g	? oz
b.	? g	4 oz

22.

	Metric Units	US Customary Units
a.	175 g	? oz
b.	? g	2.5 oz

23. Arrange the following measurements in order from largest to smallest:
    2.5 kg, 2,450 g, 5.7 lb, 80 oz

24. Arrange the following measurements in order from smallest to largest:
    4.5 kg, 4,560 g, 9.5 lb, 155 oz

25. Carol bought 2 pounds of butter and used 750 grams of it to make a cake. Calculate the remaining quantity of butter, in grams.

26. A recipe requires 600 grams of butter. Dylan bought 1.5 pounds of butter and used 600 grams of it. Calculate the remaining quantity of butter, in grams.

27. William weighs 80 kg. His brother weighs 25 pounds less than him. Calculate his brother's weight, in kg.

28. A travel bag weighs 2.25 kg. The total weight of the travel bag with its contents is 50 pounds. Calculate the weight of the contents in the bag, in kg.

For Problems 29 to 38, calculate the missing values.

29.

	Metric Units	US Customary Units
a.	50 L	? gal
b.	? L	10.5 gal

30.

	Metric Units	US Customary Units
a.	25.5 L	? gal
b.	? L	30 gal

31.

	Metric Units	US Customary Units
a.	15 L	? qt
b.	? L	14 qt

32.

	Metric Units	US Customary Units
a.	22 L	? qt
b.	? L	12 qt

33.

	Metric Units	US Customary Units
a.	7.5 L	? pt
b.	? L	14 pt

34.

	Metric Units	US Customary Units
a.	6 L	? pt
b.	? L	10.5 pt

35.

	Metric Units	US Customary Units
a.	4.5 L	? c
b.	? L	14 c

36.

	Metric Units	US Customary Units
a.	5 L	? c
b.	? L	18 c

37.

	Metric Units	US Customary Units
a.	8 mL	? fl. oz
b.	? mL	20.5 fl. oz

38.

	Metric Units	US Customary Units
a.	3.5 mL	? fl. oz
b.	? mL	15 fl. oz

39. Arrange the following measurements in order from largest to smallest:
    3.5 L, 4.8 qt, 10.5 pt, 1 gal

40. Arrange the following measurements in order from smallest to largest.
    7.5 L, 8.5 qt, 15 pt, 1.7 gal

41. The capacity of a fuel tank of a car is 54 litres. The tank is $\frac{1}{3}$ empty. Calculate the current amount of fuel in the tank, in gallons.

42. The fuel tank of a van can hold 18 gallons. It is $\frac{2}{3}$ empty. Calculate the current amount of the fuel in the tank, in litres.

43. A container had 3.5 litres of milk. Ten cups of milk were used from this container. Calculate the quantity of milk, in litres, that remains in the container.

44. A bottle contained 1.2 litres of juice. Someone drinks three cups of juice from this bottle. Calculate the remaining quantity, in litres.

For Problems 45 to 50, calculate the missing values.

45.

	Metric Units	US Customary Units
a.	100 km/h	? mi/h
b.	? km/h	50 mi/h

46.

	Metric Units	US Customary Units
a.	60 km/h	? mi/h
b.	? km/h	35 mi/h

47.

	Metric Units	US Customary Units
a.	15 km/L	? mi/gal
b.	? km/L	45 mi/gal

48.

	Metric Units	US Customary Units
a.	8 km/L	? mi/gal
b.	? km/L	30 mi/gal

49.

	Metric Units	US Customary Units
a.	80 km/h	? ft/s
b.	? km/h	20 ft/s

50.

	Metric Units	US Customary Units
a.	135 km/h	? ft/s
b.	? km/h	90 ft/s

51. The fuel efficiency of Car A is 25 mi/gal, while the fuel efficiency of Car B is 10 km/L. Which car is more fuel efficient?

52. Taylor is shopping for a new vehicle and has narrowed her search down to two models. Model A has a fuel efficiency of 13 km/L, and Model B has a fuel efficiency of 28 mi/gal. If she bases her decision on fuel efficiency, which model of vehicle should Taylor buy?

53. How long, in minutes, will it take a car to travel 15 miles if it is travelling at a constant speed of 50 km/h?

54. How long, in minutes, will it take a bus to travel 60 kilometres if it is travelling at a constant speed of 40 mi/h?

55. Gas costs C$1.40 per litre in Toronto. What is the equivalent cost expressed in US$ per gallon? Use US$1 = C$1.3342.

56. At a local grocery store, grapes are sold for C$3.25 per kilogram. Express the selling price of grapes in US$ per pound. Use US$1 = C$1.3342.

For Problems 57 to 80, convert the temperatures.

57. 21 °C = _____ °F
58. 10 °C = _____ °F
59. 98.6 °F = _____ °C
60. 85 °F = _____ °C
61. 140 °C = _____ °F
62. 180 °C = _____ °F
63. 112 °F = _____ °C
64. 400 °F = _____ °C
65. −15 °F = _____ °C
66. −40 °F = _____ °C
67. 280 K = _____ °C
68. 260 K = _____ °C
69. 19 °C = _____ K
70. −10 °C = _____ K
71. 80 °F = _____ K
72. 100 °F = _____ K
73. 300 K = _____ °C
74. 250 K = _____ °C
75. 200 K = _____ °F
76. 350 K = _____ °F
77. −20 °C = _____ K
78. 35 °C = _____ K
79. −80 °F = _____ K
80. −40 °F = _____ K

7 | Review Exercises

Answers to odd-numbered problems are available at the end of the textbook.

For the following problems, express your answers rounded to two decimal places, wherever applicable.

1. a. 7 m 5 cm = _____ cm
   b. 15 km 50 m = _____ m
   c. 75 mm = _____ cm _____ mm
   d. 905 cm = _____ m _____ cm

2. a. 37 m 2 cm = _____ cm
   b. 6 km 59 m = _____ m
   c. 1,026 mm = _____ cm _____ mm
   d. 405 cm = _____ m _____ cm

3. a. 39 yd 1 ft = _____ ft
   b. 4 ft 7 in. = _____ in.
   c. 115 in. = _____ ft _____ in.
   d. 5,290 yd = _____ mi _____ yd

4. a. 43 yd 2 ft = _____ ft
   b. 15 ft 1 in. = _____ in.
   c. 102 in. = _____ ft _____ in.
   d. 3,085 yd = _____ mi _____ yd

5. a. 10 kg 32 g = _____ g
   b. 45 g 52 mg = _____ mg
   c. 3.62 kg = _____ kg _____ g
   d. 42,007 mg = _____ g _____ mg

6. a. 3 kg 753 g = _____ g
   b. 7 g 87 mg = _____ mg
   c. 2.783 kg = _____ kg _____ g
   d. 29,005 mg = _____ g _____ mg

7. a. 6 lb 7 oz = _____ oz
   b. 14 ton 1,005 lb = _____ lb
   c. 32,000 lb = _____ ton _____ lb
   d. 120 oz = _____ lb _____ oz

8. a. 26 lb 2 oz = _____ oz
   b. 1 ton 249 lb = _____ lb
   c. 23,000 lb = _____ ton _____ lb
   d. 245 oz = _____ lb _____ oz

9. a. 6 L 49 mL = _____ mL
   b. 9,006 mL = _____ L _____ mL
   c. 9 gal 2 qt = _____ qt
   d. 75 pt = _____ qt _____ pt

10. a. 86 L 630 mL = _____ mL
    b. 2,092 mL = _____ L _____ mL
    c. 15 gal 3 qt = _____ qt
    d. 32 pt = _____ qt _____ pt

11. a. 410 °F = _____ °C
    b. 80 °C = _____ °F
    c. 125 °F = _____ °C
    d. 30 °C = _____ °F

12. a. 82 °F = _____ °C
    b. 25 °C = _____ °F
    c. 300 °F = _____ °C
    d. 5 °C = _____ °F

13. a. 240 K = _____ °C
    b. 21 °C = _____ K
    c. 42 °F = _____ K
    d. 300 K = _____ °F

14. a. 212 K = _____ °C
    b. 27 °C = _____ K
    c. 75 °F = _____ K
    d. 200 K = _____ °F

15. a. 90 km/h = _____ m/s
    b. 20 cm/s = _____ km/h
    c. 60 mi/h = _____ km/h
    d. 14 km/L = _____ mi/gal

16. a. 120 km/h = _____ m/s
    b. 30 cm/s = _____ km/h
    c. 70 mi/h = _____ km/h
    d. 18 km/L = _____ mi/gal

For Problems 17 to 22, perform the conversions.

17. a. 65 km to miles
    b. 9 m to feet
    c. 2.5 yd to centimetres
    d. 3.2 mi to metres

18. a. 89 km to miles
    b. 4 m to feet
    c. 6.5 yd to centimetres
    d. 0.5 mi to metres

19. a. 5 kg to pounds
    b. 1,250 g to ounces
    c. 0.25 lb to grams
    d. 320 oz to kilograms

20. a. 4.4 kg to pounds
    b. 750 g to ounces
    c. 1.25 lb to grams
    d. 150 oz to kilograms

21. a. 35 L to gallons
    b. 26 mL to fluid ounces
    c. 17 gal to litres
    d. 42 fl oz to litres

22. a. 115 L to gallons
    b. 12 mL to fluid ounces
    c. 45 gal to litres
    d. 75 fl oz to litres

23. Arrange the following measurements in order from largest to smallest:
    7.5 km, 9,200 yd, 5.25 mi

24. Arrange the following measurements in order from smallest to largest:
    3.75 mi, 7,000 yd, 6 km

25. Arrange the following measurements in order from largest to smallest:
    7 lb, 3 kg, 115 oz

26. Arrange the following measurements in order from smallest to largest:
    4.5 kg, 9 lb, 150 oz

27. Arrange the following measurements in order from largest to smallest:

    70 L, 18 gal, 75 qt

28. Arrange the following measurements in order from smallest to largest:

    11 gal, 40 L, 45 qt

29. Paul travelled 23 km by car to the train station in Toronto. From there, he travelled another 125 mi to Cleveland, USA, by train. Calculate the total distance travelled, in (a) kilometres and (b) miles.

30. The total distance a marathon runner needs to run to complete the race is 26 miles and 385 yards. If after completing 32 km 200 m of the distance the runner pauses for a short break, how much further would he have to run to complete the race, in (a) miles and (b) kilometres?

31. Diana went on a diet and lost 26 pounds. Her weight at the end of the dieting period was 79 kg. What was her original weight, in (a) pounds and (b) kilograms?

32. The maximum weight an elevator can carry is 340 kg. Three people with an average weight of 65 kg and 2 people with an average weight of 155 pounds are waiting to get into the elevator. Determine if the elevator will be able to carry all five of them at the same time.

33. Tracy rented a car with a full tank and used up 8.5 gallons of fuel. If the total capacity of the fuel tank is 42.5 L and she needs to return the car with a full tank, how much fuel would she need to purchase, in (a) gallons and (b) litres?

34. Jerry brought in a 31 gal barrel of fruit punch for an anniversary party. If at the end of the party, 32 L of fruit punch remained in the barrel, calculate the quantity of fruit punch consumed, in (a) gallons and (b) litres.

35. Anita is making chocolate chip cookies, and the recipe states to bake the cookies for 20 minutes at 350°F. At what temperature should she set her oven, in °C? Provide the answer rounded to the nearest degree.

36. On January 6th, the temperature in Toronto, Ontario was −12 °C. The same day, the temperature in Orlando, Florida was 85 °F. What was the difference in temperature between the two cities that day, in (a) °C and (b) °F? Provide the answers rounded to one decimal place.

Self-Test | Chapter 7

Answers to all problems are available at the end of the textbook.

For the following problems, round your answers to two decimal places, wherever applicable.

1. a. 27 cm 3 mm = _____ cm

   b. 8,105 m = _____ km _____ m

   c. 5 ft 2 in. = _____ in

   d. 5,700 yd = _____ mi _____ yd

2. a. 53 kg 107 g = _____ g

   b. 5,519 mg = _____ g _____ mg

   c. 7 lb 15 oz = _____ oz

   d. 40,000 lb = _____ ton _____ lb

3. a. 5 L 7 mL = _____ mL

   b. 9,060 mL = _____ L _____ mL

   c. 26 gal 1 qt = _____ qt

   d. 83 pt = _____ qt _____ pt

4. a. 15 °F = _____ °C

   b. −10 °C = _____ °F

   c. 350 K = _____ °C

   d. 22 °F = _____ K

For Problems 5 to 7, perform the conversions.

5. a. 250 km to miles

   b. 45 m to feet

   c. 8.75 yd to centimetres

   d. 2.5 mi to metres

6. a. 2.5 kg to pounds

   b. 400 g to ounces

   c. 1.75 lb to grams

   d. 225 oz to kilograms

7. a. 60 L to gallons

   b. 425 mL to fluid ounces

   c. 2.5 gal to litres

   d. 30 fl oz to litres

8. Arrange the following measurements in order from largest to smallest:

   65 m, 215 ft, 2,500 in.

9. Arrange the following measurements in order from smallest to largest:

   2.5 lb, 1,200 g, 45 oz

10. Arrange the following measurements in order from largest to smallest:

    84 L, 22 gal, 175 pt

11. Helicopter A is flying at an altitude of 8,250 ft above ground and Helicopter B is at 2,208 m above ground. What is the difference in altitude between the two helicopters, in (a) feet and (b) metres?

12. A baby weighed 7.3 pounds at birth and another baby weighed 2.8 kg. Calculate the difference in weight of the two babies, in (a) ounces and (b) grams.

13. A carton contains 0.75 gal of milk. After pouring five glasses of milk, each holding 250 mL, calculate the amount of milk left in the carton, in (a) gallons and (b) millilitres.

14. A car is travelling at a constant speed of 60 km/h. How long, in minutes, will it take to drive 20 miles?

15. Roger is conducting a chemistry experiment, where the solution needs to be heated to exactly 100 °C. His lab partner sets the burner at 176 °F, but Roger does not think that this is right. In °C, what should be the change in temperature setting at the burner?

Chapter 8

GRAPHS AND SYSTEMS OF LINEAR EQUATIONS

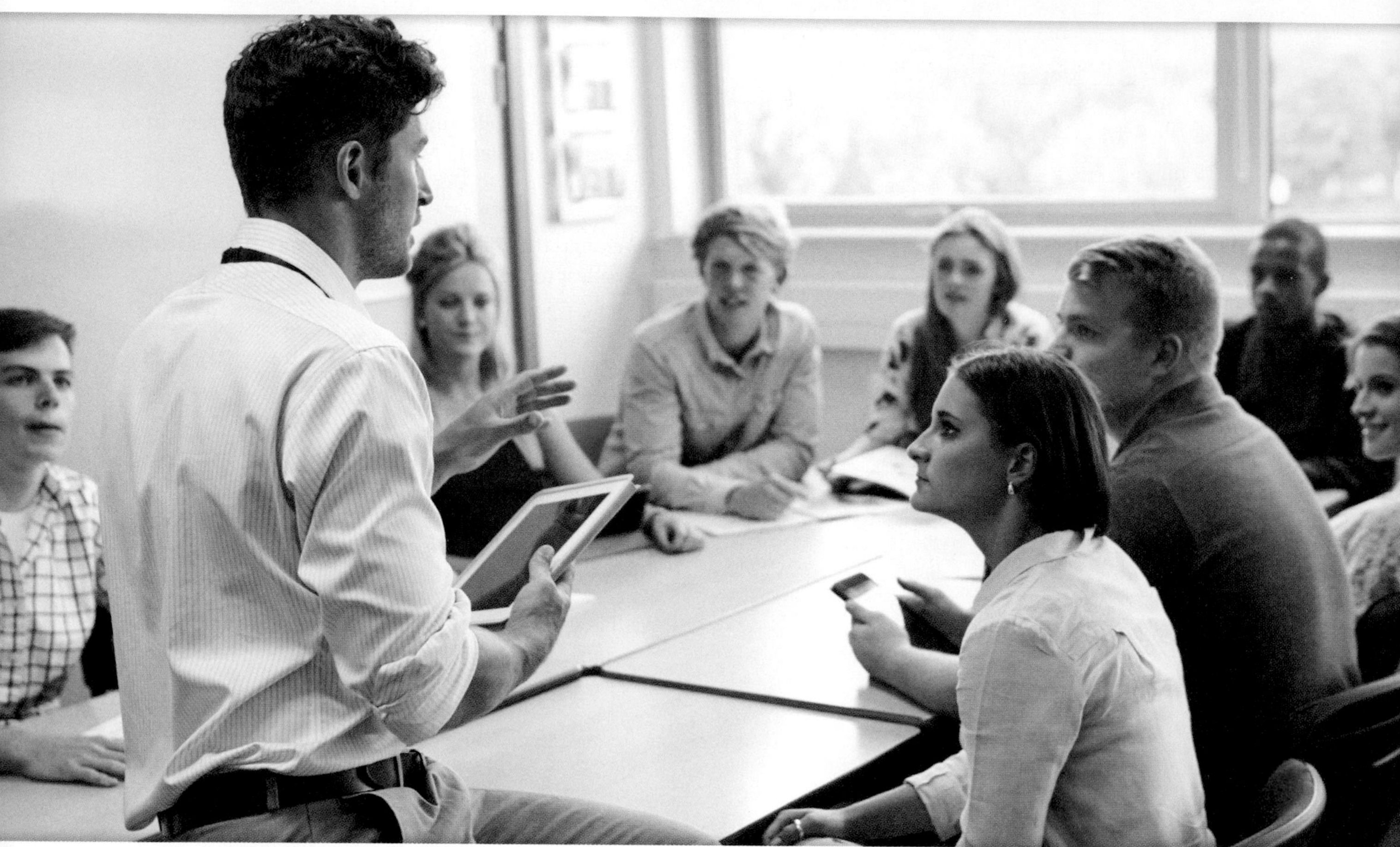

LEARNING OBJECTIVES

- Identify the basic terminology of rectangular coordinate systems.
- Express linear equations in standard form and slope-intercept form.
- Determine the slope and y-intercept of a line from its equation.
- Graph a linear equation using the table of values, slope-intercept, and x- and y-intercepts.
- Determine the equation of a line from a graph.
- Determine the equations of parallel and perpendicular lines.
- Classify systems of linear equations.
- Solve linear systems graphically and using the substitution and elimination methods.
- Write and solve systems of equations to word problems.

CHAPTER OUTLINE

Introduction

A linear equation describes a relationship in which the value of one variable depends on the value of another. The solutions to a linear equation are ordered pairs of numbers in which each number replaces one of the variables in the equation. An illustrative way to depict a linear equation with two variables is a straight line graph on a two dimensional coordinate axis system.

A 'system' of linear equations is a set of equations considered together. The simplest system of linear equations is one with two equations, each with the same two variables. These systems can be solved by several methods, including a graphical approach (by plotting the equations on the same graph) and algebraic approaches (such as the substitution and elimination methods). Many word problems in life can be solved by translating them into systems of linear equations.

In this chapter, we will learn to graph individual linear equations, and to solve systems of linear equations with two variables, both graphically and algebraically.

8.1 | Rectangular Coordinate System

Graphs drawn on a **rectangular coordinate system**, known as the Cartesian coordinate system (invented by René Descartes), help provide information in a visual form. Understanding the rectangular coordinate system is crucial in order to be able to read and draw graphs, which is essential in many branches of mathematics.

The rectangular coordinate system uses a horizontal and a vertical number line, each known as an axis. These two perpendicular axes cross at the point (O), known as the **origin**.

The horizontal number line (moving to the left or the right) is called the **X-axis** and the vertical number line (moving up or down) is called the **Y-axis**, as illustrated in Exhibit 8.1-a.

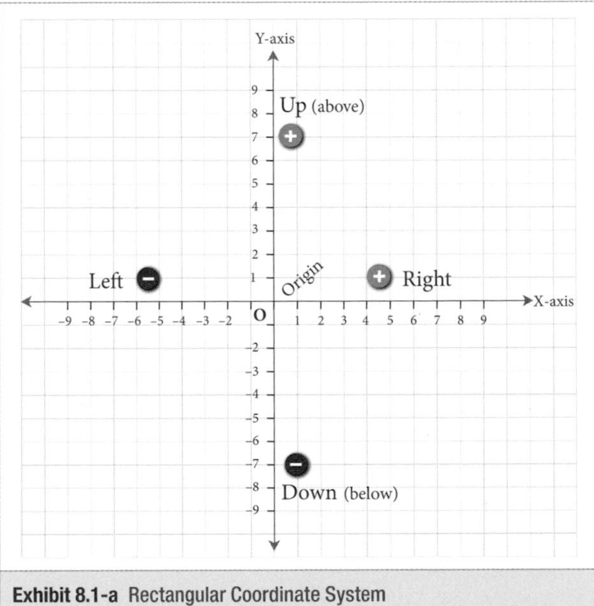

Exhibit 8.1-a Rectangular Coordinate System

The numbers to the **right** of the origin along the X-axis are **positive** (+) and those to the **left** are **negative** (–). The numbers **above** the origin along the Y-axis are **positive** (+) and those **below** are **negative** (–).

The purpose of the rectangular coordinate system and the sign convention is to locate a point relative to the X- and Y-axes and in reference to the origin 'O'.

Points in the Rectangular Coordinate System

Each ordered pair, (x, y), represents only one point on a graph. The x and y values of the ordered pair determine the location of that point.

A **point** in the Cartesian coordinate system is a location in the plane, represented as an **ordered pair** of numbers inside a set of brackets, called **coordinates.** The first number is called the ***x*-coordinate**, representing its horizontal position with respect to the origin, and the second number is called the ***y*-coordinate**, representing its vertical position with respect to the origin. The ordered pair of coordinates for a given point P is written as follows: P(x, y), or simply (x, y). For example, the origin (i.e., the point where the x-axis and y-axis intersect) is identified by the coordinates (0, 0) since both its x and y coordinates are 0.

As illustrated in Exhibit 8.1-b, the ordered pair (2, 3) refers to the coordinates of the point P which is 2 units to the right and 3 units above, in reference to the origin.

It is important to identify the coordinate numbers in their order. They are called ordered pairs because the order in which they appear determines their position on the graph. Changing the order of the coordinates will result in a different point.

For example, (2, 3) and (3, 2) are different points.

- (2, 3) refers to a point 'P', which is 2 units to the right of the origin and 3 units above the origin.
- (3, 2) refers to a point 'Q', which is 3 units to the right of the origin and 2 units above the origin.

Pay close attention to the order in which coordinate pairs are written - the first coordinate always refers to the x-coordinate (horizontal distance) and the second coordinate always refers to the y-coordinate (vertical distance).

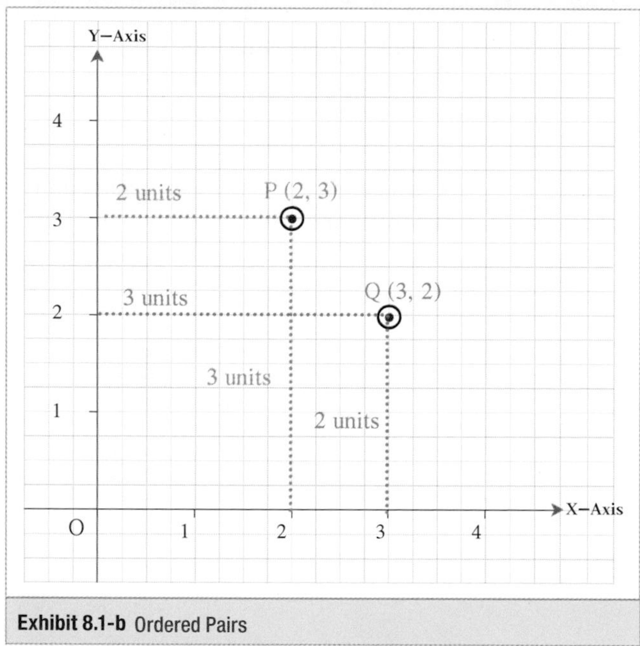

Exhibit 8.1-b Ordered Pairs

It is called a rectangular coordinate system because the x- and y-coordinates form a rectangle with the X- and Y-axes, as seen in the exhibit above.

Quadrants

The X- and Y-axes divide the coordinate plane into four regions, called **quadrants**. Quadrants are numbered counter-clockwise from one (I) to four (IV), starting from the upper-right quadrant, as illustrated in Exhibit 8.1-c.

That is, the upper-right quadrant is Quadrant I, the upper-left quadrant is Quadrant II, the lower-left quadrant is Quadrant III, and the lower-right quadrant is Quadrant IV. Table 8.1 shows the sign convention of coordinates in each of the quadrants with examples that are plotted on the graph in Exhibit 8.1-d.

Table 8.1 **Sign Convention of Coordinates in Different Quadrants, Axes, and Origin**

Quadrant, Axis, Origin	Sign of x-coordinate	Sign of y-coordinate	Example (plotted in Exhibit 8.1-d)
Quadrant I	Positive (+)	Positive (+)	A (3, 2)
Quadrant II	Negative (–)	Positive (+)	B (–3, 4)
Quadrant III	Negative (–)	Negative (–)	C (–5, –2)
Quadrant IV	Positive (+)	Negative (–)	D (5, –3)
X–Axis	Positive (+) or Negative (–)	Zero (0)	E (4, 0), F (–2, 0)
Y–Axis	Zero (0)	Positive (+) or Negative (–)	G (0, 3), H (0, –4)
Origin	Zero (0)	Zero (0)	O (0, 0)

Points with one or more zeros (0) as coordinates are on axes and not in quadrants.

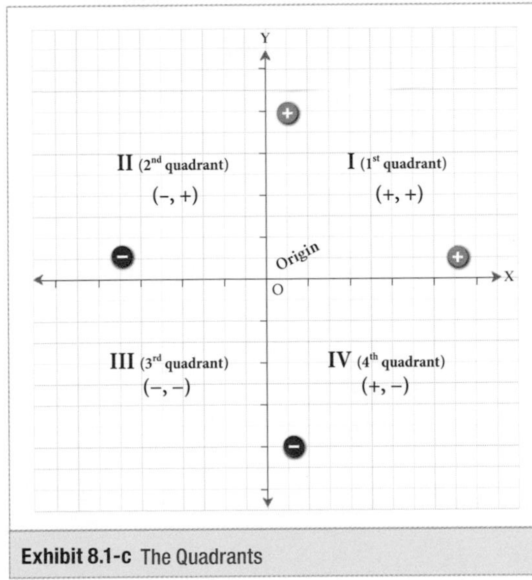

Exhibit 8.1-c The Quadrants

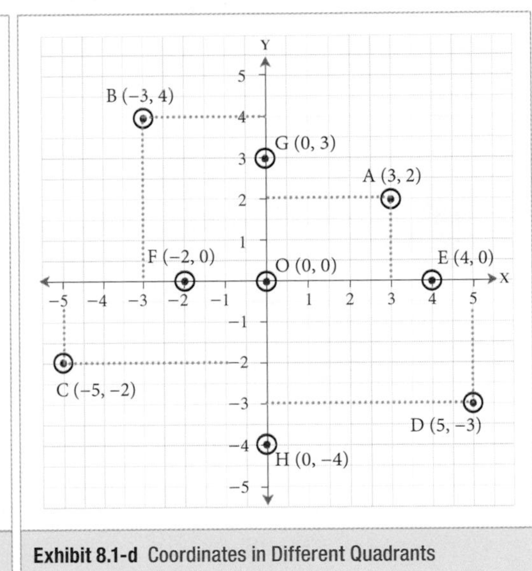

Exhibit 8.1-d Coordinates in Different Quadrants

Example 8.1-a **Identifying *x*- and *y*-Coordinates**

Determine the x- and y-coordinates of the points A, B, C, D, E, F, G, and H labelled in the graph.

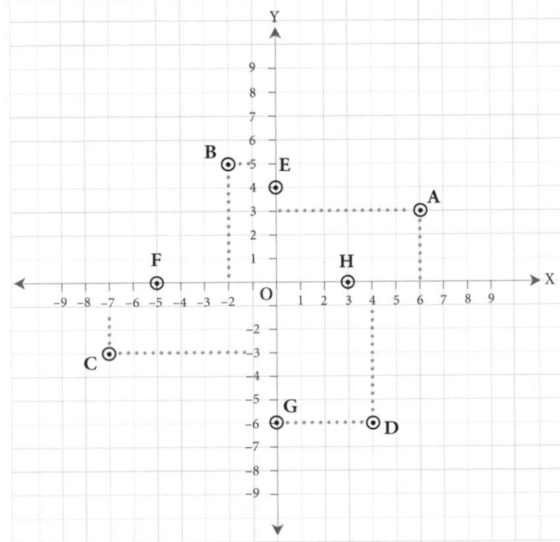

Solution

A: (6, 3)	B: (–2, 5)	C: (–7, –3)	D: (4, –6)
E: (0, 4)	F: (–5, 0)	G: (0, –6)	H: (3, 0)

Example 8.1-b Identifying the Quadrant or the Axis

Identify the quadrant or the axis in which the following points are located:

(i)	A (−15, 20)	(ii)	B (20, 5)	(iii)	C (9, 0)	(iv)	D (0, 20)
(v)	E (12, −18)	(vi)	F (0, −6)	(vii)	G (−30, −15)	(viii)	H (−1, 0)

Solution

(i)	A (−15, 20)	⟶	(−, +)	= 2nd Quadrant
(ii)	B (20, 5)	⟶	(+, +)	= 1st Quadrant
(iii)	C (9, 0)	⟶	(+, 0)	= X-Axis (Right)
(iv)	D (0, 20)	⟶	(0, +)	= Y-Axis (Up)
(v)	E (12, −18)	⟶	(+, −)	= 4th Quadrant
(vi)	F (0, −6)	⟶	(0, −)	= Y-Axis (Down)
(vii)	G (−30, −15)	⟶	(−, −)	= 3rd Quadrant
(viii)	H (−1, 0)	⟶	(−, 0)	= X-Axis (Left)

Example 8.1-c Plotting Coordinates to Form a Rectangle

Three vertices of a rectangle ABCD have points A (−3, 3), B (4, 3), and C (4, −2). Find the coordinates of the 4th vertex D.

Solution

Plotting points A, B, and C:

A (−3, 3): 3 units to the left of the origin and 3 units above the origin

B (4, 3): 4 units to the right of the origin and 3 units above the origin

C (4, −2): 4 units to the right of the origin and 2 units below the origin

Connecting point A to point B results in a horizontal line (since they share the same y-coordinate), and connecting point B to point C results in a vertical line (since they share the same x-coordinate).

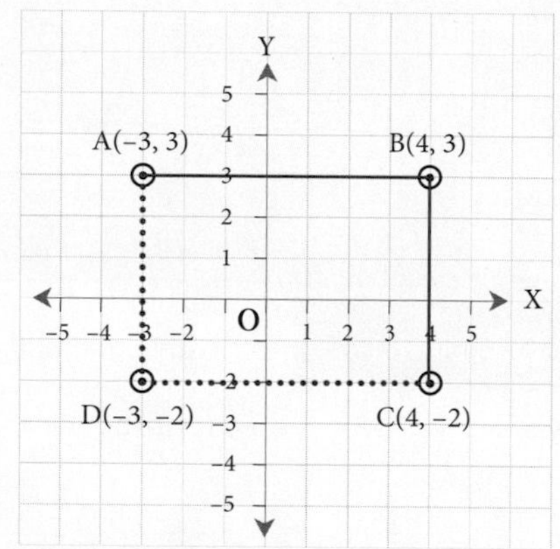

The 4th vertex of the rectangle, D, will have the same x-coordinate as point A and the same y-coordinate as point C.

Therefore, the coordinates for the 4th vertex are D (−3, −2).

Example 8.1-d Plotting Coordinates to Form a Vertical Line

A vertical line has a length of 3 units and the coordinates at one end of the line are P (−2, 1). Find the possible coordinates of the other end of the line, Q.

Solution

Plotting point P:

P (–2, 1): 2 units to the left of the origin and 1 unit above the origin

Since we are drawing a vertical line, point Q will have the same x-coordinate as point P.

One possible set of coordinates for the other end of the line is 3 units **above** point P, i.e., Q (–2, 4).

The other possible set of coordinates for the other end of the line is 3 units **below** point P, i.e., Q (–2, –2).

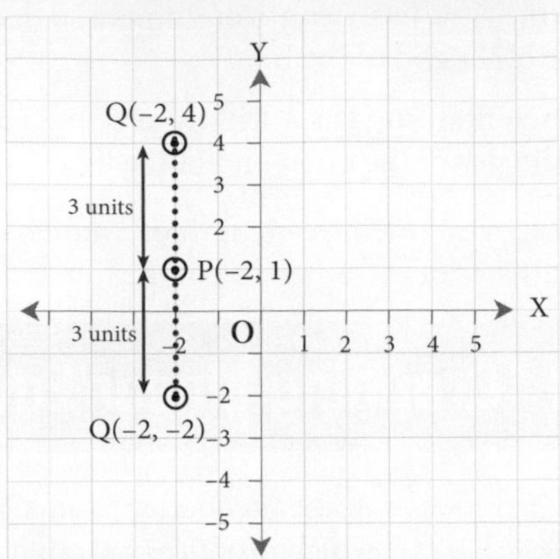

8.1 | Exercises

Answers to odd-numbered problems are available at the end of the textbook.

For Problems 1 to 4, plot the points on a graph.

1. a. A (–3, 5) b. B (5, –3) c. C (0, –4)
2. a. A (–6, 0) b. B (4, –2) c. C (0, –7)
3. a. D (6, 0) b. E (–2, 4) c. F (5, 2)
4. a. D (8, 0) b. E (–3, –5) c. F (5, 5)

For Problems 5 to 8, determine the quadrant or axis in which the points lie.

5. a. A (–1, 2) b. B (5, –1) c. C (3, 5)
6. a. A (1, 6) b. B (4, –3) c. C (–7, 3)
7. a. D (–4, 0) b. E (–2, –7) c. F (0, 5)
8. a. D (6, 0) b. E (–1, –13) c. F (0, –7)

For Problems 9 to 12, plot the pairs of points on a graph and calculate the length of each horizontal line joining the pair of points.

9. a. (3, 4) and (5, 4) b. (–7, 1) and (2, 1)
10. a. (2, –6) and (7, –6) b. (–5, –4) and (0, –4)
11. a. (–5, 3) and (0, 3) b. (–2, –2) and (6, –2)
12. a. (–6, 8) and (–1, 8) b. (7, –5) and (2, –5)

For Problems 13 to 16, plot the pairs of points on a graph and calculate the length of each vertical line joining the pair of points.

13. a. (3, 6) and (3, 1) b. (5, 2) and (5, –5)
14. a. (–3, –5) and (–3, –9) b. (–3, 0) and (–3, 6)
15. a. (5, 6) and (5, 2) b. (7, 2) and (7, –4)
16. a. (–3, 5) and (–3, –4) b. (–3, 5) and (–3, 0)
17. Three vertices of a square ABCD have points A (–3, 3), B (1, 3), and C (1, –1). Find the coordinates of the 4th vertex D.
18. Three vertices of a square EFGH have points E (–1, –2), F (6, –2), and G (6, 5). Find the coordinates of the 4th vertex H.
19. Three vertices of a rectangle PQRS have points P (–3, 4), Q (6, 4), and R (6, –1). Find the coordinates of the 4th vertex S.
20. Three vertices of a rectangle TUVW have points T (–4, 7), U (5, 7), and V (5, 4). Find the coordinates of the 4th vertex W.
21. A vertical line has a length of 7 units and the coordinates of one end of the line are (1, 5). Find the possible coordinates of the other end of the line.

22. A vertical line has a length of 5 units and the coordinates of one end of the line are (–3, 1). Find the possible coordinates of the other end of the line.

23. A horizontal line has a length of 6 units and the coordinates of one end of the line are (–1, 3). Find the possible coordinates of the other end of the line.

24. A horizontal line has a length of 8 units and the coordinates of one end of the line are (–1, –2). Find the possible coordinates of the other end of the line.

8.2 | Graphing Linear Equations

A linear equation is an algebraic equation with one or two variables (each with an exponent of one), which produces a straight line when plotted on a graph.

Examples of linear equations with one variable in the rectangular coordinate system are:

$3x - 5 = 0,\qquad x = 3,\qquad y + 2 = 0,\qquad y = -\frac{7}{5}$

Examples of linear equations with two variables in the rectangular coordinate system are:

$2x - 3y = -3,\qquad y = 2x + 3,\qquad y = -\frac{3}{4}x,\qquad x + y = 0$

The process of finding the value of the variables for which the equation is true is known as solving the equation. A linear equation with two variables has infinitely many pairs of values as solutions; therefore, it is often convenient to represent these solutions by drawing a graph.

Linear equations with two variables are generally represented by the variables x and y and are expressed either in the form of $Ax + By = C$ (where A, B, and C are integers and A is positive), known as **standard form**, or in the form of $y = mx + b$ (where m and b are integers or fractions), known as **slope-intercept form**.

Linear Equations in Standard Form

For an equation in standard form, the value of A is usually positive.

The 'standard' form for a linear equation with two variables, x and y, is written as $\mathbf{Ax + By = C}$, where A, B, and C are integers, A is positive, and A, B, and C, have no common factors other than 1.

For example, consider the following simple linear equation with two variables: $2x - y = -3$

This equation is in the standard form of $Ax + By = C$, where $A = 2$, $B = -1$, and $C = -3$.

- If a given equation has fractions, then multiply each term by the least common denominator (LCD), divide each term by any common factors, and rearrange the equation into standard form.
- If a given equation has decimals, then multiply each term by an appropriate power of 10 to eliminate the decimals, divide each term by any common factors, and rearrange the equation into standard form.
- If a given equation has no fractions or decimals, then divide each term by any common factors and rearrange it into standard form.

Example 8.2-a **Writing Linear Equations in Standard Form**

Write the following linear equations in standard form:

(i) $\frac{2}{3}x + \frac{1}{2}y - 3 = 0$ (ii) $0.3x = 1.25y - 2$ (iii) $y = \frac{2}{3}x - 5$

Solution

(i) $\frac{2}{3}x + \frac{1}{2}y - 3 = 0$ Multiplying each term by the LCD of 6 and simplifying,

$4x + 3y - 18 = 0$ Rearranging,

$4x + 3y = 18$ This is in the form $Ax + By = C$.

Therefore, the equation $\frac{2}{3}x + \frac{1}{2}y - 3 = 0$, in standard form, is $4x + 3y = 18$.

Solution *continued*

(ii) $0.3x = 1.25y - 2$ Multiplying each term by 100,

$30x = 125y - 200$ Dividing each term by the common factor 5 and simplifying,

$6x = 25y - 40$ Rearranging,

$6x - 25y = -40$ This is in the form $Ax + By = C$.

Therefore, the equation $0.3x = 1.25y - 2$, in standard form, is $6x - 25y = -40$.

(iii) $y = \frac{2}{3}x - 5$ Multiplying each term by 3 and simplifying,

$3y = 2x - 15$ Rearranging,

$-2x + 3y = -15$ Multiplying each term by –1 to make A positive,

$2x - 3y = 15$ This is in the form $Ax + By = C$.

Therefore, the equation $y = \frac{2}{3}x - 5$, in standard form, is $2x - 3y = 15$.

Linear Equations in Slope-Intercept Form

The 'slope-intercept' form for a linear equation with two variables, x and y, is written as $\boldsymbol{y = mx + b}$, where m and b are either integers or fractions. '$\boldsymbol{m}$' represents the slope and '$\boldsymbol{b}$' represents the y-coordinate of the y-intercept.

The **slope** is the steepness of the line relative to the X-axis.

The **y-intercept** is the point at which the line crosses the Y-axis and where the x-coordinate is zero.

For example, consider a simple linear equation such as $y = 2x + 3$. This equation is in the slope-intercept form of $y = mx + b$, where $m = 2$ and $b = 3$; hence, the slope is 2 and the y-intercept is (0, 3).

Example 8.2-b **Writing Linear Equations in Slope-Intercept Form**

Write the following linear equations in slope-intercept form and identify the slope and the y-intercept.

(i) $4x + 3y = 18$ (ii) $x = \frac{25}{6}y + \frac{20}{3}$

Solution

(i) $4x + 3y = 18$ Rearranging the equation with y on the left,

$3y = -4x + 18$ Dividing each term by 3 and simplifying,

$y = -\frac{4}{3}x + 6$ This is in the form $y = mx + b$.

Therefore, the slope is $m = -\frac{4}{3}$ and the y-intercept is the point (0, 6).

(ii) $x = \frac{25}{6}y + \frac{20}{3}$ Multiplying each term by the LCD of 6 and simplifying,

$6x = 25y + 40$ Rearranging the equation with y on the left,

$-25y = -6x + 40$ Multiplying each term by –1,

$25y = 6x - 40$ Dividing each term by 25 and simplifying,

$y = \frac{6}{25}x - \frac{8}{5}$ This is in the form $y = mx + b$.

Therefore, the slope is $m = \frac{6}{25}$ and the y-intercept is the point $\left(0, -\frac{8}{5}\right)$.

Determining the Solution Set of a Linear Equation

If a linear equation has two variables, x and y, then there are infinitely many solutions to the equation, and it is not possible to solve the equation for a single value of each variable. However, it is possible to create a **set** of solutions by replacing one variable (either x or y) with any value and then computing for the value of the other variable.

For example, consider the equation: $y = 2x + 3$

Choosing $x = 1$ and substituting $x = 1$ into the equation: $y = 2x + 3$

$$y = 2(1) + 3 = 5$$

Therefore, $x = 1$ and $y - 5$ is one of the infinitely many solutions to the equation; i.e., the ordered pair (1, 5) is a point that satisfies the equation.

Choosing $x = 2$ and substituting $x = 2$ into the equation: $y = 2x + 3$

$$y = 2(2) + 3 = 7$$

Therefore, $x = 2$ and $y = 7$ is another solution to the equation; i.e., the ordered pair (2, 7) is another point that satisfies the equation.

Similarly, we can obtain any number of points that satisfy the equation by choosing different values for x, and computing the corresponding value for y.

We can represent the full solution set by graphing the linear equation. The graph of the linear equation will be a line formed by all the solutions to the linear equation. Conversely, any point on the line is a solution to the linear equation.

Graphing Linear Equations Using a Table of Values

Follow these steps to graph a linear equation using a table of values:

> Drawing a linear graph requires only two points. However, at least three points will ensure that the graph of the line truly represents the given linear equation.

Step 1: Create a table of values by choosing any value for the variable x (0 is often a good first choice).

Step 2: Compute the corresponding value for the variable y (this is easiest if the equation is in slope-intercept form).

Step 3: Form the ordered pair (x, y).

Step 4: Repeat Steps 1 to 3 at least two more times to create at least three ordered pairs.

Step 5: Plot the ordered pairs (points) on the coordinate system, using an appropriate scale.

Step 6: Join the points in a straight line, continuing the line indefinitely in both directions using arrows.

Step 7: Label the graph with the equation of the line.

For example, consider the linear equation $y = 2x + 3$. We will first determine the coordinates of four ordered pairs that are on this line by choosing values for x and finding the corresponding values for y; then we will draw the graph.

- Choosing $x = 0$,
$$\begin{aligned} y &= 2x + 3 \\ &= 2(0) + 3 \\ &= 0 + 3 = 3 \end{aligned}$$
(0, 3) is a point on the line.

- Choosing $x = 1$,
$$\begin{aligned} y &= 2x + 3 \\ &= 2(1) + 3 \\ &= 2 + 3 = 5 \end{aligned}$$
(1, 5) is a point on the line.

- Choosing $x = 2$,
$$\begin{aligned} y &= 2x + 3 \\ &= 2(2) + 3 \\ &= 4 + 3 = 7 \end{aligned}$$
(2, 7) is a point on the line.

- Choosing $x = 3$,
$$\begin{aligned} y &= 2x + 3 \\ &= 2(3) + 3 \\ &= 6 + 3 = 9 \end{aligned}$$
(3, 9) is a point on the line.

$y = 2x + 3$		
x	y	(x, y)
0	3	(0, 3)
1	5	(1, 5)
2	7	(2, 7)
3	9	(3, 9)

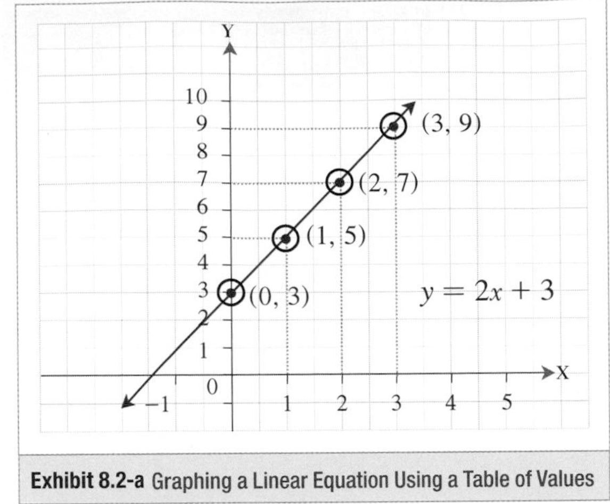

Exhibit 8.2-a Graphing a Linear Equation Using a Table of Values

Since all the points fall on a line when joined, it verifies that the plotted line represents the equation.

Graphing Linear Equations Using the *x*-intercept and the *y*-intercept

Recall that the ***y*-intercept** is the point at which the line crosses the Y-axis and where the x-coordinate is zero. Similarly, the ***x*-intercept** is the point at which the line crosses the X-axis and where the y-coordinate is zero.

If the intercepts are not at the origin (0, 0), we may use the x-intercept and y-intercept as two points to draw a linear graph and use a third point to test the drawn line.

If the intercepts are at the origin (0, 0), then we need to compute another ordered pair to use as the second point (along with the origin) with which to draw the line, and a third point to test the drawn line.

For example, consider a linear equation, $3x - y = -9$, where we will find the x-intercept, y-intercept, and another ordered pair to draw the graph.

At the x-intercept, the y-coordinate is zero.

Finding the x-intercept:

Substituting $y = 0$ into the given equation and solving for x,

$3x - 0 = -9$, thus, $x = -3$. Therefore, $(-3, 0)$ is the x-intercept.

At the y-intercept, the x-coordinate is zero.

Finding the y-intercept:

Substituting $x = 0$ into the given equation and solving for y,

$3(0) - y = -9$, thus, $y = 9$. Therefore, $(0, 9)$ is the y-intercept.

Finally, finding another ordered pair as a third point on the line to use as a test point to verify the plotted line joining the x-intercept and y-intercept:

Choosing $x = -1$, substituting this in the given equation, and solving for y,

$3(-1) - y = -9$, thus, $y = 6$. Therefore, $(-1, 6)$ is a point on the line $3x - y = -9$.

Now that we have the x-intercept, the y-intercept, and a test point:

- Plot the ordered pairs on the coordinate system using an appropriate scale.
- Draw a line to join the x-intercept and y-intercept.
- Verify that the test point falls on the graph of the plotted line.

$3x - y = -9$			
x	y	(x, y)	
-3	0	(–3, 0)	x-intercept
0	9	(0, 9)	y-intercept
-1	6	(–1, 6)	Test point

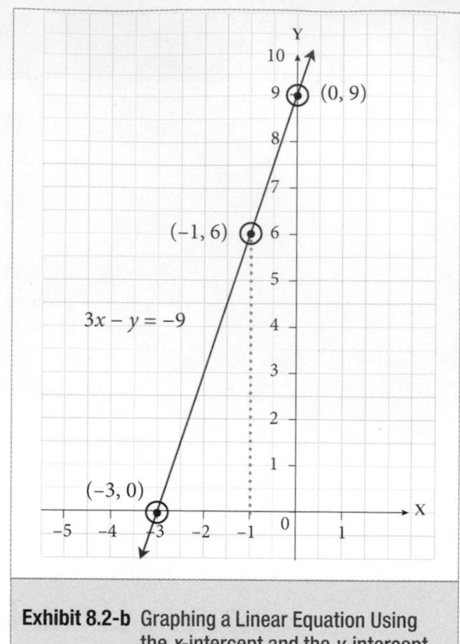

Exhibit 8.2-b Graphing a Linear Equation Using the *x*-intercept and the *y*-intercept

Since the point (–1, 6) falls on the line when plotted on the graph, it verifies that the plotted line represents the linear equation.

Graphing Linear Equations Using the Slope and the *y*-intercept

Recall that a linear equation in the form of $y = mx + b$ is known as the equation in slope-intercept form, where 'm' is the slope and 'b' is the y-coordinate of the y-intercept.

If the equation is in the standard form $Ax + By = C$, it can be rearranged to represent the slope-intercept form, as follows:

$$Ax + By = C$$

$$By = -Ax + C$$

$$y = -\frac{A}{B}x + \frac{C}{B}$$

This is in the form $y = mx + b$, where the slope $m = -\frac{A}{B}$, and the y-coordinate of the y-intercept $b = \frac{C}{B}$.

The Slope and *y*-intercept of a Line

Δ represents 'the change in'

The slope (m) is the steepness of the line relative to the X-axis. It is the ratio of the change in value of y (called the 'rise' and denoted Δy) to the corresponding change in value of x (called the 'run' and denoted Δx).

If P (x_1, y_1) and Q (x_2, y_2) are two different points on a line, then the slope of the line PQ between the two points is:

$$m = \frac{\textit{Rise}}{\textit{Run}} = \frac{\textit{Change in y value}}{\textit{Change in x value}} = \frac{\Delta y}{\Delta x} = \frac{y_2 - y_1}{x_2 - x_1}$$

This is illustrated in Exhibits 8.2-c and 8.2-d:

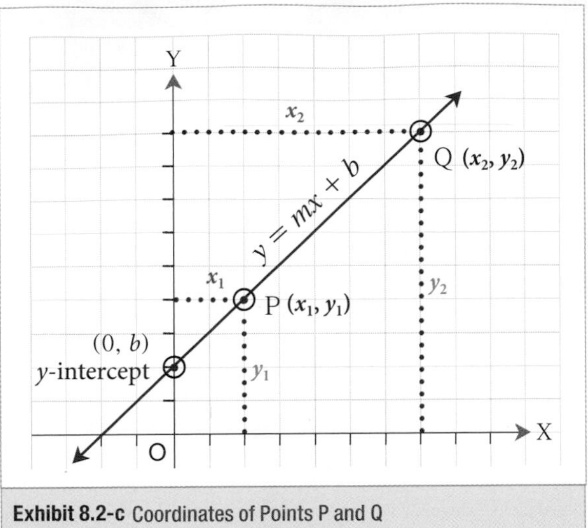

Exhibit 8.2-c Coordinates of Points P and Q

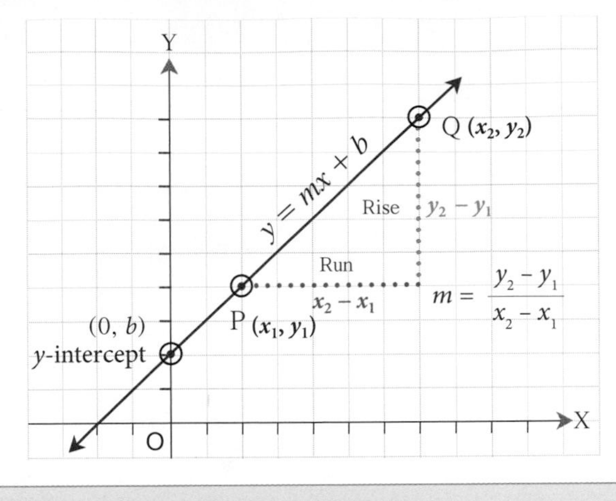

Exhibit 8.2-d Rise and Run Between Points P and Q

Example 8.2-c Finding the Slope and *y*-intercept of a Linear Equation and Graphing the Equation

Find the slope and *y*-intercept of the linear equation $-2x + 3y - 12 = 0$ and graph the equation.

Solution

$-2x + 3y - 12 = 0$	Rearranging the equation with *y* on the left,
$3y = 2x + 12$	Dividing each term by 3 and simplifying,
$y = \frac{2}{3}x + 4$	This is in the form $y = mx + b$.

Therefore, the slope is $m = \frac{2}{3}$, and the *y*-intercept is the point (0, 4).

Therefore, (0, 4) is a point on the line and the slope, $m = \frac{Rise}{Run} = \frac{\text{Change in } y \text{ value}}{\text{Change in } x \text{ value}} = \frac{2}{3}$, represents an increase of 2 in the vertical direction ('rise') for every increase of 3 in the horizontal direction ('run').

Representing this on a graph:

(i) First, plot the *y*-intercept (0, 4).

(ii) From this point, move 3 units to the right and then move 2 units up to locate the new point (3, 6).

Note: This is the same as moving 2 units up, and then 3 units to the right.

(iii) Similarly, from the point (3, 6), move 3 units to the right and 2 units up to locate another point (6, 8).

(iv) Draw the line through these points to graph the equation.

Or,

(i) First, plot the *y*-intercept (0, 4).

(ii) From this point, move 3 units to the left and then move 2 units down to locate the new point (–3, 2).

(iii) Similarly, from the point (–3, 2), move 3 units to the left and 2 units down to locate another point (–6, 0).

(iv) Draw the line through these points to graph the equation.

Solution
continued

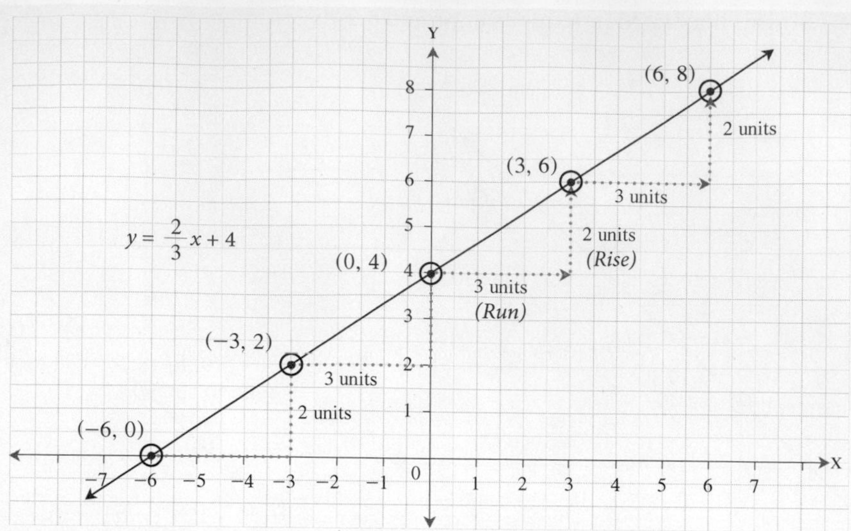

Note: All the points must lie on the same line or else a mistake has been made.

Example 8.2-d Graphing a Linear Equation in the Slope-Intercept Form

Graph the equation $y = -\frac{3}{4}x - 2$.

Solution

> $\frac{3}{4}, \frac{-3}{4}$, and $\frac{3}{-4}$ all have the same value.

The equation is in the form $y = mx + b$.

Therefore, $m = -\frac{3}{4}$ and $b = -2$, which means the y-intercept is the point (0, −2) and the slope is

$$m = \frac{Rise}{Run} = \frac{Change\ in\ y\ value}{Change\ in\ x\ value} = \frac{-3}{4} \text{ or } \frac{3}{-4}$$

First plot the point (0, −2). Then, using the slope, $m = \frac{-3}{4}$, from the point (0, −2), move 4 units to the right and 3 units down to locate the new point, (4, −5).

Alternatively, using the slope, $m = \frac{3}{-4}$, from the point (0, −2), move 4 units to the left and 3 units up to locate another point on the line, (−4, 1).

Draw a line through these points to graph the equation.

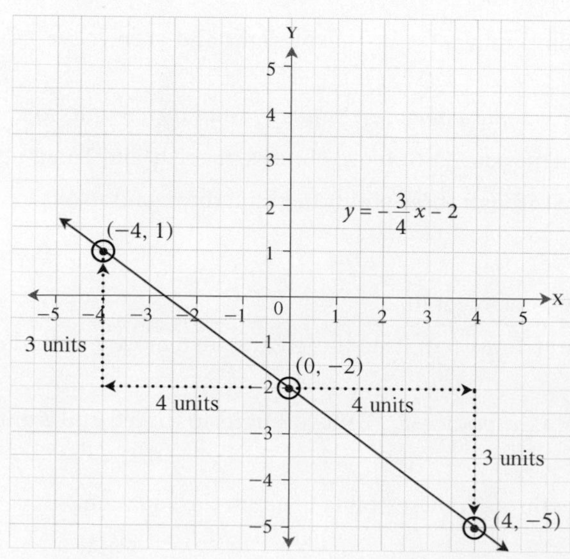

Slope and Direction of a Line

The slope, m, of a line is a number that describes the direction of the line and the steepness of the slope.

The **direction** of the line either (i) slopes upwards to the right, (ii) slopes downwards to the right, (iii) is horizontal, or (iv) is vertical, as discussed below:

If the slope of a line is positive, then the line rises to the right.

(i) If the sign of 'm' is positive, then the line slopes upwards to the right (i.e., the line rises from left to right), as illustrated in Exhibit 8.2-e.

If the slope of a line is negative, then the line falls to the right.

(ii) If the sign of 'm' is negative, then the line slopes downwards to the right (i.e., the line falls from left to right), as illustrated in Exhibit 8.2-f.

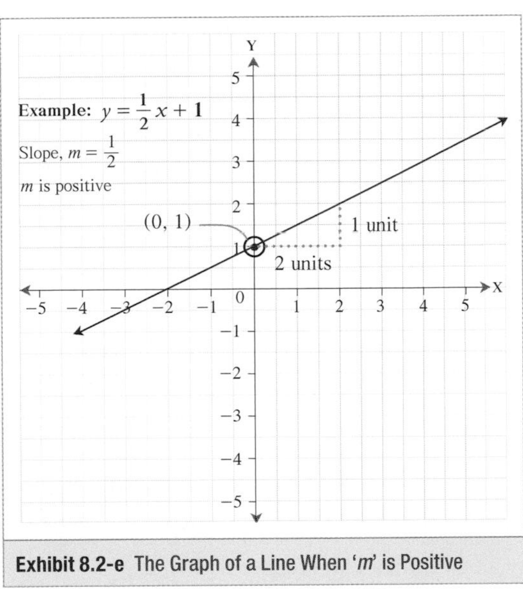

Exhibit 8.2-e The Graph of a Line When 'm' is Positive

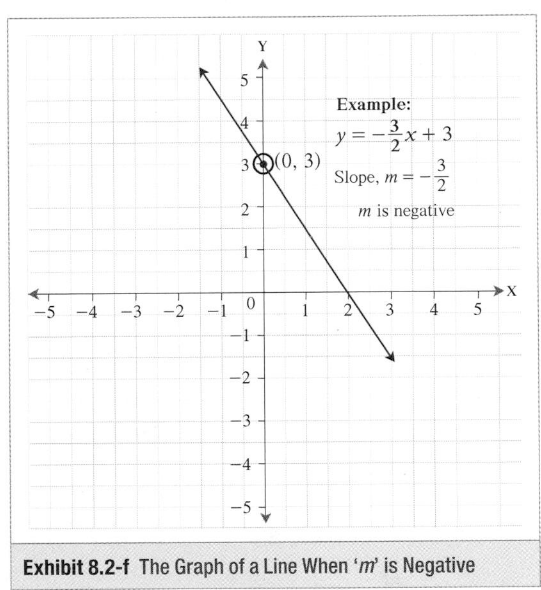

Exhibit 8.2-f The Graph of a Line When 'm' is Negative

If the slope of a line is zero, then the line is horizontal.

(iii) If 'm' is zero, then the line is horizontal (parallel to the X-axis). A slope of zero means that when the x-coordinate increases or decreases, the y-coordinate does not change (i.e., 'rise' = 0). This is a special case of the linear equation $Ax + By = C$, where the value $A = 0$.

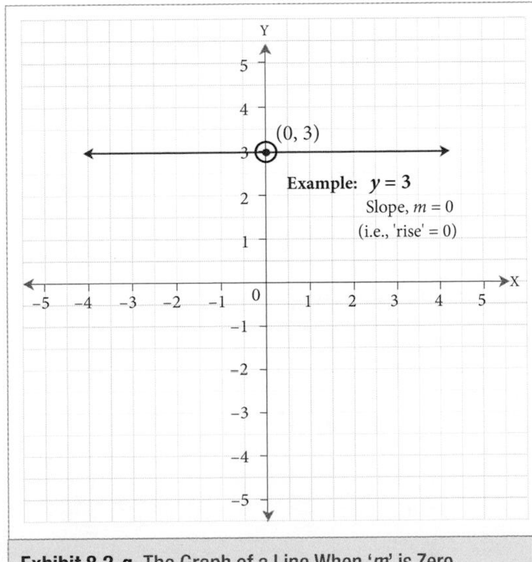

Exhibit 8.2-g The Graph of a Line When 'm' is Zero

Therefore, the equation of a horizontal line will be in the form $y = b$, and the y-intercept of the line is $(0, b)$.

For example, in the equation, $y = 3$, (i.e., $y = 0x + 3$), the slope is zero and the value of the y-coordinate is 3 for all values of x.

Therefore, the line is horizontal and passes through the y-intercept (0, 3), as illustrated in Exhibit 8.2-g.

If the slope of a line is undefined, then the line is vertical.

(iv) If 'm' is undefined, then the line is vertical (parallel to the Y-axis). An undefined slope means that when the y-coordinate increases or decreases, the x-coordinate does not change (i.e., 'run' = 0). This is a special case of the linear equation $Ax + By = C$, where the value $B = 0$.

An equation in this form cannot be rearranged into slope-intercept form, as it would require dividing by 0. As such, rather than isolating for y, we isolate for the variable x.

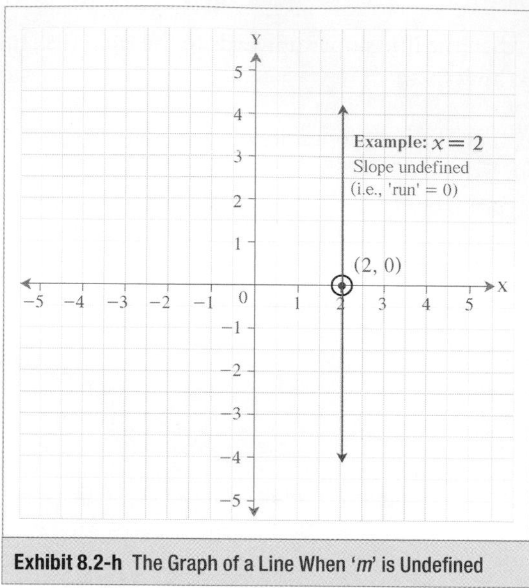

Exhibit 8.2-h The Graph of a Line When 'm' is Undefined

Therefore, the equation of a vertical line will be in the form $x = a$, and the x-intercept of the line is $(a, 0)$.

For example, in the equation, $\mathbf{x = 2}$, the slope is undefined and the value of the x-coordinate is 2 for all values of y.

Therefore, the line is vertical and passes through the x-intercept (2, 0), as illustrated in Exhibit 8.2-h.

Slope and Steepness of a Line

The **steepness** of the line is also measured by the slope ('m') of the line. The farther the coefficient 'm' is away from zero, the steeper is the slope. The closer the coefficient 'm' is to zero, the flatter is the slope.

- A greater value for a positive slope indicates a steeper rise.

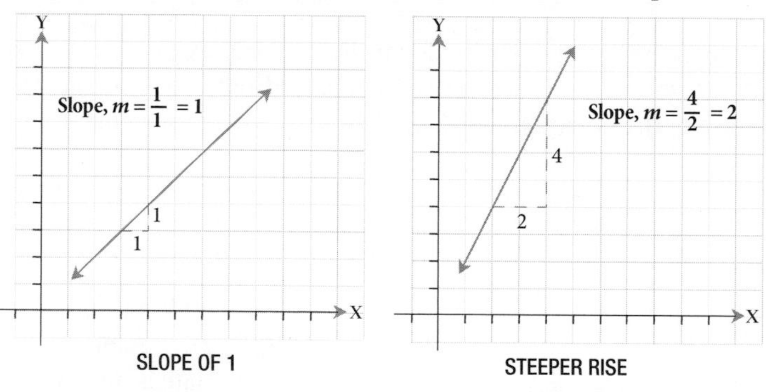

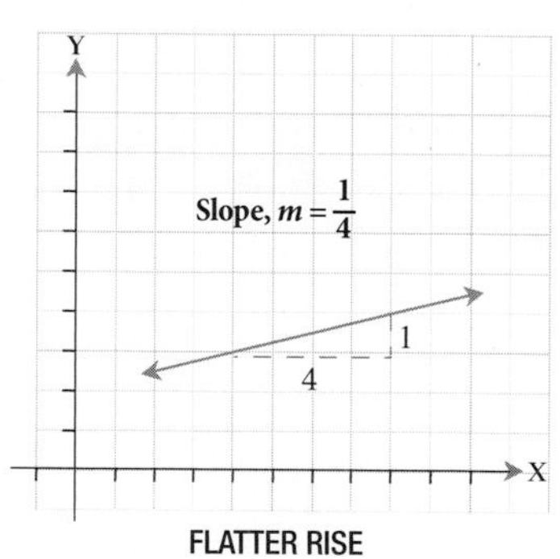

Positive slopes

- A lesser value for a negative slope indicates a steeper fall.

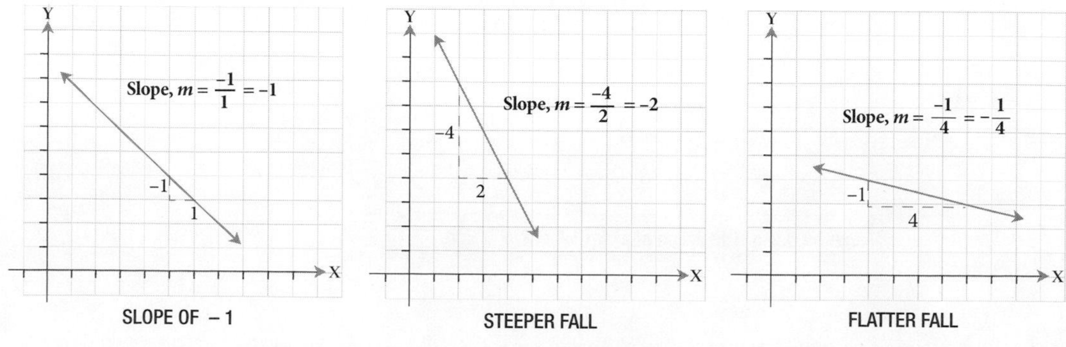

Negative slopes

- As discussed earlier, a slope of 0 indicates a horizontal line (no steepness) and an undefined slope indicates a vertical line (infinite steepness).

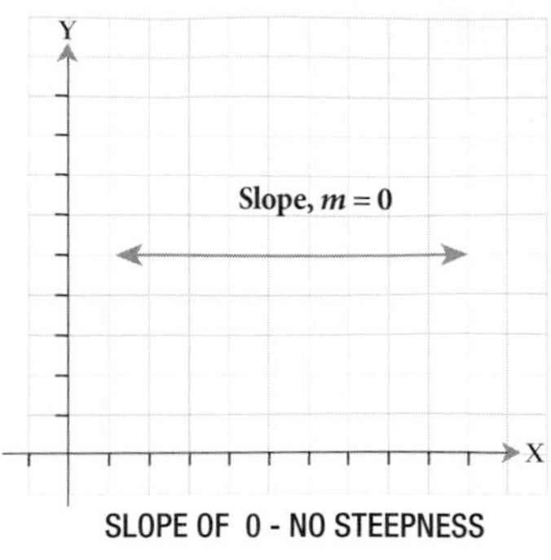

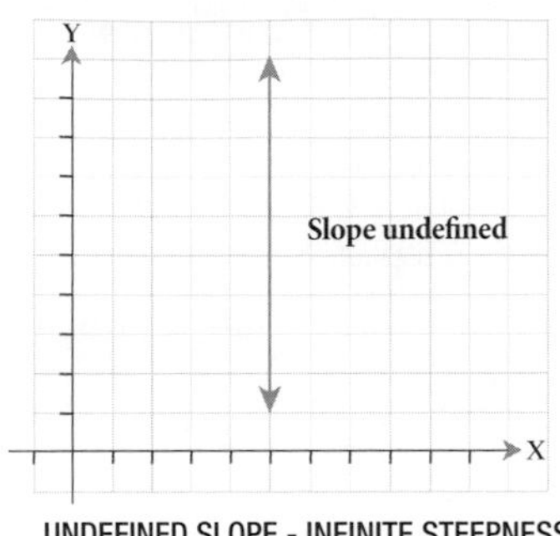

Special slopes

Lines Passing Through the Origin

An equation with a y-intercept (or x-intercept) equal to 0 will have the graph passing through the origin.

Lines passing through the origin means that the point (0, 0) is on the line. That is, the coordinates of both the x- and y-intercepts are (0, 0). Hence, the equation of a line passing through the origin will be in the form $y = mx$, with the exception of two special cases:

$y = 0$ - **the equation of the X-axis** (i.e., the horizontal line passing through the origin)

$x = 0$ - **the equation of the Y-axis** (i.e., the vertical line passing through the origin)

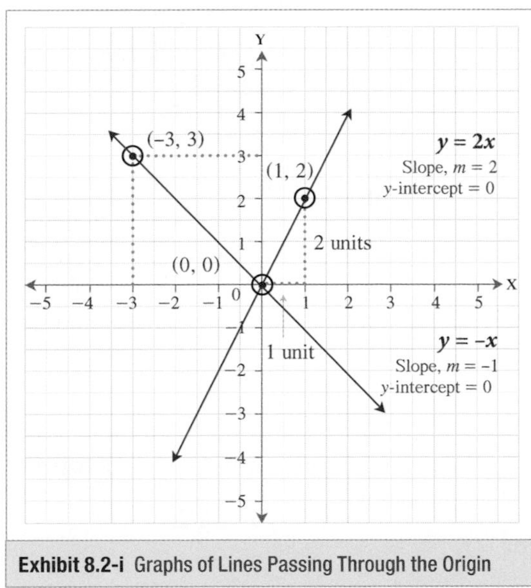

Exhibit 8.2-i Graphs of Lines Passing Through the Origin

For example, in the equation, $\mathbf{y = 2x}$, $m = 2$, and $b = 0$; hence the slope is 2 and the y-intercept is the point (0, 0).

Similarly, in the equation $\mathbf{y = -x}$, $m = -1$, and $b = 0$; hence the slope is -1 and the y-intercept is the point (0, 0).

Therefore, both of the lines above pass through the origin (0, 0), as illustrated in Exhibit 8.2-i.

Determining Equations of Lines

In order to determine the equation of a line, we need both the slope and the y-intercept. If we do not know this information, we can determine it by following these steps:

Step 1: If the slope is unknown, determine it by computing the rise and run between two points on the graph.

Step 2: Replace the unknown m in the slope-intercept form of the equation with the slope value from Step 1.

Step 3: If the y-intercept is unknown, determine it by substituting the coordinates of a point on the line in for the x and y values in the slope-intercept form of the equation from Step 2, and solve for b.

Step 4: Replace the unknown b in the slope-intercept form of the equation from Step 2 with the y-intercept value from Step 3 to arrive at the final equation of the line.

Example 8.2-e **Finding the Equation of a Line Given the Slope and One Point**

Find the equation of a line having a slope of –2 and passing through the point (3, 5).

Solution

Step 1: In this case, the slope is already known: $m = -2$.

Step 2: Replace m in the equation $y = mx + b$ with the value given.

Substituting for m in the slope-intercept equation $y = mx + b$, we obtain $y = -2x + b$.

Step 3: Substitute the coordinates of the given point into the equation to solve for b.

Substituting the x- and y-coordinates of the point (3, 5) into the above equation, we obtain,

$$5 = -2(3) + b$$

$$b = 5 + 6 = 11$$

Step 4: Write the equation in slope-intercept form, $y = mx + b$, by substituting for the values of m and b determined in the steps above.

Therefore, the equation of the line is $y = -2x + 11$.

Example 8.2-f **Finding the Slope and the Equation of a Line Given Two Points**

Find the equation of a line that passes through the points (3, 2) and (4, 5).

Solution

Step 1: Calculate the slope.

$$m = \frac{\text{Change in } y \text{ value}}{\text{Change in } x \text{ value}} = \frac{y_2 - y_1}{x_2 - x_1} = \frac{5 - 2}{4 - 3} = \frac{3}{1} = 3$$

Step 2: Replace m in the equation $y = mx + b$ with the calculated slope.

Substituting for m in the slope-intercept equation $y = mx + b$, we obtain $y = 3x + b$.

Step 3: Substitute the coordinates of one of the given points into the equation to solve for b.

Substituting the x- and y-coordinates of the point (3, 2) into the above equation, we obtain,

$$2 = 3(3) + b$$

$$b = 2 - 9 = -7$$

Step 4: Write the equation in slope-intercept form, $y = mx + b$, by substituting for the values of m and b determined in the steps above.

Therefore, the equation of the line is $y = 3x - 7$.

Note: A good check to validate the equation is to substitute the coordinates of the other point into the equation to ensure that it is a solution.

That is, substituting the x- and y-coordinates of the point (4, 5) into the equation,

$$y = 3x - 7$$

$$5 = 3(4) - 7$$

$$= 12 - 7$$

$$= 5 \text{ (True)}$$

Example 8.2-g **Finding the Equation of a Line Given a Graph**

Determine the equation of the line in standard form that is plotted on the graph shown:

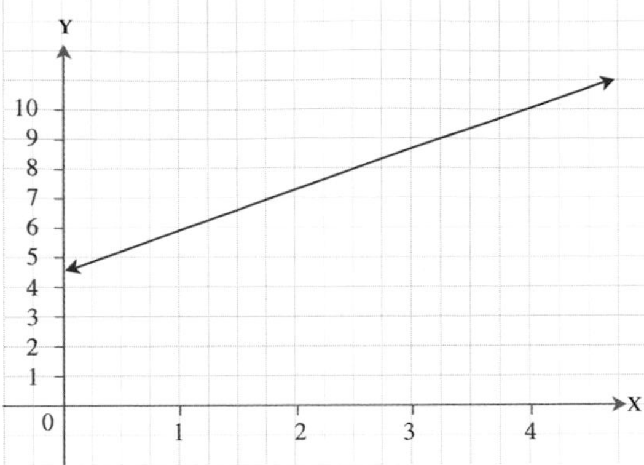

Solution

Step 1: Start by choosing any two points (with integer coordinates) on the line: e.g., (1, 6) and (4, 10).

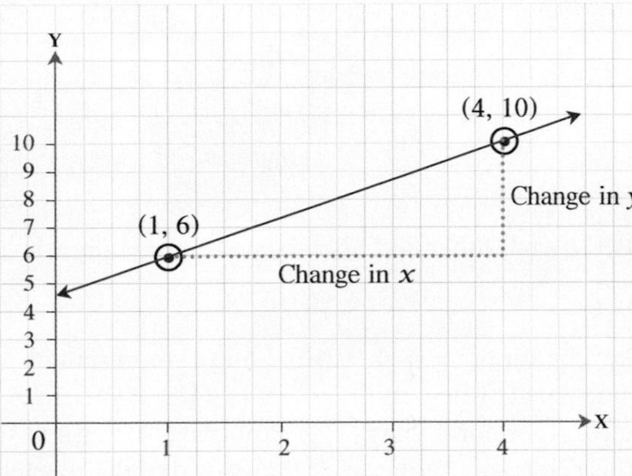

The slope of the line is, $m = \frac{y_2 - y_1}{x_2 - x_1} = \frac{10 - 6}{4 - 1} = \frac{4}{3}$.

Step 2: Let the equation of the line be $y = mx + b$ Substituting $m = \frac{4}{3}$,

Therefore, $y = \frac{4}{3}x + b$

Step 3: Substituting the coordinates of one of the points (1, 6) into the above equation and solving for b,

$$y = \frac{4}{3}x + b$$

$$6 = \frac{4}{3}(1) + b$$

$$b = 6 - \frac{4}{3} = \frac{18 - 4}{3} = \frac{14}{3}$$

Step 4: Therefore, the equation of the line in slope-intercept form is: $y = \frac{4}{3}x + \frac{14}{3}$.

$y = \frac{4}{3}x + \frac{14}{3}$ Multiplying each term by 3 and simplifying,

$3y = 4x + 14$ Rearranging, ensuring that the coefficient of the x term remains positive,

$$4x - 3y = -14$$

Therefore, the equation of the line in standard form is: $4x - 3y = -14$.

Parallel and Perpendicular Lines

Parallel Lines

Lines that never intersect are called **parallel lines**. All lines with the same slope are parallel to each other.

For example,

(i) Lines represented by the equations $y = \frac{3}{2}x + 6$, $y = \frac{3}{2}x + 3$, and $y = \frac{3}{2}x - 6$ have the same slope (equal to $\frac{3}{2}$).

Therefore, they are all parallel to each other.

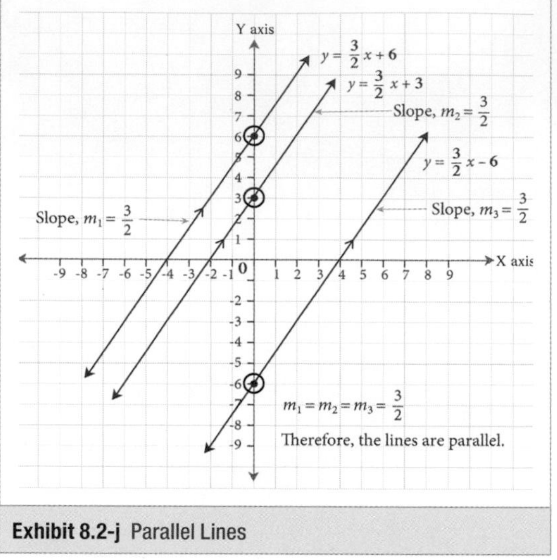

Exhibit 8.2-j Parallel Lines

All horizontal lines are parallel to each other and all vertical lines are parallel to each other.

For example,

(ii) Lines represented by the equations $y = 4$, $y = 2$, and $y = -2$ are horizontal lines and have slopes equalling zero. Therefore, they are all parallel to each other. Horizontal lines are also parallel to the X-axis (which has the equation $y = 0$).

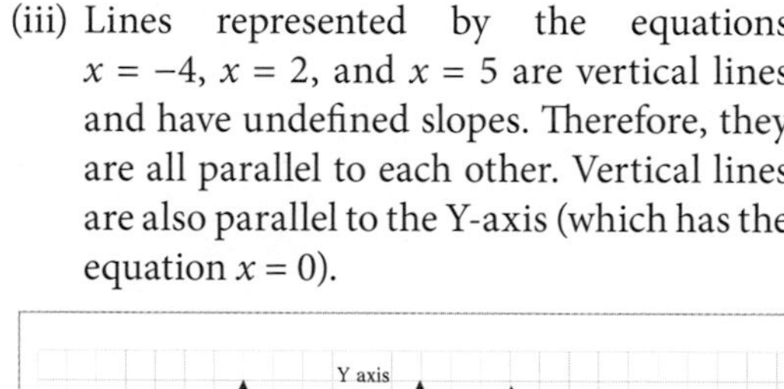

(iii) Lines represented by the equations $x = -4$, $x = 2$, and $x = 5$ are vertical lines and have undefined slopes. Therefore, they are all parallel to each other. Vertical lines are also parallel to the Y-axis (which has the equation $x = 0$).

All points on a horizontal line will have the same y-coordinate and the slope is zero.

The equation of a horizontal line is in the form $y = b$, where b represents the y-coordinate of all the points of the line.

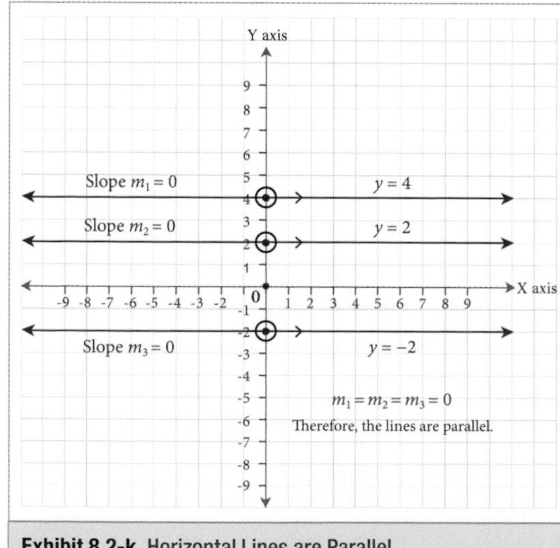

Exhibit 8.2-k Horizontal Lines are Parallel

All points on a vertical line will have the same x-coordinate and the slope is undefined.

The equation of a vertical line is in the form $x = a$, where a represents the x-coordinate of all the points on the line.

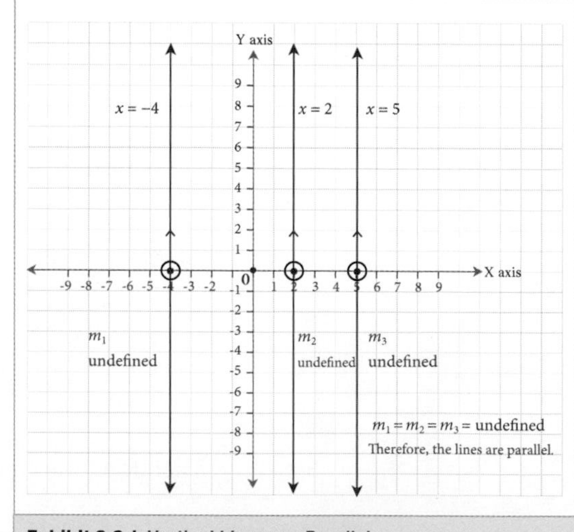

Exhibit 8.2-l Vertical Lines are Parallel

Example 8.2-h **Writing the Equation of a Line Parallel to a Given Line and Passing Through a Given Point**

Write the equation of the line that is parallel to $3x + y = 5$ and passes through the point P(2, 4).

Solution

$3x + y = 5$ Rearranging to slope-intercept form,

$y = -3x + 5$ Therefore, the slope is $m = -3$.

The slope of the line parallel to this will have the same slope, $m = -3$.

Lines that are parallel have the same slope.

Let the equation of the line parallel to $3x + y = 5$ be $y = mx + b$. It passes through (2, 4) and has a slope of $m = -3$.

$y = mx + b$ Substituting the slope $m = -3$,

$y = -3x + b$ Substituting the coordinates of the given point (2, 4),

$4 = -3(2) + b$ Solving for b,

$4 = -6 + b$

$b = 4 + 6 = 10$

Therefore, the equation of the desired line is $y = -3x + 10$, or $3x + y = 10$ in standard form.

Note: For parallel lines in standard form $Ax + By = C$, the values of A and B will always be proportional, and often will be equal.

Perpendicular Lines

Two lines that meet at a right angle are known as **perpendicular lines**. If the product of the slopes of two lines is –1, then the two lines are perpendicular to each other. This is the same as stating that if the slope of one line is the **negative reciprocal** of the other, then the two lines are perpendicular to each other.

For example,

(i) Lines represented by the equations $y = 2x + 4$ and $y = -\frac{1}{2}x + 1$ are perpendicular to each other because their slopes are negative reciprocals of each other.

$$m_1 = 2, m_2 = -\frac{1}{2}$$

$$m_1 \cdot m_2 = 2\left(-\frac{1}{2}\right) = -1$$

Two lines are perpendicular if the product of their slopes is –1.

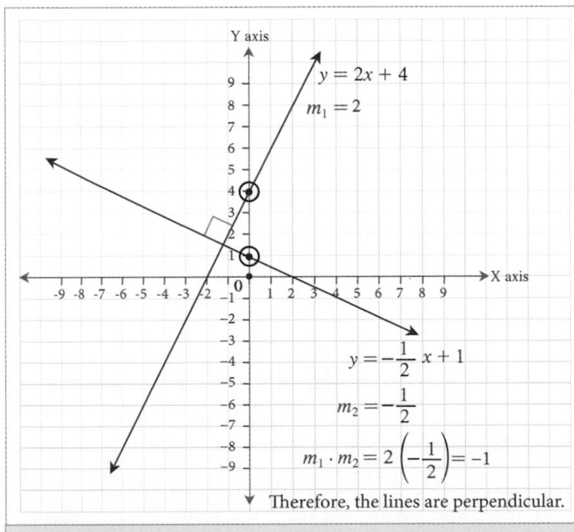

Exhibit 8.2-m Perpendicular Lines

All vertical lines (slope is undefined) and horizontal lines (slope is zero) are perpendicular to each other.

For example,

(ii) Lines represented by the equations $y = 2$ and $x = 4$ are perpendicular to each other.

Two lines are also perpendicular if one of them is vertical (parallel to Y-axis), and the other is horizontal (parallel to X-axis).

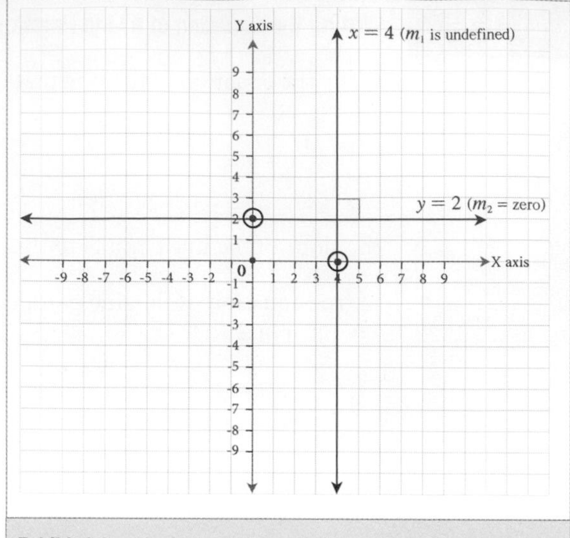

Exhibit 8.2-n Vertical and Horizontal Lines are Perpendicular

Example 8.2-i **Writing the Equation of a Line Perpendicular to a Given Line and Passing Through a Given Point**

Write the equation of the line that is perpendicular to $x + 3y = 9$ and passes through the point P(−4, 2).

Solution

$x + 3y = 9$ Rearranging to slope-intercept form,

$3y = -x + 9$

$y = -\frac{1}{3}x + 3$ Therefore, the slope is $m = -\frac{1}{3}$.

The slope of the line perpendicular to this will be the negative reciprocal of $-\frac{1}{3}$, which is 3.

Let the equation of the line perpendicular to $x + 3y = 9$ be $y = mx + b$. It passes through the point (−4, 2) and has a slope of $m = 3$.

Lines that are perpendicular have slopes that are negative reciprocals of each other.

$y = mx + b$ Substituting the slope $m = 3$,

$y = 3x + b$ Substituting the coordinates of the given point (−4, 2),

$2 = 3(-4) + b$ Solving for b,

$2 = -12 + b$

$b = 2 + 12 = 14$

Therefore, the equation of the desired line is $y = 3x + 14$, or $3x - y = -14$ in standard form.

8.2 | Exercises

Answers to odd-numbered problems are available at the end of the textbook.

1. For the equation $2x + 3y = 18$, find the missing values in the following ordered pairs:

   a. (3, ?) b. (−6, ?) c. (0, ?)

   d. (?, 0) e. (?, −4) f. (?, 2)

2. For the equation $x + 5y = 20$, find the missing values in the following ordered pairs:

   a. (0, ?) b. (−15, ?) c. (5, ?)

   d. (?, 6) e. (?, −3) f. (?, 0)

3. For the equation $y = -\frac{2}{3}x + 1$, find the missing values in the following ordered pairs:

a. (6, ?) b. (−3, ?) c. (0, ?)

d. (?, 0) e. (?, −3) f. (?, 5)

4. For the equation $y = -\frac{3}{2}x + 1$, find the missing values in the following ordered pairs:

a. (2, ?) b. (−3, ?) c. (0, ?)

d. (?, 0) e. (?, −3) f. (?, 9)

For Problems 5 to 10, write the equations in standard form.

5. $y = \frac{5}{2}x + 1$

6. $y = \frac{2}{5}x - 1$

7. $y = -\frac{3}{4}x - 3$

8. $y = -\frac{4}{3}x + 4$

9. $y = \frac{1}{2}x + \frac{3}{2}$

10. $y = \frac{3}{2}x - \frac{1}{4}$

For Problems 11 to 16, write the equations in slope-intercept form.

11. $4y + 6x = -3$

12. $9y + 2x = 18$

13. $3y - 2x = 15$

14. $5y - 2x = -20$

15. $\frac{x}{2} + \frac{y}{3} = 1$

16. $\frac{x}{4} + \frac{y}{5} = 2$

For Problems 17 to 24, graph the equations using a table of values.

17. $y = x + 3$

18. $y = 3x + 2$

19. $y = -5x + 1$

20. $y = -2x + 3$

21. $2x + y + 1 = 0$

22. $4x + y + 2 = 0$

23. $2x - y - 3 = 0$

24. $x - y - 1 = 0$

For Problems 25 to 30, determine the x- and y-intercepts for the equations and graph the equations.

25. $3x + y = -2$

26. $5x + y = -3$

27. $x + y - 3 = 4$

28. $x + y - 4 = 7$

29. $y = 2x + 4$

30. $y = 4x + 1$

For Problems 31 to 34, determine the slopes and y-intercepts of the equations and graph the equations.

31. $2x - 3y - 18 = 0$

32. $5x - 2y + 10 = 0$

33. $-4x + 7y - 21 = 0$

34. $-7x + 8y - 32 = 0$

35. Point 'A' is in the 3rd quadrant and Point 'B' is in the 1st quadrant. Determine the sign of the slope of the line AB.

36. Point 'C' is in the 4th quadrant and Point 'D' is in the 2nd quadrant. Determine the sign of the slope of the line CD.

For Problems 37 to 40, determine the slopes of the lines passing through:

37. (2, 1) and (6, 1)

38. (−6, 4) and (2, 4)

39. (−5, 4) and (3, −1)

40. (5, 6) and (5, −4)

For Problems 41 to 44, determine the equations of the lines in slope-intercept form that pass through the points.

41. (1, 2) and (5, 2)

42. (5, 0) and (4, 5)

43. (−3, −5) and (3, 1)

44. (−4, −7) and (5, 2)

For Problems 45 to 50, determine the equations of the lines in slope-intercept form that:

45. Have a slope of -2 and pass through $(2, 6)$.

46. Have a slope of 3 and pass through $(-3, -2)$.

47. Have a slope of $\frac{2}{3}$ and pass through the origin.

48. Have a slope of $-\frac{4}{5}$ and pass through the origin.

49. Have an x-intercept $= 4$ and a y-intercept $= 6$.

50. Have an x-intercept $= -4$ and a y-intercept $= 2$.

51. The slope of a line is 3. The line passes through $A(4, y)$ and $B(6, 8)$. Find y.

52. The slope of a line is 2. The line passes through $A(x, 8)$ and $B(2, 4)$. Find x.

53. Points $A(2, 3)$, $B(6, 5)$, and $C(10, y)$ are on a line. Find y.

54. Points $D(3, 2)$, $E(6, 5)$, and $F(x, 1)$ are on a line. Find x.

For Problems 55 to 58, determine the equation of the line (in standard form) for the graphs.

55.

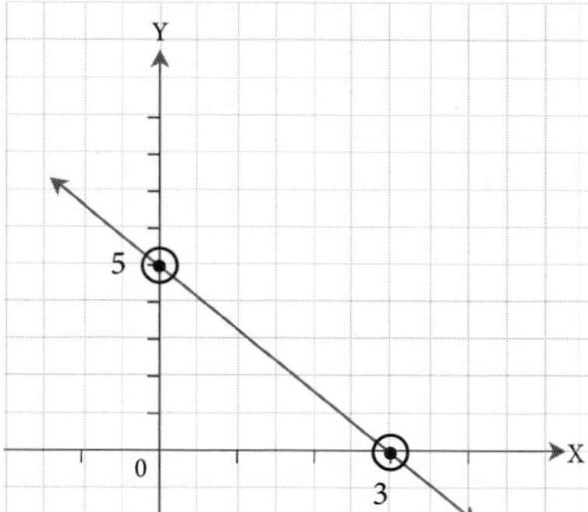

56.

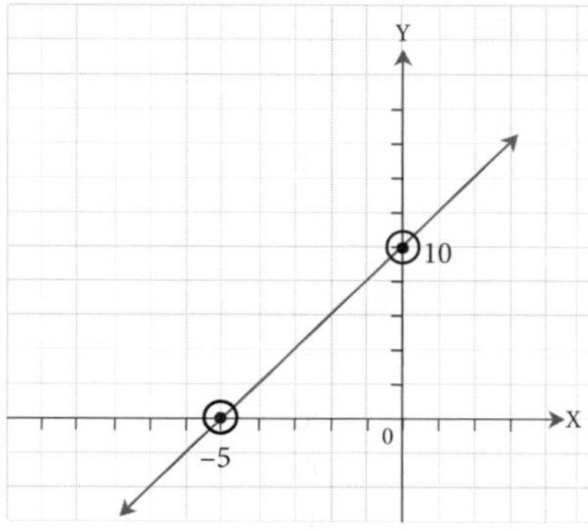

57.

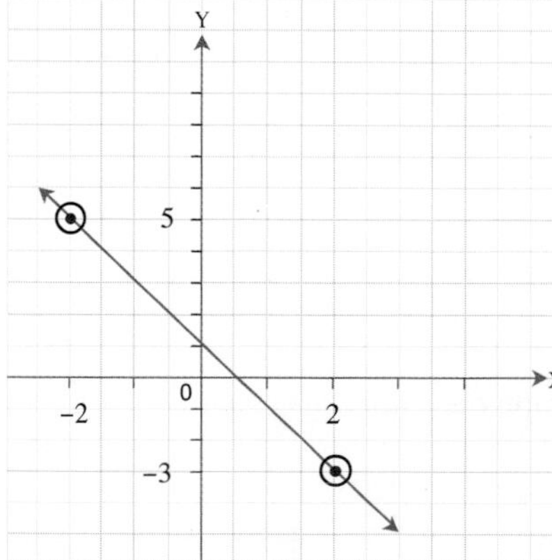

58.

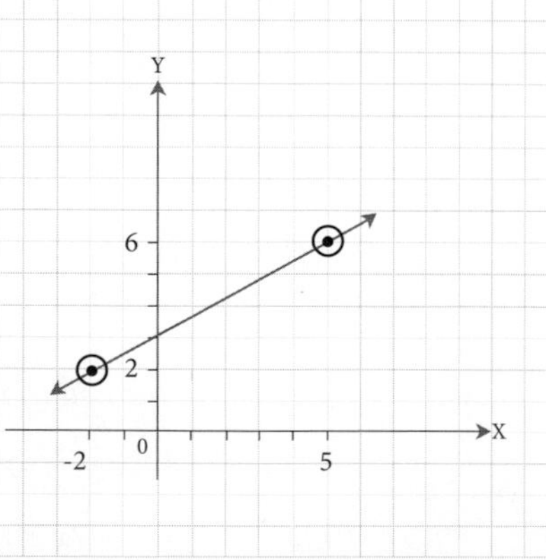

For Problems 59 to 66, use the slope property of parallel and perpendicular lines to identify whether each of the pairs of lines are parallel, perpendicular, or neither.

59. $y = x + 1$

$4x + 4y = -1$

60. $6x - 5y = 10$

$y = -\frac{6}{5}x - 12$

61. $x - 3y = -60$

$y = \frac{1}{3}x - 4$

62. $3x - 2y = -12$

$2x + 3y = -12$

63. $2x + 5y = -5$
$$y = \frac{5}{2}x - 4$$

64. $7x + 4y = 16$
$$y = -\frac{4}{7}x + 3$$

65. $3x + 2y = -24$
$$y = \frac{3}{2}x + 3$$

66. $3x - 2y = -6$
$$y = \frac{3}{2}x - 16$$

For Problems 67 to 74, determine the equations for the lines in slope-intercept form.

67. A line parallel to $3y - 2x = 6$ and passing through the point P(2, −3).

68. A line parallel to $y = 3x - 1$ and passing through the point P(−2, −4).

69. A line parallel to $3x - 9y = -2$ and passing through the y-intercept of the line $5x - y = 20$.

70. A line parallel to $3x + y = -2$ and passing through the x-intercept of the line $2x + 3y - 4 = 0$.

71. A line perpendicular to $x + y = 3$ and passing through the point P(−2, 5).

72. A line perpendicular to $4x + y + 1 = 0$ and passing through the point P(3, 4).

73. A line perpendicular to $2x - y = 5$ and passing through the x-intercept of the line $3x + 2y - 6 = 0$.

74. A line perpendicular to $3x + y + 9 = 0$ and passing through the y-intercept of the line $2x + 3y - 10 = 0$.

8.3 Solving Systems of Linear Equations with Two Variables, Graphically

In the previous section, we learned that a linear equation with two variables produces a straight line when plotted on a graph. If the graph of an equation is linear, then all the points (ordered pairs) on the line are solutions to that linear equation.

For example, $2x + y = 4$ is a linear equation with two variables, x and y. The graph of this equation is a line and all the points (ordered pairs) on this line are solutions to this equation, as shown in the diagram below.

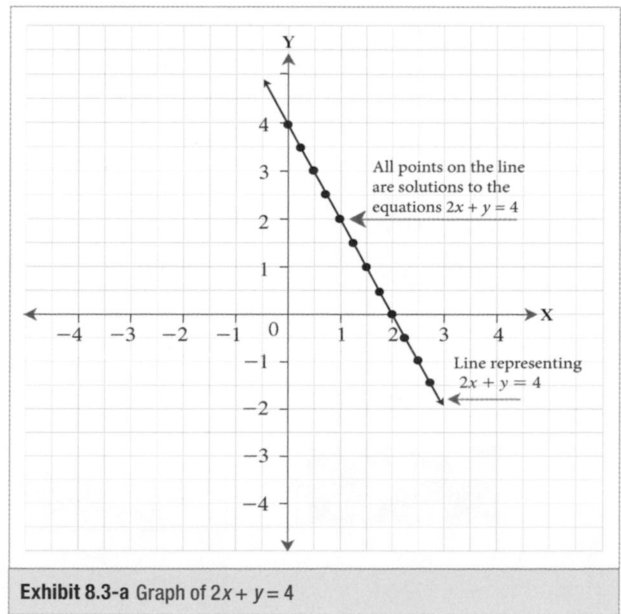

Exhibit 8.3-a Graph of $2x + y = 4$

Systems of Equations

Two or more equations analyzed together are called a **system of equations**. In this section, we will be analyzing systems of two linear equations with two variables.

The solution to a system of two equations with two variables is an ordered pair of numbers (or coordinates) that satisfy both equations. If we graph a system of two linear equations, the solution to the system (if it exists) will be the coordinates of the point at which the two linear equations intersect.

For example, $2x + y = 4$ and $x - 2y = -3$ form a system of two linear equations. The graphs of these equations intersect at the point (1, 2), as shown in the following diagram. Therefore, the point (1, 2) is the solution to the system of two linear equations.

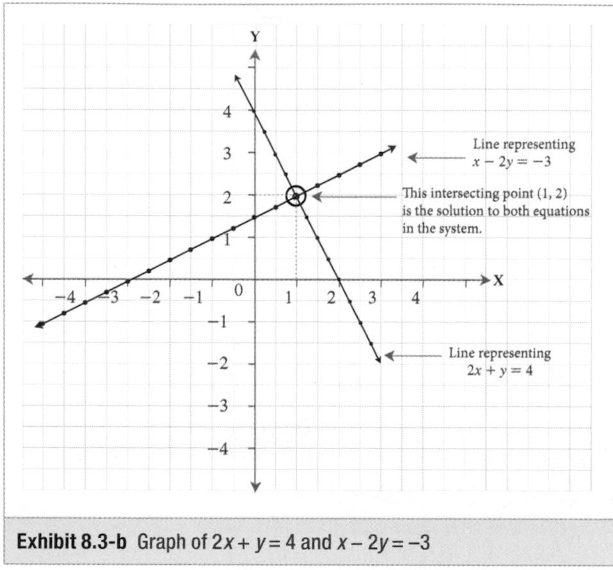

Exhibit 8.3-b Graph of $2x + y = 4$ and $x - 2y = -3$

There are three cases to be considered for a system of two linear equations with two variables:

1. If the lines **intersect** (i.e., the lines are **not parallel**), then there is only **one** solution to the system, which is the point of intersection (as seen in Exhibit 8.3-b above).
2. If the lines do **not intersect** (i.e., the lines are **parallel** and **distinct**), then there is **no** solution to the system.
3. If the lines **coincide** (i.e., the lines are the **same**), then there are an **infinite** number of solutions to the system, which are all the points on the coincident lines.

Consistent and Inconsistent Systems

A linear system of two equations that has **one** or an **infinite** number of solutions is known as a **consistent linear system.**

A linear system of two equations that has **no** solution is called an **inconsistent linear system.**

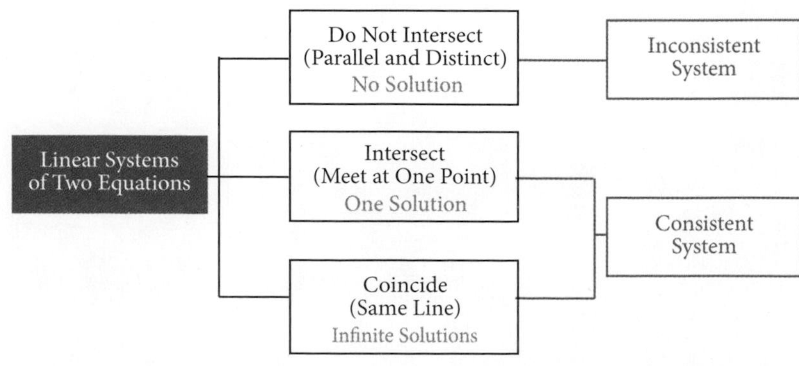

If the graphs of two linear equations intersect at one point or coincide (represent the same line), then the system is "consistent". Otherwise, the system is "inconsistent".

Dependent and Independent Equations

If a system of equations has an **infinite** number of solutions, then the equations are **dependent**. If a system of equations has **one** or **no** solution, then the equations are **independent**.

If the graphs of two linear equations coincide (represent the same line), then the equations are "dependent". Otherwise, the equations are "independent".

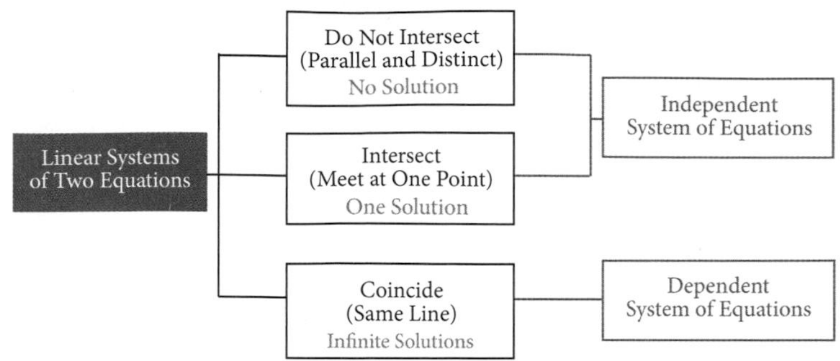

Intersecting Lines

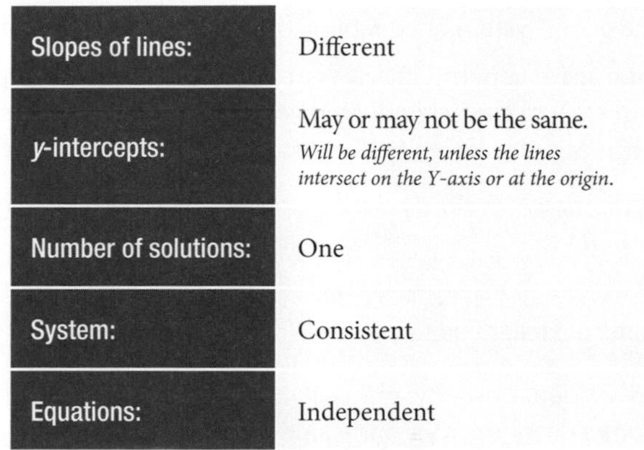

Slopes of lines:	Different
y-intercepts:	May or may not be the same. *Will be different, unless the lines intersect on the Y-axis or at the origin.*
Number of solutions:	One
System:	Consistent
Equations:	Independent

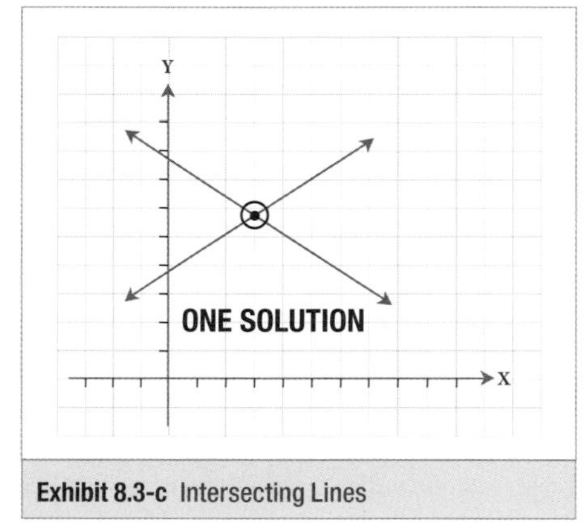

Exhibit 8.3-c Intersecting Lines

Parallel and Distinct Lines

Slopes of lines:	Same
y-intercepts:	Different
Number of solutions:	None
System:	Inconsistent
Equations:	Independent

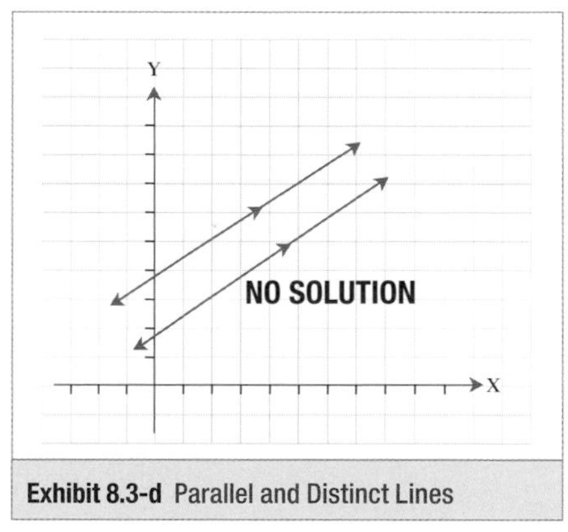

Exhibit 8.3-d Parallel and Distinct Lines

Coincident Lines

Slopes of lines:	Same
y-intercepts:	Same
Number of solutions:	Infinitely many
System:	Consistent
Equations:	Dependent

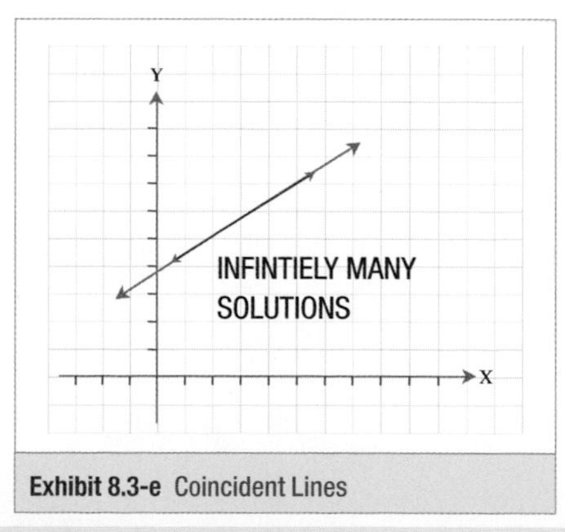

Exhibit 8.3-e Coincident Lines

Solving Linear Systems Graphically

The following steps will help to solve systems of two linear equations with two variables graphically:

Step 1: Rewrite both equations in the slope-intercept form of $y = mx + b$ (or the standard form of $Ax + By = C$).

Step 2: Graph the first equation using the slope and y-intercept method, the x- and y-intercept method, or using a table of values. The graph will be a straight line.

Step 3: Graph the second equation on the same axes as in Step 2. It will be another straight line.

Step 4: Analyze the system.

- If the two lines intersect at a point, then the point of intersection (x, y) is the solution to the given system of equations.
- If the lines are parallel and distinct, then there is no solution to the given system of equations (i.e., the system is inconsistent).
- If the lines are coincident, then all of the infinitely-many points on the lines are solutions to the given system of equations (i.e., the equations are dependent).

Step 5: If the solution obtained is a point, check your answer by substituting the values for the variables x and y in each of the original equations. If the answer satisfies **both** equations, then it is indeed the correct solution to the given system of equations.

Note: In Steps 2 and 3, the order in which the equations are graphed and the method(s) used to graph the equations does not matter.

Example 8.3-a **Solving and Classifying Systems of Linear Equations**

Solve the following system of equations by graphing, and classify the system as consistent or inconsistent and the equations as dependent or independent.

$x - y + 1 = 0$

$x + y - 3 = 0$

Solution

Step 1: $x - y + 1 = 0$ Writing the equation in $y = mx + b$ form,

$y = x + 1$ Equation (1)

$x + y - 3 = 0$ Writing the equation in $y = mx + b$ form,

$y = -x + 3$ Equation (2)

Step 2: Equation (1): $y = x + 1$

$m = 1$ and $b = 1$

Therefore, the slope is $\frac{1}{1}$ and the y-intercept is $(0, 1)$.

Step 3: Equation (2): $y = -x + 3$

$m = -1$ and $b = 3$

Therefore, the slope is $\frac{-1}{1}$ and the y-intercept is $(0, 3)$.

Solution *continued*

Graphing equations (1) and (2) using the slope-intercept method:

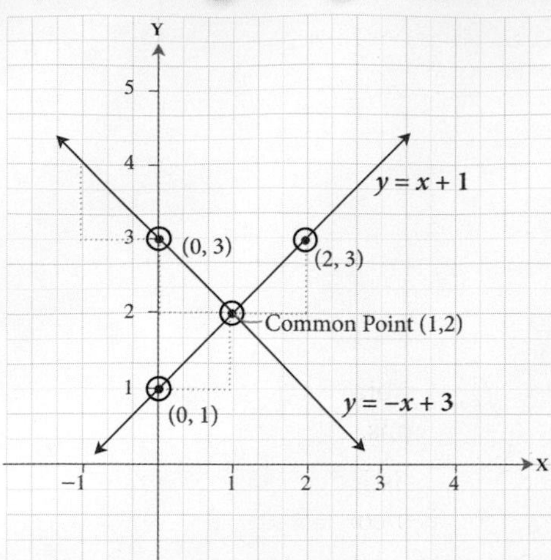

Step 4: The two lines intersect at the common point (1, 2).

Step 5: Check the solution (1, 2) in Equations (1) and (2).

Equation (1), $y = x + 1$	Equation (2), $y = -x + 3$
$LS = y = 2$	$LS = y = 2$
$RS = x + 1 = 1 + 1 = 2$	$RS = -x + 3 = -1 + 3 = 2$
Therefore, $LS = RS$	Therefore, $LS = RS$

Therefore, the solution is (1, 2). The system is consistent (has a solution) and the equations are independent (lines are not coincident).

Example 8.3-b Solving and Classifying Systems of Linear Equations

Solve the following system of equations by graphing, and classify the system as consistent or inconsistent and the equations as dependent or independent.

$3x + y - 3 = 0$
$3x + y + 2 = 0$

Solution

Step 1: $3x + y - 3 = 0$ Writing the equation in $y = mx + b$ form,

$y = -3x + 3$ Equation (1)

$3x + y + 2 = 0$ Writing the equation in $y = mx + b$ form,

$y = -3x - 2$ Equation (2)

Step 2: Equation (1): $y = -3x + 3$

$m = -3$ and $b = 3$

Therefore, the slope is $\frac{-3}{1}$ and the y-intercept is (0, 3).

Step 3: Equation (2): $y = -3x - 2$

$m = -3$ and $b = -2$

Therefore, the slope is $\frac{-3}{1}$ and the y-intercept is (0, –2).

Since the slopes are the same, the lines are parallel.

Solution *continued*

Graphing equations (1) and (2) using the slope-intercept method:

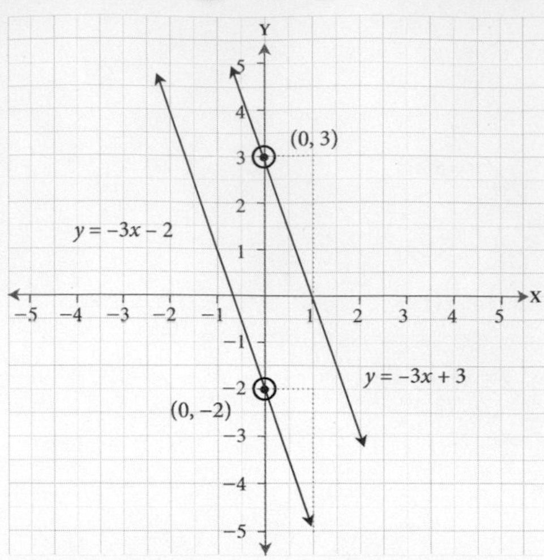

Step 4: The lines have the same slopes but different y-intercepts. Therefore, the lines are parallel and distinct; i.e., they have no solutions.

The system is inconsistent (no solution) and the equations are independent (lines are not coincident).

Note: Once we had the equations in slope-intercept form, we could already tell that they were parallel (same slope) and distinct (different y-intercept) and, therefore, that there were no solutions to the system of equations, without even needing to graph the system.

Example 8.3-c

Analyzing System of Equations

Without graphing, determine whether each system has one solution, no solution, or infinitely many solutions.

(i) $4x + y = 9$
$2x + y = 5$

(ii) $2y + x = 4$
$2x + 4y = 16$

(iii) $2x - 3y + 6 = 0$
$6x - 9y = -18$

Solution

(i) Rewrite the equations in slope-intercept form ($y = mx + b$):

$4x + y = 9$

$y = -4x + 9 \longrightarrow$ Slope (m) = −4, y-intercept (b) = 9

$2x + y = 5$

$y = -2x + 5 \longrightarrow$ Slope (m) = −2, y-intercept (b) = 5

The slopes of the lines are different (−4 and −2).

Therefore, the lines are not parallel. They will intersect at one point. The system will have one solution.

(ii) Rewrite the equations in slope-intercept form ($y = mx + b$):

$2y + x = 4$

$2y = -x + 4$

$y = -\frac{1}{2}x + 2 \longrightarrow$ Slope (m) = $-\frac{1}{2}$, y-intercept (b) = 2

$2x + 4y = 16$

$4y = -2x + 16$

$y = -\frac{1}{2}x + 4 \longrightarrow$ Slope (m) = $-\frac{1}{2}$, y-intercept (b) = 4

Solution *continued*

The slopes of the lines are the same $\left(-\frac{1}{2}\right)$ but the y-intercepts are different (2 and 4).

Therefore, the lines are parallel but distinct. The system will have no solutions.

(iii) Rewrite the equations in slope-intercept form ($y = mx + b$):

$$2x - 3y + 6 = 0$$
$$-3y = -2x - 6$$
$$y = \frac{2}{3}x + 2 \longrightarrow \text{Slope } (m) = \frac{2}{3}, y\text{-intercept } (b) = 2$$

$$6x - 9y = -18$$
$$-9y = -6x - 18$$
$$y = \frac{2}{3}x + 2 \longrightarrow \text{Slope } (m) = \frac{2}{3}, y\text{-intercept } (b) = 2$$

The slopes of the lines are the same $\left(\frac{2}{3}\right)$ and the y-intercepts are also the same (2).

Therefore, the two lines coincide. The system will have infinitely many solutions.

Example 8.3-d

Graphing a System of Linear Equations to Solve a Word Problem

A car rental company requires that you choose from one of the following two payment options when you rent a car:

- Option 1: A flat rate of $40, plus 20¢ per kilometre driven.
- Option 2: No flat rate, but 30¢ per kilometre driven.

(i) Write an equation in slope-intercept form to represent the cost of renting a car using each option.

(ii) Sketch the graphs and label the lines.

(iii) Where do the two lines intersect? What does this point represent?

(iv) Which option will be cheaper if you plan to drive 450 km?

Solution

(i) Let x represent the number of kilometres driven and y represent the total rental cost (in $). Then,

Option 1: $y = 40 + 0.20x$ $\longrightarrow$ In the form of $y = mx + b$, $y = 0.20x + 40$

Option 2: $y = 0.30x$ $\longrightarrow$ This equation is in the form of $y = mx$, i.e., it passes through the origin.

(ii) We will use a table of values to graph the system.

$y = 0.20x + 40$		
x	y	(x, y)
0	40	(0, 40)
100	60	(100, 60)
200	80	(200, 80)
300	100	(300, 100)
400	120	(400, 120)
500	140	(500, 140)

$y = 0.30x$		
x	y	(x, y)
0	0	(0, 0)
100	30	(100, 30)
200	60	(200, 60)
300	90	(300, 90)
400	120	(400, 120)
500	150	(500, 150)

Solution
continued

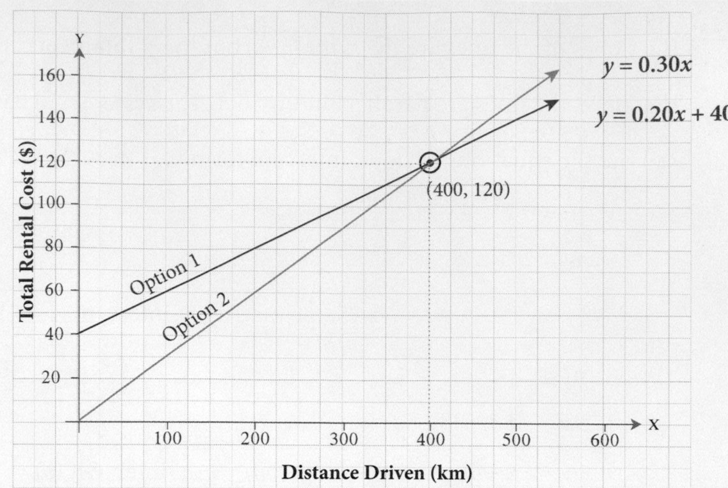

(iii) From the graph, we can see that the two lines intersect at the common point (400, 120). This means that if the car is driven 400 km, the total rental cost will be $120 under either payment option.

(iv) From the graph, we can see that when the distance driven is less than 400 km, Option 2 is cheaper than Option 1. When the distance driven is more than 400 km, Option 1 becomes cheaper than Option 2. Therefore, if you plan to drive 450 km, Option 1 will be cheaper.

8.3 | Exercises

Answers to odd-numbered problems are available at the end of the textbook.

For Problems 1 to 20, solve the systems of equations by graphing, and then classify the systems of equations as consistent or inconsistent and the equations as dependent or independent.

1. $y = 3x - 2$
   $y = -7x + 8$

2. $y = 3x + 9$
   $y = x - 4$

3. $y = -x + 2$
   $2y = -2x + 6$

4. $y = 2x + 6$
   $2y = -3x + 6$

5. $y = -4x + 7$
   $2y + 8x = 14$

6. $y = -2x + 3$
   $2y + 4x = 6$

7. $3x - y - 8 = 0$
   $6x - 2y - 1 = 0$

8. $y = 2x - 4$
   $3y = -2x + 4$

9. $y - x + 1 = 0$
   $y + 2x - 5 = 0$

10. $y = x - 2$
    $3y = -2x + 9$

11. $5x + y + 9 = 0$
    $x - 3y + 5 = 0$

12. $3x - 2y + 1 = 0$
    $y + 4x - 6 = 0$

13. $3x + 2y = -4$
    $y + \frac{3}{2}x + 2 = 0$

14. $2x - y = 6$
    $6x - 3y = 15$

15. $4x - 2y = 6$
    $-2y + 4x - 8 = 0$

16. $2y - x - 6 = 0$
    $y = \frac{1}{2}x + 3$

17. $x - y = 6$

$2x + y = 3$

18. $4x - 8y = 0$

$2x - 4y = -8$

19. $y + \frac{1}{2}x + 1 = 0$

$4y - x - 4 = 0$

20. $y = x + 5$

$x + 2y = 10$

For Problems 21 to 28, determine whether each system has one solution, no solution, or infinitely many solutions ***without*** *graphing.*

21. $3x + 4y = 4$

$2x + y = 6$

22. $3x - 2y = 6$

$x + 2y = 6$

23. $x - y = 1$

$2x + y = 5$

24. $x + y = 7$

$2x - y = 8$

25. $3y - 2x = 1$

$12y - 8x = -4$

26. $2x - y - 4 = 0$

$6x - 3y + 12 = 0$

27. $2x = 3y - 1$

$8x = 12y + 4$

28. $x + 2y = 5$

$x + 4y = 9$

29. Find the value of 'A' for which the lines $Ax - 2y - 5 = 0$ and $8x - 4y + 3 = 0$ are parallel.

30. Find the value of 'B' for which the lines $3x + 2y + 8 = 0$ and $6x - By - 3 = 0$ are parallel.

31. Find the value of 'A' for which the lines $x + 3y + 1 = 0$ and $Ay + 2x + 2 = 0$ are coincident.

32. Find the value of 'B' for which the lines $y = Bx + 3$ and $x - 2y + 6 = 0$ are coincident.

33. Louis is interested in learning to dance and is comparing two different clubs. Dance club A charges a \$60 annual fee, and \$4 for each class you attend. Dance club B charges a \$36 annual fee, and \$6 for each class you attend.

    a. Write an equation in slope-intercept form to represent the total fees charged by each dance club.

    b. Sketch the graphs and label the lines.

    c. Where do the lines intersect? What does this point represent?

    d. What does the graph indicate to Louis about which dance club he should join?

34. Shelley is looking into joining a yoga club. Yoga club A charges a \$100 annual fee and a \$5 fee for each class you attend. Yoga club B charges a \$50 annual fee and a \$7 fee for each class you attend.

    a. Write an equation in slope-intercept form to represent the total fees charged by each yoga club.

    b. Sketch the graphs and label the lines.

    c. Where do the lines intersect? What does this point represent?

    d. What does the graph indicate to Shelley about which yoga club she should join?

8.4 Solving Systems of Linear Equations with Two Variables, Algebraically

Solving systems of linear equations using algebraic methods is preferable to using graphing methods for the following reasons:

- Algebraic methods eliminate the possibility of graphing errors.
- Algebraic methods provide the exact answer for systems of equations that have solutions with fractional coordinates.

There are two algebraic methods for solving systems of linear equations:

1. The Substitution Method
2. The Elimination Method

Substitution Method

The substitution method is the preferred algebraic method if either one of the equations in the system has a variable with a coefficient of 1 or –1, which makes that variable easy to isolate in the equation.

The following steps are used to solve systems of two linear equations with two variables using the substitution method:

Step 1: Choose the simplest variable for which to isolate in either of the two equations (preferably a variable with a coefficient of 1 or –1), and isolate for that variable to find an expression for that variable in terms of the other variable.

Step 2: Substitute the expression for the variable from Step 1 into the other equation (the one not used in Step 1). This will result in an equation involving only one of the two variables.

Step 3: Solve the equation in Step 2 for the one unknown variable.

Step 4: Solve for the other variable by substituting the value of the known variable into either of the original equations (it is often easier to substitute back into the equation from Step 1 with the isolated variable).

Step 5: State the solution for the system of equations as an ordered pair of the solutions for the two variables found in Steps 3 and 4.

Step 6: Check if the solution obtained for the variables is true by substituting these values in each of the original equations. If the solution satisfies **both** of the equations, then it is the solution to the given system of equations.

Example 8.4-a **Solving a System of Equations by Substituting for the Variable '*y*'**

Solve the system of equations given below:

$y - 3x + 2 = 0$

$3y + x - 14 = 0$

Solution

Step 1: The coefficient of y in Equation 1 is one, so we isolate for y in that equation.

$$y - 3x + 2 = 0$$

$$y = 3x - 2$$

Step 2: Substituting $(3x - 2)$ for y in Equation 2 ,

$$3y + x - 14 = 0$$

$$3(3x - 2) + x - 14 = 0$$

Solution *continued*

Step 3: Solving for 'x',

$$9x - 6 + x - 14 = 0$$
$$9x + x = 14 + 6$$
$$10x = 20$$
$$x = 2$$

Step 4: Substituting for $x = 2$ back into the equation that is solved for y,

$$y = 3x - 2$$
$$y = 3(2) - 2$$
$$y = 4$$

Step 5: Therefore, the solution is (2, 4).

Step 6: Checking the solution in Equations 1 and 2,

Equation 1, $y - 3x + 2 = 0$

$$\begin{aligned} LS &= y - 3x + 2 \\ &= 4 - 3(2) + 2 \\ &= 0 \\ &= RS \text{ (True)} \end{aligned}$$

Therefore, LS = RS.

Equation 2, $3y + x - 14 = 0$

$$\begin{aligned} LS &= 3y + x - 14 \\ &= 3(4) + 2 - 14 \\ &= 0 \\ &= RS \text{ (True)} \end{aligned}$$

Therefore, LS = RS.

Example 8.4-b Solving a System of Equations by Substituting for the Variable 'x'

Solve the system of equations given below:

$x + 2y = 6$

$4x + 3y = 4$

Solution

Step 1: The coefficient of x in Equation 1 is one.

$$x + 2y = 6$$
$$x = 6 - 2y$$

Step 2: Substituting $(6 - 2y)$ for x in Equation 2,

$$4x + 3y = 4$$
$$4(6 - 2y) + 3y = 4$$

Step 3: Solving for 'y',

$$24 - 8y + 3y = 4$$
$$-8y + 3y = 4 - 24$$
$$-5y = -20$$
$$y = 4$$

Step 4: Substituting $y = 4$ back into the equation that is solved for x,

$$x = 6 - 2y$$
$$x = 6 - 2(4)$$
$$x = -2$$

Step 5: Therefore, the solution is (−2, 4).

Solution *continued*

Step 6: Checking the solution in Equations (1) and (2),

Equation (1) $x + 2y = 6$

$$\begin{aligned} LS &= x + 2y \\ &= -2 + 2(4) \\ &= 6 \\ &= RS \text{ (True)} \end{aligned}$$

Therefore, LS = RS.

Equation (2) $4x + 3y = 4$

$$\begin{aligned} LS &= 4x + 3y \\ &= 4(-2) + 3(4) \\ &= 4 \\ &= RS \text{ (True)} \end{aligned}$$

Therefore, LS = RS.

Elimination Method

The elimination method is the preferred algebraic method if neither of the equations in the system has a variable with a coefficient of 1 or –1. The elimination method is easier to use when the equations are in standard form (i.e., in the form of $Ax + By = C$).

The following steps are used to solve systems of two linear equations with two variables using the elimination method:

Step 1: Rewrite both equations in the form of $Ax + By = C$, where, A, B, and C are integers.

Step 2: Multiply one equation (or both equations) by suitable integer(s) so that the coefficients for one of the variables are the **same** (or **opposite**) in both equations.

The purpose is to eliminate one of the variables by subtracting (or adding) these two equations.

Step 3: Subtract (or add) the two equations from Step 2 to obtain one equation with only one variable.

Step 4: Solve the equation in Step 3 to find the value of that one variable.

Step 5: Solve for the other variable by substituting the value of the known variable into either of the original equations.

Step 6: State the solution for the system of equations as an ordered pair of the solutions for the two variables found in Steps 4 and 5.

Step 7: Check if the solution obtained for the variables is true by substituting these values in each of the original equations. If the solution satisfies **both** of the equations, then it is the solution to the given systems of equations.

Note:

(i) *In Step 2, it does not matter which of the variables you choose to create to have the same (or opposite) coefficient.*

(ii) *In Step 3, you will **subtract** if both equations have the same coefficient for the variable to be eliminated. If the coefficients are opposite, then you will **add** to eliminate that variable.*

Example 8.4-c **Solving a System of Equations by Eliminating the Variable 'x'**

Solve the system of equations given below:

$3x + 2y = 12$

$6x - 3y = 3$

Solution

Step 1: The equations are in the form of $Ax + By = C$,

$3x + 2y = 12$ Equation (1)

$6x - 3y = 3$ Equation (2)

Step 2: In this case, the variable 'x' will be easier to eliminate, as its coefficient in the second equation (6) is a multiple of its coefficient in the first equation (3).

Solution *continued*

Multiplying Equation (1) by 2 to make the coefficients on x the same,

$$2(3x + 2y) = 2(12)$$
$$6x + 4y = 24 \qquad \text{Equation (3)}$$

Step 3: Since the coefficients on the variable 'x' are the same, we subtract Equation (2) from Equation (3),

$$6x + 4y = 24$$
$$-\ (6x - 3y) = -\ (3)$$
$$7y = 21$$

Step 4: Solving for 'y',

$$7y = 21$$
$$y = \frac{21}{7} = 3$$

Step 5: Substituting $y = 3$ in Equation (1) and solving for 'x',

$$3x + 2y = 12$$
$$3x + 2(3) = 12$$
$$3x = 12 - 6 = 6$$
$$x = 2$$

Step 6: Therefore, the solution is (2, 3).

Step 7: Checking the solution in Equations (1) and (2),

Equation (1), $3x + 2y = 12$

$$\begin{aligned} LS &= 3x + 2y \\ &= 3(2) + 2(3) \\ &= 6 + 6 \\ &= 12 \\ &= RS \text{ (True)} \end{aligned}$$

Therefore, LS = RS.

Equation (2), $6x - 3y = 3$

$$\begin{aligned} LS &= 6x - 3y \\ &= 6(2) - 3(3) \\ &= 12 - 9 \\ &= 3 \\ &= RS \text{ (True)} \end{aligned}$$

Therefore, LS = RS.

Example 8.4-d Solving a System of Equations by Eliminating the Variable 'y'

Solve the system of equations given below:

$3x + 2y = 22$

$8x - 5y = 7$

Solution

Step 1: The equations are in the form of $Ax + By = C$,

$$3x + 2y = 22 \qquad \text{Equation (1)}$$
$$8x - 5y = 7 \qquad \text{Equation (2)}$$

Step 2: In this case, since neither of the variables have pairs of coefficients that are multiples of each other or even share a common factor, we choose the variable 'y' to eliminate, as the coefficients are smaller:

The variable 'y' in Equations (1) and (2) has coefficients of 2 and –5, respectively.

Solution *continued*

Multiplying Equation 1 by 5, and multiplying Equation 2 by 2 to make the coefficients on y the same:

$5(3x + 2y) = 5(22)$

$15x + 10y = 110$ Equation 3

$2(8x - 5y) = 2(7)$

$16x - 10y = 14$ Equation 4

Step 3: Since the coefficients on the variable 'y' are opposite, we add Equations 3 and 4,

$$\begin{array}{r} 15x + 10y = 110 \\ +\ (16x - 10y) = +(14) \\ \hline 31x \qquad\quad = 124 \end{array}$$

Step 4: Solving for 'x',

$$31x = 124$$

$$x = \frac{124}{31} = 4$$

Step 5: Substituting $x = 4$ in Equation 1 and solving for 'y',

$$3x + 2y = 22$$

$$3(4) + 2y = 22$$

$$2y = 22 - 12 = 10$$

$$y = 5$$

Step 6: Therefore, the solution is (4, 5).

Step 7: Checking the solution in Equations 1 and 2,

Equation 1, $3x + 2y = 22$

$$\begin{aligned} LS &= 3x + 2y \\ &= 3(4) + 2(5) \\ &= 12 + 10 \\ &= 22 \\ &= RS \text{ (True)} \end{aligned}$$

Therefore, LS = RS.

Equation 2, $8x - 5y = 7$

$$\begin{aligned} LS &= 8x - 5y \\ &= 8(4) - 5(5) \\ &= 32 - 25 \\ &= 7 \\ &= RS \text{ (True)} \end{aligned}$$

Therefore, LS = RS.

Solving Systems of Equations with Fractions

When one or more of the variables in a system of equations has fractional coefficients, it is often easiest to first clear the fractions by multiplying each equation by its least common denominator **(LCD)**.

For example, consider the following system of equations:

$$\frac{2}{3}x + \frac{1}{2}y = 1$$

$$\frac{1}{3}x - \frac{3}{4}y = -2$$

To clear the fractions, multiply each equation by its **LCD** (least common denominator).

$\frac{2}{3}x + \frac{1}{2}y = 1$ The LCD is 6; therefore, multiplying each term by 6,

$4x + 3y = 6$ Equation (1)

$\frac{1}{3}x - \frac{3}{4}y = -2$ The LCD is 12; therefore, multiplying each term by 12,

$4x - 9y = -24$ Equation (2)

Therefore, the equations of the given system are equivalent to:

$4x + 3y = 6$

$4x - 9y = -24$

This system can then easily be solved using the elimination method.

Solving Systems of Equations with Decimal Numbers

When one or more of the variables in a system of equations has decimal numbers as coefficients, it is often easiest to first clear the decimal numbers by multiplying each equation by an appropriate power of 10 (depending on the number of decimal places), and then dividing all the terms in the equation by any common factors.

For example, consider the following system of equations:

$0.05x + 0.15y = 2.4$

$2.5x + 0.5y = 2.2$

To clear the decimal numbers, multiply the first equation by 100 (to eliminate 2 decimal places) and the second equation by 10 (to eliminate 1 decimal place).

$0.05x + 0.15y = 2.4$ Multiplying by 100,

$5x + 15y = 240$ Dividing by 5,

$x + 3y = 48$ Equation (1)

$2.5x + 0.5y = 2.2$ Multiplying by 10,

$25x + 5y = 22$ Equation (2)

Therefore, the equations of the given system are equivalent to:

$x + 3y = 48$

$25x + 5y = 22$

This system can then easily be solved using the substitution method.

Systems with No Solutions

If a false equation is obtained (such as $0 = 4$) when solving a system of two linear equations with two variables, then the system has no solutions. That is, the graphs of the linear equations will be parallel and distinct. A system of equations with no solutions is inconsistent and independent.

Example 8.4-e **Solving a System With No Solutions**

Solve the following system of equations by using the Elimination method:

$2x + 3y = 6$

$6x + 9y = 45$

Solution

Step 1: $2x + 3y = 6$ Equation (1)

$6x + 9y = 45$ Equation (2)

Step 2: Choosing the variable to be eliminated; in this case, 'x'.

The variable 'x' in Equations (1) and (2) has coefficients of 2 and 6, respectively.

Multiplying Equation (1) by 3,

$$3(2x + 3y) = 3(6)$$

$$6x + 9y = 18 \quad \text{Equation (3)}$$

Step 3: Subtracting Equation (3) from (2),

$$6x + 9y = 45$$

$$-(6x + 9y) = -(18)$$

$$0 = 27 \quad \text{This cannot be true.}$$

Therefore, the system has no solution.

The system is inconsistent and independent. That is, the graph of the system will have parallel and distinct lines, as shown below.

Equation (1)

$2x + 3y = 6$

x-intercept: (3, 0)

y-intercept: (0, 2)

Equation (2)

$6x + 9y = 45$

x-intercept: (7.5, 0)

y-intercept: (0, 5)

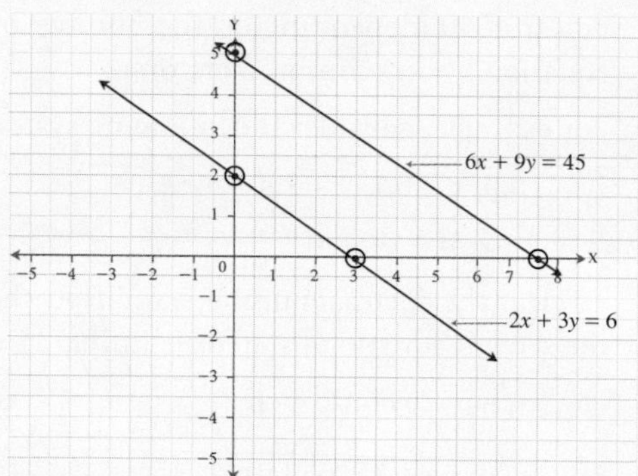

Systems with Many (Infinite) Solutions

If an identity of $0 = 0$ is obtained when solving a system of two linear equations with two variables, then the system has infinitely many solutions. That is, the graphs of the linear equations will be the same line. A system of equations with infinitely many solutions is consistent and dependent.

Example 8.4-f **Solving a System With Many (Infinite) Solutions**

Solve the following system of equations by using the Substitution method:

$2x + y = 7$

$6x + 3y = 21$

Solution

Step 1: The coefficient of y in Equation (1) is 1.

Rearranging, $2x + y = 7$

$$y = -2x + 7$$

Step 2: Substituting $(-2x + 7)$ in for y into Equation (2),

$$6x + 3y = 21$$

$$6x + 3(-2x + 7) = 21$$

Solution *continued*

Step 3: Solving for 'x',

$$6x - 6x + 21 = 21$$
$$6x - 6x = 21 - 21$$
$$0 = 0$$

Therefore, the system will have infinitely many solutions.

The system is consistent and dependent. That is, the graph of the system will have coincident lines, as shown below.

Equation 1 :
$2x + y = 7$
x-intercept: (3.5, 0)
y-intercept: (0, 7)
Equation 2 :
$6x + 3y = 21$
x-intercept: (3.5, 0)
y-intercept: (0, 7)

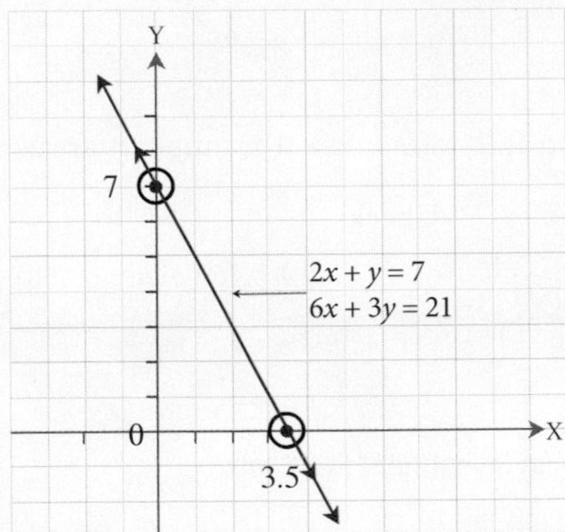

Writing a System of Linear Equations from Word Problems with Two Unknowns

In previous chapters, we solved application problems that could be modeled using only one variable. However, in many real-life application problems, we need to use two variables to model and solve the problem. If a problem can be modeled with linear equations, then we can solve the problem by setting up and solving a system of linear equations with two variables, using either the substitution or elimination method.

The following steps will assist in writing the equations:

Step 1: Choose two different variables (e.g., x and y) to represent each of the unknown quantities and specify clearly what each variable represents and its unit of measure.

Step 2: Based on the given information, translate the word expressions into mathematical equations.

Step 3: Solve the equations for the unknown variables, using either the substitution or elimination method.

Step 4: Indicate the solutions to the word problem, including units.

Step 5: Verify the solutions by substituting the values back into the original problem.

Example 8.4-g **Solving Mathematical Problems**

The sum of two numbers is 46. The difference between the numbers is 8. Find the numbers.

Solution

Step 1: Let the larger number be x and the smaller number be y.

Step 2: $x + y = 46$ Equation 1

$x - y = 8$ Equation 2

Solution *continued*

Step 3: We will use the Elimination method for this example, though the Substitution method would work just as well. Adding Equations (1) and (2),

$$2x = 54$$
$$x = 27$$

Substituting $x = 27$ into Equation (1),

$$x + y = 46$$
$$27 + y = 46$$
$$y = 46 - 27$$
$$y = 19$$

Step 4: Therefore, the numbers are 27 and 19.

Step 5: Check:

$27 + 19 = 46$ (True)

$27 - 19 = 8$ (True)

Example 8.4-h Solving Investment Problems

Steve invested \$50,000. He invested part of it in a fixed deposit paying 4% per annum and the remainder in bonds paying 6% per annum. After one year, he received \$2,700 as interest from both investments. How much did he invest at each rate?

Solution

Step 1: Let the amount invested at 4% be \$$x$.

Let the amount invested at 6% be \$$y$.

Step 2:

$x + y = 50{,}000$	Equation (1)
$0.04x + 0.06y = 2{,}700$	Multiplying by 100,
$4x + 6y = 270{,}000$	Dividing by 2,
$2x + 3y = 135{,}000$	Equation (2)

Step 3: We will use the Substitution method for this example, though the Elimination method would work just as well. From Equation (1),

$$x + y = 50{,}000$$
$$x = 50{,}000 - y$$

Substituting $(50{,}000 - y)$ for x in Equation (2),

$$2x + 3y = 135{,}000$$
$$2(50{,}000 - y) + 3y = 135{,}000$$
$$100{,}000 - 2y + 3y = 135{,}000$$
$$-2y + 3y = 135{,}000 - 100{,}000$$
$$y = 35{,}000$$

Substituting $y = 35{,}000$ into the equation that is solved for x,

$$x = 50{,}000 - y$$
$$= 50{,}000 - 35{,}000$$
$$x = 15{,}000$$

Solution *continued*

Step 4: Therefore, the amount invested in the fixed deposits at 4% interest is \$15,000 and the amount invested in bonds at 6% interest is \$35,000.

Step 5: Check:

Total invested = \$15,000 + \$35,000 = \$50,000 (True)

$$\begin{aligned}\text{Total interest} &= \$15{,}000 \times 4\% + \$35{,}000 \times 6\% \\ &= \$600 + \$2{,}100 \\ &= \$2{,}700 \text{ (True)}\end{aligned}$$

Example 8.4-i **Solving Monetary Problems**

Aran collected 81 coins in quarters (25¢) and dimes (10¢). If all the coins are worth \$15.00, find the number of quarters and dimes he collected.

Solution

Step 1: Let the number of quarters be x and the number of dimes be y.

Step 2: $x + y = 81$ Equation ①

The value of x quarters is \$0.25x and the value of y dimes is \$0.10y. Therefore,

$0.25x + 0.10y = 15.00$ Multiplying by 100,

$25x + 10y = 1{,}500$ Dividing by 5,

$5x + 2y = 300$ Equation ②

Step 3: We will use the Substitution method for this example, though the Elimination method would work just as well. From Equation ①,

$$\begin{aligned}x + y &= 81 \\ y &= 81 - x\end{aligned}$$

Substituting $(81 - x)$ for y in Equation ②,

$$\begin{aligned}5x + 2y &= 300 \\ 5x + 2(81 - x) &= 300 \\ 5x + 162 - 2x &= 300 \\ 5x - 2x &= 300 - 162 \\ 3x &= 138 \\ x &= 46\end{aligned}$$

Substituting $x = 46$ into the equation that is solved for y,

$$\begin{aligned}y &= 81 - x \\ &= 81 - 46 \\ y &= 35\end{aligned}$$

Step 4: Therefore, the number of quarters is 46 and the number of dimes is 35.

Step 5: Check:

Total coins = 46 + 35 = 81 (True)

$$\begin{aligned}\text{Total amount} &= \$0.25(46) + \$0.10(35) \\ &= \$11.50 + \$3.50 \\ &= \$15.00 \text{ (True)}\end{aligned}$$

Example 8.4-j Solving Mixture Problems

How many litres of a 50% salt solution and of a 25% salt solution are required to be mixed to produce 80 litres of a 40% salt solution?

Solution

Step 1: Let the volume of the 50% salt solution required be x L and the volume of the 25% salt solution required be y L.

Step 2: $x + y = 80$ Equation (1)

In the 80 litres of 40% salt solution, the contribution from the 50% salt solution will be $0.50x$ and from the 25% salt solution will be $0.25y$. Therefore,

$0.50x + 0.25y = 0.40(80)$

$0.50x + 0.25y = 32$ Multiplying by 100,

$50x + 25y = 3{,}200$ Dividing by 25,

$2x + y = 128$ Equation (2)

Step 3: We will use the Elimination method for this example, though the Substitution method would work just as well. Subtracting Equation (1) from Equation (2),

$x = 48$

Substituting $x = 48$ into Equation (1),

$x + y = 80$

$48 + y = 80$

$y = 80 - 48$

$y = 32$

Step 4: Therefore, 48 litres of the 50% salt solution and 32 litres of the 25% salt solution are required to be mixed to produce 80 litres of a 40% salt solution.

Step 5: Check:

Total mixture = 48 + 32 = 80 L (True)

Total salt = 0.50(48) + 0.25(32)

= 24 + 8

= 32 L (True)

Example 8.4-k Calculating Speed by Solving a System of Linear Equations

A motorboat took three hours to travel 18 km while travelling in the same direction as the current, and five hours for the return trip while travelling against the direction of the same current. Calculate the average speed of the motorboat in still water and the average speed of the current. (*Hint: Distance = Speed × Time*)

Solution

Let the average speed of the motorboat in still water be x km/h and the average speed of the current be y km/h.

When the motorboat is travelling in the same direction as the current (or **with** the current), the resultant speed is equal to the speed of the motorboat in still water plus the speed of the current.

x → , y → : $(x + y)$

When the motorboat is travelling against the direction of the current (or **against** the current), the resultant speed is equal to the speed of the motorboat in still water minus the speed of the current.

x ← , y → : $(x - y)$

Solution *continued*

Using the formula, *Distance* = *Speed* × *Time*

With the current: $18 = (x + y) \times 3$ Dividing by 3,

$6 = x + y$ Equation (1)

Against the current: $18 = (x - y) \times 5$

$18 = 5(x - y)$ Equation (2)

From Equation (1), $x = 6 - y$. Substituting $(6 - y)$ for x in Equation (2),

$$18 = 5(6 - y - y)$$

$$18 = 5(6 - 2y)$$

$$18 = 30 - 10y$$

$$10y = 30 - 18$$

$$10y = 12$$

$$y = 1.2$$

Substituting $y = 1.2$ into the equation that is solved for x:

$$x = 6 - y = 6 - 1.2 = 4.8$$

Therefore, the average speed of the motorboat in still water is 4.8 km/h and the average speed of the current is 1.2 km/h.

Example 8.4-I

Calculating the Meeting Time of Two Moving Vehicles by Solving a System of Linear Equations

Car A leaves a junction and travels at an average speed of 64 km/h. Two hours later, Car B leaves from the same junction and travels in the same direction at an average speed of 80 km/h. How many hours and how many kilometres will Car A have travelled when Car B catches up to it?

Solution

Let the number of hours travelled by Car A when the cars meet be x hours. Therefore, the number of hours travelled by Car B when the cars meet is $(x - 2)$ hours. Let the number of kilometres travelled by the cars when they meet be y km.

Using the formula, *Distance* = *Speed* × *Time*

Car A: $y = 64x$ Equation (1)

Car B: $y = 80(x - 2)$ Equation (2)

Substituting $64x$ for y (from Equation (1)) in Equation (2),

$$64x = 80(x - 2)$$

$$64x = 80x - 160$$

$$160 = 80x - 64x$$

$$160 = 16x$$

$$x = 10$$

Substituting $x = 10$ in Equation (1),

$$y = 64x = 64(10) = 640$$

Therefore, Car A will have travelled 10 hours and 640 kilometres when Car B catches up to it.

8.4 | Exercises

Answers to odd-numbered problems are available at the end of the textbook.

For Problems 1 to 12, solve the systems of equations by using the Substitution method.

1. $y - 3x + 8 = 0$
   $y - x + 4 = 0$
2. $4x - 7y + 6 = 0$
   $x - 3y + 2 = 0$
3. $3x - 2y = 8$
   $x + 3y = 15$
4. $6x - 9y + 2 = 0$
   $x - 2y - 5 = 0$
5. $x - 3y = 12$
   $5x + 2y = 9$
6. $3x + y = -8$
   $3x - 4y = -23$
7. $5x + 4y = 14$
   $x - 3y = -1$
8. $x - 9y = 6$
   $3x - 7y = 16$
9. $3x - 2y = 20$
   $y + 4x = 23$
10. $9x - 2y = 12$
    $5y + 3x = 21$
11. $7x - 5y + 3 = 0$
    $-3x + y + 1 = 0$
12. $6x - 5y + 13 = 0$
    $-3x + y - 8 = 0$

For Problems 13 to 24, solve the systems of equations by using the Elimination method.

13. $3y + 2x = 24$
    $2x - 2y = 14$
14. $7x - 3y = -5$
    $5x - 9y = 7$
15. $5x + 3y = 19$
    $3x - 5y = -9$
16. $5x - 3y = 2$
    $3x - 5y = 7$
17. $5x - 2y + 1 = 0$
    $2x - 3y - 4 = 0$
18. $4x + 5y = 11$
    $2x + 3y = 5$
19. $5x - 7y = 19$
    $2x + 3y = -4$
20. $9x + 8y = 10$
    $3x + 2y = 4$
21. $2y + 3x = 14$
    $9x - 4y = 2$
22. $3x - 5y = 4$
    $5x + 3y = -16$
23. $3y + 7x = 15$
    $3x + 5y + 1 = 0$
24. $9y + 4x - 1 = 0$
    $4x + 5y + 3 = 0$

For Problems 25 to 36, solve the systems of equations by either using the Substitution or the Elimination method.

25. $0.5x - 0.3y = -1.2$
    $0.2x - 0.7y = 0.1$
26. $1.2x + 0.6y = 0$
    $3.5x + 1.7y = 0.01$
27. $0.7x - 0.4y = 2.9$
    $0.6x - 0.3y = 2.4$
28. $1.5x + y = 1$
    $0.8x + 0.7y = 1.2$
29. $\frac{x}{5} + \frac{y}{6} = 3$
    $\frac{x}{2} - \frac{y}{3} = 3$
30. $\frac{x}{6} - \frac{y}{3} = \frac{2}{3}$
    $\frac{x}{4} - \frac{y}{12} = -\frac{3}{2}$
31. $\frac{x}{4} + \frac{y}{2} = 2\frac{1}{4}$
    $\frac{2x}{3} - \frac{y}{6} = \frac{3}{2}$
32. $\frac{3x}{10} - \frac{y}{5} = \frac{1}{2}$
    $\frac{x}{3} - \frac{y}{3} = -\frac{1}{2}$

33. $4(x - 3) + 5(y + 1) = 12$

$(y + 7) - 3(x + 2) = 1$

34. $4(x + 3) - 3(y + 4) = 21$

$2(x + 4) + 5(y - 3) = 10$

35. $2(x - 2) - 3(y - 1) = 11$

$5(x + 1) + 2(y - 4) = 8$

36. $3(x + 1) - 6(y + 2) = 6$

$5(2x - 4) + 7(y + 1) = -17$

37. Two meals for adults and three meals for children cost \$48, whereas three meals for adults and two meals for children cost \$52. How much is one adult meal?

38. Three DVDs and four movie tickets cost \$94, whereas four DVDs and three movie tickets cost \$81. How much is one DVD?

39. The sum of a son's age and of his father's age, in years, is 92. The difference in their ages is 28. How old are the son and the father?

40. The sum of two numbers is 56. When the smaller number is subtracted from the larger number, the result is 22. What are the numbers?

41. Viktor invested \$25,000, part of it at 5% per annum and the remainder at 4% per annum. If the total interest after one year was \$1,150, how much did he invest at each rate?

42. Two investments were made by Adam, totalling \$22,500. Part of it was invested at 6% per annum and the remainder at 5% per annum. The total interest received after one year was \$1,295. Find the amount invested at each rate.

43. There are 130 coins consisting of quarters (25¢) and dimes (10¢). If the coins are worth \$27.70, how many quarters and dimes are there?

44. There are 175 coins consisting of dimes (10¢) and nickels (5¢). The coins are worth \$15.00. How many dimes and nickels are there?

45. The sum of two angles is 180°. One angle is 24° less than three times the other angle. Find the measure of the angles.

46. The sum of two angles is 90°. One angle is 15° more than twice the other angle. Find the measure of the angles.

47. One canned juice drink contains 15% sugar and another contains 5% sugar. How many liters of each should be mixed together to obtain 10 liters of juice that has 10% sugar?

48. Solution A has 25% acid and Solution B has 50% acid. How many liters of a Solutions A and B should be mixed to obtain 10 liters of 40% acid?

49. A boat took 4 hours to travel 24 km with the current and 8.5 hours for the return trip against the same current. Calculate the average speed of the boat in still water and the average speed of the current.

50. A canoeist paddled 3 hours to travel 57 km against the current and 2 hours for the return trip with the current. Calculate the average speed of the canoe in still water and the average speed of the current.

51. Train A leaves a station and travels at an average speed of 90 km/h. Three hours later, Train B leaves from the same station on a parallel track and travels in the same direction at an average speed of 120 km/h. How long does Train A travel before being overtaken by Train B?

52. Flight A takes off from Toronto airport at an average speed of 650 km/h. After two hours, Flight B takes off from the same airport and travels in the same direction at an average speed of 780 km/h. How many hours later will Flight B catch up with Flight A?

53. Hanna charges \$20 for the first shirt that you purchase at her store. However, for every additional shirt, she charges \$15. Write an equation that shows the relationship between her total revenue (y) and number of shirts sold (x). If you plot a graph of y vs. x, what are the y-intercept and the slope of the line that would represent the equation?

54. An online music store charges \$2 for the first song that you download. For every additional song that you download, you will be charged only \$1.50. Write an equation that shows the relationship between the total revenue (y) and the number of songs sold (x). If you plot a graph of y vs. x, what are the y-intercept and the slope of the line that would represent the equation?

8 | Review Exercises

Answers to odd-numbered problems are available at the end of the textbook.

1. In which quadrant or on which axis do the following points lie?

   a. A (5, –1) b. B (–2, 3)
   c. C (3, 0) d. D (4, –2)
   e. E (2, 0) f. F (0, 4)

2. In which quadrant or on which axis do the following points lie?

   a. A (4, –1) b. B (–5, 0)
   c. C (–2, –7) d. D (0, –3)
   e. E (6, 6) f. F (5, 4)

3. Plot the following points and join them in the order A, B, C, D. Identify the type of quadrilateral and find its area and perimeter.

   a. A (6, –3) b. B (6, –6)
   c. C (–2, –6) d. D (–2, –3)

4. Plot the following points and join them in the order P, Q, R, S. Identify the type of quadrilateral and find its area and perimeter.

   a. P (–2, 4) b. Q (–8, 4)
   c. R (–8, –2) d. S (–2, –2)

For Problems 5 to 10, graph the equations using a table of values with four points.

5. $4x - y = 2$
6. $2x + 3y = 12$
7. $x + y - 4 = 0$
8. $x + 2y - 4 = 0$
9. $y = \frac{1}{2}x + 2$
10. $y = -\frac{1}{2}x - 2$

For Problems 11 to 16, graph the equations using the x-intercept, y-intercept, and another point.

11. $3x - 4y = 12$
12. $x - 2y = -1$
13. $x - 2y - 6 = 0$
14. $3x + y - 4 = 0$
15. $y = 4x$
16. $x = 2y$

For Problems 17 to 22, graph the equations using the slope and y-intercept method.

17. $y = 4x + 6$
18. $y = 5x + 4$
19. $3x + 2y - 12 = 0$
20. $2x + 3y + 6 = 0$
21. $y = -\frac{3}{4}x - 1$
22. $y = -\frac{1}{3}x - 1$

For Problems 23 to 28, determine the equation of the line in slope-intercept form that passes through the following points:

23. (3, 2) and (7, 5)
24. (4, 6) and (2, 4)
25. (5, –4) and (–1, 4)
26. (0, –7) and (–6, –1)
27. (1, –2) and (4, 7)
28. (3, –4) and (–1, 4)
29. Write the equation of a line parallel to $3x - 4y = 12$ and that passes through the point P(–2, 3).
30. Write the equation of a line parallel to $2x - 3y = 9$ and that passes though the point P(2, –3).
31. Write the equation of a line perpendicular to $2y = x + 4$ and that passes through the point P(–2, 5).
32. Write the equation of a line perpendicular to $3x + 4y + 6 = 0$ and that passes through the point P(4, –1).

For Problems 33 to 38, solve the systems of equations by using the Graphical method.

33. $y = -2x - 1$; $y = 3x - 11$
34. $y = 2x + 3$; $y = -2x - 1$
35. $2x - 3y - 6 = 0$; $x + 2y - 10 = 0$
36. $3x + 4y - 5 = 0$; $2x - y + 4 = 0$
37. $2y = x$; $y = -x + 3$
38. $3y = 2x$; $y = -3x + 11$
39. Paul wants to hire a plumbing company to do work on a condominium project. Company A charges $250 for the initial consultation and $40/hour for labour. Company B charges $200 for the initial consultation and $50/hour for labour.

   a. Write an equation in slope-intercept form to represent the total fees charged by each plumbing company.
   b. Sketch the graphs and label the lines.
   c. Where do the lines intersect? What does this point represent?
   d. What does the graph indicate regarding which company should be hired?

40. Paul also wants to hire an electrical company for the condominium project. Company A charges \$500 for the initial consultation and \$50/hour for labour. Company B charges \$300 for the initial consultation and \$60/hour for labour.

   a. Write an equation in slope-intercept form to represent the total fees charged by each electrical company.

   b. Sketch the graphs and label the lines.

   c. Where do the lines intersect? What does this point represent?

   d. What does the graph indicate regarding which company should be hired?

For Problems 41 to 46, determine whether each of the systems of equations has one solution, no solution, or many solutions ***without*** *graphing.*

41. $3x - 2y + 13 = 0$
    $3x + y + 7 = 0$

42. $4x + 6y - 14 = 0$
    $2x + 3y - 7 = 0$

43. $x - 3y + 2 = 0$
    $3x - 9y + 11 = 0$

44. $15x + 3y = 10$
    $5x + y = -3$

45. $2x - 4y = 6$
    $x - 2y = 3$

46. $3x - y + 2 = 0$
    $9x - 3y + 6 = 0$

For Problems 47 to 52, solve the systems of equations by using the Substitution method.

47. $x + 4y = 8$
    $2x + 5y = 13$

48. $x + y = 3$
    $2x - y = 12$

49. $x + 4y + 12 = 0$
    $9x - 2y - 32 = 0$

50. $x - y - 1 = 0$
    $2x + 3y - 12 = 0$

51. $3x + 2y = 5$
    $y = 2x - 1$

52. $4x + 3y = 12$
    $9 - 3x = y$

For Problems 53 to 58, solve the systems of equations by using the Elimination method.

53. $8x + 7y = 23$
    $7x + 8y = 22$

54. $2x + y = 8$
    $3x + 2y = 7$

55. $9x - 2y = -32$
    $x + 4y = -12$

56. $5x - 2y + 3 = 0$
    $3x - 2y - 1 = 0$

57. $4x + 3y = 12$
    $18 - 6x = 2y$

58. $2x + y + 2 = 0$
    $6x = 2y$

For Problems 59 to 64, solve the systems of equations by using either the Substitution method or the Elimination method.

59. $0.4x - 0.5y = -0.8$
    $0.3x - 0.2y = 0.1$

60. $0.2x - 0.3y = -0.6$
    $0.5x + 0.2y = 2.3$

61. $\frac{5x}{3} - \frac{5y}{2} = -5$
    $\frac{x}{3} - \frac{y}{4} = 2$

62. $\frac{x}{4} + \frac{y}{2} = 2$
    $\frac{x}{6} + \frac{2y}{3} = \frac{4}{3}$

63. $(2x + 1) - 2(y + 7) = -1$
    $4(x + 5) + 3(y - 1) = 28$

64. $2(3x + 2) + 5(2y + 7) = 13$
    $3(x + 1) - 4(y - 1) = -15$

65. Find the two numbers whose sum is 95 and the difference between the larger number and the smaller number is 35.

66. Find the two numbers whose sum is 84 and the difference between the larger number and the smaller number is 48.

67. 300 tickets were sold for a theatrical performance. The tickets cost \$28 for adults and \$15 for kids. If \$7,230 was collected, how many adults and children attended this play?

68. 640 tickets were sold for a soccer game between Toronto FC and Liverpool FC. The tickets cost \$35 for adults and \$20 for students. If \$16,250 was collected from sales, how many adults and students attended the game?

69. A fruit punch contains 30% orange juice, while another contains 15% orange juice. How many litres of each should be mixed to make 60 litres of punch that contains 21% orange juice?

70. One type of Antifreeze is 16% alcohol and a second type of Antifreeze is 9% alcohol. How many litres of each should be mixed to obtain 35 litres of Antifreeze that is 12% alcohol?

71. A canoeist paddled for four hours at a speed of 4 km/h with the current and it took ten hours for the return trip against the same current. Calculate the average speed of the canoe in still water.

72. A patrol boat travelled for five hours at a speed of 9 km/h against the current and it took three hours for the return trip with the same current. Calculate the average speed of the boat in still water.

73. Girija drove at an average speed of 60 km/h. One hour later, Aran drove from the same location in the same direction at an average speed of 100 km/h. How many hours did Girija drive before Aran catches up to her?

74. Ship A leaves the port at an average speed of 75 km/h. After two hours, Ship B leaves from the same port and heads in the same direction at an average speed of 90 km/h. How many hours later will Ship B pass Ship A?

Self-Test | Chapter 8

Answers to all problems are available at the end of the textbook.

1. Three vertices of a rectangle ABCD have the points A (–3, 4), B (5, 4), and C (5, –1). Find the coordinates of the 4th vertex, and determine the area of the rectangle.

   (Hint: Area of a rectangle = length × width)

2. Write the following equations in standard form:

   a. $y = \frac{2}{3}x - 2$ b. $6 - 2x + \frac{1}{4} = 0$

3. Write the following equations in slope-intercept form:

   a. $2x - 3y + 6 = 0$ b. $3x + 4y - 5 = 0$

4. Graph the equation $2x - 3y = 9$ using a table of values with 4 points.

5. Graph the equation $3y + 4x = 0$ using the x-intercept, y-intercept, and another point on the line.

6. Use the following slopes (m) and y-intercepts (b) to graph the equations:

   a. $m = -\frac{1}{2}, b = -4$ b. $m = \frac{2}{3}, b = -2$

7. Determine the equation of the line, in standard form, that passes through the points P (–4, 5) and Q (1, 1).

8. Determine the equation of the line, in standard form, having an x-intercept equal to 5 and y-intercept equal to –3.

9. Determine the equation of a line, in standard form, that is parallel to $3x - 2y + 9 = 0$ and that passes through the point (–6, –3).

10. Determine the equation of the line, in standard form, that passes through the origin and that is perpendicular to the line passing through the points P(–3, 5) and Q(5, –1).

11. Solve the following system of equations by using the Graphing Method:

    $y = 3x + 6$

    $6x - 2y + 12 = 0$

12. Sandra wants to join a tennis club, and is looking at two different options. Club A has a $180 membership fee, and an additional $20 fee per hour of court time. Club B doesn't have a membership fee, but has a $30 fee per hour of court time.

    a. Write an equation in slope-intercept form to represent the total fees charged by each tennis club.

    b. Sketch the graphs and label the lines.

    c. Where do the lines intersect? What does this point represent?

    d. What does the graph indicate regarding which tennis club Sandra should join?

13. Determine whether each of the following systems of equations has one solution, no solution, or infinitely many solutions **without** graphing.

    a. $4x + 3y - 16 = 0$ and $2x - y + 2 = 0$

    b. $x - 3y + 11 = 0$ and $2x - 6y + 4 = 0$

    c. $y = 4x + 8$ and $8x - 2y + 8 = 0$

14. Solve the following system of equations by using the Substitution Method:

    $2x + 4y + 6 = 0$

    $y - 3x + 9 = 0$

15. Solve the following system of equations by using the Elimination Method:

    $6x - 4y + 3 = 0$

    $4x - 6y - 3 = 0$

16. Determine the value of two numbers if their sum is 65 and the difference between the larger number and the smaller number is 5.

17. In a coin box, there are three times as many quarters (25¢) as dimes (10¢). If the total value of all these coins is $21.25, how many quarters are there?

18. The cost of admission to a concert was $75 for adults and $50 for students. If 400 tickets were sold and $28,125 was collected, how many adult tickets were sold?

19. A soybean meal contains 20% protein and a cornmeal contains 14% protein. How many pounds of each should be mixed to make a 15-pound mixture that contains 16% protein?

20. Mythili paddled a canoe for three hours at a speed of 6 km/h with the current and it took five hours for the return trip against the same current. Calculate the average speed of the canoe in still water and the average speed of the current.

Chapter 9 BASIC GEOMETRY

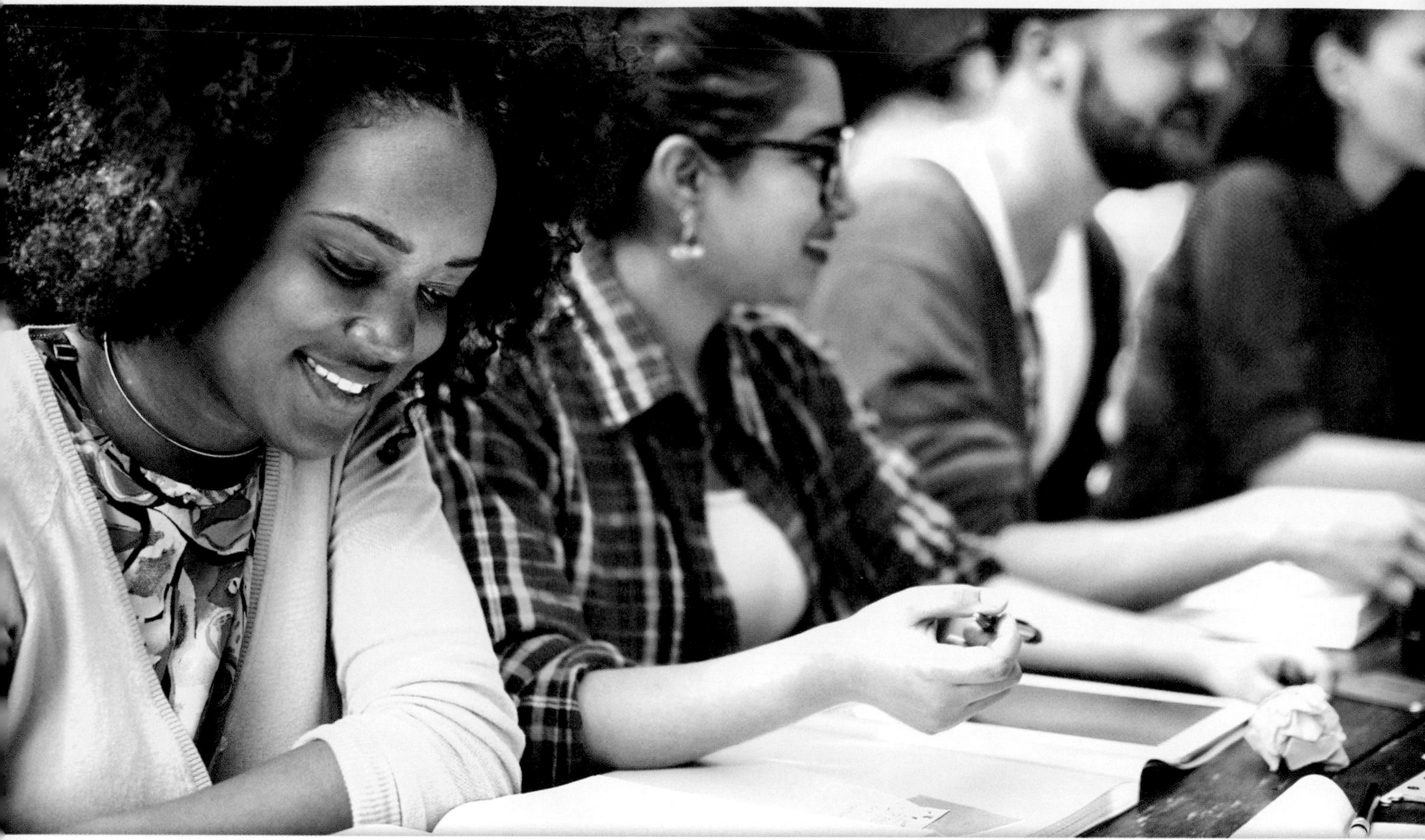

LEARNING OBJECTIVES

- Recognize and use various notations to represent points, lines, line segments, rays, and angles.
- Classify angles and determine the angle relationships between parallel lines and transversals.
- Classify triangles, quadrilaterals, and polygons based on properties of their sides and angles.
- Compute the perimeter and area of plane figures, such as triangles, quadrilaterals, and circles.
- Compute the surface area and volume of common three-dimensional solid objects.
- Use a variety of methods to maximize area or minimize perimeter of a rectangle, given a constraint.
- Use a variety of methods to maximize volume or minimize surface area for a rectangular prism or cylinder, given a constraint.

CHAPTER OUTLINE

Introduction

Geometry (which translates to "earth measurement" from Greek) is a branch of mathematics that deals with the study of relative positions, properties, and relations of geometric objects (such as points, lines, 2-dimensional plane figures, and 3-dimensional solid objects), as well as calculations involving lengths, angles, perimeters, areas, and volumes of such objects. Geometry can be traced as far back as to the ancient Egyptians and Babylonians. However, it was revolutionized by the ancient Greeks, including Pythagoras, Plato, and most notably, Euclid, who invented **Euclidean Geometry**, which is the focus of this chapter.

Geometry is linked to many other topics in mathematics, and is applied in the fields of art, architecture, engineering, land surveying, astronomy, nature, sports, machinery, and more. Furthermore, it has many practical day-to-day uses at home. For example, you use geometry to determine the quantity of paint needed to paint a wall, the amount of carpet needed to floor a room, the length of fence needed to enclose a garden, etc.

In this chapter, we will learn the most basic form of geometry, called Euclidean Geometry, involving points, lines, angles, lengths, areas, and volumes.

9.1 | Lines and Angles

Euclidean geometry begins with the notion of a point. Recall from the previous chapter that a **point** in the Cartesian plane represents a **location** in the plane, determined by its x-coordinate, (representing its horizontal position with respect to the origin), and its y-coordinate (representing its vertical position with respect to the origin). It has no dimensions; that is, it has no length, width, or height.

We label a point in the Cartesian plane using a dot, a capital letter (often P), and ordered coordinates in brackets. The point P(3, 5) in the Cartesian plane is illustrated in Exhibit 9.1-a below.

Often, when working with Euclidean Geometry, we are only concerned with the relative position of a point to other points, and not its specific position in the Cartesian plane. As such, we often omit the coordinates and label the point using a dot and a capital letter (P).

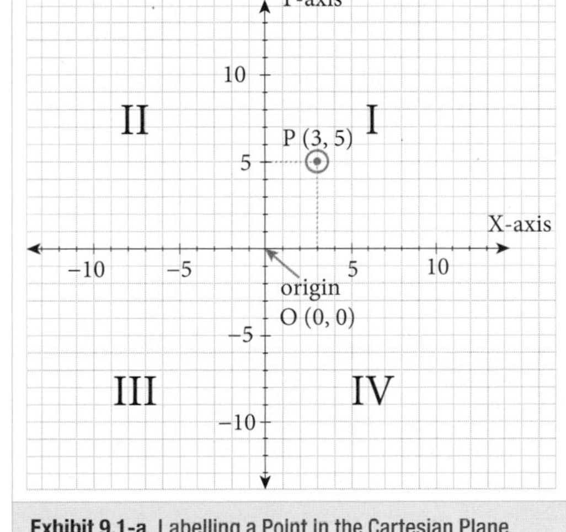

Exhibit 9.1-a Labelling a Point in the Cartesian Plane

Lines, Line Segments, and Rays

A **line** is an object that has only one dimension: length. A line is created by joining two points, includes all the points that fall directly between them, and extends indefinitely in both directions. Therefore, a line is straight, has no gaps, and has no end points. It is denoted with the names of the two points over-lined with a double-arrowhead.

Line	A B	**Line $\overleftrightarrow{AB}$ (or $\overleftrightarrow{BA}$)**

A **line segment** is the portion of a line bound between two end points. A line segment is created by joining two points, and it includes only the points that fall directly between them. It is denoted with the names of the two end points, over-lined with a straight line.

Line Segment	A ⊙———⊙ B	**Line Segment $\overline{AB}$ (or $\overline{BA}$)**

A **ray** is the portion of a line bound in one direction by a single end point. A ray is created by joining two points, and it includes all the points that fall directly between them, and extends indefinitely in one direction only. It is denoted with the names of the two points, over-lined with a single arrowhead.

Ray	A ⊙———⊙→ B	**Ray $\overrightarrow{AB}$**
	←⊙———⊙ A B	**Ray $\overrightarrow{BA}$**

Note: When labeling a ray, the order of the letters matters. For example, ray $\overrightarrow{AB}$ originates at point A and extends indefinitely in the direction of point B, while ray $\overrightarrow{BA}$ originates at point B and extends indefinitely in the direction of point A.

Example 9.1-a **Identifying Lines, Line Segments, and Rays**

Identify and label the following geometric objects:

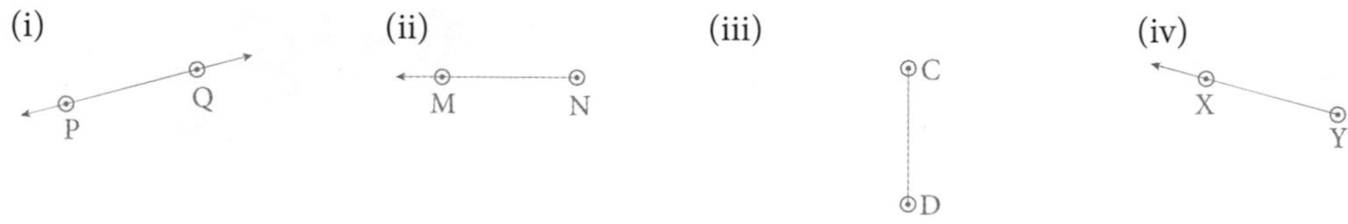

Solution

(i) Line $\overleftrightarrow{PQ}$ or $\overleftrightarrow{QP}$ (ii) Ray $\overrightarrow{NM}$ (iii) Line segment $\overline{CD}$ or $\overline{DC}$ (iv) Ray $\overrightarrow{YX}$

Angle Measures in Degrees

An angle is formed when two rays intersect at their endpoints. The point of intersection is called the **vertex** of the angle and the two rays are called the sides of the angle. The angle is identified by the symbol ∠, followed by the letters of the three points of the two rays, with the vertex in the middle. For example, rays $\overrightarrow{BA}$ and $\overrightarrow{BC}$ form the angle ∠ABC or ∠CBA. When the context is clear, we may simply refer to this angle as ∠B.

When naming an angle, the vertex is always written in the middle.

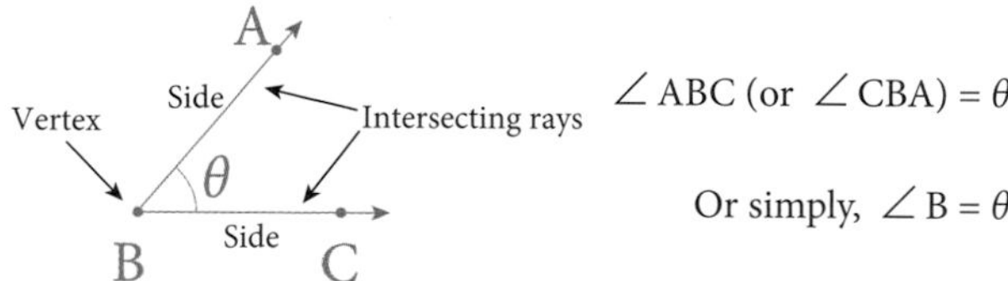

The size of the angle is measured in degrees (denoted with the symbol °), where one revolution of a circle is 360°. One degree is a $\frac{1}{360}$ slice of one revolution of a circle. Imagine a circle centered at point B, divided into 360 equal sectors through B. The degree measure of ∠ABC is the number of sectors that can fit in the wedge formed between rays $\overrightarrow{BA}$ and $\overrightarrow{BC}$. Exhibit 9.1-b shows a circle divided into 36 sectors, where each sector represents 10°, and the angle ∠ABC = 60°.

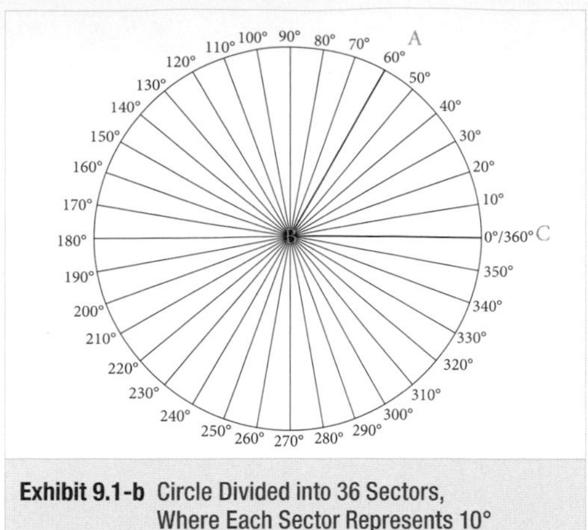

Exhibit 9.1-b Circle Divided into 36 Sectors, Where Each Sector Represents 10°

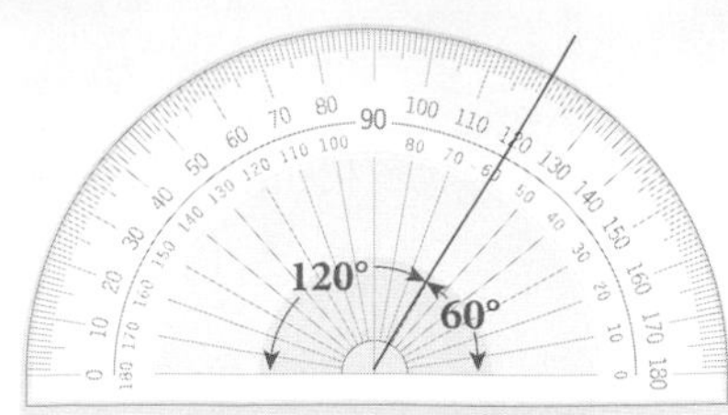

A protractor is used to measure and draw angles in degrees.

Two rays from the center of a circle extending in opposite directions create a line which divides the circle into two equal halves; thus, the angle between two opposite rays has an angle measure equal to $\frac{1}{2}$ a revolution, or $\frac{360°}{2} = 180°$.

Two perpendicular lines through the centre of a circle cut the circle into four equal quadrants; thus the angle between two perpendicular rays has an angle measure equal to $\frac{1}{4}$ a revolution, or $\frac{360°}{4} = 90°$.

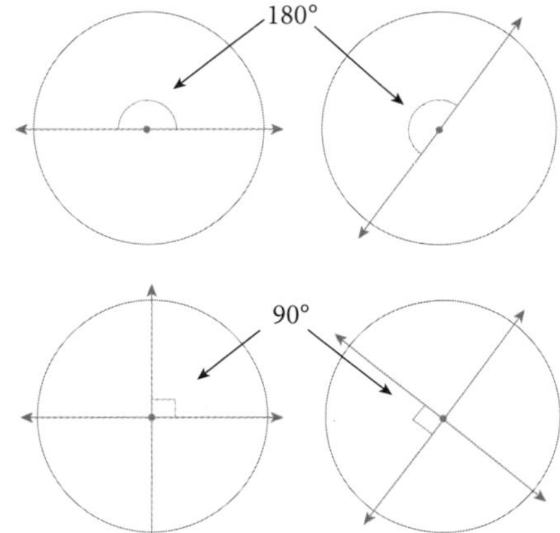

Classification of Angles

Angles are classified according to their size in degrees.

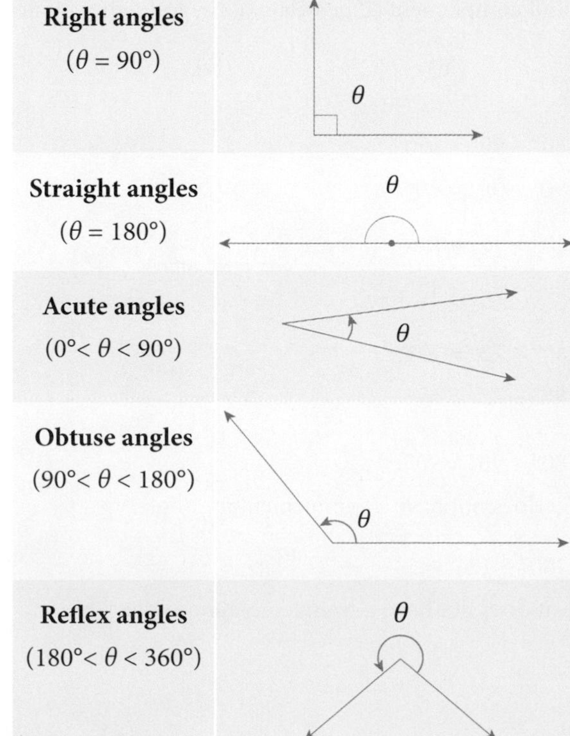

Right angles ($\theta = 90°$)	θ	Any angle measure of 90° is called a **right angle**, and is denoted with a small square at the vertex.
Straight angles ($\theta = 180°$)	θ	Any angle measure of 180° is called a **straight angle,** and is denoted with a semi-circle where the endpoints of the two rays meet.
Acute angles ($0° < \theta < 90°$)	θ	Any angle less than a right angle (i.e., with a degree measure between 0° and 90°) is called an **acute angle**.
Obtuse angles ($90° < \theta < 180°$)	θ	Any angle greater than a right angle but less than a straight angle (i.e., with a degree measure between 90° and 180°) is called an **obtuse angle**.
Reflex angles ($180° < \theta < 360°$)	θ	Any angle greater than a straight angle (i.e., with a degree measure between 180° and 360°) is called a **reflex angle**.

In any pair of rays, there is one angle that is **at most** 180° and one that is **at least** 180°.

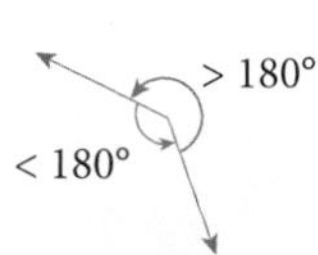

Example 9.1-b Classifying Angles

Identify the following angles as acute, right, obtuse, straight, or reflex:

(i)	(ii)	(iii)	(iv)	(v)
	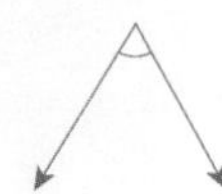	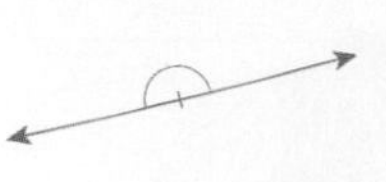		

Solution

(i) Obtuse (ii) Acute (iii) Straight (iv) Right (v) Reflex

Supplementary and Complementary Angles

Angle pairs with measures that sum to a right angle (90°) or a straight angle (180°) are given special names:

Supplementary angles ($\theta + \phi = 180°$)		Two angles are called **supplementary angles** if their sum is 180°. Each angle is called a supplement of the other.
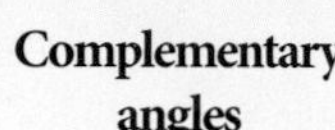 **Complementary angles** ($\theta + \phi = 90°$)	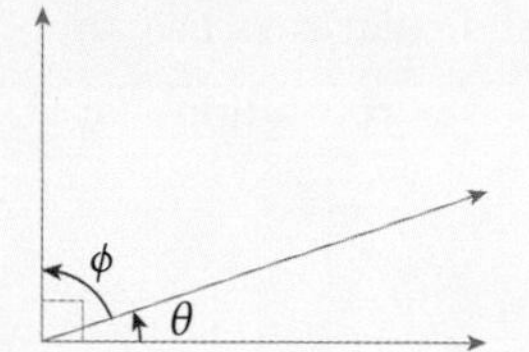	Two angles are called **complementary angles** if their sum is 90°. Each angle is called a complement of the other.

Since the sum of complementary angles is 90°, each angle must be acute (i.e., less than 90°). As a result, only acute angles have complements.

Example 9.1-c Supplementary and Complementary Angles

Determine the supplement and complement (if possible) of the following angles:

(i) 30° (ii) 45° (iii) 72° (iv) 90° (v) 126°

Solution

(i) Supplement of 30° = 180° – 30° = 150°

Complement of 30° = 90° – 30° = 60°

(ii) Supplement of 45° = 180° – 45° = 135°

Complement of 45° = 90° – 45° = 45°

A 45° angle is self-complementary.

(iii) Supplement of 72° = 180° – 72° = 108°

Complement of 72° = 90° – 72° = 18°

(iv) Supplement of 90° = 180° – 90° = 90°

Since 90° is not acute, it does not have a complementary angle.

A 90° (right) angle is self-supplementary.

(v) Supplement of 126° = 180° – 126° = 54°

Since 126° is not acute, it does not have a complementary angle.

Opposite and Adjacent Angles

When two lines intersect at a point P, they create four angles. Every pair of consecutive angles, called **adjacent angles**, is supplementary, since each line forms a straight angle (180°) at point P and the other line cuts it into two angles, which have a sum of 180°. As a result, the angles opposite to each other, called **opposite angles**, are always equal (or congruent).

When two lines intersect, the adjacent angles are supplementary (sum to 180°) and the opposite angles are congruent (equal).

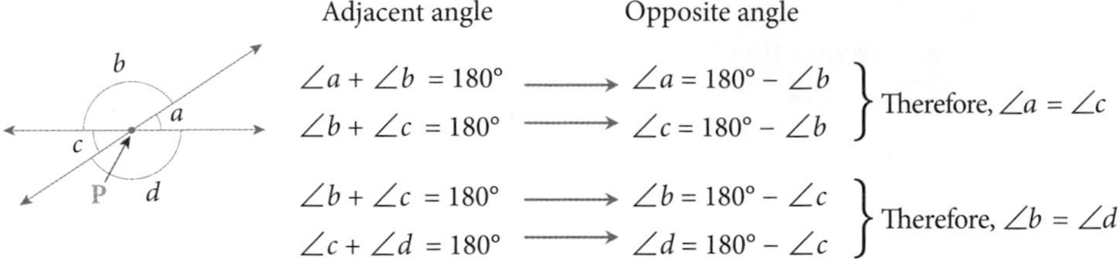

Example 9.1-d **Opposite and Adjacent Angles**

Determine the measures of the three unknown angles in the following diagram:

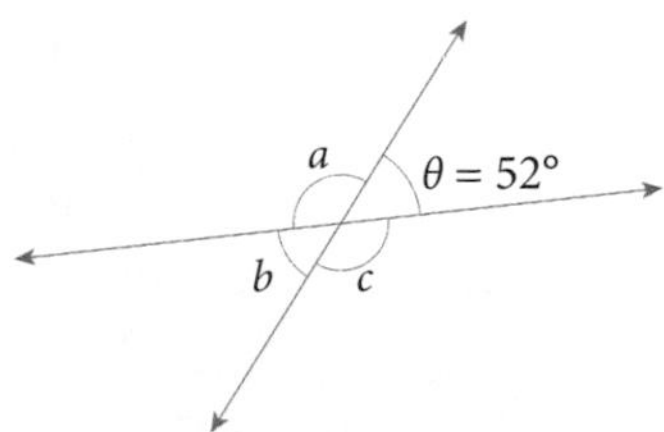

Solution

(i) Since angle a is adjacent to angle θ, it is supplementary to angle θ.
Therefore, $\angle a = 180° - 52° = 128°$.

(ii) Since angle b is opposite to angle θ, it is congruent to angle θ.
Therefore, $\angle b = 52°$.

(iii) Since angle c is adjacent to angle θ, it is supplementary to angle θ.
Therefore, $\angle c = 180° - 52° = 128°$.
Note: Angle c is also opposite to angle a, so $\angle c = \angle a = 128°$.

Parallel Lines and Transversal Angles

Parallel lines are lines in a plane which do not meet (or intersect) even when extended. To demonstrate that the lines are parallel, small arrowheads are drawn.

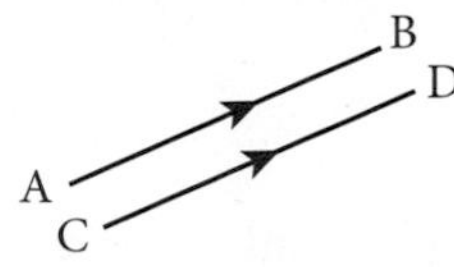

Also, the symbol "//" is used to indicate that the lines are parallel; e.g. $\overline{AB} // \overline{CD}$

A transversal is a line that intersects two distinct parallel lines, and the angles it forms with each of the two parallel lines are congruent.

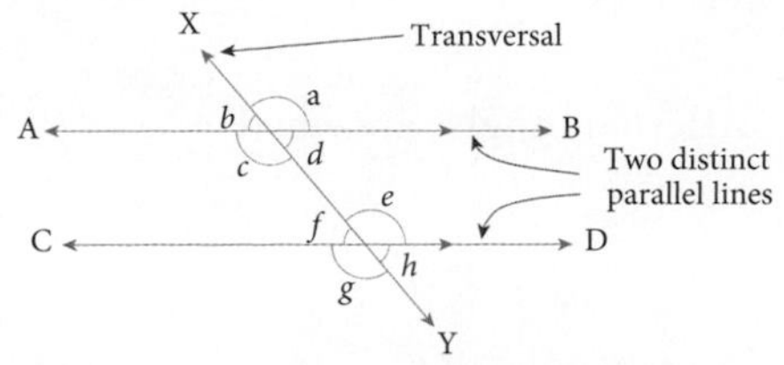

In the above diagram, $\overleftrightarrow{XY}$ is a transversal which intersects parallel lines $\overleftrightarrow{AB}$ and $\overleftrightarrow{CD}$. The four angles, a, b, c, and d are congruent to the four angles, e, f, g, and h, respectively; i.e., $\angle a = \angle e$, $\angle b = \angle f$, $\angle c = \angle g$, and $\angle d = \angle h$.

This means that there are special relationships between the angles formed by the transversal and each of the parallel lines, as classified below:

Corresponding angles have a pattern that looks like the letter F:

Co-interior angles have a pattern that looks like the letter C:

Alternate angles have a pattern that looks like the letter Z:

Opposite angles have a pattern that looks like the letter X:

Corresponding angles (e.g., $\angle d = \angle h$)	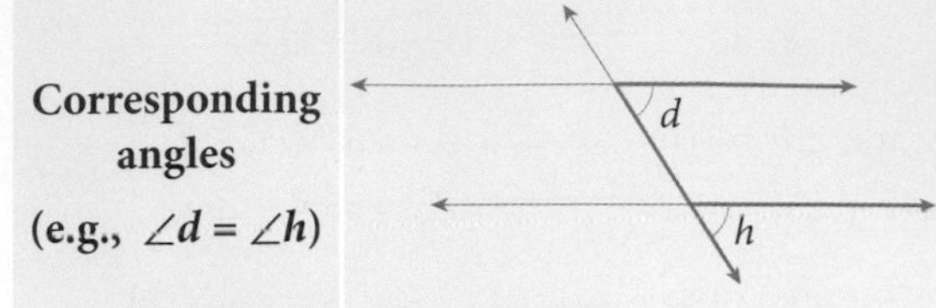	The angles formed on the same corner of the intersection between the transversal and each of the parallel lines are called **corresponding angles**, and they are *congruent*.
Co-interior angles (e.g., $\angle d + \angle e = 180°$)	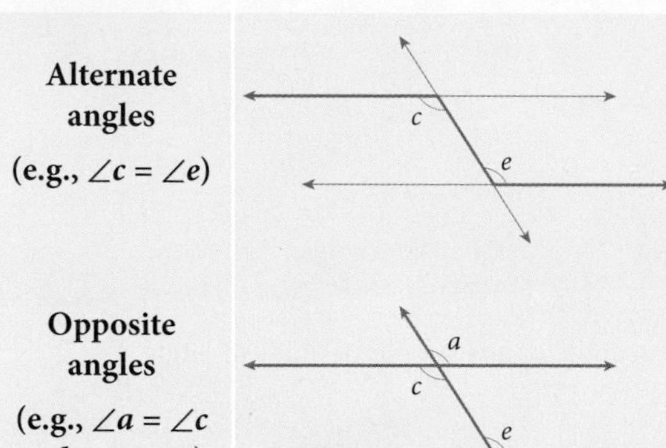	The angles formed on the same side of the transversal and on the interior of the parallel lines are called **co-interior angles**, and they are *supplementary*.
Alternate angles (e.g., $\angle c = \angle e$)		The angles formed on opposite sides of the transversal and on the interior of the parallel lines are called **alternate angles**, and they are *congruent*.
Opposite angles (e.g., $\angle a = \angle c$ and $\angle e = \angle g$)		The angles formed by any intersecting lines that are opposite to the same vertex are called **opposite angles**, and they are *congruent*.

To summarize, consider the angles formed by two distinct parallel lines $\overleftrightarrow{AB} // \overleftrightarrow{CD}$ and a transversal $\overleftrightarrow{XY}$.

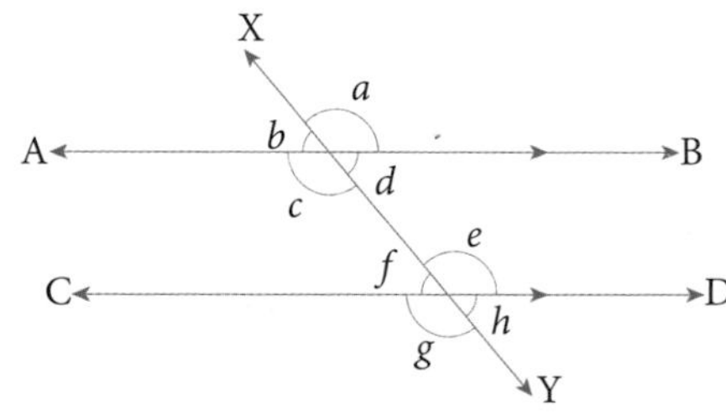

Corresponding angles are equal	Co-interior angles are supplementary
$\angle a = \angle e$ $\angle b = \angle f$ $\angle c = \angle g$ $\angle d = \angle h$	$\angle d + \angle e = 180°$ $\angle c + \angle f = 180°$

Alternate angles are equal	Opposite angles are equal
$\angle d = \angle f$ $\angle c = \angle e$	$\angle a = \angle c$ $\angle b = \angle d$ $\angle e = \angle g$ $\angle f = \angle h$

Example 9.1-e

Identifying Relationships Between Angles

State the relationship to angle θ of each of the five unknown angles a, b, c, d, and e identified in the following diagram. Then state whether the angle is congruent or supplementary to θ.

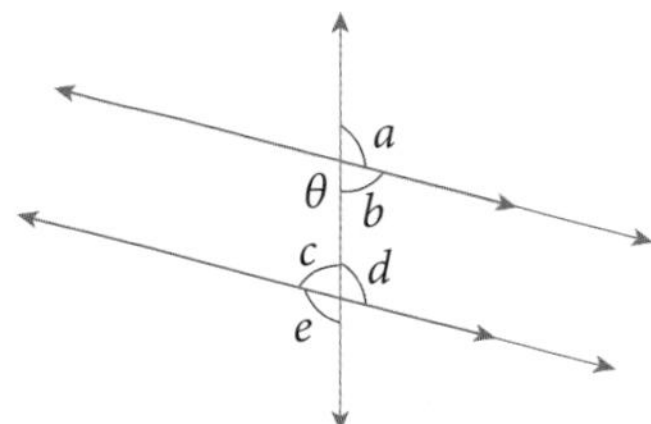

Solution

(i) Angle a is opposite angle θ; hence it is congruent to θ.

(ii) Angle b is adjacent to angle θ; hence it is supplementary to θ.

(iii) Angle c is co-interior to angle θ; hence it is supplementary to θ.

(iv) Angle d is alternate to angle θ; hence it is congruent to θ.

(v) Angle e is corresponding to angle θ; hence it is congruent to θ.

Example 9.1-f

Calculating Measure of Transversal Angles

Calculate the angle measures of the five unknown angles identified in Example 9.1-e, given that angle $\theta = 105°$.

Solution

(i) Since angle a is congruent to θ, $\angle a = \theta = 105°$.

(ii) Since angle b is supplementary to θ, $\angle b = 180° - \theta = 180° - 105° = 75°$.

(iii) Since angle c is supplementary to θ, $\angle c = 180° - \theta = 180° - 105° = 75°$.

(iv) Since angle d is congruent to θ, $\angle d = \theta = 105°$.

(v) Since angle e is congruent to θ, $\angle e = \theta = 105°$.

Example 9.1-g

Application of Transversal Angles - Intersections of Roads

Alder Road, Birch Street, and Cedar Avenue are all straight roads that run in different directions, and their intersections form a triangle. Alder Road intersects Birch Street at an angle of 72° and Cedar Avenue at an angle of 47°, both measured from within the triangle. Using the angle relationships learned in this section, determine the angle of intersection between Birch Street and Cedar Avenue.

Solution

Step 1: Draw a diagram representing the intersection of roads and mark the known angles. Name the triangle as XYZ and let θ be the angle of intersection between Birch Street and Cedar Avenue.

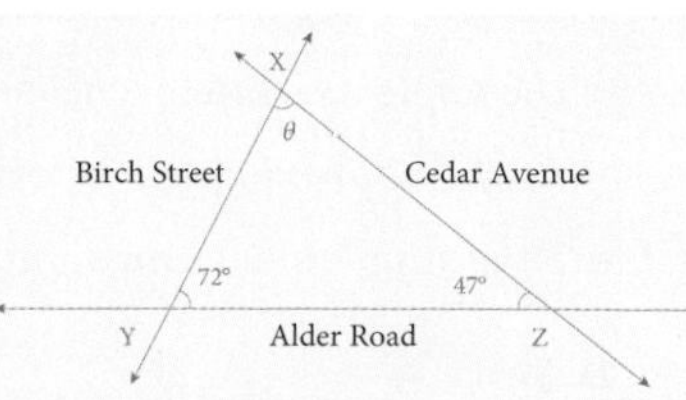

Step 2: To make use of the angle relationships that we learned in this section, draw an imaginary road, parallel to Alder Road, that runs through X, the intersection of Birch Street and Cedar Avenue. Now Birch Street and Cedar Avenue are transversals.

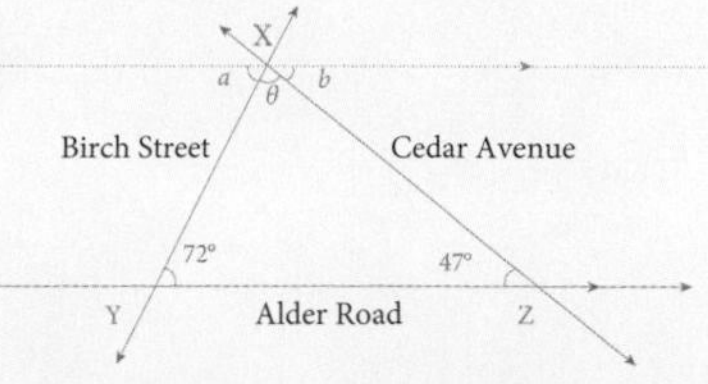

Solution *continued*

Step 3: Calculate the alternate angles that are formed, denoted as a and b on the diagram above.

$\angle a = 72°$ (Alternate Angle)

$\angle b = 47°$ (Alternate Angle)

Step 4: The three angles a, θ, and b at the vertex X must be equal to 180° (angles in a straight line).

$$\angle a + \theta + \angle b = 180°$$

$$\theta = 180° - \angle a - \angle b$$
$$= 180° - 72° - 47°$$
$$\theta = 61°$$

Therefore, the interior angle of intersection between Birch Street and Cedar Avenue is 61°.

The above example demonstrates that the three internal angles of a triangle must add up to 180°. We will examine this further as we begin to analyze plane figures in the next section.

9.1 | Exercises

Answers to odd-numbered problems are available at the end of the textbook.

1. Draw and label the following geometric objects:

   a. Line $\overleftrightarrow{EF}$ b. Line segment $\overline{GH}$ c. Ray $\overrightarrow{JK}$

2. Draw and label the following geometric objects:

   a. Line $\overleftrightarrow{ST}$ b. Line segment $\overline{UV}$ c. Ray $\overrightarrow{XW}$

3. Identify and name the following geometric objects:

   a. 

   b. 

   c. 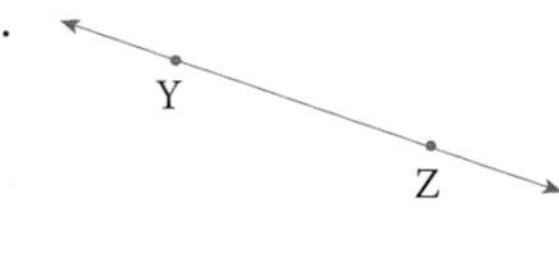

4. Identify and name the following geometric objects:

   a. 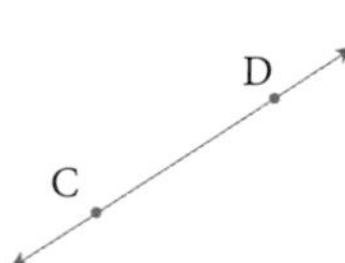

   b. 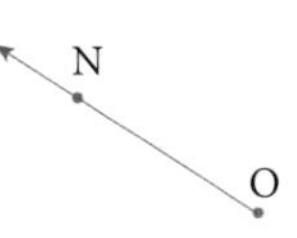

   c. 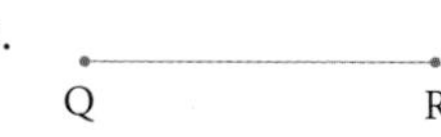

For the figures shown in Problems 5 to 8, answer the following questions:

(i) *Name the angle using the three-letter naming convention (e.g., $\angle$ ABC).*

(ii) *Classify the angle as acute, right, or obtuse.*

(iii) *Determine the approximate angle measure using a protractor.*

(iv) *Calculate the supplement and complement (if applicable) of the angle.*

5. a. 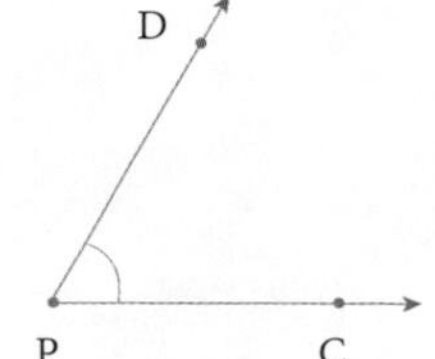

   b. 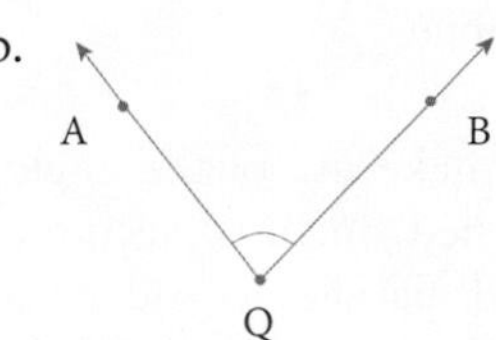

6. a.

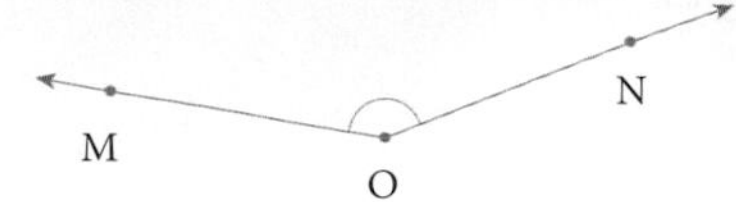

b.

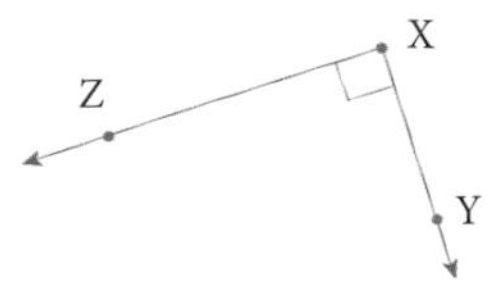

7. a.

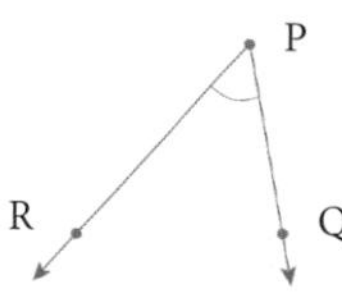

b.

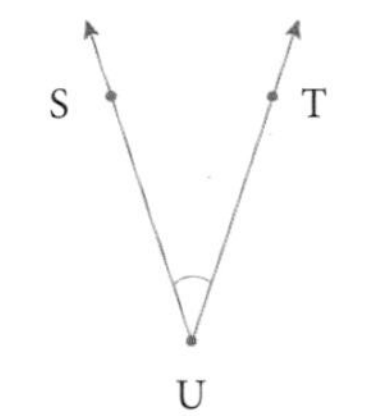

8. a.

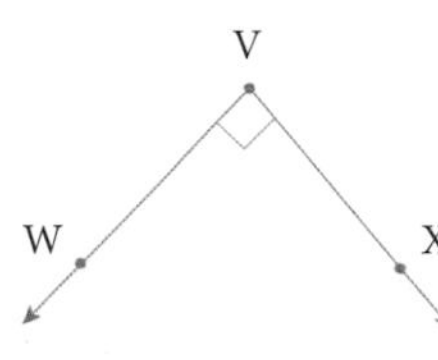

b.

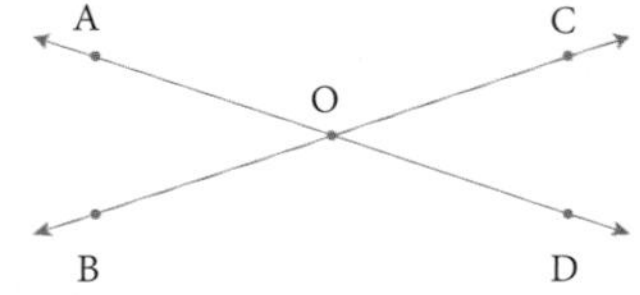

9. Determine the measure of the angle that is complementary to: a. 32.5° b. 18°

10. Determine the measure of the angle that is complementary to: a. 83.1° b. 5°

11. Determine the measure of the angle that is supplementary to: a. 123.4° b. 89°

12. Determine the measure of the angle that is supplementary to: a. 7.8° b. 92°

For the figures shown in Problems 13 to 16, determine the congruent pairs of angles.

13. a.

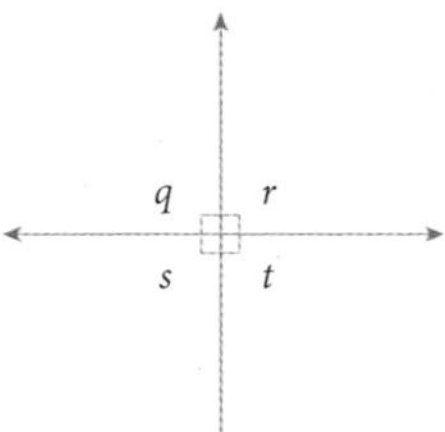

b.

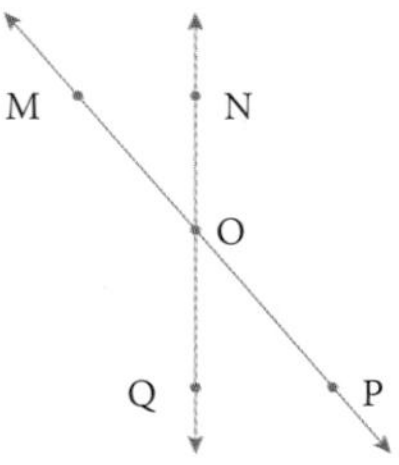

14. a.

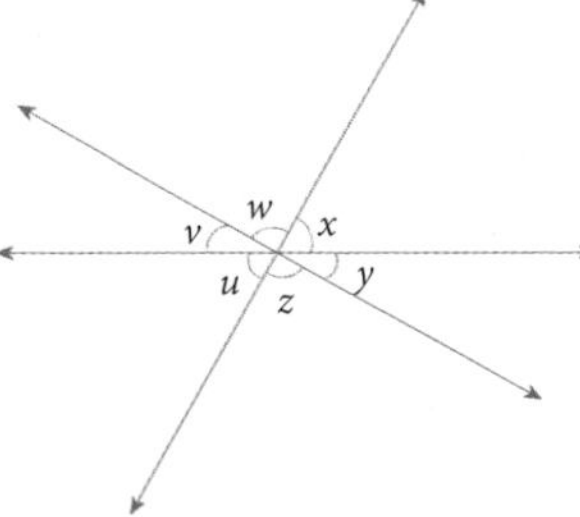

b.

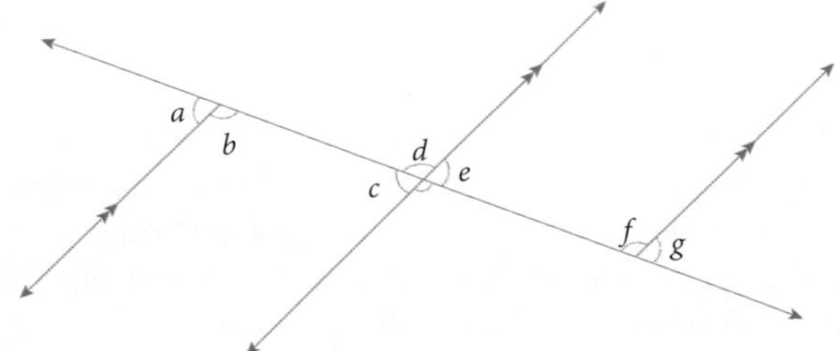

15.

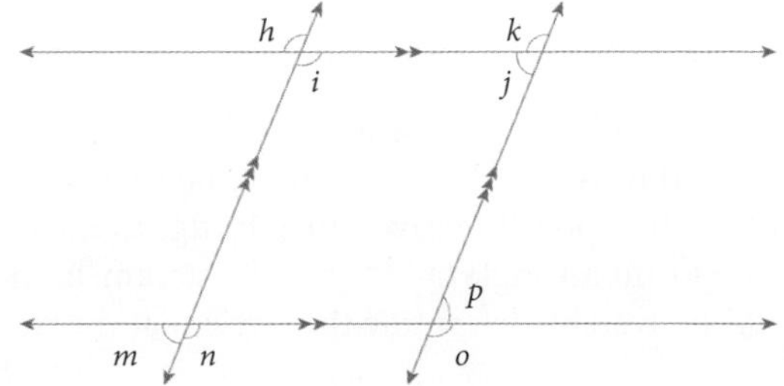

16.

For the figures shown in Problems 17 to 20, determine the values of the unknown angles.

17. a.

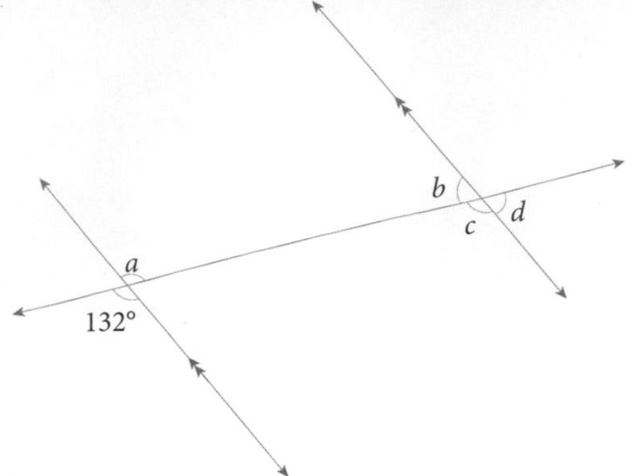

b.

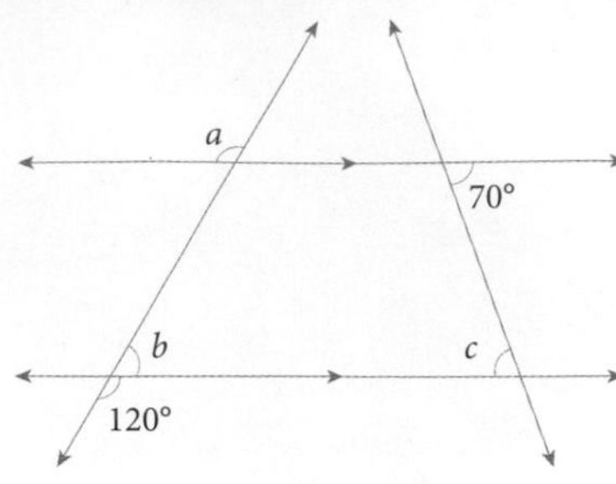

18. a.

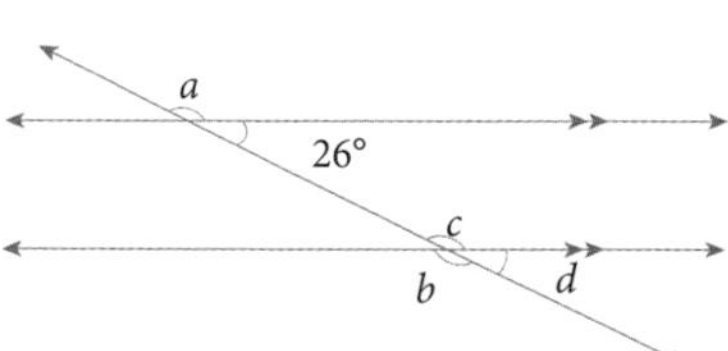

b.

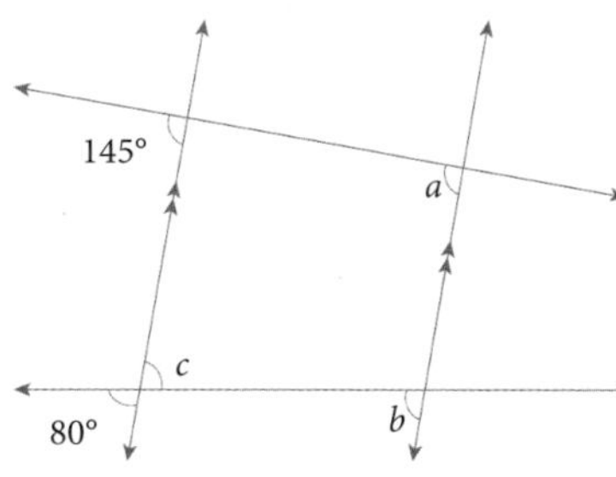

19. a.

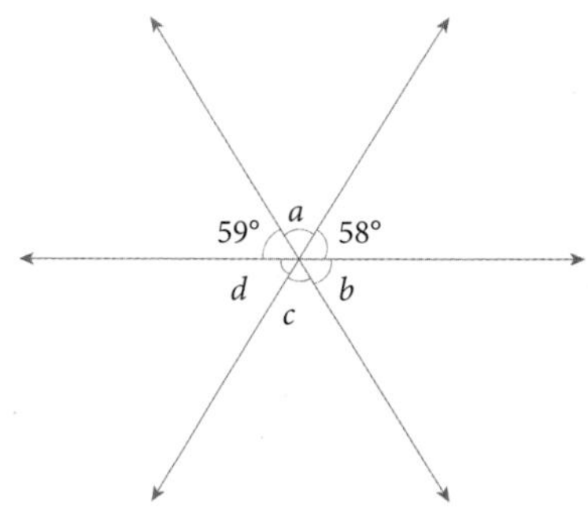

b.

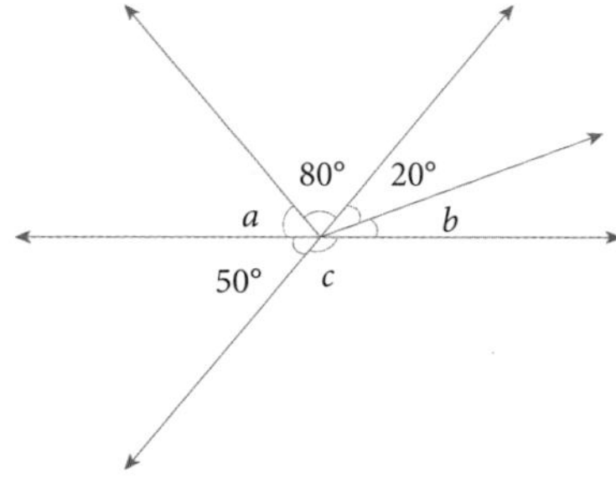

20. a.

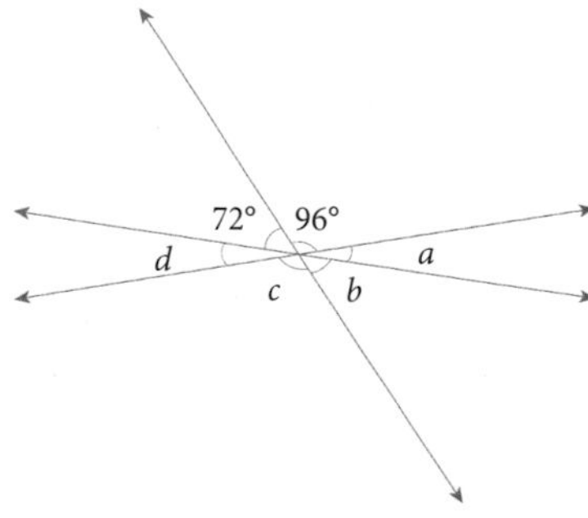

b.

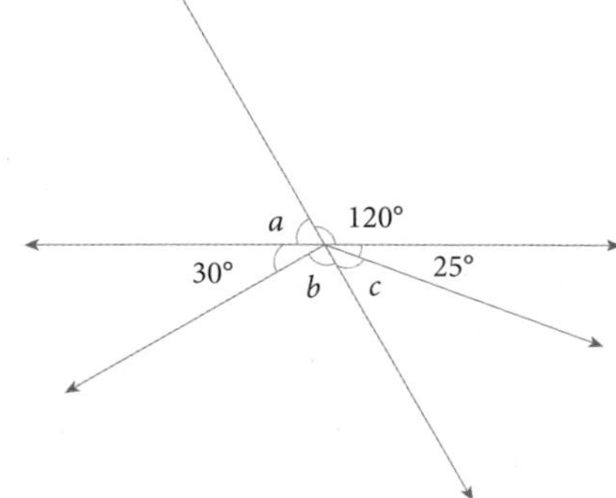

21. A small island is situated at the south of Lois Lake, separated from the mainland by two tributaries of Lois Lake: Crag Creek to the West and Slip Stream to the East. A straight highway called River Road connects the island to the mainland in either direction. The River Road bridge over Crag Creek forms an angle of 77° with the creek, and the bridge over Slip Stream forms an angle of 71° with the stream, both on the island's side. Assuming that both Crag Creek and Slip Stream are fairly straight, determine the angle that they form with each other when they branch off Lois Lake.

22. The South-West corner of the intersection of Main and Queen forms an angle of 104°. Further down Main Street, the South-West corner of the intersection of Main and King forms an angle of 63°. Determine the acute angle formed by the intersection of Queen and King, assuming that all three roads are perfectly straight.

For the figures shown in Problems 23 and 24, use transversal angles and the fact that the sum of the three internal angles of a triangle always equals 180°.

23. a. Calculate the value of θ.

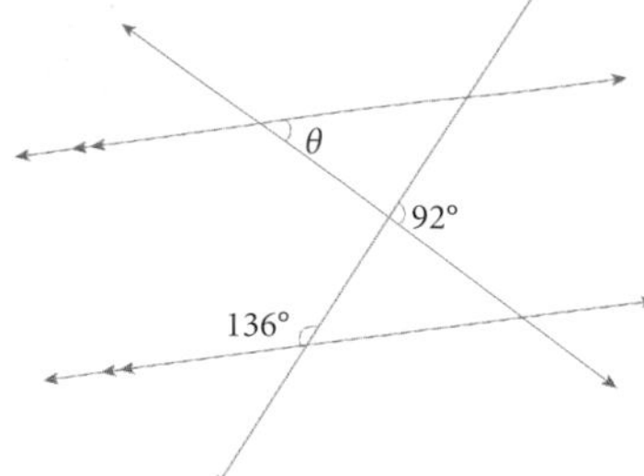

b. Calculate the values of a, b, and c.

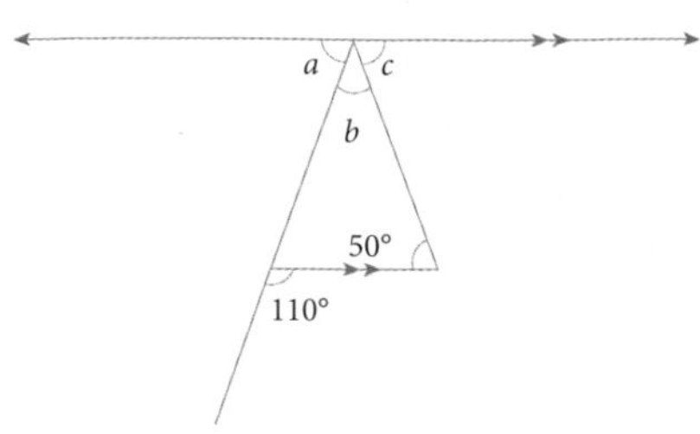

24. a. Calculate the value of θ.

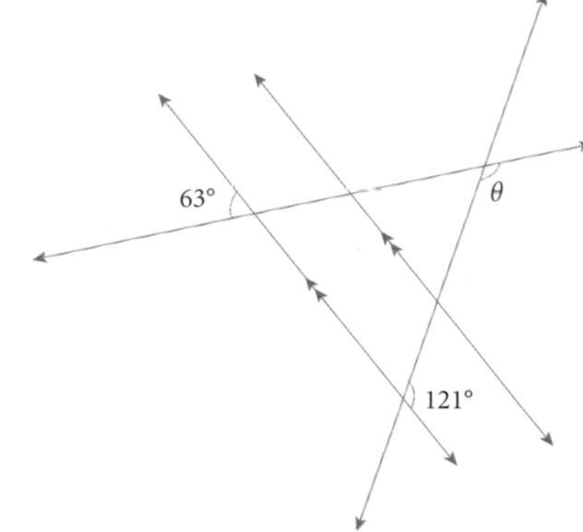

b. Calculate the values of a, b, and c.

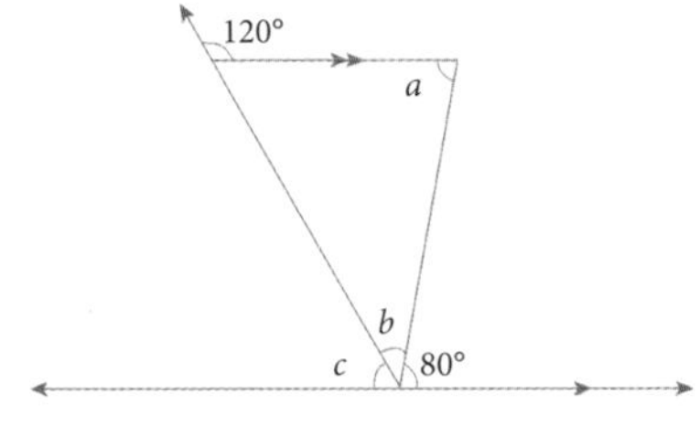

9.2 | Classification and Properties of Plane Figures

The study of geometry that deals with objects or figures that are flat (i.e., 2-dimensional) and that can be drawn in the Cartesian plane is known as **plane geometry**. In plane geometry, we study the properties and relations of plane figures such as triangles, quadrilaterals, polygons, and circles. A plane figure is continuous and closed, meaning that it can be drawn without lifting the pencil from the page and that the start-point is the same as the end-point of the object.

Some examples of plane figures are shown below:

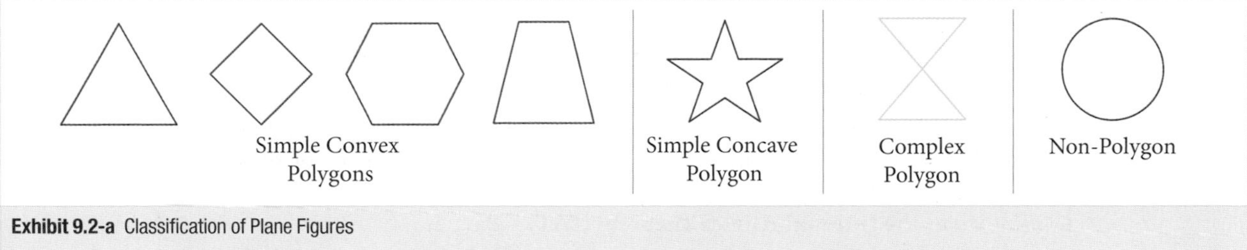

Exhibit 9.2-a Classification of Plane Figures

Polygons

A **polygon** is a plane figure that is created by joining a finite number of line segments together at their vertices; i.e., a polygon is a plane figure that is bound by three or more straight edges, known as sides. The first six shapes in Exhibit 9.2-a are polygons. The circle (i.e., the 7th shape) in Exhibit 9.2-a is not a polygon, as it is not formed by joining a finite number of line segments together. However, the circle is a special shape which we will learn about later in the chapter.

A **simple polygon** is a polygon which does not intersect itself. The first five shapes in Exhibit 9.2-a are simple polygons. A polygon that is not simple (i.e., it intersects itself) is called a **complex polygon**. The hourglass shape (i.e., the 6th shape) in Exhibit 9.2-a is an example of a complex polygon.

A **convex polygon** is a simple polygon whose internal angles are each less than 180°. The first four shapes in Exhibit 9.2-a are convex polygons. A simple polygon that is not convex (i.e., contains an internal angle greater than 180°) is called a **concave polygon**. The star shape (i.e., the 5th shape) in Exhibit 9.2-a is an example of a concave polygon.

A **regular convex polygon** is a convex polygon whose sides are all the same length and whose internal angles all have the same measure.

Polygons are named according to the number of sides that they have. The first eight regular convex polygons are shown below:

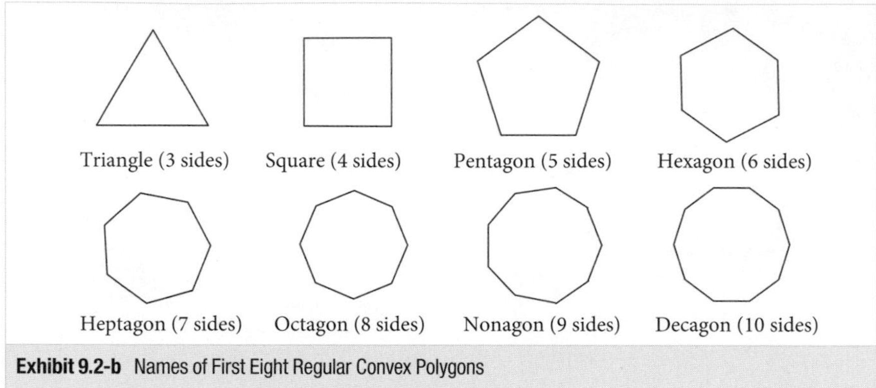

Exhibit 9.2-b Names of First Eight Regular Convex Polygons

Internal Angles of Polygons

An internal angle of a simple polygon is an angle at a vertex where two line segments meet, as measured from the inside of the simple polygon.

If lines are drawn from one vertex of an n-sided polygon to all vertices across from it, there will be $(n - 2)$ triangles that can be drawn within the polygon.

For example,

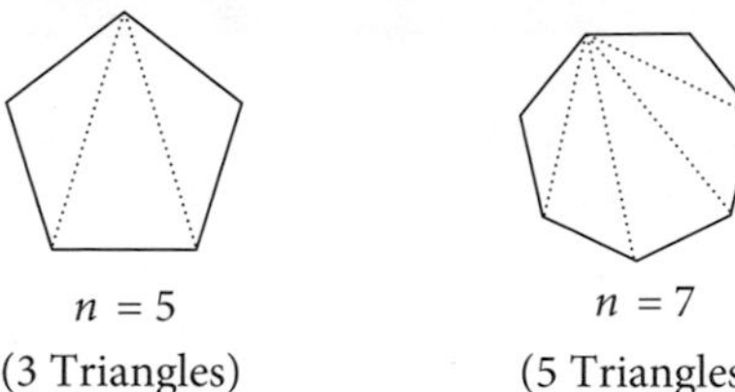

Recall from the end of the previous section that the interior angles of a triangle add up to 180°.

Therefore, the sum of the internal angles of any n-sided polygon = $(n - 2) \times 180°$. This is known as the **Internal Angles Theorem (IAT) – Part 1**.

Furthermore, every internal angle in a *regular* n-sided *convex* polygon = $\frac{(n - 2) \times 180°}{n}$. This is known as the **Internal Angles Theorem (IAT) – Part 2**.

Example 9.2-a

Internal Angles of Regular Convex Polygons

Using the Internal Angles Theorem (IAT) - Part 2, calculate the measure of each internal angle of the first eight regular convex polygons, listed in Exhibit 9.2-b.

Solution

Using $\theta = \frac{(n-2) \times 180°}{n}$,

	Name of Polygon	Number of Sides (n)	Measure of Each Internal Angle
(i)	Triangle	3	$\theta = \frac{(3-2) \times 180°}{3} = \frac{180°}{3} = 60°$
(ii)	Square	4	$\theta = \frac{(4-2) \times 180°}{4} = \frac{360°}{4} = 90°$
(iii)	Pentagon	5	$\theta = \frac{(5-2) \times 180°}{5} = \frac{540°}{5} = 108°$
(iv)	Hexagon	6	$\theta = \frac{(6-2) \times 180°}{6} = \frac{720°}{6} = 120°$
(v)	Heptagon	7	$\theta = \frac{(7-2) \times 180°}{7} = \frac{900°}{7} \approx 128.6°$
(vi)	Octagon	8	$\theta = \frac{(8-2) \times 180°}{8} = \frac{1{,}080°}{8} = 135°$
(vii)	Nonagon	9	$\theta = \frac{(9-2) \times 180°}{9} = \frac{1{,}260°}{9} = 140°$
(viii)	Decagon	10	$\theta = \frac{(10-2) \times 180°}{10} = \frac{1{,}440°}{10} = 144°$

Example 9.2-b

Verifying a Special Case of the Internal Angles Theorem

A trapezoid is any four-sided convex polygon with one pair of opposite sides that are parallel to each other (see diagram below). Use the properties of parallel lines and transversal angles to prove that the Internal Angles Theorem (IAT) - Part 1 holds true for all trapezoids.

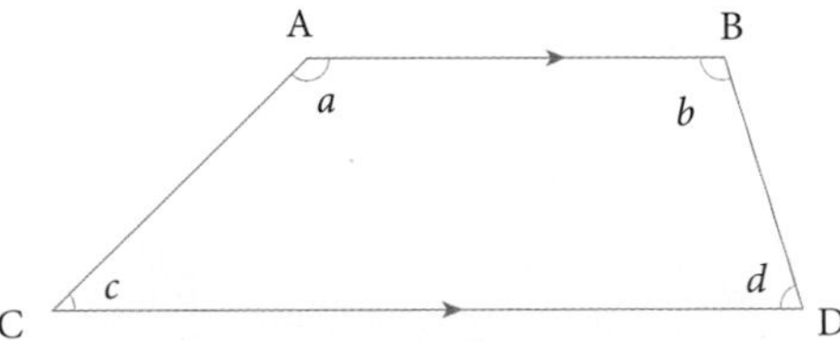

Solution

The IAT-1 states that the sum of the internal angles of any four-sided convex polygon is $(4-2) \times 180° = 360°$.

Since the line segment AB is parallel to the line segment CD, angles a and c are co-interior angles, and hence supplementary.

i.e., $\angle a + \angle c = 180°$ (1)

Similarly, angles b and d are also co-interior, and hence supplementary.

i.e., $\angle b + \angle d = 180°$ (2)

Adding (1) and (2) : $\angle a + \angle b + \angle c + \angle d = 360°$

Therefore, the sum of all four angles in the trapezoid is 360°, which validates the result of the IAT-1 formula. Hence, the formula is valid for all trapezoids.

External Angles of Polygons

An external angle of a simple polygon is the angle obtained by extending one of the sides at a vertex where two line segments meet, and measuring the angle formed outside the simple polygon. For example, an n-sided polygon will have n external angles.

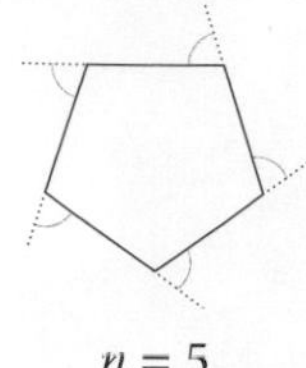

$n = 5$

(5 external angles)

The internal angle and the external angle at each vertex are supplementary i.e., the internal and external angles add to 180°. Since there are n vertices, the sum of all interior and exterior angles of an n-sided polygon = $n \times 180°$. However, we know from the Internal Angles Theorem - Part 1 that the sum of all the interior angles = $(n - 2) \times 180°$.

Putting this all together, the sum of all the exterior angles of an n-sided polygon is equal to the following:

$$n \times 180° - (n - 2)180°$$
$$= n \times 180° - n \times 180° + 2 \times 180°$$
$$= 360°$$

Therefore, the sum of the external angles formed by extending the sides of any n-sided, simple polygon = 360°. This is known as the **External Angles Theorem (EAT) – Part 1**.

Furthermore, every external angle in a *regular* n-sided *convex* polygon = $\frac{360°}{n}$. This is known as the **External Angles Theorem (EAT) – Part 2.**

Example 9.2-c External Angles of Regular Convex Polygons

Using the External Angles Theorem (EAT) - Part 2, calculate the measure of each external angle of the first eight regular convex polygons, listed in Exhibit 9.2-b.

Solution

Using $\theta = \frac{360°}{n}$,

	Name of Polygon	Number of Sides (n)	Measure of Each External Angle
(i)	Triangle	3	$\theta = \frac{360°}{3} = 120°$
(ii)	Square	4	$\theta = \frac{360°}{4} = 90°$
(iii)	Pentagon	5	$\theta = \frac{360°}{5} = 72°$
(iv)	Hexagon	6	$\theta = \frac{360°}{6} = 60°$
(v)	Heptagon	7	$\theta = \frac{360°}{7} \approx 51.4°$
(vi)	Octagon	8	$\theta = \frac{360°}{8} = 45°$
(vii)	Nonagon	9	$\theta = \frac{360°}{9} = 40°$
(viii)	Decagon	10	$\theta = \frac{360°}{10} = 36°$

Note: The internal angle and the external angle at every vertex of a convex polygon are supplementary, since each pair of internal and external angles together form a straight line.

Example 9.2-d **Application of the External Angles Theorem - Navigation**

A plane takes off, heading due west. Shortly after take-off, it turns 60° to the north (clockwise). Later on, it turns another 75° in the same (clockwise) direction. A few minutes later, it makes another turn of 80° in the same (clockwise) direction. Finally, it makes one last clockwise turn and heads back to its take-off point, flying in to the airstrip bearing due south. Find the bearing change (change in angle) of the final turn.

Solution

Based on the given information, draw a picture of the situation:

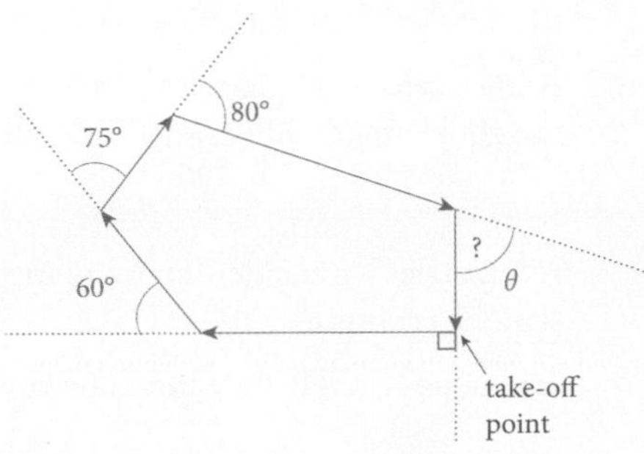

Using EAT-1, the sum of all exterior angles = 360°.

Let the final external angle be θ.

Then, $60° + 75° + 80° + \theta + 90° = 360°$

$$\theta = 360° - 305° = 55°.$$

Therefore, the bearing change of the final turn is 55°.

Classification and Properties of Triangles

We will now examine one type of convex polygon: triangles. A **triangle** (literally meaning "three-angles") is any polygon with three sides and three internal angles. We will now look at the different sub-categories and classifications of triangles and the various properties of the figures.

Using the IAT-1, the sum of the three internal angles of a triangle equals $(3 - 2) \times 180° = 1 \times 180° = 180°$. Therefore, since the sum of the internal angles equals 180°, each internal angle must be less than 180°, which means every triangle is a convex polygon.

$\angle A + \angle B + \angle C = 180°$

There are two ways to classify triangles: by angle measure and by side length.

Classification of Triangles by Angle Measures

Acute triangle (three acute angles)		A triangle with all three angles less than 90° (acute angle) is called an **acute triangle**.
Right triangle (one right angle)	$\theta = 90°$	A triangle with one angle of 90° (right angle) is called a **right triangle**. Since the sum of the three angles is 180° and one angle is 90°, this means that the other two angles must add up to 90°; therefore, they are acute and complementary.
Obtuse triangle (one obtuse angle)	$\theta > 90°$	A triangle with one angle greater than 90° (obtuse angle) is called an **obtuse triangle**. Since the sum of the three angles is 180° and one angle is greater than 90°, this means that the other two angles must add up to less than 90°; therefore, they are acute.

Classification of Triangles by Side Measures

Equilateral triangle (three equal sides)	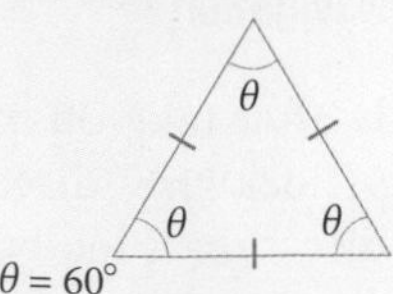	A triangle that has sides of equal length is called an **equilateral triangle**. Since an equilateral triangle is a regular polygon with 3 sides, by the IAT-2, each angle is 60°. Therefore, every equilateral triangle is also an acute triangle.
Isosceles triangle (two equal sides)	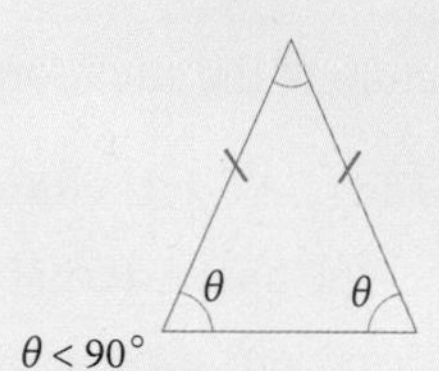	A triangle that has two sides of equal length is called an **isosceles triangle**. The angles opposite to the equal sides of an isosceles triangle will have equal measure. An isosceles triangle may be acute, right, or obtuse (but the equal angles will always be acute).
Scalene triangle (no equal sides)	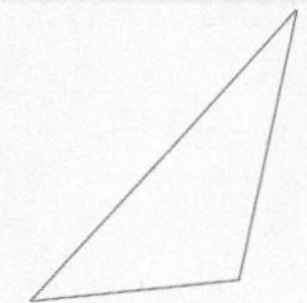	A triangle with sides of different lengths is called a **scalene triangle**. A scalene triangle may be acute, right, or obtuse.

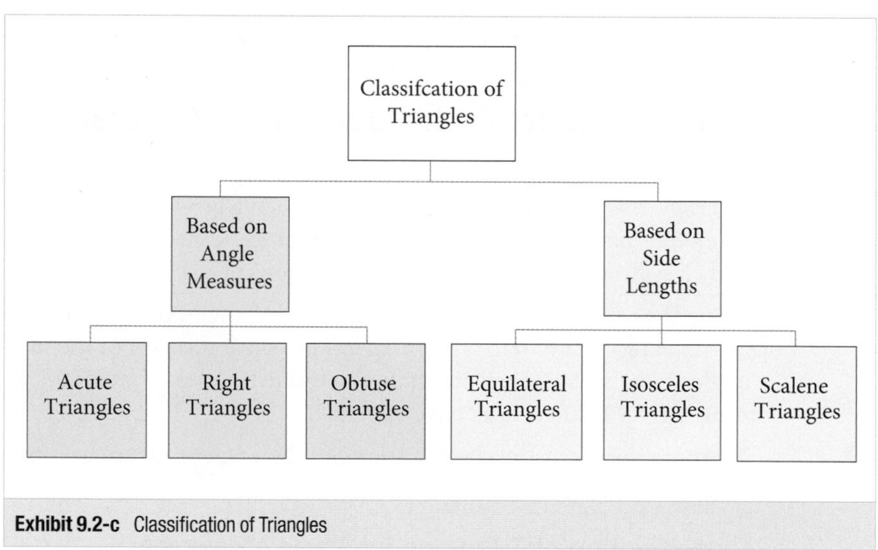

Exhibit 9.2-c Classification of Triangles

Note: It is common for the vertices to be labelled using capital letters and the sides to be labelled using lower case letters, with the capitals and lower case letters corresponding to each other on opposite sides of the triangle, as shown in the diagram.

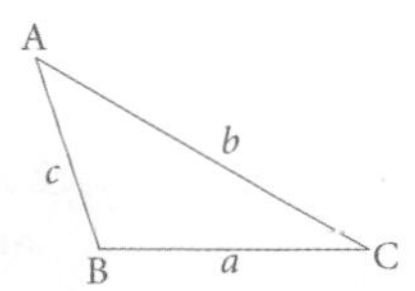

Example 9.2-e

Classifying Triangles

Classify the following triangles by angle measure and by side length:

(i)

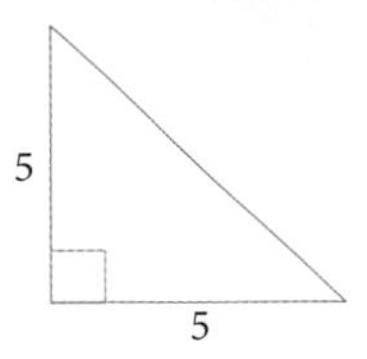

(ii)

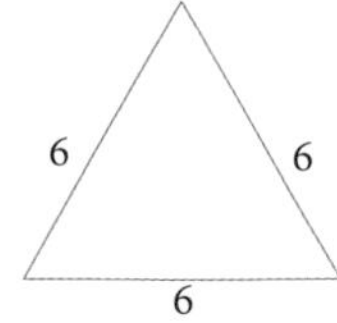

(iii)

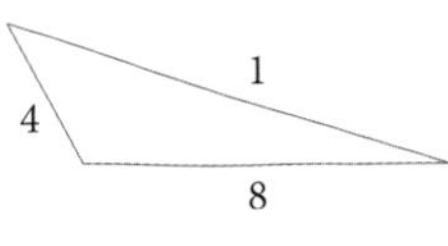

(iv)

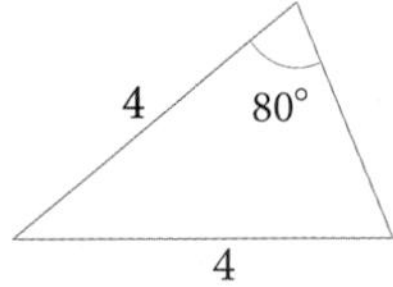

(v)

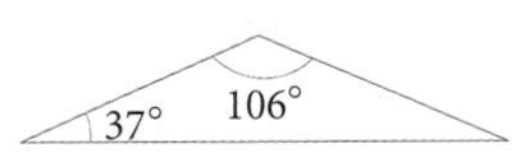

(vi)

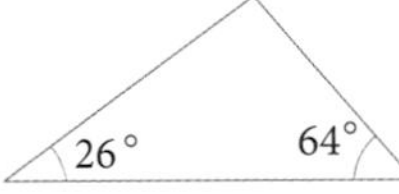

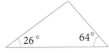

Solution

(i)	Right and Isosceles triangle	(ii)	Acute and Equilateral triangle	(iii)	Obtuse and Scalene triangle
(iv)	Acute and Isosceles triangle	(v)	Obtuse and Isosceles triangle	(vi)	Right and Scalene triangle

Example 9.2-f

Calculating Unknown Angles in a Triangle

Using the Internal Angles Theorem (IAT) - Part 1, calculate the measure of the unknown angle in each of the following triangles. Then, classify the triangle by angle measure and by side length.

(i) ΔXYZ, $\angle YXZ = 30°$, $\angle XYZ = 120°$

(ii) ΔABC, $\angle BAC = 35°$, $\angle ACB = 55°$

(iii) ΔRST, $\angle RST = 60°$, $\angle STR = 60°$

Solution

(i) $\angle Z = 180° - (30° + 120°) = 30°$

Since $\angle Y > 90°$, ΔXYZ is an **Obtuse triangle.**

Since $\angle X = \angle Z$, ΔXYZ is an **Isosceles triangle.**

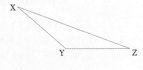

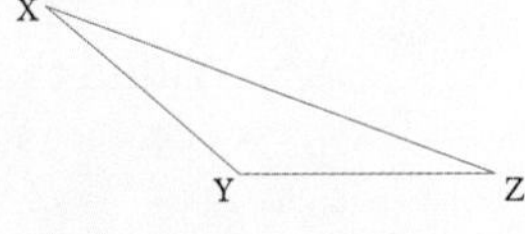

(ii) $\angle B = 180° - (35° + 55°) = 90°$

Since $\angle B = 90°$, ΔABC is a **Right triangle.**

Since no angles are equal, ΔABC is a **Scalene triangle.**

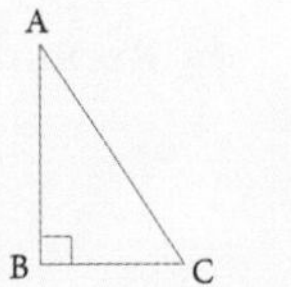

(iii) $\angle R = 180° - (60° + 60°) = 60°$

Since all angles are less than 90°, ΔRST is an **Acute triangle.**

Since all angles are equal, ΔRST is an **Equilateral triangle.**

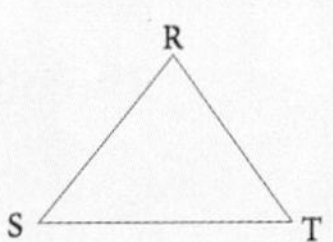

Example 9.2-g

Application of Triangles - Distances Between Cities

The flying distance from Toronto to Sudbury is the same as that of Toronto to Ottawa, which is approximately 345 km. The angle from Toronto between Sudbury and Ottawa is 76°. What kind of triangle is created between the three cities?

Solution

Since the distance between Toronto and Sudbury is equal to the distance between Toronto and Ottawa, the angles opposite to these sides are equal.

Solution *continued*

Let the equal angles be θ.

$$\theta + \theta + 76° = 180°$$
$$2\theta = 180° - 76°$$
$$2\theta = 104°$$
$$\theta = \frac{104°}{2} = 52°$$

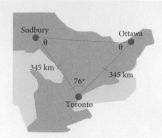

The angles are 52°, 52°, and 76°.

Two sides are equal and all three angles are less than 90°.

Therefore, the triangle created is an acute, isosceles triangle.

Classification and Properties of Quadrilaterals

We will now examine another class of convex polygons and their properties: convex quadrilaterals.

A **quadrilateral** (literally meaning "four-sided") is any polygon with four sides and four internal angles. In this section, we will examine **convex quadrilaterals** only, in which each of the internal angles is less than 180°.

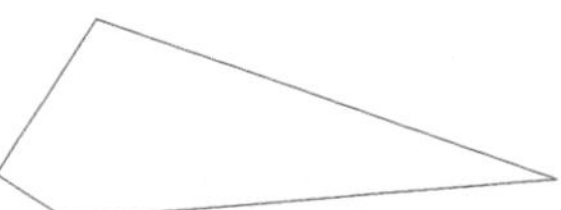

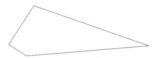

There are two main classes of quadrilaterals: parallelograms, which have special properties, and non-parallelograms.

A **parallelogram** is a quadrilateral with opposite sides that are parallel. As a result, in a parallelogram, the opposite sides are equal, the opposite angles are equal, and the adjacent angles are supplementary ($\theta + \varphi = 180°$). A **non-parallelogram** is a quadrilateral with at least one set of opposite sides that are not parallel.

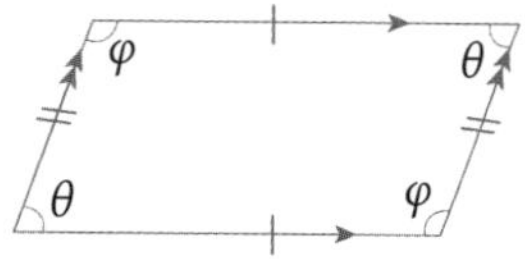

Classification of Quadrilaterals that are Parallelograms

Within the class of parallelograms, there are three sub-classes:

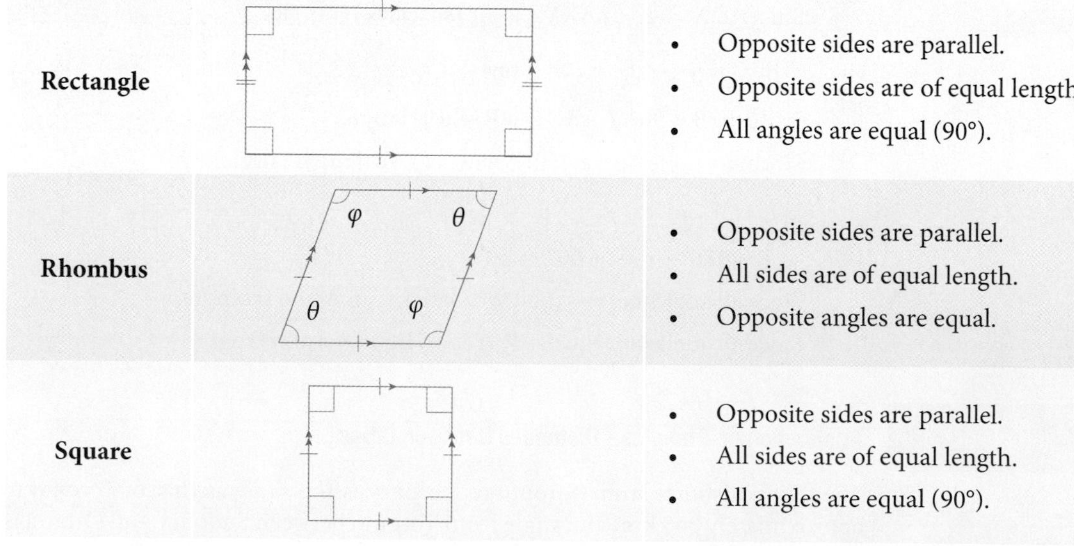

Rectangle		• Opposite sides are parallel. • Opposite sides are of equal length. • All angles are equal (90°).
Rhombus	φ θ θ φ	• Opposite sides are parallel. • All sides are of equal length. • Opposite angles are equal.
Square		• Opposite sides are parallel. • All sides are of equal length. • All angles are equal (90°).

Note: A parallelogram that is not a rectangle, square, or rhombus is known simply as a parallelogram.

Classification of Quadrilaterals that are Non-Parallelograms

Within the class of non-parallelograms, there are two sub-classes:

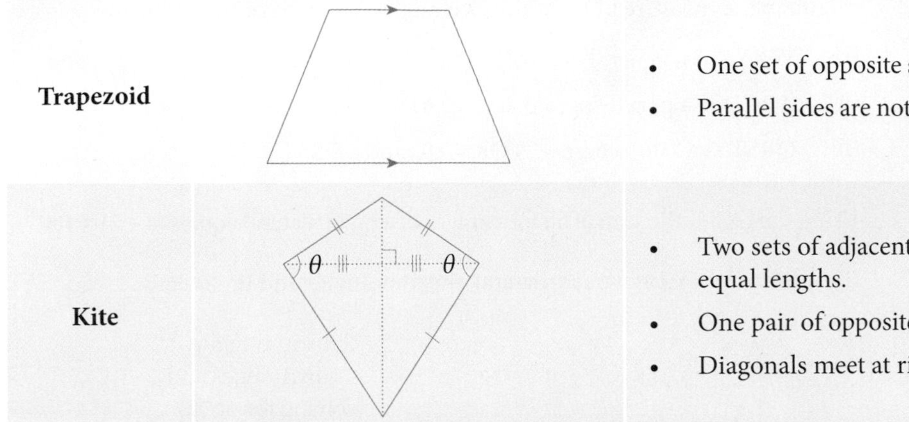

Trapezoid		• One set of opposite sides are parallel. • Parallel sides are not of equal lengths.
Kite		• Two sets of adjacent sides are of equal lengths. • One pair of opposite angles is equal. • Diagonals meet at right angles.

Note: A quadrilateral that is a non-parallelogram, which is neither a trapezoid nor a kite is known simply as a quadrilateral.

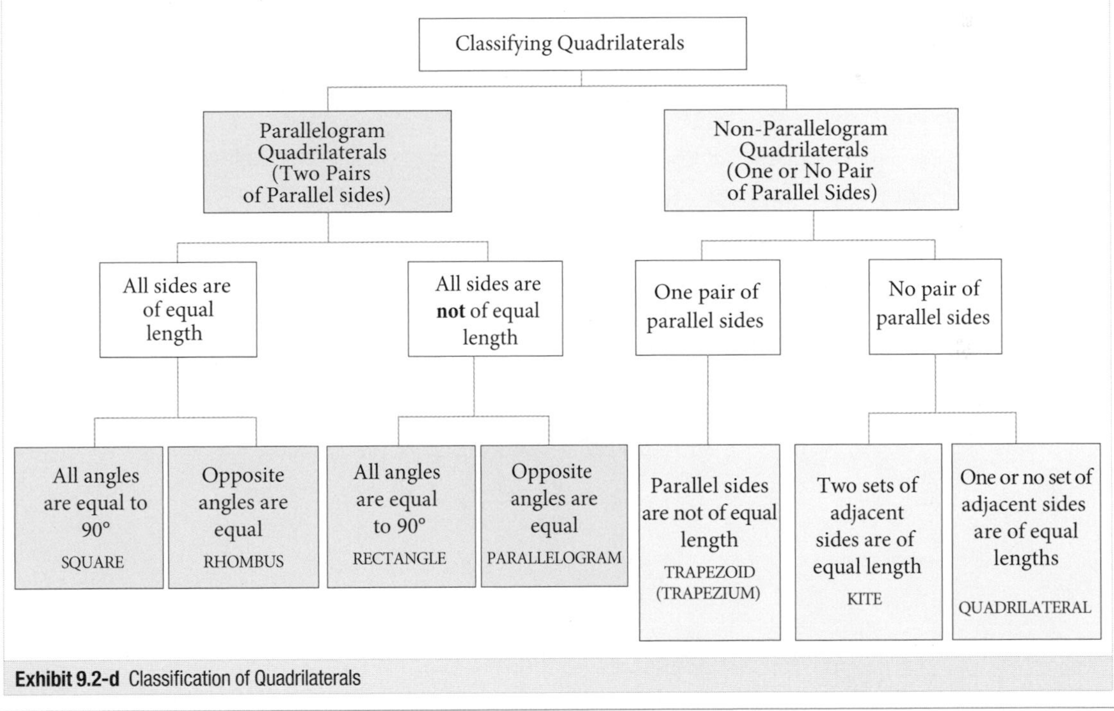

Exhibit 9.2-d Classification of Quadrilaterals

Example 9.2-h **Classifying Quadrilaterals**

Classify the following quadrilaterals:

(i)

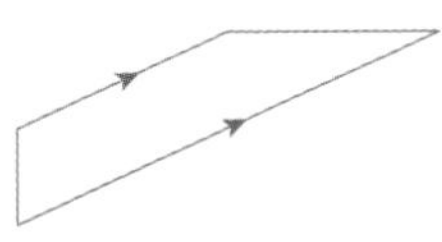

(ii)

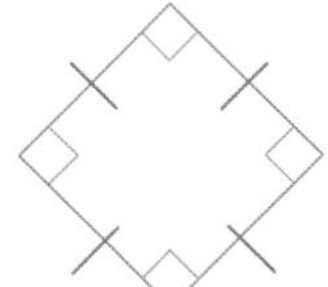

(iii)

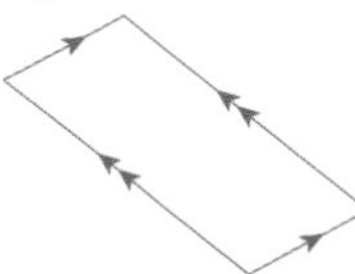

Solution

(i) One pair of opposite sides is parallel – **Trapezoid**

(ii) All sides are of equal length and all angles are equal (90°) – **Square**

(iii) Opposite sides are parallel – **Parallelogram**

Example 9.2-i Calculating Unknown Angles in a Quadrilateral

Using the Internal Angles Theorem (IAT) - Part 1 and the properties of various quadrilaterals, calculate the measure of the unknown angle(s) in each of the following:

(i) WXYZ is a general quadrilateral, $\angle XWZ = 72°$, $\angle WXY = 106°$, and $\angle XYZ = 55°$.

(ii) ABCD is a parallelogram and $\angle ADC = 25°$.

(iii) QRST is a kite, where $\angle TQR = 80°$ and $\angle RST = 50°$.

Solution

Using the IAT-1, the sum of all four angles of a quadrilateral equals $(4 - 2) \times 180° = 2 \times 180° = 360°$

(i) Since WXYZ is a quadrilateral, the four angles add up to 360°.

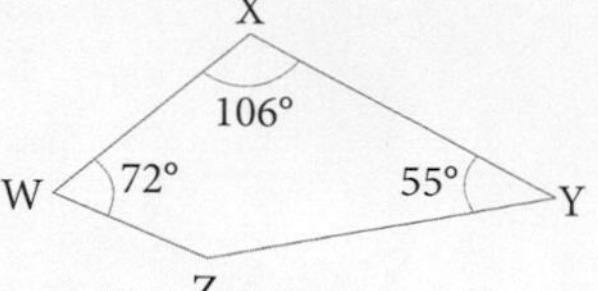

$\angle W + \angle X + \angle Y + \angle Z = 360°$ Substituting the known values and solving for $\angle Z$,

$$\angle Z = 360° - (72° + 106° + 55°) = 360° - 233° = 127°$$

(ii) Since ABCD is a parallelogram, the opposite angles are congruent and adjacent angles are supplementary. Therefore,

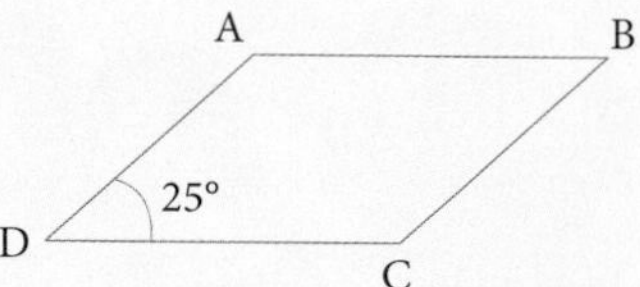

$\angle B = \angle D = 25°$ Opposite angles are equal.

$\angle A = \angle C = 180° - 25° = 155°$ Adjacent angles are supplementary.

(iii) Since QRST is a kite, one pair of opposite angles is equal, and since $\angle Q \neq \angle S$, then $\angle R = \angle T$.
Let θ represent the measure of each of the two equal angles:

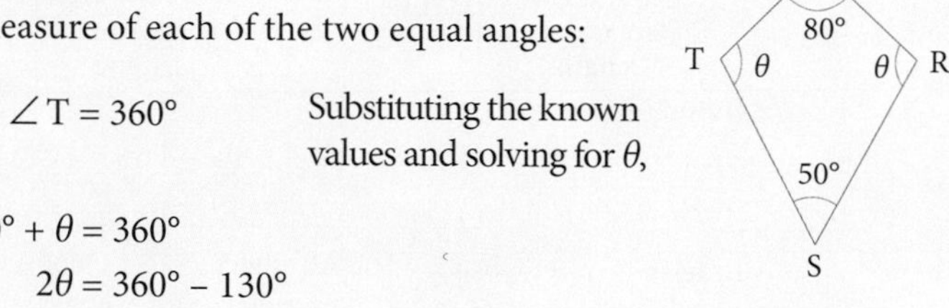

$\angle Q + \angle R + \angle S + \angle T = 360°$ Substituting the known values and solving for θ,

$$80° + \theta + 50° + \theta = 360°$$
$$2\theta = 360° - 130°$$
$$2\theta = 230°$$
$$\theta = \frac{230°}{2} = 115°$$

Therefore, $\angle R = \angle T = 115°$.

Example 9.2-j Identifying Quadrilaterals Based on Angle Measures

For the following quadrilaterals, use the Internal Angles Theorem (IAT) - Part 1 to determine the missing angle measure, and then classify the type of quadrilateral based on their angle measures:

(i) EFGH, given that $\angle E = 64°$, $\angle F = 116°$, and $\angle H = 90°$

(ii) MNOP, given that $\angle M = 112°$, $\angle N = 58°$, and $\angle O = 112°$

(iii) STUV, given that $\angle S = 45°$, $\angle U = 45°$, and $\angle V = 135°$

Solution

Using the IAT-1, the sum of all four angles of a quadrilateral is 360°.

(i) $\angle E + \angle F + \angle G + \angle H = 360°$ Substituting the known values and solving for $\angle G$,

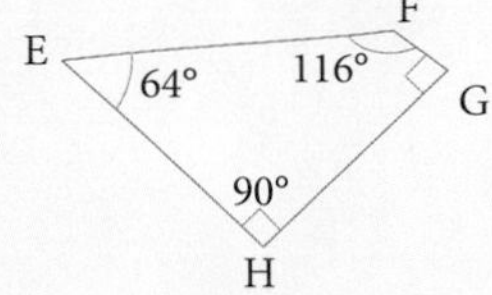

$\angle G = 360° - (64° + 116° + 90°) = 90°$

Therefore, $\angle G + \angle H = 180°$

$\angle E + \angle F = 180°$

Since adjacent angles are supplementary, one opposite pair of sides is parallel (i.e., $\overline{EH} \,//\, \overline{FG}$).

Since opposite angles are not congruent, the other opposite pair of sides, $\overline{EF}$ and $\overline{GH}$, are not parallel.

Therefore, EFGH is a trapezoid.

(ii) $\angle M + \angle N + \angle O + \angle P = 360°$ Substituting the known values and solving for $\angle P$,

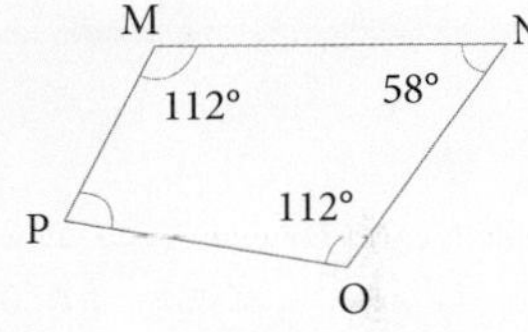

$\angle P = 360° - (112° + 58° + 112°) = 78°$

Knowing that there is one pair of congruent opposite angles is not sufficient to determine the type of quadrilateral. However, we can narrow down the choices to two: a kite or a general quadrilateral.

(iii) $\angle S + \angle T + \angle U + \angle V = 360°$ Substituting the known values and solving for $\angle T$,

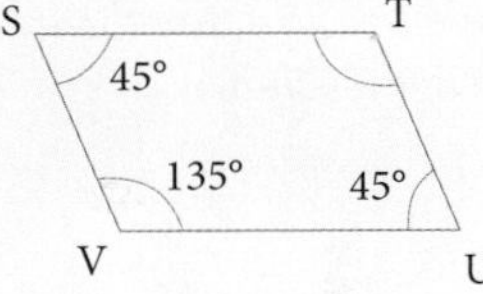

$\angle T = 360° - (45° + 45° + 135°) = 135°$

Since both pairs of opposite angles are congruent and not equal to 90°, STUV is either a parallelogram or a rhombus (we cannot tell which without knowing the side lengths).

Example 9.2-k **Constructing Quadrilaterals**

Jeremy labels a point A on his paper and draws a straight line 20 cm long to another point B. From there, he uses a compass to measure a 90° angle from $\overline{\textbf{AB}}$ and draws a line from point B to a third point C, that is perpendicular to $\overline{\textbf{AB}}$ and is 15 cm long. How many different types of quadrilaterals can Jeremy create by plotting a fourth point D and then connecting the line segments $\overline{\textbf{CD}}$ and $\overline{\textbf{DA}}$?

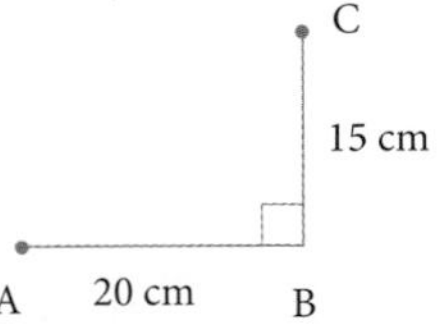

Solution

Since the lengths of two sides are different, Jeremy cannot create a square or a rhombus. Since the angle is a right angle, he cannot create a general parallelogram, either. However, he can create four other kinds of quadrilaterals:

Option A: Jeremy can create a **rectangle** by measuring out another right angle from point C and drawing a line segment $\overline{\textbf{CD}}$ parallel to $\overline{\textbf{AB}}$ and 20 cm long.

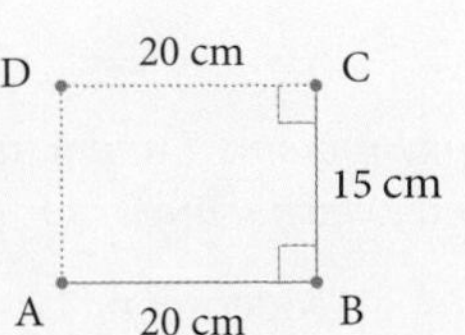

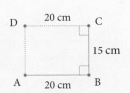

Solution
continued

Option B: Jeremy can create a **trapezoid** by measuring out another right angle from point C and drawing a line segment $\overline{CD}$ parallel to $\overline{AB}$ but of a length other than 20 cm.

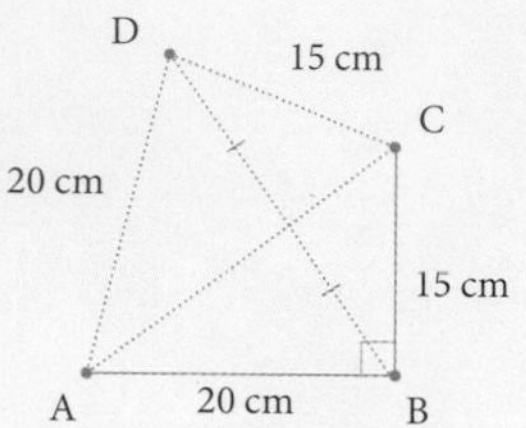

Option C: Jeremy can create a **kite** by drawing a dashed line from point A to point C, then drawing a line segment from point B to a fourth point D that is perpendicular to $\overline{AC}$ and twice the length from B to $\overline{AC}$.

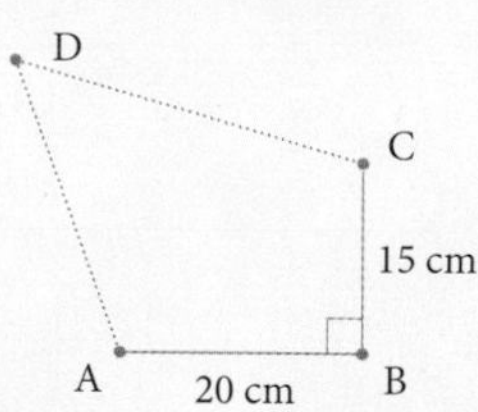

Option D: Jeremy can create a **general quadrilateral** by placing point D in any location that is any distance, other than 15 cm, away from C and not parallel to $\overline{AB}$.

D
C
15 cm
A
20 cm
B

9.2 | Exercises

Answers to odd-numbered problems are available at the end of the textbook.

For Problems 1 to 4, use the Internal or External Angle Theorems (IAT or EAT) to determine the measure of the unknown angle θ for the figures shown.

1.

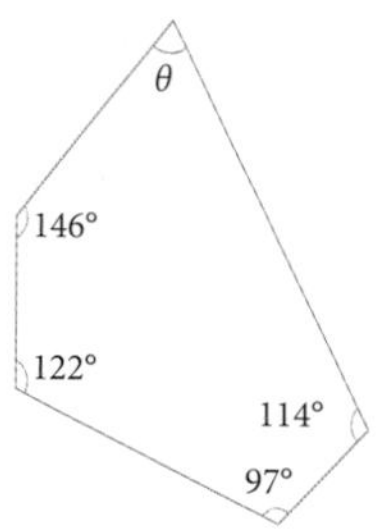

2.

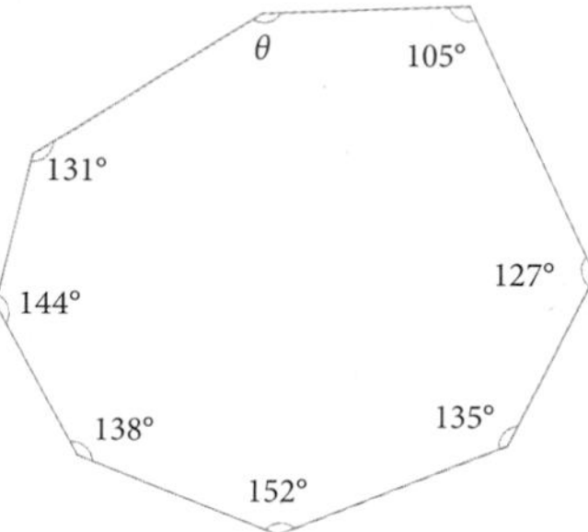

3.

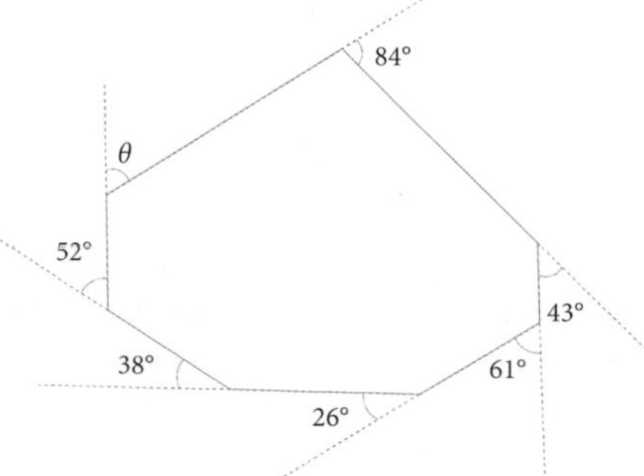

4.

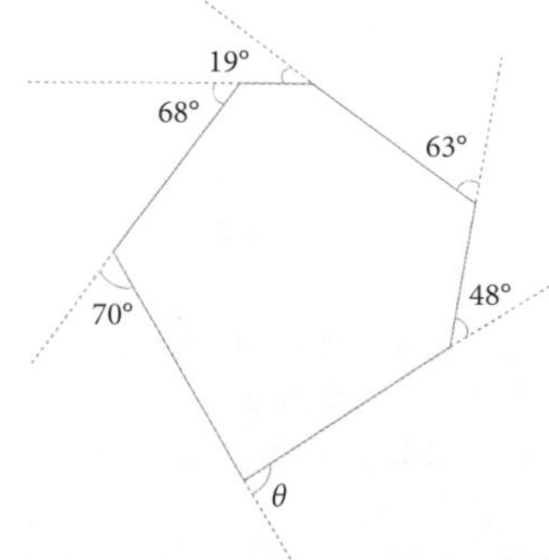

For Problems 5 and 6, use the Internal and External Angle Theorems (IAT and EAT) to determine the measure of the internal and external angles for the regular convex polygons.

5. a. Dodecagon (12 sides) b. Icosagon (20 sides)

6. a. Hexadecagon (16 sides) b. Hectogon (100 sides)

For Problems 7 and 8, the internal or external angle measure of a regular polygon is provided. Using the External Angle Theorem (EAT) - Part 2, determine the number of sides in the regular polygon.

7. a. External angle measure is 12°
   b. Internal angle measure is 175°
   Hint: first find the measure of the external angle.

8. a. External angle measure is 15°
   b. Internal angle measure is 165°
   Hint: first find the measure of the external angle.

9. A sailboat in a race heads West on the opening stretch of the race. At the first checkpoint, the boat makes a 66° turn to port (left) and sails towards the second checkpoint, where it then makes a 112° turn to port. It then continues toward the third checkpoint, makes a 75° turn to port and heads to the fourth and final checkpoint, where it makes a final turn to port until it faces due West again, and heads back toward the starting line to complete the circuit. Determine the degree measure of the final turn knowing that the fourth check point forms an angle of 150° with the port (starting point).

10. The owners of a house with a backyard in the shape of an irregular hexagon (6 sides) are putting up a fence around their yard, except for one side of their yard which is tree-lined. Using a city survey, the owners have laid down guidelines and have determined the angles at each of the corners, except where the fence meets the trees. Use the diagram and measurements below to determine the unknown angle.

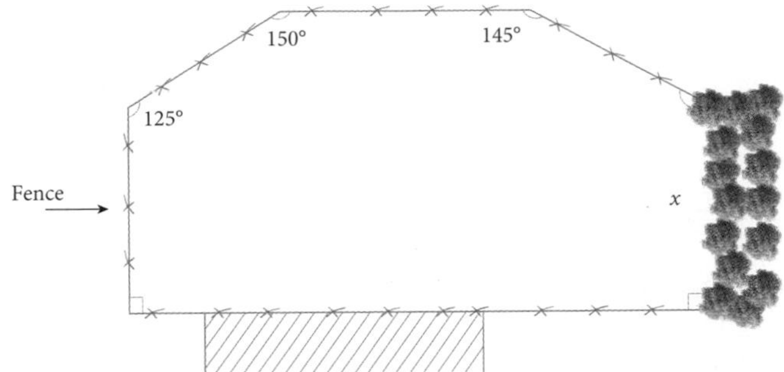

11. In an acute isosceles triangle, the measure of the unique angle is 2° less than three-fifths of the measures of each of the other two angles. Find the degree measures of all three internal angles.

12. In a parallelogram, the degree measure of the larger pair of congruent angles is 5° more than six times the degree measure of the smaller pair of congruent angles. Determine the degree measures of both pairs of congruent angles.

13. In an obtuse scalene triangle, the measure of the larger internal acute angle is 60°. The measure of the external angle to the obtuse angle is 6° greater than three times the measure of the smallest internal acute angle. Determine the measure of the internal obtuse angle.

14. Use the Internal Angle Theorem - Part 1 for triangles to show that any external angle of a triangle is equal to the sum of the two internal opposite angles.

For Problems 15 and 16, classify the triangles shown by side length and angle measure:

15. a.
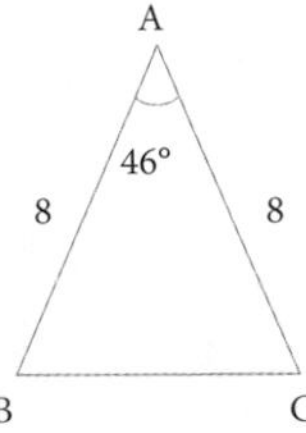

b.
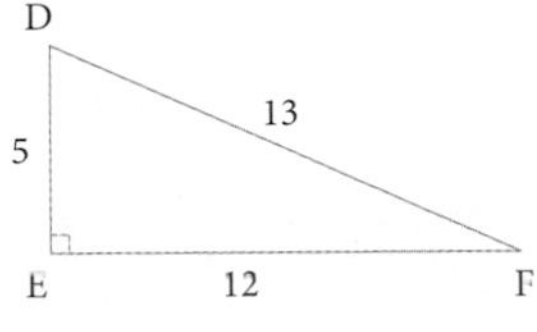

c.
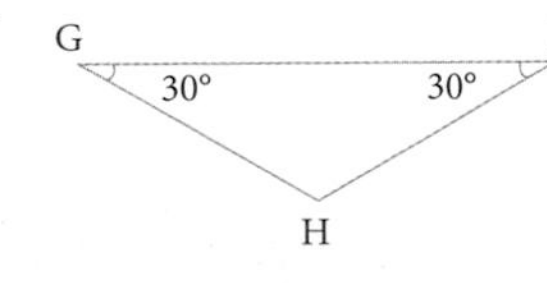

16. a.
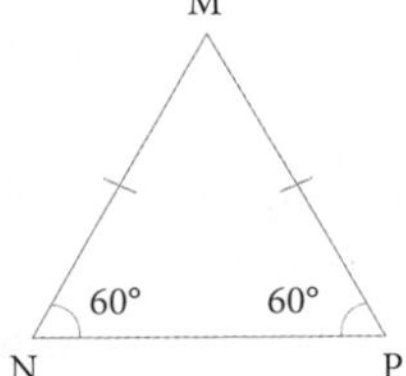

b.
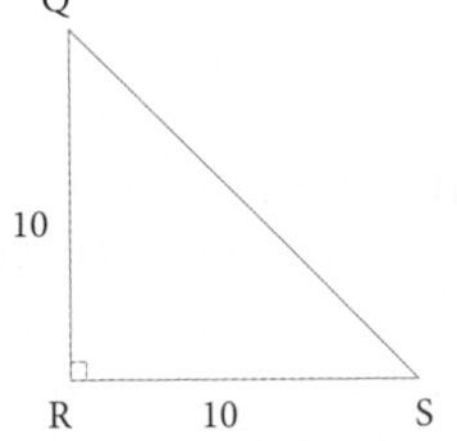

c.
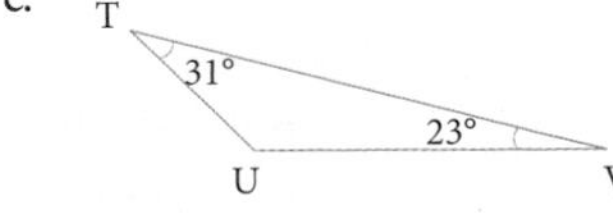

For Problems 17 and 18, classify the quadrilaterals shown:

17. a.

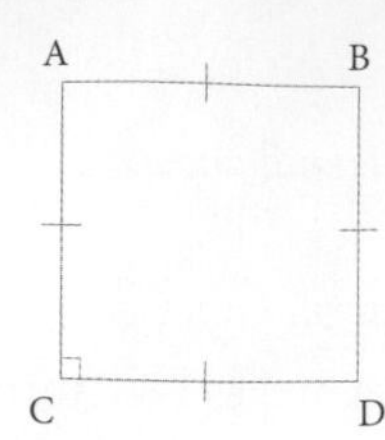

b.

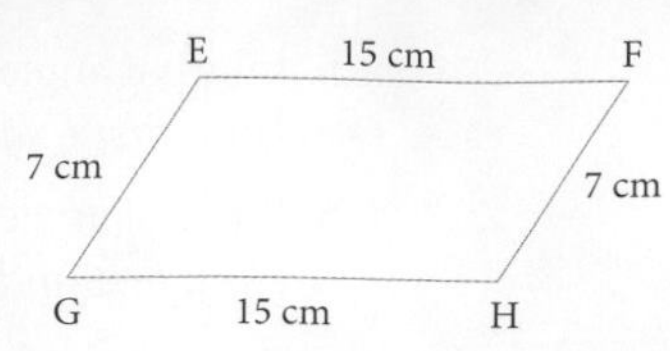

c.

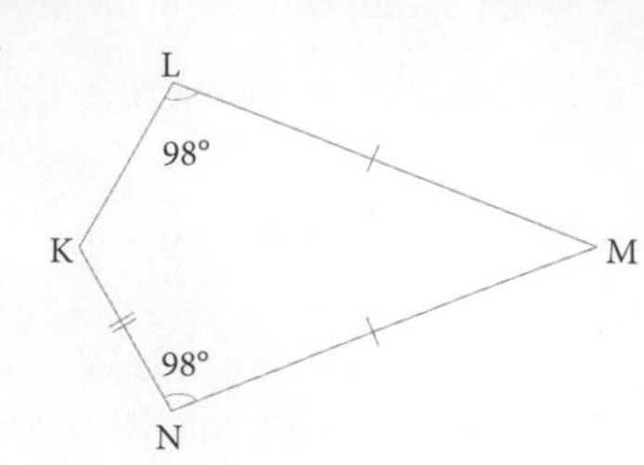

18. a.

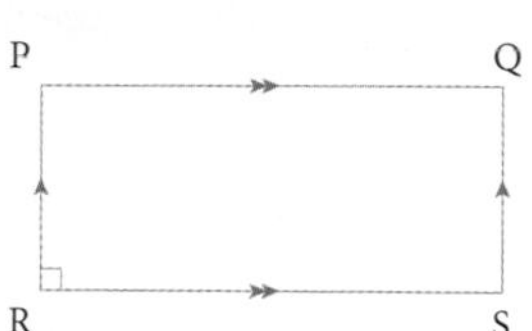

b.

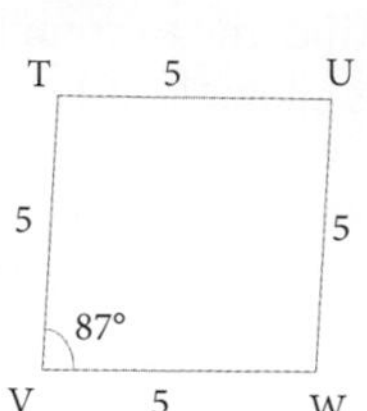

c.

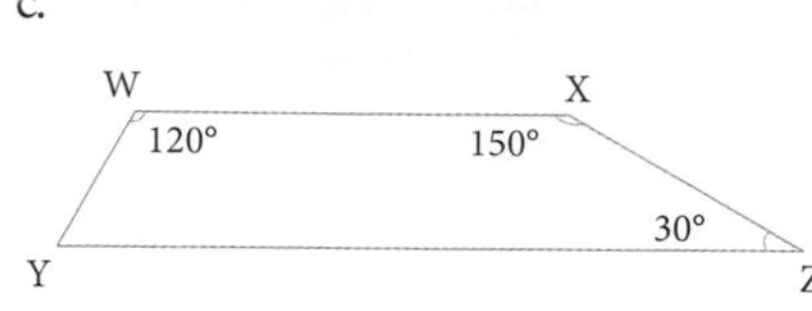

For Problems 19 to 22, determine the missing angle(s) for each quadrilateral ABCD:

19. ABCD is a rectangle

20. ABCD is a rhombus, with $\angle A = 77°$

21. ABCD is a kite, with $\overline{AB} = \overline{BC}$, $\overline{AD} = \overline{DC}$, $\angle A = 105°$, and $\angle D = 52°$

22. ABCD is a trapezoid, with $\overline{AB}$ parallel to $\overline{CD}$, $\angle A = 93°$, and $\angle B = 116°$

For Problems 23 to 26, classify the quadrilateral ABCD based on the properties given:

23. $\overline{AB} = \overline{BC} = \overline{CD} = \overline{DA}$ and $\angle A = 90°$

24. $\overline{AB} = \overline{CD}$, $\overline{BC} = \overline{DA}$, and $\angle A = 105°$

25. $\overline{AB} = \overline{BC} = \overline{CD} = 15$ cm, $\overline{DA} = 27$ cm, and $\overline{BC}$ is parallel to $\overline{DA}$

26. $\overline{AB} = \overline{BC} = 20$ cm, $\overline{AD} = \overline{DC} = 30$ cm, and $\angle A = \angle C$.

For Problems 27 to 30, state the names of all the possible quadrilaterals based on the given property:

27. a. 4 equal angles   b. 4 equal sides

28. a. 4 right angles   b. No equal sides

29. a. 2 pairs of parallel sides   b. 2 pairs of equal angles

30. a. At least 1 pair of parallel sides   b. At least 1 pair of equal angles

9.3 | Perimeters and Areas of Plane Geometric Figures

In the previous section, we introduced the concept of **plane figures**; i.e., geometric objects that can be drawn in the 2-dimensional Cartesian plane. In this section, we will introduce two important measurements of those figures: perimeter and area.

The **perimeter** (P) of a plane figure is the total length of the boundary of the plane figure. In a polygon, the perimeter is the sum of the lengths of the line segments (sides) that form the boundary of the polygon.

The **area** (A) of a plane figure is the amount of 2-dimensional surface that is enclosed within the figure. Area is measured using square units – e.g., square centimetre (cm^2), square metre (m^2), square inch (in^2), or square foot (ft^2); that is, the amount of surface occupied by squares with the respective side lengths.

Squares and Rectangles

A **square** is a quadrilateral with four sides of equal length and four right angles; therefore, it is a regular polygon. We denote the length of each equal **side** by the letter s.

A **rectangle** is a quadrilateral with four right angles and opposite sides of equal length; it is differentiated from a square by the property that the sides do not need to be the same length. We denote the longer side by the letter l (for **length**), and the shorter side by the letter w (for **width**).

		Perimeter	Area
Square	s, s	$P = 4s$	$A = s^2$
Rectangle	w, l	$P = 2l + 2w$ $P = 2(l + w)$	$A = l \times w$

Example 9.3-a **Calculating the Perimeter and Area of Squares and Rectangles**

Calculate the perimeter and area of the following figures:

(i)

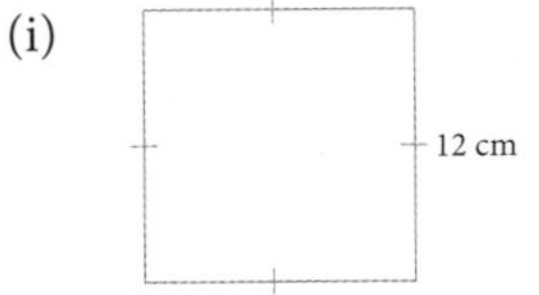

(ii)

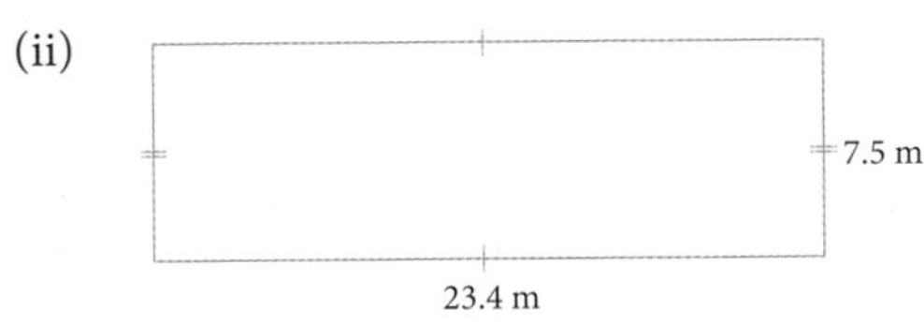

Solution

(i) The figure is a square.

Using $P = 4s$,

$$P = 4(12 \text{ cm}) = 48 \text{ cm}$$

Using $A = s^2$,

$$A = (12 \text{ cm})^2 = 144 \text{ cm}^2$$

Therefore, the perimeter is 48 cm and the area is 144 cm^2.

(ii) The figure is a rectangle.

Using $P = 2l + 2w$,

$$P = 2(23.4 \text{ m}) + 2(7.5 \text{ m}) = 61.8 \text{ m}$$

Using $A = l \times w$,

$$A = (23.4 \text{ m})(7.5 \text{ m}) = 175.5 \text{ m}^2$$

Therefore, the perimeter is 61.8 m and the area is 175.5 m^2.

Example 9.3-b **Determining the Cost to Lay a Rectangular Garden**

A rectangular garden is being built to be 6.5 m long and 3.2 m wide. The fencing for the garden costs \$2.95/m and the soil costs \$6.25/m^2. Calculate the cost to lay the garden.

Solution

Using $P = 2l + 2w$,

$$P = 2(6.5 \text{ m}) + 2(3.2 \text{ m}) = 19.4 \text{ m}$$

$$\text{Fencing cost} = \frac{\$2.95}{1 \text{ m}} \times 19.4 \text{ m} = \$57.23$$

$w = 3.2$ m

$l = 6.5$ m

Using $A = l \times w$,

$$A = (6.5 \text{ m})(3.2 \text{ m}) = 20.8 \text{ m}^2$$

$$\text{Soil cost} = \frac{\$6.25}{1 \text{ m}^2} \times 20.8 \text{ m}^2 = \$130.00$$

Total cost = \$57.23 + \$130.00 = \$187.23

Therefore, the total cost to lay the garden is \$187.23.

Example 9.3-c **Calculating the Area of a Square Given the Perimeter**

A square picture is being framed around its border with 180 cm of wood. What area of glass is needed to frame the picture?

Solution

Perimeter of the square frame, P = 180 cm.

$$P = 4s$$

Rearranging the formula for s,

$$s = \frac{P}{4}$$

Substituting P = 180 cm,

$$s = \frac{180 \text{ cm}}{4} = 45 \text{ cm}$$

Using $A = s^2$,

$$A = (45 \text{ cm})^2 = 2{,}025 \text{ cm}^2$$

Therefore, the area of glass needed to frame the picture is 2,025 cm^2.

Rhombuses and Parallelograms

A **rhombus** is a quadrilateral whose sides are all equal in length; it is differentiated from a square by the property that the angles are not right angles. We denote the length of each side by the letter b, and the perpendicular height by the letter h.

Rhombuses, like squares, have four equal sides, which makes the calculation of the perimeter of a rhombus the same as that of a square.

The area of a rhombus is determined as follows:

Draw a perpendicular line from the top corner of the rhombus to its base. This is the **height**, h, of the rhombus. "Cut" the resulting triangle that is created and "paste" it on the opposite side. The result is a rectangle with length b and width h, as shown in the diagram below:

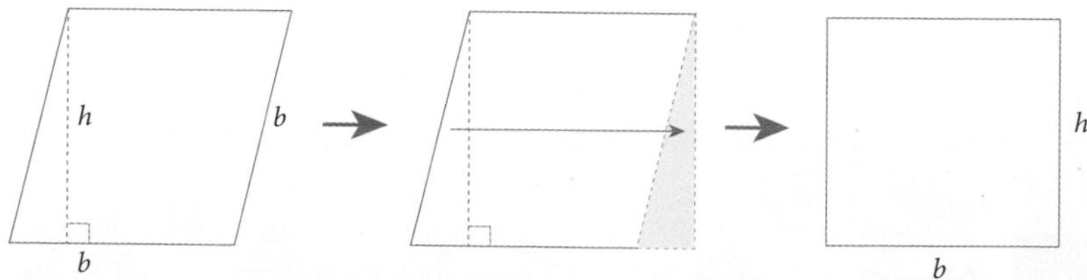

A **parallelogram** is a quadrilateral whose opposite sides are equal and parallel. It is differentiated from a rectangle by the property that the angles are not right angles. We denote the length of the **base** by the letter b, the length of the slant side by the letter a, and the perpendicular **height** by the letter h.

The calculation of the perimeter of a parallelogram is equal to that of a rectangle, replacing the letters l and w with a and b.

The area of a parallelogram is determined using the same procedure as that of a rhombus.

		Perimeter	Area
Rhombus		$P = 4b$	$A = b \times h$
Parallelogram		$P = 2a + 2b$ $P = 2(a + b)$	

Example 9.3-d

Calculating the Perimeter and Area of Rhombuses and Parallelograms

Calculate the perimeter and area of the following figures:

(i) (ii)

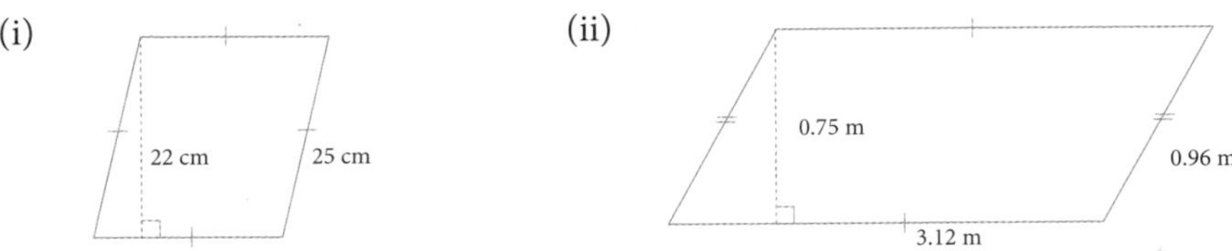

Solution

(i) The figure is a rhombus.

Using $P = 4b$,

$$P = 4(25 \text{ cm}) = 100 \text{ cm}$$

Using $A = b \times h$,

$$A = (25 \text{ cm})(22 \text{ cm}) = 550 \text{ cm}^2$$

Therefore, the perimeter is 100 cm and the area is 550 cm^2.

(ii) The figure is a parallelogram.

Using $P = 2a + 2b$,

$$P = 2(0.96 \text{ m}) + 2(3.12 \text{ m}) = 8.16 \text{ m}$$

Using $A = b \times h$,

$$A = (3.12 \text{ m})(0.75 \text{ m}) = 2.34 \text{ m}^2$$

Therefore, the perimeter is 8.16 m and the area is 2.34 m^2.

Trapezoids

A **trapezoid** is a quadrilateral with one pair of opposite sides that are parallel; it is differentiated from a parallelogram by the property that the other pair of opposite sides are not parallel. Since all four sides may have different lengths, we denote the length of the smaller parallel side by the letter a, the length of the larger parallel side by the letter b, and the lengths of the other two sides by the letters c and d. Again, we denote the perpendicular height by the letter h.

The perimeter of a trapezoid is the sum of the four side lengths, a, b, c, and d.

To calculate the area of a trapezoid, "copy" the trapezoid, rotate the image by 180°, and "paste" it to the original trapezoid, as shown below. The result will be a parallelogram with an area of $(a + b) \times h$.

The area of the trapezoid is half the area of the parallelogram $= \frac{1}{2}(a + b) \times h$.

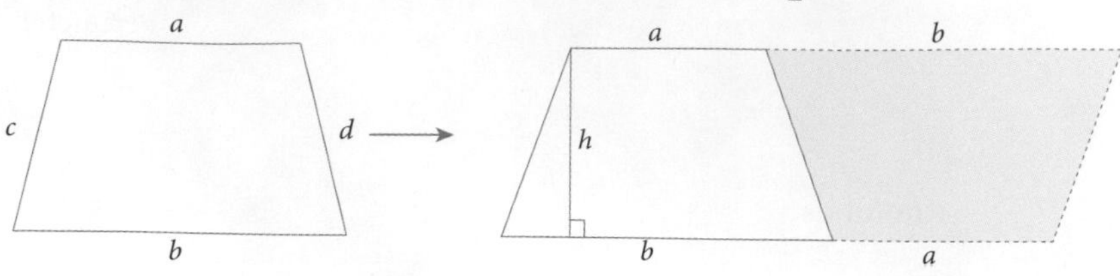

		Perimeter	Area
Trapezoid		$P = a + b + c + d$	$A = \frac{1}{2}(a + b) \times h$

Example 9.3-e Calculating the Perimeter and Area of a Trapezoid

Calculate the perimeter and area of the following trapezoid:

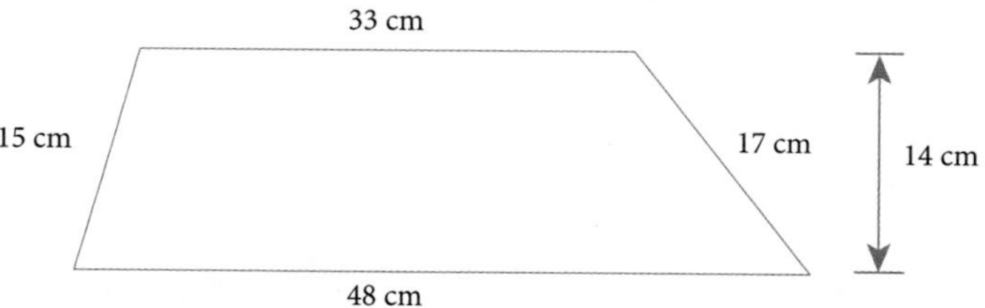

Solution

Using $P = a + b + c + d$,

$$P = 33 \text{ cm} + 48 \text{ cm} + 15 \text{ cm} + 17 \text{ cm} = 113 \text{ cm}$$

Using $A = \frac{1}{2}(a + b) \times h$,

$$A = \frac{1}{2}(33 \text{ cm} + 48 \text{ cm})(14 \text{ cm})$$

$$= \frac{1}{2}(81 \text{ cm})(14 \text{ cm}) = 567 \text{ cm}^2$$

Therefore, the perimeter of the trapezoid is 113 cm and the area of the trapezoid is 567 cm^2.

Example 9.3-f Determining the Cost of Fencing and Sodding a Trapezoidal Lawn

A house on the corner of a crescent has a backyard in the shape of a trapezoid, with the dimensions given on the figure below. If fencing costs \$25.00 per linear foot and sod costs \$0.40 per square foot, how much will it cost to fence and sod the backyard?

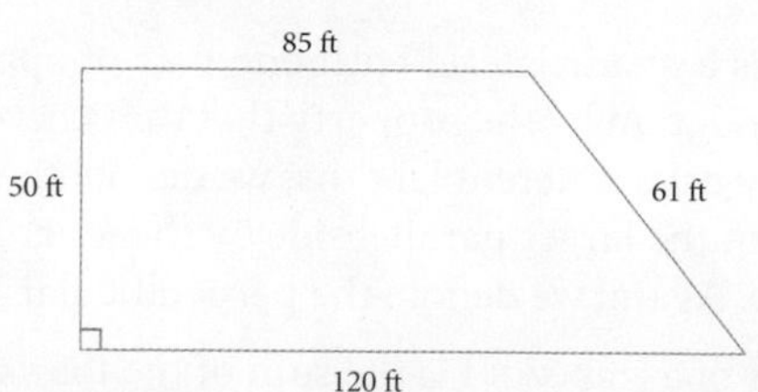

Solution

Using $P = a + b + c + d$,

$$P = 85 \text{ ft} + 120 \text{ ft} + 50 \text{ ft} + 61 \text{ ft} = 316 \text{ ft}$$

$$\text{Fencing Cost} = \frac{\$25.00}{1 \text{ ft}} \times 316 \text{ ft} = \$7{,}900.00$$

Using $A = \frac{1}{2}(a + b) \times h$,

$$A = \frac{1}{2}(85 \text{ ft} + 120 \text{ ft}) \times 50 \text{ ft} = \frac{1}{2}(205 \text{ ft})(50 \text{ ft}) = 5{,}125 \text{ ft}^2$$

$$\text{Sod cost} = \frac{\$0.40}{1 \text{ ft}^2} \times 5{,}125 \text{ ft}^2 = \$2{,}050.00$$

Total cost = \$7,900.00 + \$2,050.00 = \$9,950.00

Therefore, it will cost \$9,950 to fence and sod the backyard.

Triangles

A **triangle** is a closed figure formed by three sides and three internal angles. We use the letters a, b, and c to denote the side lengths, and h to denote the height.

The perimeter of a triangle (P), regardless of whether it is acute, right, or obtuse, is the sum of the three side lengths a, b, and c.

$$P = a + b + c$$

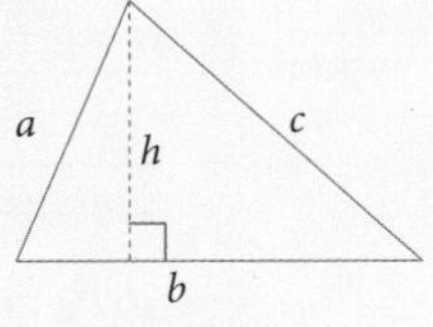

(i) Acute Triangle

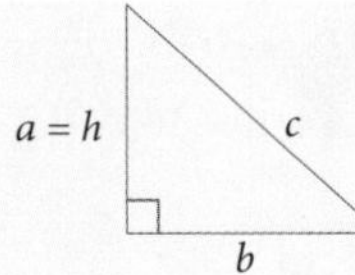

(ii) Right Triangle

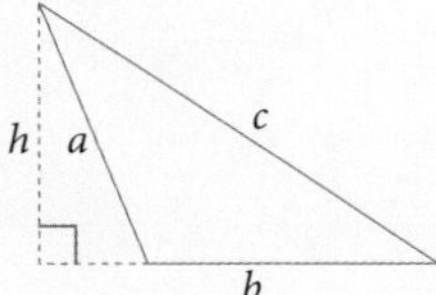

(iii) Obtuse Triangle

Calculating the area of a triangle (acute, right, or obtuse) when the lengths of the base and height are known:

To calculate the area of a triangle (regardless of whether it is acute, right, or obtuse), "copy" the triangle, rotate the image by 180°, and "paste" it to the original triangle as shown below. The result in all three cases will be a parallelogram, with base b and height h.

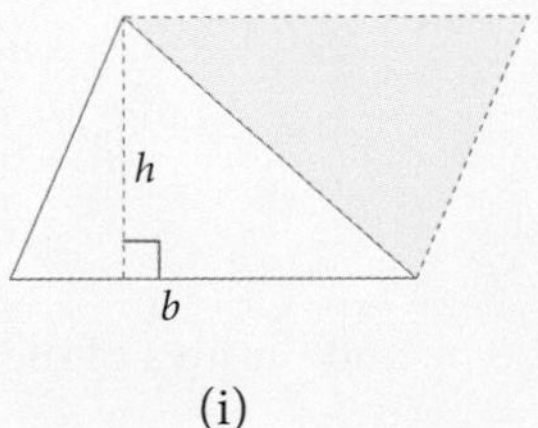

(i)

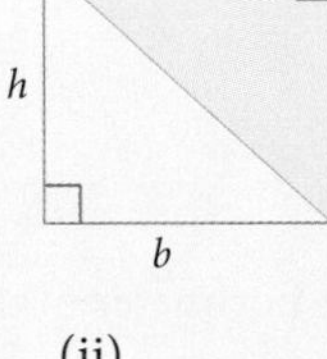

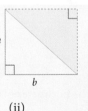

(ii)

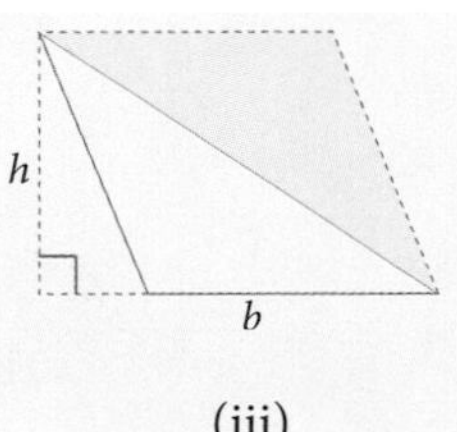

(iii)

Thus, the area of a triangle is half that of a parallelogram.

$$A = \frac{1}{2}(b \times h)$$

Calculating the area of a triangle (acute, right, or obtuse) when the lengths of all three sides are known (Using Heron's formula):

Heron's formula states that if a, b, c, are the lengths of the sides of the triangle, the area is given by:

$$A = \sqrt{p(p - a)(p - b)(p - c)}$$

Where p is half the perimeter (P), $p = \dfrac{a + b + c}{2}$

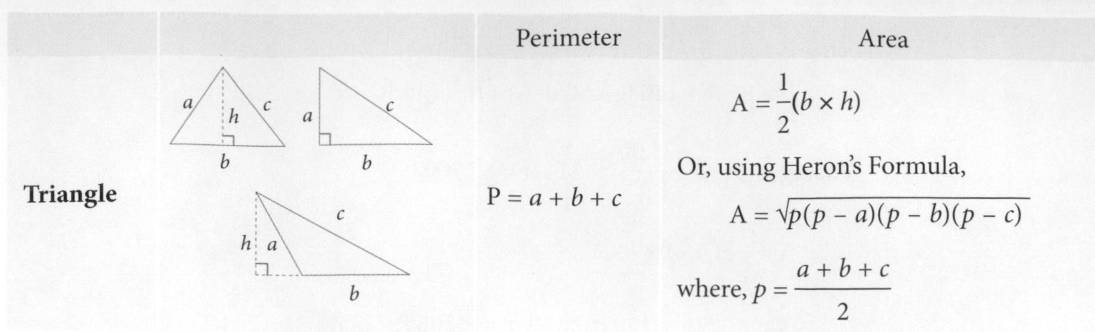

		Perimeter	Area
Triangle		$P = a + b + c$	$A = \frac{1}{2}(b \times h)$ Or, using Heron's Formula, $A = \sqrt{p(p-a)(p-b)(p-c)}$ where, $p = \frac{a+b+c}{2}$

Example 9.3-g

Calculating the Perimeter and Area of a Triangle

Calculate the perimeter and area of the following triangles:

(i) 16 cm, 41.6 cm, 38.4 cm

(ii) 27.4 in, 25.88 in, 18 in

Solution

(i) Using $P = a + b + c$,

$$P = 16 \text{ cm} + 38.4 \text{ cm} + 41.6 \text{ cm} = 96 \text{ cm}$$

Using $A = \frac{1}{2}(b \times h)$,

$$A = \frac{1}{2}(38.4 \text{ cm} \times 16 \text{ cm})$$

$$= 307.2 \text{ cm}^2$$

or

Using $A = \sqrt{p(p-a)(p-b)(p-c)}$,

where $p = \frac{a+b+c}{2} = \frac{96 \text{ cm}}{2} = 48 \text{ cm}$

$$A = \sqrt{48(48-16)(48-38.4)(48-41.6)}$$

$$= 307.2 \text{ cm}^2$$

Therefore, the perimeter of the triangle is 96 cm and the area is 307.2 cm^2.

(ii) $P = 27.4 \text{ in} + 18 \text{ in} + 27.4 \text{ in} = 72.8 \text{ in}$

$$A = \frac{1}{2}(18 \text{ in} \times 25.88 \text{ in})$$

$$= 232.92 \text{ in}^2$$

or

$$p = \frac{72.8 \text{ in}}{2} = 36.4 \text{ in}$$

$$A = \sqrt{36.4(36.4-27.4)(36.4-18)(36.4-27.4)}$$

$$= 232.917496... = 232.92 \text{ in}^2$$

Therefore, the perimeter of the triangle is 72.8 in. and the area of the triangle is 232.92 in^2.

Example 9.3-h

Calculating the Area of a Kite

Calculate the area of the kite shown in the figure below:

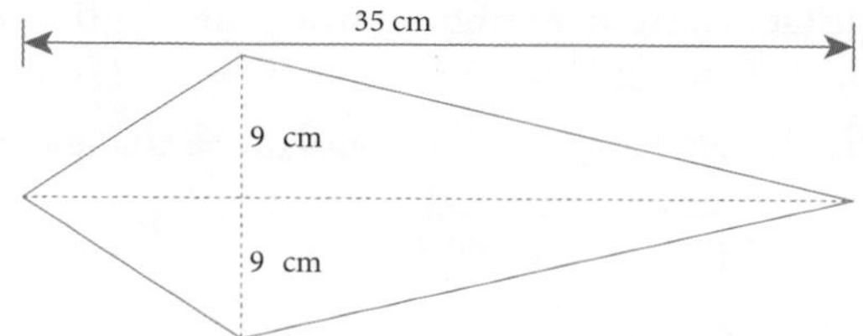

Solution

The kite consists of two identical triangles, each with a base of 35 cm and a height of 9 cm.

First, we will calculate the area of each of the two identical triangles.

Using $A = \frac{1}{2}(b \times h)$,

$$A = \frac{1}{2}(35 \text{ cm} \times 9 \text{ cm}) = 157.5 \text{ cm}^2$$

Therefore, the area of the kite is $2 \times 157.5 \text{ cm}^2 = 315 \text{ cm}^2$.

Circles and Sectors

Circles

A **circle** is a closed plane curve such that any point on the curve lies the same distance (the **radius**) from a fixed point (the centre).

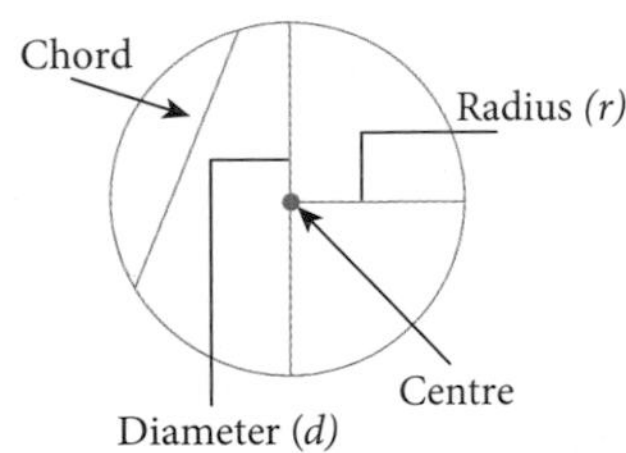

The **radius (*r*)** of the circle is the distance from the centre of the circle to the boundary of the circle.

A **chord** is a line segment that connects any two points on the boundary of the circle.

The **diameter (*d*)** of the circle is the length of the largest chord on the circle, i.e., the one that passes through the centre. Notice that the diameter is exactly twice the radius: $d = 2r$.

Exhibit 9.3 A Circle and its Components

To describe the boundary length of the circle, the word **circumference**, rather than perimeter, is used. For any circle, the ratio of the circumference, C, to its diameter, *d*, is a constant, special irrational number discovered by the ancient Greeks, known as π (pi, pronounced "pie").

$$C = \pi d$$

i.e., $\frac{C}{d} = \pi$; hence, $C = \pi(2r)$

$$C = 2\pi r$$

Note: π is an irrational number, which means that we cannot express its exact value as a decimal number; however, we can approximate: $\pi \approx 3.14159$, or more simply, $\pi \approx 3.14$. Throughout this chapter, we will use the "π" button on our calculator in examples and exercise questions involving pi, unless otherwise stated.

The area of a circle is calculated as follows:

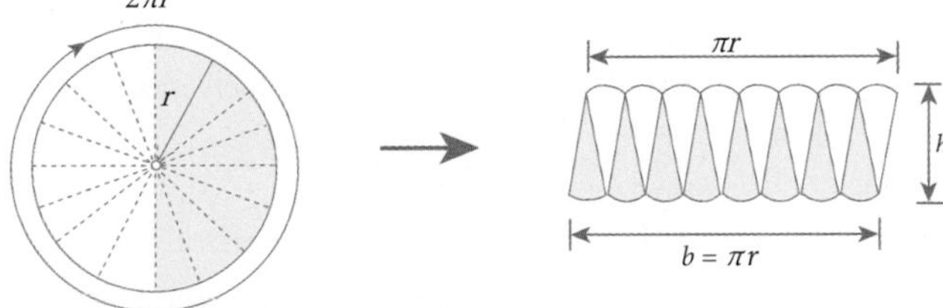

Step 1: Cut a circle into an even number of equal slices (for example, 16).

Step 2: Take half of the slices and arrange them end-to-end in the shape of "teeth". Do the same with the other half and place it on each end to make the interlocking shape symmetrical.

Step 3: The result is approximately a parallelogram. The length of the parallelogram is half of the circumference of the circle; i.e., $b = \frac{2\pi r}{2} = \pi r$. The height of the parallelogram is the distance from the boundary of the circle to the centre, which is the radius, *r*. The area of the circle, therefore, is approximately equal to the area of the parallelogram:

$A \approx b \times h = (\pi r) \times r = \pi r^2$.

Note: The more slices used in the circle, the closer the approximation gets. Therefore, the formula in Step 3 is indeed the exact formula for the area of a circle.

		Circumference	Area
Circle	(r, d)	$C = \pi d$ $C = 2\pi r$	$A = \pi r^2$

Example 9.3-i **Calculating Circumference and Area of a Circle**

Calculate the circumference and area of the following circles (round the answer to two decimal places):

(i) (ii)

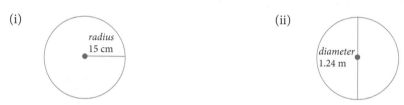

Solution

(i) Using $C = 2\pi r$ and $A = \pi r^2$,

$C = 2\pi r = 2(\pi)(15 \text{ cm}) = 94.247779... = 94.25 \text{ cm}$

$A = \pi r^2 = \pi(15 \text{ cm})^2 = 706.858347... = 706.86 \text{ cm}^2$

Therefore, the circumference of the circle is 94.25 cm and the area is 706.86 cm^2.

(ii) Using $C = \pi d$ and $A = \pi r^2$,

$C = \pi d = \pi(1.24 \text{ m}) = 3.895574... = 3.90 \text{ m}$

$$r = \frac{d}{2} = \frac{1.24 \text{ m}}{2} = 0.62 \text{ m}$$

$A = \pi r^2 = \pi(0.62 \text{ m})^2 = 1.207628... = 1.21 \text{ m}^2$

Therefore, the circumference of the circle is 3.90 m and the area is 1.21 m^2.

Example 9.3-j **Calculating the Distance Travelled on an Exercise Bicycle**

A road bike has a wheel with a 622 mm diameter. If the wheel spins at 192 rpm (revolutions per minute), determine the distance the cyclist travels in 1 hour and 20 minutes, rounded to the nearest tenth of a km.

Solution

The distance travelled in one revolution of the wheel is equivalent to the circumference of the wheel.

Distance travelled in one revolution = $C = \pi d = \pi(622 \text{ mm}) \approx 1{,}954 \text{ mm} = 1.954 \text{ m}$

Since it spins at 192 rpm (revolutions per minute), the distance travelled in 1 minute is equal to,

$$\frac{192 \text{ rev}}{1 \text{ min}} \times \frac{1.954 \text{ m}}{1 \text{ rev}} \approx 375.2 \text{ m/min}$$

The total distance travelled in 1 hour and 20 minutes (= 80 minutes) is,

$$80 \text{ min} \times \frac{375.2 \text{ m}}{1 \text{ min}} = 30{,}016 \text{ m} \approx 30.0 \text{ km}$$

Therefore, the cyclist travelled approximately 30.0 km in 1 hour and 20 minutes.

Example 9.3-k **Determining the Amount of Pizza Sauce Needed**

An extra-large pizza is circular with a diameter of 16 inches. Pizza sauce is spread on the pizza dough at a rate of 1.5 mL of pizza sauce per square inch (in^2) of crust. How much pizza sauce (rounded to the nearest 10 mL) is required to cover the entire pizza, if a 1-inch crust is to be left around the edge of the entire pizza?

Solution

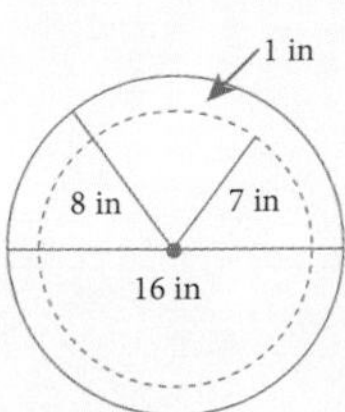

Radius of pizza dough surface $= r = \frac{d}{2} = \frac{16 \text{ in}}{2} = 8 \text{ in}$

Since there is a 1-inch crust to be left at the edge of the pizza, the radius of the surface to be covered with pizza sauce is 7 inches.

The area of the pizza dough to be covered with the sauce is:

$$A = \pi r^2 = \pi(7 \text{ in})^2 \approx 154 \text{ in}^2$$

The quantity of pizza sauce needed to cover the pizza is:

$$154 \text{ in}^2 \times \frac{1.5 \text{ mL}}{1 \text{ in}^2} \approx 230 \text{ mL}$$

Therefore, approximately 230 mL of pizza sauce is needed to cover the pizza.

Sectors

A **sector** (denoted by a capital S) is a portion of a circle that is bounded by two radii from the centre of the circle to the boundary of the circle, as shown in the diagram below. The section of the circumference that bounds the sector is known as the **arc** (denoted by a capital L). The internal angle of the sector inscribed by the two radii is known as the **angle subtended by the arc** (denoted by the Greek letter θ).

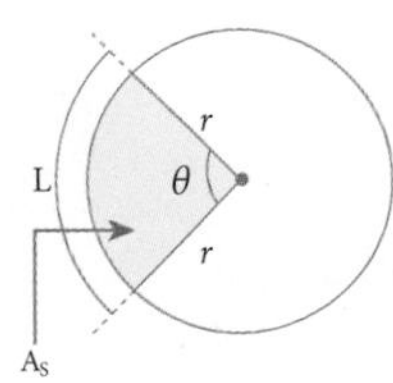

In a sector of a circle with sector angle θ:

(i) The arc length, L, of the sector is proportional to the circumference of the circle, πd, as θ is to 360°.

i.e., $\frac{\theta}{360°} = \frac{L}{\pi d} \longrightarrow L = \pi d \times \frac{\theta}{360°}$

Thus, the perimeter of the sector $P_S = r + r + L = 2r + L$

(ii) The area, A_S, of the sector is proportional to the area of the circle, πr^2, as θ is to 360°.

i.e., $\frac{\theta}{360°} = \frac{A_S}{\pi r^2} \longrightarrow A_S = \pi r^2 \times \frac{\theta}{360°}$

		Arc length	Area
Sector		$L = \pi d \times \frac{\theta}{360°}$ Perimeter $P_S = 2r + L$	$A_S = \pi r^2 \times \frac{\theta}{360°}$

Example 9.3-l **Calculating the Perimeter and Area of a Sector**

Calculate the perimeter and area (rounded to the nearest mm and mm^2, respectively) of a sector of a circle with a radius of 75 mm and an inscribed angle of 75°.

Solution

Using $P_S = 2r + L$ and $L = \pi d \times \dfrac{\theta}{360°}$,

$$P_S = 2(75 \text{ mm}) + \pi(2 \times 75 \text{ mm})\left(\frac{75°}{360°}\right) \approx 150 \text{ mm} + 98 \text{ mm} = 248 \text{ mm}$$

Using $A_S = \pi r^2 \times \dfrac{\theta}{360°}$,

$$A_S = \pi(75 \text{ mm})^2\left(\frac{75°}{360°}\right) \approx 3{,}682 \text{ mm}^2$$

Example 9.3-m

Determining the Speed of a Gondola on a Ferris Wheel

A giant ferris wheel has a diameter of 50.5 m. If it rotates at a maximum speed of 9° per second, determine the speed at which the gondolas on the rim of the wheel are moving (in km/h, rounded to the nearest tenth of a km).

Solution

Using $L = \pi d \times \dfrac{\theta}{360°}$,

$$L = \pi(50.5)\left(\frac{9°}{360°}\right) \approx 3.966 \text{ m}$$

Hence, the gondolas travel at a maximum speed of 3.966 m/s.

Converting this speed to km/h,

$$3.966 \text{ m/s} = \frac{3.966 \cancel{\text{m}}}{1 \cancel{\text{s}}} \times \frac{1 \text{ km}}{1{,}000 \cancel{\text{m}}} \times \frac{60 \times 60 \cancel{\text{s}}}{1 \text{ h}}$$

$$= \frac{3.966 \times 60 \times 60}{1{,}000} \text{ km/h}$$

$$\approx 14.3 \text{ km/h}$$

Therefore, the gondolas travel at a maximum speed of approximately 14.3 km/h.

Composite Figures

It is quite common, when solving application problems, to see a complex geometric figure constructed out of two or more simple geometric figures that have been previously described. Such figures are called **composite figures.**

- **To determine the perimeter of a composite figure,** simply calculate the length of the boundary, by adding up all the straight lengths and sector lengths along the boundary.
- **To determine the area of a composite figure,** break the figure up into simple figures and add up all the areas.

Example 9.3-n

Calculating the Perimeter and Area of a Parking Lot

A new parking lot is to be created around a commercial building (see image to the right). The edge of the parking lot is to be enclosed with concrete curbs and the surface of the parking lot is to be paved with asphalt. Determine how many linear metres of concrete curbing and square metres of asphalt are required to create the parking lot.

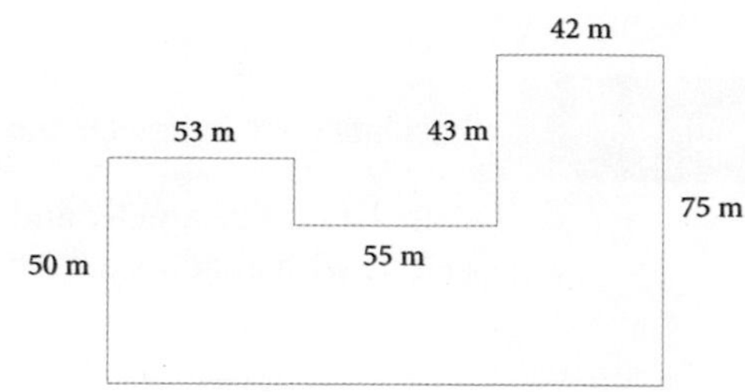

Solution

Let x, y, and z be the unknown lengths as marked in the diagram below:

To calculate the amount of asphalt needed, we calculate the area of the parking lot by breaking it up into three rectangular components, 1, 2 and 3:

$x = 53 \text{ m} + 55 \text{ m} + 42 \text{ m} = 150 \text{ m}$

$y = 75 \text{ m} - 43 \text{ m} = 32 \text{ m}$

$z = 50 \text{ m} - y = 50 \text{ m} - 32 \text{ m} = 18 \text{ m}$

$P = 50 + 53 + z + 55 + 43 + 42 + 75 + x = 486 \text{ m}$

$A_1 = (50 \text{ m})(53 \text{ m}) = 2{,}650 \text{ m}^2$

$A_2 = (y)(55 \text{ m}) = (32 \text{ m})(55 \text{ m}) = 1{,}760 \text{ m}^2$

$A_3 = (75 \text{ m})(42 \text{ m}) = 3{,}150 \text{ m}^2$

$A = 2{,}650 + 1{,}760 + 3{,}150 = 7{,}560 \text{ m}^2$

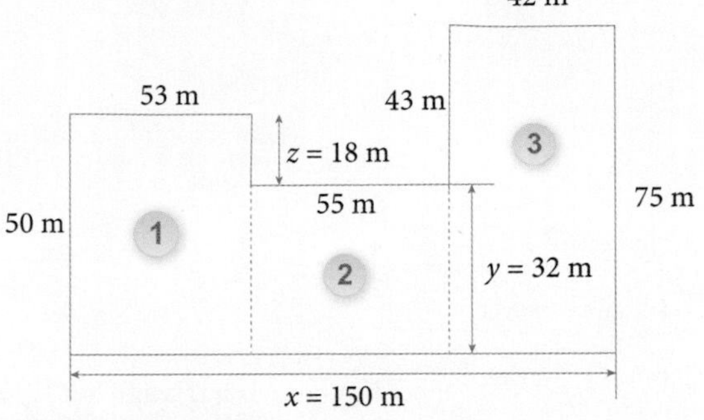

Therefore, 486 m of concrete curbing and 7,560 m² of asphalt are needed to create the parking lot.

Example 9.3-o

Calculating the Area of a Hockey Rink

A hockey rink is created that is rectangular in shape with two semi-circular ends (see sketch below). Determine the area (rounded to the nearest square metre) of the rink ice if it is 60 m from end to end at its longest and 20 m wide.

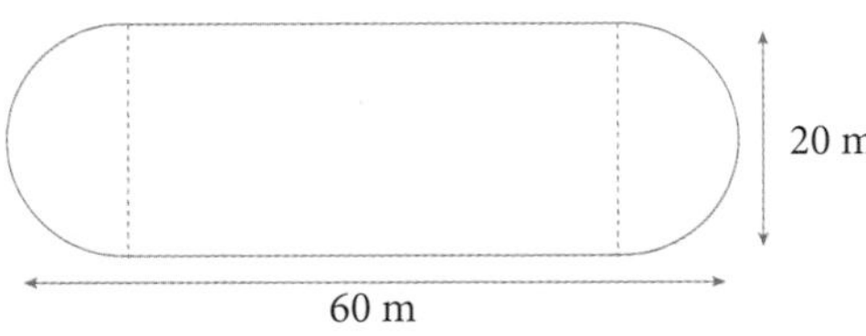

Solution

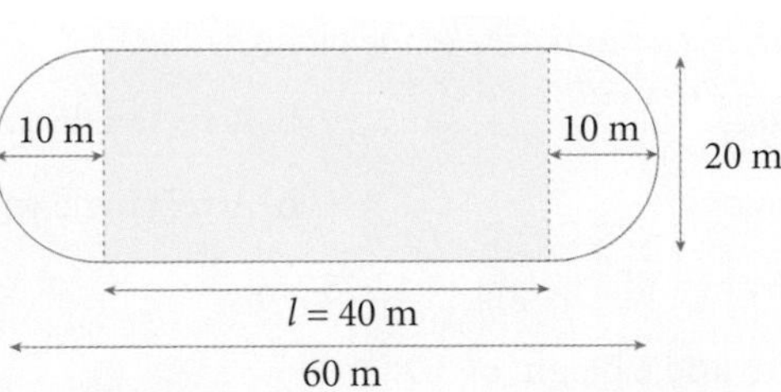

The width of the rectangle = 20 m.

Since the rink is 20 m wide, the diameters of each of the end semi-circles = 20 m; hence the radius = 10 m.

The length of the rectangle is the full length of the rink minus the radius of the two semi-circles at the end = 60 – 2(10) = 40 m.

$$A_{\text{rectangle}} = (40 \text{ m})(20 \text{ m}) = 800 \text{ m}^2$$

$$A_{\text{semi-circles at both ends}} = 2\left[\frac{1}{2}\pi(10)^2\right] \approx 314 \text{ m}^2$$

Therefore, $A \approx 800 + 314 = 1{,}114 \text{ m}^2$.

In some cases, it may be easier to think of the composite figure as a "cut-out" shape; i.e., as a simple geometric figure with another simple geometric figure cut out of it. In such cases, subtraction may be necessary to calculate the perimeter or area of the composite figure.

Example 9.3-p **Calculating the Area of a "Cut-Out" Shape**

Determine the area of the following "cut-out" shape:

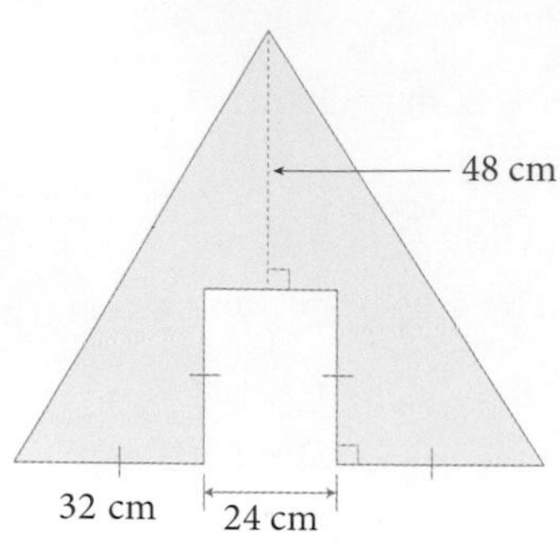

Solution

The shape is a triangle with a rectangle cut out of it. As with the previous questions, we need the dimensions of both simple shapes:

The dimensions of the rectangle at the centre are l = 32 cm and w = 24 cm.

The height of the triangle is h = 48 cm + 32 cm = 80 cm

The base of the triangle is b = 2(32 cm) + 24 cm = 88 cm

$$A_{triangle} = \frac{1}{2}(88 \text{ cm})(80 \text{ cm}) = 3{,}520 \text{ m}^2$$

$$A_{rectangle} = (32 \text{ cm})(24 \text{ cm}) = 768 \text{ cm}^2$$

Therefore, the area of the 'cut-out' shape = 3,520 cm^2 – 768 cm^2 = 2,752 cm^2

9.3 | Exercises

Answers to odd-numbered problems are available at the end of the textbook.

For Problems 1 to 10, calculate the perimeter and area of the plane figures.

1. a. A square with sides 8 mm long. b. A rectangle with sides of 6.4 m and 4.5 m.
2. a. A square with sides 22.5 cm long. b. A rectangle with sides of 15 m and 20 m.
3. A rhombus with sides of 16.25 cm and a height of 12.75 cm.
4. A rhombus with sides of 6.75 m and a height of 5.25 m.
5. A parallelogram with a base of 12 cm, slant sides of 4 cm, and a height of 3.5 cm.
6. A parallelogram with a base of 14 cm, slant sides of 7 cm, and a height of 5.5 cm.
7. A trapezoid with parallel sides of 2.45 m and 1.55 m, slant sides that are both 0.75 m, and a perpendicular height of 0.6 m.
8. A trapezoid with parallel sides of 98 mm and 73 mm, one side measuring 60 mm that is perpendicular to the parallel sides, and a slant side of 65 mm.
9. An isosceles triangle with a base of 9 cm, slant sides of 7.5 cm, and a height of 6 cm.
10. An equilateral triangle with sides of 52.5 mm and a height of 45.5 mm.

For Problems 11 to 14, calculate the circumference and area of the circles (rounded to the indicated place value).

11. A circle with a radius of 8 cm (to the nearest hundredth).
12. A circle with a radius of 25 cm (to the nearest tenth).
13. A circle with a diameter of 1.84 m (to the nearest thousandth).
14. A circle with a diameter of 95 mm (to the nearest whole number).

For Problem 15 to 18, calculate the perimeter and area of the given sectors (rounded to the indicated place value).

15. A sector of a circle with radius 72 cm, inscribed by an angle of 135° (to the nearest whole number).

16. A sector of a circle with radius 2.5 m, inscribed by an angle of 40° (to the nearest hundredth).

17. A sector of a circle with diameter 64 m, inscribed by an angle of 12° (to the nearest thousandth).

18. A sector of a circle with diameter 48 m, inscribed by an angle of 75° (to the nearest tenth).

19. A playground is being built on a rectangular piece of land, 35 m long by 28 m wide, at a local public park. If there is to be a 2 m wide walkway around the entire playground, determine the area available to build the playground.

20. A circular flower bed with diameter 3.5 m is built on a lawn 28 m long and 12.5 m wide. Calculate the remaining area of the lawn.

21. A circular pond has an area of 225 cm^2. Determine the diameter of the pond.

22. A square piece of window glass has an area of 7,225 cm^2. Determine the perimeter of the piece of glass.

23. A rectangular field that is three times as long as it is wide has a perimeter of 2.4 km. Determine the area of the field in km^2.

24. A square field has a perimeter of 144 m. Calculate the area of the field in m^2.

25. A kite is constructed using a simple frame of two pieces of bamboo, one long piece measuring 60 cm and one short piece measuring 32 cm, fashioned together in the shape of a perpendicular cross (see diagram to the right). A light-weight material is then fitted to the frame to make the kite. Determine the amount of material needed.

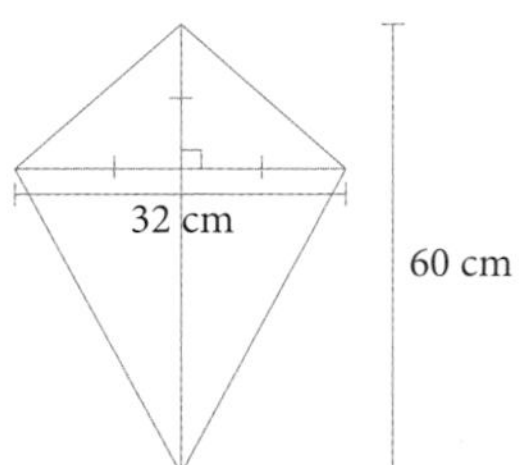

26. If the dimensions in Problem 25 were doubled, what would happen to the amount of material needed to construct the kite? What total amount of material would be required?

27. A garden is planted by a township on a right-triangular plot that is 6.5 m long and 6.5 m wide, at the corner of the main intersection coming into the town. If soil for the garden costs $2.75/$m^2$, determine the total cost to lay the soil in the garden.

28. A quilt for a new baby is constructed using triangular pieces of fabric, each 16 cm long at the base and 10 cm high. How many triangular pieces of fabric are needed to make a quilt that has an area of 1 m^2?

29. A ferris wheel with a diameter of 32 m makes a complete revolution in 40 seconds. Determine the speed of the passenger cars on the wheel, in km/h, rounded to the nearest tenth.

30. A car tire has a diameter of 68 cm and the car is travelling at a speed of 100 km/h. Determine the number of revolutions the tire makes in one minute (rpm), rounded to the nearest rpm.

For Problems 31 to 40, determine the perimeter and area of the composite plain figures. Round all answers to the nearest hundredth.

31.

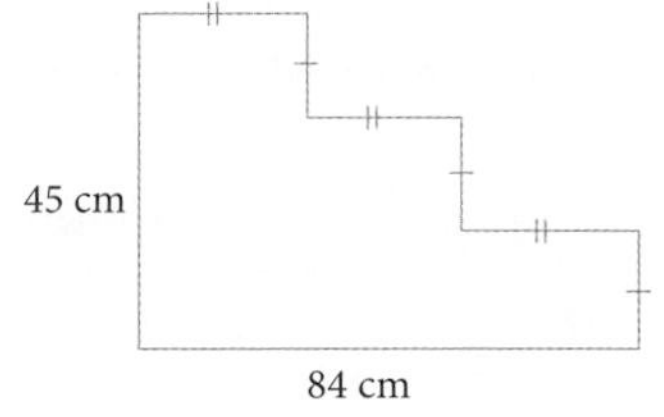

32.

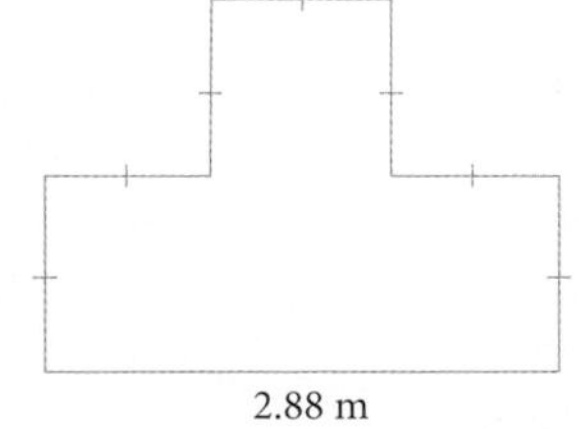

33.

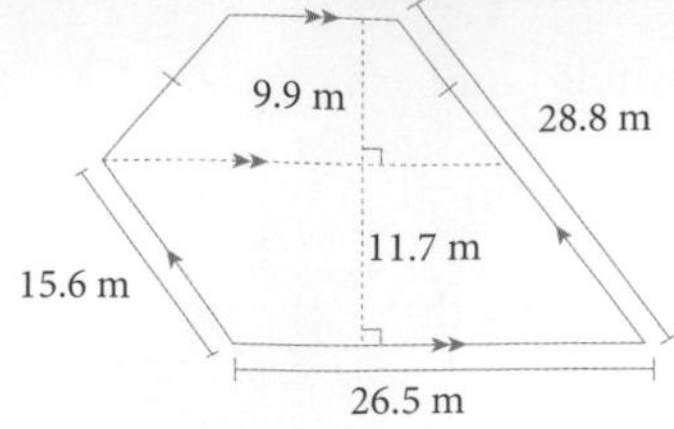

34.

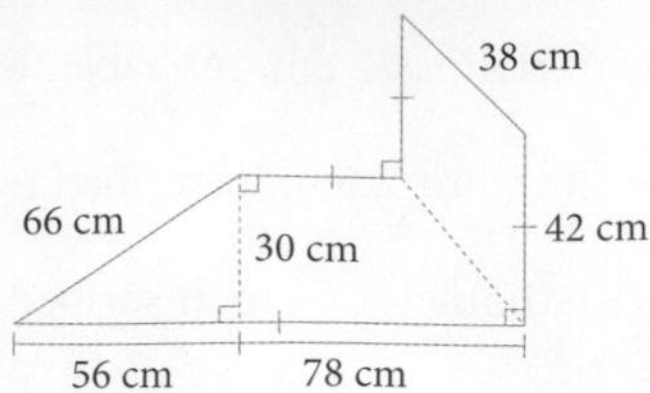

35.

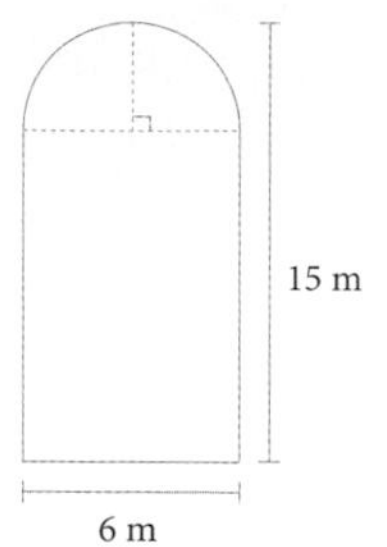

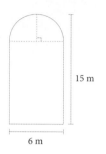

36.

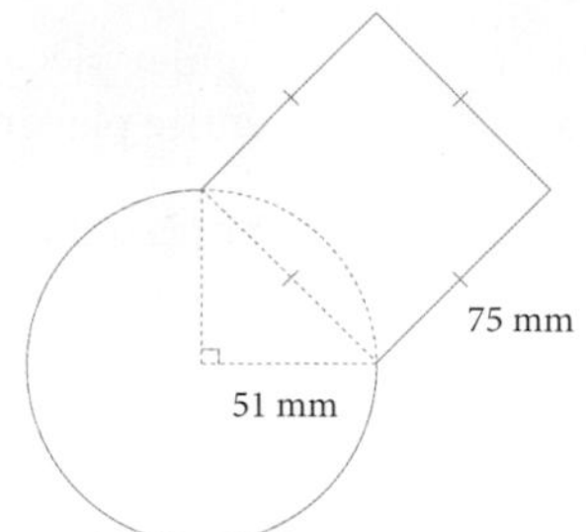

37.

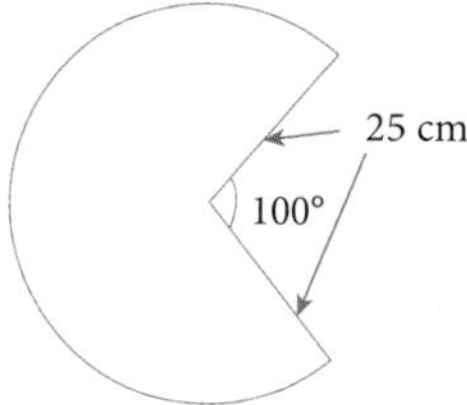

38.

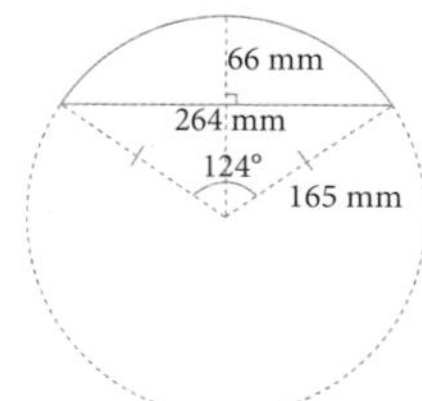

39.

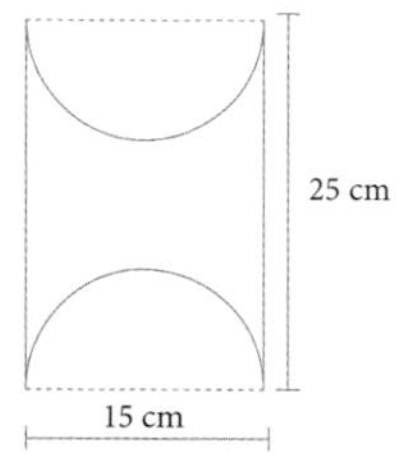

40.

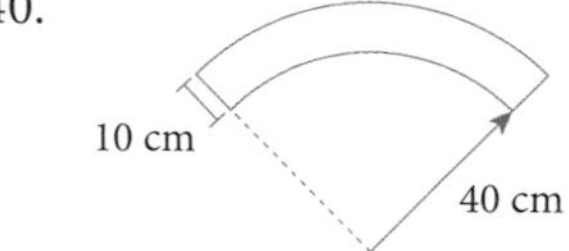

9.4 | Surface Areas and Volumes of Common Solid Objects

All the shapes and figures outlined in the previous two sections were 2-dimensional. In this section, the general classification of common solid objects that occupy 3-dimensions, and the two important measurements of these objects - surface area and volume - will be discussed. The 3-dimensions are length (l), width (w), and height (h). Sometimes, these terms are interchanged with breadth, thickness, and depth.

The **surface area** of a solid is the total area of all of the outside faces of a three dimensional object, including its ends or bases. The **lateral area** of a solid does not include the area of the base. Area measurements are expressed in square units (cm^2, m^2, ft^2, etc.).

The **volume** of a solid is a measure of the space it occupies or encloses. It is measured in cubic units (cm^3, m^3, ft^3, etc.) or in the case of liquids, in litres, gallons etc.

The different types of common solid objects that are classified based on their shapes are shown in Exhibit 9.4-a.

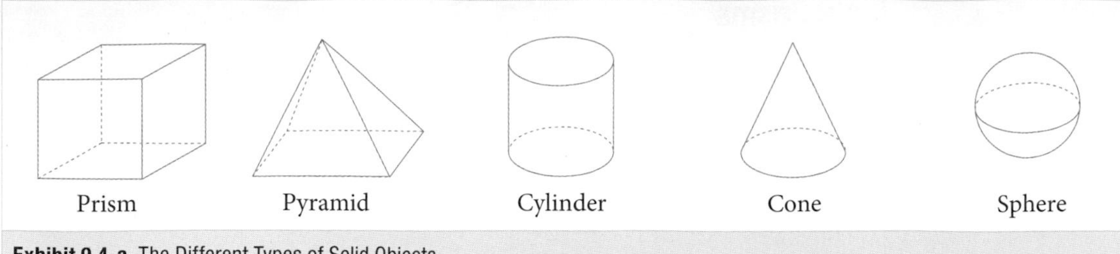

Exhibit 9.4-a The Different Types of Solid Objects

A **polyhedron** is a 3-dimensional object in which all the faces are polygons (flat surfaces with straight edges). For example, prisms and pyramids are bounded by polygons (flat surfaces), and therefore, they are polyhedrons. However, cylinders, cones, and spheres are not polyhedrons because they are formed by curved surfaces.

A polyhedron with congruent faces is known as a **platonic solid**. There are only five possible platonic solids:

- Tetrahedron: 4 faces, congruent equilateral triangles (a special type of pyramid)
- Cube: 6 faces, congruent squares (a special type of prism)
- Octahedron: 8 faces, congruent equilateral triangles
- Dodecahedron: 12 faces, congruent pentagons
- Icosahedron: 20 faces, congruent equilateral triangles

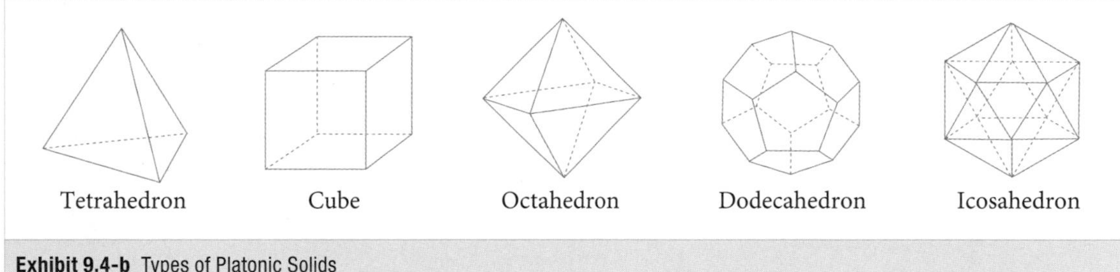

Exhibit 9.4-b Types of Platonic Solids

Prisms

A **prism** is a polyhedron with two parallel and congruent end-faces (bases). The height of a prism is the perpendicular distance between its bases.

Prisms are named according to the shape of the bases. For example, a prism with a rectangular base is a rectangular prism, while a prism with a triangular base is a triangular prism.

In a **right rectangular prism**, all the lateral faces are rectangles. The height of a right rectangular prism is the length of a lateral edge. In an **oblique rectangular prism**, all lateral faces are parallelograms.

Lateral faces are surfaces on a solid object that are not bases (top or bottom).

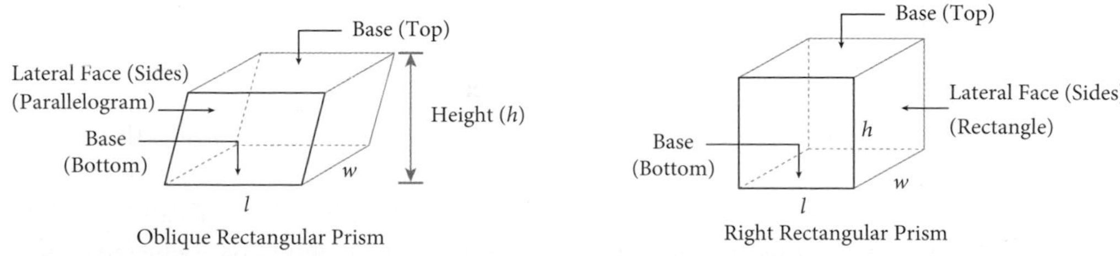

Surface Area = 2 × Base Area + Sum of the area of all lateral faces

Volume = Base Area × Height of the prism

Right Prisms

A Cube is a solid object with six congruent square faces.

A Rectangular Prism is a solid object with six rectangular faces. Opposite faces have the same area.

A Triangular Prism is a solid object with five faces. It has two triangular faces and three rectangular faces.

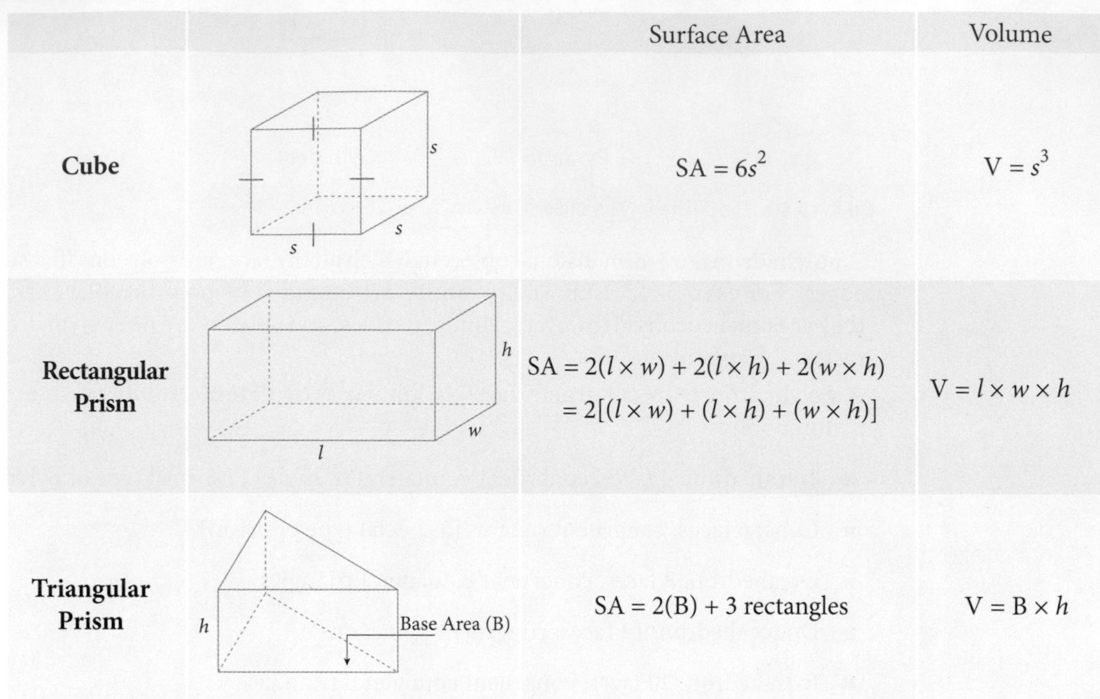

		Surface Area	Volume
Cube		$SA = 6s^2$	$V = s^3$
Rectangular Prism		$SA = 2(l \times w) + 2(l \times h) + 2(w \times h)$ $= 2[(l \times w) + (l \times h) + (w \times h)]$	$V = l \times w \times h$
Triangular Prism		$SA = 2(B) + 3$ rectangles	$V = B \times h$

Example 9.4-a **Calculating the Surface Area and Volume of Rectangular Prisms**

The dimensions of a shipping box are 45 cm by 30 cm by 12 cm. Calculate the surface area and volume of the shipping box.

Solution

Using $SA = 2(l \times w) + 2(l \times h) + 2(w \times h)$,

$$SA = 2(45 \text{ cm} \times 30 \text{ cm}) + 2(45 \text{ cm} \times 12 \text{ cm}) + 2(30 \text{ cm} \times 12 \text{ cm})$$

$$= 2{,}700 \text{ cm}^2 + 1{,}080 \text{ cm}^2 + 720 \text{ cm}^2$$

$$= 4{,}500 \text{ cm}^2$$

Using $V = l \times w \times h$,

$$V = 45 \text{ cm} \times 30 \text{ cm} \times 12 \text{ cm}$$

$$= 16{,}200 \text{ cm}^3$$

Therefore, the surface area of the shipping box is $4{,}500 \text{ cm}^2$ and the volume is $16{,}200 \text{ cm}^3$.

Pyramids

A **pyramid** is a polyhedron in which the base is a polygon and all lateral faces are triangles, meeting at a common point called the **apex** (or vertex).

A **regular right pyramid** is a pyramid whose base is a regular polygon and all the lateral faces are congruent triangles. Also, the line connecting the apex to the centre of the base forms a right-angle with the base: this is the height of the regular pyramid. If the line connecting the apex to the centre of the base does not form a right angle with the base, then this is called an **oblique pyramid**.

A **right rectangular pyramid** is a pyramid with a rectangular base (the term **rectangular pyramid** is often used to describe a right rectangular pyramid). If the base happens to be a square, then it is called a **right square pyramid**.

The slant heights of a right rectangular pyramid are usually denoted by s_1 for the slant height on the length side and s_2 for the slant height on the width side. In a right square pyramid, since all four triangular sides are identical, there is only one slant height, denoted by s.

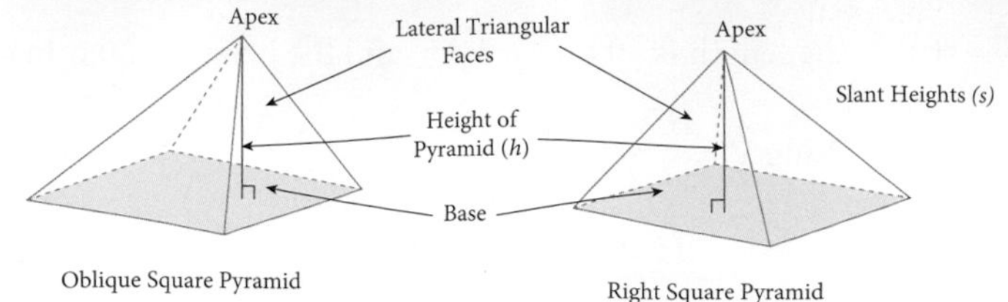

Surface Area = (Sum of the area of all lateral triangular faces) + (Base area)

Volume = $\frac{1}{3}$(Base area × Height of the pyramid)

Right Pyramids

		Surface Area	Volume
Square Pyramid		$SA = 4\left(\frac{l \times s}{2}\right) + l^2$ $= 2(l \times s) + l^2$	$V = \frac{1}{3}(l \times l)h$ $= \frac{l^2 \times h}{3}$
Rectangular Pyramid		$SA = 2\left(\frac{l \times s_1}{2} + \frac{w \times s_2}{2}\right) + l \times w$ $= (l \times s_1 + w \times s_2) + l \times w$	$V = \frac{1}{3}(l \times w)h$ $= \frac{l \times w \times h}{3}$
Triangular Pyramid		SA = Area of all 3 lateral sides + Base Area (B)	$V = \frac{1}{3}(B)h$ $= \frac{B \times h}{3}$

Note: The formulas for volume of a right pyramid are exactly the same as those for an oblique pyramid; however, the formulas for surface area are not the same!

Example 9.4-b **Calculating the Surface Area and Volume of Pyramids**

A tea bag is manufactured in the shape of a square-based pyramid, with side length 30 mm, height 20 mm, and slant height 25 mm. Calculate the following:

(i) The amount of mesh (in mm^2) needed to manufacture the tea bag

(ii) The volume of tea (in cm^3) the bag can hold

Solution

Since the tea bag has a square base, the slant heights are equal on all sides.

(i) Using $SA = 2(l \times s) + l^2$,

$$SA = 2(30 \text{ mm} \times 25 \text{ mm}) + (30 \text{ mm})^2$$
$$= 2{,}400 \text{ mm}^2$$

Therefore 2,400 mm^2 of mesh is needed to manufacture the tea bag.

Solution
continued

(ii) The length is 30 mm = 3 cm, and the height is 20 mm = 2 cm.

Using $V = \frac{l^2 \times h}{3}$,

$$V = \frac{(3\text{ cm})^2 \times (2\text{ cm})}{3}$$

$= 6\text{ cm}^3$

Therefore, the tea bag can hold 6 cm^3 of tea.

Cylinders

A **cylinder** is a prism with two parallel and congruent circular bases and a curved lateral surface connecting the two bases. The height (altitude), h, of the cylinder is the perpendicular distance between the two bases. The radius, r, of the cylinder is the radius of the base circle.

In a **right cylinder**, the line joining the centre of the bases is perpendicular to the bases. If the line joining the centre of the bases in not perpendicular to the bases, then this is an **oblique cylinder**.

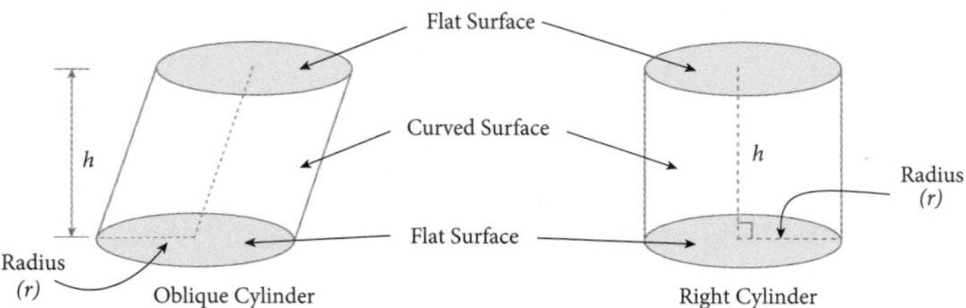

If the lateral side of a right circular cylinder is unwrapped, as in Exhibit 9.4-c, we see that it is a rectangle with a length equal to the circumference of the circular base ($C = 2\pi r$) and width equal to the height of the cylinder.

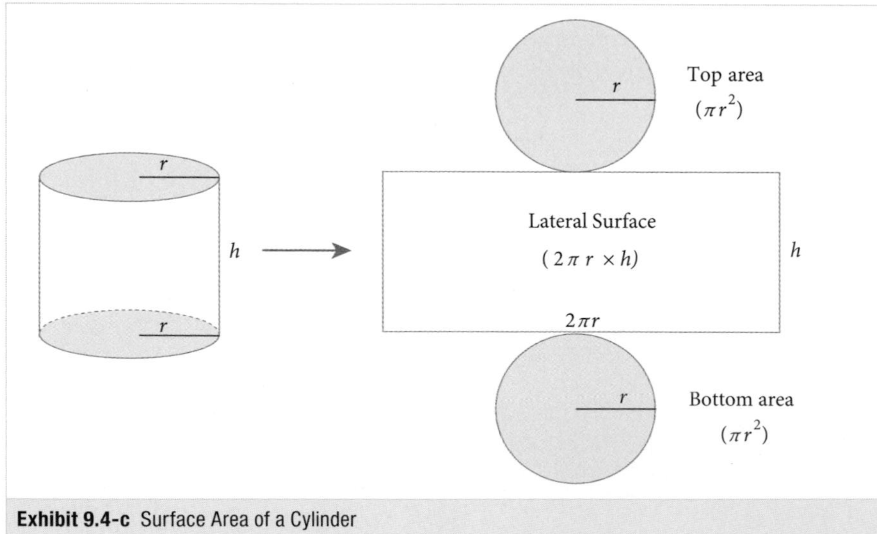

Exhibit 9.4-c Surface Area of a Cylinder

That is, we can take a rectangle and wrap it around to create a circular tube, which can then be "capped" at either or both ends with circles. This leads us to the following three definitions:

- A **closed cylinder** (or **can**) is a cylinder that has a lateral face and two end-faces.
- A **semi-closed cylinder** (or **cup**) is a cylinder that has a lateral face and one end-face.
- An **open cylinder** (or **tube**) is a cylinder that only has a lateral face with no end-faces.

Surface Area = Circular base area(s) + Area of the curved lateral face

Volume = Base area × Height of the cylinder

Right Cylinders

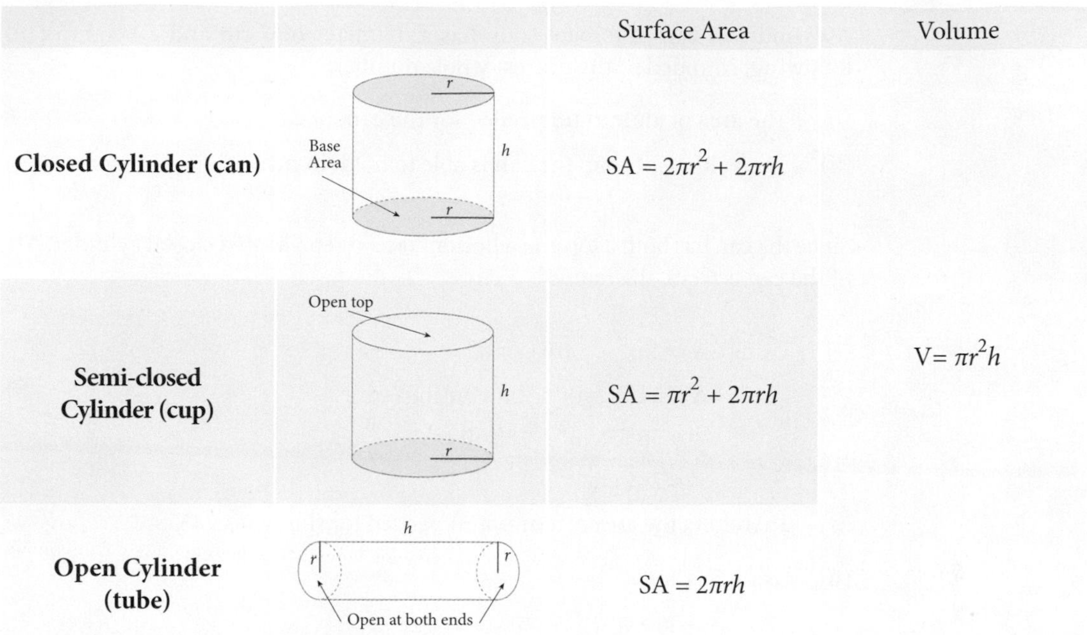

		Surface Area	Volume
Closed Cylinder (can)	Base Area; r; h	$SA = 2\pi r^2 + 2\pi rh$	$V = \pi r^2 h$
Semi-closed Cylinder (cup)	Open top; r; h	$SA = \pi r^2 + 2\pi rh$	
Open Cylinder (tube)	h; r; Open at both ends	$SA = 2\pi rh$	

Note: The formulas for surface area and volume of a right circular cylinder are exactly the same as those for an oblique circular cylinder.

If the lateral side of an oblique circular cylinder is "unwrapped", it becomes a parallelogram with the same base length and height (i.e., perpendicular height) as the rectangular lateral side in a right circular cylinder.

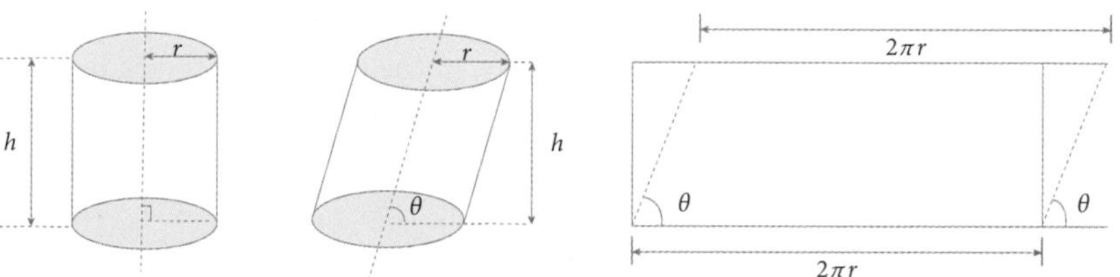

To understand the way the volume formula applies to an oblique circular cylinder, consider a stack of quarters; when stacked perfectly, they form a right cylinder. If this stack of quarters are pushed on a slant, they form an oblique cylinder; however, the volume of metal in the quarters has not changed.

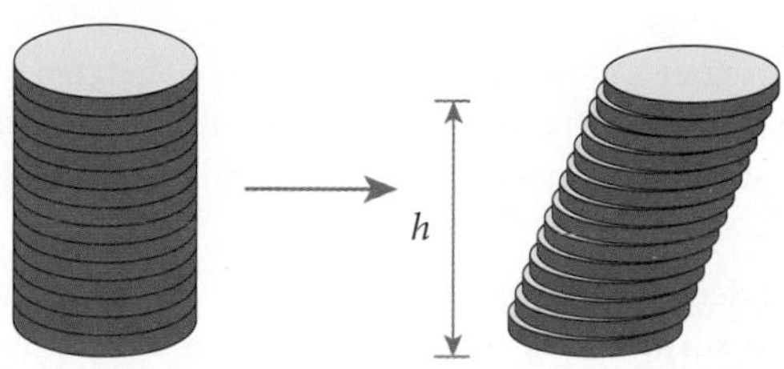

Example 9.4-c

Calculating the Surface Area and Volume of Cylinders

A cylindrical can of tomato soup has a diameter of 6 cm and a height of 10 cm. Calculate the following, rounded to the nearest whole number:

(i) The area of aluminum needed for the can, in cm^2.

(ii) The volume of soup the can is able to hold, in mL.

Solution

Since the can has both a top and a bottom face, it represents a closed cylinder. Also, since the diameter of the can is 6 cm, the radius is 3 cm.

(i) Using $SA = 2\pi r^2 + 2\pi rh$,

$$SA = 2\pi(3\text{ cm})^2 + 2\pi(3\text{ cm})(10\text{ cm})$$
$$\approx 56.55\text{ cm}^2 + 188.50\text{ cm}^2$$
$$\approx 245\text{ cm}^2$$

Therefore, the area of aluminum needed for the can is 245 cm^2.

(ii) Using $V = \pi r^2 h$,

$$V = \pi(3\text{ cm})^2(10\text{ cm})$$
$$\approx 283\text{ cm}^3$$

Recall that $1\text{ cm}^3 = 1\text{ mL}$; therefore, $V \approx 283\text{ mL}$.

Therefore, the volume of soup that the can is able to hold is 283 mL.

Cones

A **cone** is a pyramid with a circular base and a curved lateral surface, which extends from the base to a point called the vertex. The height (altitude), h, of the cone is the perpendicular distance from the vertex to the base. The radius, r, of the cylinder is the radius of the base circle. The slant height of the cone, s, is the distance from the vertex to any point on the edge of the base.

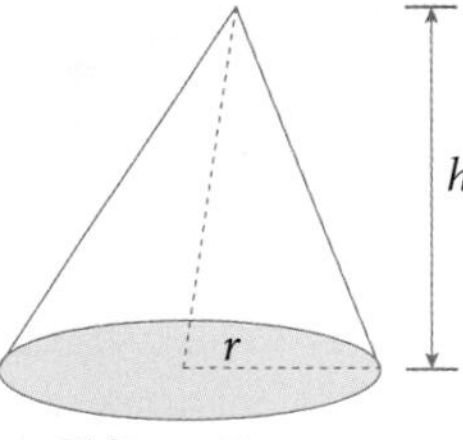

Oblique Cone

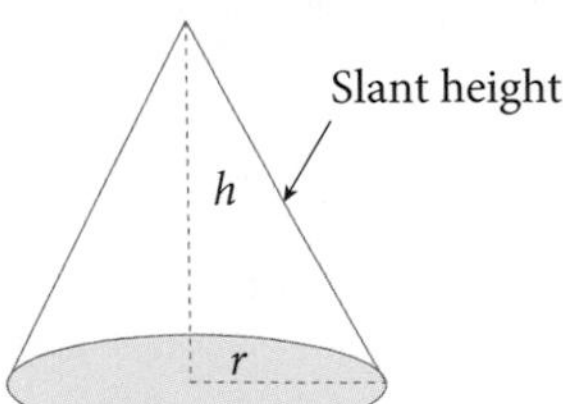

Right Cone

The surface area of a closed cone is the sum of the area of the circular base and the area of the lateral face. The area of the lateral face is $A = \pi \times r \times s$; the explanation of this formula is beyond the scope of this textbook.

As with cylinders, closed cones have "lids" while open cones do not. Therefore, the surface area of an open cone is simply the area of the lateral face.

Surface Area = (Area of the circular base) + (Area of the lateral face)

Volume $= \frac{1}{3}$ **(Area of circular base × Height of the cone)**

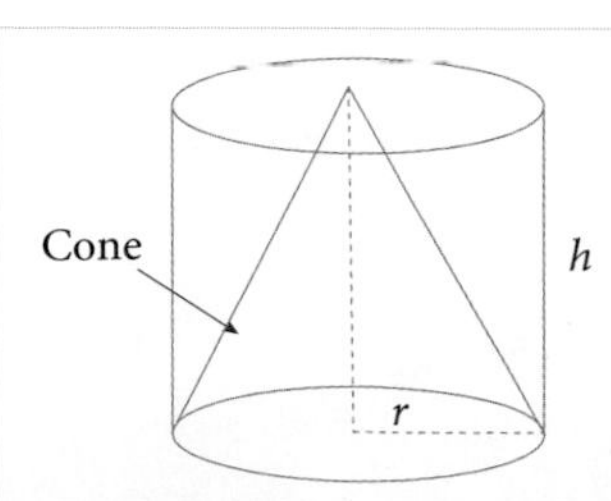

The volume of a cone is exactly one third that of the cylinder with the same base and height.

Right Cones

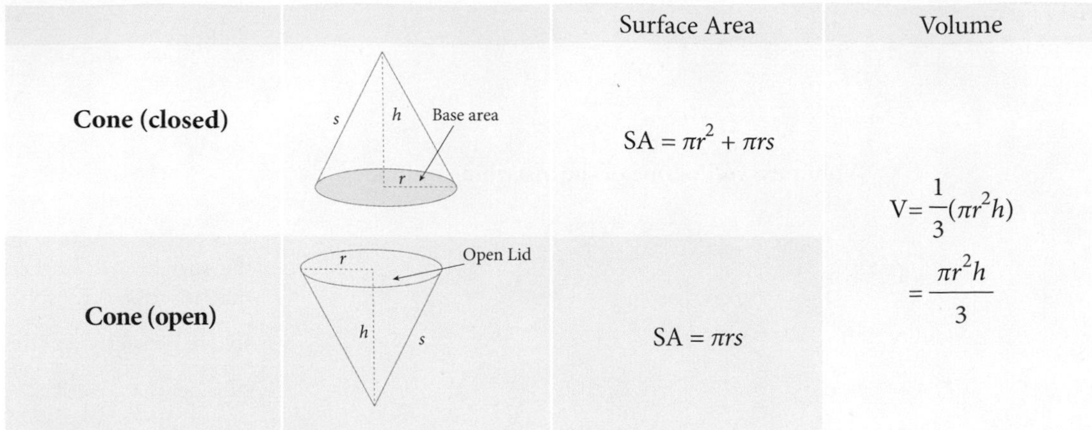

		Surface Area	Volume
Cone (closed)	(figure: s, h, r, Base area)	$SA = \pi r^2 + \pi rs$	$V = \frac{1}{3}(\pi r^2 h) = \frac{\pi r^2 h}{3}$
Cone (open)	(figure: r, h, s, Open Lid)	$SA = \pi rs$	

Note: The formulas for volume of a right cone are exactly the same as those for an oblique cone, however, the formulas for surface area are not the same!

Example 9.4-d **Calculating the Surface Area and Volume of Cones**

A paper water cup used for a water cooler is in the shape of a cone, with a diameter of 6.4 cm, a height of 10.8 cm, and a slant height of 11.3 cm. Calculate the following:

(i) The area of the paper needed to make the cup (rounded to the nearest cm^2).

(ii) The volume of water the cup can hold (rounded to the nearest mL).

Solution

Since the cup has no lid, we need the formula for an open cone. Also, since the diameter of the cup is 6.4 cm, the radius is 3.2 cm.

(i) Using $SA = \pi rs$,

$$SA = \pi(3.2 \text{ cm})(11.3 \text{ cm})$$
$$\approx 114 \text{ cm}^2$$

Therefore, the area of the paper needed to make the cup is 114 cm^2.

(ii) Using $V = \frac{\pi r^2 h}{3}$,

$$V = \frac{\pi(3.2 \text{ cm})^2(10.8 \text{ cm})}{3}$$
$$\approx 116 \text{ cm}^3$$
$$= 116 \text{ mL}$$

Therefore, the volume of water the cup can hold is 116 mL.

Spheres

A sphere is a 3-dimensional object shaped like a ball. It is a solid bounded by curved surfaces and every surface point is a fixed distance (called the **radius**) away from the centre.

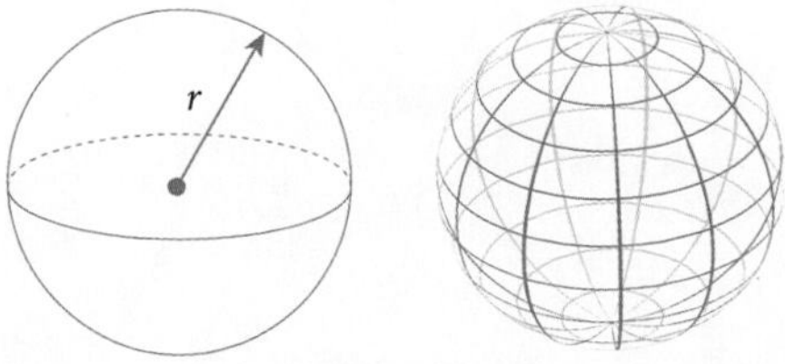

Surface Area = (Surface area of inscribing open cylinder)

$$SA = 2\pi rh$$
$$= 2\pi r(2r)$$
$$= 4\pi r^2$$

Volume $= \frac{2}{3}$ (Volume of the inscribing cyclinder)

$$V = \frac{2}{3}\pi r^2 h$$
$$= \frac{2}{3}\pi r^2(2r)$$
$$= \frac{4}{3}\pi r^3$$

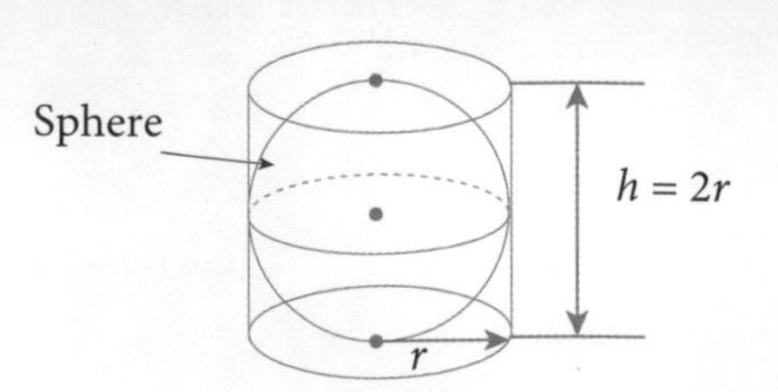

The surface area of a sphere is exactly equal to the surface area of the smallest **open** cylinder that inscribes the sphere. The volume of the sphere is exactly $\frac{2}{3}$ of the volume of the smallest cylinder that inscribes it.

		Surface Area	Volume
Sphere		$SA = 4\pi r^2$	$V = \frac{4}{3}(\pi r^3)$ $= \frac{4\pi r^3}{3}$
Half-sphere (or hemisphere)		$SA = \frac{1}{2}(4\pi r^2) + \pi r^2$ $= 3\pi r^2$	$V = \frac{1}{2}\left(\frac{4}{3}\pi r^3\right)$ $= \frac{2}{3}(\pi r^3)$ $= \frac{2\pi r^3}{3}$

Example 9.4-e

Calculating the Surface Area and Volume of Spheres

A spherical yoga ball has a height of 75 cm. Calculate the following:

(i) The amount of rubber needed to construct the ball (in m^2, rounded to the nearest thousandth).

(ii) The volume of air that the ball can hold when fully inflated (rounded to the nearest L).

Solution

The height of the yoga ball is the same as the diameter of the ball, which is twice the radius; therefore, $r = 37.5 \text{ cm} = 0.375 \text{ m}$.

(i) Using $SA = 4\pi r^2$,

$$SA = 4\pi(0.375 \text{ m})^2$$
$$\approx 1.767 \text{ m}^2$$

Therefore, the amount of rubber needed to construct the ball is 1.767 m^2.

Solution *continued*

(ii) Since 1 mL = 1 cm^3, 1 L = 1,000 mL = 1,000 cm^3.

Using $V = \frac{4\pi r^3}{3}$,

$$V = \frac{4\pi(37.5\text{ cm})^3}{3}$$

$$\approx 220{,}893\text{ cm}^3$$

$$\approx 221\text{ L}$$

Therefore, the volume of air that the ball can hold when fully inflated is 221 L.

Composite Figures

As in 2-dimensional plane geometry, there are many complex 3-dimensional solids which are composed of simpler solids like prisms, cylinders, pyramids, cones, and spheres. We will consider some examples of these below.

Example 9.4-f

Calculating the Surface Area of a Composite Shape

A greenhouse is built 5.0 m long, 3.0 m wide, 2.55 m tall at the sides and 3.2 m tall in the middle, with a roof that has a slant height of 1.6 m, as per the following diagram:

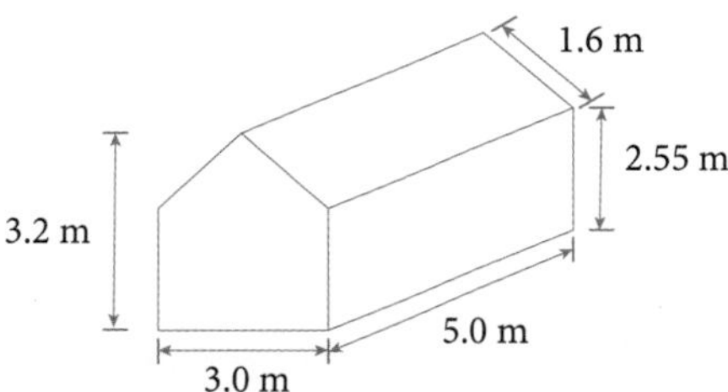

If the glass to build the greenhouse costs $3.96/$m^2$, calculate the total cost of the glass needed to build the greenhouse.

Solution

First, we need to determine the amount of glass needed to build the greenhouse, in m^2, which is the surface area of the greenhouse. This is a pentagonal prism, which we do not have a formula for. However, we can analyze the shape as a prism with two rectangular side faces, two rectangular roof faces, (no bottom face, since the floor is not constructed out of glass), and two end-faces that are each comprised of a rectangle and a triangle:

$$SA = 2A_{side} + 2A_{roof} + 2(A_{end\ rectangle} + A_{end\ triangle})$$

$$SA = 2(5.0\text{ m})(2.55\text{ m}) + 2(5.0\text{ m})(1.6\text{ m}) + 2\left((3.0\text{ m})(2.55\text{ m}) + \frac{1}{2}(3.0\text{ m})(3.2\text{ m} - 2.55\text{ m})\right)$$

$$= 25.5\text{ m}^2 + 16.0\text{ m}^2 + 2(8.625\text{ m}^2)$$

$$= 58.75\text{ m}^2$$

$$\text{Cost} = 58.75\ \cancel{\text{m}^2} \times \frac{\$3.96}{\cancel{\text{m}^2}} = \$232.65$$

Therefore, the total cost of the glass needed to build the greenhouse is $232.65.

Example 9.4-g Calculating the Volume of a Composite Shape

An ice-cream waffle-cone has a diameter of 8.5 cm at the opening, a perpendicular height of 17.5 cm, and a slant height of 18 cm. Ice-cream is scooped and packed into the waffle-cone until it is completely filled with ice cream and an additional hemisphere of ice cream sits on top, as in the figure below:

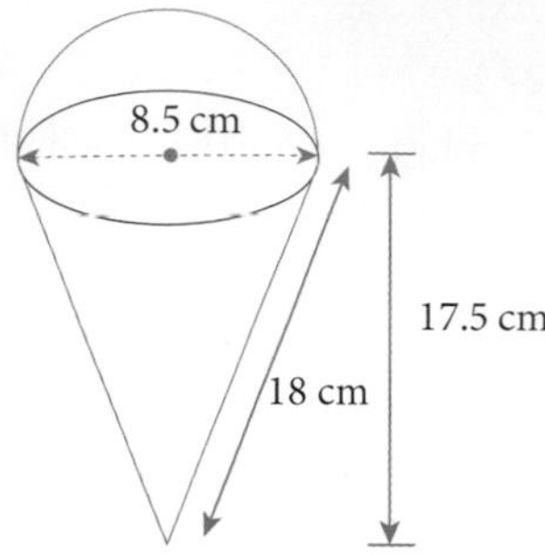

Calculate the following:

(i) The surface area of the waffle cone (rounded to the nearest cm^2).

(ii) The volume of ice-cream the cone can hold, including the hemisphere on top (rounded to the nearest mL).

Solution

(i) Since the cone does not have a lid, we use the formula for an open cone, and the radius is half of the diameter, so $r = 4.25$ cm.

Using $SA = \pi rs$

$$SA = \pi(4.25 \text{ cm})(18 \text{ cm})$$
$$\approx 240 \text{ cm}^2$$

Therefore, the surface area of the waffle cone is 240 cm^2.

(ii) The volume of ice-cream is equal to the volume of the cone, plus the volume of a hemisphere. Since the flat circular face of the hemisphere lines up with the open circular face of the cone, the radii of the two solids are equal (i.e., $r = 4.25$ cm for both the cone and hemisphere).

$$V = \frac{\pi r^2 h}{3} + \frac{2\pi r^3}{3}$$

$$V = \frac{\pi(4.25 \text{ cm})^2(17.5 \text{ cm})}{3} + \frac{2\pi(4.25 \text{ cm})^3}{3}$$

$$\approx 331.0 \text{ cm}^3 + 160.8 \text{ cm}^3$$
$$\approx 492 \text{ cm}^3$$
$$= 492 \text{ mL}$$

Therefore, the volume of ice-cream the cone can hold, including the hemisphere on top is 492 mL.

9.4 | Exercises

Answers to odd-numbered problems are available at the end of the textbook.

For the following problems, round your answers to two decimal places (unless otherwise indicated).
For Problems 1 to 14, determine the surface area and volume of the given solids.

1. A cube with sides 25 mm long.
2. A cube with sides 8 cm long.
3. A rectangular prism with sides of 3 m, 6 m, and 12.5 m.
4. A rectangular prism with sides of 40 cm, 80 cm, and 150 cm.

5. A semi-open cylinder with a height of 15 cm and a base with a diameter of 12 cm.
6. An open cylinder with a height of 51 cm and a base with a radius of 5 cm.
7. A closed cylinder with a height of 85 mm and a base with a radius of 32 mm.
8. A semi-open cylinder with a height of 1.5 m and a base with a diameter of 64 cm.
9. An open cone with a perpendicular height of 22 cm, a slant height of 22.5 cm, and a base with a radius of 4.5 cm.
10. A closed cone with a perpendicular height of 94 mm, a slant height of 98 mm, and a base with a diameter of 56 mm.
11. A sphere with a radius of 22 cm.
12. A sphere with a radius of 8 mm.
13. A sphere with a diameter of 1.3 m.
14. A sphere with a diameter of 7.5 cm.

For Problems 15 to 20, determine the volume of the given solids.

15. A cone with a base area of 140 cm^2 and a height of 40 cm.
16. A triangular pyramid with a base area of 270 m^2 and a height of 15 m.
17. A square pyramid with sides 4.5 m long and a height of 2.8 m.
18. A rectangular pyramid with side lengths of 48 cm and 60 cm, and a height of 55 cm.
19. A triangular prism with a base area of 7 cm^2 and a height of 36 cm.
20. A triangular pyramid with a base area of 270 m^2 and a height of 15 m.
21. Calculate the volume of a rectangular box that measures 1.44 m by 1.25 m by 75 cm. How much cardboard is needed to construct the box?
22. Calculate the volume of a can of beans that has a base with a diameter of 7.4 cm and a height of 11 cm. How much aluminum is needed to create the can?
23. Determine the volume of air needed in a spherical basketball that has a surface area of 1,800 cm^2.
24. A puzzle cube has a surface area of 168.54 cm^2. Determine the volume of plastic needed to make the puzzle cube.
25. A rectangular box with a width that is twice its height and two-thirds its length has a volume of 93,750 cm^3. Determine the surface area of the box.
26. A cylindrical pipe with a height that is ten times its base diameter has a volume of 2.5 m^3. Determine the surface area of the (open) cylindrical pipe, rounded to the nearest tenth of a square metre.
27. A novelty megaphone sold at all home-games of a local football team is created from an open plastic cone that has a slant height of 70 cm and a base diameter of 25 cm. Determine the amount of plastic needed to create the megaphone.
28. The smallest of the three pyramids of Giza in Egypt has a square-base with side lengths of 108.6 m, a slant height of 85.8 m, and a perpendicular height of 66.4 m. The surface of the pyramid was originally covered in white limestone. Determine the amount of white limestone that would have been needed to complete this task.
29. The circumference of the earth is approximately 40,075 km. Approximate the surface area (rounded to the nearest million km^2) and volume (rounded to the nearest billion km^3) of the earth, assuming that it is a perfect sphere.
30. A spherical bowling ball is made up of a polyurethane core and a reactive resin cover, and must have a circumference of 68 cm. Determine the cost to manufacture the ball if the polyurethane for the core costs \$0.0065/cm^3 and the reactive resin coating costs \$0.0105/cm^2. Round you answer to the nearest cent.

For Problems 31 to 34, determine the surface area and volume of the composite figures.

31. A child's playhouse consisting of a square prism base and a square-pyramid roof:

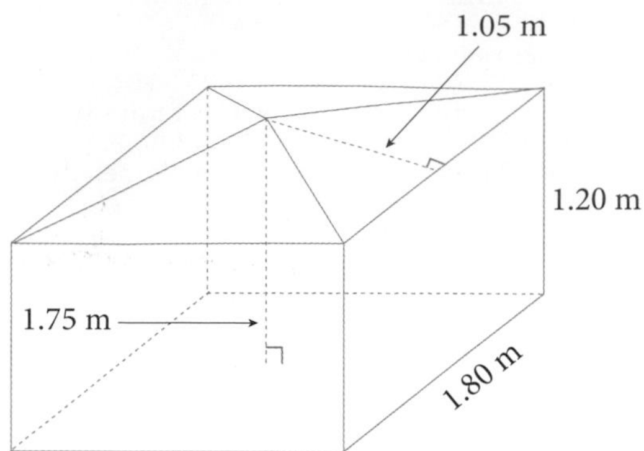

32. A greenhouse consisting of a rectangular base and a half-cylindrical roof:

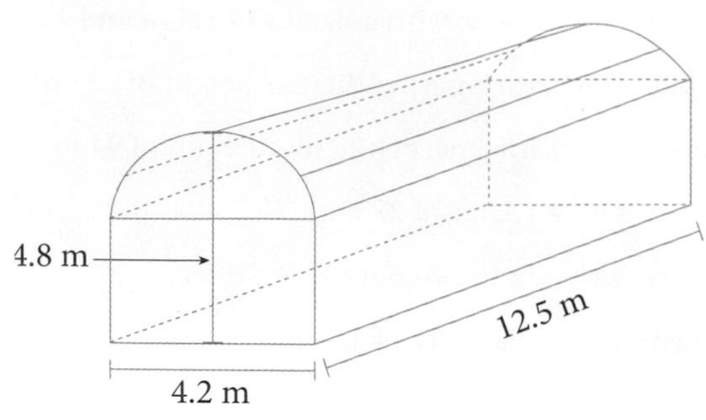

33. A silo consisting of a cylindrical base and a hemispherical roof:

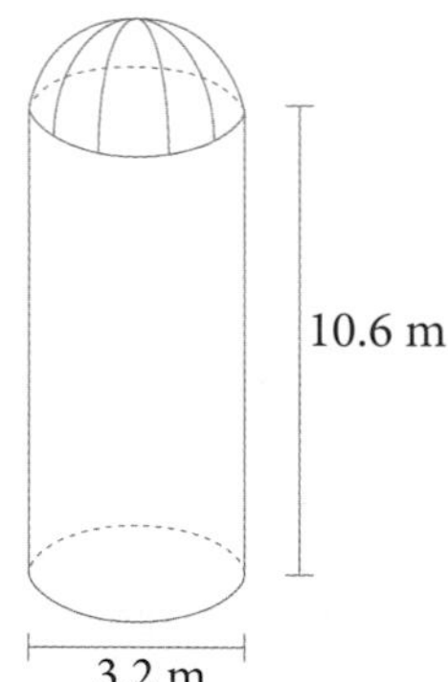

34. A gazebo consisting of a cylindrical base and a conical roof:

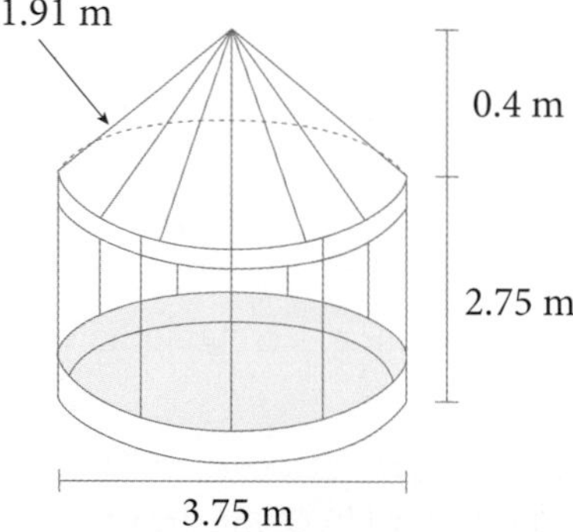

9.5 | Optimization

Optimization is the process of maximizing or minimizing a measurement, given a constraint. It is a very common and useful calculation.

For example,

- When purchasing a new cell phone plan, a customer will select the option that maximizes their data/minutes for a given budget.
- When taking a road trip, a GPS will select the path that minimizes the driving time given a specific destination.
- When building a new house, the contractor will try to maximize the square footage given the size of the lot and the building code restrictions.

There are many more examples of how optimization can be applied in every day life; similarly, there are many applications of optimization in the different branches of mathematics. This section will focus on optimization in geometry, and more specifically, maximizing/minimizing perimeter and area in two-dimensional figures, as well as surface area and volume in three-dimensional solids.

Methods of Optimization

In 2-D problems, there are a number of different methods that can be used to find optimal measurements. Since the problems involve geometrical shapes, we will need to use the formulas outlined in the previous sections of this chapter, as well as diagrams, tables of values, and graphs.

The following example will be used to illustrate these methods for a basic 2-D optimization problem.

Problem: Maximize the area of a rectangle with a perimeter of 20 m and integer side lengths

Optimize: Maximum Area

Constraint: Perimeter is 20 m, side lengths are integer values

Shape: Rectangle, with length l and width w

Formulas: $P = 2l + 2w$

$A = l \times w$

Method 1: Using Diagrams

Step 1: Draw out each possible rectangle that fits the constraints (P = 20 m, integer side lengths).

The smallest (integer) width that a rectangle can have is 1 m.

Drawing the rectangle with width 1 m and perimeter 20 m:

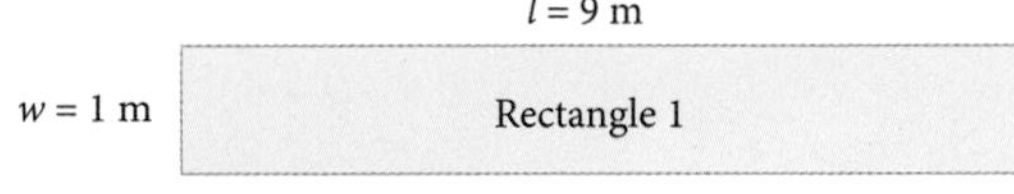

$P = 2(9\text{ m}) + 2(1\text{ m}) = 20\text{ m}$

This is the same as a rectangle with length 1 m and width 9 m.

Drawing the rest of the rectangles by increasing the width by 1 m:

$l = 8$ m
$w = 2$ m
Rectangle 2

$P = 2(8\text{ m}) + 2(2\text{ m}) = 20\text{ m}$

This is the same as a rectangle with length 2 m and width 8 m.

$l = 7$ m
$w = 3$ m
Rectangle 3

$P = 2(7\text{ m}) + 2(3\text{ m}) = 20\text{ m}$

This is the same as a rectangle with length 3 m and width 7 m.

$l = 6$ m
$w = 4$ m
Rectangle 4

$P = 2(6\text{ m}) + 2(4\text{ m}) = 20\text{ m}$

This is the same as a rectangle with length 4 m and width 6 m.

$l = 5$ m
$w = 5$ m
Rectangle 5

$P = 2(5\text{ m}) + 2(5\text{ m}) = 20\text{ m}$

Step 2: Calculate the area for each rectangle and compare to find the one with the largest area.

Calculating the areas of the five rectangles, using $A = l \times w$,

Rectangle 1: $A = (9 \text{ m})(1 \text{ m}) = 9 \text{ m}^2$

Rectangle 2: $A = (8 \text{ m})(2 \text{ m}) = 16 \text{ m}^2$

Rectangle 3: $A = (7 \text{ m})(3 \text{ m}) = 21 \text{ m}^2$

Rectangle 4: $A = (6 \text{ m})(4 \text{ m}) = 24 \text{ m}^2$

Rectangle 5: $A = (5 \text{ m})(5 \text{ m}) = 25 \text{ m}^2$

Therefore, the maximum area of a rectangle with a perimeter of 20 m and integer side lengths is 25 m^2, with dimensions of 5 m by 5 m.

Method 2: Using a Table of Values

Step 1: Identify the formula for the constraint given: P = 20 m. Isolate for one of the variables in the formula: *l* or *w*.

The constraint given in this problem is that the perimeter is 20 m. The perimeter of a rectangle is given by the formula $P = 2l + 2w$.

$P = 2l + 2w$ Substituting P = 20 m,

$20 = 2l + 2w$ Rearranging to isolate *w*,

$20 = 2(l + w)$

$10 = l + w$

$w = 10 - l$

By simplifying and rearranging the formula, we have a formula for width based on the length of the rectangle.

Note: We could have just as easily rearranged to isolate l, to create a formula for length based on the width of the rectangle.

Step 2: Using the formula created in Step 1, determine the dimensions of the possible rectangles, and create a table of values for *l* and *w*.

The smallest (integer) length that a rectangle can have is 1 m.

Substituting $l = 1$ m into the formula from Step 1:

$$w = 10 - l = 10 - 1 = 9 \text{ m}$$

Therefore, for a rectangle with P = 20 m and $l = 1$ m, $w = 9$ m.

Substitute all possible integer values for *l* into the formula to calculate *w*, and create a table of values.

Since length and width cannot be negative numbers, the values for *l* and *w* must fall between 0 and 10.

l (m)	*w* (m)
1	9
2	8
3	7
4	6
5	5
6	4
7	3
8	2
9	1

Step 3: Calculate the area for each rectangle and compare to find the one with the largest area.

Calculating the areas of the rectangles, using A = $l \times w$,

l (m)	w (m)	A (m^2) = $l \times w$
1	9	$A = (1\text{ m})(9\text{ m}) = 9\text{ m}^2$
2	8	$A = (2\text{ m})(8\text{ m}) = 16\text{ m}^2$
3	7	$A = (3\text{ m})(7\text{ m}) = 21\text{ m}^2$
4	6	$A = (4\text{ m})(6\text{ m}) = 24\text{ m}^2$
5	**5**	**$A = (5\text{ m})(5\text{ m}) = 25\text{ m}^2$**
6	4	$A = (6\text{ m})(4\text{ m}) = 24\text{ m}^2$
7	3	$A = (7\text{ m})(3\text{ m}) = 21\text{ m}^2$
8	2	$A = (8\text{ m})(2\text{ m}) = 16\text{ m}^2$
9	1	$A = (9\text{ m})(1\text{ m}) = 9\text{ m}^2$

Therefore, the maximum area of a rectangle with a perimeter of 20 m and integer side lengths is 25 m^2, with dimensions of 5 m by 5 m.

Method 3: Graphing

Step 1: Identify the formula for the constraint given: P = 20 m. Isolate for one of the variables in the formula: l or w.

Recall from Method 2, Step 1: $w = 10 - l$

Step 2: Substitute this value into the formula for the measure we are trying to optimize: area (A).

The area of a rectangle is given by the formula A = $l \times w$.

$$A = l \times w \qquad \text{Substituting } w = 10 - l \text{ (from Step 1),}$$
$$= l \times (10 - l)$$
$$= 10l - l^2$$

Step 3: Graph the new equation using a table of values. Visually identify the maximum value from the graph.

*Note: The equation from Step 2 is **not** linear, and will result in a curve rather than a straight line. As such, use a minimum of five points when creating your table of values/graphing.*

Using the equation from Step 2 to create a table of values of areas for different possible lengths:

Since length and width cannot be negative numbers, the values for l and w must fall between 0 and 10.

l (m)	A (m^2) = $10l - l^2$
1	$A = 10(1) - (1)^2 = 9\text{ m}^2$
2	$A = 10(2) - (2)^2 = 16\text{ m}^2$
3	$A = 10(3) - (3)^2 = 21\text{ m}^2$
4	$A = 10(4) - (4)^2 = 24\text{ m}^2$
5	$A = 10(5) - (5)^2 = 25\text{ m}^2$
6	$A = 10(6) - (6)^2 = 24\text{ m}^2$
7	$A = 10(7) - (7)^2 = 21\text{ m}^2$
8	$A = 10(8) - (8)^2 = 16\text{ m}^2$
9	$A = 10(9) - (9)^2 = 9\text{ m}^2$

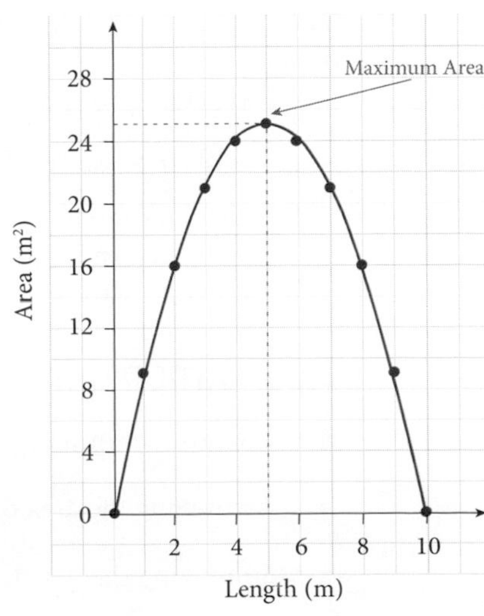

Therefore, by analyzing the graph, it can be seen that the maximum area of a rectangle with a perimeter of 20 m is 25 m^2, which occurs when $l = 5$ m and $w = 10 - 5 = 5$ m.

Determining Which Method to Use

As can be seen in the previous example, each of these methods produced the same result, but each has its own unique strengths and weaknesses. For instance, the diagram method is similar to solving by trial and error, which can be very time consuming, and inaccurate. It is difficult (if not almost impossible) to create every rectangle that fits the constraint, especially if lengths with decimal numbers may be included. In this basic example, we were constrained to integer-value side lengths, so the diagram method worked, but in real-life problems which allow for decimal-value answers, the diagram method should generally be used more as an exploratory tool.

The most accurate method is the graphing method. This method uses a combination of skills learned in the previous chapter, including graphing using a table of values.

Although the graphing method allows for the identification of non-integer solutions, those values are only an estimate when read off of a graph. The exact solution can be found by solving the equation algebraically; however, as seen in the previous example, the equation for an optimization problem is not linear, and thus solving for these types of equations is beyond the scope of this textbook. However, we can make use of **patterns** to help identify non-integer solutions.

Notice in the previous example that the curve is **symmetrical** around the maximum point (called the **vertex**). This means that the x-coordinate for the vertex is going to be exactly halfway between any pair of points with the same y-coordinate. For example, from the graph and the table of values, the points (2, 16) and (8, 16) have the same y-values (A = 16 m^2). Therefore, since the curve is symmetrical, to find the vertex using these points, we simply need to take the average of the x-values (lengths):

$$\frac{2+8}{2} = \frac{10}{2} = 5$$

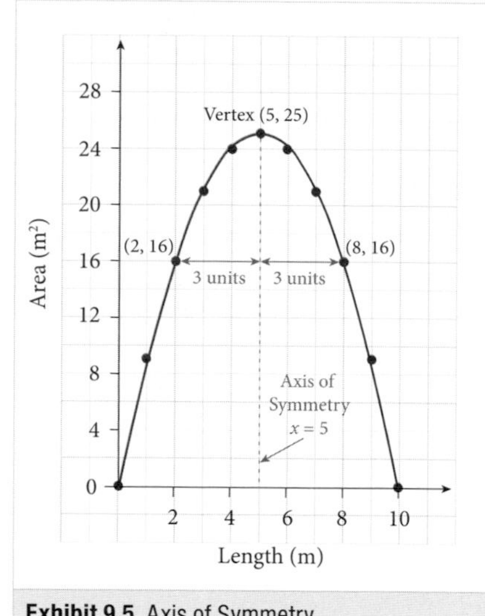

Exhibit 9.5 Axis of Symmetry

Therefore, the vertex has an x-coordinate (length) of 5 m. Substituting this into the equation from Step 2 (for area):

$$A = 10l - l^2 = 10(5) - 5^2 = 50 - 25 = 25 \text{ m}^2$$

Once we have calculated the area using the formula, double check the graph to make sure it matches with what is seen on the curve. Once this is confirmed as the maximum area, use the equation from Step 1 to determine the missing dimension, which in this case is the width:

$$w = 10 - l = 10 - 5 = 5 \text{ m}$$

Unless the question explicitly states the method to be used, it is preferable to use a combination of the three: a diagram of the shape being explored, a table of values created using the formulas, and a graph illustrating the optimal value.

Two-Dimensional Optimization Problems

The two most common types of problems in this category are:

- Maximizing the area of an object given its perimeter
- Minimizing the perimeter of an object given its area

Example 9.5-a Optimizing the Area of a Rectangle and a Circle

Which has a larger maximum area: a rectangle with a perimeter of 10 cm, or a circle with a circumference of 10 cm?

Solution

Optimizing the Rectangle

First, we will determine the maximum area of a rectangle with a perimeter of 10 cm.

w | P = 10 cm | l

The constraint is P = 10 cm. The perimeter, P, of a rectangle is given by $P = 2l + 2w$.

$P = 2l + 2w$ Substituting P = 10 cm,

$10 = 2l + 2w$ Rearranging to isolate l,

$10 = 2(l + w)$

$5 = l + w$

$l = 5 - w$ Equation 1

We are trying to maximize area. The area, A, of a rectangle is given by $A = l \times w$.

$A = l \times w$ Substituting $l = 5 - w$ (Equation 1),

$= (5 - w) \times w$

$= 5w - w^2$ Equation 2

If w is greater than 5, then from Equation 1, length would be negative.

Since length and width cannot be negative numbers, the values for w must be between 0 and 5. Creating a table of values for width and area and graphing the relationship,

w (cm)	A (cm^2) = $5w - w^2$
0	$A = 5(0) - (0)^2 = 0 \text{ cm}^2$
1	$A = 5(1) - (1)^2 = 4 \text{ cm}^2$
2	$A = 5(2) - (2)^2 = 6 \text{ cm}^2$
3	$A = 5(3) - (3)^2 = 6 \text{ cm}^2$
4	$A = 5(4) - (4)^2 = 4 \text{ cm}^2$
5	$A = 5(5) - (5)^2 = 0 \text{ cm}^2$

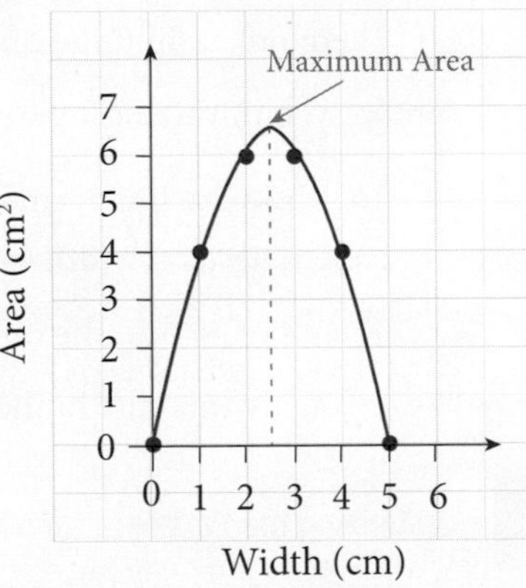

Observing the table of values and the graph, it becomes apparent that the curve is symmetrical around a maximum point (vertex), which occurs when the width is between 2 cm and 3 cm.

That is, since the curve is symmetrical and the points (2, 6) and (3, 6) have the same y-value ($A = 6 \text{ cm}^2$), the x-coordinate (width) for the vertex is $\frac{2+3}{2} = 2.5$ cm.

Using Equation 2,

$A = 5w - w^2$ Substituting $w = 2.5$ cm,

$= 5(2.5) - (2.5)^2$

$= 12.5 - 6.25$

$= 6.25 \text{ cm}^2$

or

Using Equation 1,

$l = 5 - w$ Substituting $w = 2.5$ cm,

$= 5 - 2.5$

$= 2.5$ cm

Using $A = l \times w$,

$= 2.5 \times 2.5$

$= 6.25 \text{ cm}^2$

Therefore, for a rectangle with a perimeter of 10 cm, the maximum area is equal to 6.25 cm^2.

Solution *continued*

Optimizing the Circle

Next, we determine the maximum area of a circle with a circumference of 10 cm.

The constraint is C = 10 cm. The circumference, C, of a circle is given by $C = 2\pi r$.

$C = 2\pi r$ Substituting C = 10 cm,

$10 = 2\pi r$ Rearranging to isolate r,

$r = \frac{10}{2\pi}$

$= \frac{5}{\pi} \approx 1.59$ cm There is only one possible radius for a circle with a circumference of 10 cm.

The area, A, of a circle is given by $A = \pi r^2$.

$A = \pi r^2$ Substituting r = 1.59 cm,

$= \pi(1.59)^2 \approx 7.94 \text{ cm}^2$

Therefore, for a circle with a circumference of 10 cm, the area is equal to 7.94 cm^2.

In conclusion, the circle with a circumference of 10 cm has a larger maximum area than a rectangle with a perimeter of 10 cm.

Did you notice that in the introductory example and in Example 9.5-a, the optimal dimensions to maximize the area of a rectangle formed a **square**? This result can be generalized as follows:

- To **maximize the area of a closed rectangle**, the side lengths should be equal; i.e., length (l) = width (w).

  Therefore, to find the dimensions of the sides, divide the given perimeter by four.

Similarly, minimizing a perimeter given an area can be summarized as follows:

- To **minimize the perimeter of a closed rectangle**, the side lengths should be equal; i.e., length (l) = width (w).

  Therefore, to find the dimensions of the sides, take the square root of the given area.

We will apply this rule in the next example.

Example 9.5-b **Optimizing the Perimeter of a Rectangle**

Frieda is framing a canvas and needs the area of the canvas to be 625 cm². What is the minimum length of wood that she will need to create the frame?

Solution

The constraint is A = 625 cm^2. The area, A, of a rectangle is given by $A = l \times w$.

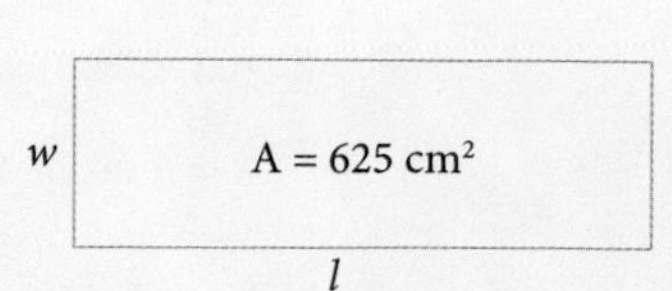

Since we are trying to minimize the perimeter of a closed rectangle, based on the rule above, the resulting shape will be a square, i.e., length (l) = width (w).

$A = l \times w$ Substituting A = 625 cm^2 and $l = w$,

$625 = w^2$ Rearranging to isolate w,

$w = \sqrt{625} = 25$ cm

Therefore, the minimum length of wood that she will need to create the frame will be:

$P = 2l + 2w = 2(25 \text{ cm}) + 2(25 \text{ cm}) = 100 \text{ cm}$

Solution *continued*

We can confirm our answer by following the graphing method.

$A = l \times w$	Substituting $A = 625 \text{ cm}^2$,
$625 = l \times w$	Rearranging to isolate l,
$l = \dfrac{625}{w}$	Equation 1

$P = 2l + 2w$	Substituting $l = \dfrac{625}{w}$,
$= 2\left(\dfrac{625}{w}\right) + 2w$	
$= \dfrac{1{,}250}{w} + 2w$	
$= \dfrac{1{,}250 + 2w^2}{w}$	Equation 2

Creating a table of values for width and perimeter and graphing the relationship to visually identify the minimum,

w (cm)	P (cm)
5	260
10	145
15	113.3
20	102.5
24	100.083
25	**100**
26	100.077
30	101.7
35	105.7
40	111.3
45	117.8
50	125

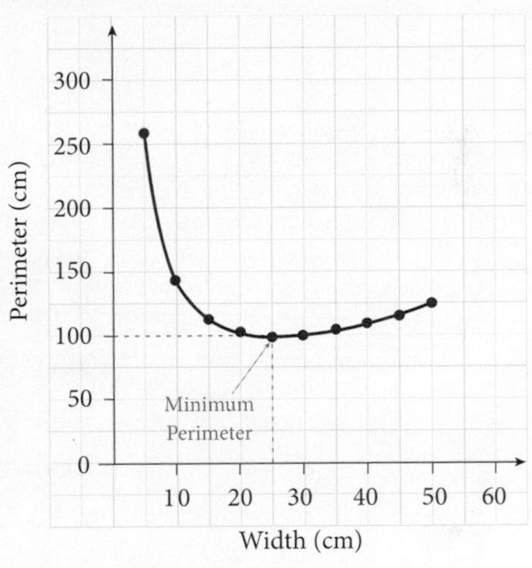

Observing the table of values and the graph, it becomes apparent that the curve in this case is **not** symmetrical. The minimum perimeter visually appears to be 100 cm, which occurs when the width is 25 cm.

Therefore, the dimensions that minimize the perimeter are $w = 25$ cm and $l = \dfrac{625}{25} = 25$ cm, forming a square as predicted.

It is important to note the word "closed" in the rules stated above, because this is only true when working with all four sides of a rectangle. In the next example, only three sides of the rectangle are needed for the problem, and the solution does not have equal sides.

Example 9.5-c

Optimizing the Area of an Un-closed Rectangle

Liv is building a garden. A shed is on one side of the garden and she wants to enclose the other three sides with wood planking in order to keep out the rabbits. What is the maximum area that she can enclose, given that she has already purchased 20 ft of wood planking? What are the dimensions of the garden?

Solution

$P = 2w + l$ — Only three sides of the garden need wood planking.

$20 = 2w + l$ — Rearranging to isolate l,

$l = 20 - 2w$ — Equation 1

$A = l \times w$ — Substituting $l = 20 - 2w$,

$= (20 - 2w) \times w$

$= 20w - 2w^2$ — Equation 2

Shed | Garden | w | l

> If w is greater than 10, then from Equation **1**, length would be negative.

Since length and width cannot be negative numbers, the values for w must be between 0 and 10.

w (ft)	A (ft^2)
0	$20(0) - 2(0)^2 = 0$ ft^2
1	$20(1) - 2(1)^2 = 18$ ft^2
2	$20(2) - 2(2)^2 = 32$ ft^2
3	$20(3) - 2(3)^2 = 42$ ft^2
4	$20(4) - 2(4)^2 = 48$ ft^2
5	$20(5) - 2(5)^2 = 50$ ft^2
6	$20(6) - 2(6)^2 = 48$ ft^2
7	$20(7) - 2(7)^2 = 42$ ft^2
8	$20(8) - 2(8)^2 = 32$ ft^2
9	$20(9) - 2(9)^2 = 18$ ft^2
10	$20(10) - 2(10)^2 = 0$ ft^2

> The graph of the curve is symmetrical around the maximum point (vertex).

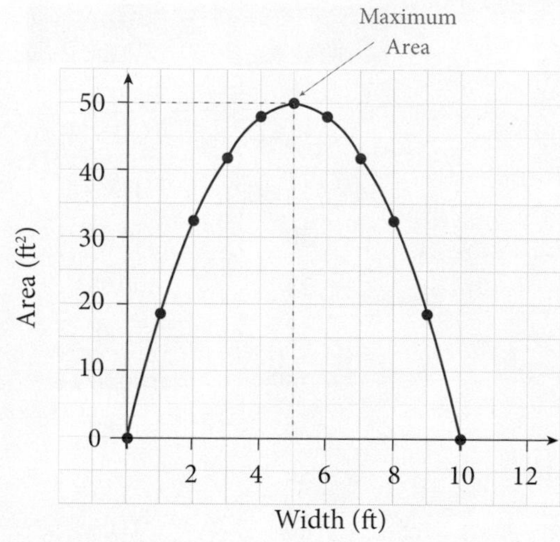

From the table of values and the graph, the maximum area is 50 ft^2 and it occurs when the width $w = 5$ ft.

Using Equation 1 : $l = 20 - 2w = 20 - 2(5) = 20 - 10 = 10$ ft

Therefore, the rectangle that optimizes the area of the garden is 10 ft by 5 ft.

Three-Dimensional Optimization Problems

Optimizing three-dimensional solids is a little more complicated than working in two-dimensions because of the additional variables involved. These types of problems are best solved using calculus, which is beyond the scope of this textbook, so the diagrams, tables, and graphs from the previous examples will not be as helpful here. However, as we discovered in working with 2-D shapes, optimal dimensions are created when the sides are all of equal length. If we apply this same rule to 3-D solids, we can solve optimization problems without using calculus.

Example 9.5-d **Optimizing the Volume of a Rectangular Prism**

Determine the maximum volume of a rectangular prism with a given surface area of 2,400 mm^2.

Solution

The constraint is SA = 2,400 mm^2. The surface area, SA, of a rectangular prism is given by SA = $2lw + 2lh + 2wh$.

Using our knowledge that volume will be maximized when all the side lengths are equal, the resulting shape will be a cube, i.e., $l = w = h$.

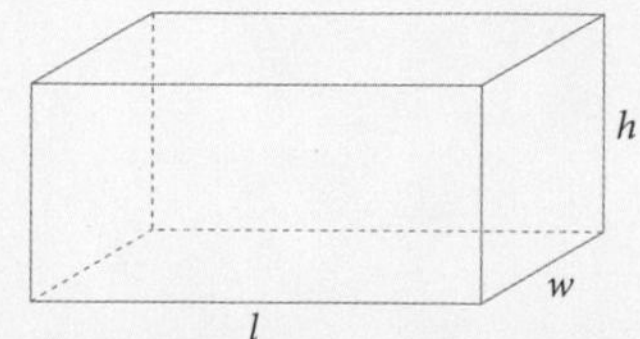

Solution
continued

$$\begin{aligned} SA &= 2lw + 2lh + 2wh && \text{Substituting SA} = 2{,}400 \text{ mm}^2 \text{ and } l = w = h, \\ 2{,}400 &= 2l^2 + 2l^2 + 2l^2 && \text{Rearranging to isolate } l, \\ 2{,}400 &= 6l^2 \\ 400 &= l^2 \\ l &= \sqrt{400} = 20 \text{ mm} \end{aligned}$$

We are trying to maximize volume. The volume, V, of a rectangular prism is given by $V = l \times w \times h$.

$$\begin{aligned} V &= l \times w \times h && \text{Substituting } l = w = h, \\ &= l^3 && \text{Substituting } l = 20 \text{ mm}, \\ &= 20^3 = 8{,}000 \text{ mm}^3 \end{aligned}$$

Therefore, the maximum volume for a rectangular prism with a surface area of 2,400 mm^2 is 8,000 mm^3, with dimensions 20 mm × 20 mm × 20 mm.

For comparison, a rectangular prism that has a SA of 2,400 mm^2 and measures 10 mm × 10 mm × 55 mm only has a volume of 5,500 mm^3.

Example 9.5-e

Optimizing the Surface Area of a Cylinder

A cylindrical water tank is designed to hold 500 m^3. What is the minimum amount of materials needed to create this water tank?

Solution

The constraint is V = 500 m^3. The volume, V, of a cylinder is given by $V = \pi r^2 h$.

In order to minimize surface area, we need the side lengths of the cylinder to be equal; that is, we need a cylinder that is as tall as it is wide, i.e., $h = d = 2r$.

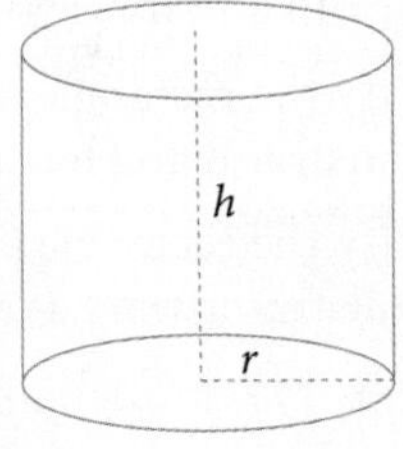

$$\begin{aligned} V &= \pi r^2 h && \text{Substituting V} = 500 \text{ m}^3 \text{ and } h = 2r, \\ 500 &= \pi r^2(2r) && \text{Solving for } r, \\ 500 &= 2\pi r^3 \\ 250 &= \pi r^3 \\ r^3 &= \frac{250}{\pi} \\ r &= \sqrt[3]{\frac{250}{\pi}} \approx 4.30 \text{ m} \end{aligned}$$

We are trying to minimize surface area. The surface area, SA, of a closed cylinder is given by $SA = 2\pi r^2 + 2\pi rh$.

$$\begin{aligned} SA &= 2\pi r^2 + 2\pi rh && \text{Substituting } h = 2r, \\ &= 2\pi r^2 + 2\pi r(2r) \\ &= 2\pi r^2 + 4\pi r^2 \\ &= 6\pi r^2 && \text{Substituting } r = 4.30 \text{ m}, \\ &= 6\pi(4.30)^2 \approx 348.5 \text{ m}^2 \end{aligned}$$

Therefore, the minimum surface area for a cylinder with a volume of 500 m^3 is approximately 348.5 m^2, with a height and diameter both equal to 4.30 × 2 = 8.60 m.

For comparison, a cylinder that has a V of 500 m^3, a height of 1.6 m, and a diameter of 20 m has a surface area of about 730 m^2.

9.5 | Exercises

Answers to odd-numbered problems are available at the end of the textbook.

For Problems 1 to 4, draw every possible rectangle with integer side lengths and the following constraints:

1. A perimeter of 36 cm.
2. A perimeter of 42 cm.
3. An area of 60 cm^2.
4. An area of 100 cm^2.

For Problems 5 to 8, fill in the following table, adding as many rows as needed to show all rectangles with integer side lengths that satisfy the constraint.

Length	Width	Perimeter	Area

5. A perimeter of 12 m.
6. A perimeter of 16 m.
7. An area of 72 m^2.
8. An area of 24 m^2.
9. Identify the rectangle in Problem 1 with the largest area. Is there another rectangle that exists that satisfies the constraint and has a larger area? If so, what are the dimensions of this rectangle?
10. Identify the rectangle in Problem 2 with the largest area. Is there another rectangle that exists that satisfies the constraint and has a larger area? If so, what are the dimensions of this rectangle?
11. Identify the rectangle in Problem 7 with the smallest perimeter. Is there another rectangle that exists that satisfies the constraint and has a smaller perimeter? If so, what are the dimensions of this rectangle?
12. Identify the rectangle in Problem 8 with the smallest perimeter. Is there another rectangle that exists that satisfies the constraint and has a smaller perimeter? If so, what are the dimensions of this rectangle?

For Problems 13 to 16, optimize the rectangles and use the graphing method to verify.

13. Determine the maximum area for a rectangle with a perimeter of 28 units.
14. Maximize the area for a rectangle with a perimeter of 8 units.
15. Given that the area of a rectangle is 36 m^2, what dimensions will minimize the perimeter?
16. What is the minimum perimeter for a rectangle with an area of 900 mm^2?
17. Carl needs to replace a window in his home. He purchased 32 ft of material to frame the window. What are the dimensions of the largest possible window?
18. A new cell phone is on the market that boasts a screen edged in a 24-carat gold border. If each phone has 30 cm of gold, what is the maximum area of the screen?
19. A rectangular building lot is for sale, and the representative is advertising that a house can be built on the lot with a 1,500 square foot ground floor. Based on this description, calculate the minimum dimensions of the lot, assuming that the house can be built right to the edges of the property. Round your answer to two decimal places.
20. A young soccer referee is trying to estimate how far he walks when he lines the outer edge of the field each week with paint. If he knows that a standard soccer pitch is approximately 7,000 m^2, what is the minimum distance that he has to walk while he paints? Round your answer to two decimal places.
21. Kristin is building a dog run for Oliver, her bulldog. She needs to buy material for only three sides of the fencing, since the fourth side will use the fence that already encloses her yard. If she wants Oliver to have an area of 300 square feet, what is the minimum amount of material that she needs to purchase? Round up to the next foot.
22. Dwayne has 80 m of rope to enclose a rectangular swimming area off of the shore of the lake for his camp group. He needs to rope off three sides of the swimming area, since the fourth side will be the beach. What is the largest area that he can enclose rounded to the nearest whole number?
23. Determine the minimum surface area of a rectangular prism with a volume of 220 m^3. Round to two decimal places.

24. Determine the maximum volume of an open cylinder with a surface area of 750 cm^2. Round to two decimal places.

25. A manufacturing company needs to reduce its costs, while still maintaining the quality and value of its product. Currently, it sells 250 cm^3 of tuna in a cylindrical can.

    a. Determine the dimensions of the can that would use the least amount of packaging material.

    b. How much packaging material is required?

26. Van wants to build a rectangular shed in his backyard, including a flat roof and a floor. According to his budget, he can afford to purchase 600 square feet of the aluminum he priced out.

    a. What are the dimensions that maximize the volume of his shed?

    b. What is the maximum volume of the shed?

27. Given a surface area constraint of 180 square units, which has a larger volume: a cylinder or a rectangular prism?

28. Given a volume constraint of 425 cubic units, which has a smaller surface area: a cylinder or a rectangular prism?

29. In a rectangular room with a perimeter of 80 feet, calculate:

    a. The dimensions that maximize the area of the room, rounded to one decimal place.

    b. The maximum area of a circular rug that touches every wall, rounded to the nearest whole number.

30. Sherman is setting up a rectangular skating rink in his backyard and the Plexiglas boarding that goes around the outside costs \$40/m. If he wants the area of the rink to be 150 m^2, calculate:

    a. The dimensions that minimize the perimeter, rounded to one decimal place.

    b. The cost of the boarding he needs, rounded to the nearest dollar.

31. The material for a shipping container costs \$0.75/square foot to build. If the size of the container is to be 1,350 cubic feet, calculate the minimum cost of the materials needed to build one of these containers, if it were in the shape of:

    a. A closed cylinder.

    b. A rectangular prism.

    Round your answers to the nearest cent.

32. The average gas tank in a car holds 12 gallons. Calculate the dimensions, in inches, that would minimize the surface area of the gas tank, if it were in the shape of:

    a. A closed cylinder.

    b. A rectangular prism.

    Hint: There are 231 cubic inches in a gallon.

9 | Review Exercises

Answers to odd-numbered problems are available at the end of the textbook.

For the following problems, round your answers to two decimal places (unless otherwise indicated).

For Problems 1 and 2, determine (i) the measure of angle θ using a protractor, and (ii) calculate the supplement and complement of the angle θ.

1. a.

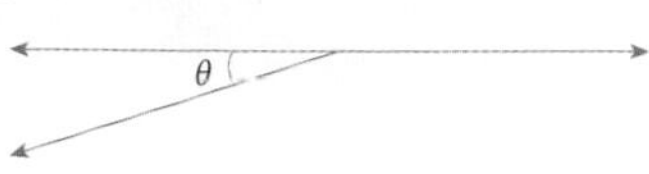

b.

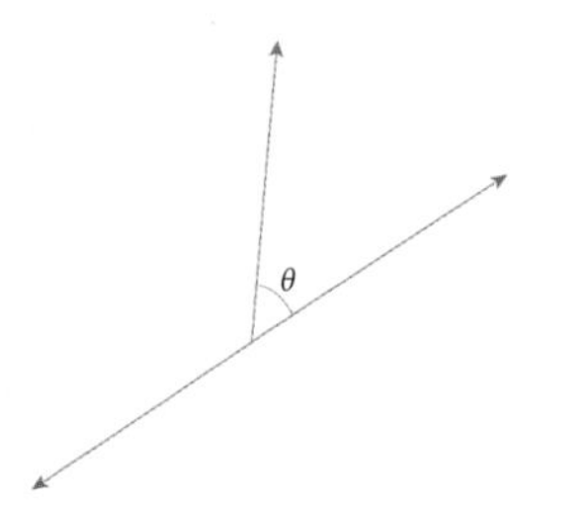

2. a.

b.

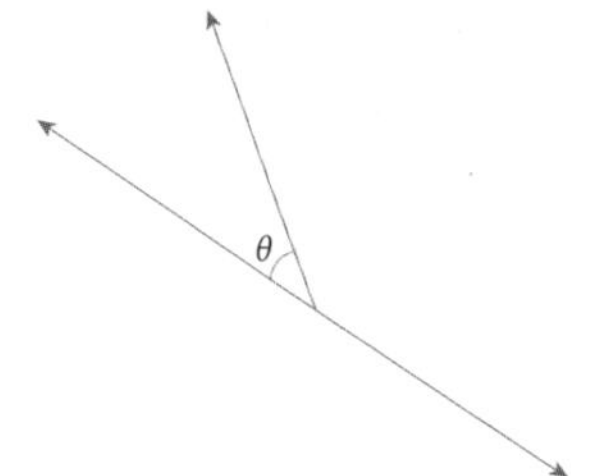

3. Given the following diagram:

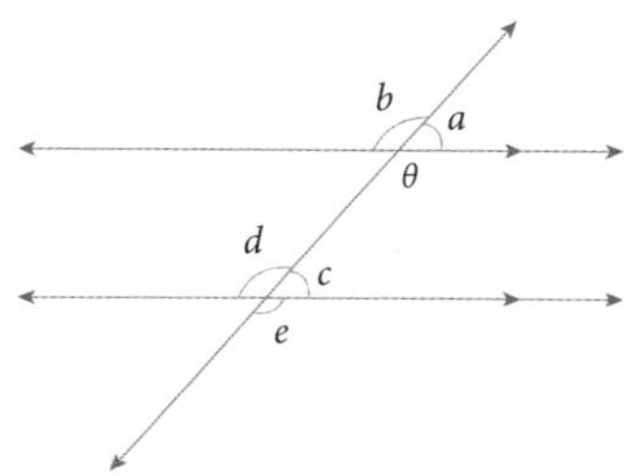

a. State the relationship of θ to each of the unknowns, *a, b, c, d,* and *e*.

b. Calculate the angle measure of each of the unknown angles, given that $\theta = 113°$.

4. Given the following diagram:

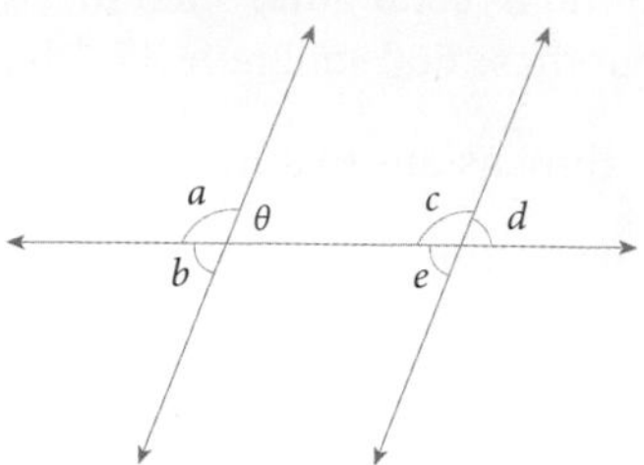

a. State the relationship of θ to each of the unknowns, *a, b, c, d,* and *e*.

b. Calculate the angle measure of each of the unknown angles, given that $\theta = 89°$.

For Problems 5 and 6, determine the unknown angles a, b, and c, in each of the diagrams.

5. a.

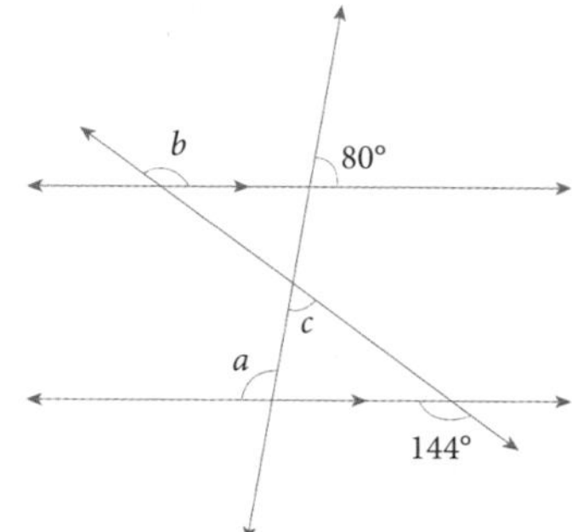

b.

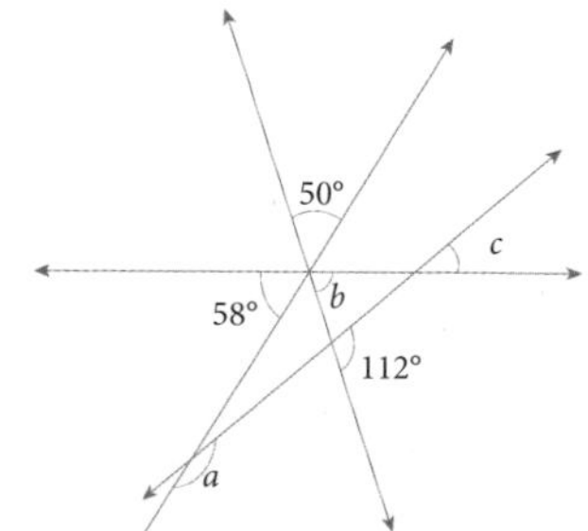

6. a.

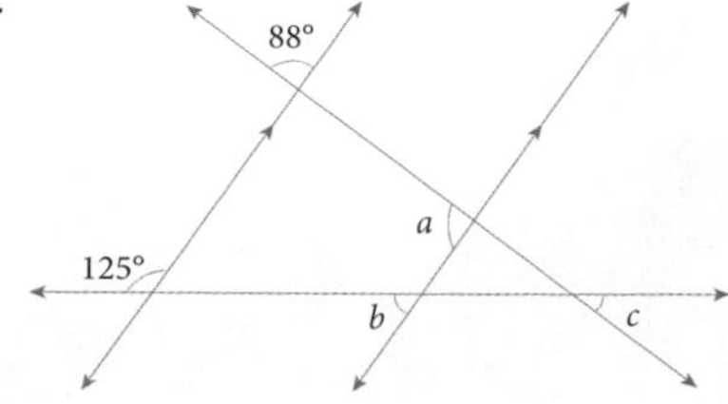

b.

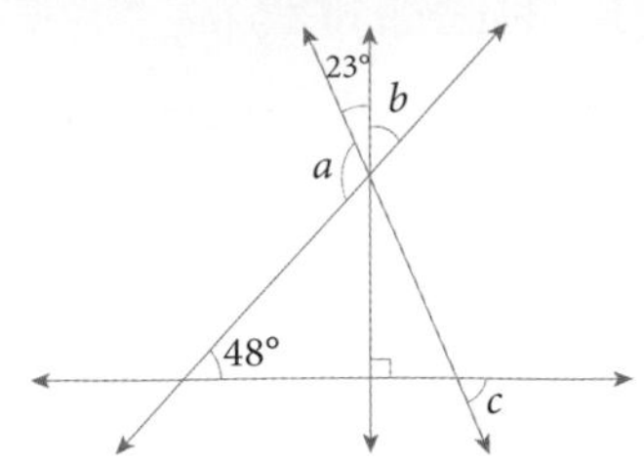

For Problems 7 and 8, classify the quadrilaterals.

7. a.

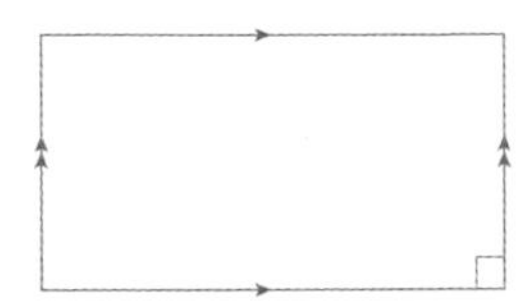

b.

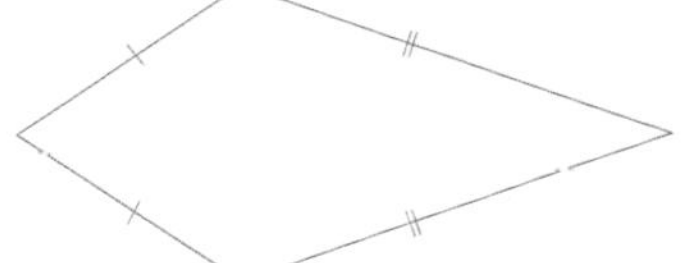

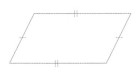

c.

8. a.

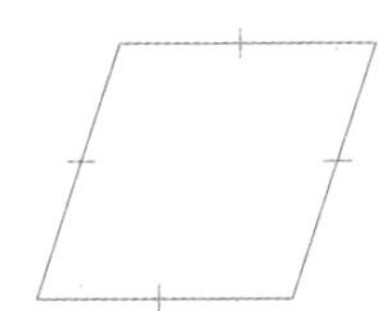

b.

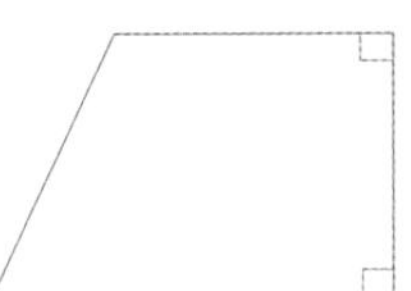

c.

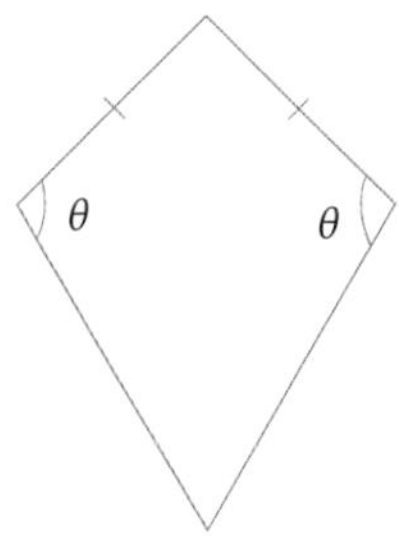

For Problems 9 and 10, use the Internal Angles Theorem (IAT) - Part 1 and the properties of various quadrilaterals to calculate the measure of the unknown angles.

9. a. ABCD is a rhombus, where $\angle DAB = 45°$.

   b. QRST is a general quadrilateral, where $\angle TQR = 112°$, $\angle RST = 68°$, $\angle STQ = 103°$.

   c. WXYZ is a trapezoid, where $\angle XYZ = 114°$, $\angle YZW = 76°$, $\angle ZWX = 68°$.

10. a. WXYZ is a parallelogram, where $\angle WXY = 63°$.

    b. ABCD is a general quadrilateral, where $\angle BAD = 128°$, $\angle ABC = 93°$, $\angle BCD = 52°$.

    c. QRST is a kite, where $\angle TQR = 93°$, $\angle SRQ = 87°$.

For the triangles in Problems 11 and 12, (i) determine all the missing angles, and (ii) classify the triangle by side length and by angle.

11. a.

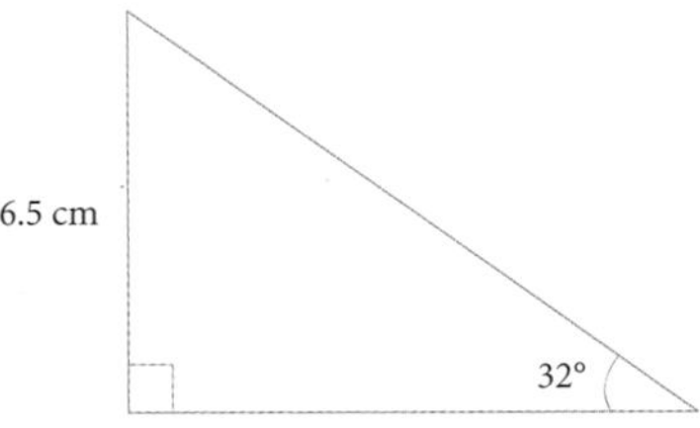

b.

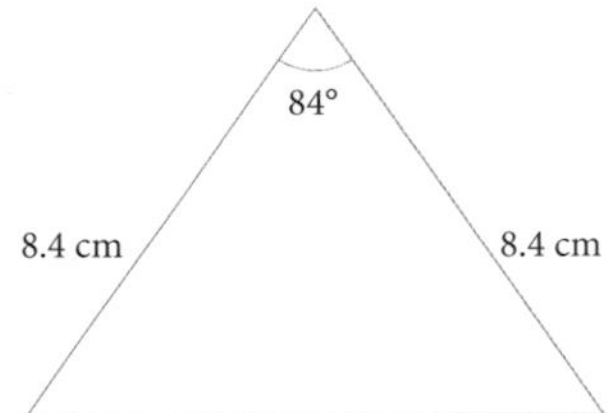

12. a.

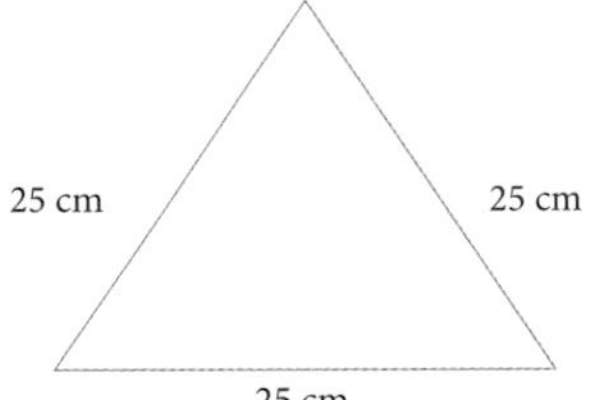

b.

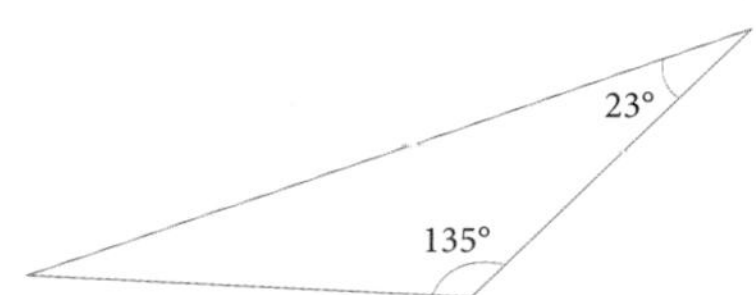

For Problems 13 and 14, calculate the perimeter and the area of the given triangles using (i) the "half-base times height" method, and (ii) Heron's formula.

13. a.

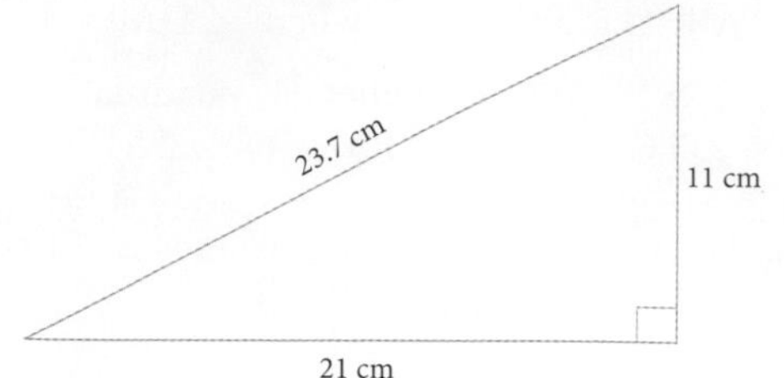

b.

13.1 in
10.08 in
33.9 in
24 in

14. a.

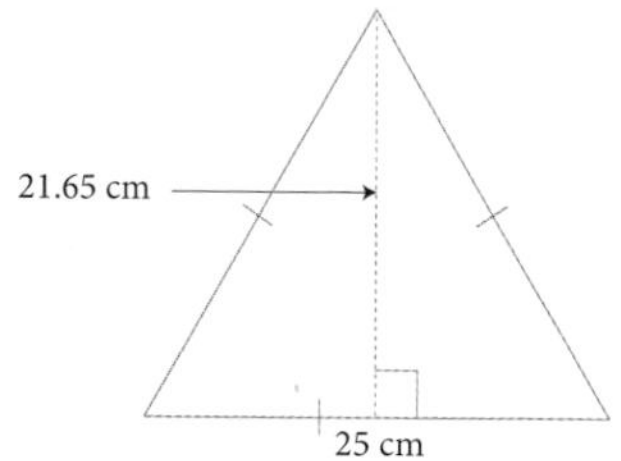

b.

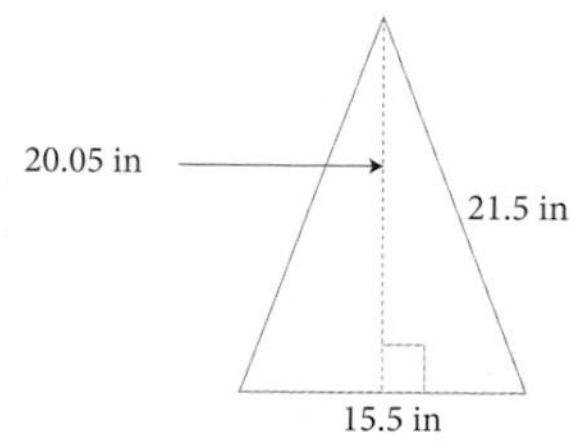

15. Calculate the perimeter of a rectangle with a length that is twice its width and an area of 392 cm^2.

16. Calculate the volume (to the nearest cm^3) of a sphere with a surface area of 452 cm^2.

For Problems 17 to 20, calculate the perimeter and area of the given shapes.

17. A parallelogram with a base of 32 cm, a perpendicular height of 15 cm, and a slant height of 18 cm.

18. A rhombus with a side length of 45 cm and a perpendicular height of 36 cm.

19. a. A circle with a radius of 23.6 m.

    b. A sector of a circle with a diameter of 125 cm and an inscribed angle of 30°.

20. a. A circle with a diameter of 3.5 m.

    b. A sector of a circle with a radius of 78 cm and an inscribed angle of 115°.

21. Calculate the surface area of a cylinder (to the nearest cm^2) that has a volume of 3,220 cm^3 and a height that is equal to its diameter.

22. A circular pane of glass is to be constructed to fit an attic window that has a diameter of 55 cm. Determine the amount of glass (in cm^2) needed to construct the window pane.

23. A medium pizza with a 10-inch diameter is cut into 8 unequal slices. The largest slice has a subtended angle of 65°, while the smallest slice has a subtended angle of 20°. Determine the difference in area between the two slices of pizza, to the nearest tenth of a square inch (in^2).

24. Sixteen spherical chocolates are stacked 4 chocolates long, 2 chocolates high, and 2 chocolates deep, and sold in a rectangular plastic box that perfectly fits the chocolates. Assuming that the box is 10 cm long, 5 cm high, and 5 cm deep, determine the volume of "wasted space" in the box (i.e., the space not occupied by the chocolates). What percent of the box does this represent? Does this seem surprising to you? Why or why not?

For Problems 25 to 28, determine the perimeter and area of the given composite shapes.

25.

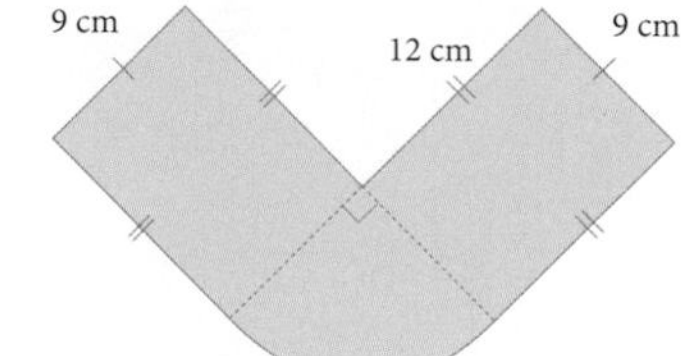

26.

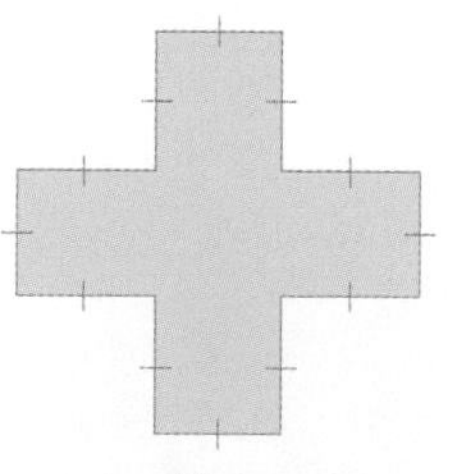

27.

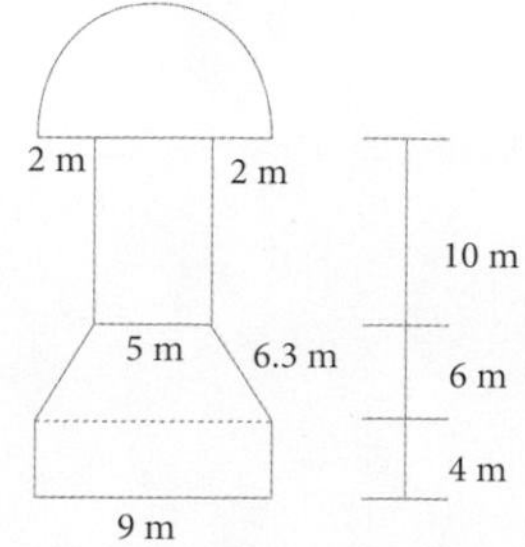

28.

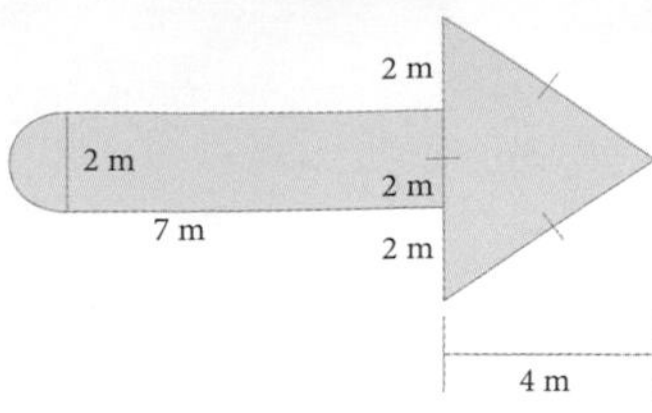

For Problems 29 to 32, determine the surface area and volume of the following 3-dimensional objects.

29. A cylindrical pop can with a radius of 32 mm and a height of 12 cm.

30. A cylindrical cardboard paper towel roll with a diameter of 38 mm and a length of 28 cm.

31. A cement monument in the shape of a square-based pyramid, with a base length of 4.2 m, a slant height of 3.5 m, and a height of 2.8 m.

32. A tetrahedral (equilateral triangular prism) die for a board game, with side lengths of 22 mm each, and a height of 18 mm.

For the composite figures in Problems 33 and 34, determine the surface area and volume.

33.

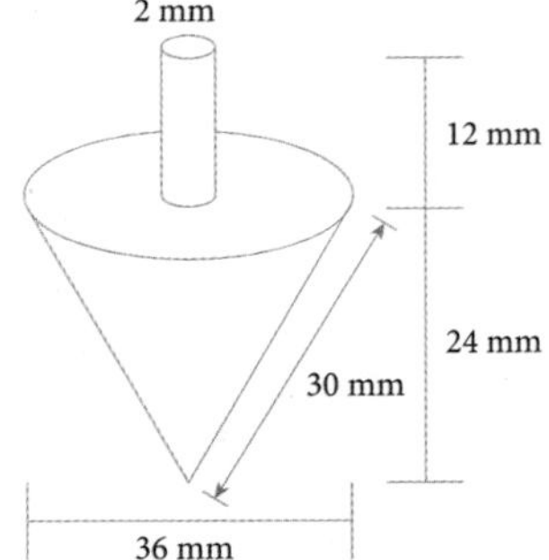

34.

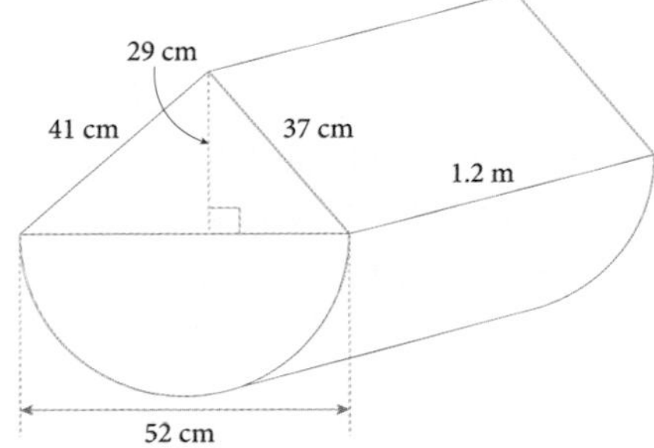

35. List all of the rectangles with integer side lengths and a perimeter of 20 metres.

    a. Identify the rectangle that has the maximum area.

    b. Use the graphing method to verify the optimal dimensions.

36. List all of the rectangles with integer side lengths and an area of 40 square metres.

    a. Identify the rectangle that has the minimum perimeter.

    b. Use the graphing method to verify the optimal dimensions.

37. Determine the optimal dimensions for:

    a. A rectangle with a perimeter of 568 cm and maximum area.

    b. A cylinder with a volume of 286.28 mm^3 and minimum surface area.

38. Determine the optimal dimensions for:

    a. A rectangle with an area of 2,704 m^2 and minimum perimeter.

    b. A rectangular prism with a surface area of 216 cm^2 and maximum volume.

39. Anita is going for a run and has the choice of running around a circular pond or a rectangular city block. The pond covers an area of 19.6 km^2, while the city block covers an area of 20.25 km^2.

    a. Calculate the minimum distance of each route.

    b. Assuming the distances calculated in part (a) are the true distances, if Anita wants to run the shorter distance, which path should she take?

40. Dino's Deli sells cylindrical cups of fresh soup, as well as soups in pre-packaged rectangular cartons. The surface area of the cup (semi-open) is 150.8 in^2 and the surface area of the carton (closed) is 150 in^2.

    a. Calculate the maximum volume of soup in each container, rounded to the nearest cubic inch.

    b. Assuming the volumes calculated in part (a) are the true volumes, if both containers of soup cost the same amount, which is the better deal?

Self-Test | Chapter 9

Answers to all problems are available at the end of the textbook.

1. For the following angles:
   (i) Classify the angle as acute, right, or obtuse.
   (ii) Calculate the supplement of the angle.
   (iii) Calculate the complement of the angle (if applicable).
   a. $\theta = 116°$ b. $\theta = 67°$ c. $\theta = 90°$

2. Determine the unknown angles for a, b, and c in the following figures:

   a.
   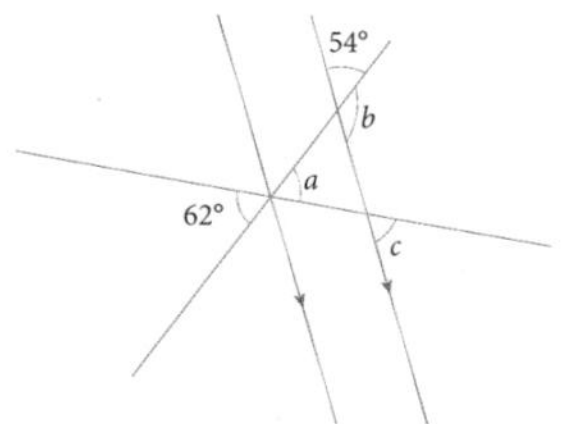

   b.
   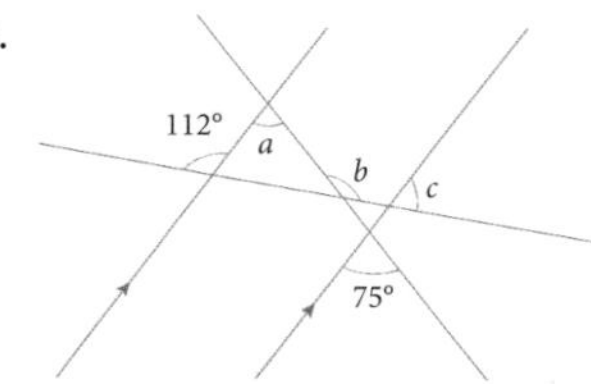

3. Classify the following triangles by angle measure and by side length:
   a.
   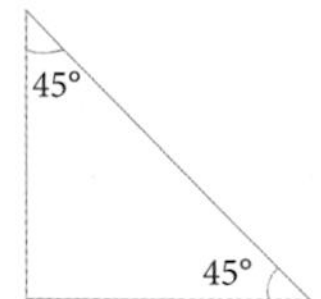

   b.
   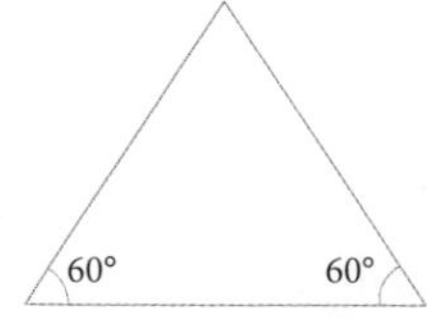

   c.
   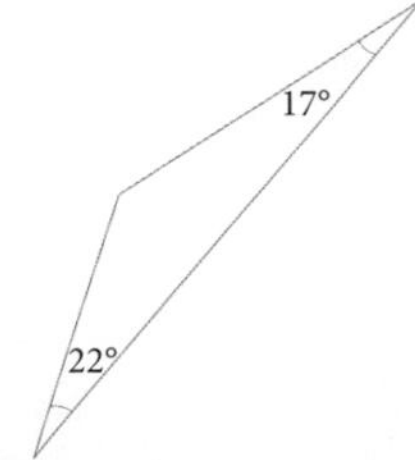

4. Classify the following quadrilaterals:
   a.
   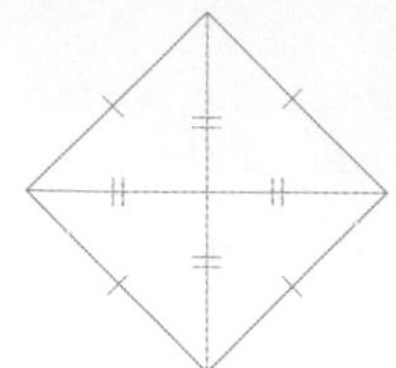
   b.
   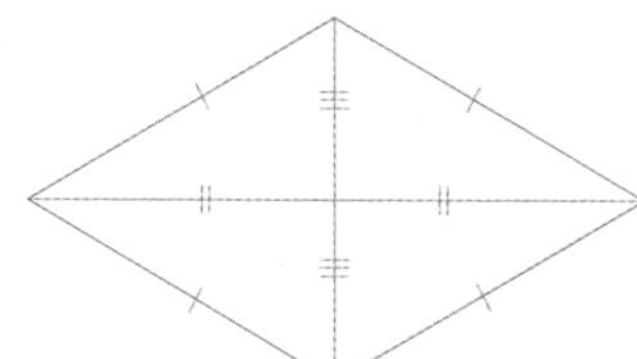
   c.
   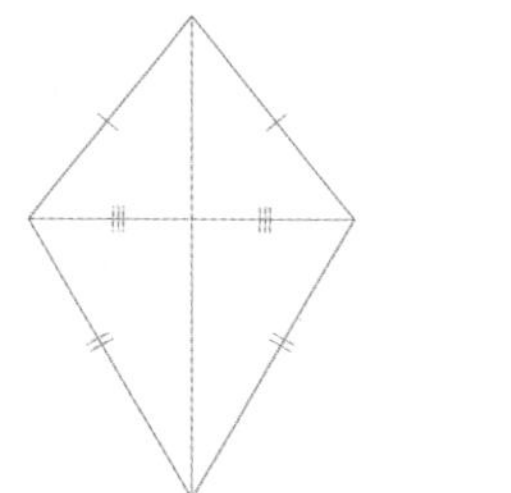

5. Calculate the area of the following triangle:
   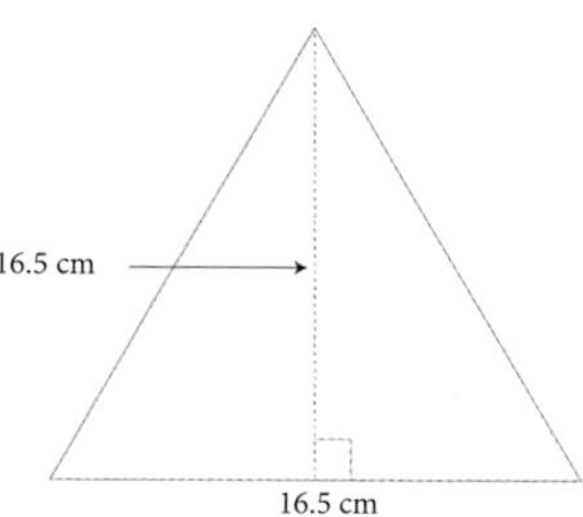

6. Calculate the area of the following figures:
   a. A rhombus with a side length of 8.5 cm and a perpendicular height of 7.2 cm.
   b. A parallelogram with a base of 1.75 m, a perpendicular height of 84 cm, and a slant height of 1.12 m.

7. Determine the circumference (or perimeter) and area of the following figures:
   a. A circle with a diameter of 2.5 m.
   b. A sector of a circle with a radius of 36 cm and an inscribed angle of 65°.

8. In order to calculate the speed to display on a vehicle's speedometer, the on-board computer must be programmed with the size of the car tire installed. Following this, it can compute the speed (in km/h) based on the number of revolutions per minute (rpm) at which the wheel turns. If the factory-installed tires on a new car have a diameter of 63 cm and the wheels are turning at a rate of 96 rpm, determine the speed displayed on the car's speedometer, in km/h.

9. Determine the area of the shaded regions in the following composite figures:

a.

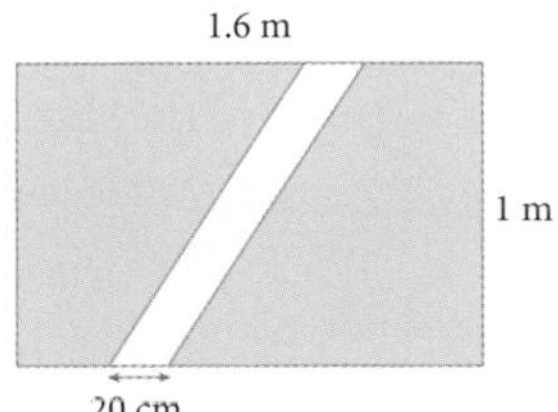

b.

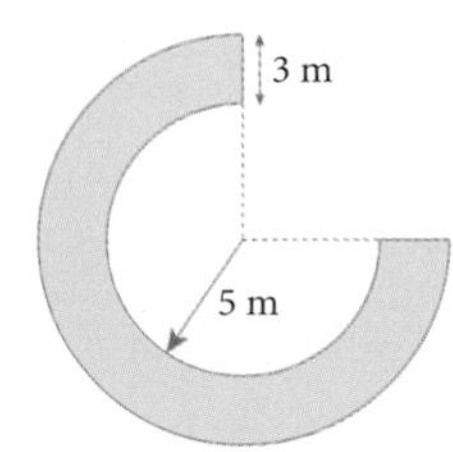

10. Calculate the volume of the following common household objects:

a. A cylindrical pipe with a radius of 18 mm and a length of 175 mm.

b. A cone-shaped paper cup with a diameter of 6.8 cm at the opening and a height of 9.2 cm.

11. A cylinder with a height of 15 cm has a volume of 3,000 cm^3.

a. Calculate its base radius, rounded to 2 decimal places.

b. Calculate its surface area, rounded to the nearest cm^2.

12. A sphere has a surface area of 450 cm^2.

a. Calculate its radius, rounded to 2 decimal places.

b. Calculate its volume, rounded to the nearest cm^3.

13. Calculate the surface area and volume of a swimming pool in the shape of a hexagonal prism, with a height of 1.5 m and six equal side lengths of 1.8 m each. *(Hint: to find the area of the hexagonal base, split it into two equal trapezoids.)*

14. Calculate the volume of the following objects:

a.

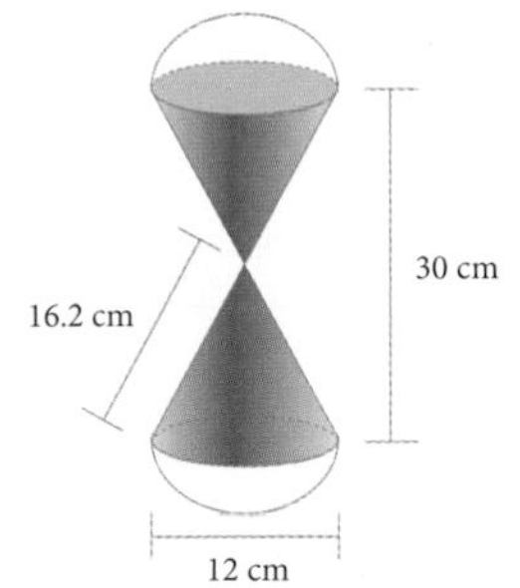

b.

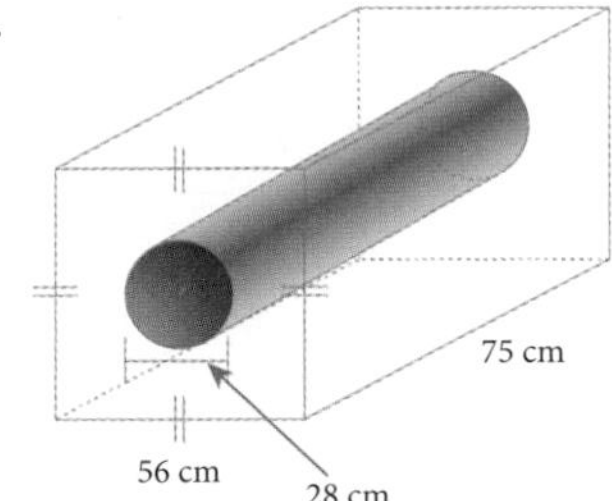

Note: The cylinder is a "cut-out".

15. Lee and Ash qualified for the championship in doubles badminton. They needed to perform calculations with the court dimensions in order to choose the best strategy for the gold medal game. They measured the outside of their half of the court (the three sides **not** including the net) to be 19.5 m. What is the maximum area of the entire court?

16. J.R. is building a rectangular toy box for his son on a budget of $200. He wants it to have a volume of 64 cubic feet and wood costs $2.25 per square foot. Can he complete the toy box under budget?

9 | Summary of Notation and Formulas

Plane Figures

FORMULAS	COMMON PLANE FIGURES	NOTATION
Square: $P = 4s$ $A = s^2$		P = Perimeter A = Area s = length of the sides
Rectangle: $P = 2l + 2w = 2(l + w)$ $A = l \times w$	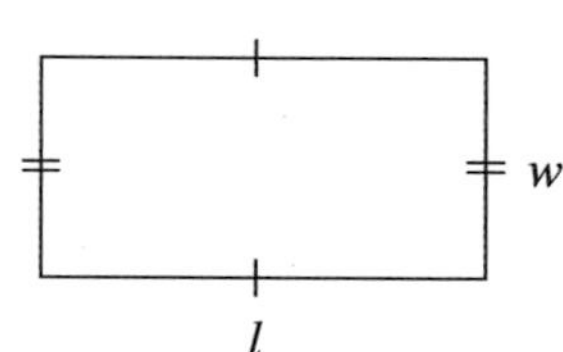	P = Perimeter A = Area l = length w = width
Rhombus: $P = 4b$ $A = b \times h$	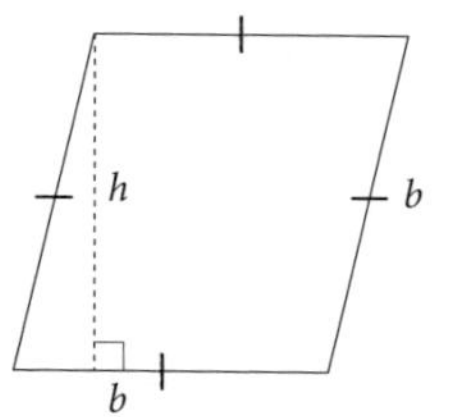	P = Perimeter A = Area b = length of each side h = perpendicular height
Parallelogram: $P = 2a + 2b = 2(a + b)$ $A = b \times h$	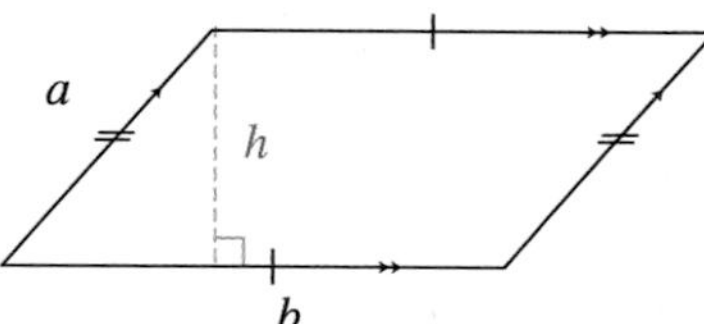	P = Perimeter A = Area a = length of the slant b = length of the base h = perpendicular height
Trapezoid $P = a + b + c + d$ $A = \frac{1}{2}(a + b) \times h$	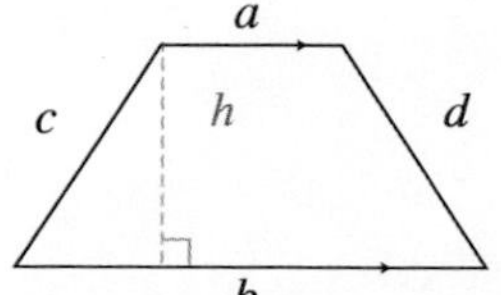	P = Perimeter A = Area a = length of the smaller parallel side b = length of the larger parallel side c, d = other sides h = perpendicular height

Triangle:

$P = a + b + c$

$A = \frac{1}{2}(b \times h)$

Heron's Formula:

$A = \sqrt{p(p-a)(p-b)(p-c)}$

where, $p = \frac{a+b+c}{2}$

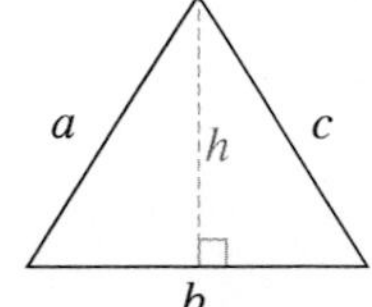

P = Perimeter

A = Area

a, b, c = side lengths

h = height

p = half of the Perimeter

Circle:

$C = \pi d = 2\pi r$

$A = \pi r^2$

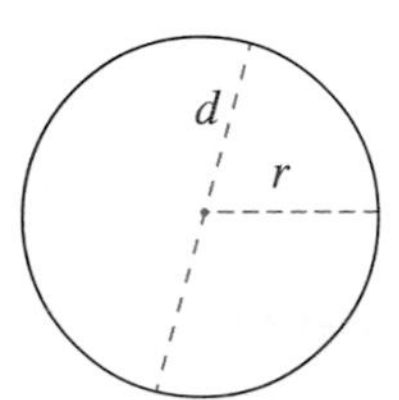

C = Circumference

A = Area

d = diameter = $2r$

r = radius

Sector:

$L = \pi d \times \frac{\theta}{360°}$

$P_S = 2r + L$

$A_S = \pi r^2 \times \frac{\theta}{360°}$

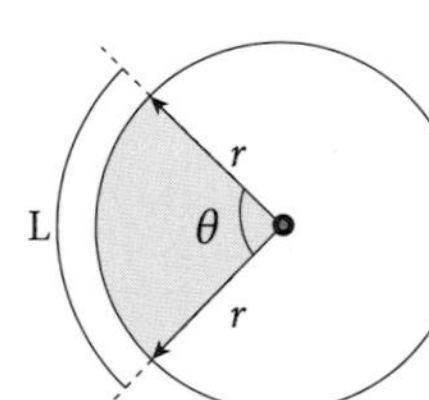

L = Arc length

P_S = Perimeter of sector

A_S = Area of sector

θ = angle subtended by the arc

d = diameter = $2r$

r = radius

Solid Objects

FORMULAS	COMMON SOLID OBJECTS	NOTATION

Cube:

$SA = 6s^2$

$V = s^3$

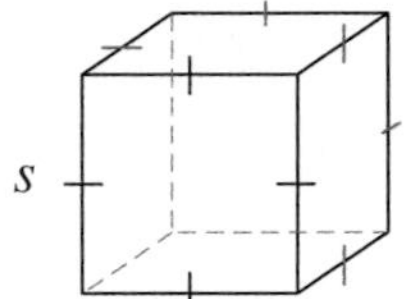

SA = Surface Area

V = Volume

s = side length

Rectangular Prism:

$SA = 2(l \times w) + 2(l \times h) + 2(w \times h)$

$= 2[(l \times w) + (l \times h) + (w \times h)]$

$V = l \times w \times h$

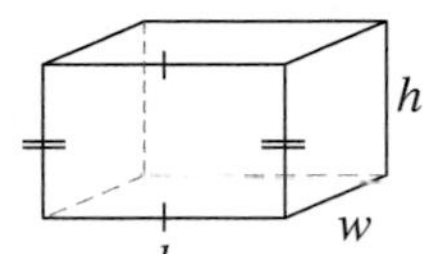

SA = Surface Area

V = Volume

l = length

w = width

h = height

Triangular Prism:

SA = 2(B) + 3 rectangles

$V = B \times h$

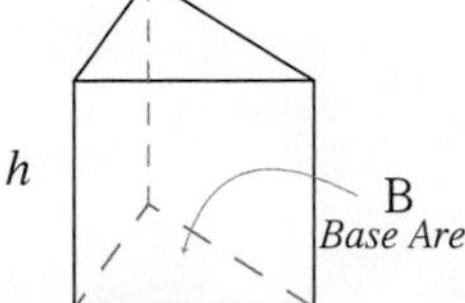

SA = Surface Area

V = Volume

B = Base Area

h = height

Square Pyramid:

$$SA = 4\left(\frac{l \times s}{2}\right) + l^2$$
$$= 2(l \times s) + l^2$$
$$V = \frac{1}{3}(l \times l)h$$
$$= \frac{l^2 \times h}{3}$$

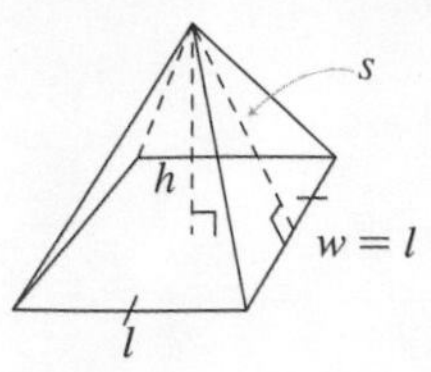

SA = Surface Area

V = Volume

s = slant height

h = height

l = length

w = width

Rectangular Pyramid:

$$SA = 2\left(\frac{l \times s_1}{2} + \frac{w \times s_2}{2}\right) + l \times w$$
$$= (l \times s_1 + w \times s_2) + l \times w$$
$$V = \frac{1}{3}(l \times w)h$$
$$= \frac{l \times w \times h}{3}$$

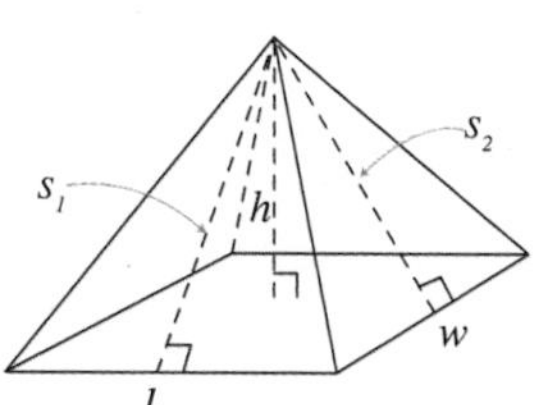

SA = Surface Area

V = Volume

h = height

l = length

w = width

s_1 = slant height on the length side

s_2 = slant height on the width side

Triangular Pyramid:

SA = Area of all 3 lateral sides + Base Area (B)

$$V = \frac{1}{3}(B)h$$
$$= \frac{B \times h}{3}$$

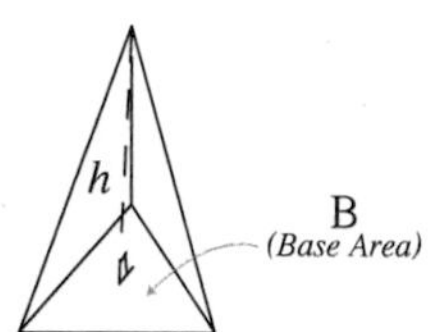

SA = Surface Area

V = Volume

B = Base Area

h = height

Cylinder:

$$SA = 2\pi r^2 + 2\pi rh \text{ (closed)}$$
$$= \pi r^2 + 2\pi rh \text{ (semi-closed)}$$
$$= 2\pi rh \text{ (open)}$$
$$V = \pi r^2 h$$

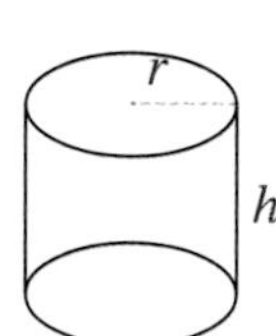

SA = Surface Area

V = Volume

r = radius

h = height

Cone:

$$SA = \pi r^2 + \pi rs \text{ (closed)}$$
$$= \pi rs \text{ (open)}$$
$$V = \frac{1}{3}\pi r^2 h = \frac{\pi r^2 h}{3}$$

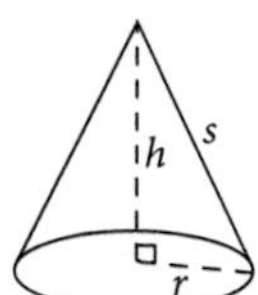

SA = Surface Area

V = Volume

r = radius

s = slant height

h = height

Sphere:

$$SA = 4\pi r^2$$
$$V = \frac{4}{3}(\pi r^3) = \frac{4\pi r^3}{3}$$

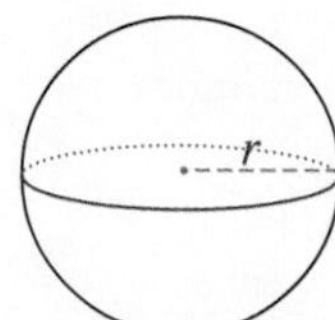

SA = Surface Area

V = Volume

r = radius

Chapter 10 BASIC TRIGONOMETRY

LEARNING OBJECTIVES

- Apply the properties of similar and congruent triangles in solving problems involving triangles.
- Use the Pythagorean Theorem to determine the length of the unknown side of a right triangle.
- Determine the basic trigonometric ratios of angles of right triangles.
- Evaluate the exact trigonometric ratios of special angles.
- Solve right triangles using the Pythagorean Theorem and trigonometric ratios.
- Solve triangles using the Sine Law and the Cosine Law.

CHAPTER OUTLINE

Introduction

The **triangle** is one of the most basic shapes in geometry because it is the simplest polygon. All triangles have three sides and three angles, but they come in many different shapes and sizes. In the previous chapter, we learned that triangles can be classified by their **side** measures (equilateral, isosceles, or scalene), as well as by their **angle** measures (acute, obtuse, or right). In this chapter, we will learn the characteristics of each of these types of triangles, and how the properties of the sides and angles can be used to solve for any missing part of a triangle and to classify pairs of triangles. Since triangles are such a common and basic shape, understanding these characteristics will allow to solve for real world application problems, such as finding immeasurable distances, calculating the slope of a ramp or a road, determining the magnitude and direction of a force, etc.

10.1 | Similar and Congruent Triangles

Geometric shapes, also known as figures, are an important part of the study of geometry. Recognizing and using similar and congruent shapes make calculations and design work easier. For example, in most design work, rather than using different shapes, a few shapes are copied and used in different positions and/or produced in different sizes to complete the design.

When a shape is obtained from another figure by means of enlargement or reduction, its size will be different from the original one, but it remains the same shape as the original one.

Similar figures have the same shape and retain the same angles at corresponding vertices. They may or may not have the same size, but the lengths of the corresponding sides will be in proportion between the figures.

Congruent figures have the same sides as well as the same angles at corresponding vertices.

It is important to note that two figures can be similar, but not congruent; however, two figures cannot be congruent and not similar.

Similar Triangles

Similar figures must have the same shape, but their sizes may be different.

Two equal-sided polygons are said to be **similar** if all the corresponding angles are equal in measure and the corresponding sides are proportional in length.

The symbol for similar is '~'.

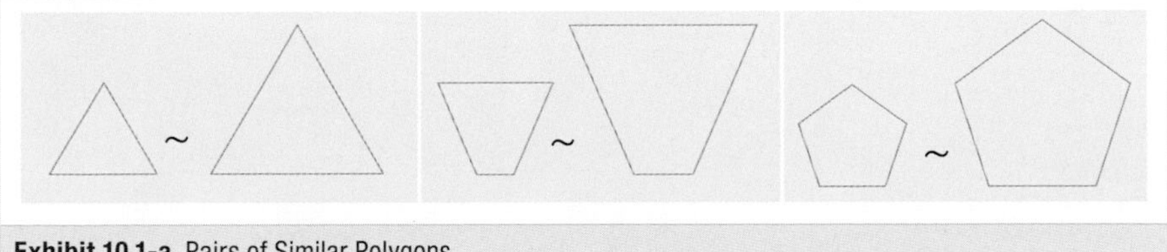

Exhibit 10.1-a Pairs of Similar Polygons

When writing the similarity relationship, the order in which the letters are written to represent the similar figures is very important.

In similar figures, the measures of corresponding angles are equal and the ratios of the lengths of corresponding sides are equal. The ratio between the corresponding sides of similar figures are expressed as a fraction and is called the "scale" or scale factor.

For example, ΔABC is similar to ΔDEF,

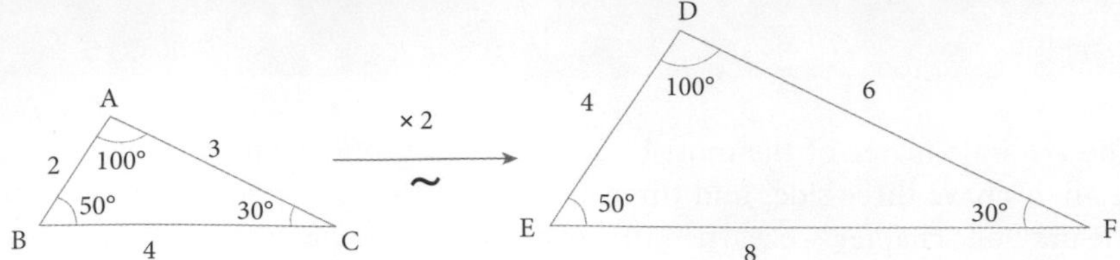

(i) ΔABC ~ ΔDEF

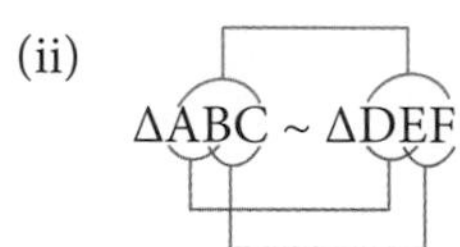

∠A = ∠D, ∠B = ∠E, and ∠C = ∠F

(Corresponding angle measures of the two triangles are equal.)

(ii) ΔABC ~ ΔDEF

$$\frac{AB}{DE} = \frac{BC}{EF} = \frac{AC}{DF} = \frac{1}{2}$$

(Corresponding side lengths of the two triangles are proportional.)

Any triangle is defined by six measures: three sides and three angles. However, it is not necessary to know all of the six measures to demonstrate that the two triangles are similar. If any one of the following four conditions are met, then the two triangles are similar:

1. AAA (angle, angle, angle)

   If all three pairs of corresponding angles are the same (equal), then the triangles are similar.

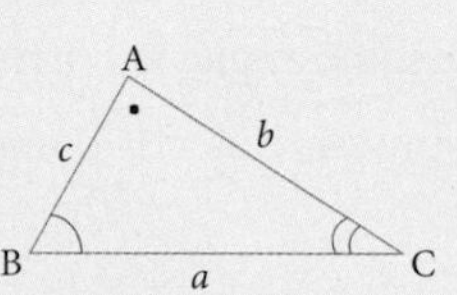

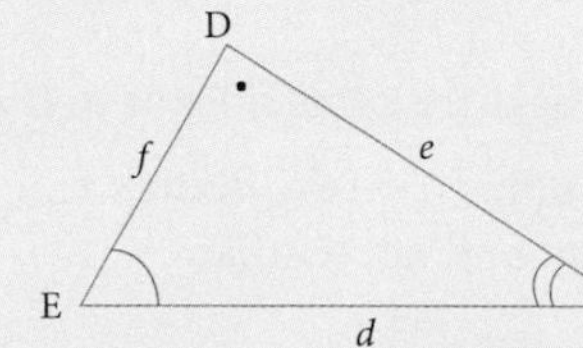

If ∠A = ∠D,
∠B = ∠E, and
∠C = ∠F,
then ΔABC ~ ΔDEF

This is the same as AA (angle, angle) because if any two angles of the two triangles are equal, then the third angle must be equal.

2. SSS (side, side, side)

   If all three pairs of corresponding side lengths of two triangles are in proportion, then the triangles are similar.

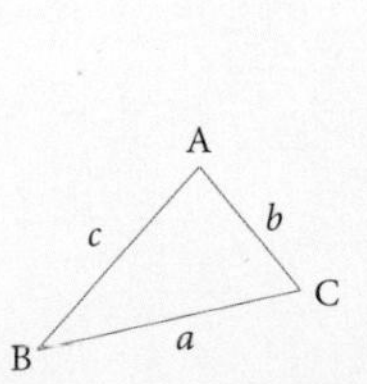

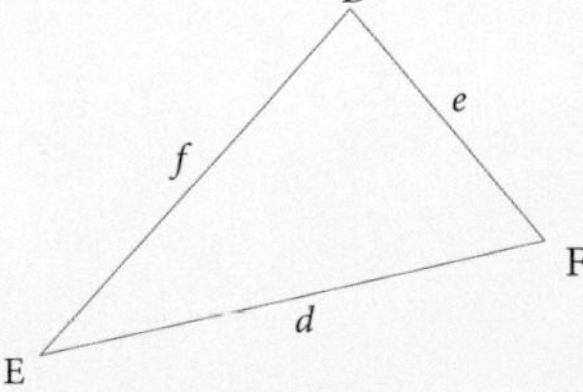

If $\frac{BC}{EF} = \frac{AC}{DF} = \frac{AB}{DE}$,

$\left(\text{i.e., } \frac{a}{d} = \frac{b}{e} = \frac{c}{f}\right)$,

then ΔABC ~ ΔDEF

3. SAS (side, angle, side)

   If two triangles have a pair of equal angle measures and the corresponding sides containing the equal angles are in proportion, then the triangles are similar.

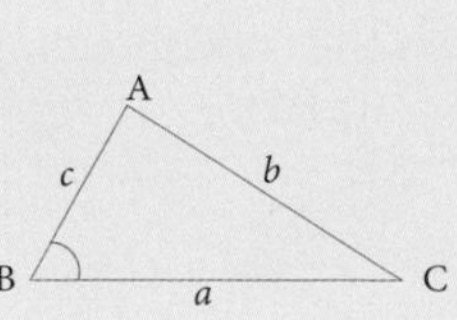

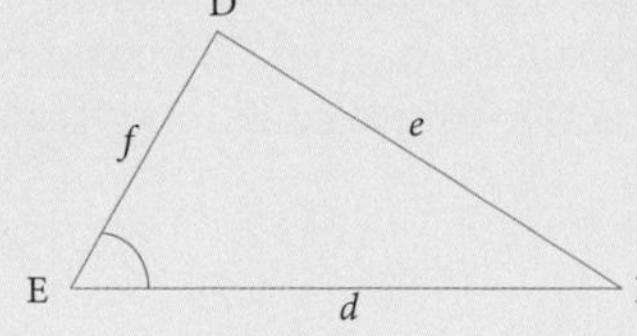

If ∠B = ∠E,

and $\frac{AB}{DE} = \frac{BC}{EF}$,

$\left(\text{i.e., } \frac{c}{f} = \frac{a}{d}\right)$,

then ΔABC ~ ΔDEF

The **hypotenuse** is the side opposite the right angle in a right triangle. This will be studied further in the next section.

4. RHS (Right angle, hypotenuse, side)

   In right-angled triangles, if the hypotenuses and lengths of one pair of corresponding sides are proportional, then the triangles are similar.

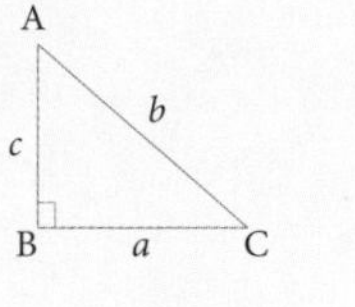

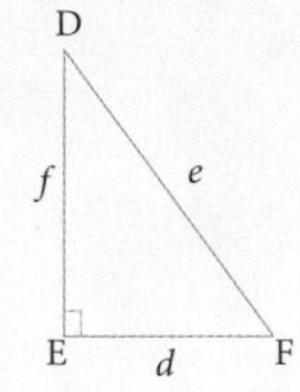

If $\angle B = \angle E = 90°$,

and $\frac{AC}{DF} = \frac{BC}{EF}$, $\left(\text{i.e., } \frac{b}{e} = \frac{a}{d}\right)$,

then $\Delta ABC \sim \Delta DEF$

Example 10.1-a **Rules for Similar Triangles**

Based on the information provided for the following pairs of triangles, state the property that will prove that they are similar.

(i)

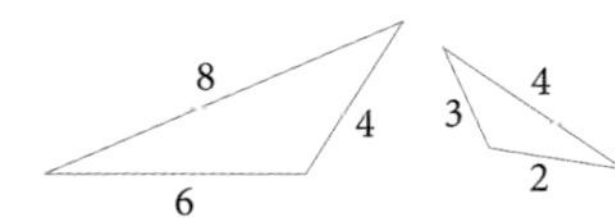

(ii)

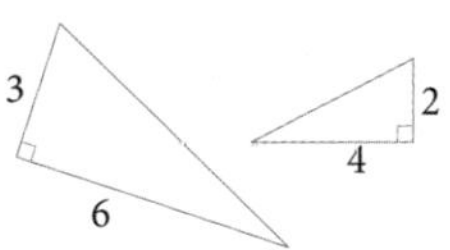

(iii)

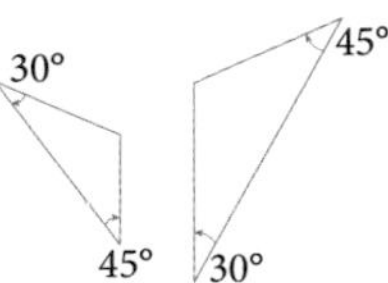

Solution (i) SSS Property (ii) SAS Property (iii) AAA Property

Example 10.1-b **Using Similar Triangles to Find the Unknown Length**

(i) If $\Delta PQR \sim \Delta XYZ$, find XY and XZ

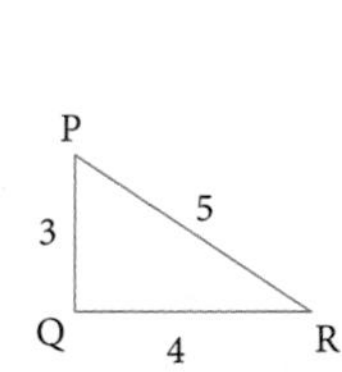

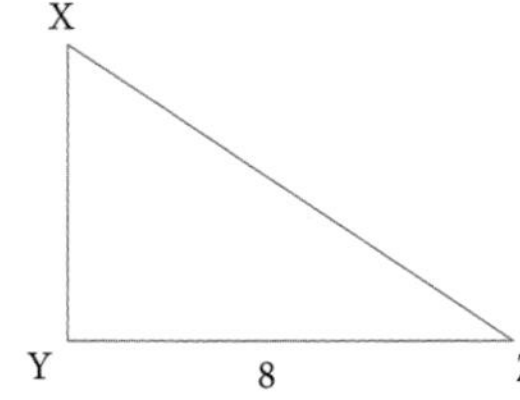

(ii) If $\Delta ABC \sim \Delta DEF$, find AB and DF

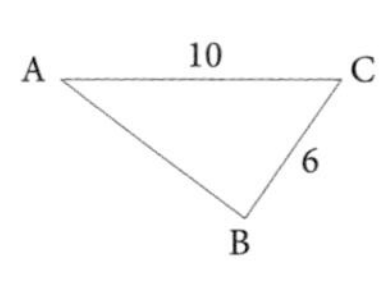

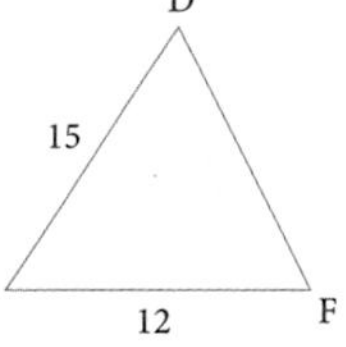

Solution

(i) $\Delta PQR \sim \Delta XYZ$

Therefore, $\frac{PQ}{XY} = \frac{QR}{YZ} = \frac{PR}{XZ}$

$\frac{3}{XY} = \frac{4}{8} = \frac{5}{XZ}$

$\frac{3}{XY} = \frac{4}{8}$

$4(XY) = 3(8)$

$XY = \frac{3(8)}{4}$

$= 6$

$\frac{4}{8} = \frac{5}{XZ}$

$4(XZ) = 5(8)$

$XZ = \frac{5(8)}{4}$

$= 10$

Therefore, XY = 6 and XZ = 10.

(ii) $\Delta ABC \sim \Delta DEF$

Therefore, $\frac{AB}{DE} = \frac{BC}{EF} = \frac{AC}{DF}$

$\frac{AB}{15} = \frac{6}{12} = \frac{10}{DF}$

$\frac{AB}{15} = \frac{6}{12}$

$12(AB) = 6(15)$

$AB = \frac{6(15)}{12}$

$= 7.5$

$\frac{6}{12} = \frac{10}{DF}$

$6(DF) = 10(12)$

$DF = \frac{10(12)}{6}$

$= 20$

Therefore, AB = 7.5 and DF = 20.

Example 10.1-c Identifying Similar Triangles

Determine whether the following pairs of triangles are similar:

(i)

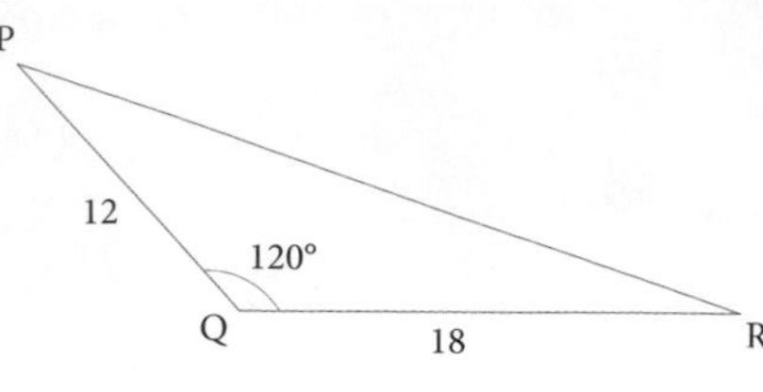

(ii)

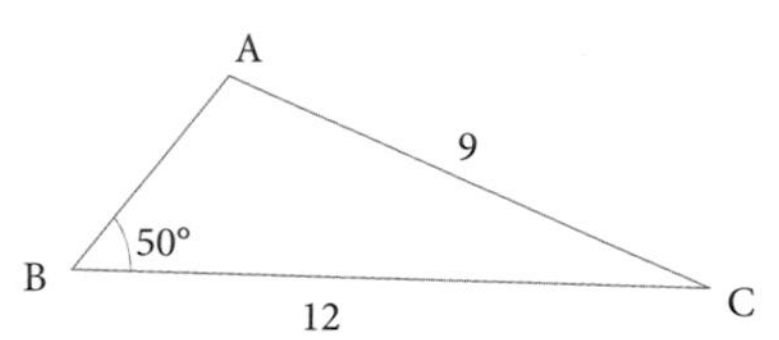

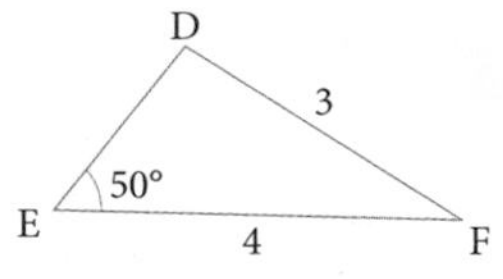

Solution

(i) $\angle Q = 120°$, $\angle Y = 180 - (40 + 20) = 120°$

Therefore, $\angle Q = \angle Y$ (Equal angle measures)

$$\frac{PQ}{XY} = \frac{12}{6} = 2$$

$$\frac{QR}{YZ} = \frac{18}{9} = 2$$

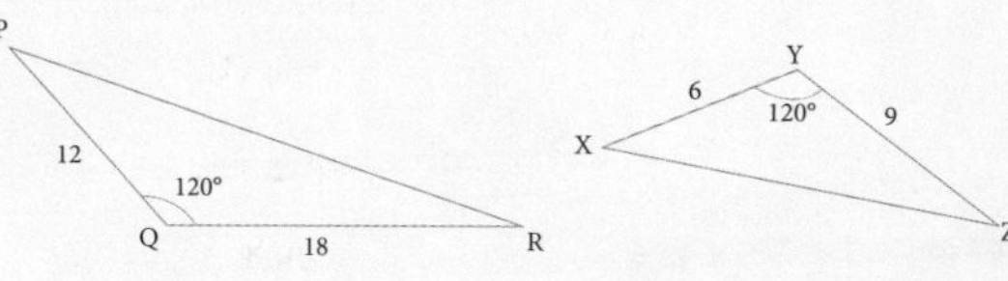

i.e., $\frac{PQ}{XY} = \frac{QR}{YZ}$ (Corresponding sides containing the equal angles are in proportion)

Therefore, by the SAS Property, $\Delta PQR \sim \Delta XYZ$

(ii) $\angle B = \angle E$ (Equal angle measures)

$$\frac{BC}{EF} = \frac{12}{4} = 3$$

$$\frac{AC}{DF} = \frac{9}{3} = 3$$

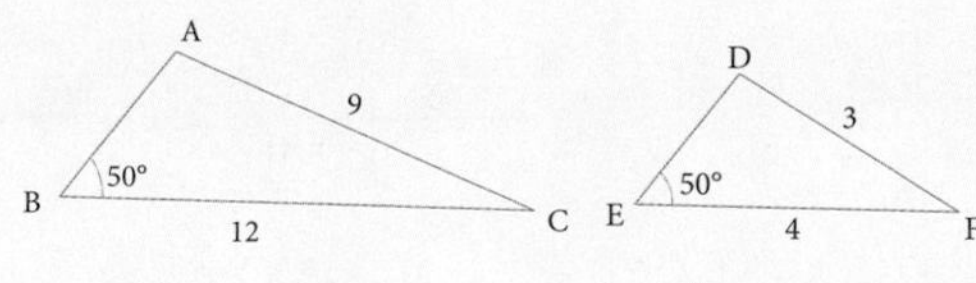

i.e., $\frac{BC}{EF} = \frac{AC}{DF}$ (Lengths of two sides are in proportion)

However, the equal angles are not contained within the sides that are proportional.

Therefore, we cannot conclude that ΔABC is similar to ΔDEF.

> SSA (side, side, angle) is **not** sufficient to conclude that two triangles are similar.

Example 10.1-d **Calculating Angle and Side Measures of Triangles**

Calculate the lengths of the unknown sides and unknown angle measures of the following triangles:

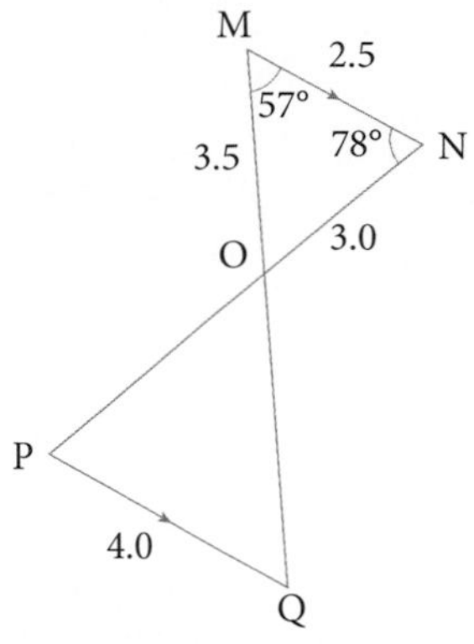

Solution

Since $\overline{MN} // \overline{PQ}$, $\angle N = \angle P$ and $\angle M = \angle Q$, because they are alternate angles.

$\angle P = 78°$ and $\angle Q = 57°$. Therefore, $\Delta MNO \sim \Delta QPO$ by the AAA Property.

Hence, the corresponding side lengths of the triangles must be proportional:

$$\frac{MN}{QP} = \frac{NO}{PO} = \frac{MO}{QO}.$$

$$\text{i.e., } \frac{2.5}{4.0} = \frac{3.0}{PO} = \frac{3.5}{QO}$$

$$\frac{2.5}{4.0} = \frac{3.0}{PO}$$

$$PO = \frac{4.0(3.0)}{2.5}$$

$$= 4.8$$

$$\frac{2.5}{4.0} = \frac{3.5}{QO}$$

$$QO = \frac{4.0(3.5)}{2.5}$$

$$= 5.6$$

Since the corresponding two angles of the triangles are known, the third angles (which are opposite angles) can be computed as follows: $\angle MON = \angle QOP = 180° - (78° + 57°) = 45°$.

Note: The angles cannot simply be referred to as $\angle O$ in this scenario, as that would create ambiguity.

Congruent Triangles

Congruent figures must have the same shape **and** size.

Two equal-sided polygons are said to be **congruent** if all the corresponding angles are equal in measure and the corresponding sides are equal in length (i.e., the polygons are similar and they have equal side lengths).

The symbol for congruent is '≅'.

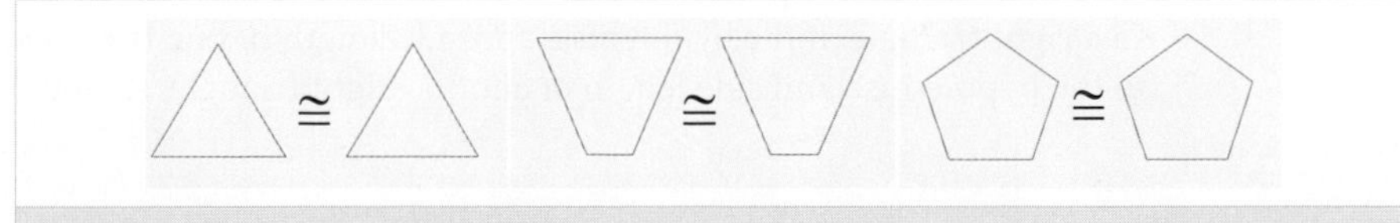

Exhibit 10.1-b Pairs of Congruent Polygons

Once again, it is important to note that when the congruent relationship is written, the order of letters representing the figures must be consistent to illustrate the equal corresponding angle measures and side lengths.

For example, ΔABC is congruent to ΔDEF,

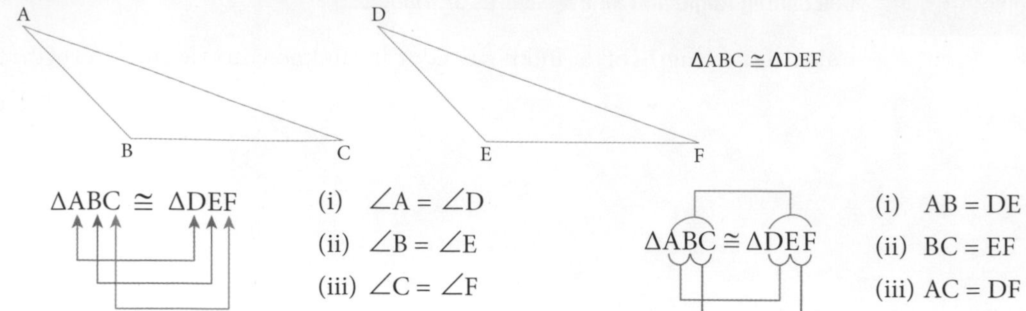

Corresponding angle measures and sides are equal.

The condition of congruence for triangles requires all three sides and all three angle measures to be congruent. However, it is not necessary to know all of the six measurements to demonstrate that the two triangles are congruent. If any of the following four conditions are met, then the triangles are congruent.

1. SSS (side, side, side)

   If all three pairs of corresponding side lengths of two triangles are equal, then the triangles are congruent.

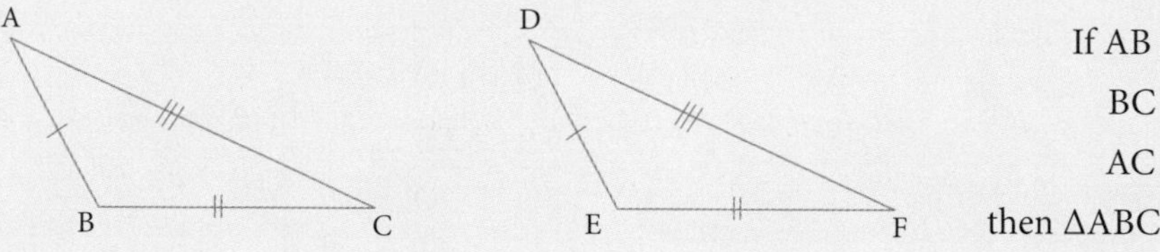

If AB = DE,
BC = EF, and
AC = DF,
then ΔABC ≅ ΔDEF

2. SAS (side, angle, side)

   If two side lengths and the contained angle measure of one triangle is correspondingly equal to two side length and the contained angle measure of another triangle, then the triangles are congruent.

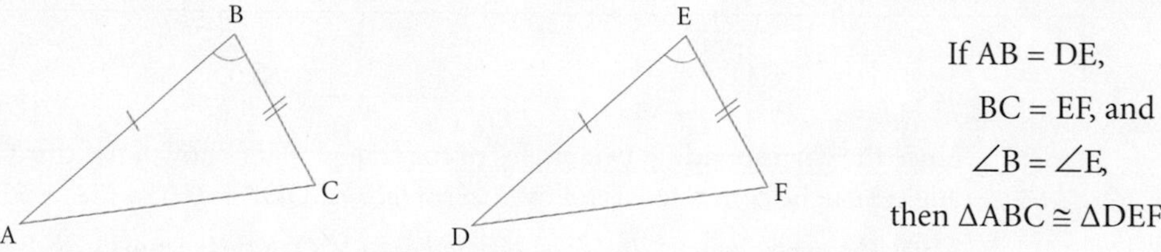

If AB = DE,
BC = EF, and
∠B = ∠E,
then ΔABC ≅ ΔDEF

3. ASA (angle, side, angle)

   If two angle measures and the contained side length of one triangle is correspondingly equal to two angle measures and the contained side length of another triangle, then the triangles are congruent.

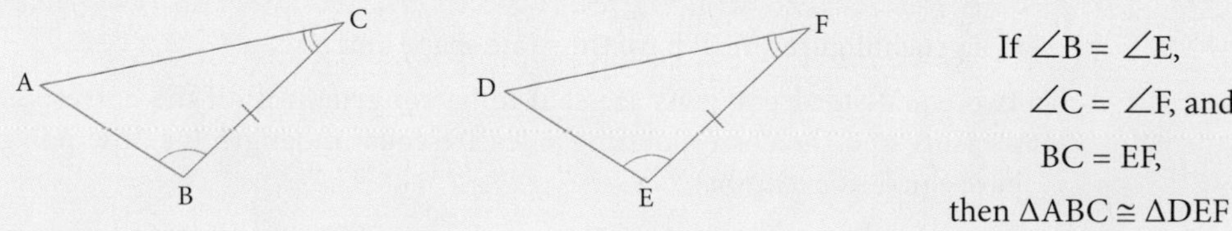

If ∠B = ∠E,
∠C = ∠F, and
BC = EF,
then ΔABC ≅ ΔDEF

4. RHS (Right angle, hypotenuse, side)

   In a right triangle, if the hypotenuse and side length of one triangle is correspondingly equal to the hypotenuse and side length of another right triangle, then the triangles are congruent.

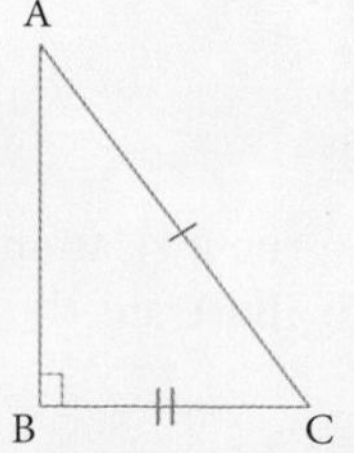

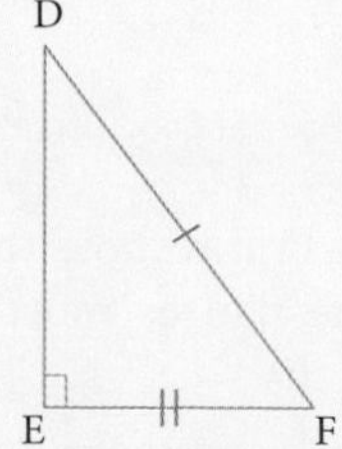

If ∠B = ∠E = 90°,
AC = DF, and
BC = EF,
then ΔABC ≅ ΔDEF

Example 10.1-e

Determining Similarity/Congruency of Triangles

In the following examples, determine whether the pairs of triangles are congruent, similar, or neither:

(i)

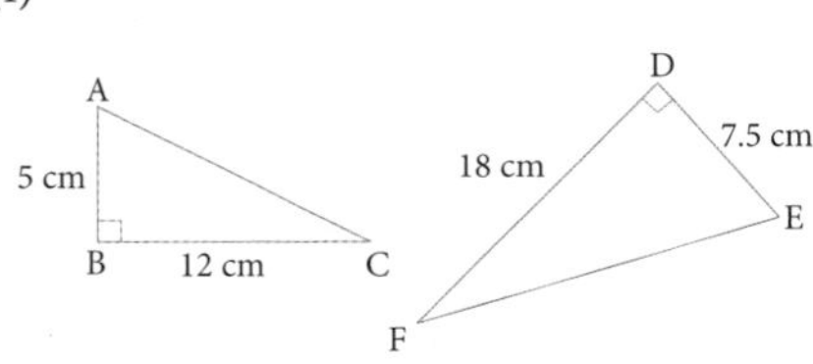

(ii)

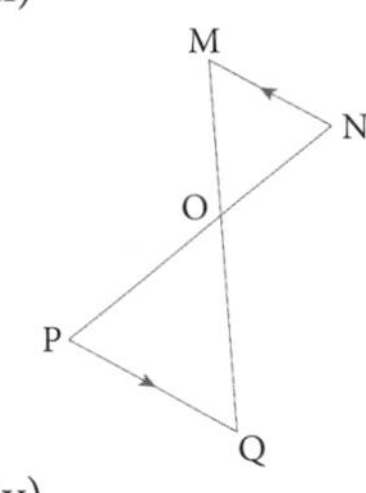

(iii)

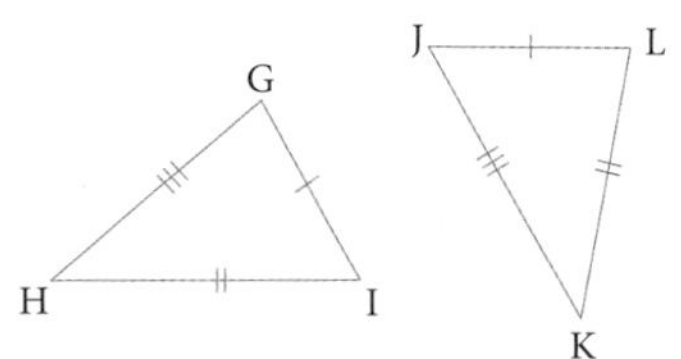

(iv)

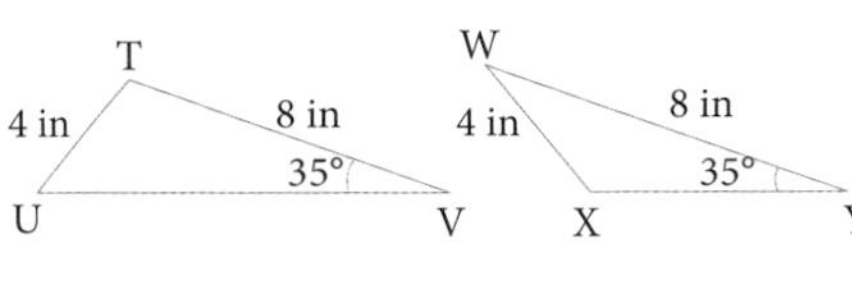

Solution

(i) Since $\frac{AB}{DE} = \frac{BC}{DF}$ and the angle measures between those two sides ($\angle B$ and $\angle D$) are equal, both right triangles, ΔABC and ΔEDF, are similar by the SAS Property (i.e., $\Delta ABC \sim \Delta EDF$). Since the corresponding lengths of the sides are different, the triangles are not congruent.

(ii) Since $\overline{MN}$ and $\overline{PQ}$ are parallel, we know that alternate angles are equal (i.e., $\angle N = \angle P$ and $\angle M = \angle Q$), and therefore, ΔMNO and ΔQPO are similar by the AAA Property (i.e., $\Delta MNO \sim \Delta QPO$).

Since the lengths of the sides are not known, we cannot determine congruency. However, judging by the scale, it appears that they are not congruent.

(iii) Since GH = JK, GI = JL, and HI = KL, the triangles ΔGHI and ΔJKL are congruent by the SSS Property.

Since the triangles are congruent, they are also similar.

(iv) Since UT = XW, TV = WY, and $\angle V = \angle Y$, it may be tempting to label ΔTVU and ΔWYX as similar triangles. However, it is obvious that UV $\neq$ XY, and therefore, they are not in proportion with the lengths of the other two sides; thus, the triangles are not similar (this is an example to demonstrate that the SSA criterion is not sufficient to demonstrate similarity).

Since the triangles are not similar, they are not congruent either.

Recall: two figures cannot be congruent and not similar.

Solving Application Problems using Similar and Congruent Triangles

Similar and/or congruent triangles can be used to solve a variety of real-life application problems when it is difficult or impossible to calculate certain angles or lengths.

Example 10.1-f Determining the Height of a Building using Similar Triangles

The new science building at a college is six stories tall. Arianna wishes to know the height of the building. She devises a method whereby, she and a friend measure the length of the shadow that the building casts at 3:00 in the afternoon. The length of this shadow is 6.24 m. She then has her friend measure her height - 165 cm - and the length of her shadow - 44 cm. Using this information, how can Arianna determine the height of the science building?

Solution

Since the sun meets all points on the ground in a close vicinity at the same angle at any given time, and it hits both the building and Arianna (standing vertically) at the same angle, the shadows created by the building and Arianna form similar triangles, as shown in the diagram.

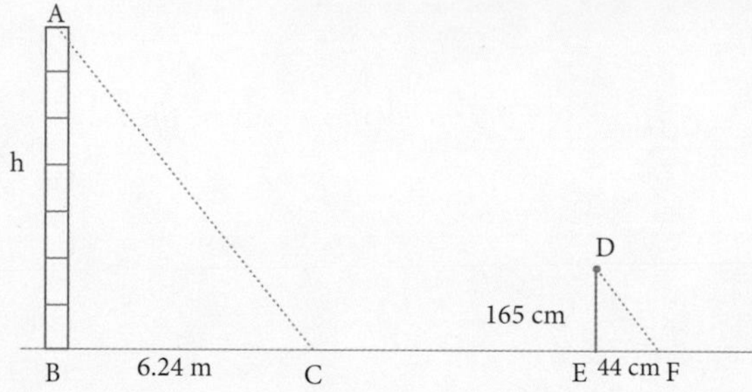

Therefore, the measurements of the building's height and length of its shadow are proportional to Arianna's respective measurements:

$$\frac{h}{6.24 \text{ m}} = \frac{165 \text{ cm}}{44 \text{ cm}}$$ Solving this ratio for h,

$$h = 6.24 \text{ m} \times \frac{165 \text{ cm}}{44 \text{ cm}}$$

$$= 23.4 \text{ m}$$

Therefore, the science building has a height of approximately 23.4 m.

Note that when performing the calculation, we are able to use measurements that are in both m and cm without having to convert to a uniform unit. In the ratio that is formed, the cm units cancel out, leaving a measurement in m. This is a review of proportions, which was covered in earlier chapters.

Example 10.1-g Calculating the Distance across a Lake using Congruent Triangles

A lake is situated on a property in the country. A couple looking to purchase the property wishes to know how long the lake is. How can they determine this (without getting wet)?

Solution

They can each mark a point on either end of the lake (denoted A and B on the diagram below), and measure the distance to a common point on one of the adjacent sides of the lake (denoted C). They can then each continue to walk the same distance in the same direction to another set of points on their property (denoted D and E respectively), creating congruent triangles (by SAS). Finally, they can measure the distance from D to E, which will be the same distance as A to B, since the triangles are congruent. In this way, they will have determined the length of the lake.

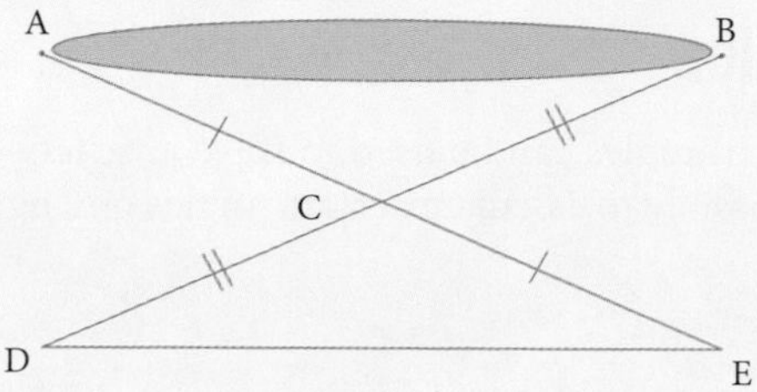

10.1 | Exercises

Answers to odd-numbered problems are available at the end of the textbook.

For Problems 1 and 2, for each pair of similar triangles, name the proportional sides and congruent angles.

1. a. $\Delta ABC \sim \Delta DEF$ b. $\Delta OPQ \sim \Delta RST$

2. a. $\Delta UVW \sim \Delta XYZ$ b. $\Delta GHI \sim \Delta JKL$

For Problems 3 and 4, for each pair of congruent triangles, name the equal sides and equal angles.

3. a. $\Delta ABC \cong \Delta XYZ$ b. $\Delta DEF \cong \Delta RST$

4. a. $\Delta UVW \cong JKL$ b. $\Delta XYZ \cong \Delta JKL$

For Problems 5 to 10, identify any pairs of similar triangles and state the rule used to determine similarity.

5. a.

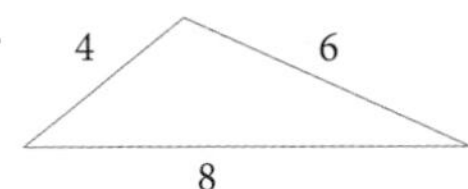

b.

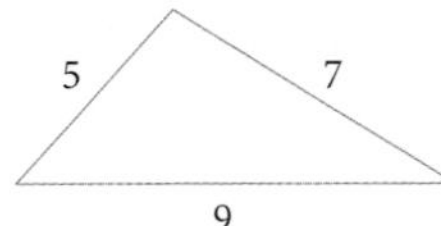

c.

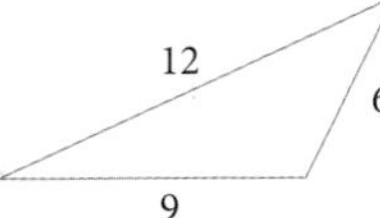

6. a.

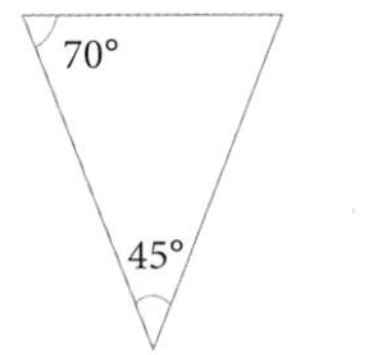

b.

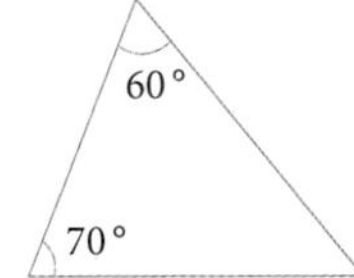

c.

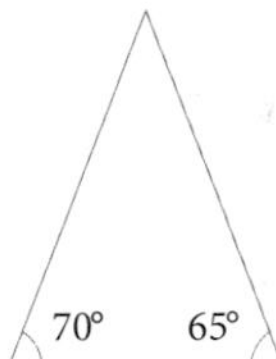

7. a.

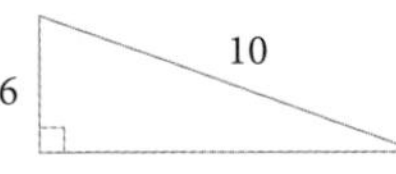

b.

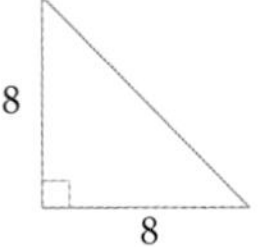

c.

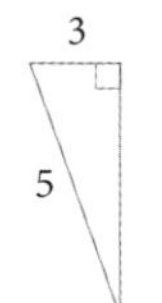

8. a.

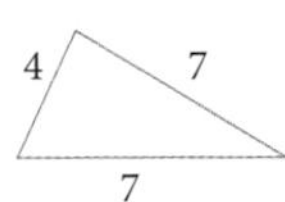

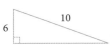

b.

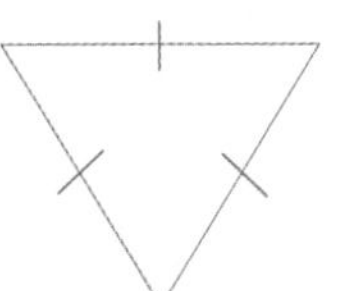

c.

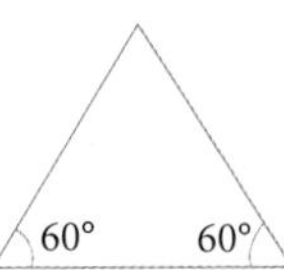

9. a.

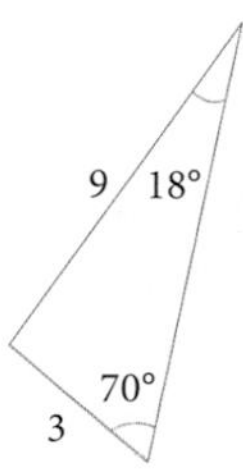

b.

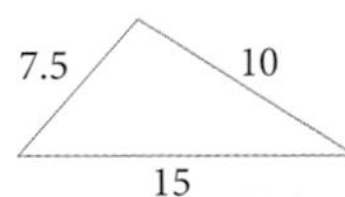

c.

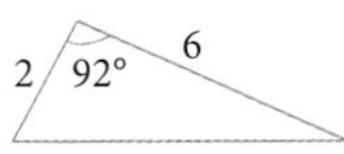

10. a.

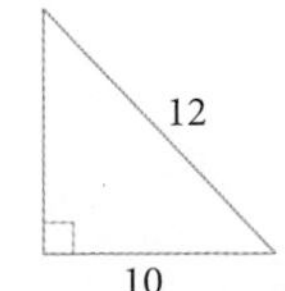

b.

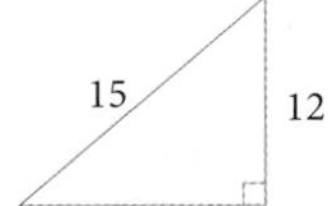

c.

8

10

For Problems 11 to 16, identify any pair of congruent triangles and state the rule used to determine congruency.

11. a. 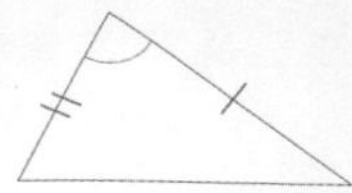 b. 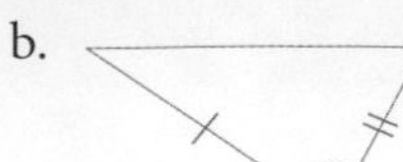 c. 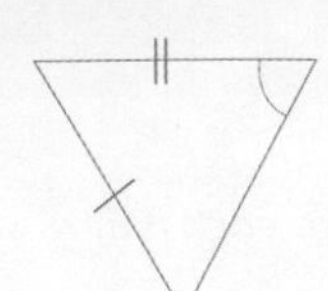

12. a. 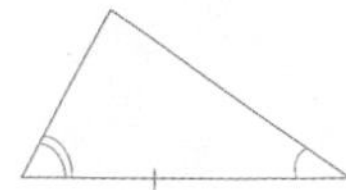 b. 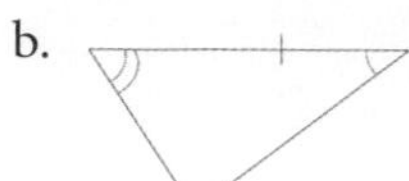 c. 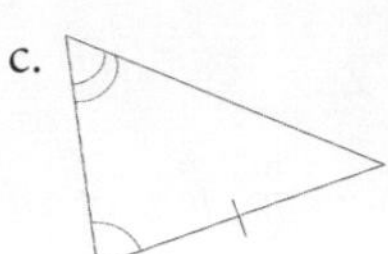

13. a. 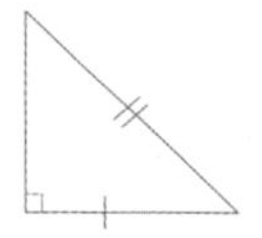 b. 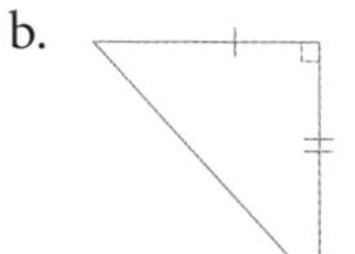 c. 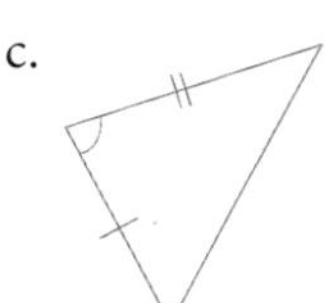

14. a. 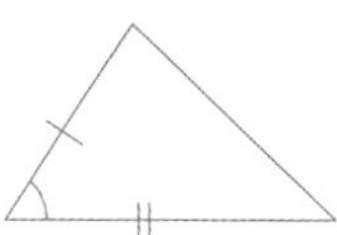 b. 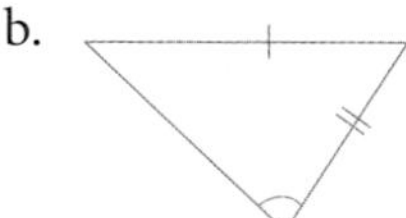 c. 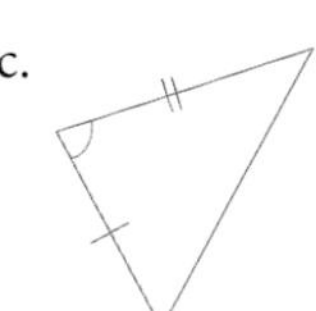

15. a. 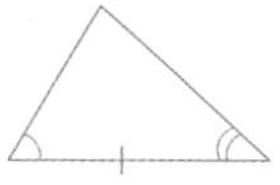 b. 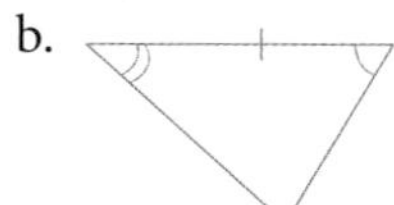 c. 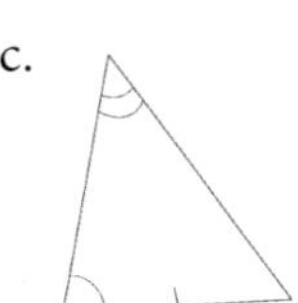

16. a. 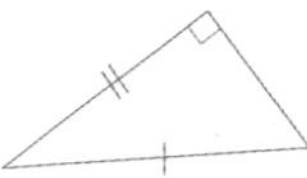 b. 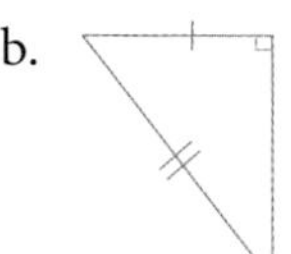 c. 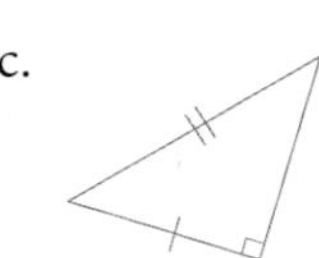

For Problems 17 to 22, determine whether each pair of triangles is congruent, similar, or neither:

17.

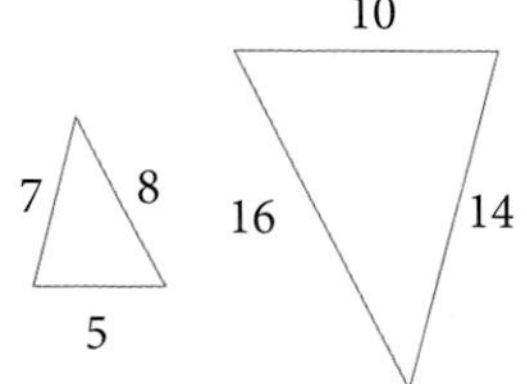

18.

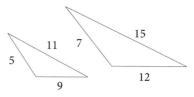

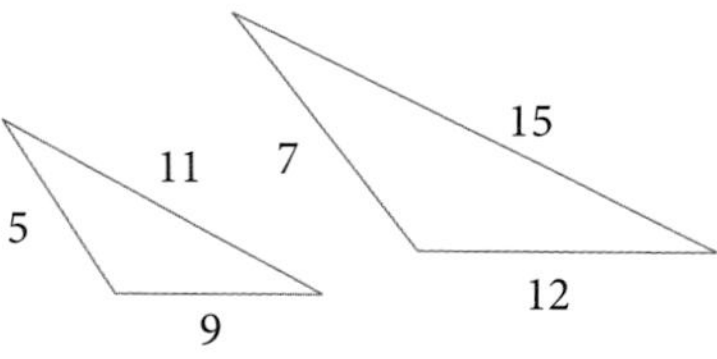

19.

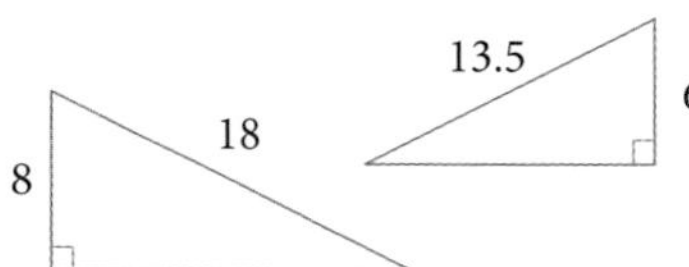

20.

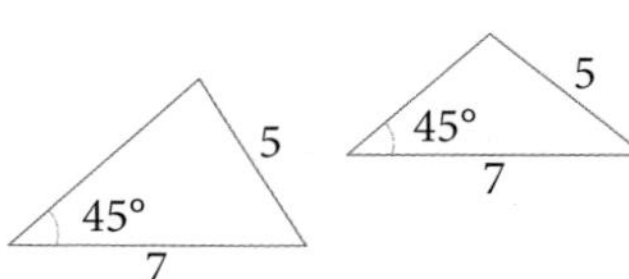

21.

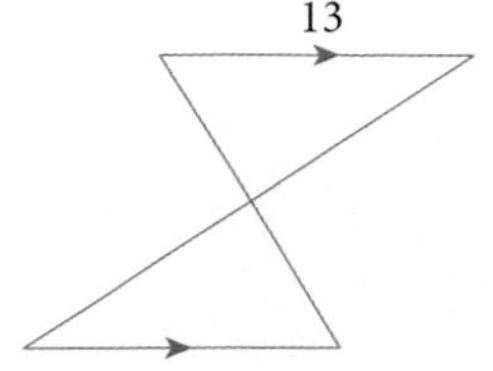

22.

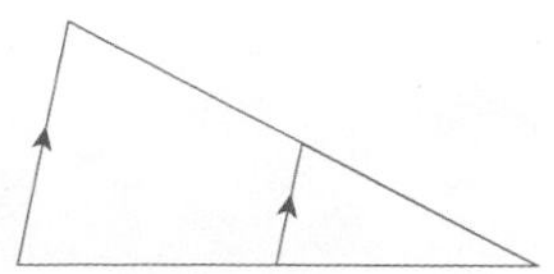

For Problems 23 to 26, triangles and quadrilaterals are divided into two triangular pieces. Determine if the resulting pieces are congruent, similar, or neither.

23.

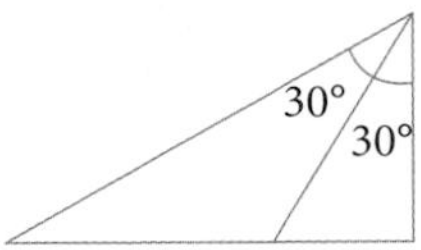

24.

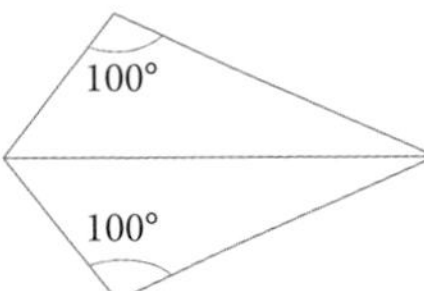

25.

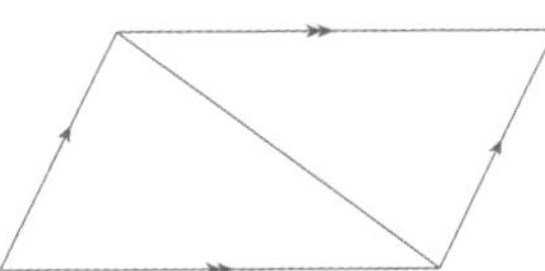

26.

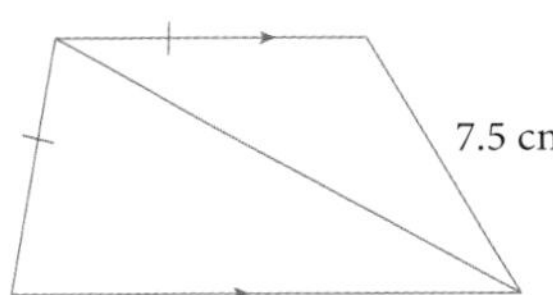

For Problems 27 to 30, solve each pair of similar triangles completely, by calculating the unknown side lengths (rounded to the nearest tenth as necessary) and angle measures.

27.

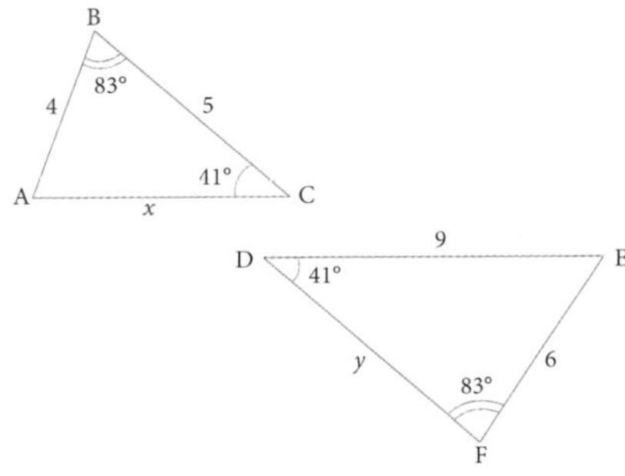

28.

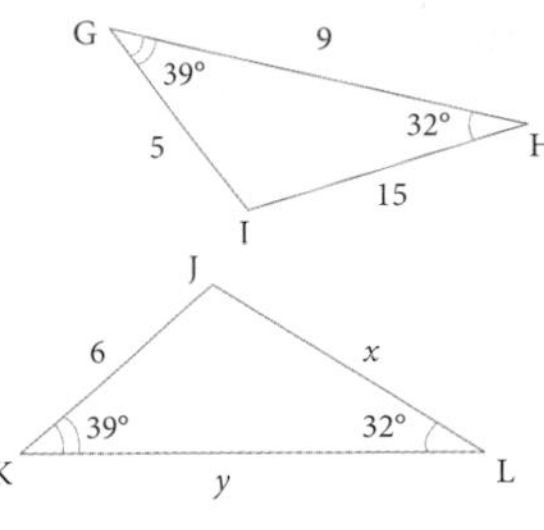

29.

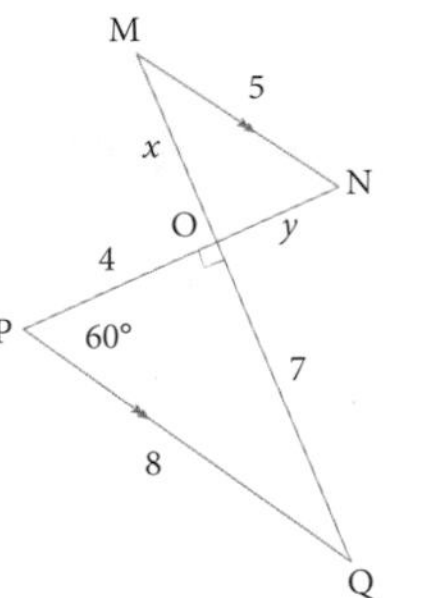

30.

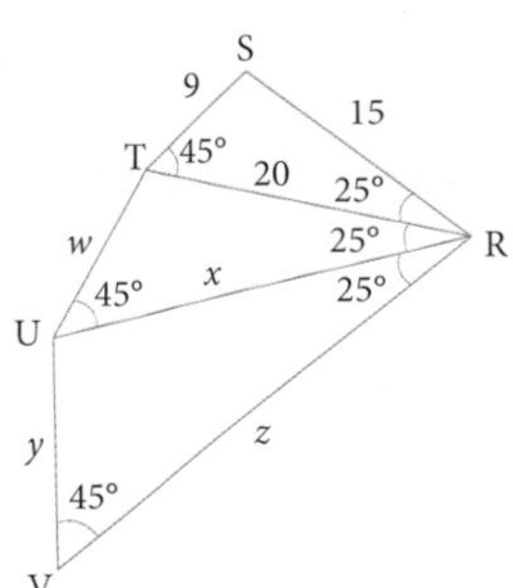

31. A flagpole casts a 3.4 m shadow. Melanie, who is 160 cm tall, stands beside the flagpole, and her shadow is 64 cm long. Draw a diagram and calculate the height of the flagpole.

32. A tree casts a 4.5 m shadow. At the same time, a stick 55 cm long casts a shadow 90 cm long. Calculate the height of the tree in metres and centimeters.

33. In an outdoor theatre at night, a spotlight is placed 8 m behind a sheet that is 5.5 m high. As an actress, who is 1.65 m tall, walks from the sheet towards the spotlight, it casts her shadow onto the wall. How far away from the spotlight is the actress when her shadow is the entire height of the sheet?

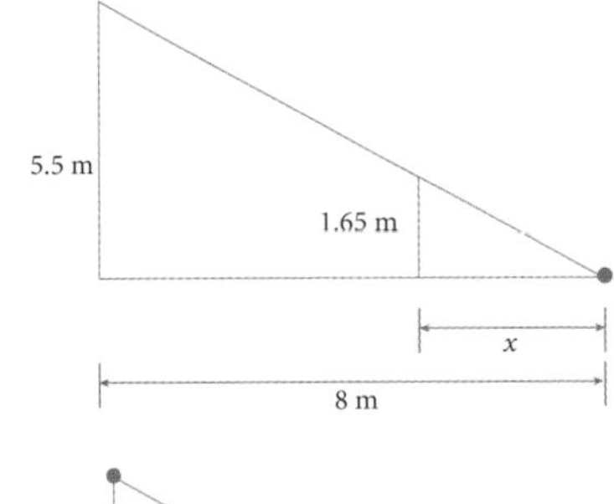

34. A streetlight situated 7.4 m above the street casts a shadow on a pedestrian, taking a late-night walk. If the pedestrian is 1.8 m tall, how long is his shadow when he is 7 m away from the streetlight?

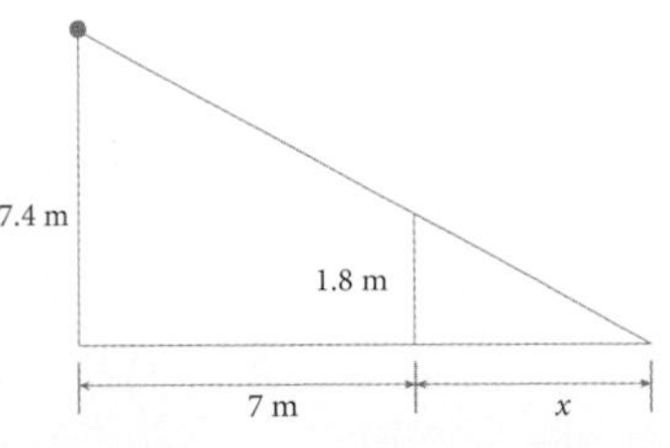

35. A man is standing 12 m away from a lamp post that is 10 m tall. If his shadow is 2.2 m long, how tall is he?

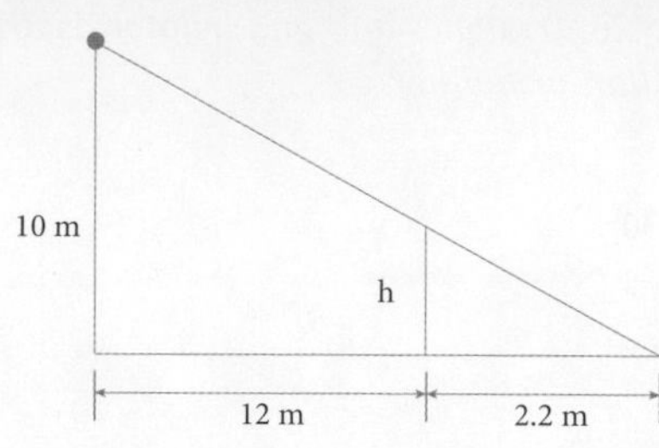

36. Two ladders of lengths 4 m and 9 m are leaning at the same angle against a wall. If the 4 m ladder reaches 3.2 m up the wall, how much further up the wall does the 9 m ladder reach?

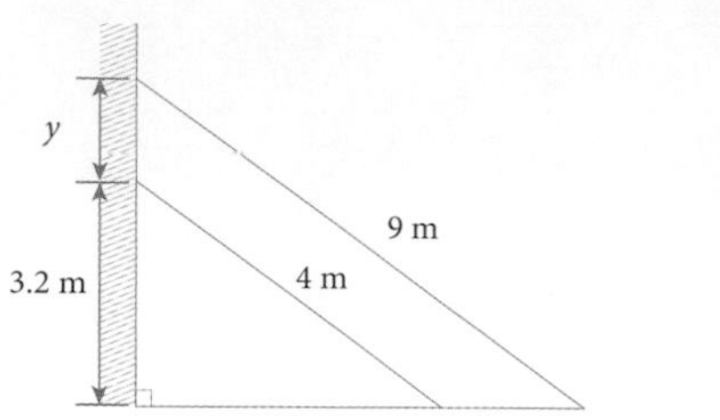

37. Calculate the height of "y" in the diagram below.

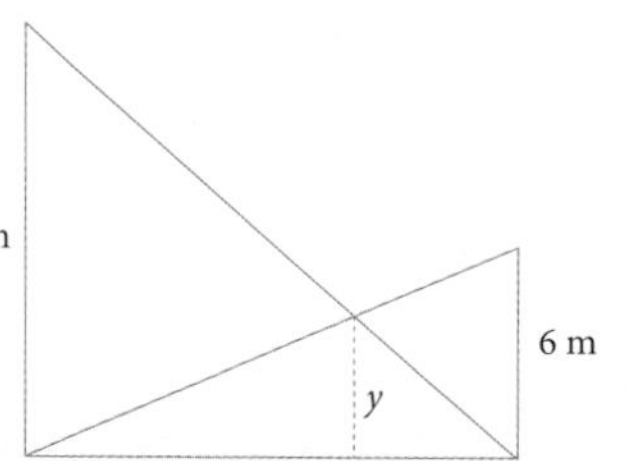

38. Calculate the length of "x" in the diagram below.

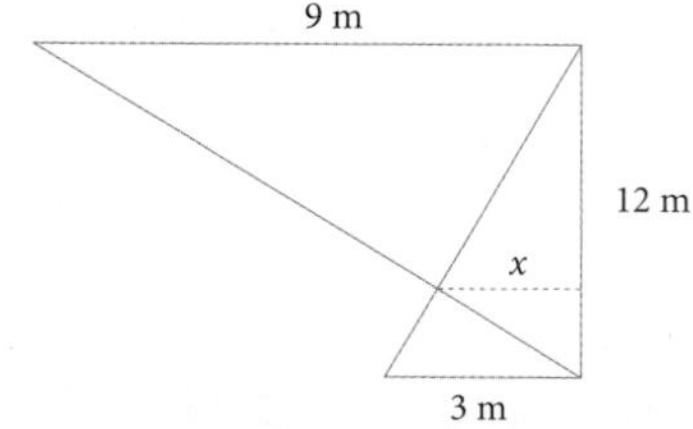

10.2 | Pythagorean Theorem

The **Pythagorean Theorem** is a famous theorem in mathematics, named after a Greek philosopher and mathematician, Pythagoras. It describes a special relationship between the lengths of the three sides of a right-triangle. The theorem states that the sum of the squares of the lengths of the two shorter sides that meet at the right-angle (called the **legs** of the right triangle) is equal to the square of the longest side opposite the right-angle (called the **hypotenuse** of the right triangle).

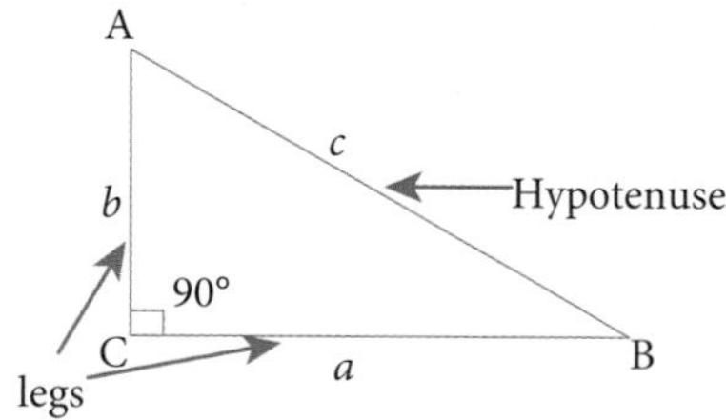

For example, in a right-triangle ABC with the right angle at C, the Pythagorean Theorem is written as an equation relating the lengths of the sides a, b, and c, where a and b represent the legs, and c represents the hypotenuse, as follows:

$$a^2 + b^2 = c^2$$

Using this equation, if the lengths of both legs (a and b) are known, then the hypotenuse (c) can be calculated as follows:

$$c = \sqrt{a^2 + b^2}$$

Exhibit 10.2-a Pythagorean Theorem

Similarly, if the lengths of the hypotenuse (c) and one leg (a or b) are known, then the length of the other leg can be calculated as follows:

$$a = \sqrt{c^2 - b^2} \quad \text{or} \quad b = \sqrt{c^2 - a^2}$$

A set of positive integers that satisfies the Pythagorean Theorem is known as a Pythagorean triple. For example, the set of integers 3, 4, and 5 is a Pythagorean triple.

$$3^2 + 4^2 = 5^2$$

$$(\text{i.e., } 9 + 16 = 25)$$

Some of the other Pythagorean triples are: (5, 12, 13), (7, 24, 25), (8, 15, 17), (9, 40, 41), (12, 35, 37), (20, 21, 29)

Proofs of the Pythagorean Theorem

The Pythagorean Theorem has numerous proofs. In this section, we will explore two proofs of the theorem, one being an application of similar triangles (review of Section 10.1), and the other being an application of geometry (review of Chapter 9).

Proof Using Similar Triangles

The symbol "⊥" represents "perpendicular to".

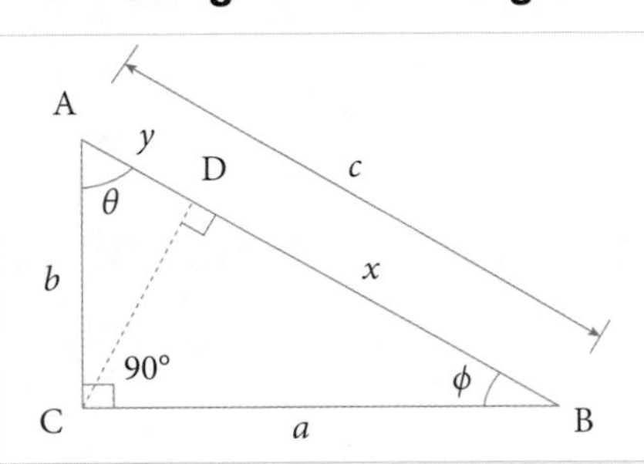

Exhibit 10.2-b Proof of Pythagorean Theorem using Similar Triangles

For this proof of the Pythagorean Theorem, start with a right-triangle, ABC, with legs a and b, and hypotenuse c.

Draw a line CD such that CD $\perp$ AB.

Let $\angle A = \theta$ and $\angle B = \phi$ (where $\theta + \phi = 90°$).

Let BD $= x$ and AD $= y$ (where $x + y = c$). Then,

ΔABC and ΔCBD are similar.

Therefore, $\dfrac{c}{a} = \dfrac{a}{x}$

i.e., $a^2 = cx$ (1)

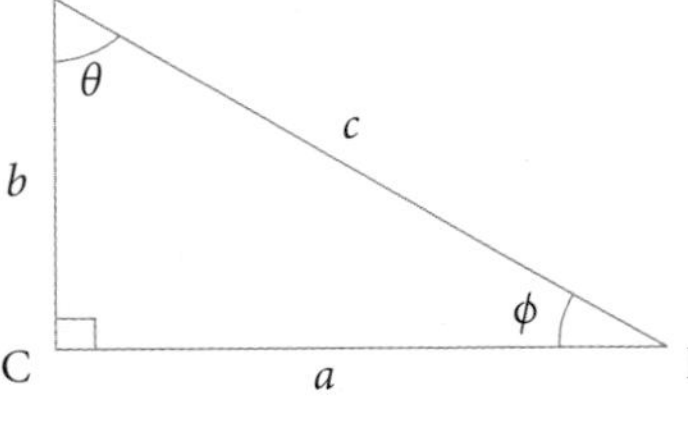

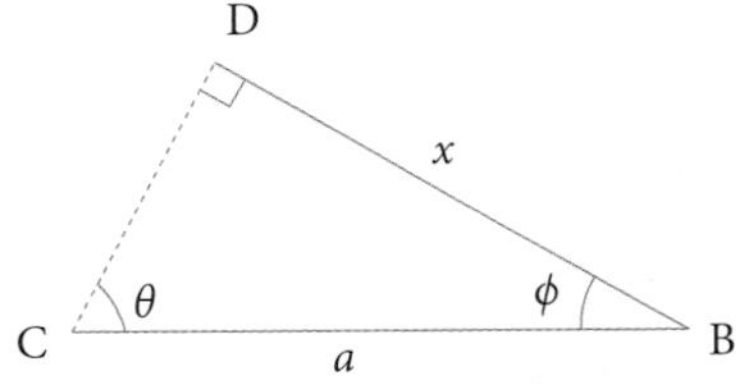

ΔABC and ΔACD are similar.

Therefore, $\dfrac{b}{c} = \dfrac{y}{b}$

i.e., $b^2 = cy$ (2)

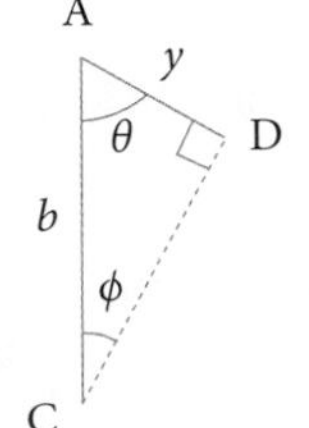

Adding (1) and (2),

$$a^2 + b^2 = cx + cy$$

$$a^2 + b^2 = c(x + y) = c(c) = c^2$$

Therefore, $a^2 + b^2 = c^2$.

Proof Using a Geometric Construction

For this proof of the Pythagorean Theorem, start with a right-triangle with legs a and b, and hypotenuse c. Then, create three additional copies of the triangle and line them up tip-to-tip so that their boundaries form a square, as shown in Exhibit 10.2-c.

The outer boundary forms a square, as all angles are right-angles and all side lengths are equal to $(a + b)$.

The inner boundary also forms a square, as all angles are right-angles (by the IAT-2 from Chapter 9) and all side lengths are equal to c.

Area of larger square = Area of smaller square + Area of each of the 4 triangles

Using the formulas for the area of a square and the area of a triangle:

$$(a + b)^2 = c^2 + 4\left[\frac{a \times b}{2}\right]$$

$$a^2 + 2ab + b^2 = c^2 + 2ab$$

$$a^2 + b^2 = c^2$$

Therefore, $a^2 + b^2 = c^2$.

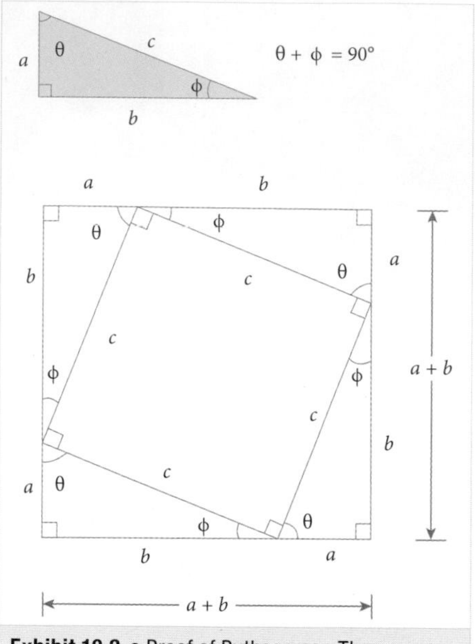

Exhibit 10.2-c Proof of Pythagorean Theorem using a Geometric Construction

Determining the Unknown Length of One Side of a Right Triangle

If we are given the lengths of any two sides of a right-triangle, we can use the Pythagorean Theorem to determine the length of the third side.

Example 10.2-a **Calculating the Length of the Hypotenuse of a Right-Triangle**

Using the Pythagorean Theorem, calculate the length (rounded to the nearest hundredth, as needed) of the hypotenuse, c, of the following right-triangles, given the lengths of the two legs, a and b.

(i) $a = 3$ m and $b = 4$ m (ii) $a = 10$ cm and $b = 12$ cm

Solution

The set 3, 4, and 5 is a Pythagorean triple.

(i) Using $a^2 + b^2 = c^2$,

$c^2 = a^2 + b^2 = 3^2 + 4^2 = 9 + 16 = 25$

$c = \sqrt{25} = 5$ m

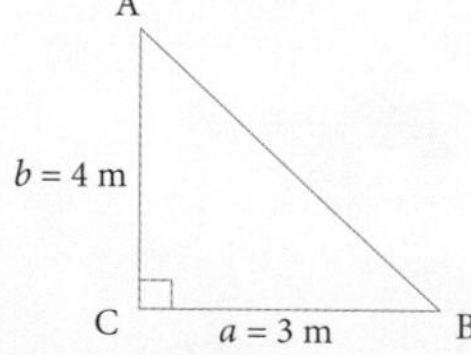

(ii) Using $a^2 + b^2 = c^2$,

$c^2 = a^2 + b^2 = 10^2 + 12^2 = 100 + 144 = 244$

$c = \sqrt{244} = 15.620499... = 15.62$ cm

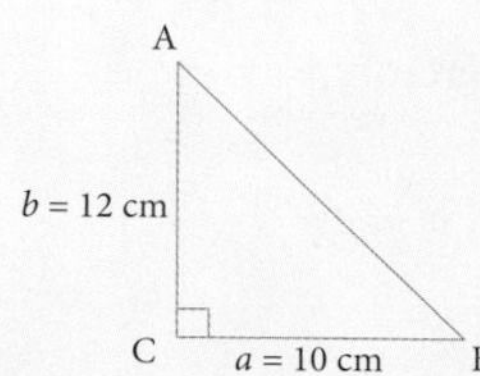

Example 10.2-b **Calculating the Length of One of the Legs of a Right-Triangle**

Using the Pythagorean Theorem, calculate the length (rounded to the nearest hundredth, as needed) of the missing leg of the following right-triangles, given the lengths of the hypotenuse, c, and one leg.

(i) $a = 5$ cm and $c = 13$ cm (ii) $b = 8$ m and $c = 16$ m

Solution

The set 5, 12, and 13 is a Pythagorean triple.

(i) Using $a^2 + b^2 = c^2$,

$$b^2 = c^2 - a^2 = 13^2 - 5^2 = 169 - 25 = 144$$

$$b = \sqrt{144} = 12 \text{ cm}$$

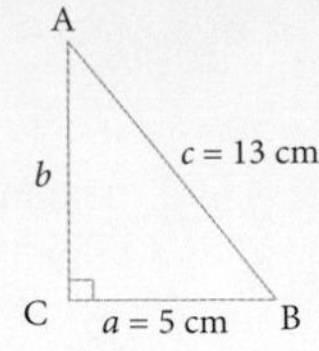

(ii) Using $a^2 + b^2 = c^2$,

$$a^2 = c^2 - b^2 = 16^2 - 8^2 = 256 - 64 = 192$$

$$a = \sqrt{192} = 13.856406... = 13.86 \text{ m}$$

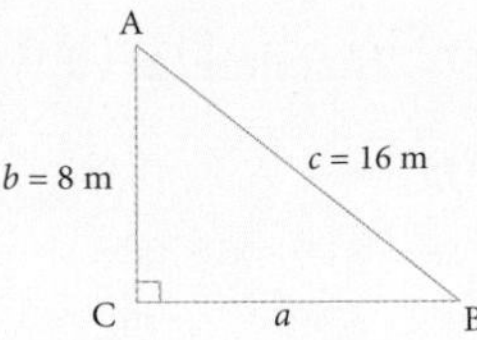

Example 10.2-c

Calculate the Unknown Lengths (x and y) in the Following Diagrams

In the following figures, calculate the lengths of x and y (rounded to the nearest tenth, as needed):

(i)

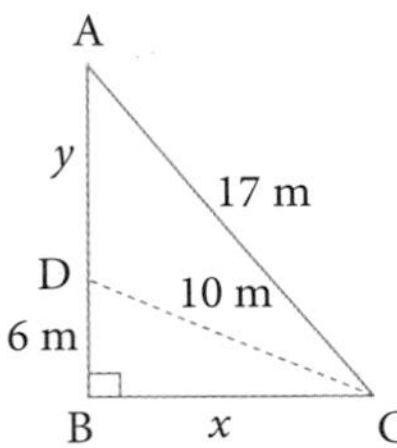

(ii)

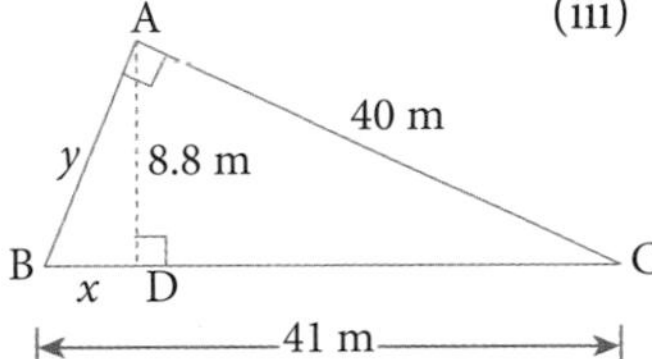

(iii)

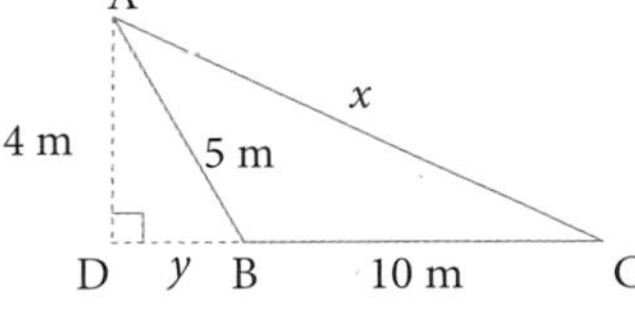

Solution

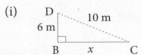

(i) In the right-triangle BCD, using the Pythagorean Theorem,

$$x^2 + 6^2 = 10^2$$

$$x^2 = 10^2 - 6^2$$

$$= 100 - 36 = 64$$

$$x = \sqrt{64} = 8 \text{ m}$$

In the right-triangle ABC, using the Pythagorean Theorem,

$$(y + 6)^2 + 8^2 = 17^2$$

$$(y + 6)^2 = 17^2 - 8^2$$

$$= 289 - 64 = 225$$

$$(y + 6) = \sqrt{225} = 15$$

$$y = 15 - 6 = 9 \text{ m}$$

Therefore, $x = 8$ m and $y = 9$ m.

(ii)

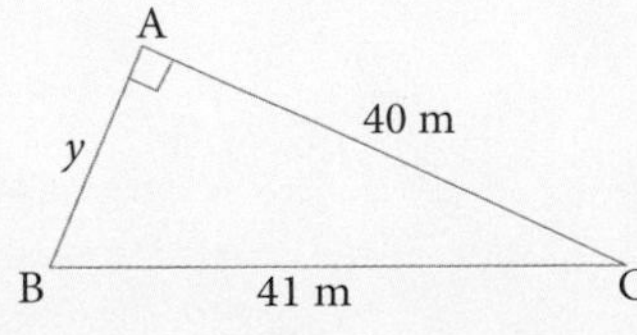

In the right-triangle ABC, using the Pythagorean Theorem,

$$y^2 + 40^2 = 41^2$$

$$y^2 = 41^2 - 40^2$$

$$= 1{,}681 - 1{,}600 = 81$$

$$y = \sqrt{81} = 9 \text{ m}$$

Solution
continued

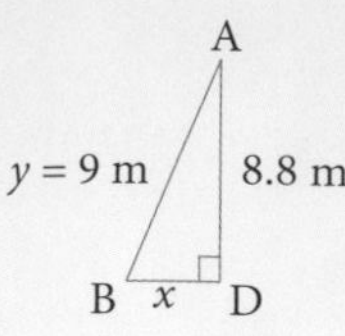

In the right-triangle ABD, using the Pythagorean Theorem,

$$x^2 + 8.8^2 = 9^2$$

$$x^2 = 9^2 - 8.8^2$$

$$= 81 - 77.44 = 3.56$$

$$x = \sqrt{3.56} = 1.886796... \approx 1.9 \text{ m}$$

Therefore, $x = 1.9$ m and $y = 9$ m.

(iii)

In the right-triangle ADB, using the Pythagorean Theorem,

$$y^2 + 4^2 = 5^2$$

$$y^2 = 5^2 - 4^2$$

$$= 25 - 16 = 9$$

$$y = \sqrt{9} = 3 \text{ m}$$

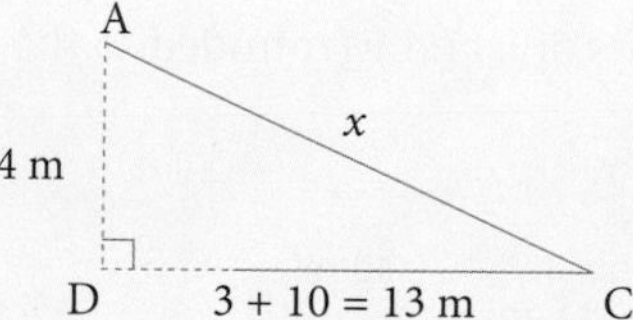

In the right-triangle ADC, using the Pythagorean Theorem,

$$4^2 + 13^2 = x^2$$

$$x^2 = 16 + 169 = 185$$

$$x = \sqrt{185} = 13.601470... \approx 13.6 \text{ m}$$

Therefore, $x = 13.6$ m and $y = 3$ m.

Calculating the Distance Between Two Points

In Chapter 8, the concept of the distance between two points on the Cartesian plane was introduced; however, it was limited to points that are on the same vertical line (sharing the same x-coordinate) or horizontal line (sharing the same y-coordinate). If the two points share neither the same x-coordinate nor y-coordinate, the calculation becomes more difficult. Certainly, the distance is at most the sum of the horizontal and vertical distances between the two points, but there is a shorter distance: the line segment joining the two points.

In this section, the method to calculate the shortest distance between two points having coordinates $P(x_1, y_1)$ and $Q(x_2, y_2)$ will be demonstrated.

In these last two chapters, Δ has been used to specify the name of a triangle (e.g., ΔABC), but this symbol has many uses. Recall from Chapter 8 that Δ is also commonly used as a short form for "the change in".

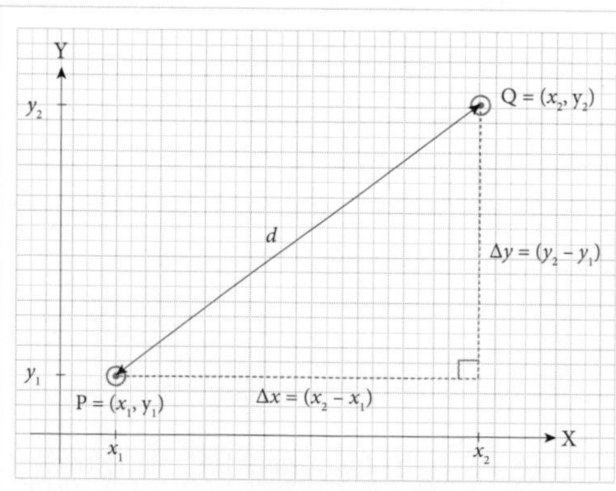

Exhibit 10.2-d The shortest distance between two points, using the Pythagorean Theorem.

Every horizontal line and every vertical line meet at a right-angle. Therefore, the shortest distance between two points is related to the horizontal and vertical distances between the points by the Pythagorean Theorem. This forms the equation for the shortest distance:

$$d^2 = (\Delta x)^2 + (\Delta y)^2$$

where Δx is the horizontal distance between the two points (i.e., change in x) and Δy is the vertical distance between the two points (i.e., change in y).

That is, using the two points $P(x_1, y_1)$ and $Q(x_2, y_2)$:

$$d^2 = (x_2 - x_1)^2 + (y_2 - y_1)^2$$

Performing the square root on both sides, the shortest distance, d, between the two points $P(x_1, y_1)$ and $Q(x_2, y_2)$ is:

$$d = \sqrt{(x_2 - x_1)^2 + (y_2 - y_1)^2}$$

Example 10.2-d

Calculating the Distance Between Two Points in the Cartesian Plane

Calculate the distance (rounded to the nearest tenth of a unit, as needed) between the following points:

(i) A(2, 1) and B(7, 8)

(ii) P(–3, 7) and Q(3, –1)

(iii) X(4.5, –1.2) and Y(–7.3, 2.8)

Solution

Using $d^2 = (x_2 - x_1)^2 + (y_2 - y_1)^2$,

(i) $d^2 = (7 - 2)^2 + (8 - 1)^2$

$= 5^2 + 7^2 = 25 + 49 = 74$

$d = \sqrt{74} = 8.602325... \approx 8.6$ units

(ii) $d^2 = [3 - (-3)]^2 + [(-1) - 7]^2$

$= 6^2 + (-8)^2 = 36 + 64 = 100$

$d = \sqrt{100} = 10$ units

(iii) $d^2 = [(-7.3) - 4.5]^2 + [2.8 - (-1.2)]^2$

$= (-11.8)^2 + (4.0)^2 = 139.24 + 16 = 155.24$

$d = \sqrt{155.24} = 12.459534... \approx 12.5$ units

Applications of the Pythagorean Theorem

Example 10.2-e

Calculating the Distance Between Two Cities

Toronto is 45 km north and 26 km east of Hamilton. Determine the shortest flying distance (rounded to the nearest kilometre) between the two cities.

Solution

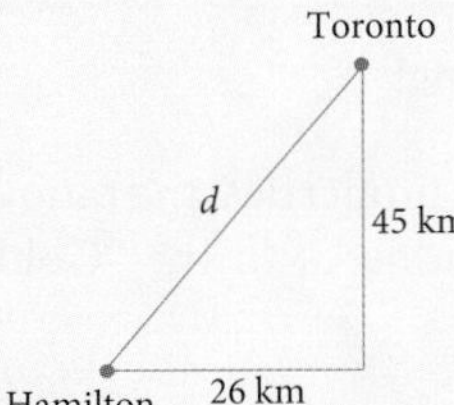

Let d be the distance between the two cities.

Using the Pythagorean theorem,

$d^2 = 45^2 + 26^2$

$= 2{,}025 + 676 = 2{,}701$

$d = \sqrt{2{,}701}$

$= 51.971145... \approx 52$ km

Therefore, the shortest flying distance between the two cities is 52 km.

Example 10.2-f

Calculating the Length of a Guy Wire

A guy wire is tied to an antenna tower 12 m above the ground and the other end of the guy wire is tied to the ground 15 m away. Determine the length of the guy wire, rounded to the nearest tenth of a metre.

Solution

Let ℓ be the length of the guy wire.

Using the Pythagorean Theorem,

$$\ell^2 = 15^2 + 12^2$$
$$= 225 + 144 = 369$$
$$\ell = \sqrt{369}$$
$$= 19.209372... \approx 19.2 \text{ m}$$

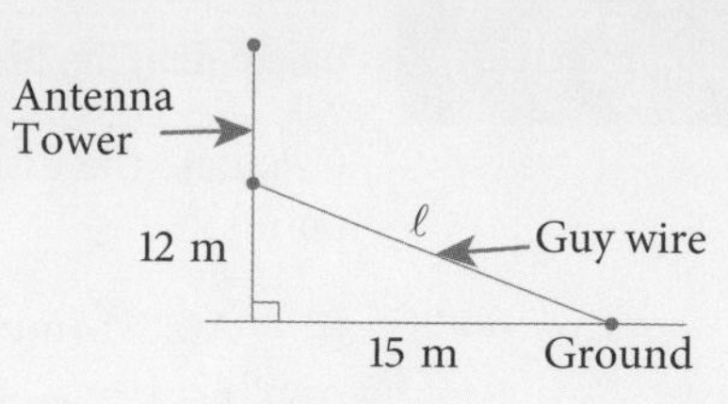

Therefore, the length of the guy wire is 19.2 m.

Example 10.2-g

Determining the Dimensions of a Television

A 42″ television, with a length to height ratio 16 : 9, measures 42 inches across the diagonal. Determine the length and the height of the TV, to the nearest tenth of an inch.

Solution

Since the ratio of the length of the TV to the height of the TV is 16 : 9, let $16x$ represent the length of the TV and $9x$ represent the height of the TV.

Using the Pythagorean Theorem,

$$42^2 = (16x)^2 + (9x)^2$$
$$1{,}764 = 256x^2 + 81x^2$$
$$1{,}764 = 337x^2$$
$$x^2 = \frac{1{,}764}{337} = 5.234421...$$
$$x = \sqrt{5.234421...} = 2.287885...$$

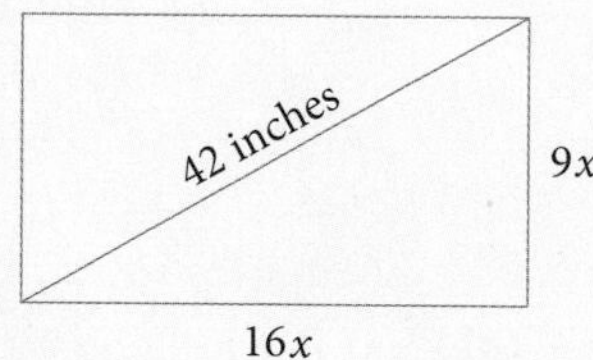

Length of the TV = $16x = 16(2.287885...) = 36.606172... \approx 36.6$ inches

Height of the TV = $9x = 9(2.287885...) = 20.590972... \approx 20.6$ inches

Therefore, the length of the TV is 36.6 inches and the height is 20.6 inches.

Example 10.2-h

Calculating the Height, Surface Area, and Volume of a Pyramid

The Great Pyramids of Giza in Egypt have certain special properties: the ratio of the slant height (s) of the pyramid to the semi-base (b_1) of the pyramid adheres to the "Golden Ratio," which is approximately 1.618 : 1.

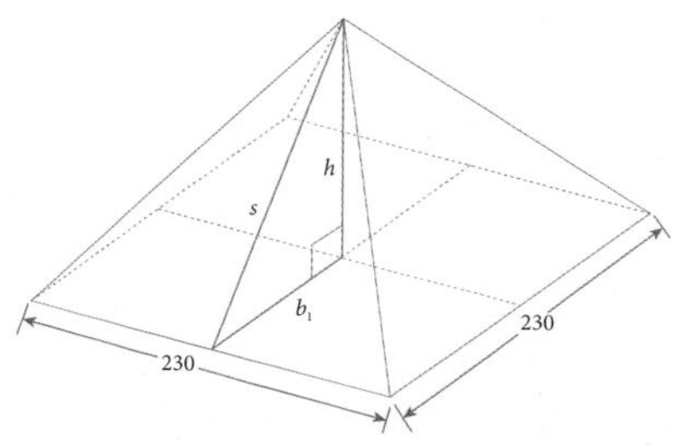

Jorge wishes to know the height (h), surface area (SA), and volume (V) of the largest pyramid. If he measures the length of one side of the base to be 230 m, find the height of the pyramid, rounded to the nearest metre. Then, find the surface area and volume of the pyramid, rounded to the nearest square metre and cubic metre, respectively.

Solution

Since the base is 230 m, $b_1 = \frac{230}{2} = 115$ m.

Step 1: Calculate the slant height of the pyramid, s, using the Golden Ratio $\frac{s}{b_1} = 1.618$,

$$s = 1.618(115) = 186.07 \approx 186 \text{ m}$$

Therefore, the slant height of the pyramid is 186 m.

Solution
continued

Step 2: Calculate the height of the pyramid using the Pythagorean Theorem.

$$s^2 = b_1^{\ 2} + h^2$$
$$(186)^2 = (115)^2 + (h)^2$$
$$34{,}596 = 13{,}225 + h^2$$
$$h^2 = 21{,}371$$
$$h = \sqrt{21{,}371} = 146.188234... \approx 146 \text{ m}$$

Therefore, the height of the pyramid is 146 m.

Step 3: Calculate the surface area of the four equal triangular sides using slant height $s = 186$ m and $b = 230$ m.

$$\text{SA} = 4 \times \left[\frac{(230 \text{ m})(186 \text{ m})}{2}\right] = 85{,}560 \text{ m}^2$$

Step 4: Calculate the volume of the pyramid using base $b = 230$ m, height $h = 146$ m, and the formula for a square-based pyramid.

$$\text{V} = \frac{(230 \text{ m})^2(146 \text{ m})}{3} \approx 2{,}574{,}467 \text{ m}^3$$

Therefore, the surface area of the pyramid is 85,560 m^2 and the volume of the pyramid is 2,574,467 m^3.

10.2 | Exercises

Answers to odd-numbered problems are available at the end of the textbook.

For Problems 1 to 4, use the Pythagorean Theorem to determine the length (rounded to the nearest hundredth, wherever applicable) of the missing side in the given right-angled triangles, where a and b represent the legs of the triangle and c represents the hypotenuse of the triangle.

1.

	a	*b*	*c*
a.	15 cm	20 cm	?
b.	2.5 cm	?	6.5 cm
c.	?	6 cm	6.25 cm

2.

	a	*b*	*c*
a.	7 cm	24 cm	?
b.	7.5 cm	?	12.5 cm
c.	?	20 cm	20.5 cm

3.

	a	*b*	*c*
a.	12 cm	15 cm	?
b.	8 cm	?	17 cm
c.	?	15 cm	16 cm

4.

	a	*b*	*c*
a.	16 cm	18 cm	?
b.	20 cm	?	29 cm
c.	?	17 cm	23 cm

For Problems 5 to 10, calculate the length of the missing side for each of the diagrams.

5.

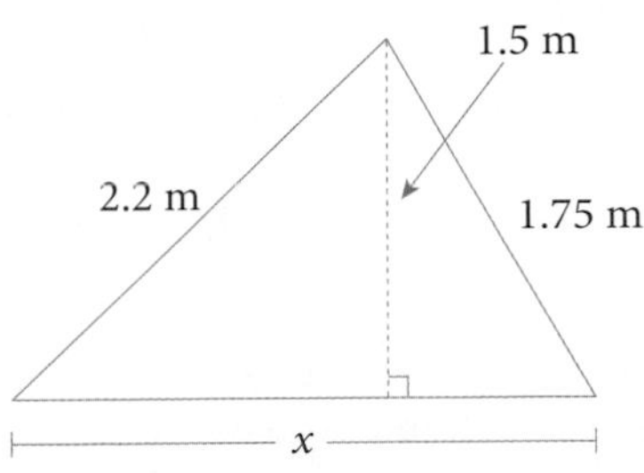

6.

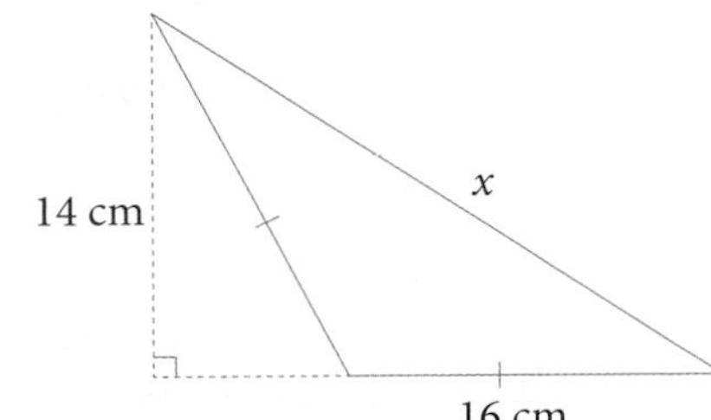

7.

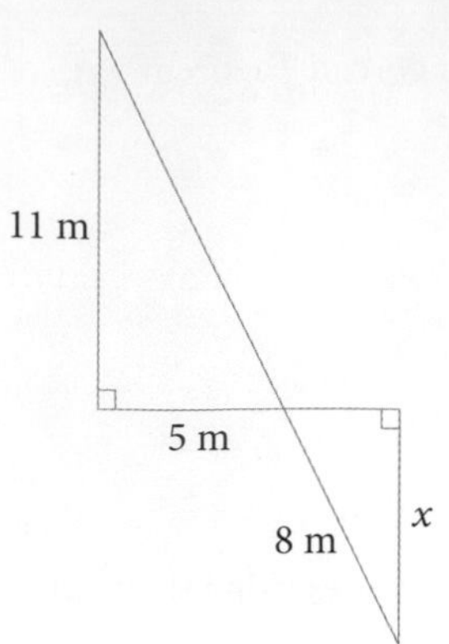

8.

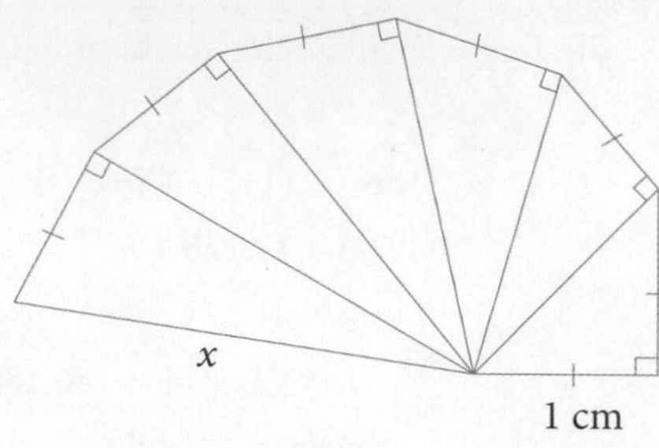

9.

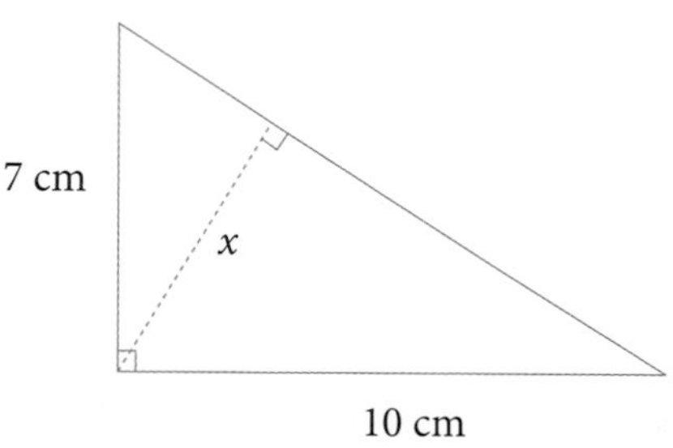

10.

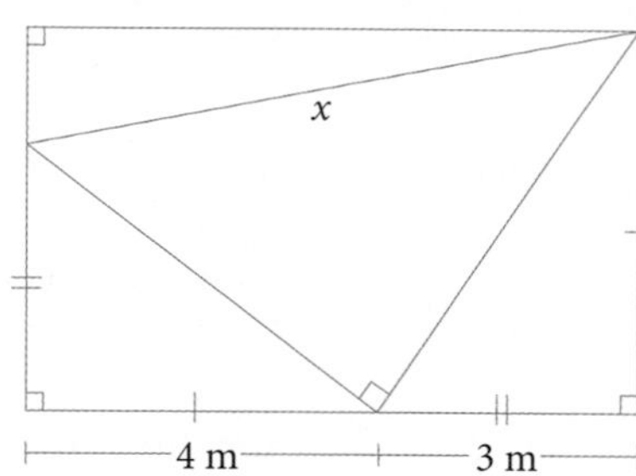

For Problems 11 to 14, calculate the perimeter and area of each of the given diagrams.

11.

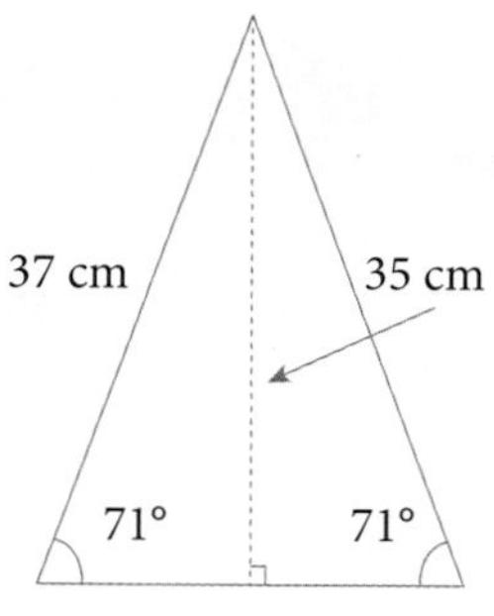

12.

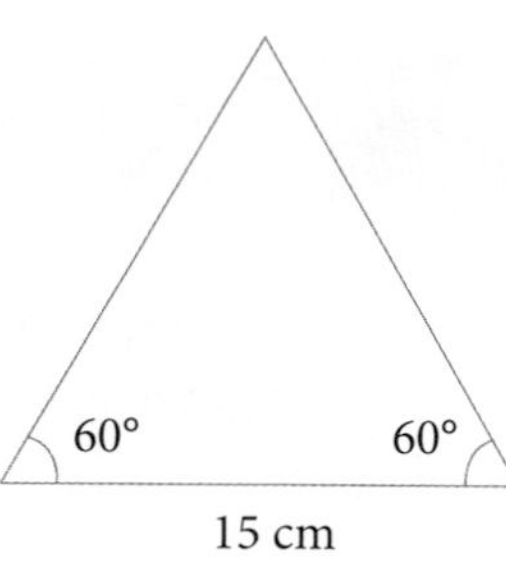

13.

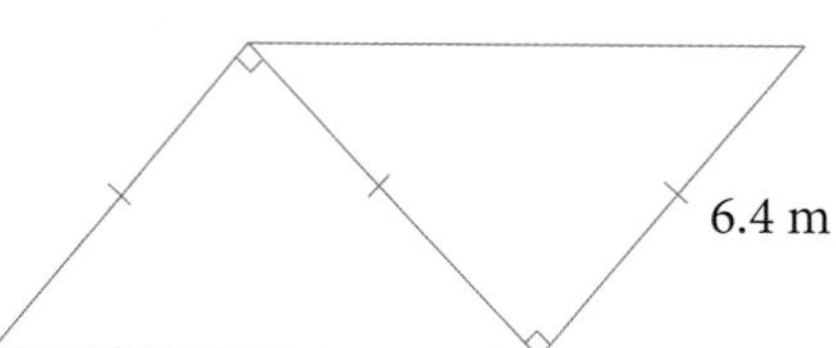

14.

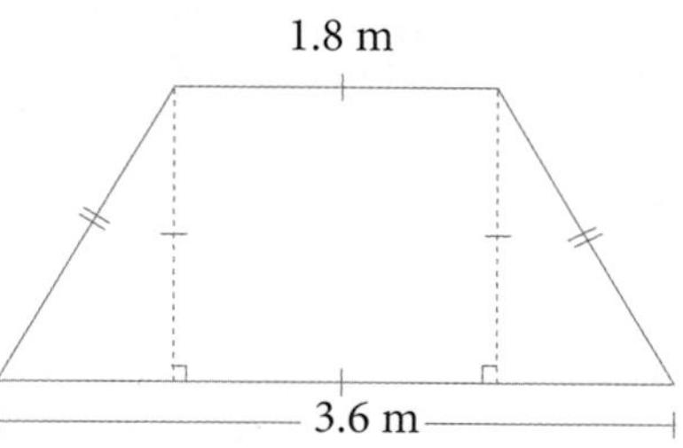

For Problems 15 to 22, calculate the length of the line segments joining the pairs of points.

15. A(−2, 5) and B(4, 7)
16. C(−6, 1) and D(2, 5)
17. E(4, −3) and F(−1, 5)
18. G(1, −6) and H(−4, 3)
19. M(−3, −3) and N(−7, 2)
20. P(−4, −1) and Q(3, −5)
21. S(0, 4) and T(−3, 0)
22. U(2, 0) and V(0, −6)

23. A laptop screen measures 31 cm long by 17.5 cm high. Determine the diagonal length of the computer screen, rounded to the nearest tenth of a cm.

24. From a point 'X', a person walked 850 m due west and then turned and walked for another 1.7 km due south to reach point 'Y'. Calculate the shortest distance between X and Y, rounded to the nearest hundredth of a km.

25. A 2.5 m tent pole is secured using a 4.3 m long guy rope from the top of the pole. How far away from the base of the pole will the rope need to be secured to the ground, assuming it is pulled taut?

26. A 5 m ladder is leaned up against a wall. If the base of the ladder is placed on the ground 1.7 m away from the wall, how high up against the wall will the ladder reach, rounded to the nearest tenth of a metre?

27. A skateboard ramp that is 3.5 m long is built with a slope of $\frac{3}{5}$. Determine the maximum height of the ramp, rounded to the nearest cm.

28. A wheelchair ramp is to be constructed to the top of a set of stairs that is 1.75 m tall, with a maximum slope of $\frac{1}{12}$.

    Determine the minimum ramp length required, in order for the ramp to be built according to specifications. Can you suggest a way to build the ramp that would save space?

29. A towel rack that is 1 m long is to be placed in a box measuring 75 cm × 60 cm × 45 cm. Will the towel rack fit along the diagonal at the bottom of the box? Will it fit in the box if placed on the 3-dimensional diagonal?

30. Will a 16-foot-long piece of lumber fit in a truck with interior cargo dimensions of 12.5 feet by 8 feet by 7.5 feet?

For Problems 31 to 36, calculate the perpendicular height (to the nearest tenth), surface area (to the nearest whole number), and volume (to the nearest whole number) of the solids.

31. A cone with a base diameter of 24 cm and a slant height of 30 cm.

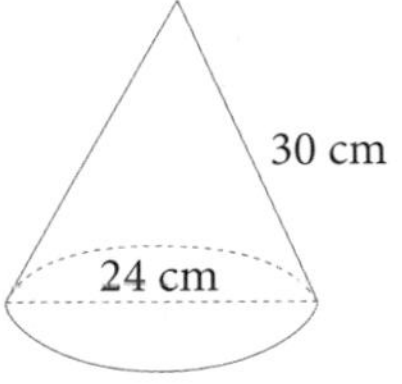

32. A cone with a base diameter of 64 mm and a slant height of 105 mm.

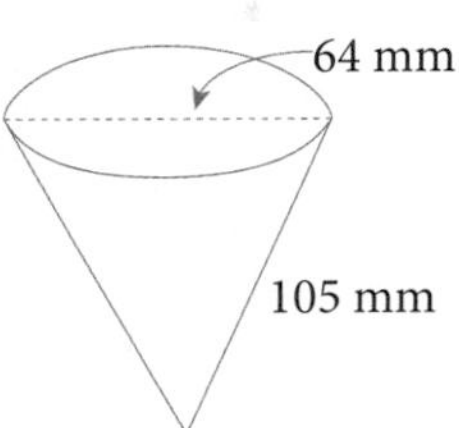

33. A square pyramid with a base length and corner edge length all equal to 98 m.

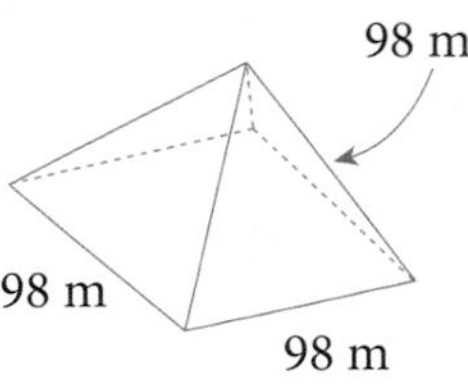

34. A pyramid with a rectangular base that has a length of 50 cm, a width of 36 cm, and a corner edge length of 45 cm.

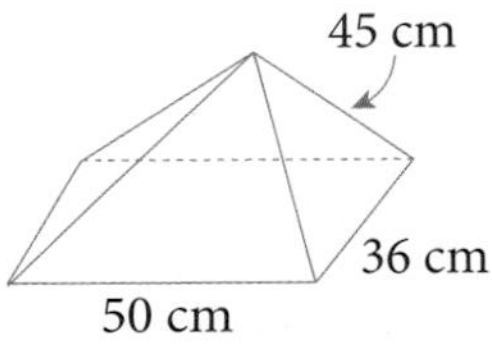

• 35. A truncated cone with a top diameter of 24 cm, a base diameter of 40 cm, and a slant height of 18 cm.

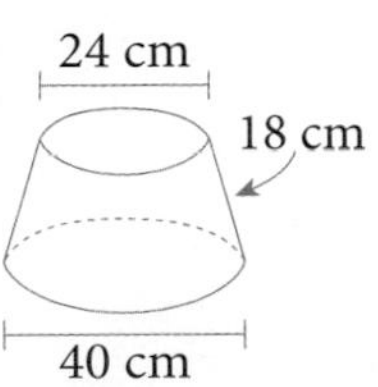

• 36. A truncated square pyramid with a top side length of 75 m, a base side length of 225 m, and a slant height of 120 m.

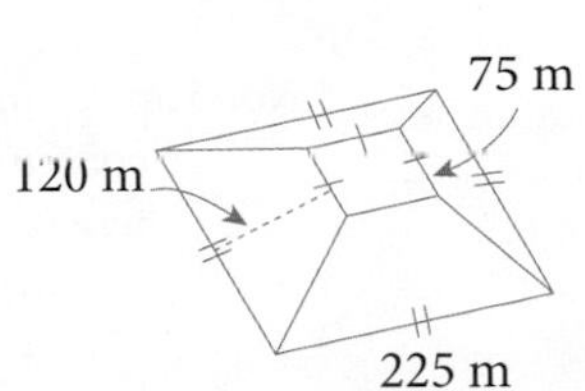

10.3 | Primary Trigonometric Ratios

In the previous section, the relationship between the side lengths of the three sides of a right triangle was examined. In this section, we will study the relationship between the side lengths of a right triangle and its acute angle measures. The core concept behind this relationship is based on the fact that if one of the two acute angles of a right triangle is known, then all right triangles with that one angle measure will be similar; therefore, their side lengths will be in proportion.

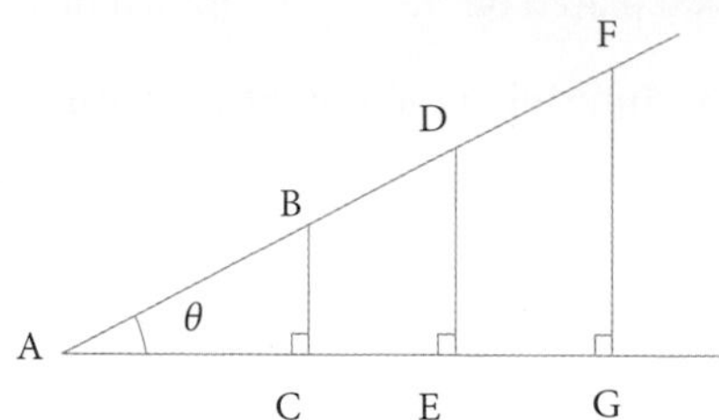

ΔABC, ΔADE, ΔAFG are similar; their side lengths are in proportion.

A **trigonometric ratio** is a ratio of the lengths of two sides of a right triangle. Mathematicians have given special names to the six ratios of the three side lengths, relative to one of the acute angles in the right triangle, known as θ. They are:

1. the sine (sin) ratio
2. the cosine (cos) ratio
3. the tangent (tan) ratio
4. the cosecant (csc) ratio
5. the secant (sec) ratio
6. the cotangent (cot) ratio

The first three ratios are known as the **primary trigonometric ratios**, and will be the focus of this section. The other three ratios, known as the **secondary trigonometric ratios**, are the reciprocal ratios of the three primary trigonometric ratios, respectively. They are not covered in this textbook.

Sine, Cosine, and Tangent Ratios of Angles in a Right Triangle

In a right triangle, recall that the **hypotenuse**, the longest side, is the side across from the right angle. In a right triangle with an acute angle θ (i.e., $0° < \theta < 90°$), the leg that forms the angle θ with the hypotenuse is known as the **adjacent** leg, and the third side, across (opposite) from angle θ, is known as the **opposite** leg. The three primary trigonometric ratios of θ are shown in Exhibit 10.3-a:

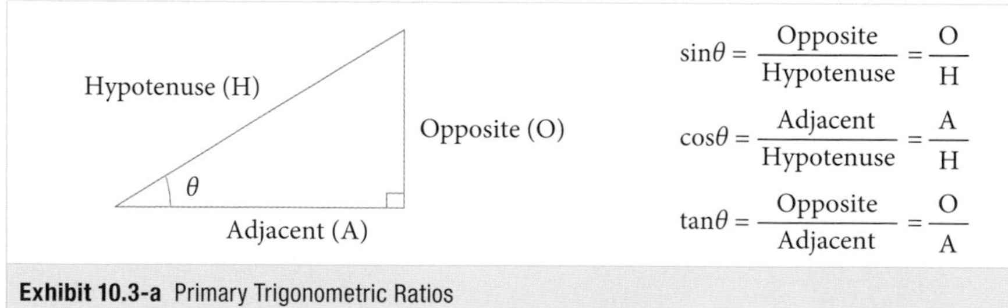

$$\sin\theta = \frac{\text{Opposite}}{\text{Hypotenuse}} = \frac{O}{H}$$

$$\cos\theta = \frac{\text{Adjacent}}{\text{Hypotenuse}} = \frac{A}{H}$$

$$\tan\theta = \frac{\text{Opposite}}{\text{Adjacent}} = \frac{O}{A}$$

Exhibit 10.3-a Primary Trigonometric Ratios

You may find it helpful to use the acronym **SOH-CAH-TOA** to remember the three primary trigonometric ratios:

SOH	Sin θ = **O**pposite/**H**ypotenuse
CAH	Cos θ = **A**djacent/**H**ypotenuse
TOA	Tan θ = **O**pposite/**A**djacent

In any acute angle,
$0 < \sin\theta < 1$
$0 < \cos\theta < 1$
$\tan\theta > 0$

Note: Since the lengths of the legs of a right triangle will be greater than 0 but always less than the hypotenuse, the sine and cosine ratios of any acute angle must be between 0 and 1. However, since there is no relationship between the opposite leg and the adjacent leg, except that they must both be greater than 0, the tangent ratio can be any positive number.

Exact Trigonometric Ratios of Special Common Angles

There are trigonometric ratios of special common angles (30°, 45°, and 60°) that can be computed from special right triangles: the **30-60-90** triangle and **45-45-90** triangle.

30 - 60 - 90 Triangle

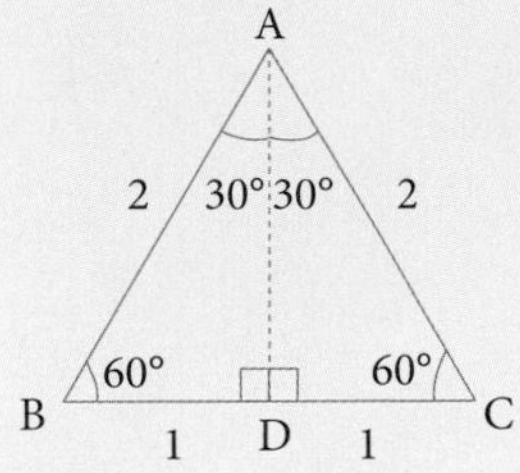

To calculate the trigonometric ratios of 30° and 60°, draw an equilateral triangle, ABC, with side lengths of 2 units each and draw AD ⊥ BC, as shown.

Since the angle measures are all 60°, the angle at the vertex A is bisected into two 30° angles and the base length 'BC' is bisected into 1 unit each.

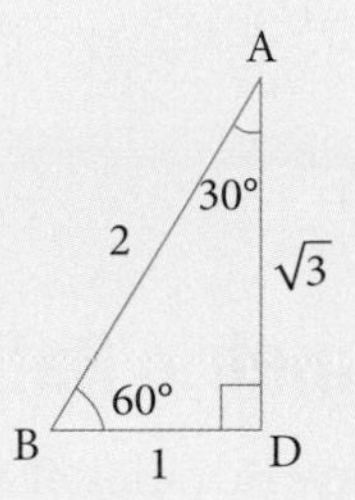

In the right triangle ABD (30 - 60 - 90), AB = 2 units, BD = 1 unit, and AD = $\sqrt{3}$ units (calculated using the Pythagorean Theorem: $AD^2 = 2^2 - 1^2 = 4 - 1 = 3$, which gives AD = $\sqrt{3}$).

Using the above measures in the right triangle ABD, the sine, cosine, and tangent ratios of 30° and 60° can be calculated exactly:

Using $\sin\theta = \dfrac{O}{H}$, $\quad \sin 30° = \dfrac{BD}{AB} = \dfrac{1}{2}$, $\quad \sin 60° = \dfrac{AD}{AB} = \dfrac{\sqrt{3}}{2}$

Using $\cos\theta = \dfrac{A}{H}$, $\quad \cos 30° = \dfrac{AD}{AB} = \dfrac{\sqrt{3}}{2}$, $\quad \cos 60° = \dfrac{BD}{AB} = \dfrac{1}{2}$

Using $\tan\theta = \dfrac{O}{A}$, $\quad \tan 30° = \dfrac{BD}{AD} = \dfrac{1}{\sqrt{3}}$, $\quad \tan 60° = \dfrac{AD}{BD} = \dfrac{\sqrt{3}}{1} = \sqrt{3}$

45 - 45 - 90 Triangle

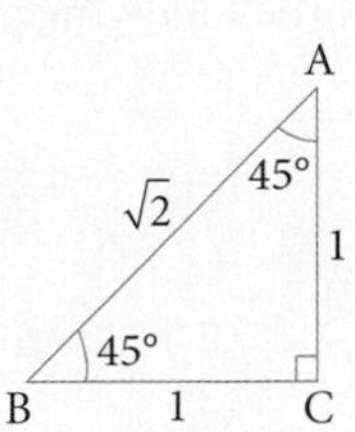

To calculate the trigonometric ratios of 45°, draw a right isosceles triangle, ABC, with leg side lengths of 1 unit each, as shown.

Since the triangle is a right isosceles, the two acute angles must be equal. Therefore, the two acute angles are each 45°.

In the right isosceles triangle ABC (45 - 45 - 90), AC = 1 unit, BC = 1 unit, and AB = $\sqrt{2}$ units (calculated using the Pythagorean Theorem: $AB^2 = 1^2 + 1^2 = 1 + 1 = 2$, which gives AB = $\sqrt{2}$).

Using the above measures in the right isosceles triangle ABC, the sine, cosine, and tangent ratios of 45° can be calculated exactly:

Using $\sin\theta = \dfrac{O}{H}$, $\quad \sin 45° = \dfrac{AC}{AB} = \dfrac{BC}{AB} = \dfrac{1}{\sqrt{2}}$

Using $\cos\theta = \dfrac{A}{H}$, $\quad \cos 45° = \dfrac{BC}{AB} = \dfrac{AC}{AB} = \dfrac{1}{\sqrt{2}}$

Using $\tan\theta = \dfrac{O}{A}$, $\quad \tan 45° = \dfrac{AC}{BC} = \dfrac{BC}{AC} = \dfrac{1}{1} = 1$

$\sin 30° = \cos 60° = \frac{1}{2}$

$\sin 60° = \cos 30° = \frac{\sqrt{3}}{2}$

$\sin 45° = \cos 45° = \frac{1}{\sqrt{2}}$

$\tan 30° = \frac{1}{\sqrt{3}}$

$\tan 45° = 1$

$\tan 60° = \sqrt{3}$

The primary trigonometric ratios of the special common angles are summarized in Exhibit 10.3-b. We refer to these as the special trig ratios.

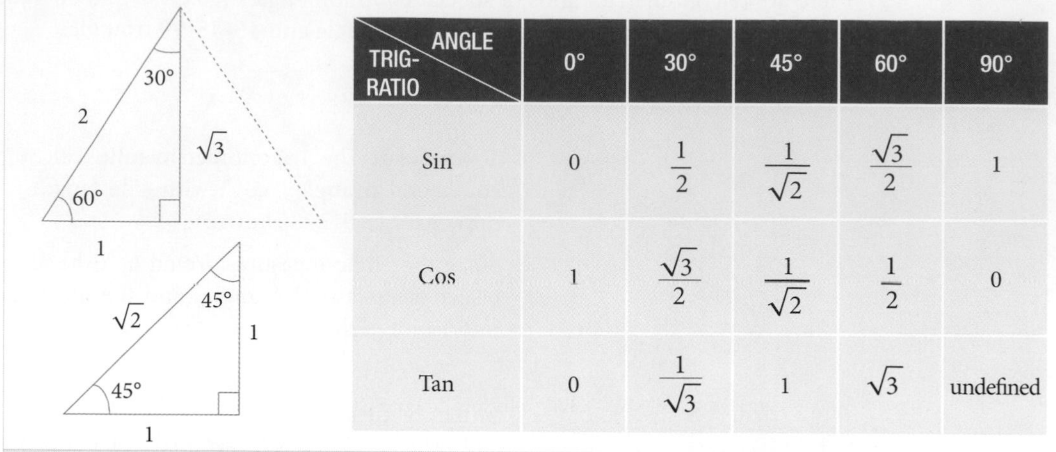

ANGLE / TRIG-RATIO	0°	30°	45°	60°	90°
Sin	0	$\frac{1}{2}$	$\frac{1}{\sqrt{2}}$	$\frac{\sqrt{3}}{2}$	1
Cos	1	$\frac{\sqrt{3}}{2}$	$\frac{1}{\sqrt{2}}$	$\frac{1}{2}$	0
Tan	0	$\frac{1}{\sqrt{3}}$	1	$\sqrt{3}$	undefined

Exhibit 10.3-b Special Trig Ratios

Using Calculators to Determine Trigonometric Ratios

A scientific calculator can be used to determine the trigonometric ratios of any angle.

When using a calculator to determine the trigonometric ratios, ensure that it is in "degree" mode.

Note: Some calculators may yield trigonometric ratios as a decimal number.

e.g., $\sin 60° = 0.866025...$ *(which is equivalent to to* $\frac{\sqrt{3}}{2}$ *).*

Example 10.3-a **Using a Calculator to Calculate sin, cos, and tan of Acute Angles**

Using a calculator, calculate the sine, cosine, and tangent of the following acute angles, rounded to four decimal places as required:

(i) $\theta = 15°$ (ii) $\theta = 72°$ (iii) $\theta = 36.87°$

Solution

(i) $\sin 15° = 0.258819... = 0.2588$

$\cos 15° = 0.965925... = 0.9659$

$\tan 15° = 0.267949.... = 0.2679$

(ii) $\sin 72° = 0.951056... = 0.9511$

$\cos 72° = 0.309016... = 0.3090$

$\tan 72° = 3.077683... = 3.0777$

(iii) $\sin 36.87° = 0.600001... = 0.6000$

$\cos 36.87° = 0.799998... = 0.8000$

$\tan 36.87° = 0.750002... = 0.7500$

Example 10.3-b **Calculating Side Lengths Using the Sine Ratio**

Calculate the unknown side lengths in the following diagrams. Round to the nearest hundredth, wherever required.

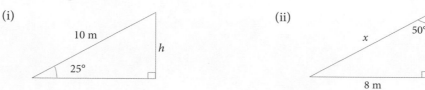

Solution

Using $\sin \theta = \frac{O}{H}$,

(i) $\sin 25° = \frac{h}{10}$

$h = 10 (\sin 25°)$

$= 4.226182... = 4.23$ m

(ii) $\sin 50° = \frac{8}{x}$

$x = \frac{8}{\sin 50°}$

$= 10.443258... = 10.44$ m

Example 10.3-c Calculating Side Lengths Using the Cosine Ratio

Calculate the unknown side lengths in the following diagrams. Round to the nearest hundredth, wherever required.

(i)

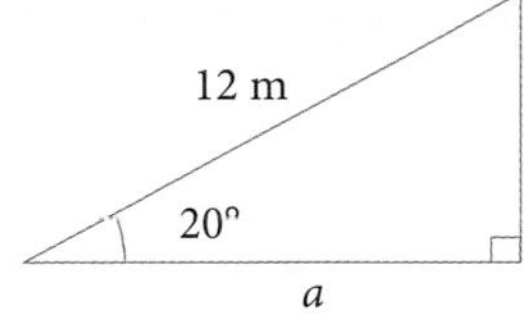

(ii)

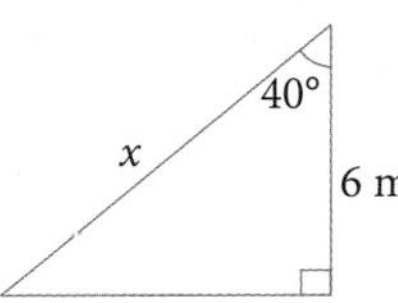

Solution

Using $\cos \theta = \frac{A}{H}$,

(i) $\cos 20° = \frac{a}{12}$

$a = 12 (\cos 20°)$

$= 11.276311... = 11.28$ m

(ii) $\cos 40° = \frac{6}{x}$

$x = \frac{6}{\cos 40°}$

$= 7.832443... = 7.83$ m

Example 10.3-d Calculating Side Lengths Using the Tangent Ratio

Calculate the unknown side lengths in the following diagrams. Round to the nearest hundredth, wherever required.

(i)

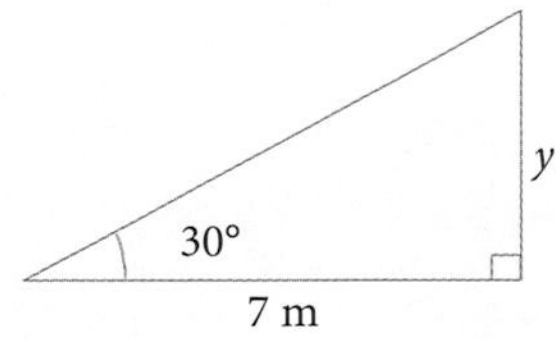

(ii)

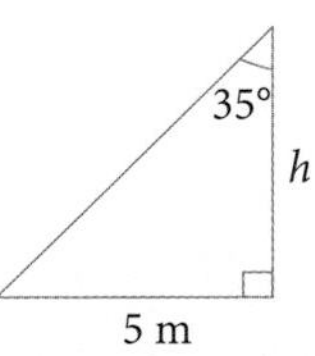

Solution

Using $\tan \theta = \frac{O}{A}$,

(i) $\tan 30° = \frac{y}{7}$

$y = 7 (\tan 30°)$

$= 4.041451... = 4.04$ m

(ii) $\tan 35° = \frac{5}{h}$

$h = \frac{5}{\tan 35°}$

$= 7.140740... = 7.14$ m

Using Calculators to Calculate Angles

If we know the ratio of the lengths of two sides of a right triangle, we can determine the angle related to that ratio using the **inverse trigonometric functions** of sine, cosine, and tangent, known as arcsine, arccosine, and arctangent, respectively. These functions often appear on scientific calculators as $\sin^{-1}$, $\cos^{-1}$, and $\tan^{-1}$.

Example 10.3-e **Using a Calculator to Calculate the Angle Given a Trig Ratio**

Using a calculator, calculate the angle measure in degrees (rounded to the nearest tenth of a degree) for each of the following trigonometric ratios:

(i) $\sin\theta = 0.9063$ (ii) $\cos\theta = 0.6$ (iii) $\tan\theta = 0.1467$

Solution

(i) $\theta = \sin^{-1}(0.9063)$

$\theta = 64.998944... = 65.0°$

(ii) $\theta = \cos^{-1}(0.6)$

$\theta = 53.130102... = 53.1°$

(iii) $\theta = \tan^{-1}(0.1467)$

$\theta = 8.345761... = 8.3°$

Example 10.3-f **Calculating Angles using the Inverse Trigonometric Ratios**

Calculate the unknown angle in the following diagrams. Round to the nearest degree, wherever required.

(i)

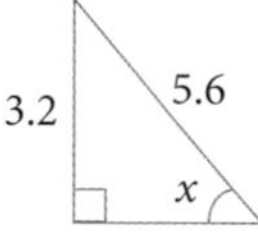

(ii)

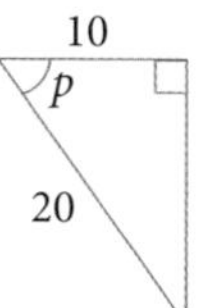

(iii)

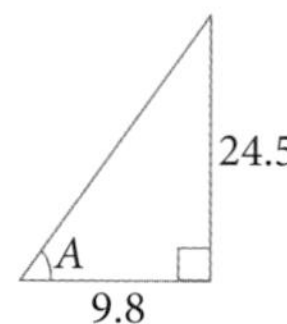

Solution

(i) Using $\sin\theta = \frac{\text{O}}{\text{H}}$,

$$\sin x = \frac{3.2}{5.6}$$

$$x = \sin^{-1}\left(\frac{3.2}{5.6}\right)$$

$$x = 34.849904... = 35°$$

(ii) Using $\cos\theta = \frac{\text{A}}{\text{H}}$,

$$\cos p = \frac{10}{20} = \frac{1}{2}$$

$$p = \cos^{-1}\left(\frac{1}{2}\right)$$

$$p = 60°$$

This is one is the special angles, since the ratio $\cos p = \frac{1}{2}$

(iii) Using $\tan\theta = \frac{\text{O}}{\text{A}}$,

$$\tan A = \frac{24.5}{9.8}$$

$$A = \tan^{-1}\left(\frac{24.5}{9.8}\right)$$

$$A = 68.198590... = 68°$$

Solving Right Triangles using Trigonometry

If one side length and one acute angle measure in a right triangle are provided, trigonometric ratios may be used to solve for the lengths of the remaining sides.

Conversely, if any two side lengths of a right triangle are given, the inverse trigonometric functions may be used to solve for the two acute angles.

When solving right triangles, there are often several ways to proceed. However, calculations should be performed using the method that requires the fewest number of steps. Whenever possible, measurements **provided in the question**, rather than measurements obtained from secondary calculations, should be used.

Example 10.3-g **Solving a Right-Triangle Given One Side Length and One Acute Angle**

Determine the unknown side lengths and missing angle of the following right triangles. Round all side lengths to the nearest hundredth and all angle measures to the nearest tenth.

(i)

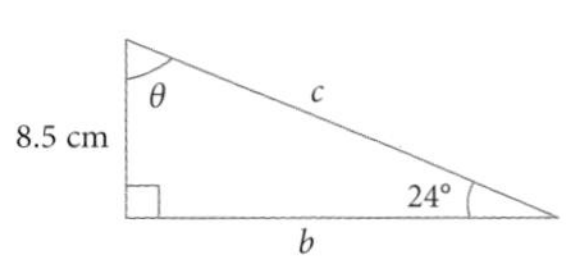

(ii)

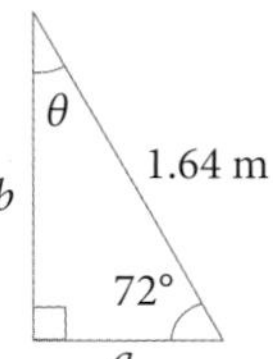

Solution

(i) Calculate the length of one of the unknown sides using a primary trig ratio. Note that either b or c can be calculated first.

$$\tan 24° = \frac{\text{O}}{\text{A}} = \frac{8.5}{b}$$

$$b = \frac{8.5}{\tan 24°} = \frac{8.5}{0.445228...}$$

$$= 19.091312... \approx 19.09 \text{ cm}$$

Then, calculate the other unknown side length using another trig ratio. Make sure to only use the information that was given in the original question.

$$\sin 24° = \frac{\text{O}}{\text{H}} = \frac{8.5}{c}$$

$$c = \frac{8.5}{\sin 24°} = \frac{8.5}{0.406736...}$$

$$= 20.898043... \approx 20.90 \text{ cm}$$

> Using the Pythagorean Theorem to calculate the length of the hypotenuse, c, could have resulted in a rounding error, or a compound calculation error had there been an error in calculating b. It is for this reason that it is important to use measurements provided in the question whenever possible.

Finally, since the acute angles in a right-triangle are complementary: $\theta = 90° - 24° = 66°$

(ii) Calculate the length of one of the unknown sides using a primary trig ratio. Note that either a or b can be calculated first.

$$\cos 72° = \frac{\text{A}}{\text{H}} = \frac{a}{1.64}$$

$$a = 1.64(\cos 72°) = 1.64(0.309016...)$$

$$= 0.506787... \approx 0.51 \text{ m}$$

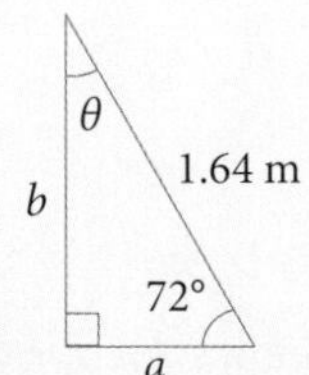

Then, calculate the other unknown side length using another trig ratio. Make sure to only use the information that was given in the original question.

$$\sin 72° = \frac{\text{O}}{\text{H}} = \frac{b}{1.64}$$

$$b = 1.64(\sin 72°) = 1.64(0.951056...)$$

$$=1.559732... \approx 1.56 \text{ m}$$

Finally, since the acute angles in a right-triangle are complementary: $\theta = 90° - 72° = 18°$

Example 10.3-h **Solving a Right-Triangle Given Two Side Lengths**

Determine the unknown side length and acute angles of the following right triangles. Round all side lengths to the nearest hundredth and all angle measures to the nearest tenth.

(i)

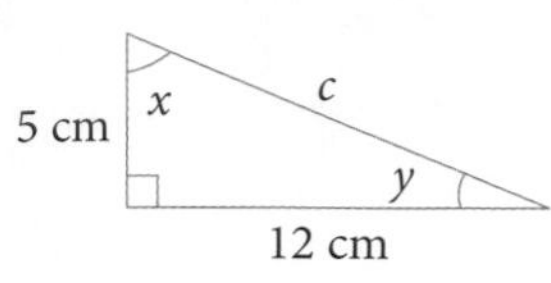

(ii)

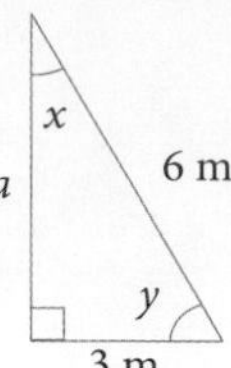

Solution

(i) Calculate the length of the hypotenuse using the Pythagorean Theorem,

$c^2 = 5^2 + 12^2 = 25 + 144 = 169$

$c = \sqrt{169} = 13$ cm

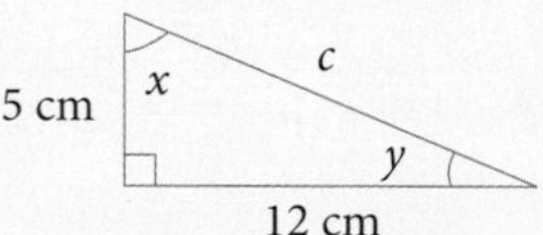

Then, solve for one of the acute angles using the inverse trig functions. Note that either x or y can be calculated first.

Notice every calculation in this example only involves those values that were given in the original question.

As the opposite and adjacent lengths are provided, we use the inverse trig function for tan (i.e., $\tan^{-1}$) to determine the angle x.

$$\tan x = \frac{12}{5}$$

$$x = \tan^{-1}\left(\frac{12}{5}\right)$$

$$= 67.380135... = 67.4°$$

Similarly, determining the angle y,

$$\tan y = \frac{5}{12}$$

$$y = \tan^{-1}\left(\frac{5}{12}\right)$$

$$= 22.619864... = 22.6°$$

(ii) Calculate the length of the unknown leg using the Pythagorean Theorem,

$a^2 = 6^2 - 3^2 = 36 - 9 = 27$

$a = \sqrt{27} = 5.196152... \approx 5.20$ m

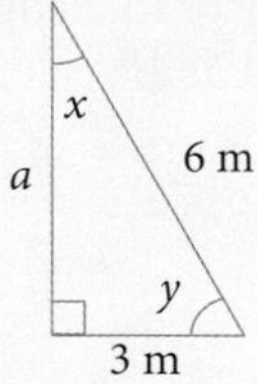

Then, solve for one of the acute angles using the inverse trig functions. Note that either x or y can be calculated first.

As the hypotenuse length and the length opposite to x are provided, we use the inverse trig function for sin (i.e., $\sin^{-1}$) to determine the angle x.

$$\sin x = \frac{3}{6}$$

$$x = \sin^{-1}\left(\frac{3}{6}\right) = \sin^{-1}\left(\frac{1}{2}\right)$$

$$= 30°$$

As the hypotenuse length and the length adjacent to y are provided, we use the inverse trig function for cos (i.e., $\cos^{-1}$) to determine the angle y.

$$\cos y = \frac{3}{6}$$

$$y = \cos^{-1}\left(\frac{3}{6}\right) = \cos^{-1}\left(\frac{1}{2}\right)$$

$$= 60°$$

Angles of Elevation and Depression

The **angle of elevation** is the angle **above** the horizontal line from the observer's eye to an object, known as the line of sight. The **angle of depression** is the angle **below** the horizontal line from the observer's eye to an object (also known as the line of sight).

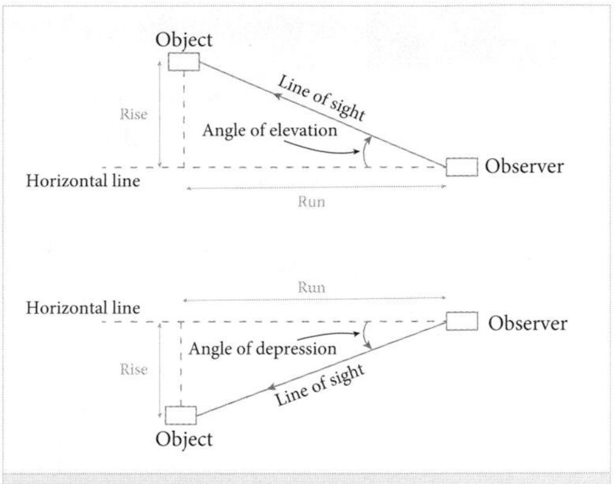

Exhibit 10.3-c Angles of Elevation and Depression

Recall the definition of slope:

$$m = \frac{Rise}{Run}$$

In problems involving angles of elevation and depression, we are usually given a **slope**. That is, in the right triangle formed by the horizontal line and the line of sight, we are given the side measure **opposite** to the angle of elevation/depression **(rise)** and the side measure **adjacent** to the angle of elevation/depression **(run)**. Therefore, **tangents** are used to solve problems involving angles of elevation and depression.

Example 10.3-i Calculating the Angle of Elevation or Depression

Determine the angle of elevation/depression of the following, rounded to the nearest tenth of a degree as required:

(i) A ramp with a rise of 1.2 m and a run of 15 m.

(ii) A road with a decline of 500 m over 8 km.

Solution

(i) The slope of the ramp is $m = \frac{Rise}{Run} = \frac{1.2}{15}$

Line of sight
1.2 m
15 m
Angle of Elevation

Therefore,

Solving for θ, the angle of elevation,

$$\tan\theta = \frac{\text{O}}{\text{A}} = \frac{1.2}{15}$$

$$\theta = \tan^{-1}\left(\frac{1.2}{15}\right)$$

$$= 4.573921... = 4.6°$$

Therefore, the angle of elevation is 4.6°.

(ii) First, convert 8 km to 8,000 m so that the units of measurement are the same.

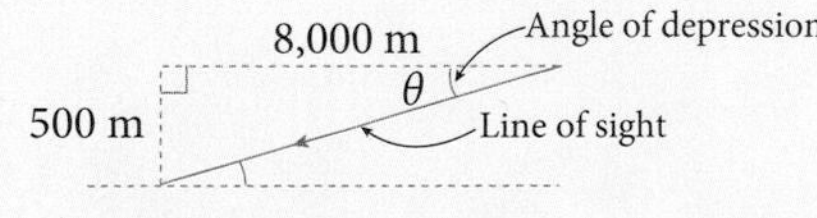

Regardless of whether you are calculating an angle of elevation or depression, use **positive** values for rise and run in your calculations.

Then, the slope of the road is $m = \frac{Rise}{Run} = \frac{500}{8{,}000}$

Therefore,

Solving for θ, the angle of depression,

$$\tan\theta = \frac{\text{O}}{\text{A}} = \frac{500}{8{,}000}$$

$$\theta = \tan^{-1}\left(\frac{500}{8{,}000}\right)$$

$$= 3.576334... = 3.6°$$

Therefore, the angle of depression is 3.6°.

Applications of the Trigonometric Ratios

Example 10.3-j

Determining the Height of the CN Tower

From a point 30 m away from the base of the CN Tower, the angle of elevation to the top of the tower is 83.5°. If the radius of the base is 33 m, determine the height of the tower, rounded to the nearest metre.

Solution

Angle of **elevation** is the angle between the horizontal line and the line from the observer's eye to the object (when the object is **above** the level of the observer).

First, draw a picture of this to better understand how to solve the question:

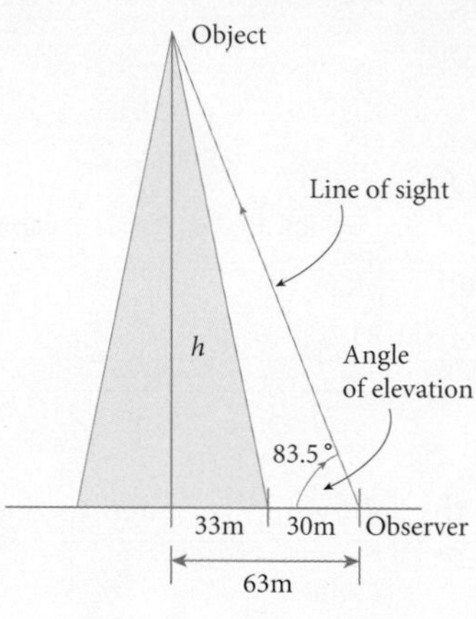

$$\tan 83.5° = \frac{O}{A} = \frac{h}{63}$$

$$h = 63(\tan 83.5°)$$
$$= 63(8.776887...)$$
$$= 552.943903...$$
$$\approx 553 \text{ m}$$

Therefore, the height of the tower is approximately 553 m.

Example 10.3-k

Determining the Distance Across a Lake

From a point 520 m above a lake in the shape of an ellipse (oval), the angle of depression to one end of the lake is 40.6° and the angle of depression to the other end of the lake is 33.5°. Determine the length of the lake, to the nearest metre.

Solution

Angle of **depression** is the angle between the horizontal line and the line from the observer's eye to the object (when the object is **below** the level of the observer).

First draw a picture of this to better understand how to solve the question:

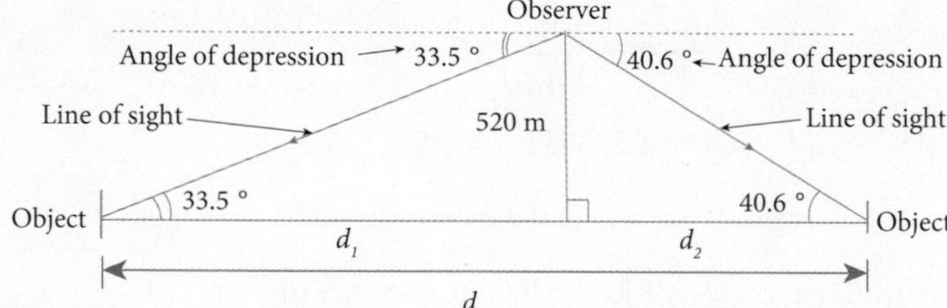

Calculating the horizontal distance from the observer to one side of the lake:

$$\tan 33.5° = \frac{O}{A} = \frac{520}{d_1}$$

$$d_1 = \frac{520}{\tan 33.5°} = \frac{520}{0.661885...} = 785.634300 \approx 785.6 \text{ m}$$

Calculating the horizontal distance from the observer to the other side of the lake:

$$\tan 40.6° = \frac{O}{A} = \frac{520}{d_2}$$

$$d_2 = \frac{520}{\tan 40.6°} = \frac{520}{0.857103...} = 606.694410... \approx 606.7 \text{ m}$$

Calculating the total length of the lake:

$$d = d_1 + d_2 = 785.6 + 606.7 \approx 1{,}392 \text{ m}$$

Therefore, the length of the lake is approximately 1,392 m.

Example 10.3-l **Calculating the Heading and Groundspeed of a Plane**

An airplane is flying at a speed of 880 km/h. The wind is blowing from due east at a speed of 132 km/h. If the airplane needs to travel due south, find the angle of its trajectory (the "heading") rounded to the nearest hundredth of a degree, and its resultant speed (the groundspeed), rounded to the nearest km/h.

Solution

If the plane were to head due south, the wind from the east would push it off course to the west. As such, the plane needs to fly into the wind (i.e., slightly east of south) in order to fly due south. First, draw a picture of this to better understand how to solve the question:

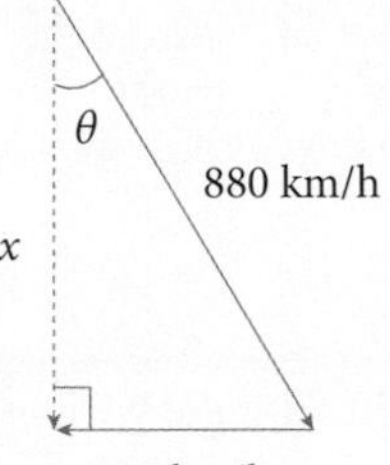

Calculating the angle of trajectory:

$$\sin\theta = \frac{O}{H} = \frac{132}{880} = 0.15$$

$$\theta = \sin^{-1}(0.15) = 8.626926... \approx 8.63°$$

Calculating the resultant speed, using the Pythagorean Theorem:

$$x^2 = 880^2 - 132^2 = 774{,}400 - 17{,}424 = 756{,}976$$

$$x = \sqrt{756{,}976} = 870.043677... \approx 870 \text{ km/h}$$

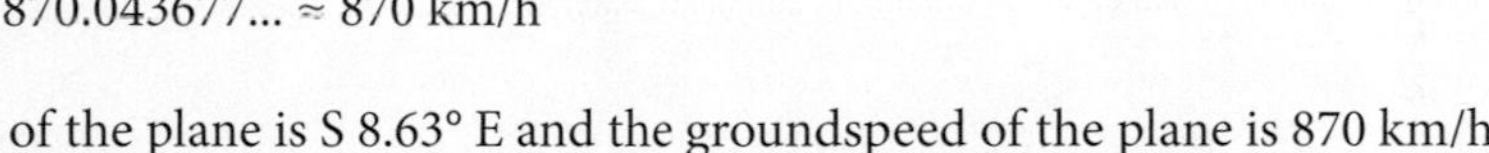

Therefore, the heading of the plane is S 8.63° E and the groundspeed of the plane is 870 km/h.

10.3 | Exercises

Answers to odd-numbered problems are available at the end of the textbook.

For Problems 1 and 2, given the values of θ, determine the three primary trigonometric ratios of θ, rounded to four decimal places.

1.

	θ	$\sin\theta$	$\cos\theta$	$\tan\theta$
a.	65°	?	?	?
b.	12.5°	?	?	?
c.	53.13°	?	?	?

2.

	θ	$\sin\theta$	$\cos\theta$	$\tan\theta$
a.	24°	?	?	?
b.	82.8°	?	?	?
c.	73.74°	?	?	?

For Problems 3 and 4, given one trigonometric ratio, determine the corresponding angle θ, rounded to the nearest degree, and the other two, primary trigonometric ratios, rounded to four decimal places.

3.

	θ	$\sin\theta$	$\cos\theta$	$\tan\theta$
a.	?	0.4540	?	?
b.	?	?	0.2924	?
c.	?	?	?	0.3639

4.

	θ	$\sin\theta$	$\cos\theta$	$\tan\theta$
a.	?	0.5591	?	?
b.	?	?	0.9743	?
c.	?	?	?	8.1443

For Problems 5 and 6, given one trigonometric ratio, determine the remaining trigonometric ratios exactly using the Pythagorean Theorem, and determine the corresponding angle, rounded to the nearest degree.

5.

	$\sin\theta$	$\cos\theta$	$\tan\theta$	θ
a.	$\frac{3}{5}$	?	?	?
b.	?	$\frac{24}{25}$	?	?
c.	?	?	$\frac{20}{21}$	?

6.

	$\sin\theta$	$\cos\theta$	$\tan\theta$	θ
a.	$\frac{5}{13}$	?	?	?
b.	?	$\frac{8}{17}$	?	?
c.	?	?	$\frac{12}{35}$	?

For Problems 7 to 12, use the special trig ratios in Exhibit 10.3-b to determine the exact values.

7. $\sin 60° \cdot \cos 45° - \sin 45° \cdot \cos 30°$

8. $\sin 60° \cdot \tan 30° - \sin 30° \cdot \tan 60°$

9. $\dfrac{\sin 45° \cdot \cos 45°}{2 \tan 45°}$

10. $\dfrac{\sin 60° - \sin 30°}{\cos 60° - \cos 30°}$

11. $\tan^2 60° - \sin^2 60° + \cos^2 60°$

12. $\sin^2 45° - \cos^2 30° + \tan^2 30°$

For Problems 13 to 18, determine the length of the unknown side, rounded to the nearest hundredth, for the given right triangles.

13. 

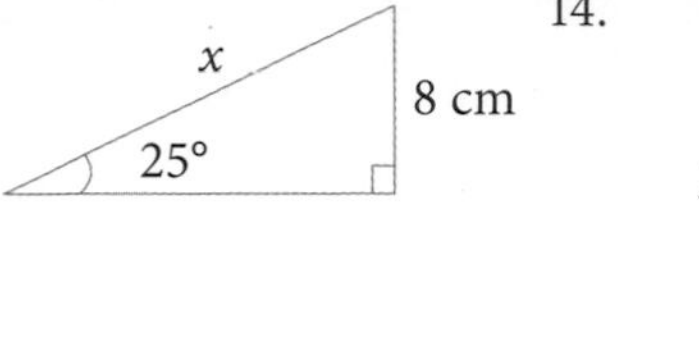

14.

15. 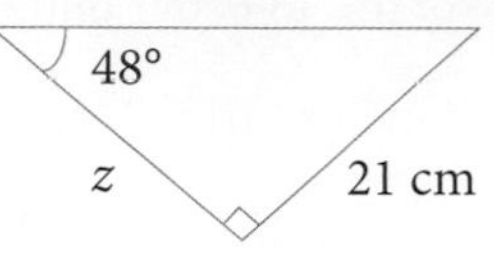

16. 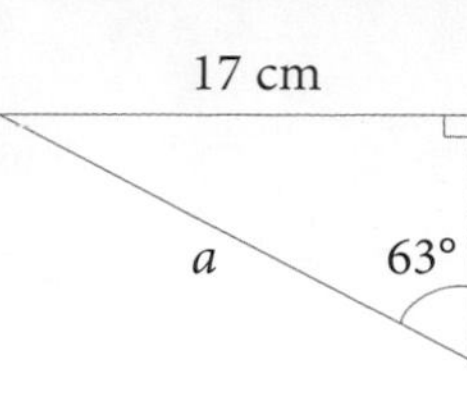

17. In a right triangle with angle $\theta = 72°$ and a hypotenuse of 27 cm, determine the length of the side adjacent to θ.

18. In a right triangle with angle $\theta = 55°$ and the side adjacent to θ equal to 4.5 cm, determine the length of the side opposite to θ.

For Problems 19 to 24 determine the value of θ, rounded to the nearest hundredth of a degree, for the given right triangles.

19. 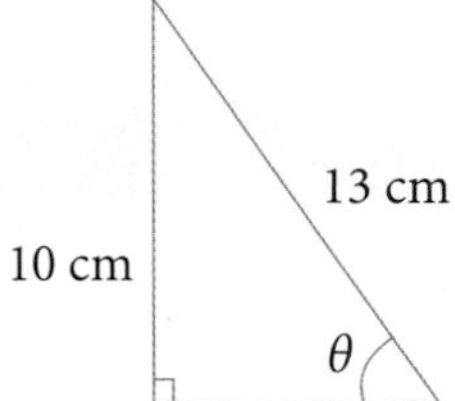

20. 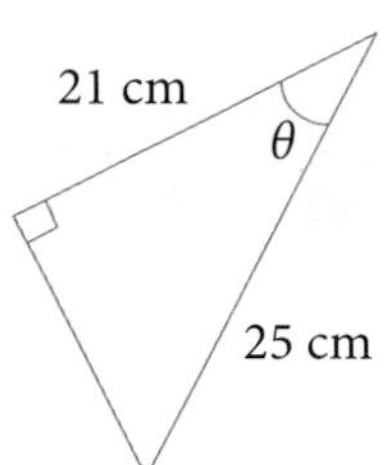

21. 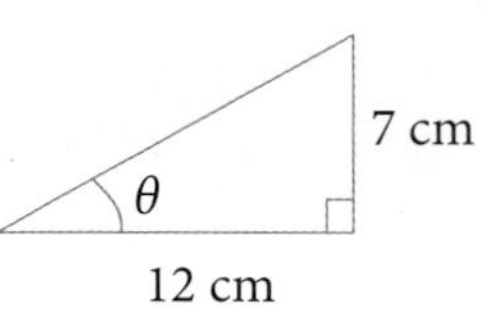

22. 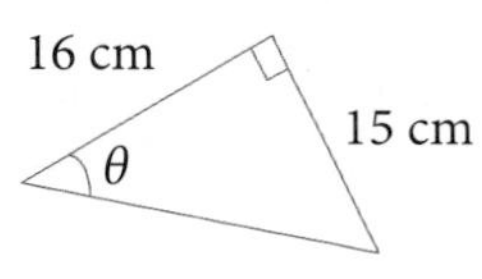

23. In a right triangle with angle θ, a hypotenuse of 30 cm, and the side adjacent to θ equal to 29 cm, determine θ.

24. In a right triangle with angle θ, a hypotenuse of 8 cm, and the side opposite to θ equal to 6 cm, determine θ.

For Problems 25 to 30, solve the given right triangles fully (i.e., identify all missing sides and angle measures).

25. 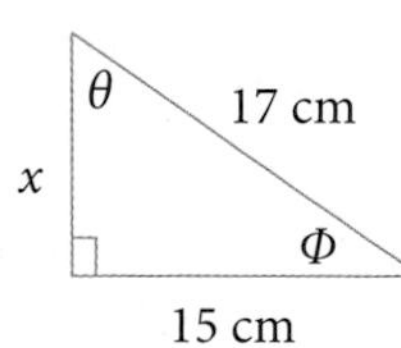

26. 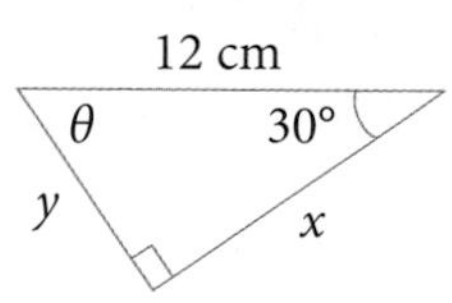

27. 28. 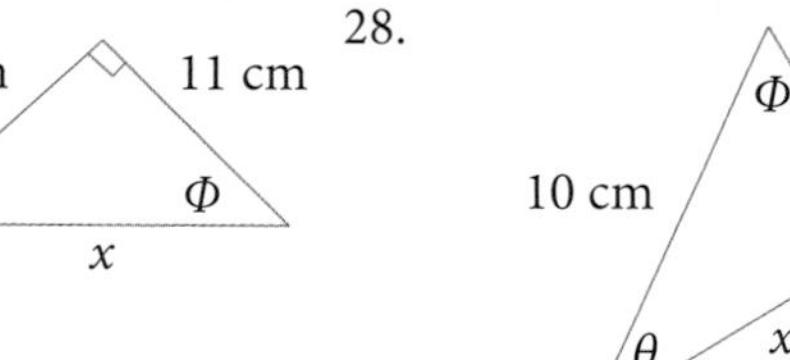

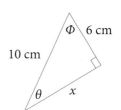

29. In a right triangle with angle $\theta = 16°$ and the side adjacent to θ equal to 14 cm, determine the missing angle measure and the two missing side lengths.

30. In a right triangle with angle $\theta = 65°$ and the side opposite to θ equal to 29 cm, determine the missing angle measure and the two missing side lengths.

For Problems 31 to 34, determine the angle of elevation/depression, rounded to the nearest degree.

31. A wheelchair ramp that rises 1 inch for every 12 inches along the ground.

32. A bicycle ramp that rises 3 feet for every 8 feet along the ground.

33. A road that descends 500 m vertically for every 6 km horizontally.

34. A ski-jump ramp that descends 7 m vertically for every 10 m horizontally.

35. The Burj Khalifa is the tallest building in the world, soaring over Dubai at a pinnacle height of approximately 830 m. From a point on the ground, an observer measures the angle of elevation to the aircraft beacon at the very top of the building to be 77.5°. He then measures the angle of elevation to the observation deck to be 67.85°. Determine the height of the observation deck, rounded to the nearest metre.

36. The distance between the CN Tower, the tallest free-standing building in Canada, and the First Canadian Place, the tallest skyscraper in Canada, is 818 m (horizontally). From the top of First Canadian Place, the angle of depression to the bottom of the CN Tower is 20.0°, and the angle of elevation to the space-deck of the CN Tower is 10.4°.

    a. Determine the height of the First Canadian Place, rounded to the nearest metre.

    b. Determine the height of the CN Tower space-deck, rounded to the nearest metre.

37. From the cockpit of a light aircraft 1,980 m above the ground, the angle of depression to the closer bank of a small lake is 52.5°, and the angle of depression to the farther bank of the same lake is 31.6°. Determine the distance across the lake, rounded to the nearest ten metres.

38. To measure the height of a hill, a surveyor records a 32.5° angle of elevation from the ground to the top of the hill. The surveyor moves 12 m closer on the flat ground and records a 43.5° angle of elevation to the top of the hill. Determine the height of the hill, rounded to the nearest tenth of a metre.

39. A goose is flying north at an air-speed of 65 km/h. There is a cross wind coming from the west, blowing at a speed of 30 km/h. Determine the goose's resulting trajectory and ground-speed.

40. A swimmer is attempting to swim across a river. She wishes to land at a point on the opposite shore, directly across from the point she is starting. She swims at a speed of 4 km/h and the current is flowing at a speed of 2.4 km/h downstream.

    a. At what angle will she need to swim upstream in order to reach her desired point on the opposite shore?

    b. If the river is 400 m wide, how long will it take her to reach the other shore?

41. Determine the area of an isosceles triangle with base length of 32 cm and an opposite angle measuring 32°. Round the answer to the nearest tenth of a cm^2.

42. A segment of a circle is the area bounded between a chord and the boundary of the circle. Determine the area of a segment bounded by a chord of length 24 cm in a circle of radius 14 cm. Round the answer to the nearest hundredth of a cm^2.

10.4 | Laws of Sine and Cosine

An **oblique triangle** does not contain a right angle (i.e., is acute or obtuse).

In the previous section, methods for solving right triangles using the primary trigonometric ratios of sine, cosine, and tangent were outlined. However, if the triangle is oblique (acute or obtuse), which does not include a right angle, the primary trigonometric ratios do not apply.

In this section, the sine and cosine ratios will be used to develop two laws, namely the **Sine Law** and the **Cosine Law**, for solving oblique triangles. One of the benefits of these laws is that they apply not only to oblique triangles, but also to right triangles.

The Sine Law

The Sine Law provides a formula that relates the sides of a triangle to the sine of its angles. It is developed as follows:

Step 1: Draw an oblique triangle ABC and name the sides opposite to angles A, B, and C as a, b, and c, respectively, as shown in the diagram.

Step 2: Draw a perpendicular line from vertex B to the opposite side, AC, to meet at D (i.e., BD $\perp$ AC).

Triangles ABD and BDC are both right triangles since BD $\perp$ AC.

Let BD = h_1

In ΔABD, $\sin A = \frac{h_1}{c} \longrightarrow h_1 = c(\sin A)$

In ΔBDC, $\sin C = \frac{h_1}{a} \longrightarrow h_1 = a(\sin C)$

Equating h_1 from both equations,

$c(\sin A) = a(\sin C)$ Dividing both sides by 'ac',

$$\frac{\sin A}{a} = \frac{\sin C}{c}$$ Equation 1

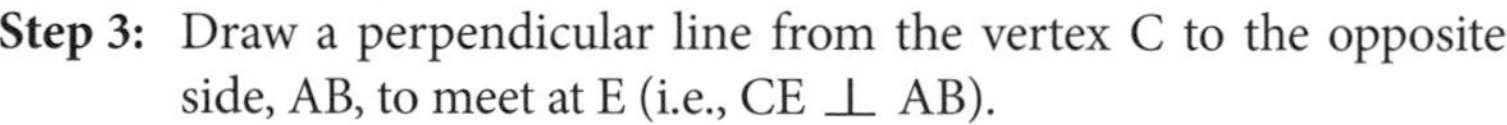

Step 3: Draw a perpendicular line from the vertex C to the opposite side, AB, to meet at E (i.e., CE $\perp$ AB).

Triangles AEC and BEC are both right triangles since CE $\perp$ AB.

Let CE = h_2

In ΔAEC, $\sin A = \frac{h_2}{b} \longrightarrow h_2 = b(\sin A)$

In ΔBEC, $\sin B = \frac{h_2}{a} \longrightarrow h_2 = a(\sin B)$

Equating h_2 from both equations,

$b(\sin A) = a(\sin B)$ Dividing both sides by 'ab',

$$\frac{\sin A}{a} = \frac{\sin B}{b}$$ Equation 2

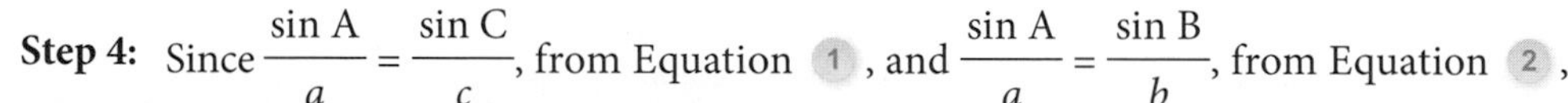

Step 4: Since $\frac{\sin A}{a} = \frac{\sin C}{c}$, from Equation 1, and $\frac{\sin A}{a} = \frac{\sin B}{b}$, from Equation 2,

we have, $\frac{\sin A}{a} = \frac{\sin B}{b} = \frac{\sin C}{c}$, which can be rearranged to, $\frac{a}{\sin A} = \frac{b}{\sin B} = \frac{c}{\sin C}$

Sine Law for Sides	Sine Law for Angles
$\frac{a}{\sin A} = \frac{b}{\sin B} = \frac{c}{\sin C}$	$\frac{\sin A}{a} = \frac{\sin B}{b} = \frac{\sin C}{c}$

Sine Law is primarily used in the following two situations:

- Two side lengths and an angle measure opposite to one of them are known (SSA).
- Two angle measures and any one side length are known (AAS or ASA).

Example 10.4-a **Calculating Side Lengths using the Sine Law, Given Two Angle Measures and a Side Length**

Given the following triangles, use the Sine Law to determine the indicated side length. Round the answers to the nearest integer.

(i) For ΔXYZ with $\angle X = 83°$, $\angle Z = 35°$, $z = 10$ cm, find x.

(ii) For ΔABC with $\angle A = 60°$, $\angle C = 54°$, $b = 16$ mm, find a.

Solution

(i) Draw and label ΔXYZ.

Two angle measures and a side length (AAS) are known.

Using the Sine Law for sides to find x,

$$\frac{x}{\sin X} = \frac{z}{\sin Z}$$ Substituting the given values,

$$\frac{x}{\sin 83°} = \frac{10}{\sin 35°}$$ Solving for x,

$$x = \frac{10 \sin 83°}{\sin 35°}$$

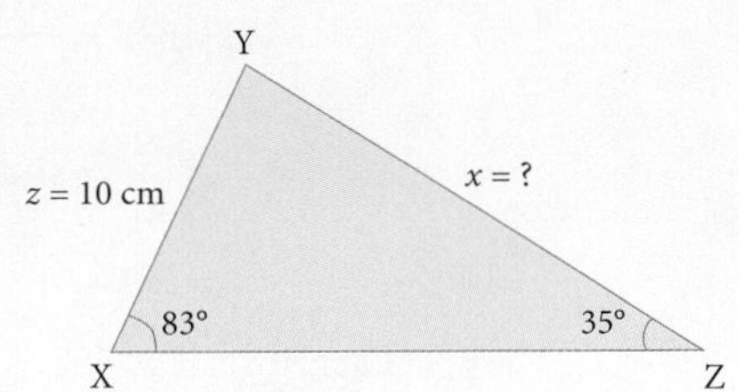

$$x = 17.304514... \approx 17 \text{ cm}$$

Therefore, $x \approx 17$ cm.

(ii) Draw and label ΔABC.

Two angle measures and a side length (ASA) are known. However, the side is not opposite to one of the known angles.

The sum of all angles in a triangle is 180° (from IAT - Part 1). Therefore, first find the third angle, $\angle B$,

$$\angle A + \angle B + \angle C = 180°$$

$$\angle B = 180° - 60° - 54°$$

$$\angle B = 66°$$

Now, using the Sine Law for sides to find a,

$$\frac{a}{\sin A} = \frac{b}{\sin B}$$ Substituting the given values,

$$\frac{a}{\sin 60°} = \frac{16}{\sin 66°}$$ Solving for a,

$$a = \frac{16 \sin 60°}{\sin 66°}$$

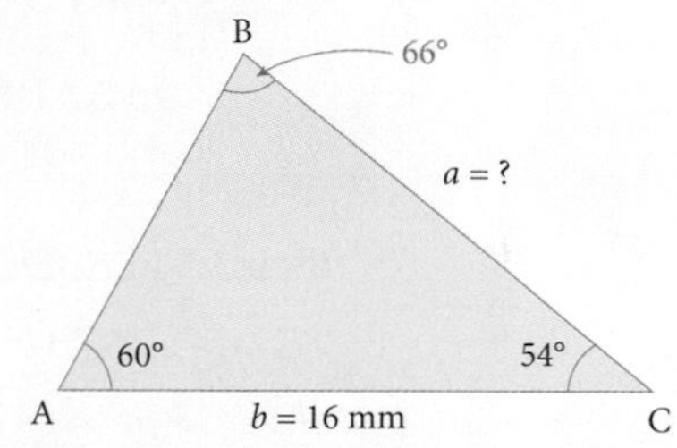

$$a = 15.167725... \approx 15 \text{ mm}$$

Therefore, $a \approx 15$ mm.

Example 10.4-b **Calculating Angle Measure using the Sine Law, Given Two Side Lengths and an Angle Measure**

Given ΔSTU with $\angle U = 95°$, $u = 22$ cm, and $t = 20$ cm, determine $\angle T$. Round the answer to the nearest degree.

Solution

Draw and label ΔSTU.

Two side lengths and the angle measure opposite to one of them (SSA) are known.

Using the Sine Law for angles to find $\angle T$,

Solution
continued

$$\frac{\sin T}{t} = \frac{\sin U}{u}$$ Substituting the given values,

$$\frac{\sin T}{20} = \frac{\sin 95°}{22}$$ Solving for T,

$$\sin T = \frac{20 \sin 95°}{22}$$

$$T = \sin^{-1}\left(\frac{20 \sin 95°}{22}\right)$$

$$T = 64.908476... \approx 65°$$

Therefore, T ≈ 65°

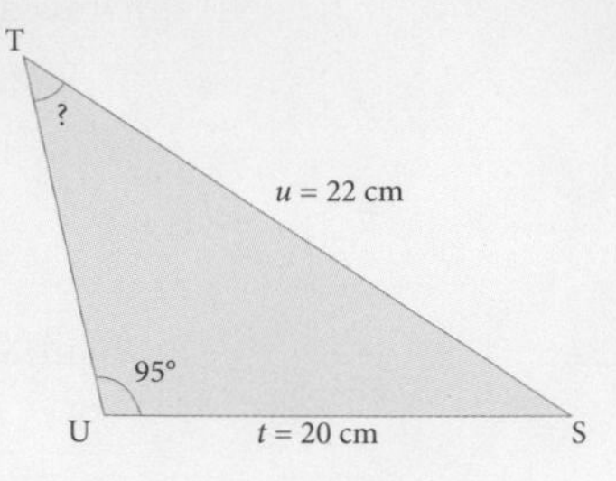

The Cosine Law

The Cosine Law provides a formula that relates the lengths of the sides of a triangle to the cosine of one of its angles. It is developed as follows:

Step 1: Draw an oblique triangle ABC and name the sides opposite to angles A, B, and C as a, b, and c, respectively, as shown in the diagram.

Step 2: Draw a perpendicular line from vertex B to the opposite side, AC, to meet at D (i.e., BD ⊥ AC).

Triangles ADB and BDC are both right triangles since BD ⊥ AC.

Let BD = h and AD = m

Since AC = b, DC = $(b - m)$

In ΔADB, $\cos A = \frac{m}{c} \rightarrow m = c(\cos A)$

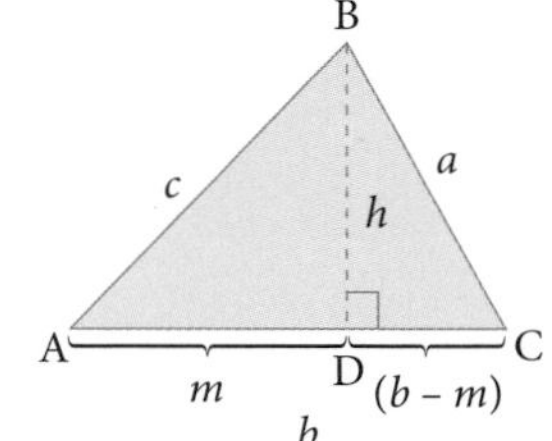

Step 3: In ΔBDC, using the Pythagorean Theorem,

$a^2 = (b - m)^2 + h^2$ Expanding,

$a^2 = b^2 - 2bm + m^2 + h^2$ Regrouping,

$a^2 = b^2 + \underbrace{m^2 + h^2} - 2bm$ Using Pythagorean Theorem, $m^2 + h^2 = c^2$, in ΔADB,

$a^2 = b^2 + c^2 - 2bm$ Substituting $m = c(\cos A)$ from Step 2,

$a^2 = b^2 + c^2 - 2bc(\cos A)$

This can be rearranged to $\cos A = \frac{b^2 + c^2 - a^2}{2bc}$

A similar procedure can be used to obtain:

$b^2 = a^2 + c^2 - 2ac(\cos B)$, and

$c^2 = a^2 + b^2 - 2ab(\cos C)$

Cosine Law for Sides	Cosine Law for Angles
$a^2 = b^2 + c^2 - 2bc(\cos A)$	$\cos A = \frac{b^2 + c^2 - a^2}{2bc}$
$b^2 = a^2 + c^2 - 2ac(\cos B)$	$\cos B = \frac{a^2 + c^2 - b^2}{2ac}$
$c^2 = a^2 + b^2 - 2ab(\cos C)$	$\cos C = \frac{a^2 + b^2 - c^2}{2ab}$

Cosine Law is primarily used in the following two situations:

- Two side lengths and the contained (included) angle measure are known (SAS).
- All three side lengths are known (SSS).

Note: If two side lengths and the contained angle measure are known, calculate the third side length using the Cosine Law, and the other two angle measures can be calculated using the Sine Law.

If three side lengths are known, calculate one of the angle measures using the Cosine Law, and the other two angle measures can be calculated using the Sine Law.

Example 10.4-c **Calculating Side Length Using the Cosine Law, Given Two Side Lengths and the Contained Angle Measure**

Given ΔQRS with $\angle S = 50°$, $q = 5.8$ m, and $r = 7.3$ m, use the Cosine Law to determine s. Round the answer to one decimal place.

Solution

Draw and label ΔQRS.

Two side lengths and the contained angle measure (SAS) are known.

Using the Cosine Law for sides to find s,

$s^2 = r^2 + q^2 - 2rq \cos S$ Substituting the given values,

$s^2 = 7.3^2 + 5.8^2 - 2(7.3)(5.8) \cos 50°$

$s^2 = 32.498745...$ Solving for s,

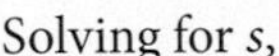

$s = \sqrt{32.498745...}$

$s = 5.700767... \approx 5.7$ m

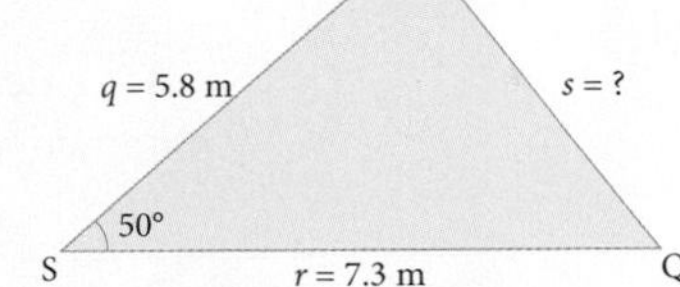

Therefore, $s \approx 5.7$ m

Example 10.4-d **Calculating Angle Measure Using the Cosine Law, Given Three Side Lengths**

Given ΔPQR with $p = 9.1$ mm, $q = 10.5$ mm, and $r = 6.0$ mm, determine $\angle R$. Round the answer to the nearest degree.

Solution

Draw and label ΔPQR.

Three side lengths (SSS) are known. Using the Cosine Law for angles to find $\angle R$,

$\cos R = \dfrac{p^2 + q^2 - r^2}{2pq}$ Substituting the given values,

$\cos R = \dfrac{9.1^2 + 10.5^2 - 6.0^2}{2(9.1)(10.5)}$

$\cos R = 0.821873...$ Solving for R,

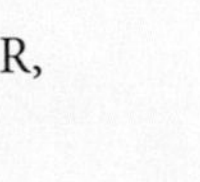

$R = \cos^{-1}(0.821873...)$

$R = 34.727233... \approx 35°$

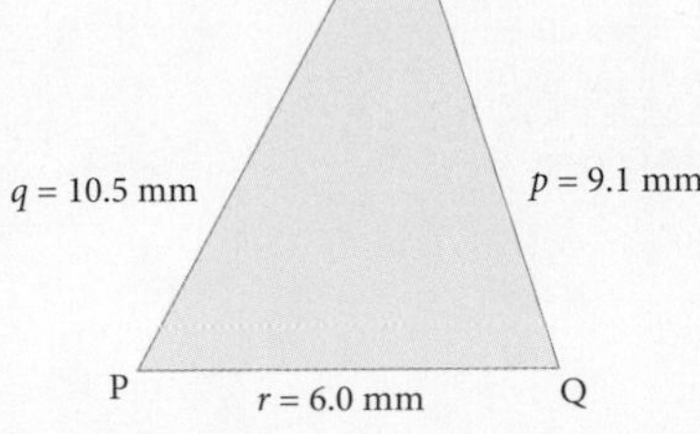

Therefore, $\angle R \approx 35°$

Solving Triangles using the Sine Law and the Cosine Law

Solving a triangle refers to finding all the measurements of unknown sides and angles of that triangle.

A triangle has six measurements, three sides and three angles. To solve a triangle, the measure of at least one side and two other measures are necessary (it is not possible to solve a triangle with three angle measures only).

As explained in the previous examples, different laws are used to solve for the measures of the unknown sides and angles of a triangle based on the given information. The following table summarizes these generalizations.

Table 10.4 **Use of Sine Law and Cosine Law in Different Situations**

Hint: use the Sine Law whenever you have a "pair" - a side and the angle opposite from it.

Given Information	Diagram	Law Required
Two angles and a side (AAS or ASA)		Sine Law
Two sides and an angle opposite to one of them (SSA)		Sine Law
Two sides and the contained angle (SAS)		Cosine Law
Three sides (SSS)		Cosine Law

Example 10.4-e **Identifying the Use of the Sine Law and the Cosine Law in Solving Triangles**

For each of the following situations, determine whether to use the Sine Law or the Cosine Law to solve the triangles. Also, explain the steps required in solving for the unknown side lengths and angle measures.

(i) ΔABC, given b, c, $\angle$C (ii) ΔABC, given $\angle$A, $\angle$B, c (iii) ΔABC, given a, b, c
(iv) ΔABC, given a, b, $\angle$C (v) ΔABC, given $\angle$B, $\angle$C, b

Solution

(i) ΔABC, given b, c, $\angle$C

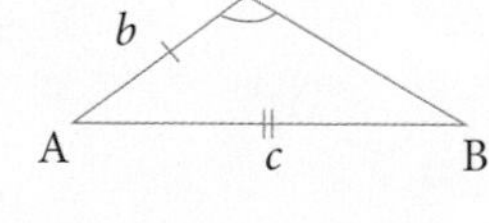

i.e., two side lengths and an angle measure opposite to one of them are known (SSA). Therefore, use the Sine Law.

In the previous section, we were able to solve right triangles using **only** the information given in the question. Unfortunately, this is not possible when performing multi-step calculations with oblique triangles. Be very careful of compound errors!

Steps to solve for the unknown measurements of the triangle:

Step 1: Solve for $\angle$B : use the Sine Law for Angles $\left(\frac{\sin B}{b} = \frac{\sin C}{c}\right)$

Step 2: Solve for $\angle$A : use IAT - Part 1 ($\angle A + \angle B + \angle C = 180°$)

Step 3: Solve for a: use the Sine Law for Sides $\left(\frac{a}{\sin A} = \frac{c}{\sin C}\right)$

(ii) ΔABC, given $\angle$A, $\angle$B, c

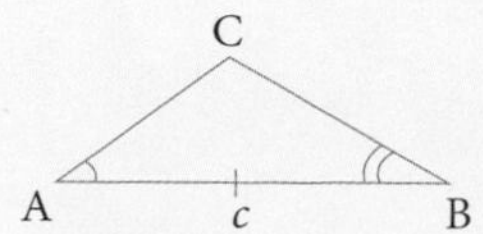

i.e., two angle measures and a side length are known (ASA).

Therefore, use the Sine Law.

Since the given side is not opposite to the known angle, we must **first** use IAT - Part 1 to find the third angle before using the Sine Law.

Steps to solve for the unknown measurements of the triangle:

Solution
continued

Step 1: Solve for $\angle C$: use IAT - Part 1 ($\angle A + \angle B + \angle C = 180°$)

Step 2: Solve for a and b: use the Sine Law for Sides
$$\left(\frac{a}{\sin A} = \frac{b}{\sin B} = \frac{c}{\sin C}\right)$$

(iii) ΔABC, given a, b, c

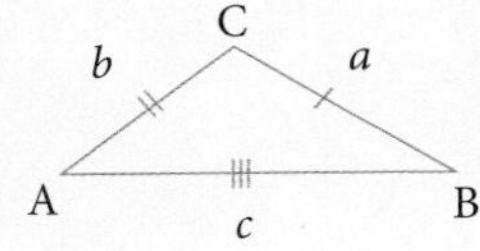

i.e., three side lengths are known (SSS).

Therefore, use the Cosine Law.

Steps to solve for the unknown measurements of the triangle:

Step 1: Solve for $\angle A$: use the Cosine Law for Angles
$$\left(\cos A = \frac{b^2 + c^2 - a^2}{2bc}\right)$$

Step 2: Solve for $\angle B$: use the Sine Law for Angles $\left(\frac{\sin A}{a} = \frac{\sin B}{b}\right)$

Step 3: Solve for $\angle C$: use IAT - Part 1 ($\angle A + \angle B + \angle C = 180°$)

(iv) ΔABC, given a, b, $\angle C$

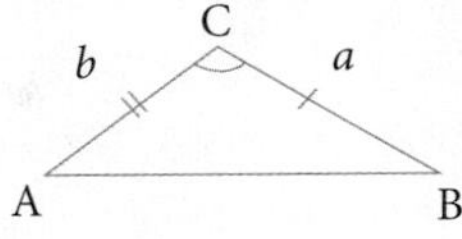

i.e., two side lengths and the contained angle measure are known (SAS).

Therefore, use the Cosine Law.

Steps to solve for the unknown measurements of the triangle:

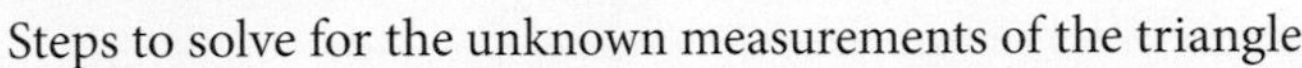

Step 1: Solve for c: use the Cosine Law for Sides
($c^2 = a^2 + b^2 - 2ab \cos C$)

Step 2: Solve for $\angle A$: use the Sine Law for Angles $\left(\frac{\sin A}{a} = \frac{\sin C}{c}\right)$

Step 3: Solve for $\angle B$: use IAT - Part 1 ($\angle A + \angle B + \angle C = 180°$)

(v) ΔABC, given $\angle B$, $\angle C$, and b

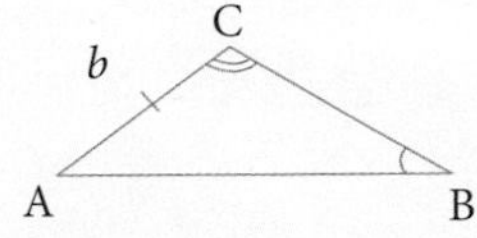

i.e., two angle measures and a side length opposite to a given angle are known (AAS). Therefore, use the Sine Law.

Steps to solve for the unknown measurements of the triangle:

Step 1: Solve for $\angle A$: use IAT - Part 1 ($\angle A + \angle B + \angle C = 180°$)

Step 2: Solve for a and c: use the Sine Law for Sides
$$\left(\frac{a}{\sin A} = \frac{b}{\sin B} = \frac{c}{\sin C}\right)$$

Identifying whether to use the Sine Law or the Cosine Law is the first step in the solution to solve the triangle. In each of the triangles listed in the above examples, there is enough information given to solve for all the unknown measures of the triangle.

These unknown measures can be determined using the Sine Law, the Cosine Law, or using IAT - Part 1 and applying the Sine and Cosine Laws repeatedly until all the unknown measures are solved.

Note: In the following examples and exercises, only acute angles will be used in calculating the solutions to angles using Sine values.

Example 10.4-f Solving a Triangle given SSA

In ΔSTU, $t = 15$ cm, $u = 12$ cm, and $\angle T = 65°$. Solve the triangle. Round angles to the nearest degree, and side lengths to one decimal place.

Solution

To solve the triangle, we need to find $\angle U$, $\angle S$, and s.

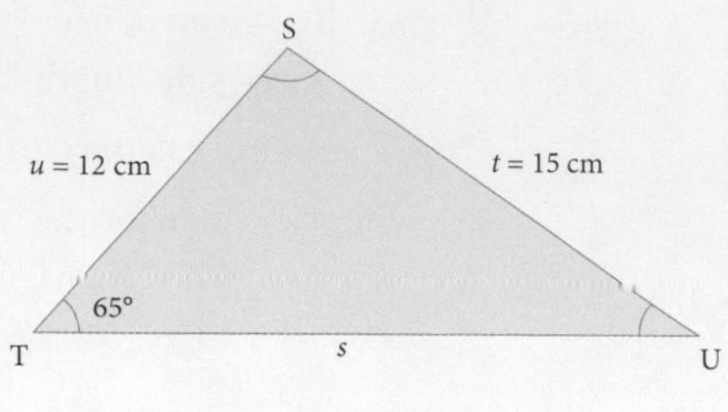

Using the Sine Law for Angles,

$$\frac{\sin T}{t} = \frac{\sin U}{u}$$ Substituting values,

$$\frac{\sin 65°}{15} = \frac{\sin U}{12}$$ Solving for U,

$$\sin U = \frac{12 \sin 65°}{15}$$

$$U = \sin^{-1}\left(\frac{12 \sin 65°}{15}\right)$$

$$U = \sin^{-1}(0.725046...)$$

$$U = 46.472693...$$

$$\angle U \approx 46°$$

Using IAT - Part 1,

$$\angle S + \angle T + \angle U = 180°$$

$$\angle S = 180° - 65° - 46°$$

$$\angle S = 69°$$

Using the Sine Law to find side s,

$$\frac{s}{\sin S} = \frac{t}{\sin T}$$

$$\frac{s}{\sin 69°} = \frac{15}{\sin 65°}$$

$$s = \frac{15 \sin 69°}{\sin 65°}$$

$$s = 15.451380... \approx 15.5 \text{ cm}$$

or

Using the Cosine Law to find side s,

$$s^2 = t^2 + u^2 - 2tu \cos S$$

$$s^2 = 15^2 + 12^2 - 2(15)(12) \cos 69°$$

$$s = \sqrt{15^2 + 12^2 - 2(15)(12) \cos 69°}$$

$$s = 15.491531... \approx 15.5 \text{ cm}$$

Example 10.4-g Solving a Triangle given SAS

In ΔXYZ, $x = 6.2$ m, $\angle Y = 50°$, and $z = 5.8$ m. Solve the triangle. Round angles to the nearest degree, and side lengths to one decimal place.

Solution

To solve the triangle, we need to find y, $\angle X$, and $\angle Z$.

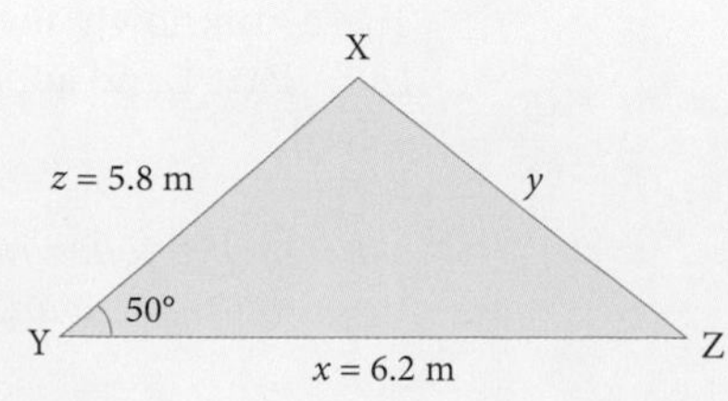

Using the Cosine Law for Sides,

$$y^2 = x^2 + z^2 - 2xz \cos Y$$

$$y^2 = (6.2)^2 + (5.8)^2 - 2(6.2)(5.8) \cos 50°$$

$$y = \sqrt{(6.2)^2 + (5.8)^2 - 2(6.2)(5.8) \cos 50°}$$

$$y = 5.084359...$$

$$y = 5.1 \text{ m}$$

Solution *continued*

Using the Cosine Law for Angles to find $\angle Z$,

$$\cos Z = \frac{x^2 + y^2 - z^2}{2xy}$$

$$\cos Z = \frac{(6.2)^2 + (5.1)^2 - (5.8)^2}{2(6.2)(5.1)}$$

$$Z = \cos^{-1}\left(\frac{(6.2)^2 + (5.1)^2 - (5.8)^2}{2(6.2)(5.1)}\right)$$

$$Z = \cos^{-1}(0.487191...)$$

$$Z = 60.843836...$$

$$\angle Z \approx 61°$$

Using IAT - Part 1 to find $\angle X$,

$$\angle X + \angle Y + \angle Z = 180°$$

$$\angle X = 180° - 50° - 61°$$

$$\angle X = 69°$$

or

Using the Sine Law for Angles to find $\angle X$,

$$\frac{\sin X}{x} = \frac{\sin Y}{y}$$

$$\frac{\sin X}{6.2} = \frac{\sin 50°}{5.1}$$

$$\sin X = \frac{6.2 \sin 50°}{5.1}$$

$$X = \sin^{-1}\left(\frac{6.2 \sin 50°}{5.1}\right)$$

$$X = \sin^{-1}(0.931269...)$$

$$X = 68.633613...$$

$$\angle X \approx 69°$$

Using IAT - Part 1 to find $\angle Z$,

$$\angle X + \angle Y + \angle Z = 180°$$

$$\angle Z = 180° - 69° - 50°$$

$$\angle Z = 61°$$

Applications of the Sine Law and the Cosine Law

Example 10.4-h **Calculating a Resultant Force**

Two forces act on an object. One force acts due north with a magnitude of 81 Newtons and the second acts N 38° E with a magnitude of 65 Newtons. Determine the magnitude and direction of the resultant force. Round the answer to two decimal places.

Solution

Draw a triangle to represent the magnitude and direction of the two forces, f_1 and f_2, and its resultant, r, as shown in the diagram.

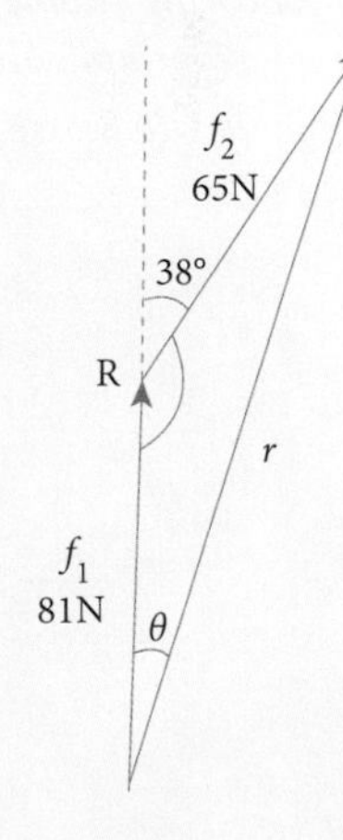

Observing the diagram, $\angle R$ is the supplement of 38°. Therefore, $\angle R = 180° - 38° = 142°$.

In the triangle, we now have known measures of two sides and the contained angle (SAS).

Therefore, use the Cosine Law for Sides in order to determine the magnitude of the resultant, r.

$$r^2 = f_1^{\,2} + f_2^{\,2} - 2f_1 f_2 \cos R$$

$$r^2 = 81^2 + 65^2 - 2(81)(65)\cos 142°$$

$$r = \sqrt{81^2 + 65^2 - 2(81)(65)\cos 142°}$$

$$r = 138.143958... = 138.14 \text{ Newtons}$$

Now, use the Sine Law for Angles to determine the direction of the resultant, θ.

$$\frac{\sin \theta}{65} = \frac{\sin 142°}{138.14}$$

$$\sin \theta = \frac{65 \sin 142°}{138.14}$$

$$\theta = \sin^{-1}\left(\frac{65 \sin 142°}{138.14}\right)$$

$$\theta = 16.839492... = 16.84°$$

Therefore, the resultant force has a magnitude of 138.14 Newtons in a direction of N 16.84° E.

Example 10.4-i **Calculating the Angle between the Hands of a Clock**

A clock has a long hand of length 5 cm and a short hand of length 3 cm. What is the distance between the tips of the hands of the clock at 4 o'clock?

Solution

In the clock face, there are 12 equal divisions in a complete turn of 360°.

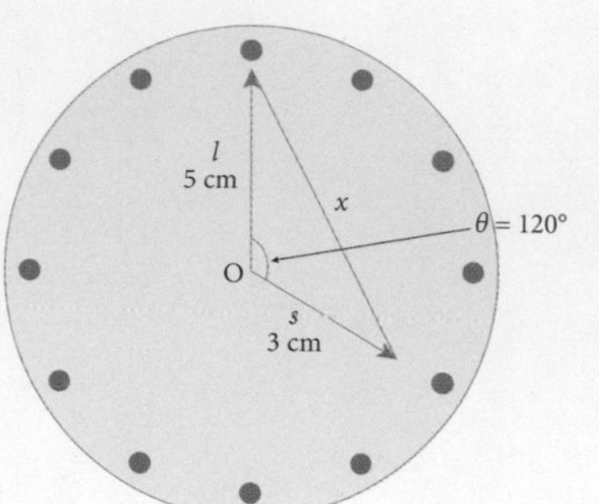

Therefore, the angle between each division at the centre is equal to $\dfrac{360°}{12} = 30°$.

At 4 o'clock, the hands are 4 divisions apart. That is, the angle between the hands of the clock at the center at 4 o'clock is $4 \times 30° = 120°$.

Using the Cosine Law for Sides to determine the length x,

$$x^2 = l^2 + s^2 - 2ls \cos \theta$$

$$x^2 = 5^2 + 3^2 - 2(5)(3) \cos 120°$$

$$x = \sqrt{5^2 + 3^2 - 2(5)(3) \cos 120°}$$

$$x = 7 \text{ cm}$$

Therefore, the length between the tips of the hands of the clock at 4 o'clock is 7 cm.

10.4 | Exercises

Answers to odd-numbered problems are available at the end of the textbook.

For the following problems, express the side lengths rounded to one decimal place and the angles rounded to the nearest degree, wherever aplicable.

For Problems 1 to 8, use the Sine Law for Sides to find the length of the indicated side in each of the triangles.

1. 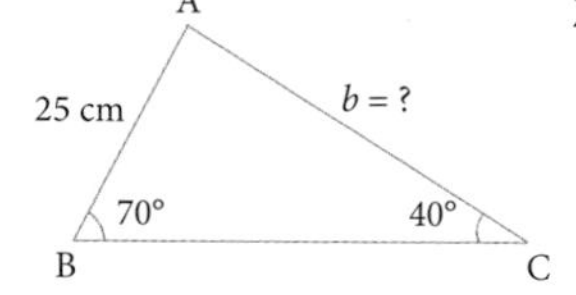

2. 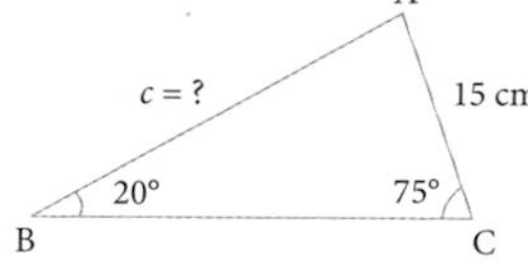

3. 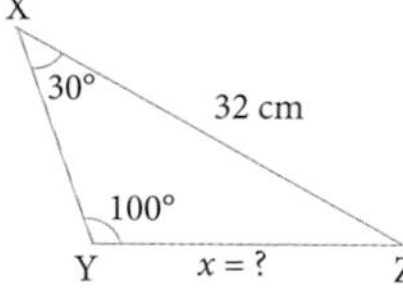

4. 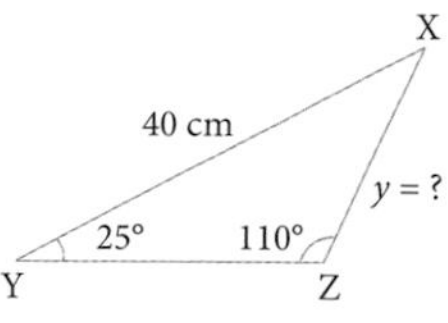

5. 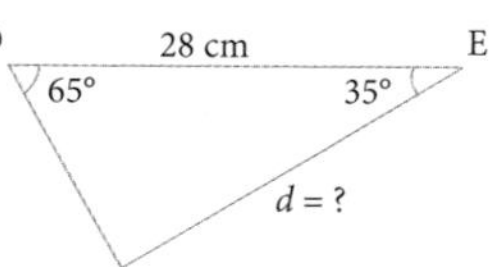

6. 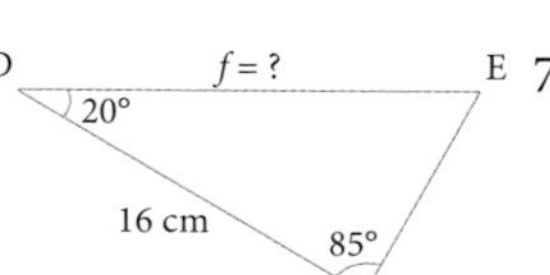

7. 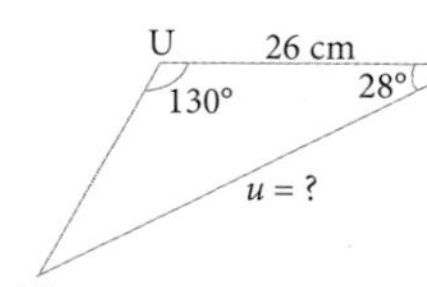

8. 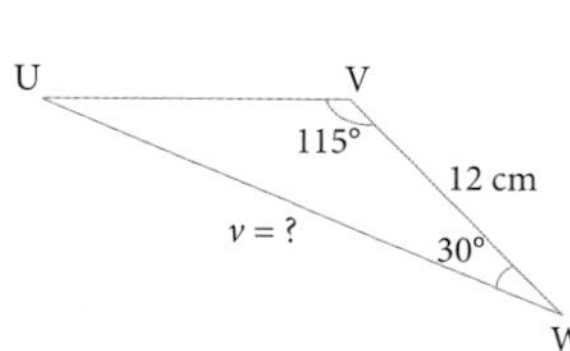

For Problems 9 to 16, use the Sine Law for Angles to find the measure of the indicated angle in each of the triangles.

9. 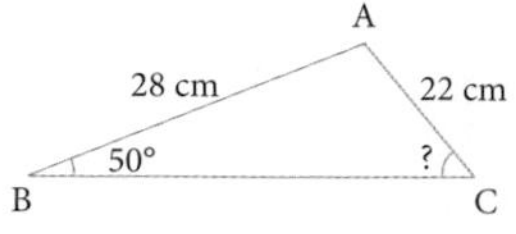

10. 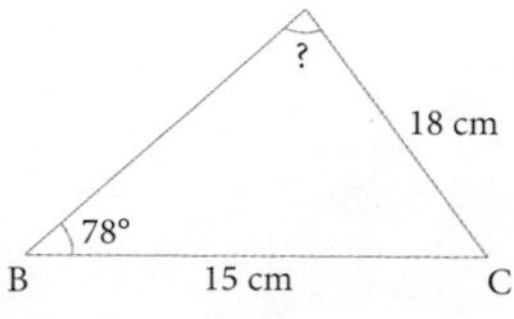

11. 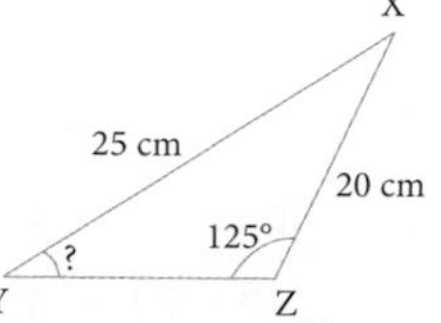

12. 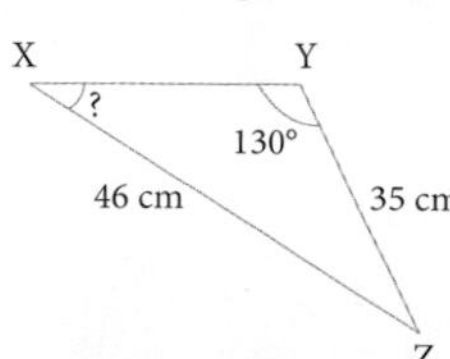

13. 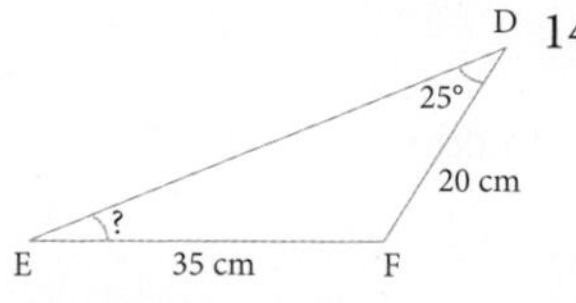

14. 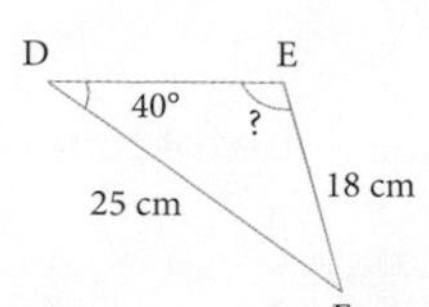

15. 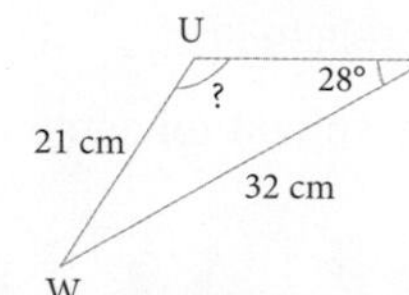

16. 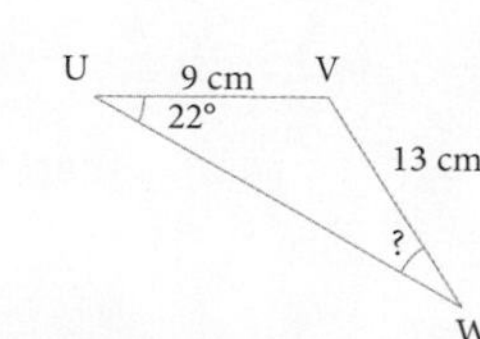

For Problems 17 to 24, use the Cosine Law for Sides to find the length of the indicated side in each of the triangles.

17. 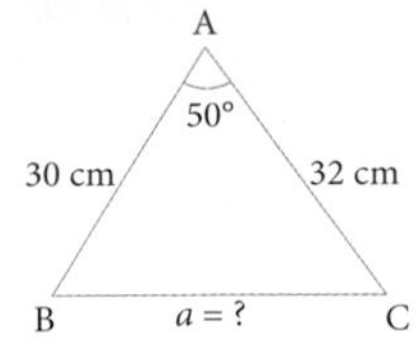

18. 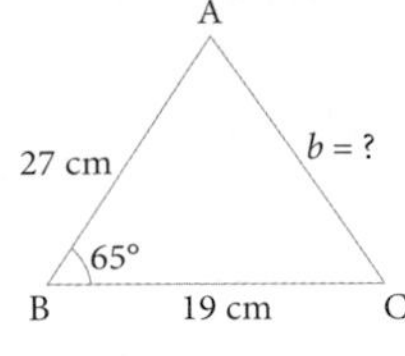

19. 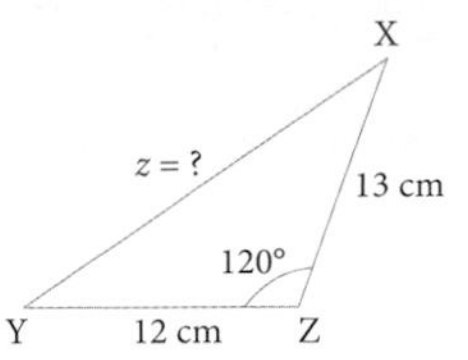

20. 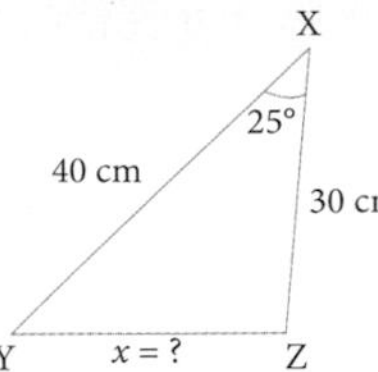

21. 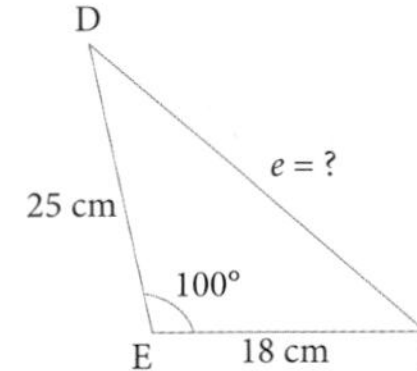

22. 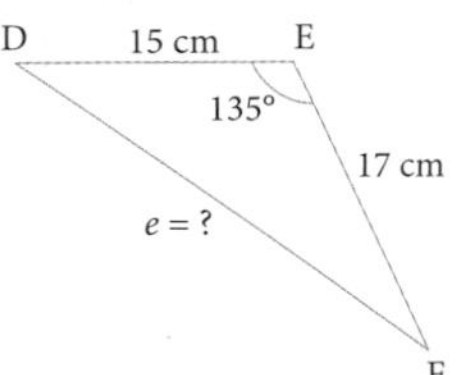

23. 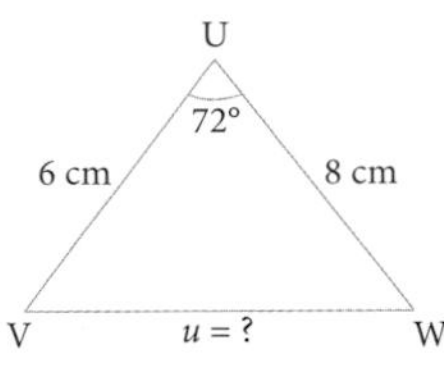

24. 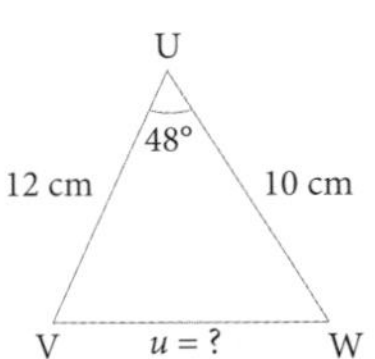

For Problems 25 to 32, use the Cosine Law for Angles to find the measure of the indicated angle in each of the triangles.

25. 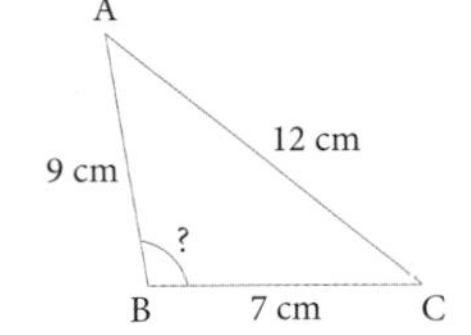

26. 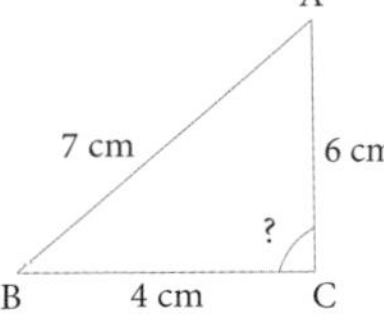

27. 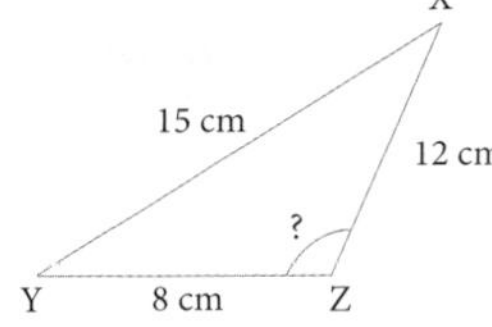

28. 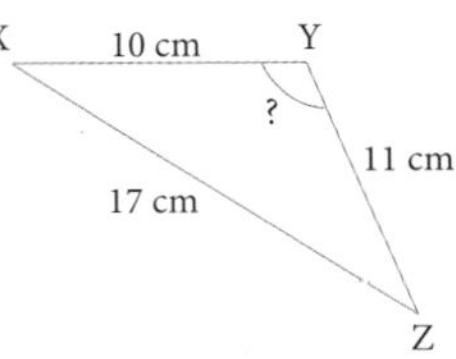

29. 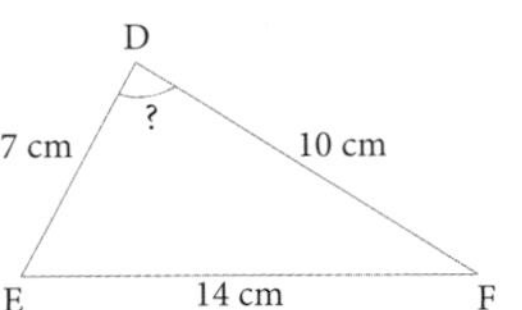

30. 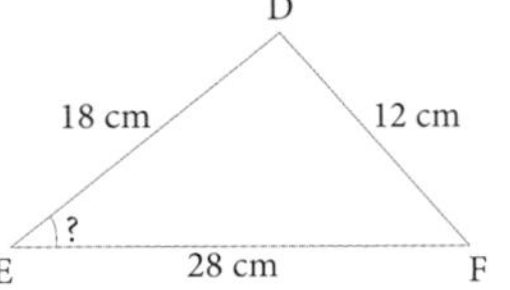

31. 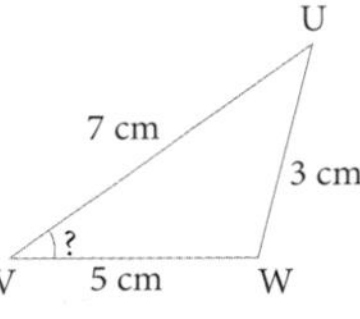

32. 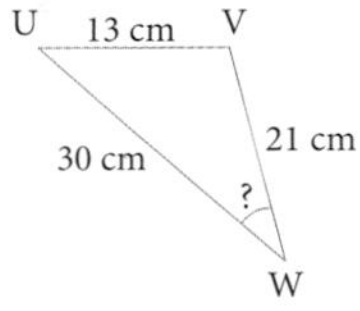

For Problems 33 to 42, state which formula, the Sine Law or the Cosine Law, would be required to begin to solve each of the triangles ABC.

33. Given $\angle A$, $\angle B$, and c

34. Given $\angle B$, $\angle C$, and b

35. Given $\angle A$, a, and b

36. Given $\angle C$, a, and b

37. Given b, $\angle A$, and c

38. Given $\angle B$, a, and b

39. Given a, b, and c

40. Given $\angle B$, $\angle C$, and a

41. Given $\angle B$, $\angle C$, and c

42. Given $\angle B$, a, and c

For Problems 43 to 54, solve the triangles fully (i.e., find all missing side lengths and angle measures). Round angles to the nearest degree and round sides to 2 decimal places.

	Angles (degrees)			Length (cm)		
	∠A	∠B	∠C	*a*	*b*	*c*
43.	35	120			12	
44.	22		81			50
45.			36	15	11.5	
46.		20		5		8
47.				13	9	6
48.	19	102				10

	Angles (degrees)			Length (cm)		
	∠A	∠B	∠C	*a*	*b*	*c*
49.		65	75			10
50.		115	45		18	
51.		85			35	25
52.			125	5	7.5	
53.				10	15	22.5
54.	25		60		16	

55. Lucy is leaving her house to run some errands. She needs to go to the grocery store and to the pet store. She knows that the grocery store is 5.6 km away and is situated N 18° E of her house, while the pet store is 3.4 km away at N 10° W of her home. What is the distance between the two stores?

56. Tabitha is sitting at one end of a soccer stadium, up in the top row of seats. She knows that the field is 110 m long, and from her seat, the angles of depression to the near and far ends of the field are 55° and 3°, respectively. How far is she from each end of the field?

57. A ship is traveling north at a speed of 10 knots in water with a current moving at 2 knots. The current flows S 60° E. What is the resultant speed and bearing of the ship?

58. Two unequal forces act on an object with an angle of 135° between them, and the resultant force has a magnitude of 62.1 Newtons. If one of the original forces had a magnitude of 55.8 Newtons, what was the magnitude of the other force?

59. From the base of a pyramid, the angle of elevation to the top of the pyramid is 47°. At a point 100 metres from the base, the angle of elevation to the top is 22°. Calculate the slant height of the pyramid.

60. From the base of a hill, the angle of elevation to the top of the hill is 65°. At a point 350 metres from the base, the angle of elevation to the top is 45°. Calculate the slant height of the hill.

10 | Review Exercises

Answers to odd-numbered problems are available at the end of the textbook.

For Problems 1 and 2, identify the two similar triangles and state the rule used to determine similarity.

1. a.

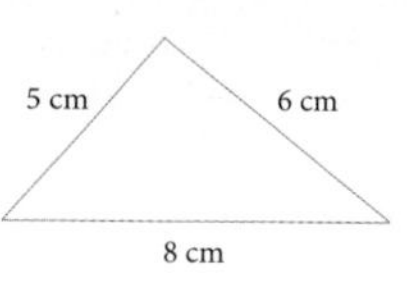

b.

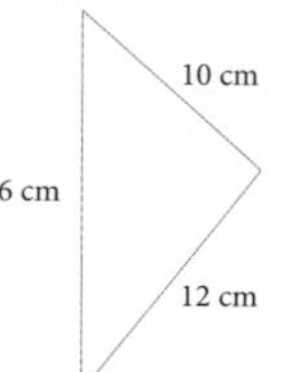

c.

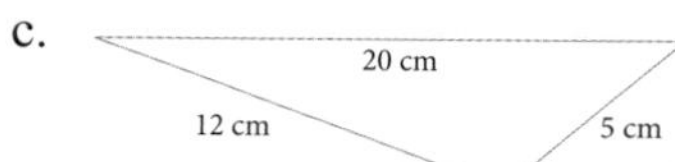

2. a.

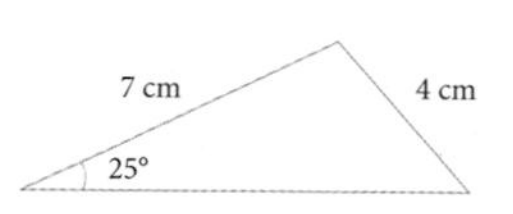

b.

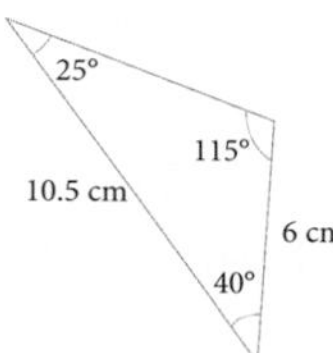

c.

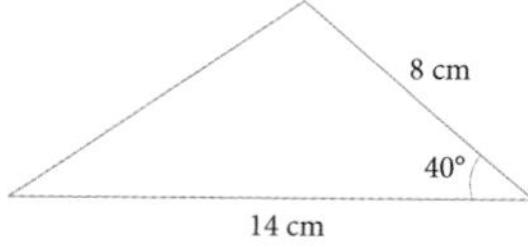

For Problems 3 and 4, identify the two congruent triangles and state the rule used to determine congruency.

3. a.

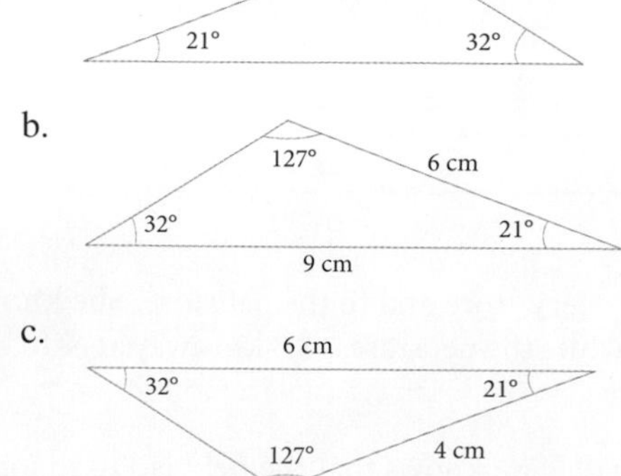

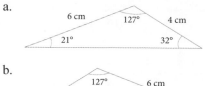

4. a.

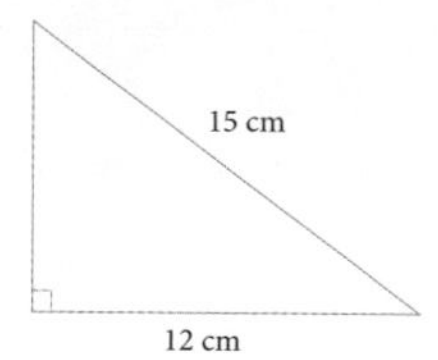

b.

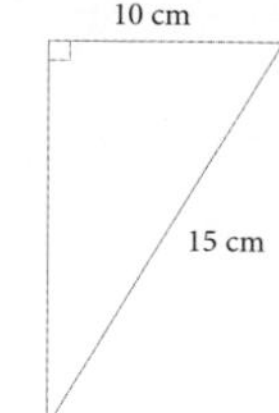

c.

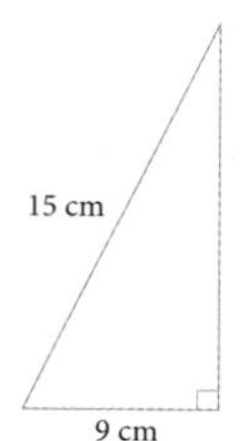

For Problems 5 and 6, determine the unknown side lengths of the given pairs of similar triangles.

5. a.

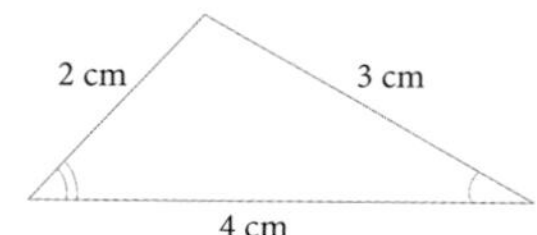

b.

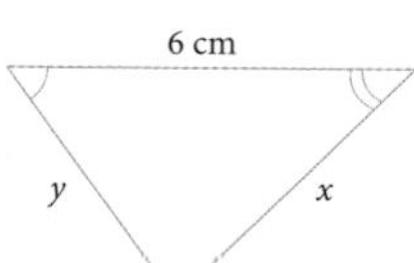

6. a.

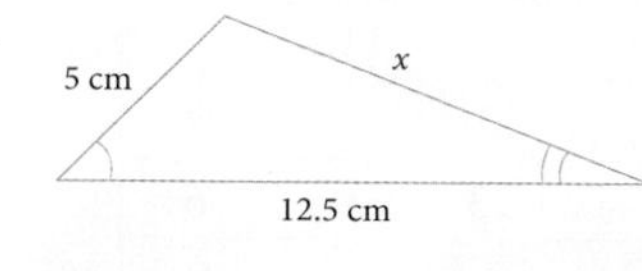

b.

y

8 cm

14 cm

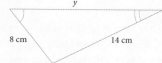

For Problems 7 and 8, calculate the unknown side length(s) and angle(s) in the given figures.

7. a.

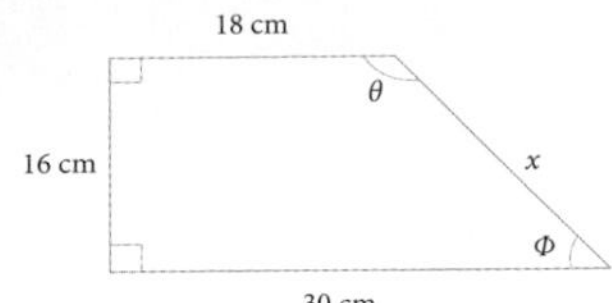

b.

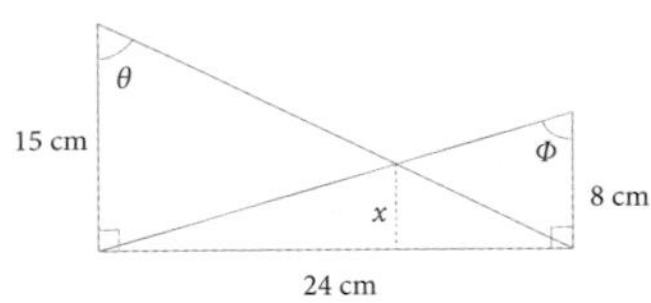

8. a.

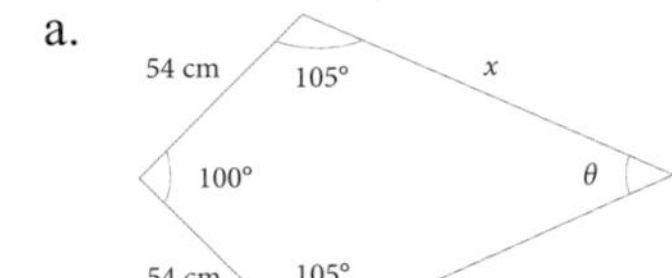

b.

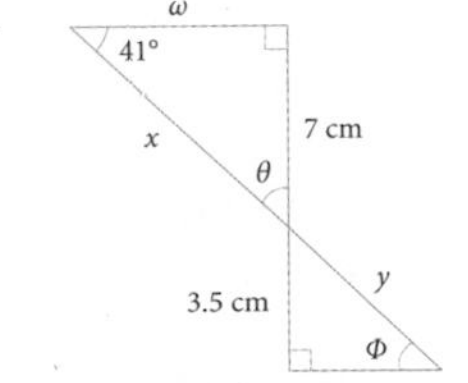

For Problems 9 and 10, calculate the distance between the given Cartesian points.

9. a. A(5, –1) and B(–2, 6) b. C(3, –2) and D(0, –4)

10. a. M(–6, 8) and N(3, –4) b. P(1, –3) and Q(4, 0)

11. Use the Pythagorean Theorem to calculate the perimeter and area of a right trapezoid, with parallel sides that are 64 cm and 40 cm long, and a perpendicular height of 18 cm.

12. Use the Pythagorean Theorem to calculate the perimeter and area of an isosceles trapezoid, with parallel sides that are 6.5 m and 4.2 m long, and slant heights that are both 2.3 m long.

For Problems 13 and 14, determine the exact value of the given trigonometric expressions. Express the answers in simplified radical form.

13. a. $\sin 45° \cos 30° - \cos 45° \sin 30°$

b. $\dfrac{\sin^2 30° + \cos^2 30°}{\tan 30°}$

14. a. $\sin 30° \sin 60° + \cos 30° \cos 60° + \tan 30° \tan 60°$

b. $\dfrac{\sin^2 60° + \cos^2 30°}{\sin 60°}$

15. Calculate the degree measures of all angles in a kite, if the two equal angles are each 10° greater than twice the smaller remaining angle, and 10° less than twice the larger, remaining angle.

16. Calculate the degree measures of all five angles in a pentagon with four equal angles and the fifth angle twice the measure of the other four.

17. A radio mast is supported by a guy wire that runs from the top of the tower to a point on the ground 55 m away from the base of the mast.

a. If the angle that the guy wire makes with the ground is 63°, determine the height of the radio mast, rounded to the nearest metre.

b. For additional support, a second guy wire is attached from the same point on the ground to the mast, two-thirds of the way to the top. Determine the length needed for the additional guy wire and the angle it will make with the ground.

18. Standing on his balcony on the 17th floor, a man observes that the angle of elevation to the top of the building next to him is 35° and the angle of depression to the bottom of the same building is 45°. He then measures the ground distance between the buildings to be 60 m.

a. Determine the height of his balcony, in metres.

b. Determine the height of the building next to him, rounded to the nearest metre.

19. On a hike, Cory and Nell walk 1.2 km west, then walk 500 m N 20° W. How far are they from their original starting position, and at what bearing? Round your answers to the nearest integer.

20. The train routes between three cities form a triangle. The distance between City A and City B is 52 km, between City A and City C is 118 km, and between City B and City C is 74 km. Find the angle between the routes at City B, rounded to the nearest integer.

For Problems 21 to 30, solve the triangles fully (i.e., identify all missing side lengths and angle measures). Round angles to the nearest degree and side lengths to two decimal places.

	Angles (degrees)			Length (cm)		
	∠A	∠B	∠C	*a*	*b*	*c*
21.		30		13.04		3.03
22.		32		43.23		53.29
23.		12	78		10.80	
24.		21	145		21.64	
25.	47			53.54	31.61	
26.	25			33.33	32.86	
27.	140				23	18
28.	50				30	28
29.				15	17	30
30.				12	18	28

Self-Test | Chapter 10

Answers to all problems are available at the end of the textbook.

For Problems 1 and 2, determine the unknown side lengths in the figures given.

1. a.

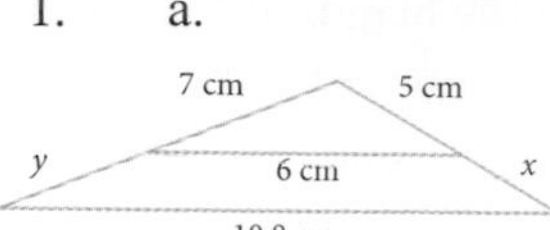

b.

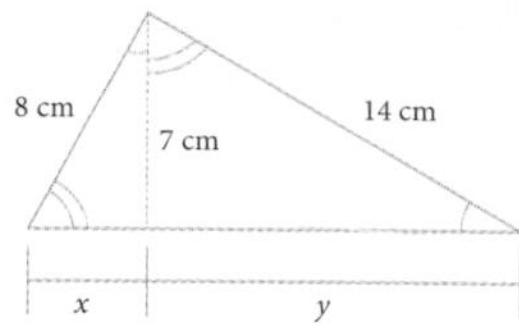

2. a.

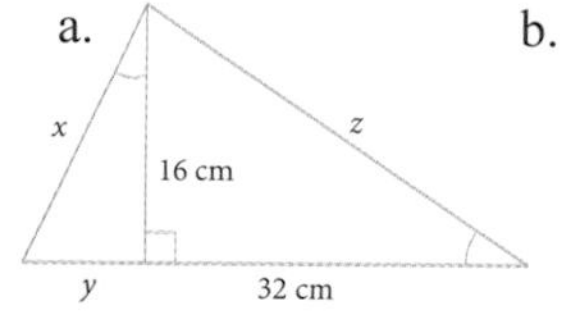

b.

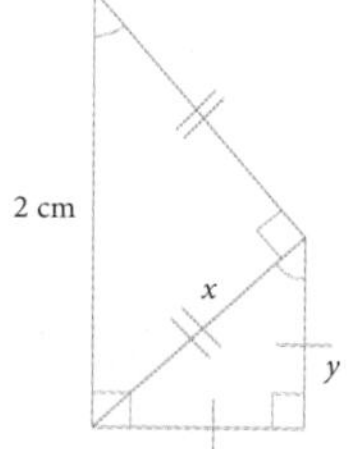

3. At 2:00 PM, a cliff with a vertical face casts a shadow 15 m long out onto the water. If, at the same time, a 72 cm buoy on the water casts a 45 cm shadow, how tall is the cliff?

4. Use the Pythagorean Theorem to determine the perimeter and area of the following figures:

   a. A right trapezoid, with parallel sides that are 5.3 m and 9.7 m long, and a perpendicular height of 2.4m.

   b. An isosceles triangle with a base length of 32 cm and slant heights that are each 34 cm.

5. Use the Pythagorean Theorem to determine the surface area and volume of the following 3-dimensional objects:

   a. An ice-cream cone with a diameter of 4.4 cm and a height of 11.8 cm.

   b. A conical candy container with a radius of 15 cm and a height of 25 cm.

6. Find the distance between the following Cartesian points:

   a. U(−4, −7) and V(4, 8)

   b. W(7, −3) and X(−1, 5)

   c. Y(0, −2.5) and Z(6, 0)

7. A house painter is using a 10 m ladder to paint the exterior wall of a house.

   a. How far back from the wall should the ladder be placed in order for it to reach a height of 8.5 m?

   b. If the maximum safe slope of the ladder is 4 : 1, what is the maximum safe height that the ladder can reach?

For Problems 8 and 9, solve the triangles completely.

8. a.

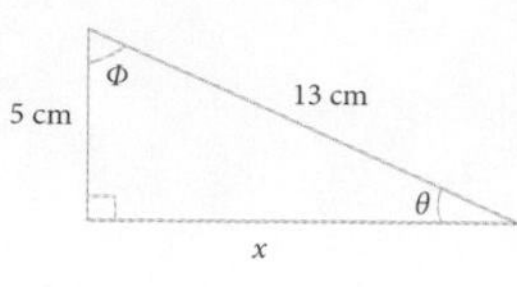

b.

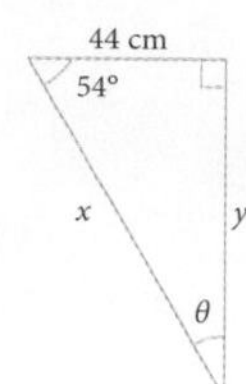

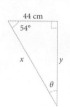

9. a.

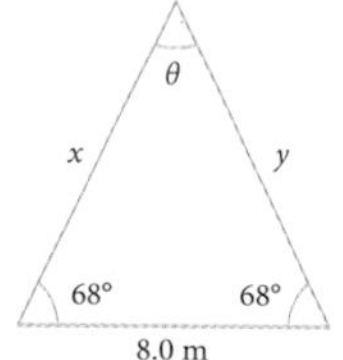

b.

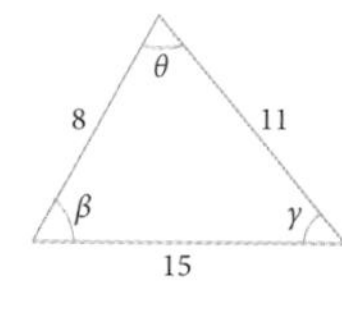

10. A mountain road has a 5° angle of depression for 7 km. How far down the mountain does the road descend? *(Hint: the distance given represents the road length, not the horizontal distance travelled.)*

11. Using only the Cosine Law, solve ΔXYZ, with $x = 12.3$ mm, $y = 8.7$ mm, and $\angle Z = 38°$. Round side lengths to one decimal place and angles to the nearest whole number.

12. Using only the Sine Law, solve ΔPQR with $\angle P = 50°$, $\angle Q = 30°$, and $q = 12$ cm. Round side lengths to one decimal place and angles to the nearest whole number.

13. Determine the following unknown values:

a.

48 cm
36 cm
x

b.

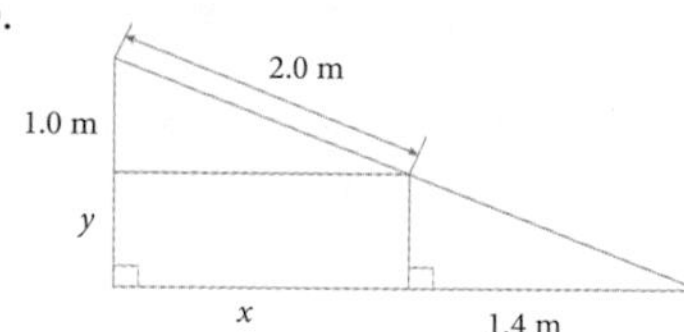

14. A family resort on a lake in Muskoka ropes off a small inlet of water at the beach to create a swimming area for children. Based on the diagram below, calculate the length of buoy rope needed for the swimming area.

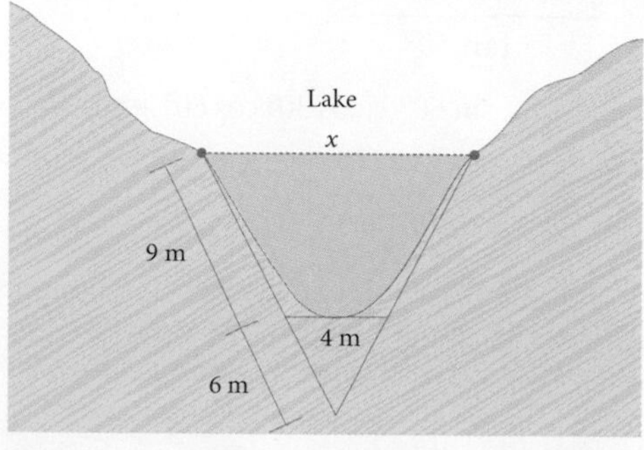

10 | Summary of Notation and Formulas

Pythagorean Theorem:

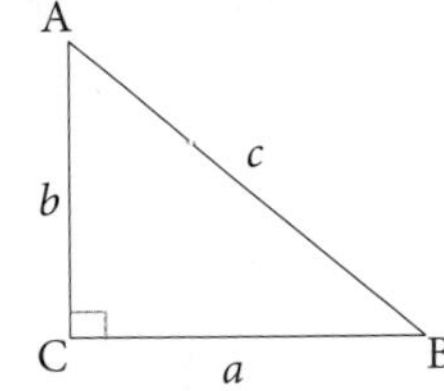

$c^2 = a^2 + b^2$

$c = \sqrt{a^2 + b^2}$

$a = \sqrt{c^2 - b^2}$

$b = \sqrt{c^2 - a^2}$

Distance (d) between two points P(x_1, y_1) and Q(x_2, y_2):

$$d = \sqrt{(x_2 - x_1)^2 + (y_2 - y_1)^2}$$

Primary Trigonometric Ratios:

$$\sin\theta = \frac{\text{Opposite}}{\text{Hypotenuse}} = \frac{\text{O}}{\text{H}}$$

$$\cos\theta = \frac{\text{Adjacent}}{\text{Hypotenuse}} = \frac{\text{A}}{\text{H}}$$

$$\tan\theta = \frac{\text{Opposite}}{\text{Adjacent}} = \frac{\text{O}}{\text{A}}$$

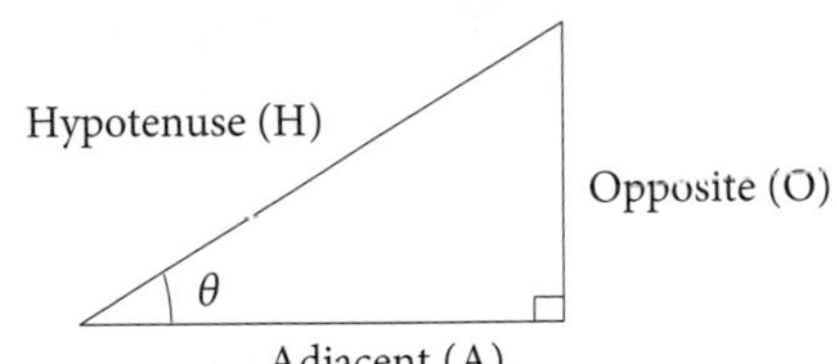

Exact Trigonometric Ratios of 30°, 45°, 60°:

$\sin 30° = \cos 60° = \frac{1}{2}$

$\sin 45° = \cos 45° = \frac{1}{\sqrt{2}}$

$\sin 60° = \cos 30° = \frac{\sqrt{3}}{2}$

$\tan 30° = \frac{1}{\sqrt{3}}$

$\tan 45° = 1$

$\tan 60° = \sqrt{3}$

Sine Laws:

Sine Law for Sides: $\frac{a}{\sin A} = \frac{b}{\sin B} = \frac{c}{\sin C}$

Sine Law for Angles: $\frac{\sin A}{a} = \frac{\sin B}{b} = \frac{\sin C}{c}$

Cosine Laws:

Cosine Law for Sides:

$a^2 = b^2 + c^2 - 2bc\,(\cos A)$

$b^2 = a^2 + c^2 - 2ac\,(\cos B)$

$c^2 = a^2 + b^2 - 2ab\,(\cos C)$

Cosine Law for Angles:

$\cos A = \frac{b^2 + c^2 - a^2}{2bc}$

$\cos B = \frac{a^2 + c^2 - b^2}{2ac}$

$\cos C = \frac{a^2 + b^2 - c^2}{2ab}$

Chapter 11 BASIC STATISTICS

LEARNING OBJECTIVES

- Understand terminology used in statistics and distinguish between types of data and levels of measurement.
- Organize data using stem-and-leaf plots, tally charts, scatter plots, and line graphs.
- Summarize data using pie charts, bar charts, and histograms.
- Construct frequency polygons, frequency distributions, and cumulative frequency distributions.
- Perform calculations involving mean (average), weighted mean, and geometric mean.
- Calculate and interpret measures of central tendency using mean, median, and mode.
- Determine range, quartiles, inter-quartile range, and construct box-and-whisker plots.
- Calculate and interpret measures of dispersion using mean deviation, variance, and standard deviation.

CHAPTER OUTLINE

Introduction

Statistics is a branch of mathematics and procedures that involves collecting, organizing, presenting, analyzing, and interpreting data for the purpose of drawing conclusions and making a decision.

The applications of statistics can be seen all around us in day-to-day life; for example, statistical information is presented to us daily in newspapers, magazines, and on radio, television, etc. Furthermore, statistics is used in nearly every industry, including business, finance, economics, science, engineering, politics, health, and more. A basic knowledge of statistics is essential in order to understand, interpret, and make decisions based on information provided or collected.

Statistics is divided into two categories: descriptive and inferential.

Descriptive statistics deals with organizing, presenting, and summarizing raw data to present meaningful information. **Inferential statistics** deals with the analysis of data to develop meaningful inferences and conclusions.

In this chapter, we will focus on descriptive statistics, and learn techniques to organize and present data using graphs, charts, tables, etc. We will also learn measures of central tendency and dispersion to describe and summarize data in a meaningful way.

11.1 | Organizing and Presenting Data

Populations and Samples

Population refers to all possible individuals, objects, or measurements of items of interest. This is usually of large or infinite quantity. For example, the ages of all college students.

Sample refers to a set of data drawn from the population. It is a subset of a population, meaning a portion or part of the population. For example, the ages of a representative sample of 200 college students.

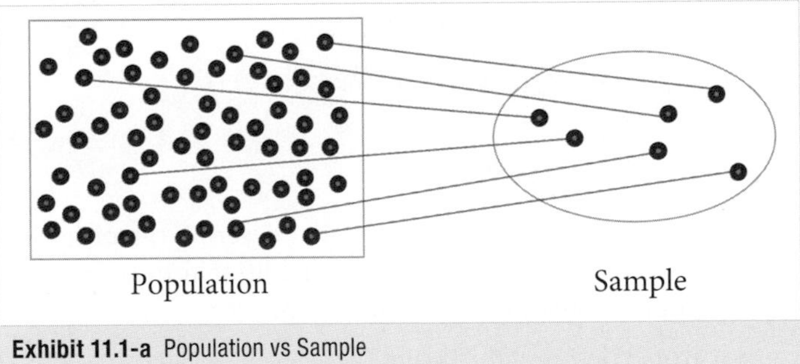

Exhibit 11.1-a Population vs Sample

The descriptive values for a population are called **parameters** and that for a sample are called **statistics**. Parameters are usually represented by Greek letters (e.g., population mean: μ, population standard deviation: σ) and statistics are usually represented by lowercase English letters (e.g., sample mean: $\overline{x}$, sample standard deviation: s).

Note: We will learn more about the descriptive values mean and standard deviation in the following two sections.

Normally, we will not have access to the whole population we are interested in investigating; therefore, population parameters are often estimated from the sample statistics. Sample statistics are calculated from the actual data observed or measured from the sample.

For example, assume that there are 40 students in a particular math class at a college. If 80% of the students passed an exam, this 80% is referred to as a "parameter", because it includes the marks of all 40 students. However, if this class is selected as the representative math class of all the math classes in the college, then the 80% is referred to as a "statistic", because it represents a sample of the population.

Types of Variables and Levels of Measurement

Types of Variables

A collection of facts and information obtained in a study is known as the data. The variables within a dataset may be numerical, called quantitative variables, or non-numerical, called qualitative variables.

Quantitative variables are data that are expressed using numbers and are known as numeric data. These data are further classified as continuous variables or discrete variables.

- **Continuous variables** are obtained by *measuring*. Measurements of length, weight, time, temperature, etc., are examples of continuous variables. These can be measured in whole units, approximated or rounded whole units, fractions, or decimal numbers (with any number of decimal places).
- **Discrete variables** are obtained by *counting*, or are data that can only take on specific values. The number of students in a class, number of chapters in a book, position in a race, etc., are examples of discrete variables.

Qualitative variables are data that cannot be obtained by measuring or counting, and are known as categorical data. Make and model of cars, colour, gender, etc., are examples of qualitative variables.

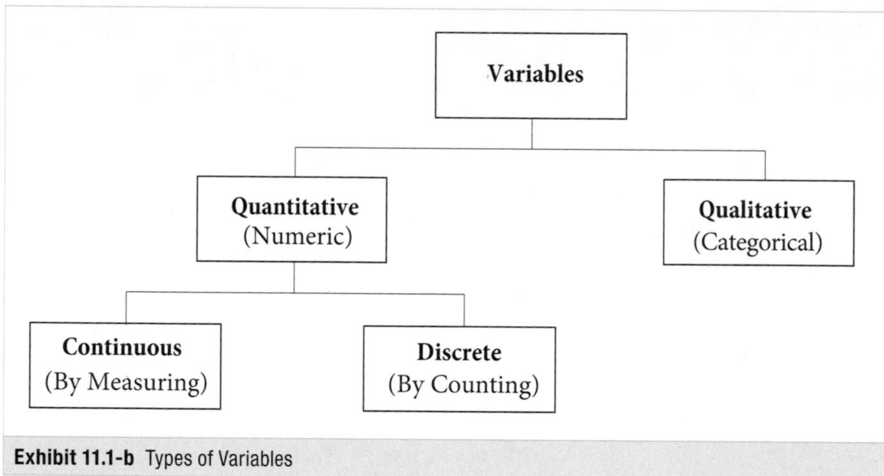

Exhibit 11.1-b Types of Variables

Levels of Measurement

Levels of measurement are rules that describe the properties of data that is collected and the way in which it can be used to provide additional information. There are four levels of measurement: Nominal, Ordinal, Interval, and Ratio.

The properties used to classify these levels of measurement are: order (rank), meaningful difference (interval between measurements), and meaningful zero point.

Table 11.1-a **Summary of Levels of Measurement**

Levels of Measurement	Order (Rank)	Meaningful Difference	Meaningful Zero
Nominal	No	No	No
Ordinal	Yes	No	No
Interval	Yes	Yes	No
Ratio	Yes	Yes	Yes

Table 11.1-b **Properties and Examples of Levels of Measurement**

Levels of Measurement	Properties	Examples
Nominal	• Have no order, but numbers may be assigned for referencing and differentiating purposes using codes. • The interval between measurements is not meaningful. • No meaningful zero point. • Qualitative data and usually classified using letters, symbols, or names.	• Gender • Religion • Country of birth • Colour
Ordinal	• Have order by their relative position. • The interval between measurements is not meaningful. • No meaningful zero point. • Qualitative data and usually classified using letters, symbols, or numbers.	• Satisfaction level • Movie rating • GPA (A = 4, B = 3, C = 2, ...) • Shoe/clothing size
Interval	• Have order by their relative position. • Meaningful intervals between measurements. • No meaningful zero point (the zero point is located arbitrarily). • Quantitative data but measurements cannot be multiplied or divided.	• Temperature • Dates • Calendar years • IQ score
Ratio	• Have order by their relative position. • Meaningful intervals between measurements. • Meaningful zero point. • Quantitative data and measurements can be multiplied or divided.	• Percent • Age • Weight • Speed

Stem-and-Leaf Plots

A **stem-and-leaf plot** is one method of displaying quantitative data to show the spread of data and the location of where most of the data points lie. The method is simply a sorting technique to arrange the data from the lowest to the highest value, which is known as an **array**.

In this display, the set of numbers is rewritten, so that the last digit (unit or ones digit) becomes the leaf and the other digits become the stem. The stems are written vertically and the leaves are written horizontally. A stem-and-leaf plot shows the exact values of individual data values.

For example, for the two-digit number 38, the stem is the tens digit 3 (written on the left side), and the leaf is the units digit 8 (written on the right side), as shown on the stem-and-leaf plot below.

For the three-digit number 156, the stem is 15 and the leaf is 6.

For the one-digit number 8, the stem is 0 and the leaf is 8.

For decimal numbers, all the digits including the decimal point will be the stem and all the decimal values will be the leaves.

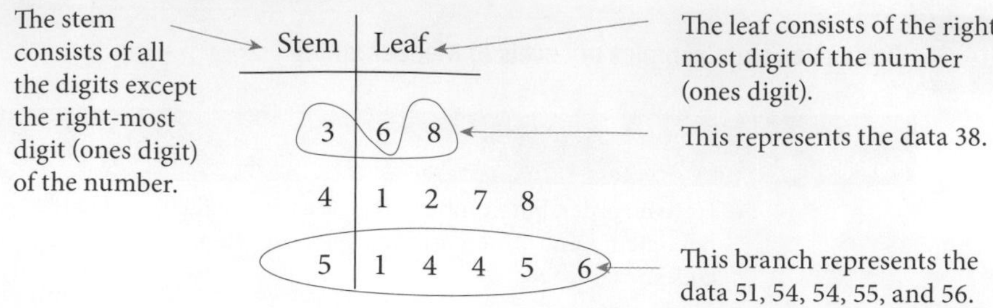

The stem consists of all the digits except the right-most digit (ones digit) of the number.

This represents the data 38.
This branch represents the data 51, 54, 54, 55, and 56.

The following example illustrates the procedure for constructing a stem-and-leaf plot.

Example 11.1-a **Constructing a Stem-and-Leaf Plot**

The marks on a statistics exam for a sample of 40 students are as follows:

63	74	42	65	51	54	36	56	68	57
62	64	76	67	79	61	81	77	59	38
84	68	71	94	71	86	69	75	97	55
48	82	83	54	79	62	68	58	41	47

(i) Construct a stem-and-leaf plot to display the data in an array.

(ii) Use the stem-and-leaf plot to determine the number of students who scored:

a. 70 marks or more.

b. less than 50 marks.

Solution

(i) Construct a stem-and-leaf plot to display the data in an array.

Step 1: Identify the lowest and highest stems of the data.
Looking at the data, the lowest stem is 3 and the highest stem is 9.

Step 2: Use Step 1 to identify the range in the stem. The stem will have the digits 3, 4, 5, 6, 7, 8, and 9. Draw a vertical line and write out the stem in this order to the left of the line.

Step 3: Starting from the first data, place each leaf of the number to the right of the vertical line on the corresponding stem, until the last data is recorded. There is no need to use commas on the leaf side.

For example,

- The first data value is 63. Therefore, the stem is 6 and the leaf is 3.
- The second data value is 74. Therefore, the stem is 7 and the leaf is 4.
- Continue until the last data, 47, where the stem is 4 and the leaf is 7.

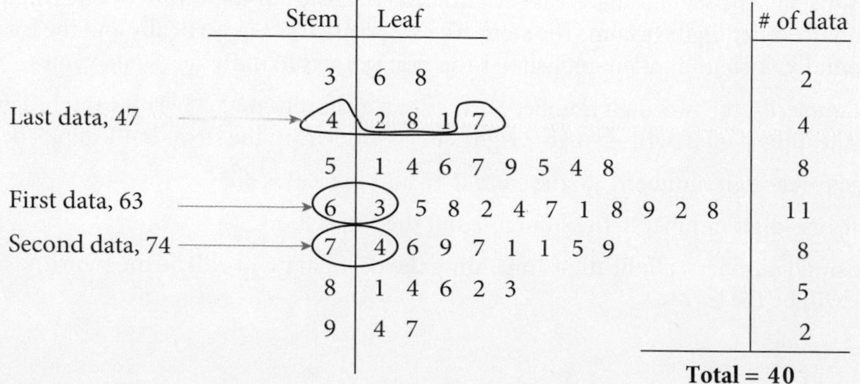

Stem | Leaf | # of data
3 | 6 8 | 2
Last data, 47
4 | 2 8 1 7 | 4
5 | 1 4 6 7 9 5 4 8 | 8
First data, 63
6 | 3 5 8 2 4 7 1 8 9 2 8 | 11
Second data, 74
7 | 4 6 9 7 1 1 5 9 | 8
8 | 1 4 6 2 3 | 5
9 | 4 7 | 2
Total = 40

Solution *continued*

Step 4: Rearrange the leaves against each stem, from the smallest to the largest number, to have the numbers displayed in an array.

Stem	Leaf	# of data
3	6 8	2
4	1 2 7 8	4
5	1 4 4 5 6 7 8 9	8
6	1 2 2 3 4 5 7 8 8 8 9	11
7	1 1 4 5 6 7 9 9	8
8	1 2 3 4 6	5
9	4 7	2
		Total = 40

Number of data less than 50 is 2 + 4 = 6.

Number of data 70 and above is 8 + 5 + 2 = 15.

(ii) The number of leaves against stem 7 is 8, against stem 8 is 5, and against stem 9 is 2. Therefore, the number of students who scored 70 marks or more is 8 + 5 + 2 = 15.

The number of leaves against stem 4 is 4 and against stem 3 is 2. Therefore, the number of students who scored less than 50 marks is 4 + 2 = 6.

Example 11.1-b

Interpreting Data in a Stem-and-Leaf Plot

A manager recorded the number of CDs sold in his store each day for the last fifteen days, and created the following stem-and-leaf plot.

Stem	Leaf
0	6 8
1	0 1 3 4
2	6 8 9
3	0 3 8 9
4	1 4

Calculate the following:

(i) Total number of CDs sold in the last 15 days.

(ii) Highest and lowest sales in a day in the last 15 days.

(iii) Number of days 30 or more CDs were sold in the last 15 days.

Solution

(i) Add all the data values in each row of the stem and leaf plot,

Sum of 1st row data	6 + 8	=	14
Sum of 2nd row data	10 + 11 + 13 + 14	=	48
Sum of 3rd row data	26 + 28 + 29	=	83
Sum of 4th row data	30 + 33 + 38 + 39	=	140
Sum of 5th row data	41 + 44	=	85
	Total	=	**370**

Therefore, the total number of CDs sold in the last 15 days = 370.

Solution *continued*

(ii) The highest data value is 44 and the lowest data value is 6.

Therefore, the highest sales in a day is 44 CDs and the lowest sales in a day is 6 CDs.

(iii) To determine the number of days in which 30 or more CDs were sold, simply count the number of leaves in the rows with stems 3 and 4.

There are 4 leaves in the row with stem 3 and 2 leaves in the row with stem 4.

Therefore, the number of days 30 or more CDs were sold = 4 + 2 = 6 days.

Tally Charts

A **tally chart** is another method of collecting and organizing data. A tally chart is used to keep count of the number of times a particular event or data occurs.

For each count, a tally mark "|", a vertical line, in the row against that event or data is used. The fifth tally mark is drawn as a diagonal line (or as a horizontal line) across the four tally marks: "𝍸". This helps to group the data in multiples of five.

For example, 12 counts of the same item is shown as "𝍸𝍸||" (two groups of five and two single tally marks = 12).

The number of times an event happens is known as the **frequency (*f*)**. Once a tally chart is completed, it may be used to produce a **frequency table**. Alternatively, if the data is organized using the stem-and-leaf method, then tallying may not be required to produce a frequency table.

Example 11.1-c Constructing a Frequency Table Using a Tally Chart

The ages of 35 students in a class were recorded as follows:

18	19	18	20	19	17	18	18	20	19
21	20	17	19	20	18	19	17	19	21
19	20	19	18	20	22	19	21	19	20
19	21	19	21	22					

Display the data using a tally chart to show the frequency distribution of ages of students in the class.

Solution

Step 1: Draw 3 columns to represent age, tally, and frequency (*f*).

Step 2: Identify the lowest and highest data values.
17 is the lowest and 22 is the highest. Therefore, the first column will have 6 entries displaying ages from 17 to 22.

Step 3: Starting with the first data value, use tally marks in Column 2 to count the frequency of each age in the dataset.

Step 4: Count the tally marks in each row to obtain the frequency of each age and enter it in Column 3.

Step 5: Add the frequencies in Column 3, noting the total at the bottom. Check that this total is the same as the number of data values in the dataset.

Age	Tally	Frequency (*f*)
17					3
18	𝍸|	6
19	𝍸𝍸||	12
20	𝍸||	7
21	𝍸	5
22				2
		Total = 35

Example 11.1-d Interpreting a Tally Chart

The tally chart below shows the height of students (in cm) in a class.

Height (cm)	Tally	Frequency (f)
140 to under 150	|||	
150 to under 160	~~||||~~ ||	
160 to under 170	~~||||~~ ~~||||~~ ~~||||~~	
170 to under 180	~~||||~~ |||	
180 to under 190	||	

(i) Complete the frequency column.

(ii) Identify the group with the highest frequency and the number of data in that group.

(iii) Calculate the number of students who are taller than 170 cm and express it as a percent of the whole class.

Solution

(i)

Height (cm)	Tally	Frequency (f)
140 to under 150	|||	3
150 to under 160	~~||||~~ ||	7
160 to under 170	~~||||~~ ~~||||~~ ~~||||~~	15
170 to under 180	~~||||~~ |||	8
180 to under 190	||	2
	Total = 35	

(ii) The group with the highest frequency is "160 to under 170" and the number of data (students) in that group is 15.

(iii) The number of students taller than 170 cm $= 8 + 2 = 10$.

The percent of students taller than 170 cm $= \frac{10}{35} \approx 28.6\%$.

Scatter Plots

The **independent variable** is the variable selected for the study. The **dependent variable** is the variable observed or measured.

A **scatter plot** is a 2-dimensional graph with two perpendicular axes used to illustrate the relationship between pairs of data values; one value is drawn from an **independent variable**, selected for study, along with a corresponding value from a **dependent variable**, which is observed or measured. It is conventional to use the horizontal axis for the scale of the independent variable and the vertical axis for the scale of the dependent variable. A dot or small circle is used to represent a single data point (i.e., one dot for each pair of data values). The scatter plot of the collection of all points illustrates the relationship between the independent and dependent variables.

Note: Since each scatter plot is only 2-dimensional, if an analysis contains more than one independent or dependent variable, then separate scatter plots are required.

The relationship between two variables is known as the **correlation** between them. If the data points follow a straight line pattern (as shown in Scatter Plots 1, 2, 4, and 5 below), then the variables are **linearly correlated**. If the points follow another pattern, such as a curve, the variables are related but not linearly correlated. Finally, if no pattern exists in the plotted points (as shown in Scatter Plot 3 below), then there is little or no relationship or correlation between the variables.

A linear correlation is **positive** when the slope of the plotted points is positive; i.e., as one variable increases, the other variable increases. This is shown in Scatter Plots 1 and 4 below.

A linear correlation is **negative** when the slope of the plotted points is negative; i.e., as one variable increases, the other variable decreases. This is shown in Scatter Plots 2 and 5 below.

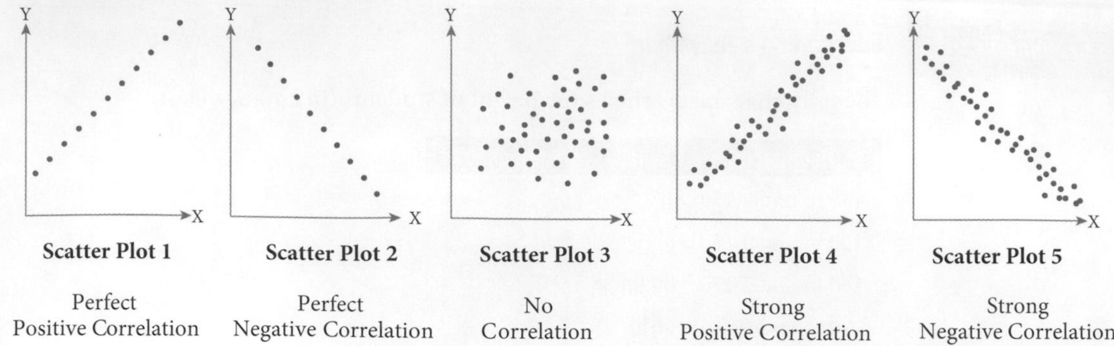

Example 11.1-e **Constructing and Interpreting a Scatter Plot of Height (cm) vs. Weight (kg)**

Construct a scatter plot for the following data and comment on the correlation between the heights and weights of these 10 students.

Student	1	2	3	4	5	6	7	8	9	10
Height (cm)	164	145	169	162	181	155	191	151	172	176
Weight (kg)	60	43	62	57	77	55	82	50	64	75

Solution

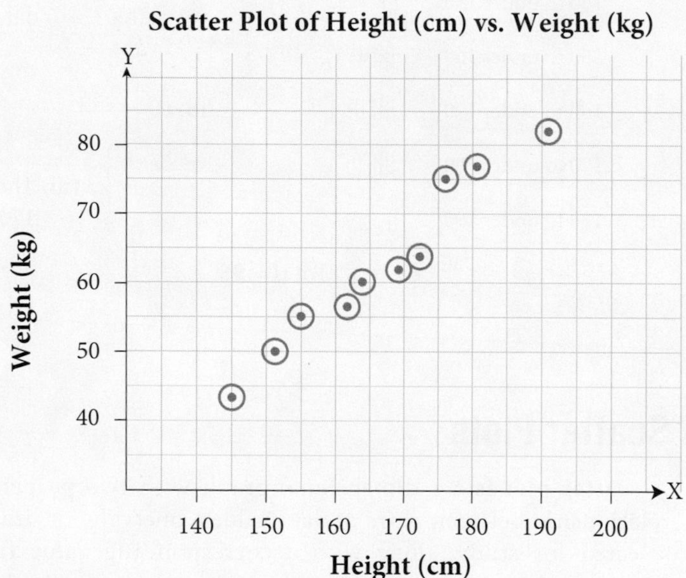

The scatter plot shows a strong positive correlation between the heights and the weights of the students; i.e., as the height increases, the weight also increases.

Example 11.1-f **Constructing and Interpreting a Scatter Plot of Price ($) vs. Items Sold (#)**

Construct a scatter plot for the following data and comment on the correlation between the price and the number of items sold.

Price ($)	15	18	20	25	27	30	35
Items Sold (#)	48	40	36	28	24	18	6

Solution

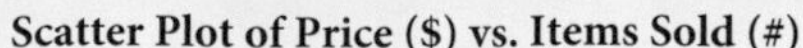

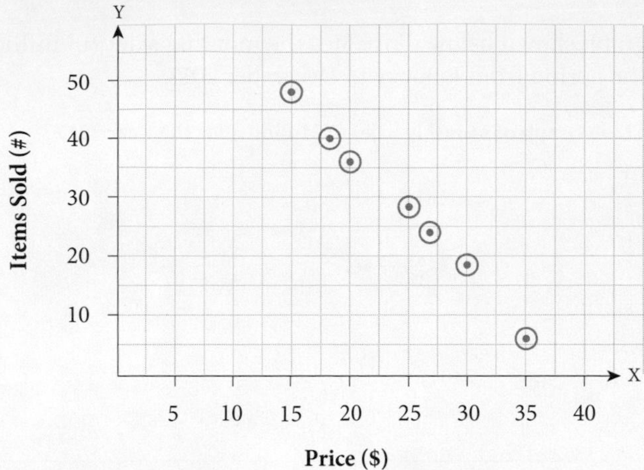

The scatter plot shows a strong negative correlation between the price and the number of items sold; i.e., as the price increases, the number of items sold decreases.

Line Graphs

Line graphs are most often used for representing continuous data; as such, consecutive points are connected using straight lines. Line graphs are an important feature of mathematics, and are similar to the graphs discussed in Chapter 8.

A line graph should include the following:

- Title of the graph, describing the purpose.
- Labelled axes to show the variables and the units of measure used.
- Position of origin: (0, 0).

Example 11.1-g

Constructing a Multi-Line Graph

The data showing the daily high and low temperature readings in Toronto for the period from September 15 to September 21 is provided below. Plot the two line graphs for the data.

Date	Sep. 15	Sep. 16	Sep. 17	Sep.18	Sep. 19	Sep. 20	Sep. 21
Temp (°C) High	20	15	16	24	21	20	18
Temp (°C) Low	11	10	8	16	15	14	12

Solution

Line Graph of Daily High and Low Temperature Readings (°C) from Sep. 15 to Sep. 21.

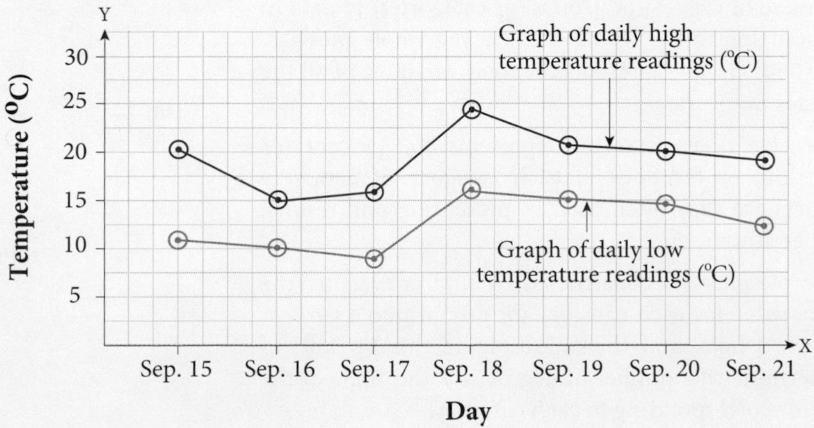

Example 11.1-h **Interpreting a Line Graph**

The line graph shown below illustrates the monthly sales (in millions of dollars) of a department store for the period from January to December 2017.

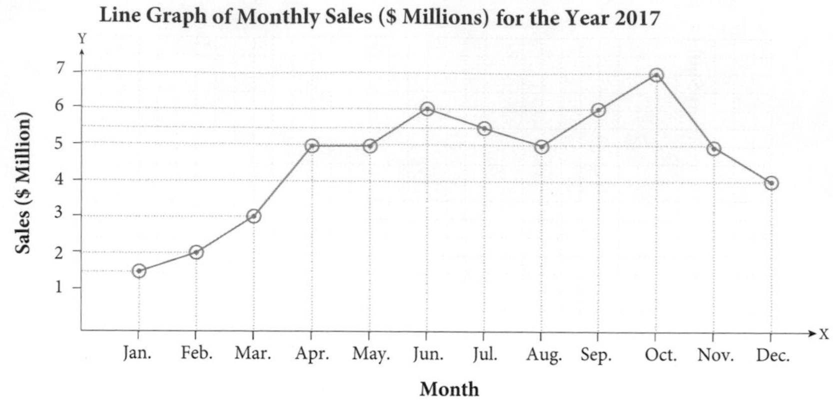

(i) Calculate the total sales for the period of May to August.

(ii) Which month had the lowest sales and what is the amount of sales for that month?

(iii) Which month had the highest sales and what is the amount of sales for that month?

Solution

(i)

Sales in May	5 Million
Sales in June	6 Million
Sales in July	5.5 Million
Sales in August	5 Million
Total =	**21.5 Million**

Therefore, the total sales for the period of May to August were $21.5 million.

(ii) The lowest sales occurred in January and the sales amount was $1.5 million.

(iii) The highest sales occurred in October and the sales amount was $7 million.

Pie Charts

Pie charts are usually used to summarize and show the size of classes (or groups, or categories) of data in proportion to the whole dataset. The whole 'pie' (i.e., the 360° circle) represents the total, or 100%, of all the values in the dataset.

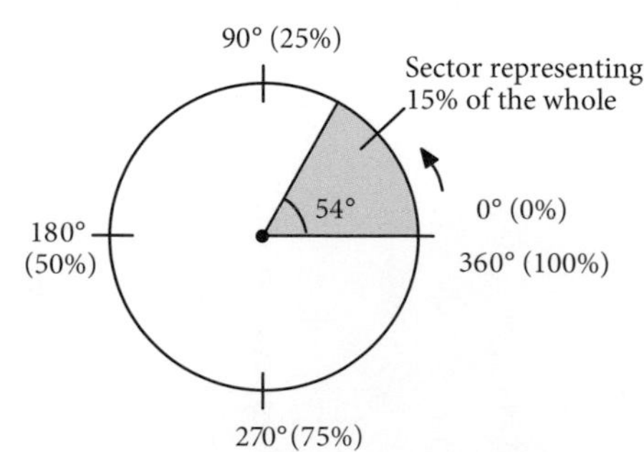

The size of each sector represents the percent (or portion, or fraction) of each category of data. Pie charts are very often used in presenting poll results, expenditures, etc.

The pie chart is constructed by first converting the data value for each category (or group) into a percent of the whole, and then multiplying this by 360° to determine the number of degrees for the angle of the sector corresponding to each category.

For example, 15% of the data is represented by a sector with an angle of 54 degrees ($0.15 \times 360° = 54°$).

The interpretation of a pie chart is based on the fact that the largest 'slice of pie' relates to the largest proportion of the data, and the smallest 'slice' to the smallest proportion. It is therefore easy to make comparisons between the relative sizes of data items.

Example 11.1-i Constructing a Pie Chart

Draw a pie chart representing the data using (i) percent and (ii) sector angles.

Item	Expense ($)
Housing	15,000
Meals	9,000
Transportation	8,000
Medicine	5,000
Miscellaneous	7,000
Savings	6,000
Total	**$50,000**

Solution

Reminder: when working with percents, you will need to convert to the decimal or fraction form before performing any calculations.

$30\% = 0.3 = \frac{3}{10}$

The expenses total $50,000 which is 100% and represents 360° in a circle (pie chart).

Calculate the percent for each listed expense.

For example, housing expense of $15,000 is $\frac{\$15,000}{\$50,000} \times 100\% = 30\%$.

Similarly, calculate the percent for all the remaining items and complete the 3rd column of the table, as shown below.

Calculate the angle that represents each sector in the pie chart by multiplying the calculated percent for each of the items by 360°.

For example, the sector angle for the housing expense is 30% of 360° = 108°.

Similarly, calculate the sector angle of all the remaining items and complete the 4th column of the table, as shown below.

Item	Expense	Percent	Sector Angle
Housing	$15,000	30%	108.0°
Meals	$9,000	18%	64.8°
Transportation	$8,000	16%	57.6°
Medicine	$5,000	10%	36.0°
Miscellaneous	$7,000	14%	50.4°
Savings	$6,000	12%	43.2°
Total	**$50,000**	**100%**	**360°**

(i) Construct the pie chart using the percent calculated for each of the items.

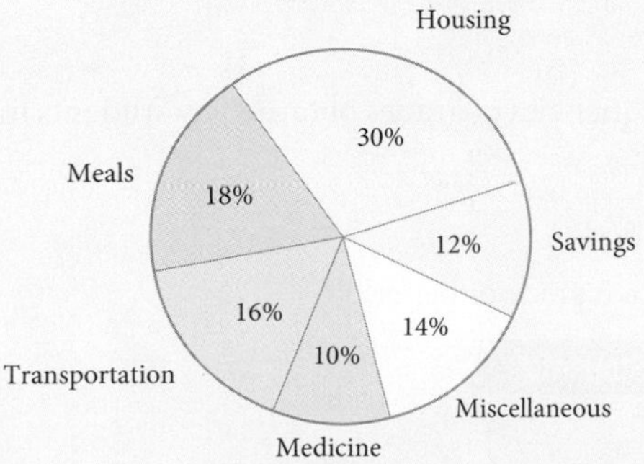

Pie Chart Using Percents

(ii) Construct the pie chart using the sector angle calculated for each of the items.

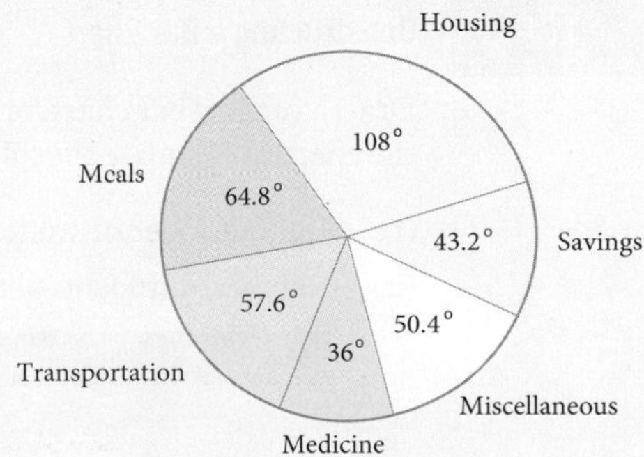

Pie Chart Using Sector Angles

Example 11.1-j

Interpreting a Pie Chart

The final grades of 40 students who passed a math exam are represented in the pie chart below. Use the pie chart to complete the table.

Grade	Number of Students	Percent	Sector Angle
A+			
A			
B			
C			
D			
Total	**40**	**100%**	**360°**

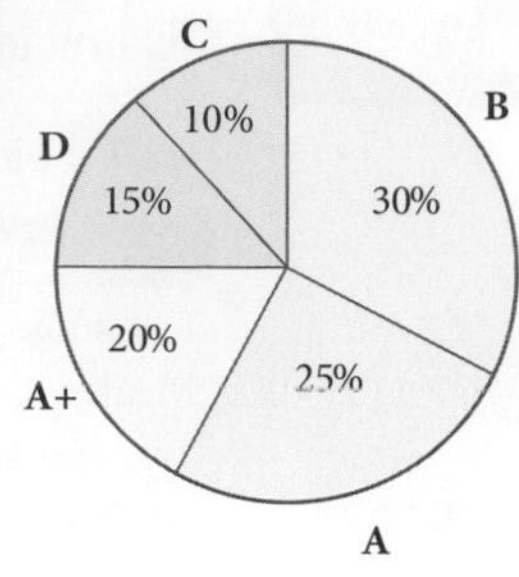

Solution

Grade	Number of Students	Percent	Sector Angle
A+	20% of 40 = 8	20%	20% of 360° = 72°
A	25% of 40 = 10	25%	25% of 360° = 90°
B	30% of 40 = 12	30%	30% of 360° = 108°
C	10% of 40 = 4	10%	10% of 360° = 36°
D	15% of 40 = 6	15%	15% of 360° = 54°
Total	**40**	**100%**	**360°**

Bar Charts

A **bar chart** is a graph that uses either vertical or horizontal bars to show the relative sizes of categories or class intervals of grouped data. On a vertical bar chart, the categories or class intervals are plotted on the X-axis, and the distribution of data in the categories (or the frequencies associated with the class intervals) can be represented by vertical bars with a scale on the Y-axis.

Bar charts are easy to produce and interpret, provided they adhere to the following two conventions:

- Classes, or intervals, of data should have no overlap.
- The width of the rectangle for each category or class interval should be the same.

The lengths (or heights) of the bars illustrate the frequency, or proportion of all data values, which exist in each category or interval.

A bar chart is also used to represent two or more sets of data having the same class interval, side-by-side, on one graph. This is called a clustered bar chart and allows for the data values in these sets to be compared easily.

Example 11.1-k

Constructing a Bar Chart

Draw a vertical bar chart for the frequencies of grades obtained by students in a math exam, and use the chart to calculate the following:

(i) Total number of students graded.

(ii) Number of students obtaining a B grade or better.

Grade	Number of Students
A+	8
A	10
B	12
C	4
D	6

Solution

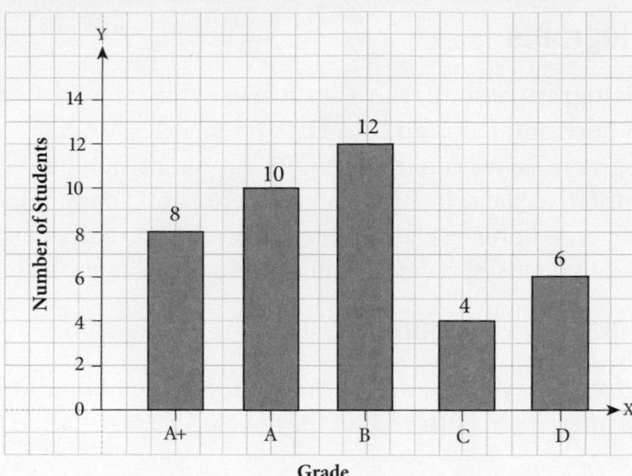

(i) Total number of students graded = 8 + 10 + 12 + 4 + 6 = 40

(ii) Number of students obtaining a B grade or better = 12 + 10 + 8 = 30

Example 11.1-I Interpreting Bar Charts

The clustered bar chart below shows the number of cellphones sold by Store A and Store B from January to June.

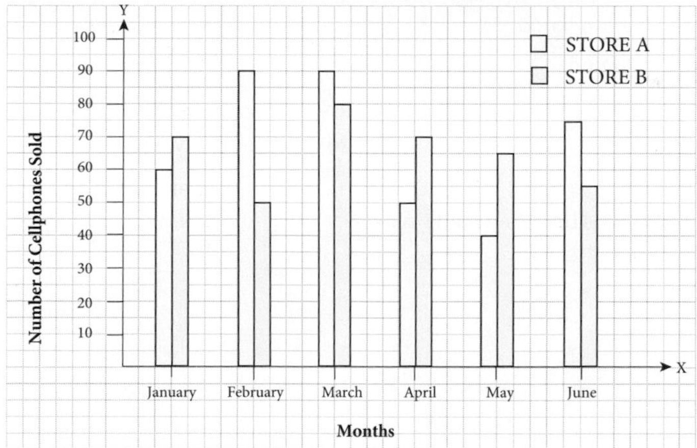

(i) What were the total cellphone sales by Stores A and B?

(ii) In which months did Store B sell more cellphones than Store A?

(iii) In which particular month was the difference in sales between Stores A and B the greatest?

Solution

(i) Total cellphone sales by Store A = 60 + 90 + 90 + 50 + 40 + 75 = 405

Total cellphone sales by Store B = 70 + 50 + 80 + 70 + 65 + 55 = 390

(ii) The months in which Store B sold more cellphones than Store A are January, April, and May.

(iii) The month in which there was the greatest difference was February. Store A sold = 90 – 50 = 40 more cellphones.

Histograms and Frequency Polygons

Histograms

A **histogram** is similar to a vertical bar chart in which the categories or class intervals are marked on a horizontal axis and the class frequencies are represented by the heights of the bars. Whereas bar graphs are primarily used to represent qualitative data, histograms are used to represent quantitative data. In histograms, there is no space between the bar of one class interval and the bar of an adjoining class interval. This is to visually demonstrate that all possible values along the horizontal axis have been grouped into exactly one of the categories/classes.

Frequency Polygons

The **frequency polygon** is the line joining the midpoints of the bars of a histogram. An additional class interval on both ends of the histogram is created so that the frequency polygon starts and ends at the X-axis.

Example 11.1-m

Constructing a Histogram and Frequency Polygon

Draw a histogram and a frequency polygon for the distribution of age groups of 200 employees in a company as shown below.

Age (Class Intervals)	Number of Employees (Frequency)
20 to under 30	35
30 to under 40	42
40 to under 50	64
50 to under 60	30
60 to under 70	24
70 to under 80	5
Total	**200**

Solution

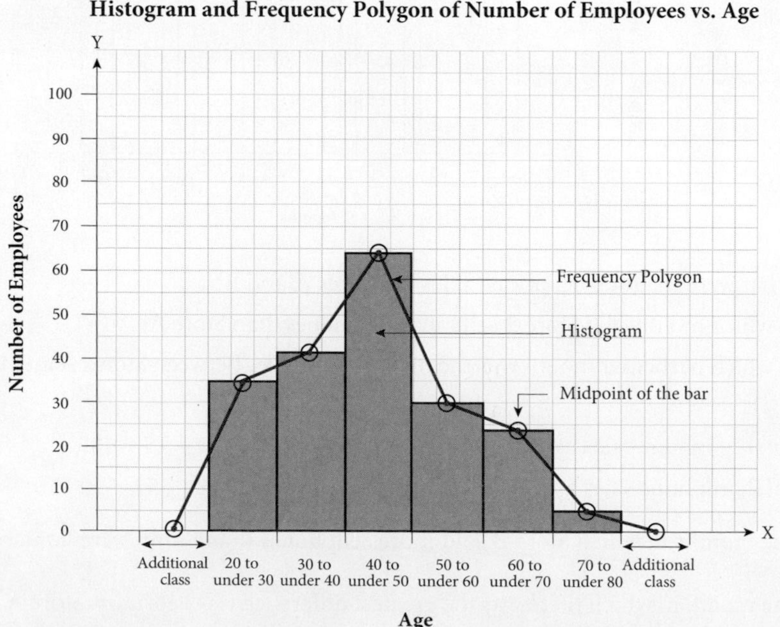

Note: Labels on the X-axis representing the class interval can be in any of the following formats: 20 to under 30, 30 to under 40, 40 to under 50, ... ; or 20-30, 30-40, 40-50, ... ; or as mid-points of class intervals (25, 35, 45, ...).

Frequency Distributions

A **frequency distribution** is a method to summarize large amounts of data without displaying each value of the observation. It groups the data into different class intervals and indicates the number of observations that fall into the given class interval, known as the frequency, *f*. In a frequency distribution, the class widths of all intervals should be the same.

The smallest value that belongs to a class interval is called the **lower class limit**, and the largest value that belongs to the class interval is called the **upper class limit**. The **class width** refers to the difference between the upper class limit and the lower class limit.

For example, in the class interval "140 to under 150", the lower class limit is 140 and the upper class limit is below 150. The class width = 150 – 140 = 10

Using the data from Example 11.1-a (shown below), the steps in constructing a frequency distribution table are as follows:

63	74	42	65	51	54	36	56	68	57
62	64	76	67	79	61	81	77	59	38
84	68	71	94	71	86	69	75	97	55
48	82	83	54	79	62	68	58	41	47

The **range** is the difference between the highest and the lowest value in a dataset.

Step 1: First, array the data using a stem-and-leaf plot and determine the number of data values, along with the highest value, lowest value, and the range.

Stem	Leaf	# of data
3	6 8	2
4	1 2 7 8	4
5	1 4 4 5 6 7 8 9	8
6	1 2 2 3 4 5 7 8 8 8 9	11
7	1 1 4 5 6 7 9 9	8
8	1 2 3 4 6	5
9	4 7	2
	Total =	**40**

There are 40 data values. The highest value is 97, and the lowest value is 36, and the range is 97 – 36 = 61.

Unless it is specified in the question, the class width/the number of classes is adaptable, depending on the question and the statistician creating the distribution. This means that there are many different correct frequency distributions for the same set of data.

Step 2: Determine the number of classes and the class intervals.

As a guideline, try to keep the number of classes between 5 and 15.

For 5 classes, the width of each class interval for the above data $= \dfrac{\text{Range}}{\text{\# of classes}} = \dfrac{61}{5} = 12.20$

For 15 classes, the width of each class interval for the above data $= \dfrac{\text{Range}}{\text{\# of classes}} = \dfrac{61}{15} \approx 4.07$

Therefore, we can use any class width between 4 and 13.

We will use a class width of 8.

The lowest class limit should accommodate the smallest value of the data. Since the smallest value is 36 and the class width is 8, we could choose the lowest class limit as any number between 29 and 36. We will use 34. Therefore, the first class interval is "34 to under 42".

The highest class limit should accommodate the largest value of the data. Since the largest value is 97 and the class width is 8, continue creating classes by adding 8 to the lower class limits, until you reach a number larger than 97.

Therefore, the class intervals are: "34 to under 42", "42 to under 50", "50 to under 58", ... "90 to under 98".

That is, there are 8 classes and each class width is 8.

Step 3: Determine the class frequencies for each class using the stem-and-leaf plot and complete the frequency distribution.

Class Interval	Frequency
34 to under 42	3
42 to under 50	3
50 to under 58	6
58 to under 66	8
66 to under 74	7
74 to under 82	7
82 to under 90	4
90 to under 98	2
Total	**40**

Example 11.1-n

Constructing a Frequency Distribution Table

The number of cars sold each month for the last two years by a car dealer is as follows:

44	58	68	27	21	55
39	15	19	16	33	25
51	52	10	26	37	48
70	75	84	73	65	80

Group the data into 5 classes and create a frequency distribution table.

Solution

Step 1: Array the data using a stem-and-leaf plot, as follows:

Stem-and-Leaf Plot (unorganized)

Stem	Leaf
1	5 9 6 0
2	7 1 5 6
3	9 3 7
4	4 8
5	8 5 1 2
6	8 5
7	0 5 3
8	4 0

Stem-and-Leaf Plot (data in array)

Stem	Leaf
1	0 5 6 9
2	1 5 6 7
3	3 7 9
4	4 8
5	1 2 5 8
6	5 8
7	0 3 5
8	0 4

Step 2: Determine the number of classes and the class intervals.

Number of classes = 5 (given)

There are 24 data values. The highest value is 84 and the lowest value is 10.

Range = 84 – 10 = 74

$$\text{Width of each class} = \frac{\text{Range}}{\text{\# of classes}} = \frac{74}{5} = 14.8 \text{ (we will use 15 for ease of presentation)}$$

Setting the class width to 15, the lowest class interval will be "10 to under 25" and the highest class interval will be "70 to under 85".

Solution *continued*

Step 3: Determine the class frequencies for each class using the stem-and-leaf plot and complete the frequency distribution, as follows:

Class Interval	Frequency
10 to under 25	5
25 to under 40	6
40 to under 55	4
55 to under 70	4
70 to under 85	5
Total	**24**

Relative Frequency Distribution and Percent Frequency Distribution

Relative Frequency Distribution

The **relative frequency** is the ratio of the frequency of a particular class interval to the total number of observations, expressed as a decimal or fraction. The **relative frequency distribution** is the entire set of relative frequencies of all of the classes. The sum of all relative frequencies of a frequency distribution should be equal to one.

Percent Frequency Distribution

The **percent frequency** is the relative frequency of each class, expressesd as a percent. The **percent frequency distribution** is the entire set of percent frequencies of all of the classes. The sum of all percent frequencies of a frequency distribution should be equal to 100%.

Example 11.1-o

Constructing Relative Frequency and Percent Frequency Distributions

Use the frequency distribution provided below to create the relative frequency distribution and the percent frequency distribution.

Class Interval	Frequency
30 to under 40	2
40 to under 50	4
50 to under 60	8
60 to under 70	11
70 to under 80	8
80 to under 90	5
90 to under 100	2
Total	**40**

Solution

Add two columns to the frequency table, one for the relative frequency distribution and one for the percent frequency distribution, as shown in the table below.

Class Interval	Frequency	Relative Frequency	Percent Frequency
30 to under 40	2	0.05	5%
40 to under 50	4	0.10	10%
50 to under 60	8	0.20	20%
60 to under 70	11	0.275	27.5%
70 to under 80	8	0.20	20%
80 to under 90	5	0.125	12.5%
90 to under 100	2	0.05	5%
Total	**40**	**1**	**100%**

Solution *continued*

The relative frequency of any class is calculated by dividing the frequency in that class by the total number of observations.

For example, the relative frequency of class "30 to under 40" is $\frac{2}{40} = 0.05$.

The relative frequencies of the remaining class intervals can be calculated similarly to complete the "Relative Frequency" column. The sum of this column should be 1.

The percent frequency of any class is calculated by multiplying the relative frequency by 100%.

For example, the percent frequency of class "30 to under 40" is $0.05 \times 100\% = 5\%$.

The percent frequencies of the remaining class intervals can be calculated similarly to complete the "Percent Frequency" column. The sum of this column should be 100%.

Cumulative Frequency Distribution and Cumulative Frequency Curve

The **cumulative frequency** value at each class is calculated by adding the frequency of that class to the frequencies of all the preceding classes. That is, it is the sum of the frequencies of all the classes up to, and including, the class in question. Simply put, it represents the running total of the frequencies up to and including that class, which means that the cumulative frequency value at the highest class is the total number of data values.

The **cumulative frequency distribution** is the entire set of cumulative values of all of the classes.

A curve showing the cumulative frequency plotted against the upper class limit of each class interval is called a **cumulative frequency curve**.

Example 11.1-p Constructing a Cumulative Frequency Distribution

Use the frequency distribution in Example 11.1-o (also provided below) to create the cumulative frequency distribution and the cumulative percent frequency distribution, and draw the cumulative frequency curve.

Class Interval	Frequency
30 to under 40	2
40 to under 50	4
50 to under 60	8
60 to under 70	11
70 to under 80	8
80 to under 90	5
90 to under 100	2
Total	**40**

Solution

Add two columns to the frequency table: one for the cumulative frequency distribution and one for the cumulative percent frequency distribution, as shown below.

Solution
continued

Class Interval	Frequency	Cumulative Frequency	Cumulative Percent Frequency
30 to under 40	2	2	5.0%
40 to under 50	4	6	15.0%
50 to under 60	8	14	35.0%
60 to under 70	11	25	62.5%
70 to under 80	8	33	82.5%
80 to under 90	5	38	95.0%
90 to under 100	2	40	100.0%
Total	**40**		

The cumulative frequency of any class is computed by calculating the total value of the frequencies up to and including that class.

For example, the cumulative frequency of class "50 to under 60" is $2 + 4 + 8 = 14$.

The cumulative percent frequency is computed by dividing the cumulative frequency of that class by the total number of observations and converting the answer to a percent.

For example, the cumulative percent frequency of class "50 to under 60" is $\frac{14}{40} \times 100\% = 35\%$.

When drawing the cumulative frequency curve, recall that it is plotted against the upper class limit of the class interval.

For example, the cumulative frequency of class "50 to under 60" (14) is plotted against 60 (the upper class limit), as shown below.

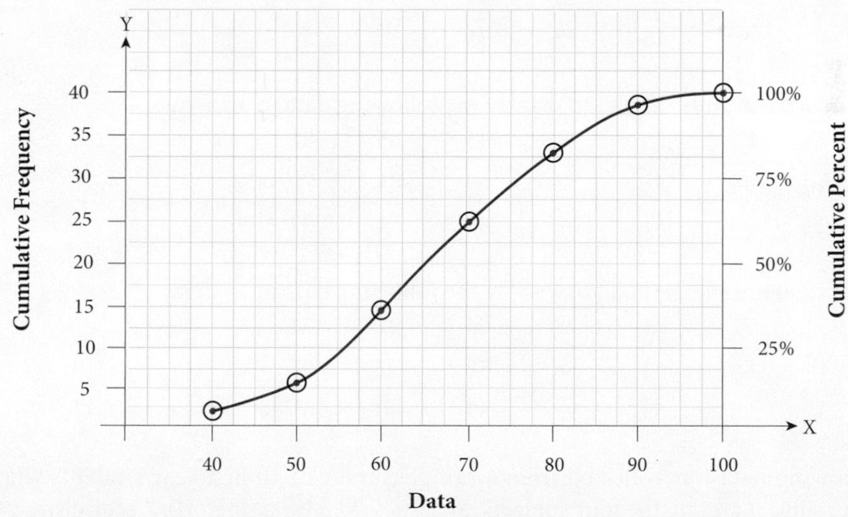

11.1 | Exercises

Answers to odd-numbered problems are available at the end of the textbook.

1. Identify the following variables as continuous or discrete:

   a. Height of students in a class
   b. Room temperature
   c. Net profit of a company
   d. Position in class

2. Identify the following variables as continuous or discrete:

   a. Number of seasons
   b. Weight of a person
   c. Time between the arrivals of two flights
   d. Air pressure

3. Identify the following variables as quantitative or qualitative:

   a. Marks on an exam b. Seasons of a year

   c. Amount of rainfall d. Mode

4. Identify the following variables as quantitative or qualitative:

   a. Height of a person b. Letter grade in an exam

   c. Median d. Model of a car

5. Identify the level of measurement (nominal, ordinal, interval, or ratio) for the following measurements:

   a. Pant size b. Mean

   c. Annual salary of individuals d. Title of a person in a company

6. Identify the level of measurement (nominal, ordinal, interval, or ratio) for the following measurements:

   a. Places of birth b. Ages of people

   c. Hours spent watching TV d. Temperature of ice in degrees Celsius

7. Construct a stem-and-leaf plot to display the following data in an array:

39	32	44	13	29	38
31	18	19	37	25	27
34	31	19	43	21	28

8. Construct a stem-and-leaf plot to display the following data in an array:

7	16	19	5	37	25
22	18	26	20	32	11
17	31	9	16	13	35

9. Construct a stem-and-leaf plot to display the following data in an array:

65	77	81	55	51	45	85	82
75	78	48	92	52	69	84	70
95	80	73	81	59	88	64	97

10. Construct a stem-and-leaf plot to display the following data in an array:

76	95	77	75	78	66	97	71
72	84	88	62	58	52	92	91
89	83	85	59	97	87	80	65

11. The following data was collected from a sample survey of 40 first-year students who were asked to indicate their favourite subject among the four subjects, Statistics (*S*), Marketing (*M*), Accounting (*A*), and Finance Math (*F*).

A	*S*	*M*	*M*	*S*	*M*	*A*	*S*	*S*	*A*
M	*M*	*S*	*F*	*A*	*M*	*M*	*S*	*S*	*A*
S	*F*	*S*	*M*	*A*	*S*	*F*	*M*	*M*	*S*

Organize the data in a frequency table using a tally chart.

12. The following data was collected from a sample survey of 40 students who were asked to indicate the mode of transportation that they normally use to get to college during the summer term. Their choices were walking *(W)*, bicycling *(B)*, taking public transportation *(P)*, and driving a car *(C)*.

C	B	C	B	C	B	P	W	P	C
W	B	P	P	B	P	C	W	W	P
W	W	P	C	B	W	W	C	C	B
P	C	P	W	B	W	B	C	P	B

Organize the data in a frequency table using a tally chart.

13. The following are the letter grades obtained by 200 students in Finance Math, in the business program of a college:

Grade	Number of Students	Percent	Cumulative Percent	Angle	Cumulative Angle
A+	24				
A	30				
B	36				
C	52				
D	42				
F	16				
Total	**200**				

a. Complete the above table for percent, cumulative percent, angle, and cumulative angle.

b. Draw a pie chart using either the percent or the angle measure.

14. Victoria kept a record of the average number of hours she spent on different activities during the weekdays. The information is provided below:

Activity	Number of Hours	Percent	Cumulative Percent	Angle	Cumulative Angle
School	7.0				
Meals	1.0				
Homework	2.0				
Travel	2.5				
Sleep	8.0				
Other	3.5				
Total	**24**				

a. Complete the above table for percent, cumulative percent, angle, and cumulative angle.

b. Draw a pie chart using either the percent or the angle measure.

15. A store's monthly sales (in thousands of dollars) for last year were as follows:

Month	Jan.	Feb.	Mar.	Apr.	May	Jun.	Jul.	Aug.	Sep.	Oct.	Nov.	Dec.
Sales ($ Thousands)	45	52	74	78	70	95	98	120	105	89	80	92

Draw a line graph representing the data.

16. The number of houses sold by a developer for the period from 2009 to 2017 is provided below:

Year	2009	2010	2011	2012	2013	2014	2015	2016	2017
Number of houses sold	82	110	130	145	90	75	128	160	180

Draw a line graph representing the data.

17. Use a scatter plot to determine the relationship (if any) between the price of an item and the number of items sold:

Price ($)	60	61	62	64	66	68
Number of items sold	190	182	176	116	104	87

18. Use a scatter plot to determine the relationship (if any) between age and income:

Age (years)	21	27	35	41	46	52	56
Income ($ Thousands)	38	51	53	64	72	76	80

19. The frequency distribution below was constructed from data collected from a sample of 100 professors at a college. Construct a histogram and a frequency polygon for the data.

Years of Teaching	Frequency
0 to under 5	10
5 to under 10	14
10 to under 15	39
15 to under 20	24
20 to under 25	13

20. The frequency distribution below was constructed from data collected from a sample of 30 students at a college. Construct a histogram and a frequency polygon for the data.

Height (in cm)	Frequency
155 to under 160	2
160 to under 165	5
165to under 170	9
170 to under 175	7
175 to under 180	4
180 to under 185	3

21. Use the frequency distribution in Problem 19 to compute the following:

    a. Relative frequency distribution.

    b. Percent frequency distribution.

22. Use the frequency distribution in Problem 20 to compute the following:

    a. Relative frequency distribution.

    b. Percent frequency distribution.

23. Use the frequency distribution in Problem 19 to compute the following:

    a. Cumulative frequency distribution.

    b. Cumulative percent frequency distribution.

    c. Cumulative frequency and cumulative percent curve.

24. Use the frequency distribution in Problem 20 to compute the following:

    a. Cumulative frequency distribution.

    b. Cumulative percent frequency distribution.

    c. Cumulative frequency and cumulative percent curve.

11.2 | Measures of Central Tendency

Central tendency is based on the concept that there are single values located in the middle region of a set of data that can be used to summarize the data set and compare data sets of similar type. The most common measures of central tendency are the 'mean' (also known as the 'arithmetic mean' or 'average'), 'median', and 'mode'. This section details the methods for computing each of these values.

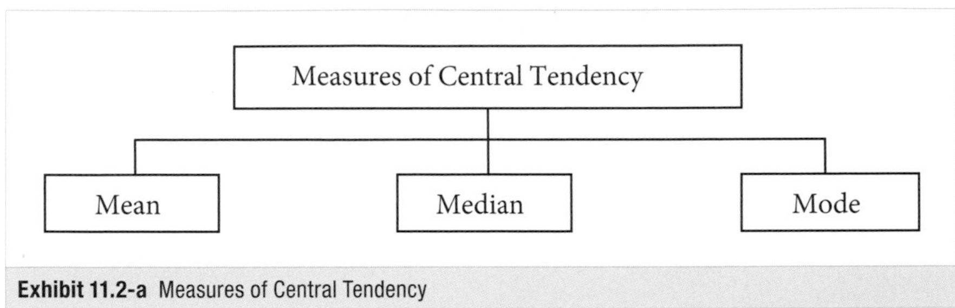

Exhibit 11.2-a Measures of Central Tendency

Mean

Arithmetic mean, or mean, is the ratio of the sum of all the terms to the number of terms, n.

The **mean** is a measure of central tendency calculated by dividing the sum of the values in a dataset by the number of values in the dataset. While the three terms 'mean', 'average', and 'arithmetic mean' are often used interchangeably, within more advanced studies of statistics, 'mean' has a formal definition related to the concept of 'expected value'.

The mean is one of the two most commonly used measures of central tendency because its calculation uses all of the data values.

$$Mean = \frac{Sum\ of\ All\ the\ Values\ of\ the\ Terms}{Number\ of\ Terms}$$

The population mean is represented by μ.

The symbol used to describe a sample mean is $\overline{x}$. The horizontal line over the 'x' is a standard way of representing a mean and it is read as 'x-bar'.

The number of terms, or observations, in a sample is represented by the letter 'n'.

Individual values are represented by 'x_i', where the subscript 'i' takes on a number to represent each individual value or measurement (i.e., i could take on any value from 1 to n).

The symbol 'Σ' is the capital form of the Greek letter *Sigma*, and is used in mathematics to represent the summation of all the individual values. Therefore, the sum of all the values of the terms can be represented by $\sum x_i$.

Putting this all together, we can formalize our definition of the mean as follows:

Formula 11.2-a **Mean**

$$\overline{x} = \frac{\sum x_i}{n} \quad \begin{array}{l} \longleftarrow \text{Sum of values of '}n\text{' observations} \\ \longleftarrow \text{Number of observations} \end{array}$$

The formula above can be rewritten as:

$$\overline{x} = \frac{x_1 + x_2 + x_3 + \ldots + x_n}{n}$$

with actual data values substituted for each of the x_i's.

By cross-multiplying the above formula, it can be seen that:

$$x_1 + x_2 + x_3 + \ldots + x_n = n \cdot \overline{x}$$

or, in other words, the total of all individual data values is equal to the number of observations times the mean.

Example 11.2-a Calculating the Mean

The number of cars sold by a sales person in the past five months is: {8, 15, 7, 11, 9}.

(i) Determine the mean number of cars sold by the sales person per month.

(ii) Explain, using a number line, what this number represents in relation to the given values.

Solution

(i) {8, 15, 7, 11, 9} There are 5 terms.

To determine the mean, add all the terms then divide by the number of terms.

$$Mean = \frac{Sum\ of\ All\ the\ Values\ of\ the\ Terms}{Number\ of\ Terms} = \frac{(8 + 15 + 7 + 11 + 9)}{5} = \frac{50}{5} = 10$$

Therefore, the mean (or average) number of cars sold by the sales person per month is 5.

(ii) If we plot these values on a number line, the number 10 represents the centre of these values.

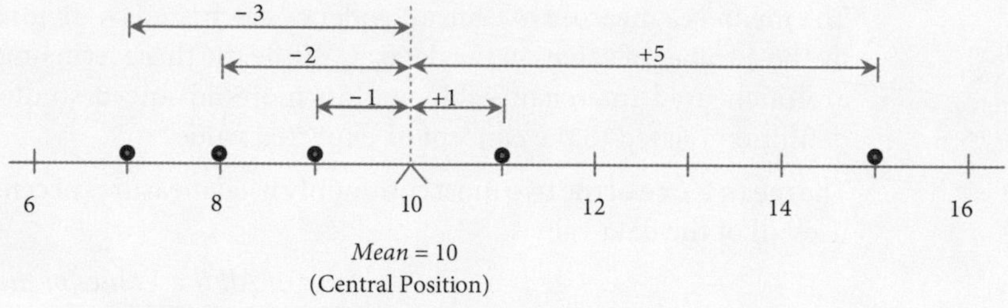

Example 11.2-b Calculating the Mean with New Data

The mean of six observations is 70. If another observation with a value of 98 is added to the above data, calculate the mean of the seven observations.

Solution

The mean of 6 observations (terms) is 70.

$$Mean = \frac{Sum\ of\ All\ the\ Values\ of\ the\ Terms}{Number\ of\ Terms}$$ Substituting values,

$$70 = \frac{\text{The sum of 6 terms}}{6}$$ Rearranging,

The sum of 6 terms = 70 × 6 = 420

Therefore, the sum of the 6 observations (terms) is 420. When a new term with a value of 98 is added,

The sum of 7 terms = 420 + 98 = 518

The mean of 7 terms $= \frac{518}{7} = 74$

Therefore, the mean of the 7 observations (terms) is 74.

Example 11.2-c

Solving for an Unknown Data Value when the Mean is Given

The mean of four terms is 12. Three of the terms are 9, 11, and 13. Find the 4th term.

Solution

Let the 4th term be x.

Using Formula 11.2-a, $\bar{x} = \frac{\Sigma x_i}{n}$

$$12 = \frac{(9 + 11 + 13 + x)}{4}$$

$$9 + 11 + 13 + x = 12 \times 4$$

$$33 + x = 48$$

$$x = 48 - 33 = 15$$

Therefore, the 4th term is 15.

Outliers

An **outlier** is a number within a dataset which has a value that is much different from the others in the set.

Including outliers in the calculation of the mean of the dataset can significantly affect its value and be misleading. Therefore, outliers are sometimes removed before calculating the mean, in which case a note should be made explaining their exclusion from the calculation.

Example 11.2-d

Showing the Effect of Extreme Values (Outliers) in the Mean

Calculate the mean (i) using all values, and (ii) after removing the outlier(s) in the dataset:

{3, 40, 45, 52, 60, 66, 70}.

Solution

(i) Mean of all seven values in the dataset:

$$\bar{x} = \frac{\Sigma x_i}{n} = \frac{3 + 40 + 45 + 52 + 60 + 66 + 70}{7} = \frac{336}{7} = 48$$

(ii) The value 3 is considered an outlier since it is significantly different from the other values in the dataset. After removing it from the mean calculation, the result for the remaining six values is:

$$\bar{x} = \frac{\Sigma x_i}{n} = \frac{40 + 45 + 52 + 60 + 66 + 70}{6} = \frac{333}{6} = 55.5$$

Therefore, the mean is greatly affected by the extreme value (or outlier) of 3, which is very different from the rest of the values in the dataset.

Weighted Mean

The **weighted mean**, also known as the weighted average, is similar to the mean, but instead of each value contributing an equal weight in the average calculation, in the weighted mean calculation, each value may contribute a different weight from that of the others.

Weightings may be used to indicate the relative importance of each value in the dataset. They may also represent the number of times, or frequency, each data value occurs in the dataset. In any case, as seen in the formula below, weightings (represented by w_i) are simply numbers which are multiplied by their respective data values. If all the weightings are equal, then the weighted mean is the same as the mean.

The weighted mean is calculated as follows:

Formula 11.2-b

Weighted Mean

$$\bar{x} = \frac{\sum(x_i \cdot w_i)}{\sum w_i}$$

$\sum(x_i \cdot w_i)$ ← Sum of the weighted values

$\sum w_i$ ← Sum of the weighting factors

x_i represents each data value ($x_1, x_2, x_3 \ldots x_n$) and w_i represents its weight or frequency ($w_1, w_2, w_3 \ldots w_n$).

i.e., $\Sigma\,(x_i \cdot w_i)$ is the sum of the weighted values, and

$\Sigma\, w_i$ is the sum of the weighting factors or the total of the frequencies.

Example 11.2-e

Calculating Weighted Mean

In a math course, the final mark is computed using a weighted average, based on the following factors (weights):

Quizzes:	1 Point
Online homework:	2 Points
Midterm test:	3 Points
Final exam:	4 Points

If a student received 80% for the quizzes, 70% for the online homework, 75% for the midterm test, and 65% for the final exam, calculate the student's final mark for the math course.

Solution

Evaluation Component	Score (x_i)	Weight (w_i)	$x_i \cdot w_i$
Quizzes	80%	1	0.80 × 1 = 0.80
Online homework	70%	2	0.70 × 2 = 1.40
Midterm test	75%	3	0.75 × 3 = 2.25
Final exam	65%	4	0.65 × 4 = 2.60
		$\Sigma\, w_i = 10$	$\Sigma\,(x_i \cdot w_i) = 7.05$

Using Formula 11.2-b, $\bar{x} = \dfrac{\sum(x_i \cdot w_i)}{\sum w_i} = \dfrac{7.05}{10} = 0.705 \times 100\% = 70.5\%$

Therefore, the student's final mark for the math course is 70.5%.

Geometric Mean

Whereas the arithmetic mean uses the sum of the numbers in the dataset to find the central tendency, the geometric mean uses the product of the numbers.

When it comes to finding the average rate at which a quantity grows over a time period, the arithmetic mean is not a good measure. Instead, a much better measure is the **geometric mean**, commonly used in accounting and finance, such as in compound interest calculations.

The geometric mean is calculated by multiplying all the values of the terms together and then taking the nth root of the product (this is the same as raising the product to the power $\frac{1}{n}$), where n is the number of terms in the dataset.

That is, if there are n terms ($x_1, x_2, x_3, \ldots x_n$), then the geometric mean, represented by G, is:

Geometric mean is the nth root of the product of n terms.

$$G = \sqrt[n]{x_1 \cdot x_2 \cdot x_3 \cdot \ldots \cdot x_n} = \left(x_1 \cdot x_2 \cdot x_3 \cdot \ldots \cdot x_n\right)^{\frac{1}{n}}$$

By rearranging the above formula, it can be seen that:

$$x_1 \cdot x_2 \cdot x_3 \cdot \ldots \cdot x_n = G^n$$

or, in other words, the product of all individual data values is equal to the geometric mean raised to the number of observations.

Example 11.2-f

Calculating Geometric Mean

Calculate the geometric mean of the following five terms: 3, 4, 6, 9, 14.

Solution

Geometric mean, $G = \left(x_1 \cdot x_2 \cdot x_3 \cdot \ldots \cdot x_n\right)^{\frac{1}{n}}$

$$= (3 \times 4 \times 6 \times 9 \times 14)^{\frac{1}{5}} = (9{,}072)^{\frac{1}{5}} = 6.187861... = 6.19$$

Therefore, the geometric mean is 6.19.

Example 11.2-g

Calculating the Average Annual Growth Rate

Sam invested $100 for four years. If the growth rate for each year was 10%, 14%, 17%, and 18%, respectively, what was the average annual growth rate?

Solution

The average growth rate using arithmetic mean $= \frac{(10\% + 14\% + 17\% + 18\%)}{4} = 14.75\%$

However, since rates of growth are multiplicative rather than additive, this is not the correct calculation in this case. The correct calculation is to determine the geometric mean, as explained below:

At the end of the first year, the value of the investment is 10% more than $100:

Value at the end of Year 1 $= 100(1 + 0.10)$

At the end of the second year, the value of the investment is 14% more than the value at the end of the first year:

Value at the end of Year 2 $= 100(1 + 0.10)(1 + 0.14)$

Continuing for the next two years:

Value at the end of Year 3 $= 100(1 + 0.10)(1 + 0.14)(1 + 0.17)$

Value at the end of Year 4 $= 100(1 + 0.10)(1 + 0.14)(1 + 0.17)(1 + 0.18)$

If 'G' is the average annual growth rate over the four-year period, then,

$$100(1 + G)^4 = (1 + 0.10)(1 + 0.14)(1 + 0.17)(1 + 0.18)$$

$$(1 + G)^4 = (1.10)(1.14)(1.17)(1.18)$$

$$(1 + G) = [(1.10)(1.14)(1.17)(1.18)]^{\frac{1}{4}} = 1.147073...$$

$$G = 0.147073... = 14.71\%$$

Therefore, the average annual growth rate was 14.71%.

Median

Median is the middle value when the data is in an array.

The **median** is the value of the middle term when the terms are in an array, arranged in an ascending order (lowest to highest value) or in a descending order (highest to lowest value). That is, half of the values are below the median and the other half of the values are above the median.

The median is not affected by extreme values (outliers). Therefore, when some measurements in the dataset are not representative of the general value of the dataset, or when the measurements contain extreme values (outliers), the median is the most preferred measure of central tendency.

The position of the median in an array is determined by $\frac{n+1}{2}$, where n is the number of terms in the dataset.

- If the number of terms is odd, the median is the value of the term in the middle, when the data is in an array.
- If the number of terms is even, the median is the average of the values of the two terms in the middle, when the data is in an array.

Example 11.2-h **Determining the Median of a Dataset with an Odd Number of Terms**

The heights (in cm) of a sample group of students are:

{198, 168, 175, 180, 171, 179, 177}

Calculate the median height for this group of students.

Solution

Arrange the data in ascending order as follows:

168 171 175 177 179 180 198

There are 7 terms in the dataset.

$$\text{Median Position} = \frac{(n+1)}{2} = \frac{(7+1)}{2} = \frac{8}{2} = 4$$

The 4th term in the array is 177.

Therefore, the median height for this group of students is 177 cm.

Example 11.2-i **Determining the Median of a Dataset with an Even Number of Terms**

The monthly rent (in $) for a sample group of two-bedroom condominium units in downtown are:

{2,700; 2,650; 2,925; 1,550; 3,050; 2,850}

Calculate the median rent for this group of two-bedroom condominium units.

Solution

Arrange the data in ascending order as follows:

1,550 2,650 2,700 2,850 2,925 3,050

There are 6 terms in the dataset.

$$\text{Median Position} = \frac{(n+1)}{2} = \frac{(6+1)}{2} = \frac{7}{2} = 3.5$$

Therefore, the median is located between the 3rd and 4th terms.

The decimal '.5' in the median position '3.5' indicates the median is located exactly halfway between the third and the fourth terms; that is, the median is the average of the two values.

3rd term = 2,700

4th term = 2,850

$$\text{Average of 3rd and 4th terms} = \frac{(2{,}700 + 2{,}850)}{2} = 2{,}775$$

Therefore, the median rent for this group of two-bedroom condominium units is $2,775.

Mode

Mode is the most frequently observed value in a data set.

The **mode** of a set of observations is the specific value which occurs most frequently (i.e., the value with the highest frequency). It is the best measure of central tendency when applied to non-numeric data (e.g., the most common colour of car on the road), or when the actual frequency is more important than the precise data value itself (e.g., the most frequently sold shirt size in a men's clothing store).

If all the observations occur with the same frequency (i.e., there is no "most frequent" measurement in the dataset), then there is no mode.

There may be more than one mode in a set of observations if there are several values that all occur with the greatest frequency. A dataset with two modes is described as bi-modal and a dataset with more than two modes is described as multimodal.

For example,

- In the dataset {1, 3, 6, 7, 12, 15, 17}, there is no mode.
- In the dataset {11, 13, **16, 16, 16,** 17, 17, 22, 22, 27}, the mode is 16 and it is unique.
- In the dataset {10, **11, 11,** 12, 13, 14, **15, 15**}, there are two modes: 11 and 15. This data is bi-modal.

Example 11.2-j

Calculating Measures of Central Tendency for a Dataset

Given the following set of data, calculate the (i) mean, (ii) median, and (iii) mode.

{14, 28, 17, 40, 26, 21, 36, 26, 27, 31}

Solution

Arrange the data in ascending order as follows:

14 17 21 26 26 27 28 31 36 40

(i) Using Formula 11.2-a, $\overline{x} = \frac{\sum x_i}{n}$

$$\overline{x} = \frac{(14 + 17 + 21 + 26 + 26 + 27 + 28 + 31 + 36 + 40)}{10} = \frac{266}{10} = 26.6$$

Therefore, the mean is 26.6.

(ii) The median position is determined by $\frac{(n + 1)}{2}$.

There are 10 terms. Therefore, the median position $= \frac{(10 + 1)}{2} = 5.5$

The median is located between the 5th and 6th terms.

$$Median = \frac{(5^{th}\text{ term} + 6^{th}\text{ term})}{2} = \frac{(26 + 27)}{2} = 26.5$$

Therefore, the median is 26.5.

(iii) The value that occurs most frequently is 26. It occurs two times in the dataset.

Therefore, the mode is 26.

Note: The mid-range is another measure of central location that is occasionally used. It is computed as the average of the smallest and largest values in a dataset.

For example, in the dataset in Example 11.2-j, the mid-range is $\frac{14 + 40}{2} = \frac{54}{2} = 27$.

Example 11.2-k

Calculating the Mean, Median, and Mode in a Frequency Distribution

The hourly wages of 30 employees are provided in the frequency distribution table below:

Hourly Wages ($) (Class)	15	20	25	30	35	40
Number of Employees (Frequency)	5	8	6	5	4	2

Calculate the (i) mean, (ii) median, and (iii) mode of the hourly wages of the employees.

Solution

(i) The frequency distribution table indicates that the number of employees earning \$15 per hour is 5, \$20 per hour is 8, ... \$40 per hour is 2.

Therefore, the mean hourly wage of all 30 employees can be computed using the weighted average formula.

Using Formula 11.2-b, $\bar{x} = \dfrac{\sum(x_i \cdot w_i)}{\sum w_i}$

$$\bar{x} = \frac{(15 \times 5) + (20 \times 8) + (25 \times 6) + (30 \times 5) + (35 \times 4) + (40 \times 2)}{(5+8+6+5+4+2)} = \frac{755}{30}$$

$$= 25.166666... = \$25.17$$

Therefore, the mean hourly wage is \$25.17.

(ii) Median position $= \dfrac{n+1}{2} = \dfrac{30+1}{2} = 15.5$

Therefore, the median is the average of the 15th and 16th terms.

There are:

- 5 terms with \$15 (i.e., terms 1 to 5)
- 8 terms with \$20 (i.e., terms 6 to 13)
- 6 terms with \$25 (i.e., terms 14 to 19)

That is, the 15th term is \$25 and the 16th term is \$25.

$$Median = \frac{25+25}{2} = 25$$

Therefore, the median hourly wage is \$25.

(iii) The value that occurs most frequently is \$20, with 8 data values.

Therefore, the mode hourly wage is \$20.

Table 11.2-a **When to Use the Mean, Median, and Mode**

Measure of Central Tendency	When to Use
Mean	Best used when the data is symmetrical or after outliers have been removed.
Median	Best used when the data is skewed (left or right) or when there are outliers in the data.
Mode	Best used when the frequency of observations is more important than the value of the observations or with qualitative data.

We will learn about skewed data later in this section.

Mean, Median, and Mode for Grouped Data

The calculation of mean, median, and mode for grouped data is different from that used for ungrouped data. In **grouped data**, the data is organised into a frequency table with class intervals and frequencies.

In grouped data, we usually do not have access to each value of the data (raw data) that lie within each class interval. Therefore, we calculate the approximate values of mean, median, and mode as follows:

Calculation of Mean for Grouped Data

Mean is defined as the arithmetic average of the values of all the terms in the dataset. Since we do not have the raw data, the midpoint of each class interval is used as an approximation of all values within that class interval. The class midpoint is represented by the symbol 'x_m' and the observed frequency within the class interval is represented by 'f'.

Therefore, the formula for calculating the mean for grouped data is:

$$\bar{x} = \frac{\Sigma(x_m \cdot f)}{\Sigma f}$$

This formula indicates that the mean for the grouped data is determined by first multiplying the midpoint of each class interval by its respective class frequency, adding the products, and finally dividing by the total number of data (i.e., sum of frequencies). That is, this formula is similar to the calculation of weighted mean (Formula 11.2-b), where the 'weights' (w) are now 'frequencies' (f).

Example 11.2-I **Calculating the Mean for Grouped Data**

The distribution of marks (out of 100) following a statistics exam for a sample of 50 students grouped in a frequency distribution is provided below. Calculate the mean mark on the statistics exam.

Class interval (Exam marks)	Frequency (f) (Number of students)
40 to under 50	4
50 to under 60	5
60 to under 70	18
70 to under 80	10
80 to under 90	6
90 to under 100	7

Solution

Class interval	Class Midpoint (x_m)	Frequency (f)	Weighted Class Midpoint ($x_m \cdot f$)
40 to under 50	45	4	180
50 to under 60	55	5	275
60 to under 70	65	18	1,170
70 to under 80	75	10	750
80 to under 90	85	6	510
90 to under 100	95	7	665
Totals		$\Sigma f = n = 50$	$\Sigma(x_m \cdot f) = 3{,}550$

The midpoint of each class interval, shown in the 2nd column, is computed by calculating the average of its lower and upper limits. The weighted class midpoint, shown in the 4th column, is the product of the midpoint and the frequency.

For example, for the first class interval, the class midpoint $x_m = \frac{40 + 50}{2} = 45$ and the weighted class midpoint $= 45 \times 4 = 180$.

$\bar{x}$ is the sum of the weighted class midpoints, divided by the total number of data.

$$\bar{x} = \frac{\Sigma(x_m \cdot f)}{\Sigma f} = \frac{3{,}550}{50} = 71$$

Therefore, the mean mark of the grouped data is 71.

Calculation of Median for Grouped Data

Recall that the median is defined as the value of the middle term in a dataset, when the data is arranged in an array. When the raw data is not available, it is not possible to determine precisely what the value of the middle term is. However, we can still determine the position of the middle term using the familiar formula $\frac{n+1}{2}$, and then obtain an approximate value for the median.

To start, construct a cumulative frequency distribution, as learned in the previous section, to determine which class the median falls in; this is referred to as the 'median class'. Once the median class is identified, use the midpoint of that class interval as the approximate median value.

Example 11.2-m **Calculating the Median for Grouped Data (using the Data in Example 11.2-l)**

For the distribution of marks (out of 100) following a statistics exam for a sample of 50 students grouped in the frequency distribution given in Example 11.2-l, calculate the median mark on the statistics exam.

Solution

Class interval	Class Midpoint (x_m)	Frequency (f)	Cumulative Frequency	
40 to under 50	45	4	4	
50 to under 60	55	5	9	
60 to under 70	65	18	27	← Median Class
70 to under 80	75	10	37	
80 to under 90	85	6	43	
90 to under 100	95	7	50	
		$\Sigma f = n = 50$		

Since there are 50 terms, the median position $= \frac{n+1}{2} = \frac{50+1}{2} = 25.5$, indicating that the median is the average of the 25th and 26th terms.

Since the cumulative frequency of class "60 to under 70" is 27 (and the cumulative frequency of the previous class interval is only 9), the 25th and 26th terms are both included in the "60 to under 70" class interval.

However, since the data is grouped, the precise values of these terms are unknown; therefore, the estimate of the median mark is the class midpoint $x_m = 65$.

Within the median class, we may also use the method of interpolation to estimate the median to a higher level of precision using the following formula:

$$Median = \ell + \left(\frac{n}{2} - m\right) \times \left(\frac{c}{f}\right)$$

where,

$\ell =$ lower limit of the median class

$n =$ total frequency

$m =$ cumulative frequency in the class one below the median class

$c =$ class width

$f =$ frequency in the median class

Using the method of interpolation to provide a more precise estimate for the median in Example 11.2-m:

$$Median = 60 + \left(\frac{50}{2} - 9\right) \times \left(\frac{10}{18}\right) \approx 68.9$$

Note: In subsequent examples and exercises, we will use the midpoint of the median class as the approximate median value.

Calculation of Mode for Grouped Data

Mode is defined as the value that occurs most often. When the raw data is not available, it is not possible to calculate the mode exactly. Therefore, we calculate an approximated modal value.

First, identify the class interval which contains the highest frequency, known as the "modal class".

Once the modal class is identified, use the midpoint of that class interval as the approximated modal value.

Example 11.2-n **Calculating the Mode of Grouped Data (using the Data in Example 11.2-l)**

For the distribution of marks (out of 100) for the statistics exam for a sample of 50 students grouped in a frequency distribution given in Example 11.2-l, estimate the mode for the statistics exam marks.

Solution

Class interval (Exam marks)	Frequency (f) (Number of students)	
40 to under 50	4	
50 to under 60	5	
60 to under 70	18	⟵ Modal Class
70 to under 80	10	
80 to under 90	6	
90 to under 100	7	

Modal class is the class interval with the highest frequency.

The class interval '60 to under 70' contains the highest frequency of 18. Therefore, it is the modal class.

The midpoint of the class is $\frac{60 + 70}{2} = 65$.

Therefore, the estimated mode is 65.

Empirical Relationship among Mean, Median, and Mode

There is a relationship among mean, median, and mode that is empirically based (i.e., based from observations of these values calculated for many sets of data).

The relationship observed most of the time is that the difference between the mean and the mode is approximately three times the difference between the mean and the median.

$$Mean - Mode = 3(Mean - Median)$$

Example 11.2-o **Estimating the Median, Given the Mean and the Mode**

The average height of the students in a college class was 172 cm and the most frequently observed height (mode) was 163 cm. What is the estimated median height of this group of students?

Solution

We can estimate the median height using the empirical relationship among mean, median, and mode.

Let the median be x.

$$Mean - Mode = 3(Mean - Median)$$

$$172 - 163 = 3(172 - x)$$

$$9 = 516 - 3x$$

$$3x = 507$$

$$x = 169$$

Therefore, the median height is estimated to be 169 cm.

Symmetry and Skewness

Data which is symmetrically distributed on either side of the centre is said to be **unskewed** or have 'zero skewness'. In such cases where there is one mode, such as in Exhibit 11.2-b, the mean, median, and mode will all be approximately equal.

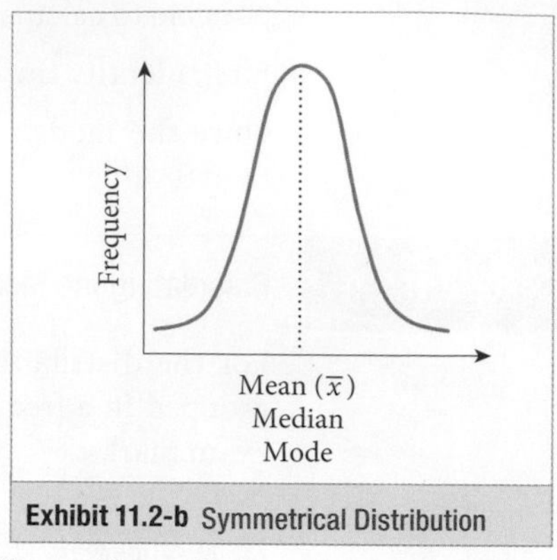

Exhibit 11.2-b Symmetrical Distribution

When data with a single mode is distributed non-symmetrically, or **'skewed'**, the mean and median will not be equal. In these cases, the mean is drawn away from the centre toward a long tail by the existence of extreme high (as in Exhibit 11.2-c) or extreme low (as in Exhibit 11.2-d) values in the dataset. The skewness of a frequency distribution is indicated by the sign of the value when the median is subtracted from the mean.

When the mean minus the median is positive (i.e., mean > median), the distribution is said to be **positively skewed**, with a long tail to the right.

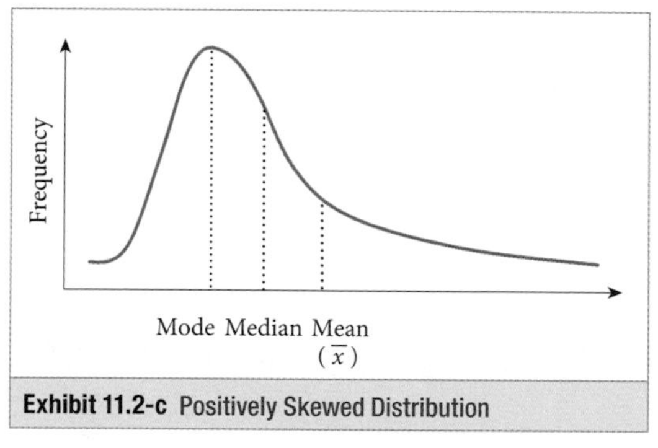

Exhibit 11.2-c Positively Skewed Distribution

When the mean minus the median is negative (i.e., mean < median), the distribution is said to be **negatively skewed**, with a long tail to the left.

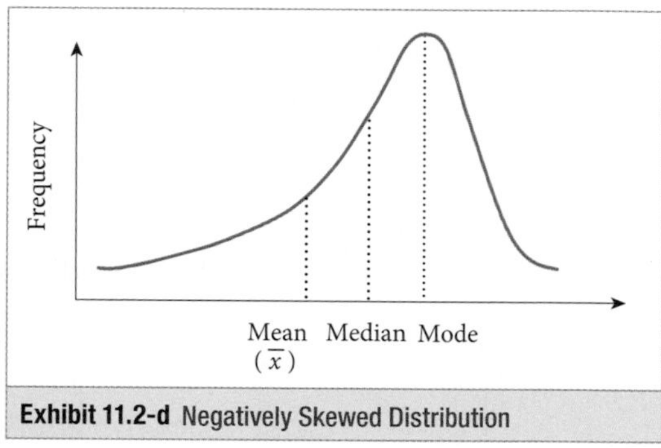

Exhibit 11.2-d Negatively Skewed Distribution

When the data is significantly skewed, either positively or negatively, then the median tends to be the best measure of central tendency.

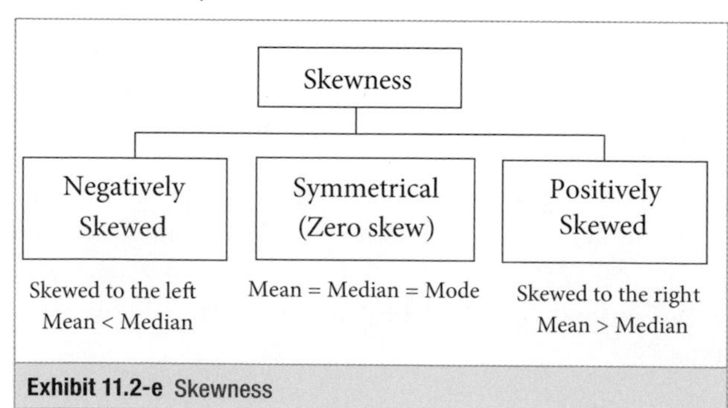

Exhibit 11.2-e Skewness

Example 11.2-p Determining the Shape of a Distribution (using Data from Example 11.2-j)

Determine the shape of the distribution of the data presented in Example 11.2-j.

Solution

In Example 11.2-j, we determined that the mean is 26.6, the median is 26.5, and the mode is 26.

The mean, median, and mode of the set of data are all close to each other. This suggests that the data is symmetrically distributed, as shown:

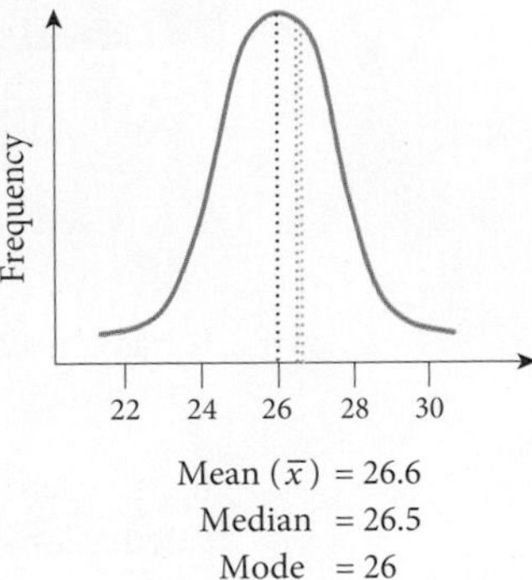

Example 11.2-q Determining the Shape of a Distribution

For a given group of students working together on a project, the average age is 22 years old, the median is 19, and the mode is 18. Based on the given measures of central tendency, determine the shape of the distribution of the students' ages.

Solution

Mean = 22

Median = 19

Mode = 18

The difference between the mean and the median is positive (i.e., Mean > Median), which suggests that there are unusually high values (i.e., outliers) in the dataset that have altered the symmetry.

Therefore, the distribution is positively skewed, and the distribution has a long right tail.

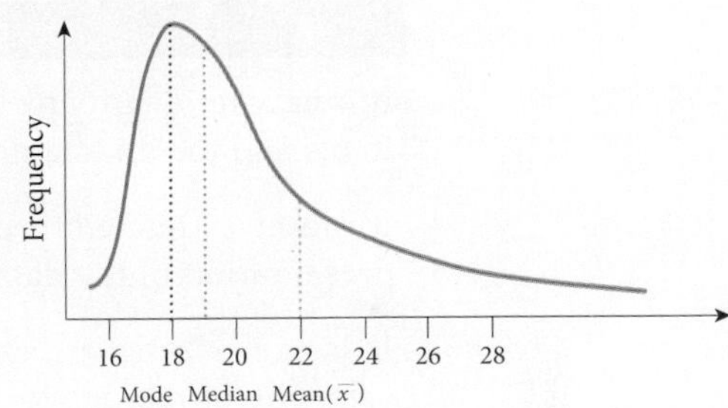

Example 11.2-r Determining the Shape of a Distribution

The average mark on a statistics test for a class of 35 students was 60, the median mark was 70, and the mode was 80. Based on these measures of central tendency, determine the shape of the distribution of the students' marks.

Solution

Mean = 60

Median = 70

Mode = 80

The difference between the mean and the median is negative (i.e., Mean < Median), which suggests that there are unusually low values (i.e., outliers) in the dataset that have altered the symmetry.

Therefore, the distribution is negatively skewed, and the distribution has a long left tail.

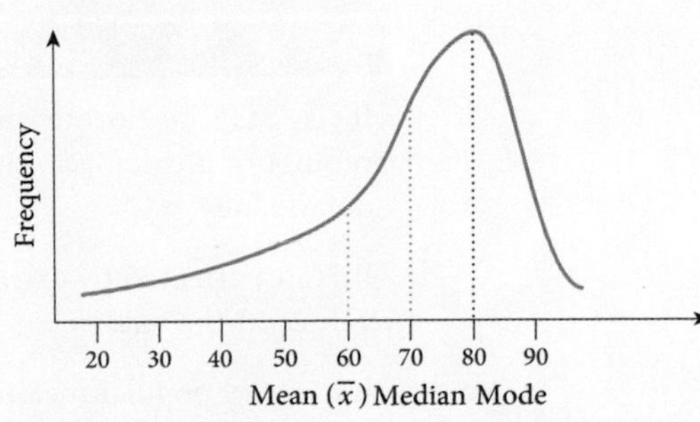

Table 11.2-b

Advantages and Disadvantages of the Mean

Mean	
Advantages	**Disadvantages**
It is defined by an algebraic formula.	It cannot be determined by inspecting the data.
It is based on all values of the given data.	It cannot be computed for qualitative data.
It has a unique value and is useful in comparing sets of data.	Its value may not be equal to any of the data values.
It is used algebraically in further statistical calculations.	It is affected by extremely large or small values in the data.
It can be multiplied by the number of items to quickly calculate the sum of the values in the dataset.	It cannot be computed when class intervals have open ends.

Table 11.2-c

Advantages and Disadvantages of the Median

Median	
Advantages	**Disadvantages**
It is easy to identify by knowing the number of items and the middle item in the data.	It is not a representative measure when the values of the data are wide apart.
It can be estimated through the graphic presentation of the data.	It is not based on all the items in the data.
It is not affected by extremely large or small values in the data.	It is an approximate measure when located between the two middle values.
It has a unique value and is useful in comparing sets of data.	It is not used in further statistical calculations.
It is a good measure of central tendency for data with skewed distribution.	It is not useful to calculate the sum of the values of the data.

Table 11.2-d

Advantages and Disadvantages of the Mode

Mode	
Advantages	**Disadvantages**
It is easy to locate in the dataset without requiring a calculation that involves all of the data values.	It is not a representative value of all the items in the data.
It is not affected by extremely large or small values in the data.	It is not possible to identify when frequencies of all items are identical.
It is a very popular measure for qualitative data.	It may have one or more values and may be difficult to interpret or compare.
It can be located graphically with the help of bar charts/histograms.	It may not reflect the centre of the distribution.
It will always be equal to a value in the dataset.	It is not used in further statistical calculations.

11.2 | Exercises

Answers to odd-numbered problems are available at the end of the textbook.

1. The final marks attained by a student in six subjects were 89, 95, 68, 86, 91, and 78. Calculate the average (arithmetic mean) mark.
2. The weights (in kilograms) of seven students were 62, 68, 65, 69, 73, 58, and 64. Calculate the average (arithmetic mean) weight.
3. Henry received the following marks on his first three math tests: 85, 94, and 89. What mark must he receive on his 4th test to have an average of exactly 90 on the four tests?
4. Giang received the following marks on her first four math tests: 87, 93, 89, and 88. What mark must she receive on her 5th test to have an average of exactly 90 on the five tests?
5. The mean of 10 observations is 20 and that of another 15 observations is 16. Determine the mean of all 25 observations.
6. A class of 25 students took a science test. Ten students had an average (arithmetic mean) score of 80. The other students had an average score of 60. What is the average score of the whole class?
7. The mean of 6 numbers is 50. If one of the numbers is excluded, the mean gets reduced by 5. Determine the excluded number.
8. The mean of 5 numbers is 27. If one of the numbers is excluded, the mean gets reduced by 2. Determine the excluded number.
9. The average monthly salary of 50 people was $4,220. The average monthly salary of 42 of them was $3,500. Calculate the average monthly salary of the remaining 8 people.
10. The average mark for a class of 40 students was 74. The 15 male students in the class had an average mark of 70. Calculate the average mark of the female students in the class.
11. In a survey, 10 people were found to have an average weight of 72 kg. When another person joined the survey, the average weight of the 11 people decreased by 2 kg. Determine the weight of the 11th person.
12. The average mark of 14 students in a class was 75. Another student took a make-up test and the class average decreased by 1 mark. What was the mark of the 15th student?
13. A class is given a quiz with 5 questions. 20% of the students got all 5 correct, 30% got 4 correct, 25% got 3 correct, 10% got 2 correct, 5% got 1 correct, and the others got them all wrong. If there are 40 students in the class, what is the mean mark on the quiz?
14. A class is given a test with 5 questions. 15% of the students got all 5 correct, 25% got 4 correct, 40% got 3 correct, 5% got 2 correct, 10% got 1 correct, and the others got them all wrong. If there are 40 students in the class, what is the mean mark on the test?
15. A student obtained marks of 75, 85, 60, 65, and 50 in the subjects of Finance, Statistics, Accounting, Marketing, and English, respectively. Assuming weights of 5, 4, 3, 2, and 1, respectively, for the above subjects, find the weighted arithmetic mean mark for the subjects.
16. In a survey of 100 people, 75 of them have an average salary of $2,500 a month. Twenty-five of them earn an average salary of $8,000 a month. What is the average monthly salary of the 100 people surveyed?

For Problems 17 and 18, calculate the geometric mean for the datasets.

17. a. 4, 36 b. 2, 4, 8 c. 1.10, 1.16, 1.13, 1.18
18. a. 9, 25 b. 4, 6, 8 c. 1.08, 1.09, 1.05, 1.12

For Problems 19 to 22, determine the median of the datasets.

19. a. 51, 56, 63, 46, 48

    b. 26, 24, 29, 24, 25, 28, 23

    c. 28, 24, 22, 24, 26, 26, 22, 28, 27

20. a. 14, 11, 19, 17, 15

    b. 30, 27, 29, 24, 22, 31, 25

    c. 93, 90, 62, 44, 75, 89, 74, 78, 72

21. a. 41, 44, 37, 39, 27, 35, 42, 40

    b. 18, 13, 5, 14, 18, 14, 19, 17, 15, 10

    c. 74, 100, 78, 61, 78, 81, 67, 93, 90, 62, 75, 89

22. a. 75, 78, 92, 69, 84, 70, 75, 89

    b. 74, 99, 78, 61, 78, 81, 67, 93, 90, 62

    c. 52, 57, 61, 64, 70, 72, 78, 79, 79, 80, 80, 81

23. The results on a recent class test out of 30 are: {30, 27, 19, 24, 22, 31, 25, 28, 26}.

    a. Determine the median mark.

    b. If a mark of 24, achieved by another student, is included in the test score, determine the new median mark.

24. The test results on a recent exam out of 100 were: {67, 62, 70, 68, 90, 84, 94}.

    a. Determine the median mark.

    b. If a mark of 75, achieved by another student, is included in the exam scores, determine the new median mark.

For Problems 25 and 26, determine the mode of the datasets.

25. a. 5, 6, 7, 10, 11, 12, 13, 15, 16

    b. 14, 16, 16, 27, 31, 31, 31, 35, 37

    c. 34, 36, 36, 36, 37, 41, 41, 41, 42

26. a. 6, 7, 8, 11, 13, 14, 16, 17

    b. 15, 15, 17, 25, 28, 29, 32, 34, 35

    c. 29, 30, 32, 34, 35, 37, 42, 42, 42

For Problems 27 and 28, calculate the mean, median, and mode for the datasets.

27. a. 8, 4, 6, 4, 10, 4, 10

    b. 72, 68, 56, 65, 72, 56, 56, 68

    c. 125, 132, 120, 118, 120, 128, 126, 120, 132

28. a. 6, 2, 4, 7, 6, 3, 8

    b. 18, 10, 21, 17, 12, 5, 9, 12

    c. 47, 50, 64, 85, 50, 47, 36, 24, 61, 48, 50, 73

29. Six employees in a restaurant earn the following weekly wages:

    $140, $220, $90, $180, $140, $200

    a. Determine the average weekly income of the six employees.

    b. What is the median wage?

    c. Determine the mode.

30. Ten employees of a department store earn the following weekly wages:

    $200, $150, $160, $125, $160, $150, $180, $130, $170, $150

    a. Determine the average weekly income of the ten employees.

    b. What is the median wage?

    c. Determine the mode.

31. The following table shows the number of TVs per household in a sample of 50 households. Compute the mean, median, and mode.

Number of TVs in household	0	1	2	3	4	5	6
Number of households	0	5	19	16	6	3	1

32. The following table shows the number of hours per day a sample of 60 people spend watching TV. Compute the mean, median, and mode.

Number of hours	0	1	2	3	4	5	6	7
Number of people	0	1	8	16	14	12	5	4

33. The hourly wages for a sample of 45 students during their summer employment were grouped into the following frequency distribution. Compute the mean, the median, and the mode.

Hourly Wages	Number (f)
$10 to under $12	3
$12 to under $14	6
$14 to under $16	12
$16 to under $18	15
$18 to under $20	7
$20 to under $22	2

34. The ages of a sample of 40 applicants for a training program are grouped into the following frequency distribution. Compute the mean, the median, and the mode.

Age	Number (f)
20 to under 22	4
22 to under 24	7
24 to under 26	10
26 to under 28	14
28 to under 30	3
30 to under 32	2

35. Using the empirical relationship among mean, median, and mode, estimate the mode if the mean is 17 and the median is 16 for a given statistical observation, and comment on the skewness of the distribution.

36. Using the empirical relationship among mean, median, and mode, estimate the mean if the median is 22 and the mode is 30 for a given statistical observation, and comment on the skewness of the distribution.

11.3 | Measures of Dispersion

In the previous section, Measures of Central Tendency, the calculation of a central number (mean, median, and mode) in order to summarize an entire set of numeric data was discussed. However, these values give no information on the **spread** or **dispersion** of data.

For example, consider the following two datasets, A and B:

Dataset A: {40, 45, **50**, 55, 60}

Dataset B: {10, 20, 30, 40, **50**, 60, 70, 80, 90}

You will notice that both the mean and the median in datasets A and B are the same and equal to 50. However, the spread of data in set A (which varies from 40 to 60) versus set B (which varies from 10 to 90) is very different.

Similarly, consider an exam in which the mean mark of a class of students is 70 out of 100. While this may represent the *average* mark of the students, not every student will have scored the mean mark (or close to the mean mark); in fact, their marks will be spread out, with some having marks lower than the mean and others higher.

To describe this spread, there are other numerical measures, known as Measures of Dispersion (or variability), which provide information on the way the other measurements are spread from the central number. In this section, we will learn about the following four measures of dispersion: the range, deviation from the mean, variance, and standard deviation.

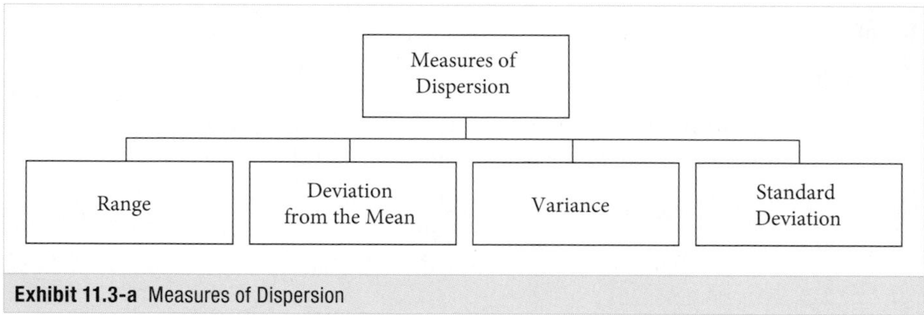

Exhibit 11.3-a Measures of Dispersion

Range

The **range (*R*)** of a dataset is the difference between the highest (*H*) and the lowest (*L*) values in a dataset. It is the simplest measure of dispersion and is easy to compute.

$$\textit{Range} = \textit{Highest value} - \textit{Lowest value}$$

$$R = H - L$$

For example, a dataset {5, 18, 19, 20, 22, 35} with low and high values of 5 and 35, respectively, results in a range, R, equal to 30 ($R = 35 - 5$).

The range provides information on the number of units between the highest and lowest data. The range does not provide information about the dispersion of values between the lowest and the highest values. The range, as in the case of the mean, is influenced by extreme values because only two values are used in the calculation.

Example 11.3-a **Determining the Range**

The following dataset provides the ages of 10 students in a class: {17, 17, 18, 18, 19, 19, 20, 21, 21, 36}.

(i) Calculate the range of the dataset.

(ii) Calculate the range if the extreme value, the age of the 36-year-old student, is removed.

Solution {17, 17, 18, 18, 19, 19, 20, 21, 21, 36}

(i) Range in age of the 10 students:

$$R = H - L$$

$$R = 36 - 17 = 19 \text{ years}$$

Therefore, the ages of the 10 students in the data are spread over a range of 19 years.

(ii) Range in age of the 9 students (after removing the age of the 10th student):

$$R = H - L$$

$$R = 21 - 17 = 4 \text{ years}$$

Therefore, the ages of the 9 students, after removing the age of the 10th student (the extreme value), are spread over a range of 4 years.

The range of the ages of students decreased from 19 years to 4 years after removing the extreme value. Therefore, the range is not a good measure of dispersion when the dataset contains outliers (extreme values).

Inter-Quartile Range

We learned in the previous section that the median is the point below which one-half of the ranked data values lie. In a similar way, we define the **first quartile** (Q_1) as the point below which the first quarter (0 - 25%) of the ranked data values lie, and the **third quartile** (Q_3) as the point above which the last quarter (75 - 100%) of the ranked data values lie. Using that definition, the **second quartile** (Q_2) is exactly equal to the median.

We can determine any percentile using the formula $(n + 1) \times \frac{P}{100}$, which gives the position of the data value in the Pth percentile for any ranked dataset.

Quartiles are specific percentiles. Q_1 is the 25th percentile, Q_2 (median) is the 50th percentile, and Q_3 is the 75th percentile.

The difference between the third quartile (Q_3) and the first quartile (Q_1) is another measure of dispersion, known as the **inter-quartile range** (**IQR**). The inter-quartile range includes the middle 50% (half) of the data. It is not affected by the extreme values of the data.

$$IQR = Q_3 - Q_1$$

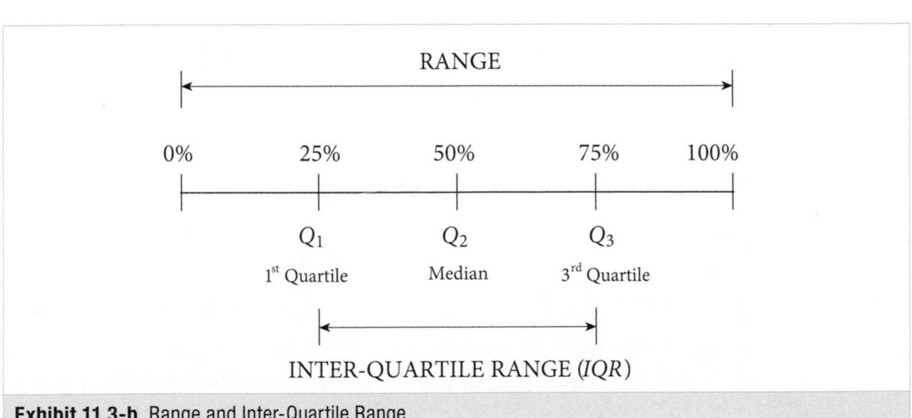

Exhibit 11.3-b Range and Inter-Quartile Range

Calculating Quartiles when there are an Even Number of Data

Step 1: Determine the median. Since there are an even number of data, the position of the median will be between the two central values in the array.

Step 2: Divide the data into low-value and high-value groups, splitting the data between the two central values in the array.

Step 3: Determine the medians of the two separate groups. The median of the low-value group is the first quartile (Q_1) and the median of the high-value group is the third quartile (Q_3).

Example 11.3-b

Calculating the Inter-Quartile Range when there are an Even Number of Data

Calculate the inter-quartile range of the dataset: {77, 65, 60, 68, 64, 80, 75, 70, 62, 68, 60, 63}

Solution

First, array the data as follows: 60, 60, 62, 63, 64, **65**, **68**, 68, 70, 75, 77, 80

There are 12 pieces of data (even number).

The median position is $\frac{12 + 1}{2} = 6.5$.

The median falls between the 6th and 7th data values in the array; therefore, the median ($Q2$) is $\frac{65 + 68}{2} = 66.5$.

Divide the dataset into two groups, each with 6 pieces of data.

Find $Q1$ and $Q3$ by determining the median in the low-value and high-value groups of data.

Low-value group: 60, 60, 62, 63, 64, 65

$$Q1 \text{ Position} = \frac{6 + 1}{2} = 3.5$$

60, 60, **62**, **63**, 64, 65

↑

Q1

$$Q1 = \frac{3^{rd} \text{ data} + 4^{th} \text{ data}}{2}$$

$$Q1 = \frac{62 + 63}{2} = 62.5$$

High-value group: 68, 68, 70, 75, 77, 80

$$Q3 \text{ Position} = \frac{6 + 1}{2} = 3.5$$

68, 68, **70**, **75**, 77, 80

↑

Q3

$$Q3 = \frac{3^{rd} \text{ data} + 4^{th} \text{ data}}{2}$$

$$Q3 = \frac{70 + 75}{2} = 72.5$$

Therefore, $Q1 = 62.5$ and $Q3 = 72.5$.

Inter-quartile range, $IQR = Q3 - Q1 = 72.5 - 62.5 = 10$

Therefore, the inter-quartile range is 10.

Calculating Quartiles when there are an Odd Number of Data

Step 1: Determine the median. Since there are an odd number of data, the position of the median will be the central value in the array.

Step 2: Divide the data into low-value and high-value groups, excluding the median from both groups.

Step 3: Determine the medians of the two separate groups. The median of the low-value group is the first quartile ($Q1$) and the median of the high-value group is the third quartile ($Q3$).

Example 11.3-c

Calculating the Inter-Quartile Range when there are an Odd Number of Data

Calculate the inter-quartile range of the dataset: {30, 28, 38, 35, 42, 26, 40, 32, 21, 23, 33}

Solution

First, array the data as follows: 21, 23, 26, 28, 30, **32**, 33, 35, 38, 40, 42

There are pieces of 11 data (odd number),

The median position is $\frac{11 + 1}{2} = 6$.

Solution *continued*

Therefore, the median ($Q2$) is the 6th data value in the array = 32.

Exclude the median and divide the dataset into two groups, each with 5 pieces of data.

Find $Q1$ and $Q3$ by determining the median in the low-value and high-value groups of data.

Low-value group: 21, 23, 26, 28, 30	**High-value group:** 33, 35, 38, 40, 42
$Q1 \text{ Position} = \frac{5+1}{2} = \frac{6}{2} = 3$	$Q3 \text{ Position} = \frac{5+1}{2} = \frac{6}{2} = 3$
21, 23, **26**, 28, 30 ↑ Q1	33, 35, **38**, 40, 42 ↑ Q3
$Q1$ = 3rd data = 26	$Q3$ = 3rd data = 38

Therefore, $Q1 = 26$ and $Q3 = 38$.

Inter-quartile range, $IQR = Q3 - Q1 = 38 - 26 = 12$

Therefore, the inter-quartile range is 12.

Box-and-Whisker Plot

A **box-and-whisker plot** is a graph that visually illustrates the full range of variation of the data (from minimum to maximum), the inter-quartile range of variation (from first quartile to third quartile), and the median; i.e., a box-and-whisker plot demonstrates the following five points:

1. Lowest data value (L)
2. First quartile ($Q1$)
3. Median ($Q2$)
4. Third quartile ($Q3$)
5. Highest data value (H)

The 'five number summary' is a list of these five points:

L, Q_1, Q_2, Q_3, H

which shows the breakdown of the data into quarters. The box-and-whisker plot is a visual display of the five number summary.

A line from the lowest data value to the highest data value is drawn to show the range, and a box with closed ends through the first and third quartile points is drawn to show the inter-quartile range, as shown in the example below.

Example 11.3-d **Graphing a Box-and-Whisker Plot**

For the dataset in Example 11.3-c, {21, 23, 26, 28, 30, 32, 33, 35, 38, 40, 42}, graph the box-and-whisker plot.

Solution

Using the solution from Example 11.3-c:

{21, 23, **26**, 28, 30, **32**, 33, 35, **38**, 40, 42}

↑ Q1 (26), ↑ Q2 (32), ↑ Q3 (38)

Lowest Data: $L = 21$

1st Quartile: $Q1 = 26$

Median: $Q2 = 32$

3rd Quartile: $Q3 = 38$

Highest Data: $H = 42$

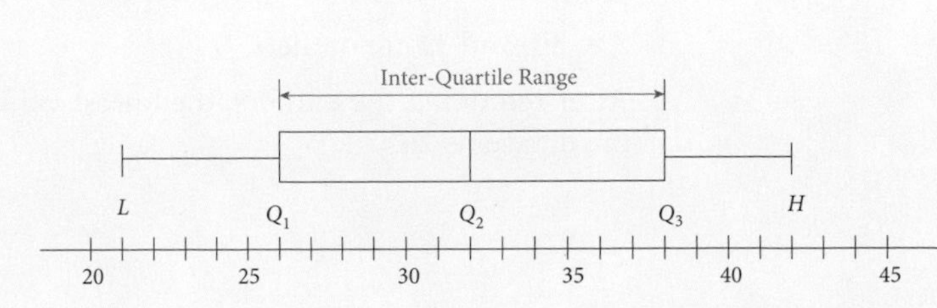

Identifying Outliers

Outliers are points that lie more than 1.5 times the inter-quartile range above $Q3$ or below $Q1$.

Step 1: Determine $Q1$ and $Q3$.

Step 2: Calculate the inter-quartile range using $IQR = Q3 - Q1$.

Step 3: Multiply the IQR by 1.5.

Step 4: Identify the points that are more than 1.5 times the IQR below $Q1$ or above $Q3$ as outliers.

Outliers are represented on a box-and-whisker plot as open dots, as shown in the example below.

Example 11.3-e Identifying Outliers and Drawing the Box-and-Whisker Plot

Identify the outlier(s) of the following dataset and draw the box-and-whisker plot.

{7, 8, 13, 16, 16, 17, 17, 18, 18, 19, 19, 20, 20, 21, 26, 30, 32}

Solution

There are 17 data (odd number of data), already arranged in an array.

$$\text{Median Position} = \frac{17+1}{2} = 9$$

Median, $Q2 = 18$

Divide the data into two groups of 8 data, excluding the median data.

Find $Q1$ and $Q3$ by determining the median in the low-value and high-value groups of data.

Low-value group: 7, 8, 13, 16, 16, 17, 17, 18

$$Q1 \text{ Position} = \frac{8+1}{2} = \frac{9}{2} = 4.5$$

7, 8, 13, **16**, **16**, 17, 17, 18

↑

Q1

$$Q1 = \frac{4^{th}\text{ data} + 5^{th}\text{ data}}{2}$$

$$Q1 = \frac{16+16}{2} = 16$$

High-value group: 19, 19, 20, 20, 21, 26, 30, 32

$$Q3 \text{ Position} = \frac{8+1}{2} = \frac{9}{2} = 4.5$$

19, 19, 20, **20**, **21**, 26, 30, 32

↑

Q3

$$Q3 = \frac{4^{th}\text{ data} + 5^{th}\text{ data}}{2}$$

$$Q3 = \frac{20+21}{2} = 20.5$$

$IQR = Q3 - Q1 = 20.5 - 16 = 4.5$

$1.5 \times IQR = 1.5 \times 4.5 = 6.75$

Outliers are:

- data below $(Q1 - 1.5 \times IQR) = (16 - 6.75) = 9.25$
- data above $(Q3 + 1.5 \times IQR) = (20.5 + 6.75) = 27.25$

Therefore, in the dataset {(7), (8), 13, 16, 16, 17, 17, 18, 18, 19, 19, 20, 20, 21, 26, (30), (32)}

7, 8, 30, and 32 are outliers.

After removing the outliers, the lowest value (L) in the dataset is 13 and the highest value (H) in the dataset is 26.

Solution
continued

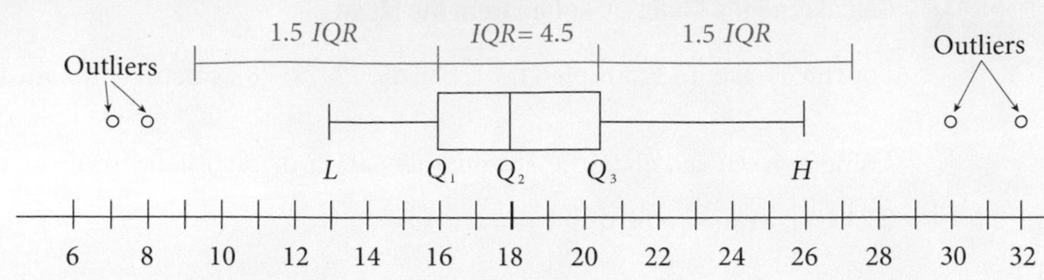

Deviation from the Mean

Different sets of data can produce the same mean. The second measure of dispersion (variability) is the **deviation from the mean**. It shows the amount by which each value or measurement in the dataset deviates from the mean. It indicates the spread of data from the mean of the data.

The deviation from the mean is calculated by subtracting the mean from each value in the dataset.

$$\textit{Deviation from mean} = x - \overline{x}$$

Example 11.3-f **Calculating the Deviation from the Mean**

Calculate the deviation from the mean in the sample dataset {55, 65, 70, 72, 78}.

Solution

First, calculate the mean.

$$\text{Mean, } \overline{x} = \frac{(55 + 65 + 70 + 72 + 78)}{5} = \frac{340}{5} = 68$$

The deviation of the first data in the dataset from the mean $= x - \overline{x} = 55 - 68 = -13$

That is, the first data in the dataset is 13 units below the mean.

Now, find the deviation of each data from the mean by subtracting the mean from each data and tabulate as follows:

x	$\overline{x}$	$(x - \overline{x})$
55	68	-13
65	68	-3
70	68	+2
72	68	+4
78	68	+10

$$\sum(x - \overline{x}) = 0$$

Average (Mean) Deviation from the Mean

In calculating the deviations from the mean, notice that some of the values are negative and others are positive; in fact, the sum of the deviations from the mean will always be zero. Therefore, to find the average deviation from the mean, we find the sum of the **absolute value** of each deviation and divide it by the number of values.

Formula 11.3-a **Average (Mean) Deviation from the Mean**

$$\textit{Mean deviation} = \frac{\sum|x - \overline{x}|}{n}$$

Example 11.3-g **Calculating the Mean Deviation from the Mean**

For the dataset in Example 11.3-f, {55, 65, 70, 72, 78}, calculate the mean deviation from the mean.

Solution

Using $\overline{x}$ = 68, calculate the absolute deviation of each data from the mean, $|x - \overline{x}|$, then calculate $\sum|x - \overline{x}|$, as shown below:

x	$\overline{x}$	$(x - \overline{x})$	$\lvert x - \overline{x}\rvert$
55	68	−13	13
65	68	−3	3
70	68	2	2
72	68	4	4
78	68	10	10
	$n = 5$	$\sum(x - \overline{x}) = 0$	$\sum\lvert x - \overline{x}\rvert = 32$

Using Formula 11.3-a, $\textit{Mean deviation} = \dfrac{\sum|x - \overline{x}|}{n} = \dfrac{32}{5} = 6.4$

Therefore, the mean deviation of the data from the mean is 6.4.

Variance

The third measure of dispersion (variability) is the **variance**. Like the average deviation from the mean, the variance is also a measure of the spread of numbers in a dataset. The greater the spread of the data values, the larger the value of the variance.

In calculating the deviations from the mean, we noticed that some of the values are negative and others are positive, resulting in a sum that is always equal to zero. To overcome this, the absolute values of the differences were used in the calculation of the average deviation. Alternatively, the variance calculates the **squares** of the differences between each data value and the mean, since the square of both negative and positive numbers is positive. Both variance and the average deviation from the mean complete their calculation by dividing by "n" to obtain an average.

Both of these calculations are better measures of dispersion of the dataset than the range, because they involve every piece of data, whereas the range calculation only uses the highest and lowest values.

The method of calculating variance depends on whether the dataset constitutes a population or is a sample. The variance of a population is represented by the symbol σ^2 (lower case Greek letter sigma, squared), and that of a sample by the symbol s^2 (lower case S, squared).

For a population, $\sigma^2 = \dfrac{\sum(x - \mu)^2}{N}$ where μ is the population mean and N is the number of data values in the population.

For a sample, $s^2 = \dfrac{\sum(x - \overline{x})^2}{n - 1}$ where $\overline{x}$ is the sample mean and n is the number of data values in the sample.

Note: For sample variance (s^2), the sum of squares of the deviations is divided by (n – 1), whereas for the population variance (σ^2), it is divided by N. The reason for dividing by (n – 1) for the sample variance is beyond the scope of this Basic Statistics chapter.

In the examples and exercises in this chapter, we will use the dataset of a sample for the calculation of variance. Follow these steps to calculate the variance of a sample:

Step 1: Determine the deviation of the data from the mean by subtracting the mean from each data item: $(x - \overline{x})$

Step 2: Square each deviation: $(x - \overline{x})^2$

Step 3: Sum the squared-deviations: $\sum(x - \overline{x})^2$

Step 4: Divide the sum of the squared deviations by the number of data minus one: $(n - 1)$

The result is the variance:

Formula 11.3-b **Variance (of a Sample)**

$$s^2 = \frac{\sum(x - \overline{x})^2}{n - 1}$$

Example 11.3-h **Calculating the Variance of a Sample Data**

Calculate the variance of the sample dataset in Example 11.3-f: {55, 65, 70, 72, 78}.

Solution

#	x	$\overline{x}$	$(x - \overline{x})$	$(x - \overline{x})^2$
1	55	68	−13	169
2	65	68	−3	9
3	70	68	+2	4
4	72	68	+4	16
5	78	68	+10	100
$n = 5$	$\sum x = 340$		$\sum(x - \overline{x}) = 0$	$\sum(x - \overline{x})^2 = 298$

$$\text{Mean, } \overline{x} = \frac{\sum x}{n} = \frac{340}{5} = 68$$

$$\text{Variance, } s^2 = \frac{\sum(x - \overline{x})^2}{n - 1} = \frac{298}{4} = 74.5$$

Therefore, the variance of the sample data is 74.5.

Standard Deviation

The fourth, and most common, measure of dispersion is the **standard deviation.** In the calculation of variance, the **square** of the deviations from the mean are totaled and divided by $(n - 1)$. Because of this, the standard deviation computes the **square root** of the variance, to obtain a measure of dispersion which is in the same units as the data.

That is,

$$\text{Population Standard Deviation, } \sigma = +\sqrt{\sigma^2} = \sqrt{\frac{\sum(x - \mu)^2}{N}}$$

$$\text{Sample Standard Deviation, } s = +\sqrt{s^2} = \sqrt{\frac{\sum(x - \overline{x})^2}{n - 1}}$$

As with variance, we will focus on datasets of samples in the calculations of standard deviation in the examples and exercises in this chapter.

Formula 11.3-c

Standard Deviation (of a Sample)

$$s = \sqrt{\frac{\sum (x - \overline{x})^2}{n - 1}}$$

Example 11.3-i

Calculating the Standard Deviation of a Sample

Calculate the standard deviation of the sample dataset in Example 11.3-h: {55, 65, 70, 72, 78}.

Solution

The variance of the sample dataset, as calculated in Example 11.3-h, is 74.5.

$$s^2 = 74.5$$
$$s = +\sqrt{74.5}$$
$$= 8.631338... = 8.63$$

Therefore, the standard deviation of the sample dataset is 8.63.

Datasets in which the values are close to each other reflect uniformity and consistency in the data. These datasets will have lower values for the average deviation from the mean, variance, and standard deviation, as well as narrower frequency distribution curves, as shown in the left-hand diagram below. Datasets in which the calculated measures of dispersion are larger, when graphed, will appear wider, as shown in the right-hand diagram below.

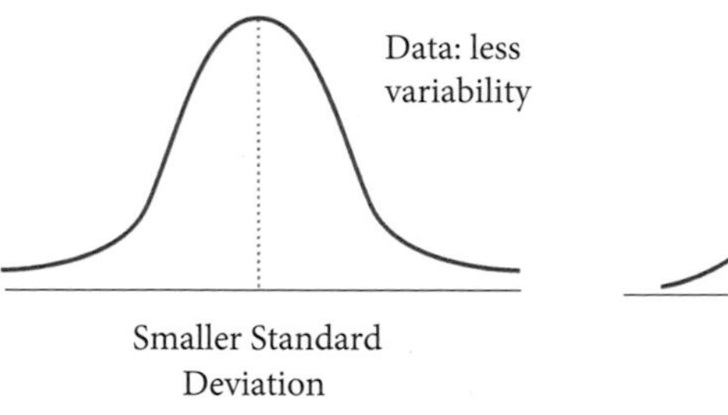

Smaller Standard Deviation

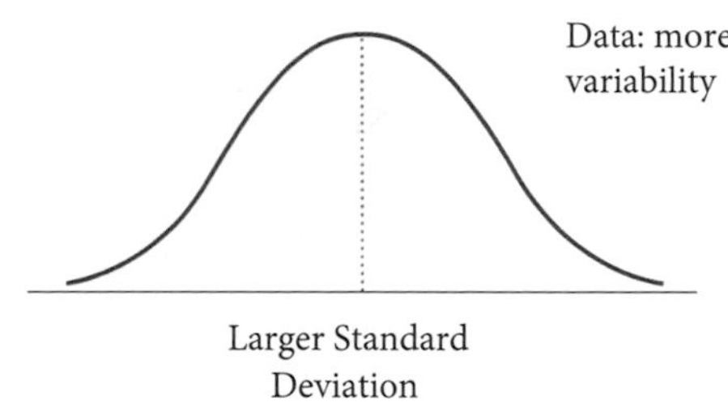

Larger Standard Deviation

Example 11.3-j

Comparing the Mean and Standard Deviation of Two Datasets

Calculate the mean and standard deviation of the following sample datasets and state which set is more uniform and consistent.

Dataset A = {10, 30, 50, 70}

Dataset B = {25, 38, 47, 58}

Solution

Dataset A

x	$\overline{x}$	$(x - \overline{x})$	$(x - \overline{x})^2$
10	40	−30	900
30	40	−10	100
50	40	+10	100
70	40	+30	900
$\sum x = 160$			$\sum(x - \overline{x})^2 = 2,000$

Dataset B

x	$\overline{x}$	$(x - \overline{x})$	$(x - \overline{x})^2$
25	42	−17	289
38	42	−4	16
47	42	+5	25
58	42	+16	256
$\sum x = 168$			$\sum(x - \overline{x})^2 = 586$

Solution
continued

Mean, $\bar{x} = \dfrac{\sum x}{n}$

$\bar{x} = \dfrac{160}{4} = 40$

Standard Deviation, $s = \sqrt{\dfrac{\sum (x - \bar{x})^2}{n - 1}}$

$s = \sqrt{\dfrac{2{,}000}{3}} \approx 25.82$

Mean, $\bar{x} = \dfrac{\sum x}{n}$

$\bar{x} = \dfrac{168}{4} = 42$

Standard Deviation, $s = \sqrt{\dfrac{\sum (x - \bar{x})^2}{n - 1}}$

$s = \sqrt{\dfrac{586}{3}} \approx 13.98$

Sample Statistic	Dataset A	Dataset B
Mean, $\bar{x}$	40	42
Standard Deviation, s	25.82	13.98

Dataset B has a lower standard deviation compared to Dataset A.

Therefore, the data in Dataset B is more uniform, consistent, and closer to the mean than the data in Dataset A.

11.3 | Exercises

Answers to odd-numbered problems are available at the end of the textbook.

1. Calculate the range for the following datasets:

   a. 56, 72, 98, 64, 87, 91, 22, 45

   b. 3, 13, 6, 12, 9, 8, 16, 15, 11, 10

   c. 72.9, 75.6, 74.3, 86.1, 80.5, 82.7

2. Calculate the range for the following datasets:

   a. 24, 15, 19, 29, 24, 22, 23, 20

   b. 113, 98, 107, 102, 123, 110

   c. 0.8, 1.3, 1.7, 2.1, 2.5, 2.8, 3.2, 3.5

3. Calculate the 1st and 3rd quartiles for the following datasets:

   a. 2, 3, 5, 7, 9, 13, 15, 18, 19, 20, 22, 23

   b. 98, 109, 123, 126, 127, 139, 139, 143, 147, 151, 175

4. Calculate the 1st and 3rd quartiles for the following datasets:

   a. 6, 7, 13, 17, 20, 25, 39, 41, 43, 49, 51, 62

   b. 50, 60, 73, 77, 80, 81, 82, 83, 84, 84, 84, 85, 88, 95, 100

5. Determine the inter-quartile range and identify the outliers, if any, for the datasets in Problem 3.

6. Determine the inter-quartile range and identify the outliers, if any, for the datasets in Problem 4.

7. In a dataset, $Q_1 = 44$, median = 48, and $Q_3 = 58$.

   a. A value greater than what number would be an outlier?

   b. A value less than what number would be an outlier?

8. In a dataset, $Q_1 = 75$, median = 80, and $Q_3 = 85$.

   a. A value greater than what number would be an outlier?

   b. A value less than what number would be an outlier?

9. For the dataset {76, 98, 102, 104, 76, 96, 57, 97, 99}, compute the following:

   a. Median

   b. 1st and 3rd quartiles

   c. Inter-quartile range

   d. Outliers, if any.

10. For the dataset {104, 139, 123, 142, 57, 104, 153, 105, 139}, compute the following:

    a. Median

    b. 1st and 3rd quartiles

    c. Inter-quartile range

    d. Outliers, if any.

11. Draw a box-and-whisker plot for the data in Problem 9.

12. Draw a box-and-whisker plot for the data in Problem 10.

13. Given the following information for a dataset, draw a box-and-whisker plot:

Lowest value	82
1st quartile	94
Median	95
3rd quartile	102
Highest value	110

14. Given the following information for a dataset, draw a box-and-whisker plot:

Lowest value	2
1st quartile	6
Median	11.5
3rd quartile	16
Highest value	30

15. Calculate the mean absolute deviation for the dataset: {92, 75, 95, 90, 98}.

16. Calculate the mean absolute deviation for the dataset: {26, 87, 34, 21, 67, 92, 74}.

17. Which of the following datasets has the greater mean absolute deviation?

    a. 1, 2, 3, 4, 5 b. 1, 4, 9, 12, 15

18. Which of the following datasets has the greater mean absolute deviation?

    a. 3, 9, 15, 21, 27 b. 3, 5, 9, 12, 18

19. Calculate the variance and standard deviation of the datasets in Problem 17.

20. Calculate the variance and standard deviation of the datasets in Problem 18.

21. Given the following information of a sample data, calculate the variance and standard deviation:

    $n = 10$, sum of the squared deviation = 40, and the sum of the data = 610.

22. Given the following information of a sample data, calculate the variance and standard deviation:

    $n = 5$, sum of the squared deviation = 46, and the sum of the data = 40.

23. The weights (in kilograms) of a group of ten randomly selected men are as follows:

    82 79 80 80 72 74 88 82 92 83

    Calculate: a. The mean b. The standard deviation

24. The marks of a group of ten students are as follows:

    77 82 43 63 59 61 66 61 76 54

    Calculate: a. The mean b. The standard deviation

25. The following are the annual incomes of five, randomly selected professors of a college: $75,000, $78,000, $72,000, $83,000, and $90,000. Compute the following:

    a. Mean
    b. Mean absolute deviation
    c. Variance
    d. Standard deviation

26. The following are the weekly incomes for a group of seven, randomly selected employees: $875, $945, $905, $885, $910, $820, $841. Compute the following:

    a. Mean
    b. Mean absolute deviation
    c. Variance
    d. Standard deviation

11 | Review Exercises

Answers to odd-numbered problems are available at the end of the textbook.

1. a. State the difference between discrete and continuous variables.

   b. State the difference between the classifications of interval and ratio in the levels of measurement.

2. a. State the difference between quantitative and qualitative variables.

   b. State the difference between the classifications of nominal and ordinal in levels of measurement.

For Problems 3 and 4, identify the data type (as quantitative or qualitative, and if quantitative, identify as discrete or continuous) and specify the appropriate measurement scale (as nominal, ordinal, interval, or ratio).

3. a. Gender
   b. Year of birth
   c. Volume of a container
   d. Number of correct answers
   e. Time to complete homework

4. a. Nationality
   b. Ranking of favourite food
   c. Average marks on an exam
   d. Number of trees in a park
   e. Distance between two cities

5. The grades on a math exam for a sample of 40 students are provided below:

   69 83 66 72 88 52 60 71 40 62
   49 58 78 74 56 45 81 65 68 91
   59 61 73 67 76 45 79 80 51 76
   96 65 55 84 44 51 63 53 65 54

   a. Construct a stem-and-leaf plot to display the data in an array.

   b. Group the above data using a class width of 10.

6. The ages of a sample of 40 students in a college are provided below:

   24 26 26 20 22 19 28 21 25 24
   19 23 21 21 20 21 23 23 27 21
   19 19 19 22 29 30 18 18 21 26
   26 25 21 22 22 20 24 26 29 23

   a. Construct a stem-and-leaf plot to display the data in an array.

   b. Group the above data using a class width of 2.

7. The five departments of a company had the following net profits last year:

Department	Profit ($ Thousands)
Dept. A	750
Dept. B	325
Dept. C	475
Dept. D	275
Dept. E	625

Represent the above information using:

a. A horizontal bar chart.

b. A line graph.

c. A pie chart.

8. The survey results of a sample of 50 students on their favourite sport is provided below:

Favourite Sport	Number of students
Swimming	10
Tennis	18
Basketball	12
Badminton	6
Volleyball	4

Represent the above information using:

a. A horizontal bar chart.

b. A line graph.

c. A pie chart.

9. The following table shows the starting salaries of a sample of recent business graduates:

Income ($ Thousands)	Number of Graduates
15 - 19	40
20 - 24	60
25 - 29	80
30 - 34	18
35 – 39	2

Calculate the percent of graduates who earn the following starting salaries:

a. At least $30,000.

b. Less than $25,000.

c. At least $20,000.

10. The following table shows the number of years of service of a group of employees at a college:

Years	Frequency
0 to under 5	10
5 to under 10	14
10 to under 15	39
15 to under 20	24
20 to under 25	13

Calculate the percent of employees with the following years of service:

a. Less than 10 years of service.

b. More than 20 years of service.

c. Between 10 and 20 years of service.

11. The following frequency distribution shows scores earned by a sample of 100 students on an Aptitude Examination marked out of 200:

Marks out of 200	Number of students
25 to under 50	5
50 to under 75	18
75 to under 100	28
100 to under 125	32
125 to under 150	8
150 to under 175	6
175 to under 200	3

Construct the following for the above data:

a. Histogram and frequency polygon.

b. Relative frequency and percent frequency distributions.

c. Relative cumulative frequency and cumulative percent frequency distributions.

d. Cumulative frequency and cumulative percent curve.

12. The following frequency distribution shows the ages of 50 employees in an organization:

Age	Number of employees
30 to under 40	3
40 to under 50	5
50 to under 60	7
60 to under 70	12
70 to under 80	16
80 to under 90	5
90 to under 100	2

Construct the following for the above data:

a. Histogram and frequency polygon.

b. Relative frequency and percent frequency distributions.

c. Relative cumulative frequency and cumulative percent frequency distributions.

d. Cumulative frequency and cumulative percent curve.

13. For the following data in ascending order {84, 89, 91, 92, 93, 93, 95, 96, 97, 98, 100}:

a. Determine the mean, median, and mode.

b. Determine the 1st and 3rd quartiles.

c. Determine the inter-quartile range.

d. Identify outliers, if any.

e. Draw a box-and-whisker plot for the data.

14. For the data given in ascending order {10, 16, 18, 20, 20, 20, 22, 22, 24, 25, 26, 29}:

a. Determine the mean, median, and mode.

b. Determine the 1st and 3rd quartiles.

c. Determine the inter-quartile range.

d. Identify outliers, if any.

e. Draw a box-and-whisker plot for the data.

15. Monthly rent (in dollars) for a sample of 18, two-bedroom condominium units in downtown Toronto are provided in the table below:

Rental amount ($)	Number of units
2,400	1
2,600	2
2,700	7
2,800	5
2,900	3

Determine the mean, median, and mode of the rent for the two-bedroom condominium units, and determine the shape of the distribution.

16. The market values of 15, four-bedroom houses in Toronto are provided in the table below:

Value of house ($)	Number of houses
550,000	1
600,000	4
650,000	3
700,000	5
850,000	2

Determine the mean, median, and mode of the market values for the four-bedroom houses, and determine the shape of the distribution.

17. For the grouped data in Problem 11:

a. Determine the mean.

b. Determine the modal class and the mode.

c. Determine the median class and the median.

18. For the grouped data in Problem 12:

a. Determine the mean.

b. Determine the modal class and the mode.

c. Determine the median class and the median.

19. For the data in Problem 13, compute the following:

a. Average (mean) deviation from the mean.

b. Variance.

c. Standard deviation.

20. For the data in Problem 14, compute the following:

a. Average (mean) deviation from the mean.

b. Variance.

c. Standard deviation.

21. In a frequency distribution, the mean is 32 and the mode is 56. Using the Empirical relationship among mean, median, and mode, estimate the median and comment on the nature of the distribution.

22. In a frequency distribution, the median is 19 and the mode is 23. Using the Empirical relationship among mean, median, and mode, estimate the mean and comment on the nature of the distribution.

23. The evaluation components for a subject are as follows: tests 20%, midterm 25%, final exam 30%, online labs 15%, and homework 10%. A student obtained the following marks: 86% (tests), 96% (midterm), 82% (final exam), 98% (online labs), and 100% (homework). Organize the scores and weights in a table to calculate the weighted mean of the scores.

24. The evaluation components for a subject are as follows: tests 40%, weekly assignments 10%, book reviews 15%, in-class exercises 5%, and final exam 30%. A student obtained the following marks: 75% (tests), 85% (weekly assignments), 98% (book reviews), 90% (in-class exercises), and 80% (final exam). Organize the scores and weights in a table to calculate the weighted mean of the scores.

25. Calculate the mean deviation from the mean of the following datasets:

a. {3, 9, 15, 21, 27}

b. {24, 37, 21, 32, 25, 36, 22, 28}

26. Calculate the mean deviation from the mean of the following datasets:

a. {7, 10, 19, 15, 28]

b. {98, 102, 107, 110, 113, 123}

27. Compute the mean, median, variance, and standard deviation of the following dataset: {17, 22, 20, 18, 23}.

28. Compute the mean, median, variance, and standard deviation of the following dataset: {30, 28, 35, 40, 25}.

Self-Test | Chapter 11

Answers to all problems are available at the end of the textbook.

1. For each of the following, identify the data type (as quantitative or qualitative, and if quantitative, as discrete or continuous) and specify the appropriate measurement scale (as nominal, ordinal, interval, or ratio):

   a. Marital status.

   b. Number of cars in a parking lot.

   c. Travel time from home to college.

   d. Letter grades in a final exam.

   e. Annual salary.

2. The grades on a math exam for a sample of 40 students are provided below:

   63 74 42 65 51 54 36 56 68 57

   62 64 76 67 79 61 81 77 59 38

   84 68 71 94 71 86 69 75 91 55

   48 82 83 54 79 62 68 58 41 47

   a. Construct a stem-and-leaf display for the data.

   b. Construct a frequency distribution and relative frequency distribution for the data, using seven class intervals of width 10.

3. The Consumer Price Index for the years 2009 to 2016 is provided below:

Year	CPI
2009	114.4
2010	116.5
2011	119.9
2012	121.7
2013	122.8
2014	125.2
2015	126.6
2016	128.4

   Represent the above information using:

   a. A horizontal bar chart.

   b. A line graph.

4. Draw a pie chart to represent the following investment funds of a corporation:

Fund	Amount ($ Thousands)
GIC	270
Bond	216
Equity	108
Fixed Income	162
Money Market	144

5. The following frequency distribution shows the hourly wages earned by a sample of 50 students during their summer employment:

Hourly wages ($)	Number of students
15 to under 20	4
20 to under 25	8
25 to under 30	12
30 to under 35	16
35 to under 40	5
40 to under 45	3
45 to under 50	2

   Construct the following for the above data:

   a. Histogram and frequency polygon.

   b. Relative frequency and percent frequency distributions.

   c. Relative cumulative frequency and cumulative percent frequency distributions.

   d. Cumulative frequency and cumulative percent curve.

6. For the following data in ascending order {40, 46, 47, 48, 49, 49, 50, 51, 52, 53, 58}:

   a. Determine the mean, median, and mode.

   b. Determine the 1st and 3rd quartiles.

   c. Determine the inter-quartile range.

   d. Identify outliers, if any.

   e. Draw a box-and-whisker plot for the data.

7. For the grouped data in Problem 5:

   a. Determine the mean.

   b. Determine the modal class and the mode.

   c. Determine the median class and the median.

8. For the data in Problem 6, compute the following:

   a. Average (mean) deviation from the mean.

   b. Variance.

   c. Standard deviation.

9. In a frequency distribution, the mode is 65 and the median is 122. Using the Empirical relationship among mean, median, and mode, estimate the mean and comment on the nature of the distribution.

10. Calculate the mean deviation from the mean of the following datasets:

    a. {1, 5, 3, 7, 6, 9} b. {80, 85, 81, 0, 85, 90, 87, 92}

11. Compute the mean, median, variance, and standard deviation of the following dataset:

    {23, 45, 49, 25, 34, 31, 19, 20, 59, 31, 21}

11 | Summary of Notation and Formulas

MEASURES OF CENTRAL TENDENCY

Mean:

$$\bar{x} = \frac{\sum x_i}{n}$$

$\sum x_i$ ← Sum of values of 'n' observations
n ← Number of observations

Weighted Mean:

$$\bar{x} = \frac{\sum (x_i \cdot w_i)}{\sum w_i}$$

$\sum (x_i \cdot w_i)$ ← Sum of the weighted values
$\sum w_i$ ← Sum of the weighting factors

Geometric Mean:

$$G = \sqrt[n]{x_1 \cdot x_2 \cdot x_3 \cdot \ldots \cdot x_n} = \left(x_1 \cdot x_2 \cdot x_3 \cdot \ldots \cdot x_n\right)^{\frac{1}{n}}$$

Median:

Median = the value of the middle term when the terms are in an array

$$\textit{Median Position} = \left(\frac{n+1}{2}\right)$$

Mode:

Mode = the most frequent value in the data

Grouped Data:

$$\bar{x} = \frac{\sum (x_m \cdot f)}{\sum f}$$

$\sum (x_m \cdot f)$ ← Sum of the class midpoints × class frequencies
$\sum f$ ← Sum of the class frequencies

Median = class midpoint of the class interval containing the middle term (median class)

$$\textit{Median Position} = \left(\frac{n+1}{2}\right)$$

Mode = class midpoint of the class interval containing the highest frequency (modal class)

Empirical Relationship among Mean, Median, and Mode:

Mean – *Mode* = 3(*Mean* – *Median*)

MEASURES OF DISPERSION

Range:

Range = *Highest value* – *Lowest value*

$$R = H - L$$

Inter-quartile Range:

$$IQR = Q_3 - Q_1$$

Average (Mean) Deviation from the Mean:

$$\textit{Mean deviation} = \frac{\sum |x - \bar{x}|}{n}$$

$\sum |x - \bar{x}|$ ← Sum of absolute deviation of terms from the mean
n ← Number of terms

Variance (of a Sample):

$$s^2 = \frac{\sum (x - \bar{x})^2}{n - 1}$$

$\bar{x}$ = Sample Mean
n = Number of terms in sample

Standard deviation (of a Sample):

$$s = \sqrt{\frac{\sum (x - \bar{x})^2}{n - 1}}$$

Chapter

12 BASIC PROBABILITY

LEARNING OBJECTIVES

- Define and differentiate between objective and subjective probability, as well as empirical and classical probability.
- Understand and use the language of inferential statistics.
- Calculate probabilities using the basic rules of probability.
- Determine odds for and odds against an event.
- Identify properties of the normal distribution and the normal curve.
- Apply the empirical rule to a set of data and draw conclusions about the data.

CHAPTER OUTLINE

Introduction

In the previous chapter, the methods for presenting data using graphs, charts, tables, etc., as well as summarizing data using measures of central tendency and dispersion, were outlined. That is, in the previous chapter, we focused on **descriptive statistics**.

The next step is to analyze the data of the sample taken from the population and use the sample evidence to make inferences about the population. This is known as **inferential statistics**. Statistical inference involves making generalizations or inferences about population parameters, based on observations in the sample statistic.

Probability theory is the basis for statistical inference. Therefore, the knowledge of probability is essential to make decisions about the population based on sample statistics. Probability involves the use of mathematics to describe the level of certainty (likelihood, chance, or possibility) that an event will occur. We hear about probabilities in everyday situations, such as in weather forecasts (probability of rain or snow), or in the lottery (probability of winning).

In this chapter, we will learn about the fundamentals of probability theory and the basic rules of probability. We will also introduce a very common probability distribution used throughout statistics: the normal distribution.

12.1 | Fundamentals of Probability Theory

Measures of Probability

The probability of an event cannot be negative or greater than 1.

Values describing the probability of an event lie between 0 and 1 (inclusive), and they can be expressed as fractions, decimals, or percents. For example, a probability of $\frac{1}{2}$ (or 0.5 or 50%) indicates that there is an equal chance that a particular event will, or will not, occur. The probability of an event which cannot (or never will) occur is 0, while the probability of an event which will definitely occur is 1 (or 100%).

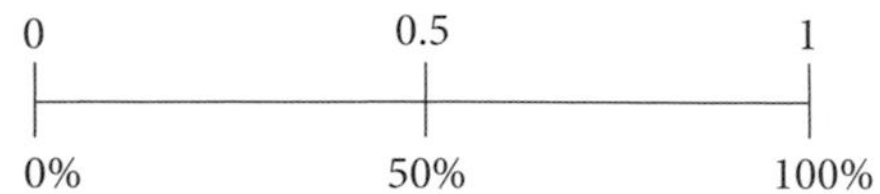

Approaches to Probability

There are two major approaches to probability theory: subjective and objective approaches.

Subjective Probability

The probability of an event, based on judgment, belief, experience, knowledge of known facts, or interpretation is known as **subjective probability**.

This approach is mostly applicable in business, finance, marketing, etc., in making quick decisions or statements without performing any formal calculations (e.g., the probability that the mortgage rate will increase next year is 90%). The disadvantage of subjective probability is that two or more persons may state different probabilities for the same event based on their judgment, knowledge on the subject, etc.

Objective Probability

The probability of an event, using theoretical methods or calculations based on observation or actual measurements, rather than personal judgment is known as **objective probability**.

In this section, the basics of probability and the methods to solve simple probability problems using objective probability will be discussed. This will help to develop a better understanding of probability in statistics to make inferences about a population, based on sample evidence.

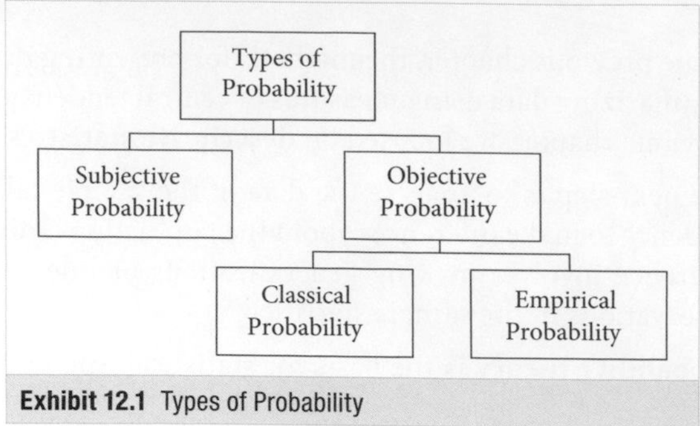

Exhibit 12.1 Types of Probability

Objective probabilities are more accurate than subjective probabilities. In objective probability, there are two approaches for finding the probabilities of events: using classical probability or empirical probability. Before we can define these approaches, we must introduce some terminology.

Terminology

We will now formally define some of the terms that are commonly used in probability: experiment, outcome, event, and sample space.

- An **experiment** is a process or action that produces one well-defined result of several possible results (i.e., the action performed).
- An **outcome** is a particular result of a single trial of an experiment (i.e., what is observed and recorded from the experiment).
- An **event** is a single outcome or a collection of outcomes of interest from an experiment (i.e., what is being looked for from the experiment). Usually, events are denoted by capital letters, e.g., A, B, E, etc.

An event is a subset of the sample space.

- The **sample space** is the set of all possible outcomes in an experiment. The symbol used for sample space is "S".

Example 12.1-a Tossing a Coin and Identifying Experiment, Outcome, Event, and Sample Space

A coin is tossed once. The result of interest is tossing Heads (H).

(i) Identify the experiment, all possible outcomes, and the sample space.

(ii) Identify the event and all possible outcomes in the event.

Solution

(i) **Experiment:** Tossing a coin once

Outcomes: Tossing either Heads H or Tails T

Sample space: $S = \{H, T\}$, the set of all possible outcomes

(ii) **Event:** Let E be the event of tossing Heads (H).

$E = \{H\}$, i.e., there is only one outcome in the sample space that will result in this event.

Example 12.1-b Tossing Two Coins and Identifying Experiment, Outcome, Event, and Sample Space

Two coins are tossed once. The result of interest is tossing one Heads (H) and one Tails (T).

(i) Identify the experiment, all possible outcomes, and the sample space.

(ii) Identify the event and all possible outcomes in the event.

Solution

(i) **Experiment:** Tossing two coins once

Outcomes: Each coin toss will result in either Heads H or Tails T

Therefore, the outcomes of tossing two coins are: Heads and Heads (H, H), Heads and Tails (H, T), Tails and Heads (T, H), or Tails and Tails (T, T)

Sample space: $S = \{(H, H), (H, T), (T, H), (T, T)\}$, the set of all possible outcomes

(ii) **Event:** Let E be the event of tossing one Heads (H) and one Tails (T).

$E = \{(H, T), (T, H)\}$, i.e., there are two outcomes in the sample space that will result in this event.

Example 12.1-c **Rolling a Die and Identifying Experiment, Outcome, Event, and Sample Space**

A standard die is rolled once. The result of interest is rolling an even number.

(i) Identify the experiment, all possible outcomes, and the sample space.

(ii) Identify the event and all possible outcomes in the event.

Solution

(i) **Experiment:** Rolling a die once

Outcomes: Rolling any of the numbers 1, 2, 3, 4, 5, or 6

Sample space: $S = \{1, 2, 3, 4, 5, 6\}$, the set of all possible outcomes

(ii) **Event:** Let E be the event of rolling an even number.

$E = \{2, 4, 6\}$, i.e., there are three outcomes in the sample space that will result in this event.

Classical Probability

Classical probability, also known as theoretical probability, is based on mathematical analysis and on the assumption that the outcomes of an experiment are equally likely.

For example, if there are "n" possible outcomes of an experiment and if all the outcomes are equally likely, then we assign a probability of $\frac{1}{n}$ for each outcome. The classical probability of an event E, denoted $P(E)$, is calculated as follows:

$P(E)$ denotes 'the probability of event E', $n(E)$ denotes 'the number of outcomes in event E', and $n(S)$ denotes 'the number of outcomes in the sample space'

$$P(E) = \frac{\textit{Number of favourable outcomes of event "E"}}{\textit{Total number of possible outcomes}}$$

$$P(E) = \frac{n(E)}{n(S)}$$

For example, as seen in Example 12.1-a, if you toss a coin once, there are two possible outcomes: Heads (H) or Tails (T). The probability of getting Heads (H) is calculated as follows:

Number of possible outcomes in the event, i.e., tossing H, is one: $n(E) = 1$

Total outcomes in the sample space, $S = \{H, T\}$, is two: $n(S) = 2$

Using $P(E) = \frac{n(E)}{n(S)}$, $\qquad P(H) = \frac{1}{2}$

Example 12.1-d

Classical Approach to Probability

A 6-sided die is rolled once. Determine the probability of the following events:

(i) Event A: Rolling the number 3.

(ii) Event B: Rolling any number less than 4.

(iii) Event C: Rolling a number 5 or more.

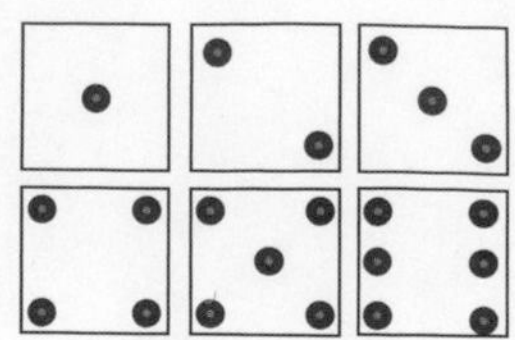

Solution

The die has 6 sides, and each number (outcome) is equally-likely to be rolled.

Therefore, using the classical approach to probability, $P(E) = \frac{n(E)}{n(S)}$, where $n(S) = 6$:

(i) There is only one outcome for the event of rolling the number 3: $A = \{3\}$. Therefore, $n(A) = 1$.

$$P(A) = \frac{1}{6}$$

Therefore, the probability of rolling the number 3 is $\frac{1}{6}$.

(ii) There are three outcomes for the event of rolling any number less than 4: $B = \{1, 2, 3\}$. Therefore, $n(B) = 3$.

$$P(B) = \frac{3}{6} = \frac{1}{2}$$

Therefore, the probability of rolling any number less than 4 is $\frac{1}{2}$.

(iii) There are two outcomes for the event of rolling a number 5 or more: $C = \{5, 6\}$. Therefore, $n(C) = 2$.

$$P(C) = \frac{2}{6} = \frac{1}{3}$$

Therefore, the probability of rolling a number 5 or more is $\frac{1}{3}$.

Empirical Probability

Empirical probability, also known as the relative frequency approach to probability, is more applicable to situations where the outcomes of an experiment are not equally likely. The empirical probability is based on results from direct observation or past results.

For example, if you conduct an experiment repeatedly, for "n" times, and observed that a particular event "E" occurs "f" times, then the empirical probability of the event E, $P(E)$, is calculated as follows:

$$\mathbf{P(E)} = \frac{\textit{Number of times (frequency) that event "E" occurs}}{\textit{Number of trials}}$$

$$\mathbf{P(E)} = \frac{f}{n}$$

The empirical probability of event E is the relative frequency of event E.

For example, if a coin is tossed 20 times and the frequency of Heads (H) is observed 7 times, then the relative frequency of obtaining Heads (H) is calculated as follows:

Number of times (frequency) of event, $f = 7$
Number of trials, $n = 20$

Using $P(E) = \frac{f}{n}$, $\quad P(H) = \frac{7}{20}$

Note: The result from empirical probability may differ from classical probability, when only a few trials are carried out. If more trials are carried out, then the result will approximate or equal that calculated from classical (theoretical) probability.

Example 12.1-e

Empirical Approach to Probability

Out of 150 LED bulbs tested, 15 of them were defective. Based on this, what is the probability that an LED bulb that you purchase will be defective?

Solution

Using $P(E) = \frac{f}{n}$,

$$P(defective) = \frac{15}{150} = \frac{1}{10}$$

Therefore, the probability of purchasing a defective bulb is $\frac{1}{10}$.

Using Tree Diagrams to Determine the Sample Space

Most of the situations examined in this chapter will use the classical approach to probability. In order to calculate probability using this approach, it is first necessary to fully determine the outcomes in the sample space, S.

The sample space for an experiment can be easily illustrated using a **tree diagram**. In a tree diagram, each outcome is represented by a branch of a tree. Below is a tree diagram to demonstrate the possible outcomes of tossing a coin twice.

Step 1: When the coin is tossed once, there are two possible outcomes: Heads (H) and Tails (T). Therefore, start drawing two branches from a point and mark the end of one branch as H and the other as T.

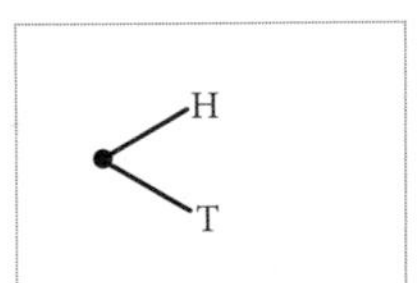

Step 2: When the coin is tossed a second time, there are two possible outcomes, H and T, as in the first toss. Draw two branches from the end point H (from Step 1) and mark the end of one branch as H and the other as T. This is to show the possible outcomes of a second toss when the outcome of the first toss is H.

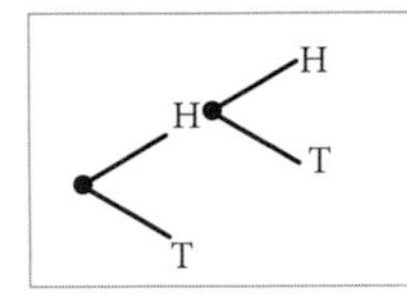

Step 3: Similarly, draw two branches from the end point T (from Step 1) and mark the end of one branch as H and the other as T. This is to show the possible outcomes of a second toss when the outcome of the first toss is T.

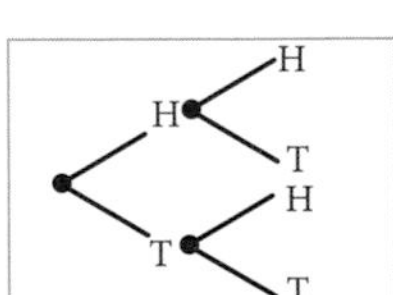

Step 4: There are 4 end points marked H, T, H, and T. To identify the outcomes in the sample space, trace through the branches to the starting point to identify all the possible outcomes.

Therefore, the sample space, $S = \{HH, TH, HT, TT\}$.

Example 12.1-f Drawing a Tree Diagram for Tossing Three Coins to Determine Sample Space

Three coins are tossed. Draw a tree diagram and list the sample space.

Solution

The possible equally-likely outcomes for each coin toss are Heads (H) or Tails (T).

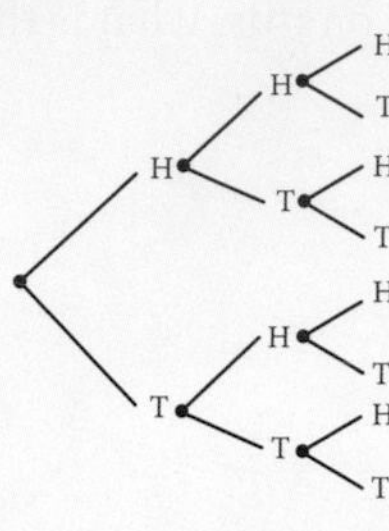

$$S = \{(H, H, H), (T, H, H), (H, T, H), (T, T, H),\\ (H, H, T), (T, H, T), (H, T, T), (T, T, T)\}$$

Example 12.1-g Identifying Events when Three Coins are Tossed

Three coins are tossed. Using the sample space generated in Example 12.1-f, list all the possible outcomes for the following events:

(i) At least two H.

(ii) Two T and one H.

Solution

(i) Let A be the event of tossing at least two H.

Using the sample space from Example 12.1-f,

$A = \{(H, H, H), (T, H, H), (H, T, H), (H, H, T)\}$

i.e., there are four outcomes in the sample space that will result in this event

(ii) Let B be the event of tossing two T and one H.

Using the sample space from Example 12.1-f,

$B = \{(T, T, H), (T, H, T), (H, T, T)\}$

i.e., there are three outcomes in the sample space that will result in this event

Example 12.1-h Calculating the Probability of an Event when Three Coins are Tossed

Three coins are tossed. Calculate the probability that at least two heads are obtained.

Solution

From Example 12.1-f, the sample space for tossing three coins is as follows:

$$S = \{(H, H, H), (T, H, H), (H, T, H), (T, T, H), (H, H, T), (T, H, T), (H, T, T), (T, T, T)\}$$

Therefore, $n(S) = 8$.

From Example 12.1-g, the event A of tossing at least two H is as follows:

$$A = \{(H, H, H), (T, H, H), (H, T, H), (H, H, T)\}$$

Therefore, $n(A) = 4$.

Using $P(E) = \dfrac{n(E)}{n(S)}$,

$$P(\text{at least 2 } H) = \frac{4}{8} = \frac{1}{2}$$

Therefore, the probability that at least two heads are obtained is $\frac{1}{2}$, or 50%.

Example 12.1-i **Drawing a Tree Diagram for Rolling Two Dice to Determine Sample Space**

Two dice are rolled simultaneously. Draw a tree diagram and list the sample space.

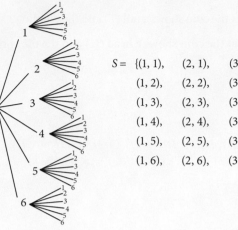

Solution

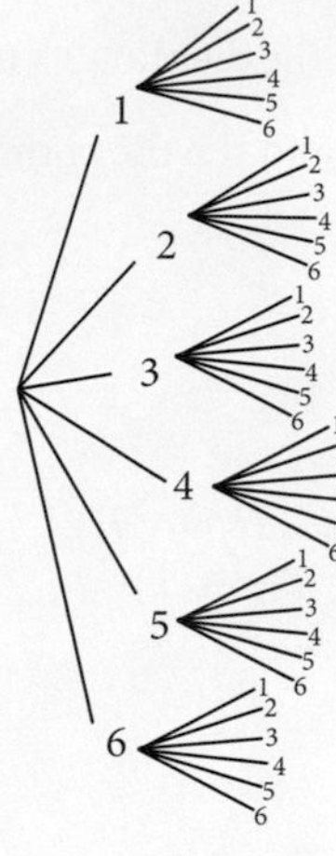

$S =$	{(1, 1),	(2, 1),	(3, 1),	(4, 1),	(5, 1),	(6, 1)
	(1, 2),	(2, 2),	(3, 2),	(4, 2),	(5, 2),	(6, 2)
	(1, 3),	(2, 3),	(3, 3),	(4, 3),	(5, 3),	(6, 3)
	(1, 4),	(2, 4),	(3, 4),	(4, 4),	(5, 4),	(6, 4)
	(1, 5),	(2, 5),	(3, 5),	(4, 5),	(5, 5),	(6, 5)
	(1, 6),	(2, 6),	(3, 6),	(4, 6),	(5, 6),	(6, 6)}

Example 12.1-j **Identifying Events when Two Dice are Rolled**

Two dice are rolled. Using the sample space generated in Example 12.1-i, list all the possible outcomes for the following events:

(i) Event A: Numbers on the faces of the dice are equal.

(ii) Event B: The sum of numbers on the faces of the dice is equal to 5.

(iii) Event C: The sum of numbers on the faces of the dice is less than 5.

(iv) Event D: The sum of numbers on the faces of the dice is more than 9.

Solution

Using the sample space from Example 12.1-i,

(i) Event A: Numbers on the faces of the dice are equal
$A = \{(1, 1), (2, 2), (3, 3), (4, 4), (5, 5), (6, 6)\}$

(ii) Event B: The sum of numbers on the faces of the dice is equal to 5
$B = \{(1, 4), (2, 3), (3, 2), (4, 1)\}$

(iii) Event C: The sum of numbers on the faces of the dice is less than 5
$C = \{(1, 1), (2, 1), (3, 1), (1, 2), (2, 2), (1, 3)\}$

(iv) Event D: The sum of numbers on the faces of the dice is more than 9
$D = \{(6, 4), (5, 5), (6, 5), (4, 6), (5, 6), (6, 6)\}$

Example 12.1-k **Calculating the Probability of an Event from Tossing a Coin and Rolling a Die**

A coin is tossed and a die is rolled.

(i) List the sample space using a tree diagram.

(ii) Determine the probability that the coin shows a tail (T) and the die shows a number less than 5.

(iii) Determine the probability that the coin shows a head (H) and the die shows an even number.

Solution

(i)

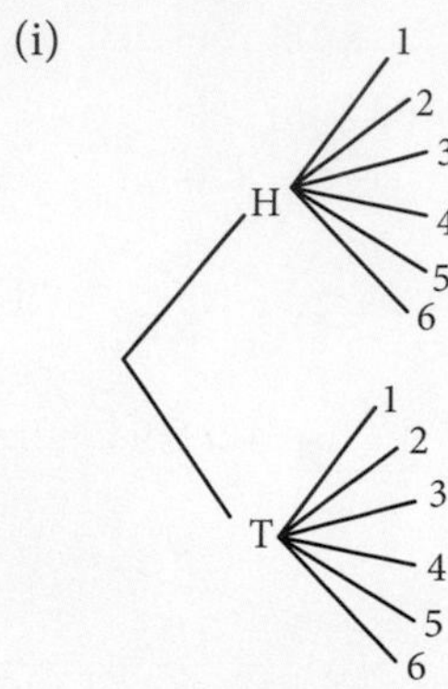

$S = \{(1, H), (2, H), (3, H), (4, H), (5, H), (6, H),$
$(1, T), (2, T), (3, T), (4, T), (5, T), (6, T)\}$

$n(S) = 12$

(ii) Let E be the event where the coin shows a tail (T) and the die shows a number less than 5.

$E = \{(1, T), (2, T), (3, T), (4, T)\}$

$n(E) = 4$

$$P(E) = \frac{n(E)}{n(S)} = \frac{4}{12} = \frac{1}{3}$$

(iii) Let E be the event where the coin shows a head (H) and the die shows an even number.

$E = \{(2, H), (4, H), (6, H)\}$

$n(E) = 3$

$$P(E) = \frac{n(E)}{n(S)} = \frac{3}{12} = \frac{1}{4}$$

Applications of Calculating Probability

Example 12.1-l **Calculating the Probability of an Event in a Game Involving a Spinning Wheel**

A game of chance involves spinning a wheel that has 10 equal sectors marked $S, T, A, T, I, S, T, I, C$, and S, as shown in the diagram.

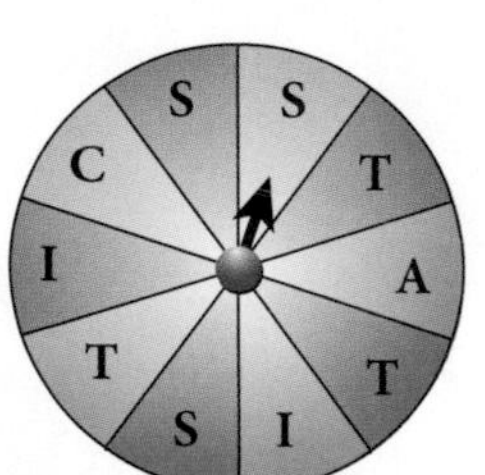

If you spin the wheel, determine the chances of landing on:

(i) S

(ii) I

(iii) Either I or S

(iv) Either S or T

Solution

Number of equal sectors = 10; i.e., $n(S) = 10$

Number of sectors of $S = 3$

Number of sectors of $T = 3$

Number of sectors of $A = 1$

Number of sectors of $I = 2$

Number of sectors of $C = 1$

Using $P(E) = \dfrac{n(E)}{n(S)}$,

(i) Let E be the event of landing on S.

$n(E) = 3$

$P(E) = \dfrac{3}{10} = 0.30 = 30\%$

(ii) Let E be the event of landing on I.

$n(E) = 2$

$P(E) = \dfrac{2}{10} = 0.20 = 20\%$

(iii) Let E be the event of landing on I or S.

$n(E) = 2 + 3 = 5$

$P(E) = \dfrac{5}{10} = 0.5 = 50\%$

(iv) Let E be the event of landing on S or T.

$n(E) = 3 + 3 = 6$

$P(E) = \dfrac{6}{10} = 0.6 = 60\%$

To solve probability problems involving cards, there are a few basic facts about a deck of cards that need to be remembered:

1. A standard deck of playing cards consists of 52 cards containing 4 suits, each with 13 cards.
2. Two suits, the spades and clubs, are black; i.e., there are 26 black cards.

Spades		Diamonds	
Clubs	♣	Hearts	♥

3. Two suits, the diamonds and hearts, are red; i.e., there are 26 red cards.
4. The 13 cards in each suit are: Ace, 2, 3, 4, 5, 6, 7, 8, 9, 10, Jack, Queen, King.
5. The Jack, Queen, and King cards from each suit are called the face (or picture) cards; i.e., there are $3 \times 4 = 12$ face cards.

"Ace" is not a face (or picture) card.

Example 12.1-m

Calculating the Probability of an Event Involving a Deck of Cards

A card is drawn at random from a standard deck of cards. Calculate the probability of obtaining the following (assume that the drawn card is put back into the deck after each draw):

(i) A red card (ii) A face card (iii) A King

Solution

$n(S) = 52$

Using $P(E) = \dfrac{n(E)}{n(S)}$,

(i) Let E be the event of obtaining a red card.

$n(E) = 13 + 13 = 26$

$P(\textit{red card}) = \dfrac{26}{52} = \dfrac{1}{2}$

Solution *continued*

(ii) Let E be the event of obtaining a face card.

$n(E) = 4 \times 3 = 12$

$P(face\ card) = \frac{12}{52} = \frac{3}{13}$

(iii) Let E be the event of obtaining a King.

$n(E) = 1 \times 4 = 4$

$P(King) = \frac{4}{52} = \frac{1}{13}$

Example 12.1-n **Calculating the Probability of an Event Involving Marbles in a Box**

A box contains 4 red marbles, 5 green marbles, 6 blue marbles, and 10 yellow marbles.

If a marble is drawn from the box at random, calculate the probability of selecting the following:

(i) A green marble.

(ii) A marble, either blue or yellow.

(iii) A marble, other than red.

Solution

(i) Let E be the event of selecting a green marble.

$n(E) = 5$

$P(E) = \frac{5}{25} = \frac{1}{5}$

(ii) Let E be the event of selecting either a blue or yellow marble.

$n(E) = 6 + 10 = 16$

$P(E) = \frac{16}{25}$

(iii) Let E be the event of selecting either a green, blue, or yellow marble.

$n(E) = 5 + 6 + 10 = 21$

$P(E) = \frac{21}{25}$

Marbles	
Red	4
Green	5
Blue	6
Yellow	10
Total : $n(S)$	25

12.1 | Exercises

Answers to odd-numbered problems are available at the end of the textbook.

1. Last semester, Ann-Marie taught Finance Math and out of 120 students, 96 students passed the subject. Based on this, what is the probability that a student will pass Finance Math in Ann-Marie's class this semester?

2. Based on past records, Kaspar established that on average, 32 out of 36 students in a Finance Math class will register for the online lessons and labs. Based on this, what is the probability that a student in a Finance Math class will register for the online lessons and labs next semester?

3. Out of the past 12 visits to a restaurant, Vera ordered fried rice 9 times. Based on this, what is the probability that she will order fried rice in her next visit to the restaurant?

4. In the last 15 times that Lily had driven to the college, she was able to find a parking space in car park "A" 12 times. Based on this, estimate the probability that there will be an empty parking space in car park "A" the next time she drives to the college.

5. There are three different models of study tables (T1, T2, and T3) and two different models of chairs (C1, C2) available in a furniture store. Draw a tree diagram to show all the possible choices for purchasing a table and a chair.

6. A first-year student at a college is required to choose one of the two math subjects (M1, M2) and one of the four general education subjects (G1, G2, G3, G4) being offered. Draw a tree diagram to show all the possible choices for choosing a math and general education subject.

7. A professor is writing a pop-quiz which will consist of four true-or-false questions. She is determining the value of each question (True or False) randomly.

   a. What are the possible combinations of answers (True or False) for the four questions? Use a tree diagram to determine the sample space.

   b. What is the probability that exactly two questions will have 'True' as the correct answer?

   c. What is the probability that there are more 'True' questions than 'False' questions?

8. Consider the following two sets of numbers: A = {1, 2, 3, 4}, and B = {5, 6, 7, 8, 9}. One number from each set is to be selected randomly.

   a. What are the possible combinations of numbers selected? Use a tree diagram to determine the sample space.

   b. What is the probability that the sum of the numbers is eight?

   c. What is the probability that the sum of the numbers is **not** six?

9. Determine the probability of choosing an odd number from the set of numbers: {1, 2, 3, 4, 5, 6, 7, 8, 9}.

10. Determine the probability of choosing an even number from the set of numbers: {11, 12, 13, 14, 15, 16, 17, 18, 19}.

11. If you choose a random two-digit number, what is the probability that the number you choose is:

    a. Divisible by 5? b. More than 50? c. Not divisible by 5?

12. If you choose a random two-digit number, what is the probability that the number you choose is:

    a. Divisible by 6? b. Between 60 and 90? c. Not divisible by 6?

13. A die is rolled once. Determine the probability that the number rolled is:

    a. Less than 3. b. Greater or equal to 2. c. Even or less than 3.

14. A die is rolled once. Determine the probability that the number rolled is:

    a. Greater than 2. b. Less than or equal to 3. c. Odd or greater than 4.

15. A card is drawn from a shuffled, standard 52-card deck of cards. Determine the probability that it is:

    a. A red card. b. A face card.

16. A card is drawn from a shuffled, standard 52-card deck of cards. Determine the probability that it is:

    a. An Ace. b. A numbered card.

17. A card is drawn from a shuffled, standard 52-card deck of cards. Determine the probability that it is:

    a. A number 5 card or a red card. b. An odd-numbered card.

18. A card is drawn from a shuffled, standard 52-card deck of cards. Determine the probability that it is:

    a. A Jack or a black card. b. An even-numbered card.

19. A spinning wheel is divided into nine equal sectors and numbered 1 to 9. Determine the probability of spinning:

    a. A number divisible by 3. b. A number less than 6. c. An odd number.

20. A spinning wheel is divided into eight equal sectors and numbered 1 to 8. Determine the probability of spinning:

    a. A number divisible by 3. b. A number greater than 5. c. An even number.

12.2 | Basic Rules of Probability

Probability rules simplify the computations of calculating the probability of an event using the known probabilities of other events.

Basic probability rules include the Complement Rule, Addition Rule, Multiplication Rule, and Conditional Probability Rule.

Definitions Used in the Rules of Probability

We begin this section with some brief definitions. We will expand upon these concepts throughout the section.

- **Complement of an event:** The set of all outcomes that are *not* contained in an event.
- **Mutually exclusive (or disjoint) events:** Two or more events that have *no* outcomes in common.
- **Mutually non-exclusive (or joint) events:** Two or more events that have *some* common outcomes.
- **Independent events:** The outcome of one event *is not* affected by the outcome of another event.
- **Dependent events:** The outcome of one event *is* affected by the outcome of another event.

Complement Rule

When the probabilities of all the possible outcomes of an experiment are added, the total will be one.

An event A will either happen, or it will not happen. Therefore, the two probabilities of event A 'happening' and event A 'not happening' always add to one.

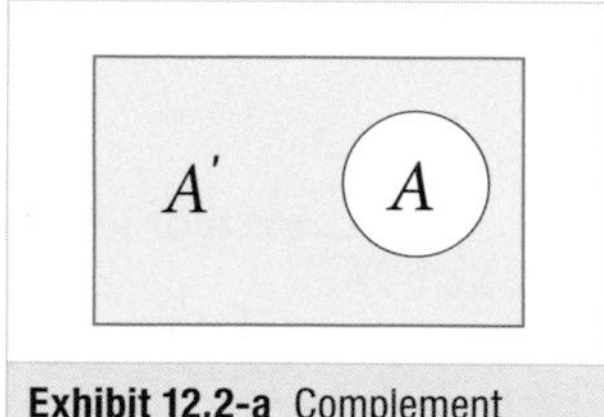

Exhibit 12.2-a Complement

The **complement** of event A, denoted by A' or $\overline{A}$, is the event that A does not happen. $P(A')$ or $P(\overline{A})$ represents the probability of the complement of A.

In Exhibit 12.2-a, the sample space, S, is represented by the entire rectangle, outlined in blue. Event A is represented by the circle, and A' is represented by the shaded area, which is the entire sample space (rectangle) except for A (circle).

That is,

$$P(A) + P(A') = 1$$

If the probability of an event is known, then it can be subtracted from 1 to determine the probability of the event's complement.

$$P(A') = 1 - P(A)$$

Similarly, if the probability of an event's complement is known, then it can be subtracted from 1 to determine the probability of the event.

$$P(A) = 1 - P(A')$$

Sometimes it is easier to determine the probability of the complement of an event rather than the probability of the event itself.

For example, consider the following scenario:

When a standard die is rolled, calculate the probability of event A: rolling any of the numbers 1, 3, 4, 5, or 6.

The complement of the event, A', is rolling a 2, the only other number on the die.

Since $n(A') = 1$ and $n(S) = 6$, $P(A') = \frac{1}{6}$

Using the complement rule, $P(A) = 1 - P(A') = 1 - \frac{1}{6} = \frac{5}{6}$

Therefore, the probability of rolling 1, 3, 4, 5, or 6 on a standard die is $\frac{5}{6}$.

Example 12.2-a **Calculating Probability Using the Complement of an Event**

A card is drawn from a standard deck of cards. Find the probability that the card is neither a red card nor a face card.

Solution

Let A be the event that the card is neither a red card nor a face card.

Then A' is the event that the card is a red card or a face card.

There are 52 cards in a deck. There are 26 red cards, which include 6 face cards in red. Also, there are 6 face cards in black.

$$n(S) = 52,\ n(A') = 26 + 6 = 32$$

$$P(A') = \frac{n(A')}{n(S)} = \frac{32}{52} = \frac{8}{13}$$

$$P(A) = 1 - P(A') = 1 - \frac{8}{13} = \frac{5}{13}$$

Therefore, the probability that the card is neither a red card nor a face card is $\frac{5}{13}$.

Addition Rule

The Addition Rule helps to solve problems that involve the probability of two or more events occurring in the same trial of an experiment. This rule can be broken down further, based on whether or not the two events can occur at the same time.

Addition Rule for Mutually Exclusive Events

If two events, A and B, are **mutually exclusive** (i.e., A and B cannot occur at the same time or there is no common outcome between them), then the probability of A or B occurring is the sum of their individual probabilities.

In general, the word "or" in a probability calculation means addition.

$$\mathbf{P(A \text{ or } B) = P(A) + P(B)}$$

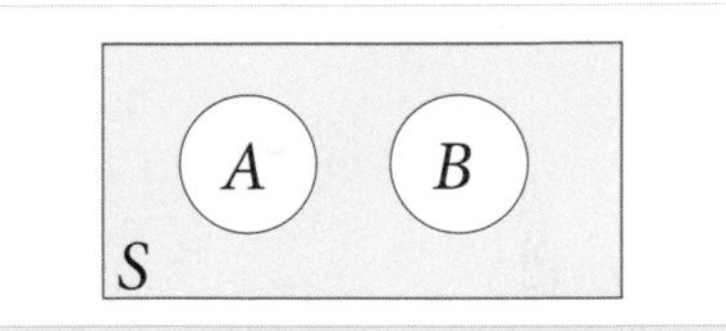

Exhibit 12.2-b Mutually Exclusive Events

For example, consider the probability of selecting a black card or a diamond from a deck of playing cards. These two events are mutually exclusive because you cannot draw a card that is both black and a diamond. Therefore,

$$\begin{aligned} P(Black \text{ or } Diamond) &= P(Black) + P(Diamond) \\ &= \frac{26}{52} + \frac{13}{52} \\ &= \frac{39}{52} = \frac{3}{4} \end{aligned}$$

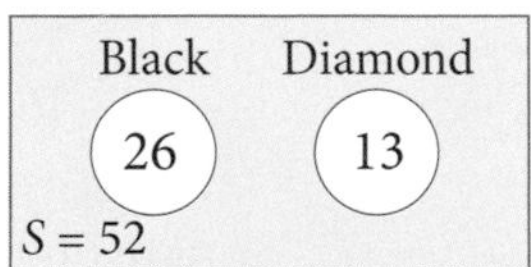

Addition Rule for Mutually Non-Exclusive Events

If two events, A and B, are **mutually non-exclusive** (i.e., A and B can occur at the same time or there is a common outcome between them), if you simply add $P(A) + P(B)$, then the region of overlap (A and B) will be accounted for twice, as depicted in Exhibit 12.2-c; therefore, the probability of A or B occurring is the sum of their individual probabilities, minus the probability of both A and B occurring, to ensure that it is only accounted for once.

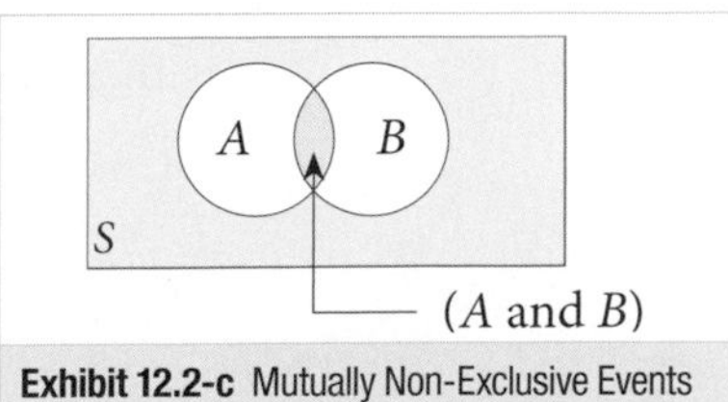

Exhibit 12.2-c Mutually Non-Exclusive Events

$$\mathbf{P(A \text{ or } B) = P(A) + P(B) - P(A \text{ and } B)}$$

For example, consider the probability of selecting a red card or a Queen from a deck of playing cards. These two events are mutually non-exclusive because it is possible to pick a card that satisfies both these requirements: the Queen of hearts and the Queen of diamonds. Therefore,

$$P(Red \text{ or } Queen) = P(Red) + P(Queen) - P(Red \text{ and } Queen)$$

$$= \frac{26}{52} + \frac{4}{52} - \frac{2}{52}$$

$$= \frac{28}{52} = \frac{7}{13}$$

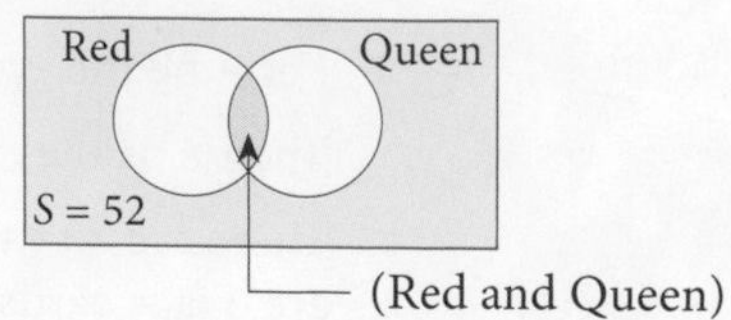

Note: There are 26 red cards and 4 Queens in the deck, 2 of which are red. By adding $\frac{26}{52} + \frac{4}{52}$*, the two red Queens are counted twice. Therefore,* $\frac{2}{52}$ *is subtracted to eliminate the double-counting.*

Example 12.2-b **Calculating the Probability of Mutually Exclusive and Mutually Non-Exclusive Events**

A standard die is rolled once. Identify which of the following events are mutually exclusive and which are mutually non-exclusive, and determine the probability of the events.

(i) Rolling a number less than 3 or greater than 4.
(ii) Rolling an even number or a number less than 4.
(iii) Rolling an odd number or the number 6.

Solution

(i) Event A: Number less than 3 $A = \{1, 2\}$

Event B: Number greater than 4 $B = \{5, 6\}$

There is no outcome common to both events.

Therefore, the events are mutually exclusive.

Using the Addition Rule for Mutually Exclusive Events,

$$P(A \text{ or } B) = P(A) + P(B)$$

$$= \frac{2}{6} + \frac{2}{6}$$

$$= \frac{4}{6} = \frac{2}{3}$$

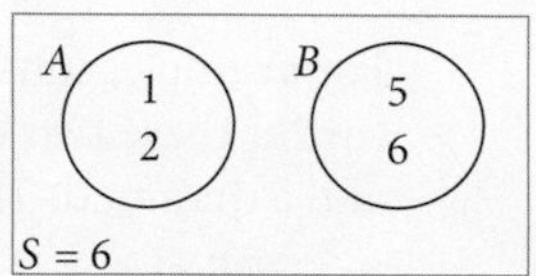

Therefore, the probability of rolling a number less than 3 or greater than 4 is $\frac{2}{3}$.

(ii) Event A: Even number $A = \{2, 4, 6\}$

Event B: Less than 4 $B = \{1, 2, 3\}$

2 is a common outcome to both events.

Therefore, the events are mutually non-exclusive.

Using the Addition Rule for Mutually Non-Exclusive Events

$$P(A \text{ or } B) = P(A) + P(B) - P(A \text{ and } B)$$

$$= \frac{3}{6} + \frac{3}{6} - \frac{1}{6}$$

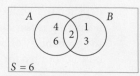

$$= \frac{5}{6}$$

A B 4 6 2 1 3 S = 6

Therefore, the probability of rolling an even number or a number less than 4 is $\frac{5}{6}$.

Solution *continued*

(iii) Event A: Odd number $A = \{1, 3, 5\}$

Event B: 6 $B = \{6\}$

There is no outcome common to both events.

Therefore, the events are mutually exclusive.

Using the Addition Rule for Mutually Exclusive Events,

$$P(A \text{ or } B) = P(A) + P(B)$$
$$= \frac{3}{6} + \frac{1}{6}$$
$$= \frac{4}{6} = \frac{2}{3}$$

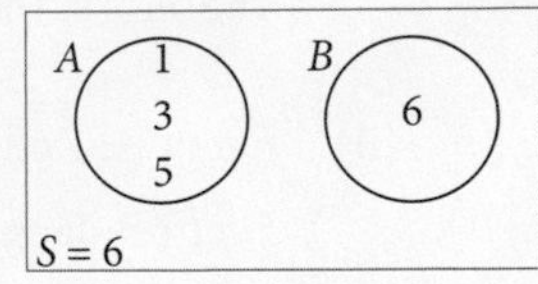

Therefore, the probability of rolling an odd number or the number 6 is $\frac{2}{3}$.

Multiplication Rule

The Multiplication Rule helps to find the probability of two or more events that occur in a sequence of tasks within a trial of an experiment. This rule can be broken down further based on whether or not the outcome of one event impacts the outcome of the other event.

Multiplication Rule for Independent Events

If two events A and B are **independent** (i.e., the occurrence of one event has no effect on the occurrence of the other event), then the probability of A and B occurring simultaneously is the product of the probability of each event.

In general, the word "and" in probability calculations means multiplication.

$$\mathbf{P(A \text{ and } B) = P(A) \times P(B)}$$

For example, if a coin is tossed and a die is rolled, the events of tossing a "Heads" and rolling a "number 4" are independent, as one does not affect the other. Therefore, the probability is,

$$P(H \text{ and } 4) = P(H) \times P(4)$$
$$= \frac{1}{2} \times \frac{1}{6}$$
$$= \frac{1}{12}$$

H
T

1
2
3
4
5
6

Example 12.2-c

Calculating the Probability of Independent Events

If two cards are selected from a standard deck of cards, and the first card is placed back in the deck before the second card is selected, calculate the probability of the following:

(i) Drawing a King and a spade.

(ii) Drawing a red card and a Jack.

(iii) Drawing an Ace and a black Queen.

Solution

All the events are independent events since the first card is placed back in the deck before the second card is selected (i.e., the probability of the second event is not affected by the first event).

Using the Multiplication Rule for Independent Events, $P(A \text{ and } B) = P(A) \times P(B)$,

Solution *continued*

(i) Event A: King - 4 cards

Event B: Spade - 13 cards

$$P(A \text{ and } B) = \frac{4}{52} \times \frac{13}{52}$$

$$= \frac{1}{52}$$

Therefore, the probability of drawing a King and a spade is $\frac{1}{52}$.

(ii) Event A: Red - 26 cards

Event B: Jack - 4 cards

$$P(A \text{ and } B) = \frac{26}{52} \times \frac{4}{52}$$

$$= \frac{1}{26}$$

Therefore, the probability of drawing a red card and a Jack is $\frac{1}{26}$.

(iii) Event A: Ace - 4 cards

Event B: Black Queen - 2 cards

$$P(A \text{ and } B) = \frac{4}{52} \times \frac{2}{52}$$

$$= \frac{1}{338}$$

Therefore, the probability of drawing an Ace and a black Queen is $\frac{1}{338}$.

Multiplication Rule for Dependent Events

If two events A and B are **dependent** (i.e., the possible outcome of one event depends on the outcome of the other event), then the probability of obtaining both events, $P(A \text{ and } B)$, is the product of the probability of event A, $P(A)$, and the probability of event B given that event A has occurred, which is denoted by $P(B|A)$ and read as "Probability of B given A".

$$\mathbf{P(A \text{ and } B) = P(A) \times \underbrace{P(B|A)}}$$

Probability of B given that event A has occured

For example, the probability of selecting a red marble R then a white marble W (without replacing the red marble) from a box containing 6 red marbles and 3 white marbles, are dependent events.

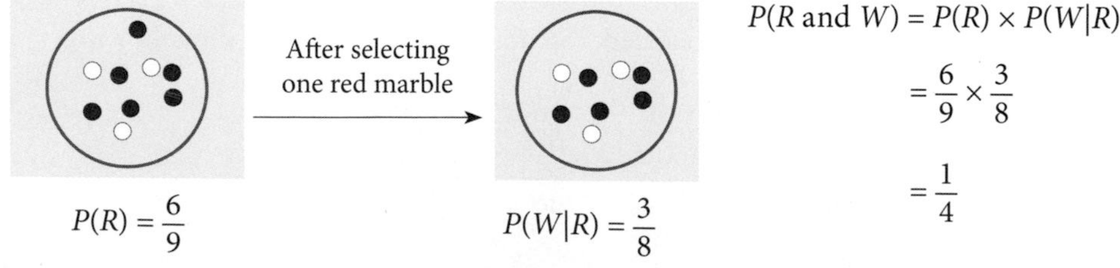

$P(R) = \frac{6}{9}$ $P(W|R) = \frac{3}{8}$

$$P(R \text{ and } W) = P(R) \times P(W|R)$$

$$= \frac{6}{9} \times \frac{3}{8}$$

$$= \frac{1}{4}$$

The probability of choosing a red marble is 6 out of 9. The probability of choosing a white marble is then 3 out of 8, because the red marble is not replaced and the white marble is chosen only from the remaining 8 marbles.

That is, the outcome of choosing the first marble has affected the outcome of choosing the second marble, making these events dependent.

Example 12.2-d

Calculating the Probability of Dependent Events

There are five defective CDs in a collection of twenty CDs. If two CDs are selected, determine the probability of the following:

(i) Both CDs are defective.

(ii) Both CDs are non-defective.

(iii) One of the CDs is defective.

Solution

$$20 \text{ CDs} \begin{cases} 5 \text{ defective} \\ 15 \text{ non-defective} \end{cases}$$

The events are dependent because the outcome of the second selection is affected by the outcome of the first.

Using the Multiplication Rule for Dependent Events, $P(A \text{ and } B) = P(A) \times P(B|A)$,

(i) $P(\textit{Both defective}) = P(1^{st}\ \textit{Def} \text{ and } 2^{nd}\ \textit{Def})$

$$= P(1^{st}\ \textit{Def}) \times P(2^{nd}\ \textit{Def} \mid 1^{st}\ \textit{Def})$$

$$= \frac{5}{20} \times \frac{4}{19}$$

$$= \frac{1}{19}$$

After the first defective CD is selected, there are 19 CDs remaining, of which 4 are defective.

Therefore, the probability that both selected CDs are defective is $\frac{1}{19}$.

(ii) $P(\textit{Both non-defective}) = P(1^{st}\ \textit{Non-Def} \text{ and } 2^{nd}\ \textit{Non-Def})$

$$= P(1^{st}\ \textit{Non-Def}) \times P(2^{nd}\ \textit{Non-Def} \mid 1^{st}\ \textit{Non-Def})$$

$$= \frac{15}{20} \times \frac{14}{19}$$

$$= \frac{21}{38}$$

After the first non-defective CD is selected, there are 19 CDs remaining, of which 14 are defective.

Therefore, the probability that both selected CDs are non-defective is $\frac{21}{38}$.

(iii) $P(\textit{One defective}) = P(1^{st}\ \textit{Def} \text{ and } 2^{nd}\ \textit{Non-Def} \textbf{ or } 1^{st}\ \textit{Non-Def} \text{ and } 2^{nd}\ \textit{Def})$

$$= P(1^{st}\ \textit{Def}) \times P(2^{nd}\ \textit{Non-Def} \mid 1^{st}\ \textit{Def}) + P(1^{st}\ \textit{Non-Def}) \times P(2^{nd}\ \textit{Def} \mid 1^{st}\ \textit{Non-Def})$$

$$= \frac{5}{20} \times \frac{15}{19} + \frac{15}{20} \times \frac{5}{19}$$

$$= \frac{15}{76} + \frac{15}{76}$$

$$= \frac{15}{38}$$

Therefore, the probability that one selected CD is defective is $\frac{15}{38}$.

Conditional Probability Rule

As introduced in the multiplication rule for dependent events, the probability of an event occurring given that another event has occurred is a **conditional probability** (i.e., the second event is conditional on the first event).

The formula for conditional probability can be derived from the multiplication rule for dependent events as follows:

$$P(A \text{ and } B) = P(A) \times P(B|A)$$ Interchange left side and right side.

$$P(A) \times P(B|A) = P(A \text{ and } B)$$ Divide both sides by $P(A)$.

$$P(B|A) = \frac{P(A \text{ and } B)}{P(A)}$$

Similarly, $$P(A|B) = \frac{P(A \text{ and } B)}{P(B)}$$

Note: $P(A|B)$ is not the same as $P(B|A)$.

Example 12.2-e Conditional Probability

Based on past results, the probability that a random student passes Finance Math is 0.85, and the probability that a random student passes Statistics is 0.70. The probability that a random student passes both subjects is 0.55.

If a student is selected at random, calculate the following:

(i) Probability that the student passes Statistics given that the student passed Finance Math.

(ii) Probability that the student passes Finance Math given that the student passed Statistics.

Solution

Both of these problems are conditional probability.

Let Event A be passing Finance Math and Event B be passing Statistics. Then,

$$P(A) = P(\textit{Passing Finance Math}) = 0.85$$

$$P(B) = P(\textit{Passing Statistics}) = 0.70$$

$$P(A \text{ and } B) = P(\textit{Passing both subjects}) = 0.55$$

(i) Using Conditional Probability, $$P(B|A) = \frac{P(A \text{ and } B)}{P(A)} = \frac{0.55}{0.85} = 0.647058... = 0.65$$

Therefore, the probability that the student passes Statistics given that the student passed Finance Math is 0.65.

(ii) Using Conditional Probability, $$P(A|B) = \frac{P(A \text{ and } B)}{P(B)} = \frac{0.55}{0.70} = 0.785714... = 0.79$$

Therefore, the probability that the student passes Finance Math given that the student passed Statistics is 0.79.

Odds In Favour and Odds Against an Event

Most probabilities in the media are stated in terms of **odds**, which relate the probability of an event to the probability of its complement. That is, the odds of an event occurring is the ratio of the probability of the event occurring to the probability of it not occurring.

For example, for an event with an 80% probability of occurring, the complement event has a 20% probability of occurring. Therefore, the odds of the event occurring are 80 to 20 (80 : 20).

Recall from Chapter 6, that like fractions, ratios are most commonly presented in their simplest terms, so the odds 80 to 20 are the same as 4 to 1 (4 : 1) in simplest terms. This indicates that the event is four times more likely to occur than not to occur.

Odds In Favour of an Event

The odds in favour of an event, A, is the ratio of the probability that event A will happen to the probability that event A will not happen (A').

If the possible number of outcomes is $n(S)$, the number of favourable outcomes in A is $n(A)$, and all outcomes are equally likely to occur, then the probability of a favourable event, A, is $P(A) = \frac{n(A)}{n(S)}$.

Since the number of possible outcomes not favourable to A is $n(S) - n(A)$, the probability of an unfavourable event, A', is: $P(A') = \frac{n(S) - n(A)}{n(S)}$

Therefore, the odds in favour of event A, $\frac{P(A)}{P(A')}$, can be rearranged to produce a second formula as follows:

$$\frac{P(A)}{P(A')} = \frac{\frac{n(A)}{n(S)}}{\frac{n(S) - n(A)}{n(S)}} = \frac{n(A)}{n(S)} \times \frac{n(S)}{n(S) - n(A)} = \frac{n(A)}{n(S) - n(A)} = \frac{n(A)}{n(A')}$$

Therefore, the odds in favour of an event, A, can also be defined as the ratio of the number of outcomes favourable to A (successes) to the number of outcomes unfavourable to A (failures).

Odds in favour of A are usually expressed as a ratio; that is, $P(A) : P(A')$, or $n(A) : n(A')$.

Example 12.2-f **Calculating the Odds in Favour of an Event**

Professors of a college reviewed the "Business and Finance Mathematics" textbook and 15 members voted for the adoption of the textbook and 3 members voted against it. What are the odds in favour of adopting the textbook?

Solution

$n(S) = 15 + 3 = 18$

Let A be the favourable event to adopt the book: $n(A) = 15$.

Therefore, $n(A') = 3$.

Method 1: $P(A) = \frac{n(A)}{n(S)} = \frac{15}{18} = \frac{5}{6}$

$P(A') = \frac{n(A')}{n(S)} = \frac{3}{18} = \frac{1}{6}$

Odds in favour of adopting the book $= \frac{P(A)}{P(A')} = \frac{\frac{5}{6}}{\frac{1}{6}} = \frac{5}{6} \times \frac{6}{1} = \frac{5}{1}$

Therefore, the odds in favour of adopting the book are 5 : 1.

Solution *continued*

Method 2: Odds in favour of adopting the book $= \frac{n(A)}{n(A')} = \frac{15}{3} = \frac{5}{1}$

Therefore, the odds in favour of adopting the book are 5 : 1.

Odds Against an Event

Sometimes odds are quoted against an event, rather than as odds in favour.

The odds against an event A is the ratio of the probability that the event, A, will not happen to the probability that the event, A, will happen.

Odds against an event $= \frac{P(A')}{P(A)} = \frac{n(A')}{n(A)}$

That is, the odds against an event, A, can also be defined as the ratio of the number of outcomes unfavourable to A (failures) to the number of outcomes favourable to A (successes).

Odds against A are usually expressed as a ratio; that is, $P(A') : P(A)$, or $n(A') : n(A)$.

In Example 12.2-f, the odds against adopting the textbook are 1 : 5.

Example 12.2-g **Odds Versus Probability**

If the odds against an event are 4 : 5, calculate the probability for the event and the probability against the event.

Solution

The odds against an event are 4 : 5.

i.e., the outcomes against the event = 4 and the outcomes for the event = 5

Total number of outcomes = 4 + 5 = 9

Therefore, the probability for the event is $\frac{5}{9}$ and the probability against the event is $\frac{4}{9}$.

12.2 | Exercises

Answers to odd-numbered problems are available at the end of the textbook.

1. A pair of 6-sided dice, one white and the other red, is rolled simultaneously.
   a. Determine the probability that the sum of the two dice is 5.
   b. Determine the probability that the sum of the two dice is not 5.

2. A pair of 6-sided dice, one black and the other white, is rolled simultaneously.
   a. Determine the probability that the sum of the two dice is 7.
   b. Determine the probability that the sum of the two dice is not 7.

For Problems 3 and 4, calculate the probability of event A ***or*** *event B occurring.*

3. a. $P(A) = 0.35$, $P(B) = 0.3$, Events A and B are mutually exclusive
   b. $P(A) = 0.2$, $P(B) = 0.45$. $P(A \text{ and } B) = 0.1$
   c. $P(A) = 0.6$, $P(B) = 0.3$, $P(A \text{ and } B) = 0.05$

4. a. $P(A) = 0.4$, $P(B) = 0.35$, Events A and B are mutually exclusive
   b. $P(A) = 0.5$, $P(B) = 0.25$, $P(A \text{ and } B) = 0.05$
   c. $P(A) = 0.75$, $P(B) = 0.35$, $P(A \text{ and } B) = 0.3$

*For Problems 5 and 6, calculate the probability of event A **and** event B occurring.*

5. a. $P(A) = 0.45$, $P(B) = 0.4$, Events A and B are independent

   b. $P(A) = 0.14$, $P(B) = 0.7$, $P(A|B) = 0.21$

   c. $P(A) = 0.62$, $P(B) = 0.33$, $P(B|A) = 0.6$

6. a. $P(A) = 0.32$, $P(B) = 0.5$, Events A and B are independent

   b. $P(A) = 0.15$, $P(B) = 0.8$, $P(A|B) = 0.55$

   c. $P(A) = 0.08$, $P(B) = 0.72$, $P(B|A) = 0.45$

7. Determine the probability of selecting a face card in each of two consecutive draws from a well-shuffled, standard 52-card deck of cards if the first card is:

   a. Replaced before the second draw. b. Not replaced before the second draw.

8. Determine the probability of selecting a red card in each of two consecutive draws from a well-shuffled, standard 52-card deck of cards if the first card is:

   a. Replaced before the second draw. b. Not replaced before the second draw.

9. The probability that a student takes Math is 0.70, English is 0.65, and both Math and English is 0.50. Determine the probability that a student selected at random takes Math or English.

10. The probability that a student learns Music is 0.75, Dance is 0.60, and both Music and Dance is 0.45. Determine the probability that a student selected at random takes Music or Dance.

11. A bag contains 8 quarters, 6 dimes, and 4 nickels. Two coins are selected (without replacement) from the bag. What is the probability that:

    a. Both coins are dimes?

    b. The first coin is a quarter and the second coin is a nickel?

12. A bag contains 12 red marbles, 8 black marbles, and 5 white marbles. Two marbles are drawn (without replacement) from the bag. What is the probability that:

    a. Both of the marbles are red?

    b. The first marble is red and the second marble is white?

13. In a class of 40 students, 15 are males. If two students are selected at random to represent the class, what is the probability that:

    a. Both are males? b. Both are females? c. One is male and the other is female?

14. A box contains 20 bulbs, out of which, 5 are defective. If two bulbs are selected at random at the same time, what is the probability that:

    a. Both are defective? b. Both are not defective? c. One is defective and the other is not?

15. In a group of 50 students, 25 take Math, 20 take English, and 15 take both Math and English.

    Determine the probability that a student selected at random:

    a. Takes Math, but not English. b. Takes English, but not Math.

    c. Takes neither Math nor English. d. Takes Math or English.

    e. Takes Math given that he/she takes English f. Takes English given that he/she takes Math

16. In a group of 40 families, 21 own a dog, 20 own a cat, and 6 own both a dog and a cat.

    If a family is selected at random, what is the probability that the family:

    a. Owns a dog, but not a cat? b. Owns a cat, but not a dog?

    c. Owns neither a dog nor a cat? d. Owns a dog or a cat?

    e. Owns a dog given that they own a cat? f. Owns a cat given that they own a dog?

17. A card is drawn from a well-shuffled, standard 52-card deck of cards.

    a. What are the odds in favour of selecting a face card?

    b. What are the odds against selecting an Ace?

18. A card is drawn from a well-shuffled, standard 52-card deck of cards.

    a. What are the odds in favour of selecting a numbered card?

    b. What are the odds against selecting a heart?

For Problems 19 to 26, consider the following scenario: randomly drawing a marble from a jar containing 12 red marbles, 10 green marbles, and 8 blue marbles.

19. What is the probability of drawing a blue marble?

20. What is the probability of not drawing a red marble?

21. What is the complement of the event in Problem 19? Calculate its probability,

22. What is the complement of the event in Problem 20? Calculate its probability,

23. What are the odds in favour of the event in Problem 19?

24. What are the odds against the event in Problem 20?

25. What is the probability of drawing two green marbles if:

    a. the first marble is replaced after being drawn?

    b. the first marble is **not** replaced after being drawn?

26. What is the probability of drawing one green marble and one red marble (in either order) if:

    a. the first marble is replaced after being drawn?

    b. the first marble is **not** replaced after being drawn?

12.3 | The Normal Distribution

As introduced in the previous chapter, a frequency distribution can be symmetrical, positively skewed, or negatively skewed. However, in most scientific and business applications, as well as natural relationships (such as weight, height, etc.), when the data is displayed using a histogram, the frequency curve takes on a bell-shape and is symmetrical; this curve is known as a **normal distribution**.

This graphical representation in statistics is called a normal curve.

Properties of a Normal Curve

A normal curve has the following properties:

- Bell-shaped
- Symmetrical at the mean
- Mean = Median = Mode
- 50% of the data is above the mean and 50% of the data is below
- The curve approaches the X-axis but never touches it.

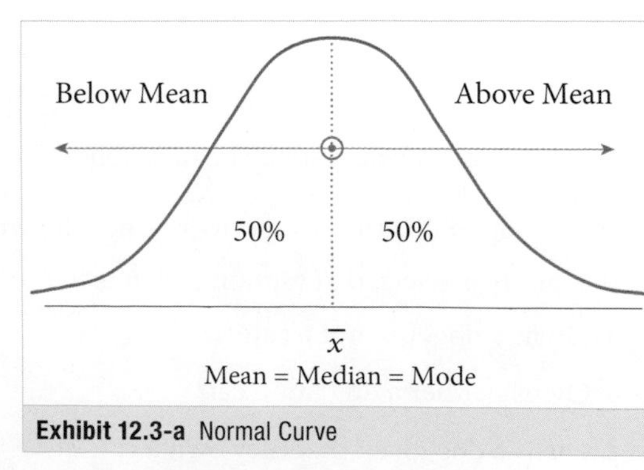

Exhibit 12.3-a Normal Curve

Empirical Rule for Normal Distribution

There is a relationship among the mean, standard deviation, and the number of data of a normal distribution. It is known as the Empirical Rule for normal distribution and is outlined below:

- Approximately 68% of the data falls within ± 1 standard deviation from the mean.
- Approximately 95% of the data falls within ± 2 standard deviations from the mean.
- Almost all (99.7%) of the data falls within ± 3 standard deviations from the mean.

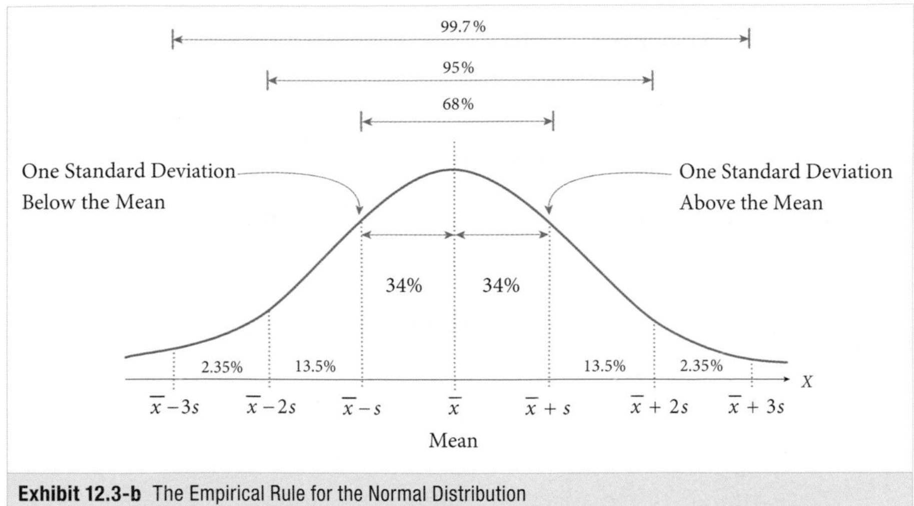

Exhibit 12.3-b The Empirical Rule for the Normal Distribution

For example, for a normal distribution, if the mean of a dataset ($\overline{x}$) is 40 and the standard deviation (s) is 12 units, then,

- 68% of the data will fall within $\overline{x} \pm s = 40 \pm 12$ units (i.e., 28 to 52 units).
- 95% of the data will fall within $\overline{x} \pm 2s = 40 \pm 2(12)$ units (i.e., 16 to 64 units).
- Almost all of the data will fall within $\overline{x} \pm 3s = 40 \pm 3(12)$ units (i.e., 4 to 76 units).

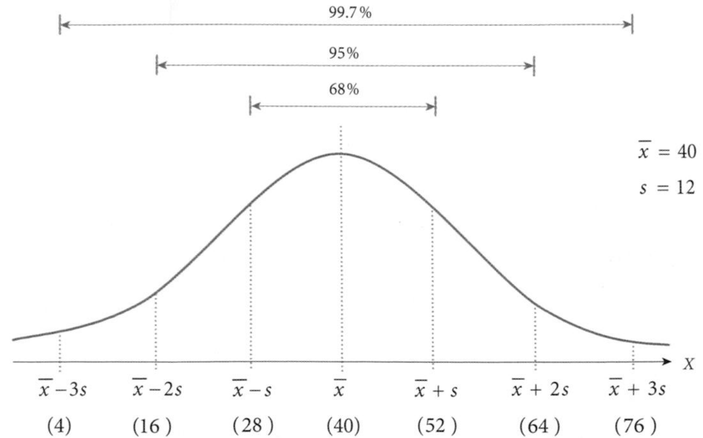

The percents associated with the Empirical Rule in the above example are based on integer multiples of the standard deviation. While it is useful to know that 68%, 95%, and 99.7% of the data in a normal distribution falls within ±1, ±2, and ±3 standard deviations from the mean, respectively, performing calculations for other percent values (50%, 75%, 90%, etc.) involves a table of values, known as ***z*-scores**, which is the next step in statistics. Although this topic is beyond the scope of this textbook, we will also use the following two common percent values:

1.28 and 1.64 are examples of *z*-scores.

- Approximately 80% of the data falls within ± 1.28 standard deviations from the mean ($\overline{x} \pm 1.28s$).
- Approximately 90% of the data falls within ± 1.64 standard deviations from the mean ($\overline{x} \pm 1.64s$).

Example 12.3-a

Calculating the Range of Values for a Percent of Normal Distribution, Given the Mean and Standard Deviation

Based on records, the average flight time from Toronto to Ottawa is 85 minutes with a standard deviation of 15 minutes. Using the Empirical Rule, estimate the maximum and minimum time for:

(i) 95% of the flights from Toronto to Ottawa.

(ii) 90% of the flights from Toronto to Ottawa.

Assume the data is normally distributed.

Solution

$\overline{x}$ = 85 minutes

s = 15 minutes

(i) Since the data is normally distributed, approximately 95% of the flights will be within ±2 standard deviations from the mean; i.e., within $\overline{x} \pm 2s$ minutes.

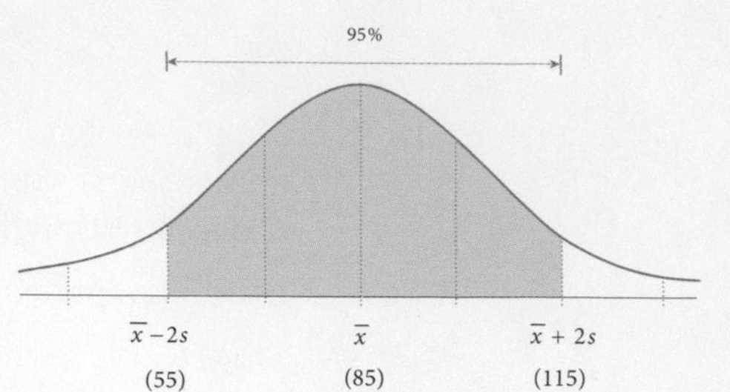

Maximum time = $\overline{x} + 2s = 85 + 2(15) = 115$ minutes

Minimum time = $\overline{x} - 2s = 85 - 2(15) = 55$ minutes

Therefore, approximately 95% of the flights from Toronto to Ottawa will take between 55 to 115 minutes.

(ii) Since the data is normally distributed, approximately 90% of the flights will be within ±1.64 standard deviations from the mean; i.e., within $\overline{x} \pm 1.64s$ minutes.

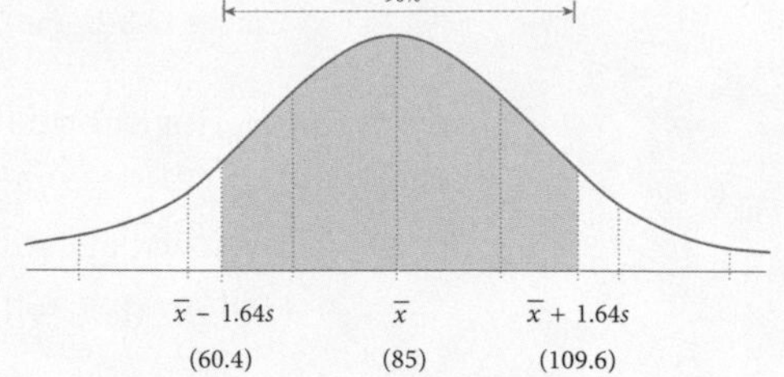

Maximum time = $\overline{x} + 1.64s = 85 + 1.64(15) = 109.6$ minutes

Minimum time = $\overline{x} - 1.64s = 85 - 1.64(15) = 60.4$ minutes

Therefore, approximately 90% of the flights from Toronto to Ottawa will take between 60 to 110 minutes.

Example 12.3-b

Calculating Percent of Normal Distribution, Given the Mean and Range of Values

160 students took a test and the test scores have a bell-shaped distribution with a mean mark of 70 and standard deviation of 10 marks. Estimate:

(i) The percent of students who scored between 60 and 80 marks.

(ii) The number of students who scored between 50 and 90 marks.

Solution

$\overline{x}$ = 70 marks

s = 10 marks

(i) 60 marks is one standard deviation below the mean; i.e., $60 = 70 - 10 = \overline{x} - s$

80 marks is one standard deviation above the mean; i.e., $80 = 70 + 10 = \overline{x} + s$

That is, 60 to 80 marks fall within ±1 standard deviation from the mean; i.e., within $\overline{x} \pm s$.

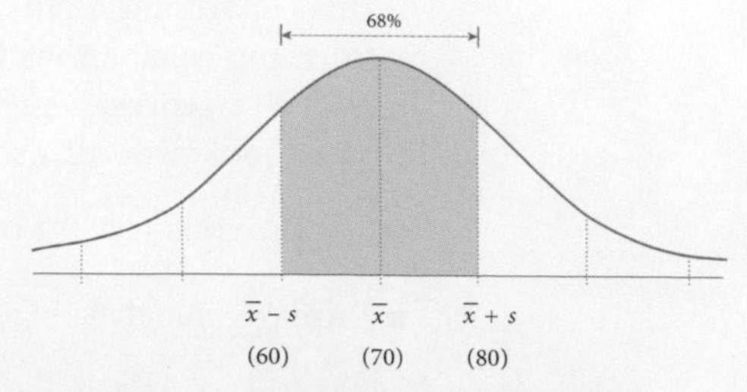

Solution
continued

We know that approximately 68% of the data for a normal distribution falls within ±1 standard deviation from the mean.

Therefore, approximately 68% of the students scored between 60 and 80 marks.

(ii) 50 marks is two standard deviations below the mean;
i.e., $50 = 70 - 20 = 70 - 2(10) = \overline{x} - 2s$

90 marks is two standard deviations above the mean;
i.e., $90 = 70 + 20 = 70 + 2(10) = \overline{x} + 2s$

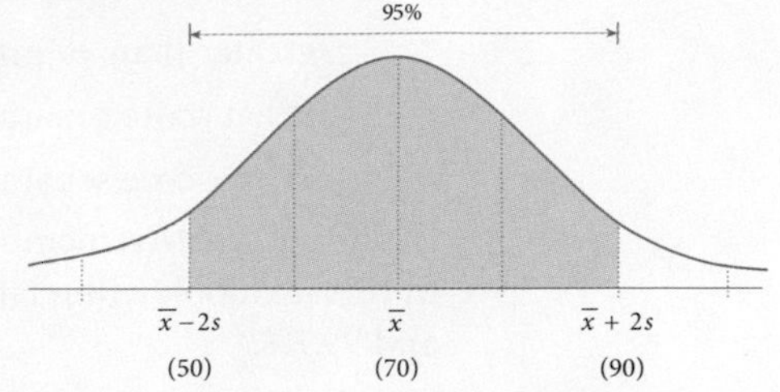

That is, 50 to 90 marks fall within ±2 standard deviations from the mean; i.e., within $\overline{x} \pm 2s$.

We know that approximately 95% of the data for a normal distribution falls within ±2 standard deviations from the mean.

Therefore, approximately 95% of the students scored between 50 and 90 marks.

Number of students = $0.95 \times 160 = 152$

Therefore, approximately 152 students scored between 50 and 90 marks.

The result from Example 12.3-b, that 95% of students scored between 50 to 90 marks, can also be interpreted as:

> For a randomly selected student, there is a 95% probability that the student scored between 50 to 90 marks.

When rewritten like this, it is clear that the Empirical Rule for the normal distribution is an application of probability; as such, the rules covered in Sections 12.1 and 12.2 apply to calculations with the normal curve.

For example, let's apply the complement rule to this problem.

Let A be the event of a randomly selected student scoring between 50 and 90 marks, so $P(A) = 95\% = 0.95$.

This means that A' refers to a randomly selected student not scoring between 50 and 90 marks; more specifically, it would mean scoring less than 50 marks or greater than 90 marks, as shaded in the diagram below.

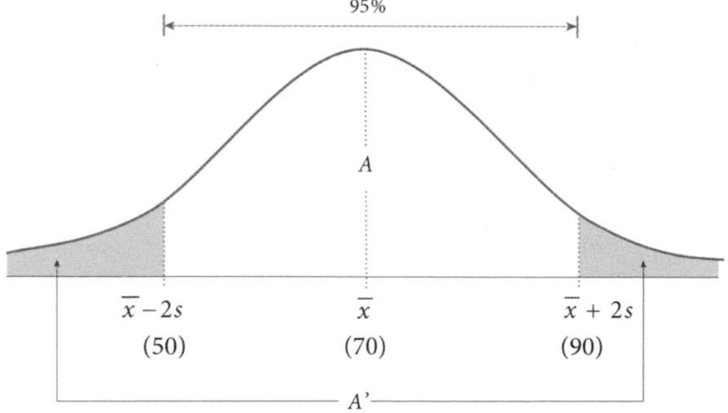

Remember, the entire sample space has a probability of 100% or 1, so $P(A') = 1 - P(A) = 1 - 0.95 = 0.05$, indicating that there is a 5% probability of a randomly selected student scoring below 50 marks or above 90 marks. Since the normal curve is symmetrical, the 0.05 is divided evenly between the two tails, and we have:

$$P(\text{scoring less than 50 marks}) = \frac{0.05}{2} = 0.025, \text{ and}$$

$$P(\text{scoring greater than 90 marks}) = \frac{0.05}{2} = 0.025$$

In addition to using the Empirical Rule to calculate percents between two values, it can also be used as a complement to calculate percents above or below certain values. These types of questions come in many forms.

For example, considering the scenario in Example 12.3-b again:

- What was the probability that a randomly selected student scored greater than 90 marks?
- What was the probability that a randomly selected student scored less than 50 marks?
- What was the probability that a randomly selected student scored less than 50 marks or greater than 90 marks?
- What score separates the lowest 2.5% of students?
- What score separates the highest 2.5% of students?

It is important to remember that all of the exercises involving probability and the normal distribution in this textbook will relate back to the five specific percents presented earlier: 68%, 80%, 90%, 95% and 99.7%.

Example 12.3-c Calculating Probability using the Empirical Rule for the Normal Distribution

A sample of college students filled out a survey about their living expenses. The monthly rental cost for this group was normally distributed with a mean of \$800 and a standard deviation of \$200. Calculate the following:

(i) The probability that a randomly selected student pays between \$472 and \$1,128.

(ii) The probability that a randomly selected student pays below \$472 *or* above \$1,128.

(iii) The probability that a randomly selected student pays above \$1,000.

(iv) The maximum rental cost for the 10% of students who pay the least.

Solution

$\overline{x} = \$800$, $s = \$200$

(i) We need to determine the number of standard deviations below and above the mean at which the given values \$472 and \$1,128 lie.

Let \$472 be z_1 standard deviations below the mean and \$1,128 be z_2 standard deviations above the mean. Then,

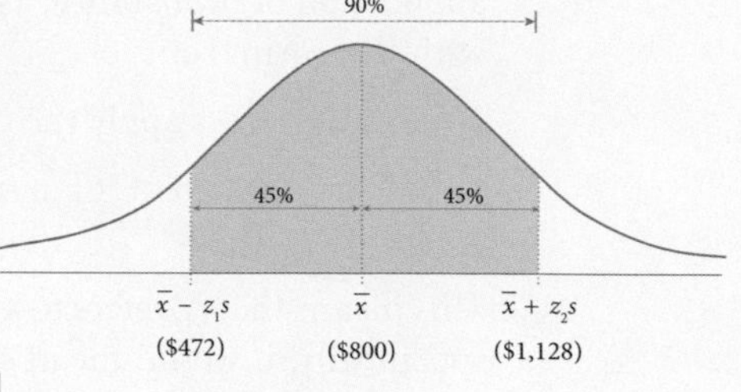

$$472 = \overline{x} - z_1 s$$
$$472 = 800 - z_1(200)$$
$$z_1(200) = 800 - 472$$
$$z_1 = \frac{328}{200} = 1.64$$

i.e., \$472 is 1.64 standard deviations below the mean

$$1{,}128 = \overline{x} + z_2 s$$
$$1{,}128 = 800 + z_2(200)$$
$$z_2(200) = 1{,}128 - 800$$
$$z_2 = \frac{328}{200} = 1.64$$

i.e., \$1,128 is 1.64 standard deviations above the mean

We know that approximately 90% of the data for a normal distribution falls within ±1.64 standard deviations from the mean.

Therefore, the probability that a randomly selected student pays between \$472 and \$1,128 is 90%.

(ii) Paying below \$472 or above \$1,128 is the complement of paying between \$472 and \$1,128.

From part (i), the probability that a randomly selected student pays between \$472 and \$1,128 is 90%

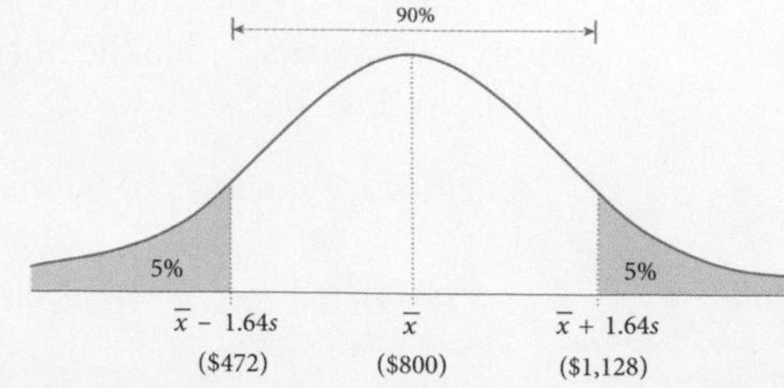

Therefore, the probability that a randomly selected student pays below \$472 or above \$1,128 is 100% – 90% = 10%.

Solution *continued*

(iii) Let $1,000 be z standard deviations above the mean. Then,

$$1{,}000 = \bar{x} + zs$$
$$1{,}000 = 800 + z(200)$$
$$z(200) = 1{,}000 - 800$$
$$z = \frac{200}{200} = 1$$

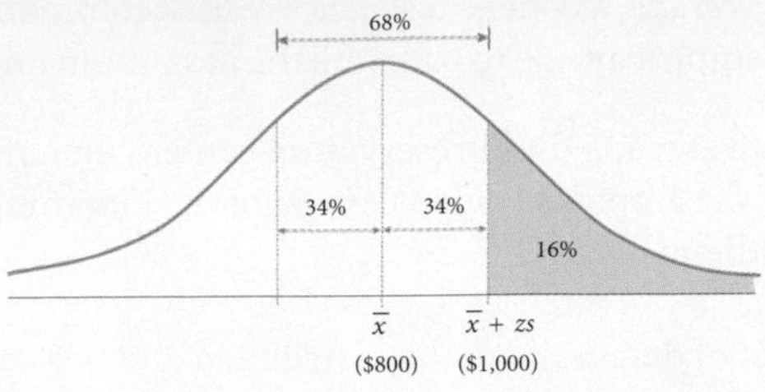

i.e., $1,000 is 1 standard deviation above the mean

We know that approximately 68% of the data for a normal distribution falls within ±1 standard deviation from the mean. Therefore, 100% – 68% = 32% of the data falls below 1 standard deviation *or* above 1 standard deviation from the mean. Since the normal curve is symmetrical, the 32% is divided evenly between the two tails.

Therefore, the probability that a randomly selected student pays above $1,000 is $\frac{32\%}{2} = 16\%$.

(iv) Since the normal distribution is symmetrical, the value that separates the lowest 10% of rental costs is the same distance from the mean as the value that separates the highest 10% of rental costs, but in the opposite direction. With 10% in each tail, this leaves 100% – 2(10%) = 80% of the data in the middle, centred around the mean.

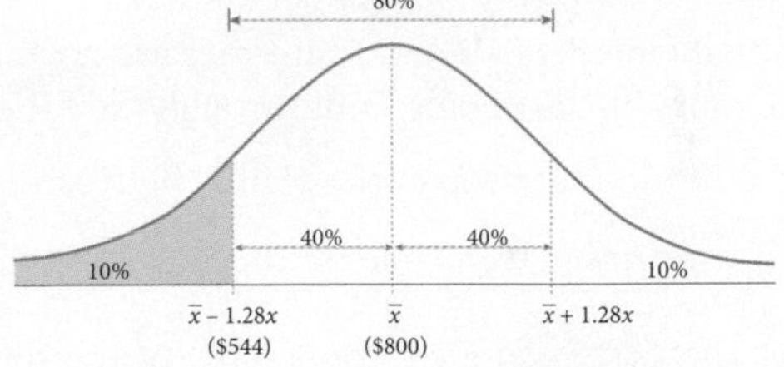

We know that 80% of the data falls within ±1.28 standard deviations from the mean.

Calculating the rental cost that separates the lowest 10% of rental costs:

$$\bar{x} - 1.28s = 800 - 1.28(200) = \$544.$$

Therefore, 10% of the students pay a maximum monthly housing cost of $544.

12.3 | Exercises

Answers to odd-numbered problems are available at the end of the textbook.

1. An aptitude test is normally distributed with a mean score of 500 and a standard deviation of 100. Use the empirical rule to answer the following:

   a. Approximately what percent of the students will have a score between 400 and 600?

   b. Randomly selected students will have a 95% chance of having scores fall between what values?

   c. Randomly selected students will have a 90% chance of having scores fall between what values?

2. A bell-shaped distribution has a mean of 550 and a standard deviation of 150. Use the empirical rule to answer the following:

   a. What percent of the data will fall between 400 and 700?

   b. Randomly selected data will have a 95% chance of falling between what values?

   c. Randomly selected data will have a 90% chance of falling between what values?

For Problems 3 to 6, assume that the data is normally distributed.

3. Out of a sample of 100 boxes of cereal, 95 boxes weigh between 780 and 820 grams. Use the empirical rule to estimate the average weight of the cereal box and the standard deviation.

4. Out of a sample of 100 juice bottles, 68 bottles contain between 975 and 1,025 millilitres of juice. Use the empirical rule to estimate the average quantity (in millilitres) in the juice bottles and the standard deviation.

5. On average, a college test center can accommodate 350 students per day with a standard deviation of 75 students. Use the empirical rule to estimate the maximum and the minimum number of students the test center can expect in a day.

6. On average, a flight reservation center can handle 200 customer calls per day with a standard deviation of 35 calls. Use the empirical rule to estimate the maximum and the minimum number of calls the flight reservation center can handle in a day.

7. A set of data is normally distributed and 90% of the data falls within a certain interval. Based on the Empirical Rule, will the interval representing 95% of the data be wider or narrower? Explain your answer and include a diagram.

8. A set of data is normally distributed and 10% of the data lies below the value A. Based on the Empirical Rule, if 5% of the data lies below the value B, then is B greater or less than A? Explain your answer and include a diagram.

9. If a set of data is normally distributed, what percentage of the data falls between the lowest 2.5% and the mean? Explain your answer and include a diagram.

10. A set of data is normally distributed and according to the Empirical Rule, 68% of the data falls in the interval $[\overline{x} - s, \overline{x} + s]$. What percentage of the data falls in the interval $[\overline{x}, \overline{x} + s]$? Explain your answer and include a diagram.

11. Hospital emergency room wait times are normally distributed with a mean of 3.5 hours and a standard deviation of 0.75 hours. If 200 people went through the ER on Friday, estimate the following:

    a. The number of people who waited between 2 hours and 5 hours.

    b. The minimum wait time for the 32 people who waited the longest.

12. Over the past year, Delia kept track of the number of kilometers she drove each day for work. She recorded 230 working days, and upon analysis, found that the distances she travelled each day was normally distributed with a mean of 115 km and a standard deviation of 28 km.

    a. Determine the number of days, approximately, where she drove more than 115 km.

    b. Determine the number of days, approximately, where she drove less than 69 km or more than 161 km.

For Problems 13 to 20, use the following set of raw data and the Empirical Rule to answer the questions. Assume that it is known that the data is normally distributed.

61.2	94.8	64.5	100.4	102.0	96.0
108.9	105.6	75.3	117.2	76.8	85.0

Hint: You will need to calculate the mean and standard deviation of the data.

13. The lowest 2.5% of the data is expected to fall below what value?

14. The highest 5% of the data is expected to fall above what value?

15. 90% of the data is expected to fall between what values?

16. 84% of the data is expected to fall below what value?

17. By using the Empirical Rule for normal distribution, how many pieces of data are expected to fall between 72.7 and 108.6? By observing the data, how many actually fall between 72.7 and 108.6?

18. By using the Empirical Rule for normal distribution, how many pieces of data are expected to lie above 113.6? By observing the data, how many actually lie above 113.6?

19. By using the Empirical Rule for normal distribution, what percent of data is expected to fall between 54.8 and 126.5? By observing the data, what percent of data actually falls between 54.8 and 126.5?

20. By using the Empirical Rule for normal distribution, what percent of data is expected to fall above 90.6? By observing the data, what percent of data actually falls above 90.6?

12 | Review Exercises

Answers to odd-numbered problems are available at the end of the textbook.

1. A baseball team played 162 games and won 72 times. Based on this, what is the probability that the team will win the next game?

2. Last month, a car salesman sold 30 cars out of the 125 cars sold at the dealership. Estimate the probability that the next car sale is by the same salesman.

3. A pair of fair, 6-sided dice is rolled. Calculate the probability that the roll:

   a. Has a sum of 5. b. Has a sum less than 7.

4. A pair of fair, 6-sided dice is rolled. Calculate the probability that the roll:

   a. Has a sum of 7. b. Has a sum more than 10.

5. A card is drawn from a well-shuffled, standard 52-card deck. Calculate the probability that it is:

   a. A Jack or a black Queen.

   b. A red card or a face card.

   c. An Ace or a heart.

6. A card is drawn from a well-shuffled, standard 52-card deck. Calculate the probability that it is:

   a. A number 10 or a black card.

   b. A King or a diamond.

   c. A spade or a face card.

7. A card is drawn from a well-shuffled, standard 52-card deck.

   a. What are the odds in favour of selecting a face card?

   b. What are the odds against selecting a heart?

8. A card is drawn from a well-shuffled, standard 52-card deck.

   a. What are the odds in favour of selecting a numbered card?

   b. What are the odds against selecting an Ace?

9. What is the probability that a randomly selected two-digit number is not divisible by 7?

10. What is the probability that randomly selected two-digit number is not divisible by 11?

11. A survey revealed that 85% of drivers wear their seatbelt while driving. If two drivers are chosen at random, what is the probability that they will not be wearing a seatbelt?

12. A survey revealed that 75% of all children like fast food. If three children are chosen at random, what is the probability that all three dislike fast food?

13. A box contains 7 white balls, 5 black balls, and 9 yellow balls. Two balls are chosen. What is the probability that both balls are black (a) with replacement, and (b) without replacement?

14. Three cards are chosen at random from a deck of 52 cards. What is the probability of choosing three face cards (a) with replacement, and (b) without replacement?

15. Nine boys and five girls apply for three scholarships. Calculate the probability that:

    a. All three scholarships go to boys.

    b. At least one scholarship goes to a girl.

16. The probability that Connor leaves for college on time is 0.60. The probability that Connor arrives at college on time is 0.80. What is the probability that he leaves on time and arrives at college on time?

17. In a normal distribution, if the mean is 35 and the standard deviation is 6, what percent of the data falls between 23 and 47?

18. In a normal distribution, if the mean is 115 and the standard deviation is 25, what percent of the data falls between 90 and 140?

19. The mean of a normally distributed group of employee income is $975 with a standard deviation of $125. Approximately, what percent of employees will have an income between $850 and $1,100?

20. The scores on an IQ test are normally distributed with a mean of 200 and a standard deviation of 17.5. A randomly selected data has a 95% chance of falling between what scores?

Self-Test | Chapter 12

Answers to all problems are available at the end of the textbook.

1. A number between 0 and 15 is randomly chosen. Calculate the probability of choosing an odd number.

2. A single letter is chosen at random from the word "Professor". What is the probability that the letter chosen is 's' or 'r'?

3. An urn contains 6 red marbles and 4 black marbles. Two marbles are drawn without replacement from the urn. What is the probability that both of the marbles are black?

4. If a fair die is rolled once, what is the probability that the roll will result in:

   a. 2 or 5? b. An odd number?

5. If a card is drawn from a well-shuffled, standard 52-card deck of cards, calculate the probability that the card is neither a spade nor a face card.

6. Two cards are drawn from a well-shuffled, standard 52-card deck without replacement. Calculate the probability of drawing:

   a. Two face cards.

   b. A King and a Queen.

   c. A face card and an Ace.

   d. Two spades.

7. There are 20 male students and 15 female students in a class. If a student is selected at random:

   a. What are the odds in favour of selecting a female student?

   b. What are the odds against selecting a male student?

8. In a survey of 160 twenty-year-olds, 80 responded that they were attending post-secondary school, 65 responded that they were working part-time, and 42 responded that they were attending school and working part-time. Determine the probability that a twenty-year-old chosen at random:

   a. Attends school, but does not work part-time

   b. Works part-time, but does not attend school

   c. Neither attends school nor works part-time

   d. Attends school or works part-time

   e. Attends school given he/she works part-time

   f. Works part-time given he/she attends school

9. In a normal distribution, if the mean is 180 and the standard deviation is 15, what percent of the data falls:

   a. Between 150 and 210?

   b. Between 135 and 225?

   c. Below 150?

   d. Above 225?

10. Given a set of data that is normally distributed with a mean of 12.2 and a standard deviation of 0.8, calculate the following:

    a. The interval that contains 95% of the data.

    b. The boundary for the lowest 5% of the data.

12 | Summary of Notation and Formulas

PROBABILITY

Classical Approach to Probability:

$$P(E) = \frac{\textit{Number of favourable outcomes of event "E"}}{\textit{Total number of possible outcomes}} = \frac{n(E)}{n(S)}$$

Empirical Approach to Probability:

$$P(E) = \frac{\textit{Number of times (frequency) that event "E" occurs}}{\textit{Number of trials}} = \frac{f}{n}$$

Complement Rule:

$P(A) + P(A') = 1$

Addition Rule for Mutually Exclusive Events:

$P(A \text{ or } B) = P(A) + P(B)$

Addition Rule for Mutually Non-Exclusive Events:

$P(A \text{ or } B) = P(A) + P(B) - P(A \text{ and } B)$

Multiplication Rule for Independent Events:

$P(A \text{ and } B) = P(A) \times P(B)$

Multiplication Rule for Dependent Events:

$P(A \text{ and } B) = P(A) \times P(B|A)$

Conditional Probability Rule:

$$P(A|B) = \frac{P(A \text{ and } B)}{P(B)}$$

Odds in Favour of an Event:

$P(A) : P(A')$, or $n(A) : n(A')$

Odds Against an Event:

$P(A') : P(A)$, or $n(A') : n(A)$

Answer Key

Chapter 1

Exercise 1.1

1. a. (i)Tens (ii) 90
   b. (i) Hundreds (ii) 300
   c. (i) Hundreds (ii) 700
3. a. (i) Ten thousands (ii) 10,000
   b. (i) Ten thousands (ii) 20,000
   c. (i) Millions (ii) 6,000,000
5. a. (i) Expanded form: 400 + 7
   (ii) Word form: Four hundred seven
   b. (i) Expanded form: 2,000 + 50 + 6
   (ii) Word form: Two thousand, fifty-six
7. a. (i) Expanded form: 20,000 + 9,000 + 100 + 80 + 6
   (ii) Word form: Twenty-nine thousand, one hundred eighty-six
   b. (i) Expanded form: 400,000 + 60,000 + 4,000 + 400 + 40 + 8
   (ii) Word form: Four hundred sixty-four thousand, four hundred forty-eight
9. a. (i) Expanded form: 2,000,000 + 600,000 + 4,000 + 300 + 20 + 5
   (ii) Word form: Two million, six hundred four thousand, three hundred twenty-five
   b. (i) Expanded form: 10,000,000 + 5,000,000 + 300,000 + 600 + 4
   (ii) Word form: Fifteen million, three hundred thousand, six hundred four
11. a. (i) Standard form: 679
   (ii) Word form: Six hundred seventy-nine
   b. (i) Standard form: 3,147
   (ii) Word form: Three thousand, one hundred forty-seven
13. a. (i) Standard form: 2,605
   (ii) Word form: Two thousand, six hundred five
   b. (i) Standard form: 9,024
   (ii) Word form: Nine thousand, twenty-four
15. a. (i) Standard form:40,990
   (ii) Word form: Forty thousand, nine hundred ninety
   b. (i) Standard form:10,053
   (ii) Word form: Ten thousand, fifty-three
17. a. (i) Standard form: 570
   (ii) Expanded form: 500 + 70
   b. (i) Standard form: 803
   (ii) Expanded form: 800 + 3
19. a. (i) Standard form: 80,630
   (ii) Expanded form: 80,000 + 600 + 30
   b. (i) Standard form: 75,025
   (ii) Expanded form: 70,000 + 5,000 + 20 + 5
21. a. (i) Standard form: 12,452,832
   (ii) Expanded form:10,000,000 + 2,000,000 + 400,000 + 50,000 + 2,000 + 800 + 30 + 2
   b. (i) Standard form: 32,684,256
   (ii) Expanded form: 30,000,000 + 2,000,000 + 600,000 + 80,000 + 4,000 + 200 + 50 + 6
23. a. (i) Standard form: 125,000
   (ii) Expanded form: 100,000 + 20,000 + 5,000
   b. (i) Standard form: 250,000
   (ii) Expanded form: 200,000 + 50,000
25. a.

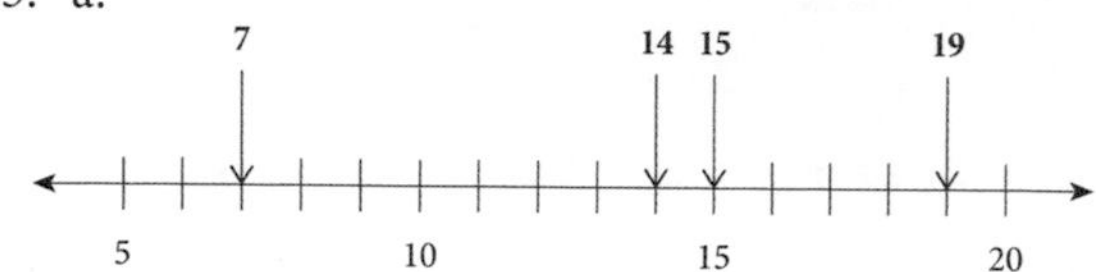

b.

27. a. 7<15 b. 19>14 c. 0<5 d.19>0
29. a. (i) 6 is less than 9 (ii) 9 is greater than 6
   b. (i)11 is less than 18 (ii)18 is greater than 11
   c. (i) 5 is less than 11 (ii) 11 is greater than 5
   d. (i) 0 is less than 11 (ii) 11 is greater than 0
31. a. 87, 96, 99, 103, 108
   b. 108, 139, 141, 159, 167
33. a. 2,040; 2,067; 2,533; 2,638
   b. 78,812; 79,468; 79,487; 79,534
35. a. (i) 259 (ii) 952
   b. (i) 1,789 (ii) 9,871
   c. (i) 3,458 (ii) 8,543
37. a. (i) 520 (ii) 500 (iii) 1,000
   b. (i) 1,650 (ii) 1,600 (iii) 2,000
   c. (i) 53,560 (ii) 53,600 (iii) 54,000
   d. (i) 235,360 (ii) 235,400 (iii) 235,000
39. a. (i) 880,000 (ii) 900,000 (iii) 1,000,000
   b. (i) 1,660,000 (ii)1,700,000 (iii) 2,000,000
   c. (i) 3,370,000 (ii) 3,400,000 (iii) 3,000,000
   d. (i) 4,570,000 (ii) 4,600,000 (iii) 5,000,000

Exercises 1.2

1. a. (i) 80 (ii) 77
   b. (i) 140 (ii) 133
3. a. (i) 930 (ii) 923
   b. (i) 650 (ii) 653

5. a. (i) 420 (ii) 410
 b. (i) 1,520 (ii) 1,511
7. a. (i) 670 (ii) 662
 b. (i) 1,830 (ii) 1,818
9. a. (i) 1,400 (ii) 1,413
 b. (i) 600 (ii) 652
11. a. (i) 7,400 (ii) 7,349
 b. (i) 5,700 (ii) 5,616
13. a. (i) 4,500 (ii) 4,531
 b. (i) 3,800 (ii) 3,732
15. a. (i) 30 (ii) 37
 b. (i) 10 (ii) 15
17. a. (i) 130 (ii) 129
 b. (i) 270 (ii) 268
19. a. (i) 610 (ii) 608
 b. (i) 490 (ii) 496
21. a. (i) 1,060 (ii)1,058
 b. (i) 2,040 (ii) 2,039
23. a. (i) 400 (ii) 494
 b. (i) 600 (ii) 604
25. a. (i) 700 (ii) 675
 b. (i) 2,200 (ii) 2,128
27. a. (i) 700 (ii) 667
 b. (i) 2,300 (ii) 2,324
29. a. (i) 4,800 (ii) 4,350
 b. (i) 3,600 (ii) 3,717
31. a. (i) 38,000 (ii) 40,492
 b. (i) 56,000 (ii) 54,332
33. a. (i) 80,000 (ii) 73,815
 b. (i) 129,000 (ii) 126,850
35. a. (i) 8 (ii) Quotient: 15 Reminder: 3
 b. (i) 4 (ii) Quotient: 4 Reminder: 4
37. a. (i) 3 (ii) Quotient: 3 Reminder: 5
 b. (i) 4 (ii) Quotient: 4 Reminder: 2
39. a. (i) 65 (ii) Quotient: 46 Reminder: 10
 b. (i) 20 (ii) Quotient: 16 Reminder: 12
41. a. (i) 128 (ii) Quotient: 142 Reminder: 6
 b. (i) 41 (ii) Quotient: 43 Reminder: 21
43. a. (i)15 (ii) Quotient: 14 Reminder: 148
 b. (i)13 (ii) Quotient: 13 Reminder: 27
45. a. 6^4 b. 12^2
47. a. 3^6 b. 9^4
49. a. Base: 2 Exponent: 9 b. Base: 5 Exponent: 7
51. a. Base: 1 Exponent: 20 b. Base: 8 Exponent: 3
53. a. $10 \times 10 \times 10 \times 10 \times 10 \times 10 = 1{,}000{,}000$
 b. $3 \times 3 \times 3 \times 3 \times 3 = 243$
55. a. $3^9 = 19{,}683$; $3^{11} = 177{,}147$
57. a. 8 b. 11
59. a. 1 b. 18
61. a. 8 b. 20
63. a. $719 b. $133
65. a. $1,362 b. $620
67. a. 360 pens b. 12 pieces
69. a. 45 weeks b. 352 chairs
71. $53 73. $2,130
75. $450 77. 42 weeks
79. 762 students 81. 125
83. $163
85. a. 24 boys b. 17 students

Exercises 1.3

1. 2, 3, 5, 7, 11, 13, 17 and 19
3. 12, 14, 15, 16, 18, 20, 21, 22, 24, 25, 26, 27 and 28
5. a. 13, 19 and 47 b. 11, 29 and 43
7. a. (i) Factors: 1, 3, 5 and 15
 (ii) Prime factors: 3 and 5
 b. (i) Factors: 1, 2, 17 and 34
 (ii) Prime factors: 2 and 17
9. a. (i) Factors: 1, 2, 4, 8, 16, 32 and 64
 (ii) Prime factors: 2
 b. (i) Factors: 1, 2, 3, 6, 9, 18, 27 and 54
 (ii) Prime factors: 2 and 3
11. a. (i) Factors: 1, 3, 7 and 21
 (ii) Prime factors: 3 and 7
 b. (i) Factors: 1, 5, 25
 (ii) Prime factors: 5
13. a. (i) Factors: 1, 2, 3, 4, 6, 9, 12, 18 and 36
 (ii) Prime factors: 2 and 3
 b. (i) Factors: 1, 5, 13 and 65
 (ii) Prime factors: 5 and 13
15. a. 6, 12, 18, 24, 30 and 36
 b. 8, 16, 24, 32, 40 and 48
17. a. 9, 18, 27, 36, 45 and 54
 b. 10, 20, 30, 40, 50 and 60
19. a. 30 b. 90 21. a. 72 b. 315
23. a. 64 b. 120 25. a. 24 b. 180
27. a. 150 b. 108 29. a. 84 b. 54
31. a. 72 b. 90
33. a. (i) Factors of 15: 1, 3, 5 and 15
 Factors of 25: 1, 5 and 25
 (ii) Common factors: 1 and 5
 (iii) GCF: 5
 b. (i) Factors of 18: 1, 2, 3, 6, 9 and 18
 Factors of 32: 1, 2, 4, 8, 16 and 32
 (ii) Common factors: 1 and 2
 (iii) GCF: 2
35. a. (i) Factors of 18: 1, 2, 3, 6, 9 and 18
 Factors of 48: 1, 2, 3, 4, 6, 8, 12, 16, 24 and 48
 (ii) Common factors: 1, 2, 3 and 6
 (iii) GCF: 6

b. (i) Factors of 32: 1, 2, 4, 8, 16 and 32
Factors of 60: 1, 2, 3, 4, 5, 6, 10, 12, 15, 20, 30 and 60
(ii) Common factors: 1, 2 and 4
(iii) GFC: 4

37. a. (i) Factors of 25: 1, 5 and 25
Factors of 80: 1, 2, 4, 5, 8, 10, 16, 20, 40 and 80
(ii) Common factors: 1 and 5
(iii) GFC: 5
b. (i) Factors of 40: 1, 2, 4, 5, 8, 10, 20 and 40
Factors of 120: 1, 2, 3, 4, 5, 6, 8, 10, 12, 15, 20, 24, 30, 40, 60 and 120
(ii) Common factors: 1, 2, 4, 5, 8, 10, 20 and 40
(iii) GFC: 40

39. a. (i) Factors of 8: 1, 2, 4 and 8
Factors of 12: 1, 2, 3, 4, 6 and 12
Factors of 15: 1, 3, 5 and 15
(ii) Common factor: 1
(iii) GFC: 1
b. (i) Factors of 6: 1, 2, 3 and 6
Factors of 15: 1, 3, 5 and 15
Factors of 20: 1, 2, 4, 5, 10 and 20
(ii) Common factor: 1
(iii) GFC: 1

41. a. (i) Factors of 12: 1, 2, 3, 4, 6 and 12
Factors of 18: 1, 2, 3, 6, 9 and 18
Factors of 24: 1, 2, 3, 4, 6, 8, 12 and 24
(ii) Common factors: 1, 2, 3 and 6
(iii) GFC: 6
b. (i) Factors of 12: 1, 2, 3, 4, 6 and 12
Factors of 30: 1, 2, 3, 5, 6, 10, 15 and 30
Factors of 42: 1, 2, 3, 6, 7, 14, 21 and 42
(ii) Common factors: 1, 2, 3 and 6
(iii) GFC: 6

43. a. (i) Factors of 40: 1, 2, 4, 5, 8, 10, 20 and 40
Factors of 50: 1, 2, 5, 10, 25 and 50
Factors of 80: 1, 2, 4, 5, 8, 10, 16, 20, 40 and 80
(ii) Common factors: 1, 2, 5 and 10
(iii) GFC: 10
b. (i) Factors of 30: 1, 2, 3, 5, 6, 10, 15 and 30
Factors of 75: 1, 3, 5, 15, 25 and 75
Factors of 90: 1, 2, 3, 5, 6, 9, 10, 15, 18, 30, 45 and 90
(ii) Common factors: 1, 3, 5 and 15
(iii) GFC:15

45. 32 cm 47. Feb 28th
49. 9 m 51. 6 minutes

Exercises 1.4

1. a. 21 b. 16 3. a. 16 b. 32
5. a. 16 b. 20 7. a. 256 b. 72
9. a. 35 b. 9 11. a. 70 b. 25
13. a. 15 b. 5 15. a. 12 b. 42
17. a. 4 b. 8 19. a. 5 b. 12
21. a. 2 b. 7 23. a. 9 b. 125
25. a. 108 b. 10 27. a. 32 b. 28
29. 126 31. 36 33. 407 35. 10
37. 4 39. 14 41. 148 43. 3
45. 11

Review Exercises 1

1. a. (i) 7,000 + 500 + 2
(ii) Seven thousand, five hundred two
b. (i) 20,000 + 5,000 + 40 + 7
(ii) Twenty-five thousand, forty-seven
c. (i) 600,000 + 20,000 + 20 + 5
(ii) Six hundred twenty thousand, twenty-five
d. (i) 3,000,000 + 50,000 + 4,000 + 700 + 5
(ii) Three million, fifty-four thousand, seven hundred five

3. a. (i) 5,607
(ii) 5,000 + 600 + 7
b. (i) 37,040
(ii) 30,000 + 7,000 + 40
c. (i) 408,105
(ii) 400,000 + 8,000 + 100 + 5
d. (i) 1,070,055
(ii) 1,000,000 + 70,000 + 50 + 5

5. a. 167 < 176 b. 2,067 < 2,097
c. 79,084 < 79,087 d. 162,555 > 162,507

7. a. (i) 3,900 (ii) 3,856
b. (i) 5,900 (ii) 5,772
c. (i) 7,100 (ii) 7,181
d. (i) 3,600 (ii) 3,636

9. a. 10,695 b. 8,760
c. 63 d. 211

11. a. 60 b. 144 c. 1,584
13. a. 4 b. 6 c. 2
15. a. 11 b. 14 17. a. 13 b. 7
19. a. 89 b. 4 21. a. 27 b. 27
23. a. 3 b. 10 25. a. 9 b. 25
27. a. 130 b. 14 29. 873 stamps
31. 850 tickets 33. $52,725
35. Babar: $875, Allan: $1,675
37. 16 boxes 39. 12 metres 41. 42 days

Self-Test Exercises 1

1. a. (i) 6900 (ii) 6,864
b. (i) 520,000 (ii) 445,900
c. (i) 67 (ii) 60
2. a. 34 b. 3 c. 2
3. a. 56 b. 36 c. 2
4. a. 7 b. 168 c. 40

5. a. 2 b. 20 c. 9
6. Hari: $1,275 Bob: $6,375
7. 25,995 kg 8. $940 9. 394 cars
10. 320 11. 1,008 sec or 16 min 48 sec
12. 6 metres

Chapter 2

Exercises 2.1

1. a. Proper fraction b. Mixed number
3. a. Improper fraction b. Mixed number
5. a. Mixed number b. Improper fraction
7. a. $\frac{16}{7}$ b. $\frac{25}{8}$
9. a. $\frac{29}{5}$ b. $\frac{27}{4}$
11. a. $2\frac{5}{7}$ b. $5\frac{5}{8}$
13. a. $7\frac{2}{3}$ b. $5\frac{1}{6}$
15. Not equivalent 17. Not equivalent
19. Equivalent 21. Equivalent
23. Not equivalent 25. Equivalent
27. Equivalent 29. Equivalent
31. a. (i) $\frac{3}{2}$ (ii) $\frac{2}{3}$ b. (i) $\frac{4}{7}$ (ii) $\frac{7}{4}$
33. a. (i) $\frac{7}{6}$ (ii) $\frac{6}{7}$ b. (i) 4 (ii) $\frac{1}{4}$
35. a. (i) $\frac{4}{7}$ (ii) $\frac{7}{4}$ b. (i) $\frac{5}{8}$ (ii) $\frac{8}{5}$
37. Equivalent 39. Not equivalent
41. Not equivalent 43. Equivalent
45. a. 12 b. 45 47. a. 24 b. 3
49. a. 8 b. 18 51. $\frac{1}{3}$ 53. $\frac{3}{4}$
55. $\frac{3}{4}$ 57. $\frac{149}{240}$

Exercises 2.2

1. $\frac{2}{5}$ 3. $\frac{12}{15}$ 5. $\frac{8}{7}$ 7. $\frac{8}{9}$
9. $\frac{5}{8}, \frac{3}{5}$ 11. a. $1\frac{1}{2}$ b. $1\frac{1}{3}$
13. a. $2\frac{1}{6}$ b. $18\frac{1}{12}$ 15. a. $15\frac{11}{12}$ b. $14\frac{5}{12}$
17. a. $\frac{309}{1000}$ b. $1\frac{9}{10}$
19. a. $\frac{5}{9}$ b. $\frac{3}{20}$
21. a. $1\frac{7}{24}$ b. $14\frac{5}{8}$
23. a. $3\frac{1}{2}$ b. $2\frac{1}{10}$
25. a. $\frac{54}{125}$ b. $\frac{11}{16}$
27. a. 4 b. $2\frac{1}{3}$
29. a. $\frac{15}{88}$ b. $12\frac{1}{2}$
31. a. $\frac{1}{14}$ b. $3\frac{1}{3}$
33. a. $1\frac{1}{2}$ b. $\frac{3}{32}$
35. a. $1\frac{5}{9}$ b. $2\frac{2}{3}$
37. a. $\frac{2}{5}$ b. $3\frac{3}{4}$
39. a. $\frac{4}{9}$ b. $12\frac{2}{3}$
41. a. $\frac{9}{25}$ b. $\frac{36}{49}$
43. a. $\frac{27}{64}$ b. $\frac{625}{81} = 7\frac{58}{81}$
45. a. $\frac{16}{9} = 1\frac{7}{9}$ b. $\frac{343}{8} = 42\frac{7}{8}$
47. a. $\frac{1}{3}$ b. $\frac{1}{7}$
49. a. $\frac{2}{5}$ b. $\frac{9}{4} = 2\frac{1}{4}$
51. a. $\frac{7}{4} = 1\frac{3}{4}$ b. $\frac{5}{2} = 2\frac{1}{2}$
53. $\frac{2}{3}$
55. $5\frac{7}{15}$ hours 57. $\frac{7}{8}$ pounds
59. $\frac{13}{28}$ kg 61. $\frac{1}{10}$
63. 1,350 textbooks 65. $3\frac{1}{2}$ km
67. 14 pieces 69. 200 doses
71. 304 bulbs 73. $2\frac{2}{5}$

Exercises 2.3

1. a. 0.6 b. 0.007 3. a. 0.12 b. 0.029
5. a. 7.5 b. 9.503 7. a. 3.67 b. 2.567
9. a. (i) 87.2 (ii) 80+7+0.2
11. a. (i) 3.04 (ii) 3+0.04
13. a. (i) 0.0401 (ii) 0.04+0.0001
15. a. (i) 89.0625
    (ii) 80 + 9 + 0.06 + 0.002 + 0.0005
17. a. (i) 1,787.025
    (ii) 1,000 + 700 + 80 + 7 + 0.02 + 0.005
19. a. (i) 412.65
    (ii) 400 + 10 + 2 + 0.6 + 0.05
21. a. (i) 1,600,000.02
    (ii) 1,000,000 + 600,000 + 0.02
23. a. (i) 23.5 (ii) 20 + 3 + 0.5
25. a. Forty-two and fifty-five hundredths
    b. Seven hundred thirty-four and one hundred twenty-five thousandths
27. a. Twenty-five hundredths
    b. Nine and five tenths

29. a. Seven and seven hundredths
    b. Fifteen and two thousandths
31. a. Sixty-two thousandths
    b. Fifty-four thousandths
33. 0.034, 0.043, 0.304, 0.403
35. 415.2   37. 264.2   39. 24.2
41. 10.4   43. 14.36   45. 181.13
47. $16.78   49. $9.99

Exercises 2.4

1. 1,716.045   3. 869.593
5. 479.444   7. 964.571
9. 240.922   11. 238.192
13. 15.88   15. 281.283
17. 229.668   19. 415.01
21. 744.606   23. 259.5571
25. 0.344   27. 319.4598
29. $7.53\overline{1}$ 31. 91.575
33. $24.\overline{3}$ 35. 12.4
37. a. 0.001   b. 0.09
39. a. 0.16   b. 0.000008
41. a. 0.5   b. 0.7   43. a. 1.1   b. 1.3
45. a. 0.1   b. 0.07   47. $378.64   49. $14.86
51. $76.38   53. $64.56
55. $1.54   57. $1,281.85
59. $187.86   61. $86.46
63. $44.21   65. $3,469.09
67. $54.45   69. 14 pieces
71. $2.55

Exercises 2.5

1. a. $\frac{1}{5}$ b. 0.75   c. $\frac{3}{50}$
3. a. 0.36   b. $\frac{1}{250}$ c. 0.14
5. a. 0.5   b. $\frac{2}{5}$ c. 0.06
7. a. $\frac{1}{200}$ b. 0.36   c. $\frac{1}{100}$
9. a. $\frac{7}{2}$ b. 1.6   c. $\frac{28}{5}$
11. a. 5.05   b. $\frac{34}{5}$ c. 2.75
13. a. $2\frac{1}{4}$ b. 1.75   c. $4\frac{1}{50}$
15. a. 8.35   b. $16\frac{1}{200}$ c. 15.5
17. a. $\frac{2}{3}$ b. $0.2\overline{5}$ c. $\frac{25}{99}$
19. a. $0.\overline{45}$ b. $\frac{2}{9}$ c. $0.\overline{285714}$
21. a. $\frac{8}{75}$ b. $\frac{3}{256}$
23 a. $\frac{27}{128}$ b. $\frac{9}{4} = 2\frac{1}{4}$

25. a. 1   b. $\frac{5}{6}$ 27. a. $\frac{2}{3}$ b. $\frac{85}{44} = 1\frac{41}{44}$
29. a. $\frac{369}{25} = 14\frac{19}{25}$ b. $\frac{707}{200} = 3\frac{107}{200}$
31. a. $\frac{55}{9} = 6\frac{1}{9}$ b. $\frac{1}{1024}$
33. a. $\frac{169}{500} = 0.338$ b. $\frac{1}{100} = 0.01$
35. $\frac{511}{192} = 2\frac{127}{192}$ 37. $\frac{12}{7} = 1\frac{5}{7}$
39. $\frac{391}{100} = 3\frac{91}{100}$ 41. $\frac{2339}{70} = 33\frac{29}{70}$
43. $\frac{1}{10} = 0.1$ 45. $\frac{3}{5} = 0.6$
47. 79   49. $\frac{73}{20} = 3\frac{13}{20} = 3.65$
51. $\frac{74}{25} = 2\frac{24}{25} = 2.96$

Review Exercises 2

1. a. 3, 48   b. 4, 60   c. 4, 15   d. 27, 24
3. a. $\frac{24}{21} < \frac{11}{5}$ b. $\frac{20}{44} > \frac{6}{15}$
   c. $\frac{18}{45} < \frac{16}{4}$ d. $\frac{15}{25} = \frac{63}{105}$
5. a. $1\frac{1}{2}$ b. $1\frac{1}{2}$ c. $7\frac{1}{3}$ d. $11\frac{1}{3}$
7. a. $\frac{5}{23}$ b. $\frac{31}{12}$ c. 5   d. $\frac{4}{5}$
9. a. Five tenths   b. Seven thousandths
   c. Twelve hundredths   d. Twenty-nine thousandths
11. a. Thirty-two and four hundredths
    b. Two hundred and two tenths
    c. Forty-five thousand, five and one thousandth
    d. One million, five thousand, seventy-one and twenty-five hundredths
13. a. 564.667   b. 40.103
    c. 79.3802   d. 9.63625
15. 0.189   17. 1.996
19. a. $\frac{1}{40}$ b. 0.625   c. $\frac{2}{25}$
    d. 0.28   e. $\frac{1}{500}$ f. 0.78
21. $13\frac{13}{24}$ kg   23. $5\frac{5}{6}$ years   25. $376\frac{1}{5}$ km
27. Alisha: $360, Beyonce: $220
29. $2,201.40   31. $870.89   33. 96 girls
35. $15\frac{27}{125}$ 37. $1\frac{1}{4} = 1.25$ 39. $\frac{21}{625}$
41. $\frac{5}{108}$ 43. $\frac{3}{4}$ 45. $1\frac{5}{11}$

Self-Test Exercises 2

1. a. 20, 24 b. 11, 30 c. 18, 96 d. 66, 24
2. a. $\frac{15}{2} = 7\frac{1}{2}$ b. $\frac{26}{3} = 8\frac{2}{3}$
   c. $\frac{16}{9} = 1\frac{7}{16}$ d. $\frac{9}{55}$
3. a. $\frac{55}{4} = 13\frac{3}{4}$ b. $\frac{28}{15} = 1\frac{13}{15}$ c. $\frac{1}{2}$ d. 6
4. a. 27.9028 b. 8.133 c. 2.13792 d. $2.297\overline{6}$
5. a. Four thousandths
   b. Six and five hundredths
   c. Three hundred and two hundredths
   d. Seven and seventy-one thousandths
6. a. $\frac{5}{8}$ b. $\frac{16}{5} = 3\frac{1}{5}$ c. $\frac{8}{11}$
   d. 0.35 e. 1.8 f. $1.0\overline{6}$
7. 593.75km; 37.8 cm 8. $1,500
9. a. $25\frac{13}{40}$ b. $8\frac{3}{4}$ c. $12\frac{17}{24} = 12.708\overline{3}$
10. a. $8\frac{16}{19}$ b. $3\frac{91}{100}$ c. $4\frac{11}{270}$
11. 13 deliveries 12. $\frac{1}{3}$; $80
13. $242.69 14. $9\frac{1}{8}$ km

Chapter 3

Exercises 3.1

1. a. Base: 7; Exponent: 4; Power: 7^4
   b. Repeated multiplication: $9 \times 9 \times 9 \times 9 \times 9$;
   Base: 9; Exponent: 5
   c. Repeated multiplication: $3 \times 3 \times 3 \times 3$; Base: 3^4
   d. Base: $\frac{2}{5}$; Exponent: 6; Power: $\left(\frac{2}{5}\right)^6$
   e. Repeated multiplication: $\frac{5}{7} \times \frac{5}{7} \times \frac{5}{7} \times \frac{5}{7} \times \frac{5}{7}$;
   Base: $\frac{5}{7}$; Exponent: 5
   f. Repeated multiplication: $\frac{4}{7} \times \frac{4}{7} \times \frac{4}{7}$; Power: $\left(\frac{4}{7}\right)^3$
   g. Base: 1.15; Exponent: 4; Power: $(1.15)^4$
   h. Repeated multiplication: $1.6 \times 1.6 \times 1.6$;
   Base: 1.6; Exponent: 3
   i. Repeated multiplication:
   $1.25 \times 1.25 \times 1.25 \times 1.25 \times 1.25$; Power: $(1.25)^5$
3. $4^9 = 262,144$ 5. $\left(\frac{1}{2}\right)^7 = 0.01$
7. $\left(\frac{5}{2}\right)^5 = 97.66$ 9. $(3.25)^6 = 1,178.42$
11. $6^5 = 7,776$ 13. $\left(\frac{2}{5}\right)^2 = 0.16$
15. $(1.4)^3 = 2.74$ 17. $6^6 = 46,656$
19. $\left(\frac{2}{3}\right)^{12} = 0.01$ 21. $(2.5)^6 = 244.14$
23. 2^{10} 25. 3^8 27. 3^6 29. 2^8
31. 10^6 33. 2^6 35. 150 37. 609
39. 240 41. 58 43. 368 45. 7
47. 609 49. 257 51. 8,000 53. 625
55. 13,168.72 57. 91 59. 96
61. $1\frac{3}{8} = 1.375$
63. 5.41 65. 5,184 67. 2.07 69. 104,976

Exercises 3.2

1. a. $\sqrt{64} = 8$ b. $\sqrt{\frac{25}{16}} = \frac{5}{4} = 1.25$
3. a. $\sqrt[3]{8} = 2$ b. $\sqrt[3]{\frac{27}{64}} = \frac{3}{4} = 0.75$
5. a. $(144)^{\frac{1}{2}} = 12$ b. $(64)^{\frac{1}{3}} = 4$
7. a. $(2)^{\frac{6}{2}} = 8$ b. $(40)^{\frac{1}{2}} = 6.32$
9. a. $(8)^{\frac{1}{2}} \times (12)^{\frac{1}{2}} = 9.80$ b. $(7)^{\frac{1}{2}} \times (14)^{\frac{1}{2}} = 9.90$
11. a. $\left(\frac{25}{49}\right)^{\frac{1}{2}} = 0.71$ b. $\left(\frac{64}{9}\right)^{\frac{1}{2}} = 2.67$
13. a. $(2)^{\frac{3}{4}} = 1.68$ b. $(5)^{\frac{3}{2}} = 11.18$
15. a. $(5)^{\frac{5}{4}} = 7.48$ b. $(3)^{\frac{103}{72}} = 4.81$
17. a. $(8)^{\frac{7}{5}} = 18.38$ b. $(5)^{\frac{5}{6}} = 3.82$
19. a. $8^2 = 64$ b. $(3)^{\frac{2}{3}} = 2.08$
21. a. $(4)^{\frac{3}{7}} = 1.81$ b. $(3)^{\frac{2}{3}} = 2.08$
23. a. $12^2 = 144$ b. $7^2 = 49$
25. a. 4.88 b. 1
27. a. 10.07 b. 0.66
29. a. 8.49 b. 51.96
31. a. $\frac{7}{6} = 1.17$ b. 0.19
33. a. $6^{-\frac{1}{2}} = \frac{1}{\sqrt{6}} = 0.41$ b. $7^{\frac{2}{3}} = \sqrt[3]{7^2} = 3.66$
35. a. $10^{-\frac{1}{5}} = \sqrt[5]{\frac{1}{10}} = 0.63$ b. $2^{-\frac{9}{7}} = \sqrt[7]{\left(\frac{1}{2}\right)^9} = 0.41$
37. a. $6^{-\frac{4}{3}} = \sqrt[3]{\left(\frac{1}{6}\right)^4} = 0.09$ b. $7^{\frac{37}{24}} = \sqrt[24]{7^{37}} = 20.08$
39. a. $5^{-\frac{8}{3}} = \sqrt[3]{\left(\frac{1}{5}\right)^8} = 0.01$ b. $6^3 = 216$
41. a. $8^4 = 4,096$ b. $7^{-3} = 0.003$
43. a. 0.67 b. 0.83 45. a. 0.33 b. 8
47. a. 0.91 b. 2.25

Exercises 3.3

1. a. $-5 < 0$ b. $-2 < 6$
3. a. $8 > -3$ b. $1 > -2$
5. a. $-6 > -8$ b. $-5 < -2$
7. a. −8, −6, −5, 2, 5, 8 b. −9, −8, −6, 3, 4, 7
9. a. −8, −5, 3, 7, 9, 10 b. −13, −8, −3, 2, 12, 15
11. a. 16 b. −3
13. a. −5 b. 9
15. a. −3 b. −5
17. a. 50 b. 5
19. a. −18 b. −4
21. a. −20 b. 6
23. a. 12 b. 14
25. a. 7 b. −3
27. a. 30 b. −24
29. a. 8 b. −9
31. a. 2 b. 17
33. a. 70 b. −72
35. a. 265 b. 30
37. −132
39. −111
41. 8
43. 9
45. a. $(-6)^8 = 1{,}679{,}616$ b. $8^3 = 512$
47. a. $(-4)^2 = 16$ b. $-5^2 = -25$
49. a. $(-2)^1 = -2$ b. $-(3^{-4}) = -0.01$
51. a. −23 b. 17
53. a. −18 b. −15

Exercises 3.4

1. a. 1 b. 3
3. a. 3 b. 4
5. a. 4 b. 6
7. a. 4 b. 5
9. a. 1 b. 3
11. a. (i) 5,060 (ii) 5,100 b. (i) 1,980 (ii) $2,\tilde{0}00$
13. a. (i) 589 (ii) 590 b. (i) 57.4 (ii) 57
15. a. (i) 48.5 (ii) 48 b. (i) 25.9 (ii) 26
17. a. (i) 0.785 (ii) 0.78 b. (i) 6.07 (ii) 6.1
19. a. (i) 0.989 (ii) 0.99 b. (i) 6.67 (ii) 6.7
21. a. 151.26 b. 353.2
23. a. 281.24 b. 412.1
25. a. 26.3 b. 42.4
27. a. 670 b. 6,960
29. a. 10 b. 8.83
31. a. $3\tilde{0}0,000$ b. 760
33. a. 2.35×10^2 b. 4.23×10^4
35. a. 5.8×10^{-1} b. 4.8×10^{-2}
37. a. 3.8×10^{-3} b. 2×10^{-4}
39. a. 6×10^6 b. 2.5×10^{-12}
41. a. 3.0×10^4 b. 3.6×10^{-7}
43. a. 46,000 b. 2.9
45. a. 3,090,000 b. 46,540
47. a. 0.89 b. 0.000216
49. a. 0.00315 b. 0.0000615
51. a. 5.6 b. 0.0004065
53. 8.884×10^5
55. 9.978×10^{-3}
57. 2.84×10^9
59. 7.215×10^{-2}
61. 2.439×10^4
63. 1.72×10^{14}
65. 3.15×10^{-6}
67. 3.2×10^{-3}
69. 5.0×10^1
71. 1.4×10^3

Review Exercises 3

1. 7
3. $(3^5)^{\frac{3}{5}} = 27$
5. a. $2^2 = 4$ b. $5^3 = 125$
7. a. $3^3 = 27$ b. $6^1 = 6$
9. a. 27 b. 0.2
11. a. 400 b. −10,000,000
13. a. $\frac{1}{5} = 0.2$ b. $\frac{1}{7} = 0.\overline{142857}$ c. $\frac{8}{9} = 0.\overline{8}$
15. a. 49 b. $\frac{5}{6} = 0.8\overline{3}$ c. $\frac{6}{5} = 1.2$
17. a. 3.97 b. 50
19. a. 96.57 b. 24
21. a. −19 b. 27
23. a. 7,180.08 b. 1,817.28
25. 164,593.54
27. −17,668.97
29. a. 0 b. −7
31. a. 13 b. −28
33. a. 5; 7.1011×10^3 b. 5; 5.4001×10^1 c. 2; 7.2×10^{-3}
35. a. 890 b. 0.056 c. 0.000964
37. a. 4.7495×10^{14} b. 7.715×10^{-2}
39. a. 3.9744×10^6 b. 2.759×10^{-3}
41. a. 2.4×10^{12} b. 4.5×10^{-10}
43. a. 5.0×10^{-4} b. 2.5×10^{-7}

Self-Test Exercises 3

1. a. 3^6 b. 2^7 c. 3^3 d. 2^3
2. a. 3^{10} b. 10^9
3. a. $\frac{3^2}{2^6} = 0.14$ b. $2 \times 3^2 = 18$
4. a. 0.01 b. 1
5. a. 0.84 b. 5.80
6. a. 13.6 b. 1
7. a. 32 b. 5.80
8. a. 1,953,125 b. 3
9. a. −26 b. 42
10. a. −61 b. −16
11. a. −3 b. 0
12. a. 2.67 b. 0.19
13. a. 1.009×10^1 b. 5.0×10^{-3} c. 6.02×10^4
14. a. 2,700 b. 0.00415 c. 0.030405
15. a. 5.009×10^4 b. -9.534×10^{-7}
16. a. 5.2×10^{-1} b. 1.4×10^{19}

Chapter 4

Exercises 4.1

1. a. $2x - 3$ b. $\frac{2x}{5}$ c. $25 + 3x$

3. a. i. 3 ii. 0 iii. 3, 7, −4
   b. i. 2 ii. 0 iii. 1, −5
   c. i. 4 ii. 2 iii. 9, 7, −6
5. a. i. 3 ii. 5 iii. 5, −3
   b. i. 3 ii. 1 iii. −2, 3
   c. i. 3 ii. 7 iii. −2, −2
7. a. $12A$ and $-7A$; $4B$ and $-B$
   b. $6x$ and $-5x$; $8y$ and $-3y$
9. a. $-2x$, $5x$ and $-12x$; 8 and −3
   b. $6xy^2$ and $2xy^2$; $-2x^2y$ and $3x^2y$; $-4x^2$ and $2x^2$
11. 24 13. 65
15. a. $\frac{23}{9}$ b. 24
17. a. 30 b. 22

Exercises 4.2

1. x^{10} 3. $8x^5$ 5. $15x^8$ 7. $-6x^8$
9. x^{14} 11. $24x^6$ 13. x^3 15. $3x^4$
17. x^3 19. x^{23} 21. 256 23. $\frac{8x^{12}}{125y^6}$
25. $\frac{4x^6}{25y^4}$ 27. 1 29. $\frac{1}{16x^8}$ 31. $\frac{x^5y}{2}$
33. $\frac{x^6}{9y^6}$ 35. $\frac{8x^6}{y^{12}}$ 37. $\frac{x}{y}$ 39. $\frac{x}{y}$
41. x^9 43. $-8x^4$ 45. $\frac{25}{64y^6}$ 47. x^4
49. $-\frac{64y^7}{x^2}$ 51. $\frac{3x^2}{y^4}$ 53. x^3y^5 55. x^8y^2
57. $x^{\frac{1}{5}}$ 59. $x^{\frac{5}{6}}$ 61. $\frac{1}{x^{\frac{1}{3}}}$ 63. $\frac{1}{x^{\frac{3}{4}}}$
65. x^6 67. $\frac{1}{(2x)^{\frac{1}{3}}}$ 69. x^4 71. x^3y^4
73. x^5 75. $3x^{\frac{2}{3}}$

Exercises 4.3

1. 30 3. 56 5. −6 7. 6,750
9. $11x^2 + 17x$ 11. $-7y^2 + y$
13. $3y^2 + 3x$ 15. $x^2y^2 + xy^2$
17. $-90x + 42$ 19. −38
21. $-5x + 7$ 23. $2x - 4$
25. $30x - 10y - 90$ 27. $-14y - 144$
29. $-7y^2 - 12y + 6$ 31. $4x + 25$
33. $-17x^2 + 58x - 36$ 35. $10x^2 - 16x - 14$
37. $-8x^2 - 16x + 15$ 39. $x^2 + 10x + 25$
41. $4x^2 + 9y^2 + 12xy$ 43. $x^2 - 6x + 9$
45. $9x^2 + 4y^2 - 12xy$ 47. $9x^2 - 6x + 1$
49. $4x^2 - 12x + 9$ 51. $x^2 - 25$
53. $-49x^2 + 9$ 55. $2x^2 + 2x + 13$
57. $8x + 25$ 59. $13x^2 - 12x - 5$
61. $4x^2 - y^2 - 16x - 6y + 7$ 63. 4
65. $\frac{3}{2}$ 67. $-x - y$
69. $5x - 3y + 1$ 71. $\frac{x^2}{2y}$

Exercises 4.4

1. $4x(2x + 1)$ 3. $7xy(1 - 5x)$
5. $3x^2y(1 + 2xy)$ 7. $5x(6x^2 + y - 3x)$
9. $10y(y + 7xy + 5x^2)$ 11. $\frac{3(x^2 + 3)}{2}$
13. $\frac{3(x - 5)}{8}$ 15. $\frac{15x(3y - 1)}{16(x + 3)}$
17. $(x - 2y)(x + 3)$ 19. $(x + 3)(x + 5)$
21. $(z^2 + 3)(2x - 3y)$ 23. $(x + 5)(x - 6y)$
25. $(5x - 3)(y + 2)$ 27. $(x + 6)(x - 6)$
29. $(1 - x)(1 + x)$
31. $(10x - 30)(10x + 30)$ 33. $(4x - 3y)(4x + 3y)$
35. $(x - 1)(x + 5)$
37. $(25 + x^2)(5 + x)(5 - x)$
39. $(x + 6)(x + 5)$ 41. $(x + 4)(x - 3)$
43. $(x - 6)(x - 1)$ 45. $(x - 6)(x + 5)$
47. $(x + 9y)(x + 7y)$ 49. $x(x + 9)(x - 2)$
51. $(5x + 3)(x + 1)$ 53. $(2x + 1)(x - 3)$
55. $(3x - 5)(x + 2)$ 57. $(5x + 3)(x - 5)$
59. $4(x + 3)(x - 5)$ 61. $(x + 6)^2$
63. $(x + 2)^2$ 65. $(5x - 1)^2$
67. $(1 - 3x)^2$ 69. $(5x + 3)^2$

Exercises 4.5

1. $x + 6 = 10$; $x = 4$ 3. $6x = 72$; $x = 12$
5. $\frac{x}{5} = 4$; $x = 20$ 7. $\frac{2}{3}x = 12$; $x = 18$
9. $x = 30$ 11. $x = 18$
13. $x = -17$ 15. $x = 6$
17. $x = 1\frac{2}{11}$ 19. $x = 1\frac{2}{5}$
21. $x = 2$ 23. $x = -\frac{3}{20}$
25. $x = 4$ 27. $x = 24$
29. $x = 16$ 31. $y = 1.72$
33. $x = 4$ 35. $x = 1.8$
37. $x = -2$ 39. $x = -2.2$
41. $x = 4.33$ 43. $x = 0.41$
45. $x = 16$ 47. $y = 42$
49. $x = 52.6$ 51. $y = 11$
53. $x = -5$ 55. 5
57. 9-metre and 16-metre long wire
59. Becky's share: \$325; Andy's share: \$175
61. Adult ticket: \$10; Child ticket: \$7
63. $A = (x + 4)(x + 3)$; $A = 182$ square metres
65. \$12.5 67. \$26
69. 30°, 70°, and 80°
71. 15 cm, 25 cm and 30 cm
73. 188.24 lb
75. Water: 2.13 L; 15% Solution: 1.87 L

Exercises 4.6

1. $x = \frac{y-5}{4}$
3. $x = \frac{y+7}{3}$
5. $C = S - M$
7. $L = \frac{N}{1-d}$
9. $E = S - C - P$
11. $x = \frac{y}{3} + 2$
13. $a = \frac{b}{c-b}$
15. $b = \frac{a}{c} - 1$
17. $a = \frac{2b+c}{b-c}$
19. $a = \frac{4c+b}{b-c}$
21. $x = a - \frac{y}{6}$
23. $x = -\frac{3}{2}a$
25. $u = \pm\sqrt{V^2 - 2as}$
27. $y = \pm\sqrt{(r^2 - x^2)}$
29. $x = \frac{y}{1-y}$
31. $x = \frac{5(y+1)}{y-1}$
33. $x = \frac{y^2+5}{2}$
35. $x = y^2 - 16y + 64$
37. $A = 4\pi r^2$
39. $y = \frac{x}{x-5}$
41. $a = \frac{2A}{h} - b$
43. $x = \pm\sqrt{y+16}$
45. $P_2 = \frac{P_1V_1T_2}{T_1V_2}$
47. a. $S = \sqrt{A}$ b. 21 cm
49. a. $r = \sqrt{\frac{A}{4\pi}}$ b. 7.98 cm

Exercises 4.7

1. a. $\log 100{,}000 = 5$ b. $\log_4 1{,}024 = 5$
3. a. $\log_2 64 = 6$ b. $\log_6 7{,}776 = 5$
5. a. $\log_3 9 = 2$ b. $\log_9 6{,}561 = 4$
7. a. $10^2 = 100$ b. $4^3 = 64$
9. a. $2^5 = 32$ b. $5^4 = 625$
11. a. $3^6 = 729$ b. $6^3 = 216$
13. a. 2.3522 b. 0.1875
15. a. 1.5441 b. −0.6021
17. a. 2.3076 b. 0.0050
19. a. −1.8018 b. 0.0198
21. a. $\ln 3 - \ln 7$
23. $\ln 4 + \ln 9$
25. $\ln A + \ln B - \ln C$
27. $\ln X - \ln Y - \ln Z$
29. $\ln 3 + \ln x - \ln 2 - \ln y - \ln z$
31. $\ln x + \ln y - \frac{1}{2}\ln z$
33. $M - N$
35. $M + 2N$
37. $2M - N$
39. $-\frac{1}{2}(M+N)$
41. $\frac{4}{5}M$
43. $-\frac{1}{3}(M+N)$
45. 5.9069
47. 5.2255
49. −3.6496
51. 1.5293
53. ln 40
55. ln 5
57. ln 675
59. $\ln \frac{32}{9}$
61. ln 25
63. ln 216
65. $\ln\left(\frac{x}{y}\right)^2$
67. $\ln (ab)^4$
69. $\ln\left(\frac{a^3b^2}{c^5}\right)$
71. $\ln\left(\frac{81}{2}\right)$
73. $\frac{3}{2} = 1.5$
75. 3
77. $\frac{4}{3}$
79. $-\frac{1}{3}$
81. 0.0688
83. 0.5163
85. 42.3316
87. 30.9989
89. 1.6234
91. 5.5345
93. 2.3258
95. 8.8275

Review Exercises 4

1. a. $3x + 12$ b. $x - 5$
3. a. $(3 + x)x$ b. $10x + 15$
5. a. $\frac{1}{x^2}$ b. $-x^7$
7. a. x^4 b. $\frac{1}{x^2}$
9. a. $x^{\frac{3}{2}} y$ b. x^2
11. a. x^2 b. 1
13. a. $3x^7$ b. x^4
15. a. $\frac{x^4}{4y^5}$ b. $\frac{2y^{10}}{x^7}$
17. a. $\frac{8x^9}{y^6}$ b. $2x^2$
19. a. x^{14} b. $\frac{y^{24}}{4x^{10}}$
21. a. 12 b. −12
23. a. −32 b. 10
25. a. −24 b. 91
27. a. $2x(3x - 2)$; 2 b. $7x(y + 2x)$; 168
29. a. $(3x - 1)(2x^2 + 5)$ b. $(x - 3)(y + 5)$
31. a. $(2x - 3)(2x + 3)$ b. $(5x - 8y)(5x + 8y)$
33. a. $(x + 9)(x - 4)$ b. $(2x + 5)(2x + 3)$
35. a. $(x + 8)(x + 8)$ b. $(3x - 4)(3x - 4)$
37. a. $5x + 17 = 42$; $x = 5$ b. $\frac{x}{15} = 45$; $x = 675$
39. a. $x - 10 = 10$; $x = 20$ b. $3(4x) = 36$; $x=3$
41. a. $x = 3$ b. $x = 18$
43. a. $x = -9$ b. $x = 2$
45. a. $= \frac{C}{2\pi}$ b. 11.94 cm
47. a. $h = \frac{3V}{\pi r^2}$ b. 35.99 cm

49. a. 28.3614 b. 55.4781

51. a. 8.9658 b. 14.2067

53. a. ln 33 b. ln 4

55. a. $\ln\left(\frac{4}{9}\right)$ b. ln 1000

57. $\ln\left(\frac{s^4t^5}{r^3}\right)$

59. a. 26.2473 b. 1,691.6285

61. a. 7 b. 4

Self-Test Exercises 4

1. a. $3x - 25$ b. $x + 18$
2. a. $2x - 6$ b. $\frac{x}{3}$
3. a. $-x^7$ b. x^2
4. a. $\frac{1}{x^2}$ b. x^2
5. a. $4y^2$ b. $-\frac{2y^4}{x^2}$
6. a. $-x^2 - 6x + 10$; 19 b. $4x - 11y + 7$; 4
7. a. $6x + 13$; 31 b. $-5x^2 + 26x + 24$; 45
8. a. $2xy(4y - 3x)$ b. $2b(5a - 4c)$
9. a. $(x - 5)(4y - x)$ b. $(1 - 11x)(1 + 11x)$
10. a. $2(x - 4)(x - 7)$ b. $(4x + 3)(x - 3)$
11. a. $(x + 5)(x + 5)$ b. $(x + 8y)(x - 2y)$
12. a. $2x - 9 = 21$; $x = 15$

    b. $3 - 5x = 22$; $x = -\frac{19}{5} = -3.8$
13. a. $(4)(8) = 16x$; $x = 2$ b. $6x = 30$; $x = 5$
14. a. $x = 4$ b. $x = 18$
15. a. $x = -\frac{4}{7}$ b. $x = 4\frac{2}{3}$
16. a. $F = \frac{9C}{5} + 32$ b. 86°F
17. a. $h = \frac{A}{2\pi r} - r$ b. 9.10 cm
18. a. 15.4545 b. 7.7527
19. $\ln\left(\frac{8}{27}\right) = \ln\left(\frac{2}{3}\right)^3$
20. a. 13.3344 b. 102.6977

Chapter 5

Exercises 5.1

1. a. 0.75, $\frac{3}{4}$

   b. 30%, $\frac{3}{10}$

   c. 25%, 0.25

3. a. 0.05, $\frac{1}{20}$

   b. 20%, $\frac{1}{5}$

   c. 60%, 0.60

5. a. 1.5, $1\frac{1}{2}$

   b. 17.5%, $\frac{7}{40}$

   c. 48%, 0.48

7. a. 0.125, $\frac{1}{8}$

   b. 5%, $\frac{1}{20}$

   c. 450%, 4.5

9. a. 0.006, $\frac{3}{500}$

   b. 0.5%, $\frac{1}{200}$

   c. 460%, 4.6

11. a. 0.0005, $\frac{1}{2,000}$

    b. 0.25%, $\frac{1}{400}$

    c. 112.5%, 1.125

13. a. 0.006, $\frac{3}{500}$

    b. 108%, $1\frac{2}{25}$

    c. $5.\overline{45}$%, $0.0\overline{54}$

15. a. 0.0175, $\frac{7}{400}$

    b. 202.5%, $2\frac{1}{40}$

    c. 0.25%, 0.0025

17. a. 0.065, $\frac{13}{200}$ b. 250%, $2\frac{1}{2}$ c. 16%, 0.16

19. a. 70 b. 100

21. a. 0.19 b. 0.5 km 23. a. 52 b.$53.33

25. 2 27. $16.50 29. $0.27 31. 7.5

33. 40% 35. 400% 37. 45.45% 39. 28%

41. 800 43. $186 45. 130

47. $2,200 49. $32.50 51. $25,000

53. 74% 55. $700,000

57. $315,723.08 59. 13%

61. $89,400

Exercises 5.2

1. a. $391.50 b. $10,687.50

   c. $480.00 d. $620.69

   e. 50% f. 170.59%

3. a. $79.75 b. –$159.38

   c. $550.00 d. $4,459.02

   e. 45.95% f. 69.23%

5. $2110.00 7. $280,000

9. 20% 11. $45.00

13. $30.53 15. 10.34%

17. $29,706.75 19. $721.78

21. 22.02% 23. $30.94

25. $60,800 27. 22.22%

29. 16.67% 31. 4.17%

33. Depreciated by 4.76% 35. –11.86%

37. 25% less 39. 13.33%

41. First Year: –13.51%; Second Year: –21.56%; Two-Year period: –32.16%

43. $450 45. Tudor

Exercises 5.3

1. I: $135; S: $1,035 3. I: $99.9; S: $1,579.9

5. I: $72; S: $5,912 7. $182

9. $126 11. $40; $1,500

13. $558; $4,158 15. r: 8%; I:$180

17. t: 2.5 years; S: $5,500 19. P: $2,540; r: 3.15%

21. t: 36 months; I: $192 23. P: $1,825; S: $1,861

25. 5% 27. 4 years 29. $2,500 31. 7%

33. $4,155.28; $304.72 35. 13.94%

37. 852 days 39. 4.32%

Exercises 5.4

1. $4,062.50; $2,031.25; $1,875.00; $937.50
3. $40,560.00; $1,690.00; $1,560.00; $780.00
5. $42,900.00; $3,575.00; $1,650.00; $825.00
7. $35,100.00; $2,925.00; $1,462.50; $675.00
9. $35,022.00; $2,918.50; $1,459.25; $1,347.00
11. Bi-weekly: $1,400.00; Monthly: $3,033.33
13. Annual: $49,725.00; Monthly: $4,143.75
15. Annual: $49,725.00; Weekly: $956.25
17. $2,145.00
19. Bi-weekly: $2,640.00; Semi-monthly:$2,860.00
21. $1,100.00; $27.50; $41.25
23. $38,870.00; $23.00; 1.50
25. $27,027.00; 33; $23.63
27. $33,540.00; $645.00; $38.70
29. a. $1,307.69 b. $56.04 c. $1,643.93
31. $39; $65,910
33. $829.50; $43,134
35. $2,047.50
37. $58,500
39. 3.0%
41. $2,612.50
43. $51,500.00
45. 6.5%

Review Exercises 5

1. a. 0.80; $\frac{4}{5}$ b. 25%; $\frac{1}{4}$ c. 150%; 1.50
   d. $0.0\overline{63}$; $\frac{19}{300}$ e. 4.8%; $\frac{6}{125}$ f. 8%; 0.08
3. a. 36 b. 20% c. $0.23
5. $460,000
7. 75%
9. $1,153,153.15
11. a. 42,875 b. 38,500,000
13. a. 306 b. $9 c. $11,250 d. 680 kg
15. a. $530 b. $7.38 c. 75% d. 25%
17. $49
19. 20%
21. 12.5%
23. $250,000
25. $41,643.84
27. $180,200
29. 13.04%
31. a. 33.33% b. 22.54%
33. 5.8%
35. $225
37. $3,125
39. 5.5%
41. Annual: $45,500; Monthly: $3,791.67
43. Hourly rate$22.5; Overtime rate: $45
45. Annual: $28,275; Semi-monthly: $1,178.13
47. Annual: $53,913.6; Bi-weekly: $2,073.6
49. $36,000

Self-Test Exercises 5

1. a. 0.106; $\frac{53}{500}$ b. 225%; $2\frac{1}{4}$
   c. 0.25%; 0.0025 d. 0.005; $\frac{1}{200}$
   e. 0.2%; $\frac{1}{500}$ f. 26.5%; 0.265
2. a. 12.5% b. $337.5 c. $500
3. $71,080.81
4. a. 60% b. 10%
5. a. 56.25% b. $819.25 c. $4.73 d. –25%
   e. $120 f. $310
6. 21
7. $85
8. –28%
9. $468,000
10. a. $18.2 b. –9%
11. a. –7.67%, –16.61% b. –23.01%
12. 4.8%
13. $4,500
14. $45.36
15. Annual: $42,120; Monthly: $3,510
16. a. $1,344 b. $19.2
17. $2,535
18. 7.5%

Chapter 6

Exercises 6.1

1. a. Not equivalent b. Equivalent
   c. Not equivalent d. Equivalent
3. a. Equivalent b. Equivalent
   c. Not equivalent d. Equivalent
5. a. (i) 3 : 8 : 5 (ii) 1 : 2.67 : 1.67
   b. (i) 7 : 2 : 5 (ii) 3.5 : 1 : 2.5
   c. (i) 9 : 20 : 40 (ii) 1 : 2.22 : 4.44
7. a. (i) 10 : 3 (ii) 3.33 : 1
   b. (i) 36 : 5 : 9 (ii) 7.2 : 1 : 1.8
   c. (i) 3 : 15 : 20 (ii) 1 : 5 : 6.67
9. a. 3 : 8 b. 1 : 4 c. 2 : 5
11. a. 12 : 2 : 1 : 4 b. 24 : 4 : 1 : 8
13. 75 km/h
15. 11 km/L
17. 75 words/min
19. 29 pages/min
21. 2 kg of flour for $3.30
23. 8 pencils for $2.88
25. 0.8 litres of juice for $1.40
27. 11:20
29. 540 km/h
31. A has a higher hourly rate
33. a. Kate's rate: $28/h; Susan's rate: $27.75/h
    b. Kate's rate is higher by $0.25 per hour.
35. Mike pays $40; Sarah pays $50.
37. Amy's share: $2,500; Gary's share: $4,000; Andrew's share: $1,000.
39. 30 cm, 16 cm, 20 cm
41. Alex: $800, Brooks: $1,200.
43. a. $\frac{4}{15}$ b. 5 : 6 : 4
    c. 25 red, 30 green, 20 blue
45. $16,875
47. 8 : 6 : 5

Exercises 6.2

1. a. Yes b. No c. Yes d. No
3. a. $x = 3$ b. $x = 36$ c. $\frac{5}{3}$ d. $x = 10$
5. a. $x = 12\frac{20}{47}$ b. $x = 3\frac{411}{475}$
   c. $x = \frac{11}{18}$ d. $x = 2\frac{5}{8}$

7. 180 L 9. $2,290.91 11. 11.63 km
13. GIC: $13,625, Fixed deposit: $8,175
15. a. B's investment: $20,000
C's investment: $15,000
b. B's profit: $24,000, C's profit: $18,000
c. A's profit: $56,250
B's profit: $45,000
C's profit: $33,750
17. A's investment: $15,000
B's investment: $18,000
C's investment: $12,000
19. 29:37:53 21. $496
23. $881.67 25. $1,730.77
27. $45,000
29. a. 26 students b. 20 girls : 13 boys
31. 360 tigers

Exercises 6.3

1. £124.44 3. €4,732.61
5. €1,773.68 7. US$22.17
9. C$1,334.12
11. a. C$2,051.33 b. C$50.03
13. C$5,988.99 15. C$6,381.64
17. Lose: C$51.26 19. 2.9%

Exercises 6.4

1. Index Number 2011: 115.63
Index Number 2016: 134.38
3. Metro Pass Adult: 143.29
Metro Pass Student: 134.53
5. Year 5: $2,558.14 Year 7: $2,790.70
7. Year 2: $1,909.09 Year 3: $1,954.55
9. $71,714.02 11. 11.93%
13. $3,647.68
15. 2015: 78.99% 2016: 77.88%
17. $28,431.15 19. $41,015.83

Review Exercises 6

1. a. Equivalent b. Not equivalent
c. Equivalent b. Not equivalent
3. 1 : 20
5. a. 18 km/hr b. 27 km
7. Gina by $0.75per hour 9. 480 grams for $3.75
11. a. $2.66/kg b. $2.50/kg
c. $2.40/kg Best offer: c
13. 9 : 15 : 5 15. 140 computers
17. a. 6 b. 18 c. 0.06
19. a. $0.7 b. $0.21
21. $1,057.69 23. $162.5
25. $13,625
27. Khan: $1,000; Thomas: $2,500
29. 17 : 20 : 23
31. Anton: $1,200; Cheryl: $2,250; Ellen: $1,800
33. £933.30 35. €886.84
37. C$3,972.65 39. $27,553.65
41. $5,596.57 43. 83.4%

Self-Test Exercises 6

1. 360 gram for $4.89 2. 74.07 km/hr
3. 9 hours 20 minutes 4. a. 12 b. 40.5
5. a. 7.5 b. $7\frac{1}{5}$ 6. 212.5 km
7. $2,668.90 8. 22.5L
9. Best offer: c 10. 6 : 10 : 15
11. $2,700 12. $208.33
13 A: $1,500; B: $2,500; C: $2,000
14. 11 : 21
15. Alice: $18,000; Bill: $12,000; Carol: $28,800
16. C$2,979.49 17. 0.40%
18. $33,849.84 19. $89,545.06
20. $9,750.78

Chapter 7

Exercises 7.1

1. a. 240 cm; 2,400 mm b. 8.6 m; 8,600 mm
c. 34.42 m; 3,442 cm
3. a. 25 cm; 250 mm b. 0.58 m; 580 mm
c. 8.47 m; 847 cm
5. a. 1,620 m; 162,000 cm b. 2.39 km; 239,000 cm
c. 0.0232 km; 23.2 m
7. a. 650 m; 65,000 cm b. 0.154 km; 15,400 cm
c. 0.0177 km; 17.7 m
9. a. 2,321 cm b. 167 mm
c. 5,252 m
11. a. 3 m 35 cm b. 60 cm 3 mm
c. 1 km 487 m
13. 0.15 km, 150,800 mm, 15,200 cm, 155 m
15. 775 metres 17. 178 centimetres
19. a. 2,620 g b. 6.75 kg
21. a. 840 g b. 0.58 kg
23. a. 1,650 g; 1,650,000 mg
b. 4.95 kg; 4,950,000 mg
c. 0.00644 kg; 6.44 g
25. a. 760 g; 760,000 mg
b. 35.76 kg; 35,760,000 mg
c. 0.0503 kg; 50.3 g
27. a. 18,079 g b. 2,000,116 mg
c. 3,074 kg
29. a. 5 kg 903 g b. 2 g 884 mg
c. 9 t 704 kg
31. 850,250 mg, 0 .075 t, 123,200 g, 125 kg
33. 200 tablespoons 35. 175 g
37. $16.25
39. a. 3,250 mL b. 5.06 L

41. a. 45 mL b. 0.22 L
43. a. 5.085 L b. 2.005 L
45. a. 2 L 708 mL b. 12 L 80 mL
47. 4.5 L 49. 790 mL

Exercises 7.2

1. a. 126 ft; 1,512 in b. 16 yd; 576 in
   c. 18 yd; 54 ft
3. a. 139.5 ft; 1,674 in b. 7.5 yd; 270 in
   c. 80 yd; 240 ft
5. a. 5,280 yd; 15,840 ft b. 3.5 mi; 18,480 ft
   c. 2 mi; 3,520 yd
7. a. 3,960 yd; 11,880 ft b. 1.25 mi; 6,600 ft
   c. 1.17 mi; 2,064 yd
9. a. 37.5 ft b. 142 in
   c. 1,881 yd
11. a. 26 yd 0 ft b. 47 ft 6 in
   c. 3 mi 425 yd
13. 15 in 15. 4.5 ft 17. 7.5 mi
19. a. 18 lb b. 128 oz
21. a. 14.5 lb b. 404 oz
23. a. 70,000 lb b. 7.25 ton
25. a. 25,500 lb b. 32.5 ton
27. a. 186 oz b. 5,250 lb
29. a. 27 ton 1,825 lb b. 9 lb 6 oz
31. 1.2 ton, 2,250 lb, 34,400 oz
33. 5 oz 35. 1,000 packages
37. a. 44 pt; 88 c b. 19 qt; 76 c c. 17 qt; 34 pt
39. a. 65 pt; 130 c b. 22.5 qt; 90 c c. 23.5 qt; 47 pt
41. a. 48 qt; 96 pt b. 4.5 gal; 36 pt c. 7 gal; 28 qt
43. a. 30 qt; 60 pt b. 3.5 gal; 28 pt c. 6.25 gal; 25 qt
45. a. 19 pt b. 33 c c. 49 qt
47. a. 9 qt 1 pt b. 19 pt 1 c c. 21 gal 2 qt
49. 6 qt,14 pt,29 c,2 gal 51. 3.75 gallons
53. 9 cups

Exercises 7.3

1. a. 155.38 mi b. 193.08 km
3. a. 19.14 yd b. 20.12 m
5. a. 820.21 ft b. 22.86 m
7. a. 39.37 in b. 8.89 cm
9. 4,250 cm, 28 yd, 82.5 ft, 24 m, 900 in
11. 2.45 m 13. 159.1 km
15. a. 3.86 tons b. 2,268 kg
17. a. 34.17 lb b. 20.41 kg
19. a. 2.65 lb b. 2,948.4 g
21. a. 7.05 oz b. 113.4 g
23. 5.7 lb, 2.5 kg, 2,450 g, 80 oz
25. 157.2 g 27. 68.66 kg
29. a. 13.21 gal b. 39.74 L
31. a. 15.85 qt b. 13.25 L
33. a. 15.85 pt b. 6.62 L
35. a. 19.02 c b. 3.31 L
37. a. 0.27 fl oz b. 606.19 mL
39. 10.5 pt, 4.8 qt, 1 gal, 3.5 L
41. 9.51 gal 43. 1.13 L
45. a. 62.15 mi/h b. 80.45 km/h
47. a. 35.29 mi/gal b. 19.13 km/L
49. a. 72.91 ft/s b. 21.95 km/h
51. Car A 53. 28.85 min
55. US$3.97per gallon 57. 69.8° F
59. 37 °C 61. 284 °F 63. 44.44 °C
65. −26.11 °C 67. 6.85 °C 69. 292.15 K
71. 299.82 K 73. 26.85 °C 75. −99.67 °F
77. 253.15 K 79. 210.93 K

Review Exercises 7

1. a. 705 cm b. 15,050 m
   c. 7 cm 5 mm d. 9 m 5 cm
3. a. 118 ft b. 55 in
   c. 9 ft 7 in d. 3 mi 10 yd
5. a. 10,032 g b. 45,052 mg
   c. 3 kg 620 g d. 42 g 7 mg
7. a. 103 oz b. 29,005 lb
   c. 16 ton 0 lb d. 7 lb 8 oz
9. a. 6,049 mL b. 9 L 6 mL
   c. 38 qt d. 37 qt 1 pt
11. a. 210 °C b. 176 °F
   c. 51.67 °C d. 86 °F
13. a. −33.15 °C b. 294.15 K
   c. 278.71 K d. 80.33 °F
15. a. 25 m/s b. 0.72 km/h
   c. 96.54 km/h d. 32.93 mi/gal
17. a. 40.40 miles b. 29.53 feet
   c. 228.6 centimetres d. 5,148.8 metres
19. a. 11.02 pounds b. 44.09 ounces
   c. 113.4 grams d. 9.07 kilograms
21. a. 9.25 gallons b. 0.88 fluid ounces
   c. 64.35 litres d. 1.24 litres
23. 5.25 mi, 9,200 yd, 7.5 km
25. 115 oz, 7 lb, 3 kg
27. 75 qt, 70 L, 18 gal
29. a. 224.13 kilometres b. 139.29 miles
31. a. 200.16 lb b. 90.79 kg
33. a. 2.73 gallons b. 10.33 litres
35. a. 177 °C

Self-Test Exercises 7

1. a. 2.73 cm b. 8 km 105 m
   c. 62 in d. 3 mi 420 yd
2. a. 53,107 g b. 5 g 519 mg
   c. 127 oz d. 20 ton 0 lb
3. a. 5,007 mL b. 9 L 60 mL
   c. 105 qt d. 41 qt 1 pt

4. a. –9.44 °C b. 14 °F
   c. 76.85 °C d. 267.59 K
5. a. 155.38 miles b. 147.64 feet
   c. 800.1 centimetres d. 4,022.5 metres
6. a. 5.51 pounds b. 14.11 ounces
   c. 793.8 grams d. 6.38 kilograms
7. a. 15.85 gallons b. 14.37 fluid ounces
   c. 9.46 litres d. 0.89 litres
8. 215 ft, 65 m, 2,500 in
9. 2.5 lb, 1,200 g, 45 oz
10. 84 L, 22 gal, 175 pt
11. a. 1,005.91 ft b. 306.6 m
12. a. 18.03 ounces b. 511.28 grams
13. a. 0.42 gallons b. 1,588.75 millilitres
14. 32.18 min
15. 20 °C higher

Chapter 8

Exercises 8.1

1.

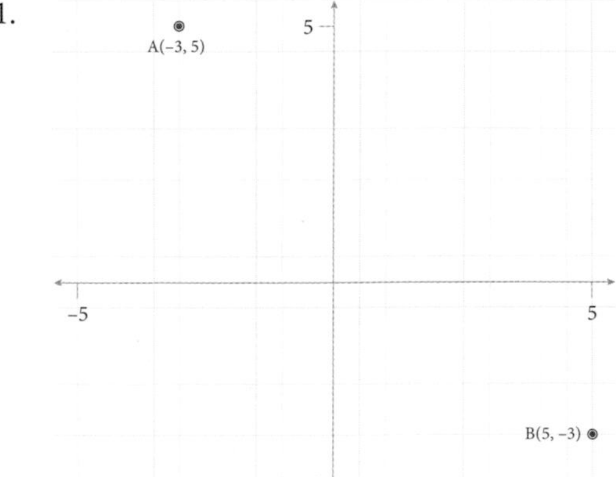

3.

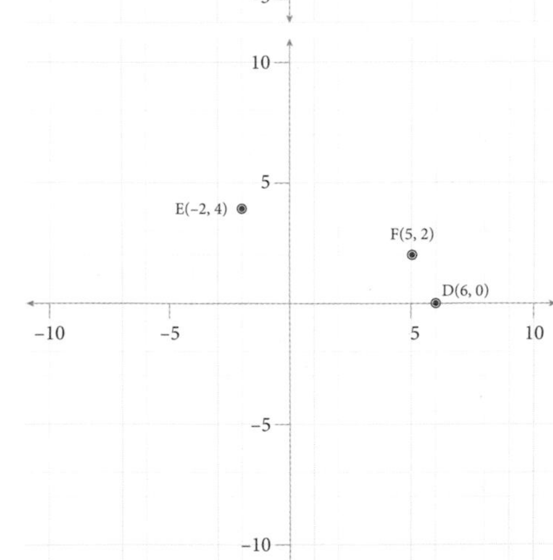

5. a. Quadrant II b. Quadrant IV
   c. Quadrant I
7. a. X-axis (left) b. Quadrant III
   c. Y-axis (up)

9. a. 2 units

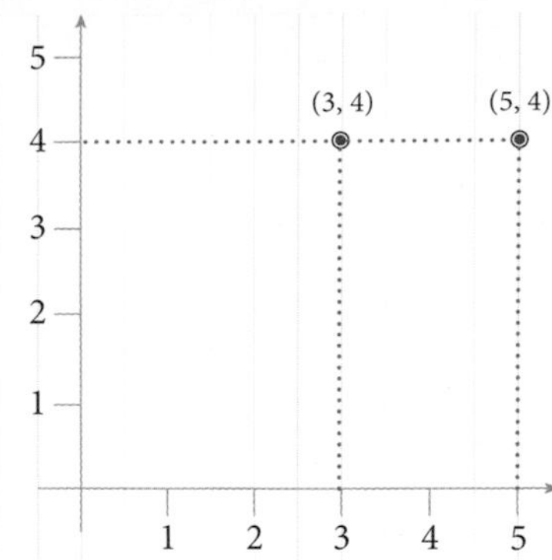

b. 9 units

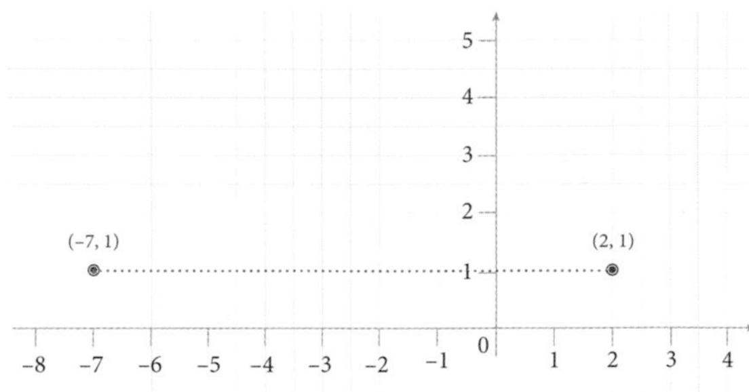

11. a. 5 units

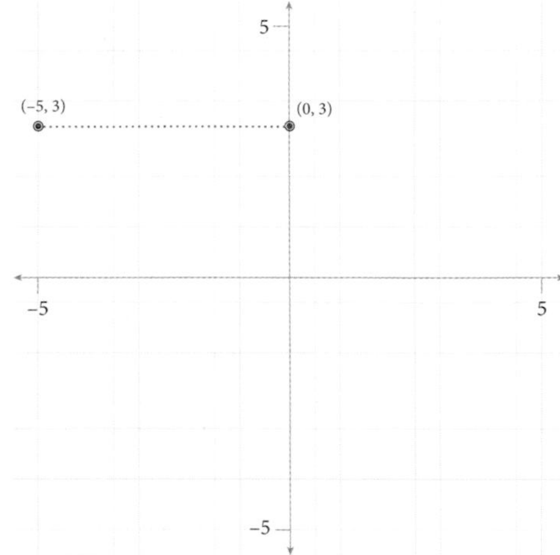

b. 8 units

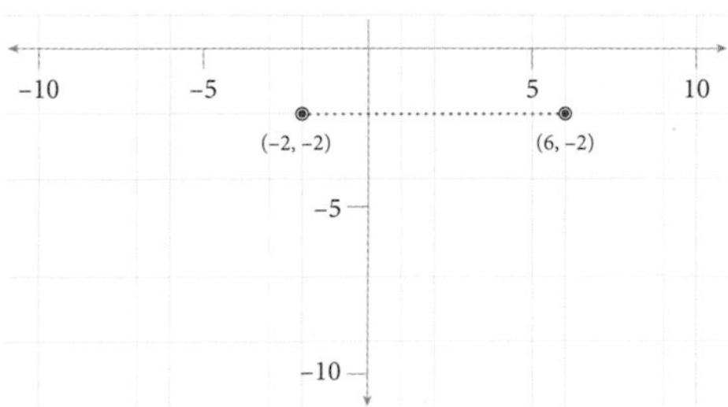

13. a. 5 units

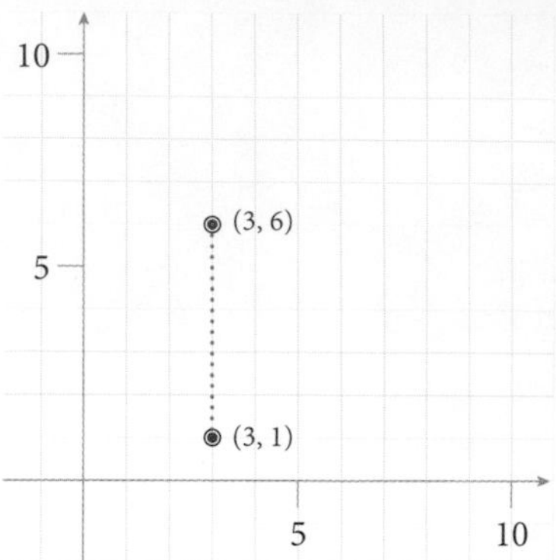

b. 7 units

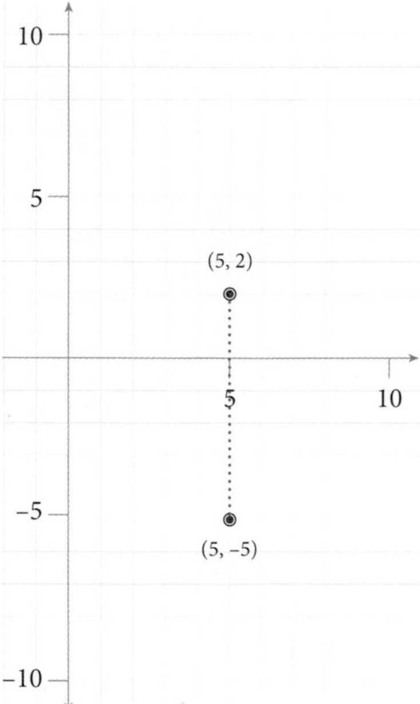

15. a. 4 units

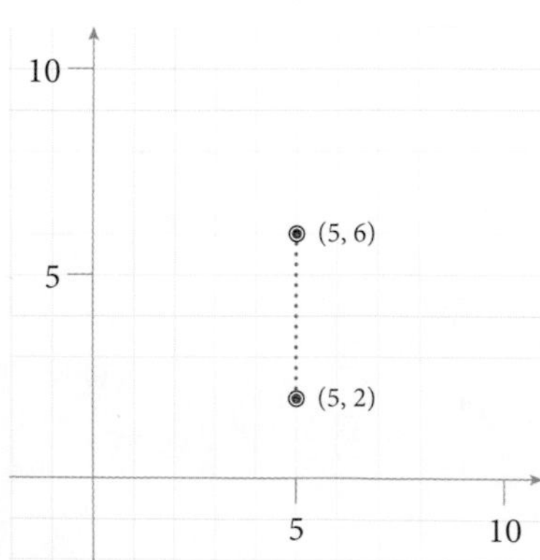

b. 6 units

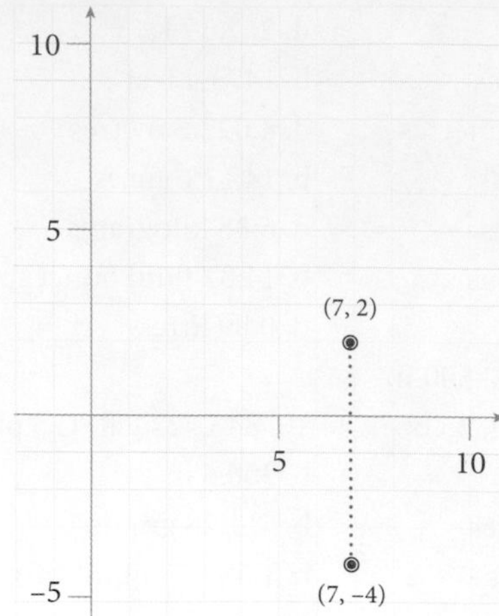

17. D (–3, –1)

19. S(–3, –1)

21. (1, 12) and (1, –2)

23. (–7, 3) and (5, 3)

Exercises 8.2

1. a. 4 b. 10 c. 6
   d. 9 e. 15 f. 6

3. a. –3 b. 3 c. 1
   d. $\frac{3}{2}$ e. 6 f. –6

5. $5x - 2y = -2$

7. $3x + 4y = -12$

9. $x - 2y = -3$

11. $y = -\frac{3}{2}x - \frac{3}{4}$

13. $y = \frac{3}{2}x + 5$

15. $y = -\frac{3}{2}x + 3$

17.

$y = x + 3$		
x	y	(x, y)
0	3	(0, 3)
1	4	(1, 4)
2	5	(2, 5)
3	6	(3, 6)

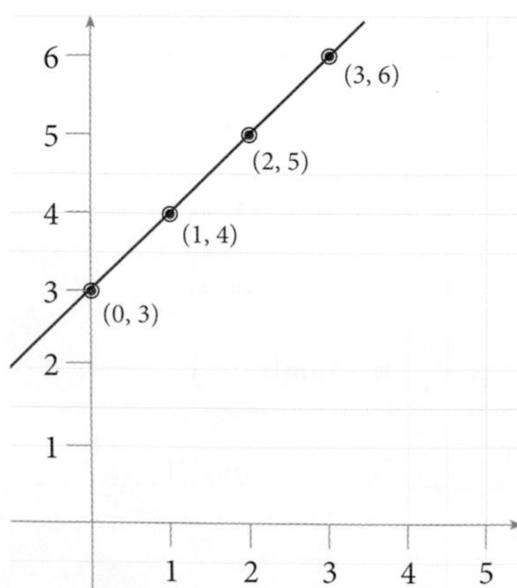

19.

$y = -5x + 1$		
x	y	(x, y)
0	1	(0, 1)
1	−4	(1, −4)
2	−9	(2, −9)
3	−14	(3, −14)

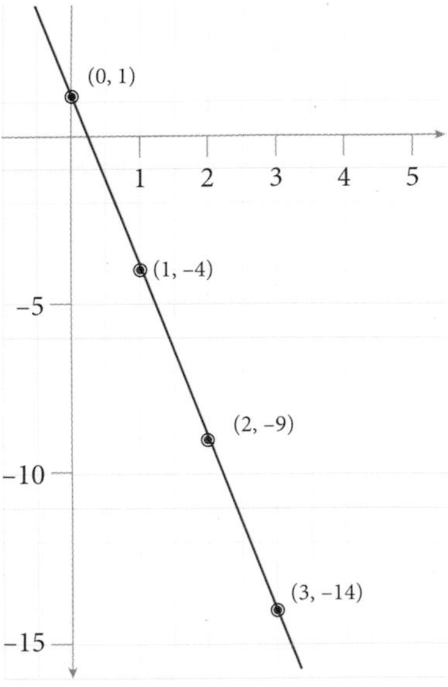

21.

$2x + y + 1 = 0$		
x	y	(x, y)
0	−1	(0, −1)
1	−3	(1, −3)
2	−5	(2, −5)
3	−7	(3, −7)

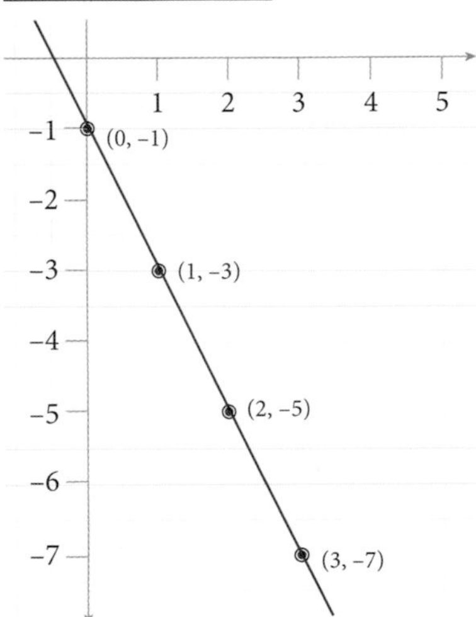

23.

$2x - y - 3 = 0$		
x	y	(x, y)
0	−3	(0, −3)
1	−1	(1, −1)
2	1	(2, 1)
3	3	(3, 3)

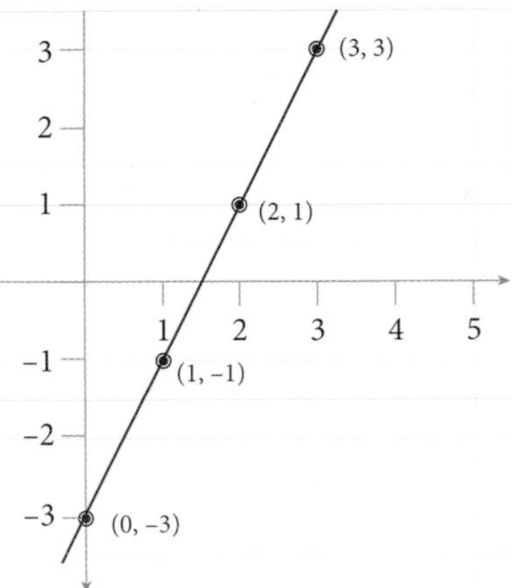

25. x-intercept: $(-\frac{2}{3}, 0)$; y-intercept:(0, −2)

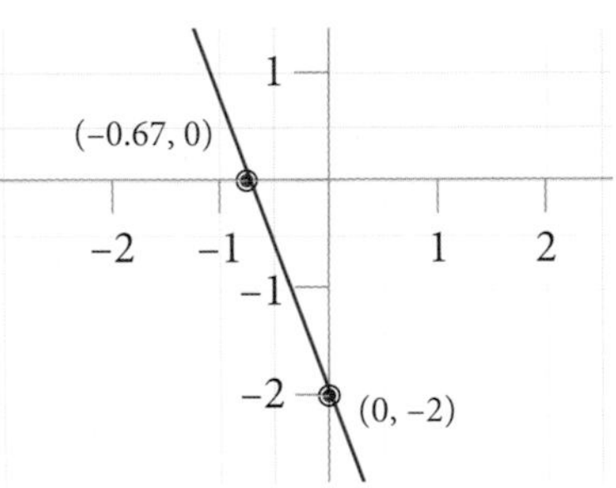

27. x-intercept: (7, 0); y-intercept: (0, 7)

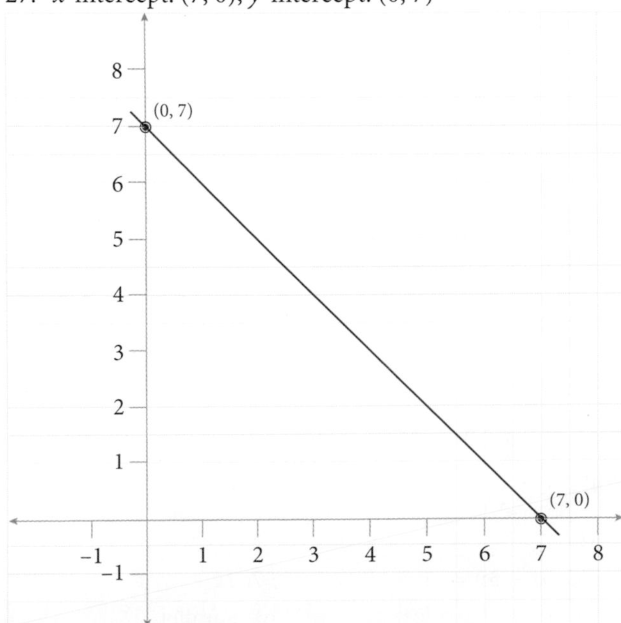

29. x-intercept:(−2, 0); y-intercept: (0, 4)

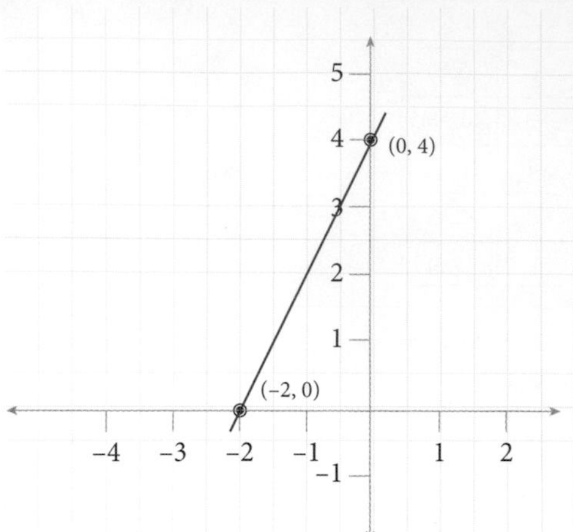

31. $m = \frac{2}{3}$; $b = -6$

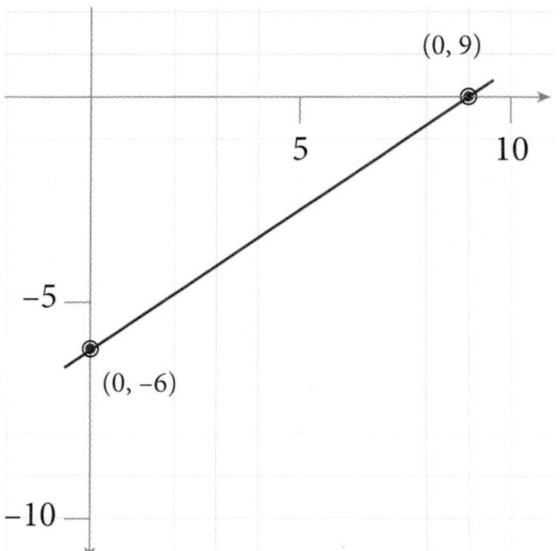

33. $m = \frac{4}{7}$; $b = 3$

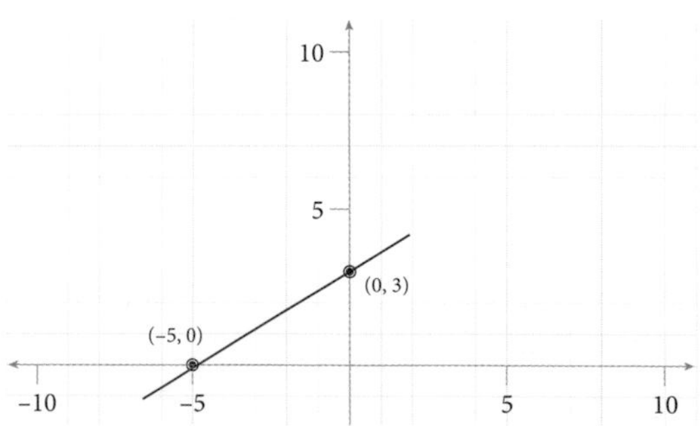

35. Positive slope

37. 0

39. $-\frac{5}{8}$

41. $y = 2$

43. $y = x - 2$

45. $y = -2x + 10$

47. $y = \frac{2}{3}x$

49. $y = -\frac{3}{2}x + 6$

51. 2

53. 7

55. $5x + 3y = 15$

57. $2x + y = 1$

59. Perpendicular

61. Parallel

63. Perpendicular

65. Neither

67. $y = \frac{2}{3}x - \frac{13}{3}$

69. $y = \frac{1}{3}x - 20$

71. $y = x + 7$

73. $y = -\frac{1}{2}x + 1$

Exercises 8.3

1. (1, 1); Consistent; Independent

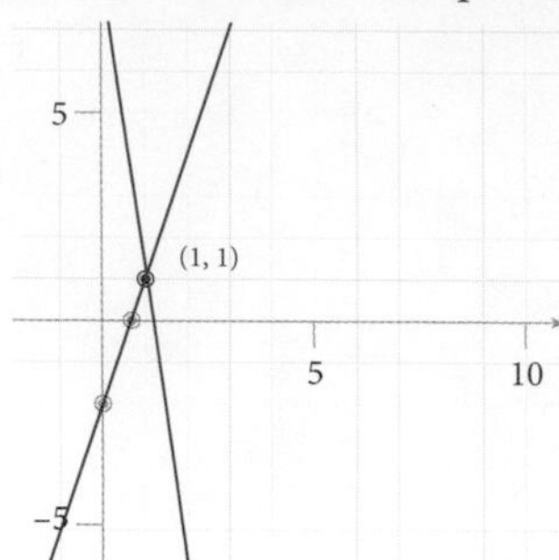

3. No solution; Inconsistent; Independent

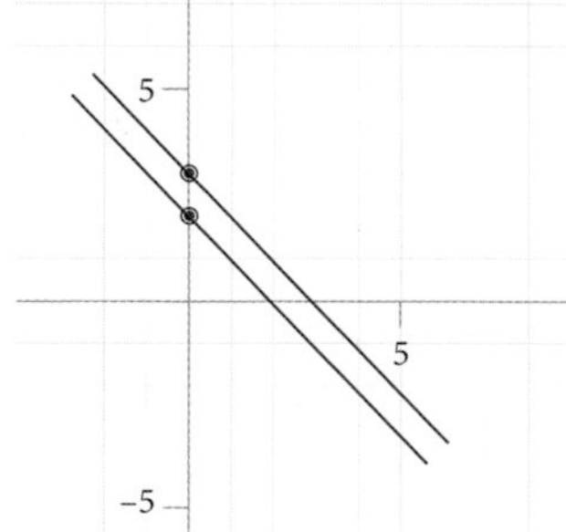

5. Infinitely many solutions; Consistent; Dependent

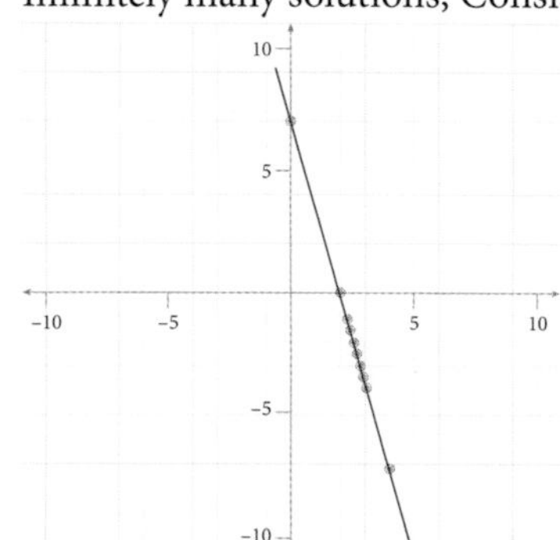

7. No solution; Inconsistent; Independent

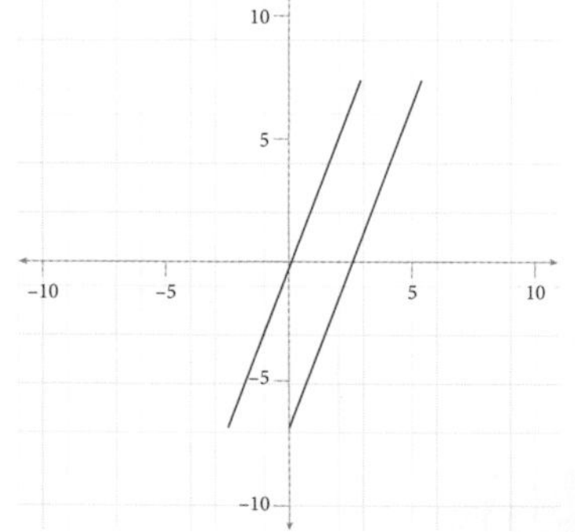

9. (2, 1); Consistent; Independent

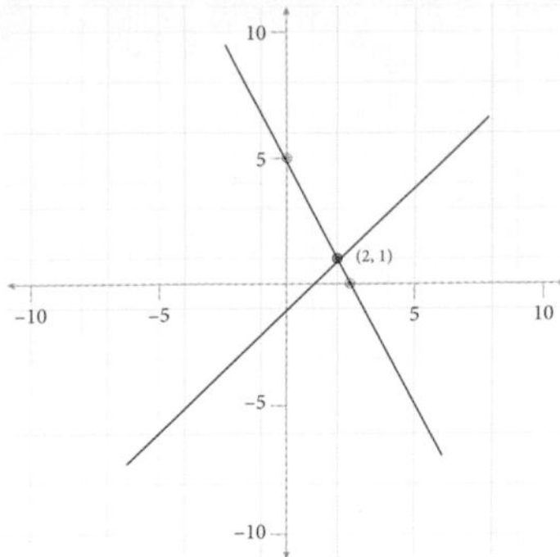

11. (−2, 1); Consistent; Independent

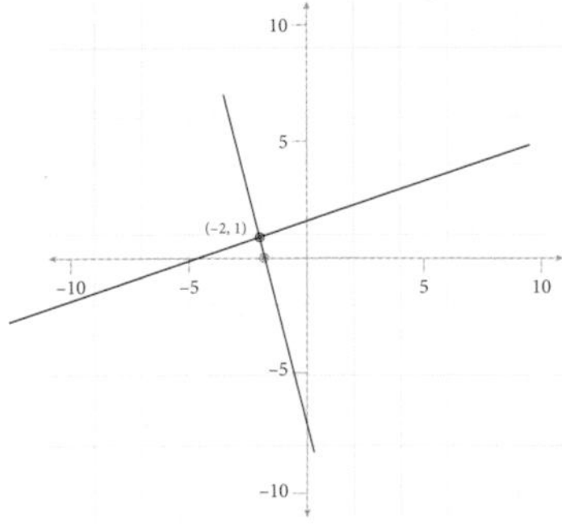

13. Infinitely many solutions; Consistent; Dependent

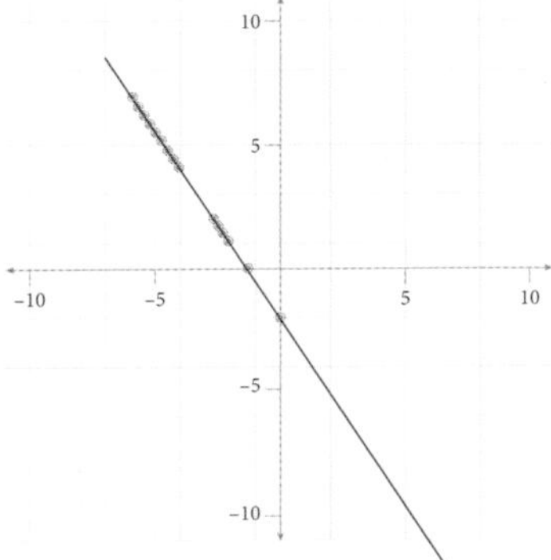

15. No solution; Inconsistent, Independent

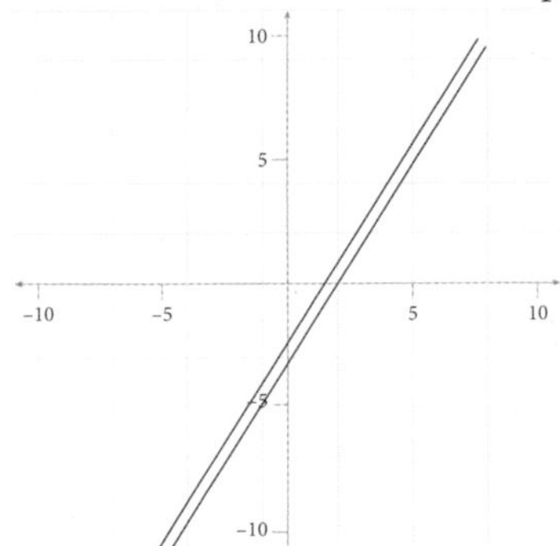

17. (3, −3); Consistent; Independent

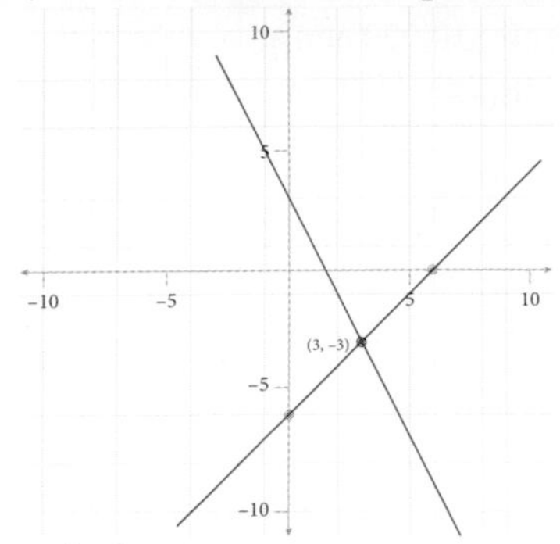

19. $(-\frac{8}{3}, \frac{1}{3})$; Consistent; Independent

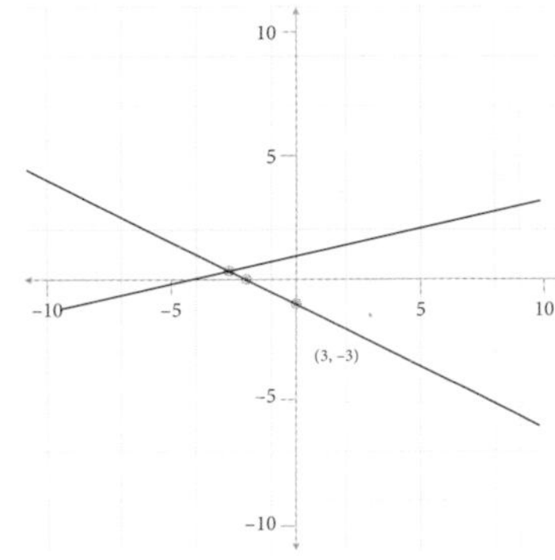

21. One solution
23. One solution
25. No solution
27. No solution
29. 4
31. 6
33. a. club A: $y = 4x + 60$; club B: $y = 6x + 36$

b.

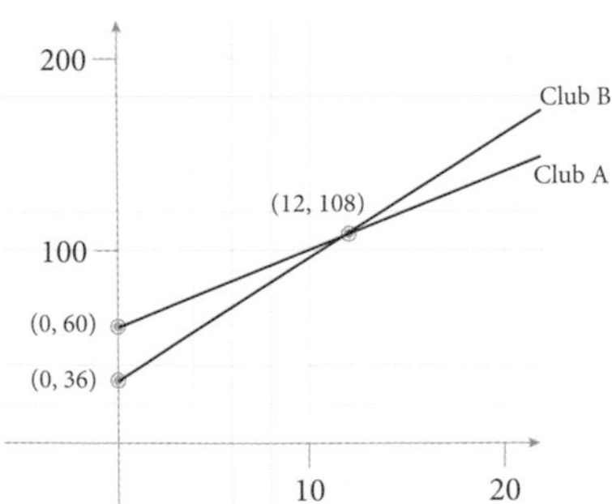

c. (12, 108); both clubs will charge $108 if Louis attends 12 classes

d. Louis should join club A if he is planning to take more than 12 classes during the year

Exercises 8.4

1. (2, −2)
3. $(\frac{54}{11}, \frac{37}{11})$
5. (3, −3)
7. (2, 1)
9. (6, −1)
11. (1, 2)
13. (9, 2)
15. (2, 3)
17. (−1, −2)
19. (1, −2)
21. (2, 4)
23. (3, −2)
25. (−3, −1)
27. (3, −2)
29. (10, 6)
31. (3, 3)
33. (1, 3)
35. (3, −2)
37. $12

39. Father' age 60 years; Son's age: 32 years
41. \$15,000 at 5% and \$10,000 at 4%
43. 98 quarters, 32 dimes
45. 129°; 51°
47. 5 litres 5% sugar and 5 litres 15% sugar
49. $y = 15x + 5$; $m = 15$; $b = 5$
51. 12 hours
53. Slope = 15 and y-intercept = 5

Review Exercises 8

1. a. Quadrant IV b. Quadrant II
   c. X-axis (right) d. Quadrant IV
   e. X-axis (right) f. Y-axis (up)
3. Rectangle
   Perimeter = 22 units; Area=24 square units

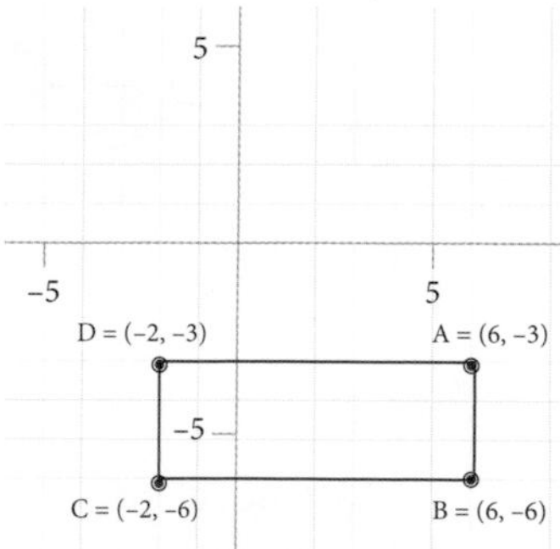

5.

$4x - y = 2$		
x	y	(x, y)
0	−2	(0, −2)
1	2	(1, 2)
2	6	(2, 6)
3	10	(3, 10)

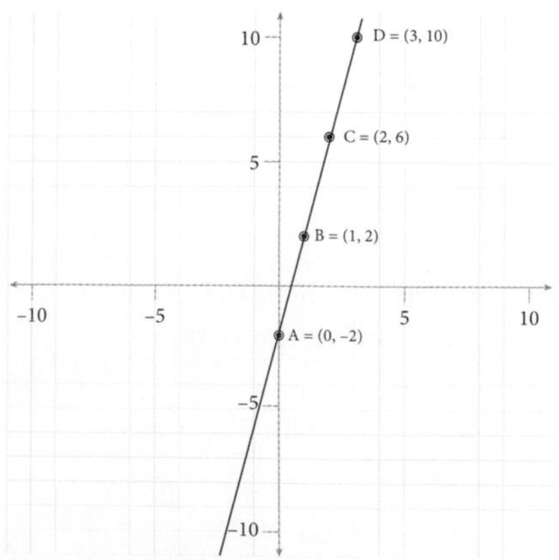

7.

$x + y - 4 = 0$		
x	y	(x, y)
0	4	(0, 4)
1	3	(1, 3)
2	2	(2, 2)
3	1	(3, 1)

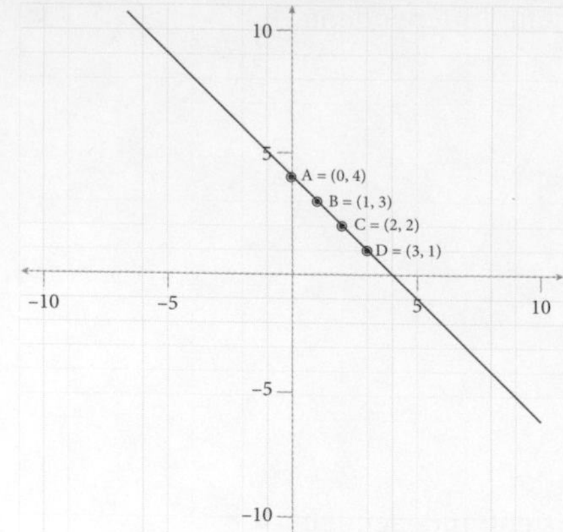

9.

$y = \frac{1}{2}x + 2$		
x	y	(x, y)
0	2	(0, 2)
2	3	(2, 3)
4	4	(4, 4)
6	5	(6, 5)

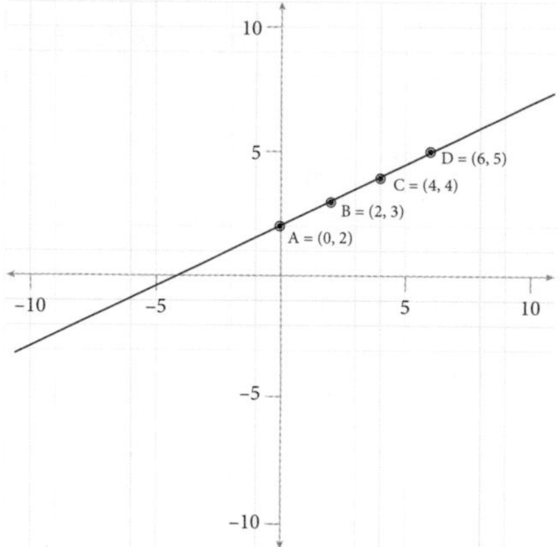

11.

$3x - 4y = 12$		
x	y	(x, y)
0	-3	(0, −3)
4	0	(4, 0)
8	3	(8, 3)

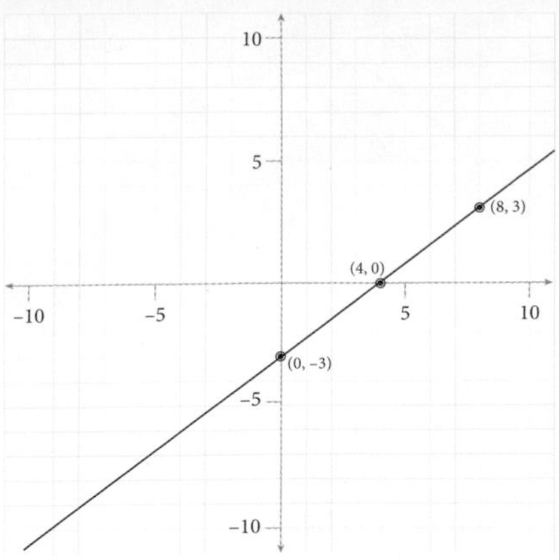

13.

$x - 2y - 6 = 0$		
x	y	(x, y)
0	-3	(0, –3)
6	0	(–1, 0)
2	-2	(2, –2)

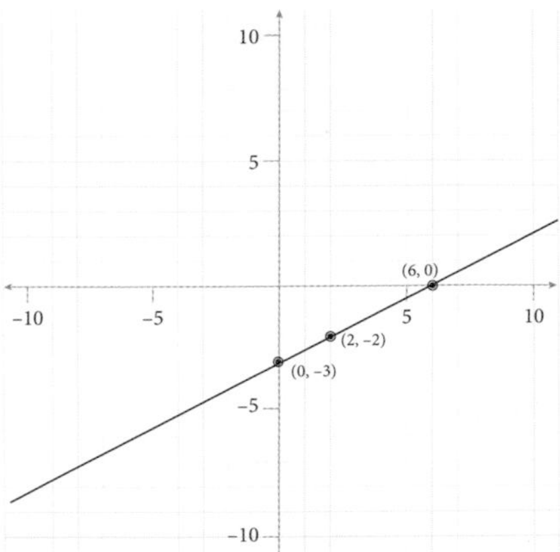

15.

$y = 4x$		
x	y	(x, y)
0	0	(0, 0)
1	4	(1, 4)

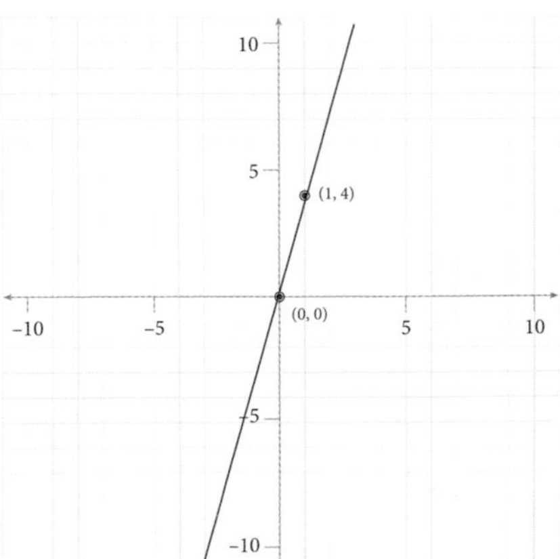

17. $m = 4$; $b = 6$

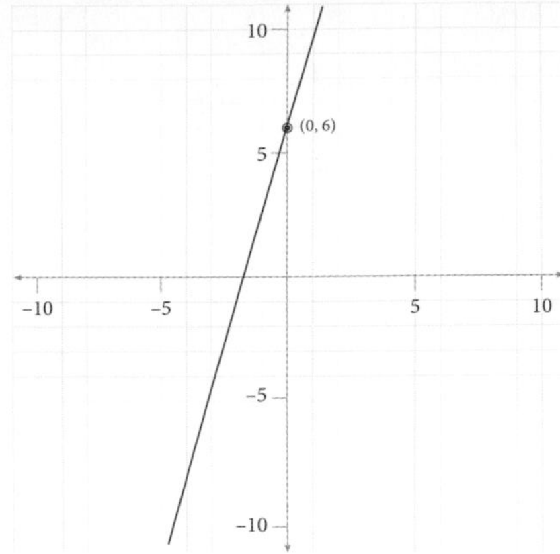

19. $m = -\frac{3}{2}$; $b = 6$

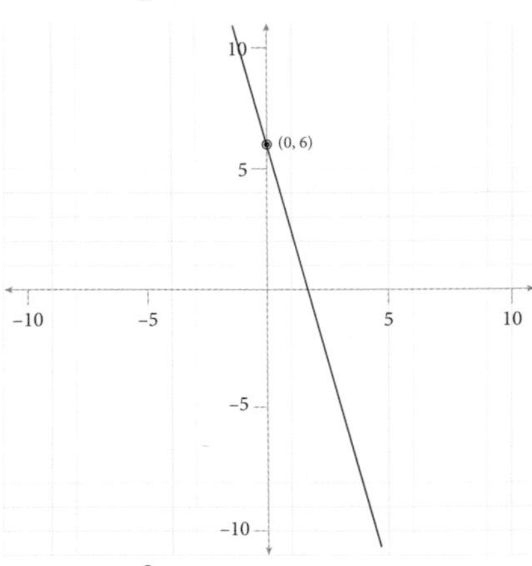

21. $m = -\frac{3}{4}$; $b = -1$

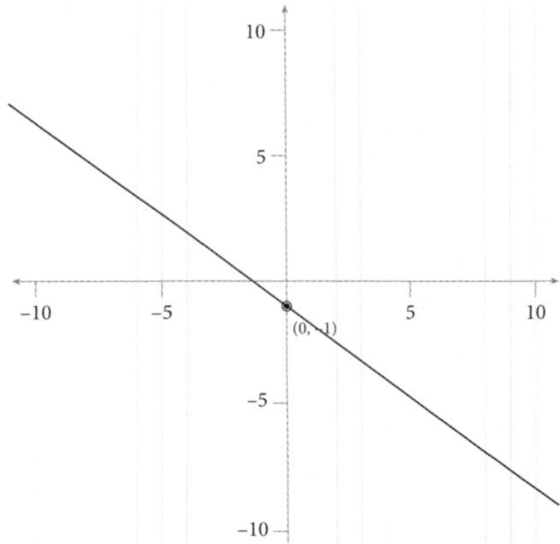

23. $y = \frac{3}{4}x - \frac{1}{4}$

25. $y = -\frac{4}{3}x + \frac{8}{3}$

27. $y = 3x - 5$

29. $y = \frac{3}{4}x + \frac{9}{2}$

31. $y = -2x + 1$

33. (2, −5)

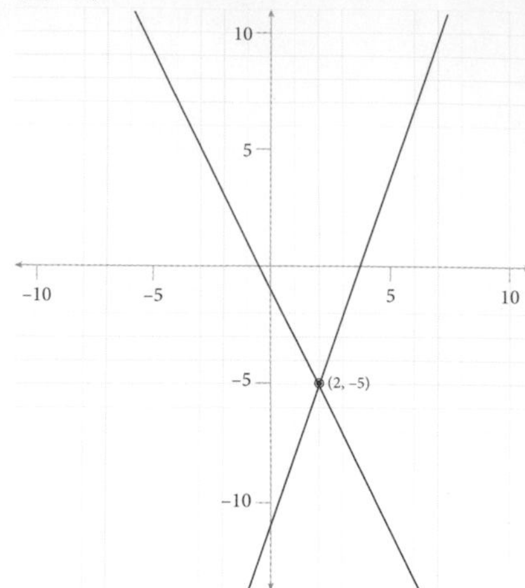

35. (6, 2)

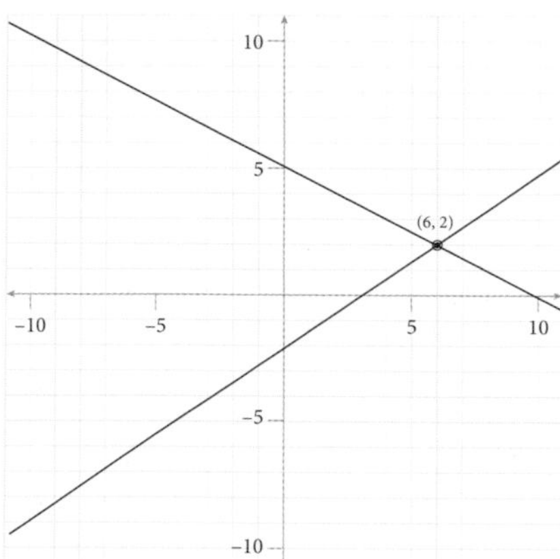

37. (2, 1)

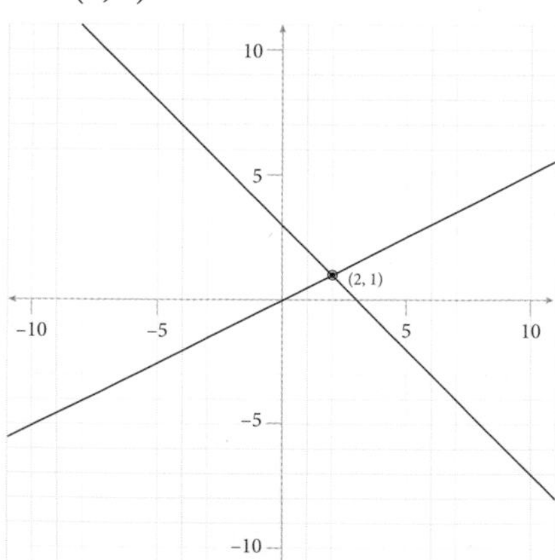

39. a. Company A: $y = 40x + 250$;
Company B: $y = 50x + 200$

b.

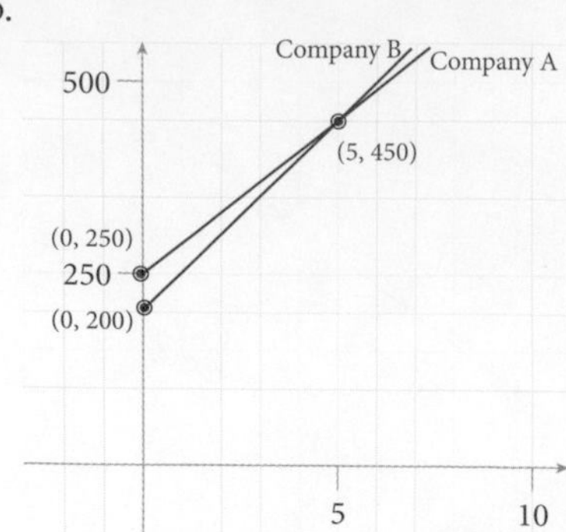

c. (5, 450); both companies charge a total fee of $450 for 5 hours of labour

d. Paul should hire Company A if the labour will take more than 5 hours

41. One solution
43. No solution
45. Infinitely many solutions
47. (4, 1)
49. $(\frac{52}{19}, -\frac{70}{19})$
51. (1, 1)
53. (2, 1)
55. (−4, −2)
57. (3, 0)
59. (3, 4)
61. (15, 12)
63. $(\frac{29}{7}, -\frac{13}{7})$
65. 65 and 30
67. 210 adults, 90 kids
69. 24 L; 36 L
71. 2.29 km/h
73. 2.5 hours

Self-Test Exercises 8

1. (−3, −1); Area = 40 square units
2. a. $2x - 3y = 6$ b. $x = \frac{25}{8}$
3. a. $y = \frac{2}{3}x + 2$ b. $y = -\frac{3}{4}x + \frac{5}{4}$
4.

$2x - 3y = 9$		
x	y	(x, y)
0	−3	(0, −3)
3	−1	(3, −1)
6	1	(6, 1)
9	3	(9, 3)

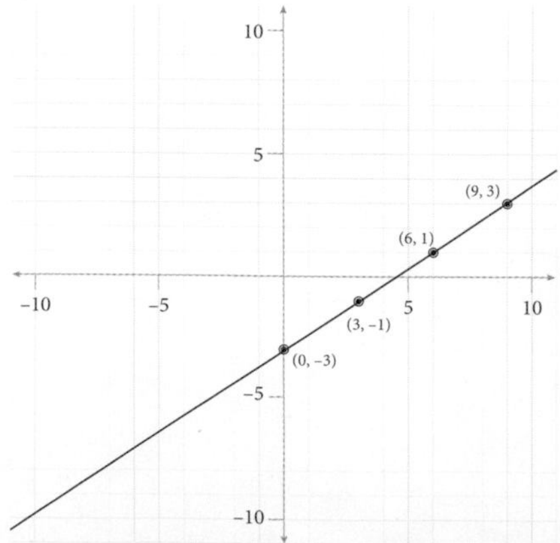

5.

$3y + 4x = 0$		
x	y	(x, y)
0	0	(0, 0)
3	−4	(3, −4)
6	1	(6, 1)

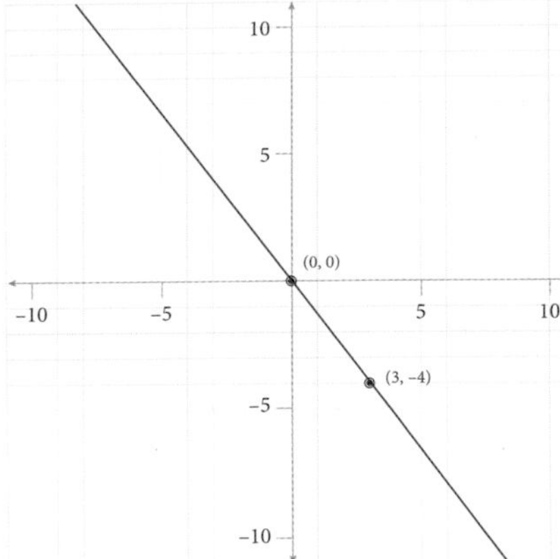

6. a.

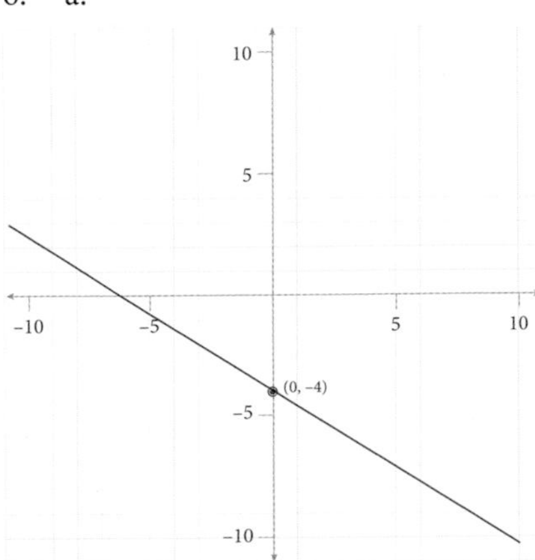

b.

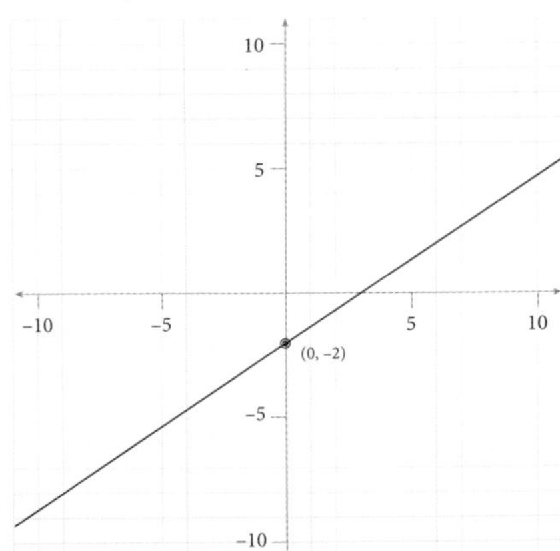

7. $4x + 5y = 9$

8. $3x - 5y = 15$

9. $3x - 2y = -12$

10. $\frac{4}{3}x - y = 0$

11. Infinitely many solutions

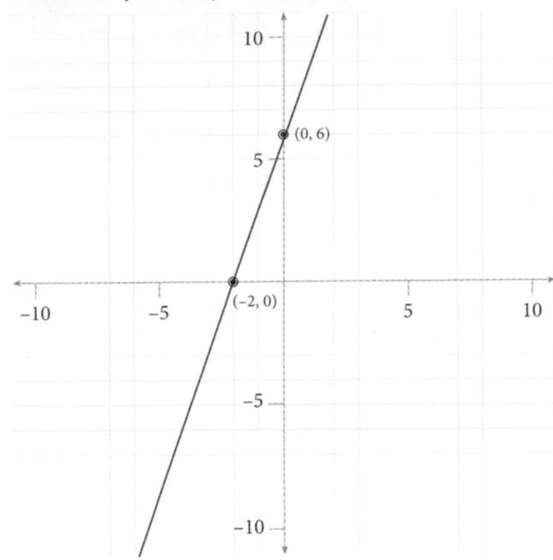

12. a. Club A: $y = 20x + 180$;
Club B: $y = 30x$

b.

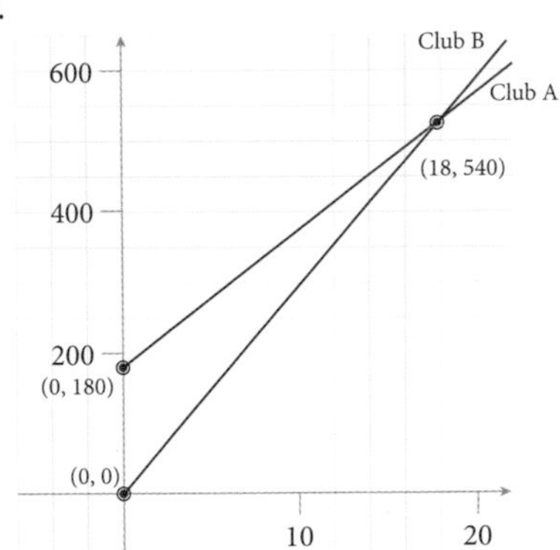

c. (18, 540); both clubs charge a fee of \$540 for 18 hours of court time

d. Sandra should join club A if she is planning to play more than 18 hours

13. a. One solution b. No solution c. No solution

14. $(\frac{15}{7}, -\frac{18}{7})$

15. $(-\frac{3}{2}, -\frac{3}{2})$

16. 35 and 30

17. 75 quarters

18. 325 adult tickets

19. 5 lb; 10 lb

20. 4.5 km/h; 1.5 km/h

Chapter 9

Exercises 9.1

1.

a. 

b. 

c. 

3. a. Ray $\overrightarrow{AB}$ b. Line segment $\overline{LM}$ c. Line $\overleftrightarrow{YZ}$

5. a. (i) ∠DPC (ii) Acute
(iii) 60° (iv) Supplement =120°
Complement = 30°

b. (i) ∠AQB (ii) Acute
(iii) 80° (iv) Supplement = 100°
Complement = 10°

7. a. (i) $\angle ZXY$ (ii) Right
(iii) 90° (iv) Supplement = 90°
b. (i) $\angle RPQ$ (ii) Acute
(iii) 50° (iv) Complement = 40°
Supplement = 130°

9. a. 57.5° b.72° 11. a. 56.6° b. 91°

13. a. $\angle AOC = \angle BOD$; $\angle AOB = \angle COD$
b. $\angle q = \angle r = \angle s = \angle t$

15. $\angle a = \angle c = \angle e = \angle g$;
$\angle b = \angle d = \angle f$

17. a. $\angle a = \angle c = 132°$
$\angle b = \angle d = 48°$
b. $\angle a = 120°$
$\angle b = 60°$
$\angle c = 70°$

19. a. $\angle a = \angle c = 63°$
$\angle b = 59°$
$\angle d = 58°$
b. $\angle a = 50°$
$\angle b = 30°$
$\angle c = 130°$

21. 32°

23. a. 48°
b. $\angle a = 70°$
$\angle b = 60°$
$\angle c = 50°$

Exercises 9.2

1. $\theta = 61°$ 3. $\theta = 56°$
5. a. Internal angles, $\theta = 150°$, external angles, $\theta = 30°$
b. Internal angles, $\theta = 162°$, external angles, $\theta = 18°$
7. a. $n = 30$ b. $n = 72$
9. 77°
11. two angles $\theta = 70°$, unique angle $\alpha = 40°$
13. 93°
15. a. Acute, isosceles
b. Right, scalene
c. Obtuse, isosceles
17. a. Square b. Parallelogram c. Kite
19. $\angle A = \angle B = \angle C = \angle D = 90°$
21. $\angle B = 98°$, $\angle C = 105°$
23. Square 25. Trapezoid
27. a. Square or rectangle b. Square or rhombus
29. a. Square, rectangle, rhombus, parallelogram
b. Square, rectangle, rhombus, parallelogram, isosceles trapezoid

Exercises 9.3

1. a. $P = 32$ mm; $A = 64$ mm^2
b. $P = 21.8$ m; $A = 28.8$m^2
3. $P = 65$ cm; $A = 207.19$ cm^2
5. $P = 32$ m; $A = 42$ m^2
7. $P = 5.5$ m; $A = 1.2$ m^2
9. $P = 24$ cm; $A = 27$ cm^2
11. $C = 50.27$ cm; $A = 201.06$ cm^2
13. $C = 5.78$ m, $A = 2.66$ m^2
15. $P = 314$ cm; $A = 6{,}107$ cm^2
17. $P = 70.702$ m; $A = 107.233$ m^2
19. $A = 744$ m^2
21. $d = 16.92$ m
23. $A = 0.27$ km^2 25. $A = 960$ cm^2
27. \$58.1 29. 9.0 km/h
31. 258 cm, $A = 2{,}520$ cm^2
33. $P = 93.14$ m, A = 485.97 m^2
35. $P = 39.42$ m, $A = 86.14$ m^2
37. $P = 163.45$ cm, $A = 1{,}418.08$ cm^2
39. $P = 97.12$ cm, $A = 198$ cm^2

Exercises 9.4

1. $SA = 3{,}750$ mm^2, $V = 15{,}625$ mm^3
3. $SA = 261$ m^2, $V = 225$ m^3
5. $SA = 678.58$ cm^2, $V = 1{,}696.46$ cm^3
7. $SA = 23{,}524.25$ cm^2, $V = 273{,}444.22$ mm^3
9. $SA = 318.09$ cm^2, $V = 466.53$ cm^3
11. $SA = 6{,}082.12$ cm^2, $V = 44{,}602.23$ cm^3
13. $SA = 5.31$ m^2, $V = 1.15$ m^3
15. $V = 1.866.67$ m^3
17. $V = 18.90$ m^3
19. 84 m^3
21. $V = 1.35$ m^3, $SA = 7.64$ m^3
23. $V = 7{,}180.96$ m^3
25. $SA = 13{,}750$ cm^3
27. $SA = 2{,}748.89$ cm^2
29. SA = 511,000,000 km^2,
V = 1,087,000,000,000 km^3
31. SA = 15.66 m^2, V = 4.48 m^3
33. SA = 130.69 m^2, V = 93.83 m^3

Exercises 9.5

1.

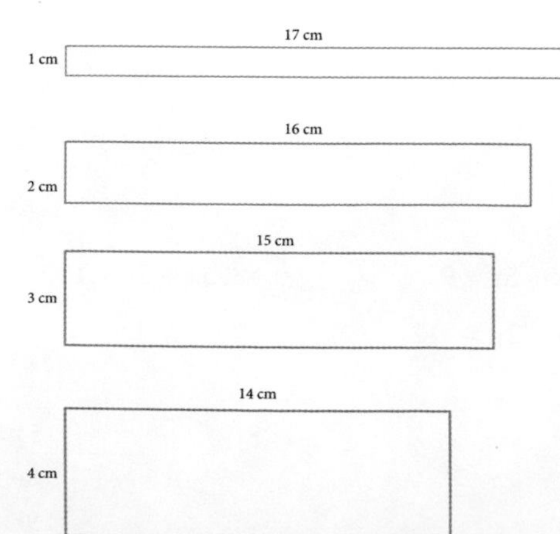

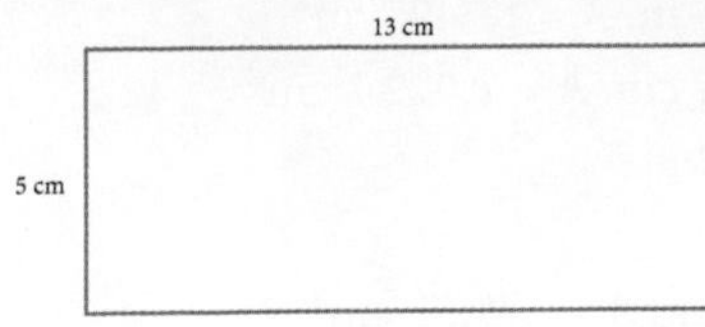

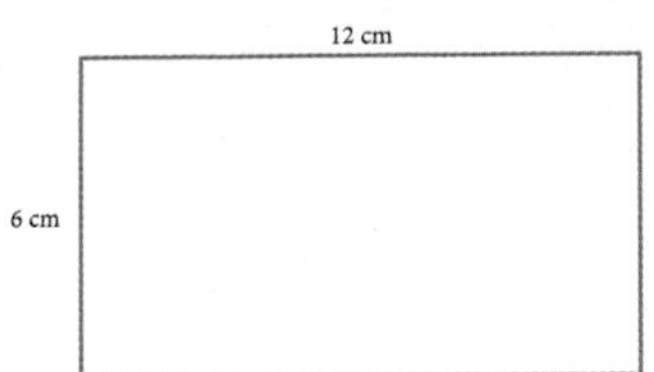

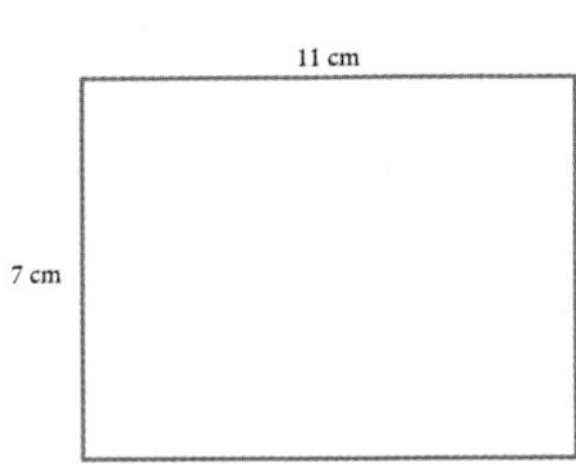

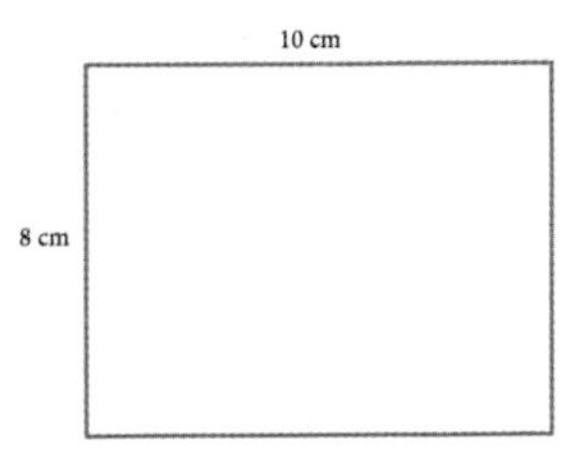

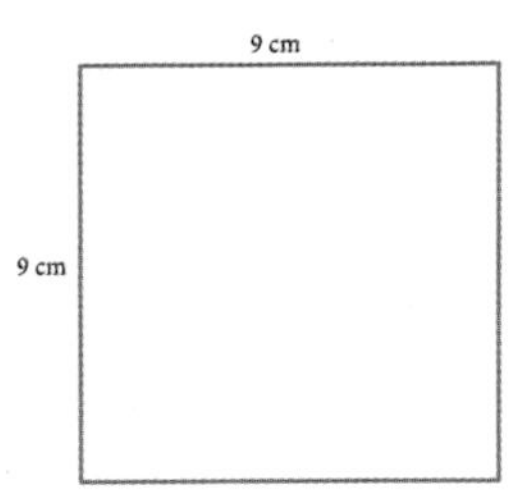

3.

1 cm × 60 cm

2 cm × 30 cm

3 cm × 20 cm

4 cm × 15 cm

5 cm × 12 cm

6 cm × 10 cm

5.

Length	Width	Perimeter	Area
5 m	1 m	12 m	5 m^2
4 m	2 m	12 m	8m^2
3 m	3 m	12 m	9m^2

7.

Length	Width	Perimeter	Area
1 m	72 m	146 m	72 m^2
2 m	36 m	76 m	72m^2
3 m	24 m	54 m	72m^2
4 m	18 m	44 m	72 m^2
6 m	12 m	36 m	72 m^2
8 m	9m	34 m	72 m^2

9. The rectangle with the largest area is the square with a side length of 9 cm. No, there is no another rectangle which has a larger area and integer side lengths.

11. The rectangle with the smallest perimeter has dimensions of 8 m by 9 m. No, there is no another rectangle which has a smaller perimeter and integer side lengths.

13. 49 m^2

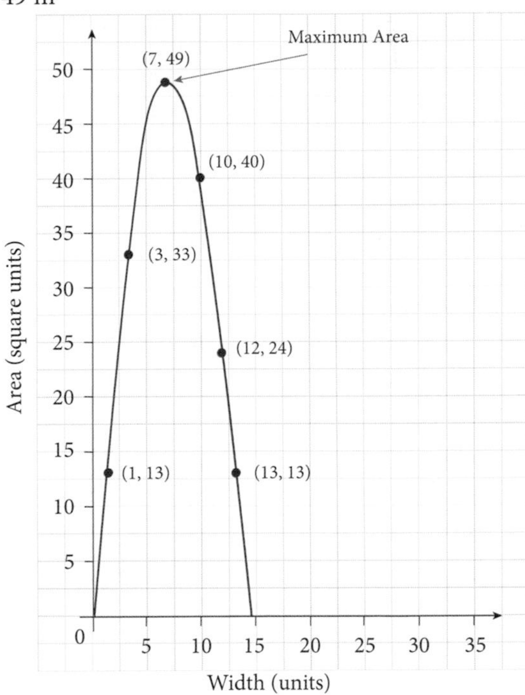

15. $l = w = 6$ m

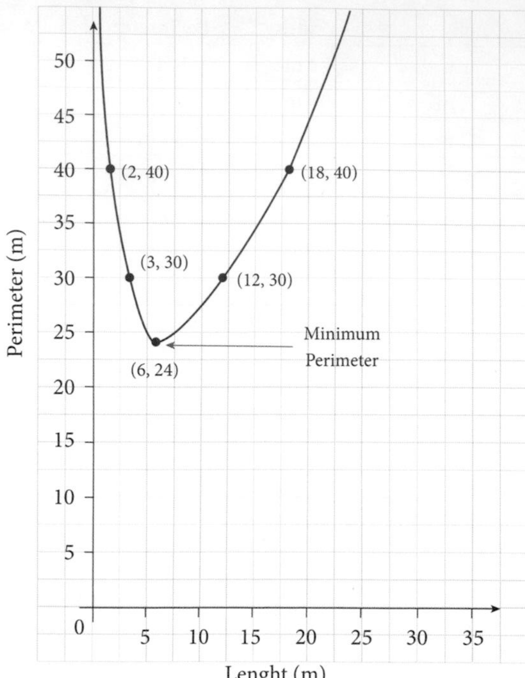

17. $l = w = 8$ ft   19. $l = w = 38.73$ ft

21. 52 ft   23. 218.89 m^2

25. a. $r = 3.41$ cm, $h = 6.82$ cm
    b. 219.18 cm^2

27. A cylinder

29. a. $l = w = 20$ ft   b. 314 ft^2

31. a. \$507.24   b. \$549.46

Review Exercises 9

1. a. (i) 20°   (ii) Supplement = 160°
   Complement = 70°
   b. (i) 50°   (ii) Supplement = 130°
   Complement = 40°

3. a. a is adjacent to $\angle\theta$.
   b is opposite to $\angle\theta$.
   c is co-interior to $\angle\theta$.
   d is alternate to $\angle\theta$.
   e is corresponding to $\angle\theta$.
   b. $a = c = 67°$, $b = d = e = 113°$

5. a. $a = 100°$, $b = 144°$, $c = 64°$
   b. $a = 162°$, $b = 72°$, $c = 40°$

7. Rectangle   b. Kite   c. Parallelogram

9. a. $\angle$CDA = 135°, $\angle$ABC = 135°, $\angle$BCD = 45°
   b. $\angle$QRS = 77°   c. $\angle$WXY = 102°

11. a. i. 58°;   ii. Right, scalene
    b. i. 48°, 48°   ii. Acute, isosceles

13. a. P = 55.7 cm, A = 115.5 cm^2
    b. P = 62.63 in, A = 120.96 in^2

15. 84 cm

17. $P = 100$ cm, $A = 480$ cm^2

19. a. $P = 148.3$ m, $A = 1{,}749.7$ m^2
    b. $P = 157.7$ cm, $A = 1{,}022.7$ cm^2

21. 1,206 cm^2

23. 9.8 in^2

25. $P = 80.14$ cm; $A = 279.59$ cm^2

27. P = 67.9 m; A = 159.8 m^2

29. SA = 305.61 cm^2; V = 386.04 cm^3

31. SA = 47.04 m^2; V = 16.46 m^3

33. SA = 2,789.73 mm^2; V = 8,180.71 mm^3

35.

Width	Length	Area
1 m	9 m	9 m^2
2 m	8 m	16 m^2
3 m	7 m	21 m^2
4 m	6 m	24 m^2
5 m	5 m	25 m^2

a. width = 5 m , length = 5 m

b.

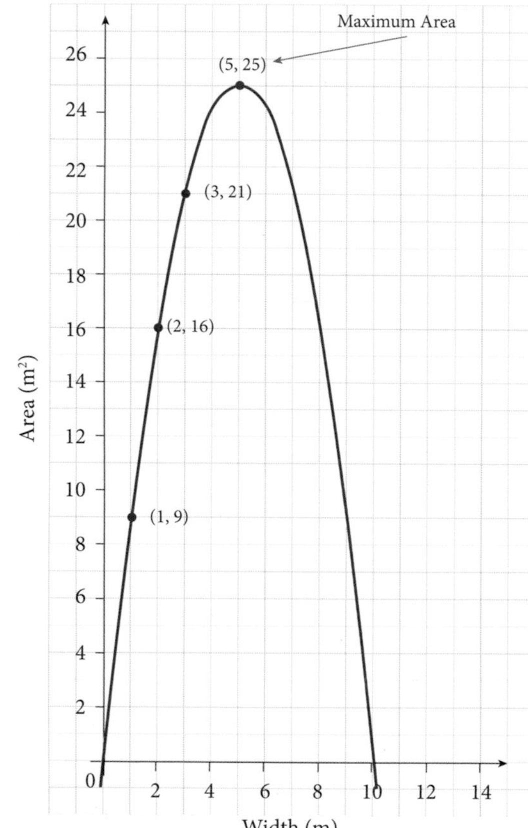

37. a. $l = w = 142$ cm   b. $d = h = 7.14$ mm

39. a. 15.7 km for the pond; 18 km for the city block
    b. the pond route

Self-Test Exercises 9

1. a. (i) Obtuse   (ii) 64°   (iii) Not applicable
   b. (i) Acute   (ii) 113°   (iii) 23°
   c. (i) Right   (ii) 90°   (iii) Not applicable

2. a. $a = 62°$ $b = 126°$ $c = 64°$
   b. $a = 75°$ $b = 143°$ $c = 68°$

3. a. Right, Isosceles
   b. Acute, Equilateral
   c. Obtuse, Scalene
4. a. square
   b. rhombus
   c. kite
5. 136.125 cm^2
6. a. 61.2 cm^2 b. 1.47 m^2
7. a. C = 7.85 m; A = 4.91 m^2
   b. C = 40.84 cm; A = 735.13 cm^2
8. 11.39 km/h
9. a. 1.4 m^2 b. 91.9 m^2
10. a. 178,128.3 mm^3 = 178 cm^3
    b. 111.37 cm^3
11. a. 7.98 cm
    b. 1,152 cm^2
12. a. 5.98 cm b. 896 cm^3
13. V = 12.63 m^3; SA = 24.62m^2
14. a. 2,035.75 cm^3 b. 189,018.6cm^3
15. 47.53 m^2
16. No, because the minimum amount of wood needed to complete the box is 96 ft^2 which cost $216.

Chapter 10

Exercises 10.1

1. a. $\frac{AB}{DE} = \frac{BC}{EF} = \frac{AC}{DF}$; $\angle A = \angle D, \angle B = \angle E, \angle C = \angle F$
   b. $\frac{OP}{RS} = \frac{PQ}{ST} = \frac{OQ}{RT}$; $\angle O = \angle R, \angle P = \angle S, \angle Q = \angle T$
3. a. AB = XY, BC = YZ, AC = XZ;
   $\angle A = \angle X, \angle B = \angle Y, \angle C = \angle Z$
   b. DE = RS, EF = ST, DF = RT;
   $\angle D = R, \angle E = \angle S, \angle F = \angle T$
5. By the SSS property, a and c are similar triangles.
7. By the RHS property, a and c are similar triangles.
9. By the SAS property, a and c are similar triangles.
11. By the SAS property, a and b are congruent triangles.
13. No pairs
15. By the ASA property, a and b are congruent triangles.
17. Similar 19. Similar
21. Similar 23. Neither
25. Congruent
27. $\angle A = \angle E = 56°, x = 6, y = 7.5$
29. $\angle Q = \angle M = 30°, \angle O = 90°, \angle N = 60°,$ $x = 4.4, y = 2.5$
31. 8.5 m

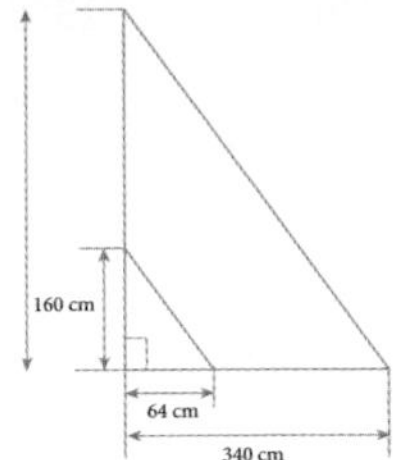

33. 2.4 m 35. 1.55 m
37. 4.29 m

Exercises 10.2

1. a. 25 cm b. 6 cm c. 1.75 cm
3. a. 19.21 cm b. 15 cm c. 5.57 cm
5. 2.51 cm 7. 7.28 m 9. 5.73 cm
11. $P = 98$ cm, $A = 420$ cm^2
13. $P = 30.9$ m, $A = 41$ m^2
15. 6.32 units 17. 9.43 units 19. 6.4 units
21. 5 units 23. 35.6 cm 25. 3.5 m
27. 180 cm
29. No, the towel rack will not fit along the diagonal at the bottom of the box, as the diagonal size is 96 cm long. Yes, the towel rack will fit in the box if placed on the 3-dimensional diagonal, as it is 106 cm long.
31. $h = 27.5$ cm, $SA = 1{,}583$ cm^2, $V = 4{,}147$ cm^3
33. $h = 69.3$ m, $SA = 26{,}244$ m^2, 221,852 m^3
35. $h = 16.1$ cm, $SA = 3{,}519$ cm^2, $V = 13{,}218$ cm^3

Exercises 10.3

1. a. 0.9063; 0.4226; 2.1445
   b. 0.2164; .9763; 0.2217
   c. 0.8000; 0.6000; 1.3333
3. a. 27°; 0.8910; 0.5095
   b. 73°; 0.9563; 3.2709
   c. 20°; 0.3420; 0.9397
5. a. $\frac{4}{5}; \frac{3}{4}$; 37° b. $\frac{7}{25}; \frac{7}{24}$; 16°
   c. $\frac{20}{29}; \frac{21}{29}$; 44°
7. 0 9. $\frac{1}{4}$ 11. $2\frac{1}{2}$
13. 18.93 cm 15.18.91 cm 17. 8.34 cm
19. 50.28° 21. 30.26° 23. 14.84°
25. $\phi = 28°, \theta = 62°, x = 8$ cm
27. $\theta = \phi = 45°, x = 15.56$ cm
29. $\phi = 74°$, hypotenuse = 14.56 cm, leg = 4.01 cm
31. 5° 33. 5° 35. 452 m
37. 1,700 m 39. N24.8°E; 71.59 km/h
41. 892.8 cm^2

Exercises 10.4

1. 36.5 cm 3. 16.2 cm 5. 25.8 cm
7. 53.2 cm 9. 77° 11. 41°

13. 14°
15. 46°
17. 26.3 cm
19. 21.7 cm
21. 33.2 cm
23. 8.4 cm
25. 96°
27. 95°
29. 110°
31. 22
33. The Sine Law
35. The Sine Law
37. The Cosine Law
39. The Cosine Law
41. The Sine Law
43. $\angle C = 25°$, $a = 7.95$, $c = 5.86$
45. c = 8.84, $\angle A = 94°$, $\angle B = 50°$
47. $\angle A = 119°$, $\angle B = 37°$, $\angle C = 24°$
49. $\angle A = 40°$, $a = 6.65$, $b = 9.38$
51. $\angle A = 50°$, $\angle C = 45°$, $a = 27$
53. $\angle A = 21°$, $\angle B = 32°$, $\angle C = 127°$
55. 8.8 km
57. 9.2 knots N11°E
59. 88.6 m

Review Exercises 10

1. By SSS property, a and b, are similar triangles
3. By AAA property, a and b are congruent triangles
5. $x = 3$cm and $y = 4.5$cm
7. $x = 20$ cm; $\phi = 53°$; $\theta = 127°$
9. a. 9.9 b. 3.6
11. Perimeter: 147.26 cm; area = 936 cm^2
13. a. $\frac{\sqrt{3} - 1}{2\sqrt{2}}$ b. $\sqrt{3}$
15. 120°; 120°; 55°; 65°
17. a.108 m b. 91 m; 53°
19. 1,449 m N 71° W
21. $\angle A = 38°$, $\angle C = 112°$, $b = 10.53$ cm
23. $\angle A = 90°$, $a = 51.95$ cm, $c = 50.81$ cm
25. $\angle B = 26°$, $\angle C = 107°$, $c = 70.01$ cm
27. $\angle B = 23°$, $\angle C = 17°$, $a = 38.57$ cm
29. $\angle A = 19°$, $\angle B = 22°$, $\angle C = 139°$

Self-Test Exercises 10

1. a. $x = 4$ cm and $y = 5.6$ cm
   b. $x = 4$ cm and $y = 12.25$ cm
2. a. $x = 17.89$ cm, $y = 8$ cm, $z = 35.78$ cm
   b. $x = \sqrt{2}$ cm, $y = 1$ cm
3. 24 m
4. a. P = 22.41 m, A = 18 m^2
   b. P = 100 cm, A = 480 cm^2
5. a. SA = 82.94 cm^2, V = 59.81cm^3
   b. SA = 2,080.52 cm^2, V = 5,890.49 cm^3
6. a. 17 b.11.3 c. 6.5
7. a. 5.27 m b. 9.68 m
8. a. $x = 12$; $\phi = 67.38°$, $\theta = 22.62°$
   b. $x = 74.86$ cm; $y = 60.56$ cm, $\theta = 36°$
9. a. $x = y = 10.68$ m, $\theta = 44°$
   b. $\theta = 103.14°$, $\gamma = 31.29°$, $\beta = 45.57°$
10. 0.61 km
11. $z = 7.6$; $\angle X = 98°$; $\angle Y = 44°$;
12. $p = 18.4$cm; $r = 23.6$cm; 100°;
13. a. $x = 14.4$ cm b. $x = 1.73$ m; $y = 0.81$ m
14. $x = 10$ m

Chapter 11

Exercises 11.1

1. a. Continuous b. Continuous
   c. Continuous d. Discrete
3. a. Quantitative b. Qualitative
   c. Quantitative d. Quantitative
5. a. Ordinal b. Ratio
   c. Ratio d. Ordinal
7.

Stem	Leaf
1	3 8 9 9
2	1 5 7 8 9
3	1 1 2 4 7 8 9
4	3 4

9.

Stem	Leaf
4	5 8
5	1 2 5 9
6	4 5 9
7	0 3 5 7 8
8	0 1 1 2 4 5 8
9	2 5 7

11. Favorite Subjects of First-year Students

Name	Tally	Value
Statistics (S)	卌 卌 |	11
Marketing (M)	卌 卌	10
Accounting (A)	卌 |	6
Finance Math (F)	|||	3

13. a.

Grade	Number of Students	Percent	Cumulative Percent	Angle	Cumulative Angle
A+	24	12%	12%	43.2°	43.2°
A	30	15%	27%	54°	97.2°
B	36	18%	45%	64.8°	162°
C	52	26%	71%	93.6°	255.6°
D	42	21%	92%	75.6°	331.2°
F	16	8%	100%	28.8°	360°
Total	200	100%	360°	360°	360°

b. Letter Grades of 200 Students in Finance Math

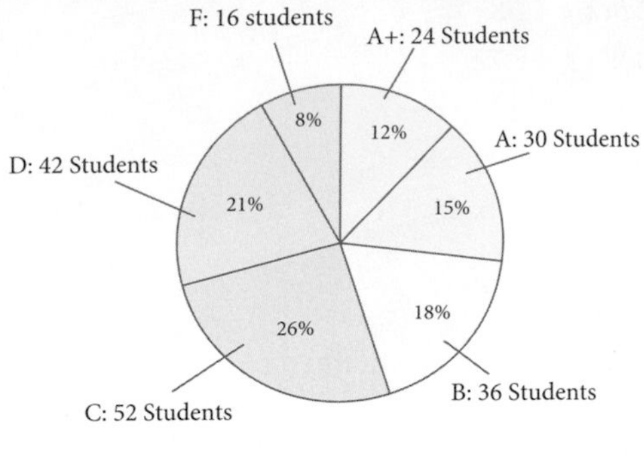

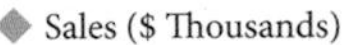

15.

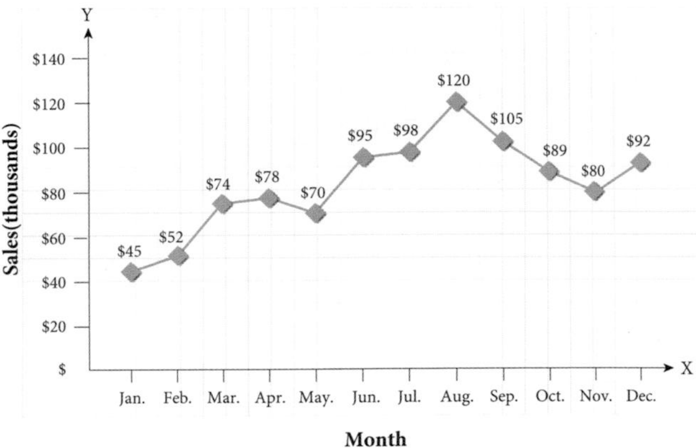

17. As price increases, number of items sold decreases

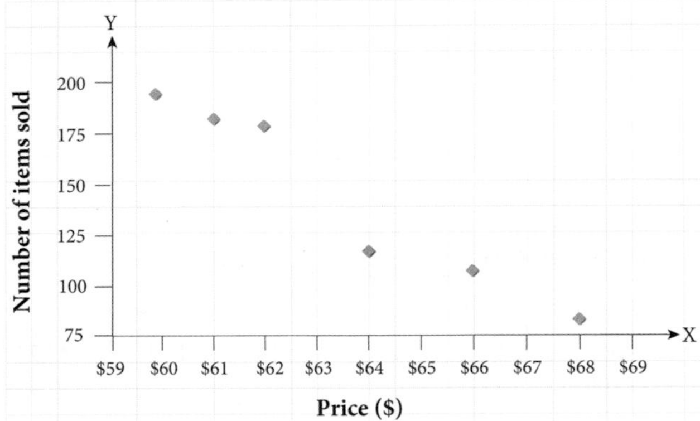

19.

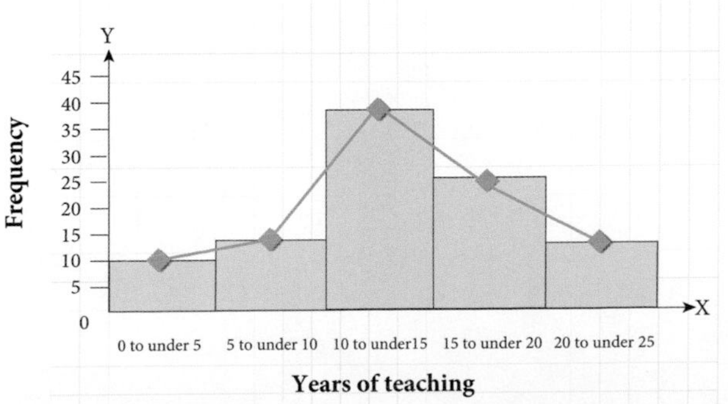

21. a.

Years of Teaching	Relative Frequency
0 to under 5	0.1
5 to under 10	0.14
10 to under 15	0.39
15 to under 20	0.24
20 to under 25	0.13

b.

Years of Teaching	Percent Frequency
0 to under 5	10%
5 to under 10	14%
10 to under 15	39%
15 to under 20	24%
20 to under 25	13%

23. a.

Years of Teaching	Cumulative Frequency
5	10
10	24
15	63
20	87
25	100

b.

Years of Teaching	Cumulative Percent Frequency
5	10.0%
10	24.0%
15	63.0%
20	87.0%
25	100%

c.

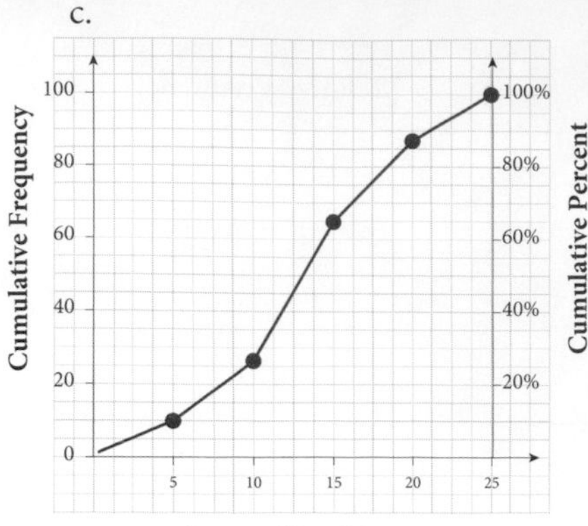

Exercises 11.2

1. 84.5 3. 92 5. 17.6
7. 75 9. $8,000 11. 50 kg
13. 3.2 15. 71.67
17. a. 12 b. 4 c. 1.14
19. a. 51 b. 25 c. 26
21. a. 39.5 b. 14.5 c. 78
23. a. 26 b. 25.5
25. a. The data has no mode
    b. 31 c. 36,41
27. a. mean = 6.57; median = 6; mode = 4
    b. mean = 64.13; median = 66.5; mode = 56
    c. mean = 124.56; median = 125; mode = 120
29. a. $161.67 b. $160 c. $140
31. mean = 2.72; median = 3; mode = 2
33. mean = 16.02 ; median = $17 ; mode = 17
35. mode = 14; positively skewed

Exercises 11.3

1. a. 76 b. 13 c. 13.2
3. a. 1st Quartile = 6; 3rd Quartile = 19.5
   b. 1st Quartile = 123; 3rd Quartile = 147
5. a. Interquartile Range = 13.5; Outliers: None
   b. Interquartile Range = 24; Outliers: None
7. a. 79 b. 23
9. a. 97
   b. 1st Quartile = 76; 3rd Quartile = 100.5
   c. 24.5 d. None
11.

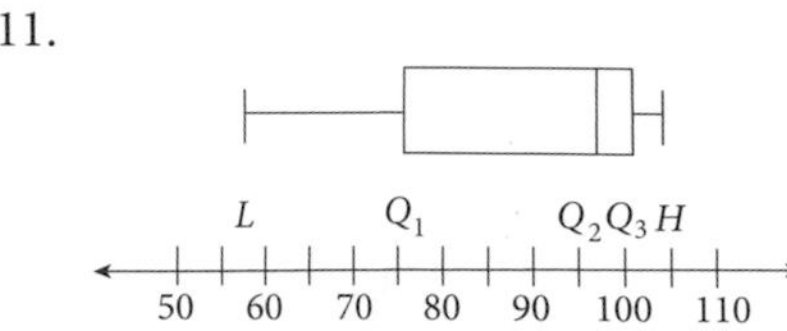

13.

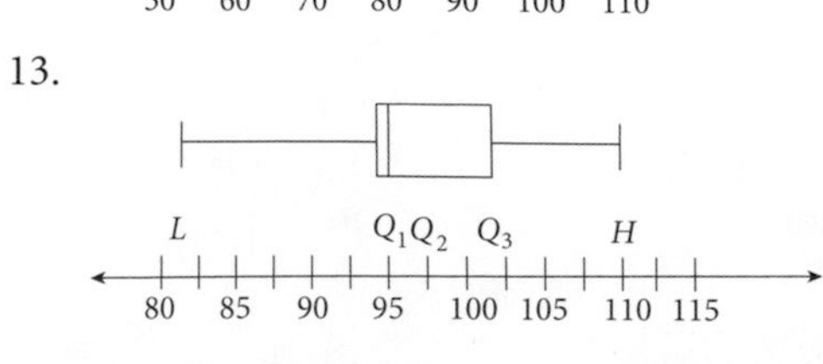

15. 6 17. Dataset in b
19. a. $s^2 = 2.5$; $s = 1.58$
    b. $s^2 = 32.7$; $s = 5.72$
21. $s^2 = 4.44$; $s = 2.11$
23. a. 81.2 kg b. 5.88 kg
25. a. $79,600 b. $5,520
    c. $50,300,000 d. $7,092.25

Review Exercises 11

1. a. Discrete variables are obtained by counting and can only take on specific values while continuous variables are obtained by measuring and can take on any value (whole numbers, approximated or rounded whole units, fractions or decimal numbers).
   b. In the interval level of measurement the zero point is located arbitrarily and the data cannot be multiplied or divided, while the ratio level of measurement has a meaningful zero point and the data can be multiplied or divided.
3. a. Qualitative, nominal
   b. Quantitative, discrete, interval
   c. Quantitative, continuous, ratio
   d. Quantitative, discrete, ratio
   e. Quantitative, continuous, ratio
5.
   a.

Stem	Leaf
4	0 4 5 5 9
5	1 1 2 3 4 5 6 8 9
6	0 1 2 3 5 5 5 6 7 8 9
7	1 2 3 4 6 6 8 9
8	0 1 3 4 8
9	1 6

   b.

Grades	Number of Students
40-49	5
50-59	9
60-69	11
70-79	8
80-89	5
90-99	2

7. a.

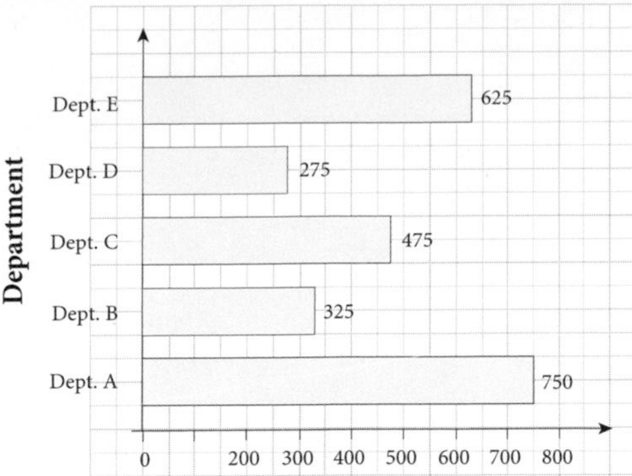

b.

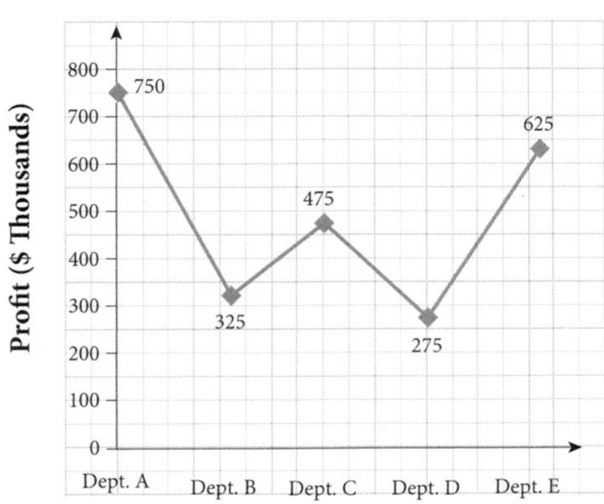

c.

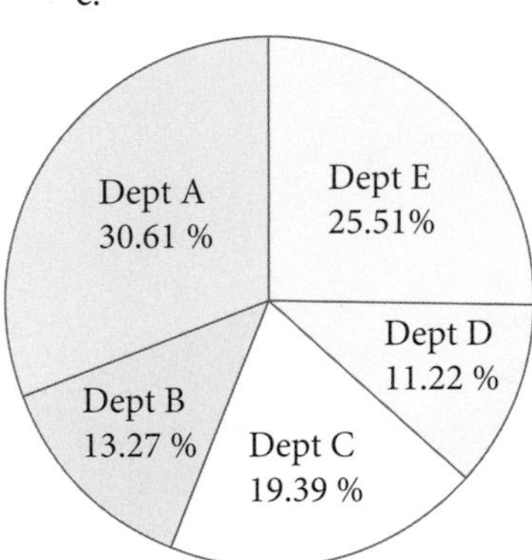

9. a. 10% b. 50% c. 80%

11. a

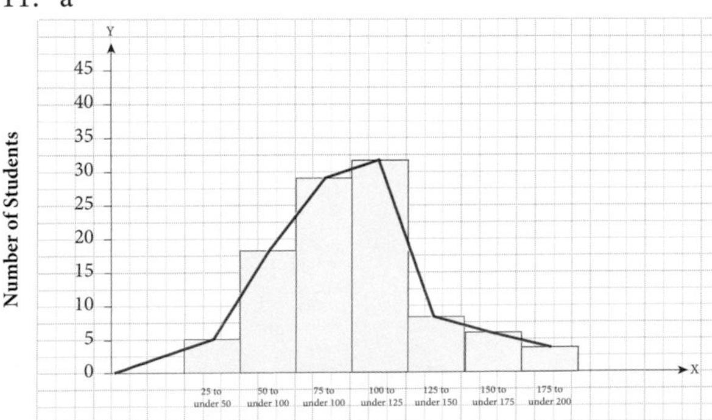

b.

Years of Teaching	Relative Frequency	Percent Frequency
25 to under 50	0.050	5.0%
50 to under 100	0.180	18.0%
75 to under 100	0.280	28.0%
100 to under 125	0.320	32.0%
125 to under 150	0.080	8.0%
150 to under 175	0.060	6.0%
175 to under 200	0.030	3.0%

c.

Years of Teaching	Relative Cumulative Frequency	Cumulative Percent Frequency
25 to under 50	5	5%
50 to under 100	23	23%
75 to under 100	51	51%
100 to under 125	83	83%
125 to under 150	91	91%
150 to under 175	97	97%
175 to under 200	100	100%

d. Cumulative Frequency Curve

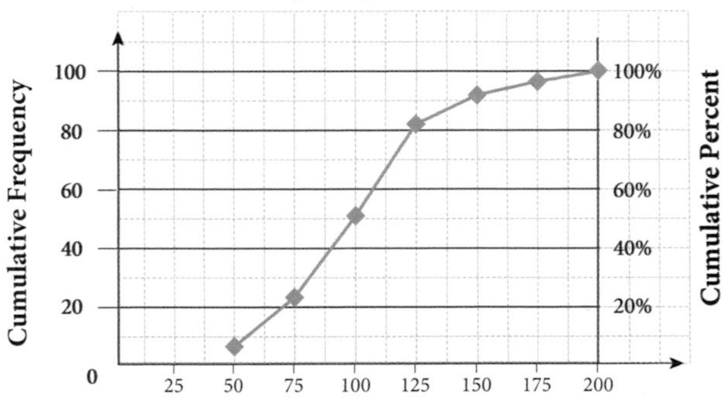

13. a. mean = 93.45; median = 93; mode = 93

b. 1st quartile = 91; 3rd quartile = 97

c. 6

d. No outliers

e.

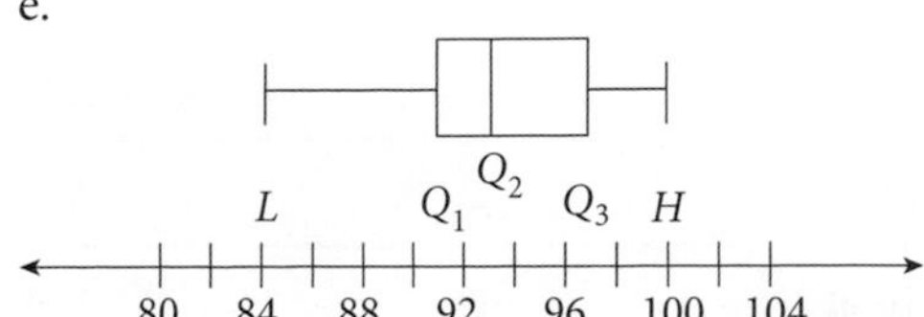

15. mean = $2,733.33; median = $2,700;
mode = $2,700; positively skewed

17. a. 100 b. 100 to under 125;112.5
c. 75 to under 100; 87.5

19. a. 3.40 b. 20.27 c. 4.50

21. 40; negatively skewed

23. weighted mean = 90.5%

Components	Weights	Score	Weighted Score
tests	20.00%	86.00%	17.20%
midterm	25.00%	96.00%	24.00%
final exam	30.00%	82.00%	24.60%
online labs	15.00%	98.00%	14.70%
homework	10.00%	100.00%	10.00%
			Σ = 90.50%

25. a. 7.2 b. 5.16

27. mean = 20,median = 20, s^2 = 6.5, s = 2.55

Self-Test Exercises 11

1. a. Qualitative, nominal
b. Quantitative, discrete, ratio
c. Quantitative, continuous, ratio
d. Qualitative, ordinal
e. Quantitative, continuous, ratio

2. a.

Stem	Leaf
3	6 8
4	1 2 7 8
5	1 4 4 5 6 7 8 9
6	1 2 2 3 4 5 7 8 8 8 9
7	1 1 4 5 6 7 9 9
8	1 2 3 4 6
9	1 4

b.

Age	Frequency	Relative Frequency
30-39	2	0.05
40-49	4	0.1
50-59	8	0.2
60-69	11	0.275
70-79	8	0.2
80-89	5	0.125
90-99	2	0.05
Total	**40**	**1**

3. a.

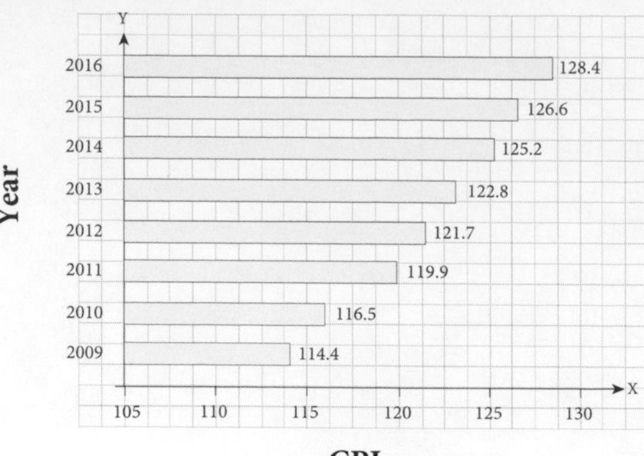

b.

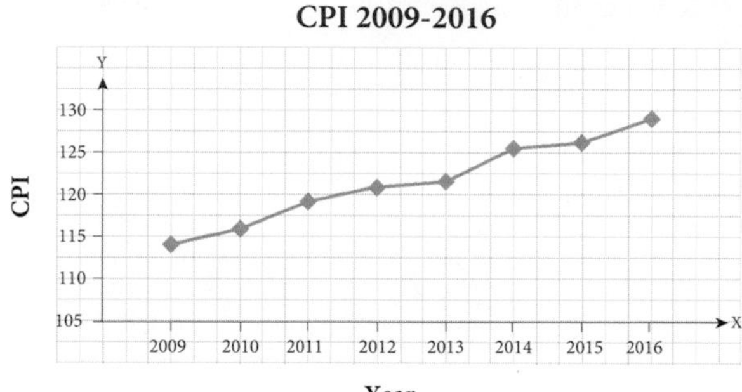

4.

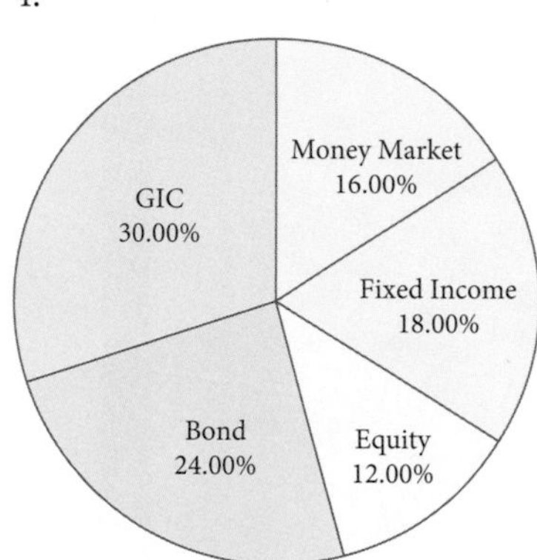

5 a.

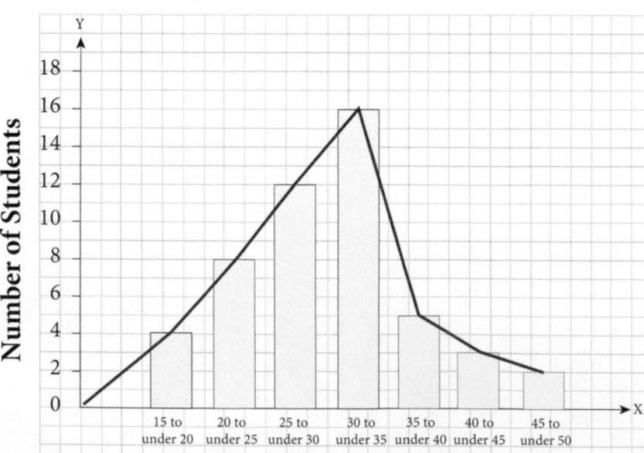

b.

Hourly Wages ($)	Relative Frequency	Percent Frequency
15 to under 20	0.080	8.0%
20 to under 25	0.160	16.0%
25 to under 30	0.240	24.0%
30 to under 35	0.320	32.0%
35 to under 40	0.100	10.0%
40 to under 45	0.060	6.0%
45 to under 50	0.040	4.0%

c.

Hourly Wages ($)	Relative Cumulative Frequency	Cumulative Percent Frequency
15 to under 20	0.08	8.0%
20 to under 25	0.240	24.0%
25 to under 30	0.480	48.0%
30 to under 35	0.800	80.0%
35 to under 40	0.900	90.0%
40 to under 45	0.960	96.0%
45 to under 50	1.000	100.0%

d. Cumulative Frequency Curve

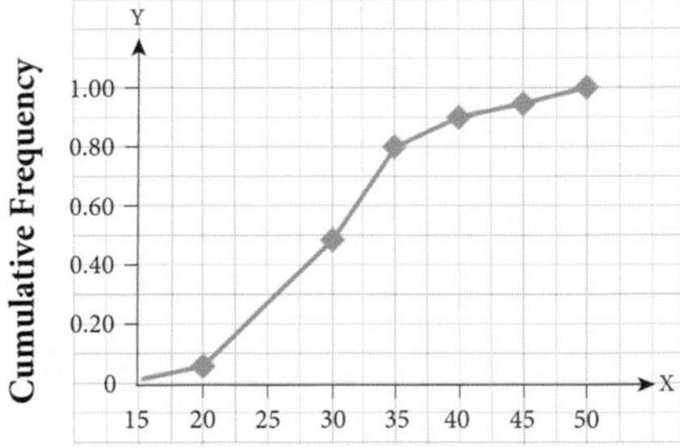

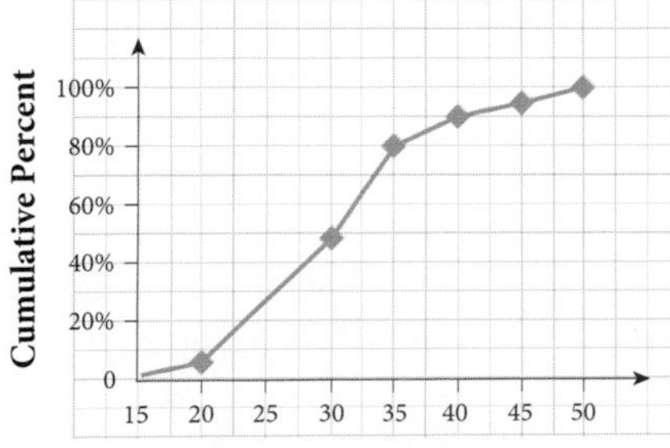

6. a. mean = 49.36, median = 49, mode = 49
   b. 1st quartile = 47, 3rd quartile = 52
   c. 5 d. No outliers
   e.

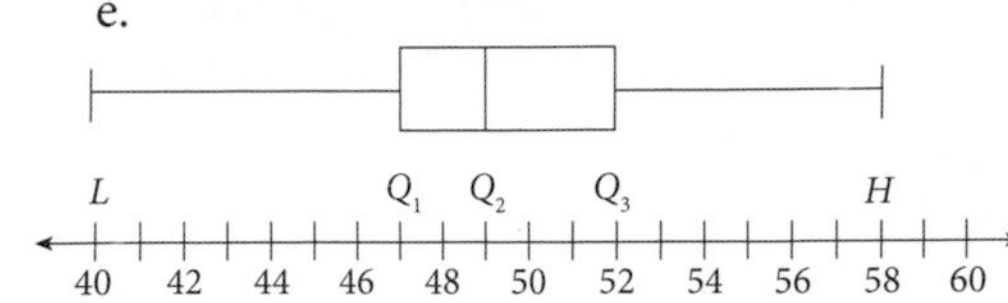

7. a. $30.2 b. 30 to under 35; $32.5
   c. 30 to under 35; $32.5
8. a. 3.12 b. $s^2 = 20.45$ c. $s = 4.52$
9. 150.5; Positively skewed
10. a. 2.17 b. 18.75
11. mean = 32.45, median = 31, $s^2 = 175.47$, $s = 13.25$

Chapter 12

Exercises 12.1

1. $\frac{4}{5} = 0.08$ 3. $\frac{3}{4} = 0.75$

5.

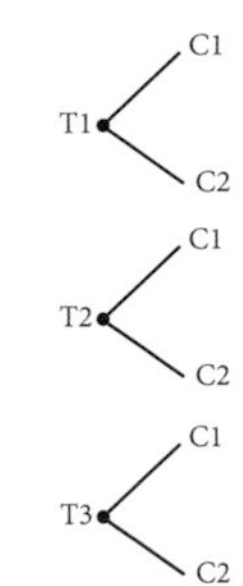

7. a.

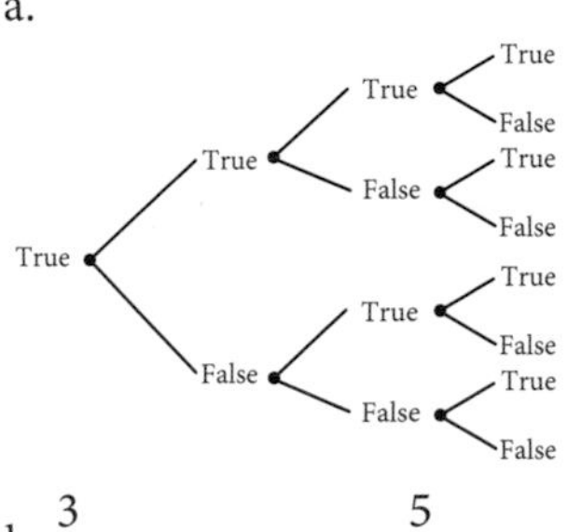

b. $\frac{3}{8}$ c. $\frac{5}{8}$

9. $\frac{5}{9} = 0.556$

11. a. $\frac{1}{5} = 0.02$ b. $\frac{5}{9} = 0.56$ c. $\frac{4}{5} = 0.44$

13. a. $\frac{1}{3} = 0.33$ b. $\frac{5}{6} = 0.83$ c. $\frac{2}{3} = 0.67$

15. a. $\frac{1}{2} = 0.5$ b. $\frac{3}{13} = 0.23$

17. a. $\frac{7}{13} = 0.54$ b. $\frac{4}{13} = 0.31$

19. a. $\frac{1}{3} = 0.33$ b. $\frac{5}{9} = 0.56$ c. $\frac{5}{9} = 0.56$

Exercises 12.2

1. a. $\frac{1}{9} = 0.11$ b. $\frac{8}{9} = 0.89$
3. a. 0.65 b. 0.55 c. 0.85
5. a. 0.18 b. 0.147 c. 0.372
7. a. $\frac{9}{169} = 0.0532$
   b. $\frac{20}{221} = 0.0498$
9. 0.85
11. a. $\frac{5}{51} = 0.98$ b. $\frac{16}{153} = 0.10$
13. a. $\frac{7}{52} = 0.13$ b. $\frac{5}{13} = 0.38$ c. $\frac{25}{104} = 0.24$
15. a. $\frac{1}{5}$ b. $\frac{1}{10}$ c. $\frac{2}{5}$ d. $\frac{3}{5}$
    e. $\frac{3}{4}$ f. $\frac{1}{5}$
17. a. 3 : 10 b. 12 : 1
19. $\frac{4}{15} = 0.27$
21. Drawing a marble that is not blue; $\frac{11}{15}$
23. 4 : 11
25. a. $\frac{1}{9} = 0.11$ b. $\frac{3}{29} = 0.10$

Exercises 12.3

1. a. 68% b. 300 and 700 c. 336 and 664
3. average weight = 800 g; standard deviation = 10 g
5. maximum = 575 students; minimum = 125 students
7. The interval representing 95% of the data will be wider than the interval representing 90% of the data, since 95% of the data will fall between $\bar{x} \pm 2s$ and 90% of the data will fall between $\bar{x} \pm 1.64s$.

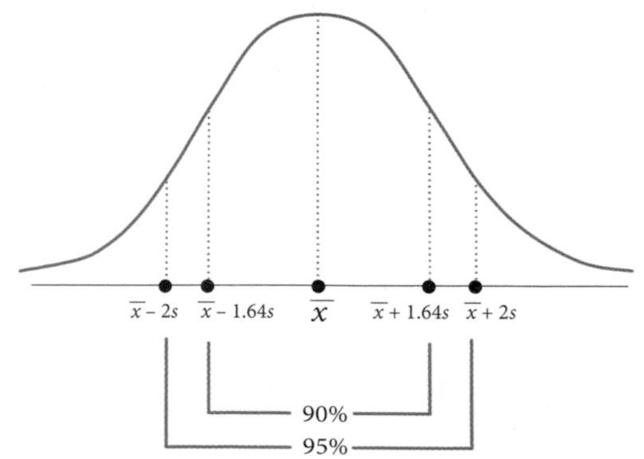

9. The mean is at the center of the curve. So, the percentage of data falling between the lowest 2.5% and the mean is: 50% – 2.5% = 47.5%.

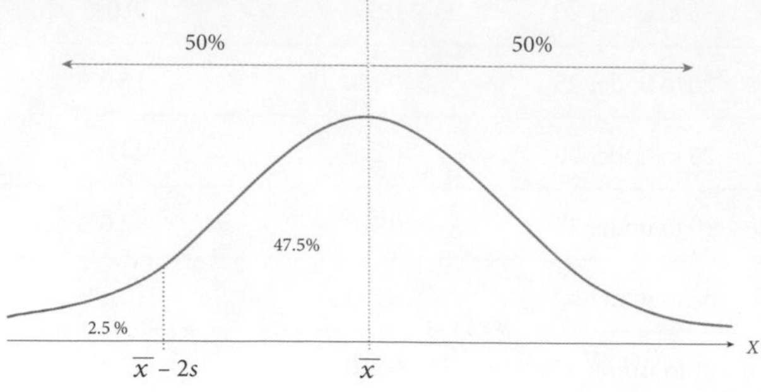

11. a. 190 people b. 4.25 hours
13. 54.76
15. (61.22, 120.06)
17. 8 pieces of data are expected to fall between 72.7 and 108.6. 8 pieces of data actually fall between 72.7 and 108.6.
19. 95% of the data is expected to fall between 54.8 and 126.5. 100% of the data actually falls between 54.8 and 126.5.

Review Exercises 12

1. $\frac{4}{9} = 0.44$
3. a. $\frac{1}{9} = 0.11$ b. $\frac{5}{12} = 0.42$
5. a. $\frac{3}{26} = 0.12$ b. $\frac{8}{13} = 0.62$ c. $\frac{4}{13} = 0.31$
7. a. 3 : 10 b. 3 : 1
9. $\frac{77}{90} = 0.86$
11. $\frac{9}{400} = 0.0225$
13. a. $\frac{25}{411} = 0.057$ b. $\frac{1}{21} = 0.048$
15. a. $\frac{3}{13} = 0.23$ b. $\frac{10}{13} = 0.77$
17. 95%
19. 68%

Self-Test Exercises 12

1. $\frac{1}{2} = 0.5$
2. $\frac{4}{9} = 0.44$
3. $\frac{2}{15} = 0.13$
4. a. $\frac{1}{3} = 0.33$ b. $\frac{1}{2} = 0.5$
5. $\frac{27}{52} = 0.52$
6. a. $\frac{11}{221} = 0.049$ b. $\frac{4}{663} = 0.006$
   c. $\frac{4}{221} = 0.018$ d. $\frac{3}{51} = 0.058$
7. a. 3 : 4 b. 3 : 4

8. a. $\frac{19}{80} = 0.2375$

   b. $\frac{23}{160} = 0.14375$

   c. $\frac{57}{160} = 0.35625$

   d. $\frac{103}{160} = 0.64375$

   e. $\frac{42}{65} = 0.65$

   f. $\frac{21}{40} = 0.525$

9. a. 95% b. 99.7% c. 2.5% d. 0.15%

10. a. (10.6, 13.8)

    b. 10.89

Glossary

Absolute value of a number is its distance from the origin '0' on the number line. Since it is a distance, it is always positive and the direction does not matter.

Addend represents each of the numbers being added.

Addition refers to combining (finding the total or sum of) numbers.

Algebra is a branch of mathematics that is used to analyze and solve day-to-day business and finance problems. It deals with different relations and operations by using letters and symbols to represent numbers, values, etc.

Algebraic expression consists of one or more terms, with a combination of variables, numbers, and operations.

Alternate angles are formed on the opposite sides of the transversal on the interior of the parallel lines.

Angle is formed when two rays intersect at their endpoints.

Area (A) of a plane figure is the amount of 2-dimensional surface that is enclosed within the figure.

Annual salary is the amount that an employee will be paid for service over a period of one year.

Bar chart is a graph that uses either horizontal or vertical bars to show comparisons among categories or class intervals of grouped data.

Base (*B*) refers to the whole quantity or value (100%) in a percent problem. It is usually followed by the word 'of', or 'percent of'.

Bi-weekly pay period refers to payment received once every two weeks. An employee will receive 26 bi-weekly payments through the year.

Billions group is the fourth group of three digits starting from the right of a whole number.

Binomial is a polynomial with two terms.

Buying rate (buy rate) is the rate at which the financial institution buys a particular foreign currency from the customers.

Celsius scale (°C) is used to measure temperature, and is part of the metric system. It derives from the basis that water freezes at 0°C and boils at 100°C.

Central tendency is based on the concept that there is a single value that best summarizes the entire set of numeric data.

Co-interior angles are formed on the same side of the transversal and on the interior of the parallel lines.

Coefficient is the numerical factor in front of the variable in a term.

Commission is the payment that an employee receives for selling a product or service.

Commission rate is used to calculate the commission payment that an employee receives for selling a product or service.

Common factor is a factor that is common to two or more numbers.

Common logarithm is a logarithm to the base 10.

Complex fraction is a fraction in which one or more fractions are found in the numerator or denominator.

Composite number is a whole number that has at least one factor other than 1 and the number itself.

Conditional equations are equations whose left side and right side are equal only for a certain value of the variable.

Consistent linear system is a linear system of two equations that has one or many solutions.

Constant is a term that has only a number, without any variables.

Consumer Price Index (CPI) is an indicator of changes in consumer prices experienced by Canadians.

Continuous variables are obtained by measuring.

Contradiction is an equation that is not true for any value of the variable.

Corresponding angles are formed on the same corner of the intersection between the transversal and each of the parallel lines.

Cosine Law provides a formula that relates the lengths of the sides of a triangle to the cosine of one of its angles.

Currency cross-rate table is used to display the currency exchange rates for quick reference.

Decimal numbers represent a part or a portion of a whole number.

Denominator represents the total number of equal parts into which the whole unit is divided.

Dependent system of equations is a system of equations that has an infinite number of solutions.

Descriptive Statistics deals with the organizing, presenting, and summarizing of raw data to present meaningful information.

Difference refers to the result of subtracting two or more numbers.

Discrete variables are obtained by counting, or are data that can only take on specific values.

Dividend refers to the number that is being divided.

Division can be thought of as repeated subtractions.

Divisor is the number by which the dividend is divided.

Elimination method is a method of solving systems of linear equations, when none of the equations in the system has a variable with a coefficient of 1 or −1.

Equivalent equations are equations that have the same solution.

Equivalent ratio is obtained when all the terms of the ratio are multiplied by the same number or divided by the same number.

Event is the specific outcome of an experiment.

Exchange rates (also called foreign exchange rates or forex rates) are used for converting currencies between countries.

Experiment is a process or action that produces one well-defined result of several possible results.

Exponent represents the number of times a number (base) is multiplied in exponential notation.

Exponential notation is used to represent a number that is multiplied by itself repeatedly.

Expression is a combination of terms. It usually refers to a statement of relations among variables.

Factor refers to each of the combinations of variables and/or numbers multiplied together in a term.

Factor of a number is a whole number that can divide the number with no remainder.

Factor tree helps to find all the prime factors of a number.

Factoring is the opposite of multiplying polynomials. It is the process of determining the factors that can be multiplied together to result in a given polynomial.

Fahrenheit scale (°F) is used to measure temperature, and is primarily used in the USA. It derives from the basis that water freezes at 32°F and boils at 212°F.

Formula is similar to an equation. In a formula, the relationship among many variables is written as a rule for performing calculations.

Fraction is a method of representing numbers, where one non-zero integer is divided by another non-zero integer.

Fraction bar represents the division sign.

Fraction in lowest terms is a fraction in which the numerator and denominator have no factors in common (other than 1).

Fractional exponent is when the exponent of a number or variable is a fraction.

Frequency (*f*) is the number of times an event happens.

Frequency distribution is a method to summarize large amounts of data without displaying each value of the observation.

Geometry is a branch of Mathematics that deals with the study of relative positions, properties, and relations of geometric objects.

Greatest Common Factor (GCF) of two or more numbers is the largest common number that divides the numbers with no remainder.

Histogram is similar to a vertical bar chart in which the categories or class intervals are marked on a horizontal axis and the class frequencies are represented by the heights of the bars.

Hourly rate of pay refers to payments received per hour for service provided.

Hypotenuse is the longest side of a right-triangle opposite the right-angle.

Identity is an equation which is true for any value of the variable.

Improper fraction is a fraction in which the numerator is greater than the denominator; i.e., the value of the entire fraction is more than 1.

Inconsistent linear system is a linear system of two equations that has no solutions.

Independent events refers to an event the occurrence of which has no effect on the occurrence of the other event.

Independent system of equations is a system of equations that has one or no solutions.

Index number is used to express the relative value of an item compared to a base value.

Inferential Statistics deals with the analysis of a sample drawn from a larger population to develop meaningful inferences about the population based on sample results.

Inflation is a rise on the general level of prices of goods and services in an economy over time.

Interest is a fee that borrowers pay to lenders for using their money temporarily for a period of time.

Irrational number is a number that cannot be expressed as a fraction.

Least Common Denominator (LCD) of a set of two or more fractions is the smallest whole number that is divisible by each of the denominators.

Least Common Multiple (LCM) of two or more numbers is the smallest multiple that is common to those numbers.

Levels of measurement are rules that describe the properties of data that are measured and the way in which they can be used to provide additional information on the data.

Like terms are terms that have the same variables and exponents.

Line is an object that has only one dimension: length.

Line segment is the portion of a line bound between two points.

Linear equation is an algebraic equation with one or two variables (each to the power of one), which produces a straight line when plotted on a graph.

Logarithm is a method of solving for an unknown exponent. It is the exponent to which the base is raised to get the number.

Maturity value (*S*) is the sum of the accumulated value of interest over time and the principal amount of the loan or investment.

Metric system of measurement uses the metre (m), gram (g), and litre (L) as the base units for the measurements of length, mass, and capacity, respectively. The Celsius (°C) scale is used for temperature.

Millions group is the third group of three digits starting from the right of a whole number.

Minuend is the number from which another number is subtracted.

Mixed number consists of both a whole number and a proper fraction, written side-by-side, which implies that the whole number and proper fraction are added.

Monomial is an algebraic expression that has only one term.

Monthly pay period refers to payment received once a month. An employee will receive 12 monthly payments through the year.

Multiple of a number is a whole number that can be divided by the number with no remainder.

Multiplication can be thought of as repeated additions.

Mutually exclusive refers to events that cannot occur at the same time or there is no common outcome.

Mutually non-exclusive refers to events that occur at the same time or there is a common outcome.

Natural logarithm is a logarithm to the base '*e*', where the constant $e = 2.718281...$

Normal Distribution is a common frequency distribution in statistics, which is bell-shaped and symmetrical about the mean.

Number line is used to represent numbers graphically as points on a horizontal line.

Numerator represents the number of equal parts in a fractional number.

Opposite angles are formed by any intersecting lines that are opposite to the same vertex.

Optimization is the process of maximizing or minimizing a measurement, given a constraint.

Order of a ratio is the order in which a ratio is presented.

Order of operations is the order in which arithmetic operations are carried out in an equation. The order that is followed is: Brackets, Exponents, Division and Multiplication, Addition and Subtraction (BEDMAS).

Ordered pair is used to locate a point in the coordinate system. The ordered pair (x, y) describes a point in the plane by its x- and y-coordinates.

Outcome is a particular result of a single trial of an experiment (i.e., what we observe and record from the experiment).

Outlier is a number that is very different from the rest of the group.

Overtime payment refers to additional payment eligible to be received for working more than the specified number of hours in a week.

Overtime rate of pay refers to the rate used to calculate the overtime payment for working more than the specified number of hours in a week.

Parallel lines are lines that have the same slope. All vertical lines are parallel to each other and all horizontal lines are parallel to each other.

Pay period refers to the frequency of payments (how often payments are being made).

Payroll is a record of the payment made to every employee of an organization.

Percent (per cent or per hundred in the literal meaning) is used to express a quantity out of 100 units and is represented by the symbol '%'.

Percent change is often used to express the ratio of the amount of change to the initial (original) value; i.e., the amount of change (increase or decrease) is calculated as a percent change (%C) of its initial value.

Perfect root is a whole number whose root is also a whole number.

Perfect square is any whole number base with an exponent of 2; i.e., a whole number multiplied by itself results in a perfect square.

Perimeter (P) of a plane figure is the total length of the boundary of the plane figure.

Perpendicular lines are lines that meet at a 90° angle; two lines are perpendicular if their slopes multiply to −1. The lines are also perpendicular if one of them is vertical and the other is horizontal.

Pie chart is usually used to summarize and show classes or groups of data in proportion to the whole dataset.

Place value is the position of each digit in a number.

Plane Geometry is the study of the properties and relations of plane figures such as triangles, quadrilaterals, circles, etc.

Polynomial is an algebraic expression that has two or more terms.

Population refers to all possible individuals, objects, or measurements of items of interest.

Portion (*P*) refers to the portion of the whole quantity or value (portion of the base) in a percent problem.

Prime number is a whole number that has only two factors: 1 and the number itself.

Principal (*P*) is the initial amount of money invested or borrowed.

Principal root is the positive root of a number.

Pro-ration is defined as sharing or allocating the quantities, usually amounts of money, on a proportional basis.

Product refers to the result from multiplying numbers.

Proper fraction is a fraction in which the numerator is less than the denominator.

Proportion is used to describe two sets of ratios that are equal.

Pythagorean Theorem is a famous theorem in Mathematics that states that the squares of the lengths of the two shorter sides that meet at the right-angle equals the square of the longest side opposite the right-angle.

Quadrant is one of the four regions that is formed by the X- and Y-axes in the rectangular coordinate system. They are numbered counter-clockwise from one (I) to four (IV).

Qualitative variables are data that are expressed non-numerically and are known as categorical data.

Quantitative variables are data that are expressed using numbers and are known as numerical data.

Quotient refers to the result of dividing numbers.

Range (*R*) is the difference between the highest and the lowest value in a dataset.

Rate is a special ratio that is used to compare two quantities or amounts having different units of measure.

Rate (*R*) refers to the percent relationship between the base and portion in a percent problem. It usually carries the percent sign (%) or the word 'percent'.

Ratio is a comparison or relationship between two or more quantities with the same unit.

Rational number is a number which can be expressed as a fraction, where one integer is divided by another non-zero integer.

Ray is the portion of a line bound in one direction by a point.

Real income is the income after adjusting for inflation.

Real numbers include all rational and irrational numbers.

Reciprocal is the fraction that is obtained by inverting the numerator and denominator in the original fraction.

Remainder refers to the number left over when the dividend cannot be divided evenly by the divisor.

Repeating decimal is a decimal that does not end but shows a repeating pattern.

Root is the inverse of exponents.

Rounding numbers makes them easier to work with and easier to remember. Rounding changes some of the digits in a number but keeps its value close to the original.

Rules of Exponents are used to simplify expressions that involve exponents.

Rules of Logarithms can be used to combine two or more logarithmic expressions into a single logarithmic expression.

S&P/TSX is an index of stock prices of the largest companies on the Toronto Stock Exchange.

Sample refers to a set of data drawn from the population.

Sample space is the set of all possible outcomes in an experiment.

Scatter Plot is a graph showing pairs of numerical data with the independent variable on a horizontal axis and the dependent variable on a vertical axis.

Scientific notation is a method of expressing numbers using decimal numbers with one non-zero digit to the left of the decimal point multiplied by a power of 10.

Selling rate (sell rate) is the rate at which the financial institution sells a particular foreign currency to the customers.

Semi-monthly pay period refers to payment received twice a month. An employee will receive 24 semi-monthly payments through the year.

Sharing quantities refers to the allocation or distribution of a quantity into two or more portions (or units) based on a given ratio.

Significant digits are used to determine the accuracy of a number.

Simplifying fractions is when you divide both the numerator and denominator of a fraction by the same number, which results in an equivalent fraction.

Sine Law provides a formula that relates the sides of a triangle to the sine of its angles.

Slope (*m*) is the steepness of the line relative to the X-axis. It is the ratio of the change in the value of y (called 'rise') to the corresponding change in the value of x (called 'run').

Statistics is a branch of Mathematics and procedures that involves collecting, organizing, presenting, analyzing, and interpreting data for the purpose of drawing conclusions and making a decision.

Stem-and-Leaf Plot is one method of displaying data to show the spread of data and the location of where most of the data points lie.

Stock index is an application of index numbers and is used to measure the performance of stock markets.

Substitution method is a method of solving systems of linear equations, when one of the equations in the system has a variable with a coefficient of 1 or −1.

Subtraction refers to finding the difference between numbers.

Subtrahend is the number that is being subtracted from another number.

Sum refers to the result from adding two or more numbers.

System of equations refers to two or more equations analyzed together.

Tally Chart is a method of collecting and organizing data, used to keep count of the number of times a particular event or data occurs.

Term is a number, variable, or a combination of numbers and variables that are multiplied and/or divided together.

Term of a ratio is the quantity in a ratio.

Terminating decimal is a decimal that ends.

Thousands group is the second group of three digits starting from the right of a whole number.

Time period (*t*) is the time taken to settle a loan or an investment.

Trigonometric ratio is a ratio of the lengths of two sides of a right-triangle.

Trigonometry is a branch of Mathematics that studies relationships involving lengths and angles of triangles.

Trillions group is the fifth group of three digits starting from the right of a whole number.

Trinomial is a polynomial with three terms.

Unit price is the unit rate when it is expressed in unit currency (dollars, cents, etc.).

Unit rate represents the number of units of the first quantity (or measurement) that corresponds to one unit of the second quantity.

Units group is the first group of three digits starting from the right of a whole number.

Unlike terms are terms that have different variables or the same variables with different exponents.

US Customary system of measurement uses the yard (yd), pound (lb), and gallon (gal) as the base units for the measurements of length, mass, and capacity, respectively. The Fahrenheit (°F) scale is used for temperature.

Variable is a letter that represents one or more numbers.

Variance is used as a measure to describe the spread of numbers from each other, in a dataset.

Vertex of an angle is the point of intersection of two rays.

Weekly pay period refers to payment received once a week. An employee will receive 52 weekly payments through the year.

Whole number include all counting numbers, also known as natural numbers or positive integers (1, 2, 3, 4...), and zero (0).

Workweek is the standard working hours per week specified by the organization.

***x*-intercept** is the point at which the line crosses the X-axis and where the y-coordinate is zero.

***y*-intercept** is the point at which the line crosses the Y-axis and where the x-coordinate is zero.

Zero is the smallest whole number.

Index

M

N

O

P

Q

R

S

T

U

V

W

Y